SUPERSEDED

D1410666

INTERNATIONAL INTELLECTUAL PROPERTY

PROBLEMS, CASES, AND MATERIALS

Second Edition

■ ■ ■

By

Daniel C.K. Chow

Joseph S. Platt–Porter, Wright, Morris & Arthur
Professor of Law
The Ohio State University Michael E. Moritz College of Law

Edward Lee

Professor of Law
Illinois Institute of Technology, Chicago–Kent College of Law

AMERICAN CASEBOOK SERIES®

WEST®
A Thomson Reuters business

Mat #40880696

American Casebook Series is a trademark registered in the U.S. Patent and Trademark Office.

© 2006 West, a Thomson business
© 2012 Thomson Reuters
    610 Opperman Drive
    St. Paul, MN 55123
    1–800–313–9378
Printed in the United States of America

ISBN: 978–0–314–20762–3

To my wife Ching and our son Alan
—DC

To my parents, Douglas and Catalina Lee
—EL

PREFACE TO THE SECOND EDITION

We are gratified by the warm reception given to the first edition of this book by our students and colleagues. *International Intellectual Property: Problems, Cases, and Materials* grew out of our belief that international intellectual property had emerged as a vital field of study for any serious student of intellectual property and that there was a need for a student friendly casebook on this growing subject.

The second edition retains the organization and approach of the first. Each chapter has been substantially updated with new cases and developments, some in replacement of existing materials. We continue to provide ample author-written explanatory text, examples, and short problems all in a concise format that can be covered in a 2 or 3 credit class. The one major structural change is that the second edition now introduces the topic of exhaustion in the Introduction and discusses the topic in depth in Chapter 6, comparing the different approaches for copyrights, trademarks, and patents.

As in the first edition, the second edition contains many short problems. We have found the problems to be an excellent pedagogical tool and have received enthusiastic feedback about their effectiveness as a tool to stimulate class discussion. Many of the problems have been updated and new ones have been added.

We have avoided the tendency to produce a second edition that is substantially longer than the first. To that end, we have assiduously pruned outdated materials from the first edition. We have designed a book of a manageable length that can be covered in its entirety in a 3 credit course. Of course, covering the entire book will require going at a fast pace and many professors may wish to emphasize certain topics. The book is designed for flexibility of use and can accommodate many different approaches. Each chapter begins with materials on core concepts that are then followed by a series of "special discussion" topics. Professors can pick and choose among these topics as a focus of extended study or can choose to cover all or the bulk of them in a survey class.

This edition, like the first, can be used by students with many different levels of background in intellectual property, including students with no previous study. We have used this book ourselves with students for whom this is the first course in intellectual property.

Many thanks to Colleen Chien, Margaret Chon, Donald Harris, Paul Heald, Tomas Gomez–Arostegui, Shubha Ghosh, Manuel Kleinemenke, Janice Mueller, John Rothchild, and John Thomas for their generous comments and suggestions related to our casebook. We also recognize the generous support of our deans, Alan Michaels and Harold Krent.

We could not have completed this edition without the incredible and untiring assistance of Matt Cooper of the Moritz Law Library and Tom Gaylord of the IIT Chicago–Kent College of Law Library and Claire Alfus.

James Baldwin, Adam Colgrove, Alan Devries, and Michael Johnson provided excellent research assistance. James Baldwin, Daniel Bujas, Adam Colgrove, Daniel D'Addario, Amy Harvey, Karen Hwang, Melanie Kibbler, Kacy King, Roberto Martell Jr., Richard Martin, Renae Resch, Alex Sklut, Smita Sarkar, Laurence Tooth, James Vergara and Filip Zucek provided invaluable help in proofreading drafts of this casebook.

DANIEL CHOW
chow.1@osu.edu
EDWARD LEE
elee@kentlaw.edu

PREFACE TO THE FIRST EDITION

Just a decade ago, only a few law schools in the United States offered courses on International Intellectual Property (IP). Today, this has changed. Courses on International IP are now part of the mainstream law school curriculum, and the study of International IP has become essential for any serious student of IP. We have written this casebook in response to the growing need for teaching materials in this emerging area.

Our casebook is designed for use by law students of all different backgrounds, including students with no prior background in IP or in international law. The casebook contains ample amounts of our own introductory and explanatory material for these students. At the same time, students who have had prior courses in IP or in international law will find our background materials and textual explanations to be useful in helping to refresh or reinforce their previous studies. Indeed, we have successfully tested the casebook in our own classes with students of all backgrounds, including in an entire class of students who had just completed their first year. Based on our own experience, we believe that professors can use this casebook in a course on International IP without requiring any prior courses in IP or international law as prerequisites.

We have made special efforts to listen to the feedback of our students, in order to make the materials on this complicated subject more "student friendly." To that end, as noted above, we have included our own explanatory text to introduce most topics we cover in the casebook. We have also added simple examples—called "Illustrations" in the casebook—to elucidate basic principles and treaty provisions, which can often be quite abstract in this area. In addition, we have included numerous problems—each of relatively short length—throughout the casebook as we have found that the use of problems works well to stimulate classroom discussion and also requires students to read the materials much as a lawyer would, with an eye to answering a legal question. We have found that having the students analyze relatively straightforward problems by applying treaty provisions, laws, and cases from the reading helps the students to obtain a much deeper understanding of these materials. Often, we have placed the problems *before* the reading materials to which they relate. Although some students and even professors may be unaccustomed to this practice, the overwhelmingly positive reaction of our students has confirmed to us the benefits of including problems before the relevant reading as a way to give students greater purpose in their reading and to hone their skills of applying legal rules and doctrines.

The casebook is designed for use in a three- or four-hour course. In a four-hour course, it should be possible to cover the bulk of the entire book at a reasonable pace of 15 to 20 pages per class for a 50–minute class. In a three-hour course, professors should be able to cover most of the casebook at a pace that should not overly burden their students. However, it is unlikely that professors using the casebook for a three-hour course will be able to cover the entire text, so some decisions on coverage will likely need to be made. To assist professors in making decisions on coverage, we have designed the casebook to provide teaching flexibility. With the exception of Chapter 1, the introductory chapter, all of the chapters in the casebook are organized as follows: the chapters begin with basic topics that most professors will want to cover. Following and interspersed with these basic topics, we often include a number of optional topics under the heading of "Special Discussion." These "Special Discussion" topics provide an in-depth treatment of current, cutting-edge topics that professors can pick and choose from in accordance with their interests and the interests of their students. We have designed the book so that professors can choose to cover or omit any of the "Special Discussion" topics without compromising on coverage of the fundamentals.

For ease of reading, we have *not* included, in most instances, any ellipses to indicate portions of text we omitted from our excerpts of articles and cases. We also have omitted most footnotes from the original sources; footnotes that we did include are numbered as they are in the original. For the most part, we have kept the spelling of words and the punctuation in foreign cases and materials as they are in the original, even though they may be different from standard U.S. conventions.

We hope that you find these materials as stimulating and as challenging as we do. We welcome your thoughts and suggestions for future editions.

DANIEL C.K. CHOW
EDWARD LEE

June, 2006
Columbus, Ohio

ACKNOWLEDGEMENTS
TO THE FIRST EDITION

We are grateful for the support of Dean Nancy H. Rogers, Associate Dean Sharon L. Davies, Professor Albert L. Clovis, and Professor David Goldberger of The Ohio State University Michael E. Moritz College of Law. Without their support, the completion of this project would not have been possible.

We also received many insightful and useful comments on these materials from Cory M. Amron, Lionel Bently, Thomas T. Moga, John Okuley, Douglas L. Rogers, and Timothy P. Trainer.

Our students in our international intellectual property classes at the Moritz College of Law have, by their responses and suggestions, helped us to write and rewrite this book in a more student-friendly way. Christopher Thiemann provided us with the photograph of the Neem tree that he took while in India. Also, the following students provided us with excellent research assistance at different stages of this book's production: Matthew Allinson, Patrick Berarducci, Erin Barker Brown, William Browne, Nicholas Kamphaus, John Hui Li, Edward Olszewski, Ajay Patel, Joseph Popp, Steven Roach, Michelle Robinson, and Derek Somogy. We would like to single out Ronald Wadlinger, who provided outstanding research assistance from start to finish.

We could not have written this book without the extraordinary help of the reference librarians at the Michael E. Moritz Law Library. We would like to thank especially Katherine Hall and Rachael Smith for their invaluable and continual assistance throughout the entire process. Finally, we are indebted to our assistant, Jennifer Pursell, for her tireless help in the production of this casebook.

D.C.

E.L.

Summary of Contents

TABLE OF CONTENTS

TABLE OF CASES

The principal cases are in bold type. Cases cited or discussed in the text are in roman type. References are to pages. Cases cited in principal cases and within other quoted materials are not included.

INTERNATIONAL INTELLECTUAL PROPERTY

PROBLEMS, CASES, AND MATERIALS

Second Edition

CHAPTER 1

INTRODUCTION

■ ■ ■

Intellectual property (IP) is a topic that cuts across virtually every country of the world. It impacts not just businesses and industries, but people in their everyday lives—at times, at the most basic level.

Consider, for example, the intense controversy that has divided the developed and developing countries over access to medicines. Patent laws allow the patent owner to enjoy a monopoly for a 20–year patent term and to charge prices far beyond what individuals in many developing countries can afford to pay. Developing and least developed nations contend that patent laws restrict or deny access to medicines necessary to combat deadly diseases such as AIDS, causing national health crises among the poorest countries of the world, especially in sub-Saharan Africa. According to one United Nations estimate, 95 percent of all people infected by HIV live in developing countries, which in turn suffer 95 percent of the total deaths resulting from AIDS. Developing countries, understandably, have argued for greater access to pharmaceuticals for treatment of AIDS and other diseases at price levels they can afford. However, pharmaceutical companies, backed by developed countries, argue that patents are necessary to allow them to receive a fair return on the medicines in order to defray research and development costs and to earn a fair profit. The inability to earn a fair return, they argue, will discourage important research and development in the future, resulting in a long-term detriment for all. Although international discussions have begun to bridge the divide between the two camps, the issue is far from resolved.

Another issue that divides countries around the world is "biopiracy." Biopiracy is a term used by some to describe the attempts by multinational enterprises (MNEs) and other entities to acquire intellectual property rights in genetic resources (GR) and in traditional knowledge (TK) indigenous to certain areas or peoples, particularly in developing countries. Developing countries are the owners of some of the world's most biologically diverse regions. MNEs are accused of "pirating" indigenous materials and traditional knowledge from developing countries by obtaining patents and other IP rights in such materials without paying adequate compensation to the developing countries or the people who first cultivated the resources and knowledge.

On the flip side, developed nations—particularly, the United States—continue to raise concerns about the level of "commercial piracy," involving infringement of copyrights and trademarks. The Internet and the advances in digital communication have greatly increased the ease with which material may be copied and disseminated. The unauthorized copying and use of trademarked and copyrighted material has become an increasingly lucrative and popular illegal activity. Some industry groups now estimate that commercial piracy results in annual losses to U.S. companies that exceed $200 billion. Some of the illegal activity may be engaged in by individuals, but some may involve well-organized international criminal organizations that are also involved in narcotics, smuggling, and prostitution. While commercial piracy problems now exist in every country in the world, some of the worst problems reportedly originate from developing countries, particularly China and southeast Asia.

These issues of intellectual property raise serious questions of international importance. Is "commercial piracy" more worthy of condemnation than "biopiracy"? Doesn't the status of a country as a developed versus a developing country, or as a net exporter versus a net importer of intellectual property, affect fundamentally that country's view on what should be the proper scope of intellectual property? After all, when the U.S. was in its early years as a nation, it refused to give foreign authors copyrights and was a leading source of "piracy" of intellectual property. What about national health concerns to combat AIDS and other diseases? To what extent should intellectual property rights give way to a country's need for potentially life-saving medicines?

In this casebook, we will explore these and other important issues related to the international aspects of intellectual property. This chapter has three purposes. First, it provides a description of the scope and approach of this casebook. Second, it sketches out an overview of international intellectual property, including an explanation why IP has become more international in scope today, much more so than it was only a couple decades ago; and a brief introduction to some of the basic principles that underlie today's international "system" of IP, including territoriality, national treatment, and the most favored nation principle. Third, this chapter provides helpful background describing the key institutions related to this area, as well as a very brief "refresher" on U.S. law of intellectual property.

A. SCOPE AND APPROACH OF OUR CASEBOOK

This book concerns "international intellectual property." The term is somewhat elusive, however, since there are no intellectual property rights that are international in scope. As we discuss in this chapter, intellectual property rights—loosely defined as exclusive rights in creations of the mind—are *territorial* in nature, meaning that they emanate from national law and they typically apply only to conduct within that nation. Yet a complex set of international IP treaties and agreements has developed over the years to establish *minimum standards* for the IP laws in countries around the world, including the very important principle of *national treatment* under which countries are obligated to extend to foreigners IP rights that are no less favorable than those granted to a country's own nationals. This nondiscrimination principle is the bedrock of international IP agreements.

Thus, by "international intellectual property," we refer to the system of international treaties and legal institutions that both facilitate the acquisition and recognition of such rights and that establish uniform obligations on the part of nations to follow minimum standards in the area of intellectual property. One of the most important of these institutions is the World Trade Organization (WTO) and its major discipline, the Agreement on the Trade Related Aspects of Intellectual Property (TRIPS). We also include within our definition of international intellectual property the national IP laws of countries that seek, as members of international IP treaties, to create ways for the international protection of IP.

No casebook or course on international intellectual property can possibly cover the vast range of issues presented in this expanding field of study. The number of international, multilateral, and bilateral agreements in IP are many, and the number of national IP laws and subtle differences in approaches to IP around the world, even more vast. Moreover, frequent developments and changes to the law in this area make study of international intellectual property an ongoing, never-ending process.

Mindful of these challenges, we have constructed our casebook to provide students with the building blocks or necessary foundation for future study and practice in international intellectual property. The material will involve a mixture of both public and private law, meaning discussion of both (i) the key "public law" international IP agreements and conventions, such as the TRIPS Agreement, that govern the relationships among nation-states and (ii) some of the "private law" national approaches to important IP issues that govern relationships among private parties. Although our primary focus will be on (i), the international agreements, we believe it is important for students of intellectual property to begin to appreciate the many international and transnational dimensions raised by national IP laws in private litigation and counseling of clients.

Several caveats should be noted. First, it is not our intention to provide a survey of IP laws around the world. The comparative materials we have chosen for discussion are not meant to be exhaustive, but instead illustrative of the complexities in IP. Second, our casebook is written based upon the assumption that most students who study this casebook will have their primary training in U.S. law. Our perspective, too, is shaped by U.S. training, so some of our materials will be arranged with an eye to how international IP intersects with U.S. law and U.S. intellectual property holders. By the same token, we have made considerable effort to prevent U.S. law or sources from dominating our casebook. This is a casebook in *international*, not U.S., intellectual property. To that end, we have included cases, sources, and authors from a number of countries besides the U.S., including Australia, Canada, the European Union, and countries in Africa, Asia, Europe, and Latin America.

Finally, our casebook is based in the problem method. We have included problems for discussion throughout each chapter that are intended to serve as a basis of classroom discussion. Many of the problems come at the start of sections and give students some key question(s) to think about before reading the section. The problems are designed to complement the readings, so students are able to think about and apply what they read in the chapter at a level of greater understanding. We hope the problems are both fun and useful to think about, and aid in your overall understanding of the legal concepts contained in the reading.

B. WHY HAS INTELLECTUAL PROPERTY GONE "INTERNATIONAL"?

To begin our study of international intellectual property, it would serve us well to ask: How did we get this way? International intellectual property is a relatively new field of study as courses devoted entirely to this subject matter were not widely offered in U.S. law schools a decade ago. Now, it is absolutely essential to any serious study of intellectual property. This section discusses some of the key forces that have made IP increasingly international in scope.

1. GLOBALIZATION, INTERNATIONAL TRADE, AND MULTI–NATIONAL ENTERPRISES

Intellectual property has always involved elements of foreign trade, dating back to the Renaissance when Venice enacted the first patent law in part to attract foreign inventors to the city. Indeed, the impetus for many of the first major international IP treaties, such as the Paris Convention and the Berne Convention, was to ensure IP protection abroad and to open up foreign markets.

But it is no exaggeration to say that, today, intellectual property plays a greater role than ever in private international business and commercial transactions of all kinds. The underlying reason can be traced to globalization, which has transformed not just intellectual property, but many other areas of law. Globalization can be defined as the relatively free movement of people, goods, money, services, and technology around the world. Globalization has occurred with amazing speed, within a single generation in the last half of the twentieth century. What are the driving forces behind globalization? Although the answer to that question deserves a book in itself, we highlight several important factors driving the process of globalization: (i) political and legal reform; (ii) international trade and multinational enterprises (MNEs); and (iii) technological advances.

Political and legal reform. At the end of World War II, the world was divided by rigid and opposing political and legal ideologies. The Soviet Union, with its eastern sphere of influence in Europe, and the People's Republic of China newly founded in 1949, with its sphere of influence in southeast Asia, competed with the United States and its allies for the allegiance of other countries around the world. An "Iron Curtain" separated the world into two opposing systems, and the Cold War froze into place both the political divisions, characterized by hostility and deep mistrust, and the physical barriers that existed in the world after World War II.

For a period of time after the War, an argument could be made that two competing economic and political models were vying for dominance in the world: free market capitalism, championed by the U.S. and its allies, and socialism, championed by the Soviet Union, China, and others. Not only were these competing economic models, they also were political systems antithetical to each other. Free market capitalism was associated with democracy, while socialism was associated with communism. These conflicting economic and political theories divided the world into two camps.

During this period, free trade (as we understand it today) occurred principally within Western developed countries. Trade between Western developed countries and the Eastern socialist countries was negligible, with trade tending to occur almost entirely within each group. Nor did developing countries play a significant role in world trade. At the end of World War II, a third group of nations—developing nations in Asia, the Middle East, and Africa—achieved independence from decades of colonial rule by European nations. Many of these countries were at such a low level of development and harbored such a deep mistrust of developed countries, that trade and economic exchanges were not considered a priority. Because of these restrictions, trade was never truly global in scope.

In the past three decades, however, with the fall of the Soviet Union and its eastern block, the rigid barriers to trade created by the Iron Curtain have collapsed. In China, the 1978 decision of the Communist Party to open China's doors to trade with the rest of the world has created one of the world's most vibrant and important economies. Free market capitalism has emerged as the dominant economic model in the world today. Even in China, the system is really socialist in name only, notwithstanding China's official policy that its economic system is "socialism with unique characteristics."

In addition, after the Cold War, many nations have shifted their national priorities from political objectives squarely to economic development. For example, in China, the national agenda for the first three decades of its existence was once a strictly political one: to further the goals of the revolution and to create a utopian political system of communism. Since 1978, this political goal has been replaced by an overtly economic one: China's national goal is one of modernization and industrialization through economic development. All around the world, other former socialist nations have adopted similar economic goals in what are referred to as "transition economies," which are in the process of discarding the vestiges of socialism and adopting the free market reforms of capitalism. Many developing countries, once wary of their former colonial oppressors, now eagerly seek out foreign capital and technology as they also strive for economic development to lift themselves out of dire poverty and backwardness. For developing nations around the world, modernization, industrialization, and economic development have now become the new national goals to help advance living standards and improve economic conditions.

International Trade. The global emphasis on economic development has led to legal reforms that facilitate trade and economic exchanges. Today, four principal channels of international trade exist: (1) trade in goods; (2) trade in services; (3) knowledge and technology transfer; and (4) foreign direct investment (FDI). Each of these channels of trade has experienced significant increases in the past several decades.

The multi-lateral world trading system has grown with the implementation of the General Agreement on Tariffs and Trade (GATT) and its successor, the WTO. Starting in 1947 in Geneva, countries have negotiated "rounds" of trade agreements to reduce tariffs. The Uruguay Round from 1986 to 1994 led to the creation of the WTO. We will detail the history of GATT and the WTO later in this chapter, but, for present purposes, it is important to note that much of the early work of the GATT was focused on lowering the barriers to trade in goods. The result of GATT was a sharp increase in the levels of international trade in goods (import/export trade transactions). Trade in merchandise exports has mushroomed from approximately $1.9 trillion in 1980 to more than $15 trillion in 2010.

Figure 1–1

Growth of World Merchandise Exports in the Past Two Decades (in $Billions) and Regional Percentage Shares

	World	*Developed Countries*	*EU*	*USA*	*Developing Countries*
1980	$1,932	65.5%	36.4	11.7	34.5
1985	1,875	68.4	35.6	11.7	31.6
1990	3,423	71.7	40.5	11.5	28.3

	World	Developed Countries	EU	USA	Developing Countries
1995	5,104	68.0	40.4	11.5	32.0
1999	5,577	66.9	39.1	12.6	33.1
2001	5,984	75.1	37.7	13.6	20.3
2005	8,975	63.1	40.4	9.1	33.5
2010	15,230	53.9	33.8	12.1	41.9

Sources: IMF and UNCTADSTAT (2011) *available at* http://unctadstat.unctad.org.

The international transfer of technology, as measured by payments for royalties and licensing fees, increased dramatically at about the same rate as foreign direct investment (FDI) in the past two decades. By technology transfer, we refer to a process by which an owner of technology protected by some form of intellectual property (e.g., patents, copyrights, trademarks, or trade secrets) will authorize use of those rights to another. Such a transfer of use can be absolute, such as in a complete assignment of intellectual property rights, or can be limited, such as in the case of a license. In a little over 15 years, technology payments rose nearly seven-fold, from $12 billion in 1983 to $80 billion in 1999. The annual growth rate for technology payments was 11.1%. *See* JORN KLEINERT, THE ROLE OF MULTINATIONAL ENTERPRISES IN GLOBALIZATION: AN EMPIRICAL OVERVIEW 9 (2001).

Another important reason for the increased international dimensions of IP is foreign direct investment (FDI). By foreign direct investment, we refer to the acquisition by an entity resident in one nation of a permanent or lasting interest in an entity resident in another nation. FDI is often the vehicle by which financial, banking, insurance, and other services are transferred to a foreign nation. A simple example of FDI is when a U.S. corporation forms a wholly-owned foreign subsidiary in a foreign nation. Because the foreign direct investment was not treated within the GATT system, most of the policy and legal liberalization occurred outside of the multi-lateral trading system. Many nations have entered into bilateral investment treaties for the purpose of liberalizing trade and encouraging foreign investment. For example, in 2001, 71 countries made 208 changes in foreign investment laws. Over 90 percent of these changes were aimed at making the investment climate more favorable in order to attract foreign investment. In addition, in 2009, 82 new bilateral investment treaties were signed, raising the total number of such treaties to over 2,750. *See* UNCTAD, WORLD INVESTMENT REPORT 2010, at 81–82.

Just as technology transfers have increased, so too has foreign direct investment. As the table below shows, the rate of growth for international trade (measured in exports) was more than double the growth rate for industrial production. The growth rate for FDI was even greater, increasing by nearly 800% from 1990 to 2010, with an average annual growth rate of 11%.

Figure 1–2
Trends in Foreign Direct Investment

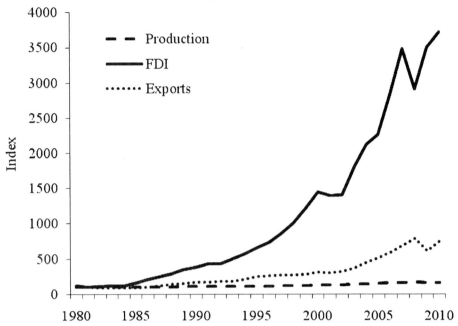

Source: UNCTAD (2011) and OECD Statistics.

Intellectual property rights play a significant role in the facilitation of all channels of international trade. Sellers of goods are more likely to sell to a nation that has a strong regime protecting intellectual property rights. Moreover, the higher the level of technology involved in the products in question, the more significant the issue of intellectual property rights becomes.

For example, in considering the sale of its goods to Country A, Mega Corporation, an owner of a portfolio of IP rights, will consider whether Country A offers protections for patents, trademarks, and copyrights. Under the principle of territoriality (discussed later in this chapter), even though Mega may have acquired intellectual property rights for its products in its home state, Country M, Mega will need to rely on the laws of Country A to provide protection within that nation. If Country A does not offer adequate protection, then Mega's products will face in Country A an environment that might lead to the unauthorized copying or piracy of the product. If Mega's product is a high technology product, such as a drug, or a product that involves a famous trademark, Mega's level of concern for the protection of its intellectual property rights might lead it to refuse to trade with Country A. Mega will be concerned not only with commercial piracy of its products in Country A, but also with the export of counterfeits from Country A to other locations around the world. Exports of counterfeit and pirated products have risen sharply in the last few decades and are a growing concern to intellectual property owners.

The same types of concerns are raised with respect to technology transfer and licensing. An owner of technology is more likely to transfer technology where the recipient nation has a strong legal regime protecting intellectual property rights. For example, imagine that Alpha Company, the owner of patents and trademarks in Country A, needs to register its patents and trademarks in Country B. Once Alpha Company acquires the patents and trademarks under Country B's laws, then Alpha Company will license the use of the patented and trademarked items to Beta Company, the licensee, for use in Country B. In this licensing arrangement, Alpha remains the owner of the intellectual property and Beta is the licensee. While providing Beta Company with some access to its intellectual property, Alpha Company, as the owner, will seek to protect its ownership interest in the technology from misuse by Beta Company or by third parties. As a result, Alpha Company will typically license those rights only if Alpha believes that Country B's intellectual property laws will adequately protect Alpha's rights in Country B. Inadequate intellectual property protection in the recipient nation tends to discourage technology transfer.

These same considerations apply with even more force in the case of foreign direct investment. In a typical FDI transaction, Gamma Company, a business in one nation, Country C, will establish a subsidiary or a joint venture in another nation, Country D. To establish a subsidiary in D, the foreign investor will inject both capital and technology into the recipient nation. In many cases, the knowledge or technology component of the foreign investment will be as important, if not even more important, to the success of the enterprise than the capital invested. Indeed, the intellectual property of the foreign investor may be its most valuable business asset.

For example, suppose that our hypothetical foreign investor, Gamma Company, is a multi-national enterprise in the pharmaceutical industry. Gamma may invest millions of dollars in capital in establishing a factory in a foreign nation, but it is the transfer of the technology—i.e., the patented inventions and material subject to other intellectual property—that is critical to the success of the foreign investment. In FDI, the level of technology that is involved can often be higher than that involved in technology licensing. In a licensing situation, the owner of the intellectual property is giving access to its proprietary technology to a third party. Many intellectual property owners are reluctant to part with their "core" technology in a licensing arrangement because giving third parties access to technology inevitably involves the risk that the technology will be misused or stolen. (Indeed, many licensees, especially those in developing countries, often complain that the licensor will only provide access to secondary technologies.)

In FDI, however, the intellectual property owner, Gamma Company in our example above, will have either full ownership of the foreign subsidiary or partial ownership of a foreign joint venture. Gamma will be able to exercise greater control over the technology and will be less concerned about its misuse. In addition, as FDI often involves a substantial commitment of capital and resources, Gamma will have a much greater stake in the success of the foreign investment. For this reason, Gamma will be more likely to transfer its core technologies to the foreign subsidiary. And Gamma may even be able to secure more favorable tax treatment by setting up a foreign subsidiary in a country with better tax rates. Of course, as the level of technology transfer in FDI may be even higher than in technology licensing, the issue of protecting the intellectual property plays an even more significant role for the foreign investor. A decision to make FDI is complex and involves many other factors, such as market conditions, political stability, and the overall strategy of the foreign investor. However, for most foreign investors, the intellectual property legal regime of the recipient nation is a major consideration.

Multi-national enterprises (MNEs). Multi-national enterprises play a crucial role in world trade of all kinds. According to some economic measures, the largest MNEs are larger than many countries. For example, in 1997, the revenues of the top 200 MNEs accounted for 26% of world Gross Domestic Product (GDP). Of the 100 largest economies in the world, 49 were countries, but 51 were MNEs. *See* SARAH D. ANDERSON & JOHN CAVANAGH, THE FIELD GUIDE TO THE GLOBAL ECONOMY 67–68 (2000). The importance of MNEs to world trade is evident in the following discussion by the United Nations Conference on Trade and Development:

> Recent estimates suggest that there are about 65,000 [MNE]s today, with about 850 foreign affiliates across the globe. Their economic impact can be measured in different ways. In 2001, foreign affiliates accounted for about 54 million employees, compared to 24 million in 1990; their sales of almost $19 trillion were more than twice as high as world exports in 2001, compared to 1990 when both were roughly equal; and the stock of outward foreign direct investment increased from $1.7 trillion to $6.6 trillion over the same period. Foreign affiliates now account for one-tenth of world GDP and one-third of world exports. Moreover, if the value of worldwide [MNE] activities associated with non-equity relationships (e.g., international subcontracting, licensing, contract manufacturers) is considered, [MNE]s would account for even larger shares in these global aggregates.

UNCTAD, WORLD INVESTMENT REPORT 2002, at xv.

As MNEs own the world's most valuable intellectual property, they have a great stake in the protection of intellectual property rights. MNEs dominate in the transfer of knowledge and technology on a worldwide basis. MNEs are also the engines that drive the world's innovation process as they have the resources to engage in research and development critical for innovation. For example, based on industry estimates, it costs an estimated $1.2 billion to successfully bring a new drug to market. *See* Christopher Paul Adams & Van Vu Bratner, *Spending on New Drug Development*, 19 Health Economics 130 (2010). Only MNEs (or governments) have resources on this scale. To protect and earn a fair return on their investments, MNEs insist on strong intellectual property rights. Although some powerful MNEs have emerged in developing countries, particularly in Asia, in recent years, most of the world's leading MNEs are located in developed countries, such as the United States, Europe, and Japan. The governments of these countries and territories have been world leaders in promoting the protection of intellectual property rights.

Technological advances. Finally, advances in technology have also facilitated globalization, which in turn fuels the pressure to secure IP protection internationally. The means of travel by air, water, and rail have made it easier to reach all parts of the world in a relatively short amount of time. Moreover, the advances in communication technology—through the Internet, computers, wireless and digital technology, and mobile phones and handheld devices—have revolutionized the daily lives of billions around the world. It is no exaggeration to say that the world is more interconnected today than it ever was before. And businesses have harnessed these advances in technology to establish highly refined production and shipping systems to enable the delivery of their goods to all parts of the world, again within a very short amount of time. This technological revolution has further enhanced the globalization of the world market and has made the international protection of intellectual property a major concern of businesses and many developed countries.

2. INTELLECTUAL PROPERTY, DEVELOPING COUNTRIES, AND ECONOMIC DEVELOPMENT

PROBLEM 1–1

You represent a group of developing and least developed countries that have recently gained their independence from decades of colonial rule. You wish to argue that developed countries have a moral, if not legal, responsibility to (1) exempt your clients from intellectual property laws of all kinds and (2) transfer technology free of charge to your clients. Develop the best arguments in favor of the developing countries' approach. How would you deal with the problem of attracting businesses to the developing and least developed countries without recognizing intellectual property rights in their products? Or should this issue be considered something akin to foreign aid? Now assume you represent a group of developed countries who deeply regret their former imperialistic aggressions but who have no desire to comply with these demands. How do you respond? What, if anything, do you offer the developing and least developed countries? Should both sides compromise on the issue of intellectual property? Consider the following discussion.

* * *

So far we have focused on the role of intellectual property in facilitating international trade and technology transfer. As we have seen, a strong intellectual property legal regime helps to attract capital, knowledge, and technology transfer to the recipient nation. Why do so many nations seek access to intellectual property and technology? We now turn to the issue of the role of intellectual property in economic development.

In the modern world, the bulk of the world's innovation and intellectual property occurs in developed countries, home to most of the world's MNEs. Developed countries dominate in innovation, exports of technology intensive goods, and technology transfer. The following figure measures technology trade by compiling information on international transactions involving royalties and license fee payments:

Figure 1–3

Receipts of Royalties and License Fees of Selected Countries, 2000–2010 (USD Billion)

	2000	2006	2007	2008	2009	2010
United States	51.8	83.5	97.8	101.1	97.2	105.6
Japan	10.2	20.1	23.2	25.7	21.7	26.7
Germany	2.9	7.0	8.5	10.8	16.3	14.4
UK	8.2	14.5	16.0	14.8	12.9	14.3
France	2.3	6.2	8.8	11.0	9.8	10.4
Singapore	0.1	1.0	1.2	1.4	1.3	1.9
South Korea	0.7	2.0	1.7	2.4	3.2	3.1
China	0.1	0.2	0.3	0.6	0.4	.8
Taiwan	0.4	0.2	0.2	.2	.2	.5
Thailand	0.0	0.0	0.1	0.1	0.1	.2

Source: UNCTADSTAT (2011) available at http://unctadstat.unctad.org.

Not only do developed countries dominate in the area of technology innovation and transfer, but most innovation occurs within a select group of developed countries, led by the United States. As of 2010, almost 75 percent of all of the royalties and licensing fees in Figure 1–3 above were received by five countries: the United States (44%), Japan (11%), Germany (6%), the United Kingdom (6%), and France (4%). These statistics indicate that in the area of knowledge and technology, developed nations are the primary innovators and exporters of intellectual property rights and developing nations are recipients and importers. Of course, this is not to say that developed countries hold a monopoly over innovation. In the past two decades, Brazil, India, and China have made incredible strides in technological development. Indeed, India's software sector may well rival the U.S.'s Silicon Valley today. And, given the comparatively cheap labor in India and China, they are popular destinations for outsourcing of work from the U.S. and other developed nations.

Developed and developing nations may have very different attitudes toward intellectual property, however. These differences constitute some of the sharpest political and legal debates in world trade today. In general, developed nations are interested in deriving full economic benefits from their innovation, knowledge, and technology while protecting their interests through strong intellectual property laws. Developing countries, by comparison, tend to favor weaker IP protection. To understand the difference in views, consider the following arguments.

Strong IP protection. Developed nations typically argue that intellectual property laws are necessary to protect the investment of significant resources in developing their products. The U.S. and other developed nations put pressure on developing countries to enact intellectual property laws that recognize and protect such rights. According to developed nations, IP protection will make a developing country an attractive place to do business. Global competitiveness in all of the four major channels of trade (goods, services, technology transfer, and FDI) is tied directly to the level of technology involved. For example, in the area of trade in goods, exports typically grow faster with higher levels of technology in the products that are less dependent on natural resources for production. The rate of export is a significant indicator of competitiveness because the exporting nation sells its products to the importing nation. The more competitive the nation, the more its exports will be attractive to buyers from other nations around the world. Every nation is interested, therefore, in increasing the level of its technology to boost its exports and to become or remain competitive on the world stage. Exports with a high technology component are in greater demand and lead to greater economic growth for the exporting nation. In the area of technology transfer and FDI, the higher the level of technology involved, the greater the demand for access to that technology by recipient nations.

To see the relationship between intellectual property and economic development, let us return to our previous FDI example. Suppose that Gamma Company, our hypothetical multi-national enterprise, proceeds with its plans to form a joint venture with Delta Company, a local company in Country D, a developing country. Gamma will inject a significant amount of capital into Country D to meet the physical needs of establishing a subsidiary and manufacturing facility. Gamma will also seek to obtain patents, trademarks, and other intellectual property for its products in Country D and then license those rights to its joint venture. In addition, Gamma will transfer a group of engineers, scientists, and managers to Country D for the purpose of managing and operating the joint venture. As part of the joint venture, Gamma will train the employees of Delta, the local company, on how to manufacture its pharmaceutical products. Gamma might even send some of the employees of Delta Company abroad for advanced training in Gamma's corporate headquarters. After several years, Gamma might decide to establish a research and development facility in Country D to support its operations rather than rely on its headquarters to provide research and development support. To establish its research and development facility in Country D, Gamma might establish another joint venture with a local university.

As Gamma Company trains local employees on how to conduct research and development, how to use the patents and trademarks in manufacturing products, and how to manage a modern and efficient business enterprise, Country D is able to absorb and assimilate the knowledge and technology transfer acquired from Gamma. If this process is repeated many times with many different joint ventures in many different industries, Country D, a developing country, might be able to close the gap between itself and developed countries. Country D will learn how to modernize and industrialize its economy and how to become globally competitive. Country D may even eventually be able to produce its own local companies that are able to manufacture products and services that can compete with Gamma's products and that can be traded in the global marketplace.

Of course, Country D can decide to develop its own technology, and modernize and industrialize on its own. But like most other developing countries, Country D realizes that the quickest way to modernize and industrialize its economy and to become globally competitive is to obtain access to the intellectual property owned by entities in advanced industrialized countries. Although we have discussed these concerns using hypothetical countries, there are also some real world examples: both Taiwan and South Korea have within the past several decades transformed themselves from countries dependent on advanced industrialized countries to technological innovators. At the same time, both Taiwan and South Korea have made significant strides in economic development and in increasing the wealth, spending power, and standard of living for their citizens. More recently, Brazil, Russia, India, and China—the so-called "BRIC countries"—have experienced rapid economic growth. Although the level of IP enforcement in these countries has often been criticized in the past, IP protection will likely figure into the long-term objectives of the BRIC countries as they produce more and more of their own IP.

Weaker IP protection. Not every developing nation buys into the developed nations' philosophy on strong intellectual property rights. Many developing nations argue that they need access to advanced technology and knowledge, which are necessary tools for industrial development, modernization, and competitiveness in the modern world economy. Developing nations also contend that intellectual property laws are used by MNEs and developed nations either to deny access altogether to advanced technology or to limit access by imposing burdensome royalties and licensing fees. Some developed nations argue that intellectual property rights are used to restrict the development of these nations and to maintain a large gap between developed and developing countries. The debate between developed and developing nations is one of the key themes that we will explore in this book.

Perhaps no nation has presented a greater challenge to the Western paradigm of intellectual property rights than the People's Republic of China (China), which has leapfrogged into the modern age through the acquisition and exploitation of foreign technology in a political and legal environment that, in the past, has shown little respect for intellectual property rights. Less than four decades ago, China was an agrarian economy mired in backwardness and poverty. At least in certain parts of the country, daily life had scarcely progressed, if at all, from medieval times. In the past three decades, however, China has emerged as an economic power and is on course, according to some experts, to surpass the United States as the world's largest economy within the near future. It is no coincidence China's surge coincided with China's emergence as one of the largest recipients of foreign direct investment. In the 1990s, China was the world's second largest recipient of foreign direct investment, second only to the United States. In 2002, China surpassed the United States to become the world's largest recipient of foreign direct investment with about $50 billion of foreign capital inflows. In another turn of events, by 2011, China became the largest creditor of the U.S. and owned $1.2 trillion of U.S. Treasury debt—further signaling a shift in the economic tides of the two countries.

The bulk of the world's largest and most successful MNEs have all now entered China's market and have established numerous joint ventures, wholly owned subsidiaries, and research and development centers. Not only have these MNEs injected massive amounts of capital, but they have provided China with unprecedented access to their technology, allowing the Chinese to acquire the world's most valuable technology. China has been able to exploit this access to technology to transform itself almost overnight into a highly competitive global player and exporter of technology intensive goods. For example, by observing and supplying the major multi-national companies with electronic goods, China has been able to absorb foreign technology and to develop Original Equipment Manufacturing (OEM) capabilities that have allowed China to manufacture those goods and to sell them directly to customers around the world. Just a few decades ago, a black-and-white television set would have been viewed as an extravagant luxury for many Chinese families. Now China has become the world's largest TV maker (including high-end plasma screen TVs). As China has OEM capabilities in many different industries as a result of FDI and has absorbed FDI through other means, China is determined to repeat the same process in every product line and to dominate in products involving ever higher levels of technology.

It is also no coincidence that China's unprecedented access to foreign technology made available by FDI has led to one of the world's serious commercial piracy problems. According to some accounts, China now accounts for up to 80% of all counterfeit and pirated goods in the world. Pirated goods from China now end up in markets around the world, and the problem shows no signs of slowing down. Commercial piracy in China and other countries has emerged as the crime of the twenty first century, rivaling drug trafficking in profits but with a much lower risk. The theft of intellectual property rights is a growing concern to MNEs. Many observers believe that China's past lack of respect for IP rights has provided China with a competitive advantage as China saves on the cost of paying for technology owned by MNEs. China's situation raises some fundamental questions concerning whether respect for IP is more beneficial in the long term for developing nations than piracy. We will return to examine this problem later in this casebook.

NOTES AND QUESTIONS

1.   The importance of MNEs in the development, creation, and transfer of intellectual property and the importance of intellectual property in world economic development raise several important questions. Given their size and power, do MNEs acquire social and ethical obligations? Do MNEs have any obligations to assist developing countries in the area of technology transfer and economic development?

2.   Given that MNEs own the bulk of the world's most commercially valuable intellectual property rights, what positions do you think they would

advocate in forums such as the WTO and TRIPS? How would the views of developing countries compare?

3. Should intellectual property be viewed in primarily economic terms? If so, do you think that international IP is a zero-sum game, meaning that some countries (net exporters of IP) will benefit at the expense of other countries (net importers of IP). Or is there a way for all countries to benefit economically from minimum standards of IP? How do welfare and public health fit into the equation, if at all?

C. THE "SYSTEM" OF INTERNATIONAL INTELLECTUAL PROPERTY

We now turn to an overview of the "system" of international intellectual property. Just as with the term "international intellectual property," calling the complex web of national IP laws and international and multilateral IP treaties around the world a "system" may be a little misleading. "System" may connote a level of uniformity or coherence that does not really apply to the territorial intellectual property laws around the world. It is probably more accurate to say that there are many intellectual property systems around the world.

With that caveat in mind, we still believe it is useful to think of laws related to international intellectual property as establishing an international system, given the over 150 countries that are subject to the Agreement on Trade Related Aspects of Intellectual Property (TRIPS) in the WTO. This international system of IP can be thought to be composed of two general types of laws: (1) individual national IP laws that establish IP rights within each nation's borders, and (2) international and multilateral IP treaties that establish the minimum standards of protection for those national IP laws. For each type of law, there typically is a body or bodies to administer certain tasks related to the IP law's enforcement. For example, for national IP laws, it is common to have copyright, patent, and trademark offices. For international IP treaties, the WTO administers the TRIPS Agreement, including disputes about a country's compliance with the minimum standards of TRIPS. This section discusses how these two parts of the system interrelate.

1. THE PRINCIPLE OF TERRITORIALITY IN A TRIPS WORLD

a. National IP Laws—Territorial in Scope

As a general matter, intellectual property rights are territorial in nature and are created, not by an international treaty, but by national law. The principle of territoriality can be viewed as a corollary to national sovereignty: a sovereign's laws, such as those creating intellectual property rights, have effect only within the territory of that nation. Thus, to take a simple example, imagine Alpha Company has developed a new invention.

If it wants to obtain patent protection in the U.S., Canada, and countries in Europe and Asia, Alpha Company must seek patents in each of those countries. Each patent would protect Alpha Company's invention from unauthorized copying within the country that granted the respective patent.

The principle of territoriality is part of a larger theory of the sovereignty of nations in the international arena, and can be traced to a more general theory of "jurisdiction to prescribe" that applies for all national laws. In this context, jurisdiction to prescribe refers to the basic authority of a nation to enact laws that are valid and binding as to the particular object of those laws.

The basic approach to prescriptive jurisdiction is an ancient one traceable to the seventeenth century Dutch theorist, Ulrich Huber. Under the modern approach, derived from Huber's theory, a nation has jurisdiction to prescribe valid and binding laws on the basis of the three principles of territoriality, nationality, and effects:

(1) Under the territoriality principle, every nation has the jurisdiction to enact laws that are valid and binding within its own territory;

(2) under the principle of nationality, every nation has jurisdiction to enact valid and binding laws with respect to its own nationals wherever in the world they may be located; and

(3) under the effects doctrine, a nation can, under some circumstances, enact valid and binding laws with respect to conduct outside of its territory that has a substantial effect within its territory.

See Restatement of Foreign Relations (Third) § 402. Of these principles, the first two, territoriality and nationality, are well accepted, whereas the third continues to be the subject of controversy. In particular, efforts by the United States to assert extraterritorial jurisdiction over a range of conduct occurring in foreign nations based upon an expanded view of the effects doctrine has caused controversy and consternation among European nations. In the area of intellectual property, jurisdiction to prescribe is most often asserted on the basis of the territoriality principle, although on occasion there may also be attempts to resort to some other basis of jurisdiction, such as the effects doctrine.

These basic principles, albeit with some variations and modifications, continue to establish the parameters for a nation's jurisdiction to prescribe all laws, including intellectual property laws. Note, however, territoriality is a principle that is not expressly required as a legal standard in any international IP agreement. It is founded more in the general principle of comity and mutual respect among nations than it is in a treaty obligation. This means that, both in theory and practice, a country could depart from the principle of territoriality and enforce its IP laws *extraterritorially*, without violating international law. But, by and large, countries follow a territorial approach in IP. The EU has been at the forefront of efforts to develop transnational IP rights that apply throughout many countries in one common market. These efforts have resulted in only mixed success, however, as will be discussed in subsequent chapters.

PROBLEM 1–2

Hyde Industries, based in Modesto, California, contacted Double Star, a manufacturing company in China known for making pirated products. Hyde asked Double Star to make copies of a popular computer game owned by another U.S. company, Microtel, for sale in international markets around the world outside the U.S. From the U.S., Hyde gave detailed information via e-mail and telephone to Double Star in China on where to procure the computer game, how to decode it, and how to reproduce it. However, all of Double Star's acts of copying the game occurred in China. Subsequently, Double Star sold large numbers of copies of the game in countries in Asia and Europe. When Microtel discovered Hyde's scheme, Microtel sued Hyde in federal district court in California alleging that Hyde violated Microtel's U.S. copyright in the game software by authorizing and providing the instructions for the illegal copying of its game. Microtel argues that the territoriality principle is satisfied because Hyde committed several acts in the United States that facilitated and contributed to the infringement of the copyright in its software by Double Star in China. What is the result? See *Subafilms* below.

SUBAFILMS, LTD. v. MGM–PATHE COMMUNICATIONS CO.

U.S. Court of Appeals for the Ninth Circuit.
24 F.3d 1088 (9th Cir. 1994) (en banc).

D.W. NELSON, CIRCUIT JUDGE:

In 1966, the musical group The Beatles, through Subafilms, Ltd., entered into a joint venture with the Hearst Corporation to produce the animated motion picture entitled "Yellow Submarine" (the "Picture"). Over the next year, Hearst, acting on behalf of the joint venture (the "Producer"), negotiated an agreement with United Artists Corporation ("UA") to distribute and finance the film. Separate distribution and financing agreements were entered into in May, 1967. Pursuant to these agreements, UA distributed the Picture in theaters beginning in 1968 and later on television.

In the early 1980s, with the advent of the home video market, UA entered into several licensing agreements to distribute a number of its films on videocassette. Although one company expressed interest in the Picture, UA refused to license "Yellow Submarine" because of uncertainty over whether home video rights had been granted by the 1967 agreements. Subsequently, in 1987, UA's successor company, MGM/UA Communications Co. ("MGM/UA"), over the Producer's objections, authorized its subsidiary MGM/UA Home Video, Inc. to distribute the Picture for the domestic home video market, and, pursuant to an earlier licensing agreement, notified Warner Bros., Inc. ("Warner") that the Picture had been cleared for international videocassette distribution. Warner, through its wholly owned subsidiary, Warner Home Video, Inc., in turn entered into agreements with third parties for distribution of the Picture on videocassette around the world.

In 1988, Subafilms and Hearst ("Appellees") brought suit against MGM/UA, Warner, and their respective subsidiaries (collectively the "Distributors" or "Appellants"), contending that the videocassette distribution of the Picture, both foreign and domestic, constituted copyright infringement and a breach of the 1967 agreements. The case was tried before a retired California Superior Court Judge acting as a special master. The special master found for Appellees on both claims, and against the Distributors on their counterclaim for fraud and reformation. Except for the award of prejudgment interest, which it reversed, the district court adopted all of the special master's factual findings and legal conclusions. Appellees were awarded $2,228,000.00 in compensatory damages, split evenly between the foreign and domestic home video distributions. In addition, Appellees received attorneys' fees and a permanent injunction that prohibited the Distributors from engaging in, or authorizing, any home video use of the Picture.

A panel of this circuit, in an unpublished disposition, affirmed the district court's judgment on the ground that both the domestic and foreign distribution of the Picture constituted infringement under the Copyright Act. With respect to the foreign distribution of the Picture, the panel concluded that it was bound by this court's prior decision in *Peter Starr Prod. Co. v. Twin Continental Films, Inc.*, 783 F.2d 1440 (9th Cir. 1986), which it held to stand for the proposition that, although " 'infringing actions that take place entirely outside the United States are not actionable' [under the Copyright Act, an] 'act of infringement within the United States' [properly is] alleged where the illegal *authorization* of international exhibitions *t[akes] place in the United States*." Because the Distributors had admitted that the initial authorization to distribute the Picture internationally occurred within the United States, the panel affirmed the district court's holding with respect to liability for extraterritorial home video distribution of the Picture.

We granted Appellants' petition for rehearing en banc to consider whether the panel's interpretation of *Peter Starr* conflicted with our subsequent decision in *Lewis Galoob Toys, Inc. v. Nintendo of Am., Inc.*, 964 F.2d 965 (9th Cir. 1992), *cert. denied*, 507 U.S. 985 (1993), which held that there could be no liability for authorizing a party to engage in an infringing act when the authorized "party's use of the work would not violate the Copyright Act," *id.* at 970.

Discussion

I. The Mere Authorization of Extraterritorial Acts of Infringement Does Not State a Claim under the Copyright Act

Since *Peter Starr* we have recognized that, when a party authorizes an activity *not* proscribed by one of the five section 106 clauses [of the

Copyright Act listing the exclusive rights of copyright], the authorizing party cannot be held liable as an infringer. In *Lewis Galoob*, we rejected the argument that "a party can unlawfully authorize another party to use a copyrighted work even if that party's use of the work would not violate the Copyright Act," *Lewis Galoob*, 964 F.2d at 970.

The apparent premise of *Lewis Galoob* was that the addition of the words "to authorize" in the Copyright Act was not meant to create a new form of liability for "authorization" that was divorced completely from the legal consequences of authorized conduct, but was intended to invoke the preexisting doctrine of contributory infringement. We agree.

Contributory infringement under the 1909 Act developed as a form of third party liability. Accordingly, there could be no liability for contributory infringement unless the authorized or otherwise encouraged activity itself could amount to infringement. As Professor Nimmer has observed:

> Accepting the proposition that a direct infringement is a prerequisite to third party liability, the further question arises whether the direct infringement on which liability is premised must take place within the United States. Given the undisputed axiom that United States copyright law has no extraterritorial application, it would seem to follow necessarily that a primary activity outside the boundaries of the United States, not constituting an infringement cognizable under the Copyright Act, cannot serve as the basis for holding liable under the Copyright Act one who is merely related to that activity within the United States.

3 Nimmer, *supra*, § 12.04[A][3][b], at 12–86.

II. The Extraterritoriality of the Copyright Act

Appellees additionally contend that, if liability for "authorizing" acts of infringement depends on finding that the authorized acts themselves are cognizable under the Copyright Act, this court should find that the United States copyright laws *do extend* to extraterritorial acts of infringement when such acts "result in adverse effects within the United States." Appellees buttress this argument with the contention that failure to apply the copyright laws extraterritorially in this case will have a disastrous effect on the American film industry, and that other remedies, such as suits in foreign jurisdictions or the application of foreign copyright laws by American courts, are not realistic alternatives.

We are not persuaded by Appellees' parade of horribles. More fundamentally, however, we are unwilling to overturn over eighty years of consistent jurisprudence on the extraterritorial reach of the copyright laws without further guidance from Congress.

There is no clear expression of congressional intent in either the 1976 Act or other relevant enactments to alter the preexisting extraterritoriality doctrine. Indeed, the *Peter Starr* court itself recognized the continuing application of the principle that "infringing actions that take place entirely outside the United States are not actionable in United States federal courts." *Peter Starr*, 783 F.2d at 1442.

Appellees, however, rely on dicta in a recent decision of the District of Columbia Circuit for the proposition that the presumption against extraterritorial application of U.S. laws may be "overcome" when denying such application would "result in adverse effects within the United States." *Environmental Defense Fund, Inc. v. Massey*, 986 F.2d 528, 531 (D.C. Cir. 1993). However, the *Massey* court did not state that extraterritoriality would be *demanded* in such circumstances, but that "the *presumption* is *generally* not *applied* where the failure to extend the scope of the statute to a foreign setting will result in adverse [domestic] effects." *Id.* at 531 (emphasis added). In each of the statutory schemes discussed by the *Massey* court, the ultimate touchstone of extraterritoriality consisted of an ascertainment of congressional intent; courts did not rest *solely* on the consequences of a failure to give a statutory scheme extraterritorial application. More importantly, as the *Massey* court conceded application of the presumption is particularly appropriate when "[i]t serves to protect against unintended clashes between our laws and those of other nations which could result in international discord," *Aramco*, 499 U.S. at 248.

We believe this latter factor is decisive in the case of the Copyright Act, and fully justifies application of the *Aramco* presumption even assuming *arguendo* that "adverse effects" within the United States "generally" would require a plenary inquiry into congressional intent. At the time that the international distribution of the videocassettes in this case took place, the United States was a member of the Universal Copyright Convention ("UCC"), and, in 1988, the United States acceded to the Berne Convention for the Protection of Literary and Artistic Works ("Berne Conv."). The central thrust of these multilateral treaties is the principle of "national treatment." A work of an American national first generated in America will receive the same protection in a foreign nation as that country accords to the works of its own nationals. *See* UCC Art. II; Berne Conv. Art. V. *See generally* 1 International Copyright Law and Practice, Intr. § 5, at 145–74 (Paul E. Geller & Melville B. Nimmer eds., 1993) [hereinafter Geller & Nimmer]; Stephen M. Stewart, International Copyright and Neighboring Rights 37–48 (2d ed. 1989). Although the treaties do not expressly discuss choice-of-law rules, *see* Geller & Nimmer, *supra,* Intr. § 6, at 181–83, 189, it is commonly acknowledged that the national treatment principle implicates a rule of territoriality. *See London Film Prods. Ltd. v. Intercontinental Communications, Inc.*, 580 F. Supp. 47, 50 n.6 (S.D.N.Y. 1984); *see also* 3 Nimmer, *supra,* § 17.05, at 17–39 ("The applicable law is the copyright law of the state in which the infringement occurred, not that of the state of which the author is a national or in which the work was first published."). *See generally* Geller & Nimmer, *supra,* Intr. § 6, at 182; Stewart, *supra,* at 46–47. Indeed, a recognition of this principle appears implicit in Congress's statements in acceding to Berne that "[t]he primary mechanism for discouraging discriminatory treatment of foreign copyright claimants is the principle of national treatment," H.R. Rep. No. 609, 100th Cong., 2d Sess. 43, and that adherence to Berne will require "careful due regard for the [ ] values" of other member nations, *id.* at 20.

In light of the *Aramco* Court's concern with preventing international discord, we think it inappropriate for the courts to act in a manner that might disrupt Congress's efforts to secure a more stable international intellectual property regime unless Congress otherwise clearly has expressed its intent. The application of American copyright law to acts of infringement that occur entirely overseas clearly could have this effect. Extraterritorial application of American law would be contrary to the spirit of the Berne Convention, and might offend other member nations by effectively displacing their law in circumstances in which previously it was assumed to govern. Consequently, an extension of extraterritoriality might undermine Congress's objective of achieving " 'effective and harmonious' copyright laws among all nations." House Report, *supra*, at 20. Indeed, it might well send the signal that the United States does not believe that the protection accorded by the laws of other member nations is adequate, which would undermine two other objectives of Congress in joining the convention: "strengthen[ing] the credibility of the U.S. position in trade negotiations with countries where piracy is not uncommon" and "rais[ing] the like[li]hood that other nations will enter the Convention." S. Rep. 352, 100th Cong., 2d Sess. 4–5, *reprinted* in 1988 U.S.C.C.A.N., 3706, 3709–10.

Accordingly, because an extension of the extraterritorial reach of the Copyright Act by the courts would in all likelihood disrupt the international regime for protecting intellectual property that Congress so recently described as essential to furthering the goal of protecting the works of American authors abroad, we conclude that the *Aramco* presumption must be applied. Because the presumption has not been overcome, we reaffirm that the United States copyright laws do not reach acts of infringement that take place entirely abroad. It is for Congress, and not the courts, to take the initiative in this field.

Conclusion

We hold that the mere authorization of acts of infringement that are not cognizable under the United States copyright laws because they occur entirely outside of the United States does not state a claim for infringement under the Copyright Act. *Peter Starr* is overruled insofar as it held to the contrary. Accordingly, we vacate Part III of the panel's disposition, in which it concluded that the international distribution of the film constituted a violation of the United States copyright laws. We also vacate that portion of the disposition that affirmed the damage award based on foreign distribution of the film and the panel's affirmance of the award of attorneys' fees. Finally, we vacate the district court's grant of injunctive relief insofar as it was based on the premise that the Distributors had violated the United States copyright laws through authorization of the foreign distribution of the Picture on videocassettes.

Vacated in Part and Remanded.

NOTES AND QUESTIONS

1. In *Subafilms*, were the plaintiffs able to assert that unauthorized foreign distribution breached U.S. copyright law? If not, do the plaintiffs have any other recourse?

2. The right of distribution is a well accepted right under the copyright law of most nations. As a result, foreign distribution, while not a violation of U.S. law, would likely be a violation of foreign copyright law of the country where the alleged infringement occurred. Assume, as was most likely the case, that Subafilms would be able to assert a violation of its copyright under foreign law. If so, why did Subafilms hope to assert a violation of United States copyright law?

3. What if *Subafilms* came out the other way and the U.S. took the position that its copyright law governed foreign conduct as long as there was some nexus to the U.S., such as an act of authorization in the U.S. for distribution of copies abroad. Do you think foreign nations would disagree with this approach? What if all countries agreed that the alleged activity was infringing under their own respective laws—would there be any harm to international relations if one country applied its law extraterritorially where all interested countries agreed that infringement had occurred?

4. Could United Artists have drafted a better contract with Hearst in 1967 to avoid the problem it faced in 1987? Or do unknown future technologies present insurmountable problems for any contract? *See* Jeffrey K. Joyner, *Future Technology Clauses: Would Their Lack of Compensation Have Discouraged Shakespeare's Creativity and Denied Society's Access to His Works in New Media?*, 31 Sw. U. L. REV. 575, 612–19 (2002) (lack of uniform approach in U.S. courts).

5. *Extraterritorial remedies?* Sometimes U.S. courts may be more receptive to imposing damages or an injunction on an infringer for both domestic *and* related foreign activities, even if the foreign activities do not constitute infringement under domestic law. Is this approach consistent with the principle of territoriality? Is there a difference between liability and remedies?

6. *Trademark cases.* U.S. courts have recognized trademark claims under the Lanham Act for extraterritorial activity with substantial effects in the United States. *See, e.g., Steele v. Bulova Watch Co.*, 344 U.S. 280, 281 (1952). What might explain the difference in approach compared to *Subafilms*?

b. Territoriality and Exhaustion of Intellectual Property Rights

National laws not only create IP rights but also determine how such rights should terminate. The principle of territoriality is tested when countries decide the issue of exhaustion, which often involves some extraterritorial activity, particularly in today's global market. We introduce this subject here, but will discuss the topic in detail in Chapter 6. For now, it is sufficient to recognize that exhaustion can be viewed as an aspect of how a nation decides the territorial scope of its IP rights.

"Exhaustion" of rights relates to the termination of distributional and importation rights over a lawfully sold item that is protected by IP. Exhaustion is also called the "first sale doctrine" because exhaustion typically arises after the item in question has been first sold in the stream of commerce. For example, suppose that Alpha Company publishes a book in Country A. Alpha has a copyright in the book under the laws of Country A and can commercially exploit its book by selling copies of the book. Under the laws of most nations, if Alpha sells copies of the book within a country, then Alpha's distribution and importation rights over the sold copies are exhausted or extinguished in that country. Lawful owners of copies of Alpha's book can freely sell, rent, or distribute their copies of the book to others. Alpha cannot prevent the second sale because Alpha's distributional rights to the sold copies have been exhausted. The first sale doctrine explains why libraries can lend books and movie rental businesses can rent movies without copyright permission.

Be careful to distinguish between the material object (e.g., a hard copy of a book) in which IP is embodied and the general exclusive rights of IP. Exhaustion applies to the particular material objects sold by the IP owner, not to the IP owner's general exclusive rights of IP. Alpha still has a valid copyright in the book, including the right of distribution, and can prohibit third parties from violating those rights, such as by distributing unauthorized copies of the book. But once Alpha sells copies of the book, its right to distribute and import those sold copies are deemed to be exhausted. The rationale for this approach is that the IP owner has reaped the benefit of the economic exploitation of the particular product from the first sale of the item and allowing the IP owner to control further sales of the same item would be anticompetitive.

Most, if not all, nations recognize a principle of exhaustion after the first sale authorized by the IP owner within the domestic country—i.e., domestic first sales—even when different IP rights, such as patents, copyrights, or trademarks, are involved. However, countries have sharply disagreed over whether exhaustion also occurs with a foreign first sale of a product protected by IP. Under *national exhaustion*, only domestic first sales give rise to exhaustion. Under *regional exhaustion*, all authorized first sales within a region—such as in the EU—give rise to exhaustion. Under *international exhaustion*, all authorized first sales anywhere give rise to exhaustion. Some countries have even adopted different approaches to this question depending on whether patents, copyrights, or trademarks are involved.

The WTO did not resolve these differences. Reflecting the diversity of views on exhaustion and the inability of WTO members to come to a consensus, Article 6 of TRIPS states: "[N]othing in this Agreement shall be used to address the issue of exhaustion of intellectual property rights."

Exhaustion rules have huge practical importance. They bear on whether a country allows so-called parallel imports or gray market goods. Gray market goods are genuine goods (made by the authority of the IP owner) that are manufactured for sale in a foreign market but that are then imported into the home market of the IP owner.

> Illustration 1–1. Alpha has an IP right from Country A in a product that it manufactures and sells in different countries. Alpha sells copies of the product to Buyer in Country B. The copies were made outside of Country A for sale in Country B. Buyer, a wholesale distributor, wishes to import the product into Country A, in order to sell it at prices cheaper than Alpha's price. Alpha now wishes to block Buyer's parallel importation of the product into Country A, where Alpha already sells the product at a higher price.

Whether a country will allow Alpha to block Buyer's importation depends on the country's view of exhaustion. Under national exhaustion, some countries may allow Alpha to block the importation on the ground that a first sale abroad does not create exhaustion. Under international exhaustion, the sale abroad constitutes exhaustion, so Alpha will not be able to block the parallel import of Alpha's goods from Country B.

Illustration 1–1 is a simple transaction, but in this age of globalization and multinational companies, scenarios involving exhaustion can be quite complex. Consider Illustration 1–2:

> Illustration 1–2. Alpha manufactures its products in the United States and also in several countries abroad, in part through its licensees. Alpha has secured various IP rights for its products in many countries, including Country B. Alpha authorizes a foreign company located in Country B to use Alpha's IP rights recognized by Country B to manufacture the products for sale in Country B. However, taking advantage of currency fluctuations, Wholesale Distributor buys Alpha's products in Country B and then attempts to export the products to buyers in Country A. When Alpha learns about the Distributor's plan, Alpha moves to block the parallel importation of the products into Country A by asserting Alpha's IP rights in Country A.

This scenario is common in international business and trade today. Indeed, some variation of this scenario is usually involved in almost every case involving exhaustion for MNEs. The goods that the Distributor seeks to import into Country A are commonly referred to as gray market goods or parallel imports. The issue is whether an importer in Country A can import the gray market goods without the prior consent of Alpha, the IP owner in Country A. Specifically, did the sale of the goods in the foreign country, Country B, exhaust Alpha's distributional rights over those goods in Country A?

Countries disagree over how this issue should be resolved. The answer may depend upon a number of factors beyond the place of first sale, including whether Alpha and the foreign manufacture are affiliated corporate entities or under a common control. Moreover, a country may apply a different rule depending whether the IP right is a patent, trademark, or copyright. The resolution of this issue is complicated by extraterritorial elements because certain acts, such as the sale or manufacture of the goods, have occurred abroad. The extraterritorial elements make the resolution of the exhaustion issue controversial, leading to a variety of approaches. We will study the differences in Chapter 6.

NOTES AND QUESTIONS

1. If a primary goal of the TRIPS Agreement is "to reduce distortions and impediments to international trade," what rule of exhaustion would best serve that goal? National, regional, or international exhaustion?

2. What rule of exhaustion do you think most IP owners prefer? Why?

3. Does it make sense for a country to have different exhaustion rules for different IP, even when dealing with the same item? For example, what if a country applied national exhaustion to copyrighted works, but international exhaustion to trademarked goods? How might trademark owners evade international exhaustion in that scenario? *See Omega v. Costco*, 541 F.3d 982 (9th Cir. 2008), aff'd by an equally divided Court, ___ U.S. ___, 131 S. Ct. 565 (2010).

4. *Contractual restraints.* One major area of controversy related to exhaustion is the extent to which IP owners can override exhaustion rules by imposing contracts or licenses that attempt to limit subsequent sales of its products. Should these contracts be enforceable? *See* Herbert Hovenkamp, *Post–Sale Restraints and Competitive Harm: The First Sale Doctrine in Perspective*, 66 N.Y.U. ANN. SURV. AM. L. 487 (2011).

c. IP Treaties and the World of TRIPS

So how do international IP treaties bear on or relate to national, territorial IP laws? International IP treaties establish basic minimum standards that member states must implement through domestic legislation, and typically require each country to follow the principle of national treatment (discussed in the next section).

Two of the oldest IP treaties are (i) the Paris Convention that applies to patents, trademarks, and industrial property (i.e., the International Convention for the Protection of Industrial Property), originally signed in Paris in 1883 and revised most recently in Stockholm in 1967; and (ii) the Berne Convention for the Protection of Literary and Artistic Works originally signed in 1886 and most recently revised in Paris in 1971, which applies to copyrights. Both of these treaties require national treatment and certain minimum standards of IP protection for their members, although as we shall see, the Paris Convention established fewer minimum standards. Most nations treat the Paris and Berne Conventions as non-self-executing treaties requiring implementation through the enactment of domestic legislation. Both of these treaties are administered by the World Intellectual Property Organization (WIPO), a specialized agency of the United Nations located in Geneva, Switzerland. We will discuss the role of WIPO and other important international institutions later in this chapter.

Both the Paris and Berne Conventions have now been superseded in importance by the Agreement on Trade Related Aspects of Intellectual Property (TRIPS), one of the major disciplines of the WTO established in 1994. Unlike Paris and Berne, TRIPS expressly links intellectual property to trade issues. Adherence to TRIPS is a basic requirement of WTO entry, although members are given different timelines to implement the TRIPS obligations depending upon their stage of economic development. TRIPS incorporates the major provisions of the Paris and Berne Conventions and adds numerous other minimum standards of its own. TRIPS is the first international treaty to establish the minimal substantive standards comprehensively for seven major categories of rights: copyright, trademarks, geographical indications, industrial designs, patents, integrated circuit designs, and trade secrets. But perhaps the crowning achievement of TRIPS over other IP agreements is its enforcement: TRIPS is subject to an elaborate Dispute Settlement Body under the auspices of the WTO. Thus, for the first time, international IP obligations can be enforced against a country in violation of its obligation with the ultimate penalty of trade sanctions under the WTO. TRIPS has added significantly to the international harmonization of intellectual property rights.

International IP treaties and agreements, such as the Patent Cooperation Treaty and the Madrid Protocol, also provide uniform procedures to simplify or make easier the obtaining of IP rights around the world. In the absence of such an international agreement, an intellectual property owner would have to comply with the laws of each nation in order to obtain intellectual property rights within a particular national legal system. Such a process entails a great deal of time and expense for filing different applications in different languages, possibly with different requirements. International treaties facilitate the process of obtaining intellectual property rights within national legal systems by streamlining the process of filing many different applications, or, in the case of copyright, prohibiting applications and filings altogether. We will revisit these issues in later chapters.

PROBLEM 1–3

You have been selected to be the Minister of Intellectual Property for Developing Country A. The President has asked you how Developing Country A should view international law, particularly the TRIPS Agreement. Developing Country A is a member of the WTO and has already signed onto the TRIPS Agreement. Should an international agreement, such as the TRIPS Agreement, be viewed as embodying an international contract that must be followed by member countries in all cases? Or should a country view the TRIPS Agreement in a more utilitarian fashion—following it or departing from it when it serves the country's self-interest? The President is particularly intrigued by the theory of Professors Jack Goldsmith and Eric Posner, who argue that international law can best be explained as "states acting rationally to maximize their interests, given their perceptions of the interests of other states and the distribution of state power." Jack L. Goldsmith & Eric A. Posner, *The Limits of International Law* 3 (2005). Under their theory, there is no moral obligation to abide by international law, *id.* at 14. Countries act in their own self-interest in deciding whether or not to abide by international law. However, weaker states simply do not have the same "freedom of action" to violate their WTO obligations as do powerful states, such as the U.S., EU, and Japan, *id.* at 162. What do you think of this theory? Would you recommend the President to follow or reject it for Developing Country A? Should Developing Country A choose not to abide by TRIPS if noncompliance would serve Developing Country A's own interest?

NOTES AND QUESTIONS

1. *Treaties as Public International Law.* International treaties belong to the field of public international law, meaning the system of laws governing the relations of nation-states, intergovernmental organizations, and, to a limited extent, the private conduct of individuals. Under the traditional view, international law is superior to national laws and where there is a conflict, international law should prevail over the individual laws of nation-states. While this principle is accepted in theory, in practice nations often find reasons not to subjugate their own laws to international legal norms in the case of conflict. In the U.S., for example, the government could not enforce an international law—even if agreed to by the Executive and ratified by the Senate—if the international law violated the U.S. Constitution.

The field of public international law traditionally consisted of treaties and customary international law. Treaties have been viewed as legally binding contracts between states. Customary international law involves states, in and by their international practice, creating rules among themselves by engaging in practices with a sense of legal obligation. Whereas treaties are evidence of an explicit agreement between nations to be bound by contract, customary international law is treated as a form of implied consent to be bound.

One other noteworthy development is that public international law was traditionally concerned with political issues, diplomatic activity, and public rights (such as determination of statehood, the rights of peoples to self-determination and independence, the justified and unjustified uses of force, and the recognition of governments). One of the hallmarks of the late twentieth century is the use of public international treaties to govern economic rights, such as intellectual property, that have direct impact on private actors, such as MNEs, in the field of international business. While IP has traditionally been viewed as a form of private law, regulating private actors, the treaties that regulate how nations frame their IP laws is a form of public international law.

2. *Bilateral, Plurilateral, and Multilateral Treaties.* Treaties can be *bilateral*, i.e., an agreement between two states, or *multilateral*, i.e., an agreement among many states. In between are *plurilateral* treaties that involve more than two states, but less than the total number of states in a given multilateral treaty. Multilateral treaties can be further categorized into two types: an *international* treaty that applies to a substantial number of countries around the world, and a *regional* treaty that applies to a more

limited number of countries. In the area of intellectual property, most of the applicable laws that we will be considering are multilateral treaties. In some areas, such as those relating to rights of developing countries to their indigenous culture, customary international law may also be applicable.

3. *The Force of International Law Under U.S. Law.* Each country must decide how an international treaty to which it has agreed becomes law in its own borders. The U.S. Constitution declares that treaties of the United States, along with the Constitution and United States law, are to be the "supreme Law of the Land." *See* U.S. CONST. art. VI. Long ago, the U.S. Supreme Court also established that customary international law is part of federal law. *See The Paquete Habana*, 175 U.S. 677, 700 (1900). While international law is thus considered to be a type of federal law, the Supreme Court established an important distinction between treaties and other types of federal law.

In *Foster v. Neilson*, 27 U.S. (2 Pet.) 253 (1829), Chief Justice Marshall established a distinction between (i) self-executing treaties and (ii) non-self-executing treaties. If the U.S. agrees to and approves a self-executing treaty, the treaty itself establishes federal law in the United States, without the need for any further action. *Id.* at 314. If the U.S. agrees to and approves a non-self-executing treaty, the treaty must await the enactment of implementing domestic legislation by Congress. *Id.* A non-self-executing treaty creates an obligation on the part of a contracting state to enact domestic legislation that implements the rights and obligations contained in the treaty. In other words, in the case of a self-executing treaty, a United States court is applying international law in the treaty that has been adopted as federal law, whereas in the case of a non-self-executing treaty, a United States court is applying federal statutory law, i.e., the implementing legislation. To determine whether a treaty is self-executing or not, courts typically examine the intent of states that are parties to the treaty, to see if the language of the treaty indicates whether it is aimed directly at the courts ("whenever it operates of itself") or Congress to enact legislation (whenever the treaty terms "import a contract" to be executed). *Id.* at 314.

To complicate matters even further, the United States recognizes a distinction between a treaty, which must be approved by two thirds of the Senate, and a congressional-executive agreement, which can be passed by a simple majority of Congress. The United States considers TRIPS to be a congressional-executive agreement, which was passed by Congress and implemented through domestic legislation. The constitutionality of the congressional-executive agreement has been much debated by U.S. legal scholars. *Compare* Bruce Ackerman & David Golove, *Is NAFTA Constitutional?*, 108 HARV. L. REV. 799 (1995) (constitutional because of unwritten amendment to Constitution with modern practice and "constitutional moment") *with* Lawrence H. Tribe, *Taking Text and Structure Seriously: Reflections on Free–Form Method in Constitutional Interpretation*, 108 HARV. L. REV. 1221 (1995) (unconstitutional violation of Treaty Power). The Supreme Court has not considered the issue.

4. A principal goal of the United States and other leading industrialized countries is the global standardization and harmonization of intellectual

property laws and procedures through the promulgation of treaties. TRIPS represents a major achievement towards these goals. Why would the U.S. go to such efforts to secure an international IP agreement such as TRIPS? What countries do you think might take a view contrary to the U.S. approach?

2. THE PRINCIPLE OF NATIONAL TREATMENT

PROBLEM 1–4

Country A has a copyright law that grants (i) a term of protection of life of the author plus 50 years to domestic authors, but (ii) a term of protection of life of the author plus 100 years to foreign authors for their works. The purpose of the latter provision is to attract foreign direct investment to Country A by providing incentives to foreign authors and multi-national corporations to market their copyrighted works in Country A. Does this law violate the principle of national treatment in TRIPS? Read the following discussion and TRIPS Art. 3(1).

* * *

The principle of territoriality raises a basic problem: how can a national who obtained IP rights under the laws of its domestic country secure IP rights in foreign countries? Because the principle of territoriality not only empowers but also limits a nation in its exercise of its lawmaking authority, the principle also operates as a potential hurdle to the international recognition of intellectual property rights. In essence, each country could decide *not* to protect any foreigners within its border. And, under a strict territorial approach, foreign countries would be powerless to stop such discrimination against their own nationals.

> Illustration 1–3. Alicia is an owner of intellectual property rights obtained and recognized under the laws of Country A. Bridget, who lives in Country B, is making unauthorized copies of Alicia's work in Country B. In the absence of an international treaty, Alicia's intellectual property rights are limited by the principle of territoriality. Country B is not required to recognize Alicia's intellectual property rights obtained in Country A or to provide Alicia with any protection under Country B's intellectual property laws. Country B can choose to allow Bridget to make unauthorized copies of Alicia's work.

As Illustration 1–3 indicates, the principle of territoriality recognizes that a nation has legitimate law-making authority within its territory and that the nation's territorial boundaries also establish a limit to the legal effectiveness of those laws. The limitations imposed by the principle of territoriality created a need on the part of nations to arrive at a method for recognizing intellectual property rights for a work across national boundaries. In Europe, in the eighteenth century, the sale of books began to cross national boundaries and unauthorized copying became a serious problem. As a result, authors began to seek international protection for their rights.

The first international copyright treaties, which were bilateral, were based upon a principle of *material reciprocity.* Under material reciprocity, Country B would grant Country A's intellectual property owners (e.g., Alicia) the same protection that Country A would grant to intellectual property owners of Country B (e.g., Bridget). This system based on a principle of material reciprocity and bilateral treaties proved to be cumbersome and ineffective for two reasons. First, this system required national courts to interpret foreign laws of other countries. For example, the courts of Country B would need to determine the scope of protection afforded by the laws of Country A to nationals of Country B—which is an issue of foreign law—in order to determine the level of reciprocity to be extended. The determination of foreign law is a complicated task, particularly if a court must interpret laws in a foreign language that were developed under a different legal system with different traditions.

Second, negotiating a separate bilateral treaty with each country in which protection was sought proved to be inefficient. It not only required laborious negotiations but also presumed that all nations would be willing to sign such bilateral agreements, even if they benefited by not granting foreigners any intellectual property rights. For example, in the 19th century, France grew frustrated with the international piracy of its books in Holland and Belgium, both of which refused to enter into a bilateral treaty with France.

Some nations adopted, as an alternative to the principle of material reciprocity, the principle of *national treatment*. France, a leading exporter of books and literature, was the first nation to adopt a principle of national treatment. In 1852, France issued a decree that rendered illegal in France copyright infringement of all works, as well as the sale or trafficking in any illegally copied works, regardless of where the works originated from. This decree established a principle of national treatment: any work of any origin was entitled to the same protection that French works received under French copyright law. This bold move by France marked the beginning of wide acceptance of the national treatment principle. France soon became a leader in forming international copyright treaties and sparked an interest in Europe in forming an international system of intellectual property rights protection.

The principle of national treatment is now firmly established as a basic principle in all areas of international trade, not just in intellectual property law. The principle of national treatment is a principle of non-discrimination, requiring each nation to accord treatment to foreign nationals that is at least as favorable as that accorded to its own nationals. For example, Article 3(1) of TRIPS provides in relevant part:

> Each Member shall accord to the nationals of other Members treatment no less favourable than that it accords to its own nationals with regard to the protection of intellectual property . . .

Here is an example of how national treatment under TRIPS operates:

Illustration 1–4. Alicia is an owner of intellectual property rights obtained and recognized under the laws of Country A. Bridget, who lives in Country B, is making unauthorized copies of Alicia's work in Country B. Countries A and B have agreed to apply the principle of national treatment to intellectual property rights belonging to the nationals of each country. Under national treatment, Country B must afford Alicia at least the same level of protection for her intellectual property rights as it would afford B's own nationals. If Country B's own nationals would be entitled to prevent Bridget from unauthorized copying, then Alicia must be given at least the same right to prevent Bridget from copying Alicia's intellectual property.

Consequently, the effect of national treatment in Country B is that the foreign national is assimilated to the national laws of Country B. In other words, Alicia, a foreign national, is treated by Country B as if Alicia were one of B's own nationals. Alicia can therefore assert a claim of IP to the same (if not greater) extent as Country B's own nationals can within its borders.

The principle of national treatment has, at least in theory, a number of advantages over the principle of material reciprocity. First, national treatment applies without regard to a condition of reciprocity. It would not matter in Illustration 1–4 that Country A did not provide nationals of Country B with protection. The sole inquiry for national treatment is whether Country B accords foreign nationals at least the same level of protection that it accords to its own nationals. As we shall see later, to avoid the problem of no protection being offered in a particular country, the major IP conventions also typically require some minimum standards of protection. Second, the national treatment principle, unlike the principle of material reciprocity, does not require national courts to apply or interpret foreign law. In Illustration 1–4, the courts of Country B will apply the laws of Country B to Alicia's intellectual property rights and will not need to engage in complicated analysis of foreign law to determine a "reciprocal" level of protection under Country A's law. As noted above, these advantages exist "at least in theory." Later in this chapter, we shall see that the contours of national treatment are not without some debate and controversy, particularly as it relates to choice of law issues. For now consider the following case, which provides a good illustration of the national treatment principle in the European Union under EU law.

PHIL COLLINS v. IMTRAT HANDELSGESELLSCHAFT GmbH

European Court of Justice.
[1993] ECR I–5145, C–92/92 (October 20, 1993).

By order of 4 March 1992, received at the Court on the following 23 March, the Landgericht Munchen I (Regional Court Munich I) referred to the Court for a preliminary ruling under Article 177 of the EEC Treaty two questions on the interpretation of the first paragraph of Article 7 of the EEC Treaty.* The questions were raised in proceedings between Phil Collins, singer and composer of British nationality, and a phonogram distributor, Imtrat Handelsgesellschaft mbH ("Imtrat") [meaning Imtrat Trading Company, a limited liability company], relating to the marketing, in Germany, of a compact disk containing the recording, made without the singer's consent, of a concert given in the United States.

---

* The Article has been renumbered three times: first, as Article 6 in the Treaty Establishing the European Community (1993); second, as Article 12 in the Treaty of Amsterdam (1997); and, third, as Article 18 of the Treaty on the Functioning of European Union (TFEU) (2009). Article 18 now states: "Within the scope of application of this Treaty, and without prejudice to any special provisions contained therein, any discrimination on grounds of nationality shall be prohibited." *Ed.*

According to Paragraphs 96(1) and 125(1) of the German Copyright Act of 9 September 1965 (Urheberrechtsgesetz, hereinafter "the UrhG") performing artists who have German nationality enjoy the protection granted by Paragraphs 73 to 84 of the UrhG in respect of all their performances. In particular, they may prohibit the distribution of those performances which are reproduced without their permission, irrespective of the place of performance. In contrast, the effect of the provisions of Paragraph 125(2) to (6) of the UrhG, relating to foreign performers, as interpreted by the Bundesgerichtshof [Federal Supreme Court**] and the Bundesverfassungsgericht [Federal Constitutional Court***], is that those performers cannot avail themselves of the provisions of Paragraph 96(1), where the performance was given outside Germany.

Phil Collins applied to the Landgericht Muenchen I for an interim injunction prohibiting the marketing of the compact disk in question. It questioned, however, the conformity of those national provisions with the principle of non-discrimination laid down by the first paragraph of Article 7 of the Treaty. [T]he Landgericht Muenchen I stayed the proceedings and referred the following questions to the Court for a preliminary ruling[.] [These] questions concern the first paragraph of Article 7 of the Treaty which lays down the general principle of non-discrimination on the grounds of nationality. As is expressly provided in that paragraph, the prohibition of discrimination contained in it applies only within the scope of application of the Treaty.

The questions referred to the Court must accordingly be regarded as seeking, essentially, to ascertain:

—whether copyright and related rights fall within the scope of application of the Treaty within the meaning of the first paragraph of Article 7, and consequently, if the general principle of non-discrimination laid down by that article applies to those rights

—if so, whether the first paragraph of Article 7 of the Treaty precludes the legislation of a Member State from denying to authors or performers from other Member States, and those claiming under them, the right, accorded by that legislation to the nationals of that State, to prohibit the marketing, in its national territory, of a phonogram manufactured without their consent, where the performance was given outside its national territory[.]

The application of the provisions of the Treaty to copyright and related rights

As Community law now stands, and in the absence of Community provisions harmonizing national laws, it is for the Member States to establish the conditions and detailed rules for the protection of literary and artistic property, subject to observance of the applicable international conventions.

** The highest federal court in Germany for courts of ordinary jurisdiction, covering basic civil and criminal matters. *Ed.*

*** The specialized federal court in Germany for constitutional matters. *Ed.*

The specific subject-matter of those rights, as governed by national legislation, is to ensure the protection of the moral and economic rights of their holders. The protection of moral rights enables authors and performers, in particular, to object to any distortion, mutilation or other modification of a work which would be prejudicial to their honour or reputation. Copyright and related rights are also economic in nature, in that they confer the right to exploit commercially the marketing of the protected work, particularly in the form of licences granted in return for payment of royalties.

As the Court pointed out in the last-mentioned judgment, whilst the commercial exploitation of copyright is a source of remuneration for the owner, it also constitutes a form of control of marketing, exercisable by the owner, the copyright management societies and the grantees of licences. From this point of view, the commercial exploitation of copyright raises the same problems as does the commercial exploitation of any other industrial and commercial property right.

Like the other industrial and commercial property rights, the exclusive rights conferred by literary and artistic property are by their nature such as to affect trade in goods and services and also competitive relationships within the Community. For that reason, and as the Court has consistently held, those rights, although governed by national legislation, are subject to the requirements of the Treaty and therefore fall within its scope of application.

It follows that copyright and related rights, which by reason in particular of their effects on intra-Community trade in goods and services, fall within the scope of application of the Treaty, are necessarily subject to the general principle of non-discrimination laid down by the first paragraph of Article 7 of the Treaty, without there even being any need to connect them with the specific provisions of Articles 30, 36, 59, and 66 of the Treaty. Accordingly, it should be stated in reply to the question put to the Court that copyright and related rights fall within the scope of application of the Treaty within the meaning of the first paragraph of Article 7 the general principle of non-discrimination laid down by that article therefore applies to those rights.

Discrimination within the meaning of the first paragraph of Article 7 of the Treaty

Imtrat and Patricia maintain that the differentiation which is made between German nationals and nationals of the other Member States in the cases referred to it by the national courts is objectively justified by the disparities which exist between national laws and by the fact that not all Member States have yet acceded to the Rome Convention [for the Protection of Performers, Producers of Phonograms and Broadcasting Organizations]. That differentiation is not, in those circumstances, contrary to the first paragraph of Article 7 of the Treaty.

It is undisputed that Article 7 is not concerned with any disparities in treatment or the distortions which may result, for the persons and undertakings subject to the jurisdiction of the Community, from divergences existing between the laws of the various Member States, so long as those laws affect all persons subject to them, in accordance with objective criteria and without regard to their nationality.

Thus, contrary to what Imtrat and Patricia maintain, neither the disparities between the national laws relating to the protection of copyright and related rights nor the fact that not all Member States have yet acceded to the Rome Convention can justify a breach of the principle of non-discrimination laid down by the first paragraph of Article 7 of the Treaty.

In prohibiting "any discrimination on the grounds of nationality," Article 7 of the Treaty requires, on the contrary, that persons in a situation governed by Community law be placed on a completely equal footing with nationals of the Member State concerned. In so far as that principle is applicable, it therefore precludes a Member State from making the grant of an exclusive right subject to the requirement that the person concerned be a national of that State.

Accordingly, it should be stated in reply to the question put to the Court that the first paragraph of Article 7 of the Treaty must be interpreted as precluding legislation of a Member State from denying, in certain circumstances, to authors and performers from other Member States, and those claiming under them, the right, accorded by that legislation the nationals of that State, to prohibit the marketing, in its national territory of a phonogram manufactured without their consent, where the performance was given outside its national territory.

NOTES AND QUESTIONS

1. Why did the provisions of Paragraph 125(2) to (6) of the UrhG, the German copyright law relating to foreign performers, violate the principle of national treatment under the EEC Treaty?

2. The *Phil Collins* case involved the application of the EU national treatment principle, which requires EU countries to treat all EU nationals the same. The EU national treatment principle does not prohibit discrimination against non-EU nationals, however. How is the EU national treatment similar to national treatment in TRIPS Article 3(1)? How is it different?

3. *Rome Convention.* The Rome Convention requires national treatment for the protection of performers' performances in other member states of Rome (among other situations). Rome Conv. art. 4. Apparently, as discussed by the ECJ, German law protected performances of foreign nationals only if they occurred in Germany, while protecting the performances of German nationals regardless of where they occurred. Germany has been a member of the Rome Convention since 1966. Was German law consistent with the Rome Convention's requirement of national treatment if foreign nationals—even those from other Rome countries—could not receive protection from unauthorized recordings of performances that took place in other Rome countries? See Rome Conv. art. 4(a). We will revisit the Rome Convention in Chapter 2.

4. How should national treatment be viewed? Primarily in economic terms, to ensure a common market? Primarily in moral or ethical terms, to prevent discrimination against foreigners? Or both?

5. *Court of Justice of the European Union (CJEU).* The Court of Justice, which is located in Luxembourg, is comprised of one judge from each of the member states in the European Union. At the time *Phil Collins* was decided, the Court was often referred to as the ECJ. In 2009, under the Lisbon Treaty, the name was changed to Court of Justice of the European Union (CJEU), although it is still common to hear the Court referred to as the ECJ. (This casebook will use both CJEU and ECJ interchangeably.) The process for referral of legal issues to the Court has remained the same. National courts in the European Union may refer a question that arises under the Treaty or Community law for a preliminary ruling from the CJEU. The *Phil Collins* case involved a "referral" by a German court to the CJEU for a "preliminary ruling." Under the Treaty on European Union, the CJEU is granted authority to interpret the Treaty and to decide issues of Community law, which is superior to the national laws of EU countries. After briefing and an oral hearing, the CJEU issues a preliminary ruling, answering only the question(s) of Community law in the referral. The CJEU does *not* rule on matters of national law, or even decide whether national law violates the EU Treaty or Community law. As apparent in the *Phil Collins* case, however, the import of the CJEU's ruling on national law may be obvious if national law is clearly inconsistent with the CJEU's ruling.

6. *Bibliographic note.* PAUL E. GELLER & MELVILLE B. NIMMER, INTERNATIONAL COPYRIGHT LAW AND PRACTICE, § 2[3][b] (2003); SAM RICKETSON, THE BERNE CONVENTION FOR THE PROTECTION OF LITERARY AND ARTISTIC WORKS: 1886–1986, at §§ 5.51–5.55 (1987); STEPHEN M. STEWART, INTERNATIONAL COPYRIGHT AND NEIGHBORING RIGHTS § 3.17 (2d ed. 1989).

3. THE MOST FAVORED NATION PRINCIPLE

PROBLEM 1–5

As permitted under TRIPS Article 27(3)(a), Country A, a WTO member, excludes all genetically engineered organisms (other than micro-organisms) from patentability. But Country A grants a special exemption to this prohibition for any country that has a bilateral agreement with Country A that requires it to grant patents to the foreign nationals of the other country for genetically engineered organisms. Country B, which is not a member of the WTO, obtained a bilateral agreement with Country A in 2001 that allows nationals of Country B to patent genetically engineered life forms in Country A. Numerous inventors from Country B have benefited from this special exemption. Caleb Crocker, a national from Country C, a WTO member, now files for a patent in Country A for a genetically engineered organism. The patent office in Country A rejects Caleb's application, citing Country A's prohibition against patenting of genetically engineered life forms. Country C does not have a bilateral agreement with Country A for any exemption to this prohibition. If Country C challenged Country A's law as violating the most favored nation principle, what should be the result be under TRIPS Article 4?

* * *

Before TRIPS, the most favored nation principle (MFN) was incorporated into all of the other major disciplines that now embody the WTO: the General Agreement on Tariffs and Trade (GATT) applicable to the trade in goods and the General Agreement on Trade in Services (GATS) applicable to the trade in services. Indeed, MFN was thought to be the "golden rule" of these trade instruments. MFN effectively prevents a country from giving preferential treatment to one foreign country over others. Under MFN, if a country gives preferential treatment to one country, it must accord the same benefits to all countries within the trading group.

Today, almost all nations enjoy MFN treatment through the operation of multi-lateral treaties, such as GATT/WTO, or through bilateral trade agreements. For example, the United States accords MFN treatment to the vast majority of nations in the world. Nations that do not enjoy MFN treatment in trade relations with the United States are often those countries, such as North Korea, that for political reasons are viewed as hostile to the national interests of the United States.

Historically, MFN was not a feature of the early international IP conventions, such as the Berne and Paris Conventions, although it was a feature of several bilateral IP agreements. TRIPS is the first international IP agreement to tie IP and trade together. TRIPS recognizes the most favored nation principle in Article 4, which states:

> With regard to the protection of intellectual property, any advantage, favour, privilege or immunity granted by a Member to the nationals of any other country shall be accorded immediately and unconditionally to the nationals of all other Members ...

MFN is subject to several exceptions. Countries can depart from MFN for items expressly not subject to national treatment under the Berne and Rome Conventions. TRIPS art. 4(b). Under a grandfather-type provision, countries can also depart from MFN based on obligations in prior international IP agreements that entered into force before the formation of the WTO, "provided that such agreements are notified to the Council for Trade–Related Aspects of Intellectual Property and do not constitute an arbitrary or unjustifiable discrimination against nationals of other Members." TRIPS art. 4(d). Also, countries do not have to apply MFN to any rights of performers, producers, and broadcasters not specifically provided under TRIPS (see Article 14), perhaps reflecting the lesser esteem traditionally accorded to those entities in IP conventions—a topic discussed later in the copyright chapter. TRIPS art. 4(c). Finally, MFN may also be exempted for "international agreements on judicial assistance and law enforcement of a general nature and not particularly confined to the protection of intellectual property." TRIPS art. 4(a).

UNITED STATES—SECTION 211 OMNIBUS APPROPRIATIONS ACT OF 1998

Report of the Appellate Body, WTO. (Ehlermann, Presiding Member; Bacchus and Lacarte–Muró, Members).
WT/DS176/AB/R (Jan. 2, 2002).

[This case involves a long-standing controversy over the mark "Havana Club." Prior to 1960, the Arechabala family produced "Havana

Club" rum in Cuba and owned the rights to the trademark. In 1960, under Fidel Castro, the Cuban government confiscated the mark and business from the Arechabalas (and other companies from others). Since 1963, the U.S. has imposed a trade embargo barring Cuban products from entering the U.S. The Cuban state company named Cubaexport (Empresa Cubana Exportadora De Alimentos y Productos Varios) registered the mark "Havana Club" in Cuba in 1974 and later began selling Havana Club rum to other countries outside the U.S. Cubaexport filed in the U.S. a Section 44 application for U.S. registration of "Havana Club" within the period of Paris priority, and received its U.S. registration in 1976. Because of the U.S. embargo, however, Cubaexport could not sell its rum in the U.S. In 1993, Cubaexport entered into a joint venture with Pernod Ricard, a French company, an international distributor of liquor. Under the agreement, the joint venture owned the trademark to Havana Club. The U.S. registration for "Havana Club" was renewed in 1996, although the embargo still bars the joint venture from selling Havana Club rum in the U.S.

Meanwhile, in 1996, another company, the Bacardi & Co., Ltd., and its subsidiary Bacardi–Martini USA, Inc. began exporting "Havana Club Rum" made in Bermuda to the U.S. Later, in 1997, Bacardi bought the rights (if any) from the Arechabala family, the original Cuban owners of the mark (before confiscation by the Cuban government), to the mark "Havana Club Rum." In response to Bacardi's sales of "Havana Club Rum," Pernod Ricard's joint venture sued Bacardi for trademark infringement in the U.S. While the suit was pending, and apparently after intense lobbying by Bacardi, Congress enacted § 211 as a part of the Omnibus Consolidated and Emergency Supplemental Appropriations Act, Pub. L. No. 105–277, § 211, 112 Stat. 2681, 2681–88 (1998).

Section 211 prohibits U.S. courts from enforcing trademarks in the U.S. of "any designated national or its successor-in-interest" (defined by regulation as "Cuba and any national thereof")—if the trademarks had been confiscated by the Cuban government and the designated national had not received the consent of the original, pre-confiscation owner of the mark. In applying this section, the Second Circuit held that § 211(b) barred the Pernod joint venture—a "designated national"—from asserting the trademark right of "Havana Club" in U.S. court. *See Havana Club Holding, S.A. v. Galleon S.A.*, 203 F.3d 116, 127 (2d Cir. 2000). Afterwards, on June 30, 2000, the European Union filed a challenge in the WTO to the U.S. law, raising numerous challenges including alleged violations of national treatment, the most favored nation principle, and the *telle quelle* provision. The Appellate Body's discussion of the most favored nation principle is excerpted below. *Ed.*]

X.   Article 4 of the TRIPS Agreement

Like the national treatment obligation, the obligation to provide most-favoured-nation treatment has long been one of the cornerstones of the world trading system. For more than fifty years, the obligation to provide most-favoured-nation treatment in Article I of the GATT 1994 has been both central and essential to assuring the success of a global rules-based system for trade in goods. Unlike the national treatment principle, there is no provision in the Paris Convention (1967) that establishes a most-favoured-nation obligation with respect to rights in trademarks or other industrial property. However, the framers of the TRIPS Agreement decided to extend the most-favoured-nation obligation to the protection of intellectual property rights covered by that Agreement. As a cornerstone of the world trading system, the most-favoured-nation obligation must be accorded the same significance with respect to intellectual property rights under the TRIPS Agreement that it has long been accorded with respect to trade in goods under the GATT. It is, in a word, fundamental.

Article 4 of the TRIPS Agreement provides, in relevant part:

> With regard to the protection of intellectual property, any advantage, favour, privilege or immunity granted by a Member to the nationals of any other country shall be accorded immediately and unconditionally to the nationals of all other Members.[3]

The European Communities appeals these findings of the Panel on both Section 211(a)(2) and Section 211(b) [concluding that they were consistent with TRIPS Article 4].

Like the situation posed by the European Communities earlier, the one set forth in the most-favoured-nation treatment involves two separate owners who acquired rights, either at common law or based on registration, in two separate United States trademarks, before the Cuban confiscation occurred. Each of these two United States trademarks is the same, or substantially similar to, signs or a combination of signs of which a trademark registered in Cuba is composed. That same or similar Cuban trademark was used in connection with a business or assets that were confiscated in Cuba. Neither of the two original owners of the two United States trademarks was the owner of that same or similar trademark that was registered in Cuba. Those two original owners each now seek to assert rights in the United States in their two respective United States trademarks. The situation of these two original owners of these two United States trademarks is identical in every relevant respect, but one. That one difference is this: one original owner is a national of Cuba, and the other original owner is a national of a country other than Cuba or the United States. We will refer, for the sake of convenience, to this other original owner as "a non-Cuban foreign national."

Pointing to this particular situation, the European Communities argues that, on the face of the statute, the original owner who is a Cuban national is subject to Sections 211(a)(2) and (b),* and the original owner

---

3. "For the purposes of Articles 3 and 4, 'protection' shall include matters affecting the availability, acquisition, scope, maintenance and enforcement of intellectual property rights as well as those matters affecting the use of intellectual property rights specifically addressed in this Agreement."

* Section 211(a)(2) and (b) state:

who is a non-Cuban foreign national is not. This alone, as the European Communities sees it, is sufficient for us to find that Sections 211(a)(2) and (b) violate the most-favoured-nation obligation of the United States.

We agree with the European Communities that the situation it describes on appeal is within the scope of the statute on its face. As we explained earlier, the term "designated national" as defined in Section 515.305 of 31 CFR and Section 211(d)(1) includes non-Cuban foreign nationals only when they are successors-in-interest to Cuba or a Cuban national. Non–Cuban foreign nationals who are original owners are not covered by the definition of "designated national" and are thereby not subject to Sections 211(a)(2) and (b).

Therefore, here too, as with national treatment, the European Communities has established a prima facie case that Sections 211(a)(2) and (b) are discriminatory on their face, as between a Cuban national and a non-Cuban foreign national both of whom are original owners of United States trademarks composed of the same or substantially similar signs as a trademark used in connection with a business or assets that were confiscated in Cuba.

[The WTO Appellate Body rejected the U.S. arguments that Section 211's facial discrimination did not discriminate against Cuban nationals in operation. *Ed.*]

We, therefore, reverse the Panel's findings in paragraphs 8.148 and 8.176 of the Panel Report, to the extent that they concern the treatment of original owners, and find, in this respect, that Section 211(a)(2) and Section 211(b) are inconsistent with Article 4 of the TRIPS Agreement.

NOTES AND QUESTIONS

1. National treatment is often referred to as a principle of *internal* non-discrimination as a nation cannot treat foreign nationals less favorably than its own nationals. How is MFN similar to national treatment? How is it different? Compared to national treatment, why might MFN be characterized as a principle of *external* non-discrimination? Can you imagine circumstances in which MFN would be violated, but national treatment would not? What about circumstances in which both MFN and national treatment would be violated?

(a)(2) No U.S. court shall recognize, enforce or otherwise validate any assertion of rights by a designated national based on common law rights or registration obtained under such section 515.527 of such a confiscated mark, trade name, or commercial name.

(b) No U.S. court shall recognize, enforce or otherwise validate any assertion of treaty rights by a designated national or its successor-in-interest under sections 44 (b) or (e) of the Trademark Act of 1946 (15 U.S.C. 1126 (b) or (e)) for a mark, trade name, or commercial name that is the same as or substantially similar to a mark, trade name, or commercial name that was used in connection with a business or assets that were confiscated unless the original owner of such mark, trade name, or commercial name, or the bona fide successor-in-interest has expressly consented.

Omnibus Consolidated and Emergency Supplemental Appropriations Act, Pub. L. No. 105–277, § 211(a)(2), (b), 112 Stat. 2681, 2681–88 (1998). *Ed.*

2. Explain the EU's argument that Section 211 of the Omnibus Appropriations Act violates the most favored nation principle. How is this infraction different from a violation of national treatment?

3. *Ongoing violation.* Under the WTO's Dispute Settlement Understanding, a country found to be in violation of its WTO obligations is given a "reasonable period of time" to correct the violation. DSU art. 21.2. Initially, the U.S. and EU agreed to a period of approximately 12 months, which is a typical amount of time allotted in the DSB. The U.S., however, did not correct the violation within that time period. Instead, the U.S. obtained from the EU several extensions of time that expired on June 30, 2005. As of 2011, over 9 years later, the U.S. still had not fixed its violation. Why do you think the U.S. has delayed, for so long, to correct its violation of TRIPS? Should the delay concern the WTO?

4. *Plight of Cuban Havana Club.* In 2006, Cubaexport's renewal of its U.S. registration became due, but Cubaexport was held to be barred from renewal because of Section 211 and its regulations. *See* Empresa Cubana Exportadora de Alimentos y Productos Varios v. U.S. Dep't of Treasury, 638 F.3d 794 (D.C. Cir. 2011). Cubaexport's failure to renew meant that it lost its federal registration of its trademark in the U.S. and rights to the mark in the U.S. Not surprisingly, in 2006, Bacardi began selling "Havana Club" rum in Florida, with a label that indicated it was made in Puerto Rico, over the protest of Cubaexport. *See* Pernod Ricard USA v. Bacardi U.S.A., Inc., 653 F.3d 241 (3d Cir. 2011). A fair result?

5. Why should countries be obligated to extend MFN treatment to all countries within a treaty if it extends a special advantage to one country? Might there be some circumstances (even beyond the narrow exemptions in Article 4 of TRIPS) in which preferential treatment in IP rights given to the nationals of one country should not be required to be extended to the nationals of all member countries?

6. *Exceptions to MFN under GATT and GATS.* As discussed above, the permissible exemptions to the MFN principle for IP rights under TRIPS Article 4 are modest. By contrast, the older trade agreements GATT and GATS recognize exemptions to MFN for "free trade areas" and for "customs unions." *See* GATT art. XXIV; GATS art. V. Under these exemptions in GATT and GATS, member nations can give certain preferential trading benefits to other countries in a "free trade" or "customs union" agreement. These exemptions apply most notably to such agreements as NAFTA, the U.S.'s free trade agreement with Mexico and Canada, and to the European Union, a customs union.

Article 4 of TRIPS does not contain a similar exemption to MFN for a free trade agreement. TRIPS art. 4(d). Therefore, a free trade agreement does not exempt a country from its obligation to apply MFN to IP rights under TRIPS. However, because the EU is itself a member of WTO, for the purposes of national treatment and MFN, all nationals of EU countries are considered as a single group of EU nationals when EU law is at issue. *See* European Communities—Protection of Trademarks and Geographical Indications for Agricultural Products and Foodstuffs, WT/DS174/R, at ¶ 7.725 (15 March 2005).

7. *Bibliographic note.* Paul Beynon, *Community Mutual Recognition Agreements, Technical Barriers to Trade and the WTO's Most Favoured Nation Principle*, E.L. REV. 28(2), 231 (2003); Sydney M. Cone, III, *The Promotion of Free–Trade Areas Viewed in Terms of Most–Favored–Nation Treatment and "Imperial Preference,"* 26 MICH. J. INT'L L. 563 (2005); Warren F. Schwartz & Alan O. Sykes, *Toward a Positive Theory of the Most Favored Nation Obligation and Its Exceptions in the WTO/GATT System*, 16 INT'L REV. L. & ECON. 27 (1996).

4. CHOICE OF LAW IN TRANSNATIONAL DISPUTES

Another consequence of the principle of territoriality is that, in IP lawsuits involving alleged conduct that occurred in several different countries, a court must decide which law or laws apply to resolve the transnational dispute. We will study private enforcement of IP rights in depth in Chapter 6, but it is useful to introduce the topic of choice of law here, given its relation to the territorial approach to IP laws. Because each nation has its own IP laws effective only within its own territory, a dispute spanning several different countries may involve several IP claims each governed by a different country's law. And, where laws from two or more jurisdictions may apply to the same legal issue and produce different results, the issue is said to raise a "conflict of laws" question. International choice of law, also called private international law, is an immense field and applies to many areas of law beyond intellectual property. *See, e.g.*, DANIEL C.K. CHOW AND THOMAS J. SCHOENBAUM, INTERNATIONAL BUSINESS TRANSACTIONS: PROBLEMS, CASES, AND MATERIALS 23–24(2d ed. 2010).

> Illustration 1–5. Alicia, a national of Country A, is seeking to enforce her intellectual property rights in a court in Country A. The alleged infringing activity occurred both in Country A and Country B. If Alicia brings a case in the courts of Country A, the court may need to decide whether the intellectual property laws of Country A or Country B, or a combination of both, will govern Alicia's rights. In the absence of an effective choice of law by the parties through contract or as a result of an international treaty, the courts of Country A will use its own domestic choice of law rules to determine whether the substantive laws of Country A or Country B, or some combination, apply to the dispute.

How will a court decide what law to apply to an IP claim in such a transnational dispute? The answer to that question, as we shall soon see, has become contested in the U.S. One approach is to take a strict territorial approach, applying the law of the protecting country to all issues raised for the IP claim recognized by that country's IP law. A strict territorial approach arguably has the virtue of simplicity: one law determines all issues for an IP infringement claim brought under that country's law. It also may serve notions of sovereignty if the law of the country that created the IP right determines the full contours of that IP right, particularly if the right arises under a statute enacted by the country's elected legislative body. However, this strict territorial approach has been challenged by one court in the following case. As you read the case, try to identify how the approach differs.

ITAR–TASS RUSSIAN NEWS AGENCY v. RUSSIAN KURIER, INC.

U.S. Court of Appeals for the Second Circuit.
153 F.3d 82 (2d Cir. 1998).

NEWMAN, CIRCUIT JUDGE:

This appeal primarily presents issues concerning the choice of law in international copyright cases and the substantive meaning of Russian copyright law as to the respective rights of newspaper reporters and newspaper publishers. The conflicts issue is which country's law applies to issues of copyright ownership and to issues of infringement.

Background

The lawsuit concerns Kurier, a Russian language weekly newspaper with a circulation in the New York area of about 20,000. It is published in New York City by defendant Kurier. Defendant Pogrebnoy is president and sole shareholder of Kurier and editor-in-chief of Kurier. The plaintiffs include corporations that publish, daily or weekly, major Russian language newspapers in Russia and Russian language magazines in Russia or Israel; Itar–Tass Russian News Agency ("Itar–Tass"), formerly known as the Telegraph Agency of the Soviet Union (TASS), a wire service and news gathering company centered in Moscow, functioning similarly to the Associated Press; and the Union of Journalists of Russia ("UJR"), the professional writers union of accredited print and broadcast journalists of the Russian Federation.

The Kurier defendants do not dispute that Kurier has copied about 500 articles that first appeared in the plaintiffs' publications or were distributed by Itar–Tass. The copied material, though extensive, was a small percentage of the total number of articles published in Kurier. The Kurier defendants also do not dispute how the copying occurred: articles from the plaintiffs' publications, sometimes containing headlines, pictures, bylines, and graphics, in addition to text, were cut out, pasted on layout sheets, and sent to Kurier's printer for photographic reproduction and printing in the pages of Kurier. Most significantly, the Kurier defendants also do not dispute that, with one exception, they had not obtained permission from any of the plaintiffs to copy the articles that appeared in Kurier. Pogrebnoy claimed at trial to have received permission from the publisher of one newspaper, but his claim was rejected by the District Court at trial.

Preliminary injunction ruling. After a hearing in May 1995, the District Court issued a preliminary injunction, prohibiting the Kurier defendants from copying the "works" of four plaintiff news organizations.

Turning to the rights of the newspapers, Judge Koeltl relied on Article 11, captioned "Copyright of Compiler of Collections and Other Works." This Article contains two sub-sections. Article 11(1) specifies the rights of compilers generally:

> The author of a collection or any other composite work (compiler) shall enjoy copyright in the selection or arrangement of subject matter that he has made insofar as that selection or arrangement is the result of a creative effort of compilation.
>
> The compiler shall enjoy copyright subject to respect for the rights of the authors of each work included in the composite work.
>
> Each of the authors of the works included in the composite work shall have the right to exploit his own work independently of the composite work unless the author's contract provides otherwise. . . .

Russian Copyright Law, Art. 11(1). Article 11(2), the interpretation of which is critical to this appeal, specifies the rights of compilers of those works that are excluded from the work-for-hire provision of Article 14(2):

> The exclusive right to exploit encyclopedias, encyclopedic dictionaries, collections of scientific works—published in either one or several installments—newspapers, reviews and other periodical publications shall belong to the editor[7] thereof. The editor shall have the right to mention his name or to demand such mention whenever the said publications are exploited.
>
> The authors of the works included in the said publications shall retain the exclusive rights to exploit their works independently of the publication of the whole work.

Id., Art. 11(2). In another translation of the Russian Copyright Law, which was in evidence at the trial, the last phrase of Article 11(2) was rendered "independently from the publication as a whole." Russian Copyright Law, Art. 11(2) (Newton Davis translation). Because the parties' experts focused on the phrase "as a whole" in the Davis translation of Article 11(2), we will rely on the Davis translation for the rendering of this key phrase of Article 11(2), but all other references to the Russian Copyright Law will be to the WIPO translation.

Expert testimony at trial. The plaintiffs' expert witness at trial was Michael Newcity, coordinator for the Center for Slavic, Eurasian and East European Studies at Duke University and an adjunct member of the faculty at the Duke University Law School. He opined that Article 11(2) gave the newspapers rights to redress copying not only of the publication "as a whole," but also of individual articles. He acknowledged that the reporters retained copyrights in the articles that they authored, but stated that Article 11(2) created a regime of parallel exclusive rights in both the newspaper publisher and the reporter.

---

7. The Newton Davis translation, which was an exhibit at trial, renders this word "publisher."

Newcity offered two considerations in support of his position. First, he cited the predecessor of Article 11(2), Article 485 of the Russian Civil Code of 1964. That provision was similar to Article 11(2), with one change that became the subject of major disagreement among the expert witnesses. Article 485 had given compilers, including newspaper publishers, the right to exploit their works "as a whole." The 1993 revision deleted "as a whole" from the first paragraph of the predecessor of Article 11(2), where it had modified the scope of the compiler's right, and moved the phrase to the second paragraph of revised Article 11(2), where it modifies the reserved right of the authors of articles within a compilation to exploit their works "independently of the publication as a whole." Though Newcity opined that even under Article 485, reprinting of "one or two or three, at most," articles from a newspaper would have constituted infringement of the copyright "as a whole," he rested his reading of Article 11(2) significantly on the fact that the 1993 revision dropped the phrase "as a whole" from the paragraph that specified the publisher's right. This deletion, he contended, eliminated whatever ambiguity might have existed in the first paragraph of Article 485.

Second, Newcity referred to an opinion of the Judicial Chamber for Informational Disputes of the President of the Russian Federation ("Informational Disputes Chamber"), issued on June 8, 1995. That opinion had been sought by the editor-in-chief of one of the plaintiffs in this litigation, Moskovskie Novosti (Moscow News), who specifically called the tribunal's attention to the pending litigation between Russian media organizations and the publisher of Kurier. The Informational Disputes Chamber stated, in response to one of the questions put to it, "In the event of a violation of its rights, including the improper printing of one or two articles, the publisher [of a newspaper] has the right to petition a court for defense of its rights."

Defendants' experts presented a very different view of the rights of newspapers. Professor Peter B. Maggs of the University of Illinois, Urbana–Champaign, College of Law, testifying by deposition, pointed out that Article 11(2) gives authors the exclusive rights to their articles and accords newspaper publishers only the "exclusive rights to the publication as a whole, because that's the only thing not reserved to the authors." He opined that a newspaper's right to use of the compiled work "as a whole" would be infringed by the copying of an entire issue of a newspaper and probably by copying a substantial part of one issue, but not by the copying of a few articles, since the copyright in the articles belongs to the reporters. He also disagreed with Newcity's contention that exclusive rights to individual articles belonged simultaneously to both the newspaper and the reporter. Exclusive rights, he maintained, cannot be held by two people, except in the case of co-authors, who have jointly held rights against the world.

Trial ruling. The District Court resolved the dispute among the experts by accepting [the plaintiff's expert] Newcity's interpretation of Russian copyright law. The District Court estimated Kurier's profits during the relevant years at $2 million and found that 25 percent of these profits were attributable to the copied articles. The Court therefore awarded the plaintiffs $500,000 in actual damages against Kurier and Pogrebnoy.

Discussion

I.   Choice of Law

Choice of law issues in international copyright cases have been largely ignored in the reported decisions and dealt with rather cursorily by most commentators.

The Nimmer treatise briefly (and perhaps optimistically) suggests that conflicts issues "have rarely proved troublesome in the law of copyright." *See* Nimmer on Copyright § 17.05 (1998) ("Nimmer"). Relying on the "national treatment" principle of the Berne Convention and the Universal Copyright Convention ("U.C.C."), Nimmer asserts, correctly in our view, that "an author who is a national of one of the member states of either Berne or the U.C.C., or one who first publishes his work in any such member state, is entitled to the same copyright protection in each other member state as such other state accords to its own nationals." Nimmer then somewhat overstates the national treatment principle: "The applicable law is the copyright law of the state in which the infringement occurred, not that of the state of which the author is a national, or in which the work is first published." The difficulty with this broad statement is that it subsumes under the phrase "applicable law" the law concerning two distinct issues—ownership and substantive rights, i.e., scope of protection.[8] Another commentator has also broadly stated the principle of national treatment, but described its application in a way that does not necessarily cover issues of ownership. "The principle of national treatment also means that both the question of whether the right exists and the question of the scope of the right are to be answered in accordance with the law of the country where the protection is claimed." S.M. Stewart, International Copyright and Neighboring Rights § 3.17 (2d ed. 1989). We agree with the view of the Amicus that the Convention's principle of national treatment simply assures that if the law of the country of infringement applies to the scope of substantive copyright protection, that law will be applied uniformly to foreign and domestic authors.

Source of conflicts rules. We start our analysis with the Copyrights [sic] Act itself, which contains no provision relevant to the pending case concerning conflicts issues. We therefore fill the interstices of the Act by developing federal common law on the conflicts issue. The choice of law

---

8. Prof. Patry's brief, as Amicus Curiae, helpfully points out that the principle of national treatment is really not a conflicts rule at all; it does not direct application of the law of any country. It simply requires that the country in which protection is claimed must treat foreign and domestic authors alike. Whether U.S. copyright law directs U.S. courts to look to foreign or domestic law as to certain issues is irrelevant to national treatment, so long as the scope of protection would be extended equally to foreign and domestic authors.

applicable to the pending case is not necessarily the same for all issues. See Restatement (Second) of Conflict of Laws § 222 ("The courts have long recognized that they are not bound to decide all issues under the local law of a single state."). We consider first the law applicable to the issue of copyright ownership.

Conflicts rule for issues of ownership. Copyright is a form of property, and the usual rule is that the interests of the parties in property are determined by the law of the state with "the most significant relationship" to the property and the parties. *See id.* The Restatement recognizes the applicability of this principle to intangibles such as "a literary idea." *Id.* Since the works at issue were created by Russian nationals and first published in Russia, Russian law is the appropriate source of law to determine issues of ownership of rights. In terms of the United States Copyrights [sic] Act and its reference to the Berne Convention, Russia is the "country of origin" of these works, see 17 U.S.C. § 101 (definition of "country of origin" of Berne Convention work); Berne Convention, Art. 5(4), although "country of origin" might not always be the appropriate country for purposes of choice of law concerning ownership.

Conflicts rule for infringement issues. On infringement issues, the governing conflicts principle is usually lex loci delicti, the doctrine generally applicable to torts. We have implicitly adopted that approach to infringement claims, applying United States copyright law to a work that was unprotected in its country of origin. In the pending case, the place of the tort is plainly the United States. To whatever extent lex loci delicti is to be considered only one part of a broader "interest" approach, United States law would still apply to infringement issues, since not only is this country the place of the tort, but also the defendant is a United States corporation.

The division of issues, for conflicts purposes, between ownership and infringement issues will not always be as easily made as the above discussion implies. [I]n some cases, including the pending one, the issue is not simply who owns the copyright but also what is the nature of the ownership interest.

II.   Determination of Ownership Rights Under Russian Law

Since United States law permits suit only by owners of "an exclusive right under a copyright," 17 U.S.C. § 501(b), we must first determine whether any of the plaintiffs own an exclusive right. That issue of ownership, as we have indicated, is to be determined by Russian law. Under Article 14 of the Russian Copyright Law, Itar–Tass is the owner of the copyright interests in the articles written by its employees. However, Article 14(4) excludes newspapers from the Russian version of the work-for-hire doctrine. The newspaper plaintiffs, therefore, must locate their ownership rights, if any, in some other source of law. They rely on Article 11. The District Court upheld their position, apparently recognizing in the newspaper publishers "exclusive" rights to the articles, even though, by virtue of Article 11(2), the reporters also retained "exclusive" rights to these articles.

Having considered all of the views presented by the expert witnesses, we conclude that the defendants' experts are far more persuasive as to the meaning of Article 11. In the first place, once Article 14 of the Russian Copyright Law explicitly denies newspapers the benefit of a work-for-hire doctrine, which, if available, would accord them rights to individual articles written by their employees, it is highly unlikely that Article 11 would confer on newspapers the very right that Article 14 has denied them. Moreover, Article 11 has an entirely reasonable scope if confined, as its caption suggests, to defining the "Copyright of Compilers of Collections and Other Works." That article accords compilers copyright "in the selection and arrangement of subject matter that he has made insofar as that selection or arrangement is the result of a creative effort of compilation." Russian Copyright Law, Art. 11(1). Article 11(2) accords publishers of compilations the right to exploit such works, including the right to insist on having its name mentioned, while expressly reserving to "authors of the works included" in compilations the "exclusive rights to exploit their works independently of the publication of the whole work." *Id.* Art. 11(2). As the defendants' experts testified, Article 11 lets authors of newspaper articles sue for infringement of their rights in the text of their articles, and lets newspaper publishers sue for wholesale copying of all of the newspaper or for copying any portions of the newspaper that embody their selection, arrangement, and presentation of articles (including headlines)—copying that infringes their ownership interest in the compilation.

Relief. Our disagreement with the District Court's interpretation of Article 11 does not mean, however, that the defendants may continue copying with impunity. In the first place, Itar–Tass, as a press agency, is within the scope of Article 14, and, unlike the excluded newspapers, enjoys the benefit of the Russian version of the work-for-hire doctrine. Itar–Tass is therefore entitled to injunctive relief to prevent unauthorized copying of its articles and to damages for such copying, and the judgment is affirmed as to this plaintiff.

Furthermore, the newspaper plaintiffs, though not entitled to relief for the copying of the text of the articles they published, may well be entitled to injunctive relief and damages if they can show that Kurier infringed the publishers' ownership interests in the newspaper compilations. Because the District Court upheld the newspapers' right to relief for copying the text of the articles, it had no occasion to consider what relief the newspapers might be entitled to by reason of Kurier's copying of the newspapers' creative efforts in the selection, arrangement, or display of the articles. On these infringement issues, as we have indicated, United States law will apply.

NOTES AND QUESTIONS

1. *U.S. copyright claim.* The Russian newspaper articles first published in Russia were entitled to copyrights both in Russia and in the United States because both countries are parties to the Berne Convention. In their lawsuit in the U.S., the Russian plaintiffs asserted a copyright infringement lawsuit under U.S. law to protect their U.S. copyrights. *See Itar–Tass Russian News Agency v. Russian Kurier, Inc.*, 1997 WL 109481, at *5 (1997) ("The plaintiffs' claims arise under the Copyright Act of 1976, as amended, 17 U.S.C. § 101 *et seq.*").

If the Russian plaintiffs were asserting a U.S. copyright claim, why did the court of appeals rely on Russian law to determine who owned the U.S. copyright? Is the court's decision consistent with a territorial approach? Is it consistent with *Subafilms*, where the court recognized: "Although the treaties do not expressly discuss choice-of-law rules, it is commonly acknowledged that the national treatment principle implicates a rule of territoriality." *Subafilms*, 24 F.3d at 1097.

2. *National treatment.* Is the result in *Itar–Tass* consistent with national treatment? Have the Russian authors been assimilated into U.S. law with the same (if not better) standing as U.S. nationals? *Cf.* WIPO, GUIDE TO THE BERNE CONVENTION 32 (1978) (under Berne national treatment, "if the copyright in a work by a Sengalese author, published for the first time in the Ivory Coast, is infringed in France, this author ... must be treated in France as if the work were one made by a French author and published on French territory"). How would the case come out if the plaintiffs' newspaper articles were written by U.S. authors and published in the U.S.?

3. Which approach is simpler to apply, Nimmer's or the Second Circuit's? Note that the Second Circuit position requires a conflict of laws analysis of both ownership and infringement and, in the event that foreign law is chosen, the examination of how the ownership issue would be decided under foreign law. How confident are you that the court of appeals' interpretation of Russian law was correct?

For further discussion, see STEPHEN P. LADAS, 1 THE INTERNATIONAL PROTECTION OF LITERARY AND ARTISTIC PROPERTY 262–69 (1938) (discussing national treatment, principle of independence, and bar on formalities as examples of Berne Union's efforts to minimize the extent to which foreign copyright law will need to be considered—"The law of the country where protection is sought, *lex loci*, is ... the primary legal source of protection in the Union.").

D. INTERNATIONAL LEGAL INSTITUTIONS

In this section, we provide a brief introduction and overview of the legal institutions that are prominent in the system of international intellectual property.

1. THE WORLD TRADE ORGANIZATION

a. History and Evolution of the WTO From GATT

The most important international body for intellectual property today is the WTO, created in 1994. GATT was the predecessor to the WTO. The origins of GATT can be traced to events occurring after World War II. During that time, the world economic situation was unstable. The world had just suffered through a global conflict of immense destruction. The War itself had been presaged by economic conflict, which eventually lead to military conflict. The disastrous and protectionist trade policies of many of the world's nations during the period immediately preceding the War were widely considered to have contributed to the eruption of widespread military conflict. The U.S. and its allies convened at Bretton Woods, New Hampshire, to establish a post-war framework for international trade, in order to prevent such a conflict from ever arising again.

The post-war institutional framework envisioned at Bretton Woods consisted of (i) the International Monetary Fund (IMF), (ii) the World Bank, and (iii) the International Trade Organization (ITO). The role of the IMF was to set up restrictions on national regulations of foreign currency controls, such as exchange rates that would impact their economic relations with other nations. In addition, the IMF provided loans, as a last resort, to developing nations if they could not repay their loans to foreign lenders. The World Bank was set up to assist the reconstruction of Europe and the economic development of the poorest nations of the world through the grant of loans. The ITO was conceived to facilitate international trade by helping to reduce trade barriers between nations. The period preceding the War witnessed some of the highest tariffs (i.e., duties or taxes that are paid upon imported goods) in history, as nations sought to protect themselves from foreign competition. The ITO was intended to help reduce tariffs to a level that would promote and facilitate trade.

The Bretton Woods countries had bold ambitions for the ITO. Its proposed charter extended well beyond the goal of free trade in goods. It encompassed trade in services, rules on employment, commodity agreements, restrictive business practices, and foreign direct investment. Many nations were anxious to remove the protectionist tariffs that had been in place since the 1930s. The result was the negotiation of a free trade agreement, the General Agreement on Tariffs and Trade, commonly referred to as "GATT."

At first, nations allowed GATT to come into existence on a provisional basis in 1948, while awaiting the final approval of the ITO charter, which would then administer GATT. However, the U.S. Congress opposed the ITO, and the ITO charter was never approved. In a remarkable metamorphosis, GATT continued its "provisional" existence for the next 47 years. Even though GATT originally came into existence as a treaty, not an international organization, the demise of the ITO left GATT to develop an administration of its own. At first, a small staff was created in Geneva to handle administrative duties. But, as the work of GATT grew in importance, GATT blossomed into an international organization, even without a formal charter.

Over the years, GATT grew in stature and importance. It served as the basis for eight "rounds" of multilateral trade negotiations that were periodically held to reduce tariffs and other barriers to international trade. Each of the rounds became more complex as GATT negotiating parties became more ambitious. The eight rounds were named after the place in which the negotiations began or, in some cases, after the person who initiated the round:

- Geneva   1947
- Annecy   1949
- Torquay   1950
- Geneva   1956
- Dillon   1960–61
- Kennedy   1962–67
- Tokyo   1973–79
- Uruguay   1986–94

The main objective of the early rounds was to reduce tariffs. By the Tokyo round, however, the GATT negotiators began to consider non-tariff barriers to trade. This trend continued and expanded considerably in the Uruguay round. Spanning eight years, the Uruguay round yielded a massive body of international trade law. The Final Act, which was signed in Marrakesh, Morocco on April 15, 1994, exceeded 26,000 pages. The Act transformed the GATT into the new World Trade Organization (WTO). The WTO now administers the three principal WTO Agreements: (1) the General Agreement on Tariffs and Trade of 1994 (the original GATT is now referred to as GATT 1947), (2) the General Agreement on Trade in Services (GATS), and (3) TRIPS. The WTO also administers the Understanding on the Settlement of Disputes (commonly known as the Dispute Settlement Understanding or DSU), which provides, for the first time, an effective dispute settlement process for international trade disputes.

During the Uruguay round, which was undeniably the longest and most complex in GATT/WTO history, several countries led by the United States sought to introduce intellectual property rights into the new WTO framework. By the time that the Uruguay round was initiated, it had become increasingly clear that intellectual property rights were playing an increasingly vital role in international trade and commerce. A number of developed countries believed that it was essential to bring intellectual property rights into the WTO framework. However, initially, many developing countries resisted the TRIPS Agreement.

This discussion brings us to a recurring theme of international IP, one which we will study throughout this casebook. In a nutshell, the theme can be characterized as the "North–South debate"—meaning a dispute between developed and developing countries. As it became clear that intellectual property rights were increasingly valuable economic rights, developed countries, which create and export the bulk of intellectual property rights, sought to protect their investments by calling for the widespread promulgation of Western style intellectual property laws.

However, developing nations were concerned that Western style intellectual property laws would limit their access to advanced technology needed by many developing nations to modernize and industrialize their economies. Developing nations were also concerned that adopting Western style IP laws would limit or deny access to technology by imposing burdensome royalty and licensing fees. Ultimately, many developing nations believed that including intellectual property rights within the WTO framework would favor developed nations, but not them.

Developing countries wished to keep intellectual property outside the scope of the WTO and within the jurisdiction of the World Intellectual Property Organization (WIPO), which was the most important international organization in the area of intellectual property before the WTO was established. Because WIPO was a specialized agency of the United Nations, it was viewed in the past as being a forum that was more receptive to the needs of developing countries on intellectual property law issues than GATT/WTO for several reasons.

First, developing nations viewed the GATT as a "rich nations' club" and as an inhospitable forum for serving the needs of developing countries. In the late 1970s and early 1980s, just prior to the initiation of the Uruguay round, many developing nations, newly independent from decades of colonial rule by developed nations mainly from western Europe, did not trust that GATT, with many developed nations as influential members, would serve their interests.

Second, GATT was an organization that was concerned about trade and commerce, whereas WIPO was an organization that was devoted solely to intellectual property. Including intellectual property within the GATT/WTO framework meant that intellectual property law would be considered a trade issue connected to other trade issues. Many developing countries did not agree with this connection.

Third, WIPO was essentially a toothless organization that did not have any real powers to impose sanctions on those countries that did not obey the treaties that it administered. As some developing countries had resisted complying with intellectual property law treaties, they felt that keeping intellectual property within WIPO and outside of the GATT/WTO framework was to their advantage.

In the end, the developed nations got their way. The Agreement on Trade Related Aspects of Intellectual Property brings IP within the scope of trade and the WTO. Membership in the WTO requires adherence to all of the WTO's major disciplines, including TRIPS. The WTO eliminated the "GATT a la carte" practice that allowed members to pick and choose which treaties of GATT to which they would adhere. Under the WTO, membership requires adherence to *all* treaties of the WTO as a package. Developing nations that sought the benefits of trade under GATT 1994 and GATS also had to adhere to TRIPS. In addition, while there were few serious consequences for failing to adhere to a treaty administered by WIPO, the situation could be quite different under the WTO. A nation that fails to comply with TRIPS might ultimately face trade sanctions in the WTO in a sector that is important to the offending country's economy. To be sure, the WTO's authorization of trade sanctions is a drastic measure that is used only as a last resort. However, the mere threat of the remedy of retaliation creates pressure on nations to comply with the WTO requirements.

The conclusion of TRIPS was viewed initially as a great triumph for developed nations as it signaled a new milestone for the global harmonization of intellectual property laws and the inclusion of intellectual property within the overall world trading system. TRIPS incorporates standards that are primarily modeled on Western intellectual property laws, which was viewed as a victory and advantage for the United States and other developed countries. However, as we shall see later, recent developments in the current Doha round of WTO negotiations indicate that the balance of influence may have shifted towards developing nations on a number of significant issues under TRIPS.

b.   The General Structure of the WTO

THE WORLD TRADE ORGANIZATION:
LAW, PRACTICE AND POLICY

Mitsuo Matsushita, Thomas J. Schoenbaum & Petros Mavroidis, at 9–12 (2d ed. 2006).*

The WTO is formally endowed with existence, legal personality, and legal capacity as an international organization. It must be accorded privileges and immunities that are in accordance with its functions.

The WTO has two governing bodies: the Ministerial Conference and the General Council. The Ministerial Conference is the supreme authority. It is composed of representatives of all WTO Members and meets at least once every two years. The General Council is the chief decision-making and policy body between meetings of the Ministerial Conference. The General Council also discharges the responsibilities of two important subsidiary bodies, namely, the Dispute Settlement Body and the Trade Policy Review body. The General Council is composed of all WTO Members and meets "as appropriate."

Specialized Councils and Committees that report to the General Council do much of the day-to-day work of the WTO. The WTO Agreement establishes these Councils: a Council for Trade in Goods; a Council for Trade in Services; and a Council for Trade–Related Aspects of Intellectual Property Rights (TRIPS). These Councils have the power to establish

---

* Reproduced with permission of Oxford University Press.

committees (or subsidiary bodies) as required. The Ministerial Conference has also established committees: a Committee on Trade and Development; a Committee on Budget, Finance and Administration; and by special action on 14 April 1994, a Committee on Trade and Environment. Additional councils and committees oversee the Plurilateral Trade Agreements. These also report to the WTO General Council.

The WTO has a Secretariat located in Geneva and presided over by a Director–General, who is appointed by the Ministerial Conference. The Ministerial Conference sets the powers and term of office of the Director–General, and the Director–General has the power to appoint the staff and direct the duties of the WTO Secretariat. Neither the Director–General nor the Members of the Secretariat may seek or accept instructions from any national governments, and both must act as international officials.

Decision–Making

There are two primary modes of decision-making: decision by consensus and voting. For general decision-making, WTO bodies continue to follow the practice of the GATT 1947 of deciding by consensus. The WTO Agreement provides that "[t]he body concerned shall be deemed to have decided by consensus if no Member, present at the meeting when the decision is taken, formally objects to the proposed decision." Thus, consensus differs from unanimity. In consensus decision-making, the minority will normally go along with the majority unless it has a serious objection. The majority will, in turn, not ramrod decision through by vote but will deal with the objections of the minority. The consensus decision-making process takes a great deal of time.

Voting occurs in the WTO only when a decision cannot be taken by consensus. In the Ministerial Conference and the General Council, decisions are taken by "a majority of the votes cast" unless otherwise specified in the relevant WTO agreement. Each Member has one vote.

c. WTO Monitoring and Enforcement of TRIPS

The Council for TRIPS ("TRIPS Council") is the most important WTO council for intellectual property. Among its major goals, the TRIPS Council is charged with monitoring the faithful implementation of TRIPS by all WTO members (although developing and least developed countries have a greater period of time within which to comply, TRIPS art. 65, discussed below). The Council engages in a detailed and systematic examination of each nation's laws by other WTO members to determine whether the laws are in full compliance. Membership in the TRIPS Council is open to all nations interested in working on the administration and implementation of TRIPS.

Under TRIPS Article 63(2), each member is to notify the Council of all of its laws and regulations implementing TRIPS. As Part III of TRIPS is concerned specifically with enforcement, some members also supply supplementary materials on how their laws are being enforced as enforcement obligations cannot be ascertained by a review of the legislative texts alone. These notifications serve as the basis for a detailed scrutiny of the implementing legislation of all member states. Indeed, TRIPS Article 63(1) specifically requires that countries have transparency in their IP laws (including statutes, decisions, and regulations) by either publishing them or making them available in a manner "to enable governments and right holders to become acquainted with them."

The review procedure under the TRIPS Council serves several purposes. First, because all WTO members are aware that they must submit their implementing legislation for extensive review, members may take greater care in drafting implementing legislation to carry out the minimum standards of TRIPS. Second, the review procedure presents an opportunity for other members to raise concerns about a country's IP law that might be resolved through discussion, clarification, or, in some cases, through the country's revision of its own law. In a number of cases, nations whose laws were under review were willing to undertake substantial additional work in order to fully satisfy the WTO's requirements. The review procedure presents essentially an informal forum for the resolution of disputes that avoids a formal dispute settlement proceeding.

Finally, outside of the review procedure, the TRIPS Council provides a forum in which any member can raise any issue relating to the compliance of TRIPS by another member. For example, after the review process concerning a nation's laws has been completed, an aggrieved nation may raise an issue concerning the continuing implementation and enforcement of the offending nation's intellectual property laws. The availability of this forum also provides a continuing alternative to the initiation of formal dispute settlement proceedings before the Dispute Settlement Body (DSB).

Consultations among countries. The DSB handles formal complaints lodged by WTO member states against another WTO country that allegedly is violating its treaty obligations. The DSB's rules are set forth in the Understanding on Rules and Procedures Governing the Settlement of Disputes, which is Annex 2 to the Agreement Establishing the WTO (Dispute Settlement Understanding or DSU). The DSB has the overriding aim of achieving a "solution mutually acceptable to the parties to a dispute and consistent with the covered agreements." DSU art. 3(7). To that end, Article 4 of the Understanding encourages member states to seek "consultations" with the member state involved in the dispute before filing any formal complaint. These consultations, which are confidential and without prejudice to any participant, are intended to foster mutually acceptable settlements of disputes among the participants. *Id.* arts. 4(4), 4(5). In addition, parties may also seek "good offices, conciliation and mediation" procedures in the DSB to resolve a dispute amicably, without the lodging of a formal complaint. *Id.* art. 5. Good offices consist of providing logistical support for the parties to reach an amicable settlement; conciliation involves an independent, neutral person to participate in the settlement negotiations; and mediation involves an independent, neutral person to propose possible solutions for a settlement.

WTO complaint. However, if no settlement results from the consultation within 60 days of receipt of the request, member states can file a formal complaint with the DSB. *Id.* art. 4(7). The country that files the complaint is known as the "complainant," while the country whose law is being challenged is known as the "respondent." Other WTO countries with a substantial interest in the dispute may also join as "third parties," with the right to be heard and offer written submissions to the WTO panel. *Id.* art. 10(2). Within 45 days of the filing, the DSB then establishes a panel to hear and rule on the dispute. The panel is supposed to complete its findings within 6 months (or, in cases of urgency, within 3 months). *Id.* art. 12(8). The WTO panel is typically composed of three panelists from countries other than those involved in the dispute who have experience in international trade law or policy. *Id.* art. 8. Members may oppose the nomination of a panelist only for "compelling reasons." *Id.* art. 8(6). If the dispute is between a developing and developed country, the developing country has a right to request a panelist from a developing country. *Id.* art. 8(10). Sometimes, countries file WTO complaints, but then later decide not to pursue them or end up settling the dispute with the other country.

WTO panel. If the complaint is pursued, a WTO panel is appointed to "make an objective assessment of the matter before it, including an objective assessment of the facts of the case and the applicability of and conformity with the relevant covered agreements." *Id.* art. 11. Each party to the dispute files written submissions to the panel. The panel then holds a first hearing in which parties make oral arguments. Afterwards, the parties have the opportunity to file written rebuttals and to make another oral argument at the second hearing of the panel. The panel has the authority to enlist the aid of experts and, for any factual issue concerning scientific or technical matter, to ask an expert advisory group to prepare a report. *Id.* art. 13(2). The panel also may seek information from any relevant source it wants. *Id.* After the two hearings, the panel will prepare an "interim report" with its findings and recommendations, and issue the interim report to both sides for their review. *Id.* art. 15(2). The parties can then file comments to the panel on the interim report. Finally, the panel issues its final report containing findings of facts and recommendations on the dispute. The report becomes the official ruling of the DSB within 60 days unless a consensus of WTO members rejects it or a party appeals the decision. *Id.* art. 16(4).

Appellate Body. Since consensus of WTO countries is difficult to obtain, most parties challenge a panel decision through appeal. Either side can appeal a WTO panel's decision to the Appellate Body (AB). The AB is composed of seven members who are appointed by the DSB based on their representativeness of the WTO and their expertise. Each member of the AB serves 4–year terms, which may be renewed once. *Id.* art. 17(2). Appeals are limited to legal issues covered in the panel report and legal interpretations of the panel; factual issues cannot be revisited. *Id.* art. 17(6). Each appeal is heard by a 3–member panel of the AB. The AB "may uphold, modify, or reverse" the panel's legal findings and conclusions. *Id.* art. 17(13). Appeals typically last 60 days. *Id.* art. 17(5). The DSB then accepts the AB's report within 30 days, or can reject it but only by a consensus of the member states.

Implementation. If the DSB finds that a WTO country has violated TRIPS, the offending country is supposed to follow the recommendations of the panel or appellate report to correct the violation. However, if following the recommendations immediately would be impractical, as is often the case, the offending country is given a reasonable period of time to comply. *Id.* art. 21(3). Typically, countries mutually agree to the period of time for implementation, such as one year from the date of adoption of the report. And, if the offending country fails to do so within that time and the complainant requests, the offending country must enter into negotiations to pay mutually-acceptable compensation for the continuing violation. If no compensation agreement is forthcoming, the complainant may request authorization from the DSB to impose trade sanctions or retaliation on the offending country—typically in the form of the complaining country's suspension of concessions or other obligations owed to the offending country. *Id.* art. 22(2). The trade sanctions sought should relate to the same sector involved in the dispute (e.g., patents in a patent dispute), unless it is not practicable or effective, in which case the trade sanctions can relate to another sector within that same agreement (e.g., TRIPS). If the latter option is also not practicable or effective, the trade sanctions can relate to a sector in another covered agreement (e.g., GATS). *Id.* art. 22(3). The offending country can object to the trade sanctions proposed, in which case the DSB refers the matter to arbitration. *Id.* art. 22(6). The arbitration is to be carried out by the original WTO panel if the members are available, but, if not, then by an arbitrator appointed by the Director–General. The arbitrator then is authorized to determine whether the level of the proposed trade sanction is equivalent to the level of nullification or impairment caused by the TRIPS violation. *Id.* art. 22(7). Trade sanctions are considered a last resort in the DSB and have been used only sparingly (only 9 instances through January 2011).

DSB surveillance. The Dispute Settlement Body keeps "under surveillance the implementation of adopted recommendations or rulings." *Id.* art. 21(6). On the WTO website, the Secretariat provides extensive information, including status reports, for every WTO dispute. At its monthly meetings, the DSB also discusses the progress of implementation—or lack thereof—by countries. The minutes of these meetings are also published on the WTO website. Finally, the WTO publishes an Annual Report that discusses the status of each dispute that is unresolved.

As should be evident by these elaborate procedures, WTO countries anticipated the possibility that some countries might be slow to correct their violations. Although perhaps one might have guessed that such "rogue" nations would be countries that are havens for commercial piracy, we will later discuss a couple disputes in which the U.S. is the offending nation that has been slow to correct its violation.

MEASURING TRIPS COMPLIANCE AND DEFIANCE: THE WTO COMPLIANCE SCORECARD

Edward Lee.
18 J. Intell. Prop. L. (2011).

II.   Statistics on the First Fifteen Years of TRIPS

The fifteenth anniversary of the TRIPS Agreement's effective date marks a good time for reflection. With the deadlock in the current Doha Round of negotiations, the WTO, as an institution, seems at a crossroads. Yet, the current stalemate cannot erase the accomplishments of the WTO over the past fifteen years in handling trade-related disputes among countries. This Part analyzes the number of IP disputes brought before the WTO since its inception in 1995 to Jan. 2011, and tracks how these IP disputes were disposed, whether by settlement[11] or WTO decision.

B.   TRIPS DISPUTES, 1995–JANUARY 2011

From 1995 to Jan. 2011, WTO countries brought 29 formal complaints involving the TRIPS Agreement out of the 419 total challenges—or just roughly 7% of all WTO disputes. Some of the complaints involved related controversies, which, if paired together, would reduce the total number to 22 different TRIPS matters. A recent set of challenges brought by India and Brazil against the EU in 2010 for seizure of generic drugs in transit was still pending in January 2011, although the dispute brought by India appears close to a settlement.[32]

1.   *Settled Cases.* Most of the TRIPS complaints were settled by the countries or were not pursued to a WTO dispute panel. Excluding the pending EU generic drug dispute, 62% of TRIPS challenges (13 of 21 completed matters) settled or were not pursued.

2.   *WTO Panel and AB Decisions.* Out of the 21 resolved TRIPS matters, only 8 went to a WTO panel for decision. In all but one dispute (DS59 Indonesia Auto) at least one violation of TRIPS was found. However, of the 7 matters in which violations were found, it is worth pointing out that 5 of those decisions also found some aspect of the respondent's challenged law was consistent with TRIPS—perhaps rendering the appearance of a Solomonic judgment. Only 3 of the 7 (43%) panel decisions in which a TRIPS violation was found were appealed to the Appellate Body. That is lower than the general rate for WTO panel decisions, for which approximately 70% of all panel reports were appealed.

3.   *Disputes by Subject Matter.* In terms of subject matter before the WTO panels, 3 decisions involved patents; 2 involved copyrights; 3 in-

---

11. For simplicity, in this Part, I include under "settlement" any dispute that was not pursued to a formal WTO panel, even if no "mutually agreed settlement" was announced by the countries to the WTO.

32. *See India–EU Generic Drug Row "Resolved" at Brussels Summit*, BBC, Dec. 10, 2010, http://www.bbc.co.uk/news/world-europe–11971568; *see also* Dispute Settlement, *European Union and a Member State—Seizure of Generic Drugs in Transit*, WT/DS408/1 (May 11, 2010) & WT/DS409/1 (May 12, 2010).

volved trademarks or geographical indications; and 1 also involved customs disposal of counterfeit and pirated goods, as well as criminal law requirements under TRIPS.

4. *Complainants and Respondents.* In the 22 TRIPS matters, the complainants and respondents were as follows:

TRIPS Disputes, 1995 to Jan. 2011 Table 1			
Complainants (some matters have multiple complainants)		Respondents (some matters have multiple respondents)	
Member	Disputes	Member	Disputes
United States	17	EU	5
EU	7	United States	4
Brazil	2	Canada	2
Australia	1	China	2
Canada	1	Argentina	1
India	1	Brazil	1
		Denmark	1
		Greece	1
		India	1
		Indonesia	1
		Ireland	1
		Japan	1
		Pakistan	1
		Portugal	1
		Sweden	1

The breakdown of complainants and respondents is interesting on several fronts. First, the U.S. is the biggest complainant, filing a challenge in 77% (17 of 22) of the TRIPS matters. The EU is the second biggest complainant, filing challenges in 32% (7 of 22) of the TRIPS matters. Only two developing countries (Brazil and India) have raised TRIPS challenges so far, which were against the U.S. and the EU. The large number of complaints by the U.S. and EU is also reflected in WTO challenges generally. According to Leitner and Lester's 2009 study, the U.S. brought the most WTO challenges (93, representing 22% of challenges) in the WTO, while the EU, the second most (81, representing 19%).

Second, the EU has the most TRIPS challenges (at 5) against it, while the U.S. has the second most at 4 challenges. A similar breakdown exists for all WTO disputes; according to Leitner and Lester's survey, the U.S. has received the most challenges at 108 (27%), with the EU second at 67 (17%). The majority of TRIPS complaints have been against developed countries. Fifteen of the 22 TRIPS disputes (68%) were against developed countries, while 7 (32%) were against developing countries. Of the 15 matters against developed countries, all but 2 were brought by developed countries. Conversely, all of the 7 disputes against developing countries were brought by developed countries. In other words, the South countries have all refrained from challenging each other's implementation of TRIPS. Thus, in the majority of TRIPS challenges, the disputes involved the North versus the North, although the North did go after the South in 7 disputes.

Third, the TRIPS challenges before the WTO are a "U.S.-EU show." Remarkably, every single TRIPS challenge in the first fifteen years of the WTO had either the U.S., EU, or both involved in the dispute either as a complainant or respondent. The heavy U.S. and EU involvement in TRIPS disputes is consistent with their dominance in WTO disputes generally. From 1995 to 2009, 43.3% of the total WTO disputes involved either the U.S. or EU as complainant, while 43.8% of the total WTO complaints involved either the U.S. or EU as respondents. Fifty disputes pitted the U.S. and EU against each other, 5 of which involved TRIPS disputes. More recent trends from 2005 to 2009 indicate, however, that the U.S. and EU have decreased their number of WTO challenges, while developing countries have increased their challenges. Also, China has become a more frequent participant in WTO disputes—mainly as a respondent, but also as a complainant. Despite the recent trends, the TRIPS disputes have been dominated by the U.S. and EU throughout the entire period.

   5. *Time to Correct Violations.* Finally, in terms of TRIPS compliance, all of the offending countries in the seven disputes with a TRIPS violation—with the notable exception of the U.S. in two of the disputes—enacted changes to their laws to bring them into compliance. The U.S. has not corrected its violations in the Section 110(5) and Havana Club Rum disputes.[55] The average time it took the offending countries, other than the U.S., to correct their violations was less than a year (10.4 months) from the DSB's adoption of the WTO decision. The breakdown by member and dispute is shown in the following Table:

Time Taken by Member to Comply with WTO Decision Table 2	
Member and Dispute	Time to Comply
India–Pharmaceutical Patents ("mailbox rule")	15 months fixed
Canada–Pharmaceutical Patents	4 months fixed
Canada–Patent Term	9 months fixed
EU–Trademark and GIs	1 year fixed
China–IP Rights	1 year fixed
U.S.–Section 110(5)	10 years + counting*
U.S.–Havana Club Rum	9 years + counting*

---

55. *See* Current Status, *United States—Section 110(5) of US Copyright Act*, WT/DS160, http://www.wto.org/english/tratop_e/dispu_e/cases_e/ds160_e.htm (last visited Feb. 7, 2011); Dispute Settlement Body, Minutes of Sept. 21, 2010, ¶¶ 21–25, Meeting WT/DSB/M/287 (Nov. 5, 2010) [hereinafter Sept. 2010 Minutes] (discussing unfixed status of Section 110(5)); Current Status, *United States—Section 211 Omnibus Appropriations Act of 1998*, WT/DS176, http://www.wto.org/english/tratop_e/dispu_e/cases_e/ds176_e.htm (last visited Feb. 7, 2011); Sept. 2010 Minutes, *supra*, ¶¶ 2–16 (discussing unfixed status of Section 211).

Thus, with the exception of the U.S., members have corrected their TRIPS violations within a short amount of time. Although the sample is small, 71% of the TRIPS violations have been fully (and timely) corrected—a number that is similar to Hudec's analysis of full correction in 68% of GATT disputes from 1948 to 1990. Davey estimates that, in the first ten years of the WTO, successful implementation occurred in 83% of the disputes.

NOTES AND QUESTIONS

1. Based on the statistics of the first fifteen years of the Dispute Settlement Body and TRIPS, do you think the DSB has been a success?

2. What do you make of the U.S.'s failure to correct two of its TRIPS violations within a reasonable time? Why do you think the EU has not sought trade sanctions in either case?

3. Major developed countries were resolved to get an enforcement mechanism for international IP treaties, in order to secure greater protection of IP particularly in developing countries. Are you surprised by the relatively few TRIPS disputes brought in the first fifteen years of its implementation? What might explain the low number of TRIPS complaints? Does it show that the U.S. and other developed countries are satisfied with the progress of IP protection around the world?

d. Transitional Provisions Under TRIPS for Developing and Least Developed Countries

The drafters of the TRIPS Agreement recognized that developing and least developed countries may need more time to implement the obligations of TRIPS. TRIPS therefore established a staggered system to provide transitional provisions to developing countries and least developed countries. Under Article 65, all countries, including developed countries, were given one year from the effective date of TRIPS to apply the provisions, meaning until January 1, 1996.

Developing countries and least developed countries were given even greater transitional periods, although the basic requirements of national treatment and most favored nation still apply during the transition. Developing countries and countries transitioning from a centrally-controlled economy to a free market economy were given an additional four years—until January 1, 2000—to apply the provisions of TRIPS. Under Article 66, least developed countries had an additional ten years—until January 1, 2006—to comply with the provisions. In late 2005, the WTO TRIPS Council voted to extend the transition period for least developed countries to 2013. Further transition periods specific to patent protection are also given to developing and least developed countries, as will be discussed later in the patent chapter. Least developed countries can make requests to the Council of TRIPS seeking extensions to the ten-year transitional period under Article 66(1).

TRIPS does not provide its own definitions for developing countries and least developed countries. Countries may designate themselves as developing countries, but this self-selection is subject to the approval of the WTO and challenge by other members. In order for a country to be considered a least developed country by the WTO, the country must have received the designation from the United Nations. According to the WTO, in 2011, the UN listed 48 least developed countries, 31 of which are members of the WTO and 12 of which are petitioning to become members.[1]

Article 65(5) is an "anti-backsliding" provision, which states that during their respective transitional periods, WTO members "shall ensure that any changes in its laws, regulations and practice made during that period do not result in a lesser degree of consistency with the provisions of this Agreement." This means that, during the transition period, developing and least developed countries cannot lower their IP protections to be even more inconsistent with the obligations of TRIPS.

In 2003, the WTO provided further guidelines for least developed countries under TRIPS Article 66. Under Article 66(2), developed member countries are to provide incentives that encourage the transfer of technology to least developed member countries. In the Implementation of Article 66(2) of the TRIPS Agreement, the TRIPS Council provided that developed member countries must submit annual reports detailing their implementation of Article 66(2).[2] The reports are released as part of a three-year cycle: every three years, the annual report is to be "new" and "detailed," and in the intervening years countries must provide updates to their most recent reports. The reports, which are to be submitted to the TRIPS Council, must contain (a) an overview of legislative, policy, or regulatory incentives regimes; (b) identification of the specific types of incentives and which government agency or entity provides the incentive; (c) who is eligible to receive these incentives; and (d) any available information on how the incentives have functioned. The Implementation also provides that the TRIPS Council may review these rules in 2006 in order to make improvements.

A final issue is whether the transitional periods apply to new members who either designate themselves as developing countries or are listed by the UN as least developed countries. The WTO has noted that new members "have generally agreed in their membership agreements (their 'accession protocols') to apply the TRIPS Agreement from the date when they officially became WTO members, without the benefit of any transition period."[3] It is open to question whether this is simply as a matter of

---

1. The World Trade Organization, *Understanding the WTO: The Organization, Least-developed countries, at* http://www.wto.org/english/thewto_e/whatis_e/tif_e/org7_e.htm.

2. World Trade Organization for TRIPS, Implementation of Article 66.2 of the TRIPS Agreement, IP/C/28 (Feb. 20, 2003).

3. The World Trade Organization, *TRIPS FAQs.*

practice—or as a matter of obligation under the terms of Articles 65 and 66 of TRIPS.

2. THE WORLD INTELLECTUAL PROPERTY ORGANIZATION

The World Intellectual Property Organization (WIPO) is an intergovernmental organization and a specialized agency of the United Nations, based in Geneva, Switzerland. In 2011, WIPO had 184 members. Before TRIPS, WIPO was the most important international forum for the development of international intellectual property treaties and norms. It also served to administer the world's most important intellectual property law treaties, such as the Paris Convention on patents and trademarks and the Berne Convention on copyrights, a role that WIPO inherited from its predecessor, the United International Bureaux for the Protection of Intellectual Property, or BIRPI, founded in 1893. With the enactment of TRIPS, however, WIPO's importance in setting the agenda for international intellectual property has been greatly eclipsed by the WTO.

Nevertheless, WIPO continues to have some relevance. With the notable exception of TRIPS, WIPO continues to administer the major intellectual property law treaties of the world (although even this function is curbed by TRIPS's incorporation of parts of the Berne and Paris Conventions). WIPO also today handles the dispute settlement procedure for the Uniform Domain–Name Dispute Resolution Policy (UDRP), which has been a popular method to resolve domain name disputes. Apart from these functions, WIPO serves as a forum for the development of new intellectual property treaties or harmonization efforts, as well as for the dissemination of international property norms based upon more informal means. In recent years, WIPO has undertaken an educational role that appears to be growing in importance and has assumed the lead role in the negotiation among countries of the Development Agenda, discussed later below.

3. THE EUROPEAN UNION

Although intellectual property harmonization is just one small facet of the European Union's (EU) role, there is no dispute that the EU has been at the forefront of efforts for regional harmonization of intellectual property laws, which have influenced not only Europe, but countries outside the EU. Below we provide a brief summary of the EU's structure and function.

The EU is a political and economic union of twenty-seven nations of Europe. In terms of economic power, the EU surpasses the United States. Just to get a sense of the scope of the EU, the countries comprising the EU have a total population of 455 million and an $11 trillion economy, which constitutes 28% of world GDP and 20% of world trade. With additional nations expected to join, the EU may add to its already formidable economic power.

The EU's roots can be traced to the 1950s when a small group of six nations decided to form a customs union, which is defined as a group of nations that agree to abolish all trade barriers within union members and to adopt a single economic policy towards non-members. The Treaty of Rome established the European Economic Community in 1957, which was amended by the Single European Act in 1986, with an eye to creating a single European union. Then, in 1993, the Mastricht Treaty on European Union created the EU, subsuming the EEC. The Treaty of Amsterdam added some further refinements and amendments in 1999. In 2009, the Lisbon Treaty amended the two main treaties of the EU, the Mastricht Treaty and the Rome Treaty. Afterwards, the Mastricht Treaty was named the Treaty on European Union (TEU), and the Rome Treaty was named the Treaty on the Functioning of the European Union (TFEU). The TEU creates the European Union, while the TFEU establishes rules for its functioning, such as the free movement of goods and EU national treatment.

From its beginnings as a customs union to the present, the EU has never waivered from its original concept—that is, to establish a common market for the free movement of goods and services in Europe and to remove all barriers that impede or hinder the common market. A common currency, the Euro, was introduced among a majority of EU member states, although it is not a mandatory obligation of EU countries. Some countries, notably the United Kingdom, have not adopted it. During the debt crisis of 2011, which severely affected the financial systems of Greece, Ireland, Portugal, and Spain, some EU countries began to doubt the viability of the Euro.

Today, goods and services can move freely across national borders of EU countries without the payment of any custom duties. For non-member states that trade with EU states, the same commercial and economic policies apply no matter which EU state is involved. For example, the same tariffs apply to goods for each member state of the EU; it makes no difference whether a party exports products to France, Germany, or any other EU state—the tariffs and duties are the same. The EU as a whole determines practically all trade and economic policy toward non-members.

The EU is comprised of three legislative bodies: (1) the EU Commission proposes all legislation, which is voted on by (2) the Council of Ministers increasingly with the consultation of (3) the Parliament, whose members are the only generally elected EU officials. The different ways in which EU legislation can be passed are complex and may vary depending on subject matter. Recently, the Parliament has attempted to assert a greater role in the process.

Legislation in the EU takes two primary forms: (i) a regulation and (ii) a directive. The difference between the two resembles the difference between a self-executing and a non-self-executing treaty that we discussed earlier. A regulation is essentially a type of EU federal law that applies directly in all member states and that supersedes any conflicting national law. (To borrow the treaty parlance, a regulation would be "self-executing.") By contrast, a directive does not have direct effect within member states (but is "non-self-executing"). Each state must enact implementing domestic legislation that gives effect to the directive, so each state has a certain amount of discretion of choosing how to achieve the directive's goal through its implementing legislation. *See* Article 249 (ex Article 189) of the Treaty of Rome.

As we have already seen in the *Phil Collins* case, the Court of Justice of the European Union (CJEU or CJ) has the ultimate authority to interpret EU laws. Courts in EU countries can refer questions about the correct interpretation of EU law to the CJEU, which then issues a preliminary ruling on the questions, setting forth the correct interpretation to be applied by the referring national court in the dispute.

In 2004, a new EU Constitution was proposed to replace the prior EU treaties, but the adoption of the proposed Constitution derailed following France's rejection of it in 2005. In the aftermath, the EU members agreed to a more modest reform in the Treaty of Lisbon (2009), which amended the existing EU treaties instead of replacing them.[1]

The EU has been actively involved in harmonizing intellectual property laws in Europe. Initially, the EU's main concern was to ensure that national intellectual property rights do not create barriers that would impede the free flow of products and services in the internal market. To take an example, suppose that a French owner of a patent wishes to obtain a patent in Germany in order to produce and sell the patented goods in the German market. If German patent law differed in significant respects from French law, then the French owner might find that it was unable to obtain a patent for the same invention in Germany because of different legal standards. The patent owner, unable to obtain intellectual property protection for its product, would then be reluctant to sell its product in Germany as the product, without a German patent, could be copied by anyone with impunity. This created a barrier to a common internal market.

To deal with this problem, the EU's initial efforts focused on harmonization directives for intellectual property law—effectively requiring certain minimum standards that all EU countries must follow under their national laws. We will study parts of some of the key IP directives in subsequent chapters.

A more recent approach adopted by the EU moves beyond harmonization towards a Community-wide recognition of intellectual property rights. Instead of the territorial approach to IP, with each country creating its own IP rights, a Community-wide IP right is created by the EU and

---

1. For a summary of these changes, see Grainne de Burca, *If at First You Don't Succeed: Vote, Vote Again: Analyzing the Second Referendum Phenomenon in EU Treaty Change*, 33 FORDHAM INT'L L. J. 1472 (2010).

applies all throughout the EU, subject to a uniform law (at least in theory). In 1994, the EU created the first of these Community-wide rights through the promulgation of the Trade Mark Regulation, which created the Community Trade Mark (CTM)—a unitary trademark that has effect in all countries in the EU. We will study the CTM in Chapter 4. There have been proposals also for a Community-wide design right and a Community-wide patent. These efforts stalled for some time, but, as discussed in Chapter 3, the proponents of the EU patent have recently gained momentum in their efforts.

NOTES AND QUESTIONS

1. *Controversy over the WTO.* In 1999, an estimated 25,000 protesters demonstrated at the ministerial meetings of the WTO in Seattle, forcing the meetings to be cancelled for one day. Some analysts attribute the reason for the protest to the intense criticism of the WTO's structure and decisionmaking under which concerns for labor, the environment, and human rights can easily be ignored. *See, e.g.*, Clyde Summers, *The Battle in Seattle: Free Trade, Labor Rights, and Societal Values*, 22 U. PA. J. INT'L ECON. L. 61 (2001). The WTO's formal decisionmaking for agreements takes place "behind closed doors," and is not subject to public participation or direct democratic accountability. Furthermore, developing countries contend that the decisionmaking process disadvantages them. Do you think the WTO should be restructured to provide greater transparency and public scrutiny and/or participation? Should the U.S. spearhead such reform efforts?

2. Although he was the President when the U.S. helped to draft the WTO agreements in 1994, Bill Clinton has become highly critical of the WTO, concluding that the Seattle protesters had legitimate grievances: "[T]he WTO would have to be more open, and more sensitive to trade and environmental issues, and the wealthy countries that benefited from globalization would have to do more to bring its benefits to the other half of the world that was still living on less than two dollars a day." *See* BILL CLINTON, MY LIFE 879–80 (2004). Do you agree?

E. RECENT DEVELOPMENTS IN INTERNATIONAL INTELLECTUAL PROPERTY

Early on, many observers viewed the TRIPS Agreement as favoring the developed countries, such as the U.S. and EU, and their efforts to seek stronger IP protections in developing countries around the world. A common perception was that TRIPS was an effort to achieve "upward harmonization" or a ratcheting up of IP laws in developing countries to the higher levels of IP protection in the U.S. and EU. However, two recent developments have contributed to a growing sentiment that TRIPS and the WTO did not give the developed world the victory they had sought for IP enforcement. First, the developing countries had some success in pushing a "development agenda" in the WTO, especially related to access to medicines, and also in WIPO. Second, the U.S. and other developed countries sought and continue to seek so-called "TRIPS plus" agreements—with higher levels of protection—outside the WTO, in bilateral and plurilateral agreements, such as the controversial Anti–Counterfeiting Trade Agreement (ACTA). Each development is discussed in turn.

1. DEVELOPMENT AGENDA IN WTO AND WIPO

Although the early perceptions of TRIPS as a one-sided victory for developed countries persist today, competing views have developed over time and have gained traction. One alternative view is that TRIPS Agreement itself contains flexibilities that recognize the importance of each country's prerogative to pursue development goals, in addition to or perhaps in lieu of the minimum standards of IP protection required by TRIPS. Grounded in the Preamble of TRIPS, as well as the Objectives and Principles of TRIPS enumerated in Articles 7 and 8, this "development" view of TRIPS became instrumental in the developing countries' successful efforts to get the WTO to recognize the Doha Declaration on the TRIPS Agreement and Public Health in November 2001 and Implementation Decision in 2003. (Both agreements will be studied in Chapter 3 on patents.) Since November 2001, the WTO has been engaged in the so-called Doha Development Round of negotiations, which began in Doha, Qatar and continued in Cancun, Hong Kong, and Geneva. However, after ten years, negotiations have stalled especially over the issues of agricultural subsidies and tariffs.

Meanwhile, as the Doha Development Round foundered, Argentina and Brazil succeeded in establishing in 2004 the Development Agenda for WIPO, with the backing of 12 other developing countries. At WIPO's General Assembly and inter-sessional intergovernmental meetings of WIPO countries, various papers with development proposals were discussed. WIPO sought also the input of NGOs, academics, and the public, in addition to UNCTAD, UNIDO, WHO, and the WTO. By 2006, the proposals ballooned to 111. These were later winnowed down to 45 adopted recommendations, as well as the establishment of the Committee on Development and Intellectual Property (CDIP) that was empowered to develop a plan for how the 45 recommendations might be implemented.

The 45 recommendations were grouped into 6 clusters: (A) Technical Assistance and Capacity Building; (B) Norm-setting, Flexibilities, Public Policy and Public Domain; (C) Technology Transfer, Information and Communication Technologies (ICT) and Access to Knowledge; (D) Assessment, Evaluation and Impact Studies; (E) Institutional Matters Including Mandate and Governance; and (F) Other Issues. Progress reports on implementation of some of the recommendations were made in 2009. Whether the Development Agenda in WIPO will eventually lead to lasting reforms remains to be seen.

PROBLEM 1–6

You have been enlisted by Argentina and Brazil to assess their strategy of pursuing the Development Agenda in WIPO, rather than the WTO. Professor Laurence Helfer has theorized about the potential strategic benefit of "regime shifting"—moving treaty discussions from one international forum to another—for developing countries. According to Helfer, "[i]ntellectual property regime shifting thus heralds the rise of a complex legal environment in which seemingly settled treaty bargains are contested and new dynamics of lawmaking and dispute settlement must be considered." Laurence R. Helfer, *Regime Shifting: The TRIPS Agreement and the New Dynamic of International Intellectual Property Law–Making*, 29 YALE J. INT'L L. 1, 14 (2004). Thus, "regime shifting provides an opportunity to generate 'counterregime norms'— binding treaty rules and nonbinding soft law standards that seek to alter the prevailing legal landscape." *Id.* Some regime shifting may lead to only incremental reforms or changes, while, in other instances, the reforms may become more fundamental. *Id.* Argentina and Brazil are particularly interested in hearing your views on (i) whether they should continue to pursue the Development Agenda in WIPO and, if so, (ii) should they also attempt to push the same development goals in the WTO. Also, (iii) would it be desirable for WIPO and WTO to be integrated themselves in some way? To help formulate your answers, read the TRIPS Preamble and Articles 7 & 8 in the Documents Supplement, the excerpt from the WIPO Development Agenda below, and the following article by Professor Margaret Chon.

The 45 Adopted Recommendations, WIPO Development Agenda (excerpt)

Cluster E: Institutional Matters including Mandate and Governance

39. To request WIPO, within its core competence and mission, to assist developing countries, especially African countries, in cooperation with relevant international organizations, by conducting studies on brain drain and make recommendations accordingly.

40. To request WIPO to intensify its cooperation on IP related issues with United Nations agencies, according to Member States' orientation, in particular UNCTAD, UNEP, WHO, UNIDO, UNESCO and other relevant international organizations, especially the WTO in order to strengthen the coordination for maximum efficiency in undertaking development programs.

41. To conduct a review of current WIPO technical assistance activities in the area of cooperation and development.

*42. To enhance measures that ensure wide participation of civil society at large in WIPO activities in accordance with its criteria regarding NGO acceptance and accreditation, keeping the issue under review.

43. To consider how to improve WIPO's role in finding partners to fund and execute projects for intellectual property-related assistance in a transparent and member-driven process and without prejudice to ongoing WIPO activities.

---

* Recommendations with an asterisk were identified by the 2007 General Assembly for immediate implementation.

*44.   In accordance with WIPO's member-driven nature as a United Nations Specialized Agency, formal and informal meetings or consultations relating to norm-setting activities in WIPO, organized by the Secretariat, upon request of the Member States, should be held primarily in Geneva, in a manner open and transparent to all Members. Where such meetings are to take place outside of Geneva, Member States shall be informed through official channels, well in advance, and consulted on the draft agenda and program.

Cluster F: Other Issues

45.   To approach intellectual property enforcement in the context of broader societal interests and especially development-oriented concerns, with a view that "the protection and enforcement of intellectual property rights should contribute to the promotion of technological innovation and to the transfer and dissemination of technology, to the mutual advantage of producers and users of technological knowledge and in a manner conducive to social and economic welfare, and to a balance of rights and obligations," in accordance with Article 7 of the TRIPS Agreement.

INTELLECTUAL PROPERTY AND THE DEVELOPMENT DIVIDE

Margaret Chon.
27 Cardozo L. Rev. 2821 (2006).

Introduction: Towards Equality in Global Intellectual Property

In the early twenty-first century, the concept of intellectual property is beginning to encounter insistently the concept of development. These recent interactions, occurring within the context of accelerating globalization, have renewed questions about the fundamental purpose of intellectual property.

This Article attempts to map the challenges raised by these encounters between intellectual property and development. It proposes a normative principle of global intellectual property—one that is responsive to development paradigms that have moved far beyond simple utilitarian measures of social welfare. This new principle of substantive equality is a necessary corollary to the formal equality principles of national treatment and minimum standards that are now imposed on virtually all countries regardless of their level of development. * * *

I.   Intellectual Property Encounters Development

A.   The WTO Encounters Development

All observers agree that intellectual property globalization was accelerated greatly by TRIPS. * * * Because so many countries, both rich and poor, have a strong interest in participating in the rules of global trading established by the WTO, intellectual property norms have now been imported into many countries that had previously little to no legal regulation in this area. Intellectual property laws through TRIPS are linked to non-intellectual property issues, such as trade in agricultural and textile goods. Termed linkage bargaining, previously unrelated areas are now linked via negotiations over universal trade rules. Linkage bargaining was critical to getting developing countries to sign on to the higher standards of intellectual property protection than they would have otherwise desired.

Furthermore, the minimum standards of TRIPS are an example of deep integration—"integration not only in the production of goods and services but also in standards and other domestic policies." In contrast to the previous trade approach of shallow integration, where the focus was on trade barriers at the borders rather than harmonization of standards across borders, under TRIPS, developing countries are no longer thought to need the special protection of high trade barriers in light of their relative economic vulnerability. The TRIPS approach abandons the special treatment approach of shallow integration and adopts a formalistic, universalistic approach of deep integration of minimum standards regardless of a country's economic status. The end of preferential treatment for poor countries is tied to the ever-pervasive process of marketization of economies across the world.

The allusions within the TRIPS Agreement to national public policy and public interest concerns related to development were placed there at the behest of the so-called "Group of 14" developing countries.[88] As stated earlier, this language includes "developmental . . . objectives" of all member states, mentioned in the Preamble, as well as a reference in TRIPS Article 8 (entitled "Principles") to member states' ability to "adopt measures necessary to protect public health and nutrition, and to promote the public interest in sectors of vital importance to their socio-economic and technological development." TRIPS Article 7 (entitled "Objectives") frames "[t]he protection and enforcement of intellectual property rights" within a framework of "mutual advantage of producers and users of technological knowledge and in a manner conducive to social and economic welfare, and to a balance of rights and obligations."

The Group of 14 pushed to include this language referencing development after it became inevitable that intellectual property rights were to be included in the global trading framework. By presenting their own text, these countries wanted

> to highlight the importance of public policy objectives underlying national IPR [Intellectual Property Rights] systems, the necessity of recognizing those objectives at the international level and . . . the need to respect and safeguard national legal systems and traditions on IPRs, in view of the diverse needs and levels of development of states participating in the IPR negotiations.

---

88. These were: Argentina, Brazil, Chile, China, Colombia, Cuba, Egypt, India, Nigeria, Pakistan, Peru, Tanzania, Uruguay and Zimbabwe. Other participants in the Uruguay round that submitted proposed drafts included the European Community, the United States, Switzerland, Japan and Australia. Gervais, supra note 31, at 73 n.1; *see also* Adronico O. Adede, *Origins and History of the TRIPS Negotiations, in Trading in Knowledge*, supra note 24, at 28; Daniel J. Gervais, *Intellectual Property, Trade & Development: The State of Play*, 74 FORDHAM L. REV. 505, 505–09 (2005).

From the perspective of developed countries, non-tariff trade barriers such as overly-lax intellectual property standards were viewed as the key challenge in a post-TRIPS environment. The resulting one-size-fits-all minimum standards of intellectual property protection contained in TRIPS apply to countries varying widely in their levels of development. Thus this language of "development" was to provide developing countries with some leeway to argue in favor of flexibilities in the minimum standards mandated by TRIPS, if these flexibilities served the purposes of development.

Partly in recognition of the inequalities permeating this global trading regime, the current "Doha Development Round" of the WTO is supposed to focus on the needs of the least developed countries. One of the most galvanizing events so far of the Doha Round, by all accounts, has been the negotiation between developed and developing countries over the relationship of TRIPS to public health. TRIPS allows for limited exceptions to the exclusive rights of patent and copyright. One of them is Article 30, which includes "exceptions to the exclusive rights conferred by a patent, provided that such exceptions do not unreasonably conflict with a normal exploitation of the patent and do not unreasonably prejudice the legitimate rights of the patent owner, taking account of the legitimate interests of third parties." Another is Article 31, which allows countries to engage in compulsory licensing under certain conditions, the most salient of which is that "any such use shall be authorized predominantly for the supply of the domestic market of the Member authorizing such use." Because many developing countries in need of pharmaceuticals do not have domestic manufacturing capacity, this condition effectively nullified any ability to invoke compulsory licensing. Essentially, governments can only override the patents as long as they order generic substitutes from domestic producers. But most of the countries that need the drugs most urgently have no pharmaceutical industry of their own.

The battle over these legal provisions culminated in various concessions: first in the so-called Doha Declaration on TRIPS and Public Health, and then in the General Council Decision that allows the most desperate countries to override patents on expensive antiretroviral drugs and order cheaper copies from generic manufacturers located in other countries. Negotiations over the implementation of these concessions are still underway.

IV. A Proposed Substantive Equality Norm

In this section, I argue that a principle of substantive equality is required. It is not enough to insist on procedural fairness or that countries adhere to formal equality in the form of national treatment coupled with minimum standards. There must also be a focus on substantive equality. At a minimum—in the absence of new multilateral agreements or amendments to TRIPS or to other multilateral instruments such as the Berne Convention, or to WIPO's governing documents—I propose that this substantive equality principle be integrated throughout intellectual property globalization decision-making via a legal rule akin to the strict scrutiny doctrine in U.S. constitutional law. This doctrine generally allows decision-makers to review and strike down government regulation under a non-deferential standard of review (also known as strict scrutiny review) where that state-granted right will interfere substantially with a suspect category. By analogy, the decision-maker will exert strict scrutiny review where the regulation (in this case, the government intervention in the form of the grant of an exclusive right over intellectual property or the withholding of an exception or limitation of that exclusive right) conflicts with a basic need (in this case, the provision of a development-sensitive human need, as defined in part by the Millennium Development Goals). This principle of equality would be applied both domestically as well as in international decision-making venues. * * *

[In an extensive discussion, Professor Chon argues that a principle of substantive equality is embedded in the term "development" recognized in the TRIPS preamble and objectives, Articles 7 and 8, the DOHA Declaration, and WTO decisions. *Ed.*]

This norm also does not defer to the goodwill or good intent of domestic policymakers to achieve the optimal resource distribution of knowledge goods, based on a utilitarian social welfare calculus. It embodies a heightened skepticism towards both domestic and global decision-makers with respect to balance-setting, at least in the context of provision of basic goods. (We may not be so concerned about agency capture when it comes to the provision of non-basic goods such as Hollywood DVDs.) At a very general level, such a principle would operate in the following directions.

Norm interpretation:

    ● Incorporating a principle of strict scrutiny into the interpretation of relevant treaty texts such as TRIPS, so as to influence the outcome of international intellectual property dispute resolution;

    ● Incorporating a strict scrutiny principle into domestic law, regardless of the context of international treaty compliance, and applicable not only to the public regulation but also to private ordering (such as licensing practices being challenged by contract law).

Norm setting:

    ● Amending existing treaties to include language allowing for the incorporation of a development-related substantive equality norm;

    ● Expanding the flexibilities, exceptions and limitations within existing treaties; expanding transitional periods;

    ● Expanding technical assistance to include development of indigenous publishing capacity;

    ● Creating new treaties within intellectual property venues such as WIPO that directly address the question of basic needs;

- Revising the Berne Appendix to include more expansive mechanisms for compulsory licensing for education, libraries, translation and other activities directed at the needs of developing countries.

Norm alternatives:

- Expanding collective licensing schemes and finding other alternative ways to compensate IP producers in developed countries;

- Facilitating the development of domestic publishing capacity;

- Advocating for TRIPS plus standstill or rollback;

- Encouraging the participation and increasing the effectiveness of indigenous social movements who could speak on or behalf of education "consumers" within their own countries, and link them with others to form a global social consensus for access to essential educational materials. In the specific context of TRIPS interpretation, the application of a general substantive equality norm might result in the following outcomes. A WTO dispute settlement panel might decide that Country A's policy to exclude copyright protection for textbooks and allow diffusion to flourish for a limited period of time in a specific field of study is acceptable under the three step test of Article 13. Or, as Ruth Okediji proposes, a dispute settlement panel might develop a proportional approach to access in the context of determining whether a country's compulsory licensing of educational materials violates TRIPS.

Conclusion: Turning Intellectual Property Swords into Development Plowshares

If the instrumental mandate of intellectual property law is truly to increase knowledge for positive purposes, then there must be fuller consideration of the provision of basic needs and other global public goods such as food security, education, and health care. Undernourished, diseased, dying, undereducated, or extremely impoverished populations are viewed by many as negative externalities both qualitatively and quantitatively more serious than the danger of under-incentivizing authors and inventors. The latter is the externality to which intellectual property law devotes its exclusive attention. This disjuncture over priorities has highlighted an increasingly untenable intellectual solipsism of the intellectual property policymaking framework, as intellectual property globalization encounters ethical concerns associated with development.

NOTES AND QUESTIONS

1. How should the WTO view the relationship between intellectual property and development issues, such as education, health, and basic living conditions in WTO countries? Does the TRIPS Agreement provide any guidance? Should TRIPS be amended in any way to take development issues into greater account?

2. Should poor countries be allowed to receive preferential treatment under IP treaties? Or should poor countries be subject to the same minimum

standard requirements as other countries? Is there a downside to a "one size fits all" approach to IP?

3.   Evaluate Professor Chon's proposal for the recognition of a substantive equality principle within international intellectual property agreements such as TRIPS? Do you agree with her proposal? How would it work in practice?

4.   Should the WTO join forces with either the UN or WIPO, a specialized agency within the UN, to coordinate efforts to promote development in developing countries?

5.   *Soft law.* "Soft law" is a term of art that refers to non-binding norms, if not obligations, on states. Although countries are under no treaty obligation to follow soft law, some theorists contend that soft law may be a more effective way to achieve greater international harmonization. For example, soft law norms may evolve into customary international law or a formal treaty that becomes binding. Soft law may offer flexibility for different norms to develop and refine over time, perhaps with eventual harmonization. Should soft law be used more in international intellectual property law? Is the WIPO Development Agenda a form of soft law?

2.   "TRIPS PLUS" AGREEMENTS: ACTA, AND BILATERAL AND PLURILATERAL TRADE AGREEMENTS

PROBLEM 1–7

Thailand has hired you to evaluate how national treatment and the most-favored nation principle affect, if at all, the bilateral FTAs and plurilateral agreements like ACTA made by some other WTO members. For example, do the WTO countries involved in ACTA have to extend to all other WTO countries the "TRIPS-plus" protections in ACTA for (i) damages in civil cases of infringement and (ii) the broader, easier-to-satisfy standard of "commercial scale" infringement for criminal prosecution of trademark counterfeiting and copyright piracy? Can Thailand benefit from ACTA protections of Thai-produced goods and works in ACTA countries without even joining ACTA? Review Articles 3 and 4 of TRIPS and the following discussion.

* * *

As the Development Agenda proceeded on one front, the U.S. and other developed countries pursued their own agenda of securing stronger protection and enforcement of copyrights and trademarks. Instead of working within the WTO or WIPO, the U.S. and other developed countries pursued bilateral and plurilateral agreements mainly with developing countries. Bilateral agreements are between two countries; plurilateral agreements are among a few (more than two) countries, but not as many countries as a multilateral agreement such as TRIPS. These bilateral and plurilateral agreements, which were made outside of the WTO, are commonly called "Free Trade Agreements" or FTAs.

Worldwide, 202 FTAs are in force among countries, 79 of which agreements contain provisions dealing with IP. The U.S. has been particularly active in this regard. The U.S. has agreed to and implemented FTAs with 20 countries, including agreements with Colombia, Korea, and Panama that were implemented in October 2011. The bilateral FTAs in force include agreements with Australia, Bahrain, Chile, Jordan, Morocco, Oman, Peru, and Singapore, all of which were adopted after the WTO's formation in 1994. Before 1994, the U.S. had a prior bilateral FTA (now still in force) with Israel, as well as a plurilateral FTA with Canada and Mexico (NAFTA). In 2004, the U.S. signed a plurilateral agreement with the Dominican Republic and five Central American countries (Costa Rica, El Salvador, Guatemala, Honduras, and Nicaragua) (the CAFTA–DR FTA). The U.S. is also pursuing a plurilateral Trans–Pacific Partnership (TPP) Agreement with the Asia–Pacific countries of Australia, Brunei, Chile, Malaysia, New Zealand, Peru, Singapore, and Vietnam.

The IP provisions in these FTAs are controversial because they typically impose higher standards of IP protection—so-called "TRIPS-plus" requirements—on the countries involved. The FTAs go above and beyond the minimum standards of protection required by TRIPS. For example, a favorite provision in FTAs of the U.S. is a copyright term that lasts the life of the author plus 70 years, 20 years more than required under the Berne Convention. Another common U.S. provision is a requirement that sound and scent be considered eligible subject matter for trademarks—something that TRIPS Article 15 does not require. The FTAs are controversial also because they often involve a developed country securing from a developing country an agreement to even higher levels of IP protection—in other words, the North versus the South. Some commentators have questioned the apparent unequal bargaining power underlying these agreements, although some developing countries like Thailand have successfully rebuffed the U.S.'s efforts to secure a "TRIPS-plus" FTA.

Even more controversial is ACTA, or the Anti–Counterfeiting Trade Agreement. ACTA is a plurilateral trade agreement—negotiated outside the WTO—that is focused on increasing measures to stop trademark counterfeiting and copyright piracy. The final text of ACTA was adopted in November 2010 and open for signature in May 2011. Led by the U.S., drafts of ACTA were negotiated in secrecy for nearly three years by mostly developed countries (Japan, Canada, EU, Australia, New Zealand, Korea, Singapore). Only two developing countries—Mexico and Morocco—took part. While negotiations remained secret, parts of drafts were reportedly leaked—which fomented fears of draconian measures being adopted.

As it played out, the final ACTA text did not contain a number of the more controversial proposals feared by its critics. The final ACTA draft made optional a controversial provision allowing countries to seize "suspect goods" while in transit to another country. ACTA art. 2.5(2). Yet ACTA does require "TRIPS-plus" levels of protection against trademark counterfeiting and copyright piracy, including requirements for injunctions and damages in civil cases, and a broader standard of "commercial scale" infringement that is subject to criminal penalties. ACTA arts. 2(1), 2(2), 2(14). The definition of "commercial scale" is one that the U.S. unsuccessfully attempted to be used in interpreting the TRIPS Agreement Article 61 in a dispute with China (discussed in Chapter 6). While the final ACTA draft was not as repressive or draconian as many critics feared from the earlier leaked drafts, ACTA remains a controversial development.

In 2012, the EU's ratification of ACTA was thrown suddenly into doubt as Poland and then Germany, Bulgaria, and the Netherlands voiced concerns about signing the treaty after thousands of people in Europe protested over ACTA.

NOTES AND QUESTIONS

1. Given the nature of minimum standards in creating only a floor and not a ceiling, is there anything inappropriate about developed countries seeking "TRIPS-plus" protections from developing countries outside of TRIPS?

2. Some scholars have proposed amending TRIPS to include maximum standards that set a limit on the level of IP protection allowed. Do you agree?

3. *Secrecy.* One of the main controversies over ACTA was the secret process in which it was drafted for nearly three years by trade representatives, outside the public's view. If the final text of ACTA turned out not to be as bad or restrictive as some feared, should we discount or dismiss the many criticisms of the secret process in which early drafts of ACTA were negotiated? Can use of "behind-closed-doors" negotiations be sometimes desirable?

4. *Sole executive agreement in U.S.* Instead of implementing ACTA as a treaty confirmed by two-thirds of the Senate or as a "congressional-executive" agreement passed by a majority of Congress, the Obama Administration bypassed Congress entirely. Amid much criticism, the Obama Administration indicated that ACTA only needs the president's approval in order to become law, based on the designation of ACTA as a "sole executive agreement." Sole executive agreements have been used in the past, such as to "settle claims of American nationals against foreign governments." *American Ins. Ass'n v. Garamendi*, 539 U.S. 396, 415 (2003). That settlement practice fell within the Executive's power to conduct foreign affairs. What about intellectual property laws? Don't they fall within Congress's powers, namely, the Copyright and Patent Clause and the Commerce Clause of the U.S. Constitution? Are you persuaded by the USTR's suggestion that ACTA is a sole executive agreement because it mostly tracks U.S. standards in existing laws and therefore is a matter of the Executive's enforcement power?

5. *Bibliographic note.* Jack Goldsmith & Lawrence Lessig, *Anti–Counterfeiting Agreement Raises Constitutional Concerns*, WASH. POST, March 26, 2010; Bryan Mercurio, *Trade Liberalisation in Asia: Why Intra–Asian Free Trade Agreements Are Not Utilised by the Business Community*, 6 ASIAN J. WTO & INT'L HEALTH L. & POL'Y 109 (2011); Free Trade Agreements, Office of the U.S. Trade Representative, http://www.ustr.gov/trade-agreements/free-trade-agreements.

F. BRIEF OVERVIEW OF U.S. INTELLECTUAL PROPERTY LAWS

This final section provides a brief overview of U.S. intellectual property laws. Although this brief discussion cannot replace individual study in courses focusing on U.S. law, we believe it would be useful to recap some of the major forms of IP under U.S. law—either as a "refresher" for students with prior study in this area, or as an introduction for students new to IP.

1. COPYRIGHT

A copyright is a bundle of exclusive rights granted to authors for their creative expression. U.S. copyright law dates all the way back to the early Republic, with the enactment of the Copyright Act of 1790, whose purpose was stated as follows: "An Act for the Encouragement of Learning, by Securing the Copies of Maps, Charts, and Books, to the Authors and Proprietors of Such Copies, during the Times Therein Mentioned." Act of May 31, 1790, 1 Stat. 124. The Act applied only to maps, charts, and books, and granted authors the "sole right and liberty of printing, reprinting, publishing and vending" the copies for a term of 14 years, renewable for a second term of 14 years.

Over the years, copyright law has expanded in scope, with each substantial revision of copyright law. Today, the Copyright Act of 1976 serves as the basic source of federal copyright law, although it has been amended numerous times. Under the Act, copyrights are granted to "all original works fixed in a tangible medium of expression." 17 U.S.C. § 102. Notice that there is no limitation anymore to maps, charts, and books. Copyright potentially applies to all creative expression, as long as it is original and fixed in a tangible medium. For example, copyrights are available to (1) literary works; (2) musical works, including any accompanying words; (3) dramatic works, including any accompanying music; (4) pantomimes and choreographic works; (5) pictorial, graphic and sculptural works; (6) motion pictures and other audiovisual works; (7) sound recordings; and (8) architectural works. *Id.*

Of all the requirements in copyright law, originality is the most fundamental in the U.S. As the Supreme Court has held, originality is not only a statutory requirement of the Copyright Act, it is a constitutional requirement under the Copyright and Patent Clause. The authority of Congress to enact copyright law emanates from the Copyright Clause, which states that Congress has the power "[t]o promote the Progress of Science and useful Arts by securing for limited Times to Authors and Inventors the exclusive Right to their respective Writings and Discoveries." U.S. CONST., art. I, § 8, cl. 8. In order to be considered an "Author" of a "Writing," a person must create some expressive work that is original. Originality means: (i) the work is independently created by the person, and (ii) the work has a minimal level of creativity. *Feist Publ'ns, Inc. v. Rural Tel. Serv. Co.*, 499 U.S. 340, 345 (1991). In most cases in which a person has independently created a work, the work probably will satisfy the second element; the level of creativity required is very low. In some cases, however, such as with the compilation of facts or uncopyrightable data, originality may be more difficult to satisfy—one must show originality in the selection, arrangement, or coordination of the material, meaning, for example, that one must show a particular listing of entries in a phone book has some minimal level of creativity beyond a common alphabetical listing. We will return to a discussion of originality in the copyright chapter.

Fixation also tends to be an easy hurdle to satisfy. This requirement is met as long as the author memorializes his or her expression in some form "sufficiently permanent or stable to permit it to be perceived, reproduced, or otherwise communicated for a period of more than transitory duration." 17 U.S.C. § 101 (definition of "fixed").

If these two requirements, originality and fixation, are met, an author receives a copyright *automatically.* There is no formality, such as filing a copyright application, in order to obtain a copyright. Although old U.S. law had required copyright notice "©" on each copy published (with forfeiture of the copyright for failing to provide copyright notice), after the U.S. joined the Berne Convention in 1989, U.S. law was amended to do away with such requirement. However, registration of a U.S. copyright (and deposit of copies of the work) in the U.S. Copyright Office in Washington, D.C., is required for U.S. works before an author can pursue a copyright infringement lawsuit. 17 U.S.C. § 411. (As discussed in Chapter 2, works of foreign origin are exempted from this requirement because of the Berne Convention's prohibition of formalities). Moreover, if an author places a "©" notice on his or her work, it can negate a defense of innocent infringement in the computation of damages. *Id.* § 401(d).

A copyright generally lasts the life of the author plus 70 years after the author's death (although there are some variations for different types of authors, such as corporate entities, that need not detain us here). A copyright gives authors the exclusive rights "to do and authorize" any of the following: (1) reproduction; (2) creation of derivative works; (3) public distribution; (4) public performance; and (5) public display of the copyrighted matter. 17 U.S.C. § 106. Of course, the right to prevent unauthorized copying is the most basic right of copyright. The Act also recognizes a right of importation for the copyright owner to exclude foreign made copies of copyrighted works from entering the U.S. without the owner's permission. 17 U.S.C. § 602(a). The copyright owner can enlist the aid of U.S. Customs in seizing any pirated or infringing products at the point of entry.

The Copyright Act also contains an elaborate set of exemptions and limitations on an author's exclusive rights. 17 U.S.C. §§ 107–122. The most well-known of these is the fair use doctrine. *Id.* § 107. The basic idea behind the fair use doctrine, which was developed first by courts and later codified in the 1976 Act, is to allow the public certain limited uses of copyrighted works, without authorization of the authors, in order to facilitate criticism, education, learning, and other First Amendment goals. Fair use is determined on a case-by-case basis, with courts analyzing a set of four factors enumerated in § 107 of the Copyright Act.

2. PATENTS

Patents are a bundle of exclusive rights granted to inventors for their inventions. Historically, federal patent law began with the Patent Act of 1790, which granted patents for inventions for a term of 14 years. Act of April 10, 1790, 1 Stat. 318. Over the years, Congress has enacted several major revisions to the Patent Code—the last in 2011 with the America Invents Act—but the expansion of patents has been relatively modest compared to copyright law. For example, the current term of patents under the Patent Code of 1952 is 20 years, only 6 years more than the original patent term in 1790. U.S. patent law is also subject to constitutional limits under the Copyright and Patent Clause.

In contrast to the relative ease with which authors may obtain copyrights for their works, obtaining a patent is a complicated process, filled with both administrative and substantive hurdles, which are briefly outlined below. Unlike obtaining a copyright, an inventor must file an application that will be reviewed by the U.S. Patent & Trademark Office (PTO), headquartered in Alexandria, Virginia. The Patent Office scrutinizes the invention disclosed in the patent application to see if it satisfies the requirements of patent law. The U.S. Patent Code establishes five basic requirements to obtain a patent: an invention must be (1) novel, (2) nonobvious, (3) useful, (4) fall within the subject matter of patentable inventions, and (5) the inventor must provide an adequate written description of the invention to enable someone skilled in the art to make it. For over 220 years, the first-to-invent an invention was entitled to the patent under U.S. law. However, almost all other countries grant patents to the first-to-file for the patent in the patent office. In 2011, the U.S finally changed its approach by passing the America Invents Act, which changed the U.S. system to a modified first-to-file system. We will discuss the key changes in Chapter 3.

The U.S. has taken a broad approach to patentable subject matter, favoring the patenting of "anything under the sun that is made by man," including genetically engineered life forms. *Diamond v. Chakrabarty*, 447 U.S. 303, 309 (1980). Patents may be given to new products and processes, as well as to new improvements on existing products and processes. We will analyze the requirements of obtaining a patent in greater depth as they relate to international IP in the patent chapter. It is worth noting here that the requirement of an adequate written description is meant to carry out the *quid pro quo* that is thought to underlie the grant of a patent: the inventor gets a 20–year monopoly on the invention (and can exclude others from making it), and, in exchange, the public gets the know-how that underlies the invention as disclosed in the patent application, which can later be freely used after the patent term expires.

A U.S. patent gives the patentee the right to exclude others from making, using, selling, offering for sale, and importing the patented invention without permission of the patent holder. 35 U.S.C. § 271. A U.S. patent has a term of 20 years from the date of application, consistent with the minimum standard under Article 33 of TRIPS. Unlike the Copyright Act, the Patent Act does not contain many (or practically, any) exemptions or limitations on the exclusive rights. There is, for example, no "fair use" of a patented invention. For this reason, a patent is seen as establishing the strongest form of IP protection, but for a limited term of 20 years. The patent owner can enforce its patent rights in federal court and obtain damages and injunctive relief. The patent owner can also prevent the entry into the United States of foreign-made goods that violate the patent by obtaining an exclusion order from the International Trade Commission under § 337 of the Tariff Act of 1930. 19 U.S.C. § 1337. These exclusion orders are enforced by the U.S. Customs Office, which has primary authority over imports into the United States. Under recent organizational changes, U.S. Customs is now part of the Department of Homeland Security.

The Patent Code also allows a special, more limited kind of "design" patent for "new, original and ornamental" designs on an article of manufacture. Such designs can qualify for a patent that lasts for 14 years from the date of grant. 35 U.S.C. §§ 171, 173. The key difference between a utility patent and a design patent is that a design patent protects the ornamental aspect of a product—meaning its look or appearance—but not its useful function. If a design feature is dictated primarily by function, it is not ornamental or eligible for design patent protection. Just as in the case of utility patents, U.S. courts also apply the requirements of novelty and nonobviousness to design patents, although the application of nonobviousness in the design context has been the source of disagreement. Some historical research suggests that the standard of nonobviousness from utility patents was not meant to be applied to designs. Despite the hurdles to obtain a design patent, the number of design patents has grown considerably starting in 2006. In 2010, the USPTO received the most design patent applications in its history (29,509). From 2006 to 2010, the USPTO granted over 20,000 design patents annually, whereas in prior years the number of design patents was several thousand less. The numbers suggest a growing attractiveness of design patents as a form of IP in the U.S.

3. TRADEMARKS AND UNFAIR COMPETITION

Trademark law is somewhat different from patent and copyright law, in the sense that a trademark does not generally create a set of exclusive rights, at least not formally. Instead, a trademark—meaning "any word, name, symbol, or device or any combination thereof" that is capable of distinguishing goods or services from those of another, 15 U.S.C. § 1127—establishes legal protection against other uses of marks by competitors that are "likely to cause confusion" or that dilute the source-identifying function of a famous trademark. Although "service mark" is sometimes used to describe a mark that is used to identify services instead of goods (such as a hair salon and spa, or restaurant), it is also fairly common today to use "trademark" to encompass both marks for goods and marks for services.

Trademark law in the U.S. began as a creature of state common law, which still remains important today. The basic tort of unfair competition, misappropriation, or "passing off" provides trademark holders who establish first or prior use of a mark in commerce (known as the "senior user") the ability to stop competitors (the "junior users") from using the mark in a way that would cause confusion among consumers. Trademarks function as a way to identify the *source* of the product or service, thus enabling consumers to judge the quality of products and services without having to do elaborate information gathering for each purchase. For example, if a consumer had a good experience with "Sarandi" products in the past, the consumer will likely be able to buy "Sarandi" products based on identification of the brand. Under common law, the rights of trademarks holders are limited to the areas in which they actually *used* their marks, plus some "reasonable zone of expansion" from that area. Thus, under common law, it is conceivable to have two different entities using the exact same trademark—one in New York and the other in Florida—without any exclusive rights to stop the other.

State common law still operates today to protect trademarks under unfair competition (although some states may have also enacted trademark statutes). In addition, federal law has provided an important overlay to trademark protection. In contrast with the Copyright and Patent Clause, the Constitution contains nothing specific relating to trademarks. The Commerce Clause, however, is the basis of power for Congress's enactment of federal trademark law in the Lanham Act of 1946, 15 U.S.C. §§ 1051–1141. The Lanham Act allows trademark holders to federally register their trademarks in the Patent & Trademark Office (PTO).

The benefit of federal registration is that it provides *constructive notice and use* of the trademark from that point forward for the goods or services specified by the registrant. 15 U.S.C. §§ 1057(c), 1072. The practical effect of constructive notice and use is that it allows a trademark holder to secure *national* rights to a trademark against junior users of the mark, without requiring the registrant to establish use of the trademark in every single state. Nevertheless, use of the mark in commerce, at least somewhere in the U.S., is still required to secure federal registration, either under the traditional avenue of a "use in commerce" application, *id.* § 1051(a), or under the alternative avenue of an "intent to use" application, *id.* § 1051(b). The latter type of "intent to use" application, which is a recent development for U.S. law, allows an applicant to file for registration without use, based on intent to use the mark in commerce. But the registration is not perfected until the applicant files a verified statement of use in commerce. *Id.* § 1051(d).

Federal registration also allows a trademark owner to seek federal remedies, including injunctive relief or damages, for trademark infringement and, in the case of famous marks, trademark dilution. Under § 526 of the Tariff Act of 1930, 19 U.S.C. § 1526, the Customs Service may seize goods with counterfeit or infringing versions of a registered trademark. These federal remedies are not available to the owner of a trademark that has not been registered with the PTO.

Trademarks have considerable importance for businesses today. Trademarks serve not only as a convenient way to guarantee the quality and source of products or services to consumers, but also as a form of marketing and "branding." Companies may invest hundreds of millions of dollars annually in marketing and advertising their trademarks for the purpose of creating a significant amount of consumer recognition and goodwill in their brands. Some trademarks are now among the most valuable business assets in the world. Trademarks such as "Coca–Cola" have achieved a level of fame and recognition that is virtually worldwide.

4. TRADE SECRETS

Trade secrets are often discussed in conjunction with patents, since both forms of intellectual property may apply to "know-how," which might be loosely defined as the practical understanding to perform or create something useful, often in the context of the production of commercially valuable items or processes. The most well-known trade secret (at least the existence of it) is the secret formula for Coke. In some respects (which we will revisit in the trade secret chapter), trade secrets provide an alternative to patents in a way that is almost opposite in approach: unlike patents, trade secrets can last indefinitely, but require the nondisclosure or secrecy of the underlying know how. Trade secret protection, therefore, is predicated on the trade secret holder undertaking reasonable secrecy measures, such as requiring nondisclosure or confidentiality agreements from employees and others, and storing trade secret materials in a locked vault, accessible only to those who "need to know."

Until recently, the law of trade secrets was governed solely by state law. More than forty states and the District of Columbia have adopted the definition of a trade secret under the Uniform Trade Secrets Act:

> "Trade Secret" means information, including a formula, pattern, compilation, program, device, method, technique, or process that (i) derives independent economic value, actual or potential, from not being generally known to, and not being readily ascertainable by proper means by, other persons who can obtain economic value from its disclosure or use; and (ii) is the subject of efforts that are reasonable under the circumstances to maintain its secrecy.

Assuming one has a trade secret and takes reasonable measures to keep it secret, one can invoke the protection of trade secret law without any formality or application. There are two general ways in which someone can breach a trade secret: (1) a breach of a duty of confidentiality, an issue that arises frequently in the case of departing employees (examples of which will be discussed in Chapter 5); and (2) engaging in improper means to steal the trade secret, such as theft, espionage, or other forms of skullduggery. Trade secret law, however, does not prevent others from trying to independently devise the trade secret on their own, or even to reverse engineer the trade secret from the original product. Thus, for example, if a competitor could come up with the precise formula for Coke by analyzing the beverage in the laboratory, such reverse engineering would be perfectly legitimate. The maker of Coke would have no trade secret claim to stop the competitor from reverse engineering, or later selling its own beverage based on the formula.

In 1996, Congress enacted the Economic Espionage Act of 1996, 18 U.S.C. §§ 1831–1839 (EEA), which makes it a federal crime to misappropriate trade secrets for the benefit of foreign governments and certain other entities. Congress's enactment of this law evidences the importance of trade secret protection to business *and* entire countries. Trade secrets can be worth millions, if not billions, of dollars. Their theft could cause serious disruption to a company, and possibly the economy of the country where it is based.

NOTES AND QUESTIONS

1. *USTR*. Another important U.S. government entity that plays a key role in international intellectual property is the United States Trade Representative (USTR), a cabinet level official who has responsibility for resolving all types of trade disputes and negotiating international trade agreements. The USTR was involved in the WTO and TRIPS negotiations and plays an active role in protecting the intellectual property rights of U.S. industries on an international level within the WTO system and on a bilateral basis in FTAs and negotiations with individual countries.

2. *U.S. law*. Other countries, especially ones with less developed IP systems, often study U.S. law as a model or reference point for their own countries. Can the U.S. benefit from studying the IP laws of other countries?

CHAPTER 2

COPYRIGHT AND NEIGHBORING RIGHTS

■ ■ ■

A. INTRODUCTION

1. THE RIGHTS OF AUTHORS

Copyright is a bundle of exclusive rights granted to authors, allowing them to control and prevent different uses of their works by others. As copyright first developed at the time of the printing press, the exclusive rights were limited to publishing and vending primarily books. Over the years, copyright has expanded in terms of both the exclusive rights and the types of works protected. Today, copyright may encompass the rights of reproduction or copying, distribution, public performance, public display, and the right to make derivative works. It may extend to virtually all forms of expression, including photographs, music, dramatic works, sculptures, architecture, works of applied art, digital files, and computer software.

Copyright laws developed around the world along two distinct traditions: (i) a copyright tradition from England and (ii) an author's right tradition from continental Europe. In 1710, the British Parliament enacted its first copyright act, the Statute of Anne,[1] which was intended for "the Encouragement of Learning" and provided a limited term of copyright to authors. Before the Statute of Anne, the publishing cartel known as the Stationers' Company had controlled for many years the publication of books in England. Because these printing rights of the Stationers' Company were unlimited, the Stationers could control in perpetuity the publication of all works in England, including classical works from long ago. Parliament enacted the Statute of Anne to end the Stationers' monopoly control of the book publishing industry by granting authors a limited term of copyright (14 years for new books, with the opportunity for a renewal term of 14 more years if the author was still living). The Statute of Anne was intended to provide authors with incentives for the creation of new works and to encourage learning in England with the greater availability of works. In England, then, copyright law was based on a utilitarian rationale—copyrights were granted to serve a larger end

---

1. 8 Anne c. 19 (1710).

for the public good. Under this tradition, providing financial reward to authors through copyrights is considered secondary to the ultimate goal of creating incentives for the production of new works for the public. The British approach to copyright heavily influenced the United States and other former British colonies. The founding fathers in the United States included a provision similarly delimiting copyright in the U.S. Constitution, drafted in 1787. Under the Copyright Clause, exclusive rights can be granted only for "limited Times" and must serve the ultimate end of "promot[ing] the Progress of Science and useful Arts."[2]

By contrast, continental European countries with civil law systems followed what may be called the tradition of author's right. These countries use the term "author's right" (e.g., in France, *droit d'auteur*) to describe what is called "copyright" in other countries, such as in the United States. The author's right tradition is based more on natural rights theory. This emphasis on the natural rights of authors may stem in part from its origin in France following the Revolution at a time when natural rights theory was influential. Although utilitarian goals also underlie the intellectual property laws in these countries, there exists— much more so than in countries in the copyright tradition—a robust theory that authors are entitled to their creations as a matter of natural right. Accordingly, continental European countries recognize *moral rights* of authors, which are inherent rights of authors. For instance, the moral right of integrity gives authors the right to prevent others from changing their works in a way that would prejudice the author's honor or reputation. The moral right of attribution gives the author the right to require attribution for his or her works. In some countries, these moral rights are perpetual and inalienable. By contrast, countries that follow the copyright tradition tend to have far less strong and less formal recognition of moral rights, if at all.

Another key difference in the author's right approach is the treatment of performances and recordings. In the U.S. and United Kingdom, the rights of performers are treated under the same general rubric of copyright (although sound recordings may receive more modest copyright protection). By contrast, in continental Europe, countries treat performers outside of copyright, under the concept of *neighboring rights* or *related rights*, a lesser form of protection than author's rights. "True" authors are considered to be flesh-and-blood creators who imbue their personality in their literary and artistic creations. Performers who merely perform someone else's work do not satisfy this standard, nor do the recording studios who record their performances. These recordings do not qualify for author's right, but instead only for the lesser form of intellectual property known as neighboring rights or related rights.

Although differences still exist between the two traditions of copyright and author's right, these differences do not vitiate the basic common starting point of both traditions in recognizing the importance of provid-

---

2. U.S. CONST. art. I, § 8, cl. 8.

ing authors with exclusive rights to their works. Indeed, it would be inaccurate to suggest that utilitarian and natural rights theories of copyright law are mutually exclusive, or that the copyright and author's right traditions are at odds. Strands of both theories and traditions may well inform the development of copyright laws in the same countries, although with varying degrees of influence. And, regardless of the tradition that most heavily influenced a country's copyright law, today the international copyright conventions require a certain set of minimum standards that will be common to all countries. The TRIPS Agreement recognizes this shared commonality by combining elements of both traditions in one section for "Copyright and Related Rights" in the English text, or *"Droit d'auteur et droits connexes"* in the French version. TRIPS thus uses interchangeably copyright and author's right (*droit d'auteur*). Accordingly, this casebook will use "copyright" to encompass both terms unless greater specificity is needed.

2. INTERNATIONAL AGREEMENTS: THE TRIPS AGREEMENT, THE BERNE CONVENTION, AND THE ROME CONVENTION

With the development of the Internet and its facilitation of the instantaneous dissemination of materials around the world, the international aspects of copyright law have assumed much greater importance, as well as challenges. As the whole controversy over music file sharing demonstrates, the Internet may routinely implicate copyright laws in all parts of the world where people transmit files over the Internet. Because there is no single world-wide copyright, however, each country must protect copyrights under its own domestic law. This territorial approach to copyright allows each country to fashion its copyright law based on its own particular cultural, social, economic, and political values.

A country's freedom to enact different copyright laws is not unlimited, however, at least not today. Copyright laws of all countries within the World Trade Organization are governed by two important international copyright agreements: (i) the TRIPS Agreement and (ii) Articles 1–21 of the Berne Convention (Paris 1971) and its Appendix.

The oldest and the most important copyright treaty is the Berne Convention for the Protection of Literary and Artistic Works, commonly known as "the Berne Convention" for short. First signed in 1886 in Berne, Switzerland, the Convention was intended to establish minimum standards of copyright law that countries must satisfy in their own domestic law.

One of the problems the Berne Convention addressed was the disparate treatment of foreign authors among countries. A developing country that was a net importer of works (with fewer authors of its own) had a greater economic incentive to refuse to recognize copyright protection for works of foreign authors. In that way, domestic publishers could freely copy such foreign works and sell them at cheaper prices, particularly of popular authors. For over one hundred years, until 1891, the United States did not grant copyrights to foreign works, but was the leading "pirate" nation of the day. Conversely, a country that was a net exporter of creative works (with greater authors of its own) had an interest in ensuring that all countries offer protection to foreign works, especially the works of its own authors. In the mid 1800s, France and England were the major producers of literary and artistic works and were, not surprisingly, the major proponents of formalizing an international copyright agreement to protect the rights of authors in other countries.

A key point in the development of international copyright norms occurred in 1852, when France unilaterally extended copyright protection to all foreign works without precondition. This unilateral move helped to position France as the leading architect for developing international copyright norms at the time. From the 1850s to 1886, France and other countries secured copyright protection for their authors abroad by entering into *bilateral agreements*. Although the agreements varied in content, they did share the limitation of binding only two countries. During this time, France had the most agreements (13), followed by Belgium (9), Spain and Italy (8 each), and Germany and the United Kingdom (5 each). Throughout the 19th century, the U.S. did not agree to any. The bilateral agreements had their shortcomings, however. Besides the two-country limitation, they also allowed varying approaches, thus potentially subjecting authors to conflicting requirements in different countries.

Starting in 1858 in Brussels, Belgium, delegates from a number of countries from Europe and elsewhere began discussions to establish international copyright standards. In 1878, France convened an international literary congress in Paris, with the author Victor Hugo as its president. The organization eventually became the International Literary and Artistic Association—or ALAI, the acronym for *l'Association litteraire et artistique internationale*. In 1886, after several years of negotiating, ten countries present at the ALAI conference in Berne, Switzerland reached the first international copyright agreement—the Berne Convention for the Protection of Literary and Artistic Works. The countries consisted of Belgium, France, Germany, Haiti, Italy, Liberia, Spain, Switzerland, Tunisia, and the United Kingdom. The United States and Japan were unofficial observers to the Conference.

The Berne Convention instituted the pattern that would be central to most intellectual property agreements. It adopted (i) the principle of *national treatment*, while also requiring (ii) certain *minimum standards* for copyright laws. National treatment repudiated the approach of material reciprocity, which had been taken by some countries in bilateral agreements to extend copyright protection to foreign authors only if the foreign country extended the same level of protection to a domestic country's own authors. As discussed in Chapter 1, under national treatment, each country must treat foreigners at least as well as its own nationals (regardless of the level of protection in the foreign country).

Since its formation, the Berne Convention has been revised six times: Paris (1896), Berlin (1908), Rome (1928), Brussels (1948), Stockholm (1967), and Paris (1971). Although the Paris text (1971) is the most recent version of Berne, technically speaking, several versions of Berne may still be in force today. The Berne Convention does not require old members that have already acceded to an earlier version of the Convention to accede to subsequent revisions; new members, however, must accede to the most recent text. *See* Berne Conv. arts. 32(1), 34(1). A few Berne countries still abide by the earlier Rome, Brussels, or Stockholm text. But the vast majority of Berne countries have agreed to the Paris text (1971). In this casebook, we shall focus on the most recent Paris text.

The TRIPS Agreement, formed in 1994, follows the Berne Convention's approach of requiring national treatment, plus minimum standards of copyright protection. It also instantiates the Paris (1971) text of Berne as the premier copyright convention by incorporating Articles 1–21 and the Appendix of the Paris text as a part of TRIPS. TRIPS art. 9. In addition to these provisions of Berne, TRIPS adds several key copyright and neighboring right articles of its own. *Id.* arts. 10–14. Together, TRIPS and the Berne Convention provide the central international agreements governing copyright today.

Unlike the Berne Convention, TRIPS also covers rights in sound recordings and broadcasts—also called neighboring or related rights. *Id.* art. 14. Several other international agreements exist specifically for sound recordings and broadcasts. The most influential is the Rome Convention (the International Convention for the Protection of Performers, Producers of Phonograms and Broadcasting Organizations), first signed in 1961. The Rome Convention follows the Berne Convention's model of requiring national treatment plus minimum standards, as applied to performers, producers of phonograms (or sound recordings), and broadcast organizations.

In this chapter, we will focus on the TRIPS Agreement and the Berne Convention, given their influence and importance today. Some attention will also be given to the Rome Convention, since it still retains significance for the protection of neighboring rights. A word of caution should be noted, however: selecting to study the international treaties or agreements that are more influential at the moment does not necessarily provide the entire universe of international IP regulations. Nor does it preclude the possibility that the significance of these (or other) international IP conventions will change dramatically over time.

It is certainly possible that even TRIPS itself could eventually diminish in importance, or at least evolve into a different iteration. For example, in 1996, the World Intellectual Property Organization (WIPO), which is a specialized agency within the United Nations that administers 23 international IP treaties, ratified two treaties designed to better address the challenges to intellectual property protection posed by the Internet. The WIPO Copyright Treaty requires member countries, among other things, to "provide adequate legal protection and effective legal remedies against the circumvention of effective technological measures that are used by authors in connection with the exercise of their rights under this Treaty or the Berne Convention and that restrict acts, in respect of their works, which are not authorized by the authors concerned or permitted by law" (art. 11). The United States implemented this provision with the controversial "anti-circumvention" provision under the Digital Millennium Copyright Act (DMCA) of 1998, which we will study at the end of this chapter. The WIPO Performances and Phonograms Treaty incorporates the Rome Convention's standard of national treatment and also sets forth more expansive minimum standards for neighboring rights. Although over 180 countries are members of WIPO, the influence of these two WIPO treaties is still weaker than the TRIPS Agreement, which enjoys the strong enforcement mechanism under the WTO's Dispute Settlement Body.

Another source of IP regulation that may provide international norms that supplement—or perhaps even supplant—the TRIPS/Berne apparatus are bilateral and multilateral agreements. The adoption of TRIPS has not diminished the resurgence of bilateral and multilateral agreements in the area of intellectual property, particularly at the initiative of the more powerful developed countries. The European Union has adopted a number of important directives related to intellectual property for its member countries—for instance, the EU Copyright Term Directive and the EU Database Directive. Likewise, since 1994, the United States has continued to secure bilateral and multilateral agreements with other countries to regulate intellectual property, including the Central American Free Trade Agreement (CAFTA) and bilateral agreements with the Andean countries, Australia, Bahrain, Cambodia, Chile, Israel, Jordan, Morocco, Panama, Singapore, Southern African countries, Sri Lanka, and Trinidad & Tobago. These U.S. bilateral agreements have proved to be controversial. Some countries have complained that, in these bilateral agreements, the U.S. is seeking to impose on developing countries higher, "TRIPS-plus" requirements for even broader IP rights than required by TRIPS.

Although these other sources of transnational IP regulation are important, they will not be the focus of this casebook. The TRIPS Agreement and the Berne Convention, (and, to some extent, the Rome Convention) still provide the overall international apparatus within which all other copyright and neighboring rights agreements operate. To study international intellectual property, it is better to be able to see the forest from the trees, at least at the outset.

PROBLEM 2–1

You represent Too Spice, a new band that performs versions of ballads from the big band era of the 1940s, but attempts to give them a modern twist. Too Spice is careful to get permission from the copyright holder to perform and record the ballads, but it believes that it should be entitled to a full copyright for Too Spice's own performances. Too Spice takes issue with the lower level of legal protection for performers' rights recognized in some countries where performances do not receive full copyrights, but instead neighboring or less extensive rights. These neighboring rights laws are based in part on the historical perception that performers were not true authors. In these countries, "true" authors, such as the composers of the big band songs, receive full copyright protection for the lyrics to the songs and the underlying music, but the recording artists, such as Too Spice, receive less extensive protection in their recordings. Can you develop arguments on behalf of Too Spice why performers and recording artists should also be treated as "authors" even if the underlying musical works being performed have been composed by others? Would recognizing performers and recording artists as "authors" of their performances be consistent with the underpinnings of copyright law? Who should be considered an "author"?

NOTES AND QUESTIONS

1. Should the historical development of copyright along two different traditions (i.e., copyright and author's right) be relevant to the drafters of an international copyright agreement? Does the existence of two traditions among countries pose possible challenges for reaching agreement on international standards of copyright?

2. *Utilitarian theories of copyright.* Under U.S. copyright law, the traditional justification of copyright law is perhaps best encapsulated by this passage from the Supreme Court:

> The limited scope of the copyright holder's statutory monopoly, like the limited copyright duration required by the Constitution, reflects a balance of competing claims upon the public interest: Creative work is to be encouraged and rewarded, but private motivation must ultimately serve the cause of promoting broad public availability of literature, music, and the other arts. The immediate effect of our copyright law is to secure a fair return for an "author's" creative labor. But the ultimate aim is, by this incentive, to stimulate artistic creativity for the general public good. "The sole interest of the United States and the primary object in conferring the monopoly," this Court has said, "lie in the general benefits derived from the public from the labors of authors."

Sony Corp. of America v. Universal City Studios, Inc., 464 U.S. 417, 431–32 (1984) (quoting *Fox Film Corp. v. Doyal*, 286 U.S. 123, 127 (1932)).

This incentive-based justification of copyright is an example of a utilitarian theory, in which a practice is favored or protected for the utility it serves. Economists often defend copyright on the ground that creative works are *public goods*, meaning that they are nonexcludable and nonrivalrous. They are nonexcludable in that, once disclosed to others, creative works can be copied and disseminated to others. They are nonrivalrous in that copying of the work does not diminish the use of the work by any one person. This contrasts with real property in which over-use of the same land by different individuals will deplete the use of the land. Because creative works are nonexcludable, authors who invest time and labor into their creation might not be able to recoup money for their investment absent legal protection, thus diminishing incentives to create. Copyright helps to solve this potential problem, it is argued, by ensuring that authors have certain exclusive rights to their works, at least for a limited time.

Part of the challenge for an economic or instrumental theory of copyright is determining how much copyright protection in terms of scope and duration would be optimal for creating sufficient incentives for the production of works. *See* David McGowan, *Copyright Nonconsequentialism*, 69 Mo. L. REV. 1, 2 (2004) (arguing that utilitarian and instrumental theories are indeterminate); *see also* Margaret Jane Radin, *Regulation by Contract, Regulation by Machine*, 160 J. INST'L & THEORETICAL ECON. 1, 7 (2004) ("How much propertization is too much? That is an empirical question to which no one knows the answer."). Are you comfortable with basing a system of copyright on what amounts to guesswork?

3. *Natural rights theories of copyright.* The natural rights view of copyright largely avoids the calculus problems faced by utilitarian theories in attempting to establish a proper balance in copyright law. If authors are entitled to their creations as a matter of right, no calibration or balancing is needed. Some commentators, for example, attempt to justify copyright on Lockean labor theory, under which people are entitled to the fruits of their labors subject to the Lockean proviso that such entitlements are allowed "where there is enough, and as good left in common for others." McGowan, *supra*, at 38–39. The natural rights view of copyright, however, would appear to justify the grant of an unlimited property right—or a perpetual copyright—in a work. Would there be any harm to society if copyrights could last forever?

4. *Non–Western theories.* The development of copyright law has been an almost exclusively Western endeavor. However, other traditions associated with the development of the printing industry were historically significant. For example, long before the Western traditions discussed above, Confucianism was already established as a social and political theory that had a profound influence on not only its country of origin—China—but also on Japan, Korea, Vietnam, and other parts of Asia. At least in terms of sheer populations involved, Confucianism had a much more significant impact than either utilitarianism or natural rights theory. Confucianism was a broad social theory that was based upon respect for the past and for tradition. The norms of the past established by the masters of Chinese civilization were fundamental and constitutive of any Chinese society in any era. These norms and the works that embodied them were viewed not as private property, but as the common heritage of all Chinese, that was necessary for proper socialization through broad access to intellectual endeavors. It followed from Confucianism that propagation of the past through copying the masters in painting and poetry was beneficial to society. When the printing industry in China was developed, it led to a desire to propagate copies rather than to a system that limited copies as in countries such as England. The importance and vitality of propagating the past is summed up by a passage in the Analects, one of the Confucian classics, in which Confucius himself says, "I transmit rather than create; I believe in and I love the Ancients." Under Confucianism, copying was not viewed as wrongful but as virtuous.

5. Why was Confucianism not reflected in the Berne Convention or in TRIPS, even though Confucianism, at least in terms of sheer numbers of people affected, was far more significant than either utilitarianism or natural rights theory? Was China even at the bargaining table either for the drafting of Berne or TRIPS?

6. *Geneva Phonograms Convention and Brussels Satellite Broadcast Convention.* Two other treaties deal with recordings and broadcasts, although their influence is less extensive than the Rome Convention. The Geneva Phonograms Convention (Convention for the Protection of Producers of Phonograms Against Unauthorized Duplication of Their Phonograms of October 29, 1971) provides minimum standards of protection against unauthorized copying of sound recordings and importation of such copies. Its main provision covers only producers of phonograms, however, requiring protection—for a minimum of 20 years—against the copying and importation of their phonograms. Member countries are given the discretion to offer protection against such piracy by copyright, neighboring rights, or other law. The Geneva Phonograms Convention has diminished in importance because most of its members are also members of TRIPS and the Rome Convention, which require more extensive protection for sound recordings. Notably, Article 7(2) of Geneva leaves it up to member countries to decide "the extent, if any, to which performers whose performances are fixed in a phonogram are entitled to enjoy protection and the conditions for enjoying any such protection." Because the U.S. is a member of Geneva, but not Rome, the Geneva Phonograms Convention may retain some continuing relevance. The Brussels Satellite Broadcast Convention deals with the problem of "signal theft" of satellite transmissions by requiring countries "to take adequate measures to prevent the distribution on or from its territory of any programme-carrying signal by any distributor for whom the signal emitted to or passing through the satellite is not intended" (art. 2).

7. *Bibliographic Note.* PAUL GOLDSTEIN, INTERNATIONAL COPYRIGHT (2001); LYMAN RAY PATTERSON, COPYRIGHT IN HISTORICAL PERSPECTIVE (1968); SAM RICKETSON, THE BERNE CONVENTION FOR THE PROTECTION OF LITERARY AND ARTISTIC WORKS: 1886–1986 (1987); MARK ROSE, AUTHORS AND OWNERS: THE INVENTION OF COPYRIGHT (1993); EDWARD WALTERSCHEID, THE NATURE OF THE INTELLECTUAL PROPERTY CLAUSE: A STUDY IN HISTORICAL PERSPECTIVE (2002); Lionel Bentley & Brad Sherman, *Great Britain and the Signing of the Berne Convention in 1886*, 48 J. COPYRIGHT SOC'Y USA 311 (2001); Jane C. Ginsburg, *A Tale of Two Copyrights: Literary Property in Revolutionary France and America*, 64 TUL. L. REV. 991 (1990); J.H. Reichman, *Universal Minimum Standards of Intellectual Property Protection Under the TRIPS Component of the WTO Agreement*, in INTELLECTUAL PROPERTY AND INTERNATIONAL TRADE: THE TRIPS AGREEMENT 21 (Carlos M. Correa & Abdulqawi A. Yusuf eds., 1998).

B. FOREIGN NATIONALS ACQUIRING COPYRIGHTS AND NEIGHBORING RIGHTS

1. POINTS OF ATTACHMENT AND NATIONAL TREATMENT FOR COPYRIGHT

Imagine you are an author in the U.S. and have just finished writing a novel, although it remains unpublished. After consulting U.S. copyright law, you learn that you are automatically entitled to a U.S. copyright in your work as soon as you have fixed it in a tangible medium, such as by storing it on your computer's hard drive. There is no administrative prerequisite to your receipt of the U.S. copyright (although enforcement of a U.S. work ultimately requires registration of the copyright, 17 U.S.C. § 411, a requirement that is exempted for foreign works as discussed in the next section). You wonder, though: how do I receive copyrights in other countries? The short answer is that you *automatically* receive copyrights from all countries in the Berne Convention and the WTO by virtue of being a U.S. national. To understand why, we must examine the interrelationship between points of attachment and national treatment under Berne.

Points of attachment. Articles 3 and 4 of the Berne Convention deal with the fundamental issue of when authors and their works qualify for the protection in countries of the Berne Convention. All of the contracting states to the Berne Convention form a Union, commonly called the Berne Union or simply the Union. An author is entitled to the protection of the Berne Convention when a "point of attachment" (also called a connecting factor) exists. The basic concept behind a point of attachment is that the author and/or the work must have some connection with a contracting state to the Berne Convention in order to trigger Berne protection. This connection or nexus is commonly referred to as a "point of attachment," although that term is not expressly adopted by Berne itself. Carefully read Articles 3 and 4 below.

Berne Convention (Paris, 1971)

Article 3

(1) The protection of this Convention shall apply to:

> (a) authors who are nationals of one of the countries of the Union, for their works, whether published or not;

> (b) authors who are not nationals of one of the countries of the Union, for their works first published in one of those countries, or simultaneously in a country outside the Union and in a country of the Union.

(2) Authors who are not nationals of one of the countries of the Union but who have their habitual residence in one of them shall, for

the purposes of this Convention, be assimilated to nationals of that country.

(3) The expression *"published works"* means works published with the consent of their authors, whatever may be the means of manufacture of the copies, provided that the availability of such copies has been such as to satisfy the reasonable requirements of the public, having regard to the nature of the work. The performance of a dramatic, dramatico-musical, cinematographic or musical work, the public recitation of a literary work, the communication by wire or the broadcasting of literary or artistic works, the exhibition of a work of art and the construction of a work of architecture shall not constitute publication.

(4) A work shall be considered as having been published simultaneously in several countries if it has been published in two or more countries within thirty days of its first publication.

Article 4

The protection of this Convention shall apply, even if the conditions of Article 3 are not fulfilled, to:

> (a) authors of cinematographic works the maker of which has his headquarters or habitual residence in one of the countries of the Union;

> (b) authors of works of architecture, erected in a country of the Union or of other artistic works incorporated in a building or other structure located in a country of the Union.

As should be evident, the Berne Convention divides authors who are entitled to protection under the Convention into two categories: (i) nationals of a Berne country and (ii) others who are not nationals of a Berne country. Different points of attachment are created for each. Under Article 3(1)(a), nationals of Berne countries establish a point of attachment for their works, whether published or unpublished, immediately upon creation of the work. In other words, a point of attachment for Berne nationals is established by virtue of being a Berne national and creating a work. However, for non-Berne nationals, a point of attachment can only be established if: (i) the author publishes a work in a Berne country first or "simultaneously" (within 30 days) of publishing it in a non-Berne country (publication criterion); or (ii) the author becomes a habitual resident of a Berne country, in which case the author is to be treated in the same way as a Berne national (habitual residence criterion).

Because the TRIPS Agreement Article 9 incorporates these provisions of Berne, the obligations have effectively been extended to all WTO countries (a handful of which are not members also of Berne). Because of this incorporation of Berne, nationals of WTO countries establish a point of attachment by virtue of their nationality from a WTO country. Others who are nationals in the relatively few countries that are not members of either Berne or the WTO can establish a point of attachment under Berne in the same way as any other national of a non-Union country: first or simultaneous publication in a Berne country, or habitual residence in a Berne country.

Let us now consider a basic problem in identifying points of attachment under Berne. As you analyze the problem, keep in mind whether the author is treated as a national or non-national of a Berne country and the keys for each to establish a point of attachment.

PROBLEM 2–2

In which of the following situations is the author entitled to the protection of the Berne Convention, i.e., when does a point of attachment under the Berne Convention exist?

(a) Al, a national of a Berne Union country, writes a novel in secret showing it to no one.

(b) Bob, a national of a non-Union country, writes a novel in a non-Union country and first publishes the novel in a Union country.

(c) Cris, a national of a non-Union country, lives in a Union country and writes a novel there, but first publishes the novel in a non-Union country.

(d) David, a national of a Union country, lives in a non-Union country, and writes and publishes a novel in the non-Union country.

* * *

Supplementary points for cinematographic and architectural works. Article 4 provides two other points of attachment. Under Article 4, even if the conditions of Article 3 are not satisfied—the author is not a national of a Union country, does not habitually reside in a Union country, or has not first published the work in a Union country—the author is nevertheless entitled to Berne protection for certain cinematographic and architectural works. In the case of cinematographic works, the author or maker of the film can establish a point of attachment based on having its headquarters or habitual residence in a Berne country—regardless of whether the author can satisfy the conditions of Article 3. This provision effectively avoids any question about the nationality of a film production company that might be raised under Article 3. For architectural works, an author from a non-Union country (who does not habitually reside in a Union country) can receive protection for an architectural work if it is erected in a Union country. The erection or incorporation of the work in a Union country establishes a lasting connection with the Union country.

A point of attachment under Berne does not, in itself, create any copyright. Although Berne obligates countries to provide copyright protection (with certain minimum standards of rights) based on these points of attachment, the principle of territoriality means that each country's laws create copyright protection. Analysis of the type of protection given to works of the author in Union countries is not complete until one consults the laws of each country where copyright protection is sought. Suppose, for example, that a U.S. author seeks protection for its work in Germany, another Union member. A complete analysis of the rights afforded to the work of the U.S. author in Germany will depend on German law and the extent to which Germany has met or exceeded the minimum standards of the Berne Convention. Of course, a country is free to decide that the terms of the Berne Convention are self-executing, or otherwise establish substantive rights that are enforceable in that country based on the treaty itself without the need of any implementing legislation.

National treatment. So what is the benefit of establishing a point of attachment? Under Article 5, eligible authors and their works are entitled to national treatment in all other Union countries. Once a point of attachment exists under Article 3, the effect of Article 5 is that the work is now entitled to copyright protection in every country of the Union under the principle of national treatment. Article 5(1) of Berne states:

> Authors shall enjoy, in respect of works for which they are protected under this Convention, in countries of the Union other than the country of origin, the rights which their respective laws do now or may hereafter grant to their nationals, as well as the rights specially granted by this Convention.

The combined effect of Articles 3 and 5 is that a work entitled to protection under the Berne Convention (through a point of attachment) gives its author the right to a copyright under the domestic law in every country of the Union. Assuming all Berne members have faithfully implemented the requirements of Berne in their copyright laws, an author who is a national of a Berne Union country and who has created a work (whether published or not) automatically obtains a copyright for that work throughout the entire Berne Union under the respective laws of each country of the Union. This is a significant benefit to authors in Union countries as it assures widespread and automatic protection for all of their eligible works. Consider the following examples:

> Illustration 2–1. Alfred is the author of a work whose country of origin is Country Z, which is not a Berne Union country. Alfred first publishes his work in Country Z. In the absence of obligations created by treaty or other legally effective means, the rights granted to Alfred under the copyright law of Country Z are limited by the principle of territoriality to Country Z. Other countries are not obligated to extend Alfred copyright protection.

> Illustration 2–2. Under the same facts as contained in Illustration 2–1, but Country Z is now a contracting state to the Berne Convention. Under Article 3, Alfred's nationality establishes a point of attachment. Under the principle of national treatment as set forth in Article 5(1) and assuming all Berne countries have adequately implemented Berne in their own copyright laws, Alfred would automatically receive a copyright under the domestic copyright law of every other country in Berne. For example, in the United States, Alfred has a U.S. copyright under U.S. law; in Germany, Alfred has a German copyright under German law; and in Japan, Alfred has a Japanese copyright under Japanese law and so forth for each Berne Union country. Once a point of attachment exists, the effect of the principle of national treatment under Article 5(1) is that

Alfred now has a "basket" of national copyrights consisting of copyrights from each Union country. Each copyright, however, may vary in some respects depending upon the law of the contracting state to the Union.

As should be evident, the concept of a point of attachment is closely related to the principle of national treatment. Once a point of attachment for a foreign author is established under Berne, a country within Berne must offer national treatment to the foreign national. One way to think of the relationship between points of attachment and national treatment is to liken a Berne country to a house. The country's territorial borders are akin to the house's exterior. Foreign authors are not allowed into the house (to get copyright protection), unless the foreign authors have a key (or a point of attachment) to the house. Thus, the "keys" for a foreign national to get copyright protection within Berne countries are contained in the points of attachment.

Nationals of Berne Union countries. To build on our analogy, one way to understand a point of attachment is that Berne nationals have a key to the front doors of all the houses (countries) within Berne (for copyright protection). By virtue of their nationality, Union authors are automatically entitled to Berne protection for their works—both published and unpublished—as soon as the work has been created. Berne Conv. art. 3(1)(a). In other words, for Union authors, their nationality suffices for all purposes. A U.S. national, for example, is entitled to prohibit the unauthorized copying of its work in Germany, another Union country, regardless of whether the work has been published in the United States, another Union country, a non-Union country, or not published at all. Nationals from non-Berne countries who habitually reside in a Berne country can also invoke this same treatment. Under Article 3(2), authors who are not nationals of one of the countries of the Union but who have their habitual residence there are "assimilated to nationals of that country," i.e., given the same treatment as an author of the Union country. An author from a non-Union country who lives in the United States, for example, is treated as a national of the United States under Berne.

Others in non-Berne Union country. Apart from habitual residence in a Berne country, the only other way for non-Union authors to establish a point of attachment is to first publish the work in a Union country or simultaneously publish it in a Union and in a non-Union country. Simultaneous publication is defined as publication in two or more countries within thirty days of its first publication. Berne Conv. art. 3(4). Unlike a Union author, a non-Union author who does not habitually reside in a Berne country cannot claim the protection of the Berne Convention for an unpublished work. If a non-Union author wishes to establish a point of attachment under Berne, the author must first or simultaneously publish the work in a Union country. This is known as the "backdoor to Berne." This provision enabled U.S. authors before the U.S.'s entry into Berne in 1989 to claim copyright protection in Berne countries based on first publication of their works in a Berne country, or simultaneous publication of their works in a Berne country and the U.S. It was a simple matter, for example, for U.S. authors to simultaneously publish their works in the United States and Canada and enjoy the protection of the Berne Convention. To return to our analogy, a non-Union author can utilize the "backdoor to Berne" by using the "key" of first or simultaneously publishing in a Berne country. If the non-Union author first publishes the work in a non-Union country, however, it then becomes impossible for the author to later obtain Berne protection—except in the rare case when the country joins Berne and the work is subject to retroactive protection under Article 18, discussed later in this chapter.

Why would Union countries agree to protect the works of non-Union authors at all? During the drafting of this provision, some opponents of this position argued that granting such recognition might discourage nations from joining the Berne Convention. On the other hand, denying individuals from non-Union countries the protections of Berne might seem in tension with the spirit of nondiscrimination in the national treatment principle and of the basic concept of territoriality. A non-Union author who publishes in a Union country has established a territorial nexus with the Union country and is subject to the Union country's laws.

PROBLEM 2–3

Country X is neither a Berne Union country nor a member of TRIPS. Sigmund, a national of X, is an author who has written, but not yet published a novel that he hopes to obtain a copyright for in the United States, which has enacted copyright provisions to implement Article 3 of Berne. (i) What possible steps could Sigmund take to secure a U.S. copyright? (ii) What if he decided to post his book as an e-book online that was available to all countries on the Internet—would he be able to secure a U.S. copyright? What steps might he take to ensure that online posting of his e-book obtained a U.S. copyright?

PROBLEM 2–4

Samantha is a national of Z, a Berne Union country, who has written and published a novel in Z. Troy, a national of the United States, is making unauthorized copies of the novel in the U.S. Samantha now brings a lawsuit against Troy in United States federal district court asserting that Troy is violating Samantha's U.S. copyright in the novel. Troy moves to dismiss the case on the grounds that no U.S. copyright in the work exists because the work was written and published abroad. Assume that U.S. copyright law has adequately implemented the approach to points of attachment under Berne Convention Article 3 and follows the principle of national treatment required by Article 5? What result?

NOTES AND QUESTIONS

1. *Comparison with Patent and Trademark.* Points of attachment are more relevant to copyright analysis under Berne than under patent or trademark analysis under the Paris Convention. Why is this so? Patent and trademark typically involve some formality—such as the filing of the application—for which the patent or trademark office issues a patent or trademark registration. The effect of such an issuance is that a patent or trademark holder seeking enforcement in a country will have already received confirma-

tion of a point of attachment manifested in the patent or trademark office's issuance of a patent or a trademark registration.

2. *Post–TRIPS.* Given the vast number of countries in the WTO, points of attachment may also be diminishing in analytical importance under Berne. TRIPS incorporates the obligations of Articles 1 through 21 of Berne to WTO countries. TRIPS art. 9(1). As a result, more authors are protected today by Berne by virtue of nationality than ever before.

3. *National treatment.* The principle of national treatment, as we have discussed already, is the bedrock to many international IP agreements. It establishes a general level of nondiscrimination against foreign nationals that would seem laudable as a goal under any substantive law. Should countries ever be allowed to treat foreign nationals worse than domestic nationals?

4. *Berne Article 6 and abuses of the "back door to Berne."* Article 6 helps to control for abuses of the "back door to Berne" technique (in which simultaneous or first publication in Berne countries allowed authors from non-Union countries to invoke the protections of Berne). Article 6 allows Union countries to penalize a non-Union country that "fails to protect in an adequate manner the works of authors who are nationals of the countries of the Union." In such case, Berne Union countries are allowed under Article 6(1) to "restrict the protection given to works of authors who are, at the date of first publication thereof, nationals of the other [non-Berne] country," provided that a notice of such restriction is filed with the Director General of WIPO.

5. *Independent treatment.* Article 5(2) of Berne establishes a principle of independent treatment of copyrights: the enjoyment and exercise of rights under the Berne Convention "shall be independent of the existence of protection in the country of origin of the work." Berne Conv. art. 5(2). This limitation highlights a basic feature of territoriality and national treatment. Each country's law determines the existence of copyright within its borders, not based on material reciprocity but on national treatment.

> Illustration 2–3: Alfred is a national of Country Z, a Berne Union country. Alfred writes and publishes a novel in Country Z, which imposes a registration requirement on its own nationals (but not on foreign authors) in order to obtain copyright protection. Alfred does not register the work in Country Z and is not entitled to copyright protection. Under Article 3, a point of attachment has been established and every Berne Union country must grant Alfred copyrights under national law under Article 5(2). Such treatment is independent of whether Alfred receives any copyright protection in Country Z.

6. *Bibliographic note.* Jane C. Ginsburg, *Berne Without Borders: A Geographic Indiscretion and Digital Communications,* 2002 I.P.Q. 111 (2002) (discussing difficulties of determining place of publication in online environment); S.M. STEWART, INTERNATIONAL COPYRIGHT AND NEIGHBORING RIGHTS § 5.33, at 116–17 (2d ed. 1989).

2. BERNE PROHIBITION ON FORMALITIES

PROBLEM 2–5

Amanda is an author in Country Z, a Union country. She has published a novel Country Z. Amanda wishes to obtain copyright protection in Country X, also a Union country. Under X's laws, however, all domestic authors must first file their copyrights in a national registry and pay a small fee. Amanda does not register the work in Country X, however. Country X refuses Amanda copyright protection because of her failure to register. Country X maintains that it is not discriminating against Amanda because X has a long record of denying copyright to its own nationals who fail to register their published works. (i) Under Berne, should Amanda be entitled to receive a copyright in Country X? Is Country X in compliance with Berne? (ii) What about X's own authors who fail to register? Is X in violation of Berne by imposing registration requirements on its own domestic authors? Consider the following provision of Berne and discussion.

Berne Convention (Paris 1971)

Article 5

(1) Authors shall enjoy, in respect of works for which they are protected under this Convention, in countries of the Union other than the country of origin, the rights which their respective laws do now or may hereafter grant to their nationals, as well as the rights specially granted by this Convention.

(2) The enjoyment and the exercise of these rights shall not be subject to any formality; such enjoyment and such exercise shall be independent of the existence of protection in the country of origin of the work. Consequently, apart from the provisions of this Convention, the extent of protection, as well as the means of redress afforded to the author to protect his rights, shall be governed exclusively by the laws of the country where protection is claimed.

(3) Protection in the country of origin is governed by domestic law. However, when the author is not a national of the country of origin of the work for which he is protected under this Convention, he shall enjoy in that country the same rights as national authors.

(4) The country of origin shall be considered to be

   (a) in the case of works first published in a country of the Union, that country; in the case of works published simultaneously in several countries of the Union which grant different terms of protection, the country whose legislation grants the shortest term of protection;

   (b) in the case of works published simultaneously in a country outside the Union and in a country of the Union, the latter country;

   (c) in the case of unpublished works or of works first published in a country outside the Union, without simultaneous publication in a country of the Union, the country of the Union of which the author is a national, provided that:

> (i) when these are cinematographic works the maker of which has his headquarters or his habitual residence in a country of the Union, the country of origin shall be that country, and

> (ii) when these are works of architecture erected in a country of the Union or other artistic works incorporated in a building or other structure located in a country of the Union, the country of origin shall be that country.

* * *

Article 5(2) of Berne bars countries from imposing formalities on foreign nationals of Berne countries for their foreign works, stating: "The enjoyment and exercise of these rights shall not be subject to any formality." Formalities are procedural or administrative requirements that are imposed as a precondition to the exercise or enjoyment of a copyright. For example, under the Berne Convention, the U.S. cannot require Arthur, a foreign national from Germany who has published a work there, to file or register its copyright with the U.S. Copyright Office as a condition of obtaining U.S. copyright protection.

Berne's prohibition on formalities applies to "these rights" regulated by Article 5(1)—meaning copyrights for nationals of Berne countries "in respect of works for which they are protected under this Convention, in countries of the Union *other than the country of origin.*" Therefore, the key to determining whether formalities can or cannot be imposed under Berne is identifying the country of origin, as defined in Article 5(4). The country of origin can impose formalities on works originating there. But other countries within Berne that are not the country of origin for the work in question cannot impose formalities on the work.

Thus, a country in Berne can impose formalities on works of its own nationals if the domestic country is the "country of origin" of the work. For example, the United Kingdom, a Union country, can impose formalities on its own nationals for the works they produce or first publish within the country, so long as the formalities do not apply to foreign authors and their foreign works. Most Berne Union countries, however, do not wish to disadvantage their own authors, so they have abolished formalities for both foreign and domestic authors in the acquisition of copyrights. The U.S. is an exception, however, in requiring the registration of copyright for U.S. works before a copyright infringement suit can be commenced. 17 U.S.C. § 411.

A Berne country can also impose formalities on foreign authors if that country is the country of origin. Remember the key for Article 5(2) is not the distinction between nationals and foreigners, but rather, the distinction between the country of origin of the work and other countries. For example, if a foreign national from France first publishes in the U.S., the U.S. is the country of origin. Under Berne, the foreign national can be subject to a formality requirement just as any U.S. national would be for publishing first in the U.S., which then is the country of origin. *See* Berne Conv. art. 5(4)(a).

The international prohibition against formalities in the acquisition of intellectual property rights by foreign authors appears to be unique to copyright. As will be discussed in subsequent chapters, it is customary that, in order to obtain a patent, an inventor must file an application, which is typically subject to review by a patent office. Similarly, many countries require a foreign owner to register a trademark in a public trademark authority in order to obtain trademark protection. Copyright, however, is different. Article 5(2) of the Berne Convention prohibits a country from imposing formalities on works that originate in other Berne countries. Such foreign works cannot be subject to formalities, such as requirements for registration, fees, copyright notice, renewal, or manufacturing requirements by domestic publishers.

Berne did not always contain a prohibition on formalities. In fact, the first text signed in Berne in 1886 required them, stating that "[t]he enjoyment of these rights is subject to the accomplishment of the conditions and formalities prescribed by law in the country of origin of the work."[4] This was perhaps understandable, given that a majority of Berne countries at the time required some formalities. Even France had a requirement of copyright registration for French authors as a condition for filing an infringement suit. Little discussion remains, however, as to why the delegates decided to adopt a limited formality requirement in the first text of Berne. Perhaps the original Berne countries felt that limiting the formality requirement to just one country—the country of origin—could help to avoid the many burdens that would be created if the author had to comply with different formality requirements in various countries. Under this approach, authors would not be entitled to claim national treatment under Berne if they failed to satisfy any formalities required by the law of the country of origin.

The formality requirement was repealed by the 1908 Berlin revision of the Convention, which instituted the prohibition on formalities that has been carried in each subsequent version of the Convention. One thing to notice is that the current provision still hinges on the country of origin, as did the original provision. Under the old approach, the country of origin's law of formalities served effectively as a precondition for international protection of a work in other Berne countries. Now, under the current approach in Article 5, only the country of origin can impose formalities on works originating there; however, compliance with such formalities cannot be a precondition of copyright protection elsewhere. An author of a Union country has the right to demand no formalities in Union countries outside the country of origin of the work.

One reason for the change appears to have been a desire to limit the extent to which a court would have to interpret foreign law—here, the law related to formalities from the country of origin—in cases involving copyrights granted to foreign authors. Another reason was the Union's recognition of the principle of independent treatment in the same provision: copyrights in other countries existed independently of copyrights in the country of origin. These two reasons argue against relying upon formalities from the country of origin. They do not necessarily argue against formalities altogether, such as a matter of domestic law for domestic works, which Berne does not regulate. However, a country might attempt to justify a complete ban on copyright formalities

---

4.   Berne Conv. art. 1 (Berne 1886).

even for domestic works as a matter of convenience in treating domestic and foreign works the same, or as a matter of natural rights theory. A formality could be seen as an unnatural impediment to the author's natural right.

PROBLEM 2–6

Country Y imposes formalities on its own domestic nationals for their works but not on foreign nationals in order to obtain copyright. Alan, a national of Country Y, writes a novel in Y and first publishes the novel in Country Z, which is a Berne Union country. Alan now attempts to enforce a copyright for the novel in Country Y but the authorities in Country Y insist that Alan must first comply with the formalities required of all domestic authors in Country Y. Does Berne allow Country Y to require Alan to comply with these formalities in order to obtain protection in Country Y? Hint: determine the country of origin of the work. *See* Berne Conv., art. 5(1) & 5(4).

PROBLEM 2–7

Section 411 requires a U.S. copyright holder for any "United States work" to register the copyright in the Copyright Office before a copyright infringement suit can be instituted in federal court. 17 U.S.C. § 411. The Copyright Act (*id.* § 101) defines "United States work" as follows:

(1) in the case of a published work, the work is first published—

(A) in the United States;

(B) simultaneously in the United States and another treaty party or parties, whose law grants a term of copyright protection that is the same as or longer than the term provided in the United States;

(C) simultaneously in the United States and a foreign nation that is not a treaty party; or

(D) in a foreign nation that is not a treaty party, and all of the authors of the work are nationals, domiciliaries, or habitual residents of, or in the case of an audiovisual work legal entities with headquarters in, the United States;

(2) in the case of an unpublished work, all the authors of the work are nationals, domiciliaries, or habitual residents of the United States, or, in the case of an unpublished audiovisual work, all the authors are legal entities with headquarters in the United States; or

(3) in the case of a pictorial, graphic, or sculptural work incorporated in a building or structure, the building or structure is located in the United States.

Are these provisions consistent with Berne's prohibition on formalities under Article 5? Why or why not?

NOTES AND QUESTIONS

1. Can the prohibition on formalities for copyright under Berne be squared with the requirement of formalities for patents? Why do WTO

countries accept the burdens of filing for patents, but not for copyrights? To the extent "natural rights" arguments are made to justify Berne's ban on formalities, do inventors have any less of a moral claim to their inventions than authors to their creations?

2. *The U.S.'s historical reluctance to join Berne.* For most of the 20th century, the Berne Convention lacked one key country: the United States. Not until 1989 did the U.S. enter the Convention, which at the time had 77 other members. The U.S. did not join the Berne Convention in part due to the U.S.'s opposition to Berne's prohibition against formalities and requirement of protection of moral rights. The U.S. had required some formality (such as renewal registration and copyright notice) under copyright law, starting with the first U.S. copyright statute in 1790 and continuing with each copyright act before the 1989 amendment to the 1976 Copyright Act. In 1989, in the Berne Convention Implementation Act, Congress did away with the copyright notice requirement for all works. 17 U.S.C. § 401. It also exempted works from Berne countries of the requirement of registration of a work in the Copyright Office as a precondition of filing an infringement suit—a requirement that now only applies to U.S. works. 17 U.S.C. § 411.

3. Is a prohibition on all copyright formalities, including a requirement of registration and periodic renewal, desirable from a market or societal point of view? What are the benefits of such a system? Are there any costs?

4. *Bibliographic note.* WIPO, GUIDE TO THE BERNE CONVENTION 33–38 (1978) ("outside the country of origin, a Union author may demand protection throughout Union countries free of the need to comply with any formality there"); SAM RICKETSON, THE BERNE CONVENTION FOR THE PROTECTION OF LITERARY AND ARTISTIC WORKS: 1886–1986, at §§ 5.81–5.85, at 219–24 (1987); STEPHEN P. LADAS, 1 THE INTERNATIONAL PROTECTION OF LITERARY AND ARTISTIC PROPERTY 35–40 (1938).

3. BERNE RETROACTIVITY

Berne Convention (Paris, 1971)

Article 18

1. This Convention shall apply to all works which, at the moment of its coming into force, have not yet fallen into the public domain in the country of origin through the expiry of the term of protection.

2. If, however, through the expiry of the term of protection which was previously granted, a work has fallen into the public domain of the country where protection is claimed, that work shall not be protected anew.

3. The application of this principle shall be subject to any provisions contained in special conventions to that effect existing or to be concluded between countries of the Union. In the absence of such provisions, the respective countries shall determine, each in so far as it is concerned, the conditions of application of this principle.

4. The preceding provisions shall also apply in the case of new accessions to the Union and to cases in which protection is extended by the application of Article 7 or by the abandonment of reservations.

TRIPS Article 70

Protection of Existing Subject Matter

1. This Agreement does not give rise to obligations in respect of acts which occurred before the date of application of the Agreement for the Member in question.

2. Except as otherwise provided for in this Agreement, this Agreement gives rise to obligations in respect of all subject matter existing at the date of application of this Agreement for the Member in question, and which is protected in that Member on the said date, or which meets or comes subsequently to meet the criteria for protection under the terms of this Agreement. In respect of this paragraph and paragraphs 3 and 4, copyright obligations with respect to existing works shall be solely determined under Article 18 of the Berne Convention (1971), and obligations with respect to the rights of producers of phonograms and performers in existing phonograms shall be determined solely under Article 18 of the Berne Convention (1971) as made applicable under paragraph 6 of Article 14 of this Agreement.

3. There shall be no obligation to restore protection to subject matter which on the date of application of this Agreement for the Member in question has fallen into the public domain.

4. In respect of any acts in respect of specific objects embodying protected subject matter which become infringing under the terms of legislation in conformity with this Agreement, and which were commenced, or in respect of which a significant investment was made, before the date of acceptance of the WTO Agreement by that Member, any Member may provide for a limitation of the remedies available to the right holder as to the continued performance of such acts after the date of application of this Agreement for that Member. In such cases the Member shall, however, at least provide for the payment of equitable remuneration.

5. A Member is not obliged to apply the provisions of Article 11 and of paragraph 4 of Article 14 with respect to originals or copies purchased prior to the date of application of this Agreement for that Member. * * *

New accessions. A recurring question for IP agreements is raised for new accessions: what happens when a country agrees to join either an existing or a new IP treaty? Should the country be required to grant IP protection to existing material that has already entered into the public domain in that country? What happens if people there have come to rely on access to the material in the public domain? As more and more countries become members of TRIPS or international IP agreements, the question of retroactive protection will recede in frequency. But it still retains importance today.

The default rule for international treaties is that, absent express indication to the contrary, a treaty is not intended to apply retroactively. The Vienna Convention on the Law of Treaties (an influential treaty organized under the auspices of the United Nations for the establishment of principles of treaty interpretation) recognizes this principle of non-retroactivity under Article 28, which states: "Unless a different intention appears from the treaty or is otherwise established, its provisions do not bind a party in relation to any act or fact which took place or any situation which ceased to exist before the date of the entry into force of the treaty with respect to that party."

TRIPS Article 70(3) follows this principle of nonretroactivity as well, stating: "There shall be no obligation to restore protection to subject matter which on the date of application of this Agreement for the Member in question has fallen into the public domain." In fact, most IP agreements—e.g., the Universal Copyright Convention, the Rome Convention, and the Geneva Phonograms Convention—also follow this principle of non-retroactivity.

TRIPS Article 70(2), however, recognizes an exception for copyright and neighboring rights, incorporating the retroactive approach of the Berne Convention. Article 18(1) of Berne states that the "Convention shall apply to all works which, at the moment of its coming into force, have not yet fallen into the public domain in the country of origin through the expiry of the term of protection." This means that a country that newly joins Berne must extend copyrights to both (i) future works from Union countries and (ii) all existing foreign works from Union countries that are still under copyright in the country of origin (or at least not in the public domain there due to the end of the term of copyright protection).

Because the Berne countries recognized the potential harshness of requiring new members to remove works from the public domain, Article 18(3) gives countries some discretion in how they implement their obligation of retroactivity: "the respective countries shall determine, each in so far as it is concerned, the conditions of application of this principle." As the WIPO Guide to the Berne Convention (1981) explains (p. 101):

> This matter of retroactivity can be of considerable importance when a new country joins the Union since there may be, in such a country, many works in the public domain, not because of the expiry of the term of protection but, for example, by reason of the failure of their authors to observe the formalities demanded for their protection. That being so, thought must be given to those who have, quite properly, taken steps to exploit these works and who would be financially embarrassed, to say the least, if the authors suddenly acquired exclusive rights to control what they had been freely doing (publishing, performing, adapting, etc.). It is a matter therefore for each member country to decide on the limits of this retroactivity and, in litigation, for the courts to take into account these acquired rights.

Devising a system of retroactive copyright protection—and its proper limits—under Berne may be easier said than done. Consider the following problem and case.

PROBLEM 2–8

You are the Secretary of Commerce for Developing Country A. In the past, Developing Country A has not protected foreign works under copyright. Tens of thousands of foreign works are presently in the public domain in A, and sold at very cheap prices by domestic publishers and distributors. Developing Country A has prided itself on its sharing of works and its relatively well-educated populace. Developing Country A, however, is considering joining the Berne Convention. The President has asked you to prepare a report analyzing the measures that Developing Country A would have to undertake to implement Article 18 of the Berne Convention. The President is particularly concerned about causing a backlash among the local publishers and distributors, as well as the general populace, if tens of thousands of works are removed from the public domain. Please advise the President on (i) the measures needed to implement Article 18, (ii) the overall desirability and trade-offs of joining the Berne Convention, in light of the concerns about its effect on domestic producers and the general populace, and (iii) whether there would be any difference in joining Berne, but not TRIPS?

DAM THINGS FROM DENMARK, A/K/A TROLL COMPANY APS v. RUSS BERRIE & COMPANY, INC.

U.S. Court of Appeals for the Third Circuit.
290 F.3d 548 (3d Cir. 2002).

RENDELL, J.: We consider this case on an expedited appeal from the United States District Court for the District of New Jersey. The parties to this appeal, Dam Things from Denmark, a/k/a Troll Company ApS (together "Dam Things"), and Russ Berrie and Company, Inc. ("Russ"), are purveyors of trolls—short, pudgy, plastic dolls with big grins and wild hair. Dam Things, a Danish company, asserts that its copyright in its original troll design, the "Basic Good Luck Troll," has been restored pursuant to 17 U.S.C. § 104A. Section 104A is a highly unusual provision which has restored copyright protection in a vast number of foreign works previously in the public domain. Dam Things brought this action against Russ alleging infringement of its restored copyright. If restoration is proper under the statute, the key remaining issues are whether there is infringement, and if so, whether the infringing works will be totally prohibited or will be entitled to mandatory licenses under § 104A's safe harbor for derivative works.

We believe that the District Court properly determined that Dam Things was likely to establish that . . . the copyright [for its troll doll, which we refer to as P1] qualified for restoration and that this copyright was not abandoned by Dam Things. We find, however, that the District

Court's subsequent analysis was flawed in two ways. First, the District Court conflated the tests for infringement and derivative works, and it therefore did not properly consider the possibility that any of the Russ trolls qualified for § 104A's safe harbor for derivative works. Second, the District Court did not conduct the proper comparison of each of the allegedly infringing Russ trolls against the restored Dam Things troll–P1. As we believe that the District Court based its grant of the injunction on an incomplete factual and legal analysis, we will vacate the injunction and remand for further consideration by the District Court in light of this opinion.

I.

In the 1950s, Thomas Dam, a Danish woodcarver, created a troll figure for his daughter out of rubber. He called it the "Good Luck Troll," claiming that it had the ability to bring good luck to whomever possessed it. Apparently, his creation garnered much attention from the community and Dam decided to sell trolls to the public. As the troll's success continued, Dam began selling his trolls in other countries. According to Dam Things, the Dam trolls were first sold in the United States in 1961.

In 1960, Thomas Dam applied for a United States design patent for a troll doll, and the patent was issued in 1961. This troll doll was later described by Thomas Dam as "girl-like" as opposed to the original "boy-like" troll, and certain photographs of the troll submitted with the application reflect that the troll has hair pulled back in a ponytail. Dam Things filed applications for U.S. copyright registration of both the boy-like and girl-like trolls in 1964 and then again in 1965 after its initial applications were rejected for improperly designating the copyright holder as Denmark. Dam Things has held and continues to hold a valid Danish copyright in the trolls. In 1965, the District Court for the District of Columbia held that the Dam Things' trolls submitted for patent and copyright protection were in the public domain, because they were published in the United States with improper notice—they were marked with "Denmark" and the date or with just the date, instead of with the company's name and date—or with no notice at all. *Scandia House Enters., Inc. v. Dam Things Establishment*, 243 F. Supp. 450, 453–54 (D.D.C. 1965).

In the early 1950s, Russell Berrie was a manufacturer's representative for two companies who sold Dam Things trolls. Berrie started his own company, Russ Berrie and Company, Inc. in 1963 and began to sell trolls manufactured by Dam Things' U.S. licensee, Royalty Design, using the Dam Things molds, in 1967. When Royalty Design went bankrupt, Russ then used the Dam Things molds to manufacture trolls. Berrie claims that in 1987 his company began to modify the trolls. In 1988, Russ sent a Dam Things troll "pencil topper" to be used to make a mold and to manufacture trolls in China. In 1988 Russ also sent to China a photo of a Dam Things troll from the Russ catalog for the purpose of making a mold and manufacturing trolls. In the 1990s, Russ obtained fifteen copyright registrations for trolls—registered as derivative works of the photographs of the Dam Things trolls in the Russ catalogs.

Dam Things now claims copyright infringement of its public domain troll. This unusual claim is made possible by an act of Congress and is grounded on Dam Things' assertion that its copyright in its original troll has been restored pursuant to 17 U.S.C. § 104A. In this legislation, Congress declared that a wide range of foreign works previously in the public domain in this country, perhaps for many years, are once again afforded copyright protection. Although Russ points out the "extraordinary windfall" Dam Things will receive, and the "extraordinary burden" it will bear, if Dam Things' copyright is restored, the legislature's purpose in providing these protections for foreign copyright holders was to ensure greater protection for American copyright holders abroad.

This protection results from the United States' promise, in the context of the TRIPS Agreement to adhere to the Berne Convention, which the United States had entered in 1989. 3 Melville B. Nimmer & David Nimmer, *Nimmer on Copyright* § 9A.04 (2001) [hereinafter *Nimmer*]. In order to comply with the Berne Convention's "Rule of Retroactivity" contained in Article 18, Congress enacted the Uruguay Round Agreements Act. *Id.* Section 104A of the Copyright Act now provides for automatic restoration of copyright, as of January 1, 1996, for "an original work of authorship" which meets the following requirements:

(A) is protected under subsection (a) [which provides for a term of protection equal to what the work would have received "if the work had never entered the public domain in the United States," and excepts certain works which were "ever owned or administered by the Alien Property Custodian"];

(B) is not in the public domain in its source country through expiration of term of protection;

(C) is in the public domain in the United States due to—

(i) noncompliance with formalities imposed at any time by United States copyright law, including failure of renewal, lack of proper notice, or failure to comply with any manufacturing requirements;

(ii) lack of subject matter protection in the case of sound recordings fixed before February 15, 1972; or

(iii) lack of national eligibility; and

(D) has at least one author or rightholder who was, at the time the work was created, a national or domiciliary of an eligible country, and if published, was first published in an eligible country and not published in the United States during the 30–day period following publication in such eligible country.

Dam Things claims that its copyright in its original troll qualifies for automatic restoration in accordance with § 104A. If it does, then the copyright "shall subsist for the remainder of the term of copyright that the work would have otherwise been granted in the United States if the work never entered the public domain in the United States."

Section 104A also provides some relief for "reliance parties"—American authors who copied the restored works while they were in the public domain in the United States. 17 U.S.C. § 104A(d)(2)–(3). Parties who were in fact copying the restored work are given one year to sell the now infringing works after being given a "notice of intent to enforce" ("NIE") by the author of the restored work. 17 U.S.C. § 104A(d)(2). But, the statute also provides a safe harbor in the form of a mandatory license for authors of "derivative works"; they are allowed to continue manufacturing and selling their work, but must pay the author of the restored work reasonable compensation. 17 U.S.C. § 104A (d)(3).

The District Court concluded that Dam Things had "demonstrated a likelihood of success on its copyright infringement claim" and on December 20, 2001 it entered a Second Amended Order granting Dam Things a preliminary injunction and detailing its terms. Part of this order instructs that Russ will be entirely prohibited from selling its troll dolls as of February 13, 2002—one year after the date of the NIE.

II.

[W]e will review the District Court's legal determinations and its application of the law to the facts de novo. [W]e will examine the merits of Dam Things' claim under the statute and the District Court's treatment of it. This requires a three-step inquiry: first, does Dam Things hold a restored copyright, second, did Russ infringe Dam Things' copyright, and, third, is Russ protected by the 104A safe harbor for creators of derivative works?

A. Eligibility for Restoration

As set forth above, 17 U.S.C. § 104A provides essentially four requirements for restoration of a foreign work's copyright that are relevant here. First, the copyright has not expired in its source country. Second, it is in the public domain in the United States because of failure to comply with formalities. Third, the author of the work was a national or domiciliary of an eligible country. Fourth, the work was first published in an eligible country not less than thirty days prior to being published in the United States. The first two requirements regarding the continued existence of foreign copyright protection and the reason for the work's presence in the public domain were challenged by Russ before the District Court. However, we believe that they were properly disposed of in the Court's opinion. As to the third requirement, Russ has not challenged the fact that Thomas Dam is a national of an eligible country. We will therefore limit our discussion, as the parties did their arguments before us, to the place of first publication.

While Dam Things claims that the troll for which it seeks restoration was first published in Denmark, Russ contends that it was actually first published in the United States. Underlying this argument is the preliminary question in this case—which troll is at issue here? Dam Things has presented one troll to the Copyright Office, to the District Court, and to us as the troll whose copyright has been restored—Plaintiff's Exhibit 1 ("Pl"). Dam Things represents this doll as "an original Good Luck troll." It was reportedly manufactured in 1959, confirmed by the fact that it is made of rubber and later dolls were made of PVC. Further, it is shown in a September, 1959 magazine being held by Thomas Dam's daughter. The doll was presented to us in a box to protect it, as the rubber doll stuffed with sawdust has become very fragile with age. Although not required by statute, Dam Things applied for restoration of the copyright in this troll doll on March 9, 2000.

Russ, on the other hand, focuses its attention on what it terms "the 1961" or "Public Domain Troll." This is the troll that was the subject of Dam Things' 1961 design patent. Dam Things has referred to this at various times as a girl-like version of P1 and has also applied for a new registration for this troll in 2000 as being an "adaptation of previously published boy doll." Dam Things has not agreed that this troll was first published in 1961, and, in fact, on its 2000 copyright application it claimed it was first published in 1958. The girl-like troll that was the subject of the design patent was presented to the District Court and us as Plaintiff's Exhibit 4 ("P4"). This troll doll appears much like the first—it has four fingers on each hand and four toes on each foot, a large smile, broad nose, and large round eyes. It also stands erect with its arms outstretched, and it has a short, pudgy figure. The one difference which has been pointed to and was relied on by the Copyright Office in considering P4 as a derivative work for copyright registration purposes was its rounded ears in contrast to the pointy ears of P1.

Russ does not contest before us the fact that P1 was first published in Denmark. Instead, it argues that P4 is the relevant troll because it is really the troll that Dam Things contends Russ infringed. Dam Things, on the other hand, suggests that P4 is not a distinct work from P1 and therefore if one of them is infringed then the other is as well. Neither party argues that all of Dam Things' trolls are identical in appearance, and both seem to concede that restoration of a copyright in a troll must of necessity be linked to a specific troll which was first used in its nation of origin other than the United States. Here, Dam Things made clear at oral argument that P1 was the only specific item as to which restoration was sought.

Our holding today as to restoration is therefore limited to P1, and our discussion of Appellant's arguments will be limited accordingly. All that we need to decide is whether, as Dam Things urges, the copyright in P1 was restored. Therefore the place where P1 was first published is what matters.

The District Court concluded "that [Dam Things] can prove all of the requisite elements of § 104A and is therefore likely to succeed on the merits of its restoration claim." We agree with this aspect of the District Court's ruling, as it appears that Dam Things will be able to establish that P1 satisfies all four requirements for restoration, including first publication in an eligible country.

B. Copyright Infringement

Upon determining that the restoration of the Dam Things copyright was likely, the District Court focused on the merits of Dam Things' claim—the likelihood of success on the copyright infringement claim. We believe that the District Court's analysis was too conclusory, given the complex issues of infringement and originality before it, and particularly in light of the unique challenges presented by § 104A. We are specifically concerned with the District Court's incomplete consideration of Russ's contention that its trolls would qualify as derivative works.

The District Court should have compared the relevant trolls against one another to determine whether the various Russ trolls are derivatives of P1. Without detailed consideration of the Russ trolls as against P1, the District Court determined that all of the Russ trolls and all of the Dam Things trolls are too similar to be distinguishable. It explained: "A finder of fact who compares Russ's trolls with Dam's could not reasonably conclude that the [sic] Russ's trolls are original designs or that they comprise original expression of the idea of a troll." This blanket treatment relating to the trolls fell short of what is required. As we saw firsthand, these trolls come in all shapes and sizes—small pencil-toppers, and nine inch "giants," as well as grandparents, teenagers, and babies. Perhaps in the abstract one can believe that "a troll is a troll," but it is clear that all trolls cannot simply be judged alike, particularly when the inquiry must focus on distinct aspects of each. It is certainly possible that some of the Russ trolls could be considered to be derivative works while others would not. This exacting comparison needs to be made. Therefore, on remand, the District Court should look at the infringing Russ trolls and individually compare each one to P1 to determine whether it constitutes a derivative work of the Dam Things troll.

NOTES AND QUESTIONS

1. The U.S. provision, 17 U.S.C. § 104A, did not grant restored copyrights to works first published in the U.S. Thus, had Dam Things first published its Good Luck troll doll in the U.S., the troll doll would not be eligible for restored copyright. Why do you think the U.S. excluded works first published in the U.S. from restored copyright protection?

2. What exactly is at stake with the issue of retroactive application of treaty obligations? Who stands to benefit or lose from retroactive application? In *Dam Things*, doesn't the U.S. company have a legitimate reliance interest in being able to continue selling troll dolls, which was a part of its business for over 30 years?

Section 104A of the U.S. Copyright Act attempts to accommodate "reliance parties" in two ways. First, all reliance parties who acquired affected works before the enactment of the law are given a 12–month grace period (starting from the filing or serving of a Notice of Intent to Enforce a restored copyright in the work) before the copyright restoration becomes effective. 17 U.S.C. § 104A(d)(2). After the grace period, reliance parties lose their unrestricted rights to the works. Second, reliance parties who developed derivative works based on works § 104A has removed from the public domain are allowed to "continue to exploit that derivative work for the duration of the restored copyright if the reliance party pays to the owner of the restored copyright reasonable compensation." *Id.* § 104A(d)(3). Should a reliance party be made to pay compensation for making a derivative work that was first made on the legally correct understanding that the original work was in the public domain and free of copyright? In the *Dam Things* case, the U.S. company eventually settled the case and stopped making troll dolls forever. *See Russ Berrie Gives Up Fight to Make Troll Dolls*, N.J. REC., March 5, 2004, at B3.

3.   Troll dolls were not the only works removed from the public domain in the U.S. Many famous and important works of art and music were also removed, including the works of the Russian composers Shostakovich, Prokofiev, and Stravinsky, and films of Alfred Hitchcock and Fritz Lang. A number of orchestras in the U.S. have stopped performing Prokofiev's *Peter and the Wolf* for children because the restored copyright in the work has made the rental of the sheet music cost prohibitive. In a survey conducted by The Conductors Guild, 70% of orchestral conductors polled stated that, because of copyright restoration, they had to forego performing works that used to be in the public domain, but are now subject to restored copyrights. What theory of copyright might justify this result? How should the international dimensions of copyright factor into the analysis, if at all?

4.   Are there any constitutional concerns about removing works from the public domain under the First Amendment or the Copyright Clause of the U.S. Constitution? In 2011, the U.S. Supreme Court agreed to review the constitutionality of § 514 of the Uruguay Round Agreements Act (codified at §§ 104A and 109(a) of the Copyright Act). The challenge was brought by Lawrence Golan, a conductor and professor of orchestral conducting at the University of Denver, who—along with other conductors, orchestras, educators, and film archivists in the case—had relied on the public domain works in their artistic, business, and professional pursuits. In *Golan v. Holder*, the Court decided two questions: (1) Does the Copyright Clause of the United States Constitution, Article I, § 8, cl. 8, prohibit Congress from taking works out of the public domain? (2) Does Section 514 of the Uruguay Round Agreements Act violate the First Amendment of the United States Constitution?

The district court initially rejected both challenges but, on appeal, the Tenth Circuit ruled that § 514 restricted people's speech—limiting their use of works once in the public domain—in a way that required First Amendment scrutiny. *See Golan v. Gonzales*, 501 F.3d 1179, 1187–88 (10th Cir. 2007). This marked the first time a U.S. court has ever held that a copyright law restricted speech in a way that required First Amendment scrutiny.

On remand, the district court ruled that § 514 violated the First Amendment. *See Golan v. Holder*, 611 F. Supp. 2d 1165 (2009). The district court explained: "The Berne Convention . . . affords each member nation discretion to restore the copyrights of foreign authors in a manner consistent with that member nation's own body of copyright law. In the United States, that body of law includes the bedrock principle that works in the public domain remain in the public domain. * * * In light of the discretion afforded it by the Berne Convention, Congress could have complied with the Convention without interfering with Plaintiffs' protected speech." *Id.* at 1177. However, on appeal, a different panel of the Tenth Circuit reversed, holding that "it is immaterial whether, as plaintiffs contend, the government could have complied with the minimal obligations of the Berne Convention and granted stronger protections for American reliance parties." *Golan v. Holder*, 609 F.3d at 1091. In the Tenth Circuit's view, the U.S. government had a legitimate interest in "securing protections for American copyright owners in foreign countries," irrespective of what Berne allows or requires. *Id.* Therefore, the Tenth Circuit upheld § 514 as constitutional. Given the importance of the issue, the U.S. Supreme Court decided to hear the constitutional challenge of the petitioners. The Supreme Court upheld the law as constitutional, ruling that the Copyright Clause did not bar removal of works from the public domain and the First Amendment did not require any further scrutiny. *See Golan v. Holder*, 132 S. Ct. 873, 889–90 (2012).

5. Article 18 of the Berne Convention is commonly known as the Rule of Retroactivity. Berne qualifies the Rule of Retroactivity in Article 18 in two ways. First, "[t]he application of this principle shall be subject to any provisions contained in special conventions to that effect existing or to be concluded between countries of the Union." Second, "[i]n the absence of such provisions, the respective countries shall determine, each in so far as it is concerned, the conditions of application of this principle." Berne Conv. art. 18(3).

As Sam Ricketson describes, "These provisions leave considerable latitude to countries as to how they will implement the principle of retroactivity, enabling them to safeguard any rights which have been acquired in the previous situation where no legal protection applied." SAM RICKETSON, THE BERNE CONVENTION FOR THE PROTECTION OF LITERARY AND ARTISTIC WORKS: 1886–1986, at 674 (1987). Could the U.S. have implemented Article 18 differently than § 104A? For example, could the U.S. have implemented Berne without abrogating the first sale doctrine for affected works (see 17 U.S.C. § 109(a))? The first sale doctrine, which has been recognized in the U.S. for over 100 years, enables a lawful owner of a copy of a work to freely distribute that copy after its first sale.

6. *The United Kingdom's Implementation of Article 18*. The United Kingdom, which was a founding member of the Berne Convention, implements Article 18 of the Berne Convention in a different manner—one that is far more protective of reliance parties. Under UK copyright law, if a person "has incurred any expenditure or liability in connection with the act" of using a foreign work not before subject to UK copyright, the person *retains* the right to exploit that work even after it has been subject to a restored UK copyright because of the implementation of Berne Article 18. *See* Copyright and Per-

formances (Application to Other Countries) Order § 7, 2005 SI 2005/852 (UK). UK law protects the rights of reliance parties to continue to exploit the affected works as they had originally planned or intended. The safe harbor or "savings" clause applies not only to reliance parties who used the foreign works in good faith before the foreign country's accession to Berne, but also to reliance parties who "made in good faith effective and serious preparations to" use the foreign works when they were not subject to UK copyrights. *Id.* § 7(1)(b). These rights of reliance parties are subject to a "buy out" provision, under which the copyright holder can pay the reliance party compensation to forgo using the work. *Id.* § 7(3). If the parties cannot agree on reasonable compensation, either party can refer the matter to arbitration. *Id.* § 7(4).

The United Kingdom's implementation of Article 18, which can be traced back nearly to the beginning of the Berne Convention, has been influential in other commonwealth countries, such as Australia and New Zealand. Which approach is better—the United States' approach or the United Kingdom's?

4. POINTS OF ATTACHMENT AND NATIONAL TREATMENT FOR NEIGHBORING RIGHTS

Berne. The Berne Convention does not speak directly to rights for performers or their sound recordings. As a result, the Berne Convention leaves it up to each country to decide for itself whether to include performers' rights within the rubric of copyright; if a country decides to treat performance or sound recording rights as part of copyright law, then such rights become subject to the obligations of the Berne Convention, including national treatment. For example:

> Illustration 2–4. Country Z, a Berne Union country, treats rights for sound recordings under copyright law. By contrast, Country X, also a Union country, treats sound recordings under a lesser regime of neighboring or related rights. Alpha is a record production company located in Country X that first publishes a CD in Country X. Under the national treatment principle, because Country Z gives its own nationals copyright protection for sound recordings, Alpha is entitled to the same copyright protection for its sound recording in Country Z (even though Alpha only received a neighboring right in Country X, the country of origin). Under Berne Article 5(1), countries other than the country of origin are to grant foreign authors the same rights as their own nationals receive. Here, because Country Z gives its own nationals a copyright for domestic sound recordings, Country Z must extend copyrights to foreign sound recordings from other Berne countries.

However, for Berne Union countries that do not include performance or sound recording rights within the scope of copyright, such as Country X in the example above, the Berne Convention simply does not apply to performance rights. Consequently, other Berne countries that recognize only neighboring rights for recordings would not have to extend copyright protection to Alpha's recording. Such performance rights are subject to the principle of territoriality and would not be recognized in other countries without a treaty obligation.

Rome. To further the international recognition of performance rights, the International Convention for the Protection of Performers, Producers of Phonograms and Broadcasting Organisations (the Rome Convention) was signed in Rome in 1961. Aside from TRIPS, the Rome Convention is the most significant treaty concerning neighboring or related rights. In 2011, the Rome Convention had 91 members, although the U.S. remains a key country that has not joined Rome. While TRIPS requires some recognition of performance rights under Article 14, the protections of the Rome Convention are broader. As a result, membership in the Rome Convention can still confer benefits above and beyond what is required by TRIPS, although the Rome Convention lacks the strong enforcement mechanism of the WTO.

The same type of analysis that we encountered under Berne—points of attachment and national treatment—can also be found in the Rome Convention. The points of attachment under Rome are even more complicated, however, as it treats separately three types of entities: (i) performers, (ii) producers of phonograms or recordings, and (iii) broadcast organizations. Carefully read through the provisions and the explanation that follows.

Rome Convention

Article 2

1. For the purposes of this Convention, national treatment shall mean the treatment accorded by the domestic law of the Contracting State in which protection is claimed:

> (a) to performers who are its nationals, as regards performances taking place, broadcast, or first fixed, on its territory;

> (b) to producers of phonograms who are its nationals, as regards phonograms first fixed or first published on its territory;

> (c) to broadcasting organisations which have their headquarters on its territory, as regards broadcasts transmitted from transmitters situated on its territory.

2. National treatment shall be subject to the protection specifically guaranteed, and the limitations specifically provided for, in this Convention. * * *

Article 3

For the purposes of this Convention:

> (a) "performers" means actors, singers, musicians, dancers, and other persons who act, sing, deliver, declaim, play in, or otherwise perform literary or artistic works;

> (b) "phonogram" means any exclusively aural fixation of sounds of a performance or of other sounds;

(c) "producer of phonograms" means the person who, or the legal entity which, first fixes the sounds of a performance or other sounds;

* * *

(f) "broadcasting" means the transmission by wireless means for public reception of sounds or of images and sounds; * * *

Article 4

Each Contracting State shall grant national treatment to performers if any of the following conditions is met:

(a) the performance takes place in another Contracting State;

(b) the performance is incorporated in a phonogram which is protected under Article 5 of this Convention;

(c) the performance, not being fixed on a phonogram, is carried by a broadcast which is protected by Article 6 of this Convention.

* * *

Article 3 of the Rome Convention establishes who and what type of works are covered: performers, producers of phonograms, and broadcasting companies, and their respective rights relating to performances. Each of these persons or entities is entitled to a specific set of rights. *See* Article 7 (performers), Article 10 (producers of phonograms), Article 13 (broadcasters). The basic structure of the Rome Convention is identical to that of the Berne Convention: once a point of attachment exists, then the person or entity entitled to protection under the Rome Convention is entitled to receive performance rights under the domestic laws of every contracting state to the Rome Convention. As in the case of the Berne Convention, the Rome Convention is concerned with foreign protection—not with the protections afforded under the domestic law of the state where the performance took place, where the phonogram produced was first fixed or published, or where the broadcasting company has its headquarters or transmitter. The concern of the Rome Convention is with treatment of foreign performances, recordings, and broadcasts in *other* contracting states under the standard of national treatment, although, as a practical matter, it would be unlikely that a Rome country does not provide equivalent domestic protection. Indeed, the drafters of the Rome Convention considered requiring domestic protection, but agreed to drop the issue based on the understanding that most countries would protect domestic performances, recordings, and broadcasts at least as well as foreign ones.

Articles 4, 5, and 6 set forth the points of attachment under the Rome Convention, i.e., the conditions under which protection and national treatment under the Rome Convention becomes available. Let us start with Article 4, which sets forth the points of attachment for performers. Regardless of their nationality, performers can establish a point of attachment if the performance is in a Rome Convention country. This is particularly beneficial to U.S. performers, who can effectively "back door" to Rome protection even though the U.S. is not a party to Rome. If a U.S. performer gives a concert in a contracting state such as Germany, the U.S. performer is entitled to national treatment in all other contracting states by virtue of the performance taking place in a Rome country.

> Illustration 2–5. Carrie is a musician who gives a concert in Germany, a contracting state. Carrie is entitled to the protection of the Rome Convention in all other contracting states. If Boog makes unauthorized "bootleg" copies of Carrie's performance in Colombia, another Rome country, Carrie should be given national treatment in Colombia and the ability to prevent Boog's bootleg copies in Colombia. (As will be discussed in a later section, the Rome Convention Article 7 only requires the "possibility of preventing" such bootlegging, leaving it to countries how to carry out this obligation.)

One major difference between the Berne Convention and the Rome Convention is that the nationality of the author suffices for all purposes under the Berne Convention, whereas place of performance is the decisive element under the Rome Convention. Although a performer is a national of a contracting state to the Rome Convention, the performer must nevertheless perform in a Rome country to gain the protections of Rome. By contrast, under the Berne Convention, if the author is a national of a contracting state, the author is automatically protected regardless of whether the author wrote the work in a Berne country, and regardless of whether the author first publishes in a Berne country or even publishes the work at all. One explanation for this distinction may be that, historically, performers who merely performed someone else's work were often viewed as inferior (meaning less deserving of the societal reward of intellectual property) to authors who created the work.

Article 4(b) and 4(c) of Rome create two other points of attachment for performers. If the performance takes place in a non-contracting state, a performer can still enjoy the protection of the Rome Convention if (1) the producer of the phonograms or recording of the performance in question is entitled to protection under the Rome Convention under Article 5, or (2) a broadcasting organization that broadcast the performance is entitled to the protection of the Rome Convention under Article 6. In other words, the performer "piggybacks" onto the Rome point of attachment of any producer of a recording of the performance or any organization that broadcasts the performance. So, in order to determine if a performer is protected under Rome where the performance in question was not in a Rome country, one must typically consult Articles 5 and 6 to see if (i) any producer of a recording of the performance or (ii) any broadcaster of the performance might have established a point of attachment. Carefully read the provisions below:

Rome Convention

Article 5

1. Each Contracting State shall grant national treatment to producers of phonograms if any of the following conditions is met:

(a) the producer of the phonogram is a national of another Contracting State (criterion of nationality);

(b) the first fixation of the sound was made in another Contracting State (criterion of fixation);

(c) the phonogram was first published in another Contracting State (criterion of publication).

2. If a phonogram was first published in a non-contracting State but if it was also published, within thirty days of its first publication, in a Contracting State (simultaneous publication), it shall be considered as first published in the Contracting State.

3. By means of a notification deposited with the Secretary–General of the United Nations, any Contracting State may declare that it will not apply the criterion of publication or, alternatively, the criterion of fixation. Such notification may be deposited at the time of ratification, acceptance or accession, or at any time thereafter; in the last case, it shall become effective six months after it has been deposited.

Article 6

1. Each Contracting State shall grant national treatment to broadcasting organisations if either of the following conditions is met:

(a) the headquarters of the broadcasting organisation is situated in another Contracting State;

(b) the broadcast was transmitted from a transmitter situated in another Contracting State.

2. By means of a notification deposited with the Secretary–General of the United Nations, any Contracting State may declare that it will protect broadcasts only if the headquarters of the broadcasting organisation is situated in another Contracting State and the broadcast was transmitted from a transmitter situated in the same Contracting State. Such notification may be deposited at the time of ratification, acceptance or accession, or at any time thereafter; in the last case, it shall become effective six months after it has been deposited.

* * *

As set forth in Article 5, producers of phonograms or recordings can establish a point of attachment based on any of the following: (i) being a national of a Rome country, (ii) fixing the recording first in a Rome country, or (iii) first or simultaneously publishing the recording in a Rome country. Article 3 defines "producer of phonogram" as "the person who, or the legal entity which, first fixes the sounds of a performance or other sounds." Thus, when an employee of a corporation first fixes a performance in the course of employment, the corporation is treated as the producer of the phonogram.

Article 5 also redounds to the benefit of performers. Once the producer qualifies for protection, the performer also is entitled to national treatment for that recording from Rome countries. For example:

Illustration 2–6. Carrie gives a concert in a non-Rome state. Digitex, Carrie's recording company, produces a phonogram of the performance. Both Carrie and Digitex are entitled to national treatment under the Rome Convention if Digitex (i) is a national of a Rome state; (ii) has first fixed the concert into a phonogram in a Rome state; or (iii) has first or simultaneously published the phonogram of the concert in a Rome state. Let's assume that Digitex is not a national of a Rome country and did not fix the recording first in a Rome country. Even then, Digitex could still create a point of attachment under Rome if it first publishes the recording in a Rome country. If Digitex does so, Carrie, too, establishes a point of attachment under Rome, piggybacking onto Digitex's point of attachment. *See* Rome Conv. art. 4(b).

Illustration 2–7. Carrie gives a concert in a non-Rome state that is not fixed in a phonogram. Electra is a broadcasting company that broadcasts a live performance of Carrie's concert. Both Carrie and Electra are entitled to national treatment under the Rome Convention if (i) Electra has its headquarters in a Rome state or (ii) Electra transmitted the performance from a transmitter located in a Rome state.

The basic idea behind Illustrations 2–6 and 2–7 is to treat performers comparably to the producers of their recordings or broadcasters of their performances, at least with respect to performances that take place outside Rome countries. If a performance is the basis of a point of attachment for a recording producer or broadcasting organization, then the performer herself also receives a Rome point of attachment. Rome does not treat performers on par with producers and broadcasters in all respects. While the nationality of the performer does not establish a point of attachment under Rome, the nationality or its equivalent (i.e., the location of a recording or broadcasting company in a contracting state) is sufficient to establish a point of attachment in the case of phonogram producers and broadcasters. This difference might be attributable to the greater lobbying power and influence of the music and broadcasting industries. However, Article 4 ensures that phonogram producers and broadcasting companies are not placed in a better position than performers whose performances occur in a non-Rome state: the performer can piggyback whatever point of attachment is established by recording producers and broadcasting organizations for the performance.

Once a point of attachment is established, Rome entitles the respective party certain protections. For performers, Article 7 of the Rome Convention requires member countries to give performers "the possibility of preventing" certain prohibited acts that parallel those now designated in Article 14(1) of TRIPS. Rome Conv. art. 7(1); TRIPS art. 14(1). The language "the possibility of preventing" does not explicitly create an exclusive right, but instead gives countries flexibility to enforce such protection through criminal laws.

For producers of sound recordings, Article 10 of Rome recognizes "the right to authorize or prohibit the direct or indirect reproduction of their phonograms." Rome Conv. art. 10. Article 14(2) of TRIPS recognizes the same. TRIPS art. 14(2). TRIPS Article 14(4) also recognizes a rental right for producer of phonograms comparable to the one for computer programs in Article 11. *Id.* art. 14(4).

For broadcasting organizations, Article 13 of Rome recognizes several exclusive rights against unauthorized rebroadcasting, fixation, and reproduction of their broadcasts. Rome Conv. art. 13. Article 14(3) of TRIPS is similar. TRIPS art. 14(3).

The Rome Convention contains a provision recognizing a performance right entitling the performers and/or producers of phonograms an "equitable remuneration" for public performances. Rome Conv. art. 12. This provision has been a huge obstacle to the U.S.'s consideration of joining Rome. U.S. copyright law does not recognize a right of public performance for sound recordings (except in the case of digital transmissions), although Congress is now considering such an amendment.

The WIPO Phonograms Treaty was intended to strengthen rights for performers and producers of phonograms. One major advancement is that the WIPO Treaty recognizes a number of "exclusive rights" for both performers and producers of phonograms, including reproduction, distribution, rental, and the right of making available fixed performances. Performers also are accorded exclusive rights in their unfixed performances under the Treaty. Like Article 12 of Rome, the WIPO Phonograms Treaty recognizes a right of public performance in Article 15 (called the "right to remuneration for broadcasting and communication to the public"). WIPO Performances and Phonograms Treaty art. 15. Under the Treaty, "[p]erformers and producers of phonograms shall enjoy the right to a single equitable remuneration for the direct or indirect use of phonograms published for commercial purposes for broadcasting or for any communication to the public." *Id.* art. 15(1). The significance of this provision is undermined, however, by the fact that, by its own terms, it is purely optional for countries. The U.S. notably has not recognized such a performance right for performers.

PROBLEM 2–9

In which of the following cases is a point of attachment established under the Rome Convention for the performance in question? If a point of attachment is established, who is entitled to protection under the Rome Convention?

(a) Andrea, a national of Country Z, a contracting state to the Rome Convention, gives a concert in Country X, a non-contracting state.

(b) Brianna, a national of Country Y, a non-contracting state to the Rome Convention, gives a concert in Country Z, a contracting state.

(c) Creola, a national of Country X, a non-contracting state to the Rome Convention, gives a concert in Country W, also a non-contracting state.

The concert is broadcast live in Country W by WBC, which has its headquarters in Country Z, a contracting state.

(d) Diana, a national of country W, a non-contracting state to the Rome Convention gives a concert in Country X, also a non-contracting state. The concert is recorded live on a CD by Diana's producer Elvira, who is a national of Country Z, a contracting state.

In answering this problem, review the provisions of the Rome Convention and the related discussion above.

* * *

Other laws and treaties may further complicate the analysis of performing rights. Consider the following case involving Article 7 of the Treaty Establishing the European Economic Community (EEC), which prohibits "any discrimination on grounds of nationality" in European Community states.*

BRUCE SPRINGSTEEN AND HIS BAND

Federal Supreme Court of Germany (Bundesgerichtshof).
Case No. I ZR 205/95 (April 23, 1998).**

On June 5, 1992, during a world tour, the U.S. performer and singer Bruce Springsteen gave a performance in Los Angeles. The first plaintiff [Shane Fontayne], a British national, was the lead guitarist of the accompanying band. The concert was transmitted live by a number of radio broadcasting companies, including a broadcasting company in Los Angeles and companies in Argentina, Brazil, Austria, Paraguay, and Uruguay. In November 1992, the first defendant, whose managing director is the second defendant, launched a CD on the German market under the name "Bruce Springsteen—Live Los Angeles June 5th, 1992" containing recordings made during the concert on June 5, 1992.

The second plaintiff is the German subsidiary of S. asserting that the corresponding neighboring rights had been assigned to them, the plaintiffs filed an action against the defendants for infringement of the first plaintiff's neighboring rights.

[After the district court allowed the claim in full,] the court of appeals denied the plaintiffs' claims for damages for infringement of the first plaintiff's neighboring rights for lack of fault. On the other hand, the court largely upheld the claims for information to the extent that they assist the first plaintiff to quantify a claim for unjust enrichment.

The decision of the court of appeals cannot be upheld on appeal on the law. Contrary to the opinion of the court of appeals, there can be no doubt that the first plaintiff's neighboring rights were culpably infringed.

---

* The article was renumbered as Article 6 in Treaty Establishing the European Community (EC), ratified in 1993; as Article 12 of the Treaty of Amsterdam in 1997; and as Article 18 of the Treaty on the Functioning of the European Union in 2009.

** Translation originally published in 31 IIC 107, 107–11 (2000). Reproduced with permission.

The court of appeals wrongly dismissed the first plaintiff's claim for damages under Sec. 97(1) in conjunction with Secs. 75, first sent., and 95(1), of the former Copyright Act.

Nevertheless, the court of appeals rightly assumed an unlawful infringement of the neighboring rights to which the first plaintiff is entitled as performer according to German copyright law.

However, this does not derive, as the court of appeals ultimately rightly assumed, from a prejudicial legal effect enjoyed by the district court's finding by virtue of the fact that it was not contested by the defendants on appeal with respect to the injunction.

Equally unjustified is the objection of the appellants that the national treatment to the benefit of the plaintiff—irrespective of the effects of the EC-law prohibition on discrimination (see below)—derives from the International Convention on the Protection of Performers, Producers of Phonograms and Broadcasting Organizations dated October 26, 1961—the Rome Convention.

In this connection, the appellants object that the court of appeals denied that there was a jurisdictional basis in Art. 4(c), in conjunction with Art. 6(1), of the Rome Convention. According to this provision, each contracting state grants performing artists national treatment if their performance is not recorded on a phonogram and is transmitted by a radio or television broadcast pursuant to Art. 6 of the Rome Convention.

The appellants point out that the concert in question was transmitted live by broadcasting organizations in a number of contracting states of the Rome Convention. Even if the performance—as the appellants argue, relying on the legal expertise by Raushcer auf Weeg submitted during the proceedings—was only transmitted in one contracting state, the performing artists must be granted national treatment in Germany, irrespective of whether the contested reproduction derived from this transmission. The court of appeals, however, rightly assumed that Art. 4(c) of the Rome Convention only provides national treatment if the performance has been copied from a broadcast pursuant to Art. 6 of the Convention. However, this cannot be assumed in the case at issue.

According to the Rome Convention, performers primarily enjoy national treatment if their performance has taken place in a contracting state. In addition, the performers are always to be granted national treatment if the performance is fixed on a phonogram or transmitted by a broadcast for which the producers of phonograms can claim protection pursuant to Art. 5 or the broadcasting organization can claim protection according to Art. 6 of the Convention (Art 4(b) and (c) of the Convention). The purpose of this regulation is to create a system in which a performance fixed on a phonogram is always protected if the producer of the phonogram enjoys protection, and in which a transmitted performance (except for that fixed on a phonogram) is always protected if the broadcasting organization arranging the transmission enjoys protection. This regulation means that the producers of phonograms or broadcasting organizations whose performance is protected by the Rome Convention are not placed in a better position than the performing artists whose performances are fixed on the protected phonograms or transmitted by the protected broadcast. On the contrary, in such a case, the performing artists also enjoy protection for performances that did not take place in a contracting state. The reference to the protected performance by the producer of the phonogram or the broadcasting organization makes it clear that, unlike for instance the jurisdictional basis of the place of the first publication of a work in Art. 3(1)(b) of the RBC (Revised Berne Convention), this is a dependent protection that covers uses for which the producer of the phonograms or the broadcasting organization could also assert claims. The national treatment of performing artists in such cases avoids a producer of phonograms or a broadcasting organization being entitled to claim protection while the performing artist whose artistic achievement is fixed on the phonogram or is transmitted in the broadcast remains without protection. A similar linking of the protection of the performing artist to the protection of the producer of phonograms and broadcasting organizations is also to be found in the foreign law provisions of Sec. 125(3) and (4) of the [German] Copyright Act; there, too, the protection of foreign performing artists is tied to the protection of the producers of phonograms and broadcasting organizations, and is restricted to further use of the sound or visual recording in question or the radio broadcast.

As the court of appeals rightly assumed, the first plaintiff can, however, claim national treatment pursuant to Art. 7(1) of the EEC Treaty (now Art. 6(1) of the EC Treaty) as a national of a Member State of the European Union. This follows from the *Phil Collins* decision of the Court of Justice of the European Communities, according to which it is an infringement of the EC law prohibition on discrimination for a Member State to deny an author or a performing artist of another Member State a right of prohibition that it grants to national authors or performing artists. Since this is a description of current law, the decision—as the court of appeals rightly assumed—has retrospective effect.

NOTES AND QUESTIONS

1. Even though the performance in the *Bruce Springsteen* case occurred in the U.S., which is not a signatory of the Rome Convention, the first plaintiff (Shane Fontayne, a British national and then-lead guitarist of Springsteen's band) claimed that the performance was nevertheless entitled to national treatment under the Rome Convention. Can you explain Fontayne's argument? Did the German Federal Supreme Court accept or reject the plaintiff's interpretation of the Rome Convention? Do you agree?

2. Did the German court ultimately find that Springsteen's band was entitled to national treatment and protection in Germany? If so, was it required by the Rome Convention or some other legal obligation?

3. *Formalities for Neighboring Rights*. Since the Berne Convention does not apply to neighboring rights, and the TRIPS Agreement does not prohibit

formalities for the obtaining of neighboring rights, it is conceivable that a country could impose formalities on such rights. Most, if not all, countries do not, however. Moreover, for countries in the Rome Convention, Article 11 provides that any formality requirement for sound recordings must be considered satisfied if the copies bear the phonogram notice "(P)" with the year date of first publication on all copies or their containers.

4. *Bibliographic note.* RECORDS OF THE DIPLOMATIC CONFERENCE ON THE INTERNATIONAL PROTECTION OF PERFORMERS, PRODUCERS OF PHONOGRAMS AND BROADCASTING ORGANIZATIONS (1968); WIPO GUIDE TO THE ROME CONVENTION AND TO THE PHONOGRAMS CONVENTION (1981).

PROBLEM 2–10

Anastasia is a singer from Chapel Hill, North Carolina. She performed a concert in New York on July 4. Her record studio Too Live (TL), a U.S. corporation, taped the performance for inclusion on a future CD. Both Anastasia and TL are concerned about the sale of bootleg copies in Europe and other international markets. TL has 25 employees, one of whom is a Canadian national, Warwick, the vice president of the company. He rarely assists in the production of recordings given his many other duties, and he was not on the scene at Anastasia's July 4th concert when it was first recorded. Thus far, Warwick has not been involved in Anastasia's recordings. The production of the CD of Anastasia's concert is still in its beginning stages and won't be completed for several months. Canada is a member of the Rome Convention. You are the attorney for TL. Can you provide advice for Anastasia and TL on how, if at all, to obtain protection in Rome countries for (i) the July 4th concert and (ii) for future concerts?

5. OWNERSHIP AND TRANSFER OF COPYRIGHTS

Related to points of attachment and the national treatment is the issue of ownership of rights—who is vested with the initial ownership of exclusive rights. Unlike points of attachment and national treatment, however, ownership is left largely unaddressed by international IP treaties. This section discusses the ownership issues related to copyright, while a later section will discuss such issues as applied to an author's moral rights in copyrighted works.

PROBLEM 2–11

You are the General Counsel for Alphavex Co., headquartered in Silicon Valley, but with offices in the UK and Germany. Alphavex produces both synthesized techno music and computer software. You want to make sure that the Company owns whatever rights to the written music and software that is developed by employees at Alphavex within the scope of their employment. Is a contract necessary to obtain copyright ownership over the music and software for employees from the U.S., the UK, and Germany?

Berne Convention (Paris, 1971)

Article 14*bis*

(1) Without prejudice to the copyright in any work which may have been adapted or reproduced, a cinematographic work shall be protected as an original work. The owner of copyright in a cinematographic work shall enjoy the same rights as the author of an original work, including the rights referred to in the preceding Article.

(2) (a) Ownership of copyright in a cinematographic work shall be a matter for legislation in the country where protection is claimed.

Article 15

(1) In order that the author of a literary or artistic work protected by this Convention shall, in the absence of proof to the contrary, be regarded as such, and consequently be entitled to institute infringement proceedings in the countries of the Union, it shall be sufficient for his name to appear on the work in the usual manner. This paragraph shall be applicable even if this name is a pseudonym, where the pseudonym adopted by the author leaves no doubt as to his identity.

(2) The person or body corporate whose name appears on a cinematographic work in the usual manner shall, in the absence of proof to the contrary, be presumed to be the maker of the said work.

(3) In the case of anonymous and pseudonymous works, other than those referred to in paragraph (1) above, the publisher whose name appears on the work shall, in the absence of proof to the contrary, be deemed to represent the author, and in this capacity he shall be entitled to protect and enforce the author's rights. The provisions of this paragraph shall cease to apply when the author reveals his identity and establishes his claim to authorship of the work.

(4) (a) In the case of unpublished works where the identity of the author is unknown, but where there is every ground to presume that he is a national of a country of the Union, it shall be a matter for legislation in that country to designate the competent authority who shall represent the author and shall be entitled to protect and enforce his rights in the countries of the Union.

(b) Countries of the Union which make such designation under the terms of this provision shall notify the Director General by means of a written declaration giving full information concerning the authority thus designated. The Director General shall at once communicate this declaration to all other countries of the Union.

* * *

Under Article 5(1) of the Berne Convention, countries are obligated to vest initial ownership of copyright to the "author" of a literary or artistic work. Article 15 creates a presumption that the author is the person whose name appears on the work "in the usual manner." The Convention, however, does not provide a definition of author. Likewise, the Rome Convention establishes minimum standards for "performers," "producers of phonograms," and "broadcasting organizations" as defined in Article 3, obligating countries to provide certain protections against unauthorized fixation, recordings, and broadcast of performances.

For the ownership of copyrights, the central fault line that divides countries is over the treatment of corporate entities and the employer-employee relationship under copyright law. We have already discussed one case of copyright ownership, *Itar–Tass,* in the first chapter, and the different treatment of newspapers invoking the work-made-for-hire doctrine in the U.S. and Russia. The Berne Convention does not expressly address whether corporations can be treated as authors for all works generally. Berne does mention the possibility of corporate authors in cinematographic works. Article 14*bis* leaves the issue of ownership of copyright in a cinematographic work for each country to decide under its national law, while Article 15 contemplates the possibility that a country may choose to vest ownership of cinematographic works in a corporate entity. The ambiguity in Berne over whether corporate entities may be treated as authors of other works has sparked considerable debate. Efforts by WIPO to address this issue has resulted in far more disagreement than consensus.

Given this disagreement, it is likely that differences in national approaches will remain. Continental European countries have historically limited the author's right to flesh-and-blood authors (meaning natural persons), although this approach is by no means uniform today. France, for example, does not recognize the work-made-for-hire doctrine, except that (i) it does allow copyrights for collective works to vest initially in a corporate entity and (ii) it also recognizes the work-made-for-hire doctrine for computer software, vesting the ownership of copyright to the employer for programs created by employees within the scope of the employment. Germany also does not generally recognize the work-made-for-hire doctrine either, but it allows the work-made-for-hire doctrine for an employer of software developers to obtain copyright in software programs developed in the course of employment. Germany's general protection of flesh-and-blood authors is so strong (if not paternalistic), it even prohibits authors from completely assigning away their author's right. The prohibition is based on the monist ideal that the author's right (including both economic and moral rights) is unitary and personal to the author. Germany does allow, however, the author to grant both exclusive and nonexclusive licenses granting another party the permission to exploit the economic rights of copyright. The license is viewed, not as a transfer of the author's own right, but as the creation of a new "right of use" for the licensee. Practically speaking, an author's licensing of all exploitation rights may achieve close to what a complete assignment would achieve if it were formally permitted. However, even with licensing, an author retains statutory rights in Germany. For example, in 2002, Germany enacted a controversial measure that provides authors with a statutory right to "equitable remuneration" in contracts involving use of their copyrighted works.

The German prohibition against the complete assignment of copyrights is probably the most protective of authors. Other continental European countries, such as France, that take a dualist view to author's right—recognizing that economic rights are separable from moral rights—also may recognize inalienable statutory protections for authors, but typically of more limited scope. Most countries outside of continental Europe (and the author's right tradition) recognize much greater freedom of contract in assignment of copyrights. But measures protecting authors can be found even in countries that generally allow the freedom of contract. The U.S., for example, recognizes a "termination right," which allows authors to void transfers and licenses of their copyrights during a five year period beginning at the end of 35 years from the execution of the transfer or license. 17 U.S.C. § 203. The diversity of approaches to copyright assignments and licenses underscores the fact that neither TRIPS nor the Berne Convention speaks to these issues.

Returning to the question of corporate authors, the United States and United Kingdom typify the approach of common law countries in recognizing the work-made-for-hire doctrine generally. Under this approach, the default position is that an employee who creates a work within the scope of his or her employment does not own the copyright to the work. The employer does. Indeed, in some countries such as the U.S., the employee is not even considered the author of the work. This approach allows corporate entities—such as movie studios—to own the copyrights to their productions by operation of law, without the need for any assignment of rights. However, the work-made-for-hire doctrine, which is codified by statute in both the U.S. and UK,[5] only establishes a baseline or default approach. An employer and employee may agree to a different understanding of copyright ownership by contract—which, under U.S. law, must be formalized in a written instrument signed by both parties. 17 U.S.C. § 201(b).

NOTES AND QUESTIONS

1. Do you think the difference between the positions of countries like France and Germany on the one hand and countries such as the United States and the UK on the other hand concerning the work-made-for-hire doctrine can be traced to the level of acceptance of natural rights versus utilitarian theory of copyright in those countries? Can you suggest a possible correlation?

2. The work-made-for-hire doctrine is well-established in U.S. law. Who stands to benefit from the doctrine? How?

3. What do you think of Germany's prohibition on the assignment of copyrights?

4. *Bibliographic Note.* Adolf Dietz, *Germany*, in INTERNATIONAL COPYRIGHT LAW AND PRACTICE § 4[1][b] (Paul Edward Geller & Melville B. Nimmer eds., 2003); Paul Edward Geller, *Conflicts of Laws in Copyright Cases: Infringement and Ownership Issues*, 51 J. COPYRIGHT SOC'Y USA 315, 364 & n.221 (2004); Reto M. Hilty & Alexander Peukert, *"Equitable Remuneration" in Copyright Law: The Amended German Copyright Act as a Trap for the Entertainment Industry in the U.S.?*, 22 CARDOZO ARTS & ENT. L.J. 401 (2004); Andre Lucas and Pascal Kamina, *France*, in INTERNATIONAL COPYRIGHT LAW AND PRACTICE § 4[1][b] (Paul Edward Geller & Melville B. Nimmer eds., 2003); Neil Netanel, *Alienability Restrictions and the Enhancement of Author Autonomy in United States and Continental Copyright Law*, 12 CARDOZO ARTS & ENT. L.J. 1, 20–23 (1994); Andreas Rahmatian, *Non–Assignability of Author's*

---

5. *See* U.S. Copyright Act of 1976, 17 U.S.C. § 201; UK Copyright, Design and Patents Act § 11.

Rights in Austria and Germany and Its Relation to the Concept of Creativity in Civil Law Jurisdictions Generally: A Comparison with UK Copyright Law, 11(5) ENT. L. REV. 95 (2000); Eugen Ulmer, *Some Thoughts on the Law of Copyright Contracts*, 7 I.I.C. 202 (1976).

C. SUBJECT MATTER

What types of works are entitled to copyright protection? Traditionally, copyright has protected literary and artistic works, such as novels, plays, paintings, and music. With technological changes and the impact of globalization, new challenges have been raised concerning possible copyright protection for databases, and for folklore and traditional knowledge of indigenous peoples in developing countries. In this part, we examine the basic doctrine and the new challenges.

1. PROTECTED WORKS

TRIPS Agreement

Article 9

2. Copyright protection shall extend to expressions and not to ideas, procedures, methods of operation or mathematical concepts as such.

Article 10

Computer Programs and Compilations of Data

1. Computer programs, whether in source or object code, shall be protected as literary works under the Berne Convention (1971).

2. Compilations of data or other material, whether in machine readable or other form, which by reason of the selection or arrangement of their contents constitute intellectual creations shall be protected as such. Such protection, which shall not extend to the data or material itself, shall be without prejudice to any copyright subsisting in the data or material itself.

Berne Convention (Paris, 1971)

Article 2

(1) The expression "literary and artistic works" shall include every production in the literary, scientific and artistic domain, whatever may be the mode or form of its expression, such as books, pamphlets and other writings; lectures, addresses, sermons and other works of the same nature; dramatic or dramatico-musical works; choreographic works and entertainments in dumb show; musical compositions with or without words; cinematographic works to which are assimilated works expressed by a process analogous to cinematography; works of drawing, painting, architecture, sculpture, engraving and lithography; photographic works to which are assimilated works expressed by a process analogous to photography; works of applied art; illustrations,

maps, plans, sketches and three-dimensional works relative to geography, topography, architecture or science.

(2) It shall, however, be a matter for legislation in the countries of the Union to prescribe that works in general or any specified categories of works shall not be protected unless they have been fixed in some material form.

(3) Translations, adaptations, arrangements of music and other alterations of a literary or artistic work shall be protected as original works without prejudice to the copyright in the original work.

(4) It shall be a matter for legislation in the countries of the Union to determine the protection to be granted to official texts of a legislative, administrative and legal nature, and to official translations of such texts.

(5) Collections of literary or artistic works such as encyclopaedias and anthologies which, by reason of the selection and arrangement of their contents, constitute intellectual creations shall be protected as such, without prejudice to the copyright in each of the works forming part of such collections.

(6) The works mentioned in this article shall enjoy protection in all countries of the Union. This protection shall operate for the benefit of the author and his successors in title. . . .

(8) The protection of this Convention shall not apply to news of the day or to miscellaneous facts having the character of mere items of press information.

Article 2*bis*

(1) It shall be a matter for legislation in the countries of the Union to exclude, wholly or in part, from the protection provided by the preceding Article political speeches and speeches delivered in the course of legal proceedings.

(2) It shall also be a matter for legislation in the countries of the Union to determine the conditions under which lectures, addresses and other works of the same nature which are delivered in public may be reproduced by the press, broadcast, communicated to the public by wire and made the subject of public communication as envisaged in Article 11bis(1) of this Convention, when such use is justified by the informatory purpose.

(3) Nevertheless, the author shall enjoy the exclusive right of making a collection of his works mentioned in the preceding paragraphs.

Expression. Copyright protects the works of authors. Although "author" is not defined anywhere in the Berne Convention or TRIPS, one can infer from their provisions that an "author" creates "expression." Article 9 of TRIPS sets forth the fundamental dividing line between protectable and non-protectable subject matter: copyright extends only to expression, but not to the underlying ideas. An author who wrote a tragic novel about star-crossed lovers could claim copyright for the entire expression in the novel (i.e., the particular words used), but could not assert copyright protection for the basic idea of a tragic love tale. As courts have often recognized, however, drawing the line between expression and the underlying idea is not always easy or certain. An author is typically afforded copyright protection beyond the literal words to encompass "substantially similar" works. But at what level beyond the literal words does protection sweep in the underlying idea itself? Courts struggle in individual cases to draw the right dividing line.

"Expression" can come in many different forms. Article 2(1) of the Berne Convention sets forth an expansive definition of "literary and artistic" works that fall within the scope of copyright protection: "every production in the literary, scientific and artistic domain, whatever may be the mode or form of its expression" is eligible for copyright. Article 2(3) encompasses "[t]ranslations, adaptations, arrangements of music and other alterations of a literary or artistic work," which are also commonly called derivative works (being in part "derived" from existing works). Article 2(5) encompasses compilations, "such as encyclopaedias and anthologies which, by reason of the selection and arrangement of their contents, constitute intellectual creations shall be protected as such." Like derivative works, compilations are to be protected "without prejudice to the copyright in each of the works forming part of such collections"—meaning that separate copyrights may be granted to the author of each individual part (e.g., copyright in the article) and to the author of the collective whole (e.g., copyright for the entire journal).

Fixation (or not). Article 2(2) of Berne leaves it up to countries to decide whether copyright should apply only to works "fixed in some material form," as is required, for example, under the U.S. Copyright Act. 17 U.S.C. § 102. Thus, countries within Berne have the discretion to grant copyrights even to *unfixed* works, such as an unfixed dance or pantomime, jazz improvisation, or live broadcast. The U.S., however, requires a fixation for federal copyright.

NOTES AND QUESTIONS

1. *Copyrightable subject matter.* Under Berne and TRIPS, for what subject matter do countries have the discretion *not* to offer copyrights? What subject matter are countries *forbidden* from extending copyright to? What might explain why certain subject matter is deemed categorically ineligible for copyright?

2. *Computer Programs.* Although TRIPS incorporates the Berne Convention's provisions dealing with subject matter of "literary and artistic works," TRIPS contains its own provision for computer programs in Article 10. Countries are now required under TRIPS to treat computer programs, "whether in source or object code," as literary works within the coverage of copyright. A computer program typically is written in a human-readable computer language that constitutes the *source code* for the program. The

source code is translated by a computer into *object code*, which is in binary language consisting of a bunch of 1s and 0s.

The United States was a strong proponent of including computer programs within the coverage of copyright under TRIPS. The inclusion of computer programs within copyright has sparked considerable debate and legal commentary, ever since the U.S. first recognized such protection under its copyright law in 1980. Critics of such protection have argued that the functional nature of a computer program (which is a series of instructions to a computer) makes it a poor fit for treatment under copyright, which protects creative, not functional, elements. *See* Pamela Samuelson, Randall Davis, Mitchell D. Kapor, & J.H. Reichman, *A Manifesto Concerning the Legal Protection of Computer Programs*, 94 COLUM. L. REV. 2348 (1994).

3. *Graphical User Interfaces (GUIs)*. Graphical user interfaces (GUIs) are visual representations, such as icons, that enable a user to interact with a computer program. In 2010, the Court of Justice ruled that GUIs are not computer programs; however, they may be protected as a work if "it is its author's own intellectual creation." *Bezpečnostní softwarová asociace—Svaz softwarové ochrany v. Ministerstvo kultury*, C–393/09 (Dec. 22, 2010), ¶ 46. Controversially, the CJEU also ruled that a TV broadcast including a GUI on a display viewable to the public would not implicate the copyright holder's right of public communication of the GUI if "television viewers receive a communication of that graphic user interface solely in a passive manner, without the possibility of intervening." *Id.* ¶ 57. The CJEU reasoned: "Having regard to the fact that, by television broadcasting, the graphic user interface is not communicated to the public in such a way that individuals can have access to the essential element characterising the interface, that is to say, interaction with the user, there is no communication to the public of the graphic user interface within the meaning of Article 3(1) of Directive 2001/29." *Id.*

2. ORIGINALITY OR CREATIVITY REQUIREMENTS

Originality is often thought to be the touchstone of copyright requirements, although curiously it is not expressly mentioned in either TRIPS or the Berne Convention. Instead, both TRIPS and Berne require "intellectual creation," but only specifically for compilations of data (TRIPS art. 10(2)) or for collections of works (Berne Conv. art. 2(5)). It is commonly understood, however, that *all* works under the Berne Convention must possess some "intellectual creation," which is often used interchangeably with "originality." For compilations or collections, Berne and TRIPS appear to leave much discretion to individual nations to establish how much intellectual creation is necessary. Consider the following two cases from the United States and Canada.

FEIST PUBLICATIONS, INC. v. RURAL TELEPHONE SERVICE COMPANY, INC.

Supreme Court of the United States.
499 U.S. 340 (1991).

JUSTICE O'CONNOR delivered the opinion of the Court.

This case requires us to clarify the extent of copyright protection available to telephone directory white pages.

I

Rural Telephone Service Company, Inc., is a certified public utility that provides telephone service to several communities in northwest Kansas. It is subject to a state regulation that requires all telephone companies operating in Kansas to issue annually an updated telephone directory. Accordingly, as a condition of its monopoly franchise, Rural publishes a typical telephone directory, consisting of white pages and yellow pages. The white pages list in alphabetical order the names of Rural's subscribers, together with their towns and telephone numbers. The yellow pages list Rural's business subscribers alphabetically by category and feature classified advertisements of various sizes. Rural distributes its directory free of charge to its subscribers, but earns revenue by selling yellow pages advertisements.

Feist Publications, Inc., is a publishing company that specializes in area-wide telephone directories. Unlike a typical directory, which covers only a particular calling area, Feist's area-wide directories cover a much larger geographical range, reducing the need to call directory assistance or consult multiple directories. The Feist directory that is the subject of this litigation covers 11 different telephone service areas in 15 counties and contains 46,878 white pages listings—compared to Rural's approximately 7,700 listings. Like Rural's directory, Feist's is distributed free of charge and includes both white pages and yellow pages. Feist and Rural compete vigorously for yellow pages advertising.

Feist is not a telephone company, let alone one with monopoly status, and therefore lacks independent access to any subscriber information. To obtain white pages listings for its area-wide directory, Feist approached each of the 11 telephone companies operating in northwest Kansas and offered to pay for the right to use its white pages listings.

Of the 11 telephone companies, only Rural refused to license its listings to Feist. Rural's refusal created a problem for Feist, as omitting these listings would have left a gaping hole in its area-wide directory, rendering it less attractive to potential yellow pages advertisers. In a decision subsequent to that which we review here, the District Court determined that this was precisely the reason Rural refused to license its listings. The refusal was motivated by an unlawful purpose "to extend its monopoly in telephone service to a monopoly in yellow pages advertising."

Unable to license Rural's white pages listings, Feist used them without Rural's consent. Feist began by removing several thousand listings that fell outside the geographic range of its area-wide directory, then hired personnel to investigate the 4,935 that remained. These employees verified the data reported by Rural and sought to obtain additional information. As a result, a typical Feist listing includes the individual's street address; most of Rural's listings do not. Notwithstanding these additions, however, 1,309 of the 46,878 listings in Feist's 1983 directory were identical to listings in Rural's 1982–1983 white pages. Four of these were fictitious listings that Rural had inserted into its directory to detect copying.

Rural sued for copyright infringement in the District Court for the District of Kansas taking the position that Feist, in compiling its own directory, could not use the information contained in Rural's white pages. The District Court granted summary judgment to Rural. In an unpublished opinion, the Court of Appeals for the Tenth Circuit affirmed "for substantially the reasons given by the district court." We granted certiorari to determine whether the copyright in Rural's directory protects the names, towns, and telephone numbers copied by Feist.

II

A

This case concerns the interaction of two well-established propositions. The first is that facts are not copyrightable; the other, that compilations of facts generally are. Each of these propositions possesses an impeccable pedigree. That there can be no valid copyright in facts is universally understood. The most fundamental axiom of copyright law is that "[n]o author may copyright his ideas or the facts he narrates." *Harper & Row, Publishers, Inc. v. Nation Enters.*, 471 U.S. 539, 556 (1985). Rural wisely concedes this point. At the same time, however, it is beyond dispute that compilations of facts are within the subject matter of copyright. Compilations were expressly mentioned in the Copyright Act of 1909, and again in the Copyright Act of 1976.

The key to resolving the tension lies in understanding why facts are not copyrightable. The *sine qua non* of copyright is originality. To qualify for copyright protection, a work must be original to the author. See *Harper & Row, supra*, at 547–549. Original, as the term is used in copyright, means only that the work was independently created by the author (as opposed to copied from other works), and that it possesses at least some minimal degree of creativity. 1 M. Nimmer & D. Nimmer, Copyright §§ 2.01[A], [B] (1990) (hereinafter Nimmer). To be sure, the requisite level of creativity is extremely low; even a slight amount will suffice. The vast majority of works make the grade quite easily, as they possess some creative spark, "no matter how crude, humble or obvious" it might be. *Id.,* § 1.08[C][1]. Originality does not signify novelty; a work may be original even though it closely resembles other works so long as the similarity is fortuitous, not the result of copying. To illustrate, assume that two poets, each ignorant of the other, compose identical poems. Neither work is novel, yet both are original and, hence, copyrightable.

Originality is a constitutional requirement. The source of Congress' power to enact copyright laws is Article I, § 8, cl. 8, of the Constitution, which authorizes Congress to "secur[e] for limited Times to Authors ... the exclusive Right to their respective Writings." In two decisions from the late 19th century—*The Trade–Mark Cases*, 100 U.S. 82 (1879); and *Burrow–Giles Lithographic Co. v. Sarony*, 111 U.S. 53 (1884)—this Court defined the crucial terms "authors" and "writings." In so doing, the Court made it unmistakably clear that these terms presuppose a degree of originality.

In *The Trade–Mark Cases,* the Court addressed the constitutional scope of "writings." For a particular work to be classified "under the head of writings of authors," the Court determined, "originality is required." 100 U.S. at 94. The Court explained that originality requires independent creation plus a modicum of creativity: "[W]hile the word *writings* may be liberally construed, as it has been, to include original designs for engraving, prints, etc., it is only such as are *original,* and are founded in the creative powers of the mind. The writings which are to be protected are *the fruits of intellectual labor,* embodied in the form of books, prints, engravings, and the like." *Ibid.*

In *Burrow–Giles,* the Court distilled the same requirement from the Constitution's use of the word "authors." The Court defined "author," in a constitutional sense, to mean "he to whom anything owes its origin; originator; maker." 111 U.S. at 58. As in *The Trade–Mark Cases,* the Court emphasized the creative component of originality. It described copyright as being limited to "original intellectual conceptions of the author," and stressed the importance of requiring an author who accuses another of infringement to prove "the existence of those facts of originality, of intellectual production, of thought, and conception." 111 U.S. at 59–60.

It is this bedrock principle of copyright that mandates the law's seemingly disparate treatment of facts and factual compilations. "No one may claim originality as to facts." Nimmer, § 2.11[A], p. 2–157. This is because facts do not owe their origin to an act of authorship. The distinction is one between creation and discovery: The first person to find and report a particular fact has not created the fact; he or she has merely discovered its existence. To borrow from *Burrow–Giles,* one who discovers a fact is not its "maker" or "originator." "The discoverer merely finds and records." Nimmer § 2.03[E]. Census takers, for example, do not "create" the population figures that emerge from their efforts; in a sense, they copy these figures from the world around them. Census data therefore do not trigger copyright because these data are not "original" in the constitutional sense. Nimmer § 2.03[E]. The same is true of all facts—scientific, historical, biographical, and news of the day. "[T]hey may not be copyrighted and are part of the public domain available to every person." *Miller, supra,* at 1369.

Factual compilations, on the other hand, may possess the requisite originality. The compilation author typically chooses which facts to include, in what order to place them, and how to arrange the collected data so that they may be used effectively by readers. These choices as to selection and arrangement, so long as they are made independently by the compiler and entail a minimal degree of creativity, are sufficiently original that Congress may protect such compilations through the copyright laws. Thus, even a directory that contains absolutely no protectible written expression, only facts, meets the constitutional minimum for copyright protection if it features an original selection or arrangement.

This inevitably means that the copyright in a factual compilation is thin. Notwithstanding a valid copyright, a subsequent compiler remains free to use the facts contained in another's publication to aid in preparing a competing work, so long as the competing work does not feature the same selection and arrangement.

This, then, resolves the doctrinal tension: Copyright treats facts and factual compilations in a wholly consistent manner. Facts, whether alone or as part of a compilation, are not original and therefore may not be copyrighted. A factual compilation is eligible for copyright if it features an original selection or arrangement of facts, but the copyright is limited to the particular selection or arrangement. In no event may copyright extend to the facts themselves.

III

The selection, coordination, and arrangement of Rural's white pages do not satisfy the minimum constitutional standards for copyright protection. As mentioned at the outset, Rural's white pages are entirely typical. Persons desiring telephone service in Rural's service area fill out an application and Rural issues them a telephone number. In preparing its white pages, Rural simply takes the data provided by its subscribers and lists it alphabetically by surname. The end product is a garden-variety white pages directory, devoid of even the slightest trace of creativity.

Rural's selection of listings could not be more obvious: It publishes the most basic information—name, town, and telephone number—about each person who applies to it for telephone service. This is "selection" of a sort, but it lacks the modicum of creativity necessary to transform mere selection into copyrightable expression. Rural expended sufficient effort to make the white pages directory useful, but insufficient creativity to make it original.

Nor can Rural claim originality in its coordination and arrangement of facts. The white pages do nothing more than list Rural's subscribers in alphabetical order. This arrangement may, technically speaking, owe its origin to Rural; no one disputes that Rural undertook the task of alphabetizing the names itself. But there is nothing remotely creative about arranging names alphabetically in a white pages directory. It is an age-old practice, firmly rooted in tradition and so commonplace that it has come to be expected as a matter of course. It is not only unoriginal, it is practically inevitable. This time-honored tradition does not possess the minimal creative spark required by the Copyright Act and the Constitution.

We conclude that the names, towns, and telephone numbers copied by Feist were not original to Rural and therefore were not protected by the copyright in Rural's combined white and yellow pages directory. As a constitutional matter, copyright protects only those constituent elements of a work that possess more than a *de minimis* quantum of creativity. Rural's white pages, limited to basic subscriber information and arranged alphabetically, fall short of the mark. As a statutory matter, 17 U.S.C. § 101 does not afford protection from copying to a collection of facts that are selected, coordinated, and arranged in a way that utterly lacks originality. Given that some works must fail, we cannot imagine a more likely candidate. Indeed, were we to hold that Rural's white pages pass muster, it is hard to believe that any collection of facts could fail.

The judgment of the Court of Appeals is *Reversed.*

CCH CANADIAN LTD. v. LAW SOCIETY OF UPPER CANADA

Supreme Court of Canada.
2004 SCC 13 (March 4, 2004).

THE CHIEF JUSTICE [MCLACHLIN]:

I. Introduction—The Issues to Be Determined

The appellant, the Law Society of Upper Canada, is a statutory non-profit corporation that has regulated the legal profession in Ontario since 1822. Since 1845, the Law Society has maintained and operated the Great Library at Osgoode Hall in Toronto, a reference and research library with one of the largest collections of legal materials in Canada. The Great Library provides a request-based photocopy service (the "custom photocopy service") for Law Society members, the judiciary and other authorized researchers. Under the custom photocopy service, legal materials are reproduced by Great Library staff and delivered in person, by mail or by facsimile transmission to requesters. The Law Society also maintains self-service photocopiers in the Great Library for use by its patrons.

The respondents, CCH Canadian Ltd., Thomson Canada Ltd. and Canada Law Book Inc., publish law reports and other legal materials. In 1993, the respondent publishers commenced copyright infringement actions against the Law Society, seeking a declaration of subsistence and ownership of copyright in eleven specific works and a declaration that the Law Society had infringed copyright when the Great Library reproduced a copy of each of the works. The publishers also sought a permanent injunction prohibiting the Law Society from reproducing these eleven works as well as any other works that they published.

The Law Society denied liability and counterclaimed for a declaration that copyright is not infringed when a single copy of a reported decision, case summary, statute, regulation or a limited selection of text from a treatise is made by the Great Library staff or one of its patrons on a self-service photocopier for the purpose of research.

The key question that must be answered in this appeal is whether the Law Society has breached copyright by either (1) providing the custom photocopy service in which single copies of the publishers' works are reproduced and sent to patrons upon their request or by (2) maintaining self-service photocopiers and copies of the publishers' works in the Great Library for use by its patrons. To answer this question, the Court must address the following sub-issues:

(1) Are the publishers' materials "original works" protected by copyright?

(2) Did the Great Library authorize copyright infringement by maintaining self-service photocopiers and copies of the publishers' works for its patrons' use?

I find that the Law Society did not authorize infringement by maintaining self-service photocopiers in the Great Library for use by its patrons. I would therefore allow the appeal.

II. Analysis on Appeal

(1) Are the Publishers' Materials "Original Works" Covered by Copyright?

(a) The Law

Section 5 of the *Copyright Act* states that, in Canada, copyright shall subsist "in every *original* literary, dramatic, musical and artistic work" (emphasis added). Although originality sets the boundaries of copyright law, it is not defined in the *Copyright Act*. Section 2 of the *Copyright Act* defines "every original literary ... work" as including "every original production in the literary ... domain, whatever may be the mode or form of its expression." Since copyright protects only the expression or form of ideas, "the originality requirement must apply to the expressive element of the work and not the idea": S. Handa, *Copyright Law in Canada* (2002), at p. 209.

There are competing views on the meaning of "original" in copyright law. Some courts have found that a work that originates from an author and is more than a mere copy of a work is sufficient to ground copyright. See, for example, *University of London Press v. University Tutorial Press Ltd.*, [1916] 2 Ch. 601 (Eng. Ch. Div.); *U & R Tax Services Ltd. v. H & R Block Canada Inc.* (1995), 62 C.P.R. (3d) 257 (Fed. T.D.). This approach is consistent with the "sweat of the brow" or "industriousness" standard of originality, which is premised on a natural rights or Lockean theory of "just desserts," namely that an author deserves to have his or her efforts in producing a work rewarded. Other courts have required that a work must be creative to be "original" and thus protected by copyright. See, for example, *Feist Publications, Inc. v. Rural Telephone Service Co.* (1991), 499 U.S. 340 (U.S. Kan.); *Tele–Direct (Publications) Inc. v. American Business Information Inc.* (1997), [1988] 2 F.C. 22 (Fed. C.A.). This approach is also consistent with a natural rights theory of property law; however it is less absolute in that only those works that are the product of creativity will be rewarded with copyright protection. It has been suggested that the "creativity" approach to originality helps ensure that copyright protection only extends to the expression of ideas as opposed to the underlying ideas or facts. See *Feist Publications Inc.*, *supra*, at p. 353.

I conclude that the correct position falls between these extremes. For a work to be "original" within the meaning of the *Copyright Act*, it must be more than a mere copy of another work. At the same time, it need not be creative, in the sense of being novel or unique. What is required to attract copyright protection in the expression of an idea is an exercise of skill and judgment. By skill, I mean the use of one's knowledge, developed aptitude or practised ability in producing the work. By judgment, I mean the use of one's capacity for discernment or ability to form an opinion or evaluation by comparing different possible options in producing the work. This exercise of skill and judgment will necessarily involve intellectual effort. The exercise of skill and judgment required to produce the work must not be so trivial that it could be characterized as a purely mechanical exercise. For example, any skill and judgment that might be involved in simply changing the font of a work to produce "another" work would be too trivial to merit copyright protection as an "original" work.

In reaching this conclusion, I have had regard to: (1) the plain meaning of "original"; (2) the history of copyright law; (3) recent jurisprudence; (4) the purpose of the *Copyright Act*; and (5) that this constitutes a workable yet fair standard.

(i) The Plain Meaning of "Original"

The plain meaning of the word "original" suggests at least some intellectual effort, as is necessarily involved in the exercise of skill and judgment. The *Concise Oxford Dictionary* (7th ed. 1982), at p. 720, defines "original" as follows:

> 1. *a*.... existing from the first, primitive, innate, initial, earliest; ... 2. that has served as pattern, of which copy or translation has been made, not derivative or dependant, first-hand, not imitative, novel in character or style, inventive, creative, thinking or acting for oneself.

The plain meaning of "original" implies not just that something is not a copy. It includes, if not creativity *per se*, at least some sort of intellectual effort. As Professor Gervais has noted, "[w]hen used to mean simply that the work must originate from the author, originality is eviscerated of its core meaning. It becomes a synonym of 'originated,' and fails to reflect the ordinary sense of the word": D.J. Gervais, "*Feist* Goes Global: A Comparative Analysis of the Notion of Originality in Copyright Law" (2002), 49 *J. Copyright Soc'y U.S.A.* 949, at p. 961. * * *

(iii) Recent Jurisprudence

The United States Supreme Court explicitly rejected the "sweat of the brow" approach to originality in *Feist Publications Inc., supra*. In so doing, O'Connor J. explained that, in her view, the "sweat of the brow" approach was not consistent with the underlying tenets of copyright law:

> The "sweat of the brow" doctrine had numerous flaws, the most glaring being that it extended copyright protection in a compilation beyond selection and arrangement—the compiler's original contributions—to the facts themselves. Under the doctrine, the only defense to infringement was independent creation. A subsequent compiler was "not entitled to take one word of information previously published," but rather had to "independently wor[k] out the matter for himself, so as to arrive at the same result from the same common sources of information." ... "Sweat of the brow" courts thereby eschewed the most fundamental axiom of copyright law—that no one may copyright facts or ideas.

As this Court recognized in *Compo Co.*, U.S. copyright cases may not be easily transferable to Canada given the key differences in the copyright concepts in Canadian and American copyright legislation. This said, in Canada, as in the United States, copyright protection does not extend to facts or ideas but is limited to the expression of ideas. As such, O'Connor's J. concerns about the "sweat of the brow" doctrine's improper extension of copyright over facts also resonate in Canada. I would not, however, go as far as O'Connor J. in requiring that a work possess a minimal degree of creativity to be considered original.

(iv) Purpose of the Copyright Act

As mentioned, in *Galerie d'art du Petit Champlain inc. c. Théberge, supra*, this Court stated that the purpose of copyright law was to balance the public interest in promoting the encouragement and dissemination of works of the arts and intellect and obtaining a just reward for the creator. When courts adopt a standard of originality requiring only that something be more than a mere copy or that someone simply show industriousness to ground copyright in a work, they tip the scale in favour of the author's or creator's rights, at the loss of society's interest in maintaining a robust public domain that could help foster future creative innovation. By way of contrast, when an author must exercise skill and judgment to ground originality in a work, there is a safeguard against the author being overcompensated for his or her work. This helps ensure that there is room for the public domain to flourish as others are able to produce new works by building on the ideas and information contained in the works of others.

(v) Workable, Yet Fair Standard

Requiring that an original work be the product of an exercise of skill and judgment is a workable yet fair standard. The "sweat of the brow" approach to originality is too low a standard. It shifts the balance of copyright protection too far in favour of the owner's rights, and fails to allow copyright to protect the public's interest in maximizing the production and dissemination of intellectual works. On the other hand, the creativity standard of originality is too high. A creativity standard implies that something must be novel or non-obvious—concepts more properly associated with patent law than copyright law. By way of contrast, a standard requiring the exercise of skill and judgment in the production of a work avoids these difficulties and provides a workable and appropriate standard for copyright protection that is consistent with the policy objectives of the *Copyright Act*.

(vi) Conclusion

For these reasons, I conclude that an "original" work under the *Copyright Act* is one that originates from an author and is not copied from another work. That alone, however, is not sufficient to find that something is original. In addition, an original work must be the product of an author's exercise of skill and judgment. The exercise of skill and judgment required to produce the work must not be so trivial that it could be characterized as a purely mechanical exercise. While creative works will by definition be "original" and covered by copyright, creativity is not required to make a work "original."

(b) Application of the Law to these Facts

At trial, the respondent publishers claimed copyright in eleven works: three reported judicial decisions; the three headnotes preceding these decisions; the Annotated *Martin's Ontario Criminal Practice 1999*; a case summary; a topical index; the textbook *Economic Negligence* (1989); and the monograph "Dental Evidence," being chapter 13 in *Forensic Evidence in Canada* (1991).

On appeal, the Law Society did not challenge the trial judge's findings with respect to the three works in which he found copyright did exist, with the exception of questioning whether the monograph constituted a "work" within the meaning of the *Copyright Act*. The Federal Court of Appeal adopted the "sweat of the brow" approach to originality and found that if a work was more than a mere copy, it would be original. On this basis, Linden J.A., writing for the majority, held that all of the remaining works were original and therefore covered by copyright. The Law Society appeals, contending that the headnotes, case summary, topical index and reported judicial decisions are not "original" within the meaning of the *Copyright Act* and, therefore, are not covered by copyright.

(i) Headnotes

The Federal Court of Appeal held that "headnotes," defined as including the summary of the case, catchlines, statement of the case, case title and case information, are more than mere copies and hence "original" works in which copyright subsists. It found that the headnotes are more than simply an abridged version of the reasons; they consist of independently composed features. As Linden J.A. explained, the authors of the headnotes could have chosen to make the summaries "long or short, technical or simple, dull or dramatic, well written or confusing; the organization and presentation might have varied greatly."

Although headnotes are inspired in large part by the judgment which they summarize and refer to, they are clearly not an identical copy of the reasons. The authors must select specific elements of the decision and can arrange them in numerous different ways. Making these decisions requires the exercise of skill and judgment. The authors must use their knowledge about the law and developed ability to determine legal *ratios* to produce the headnotes. They must also use their capacity for discernment to decide which parts of the judgment warrant inclusion in the headnotes. This process is more than just a mechanical exercise. Thus the headnotes constitute "original" works in which copyright subsists.

(ii) Case Summary

For substantially the same reasons as given for headnotes, the case summary is also covered by copyright. A summary of judicial reasons is not simply a copy of the original reasons. Even if the summary often contains the same language as the judicial reasons, the act of choosing which portions to extract and how to arrange them in the summary requires an exercise of skill and judgment.

(iii) Topical Index

The topical index is part of the book *Canada GST Cases*, (1997). It provides a listing of cases with short headings to indicate the main topics covered by the decision and very brief summaries of the decisions. The Federal Court of Appeal held that the index was original in that it required skill and effort to compile. I agree. The author of the index had to make an initial decision as to which cases were authorities on GST. This alone is a decision that would require the exercise of skill and judgment. The author also had to decide which headings to include and which cases should fall under which headings. He or she had to distill the essence of the decisions down to a succinct one-phrase summary. All of these tasks require skill and judgment that are sufficient to conclude that the topical index is an "original" work in which copyright subsists.

(iv) Reported Judicial Decisions

The reported judicial decisions, when properly understood as a *compilation* of the headnote and the accompanying edited judicial reasons, are "original" works covered by copyright. Copyright protects originality of *form* or expression. A compilation takes existing material and casts it in a different form. The arranger does not have copyright in the individual components. However, the arranger may have copyright in the form represented by the compilation.

The reported judicial decisions here at issue meet the test for originality. The authors have arranged the case summary, catchlines, case title, case information (the headnotes) and the judicial reasons in a specific manner. The arrangement of these different components requires the exercise of skill and judgment. The compilation, viewed globally, attracts copyright protection.

This said, the judicial reasons in and of themselves, without the headnotes, are not original works in which the publishers could claim copyright. The changes made to judicial reasons are relatively trivial; the publishers add only basic factual information about the date of the judgment, the court and the panel hearing the case, counsel for each party, lists of cases, statutes and parallel citations. The publishers also correct minor grammatical errors and spelling mistakes. Any skill and judgment that might be involved in making these minor changes and additions to the judicial reasons are too trivial to warrant copyright protection.

In summary, the headnotes, case summary, topical index and compilation of reported judicial decisions are all works that have originated from their authors and are not mere copies. They are the product of the exercise of skill and judgment that is not trivial. As such, they are all "original" works in which copyright subsists. The appeal of these findings should be dismissed.

NOTES AND QUESTIONS

1. *Originality or Intellectual Creation.* Neither TRIPS nor the Berne Convention speaks in terms of originality. Instead, they both use the term "intellectual creation" as a requirement for a compilation of data (TRIPS art. 10(2)) or collection of works (Berne Conv. art. 2(5)) to receive protection as a literary and artistic work. The concept of "intellectual creation" correlates to what some courts in different countries, such as in *Feist* and *CCH Canadian Ltd.*, call "originality." Given that TRIPS and Berne only use the "intellectual creation" standard for compilations of data and collective works, does this mean other kinds of works that lacked intellectual creation may obtain copyrights consistent with TRIPS? Although the *expressio unius* canon of construction might suggest so, the General Report to the 1928 Berne Convention indicates the contrary. *See* Daniel J. Gervais, Feist *Goes Global: A Comparative Analysis of the Notion of Originality in Copyright Law*, 49 J. COPYRIGHT SOC'Y U.S.A. 949, 971 n.150 (2002)("originality with which every work of the mind must be endowed").

2. Does the Supreme Court of Canada in *CCH Canadian* agree with *Feist*? Was the Canadian Supreme Court's understanding of *Feist* an accurate description of the *Feist* test of originality? Is *Feist* consistent with a "natural rights theory of property" as suggested by the Canadian Supreme Court?

3. *Reliance on foreign law.* The Canadian Supreme Court in *CCH Canadian* relies on foreign cases and sources in its interpretation of Canadian law. Can you identify the different types of foreign materials the Court relied on? Of what relevance are these foreign sources to interpreting an enactment of the Canadian Parliament? For a discussion of this issue, see Edward Lee, *The New Canon: Using or Misusing Foreign Law to Decide Domestic Intellectual Property Claims*, 46 HARV. INT'L L.J. 1, 57–58 (2005).

4. *Other countries.* Commentators have often characterized common law countries, such as the United Kingdom, as having low standards for originality, allowing copyright if there is "skill, labour, and judgment" exercised in the preparation of a work. By contrast, civil law countries, such as France, have often been characterized as having high standards of originality, requiring the work to reflect "the author's personality" through "creative choices" in order to be eligible for author's right. In practice, however, the test of originality in France may not be all that difficult to satisfy. French legal commentators suggest that the test is not onerous and originality is often assumed in cases; courts tend to find originality as long as the author shows the exercise of some creative choice, not slavish copying. PAUL E. GELLER & MELVILLE B. NIMMER, INTERNATIONAL COPYRIGHT LAW AND PRACTICE § 2[1][b][iii] (France) (2004). In most cases do you think there is any difference in result applying the U.S., Canadian, and French standards for originality? How about compared to the sweat of the brow standard?

5. *Judicial decisions and laws.* Article 2(4) of Berne gives member countries the discretion "to determine the protection to be granted to official texts of a legislative, administrative and legal nature, and to official translations of such texts." The U.S. has long recognized that judicial decisions, statutes, and government works cannot be copyrighted under U.S. law. *See Wheaton v. Peters*, 33 U.S. (8 Pet.) 591, 668 (1834); 17 U.S.C. § 105. As one court explained, "public ownership of the law means precisely that 'the law' is in the 'public domain' for whatever use the citizens choose to make of it." *Veeck v. Southern Building Code Congress Int'l, Inc.*, 293 F.3d 791, 799 (5th Cir. 2002) (en banc). By contrast, in the United Kingdom, Crown copyright protects works (including laws or official decisions) made by officers or employees of the Crown in the course of their employment, while Parliamentary copyright protects works created by Parliament. Her Majesty's Stationery Office (H.M.S.O.) administers the government's copyrights, while adopting a policy to encourage wide dissemination of government material. *See* Lionel Bently & William R. Cornish, *United Kingdom*, in PAUL E. GELLER & MELVILLE B. NIMMER, INTERNATIONAL COPYRIGHT LAW AND PRACTICE, § 2[4][e] (2003). Which approach to copyrighting government material is better?

3. SPECIAL DISCUSSION: DATABASE PROTECTION

Article 10 of TRIPS specifically includes compilations of data within the coverage of copyright. The protection accorded to databases under TRIPS, however, is limited by the general principles of copyright law. Article 10 protects only those compilations "which by reason of the selection or arrangement of their contents constitute intellectual creations." Moreover, "[s]uch protection ... shall not extend to the data or material itself" and "shall be without prejudice to any copyright subsisting in the data or material itself." In other words, the protection afforded to databases under TRIPS is consistent with a copyright theory that requires some intellectual creativity and that recognizes the fact/expression dichotomy as set forth in cases such as *Feist, supra*.

A number of European countries, however, decided that databases needed additional protection beyond copyright laws. In 1996, the European Union issued a Directive on the Legal Protection of Databases, Directive 96/9/EC of the European Parliament and of the Council of 11 March 1996 on the Legal Protection of Databases. The Database Directive is one of the most significant developments for the protection of databases in Europe. It was adopted based on the view that copyright protection for databases had varied in member states, and "such unharmonized intellectual property rights can have the effect of preventing the free movement of goods or services within the Community." Although the EU Directive provides for copyright protection in databases, perhaps the most significant aspect of the EU Directive is the recognition in Article 7 of a *sui generis* right in databases independent of any copyright protection. In the discussion below, we first review the copyright provisions of the EU Directive, followed by the more controversial *sui generis* right contained in Article 7.

Copyright. Article 3 of the Database Directive follows the standard, based in copyright law, for protecting compilations of data under Article 10 of TRIPS. Under Article 3 of the EU Directive, "databases which, by reason of the selection or arrangement of their contents, constitute the author's own intellectual creation shall be protected as such by copyright." The protection for the database does not extend to the underlying content or prejudice "any rights subsisting in those contents."

The rights protected under the copyright section of the Database Directive are set forth in Article 5. The author of a database that is protectable by copyright has the exclusive right to carry out or to authorize: "(a) temporary or permanent reproduction by any means and in any form, in whole or in part; (b) translation, adaptation, arrangement and any other alteration; (c) any form of distribution to the public of the database or of copies thereof. The first sale in the Community of a copy of the database by the rightholder or with his consent shall exhaust the right to control resale of that copy within the Community; (d) any communication, display or performance to the public; (e) any reproduction, distribution, communication, display or performance to the public of the results of the acts referred to in (b)."

Article 6 sets forth exceptions to these rights. A lawful user of a database is allowed to perform any of the acts in Article 5 "for the purposes of access to the contents of the databases and normal use of the contents by the lawful user." Countries are given the option of also exempting four other uses: (i) reproduction for private purposes of a non-electronic database; (ii) use for the sole purpose of illustration for teaching or scientific research, as long as the source is indicated and to the extent justified by the non-commercial purpose; (iii) use for the purpose of public security or for the purposes of an administrative or judicial procedure; and (iv) uses based on other exceptions to copyright traditionally authorized under national law.

Sui generis database right. The EU Database Directive goes beyond TRIPS by providing a *sui generis* right for database makers, which lasts for a more limited term of 15 years (although it can, under some circumstances, be renewed indefinitely). Under Article 7, the *sui generis* right is described as "a right for the maker of a database which shows that there has been qualitatively and/or quantitatively a substantial investment in either the obtaining, verification or presentation of the contents to prevent extraction and/or re-utilization of the whole or of a substantial part, evaluated qualitatively and/or quantitatively, of the contents of that database." Extraction means "the permanent or temporary transfer of all or a substantial part of the contents of a database to another medium by any means or in any form." Re-utilization means "any form of making available to the public all or a substantial part of the contents of a database by the distribution of copies, by renting, by on-line or other forms of transmission." Note that these rights are discrete from and independent of any copyright law requirements.

Under Article 8, a lawful user of a database that is made public is allowed, however, to use "insubstantial parts of its contents, evaluated qualitatively and/or quantitatively, for any purposes whatsoever." Article 9 allows EU countries to have exceptions to the *sui generis* right comparable to the first three kinds of exceptions permitted for copyright under Article 6. Under Article 11, the EU database right applies only to nationals or habitual residents of EU countries. Businesses can fall within such protection if its "registered office, central administration or principal place of business [is] within the Community; however, where such a company or firm has only its registered office in the territory of the Community, its operations must be genuinely linked on an ongoing basis with the economy of a Member State." The *sui generis* database right can be extended to a foreign national or business only if (i) the EU Council approves it acting upon a proposal from the EU Commission; and (ii) the foreign national's country has a reciprocal database right for EU nationals who habitually reside in that country. This is an example of material reciprocity, hearkening back to the days of the first bilateral agreements before the Berne Convention.

PROBLEM 2–12

Genitech is a Belgian pharmaceutical company that has recently invested $200 million in generating a scientific database containing new data and information gathered through experiments conducted by Genitech scientists.

The information contained in the database has a number of applications that can be used in creating a whole new generation of drugs that could potentially net Genitech billions of dollars in revenues. The information is contained in a carefully designed and user-friendly format in an electronic database that Genitech will allow subscribers to consult for a hefty fee. Genitech paid a graduate student in computer science $2,500 to set up the electronic database and to enter the data generated by the scientific experiments. The graduate student, a diligent worker, finished the entire project in six days using methods taught in most basic level computer science courses. Two of Genitech's salaried secretaries assisted in the uploading of files onto the database. They also spent approximately six days on the project. They received no extra compensation for this project.

Fizer is a U.S. multi-national pharmaceutical company that is a subscriber to the Genitech database. Fizer extracted some of the data from the Genitech database and has combined the data with Fizer's own data in a database of its own, which Fizer plans on making public in a completely different selection and arrangement. Genitech now threatens to sue Fizer for unauthorized extraction and/or re-utilization of Genitech's database. Genitech's license with Fizer as its subscriber did not authorize Fizer to incorporate Genitech's data into a new database. Genitech has hired a Belgian law firm to evaluate the potential contract claim, but Genitech wants you to evaluate its potential EU database right claims.

(1) Is Genitech's database protected by the EU Database Directive under the copyright or sui generis provisions? Suppose Genitech had copyright protection only for the database. Would Fizer be liable?

(2) Assume that under Belgian applicable law, copyright protection would last for a flat 70 year period. Why would Genitech seek sui generis protection, which provides a 15 year term, when copyright provides for a much longer term?

To answer this problem, consult the EU Database Directive and the *British Horseracing Board* case below.

EU Database Directive 96/9/EC (excerpt)
CHAPTER I: SCOPE
Article 1
Scope

1. This Directive concerns the legal protection of databases in any form.

2. For the purposes of this Directive, "database" shall mean a collection of independent works, data or other materials arranged in a systematic or methodical way and individually accessible by electronic or other means.

3. Protection under this Directive shall not apply to computer programs used in the making or operation of databases accessible by electronic means.

CHAPTER II: COPYRIGHT
Article 3
Object of protection

1. In accordance with this Directive, databases which, by reason of the selection or arrangement of their contents, constitute the author's own

intellectual creation shall be protected as such by copyright. No other criteria shall be applied to determine their eligibility for that protection.

2. The copyright protection of databases provided for by this Directive shall not extend to their contents and shall be without prejudice to any rights subsisting in those contents themselves. * * *

CHAPTER III : SUI GENERIS RIGHT

Article 7

Object of protection

1. Member States shall provide for a right for the maker of a database which shows that there has been qualitatively and/or quantitatively a substantial investment in either the obtaining, verification or presentation of the contents to prevent extraction and/or re-utilisation of the whole or of a substantial part, evaluated qualitatively and/or quantitatively, of the contents of that database.

2. For the purposes of this Chapter:

> (a) ''extraction'' shall mean the permanent or temporary transfer of all or a substantial part of the contents of a database to another medium by any means or in any form;

> (b) ''re-utilisation'' shall mean any form of making available to the public all or a substantial part of the contents of a database by the distribution of copies, by renting, by on-line or other forms of transmission. The first sale of a copy of a database within the Community by the rightholder or with his consent shall exhaust the right to control resale of that copy within the Community; public lending is not an act of extraction or re-utilisation.

3. The right referred to in paragraph 1 may be transferred, assigned or granted under contractual licence.

4. The right provided for in paragraph 1 shall apply irrespective of the eligibility of that database for protection by copyright or by other rights. Moreover, it shall apply irrespective of eligibility of the contents of that database for protection by copyright or by other rights. Protection of databases under the right provided for in paragraph 1 shall be without prejudice to rights existing in respect of their content.

5. The repeated and systematic extraction and/or re-utilisation of insubstantial parts of the contents of the database implying acts which conflict with a normal exploitation of that database or which unreasonably prejudice the legitimate interests of the maker of the database shall not be permitted.

Article 10

Term of protection

1. The right provided for in Article 7 shall run from the date of completion of the making of the database. It shall expire fifteen years from the first of January of the year following the date of completion.

2. In the case of a database which is made available to the public in whatever manner before expiry of the period provided for in paragraph 1,

the term of protection by that right shall expire fifteen years from the first of January of the year following the date when the database was first made available to the public.

3. Any substantial change, evaluated qualitatively or quantitatively, to the contents of a database, including any substantial change resulting from the accumulation of successive additions, deletions or alterations, which would result in the database being considered to be a substantial new investment, evaluated qualitatively or quantitatively, shall qualify the database resulting from that investment for its own term of protection.

* * *

The *sui generis* rights created by the EU Database Directive and the database industry's efforts to create similar rights in the U.S. generated a great deal of controversy. Some legal commentators have sharply criticized the *sui generis* right:

> The Final E.C. Directive does not condition *sui generis* protection on any showing of a creative achievement or of a novel contribution to the prior art, the classical bases for justifying legal derogation from free competition. Rather, it merely requires the database maker to prove that "there has been qualitatively and/or quantitatively a substantial investment in either the obtaining, verification or presentation of the contents" or in "any substantial change resulting from the accumulation of successive additions, deletions or alterations." Because the E.C. Directive itself provides no further guidelines for evaluating the requisite level of investment in either case, this threshold will remain uncertain, pending decisions by European courts applying the still to be drafted domestic database laws. Nevertheless, there are no limits to the number of quantitative or qualitative changes that will qualify for such extensions, and any publisher who continues to make a substantial investment in updating, improving, or expanding an existing database can look forward to perpetual protection.

> On closer inspection, indeed, the investor's scope of protection under the hybrid extraction right appears paradoxically to exceed even that afforded authors of traditional literary and artistic works under the classical copyright paradigm of the Berne Convention. [I]t ignores the important distinction that copyright law makes between "ideas" (a legal metaphor for the noncopyrightable components of protected works, including among other things, the facts or data they contain) and the author's "expression" (a legal metaphor for the protectable elements of style in an otherwise eligible work). The TRIPS Agreement makes this distinction universally applicable to all copyrightable works, including such borderline works as computer programs and factual compilations. Yet, the database law contains no such distinction. This means that, in the universe of data generators, there is no evolving public domain substratum from which either research workers or second comers are progressively entitled to withdraw previously generated data without seeking licenses that may or may not be granted.

A deeper point is that, regardless of whether it is theoretically possible to regenerate the data from publicly available sources, investors in database production can always deny third parties the right to use pre-existing data in value-adding applications, even when the latter are willing to pay royalty-bearing licenses; and there is no escaping such licenses unless the database publisher either declines to exercise his or her rights or engages in an abusive exercise of market power. In other words, except when the new proprietary rights are abandoned or misused, the concept of incremental or "cumulative and sequential innovation," which is central to the development of modern technological paradigms, has been banished from the universe of database production, despite the economic waste and inefficiency inherent in such policies.

J.H. Reichman & Pamela Samuelson, *Intellectual Property Rights in Data?*, 50 VAND. L. REV. 51, 85–90 (1997). In *British Horseracing Board,* set forth below, the European Court of Justice clarified various aspects of the EU Database Directive. As you read these materials, consider whether some of the concerns expressed in the excerpt of Professors Reichman and Samuelson's article have been mollified after *British Horseracing Board.*

THE BRITISH HORSERACING BOARD LTD. v. WILLIAM HILL ORGANIZATION LTD.

European Court of Justice (Grand Chamber).
[2004] ECR I–10415, Case C–203/02 (Nov. 9, 2004).

Grounds

This reference for a preliminary ruling concerns the interpretation of Article 7 and Article 10(3) of Directive 96/9EC of the European Parliament and of the Council of 11 March 1996 on the legal protection of databases.

The reference was made in the course of proceedings brought by The British Horseracing Board Ltd, the Jockey Club and Weatherbys Group Ltd (the BHB and Others) against William Hill Organization Ltd (William Hill). The litigation arose over the use by William Hill, for the purpose of organising betting on horse racing, of information taken from the BHB database.

The main proceedings and the questions referred for a preliminary ruling

The BHB and Others manage the horse racing industry in the United Kingdom and in various capacities compile and maintain the BHB database which contains a large amount of information supplied by horse owners, trainers, horse race organisers and others involved in the racing industry. The database contains information on inter alia the pedigrees of some one million horses, and prerace information on races to be held in the United Kingdom. That information includes the name, place and date of the race concerned, the distance over which the race is to be run, the criteria for eligibility to enter the race, the date by which entries must be received, the entry fee payable and the amount of money the racecourse is to contribute to the prize money for the race.

Weatherbys Group Ltd, the company which compiles and maintains the BHB database, performs three principal functions, which lead up to the issue of pre-race information.

First, it registers information concerning owners, trainers, jockeys and horses and records the performances of those horses in each race.

Second, it decides on weight adding and handicapping for the horses entered for the various races.

Third, it compiles the lists of horses running in the races. This activity is carried out by its own call centre, manned by about 30 operators. They record telephone calls entering horses in each race organised. The identity and status of the person entering the horse and whether the characteristics of the horse meet the criteria for entry to the race are then checked. Following those checks the entries are published provisionally. To take part in the race, the trainer must confirm the horse's participation by telephone by declaring it the day before the race at the latest. The operators must then ascertain whether the horse can be authorised to run the race in the light of the number of declarations already recorded. A central computer then allocates a saddle cloth number to each horse and determines the stall from which it will start. The final list of runners is published the day before the race.

The BHB database contains essential information not only for those directly involved in horse racing but also for radio and television broadcasters and for bookmakers and their clients. The cost of running the BHB database is approximately £4 million per annum. The fees charged to third parties for the use of the information in the database cover about a quarter of that amount.

The database is accessible on the internet site operated jointly by BHB and Weatherbys Group Ltd. Some of its contents are also published each week in the BHB's official journal. The contents of the database, or of certain parts of it, are also made available to Racing Pages Ltd, a company jointly controlled by Weatherbys Group Ltd and the Press Association, which then forwards data to its various subscribers, including some bookmakers, in the form of a "Declarations Feed," the day before a race. Satellite Information Services Limited ("SIS") is authorised by Racing Pages to transmit data to its own subscribers in the form of a "raw data feed" ("RDF"). The RDF includes a large amount of information, in particular, the names of the horses running in the races, the names of the jockeys, the saddle cloth numbers and the weight for each horse. Through the newspapers and the Ceefax and Teletext services, the names of the runners in a particular race are made available to the public during the course of the afternoon before the race.

William Hill, which is a subscriber to both the Declarations Feed and the RDF, is one of the leading providers of offcourse bookmaking services in the United Kingdom, to both UK and international customers. It launched an on-line betting service on two internet sites. Those interested can use these sites to find out what horses are running in which races at which racecourses and what odds are offered by William Hill.

The information displayed on William Hill's internet sites is obtained, first, from newspapers published the day before the race and, second, from the RDF supplied by SIS on the morning of the race.

According to the order for reference, the information displayed on William Hill's internet sites represents a very small proportion of the total amount of data on the BHB database, given that it concerns only the following matters: the names of all the horses in the race, the date, time and/or name of the race and the name of the racecourse where the race will be held. Also according to the order for reference, the horse races and the lists of runners are not arranged on William Hill's internet sites in the same way as in the BHB database.

In March 2000 the BHB and Others brought proceedings against William Hill in the High Court of Justice of England and Wales, Chancery Division, alleging infringement of their *sui generis* right. They contend, first, that each day's use by William Hill of racing data taken from the newspapers or the RDF is an extraction or re-utilisation of a substantial part of the contents of the BHB database, contrary to Article 7(1) of the Directive. Secondly, they say that even if the individual extracts made by William Hill are not substantial they should be prohibited under Article 7(5) of the Directive.

The High Court of Justice ruled in a judgment of 9 February 2001 that the action of BHB and Others was well founded. William Hill appealed to the referring court.

In the light of the problems of interpretation of the Directive, the Court of Appeal decided to stay proceedings and refer the following questions to the Court of Justice for a preliminary ruling:

The questions referred

By its second and third questions the referring court seeks clarification of the concept of investment in the obtaining and verification of the contents of a database within the meaning of Article 7(1) of the Directive.

Article 7(1) of the Directive reserves the protection of the *sui generis* right to databases which meet a specific criterion, namely to those which show that there has been qualitatively and/or quantitatively a substantial investment in the obtaining, verification or presentation of their contents.

Under the 9th, 10th and 12th recitals of the preamble to the Directive, its purpose, as William Hill points out, is to promote and protect investment in data storage and "processing" systems which contribute to the development of an information market against a background of exponential growth in the amount of information generated and processed annually in all sectors of activity. It follows that the expression "investment in ... the obtaining, verification or presentation of the contents" of a database must be understood, generally, to refer to investment in the creation of that database as such.

Against that background, the expression "investment in ... the obtaining ... of the contents" of a database must, as William Hill and the Belgian, German and Portuguese Governments point out, be understood to refer to the resources used to seek out existing independent materials and collect them in the database, and not to the resources used for the creation as such of independent materials. The purpose of the protection by the *sui generis* right provided for by the directive is to promote the establishment of storage and processing systems for existing information and not the creation of materials capable of being collected subsequently in a database.

That interpretation is backed up by the 39th recital of the preamble to the Directive, according to which the aim of the *sui generis* right is to safeguard the results of the financial and professional investment made in obtaining and collection of "the contents" of a database. As the Advocate General notes in points 41 to 46 of her Opinion, despite slight variations in wording, all the language versions of the 39th recital support an interpretation which excludes the creation of the materials contained in a database from the definition of obtaining.

The 19th recital of the preamble to the directive, according to which the compilation of several recordings of musical performances on a CD does not represent a substantial enough investment to be eligible under the *sui generis* right, provides an additional argument in support of that interpretation. Indeed, it appears from that recital that the resources used for the creation as such of works or materials included in the database, in this case on a CD, cannot be deemed equivalent to investment in the obtaining of the contents of that database and cannot, therefore, be taken into account in assessing whether the investment in the creation of the database was substantial.

The expression "investment in ... the ... verification ... of the contents" of a database must be understood to refer to the resources used, with a view to ensuring the reliability of the information contained in that database, to monitor the accuracy of the materials collected when the database was created and during its operation. The resources used for verification during the stage of creation of data or other materials which are subsequently collected in a database, on the other hand, are resources used in creating a database and cannot therefore be taken into account in order to assess whether there was substantial investment in the terms of Article 7(1) of the Directive.

In that light, the fact that the creation of a database is linked to the exercise of a principal activity in which the person creating the database is also the creator of the materials contained in the database does not, as such, preclude that person from claiming the protection of the *sui generis* right, provided that he establishes that the obtaining of those materials, their verification or their presentation, in the sense described [above], required substantial investment in quantitative or qualitative terms, which was independent of the resources used to create those materials.

Thus, although the search for data and the verification of their accuracy at the time a database is created do not require the maker of that database to use particular resources because the data are those he created and are available to him, the fact remains that the collection of those data, their systematic or methodical arrangement in the database, the organisation of their individual accessibility and the verification of their accuracy throughout the operation of the database may require substantial investment in quantitative and/or qualitative terms within the meaning of Article 7(1) of the Directive.

In the case in the main proceedings, the referring court seeks to know whether the investments described in paragraph 14 of this judgment can be considered to amount to investment in obtaining the contents of the BHB database. The plaintiffs in the main proceedings stress, in that connection, the substantial nature of the above investment.

However, investment in the selection, for the purpose of organising horse racing, of the horses admitted to run in the race concerned relates to the creation of the data which make up the lists for those races which appear in the BHB database. It does not constitute investment in obtaining the contents of the database. It cannot, therefore, be taken into account in assessing whether the investment in the creation of the database was substantial.

Admittedly, the process of entering a horse on a list for a race requires a number of prior checks as to the identity of the person making the entry, the characteristics of the horse and the classification of the horse, its owner and the jockey.

However, such prior checks are made at the stage of creating the list for the race in question. They thus constitute investment in the creation of data and not in the verification of the contents of the database.

It follows that the resources used to draw up a list of horses in a race and to carry out checks in that connection do not represent investment in the obtaining and verification of the contents of the database in which that list appears.

In the light of the foregoing, the second and third questions referred should be answered as follows:

—The expression "investment in ... the obtaining ... of the contents" of a database in Article 7(1) of the Directive must be understood to refer to the resources used to seek out existing independent materials and collect them in the database. It does not cover the resources used for the creation of materials which make up the contents of a database.

—The expression "investment in ... the ... verification ... of the contents" of a database in Article 7(1) of the Directive must be understood to refer to the resources used, with a view to ensuring the reliability of the information contained in that database, to monitor the accuracy of the materials collected when the database was created and during its operation. The resources used for verification during the stage of creation of materials which are subsequently collected in a database do not fall within that definition.

—The resources used to draw up a list of horses in a race and to carry out checks in that connection do not constitute investment in the obtaining and verification of the contents of the database in which that list appears.

[The ECJ's analysis of questions related to the alleged infringement of the *sui generis* database right is omitted. *Ed.*]

NOTES AND QUESTIONS

1. Did the ECJ adopt a broad or narrow view of the *sui generis* database right in the *British Horseracing Board*? How does one qualify for the *sui generis* database right? Does the test drawn by the ECJ seem to you to be a sensible approach? What class of databases might have difficulty qualifying for protection under the ECJ's ruling?

2. *Foreign (non-EU) databases.* The EU Database Directive does not provide the *sui generis* right in databases to foreign database makers located outside the EU. Under Article 11(2), such businesses can obtain EU protection only if its "registered office, central administration or principal place of business [is] within the Community; however, where such a company or firm has only its registered office in the territory of the Community, its operations must be genuinely linked on an ongoing basis with the economy of a Member State." Absent such a physical presence in an EU country, a foreign business's only hope of obtaining a *sui generis* database right in the EU is by official action by the EU Council, but the EU Council will grant *sui generis* protection only if the country of the foreign national provides reciprocal protection to nationals of the EU. Is this aspect of the EU Directive consistent with TRIPS Article 3's principle of national treatment or most favored nation treatment concerning intellectual property? Hint: the answer depends on how TRIPS defines "intellectual property"? *See* TRIPS Article 1(2).

3. In the *British Horseracing* case, what kind of database did the British Horseracing Board claim protection for? What kind of information did it contain? Were these facts or something more? Did William Hill Organization have permission to use the database? In what way did William Hill use the database?

4. Under the ruling of the European Court of Justice, what kind of investment in the database must a database owner be able to show in order to invoke the protections of the EU Database Directive? How much money did the British Horseracing Board spend to run its database? Was this sufficient to invoke the *sui generis* right under the EU Database Directive?

5. Do you agree with Professors Reichman and Samuelson's early critique of the EU Database Directive in 1997? Does the European Court of

Justice's subsequent interpretation of the EU Database Directive in the *British Horseracing* case in 2004 ameliorate any of Professors Reichman and Samuelson's concerns?

6. *Other Database Protection Initiatives.* Database makers in the U.S. have lobbied heavily for the recognition of *sui generis* database protection comparable to the EU. Several bills have been considered in Congress, but, as of 2011, none has been enacted. A number of legal scholars and public interest groups have argued that such protection would restrict the public's access to information, create monopolies over facts and data, and impede scientific research. Some U.S. legal scholars also contend that such protection in the U.S. would violate the Copyright Clause's requirement of originality as elaborated in *Feist.* Putting aside these constitutional concerns, do you think it is a good or bad idea for intellectual property rights to be accorded to databases based on the "sweat of the brow," through the investment of resources and labor in compiling a database?

4. SPECIAL DISCUSSION: FOLKLORE AND TRADITIONAL CULTURAL EXPRESSION

As noted earlier, copyright is essentially a western concept that developed with a model of authors of books. This approach has ignored non-western traditions, including folklore or traditional cultural expression (TCE), which involves art forms such as poetry, songs, drawings, paintings, oral stories, and dance that are associated with indigenous peoples and cultures and that are often passed down from generation to generation. WIPO's Intergovernmental Committee's draft articles (WIPO/GRTKF/IC/19/4) define folklore or TCE as follows:*

1. "Traditional cultural expressions"[1] are any form, tangible or intangible, or a combination thereof, in which traditional culture and knowledge are embodied and have been passed on [from generation to generation], / tangible or intangible forms of creativity of the beneficiaries, as defined in Article 2 including, but not limited to:

(a) phonetic or verbal expressions, such as stories, epics, legends, poetry, riddles and other narratives; words, [signs,] names, [and symbols];

(b) musical or sound expressions, such as songs, [rhythms,] and instrumental music, the sounds which are the expression of rituals;

(c) expressions by action, such as dances, plays, ceremonies, rituals, rituals in sacred places and peregrinations, [sports and

---

* Material originally provided by the World Intellectual Property Organization (WIPO). The Secretariat of WIPO assumes no liability or responsibility with regard to the transformation of this data.

1. "Traditional cultural expressions" and "expressions of folklore" are synonymous for the purposes of this text.

[traditional]] games, puppet performances, and other performances, whether fixed or unfixed;

(d) tangible expressions, such as material expressions of art, [handicrafts,] [works of mas,] [architecture,] and tangible [spiritual forms], and sacred places.]**

Countries have debated whether to protect folklore from commercialization or "piracy" by third parties who do not offer compensation or credit to the indigenous groups from which the folklore is taken. The issue often involves the North taking from the South, although China's emergence as a source of appropriated folklore defies the North–South categorization. Countries and commentators have debated whether copyright law can provide an adequate protection. Some question the appropriateness of using intellectual property at all for folklore, which, in some communities, is considered sacred or religious. Protecting folklore under copyright faces at least three separate issues:

- copyright requires identifying the "authors" of the work; in many cases, folklore belongs to a group or are communally owned by an entire population;

- copyright requires that the work be original, i.e., the result of the independent efforts of the author; originality can be difficult to establish because the folklore may have passed through many generations without any records so it becomes difficult to prove originality by an author;

- copyright laws usually require fixation in a tangible medium; some folklore is oral or intangible (such as songs, dance, and other rituals).

For these reasons, folklore may be difficult to protect under western concepts of copyright law, which thereby may result in their exploitation by third parties for commercial gain. Some commentators favor a *sui generis* right to protect folklore. *See* Paul Kuruk, *Protecting Folklore Under Modern Intellectual Property Regimes: A Reappraisal of the Tensions Between Individual and Communal Rights in Africa and the United States*, 48 AM. U. L. REV. 769, 837–48 (1999). The IC of WIPO has proposed draft articles with different alternatives to provide greater international protection for folklore. *See* The Protection of Traditional Cultural Expressions: Draft Articles (July 18–22, 2011), at http://www.wipo.int/tk/en/igc/.

Is there a basic tension between folklore and western concepts of copyright law such that is impossible or impracticable to use copyright to protect folklore? Consider the following problem and case.

PROBLEM 2–13

A group of African countries have agreed to the African Folklore Protection Directive. Under the Directive, two different types of protection are

---

** N.B. Proposed insertions are underlined, while words or phrases that a Member State has proposed be deleted or has questioned are put between square brackets. Drafting proposals from observers which received Member State support are included.

offered for folklore and traditional knowledge: (i) copyright protection is extended to all works containing folklore and traditional knowledge, if created within the past 100 years or in the future, that can satisfy originality; and (ii) *sui generis* protection with a term of 15 years is offered to nationals and habitual residents of the African countries for all folklore and works containing traditional knowledge, no matter when created and regardless of whether originality is satisfied. The *sui generis* right gives the rights holder—to be determined by the law of the country of origin—the right to prevent re-utilization of the folklore without authorization. The *sui generis* right is renewable every fifteen years upon the payment of a small registration fee. A fixation is not a requirement for either copyright or the *sui generis* right. Foreign authors are eligible for copyright protection, but not the *sui generis* protection, unless they are habitual residents of the African nations. Does the Directive provide a good solution to the problem of protecting folklore? Is the Directive consistent with TRIPS and Berne?

MILPURRURRU AND OTHERS v. INDOFURN PTY LTD AND OTHERS

General Division: Northern Territory District Registry, Australia.
[1994] 54 FCR 240.

[The respondents, Mr. and Mrs. Bethune owned Beechow Pty Ltd. [Beechow], an Australian import trading company. Beechow imported carpets from Vietnam made in factories under agreement with Beechow. The carpets were copies of aboriginal artworks protected under copyright law in Australia. Mr. and Mrs. Bethune believed that the artworks were not subject to copyright protection or that permission to make copies could be obtained after the carpets were imported. After the carpets were imported, Beechow held a public exhibition of the carpets to generate commercial interest. Aboriginal Arts Management Association is a statutory body and a public trustee established under Australian law to represent the interests of the aboriginal artists. Under Australian copyright law, the copyright owner has the right to prohibit importation of unauthorized copies of the copyrighted work. AAMA sued on behalf of the artists for copyright violation and to block further importation of the carpets.]

VON DOUSSA J.

This is a claim for remedies under the Copyright Act 1968 (Cth) for copyright infringement and under the Trade Practices Act 1974 (Cth) for alleged contraventions of §§ 52, 53I and (d) and 55.

The first three applicants are Aboriginal artists. The fourth applicant, the Public Trustee, represents the estates of five deceased Aboriginal artists. The skill of each of the artists is recognised nationally and internationally as exceptional; their works are represented in national, State and other major collections of Australian artworks. The pleadings allege that since about October 1992 the respondents have manufactured, imported into Australia, offered for sale and sold woolen carpets which reproduce artwork, or substantial parts thereof, of each of the artists without the licence of the owners of the copyright.

In accordance with Aboriginal custom, and out of respect for the deceased artists, their names have not been spoken in the course of the trial. They have been referred to throughout by their appropriate skin names. It is however necessary to adequately identify the artworks in question to refer once in the judgment to these artists by name, but having done so the skin names will be used thereafter. Particulars of the artworks and the artists are as follows:

	Artist	Skin Name	Artwork
1.	George Milpurrurru		Goose Egg Hunt
2.	George Garrawun (died August 1993)	Ngaritj	Freshwater Fish
3.	Paddy Dhatanga (died 23 March 1993)	Gamarang	Wititj (olive python)
4.	Fred Nanganaralil (died 28 August 1993)	Wamut	Crow and Praying-mantis
5.	Banduk Marika		Djanda and the Sacred Water hole
6.	Tim Leura Tjapaltjarri (died 18 June 1984)	Tjapaltjarri	The Seven Sisters

The first four artists are from Central Arnhem Land. The artworks in question are bark paintings. The first three paintings are presently owned by the Australian National Gallery (the ANG). In 1993 in recognition of the International Year for the World's Indigenous People the ANG held the first solo exhibition of the works of an Aboriginal artist. The exhibition was a retrospective look at the works of Mr. Milpurrurru, and included the Goose Egg Hunt which is also featured in the publication "The Art of George Milpurrurru" which was published by the ANG at the same time. As part of the program for the 1993 International Year for the World's Indigenous People, Goose Egg Hunt was adopted as the design for the 85 cent Australian stamp issued on 4 February 1993. A large number of these stamps were put into circulation, perhaps as many as two to three million. Freshwater Fish is recognised as one of the major works of Ngaritj, and was one of two paintings hung in the foyer of the ANG when it was opened by Her Majesty the Queen.

The first three paintings, together with the work of Ms. Marika were included in a portfolio of 12 Aboriginal artworks which was published by the ANG in 1988 under the auspices of the ANG's Education staff. One of the purposes of the portfolio was to provide a resource item for teachers and students. The portfolio was intended to be representative of the best Aboriginal artworks in the ANG collection. The artwork of Wamut is in the National Museum of Australia collection, and was reproduced in a portfolio of Aboriginal art published for the Australian Information Service (AIS) by the Australian Government Printer. It was also reproduced in a calendar for the month of June 1982 similarly published for the AIS.

In both the ANG portfolio, and the AIS publications the reproduction of the artworks were published over the name of the artist. Amongst the carpets the subject of this action seven of the eight artworks were reproduced in virtually identical form and colour. It is common ground that the source of the artwork reproduced was these publications.

The reproduction of the artworks in the ANG and AIS portfolios, and on the postage stamp followed formal approval and royalty agreements with the artists or their representatives. The evidence is to the effect that reproductions of this kind are permitted by Aboriginal artists, including those involved in this case, and by traditional owners, where the reproduction is in a prestigious publication for the purposes of educating members of the white community about Aboriginal culture. In each of the ANG and AIS publications the artworks were accompanied by brief descriptions of the subject matter of the artist's work. However the introduction page to the 1986 calendar makes the following clear statement about the significance of the works in that publication:

> "The paintings have been acclaimed as 'statements of great value to the people who made them'. They express concepts that are intensely personal. These are very often private expressions concerned with ownership, ownership of land, ownership of stories, stories of the Dreamtime, that indefinable period of past time which to the Aboriginals is the source of all knowledge and of all living things.
>
> Sacred ceremonies, generally restricted to the initiated members of the tribe or those undergoing initiation, and their related celebrations in dance, song and design, form the basis of what may seem nothing more than complex abstract patterns in the paintings. The patterns in fact represent explicit visual descriptions, stylised maps of identifiable locations and myths, though the full meaning of each painting may not be clear to non-Aboriginal viewers. Nevertheless, the paintings are eloquent witnesses to the rich and enduring nature of Aboriginal culture."

The right to create paintings and other artworks depicting creation and dreaming stories, and to use pre-existing designs and well recognized totems of the clan, resides in the traditional owners (or custodians) of the stories or images. Usually that right will not be with only one person, but with a group of people who together have the authority to determine whether the story and images may be used in an artwork, by whom the artwork may be created, to whom it may be published, and the terms, if any, on which the artwork may be reproduced.

If reproduction of a story or imagery occurs, under Aboriginal law it is the responsibility of the traditional owners to take action to preserve the dreaming, and to punish those considered responsible for the breach. Notions of responsibility under Aboriginal law differ from those of the

English common law. If permission has been given by the traditional owners to a particular artist to create a picture of the dreaming, and that artwork is later inappropriately used or reproduced by a third party the artist is held responsible for the breach which has occurred, even if the artist had no control over or knowledge of what occurred. The evidence of Ms. Marika, which I accept without hesitation, illustrates the severe consequences which may occur even in a case where plainly the misuse of the artwork was without permission, and contrary to Australian statute law. In times past the "offender" could be put to death. Now other forms of punishment are more likely such as preclusion from the right to participate in ceremonies, removal of the right to reproduce paintings of that or any other story of the clan, being outcast from the community, or being required to make a payment of money; but the possibility of spearing was mentioned by Mr. Wangurra as a continuing sanction in serious cases.

Ms. Marika has endeavoured to conceal the unauthorised reproduction on carpets of Djanda and the Sacred Waterhole from her community as she will be held responsible. Her artwork expresses pictorially the creation when her ancestral creator Djang'Kawu and his two sisters, the Wagilag sisters, at the end of their journey from Burralku, landed at Yelangbara, south of Port Bradshaw, the site of their first journey. The image which she utilised in the artwork is associated with this place. Her rights to use the image arise by virtue of her membership of the land owner group in that area, and is an incident arising out of land ownership. She explained in an affidavit:

"As an artist whilst I may own the copyright in a particular artwork under western law, under Aboriginal law I must not use an image or story in such a way as to undermine the rights of all the other Yolngu (her clan) who have an interest whether direct or indirect in it. In this way I hold the image on trust for all the other Yolngu with an interest in the story."

Her creation of the artwork contemplated that it would be displayed with appropriate sensitivity in art galleries and for education purposes to help bring about a greater awareness of Aboriginal culture. The reproduction of the artwork in circumstances where the dreaming would be walked on, is totally opposed to the cultural use of the imagery employed in her artwork.

This misuse of her artwork has caused her great upset. If it had become widely known in her community at the time she believes that her family could have ordered her to stop producing any works of art; they might have stopped her participating in ceremonies; they might have outcast her, and they may have sought recompense from her—nowadays in money terms.

The reproduction of paintings which depict dreaming stories and designs of cultural significance has been a matter of great concern to the Aboriginal community. Pirating of Aboriginal designs and paintings for commercial use without the consent of the artist or the traditional owners was common for a long time. The recognition of the sacred and religious significance of these paintings, and the restrictions which Aboriginal law and culture imposes on their reproduction is only now being understood by the white community.

[A] problem [was] perceived to exist at one time in relation to the application of the Copyright Act to Aboriginal artworks based on pre-existing tradition and images. That problem was whether works incorporating them satisfied the requirement of originality so to attract copyright protection. In the present case that issue has not arisen, and by the end of the trial the copyright ownership of the artists in each of the eight works was admitted. Although the artworks follow traditional Aboriginal form and are based on dreaming themes, each artwork is one of intricate detail and complexity reflecting great skill and originality.

Copyright infringement by Beechrow

The infringements pleaded by the applicants included direct infringement contrary to § 36 of the Copyright Act and indirect infringements under §§ 37 and 38. In light of the way the trial has been conducted, and concessions made in the course of the respondents' case as to the basis on which conversion damages should be assessed in respect of any infringement found to have occurred, it is appropriate to concentrate on § 37. That section relevantly reads:

"37 . . . the copyright in a literary, dramatic, musical or artistic work is infringed by a person who, without the licence of the owner of the copyright, imports an article into Australia for the purpose of:

(a) selling, letting for hire, or by way of trade offering or exposing for sale or hire, the article;

(b) distributing the article:

(i) for the purpose of trade; or

(ii) for any other purpose to an extent that will affect prejudicially the owner of the copyright; or

(c) by way of trade exhibiting the article in public;

if the importer knew, or ought reasonably to have known, that the making of the article would, if the article had been made in Australia by the importer, have constituted an infringement of the copyright."

I am not left in any doubt by the evidence that Beechrow through Mr. Bethune knew or ought to have known at the time when the import of the carpets into Australia occurred that the making of the carpets which are exact reproductions of the artworks, if they had been made in Australia by Beechrow, would have constituted an infringement of copyright. Mr. Bethune knew whilst he was at the carpet factory in Vietnam that the artwork came from the portfolios. The source of the artwork should have suggested to him that a breach of copyright would have been committed if the carpets were made in Australia. The artworks were plainly major artworks by identified artists. By the time the carpets ordered following the samples entered Australia, the existence of copyright and the implications of Beechrow's proposed course of conduct had been made plain to Mr. Bethune. He was at no time told that copyright approval had been given, nor did he inquire as to the position at any time after the letter seeking approval was despatched to AAMA.

In the case of the 115 carpets which are exact reproductions of seven of the artworks, infringement plainly occurred under § 37.

Whether the carpets which are not exact reproductions of the artwork infringe the relevant artwork, and the requirements in § 37 as to knowledge in relation to those carpets if they constitute substantial reproductions raise more difficult questions. I shall consider each of the disputed designs separately.

For claims of infringement under § 37 to be made out by the importation of the snake, the green centre and the waterholes carpets it must be established that the importer, Beechrow, knew or ought reasonably to have known that the carpets would, if made in Australia by Beechrow, have constituted an infringement of the copyright. Notwithstanding the protestations by the respondents that they do not think the carpets are substantial copies of the artworks, and did not think this was being alleged until part way through the trial, I think, as a matter of probability, that Beechrow through Mr. Bethune, realised from the outset that the artworks from which the carpets were derived were the subject of copyright, and that the carpets reproduced those artworks in substantial parts. But it is not necessary to go that far. Actual knowledge is not necessary. I am satisfied that Beechrow and Mr. Bethune had constructive knowledge, that is knowledge of facts that would suggest to a reasonable person, particularly one about to engage in the business of distributing carpets in Australia, that a breach of the copyright law would be committed if the carpets were to be made in Australia.

In summary, I am satisfied that the import into Australia of all 246 carpets which the applicants allege to be infringing reproductions of the artworks constituted infringements by Beechrow.

I turn now to the remedies sought by the applicants.

Principles discussed in the authorities on the assessment of damages under § 115(2) concentrate upon aspects of monetary loss likely to flow from the impaired commercial potential of the copyright. That is hardly surprising as infringement actions usually arise in the commercial context of our market economy. In the circumstances of this case the damages sustained, at least by the living artists, extend beyond the commercial potential for monetary return from the copyright. The assessment of damages under § 115(2) may include compensation for personal suffering, for example for insulting behavior; and for humiliation. In the present case the infringements have caused personal distress and, potentially at least, have exposed the artists to embarrassment and contempt within their communities if not to the risk of diminished earning potential and physical harm. The losses arising from these risks are a reflection of the cultural environment in which the artists reside and conduct their daily affairs. Losses resulting from tortious wrongdoing experienced by Aborigines in their particular environments are properly to be brought to account: see Napaluma v Baker (1982) 29 SASR 192; Weston v Woodroffe (1985) 36 NTR 34; Dixon v Davies (1982) 17 NTR 31.

The applicants contend that the infringing use of the artwork was in effect the pirating of cultural heritage. That is so, but under copyright law damages can be awarded only in so far as the "pirating" causes a loss to the copyright owner resulting from infringement of copyright. Nevertheless, in the cultural environment of the artists the infringement of those rights has, or is likely to have, far reaching effects upon the copyright owner. Anger and distress suffered by those around the copyright owner constitute part of that person's injury and suffering.

There is in the circumstances of this case another avenue by which damages over and above the depreciation in the commercial value of the copyright can be awarded, namely as additional damages for flagrant infringement under § 115(4). That avenue may not be available in other cases, but I am satisfied that this is an appropriate case to make an order of additional damages having regard to the matters referred to in § 115(4)(b). In Ravenscroft v Herbert & New English Library Ltd (at 208), Brightman J described "flagrancy" as implying "the existence of scandalous conduct, deceit and such like; it includes deliberate and calculated copyright infringements." In the present case the copyright infringement was plainly deliberate and calculated by Beechrow and Mr. Bethune. From the outset the source of the imagery on the carpets was known. With that knowledge it was a calculated decision on his part to proceed with the manufacture and import of the carpets in the hopeful expectation that copyright permission would be granted. Then, when copyright permission was not immediately forthcoming through AAMA, Beechrow through Mr. and Mrs. Bethune, instead of complying with the law, and apologising to the copyright owners, sought to question the authority of AAMA and to accuse it of acting otherwise than in the interests of the artists. Thereafter they continued importing and distributing the snake, the green centre and the waterholes carpets, even after service of the proceedings. I cannot accept their assertion that they did not realise these carpets were alleged to be infringements.

In summary the applicants have established entitlements to the following orders:

1. Injunctions against all respondents against further infringement of the artworks.

2. Injunctions against Beechrow and Mr. Bethune against further contraventions of the Trade Practices Act.

3. An order against Beechrow for delivery up of the carpets identified in Exhibit A69.

4. Judgment in favour of the applicants jointly against Beechrow and Mr. Bethune for $188,640.52.

6. Liberty to the applicants to apply to have the judgment sums increased in the event that any of the carpets in Exhibit A69 are not delivered up.

Orders accordingly.

NOTES AND QUESTIONS

1. Does *Milpurrurru* address all of the concerns raised at the beginning of this section on why folklore may not be protectable under copyright laws? What were the specific works of folklore that received copyright protection in *Milpurrurru*? What about other types of folklore?

2. Based on the result in the Australian case, do you think copyright is adequate to protect folklore? For a critical view, see BOATEMA BOATENG, THE COPYRIGHT THING DOESN'T WORK HERE: ADINKRA AND KENTE CLOTH AND INTELLECTUAL PROPERTY IN GHANA (2011).

3. Did the use of the artworks for carpets play an important role in the outcome of this case? For example, suppose that the artworks were used for posters instead. Would this have made a difference in the outcome of the case or the remedy issued by the court? Was this concern based on a concept of western copyright law or based upon aboriginal law?

4. An effective means to protect all forms of folklore from piracy and exploitation would be to create a multilateral treaty that recognizes folklore as a *sui generis* intellectual property right. This treaty can be created within the auspices of the WTO, WIPO, or independently. But many nations, especially those with large indigenous populations, oppose such a treaty for political and legal reasons and it does not appear likely that such a treaty will be enacted any time in the near future. What might be their reasons for opposing such a treaty?

D. EXCLUSIVE RIGHTS OF COPYRIGHT (ECONOMIC)

PROBLEM 2–14

Section 106 of the U.S. Copyright Act sets forth the exclusive rights granted under copyright. The owner of a copyright has "the exclusive rights to do and to authorize any of the following":

(1) to reproduce the copyrighted work in copies or phonorecords;

(2) to prepare derivative works based upon the copyrighted work;

(3) to distribute copies or phonorecords of the copyrighted work to the public by sale or other transfer of ownership, or by rental, lease, or lending;

(4) in the case of literary, musical, dramatic, and choreographic works, pantomimes, and motion pictures and other audiovisual works, to perform the copyrighted work publicly;

(5) in the case of literary, musical, dramatic, and choreographic works, pantomimes, and pictorial, graphic, or sculptural works, including the individual images of a motion picture or other audiovisual work, to display the copyrighted work publicly; and

(6) in the case of sound recordings, to perform the copyrighted work publicly by means of a digital audio transmission.

Identify the article in the Berne Convention that corresponds with each of these rights. Are some of these rights not required by the Berne Convention? Which ones? See discussion below.

* * *

The Berne Convention requires member countries to provide authors with certain exclusive rights under the copyright laws of each Union country. These rights are commonly referred to as "economic rights" and are to be contrasted with the moral rights of authors contained in Article 6*bis*, which will be discussed in a later section. The economic rights involve rights of (i) reproduction; (ii) adaptation and translation; (iii) public performance, communication, and broadcast; and (iv) public distribution for cinematographic adaptations.

Although Berne provides international standards governing these economic rights, it is important to remember that the laws of each individual country create and determine the scope of the rights (unless the country's law considers the Berne Convention a self-executing treaty giving rise to substantive rights). Thus, it is possible for countries to recognize *additional* rights under copyright that are not expressly covered by the Berne Convention, such as the right to publicly display a work or the general right of distribution.

The minimum standards governing economic rights under Berne are contained in the following Articles:

Article 2*bis* (collection of speeches),

Article 8 (translations),

Article 9 (reproduction),

Article 11 (public performance of musical works),

Article 11*bis* (public communication),

Article 11*ter* (public recitation),

Article 12 (adaptations, arrangements, and alterations),

Article 14 (cinematographic adaptations), and

Article 14*ter* (droit de suite, or resale right).

The scattered organization of these rights in Berne is attributable to the fact that the provisions were added in piecemeal with successive revisions of Berne, as the member countries could reach agreement in spite of what may have been differing views of the exclusive rights. The original Berne Act in 1886 focused only on rights for translations of works, both in their making and public performances of the translated works. This focus on translation rights was to be expected, given the preeminence of the book trade for international copyright in the late nineteenth century. Translation of books into foreign languages in Europe and elsewhere provided the primary international issue for copyright at the time. With each successive revision of Berne, a minimum standard for an additional right or set of rights was added.

To these minimum standards for rights under Berne, the TRIPS Agreement adds a provision for rental rights in computer program and cinematographic works, although in a conditional way (Article 11). The rights are summarized briefly below, leaving a discussion of exceptions to such rights for a following section.

1. REPRODUCTION (COPYING)

Article 9(1) of Berne recognizes that "[a]uthors of literary and artistic works protected by this Convention shall have the exclusive right of authorizing the reproduction of these works, *in any manner or form*." Berne Conv. art. 9(1). The right of reproduction is typically viewed as the basic, core right under copyright—the right to copy. Although Berne did not expressly recognize a reproduction right until the Stockholm Act of 1967, countries had long recognized such a right of authors under their national laws. Differences in countries' views on the scope of the reproduction right (including any exceptions)—such as to copying in different formats brought about by technological advances—may explain the long delay in the Convention's formal recognition of this basic right of copyright. Article 9(1) resolves the question about scope in favor of a broad approach: the right encompasses authorizing the copying of works "in any manner or form." *Id.* There is no doubt that the exclusive right of reproduction contemplated by Article 9(1) requires countries to recognize rights of authors to proscribe the blanket, verbatim copying of their entire works. Less clear, however, is the extent to which Berne addresses lesser forms of copying, such as a substantially similar plot or character of a work. The TRIPS Agreement Article 9 addresses one of these lesser forms of copying. Drawing upon the distinction recognized in the U.S. and elsewhere between an author's expression and an author's ideas, TRIPS prohibits countries from copyrighting ideas. TRIPS art. 9(2). Under the idea-expression dichotomy, people are free to copy ideas contained in expressive works, as long as they do not copy the author's particular expression in the works.

Article 14(1)(i) deals with cinematographic reproductions. The article recognizes a minimum standard for a reproduction right for authors of literary or artistic works that have been adapted into a cinematographic work, more commonly known as a film. Authors have the right to authorize "the cinematographic adaptation and reproduction of these works, and the distribution of the works thus adapted and reproduced." Berne Conv. art. 14(1)(i). The reproduction right for cinematographic works, which has been recognized under Berne since the 1908 Berlin revision, in fact preceded the recognition of the general right of reproduction in Article 9. Intent on protecting authors from uses of their works in the then-new medium of cinematography, the French delegation was instrumental in securing the protections set forth in Article 14.

2. DISTRIBUTION

The Berne Convention does not specifically recognize a general right of distribution, although it does recognize a right of distribution for cinematographic adaptations under Article 14(1). Berne Conv. art. 14(1)(i). Even though most countries do recognize an author's interest in distribution of their works, the scope is varied among countries. Some countries, such as France, treat the right of distribution of copies of a work as a part of the right of reproduction. *See* Paul E. Geller & Melville B. Nimmer, International Copyright Law and Practice § 8[1][b][i][A] (France) (2004) (analysis of Professors Lucas, Kamina, and Plaisant). Other countries, such as the United States, treat the distribution right as a separate right. *See* 17 U.S.C. § 106(3).

Berne does not contain a general distribution right in part because the distribution right implicates a number of issues on which countries have failed to achieve international agreement. Perhaps the biggest issue is the exhaustion of rights after a first sale of a copy of a work, which still continues to divide countries. Exhaustion refers to the termination of the rights of the author to control the distribution of a copy of the work after its first sale. For example, if a U.S. author sells a book to a purchaser in the U.S., then the purchaser is free to resell the book or to donate it to a local library, all without the permission of the author. Countries disagree, however, on whether exhaustion occurs when the first sale of the work occurs abroad. Some countries find that the right of the author is exhausted by a sale anywhere in the world (international exhaustion), while other countries hold that the right of the author is exhausted only if the book is sold within the nation of the origin of the work (national exhaustion). The drafters of TRIPS expressly left the issue of exhaustion unresolved (Article 6). Disagreement over a public lending right (to compensate for borrowing of copyrighted works at public libraries) and the *droit de suite* or resale right (discussed below) has also made the distribution right a difficult issue for countries to agree upon. Berne does, however, regulate distribution of unlawful copies by requiring countries to recognize that "[i]nfringing copies of a work shall be liable to seizure in any country of the Union where the work enjoys legal protection." Berne Conv. art. 16.

3. ADAPTATION AND TRANSLATION (DERIVATIVE WORKS)

Article 12 of Berne encompasses the adaptation right. Authors "shall enjoy the exclusive right of authorizing adaptations, arrangements and other alterations of their works." Berne Conv. art. 12. Article 8 recognizes a right of authors to authorize the translation of their works into other languages. *Id.* art. 8. In some countries, such as the U.S., both adaptations and translations are encompassed under the general rubric of "derivative work," which is a work based upon or derived from one or more preexisting works. *See* 17 U.S.C. § 101 (definition of "derivative work").

Article 14 of Berne deals specifically with the right of adaptation of works into cinematographic works. Authors have the right to authorize cinematographic adaptations of their works, which encompasses both the first cinematographic adaptation and any other adaptations of that cinematographic work. Thus, if the cinematographic adaptation based on a literary or artistic work is to be subsequently adapted into another artistic form, the author of the original work retains the right to authorize the subsequent adaptation "without prejudice to the authorization of the author of the cinematographic production." Berne Conv. art. 14(2). Thus, if a copyrighted novel is turned into a movie and then later a playwright wanted to make a Broadway musical based on the movie, the playwright would need authorization of both the novelist and the author of the movie. Under Article 14, the author of the copyrighted novel retains a right to authorize subsequent adaptations of the film "into any other artistic form." *Id.*

4. PUBLIC COMMUNICATION, PERFORMANCE, AND BROADCAST (PUBLIC PERFORMANCE)

The most complicated set of provisions governing rights in Berne deal with the rights of authors to communicate their works to the public, including the important right of public performance. These rights are contained in Articles 11, 11*bis*, 11*ter*, and 14, which are summarized below. One way of thinking about these rights is in relation to a distribution right. Distribution pertains to the dissemination of a copyrighted work that is embodied in a physical copy. The communication, performance, or broadcast of a work, by contrast, need not be transmitted or recorded in any physical copy. A teacher can read a book aloud to the class, an orchestra can perform a symphony to an audience of classical music lovers, and a radio can broadcast music to the public, all without any permanent recording of the communications. Under Berne, an author has the right to authorize the dissemination of a copyrighted work whether in a tangible or intangible form.

Article 11 recognizes a public performance right for dramatic, dramatico-musical, and musical works, such as an opera, play, musical, or symphony. Authors of such works shall enjoy the exclusive right to authorize the public performance of their works by any means or process, and any further communication of such performances to the public. The author of a dramatic or dramatico-musical work, such as a musical, has the right to public performance of any translated version of the work in a different language. Berne Conv. art. 11.

Article 11*bis* pertains to all literary and artistic works. Authors shall enjoy the exclusive right of authorizing the broadcasting of their works to the public by wireless means, the rebroadcast and cable transmission of broadcast programs, and the public communication of their works by loudspeaker (or other analogous instrument). The author's rights extend also to rebroadcasts and cable transmissions of authorized broadcast programs if "this communication is made by an organization other than the original one" that broadcast the programs with authorization. Countries are allowed "to determine the conditions under which the rights [under Article 11*bis*] ... may be exercised"—meaning the possibility of adopting a system of compulsory licenses. Berne Conv. art. 11*bis*.

Article 11*ter* recognizes a public recitation right for literary works. Authors of such works shall enjoy the exclusive right of authorizing the public recitation of their work by any means or process and any further communication of such recitation to the public. Berne Conv. art. 11*ter*.

Article 14 again provides a specific provision for cinematographic adaptations. The author of a literary or artistic work that has been adapted into cinematographic work shall enjoy the exclusive right of authorizing "the public performance and communication to the public by wire of the works thus adapted or reproduced." Berne Conv. art. 14(1)(ii).

5. DROIT DE SUITE (RESALE RIGHT)

Article 14*ter* recognizes a right for authors in the resale of their original works of art and original manuscripts of writers and composers. Berne Conv. art. 14*ter*. The right, known as *droit de suite* (from the French meaning the right of follow-up), allows authors to recoup compensation for resales of the original works of art or manuscripts. "Original" denotes here the *first* work of art or manuscript composed (such as an original painting of an artist), rather than the requirement of originality or intellectual creation. The resale right developed in France to address the concerns of visual artists, whose paintings and other works of visual art had greater value in the original work, which might not attain commercial success until years after the artist died. As recognized by the Berne Convention, *droit de suite* also includes original manuscripts of writers and composers. Under Berne, the resale right is to be inalienable, creating "an interest in any sale of the work subsequent to the first transfer by the author of the work." *Id.* art. 14*ter*(1). The resale right is essentially an exception to the principle of exhaustion: in countries that recognize such a right, the artist's right to recoup proceeds from subsequent sales of the original work is inexhaustible (at least until the term expires). Each country may decide the amount of resale interest and the procedure for collection.

It is important to note, however, that the *droit de suite* provision is optional for Berne countries. Article 14*ter*(2) requires the recognition of such right "only if legislation in the country to which the author belongs so permits, and to the extent permitted by the country where this protection is claimed." Berne Conv. art. 14*ter*(2). This provision is a departure from national treatment, authorizing countries to require material reciprocity for the enjoyment of *droit de suite*. A country that recognizes *droit de suite* does not have to offer the right to nationals of another country that does not recognize such a right.

6.   TRIPS RENTAL RIGHTS

In addition to incorporating the rights contained in Berne, TRIPS recognizes rental rights for authors of computer programs and cinematographic works. Under Article 11, the right encompasses the "right to authorize or to prohibit the commercial rental to the public of originals or copies of their copyright works." TRIPS art. 11. For cinematographic works, TRIPS makes this obligation optional for countries, "unless such rental has led to widespread copying of such works which is materially impairing the exclusive right of reproduction conferred in that Member [country] on authors." *Id.* For computer programs, the rental right does not apply if "the program itself is not the essential object of the rental," such as if, for example, a person rents a house that operates in some capacity with computer programs. *Id.*

PROBLEM 2–15

Country A has enacted a new law creating a public lending right for authors. Under this right, authors are entitled to royalties for the lending of their works by public libraries based on a proportional sampling of the times their works have been borrowed. The law is entitled Public Lending Right Act and is separate from Country A's Copyright Act. Country A extends the public lending right only to its own nationals and individuals with their habitual residence in Country A.

Country B also recognizes a public lending right for authors, but it does so as an exclusive right for authors within its Copyright Act. Like Country A, Country B has extended the public lending right only to its own nationals and individuals with their habitual residence in Country B.

Country C also recognizes a public lending right for authors under a separate system outside of its copyright law. It has extended coverage of the right to its own nationals and individuals with their habitual residence in Country C, as well as to nationals of Country D who first publish their works simultaneously in Country C (but to no other foreign nationals).

Countries A, B, and C are all members of TRIPS and the Berne Union (Paris, 1971). Country D is not a member of either. Do the public lending right laws of Countries A, B, and C violate any of their obligations under TRIPS and the Berne Convention?

NOTES AND QUESTIONS

1.   Contrast the organizational structure of § 106 of the U.S. Copyright Act with the various provisions governing exclusive rights scattered in the

Berne Convention. Of course, it is easier to achieve a more organized discussion of rights when one settles upon all of the rights to include, instead of adding them in piecemeal as was the case with Berne. Several other countries, such as Germany and France, have adopted an alternative way of setting forth exclusive rights. Each has a general provision recognizing a property right of authors in their works, encompassing both moral and economic aspects. For example, Article 111–1 of the French author's right statute states: "The author of a work of the mind shall enjoy in that work, by the mere fact of its creation, an exclusive incorporeal property right which shall be enforceable against all persons. This right shall include attributes of an intellectual and moral nature as also attributes of an economic nature, as determined by Books I and III of this Code...." Subsequent sections then provide the specific moral and economic rights protected. For example, Article 122–1 recognizes: "The right of exploitation belonging to the author shall comprise the right of performance and the right of reproduction." The rights of performance and reproduction are then further delineated in subsequent sections.

The difference in approaches in designating exclusive rights might be attributable to differences in philosophical views of authors. The U.S. tends to follow a positivist utilitarian approach holding that rights exist only if they are created by law, whereas the author's right tradition in France tends more to embrace a natural rights theory holding that rights exist independently of law "by the mere fact of [a work's] creation."

2. *Adaptation.* The Berne Convention does not define what constitutes an "adaptation," "arrangement," or "other alteration" of a work. Professor Paul Goldstein suggests that an "adaptation" refers to "the recasting of a work from one format to another, as from a short story into a dramatic play," while "arrangement" probably means "modification within the same format, such as an orchestral arrangement of a popular song." PAUL GOLDSTEIN, INTERNATIONAL COPYRIGHT 252 (2001). Other changes to a work, such as an edited version or an abridgment of a work, might fall within the catch-all term of "other alteration."

However, unless a country's copyright law contains differences in protection based on whether a work is an "adaptation" versus "arrangement" or "other alteration," there probably is little, if any, need to define with precision what is meant by these terms. What is important to recognize is that "adaptations, arrangements, and other alteration" encompass a broad category of derivative works. The adaptation right thus enables authors to control alterations of their works. In this respect, the adaptation right may serve a similar or complementary function to the moral right of integrity, which gives an author the right "to object to any distortion, mutilation or other modification of, or other derogatory action in relation to, the said work, which would be prejudicial to his honor or reputation." Berne Conv. art. 6*bis*; see Goldstein, *supra*, at 253.

3. *Translations and compulsory licenses in developing countries under Berne.* As mentioned above, the translation right was the first right recognized under the Berne Convention, given its importance to authors in having their works protected in foreign countries (and foreign languages). For some

time, and as allowed by earlier acts of the Berne Convention, several developing countries continued to join Berne with reservations that were meant to absolve them of recognizing the translation right. The reservations were based on the policy of helping to promote the introduction and dissemination of learned works in the developing countries. The most recent Paris version of Berne also has a special provision under Article II (contained in the Appendix to Berne) for developing countries to "substitute for the exclusive right of translation ... a system of non-exclusive and non-transferable licenses" under a highly regulated set of circumstances. TRIPS Article 9 also incorporates the Appendix of Berne within the terms of TRIPS. *See* WIPO, GUIDE TO THE BERNE CONVENTION 146–47 (1978).

4. *The meaning of "public."* The linchpin of the various rights under Articles 11, 11*bis*, 11*ter*, and 14 is some form of performance or communication of a copyrighted work to the "public." The Berne Convention, however, does not define the meaning of public, apparently leaving that issue for countries to decide under their national laws. Under the U.S. Copyright Act, to perform a work publicly means "[t]o perform ... it at a place open to the public or at any place where a substantial number of persons outside of a normal circle of a family and its social acquaintances is gathered," as well as a transmission of a performance to such places. 17 U.S.C. § 101. Under the U.S. definition, would the singing of "Happy Birthday to You" by five friends at a table in a crowded public restaurant constitute a public performance?

5. *Distribution and Exhaustion.* By not including a general distribution right, the Berne Union avoided the ongoing controversy over the issue of exhaustion of distribution rights after first sale. Does the absence of a general right of distribution under Berne have any practical significance among Berne countries, if most countries at least to some degree recognize protection against unauthorized distribution?

6. *Right to make a collection of speeches.* Article 2*bis* of the Berne Convention gives countries the discretion to "exclude, wholly or in part, from" copyright protection "political speeches and speeches delivered in the course of legal proceedings." Countries are also given the discretion "to determine the conditions under which lectures, addresses and other works of the same nature which are delivered in public may be reproduced by the press, broadcast, communicated to the public by wire and made subject of public communication as envisaged in Article 11*bis*(1) ... when such use is justified by the informatory purpose." Article 2*bis* also recognizes, however, that the "author shall enjoy the exclusive right of making a collection of" such speeches and lectures.

7. *Right of public display.* Berne does not recognize a right of publicly displaying or exhibiting a work. It does mention, however, that countries are allowed "to permit, to control, or to prohibit, by legislation or regulation, the circulation, presentation, or exhibition of any work or production in regard to which the competent authority may find it necessary to exercise that right." Berne Conv. art. 17. Comparatively few countries in Berne formally recognize such a display right under copyright law. The U.S. is one of the minority. 17 U.S.C. § 106(5) (exclusive right "in the case of literary, musical, dramatic, and choreographic works, pantomimes, and pictorial, graphic, or sculptural

works, including the individual images of a motion picture or other audiovisual work, to display the copyrighted work publicly"). What are the pros and cons in recognizing a public display right? Do you believe it is good idea to include it as a part of an author's exclusive rights? To what extent does the Internet affect your analysis? *Cf. Kelly v. Arriba Soft Corp.*, 336 F.3d 811, 822 (9th Cir. 2003) (website's importing photograph from another site to display on own site allegedly violated right of public display).

8. *Bibliographic note.* Sam Ricketson, The Berne Convention for the Protection of Literary and Artistic Works: 1886–1986, at 364–476 (1987); Paul Goldstein, International Copyright (2001); S.M. Stewart, International Copyright and Neighboring Rights §§ 5.37–5.53 (2d ed. 1989); WIPO, Guide to the Berne Convention 54–89 (1978).

7. WTO DECISION

Can a country deny copyright protection based on the content of the work under the standards set out in the Berne Convention and TRIPS? The following case addresses this issue.

CHINA—MEASURES AFFECTING THE PROTECTION AND ENFORCEMENT OF INTELLECTUAL PROPERTY RIGHTS

Report of the Panel, WTO.
(Macey, Chairperson; Porzio and Tiwari, Members).
WT/DS362/R (January 26, 2009).

On 13 August 2007, the United States requested the Dispute Settlement Body ("DSB") to establish a panel pursuant to Article 6 of the DSU, with standard terms of reference. [The U.S. challenged China's law in three different areas: (1) thresholds for criminal procedures and penalties, (2) disposal of goods confiscated by customs authorities that infringe intellectual property rights, and (3) denial of copyright and related rights protection and enforcement to works that have not been authorized for publication or distribution within China. The excerpt below discusses the third issue. *Ed.*]

I. FINDINGS

A. Copyright Law

1. Description of the measure at issue

This Section of the Panel's findings concerns China's Copyright Law. The claims concerning the Copyright Law address, in particular, the first sentence of Article 4. The parties agreed to translate that sentence as follows:

> "Works the publication and/or dissemination of which are prohibited by law shall not be protected by this Law."

This Report refers to the first sentence of Article 4 as "Article 4(1)" for ease of reference.

2.   Claim under Article 5(1) of the Berne Convention (1971), as incorporated by Article 9.1 of the TRIPS Agreement

The United States claims that Article 4(1) of China's Copyright Law denies the protection of the Copyright Law to certain categories of works, and refers to the text of that sentence. The United States recalls that China, during a review of its legislation in the Council for TRIPS in 2002, explained that this sentence referred to works of which the publication or distribution was prohibited by such laws and regulations as the Criminal Law, the Regulation on the Administration of Publishing Industry, the Regulation on the Administration of Broadcasting, the Regulation on the Administration of Audiovisual Products, the Regulation on the Administration of Films and the Regulations on the Administration of Telecommunication. The United States gives examples of four regulations that prohibit the publication or distribution of works under various circumstances. The United States claims that Article 4(1) of China's Copyright Law denies to the authors of works "the publication or distribution of which is prohibited by law" the broad set of rights enumerated in Article 10 of the Copyright Law, which largely encompasses the rights contemplated by the provisions of the Berne Convention (1971). Nor do authors of works denied protection of the Copyright Law benefit from the remedies specified in Articles 46 and 47 of the Copyright Law. Consequently, the authors of such works do not enjoy the minimum rights that are "specially granted" by the Berne Convention, inconsistently with Article 5(1) of that Convention.

China responds that copyright vests upon creation and is independent of publication. Article 2 of the Copyright Law grants full copyright protection by expressly incorporating into Chinese law the rights conferred under international agreements, including the Berne Convention and the TRIPS Agreement. In contrast, Article 4(1) of the Copyright Law is extremely limited in scope. China, like many other countries in the world, bans from publication and dissemination such works as those that consist entirely of unconstitutional or immoral content. Article 4(1) simply provides that such a work shall not be protected by the Copyright Law. China argued in its first written submission that the application of Article 4(1) was not dependent on content review or any other regulatory regime related to publication and that the only result of a finding of prohibited content in that process was a denial of authority to publish, not a denial of copyright. Specifically, China argued that works that fail content review were not denied copyright protection. Article 17 of the Berne Convention (1971) subjects to the sovereign power of governments all of the rights otherwise granted by that Convention.

The Panel begins its assessment by observing that Chapter I of the Copyright Law comprises eight articles.

Article 2 sets out criteria of eligibility for protection. The first paragraph (to which the Panel will refer as "Article 2(1)") may be translated as follows:

"Chinese citizens, legal entities or other organizations shall enjoy copyright in their works in accordance with this Law, whether published or not."

The second (to which the Panel will refer as "Article 2(2)") may be translated as follows:

"The copyright enjoyed by foreigners or stateless persons in any of their works under an agreement concluded between China and the country to which the author belongs or in which the author has his habitual residence, or under an international treaty to which both countries are parties, shall be protected by this Law."

The Berne Convention (1971) is defined as an "international copyright treaty" for the purposes of the Provisions on the Implementation of International Copyright Treaties.

A link can be observed between Article 2(2) and 4(1). Article 2(2) provides that the copyright enjoyed by certain foreigners in any of their works "shall be protected by this Law" whilst Article 4(1) uses identical language with the addition of a negative to provide that certain works "shall not be protected by this Law." This suggests that Article 4(1) denies what Article 2(2) grants.

The term "works" is defined in the previous article, Article 3.

The term "publication and/or dissemination" was agreed between the parties as an appropriate translation. The parties had earlier used the phrases "publication or distribution" and "publication and dissemination." China alleges that the word translated as "dissemination" has a distinct, and wider, meaning than a word commonly used in its content review regulations, which may be translated as "distribution."

The term "prohibited by law," on its face, is not limited to any particular piece of legislation but could apply to any law that prohibits the publication and/or dissemination of a work. The United States alleges that it refers to "other laws and regulations." In any event, it is clear from its wording that the provision applies to a class of "works," the class being defined as those the publication and/or dissemination of which are, in some way, prohibited by law.

The phrase translated as "shall not be protected by this Law" does not include the word "shall" in the original, as it uses no modal verb. However, it is not disputed that Article 4(1) of the Copyright Law is mandatory. The reference to "this Law" is evidently a reference to the Copyright Law. On its face, it refers to the protection of the Copyright Law and not to any subset of its protection.

The United States explained that this phrase provided for the denial of the rights enumerated in Article 10 of the Copyright Law and the remedies in Articles 46 and 47 of the Copyright Law. China agreed that it included all the rights listed in Article 10.

The Panel observes that the protection provided by the Copyright Law is addressed *inter alia* in Chapter II, Section 1 titled "Copyright Owners and Their Rights." That Section includes Article 10, which provides that "copyright" includes a list of four moral rights and 13 economic rights set out in the first paragraph of that Article.

The economic rights appear to be exclusive rights in light of, *inter alia*, Article 11, which provides that the copyright in a work shall belong to its author, and Article 24, which provides that anyone who exploits another person's work shall conclude a copyright licensing contract with the copyright owner, subject to exceptions.

The Panel finds that the Copyright Law is sufficiently clear, on its face, to show that Article 4(1) denies the protection of Article 10 to certain works, including those of WTO Member nationals, as the United States claims.

This interpretation is consistent with, and clarified by, the view expressed by the Supreme People's Court of China in the course of domestic litigation in 1998, to which the Panel will refer as "the *Inside Story* case."[1] The United States submitted a letter sent from the Supreme People's Court to a provincial Higher People's Court during that case, which the Supreme People's Court reissued in 2000.[2] This letter, from China's highest judicial body, is instructive in the interpretation of Article 4(1) of the Copyright Law.[3] That case concerned a book, the publication of which violated administrative regulations but the content of which did not violate any laws. In the letter, the Court ruled that it was correct for the courts of the first and second instances to provide protection under the Copyright Law to the book at issue for the following reason:

> "The *Inside Story* was originally published in the magazine 'Yanhuang Chunqiu' (1994, No. 2). In May of the same year, the United Front Department of the Sichuan Provincial Communist Party Committee reviewed the book and approved its publication. Nothing was found in the text of the *Inside Story* to violate any laws. Therefore, it is correct for the courts of the first and second instances to provide it protection under the Copyright Law."

The Panel finds that the Supreme People's Court letter confirms that Article 4(1) of the Copyright Law denies copyright protection and clarifies that Article 4(1) applies where the publication and/or dissemination of a work is prohibited due to its content.

---

1. The title of the book that was the subject of the dispute begins with the words "Inside Story."

2. Letter from the Supreme People's Court to the Hunan Province Higher People's Court in *Zheng Haijin v Xu Zheng Xiong and Tianjin People's Publishing House* ([1998] Letter no. 33). The letter was redistributed by the Supreme People's Court on 9 March 2000 in an intellectual property document series. It is now listed on the website of the State Intellectual Property Office under the heading "judicial interpretation."

3. The Panel notes that judicial decisions in China do not have a binding effect for other courts but serve as a reference only.

3. Article 17 of the Berne Convention (1971) as incorporated by Article 9.1 of the TRIPS Agreement

China raises a defence under Article 17 of the Berne Convention (1971), as incorporated by Article 9.1 of the TRIPS Agreement. China submits that all rights granted to authors under the Berne Convention (1971) are limited by Article 17 of that Convention, that Article 17 is not an exhaustive codification of the sovereign right to censor and that Article 17 is drafted using very expansive language "that effectively denies WTO jurisdiction in this area."

The Panel recalls that Article 9.1 of the TRIPS Agreement incorporates Article 17 of the Berne Convention (1971). Article 17 of the Berne Convention (1971) provides as follows:

> "The provisions of this Convention cannot in any way affect the right of the Government of each country of the Union to permit, to control, or to prohibit, by legislation or regulation, the circulation, presentation, or exhibition of any work or production in regard to which the competent authority may find it necessary to exercise that right."

"The provisions of this Convention" as referred to in Article 17 include Article 5(1) of the Berne Convention (1971).

The parties agree that Article 17 confirms that governments have certain rights to control the exploitation of works. They do not agree as to whether those rights include a denial of all copyright protection with respect to particular works.

The Panel observes that the terms of Article 17 include certain broad phrases, notably "cannot in any way affect" and "any work or production." The use of the words "any work" (although it is slightly different in the French text) confirms that the subject-matter dealt with by Article 17 is the same as that addressed by the other substantive provisions of the Convention. However, these phrases are not used in isolation but refer to the right of a government to "permit, to control, or to prohibit ... the circulation, presentation, or exhibition" of any work or production.

The right of a government "to control, or to prohibit" the "circulation, presentation, or exhibition" of any work or production clearly includes censorship for reasons of public order. Both China and the United States referred to the records of the diplomatic conferences of the Berne Convention, opinions in the academic literature and (in the case of China) to the WIPO Guide to the Berne Convention, that explained that Article 17 relates mainly to censorship and public order.

The Panel accepts that the three terms "circulation, presentation, or exhibition" are not necessarily an exhaustive list of the forms of exploitation of works covered by Article 17. However, a noticeable feature of these three terms is that they do not correspond to the terms used to define the substantive rights granted by the Berne Convention (1971), although they may be included within some of those rights or they may refer to acts incidental to the exercise of some of those rights. The word "exhibition" is not even used in the provisions setting out the substantive rights granted by the Convention. Therefore, it cannot be inferred that Article 17 authorizes the denial of all copyright protection in any work.

China draws the Panel's attention to the WIPO Guide to the Berne Convention, which states as follows regarding Article 17 of the Berne Convention (1971):

> "It covers the right of governments to take the necessary steps to maintain public order. On this point, the sovereignty of member countries is not affected by the rights given by the Convention. Authors may exercise their rights only if that exercise does not conflict with public order. The former must give way to the latter. The Article therefore gives Union countries certain powers to control."[4]

The Panel agrees with this interpretation. A government's right to permit, to control, or to prohibit the circulation, presentation, or exhibition of a work may interfere with the exercise of certain rights with respect to a protected work by the copyright owner or a third party authorized by the copyright owner. However, there is no reason to suppose that censorship will eliminate those rights entirely with respect to a particular work.

For the above reasons, the Panel confirms its finding above and concludes that, notwithstanding China's rights recognized in Article 17 of the Berne Convention (1971), the Copyright Law, specifically Article 4(1), is inconsistent with Article 5(1) of the Berne Convention (1971), as incorporated by Article 9.1 of the TRIPS Agreement. [The WTO panel's conclusion that China's copyright law also violated TRIPS art. 41(1) is omitted. *Ed.*]

In light of these conclusions, the Panel recommends pursuant to Article 19.1 of the DSU that China bring the Copyright Law [and the Customs measures] into conformity with its obligations under the TRIPS Agreement.

NOTES AND QUESTIONS

1. The WTO panel reviewed Article 4(1) of China's Copyright Law, which states: "Works the publication and/or dissemination of which are prohibited by law shall not be protected by this Law." What exactly did this section regulate?

2. Explain the basis for the U.S.'s challenge under Article 5(1) of the Berne Convention? Could a similar challenge have been successfully brought under Article 3(1) of TRIPS?

3. Practically speaking, why would it matter to the United States whether censored works received copyright protection in China? Might the reason relate to the numerous pirated movies in China, including ones that

---

4. WIPO Guide to the Berne Convention, at para. 17.2.

are censored by the government? *See Censorship in China, Caution: Lust*, THE ECONOMIST, Jan. 10, 2008.

4. In the U.S., some circuits have held that copyrights can extend even to illegal, obscene works, while other courts have questioned the soundness of that line of decisions. *Compare Mitchell Bros. Film Group v. Cinema Adult Theater*, 604 F.2d 852, 863 (5th Cir. 1979); *Jartech v. Clancy*, 666 F.2d 403, 406 (9th Cir. 1982) (obscenity no defense to copyright infringement claim) with *Devils Films, Inc. v. Nectar Video*, 29 F. Supp. 2d 174, 175–76 (S.D.N.Y. 1998) (questioning that line of cases); *Barnes v. Miner*, 122 F. 480, 490 (S.D.N.Y. 1903). Could U.S. law deny copyrights to all obscene works for both U.S. and foreign works, consistent with Berne Convention Article 5(1)?

8. EU LAW

The European Union Directive on Copyright and Related Rights in the Information Society, 2001/29/EC ("Information Society Directive"), attempts to harmonize copyright laws—including exclusive rights, exceptions, anti-circumvention rights, and private copy levies—among EU states. The Directive recognizes rights of reproduction (Art. 2), communication to the public of works and making available to the public other subject matter (Art. 3), and distribution (Art. 4).

In 2009, the European Court of Justice considered the scope of the reproduction right in the following case upon referral from the Danish Supreme Court.

INFOPAQ INTERNATIONAL A/S v. DANSKE DAGBLADES FORENING

Court of Justice of the European Union.
Case C–302/10 (2010/C 221/49).

Judgment

This reference for a preliminary ruling concerns, first, the interpretation of Article 2(a) of Directive 2001/29/EC of the European Parliament and of the Council of 22 May 2001 on the harmonisation of certain aspects of copyright and related rights in the information society (OJ 2001 L 167, p. 10) and, secondly, the conditions for exemption of temporary acts of reproduction within the meaning of Article 5 of that directive.

The reference was made in the context of proceedings between Infopaq International A/S ('Infopaq') and Danske Dagblades Forening ('DDF') concerning the dismissal of its application for a declaration that it was not required to obtain the consent of the rightholders for acts of reproduction of newspaper articles using an automated process consisting in the scanning and then conversion into digital files followed by electronic processing of that file.

Legal context

International law

Under Article 9(1) [of TRIPS]: 'Members shall comply with Articles 1 through 21 of the Berne Convention (1971) and the Appendix thereto. . . .'

Article 2 of the Berne Convention for the Protection of Literary and Artistic Works (Paris Act of 24 July 1971), as amended on 28 September 1979 ('the Berne Convention') reads as follows:

'(1) The expression "literary and artistic works" shall include every production in the literary, scientific and artistic domain, whatever may be the mode or form of its expression, such as books, pamphlets and other writings; . . .

(5) Collections of literary or artistic works such as encyclopaedias and anthologies which, by reason of the selection and arrangement of their contents, constitute intellectual creations shall be protected as such, without prejudice to the copyright in each of the works forming part of such collections. . . .

(8) The protection of this Convention shall not apply to news of the day or to miscellaneous facts having the character of mere items of press information.'

The dispute in the main proceedings and the questions referred for a preliminary ruling

Infopaq operates a media monitoring and analysis business which consists primarily in drawing up summaries of selected articles from Danish daily newspapers and other periodicals. The articles are selected on the basis of certain subject criteria agreed with customers and the selection is made by means of a 'data capture process.' The summaries are sent to customers by email.

DDF is a professional association of Danish daily newspaper publishers, whose function is inter alia to assist its members with copyright issues. In 2005 DDF became aware that Infopaq was scanning newspaper articles for commercial purposes without authorisation from the relevant rightholders. Taking the view that such consent was necessary for processing articles using the process in question, DDF complained to Infopaq about this procedure.

[Infopaq scanned copies of DDF's works into a database and then ran an automated software program to pull out 11–word extracts from those articles based on pre-selected search terms. The extracts consisted of the search term, plus the 5 words immediately preceding and following the term. *Ed.*] [T]he data capture process described above involves two acts of reproduction: the creation of a TIFF file when the printed articles are scanned and the conversion of the TIFF file into a text file. In addition, it is common ground that this procedure entails the reproduction of parts of the scanned printed articles since the extract of 11 words is stored and those 11 words are printed out on paper.

There is, however, disagreement between the parties as to whether there is reproduction as contemplated by Article 2 of Directive 2001/29. Likewise, they disagree as to whether, if there is reproduction, the acts in question, taken as a whole, are covered by the exemption from the right.

The questions referred for a preliminary ruling

The first question

By its first question, the national court asks, essentially, whether the concept of 'reproduction in part' within the meaning of Directive 2001/29 is to be interpreted as meaning that it encompasses the storing and subsequent printing out on paper of a text extract consisting of 11 words.

It is clear that Directive 2001/29 does not define the concept of either 'reproduction' or 'reproduction in part.' Article 2(a) of Directive 2001/29 provides that authors have the exclusive right to authorise or prohibit reproduction, in whole or in part, of their works. It follows that protection of the author's right to authorise or prohibit reproduction is intended to cover 'work.'

It is, moreover, apparent from the general scheme of the Berne Convention, in particular Article 2(5) and (8), that the protection of certain subject-matters as artistic or literary works presupposes that they are intellectual creations. Similarly, under Articles 1(3) of Directive 91/250, 3(1) of Directive 96/9 and 6 of Directive 2006/116, works such as computer programs, databases or photographs are protected by copyright only if they are original in the sense that they are their author's own intellectual creation.

In establishing a harmonised legal framework for copyright, Directive 2001/29 is based on the same principle, as evidenced by recitals 4, 9 to 11 and 20 in the preamble thereto. In those circumstances, copyright within the meaning of Article 2(a) of Directive 2001/29 is liable to apply only in relation to a subject-matter which is original in the sense that it is its author's own intellectual creation.

As regards the parts of a work, it should be borne in mind that there is nothing in Directive 2001/29 or any other relevant directive indicating that those parts are to be treated any differently from the work as a whole. It follows that they are protected by copyright since, as such, they share the originality of the whole work. In the light of the considerations referred to in paragraph 37 of this judgment, the various parts of a work thus enjoy protection under Article 2(a) of Directive 2001/29, provided that they contain elements which are the expression of the intellectual creation of the author of the work.

With respect to the scope of such protection of a work, it follows from recitals 9 to 11 in the preamble to Directive 2001/29 that its main objective is to introduce a high level of protection, in particular for authors to enable them to receive an appropriate reward for the use of their works, including at the time of reproduction of those works, in order to be able to pursue their creative and artistic work. Consequently, the protection conferred by Article 2 of Directive 2001/29 must be given a broad interpretation.

As regards newspaper articles, their author's own intellectual creation, referred to in paragraph 37 of this judgment, is evidenced clearly from the form, the manner in which the subject is presented and the linguistic expression. In the main proceedings, moreover, it is common ground that newspaper articles, as such, are literary works covered by Directive 2001/29.

Regarding the elements of such works covered by the protection, it should be observed that they consist of words which, considered in isolation, are not as such an intellectual creation of the author who employs them. It is only through the choice, sequence and combination of those words that the author may express his creativity in an original manner and achieve a result which is an intellectual creation.

Words as such do not, therefore, constitute elements covered by the protection. That being so, given the requirement of a broad interpretation of the scope of the protection conferred by Article 2 of Directive 2001/29, the possibility may not be ruled out that certain isolated sentences, or even certain parts of sentences in the text in question, may be suitable for conveying to the reader the originality of a publication such as a newspaper article, by communicating to that reader an element which is, in itself, the expression of the intellectual creation of the author of that article. Such sentences or parts of sentences are, therefore, liable to come within the scope of the protection provided for in Article 2(a) of that directive.

In the light of those considerations, the reproduction of an extract of a protected work which, like those at issue in the main proceedings, comprises 11 consecutive words thereof, is such as to constitute reproduction in part within the meaning of Article 2 of Directive 2001/29, if that extract contains an element of the work which, as such, expresses the author's own intellectual creation; it is for the national court to make this determination.

It must be remembered also that the data capture process used by Infopaq allows for the reproduction of multiple extracts of protected works. That process reproduces an extract of 11 words each time a search word appears in the relevant work and, moreover, often operates using a number of search words because some clients ask Infopaq to draw up summaries based on a number of criteria. In so doing, that process increases the likelihood that Infopaq will make reproductions in part within the meaning of Article 2(a) of Directive 2001/29 because the cumulative effect of those extracts may lead to the reconstitution of lengthy fragments which are liable to reflect the originality of the work in question, with the result that they contain a number of elements which are such as to express the intellectual creation of the author of that work.

In the light of the foregoing, the answer to the first question is that an act occurring during a data capture process, which consists of storing an extract of a protected work comprising 11 words and printing out that extract, is such as to come within the concept of reproduction in part within the meaning of Article 2 of Directive 2001/29, if the elements thus reproduced are the expression of the intellectual creation of their author; it is for the national court to make this determination.

[The CJEU also ruled: The act of printing out an extract of 11 words, during a data capture process such as that at issue in the main proceedings, does not fulfil the condition of being transient in nature as required by Article 5(1) of Directive 2001/29 and, therefore, that process cannot be carried out without the consent of the relevant rightholders.]

NOTES AND QUESTIONS

1. Under the *Infopaq* ruling, can copying an 11–word fragment from a news article without authorization of the author constitute copyright infringement? What if the 11–word fragment is not a complete sentence?

2. How does the requirement of intellectual creation (or originality) factor into the ECJ's decision? Is it easy or difficult to satisfy the requirement under the ECJ's analysis?

3. *News aggregators.* What impact might *Infopaq* have on news aggregators, like Google News, in Europe? Google News collects titles and a sentence or two from news articles, and presents them on a home page aggregating news from different sites. Should Google change its business model in Europe?

4. *U.S. approach.* A copy or quotation of only 11 words from a news article would probably be considered fair use or de minimis in the U.S. Which approach do you like better—the United States or EU's?

E. EXCEPTIONS TO EXCLUSIVE RIGHTS

1. BERNE CONVENTION AND TRIPS AGREEMENT

Both the Berne Convention Article 9(2) and the TRIPS Agreement Article 13 regulate the extent to which countries can have exceptions to copyright. The WTO clarified the meaning of Article 13 in the dispute below, elaborating what is known as the "3–step test." The 3–step test has become incredibly important in debates over copyright exceptions. Study the decision carefully.

Berne Convention (Paris 1971)

Article 9(2)

(2) It shall be a matter for legislation in the countries of the Union to permit the reproduction of such works in certain special cases, provided that such reproduction does not conflict with a normal exploitation of the work and does not unreasonably prejudice the legitimate interests of the author.

TRIPS

Article 13

Exceptions and limitations

Members shall confine limitations or exceptions to exclusive rights to certain special cases which do not conflict with a normal exploitation of the work and do not unreasonably prejudice the legitimate interests of the right holder.

From the beginning of copyright and international copyright agreements, countries have recognized a need to allow for some exceptions to exclusive rights of authors, in order to balance the interests of the public. Striking the right balance has never been uncontroversial, however. One country's view of the right balance may differ from another country's, depending on its economic position as well as its social and cultural heritage. For example, U.S. law has a relatively broad understanding of fair use that is consistent with its First Amendment tradition and protections. Advances in technology have continually created pressures for reexamining the internal balances of copyright systems. Today, the Internet and digital technology have forced such a reexamination.

In addressing exceptions to copyright, the major conventions typically do not require countries to adopt a certain kind of exception. Instead, they usually set forth general conditions to delimit when an exception may be permitted. Article 13 of TRIPS, for example, allows countries to have limitations or exceptions to exclusive rights, but only if confined "to certain special cases which do not conflict with a normal exploitation of the work and do not unreasonably prejudice the legitimate interests of the right holder." We will study below the WTO's test for determining whether an exception satisfies Article 13.

With similar language, Article 9 of the Berne Convention recognizes that countries may allow exceptions to the right of reproduction. Berne also contains other possible exemptions under Articles 2*bis* (political speeches and speeches in legal proceedings; reporting and broadcasting of public speeches), 10 (quotations consistent with fair practice; using works for illustration in teaching consistent with fair practice), 10*bis* (news related exemptions), 11*bis*(2) (compulsory licenses for public broadcasts and performances), and 13 (compulsory licenses for making of "cover" recordings). As should be evident, these provisions cover a medley of possible exceptions to copyright. Developing countries also have available the option of pursuing compulsory licenses to produce translations of copyrighted works under strict regulations set forth in the Appendix of Berne. Since TRIPS Article 9 incorporates these provisions of Berne, WTO countries also can adopt these Berne exemptions.

The Rome Convention allows several specific exceptions under Article 15, such as for private use, use of short excerpts in connection with the reporting of current events, and uses solely for the purposes of teaching and scientific research. Compare these provisions of the Berne and Rome Conventions, which are reproduced in the Documents Supplement.

PROBLEM 2–16

As the representative of Developed Country A, an economic competitor to the U.S., you have been enlisted by your country's government to consider whether your country should file a complaint with the WTO over the fair use provision under the U.S. Copyright Act, which states:

§ 107.   Limitations on exclusive rights: fair use

Notwithstanding the provisions of sections 106 and 106A, the fair use of a copyrighted work, including such use by reproduction in copies or phono-records or by any other means specified by that section, for purposes such as criticism, comment, news reporting, teaching (including multiple copies for classroom use), scholarship, or research, is not an infringement of copyright. In determining whether the use made of a work in any particular case is a fair use the factors to be considered shall include:

1.   The purpose and character of the use, including whether such use is of a commercial nature or is for nonprofit educational purposes;

2.   The nature of the copyrighted work;

3.   The amount and substantiality of the portion used in relation to the copyrighted work as a whole;

4.   The effect of the use upon the potential market for or value of the copyrighted work.

The fact that a work is unpublished shall not itself bar a finding of fair use if such finding is made upon consideration of all the above factors.

After doing some research of the U.S. fair use doctrine, you learn that fair use could be potentially made of every single copyrighted work by anyone. In other words, fair use is potentially available to 100% of the U.S. population for 100% of copyrighted works, at least in theory. As far as you can tell, there are no official statistics on the number of fair uses that take place in the U.S. each year, but you imagine that it is quite large. Although typically a fair use involves copying only a selected portion of a work, sometimes, as in the case of home recording of movies broadcast on TV for "time shifting" purposes for later viewing, a person may make a copy of the entire work for fair use. *Sony Corp. v. Universal City Studios, Inc.,* 464 U.S. 417 (1984); *see also Kelly v. Arriba Soft,* 336 F.3d 811 (9th Cir. 2003) (search engine's copying of photographs on websites and reproducing them in thumbnail version was fair use); *Sega Enters. Ltd. v. Accolade, Inc.,* 977 F.2d 1510 (9th Cir. 1992) (software developer's copying of video game to identify features necessary to write programs interoperable with competitor's machine was fair use). And, in describing what constitutes a fair use, the U.S. Supreme Court has said: fair use cannot "be simplified with bright-line rules, for the statute, like the doctrine it recognizes, calls for case-by-case analysis." *Campbell v. Acuff–Rose Music, Inc.,* 510 U.S. 569, 577 (1994).

As the representative of Developed Country A, evaluate the arguments that could be made to challenge the U.S. fair use doctrine as violating TRIPS Article 13. In doing so, consider whether the elements contained in Article 13 might be reflected or embodied in § 107. Are there other legal or factual issues that could bolster such a challenge that you would like to investigate? How might the U.S. respond to such a challenge? In deciding whether to recommend to Developed Country A to raise a challenge in the WTO, what factors would you consider? To answer this problem, consider the following WTO case on Article 13 of TRIPS.

UNITED STATES—SECTION 110(5) OF THE US COPYRIGHT ACT

Report of the Panel, WTO. (Carmen Luz Guarda, Chairperson; Arumugamangalam V. Ganesan, and Ian F. Sheppard, Members).
WT/DS160/R (June 15, 2000).

[On April 12, 1999 the European Communities initiated a dispute settlement proceeding under the auspices of the WTO against the United States concerning whether Section 110(5) of the U.S. Copyright Act of 1976, as amended by the Fairness in Music Licensing Act of 1998, was consistent with Article 13 of TRIPS. Section 110(5) placed certain limitations on the exclusive rights provided to owners in respect of certain performances and displays.[6] *Ed.*]

---

6. "§ 110. Limitations on exclusive rights: Exemption of certain performances and displays

Notwithstanding the provisions of section 106, the following are not infringements of copyright:

. . .

(5)(A) except as provided in subparagraph (B), communication of a transmission embodying a performance or display of a work by the public reception of the transmission on a single receiving apparatus of a kind commonly used in private homes, unless—

(i) a direct charge is made to see or hear the transmission; or

(ii) the transmission thus received is further transmitted to the public;

(B) communication by an establishment of a transmission or retransmission embodying a performance or display of a nondramatic musical work intended to be received by the general public, originated by a radio or television broadcast station licensed as such by the Federal Communications Commission, or, if an audiovisual transmission, by a cable system or satellite carrier, if—

(i) in the case of an establishment other than a food service or drinking establishment, either the establishment in which the communication occurs has less than 2,000 gross square feet of space (excluding space used for customer parking and for no other purpose), or the establishment in which the communication occurs has 2,000 or more gross square feet of space (excluding space used for customer parking and for no other purpose) and—

(I) if the performance is by audio means only, the performance is communicated by means of a total of not more than 6 loudspeakers, of which not more than 4 loudspeakers are located in any 1 room or adjoining outdoor space; or

(II) if the performance or display is by audiovisual means, any visual portion of the performance or display is communicated by means of a total of not more than 4 audiovisual devices, of which not more than 1 audiovisual device is located in any 1 room, and no such audiovisual device has a diagonal screen size greater than 55 inches, and any audio portion of the performance or display is communicated by means of a total of not more than 6 loudspeakers, of which not more than 4 loudspeakers are located in any 1 room or adjoining outdoor space;

(ii) in the case of a food service or drinking establishment, either the establishment in which the communication occurs has less than 3,750 gross square feet of space (excluding space used for customer parking and for no other purpose), or the establishment in which the communica-

2.   The three criteria test under Article 13 of the TRIPS Agreement

(a) General introduction

Article 13 of the TRIPS Agreement requires that limitations and exceptions to exclusive rights (1) be confined to certain special cases, (2) do not conflict with a normal exploitation of the work, and (3) do not unreasonably prejudice the legitimate interests of the right holder. The three conditions apply on a cumulative basis, each being a separate and independent requirement that must be satisfied. Failure to comply with any one of the three conditions results in the Article 13 exception being disallowed.

(b) "Certain special cases"

(i) General interpretative analysis

We start our analysis of the first condition of Article 13 by referring to the ordinary meaning of the terms in their context and in the light of its object and purpose. It appears that the notions of "exceptions" and "limitations" in the introductory words of Article 13 overlap in part in the sense that an "exception" refers to a derogation from an exclusive right provided under national legislation in some respect, while a "limitation" refers to a reduction of such right to a certain extent.

The ordinary meaning of "certain" is "known and particularised, but not explicitly identified," "determined, fixed, not variable; definitive, precise, exact." The New Shorter Oxford English Dictionary, Oxford (1993), p. 364. In other words, this term means that, under the first condition, an exception or limitation in national legislation must be clearly defined. However, there is no need to identify explicitly each and every possible situation to which the exception could apply, provided that the scope of the exception is known and particularised. This guarantees a sufficient degree of legal certainty.

We also have to give full effect to the ordinary meaning of the second word of the first condition. The term "special" connotes "having an individual or limited application or purpose", "containing details; precise,

---

tion occurs has 3,750 gross square feet of space or more (excluding space used for customer parking and for no other purpose) and—

   (I) if the performance is by audio means only, the performance is communicated by means of a total of not more than 6 loudspeakers, of which not more than 4 loudspeakers are located in any 1 room or adjoining outdoor space; or

   (II) if the performance or display is by audiovisual means, any visual portion of the performance or display is communicated by means of a total of not more than 4 audiovisual devices, of which not more than one audiovisual device is located in any 1 room, and no such audiovisual device has a diagonal screen size greater than 55 inches, and any audio portion of the performance or display is communicated by means of a total of not more than 6 loudspeakers, of which not more than 4 loudspeakers are located in any 1 room or adjoining outdoor space;

   (iii) no direct charge is made to see or hear the transmission or retransmission;

   (iv) the transmission or retransmission is not further transmitted beyond the establishment where it is received; and

   (v) the transmission or retransmission is licensed by the copyright owner of the work so publicly performed or displayed; and . . ."

specific", "exceptional in quality or degree; unusual; out of th
or "distinctive in some way." Oxford English Dictionary, p.
term means that more is needed than a clear definition in or
the standard of the first condition. In addition, an exception c
must be limited in its field of application or exceptional in i
other words, an exception or limitation should be narrow in (
as well as a qualitative sense. This suggests a narrow scope a
exceptional or distinctive objective. To put this aspect of the fir
into the context of the second condition ("no conflict witl
exploitation"), an exception or limitation should be the opposi
special, i.e., a normal case.

Footnote 68 in unedited version

(ii) The business exemption of subparagraph (B)

It appears that the European Communities does not dispu
that subparagraph (B) is clearly defined in respect of the si,
establishments and the type of equipment that may be used b
ments above the applicable limits. The primary bone of contention between the parties is whether the business exemption, given its scope and
reach, can be considered as a "special" case within the meaning of the
first condition of Article 13.

The Congressional Research Service ("CRS") estimated in 1995 the
percentage of the US eating and drinking establishments and retail
establishments that would have fallen at that time below the size limits of
3,500 square feet and 1,500 square feet respectively. Its study found that:

(d) 65.2 per cent of all eating establishments;

(e) 71.8 per cent of all drinking establishments; and

(f) 27 per cent of all retail establishments

would have fallen below these size limits.

The United States confirms these figures as far as eating and drinking establishments are concerned.

We note that this study was made in 1995 using the size limit of 3,500
square feet for eating and drinking establishments, and the size limit of
1,500 square feet for retail establishments, while the size limits under
subparagraph (B) now are 3,750 square feet for eating and drinking
establishments and 2,000 square feet for retail establishments. Therefore,
in our view, it is safe to assume that the actual percentage of establishments which may fall within the finally enacted business exemption in the
Fairness in Music Licensing Act of 1998 is higher than the above percent-
ages.

Referring to these studies, the European Communities points out that
these 70 per cent of eating and drinking establishments and 45 per cent of
retail establishments are all potential users of the business exemption,
because they can at any time, without permission of the right holders,
begin to play amplified music broadcasts.

The factual information presented to us indicates that a substantial majority of eating and drinking establishments and close to half of retail establishments are covered by the exemption contained in subparagraph (B) of Section 110(5) of the US Copyright Act. Therefore, we conclude that the exemption does not qualify as a "certain special case" in the meaning of the first condition of Article 13.

(iii) The homestyle exemption of subparagraph (A)

We examine now whether the homestyle exemption in subparagraph (A), in the form in which it is currently in force in the United States, is a "certain special case" in the meaning of the first condition of Article 13 of the TRIPS Agreement.

The United States submits that the exemption of subparagraph (A) is confined to "certain special cases," because its scope is limited to the use involving a "homestyle" receiving apparatus. In the US view, in the amended version of 1998 as well, this is a well-defined fact-specific standard. The essentially identical description of the homestyle exemption in the original Section 110(5) of 1976 was sufficiently clear and narrow for US courts to reasonably and consistently apply the exception—including square footage limitation since the *Aiken* case—in a number of individual decisions. For the United States, the fact that judges have weighed the various factors slightly differently in making their individual decisions is simply a typical feature of a common-law system.

The European Communities contends that the criteria of the homestyle exemption in subparagraph (A) are ambiguously worded because the expression "a single receiving apparatus of a kind commonly used in private homes" is in itself imprecise and a "moving target" due to technological development. Also the variety of approaches and factors used by US courts in applying the original version of the homestyle exemption are proof for the European Communities that the wording of subparagraph (A) of Section 110(5) is vague and open-ended.

Beneficiaries of the homestyle exemption

The wording of the amended version of Section 110(5)(A) is essentially identical to the wording of Section 110(5) in its previous version of 1976, apart from the introductory phrase "except as provided in subparagraph (B)." Therefore, we consider that the practice as reflected in the judgments rendered by US courts after 1976 concerning the original homestyle exemption may be regarded as factually indicative of the reach of the homestyle exemption even after the 1998 Amendment.

We recall that in *Twentieth Century Music Corp. v. Aiken*, the Court held that an owner of a small fast food restaurant was not liable for playing music by means of a radio with outlets to four speakers in the ceiling. The size of the shop was 1,055 square feet (98m^2), of which 620 square feet (56m^2) were open to the public. In the evolution of case law, subsequent to the inclusion of the original homestyle exemption in the

Copyright Act of 1976 in reaction to the *Aiken* judgment, US courts have considered a number of factors to determine whether a shop or restaurant could benefit from the exemption. These factors have included: (i) physical size of an establishment in terms of square footage (in comparison to the size of the *Aiken* restaurant); (ii) extent to which the receiving apparatus was to be considered as one commonly used in private homes; (iii) distance between the receiver and the speakers; (iv) number of speakers; (v) whether the speakers were free-standing or built into the ceiling; (vi) whether, depending on its revenue, the establishment was of a type that would normally subscribe to a background music service; (vii) noise level of the areas within the establishment where the transmissions were made audible or visible; and (viii) configuration of the installation. In some federal circuits, US courts have focused primarily on the plain language of the homestyle exemption that refers to "a single receiving apparatus of a kind commonly used in private homes."

We note that the parties have submitted quantitative information on the coverage of subparagraph (A) with respect to eating, drinking and other establishments. The 1995 CRS study found that:

(a) 16 per cent of all US eating establishments;

(b) 13.5 per cent of all US drinking establishments; and

(c) 18 per cent of all US retail establishments

were as big as or smaller than the *Aiken* restaurant (1,055 square feet of total space), and could thus benefit from the homestyle exemption. These figures are not disputed between the parties. The United States expressly confirms these figures as far as eating and drinking establishments are concerned.

We believe that from a quantitative perspective the reach of subparagraph (A) in respect of potential users is limited to a comparably small percentage of all eating, drinking and retail establishments in the United States.

Homestyle equipment

We note that what is referred to as homestyle equipment might vary between different countries, is subject to changing consumer preferences in a given country, and may evolve as a result of technological development. We thus agree in principle with the European Communities that the homestyle equipment that was used in US households in 1976 (when the original homestyle exemption was enacted) is not necessarily identical to the equipment used in 1998 (when US copyright legislation was amended) or at a future point in time. However, we recall that the term "*certain special case*" connotes "known and particularised, but not explicitly identified." In our view, the term "homestyle equipment" expresses the degree of clarity in definition required under Article 13's first condition. In our view, a Member is not required to identify homestyle equipment in terms of exceedingly detailed technical specifications in order to meet the standard of clarity set by the first condition.

Musical works covered by subparagraph (A)

We have noted the common view of the parties that the addition of the introductory phrase "except as provided in subparagraph (B)" to the homestyle exemption in the 1998 Amendment should be understood by way of an *a contrario* argument as limiting the coverage of the exemption to works other than "nondramatic" musical works. As regards musical works, the currently applicable version of the homestyle exemption is thus understood to apply to the communication of music that is part of an opera, operetta, musical or other similar dramatic work when performed in a dramatic context. All other musical works are covered by the expression "nondramatic" musical works, including individual songs taken from dramatic works when performed outside any dramatic context. Subparagraph (B) would, therefore, apply for example to an individual song taken from a musical and played on the radio. Consequently, given the common view of the parties, the operation of subparagraph (A) is limited to such musical works as are not covered by subparagraph (B), for example a communication of a broadcast of a dramatic rendition of the music written for an opera, operetta, musical or other similar works.

In practice, this means that most if not virtually all music played on the radio or television is covered by subparagraph (B). Subparagraph (A) covers, in accordance with the common understanding of the parties, dramatic renditions of operas, operettas, musicals and other similar dramatic works. We consider that limiting the application of subparagraph (A) to the public communication of transmissions embodying such works, gives its provisions a quite narrow scope of application in practice.

Taking into account the specific limits imposed in subparagraph (A) and its legislative history, as well as in its considerably narrow application in the subsequent court practice on the beneficiaries of the exemption, permissible equipment and categories of works, we are of the view that the homestyle exemption in subparagraph (A) of Section 110(5) as amended in 1998 is well-defined and limited in its scope and reach. We, therefore, conclude that the exemption is confined to certain special cases within the meaning of the first condition of Article 13 of the TRIPS Agreement.

(c) "Not conflict with a normal exploitation of the work"

(i) General interpretative analysis

In interpreting the second condition of Article 13, we first need to define what "exploitation" of a "work" means. More importantly, we have to determine what constitutes a "normal" exploitation, with which a derogation is not supposed to "conflict."

The ordinary meaning of the term "exploit" connotes "making use of" or "utilising for one's own ends." Oxford English Dictionary, p. 888. We believe that "exploitation" of musical works thus refers to the activity by which copyright owners employ the exclusive rights conferred on them to extract economic value from their rights to those works.

We note that the ordinary meaning of the term "normal" can be defined as "constituting or conforming to a type or standard; regular, usual, typical, ordinary, conventional ..." Oxford English Dictionary, p. 1940. In our opinion, these definitions appear to reflect two connotations: the first one appears to be of an empirical nature, i.e., what is regular, usual, typical or ordinary. The other one reflects a somewhat more normative, if not dynamic, approach, i.e., conforming to a type or standard. We do not feel compelled to pass a judgment on which one of these connotations could be more relevant. Based on Article 31 of the Vienna Convention, we will attempt to develop a harmonious interpretation which gives meaning and effect to both connotations of "normal."

If "normal" exploitation were equated with full use of all exclusive rights conferred by copyrights, the exception clause of Article 13 would be left devoid of meaning. Therefore, "normal" exploitation clearly means something less than full use of an exclusive right.

We believe that an exception or limitation to an exclusiv[e] domestic legislation rises to the level of a conflict with a norma[l exploita]tion of the work (i.e., the copyright or rather the whole bundle o[f exclusive] rights conferred by the ownership of the copyright), if use[s that, in] principle are covered by that right but exempted under the ex[ception or] limitation, enter into economic competition with the ways t[hat the right] holders normally extract economic value from that right to the [work (i.e.,] the copyright) and thereby deprive them of significant or tang[ible com]mercial gains.

Footnote 71 on unedited version of Article

(iii) The homestyle exemption of subparagraph (A)*

It is our understanding that the parties agree that the right holders do not normally license or attempt to license the public communication of transmissions embodying dramatic renditions of "dramatic" musical works in the sense of Article 11*bis*(1)(iii) and/or 11(1)(ii). We have not been provided with information about any existing licensing practices concerning the communication to the public of broadcasts of performances of dramatic works (e.g., operas, operettas, musicals) by eating, drinking or retail establishments in the United States or any other country. In this respect, we fail to see how the homestyle exemption, as limited to works other than nondramatic musical works in its revised form, could acquire economic or practical importance of any considerable dimension for the right holders of musical works.

Therefore, we conclude that the homestyle exemption contained in subparagraph (A) of Section 110(5) does not conflict with a normal exploitation of works within the meaning of the second condition of Article 13.

---

* The WIPO panel's application of the two remaining factors of the 3–part test to the business exemption under 110(5)(B) is omitted. *Ed.*

(d) "Not unreasonably prejudice the legitimate interests of the right holder"

(i) General interpretative analysis

Given that the parties do not question the "legitimacy" of the interest of right holders to exercise their rights for economic gain, the crucial question becomes which degree or level of "prejudice" may be considered as "unreasonable." Before dealing with the question of what amount or which kind of prejudice reaches a level beyond reasonable, we need to find a way to measure or quantify legitimate interests.

In our view, one—albeit incomplete and thus conservative—way of looking at legitimate interests is the economic value of the exclusive rights conferred by copyright on their holders. It is possible to estimate in ecᵒⁿᵒmic terms the value of exercising, e.g., by licensing, such rights. That ᵢ̣t to say that legitimate interests are necessarily limited to this ᵒmic value.

ᵗhe crucial question is which degree or level of "prejudice" may be ᵈered as "unreasonable," given that, under the third condition, a ᵢn amount of "prejudice" has to be presumed justified as "not ᵢsonable." In our view, prejudice to the legitimate interests of right ᵣs reaches an unreasonable level if an exception or limitation causes ᵢs the potential to cause an unreasonable loss of income to the ᵢght owner.

mate interests of right holders of EC, US and third-country origin

We note the EC argument that, in respect of all conditions of Article 13, the effect on all right holders from all WTO Members must be taken into account.

In this case, both parties have provided estimations on the market share of music of EC right holders. The European Communities submits that at least 25 per cent of all music played in the United States belongs to EC copyright owners. This figure is based on an industry estimate according to which the United Kingdom performing artists had a 23 per cent share of the US record sales in 1988. The European Communities appears to imply that this figure concerning United Kingdom performing artists would be indicative of the share due to EC composers and other copyright holders of the royalties collected for the amplification of music transmissions. The European Communities adds that another way to estimate EC authors' market share is to look at the royalty distributions by the US CMOs. The European Communities gives a figure, provided by ASCAP for 1998, indicating what percentage of its total distributions were paid to EC right holders; this figure is not reproduced here, given that the figure was given to the European Communities in confidence.

The United States disagrees with the EC's implication that 25 per cent of royalties collected in the United States are due to EC right holders. According to the United States, a 1998 internal EC analysis of the economic effect of the homestyle exemption on EC right holders estimated that just 6.2 per cent of ASCAP revenues were distributed to all foreign CMOs, and that just 5.6 per cent of BMI revenues were due to all foreign CMOs. Obviously, the percentage payable to the EC collecting societies would be significantly less than these figures for total payments to all foreign CMOs.

The United States submits that the economic effect of the original homestyle exemption of Section 110(5) of 1976 was minimal. Its intent was to exempt from liability small shop and restaurant owners whose establishments would not have justified a commercial licence. Given that such establishments are not a significant licensing market, they could not be significant sources of revenue for right holders. Where no licences would be sought or issued in the absence of an exception, there was literally no economic detriment to the right holder from an explicit exception. Exempted establishments with small square footage and elementary sound equipment are the least likely to be aggressively licensed by the CMOs and licensing fees for these establishments would likely be the lowest in the range. Given their size and that the playing of music is often incidental to their services, these establishments are among those most likely simply to turn off the radio if pressed to pay licensing fees. The 1998 Amendment has only decreased the economic relevance of the exemption by reducing its scope to "dramatic" musical works. Therefore, in the US view, the homestyle exemption as contained in subparagraph (A) of Section 110(5) does not prejudice the legitimate interests of the right holder.

In the light of the considerations above, we conclude that the homestyle exemption contained in subparagraph (A) of Section 110(5) does not cause unreasonable prejudice to the legitimate interests of the right holders within the meaning of the third condition of Article 13.

VII. CONCLUSIONS AND RECOMMENDATIONS

In the light of the findings above, the Panel concludes that:

(a) Subparagraph (A) of Section 110(5) of the US Copyright Act meets the requirements of Article 13 of the TRIPS Agreement and is thus consistent with Articles 11*bis*(1)(iii) and 11(1)(ii) of the Berne Convention (1971) as incorporated into the TRIPS Agreement by Article 9.1 of that Agreement.

(b) Subparagraph (B) of Section 110(5) of the US Copyright Act does not meet the requirements of Article 13 of the TRIPS Agreement and is thus inconsistent with Articles 11*bis*(1)(iii) and 11(1)(ii) of the Berne Convention (1971) as incorporated into the TRIPS Agreement by Article 9.1 of that Agreement.

The Panel *recommends* that the Dispute Settlement Body request the United States to bring subparagraph (B) of Section 110(5) into conformity with its obligations under the TRIPS Agreement.

NOTES AND QUESTIONS

1. *TRIPS Article 13.* Does TRIPS Article 13 give countries sufficient flexibility to allow countries to have exceptions to copyright that can accommodate the public's interest? What are the public's interests with respect to creative works? If some members of the public have complaints that TRIPS is too limited in recognizing copyright exceptions, how would such members of the public go about airing their concerns?

2. *Three-step test.* Explain the 3–step test and how it operates. How, if at all, are steps 2 and 3 different?

3. *The Aiken "homestyle" exception.* The WTO panel in the *110(5)* case based its analysis of § 110(5)(A), the homestyle exception, on the understanding—agreed to by both the U.S. and European representatives—that the homestyle exception applies only to *dramatic* musical works, such as an opera. Is this interpretation of § 110(5)(A) correct? Is there support in the language of the statute for such a limitation?

In *Aiken*, the Supreme Court dealt with copyrighted works—specifically, two nondramatic musical works—received on a homestyle device such as the radio. *See Twentieth Century Music Corp. v. Aiken*, 422 U.S. 151, 152–53 (1975). When Congress codified the rule of *Aiken* as an exemption in § 110(5) of the Copyright Act of 1976, the exemption applied generally to "a work" without limitation. Leading commentators agree that § 110(5)(A) still applies to all works generally, including nondramatic musical works, such as contemporary songs aired on the radio. *See* PAUL GOLDSTEIN, GOLDSTEIN ON COPYRIGHT § 7.8.1.5, at 7:183 (3d ed. 2005); 2 MELVILLE B. NIMMER & DAVID NIMMER, NIMMER ON COPYRIGHT § 8.18[C][2][c] (2004); Lawrence R. Helfer, *World Music on a U.S. Stage: A Berne/TRIPS and Economic Analysis of The Fairness in Music Licensing Act*, 80 B.U. L. REV. 93, 96 n.7 (2000). No U.S. court has interpreted § 110(5)(A) to be limited to dramatic musical works. And nothing in the legislative history in the 1998 amendment to § 110(5)(A) supports such a limitation being read into the text of the provision. *See* Helfer, *supra*, at 96 n.7. Would such a limited exception for homestyle devices make sense? After all, how often do radio stations even play operas and musicals, and how often do people listen to them in public establishments, such as bars and "ma and pa" eateries like the chicken carry-out restaurant in *Aiken*?

Would the outcome in the *110(5)* case be different if the WTO panel interpreted the homestyle provision to apply to all musical works—and, indeed, to all works generally, including public broadcasts of movies, shows, and sporting events? Why did the U.S. Trade Representative propound to the WTO panel an interpretation of the homestyle exception that is unsupported by any case law and that is almost certainly wrong? Should a WTO panel rely on a legal interpretation of parties that is not disputed, or should a panel make an independent assessment of its own, perhaps with the enlistment of legal experts? Under Article 13(2) of the Dispute Settlement Understanding, a panel "may seek information from any relevant source and may consult experts to obtain their opinion on certain aspects of the matter."

4. *The business establishment exemption.* Section 110(5)(B) attempted to exempt certain food or drinking establishments from airing of transmissions of nondramatic musical works based on the square footage of the establishment and kind of equipment used. What did the WTO panel find was wrong with this section? Could the U.S. Congress rewrite the provision in a way to address the WTO panel's concerns?

5. *Violating TRIPS—at what cost?* Following the WTO decision, the U.S. has refused to change its law (§ 110(5)(B)) that was found to be in violation of TRIPS. Instead, the U.S. and EU agreed to have their differences submitted to WTO Arbitration under the authority of Article 25 of the Dispute Settlement Understanding. The WTO arbitration determined that the U.S. should pay the EU countries over $1 million damages for every year the U.S. law is not changed; eventually, the U.S. agreed to pay the EU countries a total of $3.3 million for a three-year period ending on December 2004. Still, the U.S. has not changed the provision that violates TRIPS. *See* Alain J. Lapter, *The WTO's Dispute Resolution Mechanism: Does the United States Take It Seriously? A TRIPS Analysis*, 4 CHI.-KENT J. INTELL. PROP. 217, 251 (2005). What does the U.S.'s refusal to change its noncompliant law suggest? Does it support the view of Professors Goldsmith and Posner, discussed in Chapter 1, that countries follow international law only out of self-interest?

2. COUNTRIES' APPROACHES TO COPYRIGHT EXCEPTIONS

PROBLEM 2–17

The WTO has commissioned you to prepare a report discussing whether the TRIPS Agreement should be amended to include copyright exceptions that either must be recognized by countries or that may be recognized at their discretion. As discussed earlier, Berne contains such exceptions to copyright, but TRIPS does not—instead opting for a general provision limiting exceptions in Article 13. By contrast, the 2001 EU Information Society Directive, 2001/29/EC, recognizes a list of 15 specific copyright exceptions that EU members may adopt, subject to the proviso that they "shall only be applied in certain special cases which do not conflict with a normal exploitation of the work or other subject-matter and do not unreasonably prejudice the legitimate interests of the rightholder." In preparing your report, analyze: (i) the merits of recognizing specific copyright exceptions in TRIPS, (ii) whether payment to copyright holders should be required, and (iii) whether the 3–step test under TRIPS Article 13 should apply to your proposed exceptions or whether the WTO should make such inquiry unnecessary for any enumerated exceptions in TRIPS. Consider the following discussion.

* * *

Over the years, countries have developed various exceptions to copyright, often in a style distinctive to a particular country. Article 13 of TRIPS and the 3–step test formulated by the WTO panel in *Section 110(5)* appear to gloss over the fact that copyright exceptions come in many shapes and sizes—which is not surprising given the different cultures, traditions, and economies among countries.

There are several different ways copyright exceptions may be categorized. One way would be to focus on the divide between common law and civil law countries. That distinction, however, crumbles in analysis, given the considerable overlap in approach among countries. While the former British colonies were influenced by Britain's fair dealing exception, today the level of influence varies. Australia, Canada, and Caribbean countries that were in the British Commonwealth tend to follow the British mold closely, whereas the U.S. has developed its own distinctive brand of fair use. Likewise, civil law countries typically recognize specific, enumerated copyright exceptions, but so do all common law countries as well. Given this overlap, a more fruitful comparison would focus instead on factors related to the style and content of the exceptions.

Specific, enumerated exceptions v. general exceptions. The first factor to consider in categorizing copyright exceptions is how specific they are. Some copyright exceptions set forth in detail the specific activity that is exempted. For example, Argentina has an exemption stating: "Any person may publish, for didactic or scientific purposes, comments, criticisms or notes referring to intellectual works, including up to 1,000 words for literary or scientific works, or eight bars in musical works and, in all cases, only the parts of the text essential for that purpose." Argentina Law of Sept. 28, 1933, § 10. Argentina's exception is a rule that sets forth *ex ante* exactly what is permitted.

By contrast, other copyright exceptions incorporate open-ended standards that require case-by-case analysis of the particular circumstances of each use. The U.S. fair use exception is a good example of a standard. To determine whether something is a fair use typically requires consideration of four statutory factors as applied to the particular facts of a case. Sometimes, countries incorporate both a rule and a standard together. The UK fair dealing exceptions specify three purposes that are allowed for fair dealing (research or private study, criticism or review, or reporting current events), but whether a use of a copyrighted work for these purposes is "fair" ultimately depends on a case-by-case analysis. In some instances, the UK Copyright Act even specifies, in rule-like fashion, what is *not* fair dealing. *See* UK Copyright, Designs and Patents Act 1988, §§ 28–30.

Applying the specific versus general factor, countries fall along the following fault line. All countries enumerate specific exceptions to copyright. The number of exceptions in a country ranges from a low of 2 (Micronesia) to a high of 53 (Ireland). For some countries, especially civil law countries, specific exceptions are the only form recognized. By contrast, the U.S., UK, Israel, and Commonwealth countries, recognize not only specific exceptions, but also some exception(s) that incorporate a more open-ended standard of "fair use" or "fair dealing." As noted earlier, the two concepts, fair use and fair dealing, are not the same. Fair use is more general than fair dealing and hence may apply to a much broader set of uses in a greater number of circumstances. Thus, one advantage of the fair use provision is that it can be applied to deal with new circumstances, such as new technologies, without requiring legislative action for every single new development. Several commentators in continental Europe have recognized this advantage of fair use and have proposed incorporating fair use principles in some fashion in their own laws. European commentators disagree on whether current EU law would allow countries to recognize fair use in the EU, however. *See* Ian Hargreaves, *Digital Opportunity: A Review of Intellectual Property and Growth* (May 2011). One downside to the open-endedness of fair use is that it may not give enough guidance to the public on what is permissible. To deal with this problem, Israel's Copyright Act gives the Minister of Justice the power to "make regulations prescribing conditions under which a use shall be deemed a fair use." Israel Copyright Act, § 19 (2007). Some scholars argue that the U.S. Copyright Office should be given a similar administrative power in the United States.

Payment v. free uses. The second factor that distinguishes various copyright exceptions is whether payment to the copyright holders is required. U.S. copyright exceptions allow free uses without any payment required to the copyright holders, although the U.S. does also recognize several compulsory licenses. Most copyright exceptions among countries follow the free use approach. By contrast, Germany has several copyright exceptions that require payment of "equitable remuneration" to the author. *See, e.g.*, German Copyright Law, §§ 46(4), 47(2), 49(1), 52(2).

The decision whether to allow a copyright exception does not have to be all-or-nothing. A country might recognize an exemption to copyright, such as for private copying, while, at the same time, impose a fee or a levy on the public, such as on the purchase or use of copying technology, in order to compensate copyright holders for private copying of their works. For example, the European Union Directive on Copyright and Related Rights in the Information Society, 2001/29/EC ("Information Society Directive") allows, in Article 5(2)(b), EU countries to recognize a copyright exception for private copying, but only on "the condition that the rightholders receive fair compensation which takes account of the application or non-application of technological measures referred to in Article 6 to the work or subject-matter concerned."

How to determine what constitutes "fair compensation" is not defined in the Information Society Directive. Not surprisingly, disagreement arose over the meaning of the term. Spain enacted a copyright levy for private copying equipment that imposed a flat fee on copying equipment sold, irrespective of whether the purchaser was a private individual, or commercial entity or business. A Spanish manufacturer of CD, DVD, and MP3 devices refused to pay the levy to the collecting society SGAE (Sociedad General de Autores y Editores de Espana), on the ground that the levy violated the EU Directive's standard of "fair compensation." Below is the CJEU's decision after a referral from the Barcelona Court of Appeal.

PADAWAN SL v. SOCIEDAD GENERAL DE AUTORES Y EDITORES DE ESPAÑA (SGAE)

Court of Justice of the European Union.
C–467/08 (Oct. 21, 2010).

This reference for a preliminary ruling concerns the interpretation of the concept of 'fair compensation' in Article 5(2)(b) of Directive

2001/29/EC of the European Parliament and of the Council of 22 May 2001 on the harmonisation of certain aspects of copyright and related rights in the information society (OJ 2001 L 167, p. 10) paid to copyright holders in respect of the 'private copying exception.'

The questions referred for a preliminary ruling

The first question

By its first question, the national court asks, in essence, whether the concept of 'fair compensation', within the meaning of Article 5(2)(b) of Directive 2001/29, is an autonomous concept of European Union law which must be interpreted in a uniform manner in all Member States, irrespective of the Member States' right to choose the system of collection.

It is clear from that case-law that the concept of 'fair compensation' which appears in a provision of a directive which does not contain any reference to national laws must be regarded as an autonomous concept of European Union law and interpreted uniformly throughout the European Union.

That conclusion is supported by the objective pursued by the legislation in which the concept of fair compensation appears.

The objective of Directive 2001/29, based, in particular, on Article 95 EC and intended to harmonise certain aspects of the law on copyright and related rights in the information society and to ensure competition in the internal market is not distorted as a result of Member States' different legislation requires the elaboration of autonomous concepts of European Union law. The European Union legislature's aim of achieving the most uniform interpretation possible of Directive 2001/29 is apparent in particular from recital 32 in the preamble thereto, which calls on the Member States to arrive at a coherent application of the exceptions to and limitations on reproduction rights, with the aim of ensuring a functioning internal market. * * * [The CJEU's analysis of the second question is omitted. *Ed.*]

The third and fourth questions

By its third and fourth questions, which it is appropriate to examine together, the national court asks essentially whether, under Article 5(2)(b) of Directive 2001/29, there is a necessary link between the application of the levy intended to finance fair compensation with respect to digital reproduction equipment, devices and media, and the deemed use of the latter for the purposes of private copying. It also asks whether the indiscriminate application of the private copying levy, in particular with respect to digital reproduction equipment, devices and media clearly intended for uses other than the production of private copies, complies with Directive 2001/29.

It must be held from the outset that a system for financing fair compensation such as that described in paragraphs 46 and 48 of this judgment is compatible with the requirements of a 'fair balance' only if the digital reproduction equipment, devices and media concerned are liable to be used for private copying and, therefore, are likely to cause harm to the author of the protected work. There is therefore, having regard to those requirements, a necessary link between the application of the private copying levy to the digital reproduction equipment, devices and media and their use for private copying.

Consequently, the indiscriminate application of the private copying levy to all types of digital reproduction equipment, devices and media, including in the case expressly mentioned by the national court in which they are acquired by persons other than natural persons for purposes clearly unrelated to private copying, does not comply with Article 5(2)(b) of Directive 2001/29.

On the other hand, where the equipment at issue has been made available to natural persons for private purposes it is unnecessary to show that they have in fact made private copies with the help of that equipment and have therefore actually caused harm to the author of the protected work.

Those natural persons are rightly presumed to benefit fully from the making available of that equipment, that is to say that they are deemed to take full advantage of the functions associated with that equipment, including copying.

It follows that the fact that that equipment or devices are able to make copies is sufficient in itself to justify the application of the private copying levy, provided that the equipment or devices have been made available to natural persons as private users.

Such an interpretation is supported by the wording of recital 35 in the preamble to Directive 2001/29. That recital mentions, as a valuable criterion for the determination of the level of fair compensation, not only the 'harm' as such but also the 'possible' harm. The 'possibility' of causing harm to the author of the protected work depends on the fulfilment of the necessary pre-condition that equipment or devices which allow copying have been made available to natural persons, which need not necessarily be followed by the actual production of private copies.

Furthermore, the Court has already held that, from the copyright point of view, account must be taken of the mere possibility for the ultimate user, in that case customers of a hotel, to watch programmes broadcast by means of a television set and a television signal made available to them by that establishment, and not the actual access of the customers to those works (Case C–306/05 *SGAE* [2006] ECR I–11519, paragraphs 43 and 44).

On those grounds, the Court (Third Chamber) hereby rules:

Article 5(2)(b) of Directive 2001/29 must be interpreted as meaning that the 'fair balance' between the persons concerned means that fair compensation must be calculated on the basis of the criterion of the harm caused to authors of protected works by the introduction of the private copying exception. It is consistent with the requirements of that 'fair balance' to provide that persons who have digital reproduction equipment, devices and media and who on that basis, in law or in fact, make that equipment available to private users or provide them with copying services are the persons liable to finance the fair compensation, inasmuch as they are able to pass on to private users the actual burden of financing it.

Article 5(2)(b) of Directive 2001/29 must be interpreted as meaning that a link is necessary between the application of the levy intended to finance fair compensation with respect to digital reproduction equipment, devices and media and the deemed use of them for the purposes of private copying. Consequently, the indiscriminate application of the private copying levy, in particular with respect to digital reproduction equipment, devices and media not made available to private users and clearly reserved for uses other than private copying, is incompatible with Directive 2001/29.

NOTES AND QUESTIONS

1. Based on the CJEU's ruling, do you think Spain's private copying levy violated Article 5(2)(b) of the EU Information Society Directive? Assuming there was a violation, how could Spain draft a levy provision that complies with Article 5(2)(b)?

2. What did Padawan, the Spanish manufacturer, have to gain by challenging the Spanish copyright levy? Was the CJEU ruling a victory for Padawan? What about other copy equipment manufacturers in Europe?

3. The *Padawan* case has importance for other countries in the EU, such as Germany and the Netherlands, which had copyright levy laws similar to Spain's. One can expect similar challenges to copyright levy laws based on the "fair compensation" principle. Do you expect copyright holders or equipment manufacturers to raise these challenges?

4. *Cross-border sales.* In *Stichting de Thuiskopie v. Opus Supplies Deutschland GmbH*, C–462/09 (June 16, 2011), the CJEU ruled that one EU state (Netherlands) could impose a copyright levy on a manufacturer located in another EU state (Germany) that sold copy equipment to a person in the first EU state. The CJEU ruled: "Directive 2001/29, in particular Article 5(2)(b) and (5) thereof, must be interpreted as meaning that it is for the Member State which has introduced a system of private copying levies chargeable to the manufacturer or importer of media for reproduction of protected works, and on the territory of which the harm caused to authors by the use for private purposes of their work by purchasers who reside there occurs, to ensure that those authors actually receive the fair compensation intended to compensate them for that harm. In that regard, the mere fact that the commercial seller of reproduction equipment, devices and media is established in a Member State other than that in which the purchasers reside has no bearing on that obligation to achieve a certain result." *Id.* ¶ 42.

F. COPYRIGHT TERM AND NEIGHBORING RIGHT TERM

1. BASIC APPROACH AND RULE OF THE SHORTER TERM

Berne Convention (Paris 1971)

Article 7

(1) The term of protection granted by this Convention shall be the life of the author and fifty years after his death.

(2) However, in the case of cinematographic works, the countries of the Union may provide that the term of protection shall expire fifty years after the work has been made available to the public with the consent of the author, or, failing such an event within fifty years from the making of such a work, fifty years after the making.

(3) In the case of anonymous or pseudonymous works, the term of protection granted by this Convention shall expire fifty years after the work has been lawfully made available to the public. However, when the pseudonym adopted by the author leaves no doubt as to his identity, the term of protection shall be that provided in paragraph (1). If the author of an anonymous or pseudonymous work discloses his identity during the above-mentioned period, the term of protection applicable shall be that provided in paragraph (1). The countries of the Union shall not be required to protect anonymous or pseudonymous works in respect of which it is reasonable to presume that their author has been dead for fifty years.

(4) It shall be a matter for legislation in the countries of the Union to determine the term of protection of photographic works and that of works of applied art in so far as they are protected as artistic works; however, this term shall last at least until the end of a period of twenty-five years from the making of such a work.

(5) The term of protection subsequent to the death of the author and the terms provided by paragraphs (2), (3), and (4) shall run from the date of death or of the event referred to in those paragraphs, but such terms shall always be deemed to begin on the first of January of the year following the death or such event.

(6) The countries of the Union may grant a term of protection in excess of those provided by the preceding paragraphs.

(7) Those countries of the Union bound by the Rome Act of this Convention which grant, in their national legislation in force at the time of signature of the present Act, shorter terms of protection than those provided for in the preceding paragraphs shall have the right to maintain such terms when ratifying or acceding to the present Act.

(8) In any case, the term shall be governed by the legislation of the country where protection is claimed; however, unless the legislation of that country otherwise provides, the term shall not exceed the term fixed in the country of origin of the work.

Article 7bis

The provisions of * * * Article [7] shall also apply in the case of a work of joint authorship, provided that the terms measured from the death of the author shall be calculated from the death of the last surviving author.

TRIPS

Article 12

Term of Protection

Whenever the term of protection of a work, other than a photographic work or a work of applied art, is calculated on a basis other than the life of a natural person, such term shall be no less than 50 years from the end of the calendar year of authorized publication, or, failing such authorized publication within 50 years from the making of the work, 50 years from the end of the calendar year of making.

* * *

Basic terms. One of the most basic questions for any grant of intellectual property right is deciding how long it should last. Theoretically, one might decide that the right should last forever. The early development of copyright in England—i.e., the monopoly rights held by the Stationers' Company—provides one example of an unlimited right. Perpetual copyrights, however, are hard to justify from a utilitarian view because they more than likely compensate the author far beyond any incentive needed to create. Moreover, perpetual copyrights impose considerable costs in terms of diminishing or retarding the ability of others to disseminate, use, and build on existing works, even well after the authors are long dead. For example, there would be far fewer performances and derivative works of Shakespeare, arguably, if all of his works were still copyrighted today. For this reason, starting with the Statute of Anne in 1710, countries have recognized the need for limited terms of copyright. A limited term ensures the existence of a public domain, in which people can freely use the works.

The Berne Convention and TRIPS Agreement set forth minimum requirements on the term of copyright. Article 7(1) of Berne establishes the general minimum standard of life of the author plus 50 years—which is sometimes referred to as 50 years p.m.a. or *post mortem auctoris*. The term was viewed as allowing authors and their direct descendants (a perceived span of three generations, including the author and two generations of descendants) to benefit from income earned through their copyrighted works. Of course, countries are free to exceed these requirements (see Berne Conv. art. 7(5)); the EU and U.S. have already done so in recognizing a term of life of the author plus 70 years. A single work may be subject, therefore, to different copyright terms in different Berne countries. Article 7(5) of Berne makes clear that the term of protection runs from the 1st of January in the year *following* the author's death. For example, if an author dies on January 15, 2000, the starting point for the 50 additional years of copyright begins on January 1, 2001. In such case, the copyright is effectively receiving close to one extra year beyond the life of the author plus 50 years. The January 1st starting point, however, provides a uniform date on which all works will expire.

Article 7(2) of Berne allows countries to adopt an alternative copyright term for films: "the countries of the Union may provide that the term of protection shall expire fifty years after the work has been made available to the public with the consent of the author, or, failing such an event fifty years from the making of such a work, fifty years after the making." The rule was adopted based on the recognition that there may be numerous authors or a corporate author of a film for which the "life of the author" standard might present difficulties. As Article 7*bis* indicates, the minimum term for works of joint authors under the standard approach of Article 7(1) is the life of the *last* surviving author plus 50 years. Thus, the alternative standard in Article 7(2) avoids the complexity of having to determine who the last surviving author of a film is.

Anonymous and pseudonymous works also have a special term under Article 7(3) of Berne: 50 years after the work has been lawfully made available to the public (unless the true identity of the author is known, in which case the standard life of the author plus 50 years applies). This provision was adopted in part to deal with the problem of folklore, for which at times the author's identity is unknown. Article 7(3), however, sets a limit for authors presumed to be long dead: countries "shall not be required to protect anonymous or pseudonymous works in respect of which it is reasonable to presume that their author has been dead for fifty years."

Given prior disagreements among countries about the copyrighting of photographs and works of applied art as a class of works, Berne Article 7(4) allows countries to adopt the minimum standard of 25 years from the making of such works if they are protected as artistic works in a particular country.

Article 12 of TRIPS clarifies how to compute copyright terms for works that are not based on the life of the author: "[S]uch term shall be no less than 50 years from the end of the calendar year of authorized publication, or, failing such authorized publication within 50 years from the making of the work, 50 years from the end of the calendar year of making." This effectively closed a gap left open by Berne in not specifically addressing corporate authors, which had left countries at somewhat of a loss on how to treat corporations, if at all. A number of continental European countries recognize that only natural persons can be authors, at least in most cases. TRIPS Article 12 appears to tacitly recognize that some countries may choose to treat corporations as authors—if they do so, they can grant copyrights of at least 50 years duration. However, photographic works and works of applied art are not included within this 50–year minimum standard—the 25 years of Berne still applies for these kinds of works.

Rule of the shorter term. One of the most important principles used by countries to resolve discrepancies in copyright terms is contained in Article 7(8), called the "rule of the shorter term." Under this rule, a country with a longer copyright term does not have to grant authors any term longer than the term set by the country of origin for the work as defined in Article 5(4). Instead, "unless the legislation of that country otherwise provides, the term shall not exceed the term fixed in the country of origin of the work." The rule of the shorter term, as applied, is treated as an exception to the principle of national treatment under the Berne Convention. TRIPS Article 3(1) allows its national treatment principle to be subject to the "exceptions ... provided in ... the Berne Convention." The rule of the shorter term also is an exception to the rule of independent treatment of copyrights under Article 5(2) of Berne—the term of copyright established by the country of origin may be applied to limit copyright terms for the same work in other Berne countries.

> Illustration 2–8. Country Z, a Berne Union country and a member of TRIPS, has a copyright term of life of the author plus 70 years. Abigail is a national of Country Y, also a Berne Union country and a member of TRIPS, which has a copyright term of life of the author plus 50 years. Abigail has written and first published a novel in Country Y, which is therefore the country of origin. Under the principle of national treatment, Country Z must normally grant rights to authors from Country Y that are at least as extensive as Country Z grants its own authors. However, under the rule of the shorter term, Country Z is permitted to grant Abigail a copyright term of life of the author plus 50 years, i.e., the shorter term set by the country of origin for Abigail's work. Indeed, if Country Z's copyright law is silent on the issue, the default rule under Article 7(8) of Berne is that the shorter term should be applied.

PROBLEM 2–18

Country A's copyright term lasts for the life of the author plus 50 years. Country B's copyright term lasts for the life of the author plus 80 years. Both A and B are contracting states to the Berne Convention. Neither country's copyright law speaks to the issue of the rule of the shorter term. Jackson was an author and national of Country A. He published a novel, *The Ambiguity*, in 1924 in Country A. In 1925, he published the work in Country B. Jackson died on February 1, 2000. Under the Berne Convention, when will his copyright expire in Country A? In Country B?

PROBLEM 2–19

Ricardo is a national of Country W, which provides for a term of copyright protection of life of the author plus 50 years. Ricardo writes a novel, *Love and Obscurity*, in Country X, which has a copyright term of life of the author plus 60 years and Ricardo first publishes the novel in Country Y, which recognizes a copyright term of life of the author plus 100 years. The United States recognizes a copyright term of life of the author plus 70 years. Assume that Countries W and X are Berne Union countries but Country Y is not. What is the shortest term that the U.S. is permitted to give to Ricardo's work under the Berne Convention?

PROBLEM 2–20

Sheila is a national of Country A and simultaneously publishes a play *The Connections* in Countries A, B, and C. Country A provides for a term of copyright protection of life of the author plus 50 years, Country B provides for a term of life of the author plus 60 years, and Country C provides for a term of life of the author plus 80 years. A year later, Sheila publishes the novel in the U.S. The United States provides for a term of life of the author plus 70 years. Countries B, C, and the United States are contracting states to the Berne Convention, but Country A is not. Under the Berne Convention, what is the shortest term of protection that the United States is permitted to give to Sheila? If Sheila could go back and do things differently, would there be any way she could ensure that neither the U.S. nor Country C could apply the rule of the shorter term to her work?

NOTES AND QUESTIONS

1. What policy today might justify the departure from national treatment in Berne's rule of the shorter term? Historically, the rule of the shorter term might have been justified as a way to give countries the incentive to raise their terms to the life of the author plus 50 years, since the Berlin revision of the Berne Convention in 1908 specifically allowed countries to have terms shorter than 50 years p.m.a.—and several countries did. The rule of the shorter term thus was designed to give those countries the incentive to change their terms to 50 years p.m.a., consistent with the majority of Berne countries. The current (Paris 1971) version of Berne, however, does not allow such an exception for countries to depart lower than 50 years p.m.a. (other than for prescribed categories of works). Why then should the rule of the shorter term still survive if countries no longer need "extra" incentive to raise their terms to 50 years p.m.a., which is now the minimum standard of Berne? Should the rule of the shorter term be abolished?

2. *The U.S. Copyright Term Extension Act.* In 1998, in response to the EU's term extension, the U.S. Congress enacted a comparable term extension under the Sonny Bono Copyright Term Extension Act (CTEA), Pub. L. No. 105–298, with one of the basic increases from 50 years p.m.a. to 70 years p.m.a. Because of complexities of the U.S. copyright system, there are several different types of terms of copyright besides the 70 years p.m.a. for works-

made-for-hire and for older works governed by the old 1909 Copyright Act. *See* 17 U.S.C. §§ 302–305. Consequently, even with CTEA, U.S. copyright terms are not the same as the terms of the EU copyright terms in every respect. Nevertheless, proponents of the CTEA defended the law as necessary to achieve greater harmonization, so that U.S. authors would not be disadvantaged by the rule of the shorter term.

3. *Copyright term inflation?* Is there any danger that powerful lobbying groups of authors will always seek an extension of their copyright terms in any number of countries, in order to prevent their copyrights from expiring? And, if such efforts are successful in one country, doesn't it give the lobbying groups for term extensions an advantage in seeking to ratchet up copyright terms in other countries, given the rule of the shorter term? The U.S. convinced Australia to extend its term to the life of the author plus 70 years as a part of the Australian–U.S. Free Trade Agreement, and has tried unsuccessfully to convince Taiwan to do the same. Mexico has extended its copyright term to the life of the author plus 100 years.

4. *Sound recordings and performances.* The minimum standard for the term of protection of the rights of performers and producers under TRIPS Article 14(5) is a period of 50 years, while the minimum term is only 20 years for broadcasters under TRIPS Article 14(5). The WIPO Performances and Phonograms Treaty Article 17 recognizes a minimum term of 50 years for performances. Under the Rome Convention Article 14, however, the minimum term is only 20 years. Related rights for performances are not subject to Berne's rule of the shorter term.

5. *Bibliographic note.* SAM RICKETSON, THE BERNE CONVENTION FOR THE PROTECTION OF LITERARY AND ARTISTIC WORKS: 1886–1986, at 318–363 (1987); S.M. STEWART, INTERNATIONAL COPYRIGHT AND NEIGHBORING RIGHTS § 5.54, at 134–35 (2d ed. 1989); WIPO, GUIDE TO THE BERNE CONVENTION 45–52 (1978).

2. EU COPYRIGHT TERM DIRECTIVE

PROBLEM 2–21

Jean Claude was a French performer who recorded and first released an album, *Fall Back*, in 1950 in France. Assume that back then, France accorded such recordings only 20 years of protection under neighboring rights. The album was an immediate success, and Jean Claude released international versions in 1951 in the United Kingdom, which then had a term of copyright protection of 50 years for the work, and in Germany, which then only offered 25 years of protection under neighboring rights. For the following questions, assume the year is now July 1, 1995. (1) After the *Phil Collins* decision, can the United Kingdom apply the rule of the shorter term to limit Jean Claude's term of U.K. copyright to 20 years? (2) After the EU Term Directive, do Germany and France need to protect *Fall Back* again, even though the original grant of protection has expired in those countries? To answer this problem, consult the following discussion.

* * *

The EU has been the agenda-setter in several areas of IP. We have already discussed one such area: database protection. Another has been in the area of extending copyright terms. There, too, the EU was the first to switch to the longer term of life of the author plus 70 years. In 1993, the Council for the European Communities issued the EU Directive on Harmonizing the Term of Protection of Copyright and Certain Related Rights (also known as the EU Copyright Term Directive) requiring an increase in copyright terms for both existing and future works in EU countries from the standard of the life of the author plus 50 years. Germany had increased its term to the life of the author plus 70 years, prompting efforts in the European Council to increase the copyright terms throughout Europe. Article 13(1) of the EU Directive provides that all member states must comply with the Directive by July 1, 1995. For newer works or subject matter created after July 1, 1995, the issue of protection in the EU should be straightforward as the Directive requires that they are to be given a uniform standard of protection—the life of the author plus 70 years—in every EU country. If an EU country recognizes corporate authors as eligible for copyrights (not all countries do), Article 1(4) allows a copyright term of 70 years after the work is lawfully made to the public. The EU Directive treats the "principal director" of a film as the author or one of the authors of the film, but allows countries to recognize other authors of the film as well. EU Term Directive art. 2(1). Somewhat curiously, Article 2(1) makes the term of copyright for cinematographic or audiovisual works "70 years after the death of the last of the following persons to survive, *whether or not these persons are designated as co-authors*: the principal director, the author of the screenplay, the author of the dialogue and the composer of music specifically created for use in the cinematographic or audiovisual work."

After a term extension in 2011, related rights for performers receive 70 years of protection, measured either from (i) the date of performance or (ii) "if a fixation of the performance is lawfully published or lawfully communicated to the public within this period, the rights shall expire 70 years from the date of the first such publication or the first such communication to the public, whichever is the earlier." EU Term Directive art. 3; Directive 2011/77/EU. Like the Berne Convention, the EU Directive calculates the term "from the first day of January of the year following the event which gives rise to them." EU Term Directive art. 8.

However, for older works or subject matter dating from prior to July 1, 1995, determining whether extended protection exists can be more complicated. Article 10(2) of the EU Directive provides that its terms of protection are in some cases to be applied retroactively:

> The terms of protection provided for in this Directive shall apply to all works and subject matter which are protected in at least one Member State, on the date referred to Article 13(1).

The effect of Article 10(2) is that so long as a work is still entitled to protection anywhere in the EU as of July 1, 1995, it must be protected in every other country of the EU, even if the work has already fallen into the public domain in those other EU countries. In countries where the work has fallen into the public domain, it must be restored to protection. In these circumstances, Article 10(2) has a retroactive effect. As a result of Article 10(2), in determining whether any particular work or subject matter is entitled to protection under the EU Directive, it is not enough to determine whether the work is still entitled to protection in its country of origin. A determination must be made as to whether the work is subject to protection in any EU country as of July 1, 1995. If the work or subject matter is entitled to protection in any one EU country, then protection must be extended or restored to the work in every other EU country.

This "EU-wide" application of term extensions is required by EU national treatment. EU countries are subject to not only the national treatment principle contained in Berne and TRIPS, but also to the national treatment principle contained in Article 18 of the Treaty on the Functioning of the European Union, which provides in relevant part: "Within the scope of the application of this Treaty ... any discrimination on grounds of nationality shall be prohibited." In *Phil Collins v. Imtrat Handelsgesellschaft GmbH*, 3 C.M.L.R. 773 (E.C.J. 1993), excerpted in Chapter 1 at pp. 32–35, the European Court of Justice interpreted the predecessor version of Article 18 to require full national treatment for intellectual property rights that *cannot* be subject to exceptions for EU nationals. As a result, EU countries cannot apply the rule of the shorter term to nationals from other EU countries. Of course, EU countries can still apply the rule of the shorter term to nationals from non-EU countries such as the United States.

For older works, the combination of Article 10(2) of the EU Directive and the EU national treatment principle may result in (re)copyrighting works that had fallen into the public domain.

> Illustration 2–9. On July 1, 1966, Germany enacted a copyright term of life of the author plus 70 years. Charlotta published a novel in France in 1937 and died in 1940. In 1940, France provided for a term of protection of life of the author plus 50 years. On January 1, 1991, the copyright in Charlotta's novel expired and the work entered the public domain in France. Germany is bound under the full national treatment principle of the EC Treaty to provide to Charlotta, a national of another member of the EU, a term of protection of life of the author plus 70 years. Charlotta's German copyright does not expire until 2010. As Charlotta's novel is still in copyright in Germany as of July 1, 1995, Charlotta is entitled under Article 10(2) to a term of protection of life plus 70 years as required by the EU Directive in every country of the EU, including France, the country of origin. Charlotta's copyright in France must be restored on July 1, 1995.

As the example shows, if a work is still protected by copyright or neighboring right as of July 1, 1995 in at least one EU country, then the work is entitled to extended protection in all countries of the EU.

EU Directive on Harmonizing the Term of Protection of Copyright and Certain Related Rights (93/98/EEC) (excerpt)

Article 1

Duration of authors' rights

1. The rights of an author of a literary or artistic work within the meaning of Article 2 of the Berne Convention shall run for the life of the

author and for 70 years after his death, irrespective of the date when the work is lawfully made available to the public. * * *

Article 2

Cinematographic or audiovisual works

1. The principal director of a cinematographic or audiovisual work shall be considered as its author or one of its authors. Member States shall be free to designate other co-authors.

2. The term of protection of cinematographic or audiovisual works shall expire 70 years after the death of the last of the following persons to survive, whether or not these persons are designated as co-authors: the principal director, the author of the screenplay, the author of the dialogue and the composer of music specifically created for use in the cinematographic or audiovisual work.

Article 3

Duration of related rights

1. The rights of performers shall expire 50 years after the date of the performance. However, if a fixation of the performance is lawfully published or lawfully communicated to the public within this period, the rights shall expire 50 years from the date of the first such publication or the first such communication to the public, whichever is the earlier.

2. The rights of producers of phonograms shall expire 50 years after the fixation is made. However, if the phonogram is lawfully published or lawfully communicated to the public during this period, the rights shall expire 50 years from the date of the first such publication or the first such communication to the public, whichever is the earlier.

3. The rights of producers of the first fixation of a film shall expire 50 years after the fixation is made. However, if the film is lawfully published or lawfully communicated to the public during this period, the rights shall expire 50 years from the date of the first such publication or the first such communication to the public, whichever is the earlier. The term 'film' shall designate a cinematographic or audiovisual work or moving images, whether or not accompanied by sound.

4. The rights of broadcasting organizations shall expire 50 years after the first transmission of a broadcast, whether this broadcast is transmitted by wire or over the air, including by cable or satellite.

Article 10

Application in time

1. Where a term of protection, which is longer than the corresponding term provided for by this Directive, is already running in a Member State on the date referred to in Article 13(1) [1 July 1995, *ed.*], this Directive shall not have the effect of shortening that term of protection in that Member State.

2. The terms of protection provided for in this Directive shall apply to all works and subject matter which are protected in at least one Member State, on the date referred to in Article 13(1) [1 July 1995, *ed.*], pursuant

to national provisions on copyright or related rights or which meet the criteria for protection under Directive 92/100/EEC.

3.   This Directive shall be without prejudice to any acts of exploitation performed before the date referred to in Article 13(1). Member States shall adopt the necessary provisions to protect in particular acquired rights of third parties.

4.   Member States need not apply the provisions of Article 2(1) to cinematographic or audiovisual works created before 1 July 1994.

5.   Member States may determine the date as from which Article 2(1) shall apply, provided that date is no later than 1 July 1997.

Notes and Questions

1.   *Retroactivity*. Does retroactivity make things simpler or more complicated when copyrights are brought back to life? Should there be any limit on the power of a legislature to extend the terms of copyright to works in the public domain?

2.   *Reliance parties*. Paragraph 27 of the Preamble to the EU Term Directive recognizes that countries may protect the interests of parties who have relied on works being in the public domain before being subject to a revived copyright. Paragraph 27 states: "Member States may provide ... that in certain circumstances the copyright and related rights which are revived pursuant to this Directive may not give rise to payments by persons who undertook in good faith the exploitation of the works at the time when such works lay within the public domain." This level of protection contemplated for reliance parties in the EU appears to be greater than the relatively modest protection U.S. law affords to reliance parties under 17 U.S.C. § 104A (discussed in the troll doll case). Article 10 of the Term Directive states that it is intended to be applied "without prejudice to any acts of exploitation performed before" July 1, 1995 and that "Member States shall adopt the necessary provisions to protect in particular acquired rights of third parties."

3.   *Moral rights*. The EU Term Directive Article 9 expressly excludes an author's moral rights from coverage. Accordingly, EU countries can recognize different terms of protection for moral rights, which are discussed in the next section.

4.   *EU Extension of Term of Neighboring Rights*. The EU Directive on the Term of Protection of Copyright and Certain Related Rights ("Copyright Term Directive"), 2006/116/EC, set the term of neighboring rights in the EU at 50 years. In 2011, the EU passed a Directive to extend the term to 70 years. *See* Directive, 2011/77/EU.

The Directive followed a contentious debate. Proposals were floated— pushed by the recording industry—to extend the term to 95 years, in order to make the term more in line with the longer term of copyright. In December 2006, Andrew Gowers issued a report titled the Gowers Review of Intellectual Property, commissioned by the UK government. The Gowers Review concluded that the EU "should retain the length of protection on sound recording and performers' rights at 50 years." *Id.* at 56 (recommendation 3). The

Gowers Review noted two chief economic concerns: First, the term extension would cost an estimated £240 million to £480 million to consumers, as applied to existing recordings, while adding no incentives to create those recordings. Second, "[g]iven that a low number of sound recordings or performances retain any commercial value beyond 50 years, extending term to all these would lock up the majority of recordings that are not generating income, rendering them unavailable for consumers and future creators." *Id.* at 76. Despite the Gowers Review's recommendation, the European Commission (the executive of the EU) proposed in 2008 to extend the neighboring rights term to 95 years. In 2009, the European Parliament voted in favor of extending the term to 70 years. After several years of opposition, the proposal secured passage by the European Council of Ministers.

G. MORAL RIGHTS

In an earlier section, we examined economic rights in copyrighted works, which are primarily concerned with the right of the author to economically exploit the work. In this section, we turn to a different set of rights—moral rights—that are designed to protect the interests of the author in the paternity and integrity of the work.

PROBLEM 2–22

Family Entertainment Productions is a corporation headquartered in Utah. Family Entertainment edits out all sex, profanity, and gratuitous violence from copyrighted movies it purchases on tapes for the VCR. Family Entertainment has lawfully purchased the tapes from the movie studios, which are the copyright holders for the movies in the U.S. To edit out the "offensive" content, Family Entertainment simply cuts and splices the tape, so the portion of the tape containing the "offensive" material is removed. Family Entertainment has not asked permission from copyright holders to edit the scenes, but Family Entertainment does not make any copy of the original tape it lawfully purchased. Most of the movies rented or sold by Family Entertainment are produced by U.S. movie studios with U.S. directors. But a number of the movies are foreign productions by foreign movie studios with foreign directors. In the small town community where it has its principal place of business, Family Entertainment's business is in high demand. The edited tapes are both rented and sold, although most families merely rent the movies for personal home viewing. Family Entertainment's profits have soared, and it is now considering expanding online sales and rentals to other countries, including France and other parts of Europe.

Family Entertainment has just hired you to provide legal advice. Some customer told Family Entertainment that it might have a "moral rights" problem. John Ryland, the owner of Family Entertainment, thought the customer was talking about morality, so he replied: "We stand on the side of morality." His wife, however, convinced Ryland to consult a lawyer, even though the movie studios have yet to complain about what Family Entertainment is doing. Please advise Family Entertainment about whether it has a "moral rights" problem. Should it change any of its business practices now?

And what about going online with its business? Consult the following provisions from the Berne Convention and accompanying readings.

Berne Convention (Paris, 1971)

Article 6*bis*

(1) Independently of the author's economic rights, and even after the transfer of the said rights, the author shall have the right to claim authorship of the work and to object to any distortion, mutilation or other modification of, or other derogatory action in relation to, the said work, which would be prejudicial to his honor or reputation.

(2) The rights granted to the author in accordance with the preceding paragraph shall, after his death, be maintained, at least until the expiry of the economic rights, and shall be exercisable by the persons or institutions authorized by the legislation of the country where protection is claimed. However, those countries whose legislation, at the moment of their ratification of or accession to this Act, does not provide for the protection after the death of the author of all the rights set out in the preceding paragraph may provide that some of these rights may, after his death, cease to be maintained.

(3) The means of redress for safeguarding the rights granted by this Article shall be governed by the legislation of the country where protection is claimed.

TRIPS

Article 9

1. Members shall comply with Articles 1 through 21 of the Berne Convention (1971) and the Appendix thereto. However, Members shall not have rights or obligations under this Agreement in respect of the rights conferred under Article 6*bis* of that Convention or of the rights derived therefrom.

HUSTON v. SOCIÉTÉ TURNER ENTERTAINMENT

Cour de Cassation (France).
1991 Bull. Civ. I, No. 172 (May 28, 1991).*

[John Huston was the director of *The Asphalt Jungle*, a black-and-white film made in 1950 in the U.S. Apparently under the production contract, Huston agreed that the original movie studio would own all copyrights to the movie and that Huston would have no claim of authorship or moral rights in the movie. Turner Entertainment eventually acquired the copyrights to *The Asphalt Jungle* from the movie studio and made a colorized version of the movie. The estate of John Huston, along with the screen writer Ben Maddow, objected and sued to stop the dissemination of the colorized movie in France. *Ed.*]

According to Art. 1(2) of Act No.64–689 of July 8, 1964, the integrity of a literary or artistic work in France must not be impaired; this applies

---

* Translation originally published in 23 IIC 702, 702–03 (1991). Reproduced with permission.

independently of the state in which the work was first published. On the basis of Art. 6 of the Copyright Act of March 11, 1957, the person who is the author of the work is entitled to claim *droit moral* merely due to the actual creation of the work; this right was specifically provided for in this Article in order to benefit authors. The provisions are to be strictly applied.

The joint plaintiffs, the Hustons, are the heirs of John Huston, co-director of the film "Asphalt Jungle." This film was produced in black-and-white form, yet the first defendant, the Turner company, holder of the rights as producer, made a colourized version thereof. The plaintiffs, who were also joined by various other legal persons in the appeal on the law, requested enforcement of their right to recognize the integrity of John Huston's work at the trial stage, and thus to prohibit the televising of this new version by the second defendant, "La Cinq." The court of appeal rejected the plaintiff's claim with the argument that the facts described and the legal merits of the case "forbade the supplantation of U.S. law and the disregard of the contracts"—contracts concluded between the producer and the director, which denied the latter the status as author of the film "Asphalt Jungle."

In deciding on these grounds, the court of appeal has misinterpreted the above-named provisions by non-application.

For these reasons, the decision of the Paris Court of Appeal is set aside in all its inferences and declared null and void. The dispute is therefore remanded to the Versailles Court of Appeal.

ALAI CONGRESS: ANTWERP 1993 THE MORAL RIGHT OF THE AUTHOR: MORAL RIGHTS AND THE CIVIL LAW COUNTRIES

Adolf Dietz.
19 Colum.–VLA J.L. & Arts 199, 203–05, 213–27 (1995).

The new systematization of the provisions on *droit moral* or, better, *droits moraux* in the French Intellectual Property Code as well as the comprehensive regulations in Germany, Italy and Spain make it very clear that Article 6*bis* of the Berne Convention represents a minimalist approach, indeed. Apart from the paternity right and the integrity right of the author, *droit moral* in those countries covers at least two additional rights, namely the divulgation right (*le droit de divulgation*) and its natural corollary, the right to repent or to withdraw (*droit de repentir ou de retrait*). The Spanish regulation in Article 14 of the Act—as is also explained in the Spanish report—in a specific way differentiates between the negative and the positive aspects of the individual faculties of *droit moral*, including also "the right of access to the sole or a rare copy . . . in another person's possession," so that the concept of *droit moral* seems to comprise as many as seven separate faculties in Spain.

A clear comprehensive concept of moral rights protection, going beyond the minimal approach of Article 6*bis* of the Berne Convention, thus exists in a number of civil law countries.

Other Topical Questions

A. *Time Limit or Perpetuity of Droit moral*

French theory sees a clear consequence of the preeminence of moral rights over economic rights also in the fact that protection is declared perpetual by the law itself. It continues after protection of pecuniary rights has run out fifty years, or even seventy years, after the author's death. According to the French national report, this solution corresponds to the fundamental concept of moral right in French law, even if theoretically other solutions to the problem of duration were conceivable. The other solutions, however, would misunderstand the originality of moral rights as compared to other personality rights. Since, according to the French concept, the link between the author and his work exists as long as the work is capable of being communicated to the public, in a certain way, the personality of the author lives as long as the work itself exists. On the other hand, at first sight it also appears to be a consequence of the monistic or synthetic interpretation of copyright in German doctrine[7] that moral rights, being an integral part of copyright as a whole, end together with it seventy years after the death of the author. This result is confirmed by the majority interpretation of the legal situation in German copyright law.

A closer and, in particular, comparative look at this question, however, tells us that there is no necessary correlation of dualism and perpetuity, on the one hand, and monism and *droit moral* protection limited in time, on the other hand. If, apart from Germany (and perhaps—according to my own interpretation of its new law—Switzerland), almost all other countries covered by this analysis, namely Belgium, Denmark, Italy, Netherlands, Spain and Sweden, according to the relevant national reports, can be more or less counted as dualistic countries, there is no unanimity as to whether perpetuity of moral rights protection exists or should exist.

[A]s underlined by the Spanish report, Spain expressly provides for perpetuity of moral rights, but restricts it to the right of paternity and of integrity of the work in its negative or defensive aspects. However, more precisely than in the case of France, there is also a general subsidiary competence of the State and of other public authorities—but not of private associations such as collecting societies—to enforce these rights. The Italian report also is more positive about perpetuity, since the copyright law itself (once more with the exception of the right to repent) grants moral rights protection after the author's death without time limit: they can be exercised by the members of the author's family as determined by the law, but in cases of public interest, public authorities can also intervene. The Italian report characteristically thinks that this could be particularly relevant for the utilization of the works of so-called "serious"

---

7. France follows a "dualist" theory, which posits that moral rights are separate from and prior to economic rights in copyright and must be treated under different legal rules whereas German follows a "monist" theory, which holds that both types of rights must be treated under a single set of legal rules.

music (lyric, opera, symphonic and other music), but gives no examples in case law.

If the German and, perhaps, also the Swiss example demonstrate that monistic or unitary interpretation of copyright shows a natural tendency to stop moral right protection together with copyright as a whole, there exists no necessary correlation. Duration of moral rights longer than the period of protection for the economic rights is rather a question of culture and policy. Perhaps there is no general answer to this problem and we should leave it to the legal and cultural traditions of the individual countries.

B.   Determination and Legal Position of the Author's Legal Successors in his Moral Rights

The problem of who shall decide, and in whose interest, about questions of moral right after the author's death is also of relevance during the normal period of protection of copyright. In some countries, in particular in France, but also in Belgium, Italy and Spain the legal successors of the author (his family members or other persons as determined by the laws) clearly have to enforce the moral rights in *nomine auctoris*—an expression used in the Belgian report. Consequently, the moral rights in their hands are subject to a total change of character. The legal successors receive *droit moral* only, as is stated in the French report, in order to respect the work and the person of the author. They must not exercise it in their own personal interests; this is why *droit moral* after the author's death is called a functional right (*droit-fonction*). This concept also explains why—as in other countries—the right to repent expires at the death of the author. In addition, misuse of moral rights by legal successors in the sense that they do not fulfill their duties in respecting the author's name and work could even be subject to judicial control in accordance with Article L.121–3 of the Code.

In the interest of such a concept, some countries even provide different rules for transmission of moral rights—as contrasted to economic rights—to the author's legal successors, since the family members or those persons whom the author has specifically entrusted with exercise of his moral rights normally are supposed to exercise them as the author himself would have. There is of course no legal guaranty for that, unless the law also provides for some means of control of those persons as the French Code does for the divulgation right.

German copyright law does not provide for specific rules on transmission of moral rights at the author's death, apart from the fact that, according to Section 28(2) of the Copyright Act, exercise of the copyright (and, of course, also of individual faculties of it) can be transmitted to an executor by testamentary disposition. That copyright as a whole, comprising its economic as well as its moral faculties, therefore passes over to the regular legal successors, also appears as a logical consequence of the monistic interpretation of copyright which always stresses its unity. But the true reason seems to be that German legal doctrine rejects a concept of *droit-fonction* or of special obligations of the legal successors as against the dead author. Accordingly, apart from concrete and legally binding testamentary dispositions of the author, the legal successors are able to exercise moral right protection as they think fit, even in their own interests. Of course in Germany, too, widows and widowers as well as children and other family members of dead authors de facto will normally act, to the best of their knowledge, in accordance with the dead author's interests and wishes. There is simply no control.

We also have to think of the realities of modern cultural industries where, for example, the question of whether a novel or a piece of theater can be filmed has to be decided by the legal successors of the author years after his death. Would it really make sense, in particular when there is certain actual or public interest in such a film production, to hinder the legal successors with the interference of state authorities simply because the author, many years ago, had expressed some doubts about such a filming? Think of Franz Kafka who, according to his friend Max Brod, wanted to have his work destroyed after his death. Would Max Brod have really rendered a service to mankind if he had followed this desperate decision and had not published it, as he finally did? *Tempora mutantur, nos et mutamur in illis!**

C. Exercise of the Paternity and the Integrity Rights— Waiver of Rights and Balance of Interests

As stated at the beginning, there is no unanimity even within the group of civil law countries as to how far moral rights protection extends and what individual faculties it should cover. However, unanimity exists, at least in principle, as far as the paternity right and the integrity right are concerned. In all countries as reported here statutory provisions regulate these two faculties. In Belgium the provisions of Article 6*bis* of the Berne Convention are directly applied.

1. Paternity Right

The reports generally state that the paternity right has two facets: the author can not only claim recognition of his authorship by third parties in a negative or defensive way, but also determine in a positive way whether a work is to bear an author's designation and what designation is to be used. The latter possibility also involves a right of non-paternity, which allows the author to opt for an anonymous form of publication of his work in the same way that he can decide to use a pseudonym instead of his true name. But, as most laws directly or indirectly recognize, the author always has the possibility of disclosing and claiming his paternity.

The real problem in the context of the paternity right therefore concerns the question of how far contractual arrangements concerning naming or not naming the author are enforceable and whether the right of

---

* "Times are changing, and we are changing with them." *Ed.*

attribution can be waived, in particular, within so-called ghostwriter agreements. The clearest provision that the author can always insist on an attribution of his name is contained in Article 21(2) of the Italian Act, whereas Article 25(3) of the Netherlands Act generally allows waiver of the right to be named (which itself is already granted only within the limits of reasonableness) as well as of the right to object to modification of the designation.

An intermediate position is taken by the Danish and Swedish Copyright Acts which, first, like the Dutch law, grant the right to be named only in accordance with the requirements of proper usage, but, second, exclude waiver of moral rights in a general way, while still allowing it in respect of a use of the work which is limited in nature and extent. In spite of a relatively strict formulation in Article 13 of its Copyright Act, German practice also allows waiver within certain limits, determined partly by proper usage and partly by a balancing of interests. Finally, a special situation exists under the new Swiss Act since there is no express exclusion of moral rights from the general rule in its Article 16(1) that copyright can be ceded and transmitted. The Swiss national report underlines, however, that a general waiver of the right to be named as author for all future creations would be judged as against honest practices.

As a result, the legal situation in the individual countries is far from being uniform.

2. *Integrity Right*

In the field of the integrity right, that is the right to object to distortion, mutilation or other modifications of the author's work, the question of admissibility of transfer or waiver is even more difficult to answer. There are countries such as France, Italy and Spain that strictly stress the inalienability of this special faculty of moral right. Legal provisions in other countries, on the contrary, admit at least some restrictions of the integrity right by contract or waiver. In addition, the question of whether modifications are absolutely forbidden without the author's consent, or whether infringement of this moral right depends on certain conditions or qualifications such as prejudice to the author's honor or reputation, is also answered differently in the individual countries.

Of course, in modern cultural industry and modern media, modification and adaptation of works in the framework of their exploitation is often more the rule than the exception. The laws themselves, when granting the author the economic right of adaptation, necessarily imply that the author who allows adaptation of his work must give the adaptor certain room to maneuver, as the French report rightly states. The very provisions concerning adaptation right and adaption contract therefore demonstrate that a concept of absolute inalienability and of exclusion of waiver is not compatible with the laws of even the most fundamental moral rights countries.

Totally different is the question of whether the exercise of the right of integrity has an unconditional or discretionary character or whether it is conditioned or qualified by certain elements. At least in theory, the protection of authors in France is the most absolute and unconditional; French law, according to Article L.121–1 of the Intellectual Property Code, does not make the right of respect for the author's name, authorship and work dependent on any condition. In the other countries the condition provided in Article 6*bis* of the Berne Convention, namely that modification of his work must be prejudicial to the author's honor or reputation, in one form or another is repeated in the provisions on moral rights, a result which in Belgium once more is obtained by direct application of the Berne Convention.

The French national report criticizes this approach, prefigured by the Berne Convention, as minimalist. This critique is based on the "personalistic" view of moral rights protection in French law which, without applying the criterium of honor or reputation, totally respects the subjectivity of the author, his aesthetic, moral and philosophic convictions. I think this critical position is right insofar as the formula of honor and reputation is too narrow; indeed, modification of an author's work can conflict with his fundamental artistic and moral convictions without, judging from outside, prejudicing his honor or reputation. This problem is avoided, to a certain extent, by the formulation in Section 14 of the German Act and in Article 14 (iv) of the Spanish Act, which applies the criterium of prejudice to the lawful (intellectual or personal) interests of the author in his work. Article 25 of the Dutch Copyright Act, which applies a rule of reason to modifications not amounting to distortions, applies the criterium of the value or dignity of the author in addition to prejudice to his honor or reputation in case of distortions of the work, and hence adopts a broader concept.

On the other hand, I do not agree with the French critique that all of these formulas would allow the author's aesthetic, moral or philosophic convictions and judgments to be replaced unacceptably by judgments of other persons, be it the general public or the courts. The question, in my view, is not whether the author's convictions are respected or replaced, but whether the author has to accept certain changes and modifications of his works in view of the counter-interests of the work users. This criterium, which finally leads to a concept of balancing of interests, is clearly recognizable in those countries like Germany, Spain, and the Netherlands, where the relevant provisions speak of "lawful" interests or apply a rule of reason.

A special problem within the integrity right is raised by the question of unauthorized destruction of works, especially in the field of visual arts and architecture. If in the past there was some controversy over whether destruction of a work could or could not amount to distortion of it, the opinion gains ground today that destruction of a work appears as the most intensive form of its distortion, depriving the author of the authentic means of proof for his artistic and professional skills and self-conscience.

According to the report of Professors Kernochan and Ginsburg, the United States legislators of the Visual Artists Rights Act of 1990 played a pioneer role in introducing provisions barring intentional or grossly negligent destruction of a covered work "of recognized stature." We will not discuss further details of these very interesting provisions of the U.S. legislation, not being civil law legislation; however, they demonstrate, once more, how legislators try to find adequate solutions that will be viable also in the years to come by differentiating the rules according to categories or groups of works.

Surprisingly, the very recent Copyright Act of Switzerland, fulfilling a similar pioneer function for a civil law country, provided in its Article 15 that under certain circumstances the owner of the unique original exemplar of a work may not destroy it without first offering it to the author. In the case of a work of architecture, however, the author is only entitled to take photographs of it and to make copies of the architectural plans. On the other hand, similarly to the Italian law, a work of architecture may be modified by its owner as long as there is no distortion or mutilation of the work, meaning an attack on its author's personality. These bold, if nuanced provisions, once more show the necessity of differentiation in the delicate field of moral rights protection.

In a general way, all of these legislative solutions, in my view, only exemplify the concept that moral rights questions always have to be judged in their individual context and that correspondingly different solutions have to be found for different categories of works and manners of work uses.

NOTES AND QUESTIONS

1. Under the ruling of the French Court of Cassation, did John Huston still retain his moral right of integrity to stop the airing of the colorized version of *The Asphalt Jungle* in France? Do you like the French approach to moral rights?

2. *Conflicts of Laws.* Had U.S. law applied in the *Huston* case, Turner Entertainment (through its predecessor in interest) would have owned all rights to *The Asphalt Jungle* by assignment from the director John Huston. Unlike French law, U.S. law does not recognize a moral right of integrity for authors (except in a narrow class of works of visual art not present here), and U.S. law would presumably allow authors to contract away whatever moral rights they may have under foreign laws. If both the film and contract between Huston and the movie studio had been made in the U.S., why did the Court of Cassation (the highest appellate court in France for private cases) apply French law to the case?

3. Article 6*bis* of the Berne Convention requires countries to recognize two moral rights: (1) the right of integrity of the work from "any distortion, mutilation or other modification," or any "other derogatory action in relation thereto, . . . which would be prejudicial to [the author's] honor or reputation," and (2) the right of attribution or paternity to the work, meaning the right to

be identified as the author of the work. As the Dietz article discusses, civil law countries may also formally recognize two other moral rights: (3) the right of divulgation or disclosure of a work to the public, and (4) the right of withdrawal of the work. Do you favor a broad or maximalist protection of these moral rights, or a narrow or minimalist protection? Why?

Article 6*bis* does not contain any express prohibition against the destruction of the entire work (e.g., a statue), presumably allowing countries to decide whether or not to include such a right. Why might Berne recognize a minimum standard that forbids certain kinds of distortions, mutilations, or other modifications, but allows the complete destruction of a work? Is a destruction of a work less troublesome to an author's reputation? Or is there some other way to distinguish destruction from a partial modification? If not, should Berne be amended (or interpreted) to recognize destruction as the "most intensive form of ... distortion" as suggested by Professor Dietz?

4. *Prejudicial to the author's honor or reputation.* The minimum standard under Berne Article 6*bis* seeks to protect an author's work from "any distortion, mutilation or other modification of, or any other derogatory action in relation to, the said work, which would be prejudicial to his honor or reputation." How should one determine if a modification would prejudice an author's honor or reputation? Based on the author's own personal feeling? Or the views of members of the public who are familiar with the author's work? Or should the standard be what a reasonable person would feel? What do you think of the multi-factor balancing test suggested by Dietz?

5. *Inalienability.* Berne Article 6*bis* does not address whether moral rights can be freely transferred; the silence presumably means that countries can decide the issues however they see fit. However, many civil law countries, such as France and Germany, treat moral rights as inalienable from the author (although transferable by will upon death). What might justify the bar against transferring an author's moral right? Is it merely a paternalistic provision to protect authors from bad judgment in assigning away their rights? Do you agree with this exception to the freedom to contract?

6. *Term of moral rights.* Under Berne, moral rights must last, at a minimum, the lifetime of the author and until the expiry of the economic rights. As Professor Dietz relates, a number of civil law countries recognize perpetual moral rights. In a transition provision, Article 6*bis* also provides that "those countries whose legislation, at the moment of their ratification of or accession to this Act, does not provide for the protection after the death of the author of all" the required moral rights may instead provide a term of moral rights that expires at the author's death.

7. *Performers.* Historically, countries did not recognize any moral rights for performers. Nor did any of the international conventions. For the first time, in 1996, Article 5 of the WIPO Performances and Phonograms Treaty recognized the moral rights of integrity and paternity for *aural* performers for their "live aural performances or performances fixed in phonograms." The right of paternity does not apply "where omission is dictated by manner of use of the performance." Article 5 has yet to spark widespread recognition of such rights among countries, however.

Another limitation of the WIPO Treaty is that it does not encompass moral rights for *audiovisual* performers, such as actors in films—an issue that has sparked considerable controversy internationally, particularly with the Screen Actors Guild in the United States.

WIPO has considered a proposal for protecting rights of audiovisual performers, but one key issue that has divided countries is whether and how any such rights should be deemed transferable to producers to allow for ease in licensing of audiovisual works, such as movies. The European Union advocated for a requirement of express consent by the performer for any transfer of rights; the United States sought the allowance of an automatic transfer of rights to the producer under the work-made-for-hire doctrine and collective bargaining agreements. The two sides reached an impasse that has yet to be bridged.

Today, the status of moral rights for performers, both aural and audiovisual, remains uncertain. What arguments can be made for and against the greater recognition of moral rights for performers? Is there a difference between authors and performers, or between aural and audiovisual performers, that would justify differential treatment in according moral rights? In the case of an audiovisual work, who, if anyone, should be entitled to a moral right?

8. *Bibliographic note.* Paul Edward Geller, *French High Court Remands Huston* Colorization Case, 39 J. COPYRIGHT SOC'Y U.S.A. 252 (1992); Jane C. Ginsburg, *International Copyright: From a "Bundle" of National Copyright Laws to a Supranational Code?*, 47 J. COPYRIGHT SOC'Y U.S.A. 265, 281 n.78 (2000) ("foreign authors enjoy moral rights in France, regardless of whether authors enjoyed or waived moral rights in the work's country of origin").

GILLIAM v. AMERICAN BROADCASTING COMPANIES, INC.

U.S. Court of Appeals for the Second Circuit.
538 F.2d 14 (2d Cir. 1976).

LUMBARD, CIRCUIT JUDGE:

Plaintiffs, a group of British writers and performers known as "Monty Python," appeal from a denial by Judge Lasker in the Southern District of a preliminary injunction to restrain the American Broadcasting Company (ABC) from broadcasting edited versions of three separate programs originally written and performed by Monty Python for broadcast by the British Broadcasting Corporation (BBC). We agree with Judge Lasker that the appellants have demonstrated that the excising done for ABC impairs the integrity of the original work. We further find that the countervailing injuries that Judge Lasker found might have accrued to ABC as a result of an injunction at a prior date no longer exist. We therefore direct the issuance of a preliminary injunction by the district court.

Since its formation in 1969, the Monty Python group has gained popularity primarily through its thirty-minute television programs created for BBC as part of a comedy series entitled "Monty Python's Flying

Circus." In accordance with an agreement between Monty Python and BBC, the group writes and delivers to BBC scripts for use in the television series. This scriptwriters' agreement recites in great detail the procedure to be followed when any alterations are to be made in the script prior to recording of the program. The essence of this section of the agreement is that, while BBC retains final authority to make changes, appellants or their representatives exercise optimum control over the scripts consistent with BBC's authority and only minor changes may be made without prior consultation with the writers. Nothing in the scriptwriters' agreement entitles BBC to alter a program once it has been recorded. The agreement further provides that, subject to the terms therein, the group retains all rights in the script.

Under the agreement, BBC may license the transmission of recordings of the television programs in any overseas territory.

In October 1973, Time–Life Films acquired the right to distribute in the United States certain BBC television programs, including the Monty Python series. Time–Life was permitted to edit the programs only "for insertion of commercials, applicable censorship or governmental ... rules and regulations, and National Association of Broadcasters and time segment requirements." No similar clause was included in the scriptwriters' agreement between appellants and BBC. Prior to this time, ABC had sought to acquire the right to broadcast excerpts from various Monty Python programs in the spring of 1975, but the group rejected the proposal for such a disjoined format. Thereafter, in July 1975, ABC agreed with Time–Life to broadcast two ninety-minute specials each comprising three thirty-minute Monty Python programs that had not previously been shown in this country.

Correspondence between representatives of BBC and Monty Python reveals that these parties assumed that ABC would broadcast each of the Monty Python programs "in its entirety." On September 5, 1975, however, the group's British representative inquired of BBC how ABC planned to show the programs in their entirety if approximately 24 minutes of each 90 minute program were to be devoted to commercials. BBC replied on September 12, "we can only reassure you that ABC have decided to run the programmes 'back to back,' and that there is a firm undertaking not to segment them."

ABC broadcast the first of the specials on October 3, 1975. Appellants did not see a tape of the program until late November and were allegedly "appalled" at the discontinuity and "mutilation" that had resulted from the editing done by Time–Life for ABC. Twenty-four minutes of the original 90 minutes of recording had been omitted. Some of the editing had been done in order to make time for commercials; other material had been edited, according to ABC, because the original programs contained offensive or obscene matter.

In early December, Monty Python learned that ABC planned to broadcast the second special on December 26, 1975. The parties began negotiations concerning editing of that program and a delay of the broadcast until Monty Python could view it. These negotiations were futile, however, and on December 15 the group filed this action to enjoin the broadcast and for damages. Following an evidentiary hearing, Judge Lasker found that "the plaintiffs have established an impairment of the integrity of their work" which "caused the film or program ... to lose its iconoclastic verve." According to Judge Lasker, "the damage that has been caused to the plaintiffs is irreparable by its nature." Nevertheless, the judge denied the motion for the preliminary injunction on the grounds that it was unclear who owned the copyright in the programs produced by BBC from the scripts written by Monty Python; that there was a question of whether Time–Life and BBC were indispensable parties to the litigation; that ABC would suffer significant financial loss if it were enjoined a week before the scheduled broadcast; and that Monty Python had displayed a "somewhat disturbing casualness" in their pursuance of the matter.

Judge Lasker granted Monty Python's request for more limited relief by requiring ABC to broadcast a disclaimer during the December 26 special to the effect that the group dissociated itself from the program because of the editing. A panel of this court, however, granted a stay of that order until this appeal could be heard and permitted ABC to broadcast, at the beginning of the special, only the legend that the program had been edited by ABC. We heard argument on April 13 and, at that time, enjoined ABC from any further broadcast of edited Monty Python programs pending the decision of the court.

In determining the availability of injunctive relief at this early stage of the proceedings, Judge Lasker properly considered the harm that would inure to the plaintiffs if the injunction were denied, the harm that defendant would suffer if the injunction were granted, and the likelihood that plaintiffs would ultimately succeed on the merits. We direct the issuance of a preliminary injunction because we find that all these factors weigh in favor of appellants. [The Second Circuit then agreed with the district court's finding that the balance of harms weighed in favour of granting an injunction to the plaintiffs. *Ed.*]

We then reach the question whether there is a likelihood that appellants will succeed on the merits. In concluding that there is a likelihood of infringement here, we rely especially on the fact that the editing was substantial, i.e., approximately 27 per cent of the original program was omitted, and the editing contravened contractual provisions that limited the right to edit Monty Python material. It should be emphasized that our discussion of these matters refers only to such facts as have been developed upon the hearing for a preliminary injunction. Modified or contrary findings may become appropriate after a plenary trial.

Judge Lasker denied the preliminary injunction in part because he was unsure of the ownership of the copyright in the recorded program. Appellants first contend that the question of ownership is irrelevant because the recorded program was merely a derivative work taken from the script in which they hold the uncontested copyright. Thus, even if BBC owned the copyright in the recorded program, its use of that work would be limited by the license granted to BBC by Monty Python for use of the underlying script. We agree.

Section 7 of the Copyright Law, 17 U.S.C. § 7,* provides in part that "adaptations, arrangements, dramatizations ... or other versions of ... copyrighted works when produced with the consent of the proprietor of the copyright in such works ... shall be regarded as new works subject to copyright...." Manifestly, the recorded program falls into this category as a dramatization of the script, and thus the program was itself entitled to copyright protection. However, section 7 limits the copyright protection of the derivative work, as works adapted from previously existing scripts have become known, to the novel additions made to the underlying work, and the derivative work does not affect the "force or validity" of the copyright in the matter from which it is derived. Thus, any ownership by BBC of the copyright in the recorded program would not affect the scope or ownership of the copyright in the underlying script.

Since the copyright in the underlying script survives intact despite the incorporation of that work into a derivative work, one who uses the script, even with the permission of the proprietor of the derivative work, may infringe the underlying copyright.

If the proprietor of the derivative work is licensed by the proprietor of the copyright in the underlying work to vend or distribute the derivative work to third parties, those parties will, of course, suffer no liability for their use of the underlying work consistent with the license to the proprietor of the derivative work. Obviously, it was just this type of arrangement that was contemplated in this instance. The scriptwriters' agreement between Monty Python and BBC specifically permitted the latter to license the transmission of the recordings made by BBC to distributors such as Time–Life for broadcast in overseas territories.

One who obtains permission to use a copyrighted script in the production of a derivative work, however, may not exceed the specific purpose for which permission was granted. Most of the decisions that have reached this conclusion have dealt with the improper extension of the underlying work into media or time, i.e., duration of the license, not covered by the grant of permission to the derivative work proprietor. Appellants herein do not claim that the broadcast by ABC violated media or time restrictions contained in the license of the script to BBC. Rather, they claim that revisions in the script, and ultimately in the program, could be made only after consultation with Monty Python, and that ABC's broadcast of a program edited after recording and without consultation with Monty Python exceeded the scope of any license that BBC was entitled to grant.

---

* This section was a part of the prior 1909 Copyright Act. *Ed.*

The rationale for finding infringement when a licensee exceeds time or media restrictions on his license the need to allow the proprietor of the underlying copyright to control the method in which his work is presented to the public applies equally to the situation in which a licensee makes an unauthorized use of the underlying work by publishing it in a truncated version. Whether intended to allow greater economic exploitation of the work, as in the media and time cases, or to ensure that the copyright proprietor retains a veto power over revisions desired for the derivative work, the ability of the copyright holder to control his work remains paramount in our copyright law. We find, therefore, that unauthorized editing of the underlying work, if proven, would constitute an infringement of the copyright in that work similar to any other use of a work that exceeded the license granted by the proprietor of the copyright.

If the broadcast of an edited version of the Monty Python program infringed the group's copyright in the script, ABC may obtain no solace from the fact that editing was permitted in the agreements between BBC and Time–Life or Time–Life and ABC. BBC was not entitled to make unilateral changes in the script and was not specifically empowered to alter the recordings once made; Monty Python, moreover, had reserved to itself any rights not granted to BBC. Since a grantor may not convey greater rights than it owns, BBC's permission to allow Time–Life, and hence ABC, to edit appears to have been a nullity.

Our resolution of these technical arguments serves to reinforce our initial inclination that the copyright law should be used to recognize the important role of the artist in our society and the need to encourage production and dissemination of artistic works by providing adequate legal protection for one who submits his work to the public. We therefore conclude that there is a substantial likelihood that, after a full trial, appellants will succeed in proving infringement of their copyright by ABC's broadcast of edited versions of Monty Python programs.

II

It also seems likely that appellants will succeed on the theory that, regardless of the right ABC had to broadcast an edited program, the cuts made constituted an actionable mutilation of Monty Python's work. This cause of action, which seeks redress for deformation of an artist's work, finds its roots in the continental concept of droit moral or moral right.

American copyright law, as presently written, does not recognize moral rights or provide a cause of action for their violation, since the law seeks to vindicate the economic, rather than the personal, rights of authors. Nevertheless, the economic incentive for artistic and intellectual creation that serves as the foundation for American copyright law, cannot be reconciled with the inability of artists to obtain relief for mutilation or misrepresentation of their work to the public on which the artists are financially dependent. Thus courts have long granted relief for misrepresentation of an artist's work by relying on theories outside the statutory law of copyright, such as contract law, or the tort of unfair competition.

Although such decisions are clothed in terms of proprietary right in one's creation, they also properly vindicate the author's personal right to prevent the presentation of his work to the public in a distorted form.

Here, the appellants claim that the editing done for ABC mutilated the original work and that consequently the broadcast of those programs as the creation of Monty Python violated the Lanham Act § 43(a), 15 U.S.C. § 1125(a).[10] This statute, the federal counterpart to state unfair competition laws, has been invoked to prevent misrepresentations that may injure plaintiff's business or personal reputation, even where no registered trademark is concerned. It is sufficient to violate the Act that a representation of a product, although technically true, creates a false impression of the product's origin.

These cases cannot be distinguished from the situation in which a television network broadcasts a program properly designated as having been written and performed by a group, but which has been edited, without the writer's consent, into a form that departs substantially from the original work. "To deform his work is to present him to the public as the creator of a work not his own, and thus makes him subject to criticism for work he has not done." Roeder, [53 Harv. L. Rev.] at 569. In such a case, it is the writer or performer, rather than the network, who suffers the consequences of the mutilation, for the public will have only the final product by which to evaluate the work. Thus, an allegation that a defendant has presented to the public a "garbled," distorted version of plaintiff's work seeks to redress the very rights sought to be protected by the Lanham Act, and should be recognized as stating a cause of action under that statute.

During the hearing on the preliminary injunction, Judge Lasker viewed the edited version of the Monty Python program broadcast on December 26 and the original, unedited version. After hearing argument of this appeal, this panel also viewed and compared the two versions. We find that the truncated version at times omitted the climax of the skits to which appellants' rare brand of humor was leading and at other times deleted essential elements in the schematic development of a story line. We therefore agree with Judge Lasker's conclusion that the edited version broadcast by ABC impaired the integrity of appellants' work and represented to the public as the product of appellants what was actually a mere caricature of their talents. We believe that a valid cause of action for such distortion exists and that therefore a preliminary injunction may issue to prevent repetition of the broadcast prior to final determination of the issues.

---

10. That statute provides in part:

Any person who shall affix, apply, or annex, or use in connection with any goods or services, . . . a false designation of origin, or any false description or representation . . . and shall cause such goods or services to enter into commerce . . . shall be liable to a civil action by any person . . . who believes that he is or is likely to be damaged by the use of any such false description or representation.

For these reasons we direct that the district court issue the preliminary injunction sought by the appellants.

GURFEIN, CIRCUIT JUDGE (concurring):

The Copyright Act provides no recognition of the so-called droit moral, or moral right of authors. Nor are such rights recognized in the field of copyright law in the United States. If a distortion or truncation in connection with a use constitutes an infringement of copyright, there is no need for an additional cause of action beyond copyright infringement.

So far as the Lanham Act is concerned, it is not a substitute for droit moral which authors in Europe enjoy. If the licensee may, by contract, distort the recorded work, the Lanham Act does not come into play. If the licensee has no such right by contract, there will be a violation in breach of contract. The Lanham Act can hardly apply literally when the credit line correctly states the work to be that of the plaintiffs which, indeed it is, so far as it goes. The vice complained of is that the truncated version is not what the plaintiffs wrote. But the Lanham Act does not deal with artistic integrity. It only goes to misdescription of origin and the like. The misdescription of origin can be dealt with, as Judge Lasker did below, by devising an appropriate legend to indicate that the plaintiffs had not approved the editing of the ABC version.

* * *

Berne Convention Implementation Act of 1988

Senate Report No. 100–352, reprinted in 1988 U.S.C.C.A.N. 3714–15.

MORAL RIGHTS

The statutes and decisions under which these rights are protected in Berne States are commonly referred to as comprising the "moral rights" in that sense [sic] are not provided in U.S. statutes, and various decisions of state and federal courts have rejected claims that were denominated specifically as "moral rights" or that sought relief under the "moral rights" doctrine.

However, protection is provided under existing U.S. law for the rights of authors listed in Article 6*bis*: (1) to claim authorship of their works ("the right of paternity"); and (2) to object to distortion, mutilation or other modification of their works, or other derogatory action with respect thereto, that would prejudice their honor or reputation ("the right of integrity"). This existing U.S. law includes various provisions of the Copyright Act and Lanham Act, various state statutes, and common law principles such as libel, defamation, misrepresentation, and unfair competition, which have been applied by courts to redress authors' invocation of the right to claim authorship or the right to object to distortion.

Section 2(3) of the Act clarifies that the amendments made by this Act, together with the law as it exists on the date of enactment of the Act, satisfy U.S. obligations under Article 6*bis* and that no further rights or interests shall be recognized or created for that purpose. The committee notes that Dr. Arpad Bogsch, Director General of WIPO, has given his opinion that the United States may become a member of the Berne Convention without making any changes to U.S. law for the purposes of Article 6*bis*. Consequently, the "moral rights" doctrine is not incorporated into the U.S. law by this statute.

NOTES AND QUESTIONS

1. *The U.S. Reluctance to Formally Recognize Moral Rights.* For the most part, the U.S. has resisted any formal recognition of moral rights for authors, even to the point of successfully obtaining the express exclusion of Berne Article 6*bis* from incorporation into TRIPS Article 9. As discussed in the Senate Report, the U.S. has taken the position that other federal and state laws outside of copyright approximate the moral rights of integrity and attribution required by the Berne Convention. If U.S. law already encompasses protections that are functionally similar or equivalent to moral rights as concluded by Congress, what would the harm be in giving moral rights of authors more formal recognition in copyright law? Who might be opposed to formally recognizing moral rights, and why? Is the U.S. approach consistent with Berne? Could it be justified by Berne Article 6*bis*(3), which states that "[t]he means of redress for safeguarding the rights granted by this Article shall be governed by the legislation of the country where protection is claimed."

The U.S. has recognized moral rights for a limited class of "works of visual art" under The Visual Artists Rights Act (VARA), codified in relevant part at 17 U.S.C. § 106A. This statutory right is very limited, applying only to a single copy of "a painting, drawing, print, or sculpture," or a "still photographic image produced for exhibition purposes only," or to a limited edition of 200 copies or fewer of such works, signed and consecutively numbered by the author. *Id.* § 101 (definition of "work of visual art"). However, VARA does not protect any works-made-for-hire, motion pictures, and many other kinds of works. Section 106A(c) also exempts offending works that are not themselves works of visual art. VARA would not protect, for example, an artist whose work was reproduced in a poster or advertisement without attribution or in a distorted way, since posters and advertisements are not themselves works of visual art. (The exclusive rights under copyright, however, may apply in such circumstances.)

2. *European versus U.S. approach.* Which approach to moral rights—the European or the U.S.—is better for authors? Had the U.S. approach to moral rights applied to John Huston in the *Huston* case, would the result have been the same for the airing of a colorized version of *The Asphalt Jungle* in the U.S.?

3. Could a country bring a challenge to the adequacy of U.S.'s protection of moral rights (or lack thereof) before the WTO?

4. *The "Moral Rights" interpretation of the Lanham Act.* In *Dastar Corp. v. Twentieth Century Fox Film Corp.*, 539 U.S. 23 (2003), the U.S. Supreme Court appeared to cast some doubt on interpreting § 43(a) of the Lanham Act to establish a moral right equivalent, rejecting a claim similar to

an attribution claim for a movie whose copyright had expired. The Court did not specifically address the moral right argument made by Twentieth Century Fox Film and its amici, but chose to take a plain language approach to the Lanham Act. Whether this means that the Lanham Act should not be interpreted to encompass any moral rights is unclear, since *Dastar* involved an expired copyright (and moral rights under Berne need not extend beyond such point). A future case involving a subsisting copyright might present a more attractive case to revisit the *Gilliam* type analysis. *See, e.g., Zyla v. Wadsworth, Div. of Thomson Corp.*, 360 F.3d 243 (1st Cir. 2004) (rejecting § 43(a) claim of co-author for attribution right on copyrighted work).

Compare Edward Lee, *The New Canon: Using or Misusing Foreign Law to Decide Domestic Intellectual Property Claims*, 46 HARV. INT'L L.J. 1, 42–44 (2005) (defending the Supreme Court's approach) with Graeme W. Austin, *The Berne Convention as a Canon of Construction: Moral Rights after* Dastar, 61 N.Y.U. ANN. SURV. AM. L. 111 (2005) (criticizing the *Dastar* decision); Jane C. Ginsburg, *The Right to Claim Authorship in U.S. Copyright and Trademarks Law*, 41 HOUS. L. REV. 263 (2004).

5. *Debate Over Moral Rights in Remix Culture.* The digital age has sparked renewed debate over moral rights. Digital technologies allow people to "remix" content and create their own adaptations of works, including literature, music, and videos. Should an author be able to object to a remixed version of her work as a violation of her right of integrity? Roberta Rosenthal Kwall argues that, in order to protect the author's intrinsic, non-economic motivations to create, the U.S. should formally recognize the moral rights of attribution and integrity for copyrighted works. ROBERTA ROSENTHAL KWALL, THE SOUL OF CREATIVITY: FORGING A MORAL RIGHTS LAW FOR THE UNITED STATES 149–51 (2010). But to accommodate free speech interests in the U.S., Kwall proposes that the moral right of integrity encompass the limited right of an author to require people to include, on remixes of an author's work, a disclaimer "adequate to inform the public of the author's objection to modification or contextual usage" of the author's work. *Id.* at 151. On the other side, Professor Amy Adler attacks moral rights as "obstruct[ing] rather than enabl[ing] the creation of art because the law fails to recognize the defining role that destruction has come to play in contemporary artistic practice." Amy M. Adler, *Against Moral Rights*, 97 CAL. L. REV. 263, 265 (2009). Adler contends that "metaphorical destruction lies at the heart of contemporary art." *Id.* at 284. *See also* Jacqueline D. Lipton, *Moral Rights and Supernatural Fiction: Authorial Dignity and the New Moral Rights Agendas*, 21 FORDHAM INTELL. PROP. & MEDIA & ENT. L.J. 537 (2011). Which view of moral rights do you favor?

6. *Bibliographic note.* Roberta Rosenthal Kwall, *Copyright and the Moral Right: Is an American Marriage Possible?*, 38 VAND. L. REV. 1 (1985); John H. Merryman, *The Refrigerator of Bernard Buffet*, 27 HASTINGS L.J. 1023 (1976); Burton Ong, *Why Moral Rights Matter: Recognizing the Intrinsic Value of Integrity Rights*, 26 COLUM. J.L. & ARTS 297 (2003); Martin A. Roeder, *The Doctrine of Moral Rights: A Study in the Law of Artists, Authors and Creators*, 53 HARV. L. REV. 554 (1940).

H. SPECIAL DISCUSSION: ANTI–CIRCUMVENTION RIGHTS IN THE DIGITAL AGE

The emergence of new technologies such as the Internet has posed new challenges for copyright law. The Internet allows nearly instantaneous copying and dissemination of digital files around the world. When such files are copyrighted and copied without permission, large amounts of infringement may occur. We examine below some of the responses of the international legal community.

PROBLEM 2–23

Professor Hewitt, a professor of American history at a private University, wanted to show parts of the assassination of President John F. Kennedy, Jr., as recorded on the now famous Zapruder film, which was the only live footage of the Nov. 22, 1963 tragic event. Assume that Abraham Zapruder copyrighted the film and later transferred the copyright in the film to Documentary Productions, Inc. In 2008, to commemorate the 45th anniversary of President Kennedy's death, Documentary Productions re-released the Zapruder film on DVD, adding new commentary of historians interviewed in 2008 about the presidency of Kennedy. The DVD has encryption on it that is intended to make it difficult for users to make copies of the copyrighted files stored on the DVD. Documentary Productions now makes the only publicly available copies of the Zapruder film.

In January of 2011, Professor Hewitt asked his research assistant to see if he could "hack around" the encryption on Documentary Productions' DVD that he purchased, in order to copy a brief portion of the Zapruder footage of President Kennedy's assassination. Professor Hewitt wanted to get the clip, in order to incorporate it into a PowerPoint presentation for his history class. This way Professor Hewitt wouldn't have to waste valuable class time, just to turn off his PowerPoint slide, turn on the DVD, and then skip through to the relevant portion of the DVD where the Zapruder footage was located. The research assistant "hacked around" the encryption pretty easily, and Professor Hewitt used it in his PowerPoint presentation to his history class. Because the class was webcast by the University, however, Documentary Productions later found out about Hewitt's presentation after an anonymous person emailed the company about Hewitt's presentation.

In June 2011, Documentary Productions sues Professor Hewitt for violations of the Digital Millennium Copyright Act, 17 U.S.C. § 1201 et seq. As a defense, Professor Hewitt invokes the fair use doctrine contained in § 107 of the Copyright Act. You may assume that Professor Hewitt would be held responsible for the conduct of his research assistant, and that Documentary Productions successfully proved that Hewitt's research assistant had "hacked around" its encryption on the DVD. What result? Consider the following provision and discussion, including the accompanying note on the DMCA exemptions allowed by the Librarian of Congress.

WIPO Copyright Treaty

Article 11

Obligations concerning Technological Measures

Contracting Parties shall provide adequate legal protection and effective legal remedies against the circumvention of effective technological measures that are used by authors in connection with the exercise of their rights under this Treaty or the Berne Convention and that restrict acts, in respect of their works, which are not authorized by the authors concerned or permitted by law.

Agreed statement concerning Article 10: It is understood that the provisions of Article 10 permit Contracting Parties to carry forward and appropriately extend into the digital environment limitations and exceptions in their national laws which have been considered acceptable under the Berne Convention. Similarly, these provisions should be understood to permit Contracting Parties to devise new exceptions and limitations that are appropriate in the digital network environment.

It is also understood that Article 10(2) neither reduces nor extends the scope of applicability of the limitations and exceptions permitted by the Berne Convention.

UNIVERSAL CITY STUDIOS, INC. v. CORLEY

U.S. Court of Appeals for the Second Circuit.
273 F.3d 429 (2d Cir. 2001).

NEWMAN, CIRCUIT JUDGE.

Th[is] appeal challenges the constitutionality of the Digital Millennium Copyright Act ("DMCA"), 17 U.S.C. § 1201 *et seq.* (Supp. V 1999) and the validity of an injunction entered to enforce the DMCA.

Defendant–Appellant Eric C. Corley and his company, 2600 Enterprises, Inc., (collectively "Corley," "the Defendants," or "the Appellants") appeal from the amended final judgment of the United States District Court for the Southern District of New York (Lewis A. Kaplan, District Judge), entered August 23, 2000, enjoining them from various actions concerning a decryption program known as "DeCSS." The injunction primarily bars the Appellants from posting DeCSS on their web site and from knowingly linking their web site to any other web site on which DeCSS is posted. We affirm.

Introduction

This appeal concerns the anti-trafficking provisions of the DMCA, which Congress enacted in 1998 to strengthen copyright protection in the digital age. Fearful that the ease with which pirates could copy and distribute a copyrightable work in digital form was overwhelming the capacity of conventional copyright enforcement to find and enjoin unlawfully copied material, Congress sought to combat copyright piracy in its earlier stages, before the work was even copied. The DMCA therefore backed with legal sanctions the efforts of copyright owners to protect their works from piracy behind digital walls such as encryption codes or password protections. In so doing, Congress targeted not only those pirates who would *circumvent* these digital walls (the "anti-circumvention provisions," contained in 17 U.S.C. § 1201(a)(1)), but also anyone who would *traffic* in a technology primarily designed to circumvent a digital wall (the "anti-trafficking provisions," contained in 17 U.S.C. § 1201(a)(2), (b)(1)).

Corley publishes a print magazine and maintains an affiliated web site geared towards "hackers," a digital-era term often applied to those interested in techniques for circumventing protections of computers and computer data from unauthorized access. The so-called hacker community includes serious computer-science scholars conducting research on protection techniques, computer buffs intrigued by the challenge of trying to circumvent access-limiting devices or perhaps hoping to promote security by exposing flaws in protection techniques, mischief-makers interested in disrupting computer operations, and thieves, including copyright infringers who want to acquire copyrighted material (for personal use or resale) without paying for it.

In November 1999, Corley posted a copy of the decryption computer program "DeCSS" on his web site, http://www.2600.com ("2600.com"). DeCSS is designed to circumvent "CSS," the encryption technology that motion picture studios place on DVDs to prevent the unauthorized viewing and copying of motion pictures. Corley also posted on his web site links to other web sites where DeCSS could be found.

Plaintiffs–Appellees are eight motion picture studios that brought an action in the Southern District of New York seeking injunctive relief against Corley under the DMCA. Following a full non-jury trial, the District Court entered a permanent injunction barring Corley from posting DeCSS on his web site or from knowingly linking via a hyperlink to any other web site containing DeCSS. The District Court rejected Corley's constitutional attacks on the statute and the injunction.

Background

II. DeCSS

In September 1999, Jon Johansen, a Norwegian teenager, collaborating with two unidentified individuals he met on the Internet, reverse-engineered a licensed DVD player designed to operate on the Microsoft operating system, and culled from it the player keys and other information necessary to decrypt CSS. The record suggests that Johansen was trying to develop a DVD player operable on Linux, an alternative operating system that did not support any licensed DVD players at that time. In order to accomplish this task, Johansen wrote a decryption program executable on Microsoft's operating system. That program was called, appropriately enough, "DeCSS."

If a user runs the DeCSS program (for example, by clicking on the DeCSS icon on a Microsoft operating system platform) with a DVD in the computer's disk drive, DeCSS will decrypt the DVD's CSS protection, allowing the user to copy the DVD's files and place the copy on the user's hard drive. The result is a very large computer file that can be played on a non-CSS-compliant player and copied, manipulated, and transferred just like any other computer file. Within months of its appearance on Johansen's web site, DeCSS was widely available on the Internet.

In November 1999, Corley wrote and placed on his web site, 2600.com, an article about the DeCSS phenomenon. Corley's article about DeCSS detailed how CSS was cracked, and described the movie industry's efforts to shut down web sites posting DeCSS. It also explained that DeCSS could be used to copy DVDs. At the end of the article, the Defendants posted copies of the object and source code of DeCSS. Corley also added to the article links that he explained would take the reader to other web sites where DeCSS could be found.

III. The DMCA

The DMCA was enacted in 1998 to implement the World Intellectual Property Organization Copyright Treaty ("WIPO Treaty"), which requires contracting parties to "provide adequate legal protection and effective legal remedies against the circumvention of effective technological measures that are used by authors in connection with the exercise of their rights under this Treaty or the Berne Convention and that restrict acts, in respect of their works, which are not authorized by the authors concerned or permitted by law." WIPO Treaty, Apr. 12, 1997, art. 11, S. Treaty Doc. No. 105–17 (1997).

The Act contains three provisions targeted at the circumvention of technological protections. The first is subsection 1201(a)(1)(A), the anti-circumvention provision. This provision prohibits a person from "circumvent[ing] a technological measure that effectively controls access to a work protected under [Title 17, governing copyright]." The Librarian of Congress is required to promulgate regulations every three years exempting from this subsection individuals who would otherwise be "adversely affected" in "their ability to make noninfringing uses." 17 U.S.C. § 1201(a)(1)(B)–(E).

The second and third provisions are subsections 1201(a)(2) and 1201(b)(1), the "anti-trafficking provisions." Subsection 1201(a)(2), the provision at issue in this case, provides:

> No person shall manufacture, import, offer to the public, provide, or otherwise traffic in any technology, product, service, device, component, or part thereof, that—
>
> (A) is primarily designed or produced for the purpose of circumventing a technological measure that effectively controls access to a work protected under this title;

(B) has only limited commercially significant purpose or use other than to circumvent a technological measure that effectively controls access to a work protected under this title; or

(C) is marketed by that person or another acting in concert with that person with that person's knowledge for use in circumventing a technological measure that effectively controls access to a work protected under this title.

Id. § 1201(a)(2). To "circumvent a technological measure" is defined, in pertinent part, as "to descramble a scrambled work ... or otherwise to ... bypass ... a technological measure, without the authority of the copyright owner." *Id.* § 1201(a)(3)(A).

Subsection 1201(b)(1) is similar to subsection 1201(a)(2), except that subsection 1201(a)(2) covers those who traffic in technology that can circumvent "a technological measure *that effectively controls access* to a work protected under" Title 17, whereas subsection 1201(b)(1) covers those who traffic in technology that can circumvent "protection afforded by a technological measure *that effectively protects a right of a copyright owner* under" Title 17. *Id.* § 1201(a)(2), (b)(1) (emphases added). In other words, although both subsections prohibit trafficking in a circumvention technology, the focus of subsection 1201(a)(2) is circumvention of technologies designed to *prevent access* to a work, and the focus of subsection 1201(b)(1) is circumvention of technologies designed to *permit access* to a work but *prevent copying* of the work or some other act that infringes a copyright. Subsection 1201(a)(1) differs from both of these anti-trafficking subsections in that it targets the use of a circumvention technology, not the trafficking in such a technology.

The DMCA contains exceptions for schools and libraries that want to use circumvention technologies to determine whether to purchase a copyrighted product, 17 U.S.C. § 1201(d); individuals using circumvention technology "for the sole purpose" of trying to achieve "interoperability" of computer programs through reverse-engineering, *id.* § 1201(f); encryption research aimed at identifying flaws in encryption technology, if the research is conducted to advance the state of knowledge in the field, *id.* § 1201(g); and several other exceptions not relevant here.

The DMCA creates civil remedies, *id.* § 1203, and criminal sanctions, *id.* § 1204. It specifically authorizes a court to "grant temporary and permanent injunctions on such terms as it deems reasonable to prevent or restrain a violation." *Id.* § 1203(b)(1).

Discussion

I. Narrow Construction to Avoid Constitutional Doubt

The Appellants first argue that, because their constitutional arguments are at least substantial, we should interpret the statute narrowly so as to avoid constitutional problems. They identify three different instances of alleged ambiguity in the statute that they claim provide an opportunity for such a narrow interpretation.

First, they contend that subsection 1201(c)(1), which provides that "[n]othing in this section shall affect rights, remedies, limitations or defenses to copyright infringement, including fair use, under this title," can be read to allow the circumvention of encryption technology protecting copyrighted material when the material will be put to "fair uses" exempt from copyright liability. We disagree that subsection 1201(c)(1) permits such a reading. Instead, it simply clarifies that the DMCA targets the *circumvention* of digital walls guarding copyrighted material (and trafficking in circumvention tools), but does not concern itself with the *use* of those materials after circumvention has occurred. Subsection 1201(c)(1) ensures that the DMCA is not read to prohibit the "fair use" of information just because that information was obtained in a manner made illegal by the DMCA.

Second, the Appellants urge a narrow construction of the DMCA because of subsection 1201(c)(4), which provides that "[n]othing in this section shall enlarge or diminish any rights of free speech or the press for activities using consumer electronics, telecommunications, or computing products." This language is clearly precatory: Congress could not "diminish" constitutional rights of free speech even if it wished to, and the fact that Congress also expressed a reluctance to "enlarge" those rights cuts against the Appellants' effort to infer a narrowing construction of the Act from this provision.

Third, the Appellants argue that an individual who buys a DVD has the "authority of the copyright owner" to view the DVD, and therefore is exempted from the DMCA pursuant to subsection 1201(a)(3)(A) when the buyer circumvents an encryption technology in order to view the DVD on a competing platform (such as Linux). The basic flaw in this argument is that it misreads subsection 1201(a)(3)(A). That provision exempts from liability those who would "decrypt" an encrypted DVD with the authority of a copyright owner, not those who would "view" a DVD with the authority of a copyright owner. In any event, the Defendants offered no evidence that the Plaintiffs have either explicitly or implicitly authorized DVD buyers to circumvent encryption technology to support use on multiple platforms.

This is actually what subsection 1201(a)(3)(A) means when read in conjunction with the *anti-circumvention* provisions. When read together with the *anti-trafficking* provisions, subsection 1201(a)(3)(A) frees an individual to traffic in encryption technology designed or marketed to circumvent an encryption measure if the owner of the material protected by the encryption measure authorizes that circumvention.

We conclude that the anti-trafficking and anti-circumvention provisions of the DMCA are not susceptible to the narrow interpretations urged by the Appellants. [The Second Circuit then rejected the appellants' challenge to the DCMA based on the First Amendment and refused to consider a challenge based on the Copyright Clause as not properly raised below. *Ed.*]

IV. Constitutional Challenge Based on Claimed Restriction of Fair Use

Asserting that fair use "is rooted in and required by both the Copyright Clause and the First Amendment," the Appellants contend that the DMCA, as applied by the District Court, unconstitutionally "*eliminates* fair use" of copyrighted materials, *id.* at 41 (emphasis added). We reject this extravagant claim.

Preliminarily, we note that the Supreme Court has never held that fair use is constitutionally required, although some isolated statements in its opinions might arguably be enlisted for such a requirement. [The court noted the cases. *Ed.*] We need not explore the extent to which fair use might have constitutional protection, grounded on either the First Amendment or the Copyright Clause, because whatever validity a constitutional claim might have as to an application of the DMCA that impairs fair use of copyrighted materials, such matters are far beyond the scope of this lawsuit for several reasons. In the first place, the Appellants do not claim to be making fair use of any copyrighted materials, and nothing in the injunction prohibits them from making such fair use. They are barred from trafficking in a decryption code that enables unauthorized access to copyrighted materials.

Second, as the District Court properly noted, to whatever extent the anti-trafficking provisions of the DMCA might prevent others from copying portions of DVD movies in order to make fair use of them, "the evidence as to the impact of the anti-trafficking provision[s] of the DMCA on prospective fair users is scanty and fails adequately to address the issues."

Third, the Appellants have provided no support for their premise that fair use of DVD movies is constitutionally required to be made by copying the original work in its original format. Their examples of the fair uses that they believe others will be prevented from making all involve copying in a digital format those portions of a DVD movie amenable to fair use, a copying that would enable the fair user to manipulate the digitally copied portions. One example is that of a school child who wishes to copy images from a DVD movie to insert into the student's documentary film. We know of no authority for the proposition that fair use, as protected by the Copyright Act, much less the Constitution, guarantees copying by the optimum method or in the identical format of the original. Although the Appellants insisted at oral argument that they should not be relegated to a "horse and buggy" technique in making fair use of DVD movies, the DMCA does not impose even an arguable limitation on the opportunity to make a variety of traditional fair uses of DVD movies, such as commenting on their content, quoting excerpts from their screenplays, and even recording portions of the video images and sounds on film or tape by pointing a camera, a camcorder, or a microphone at a monitor as it displays the DVD movie. The fact that the resulting copy will not be as perfect or as manipulable as a digital copy obtained by having direct access to the DVD movie in its digital form, provides no basis for a claim of unconstitutional limitation of fair use. A film critic making fair use of a movie by quoting selected lines of dialogue has no constitutionally valid claim that the review (in print or on television) would be technologically superior if the reviewer had not been prevented from using a movie camera in the theater, nor has an art student a valid constitutional claim to fair use of a painting by photographing it in a museum. Fair use has never been held to be a guarantee of access to copyrighted material in order to copy it by the fair user's preferred technique or in the format of the original. [A]ffirmed.

NOTES AND QUESTIONS

1. What is the difference between the "anti-circumvention" and "anti-trafficking" provisions in § 1201 in terms of their prohibitions? Are the protections afforded to copyright holders under the Digital Millennium Copyright Act (DMCA), § 1201, greater than the minimum standard required by Article 11 of the WIPO Copyright Treaty?

2. Can you explain the relationship between a copyright and the DMCA anti-circumvention rights under § 1201? Why do you think countries in WIPO believed it necessary to add anti-circumvention protections for copyright holders in 1996? Under the WIPO Copyright Treaty, can countries have exceptions to anti-circumvention protections?

3. *Fair use.* Regarding fair use under the DMCA, the U.S. Copyright Office has stated:

> Since copying of a work may be a fair use under appropriate circumstances, section 1201 does not prohibit the act of circumventing a technological measure that prevents copying. By contrast, since the fair use doctrine is not a defense to the act of gaining unauthorized access to a work, the act of circumventing a technological measure in order to gain access is prohibited [under § 1201(a)(1)].

U.S. Copyright Office, The Digital Millennium Copyright Act of 1998 at 3–4 (1998) at http://www.loc.gov/copyright/legislation/dmca.pdf. According to the Copyright Office, a user who circumvents an access control measure is not allowed to assert a fair use defense, but a user who has already obtained lawful access to a copyrighted work and who circumvents a copying control measure may be able to assert the fair use doctrine as a defense. Practically speaking, this fine distinction may not matter much because encryption or DRM commonly aims to prevent access to the work. For example, in *Corley*, CSS encryption was found to be an "access control" technology because the encryption is designed to deny access to the work without the proper "keys" from a licensed DVD player. *Universal City Studios, Inc. v. Reimerdes*, 111 F. Supp. 2d 294, 317–18 (S.D.N.Y. 2000).

4. *Agency exemptions to the DMCA.* Congress recognized the danger that the DMCA might unduly restrict fair uses by effectively "locking" people out of such uses. Under the DMCA, Congress authorized the Librarian of Congress, upon the recommendation of the Register of Copyrights, to issue exemptions to the anti-circumvention provision that last for a 3–year period. *See* 17 U.S.C. § 1201(a)(1)(C). Typically, the Register of Copyrights entertains

comments and submissions from the public as to possible exemptions. In 2010, the Librarian issued its fourth set of exemptions, this time recognizing 6 exemptions to the DMCA anti-circumvention provision. *See* Exemption to Prohibition on Circumvention of Copyright Protection Systems for Access Control Technologies, 75 Fed. Reg. 43825 (July 27, 2010).

Two exemptions deal with mobile phones and consumer choice. The Librarian renewed the 2006 exemption that allows people to circumvent encryption on their phones in order to switch to another mobile service provider, such as from AT&T to Verizon. *Id.* at 43830. The new "jailbreaking" exemption goes further by allowing people to circumvent the technological measures on their iPhones or other mobile devices, in order to allow the devices to run third-party software applications of the user's choice—even against the wishes of Apple or the device manufacturer. The Register of Copyrights found the argument for fair use in jailbreaking iPhones was "compelling and consistent with congressional interest in interoperability." *Id.* at 43829.

The other key exemption recognized by the Librarian is a "remix" exemption that expands a prior exemption for circumventing the encryption on movies on DVDs, in order to make a fair use of a film. The new "remix" exemption applies not only to "educational use in the classroom by media studies or film professors," as was the case under the previous exemption, but now also to documentary filmmaking and noncommercial videos—the latter class popular among "vidders." *Id.* at 43828. The "remix" exemption is limited to "relatively short portions of motion pictures" for use in creating a new work "for purposes of criticism or commentary." *Id.*

Is the administrative process for getting exemptions to the DMCA anti-circumvention provision adequate? Is the 3–year duration of the exemption a reasonable time period? Or should the exemptions have a longer life? What changes, if any, would you make to the process?

5. *Multi-use technologies.* The anti-circumvention provisions of the DMCA and the WIPO Copyright Treaty raise fundamental questions about the law's stance with respect to "multi-use" technologies that may be used for both legitimate and illegitimate uses. Should the law prohibit such a multi-use technology because it is capable of illegitimate uses such as copyright infringement? Or should the law allow for the development of the technology because it has legitimate uses that can benefit society, such as a technology that enables others to make fair uses of copyrighted works? How should the proper balance be struck?

It is worth noting that in Norway, the actual developer of DeCSS, Jon Johansen, who was a teenager at the time, was acquitted of criminal charges for his design and distribution of DeCSS. (In fact, Johansen received an award from his high school for his software development, although he later dropped out of school to focus on computer programming and reverse engineering.) In the criminal case, an Oslo trial court and appeals court both held that distribution of goods that have legal uses cannot constitute criminal cooperation under the criminal law of Norway, even though the goods may also be used for illegal purposes. *See The Public Prosecution v. Johansen*, No. 02–507 M/94 (Jan. 7, 2003). The appeals court recognized that Johansen's intent in designing his software was to make DVDs compatible with and operable on a Linux-operating system. According to the court, the DeCSS software enabled a fair use—to make backup copies—and thus was legal, even if it could also be used for illegal purposes. Do you agree with the Norwegian court's approach? If this approach were applied to the defendants in *Corley*, would the result there have been different?

6. *EU approach*. Articles 6 and 7 of the EU Information Society Directive, 2001/29/EC, set forth the EU's implementation of Articles 11 and 12 of the WIPO Copyright Treaty (WCT). Unlike the U.S. DMCA law, the EU Directive has a provision to protect the rights of users in making lawful exempted uses of copyrighted works. The safe harbor states: "Notwithstanding the legal protection provided for in paragraph 1, in the absence of voluntary measures taken by rightholders, including agreements between rightholders and other parties concerned, Member States shall take appropriate measures to ensure that rightholders make available to the beneficiary of an exception or limitation provided for in national law in accordance with Article 5(2)(a), (2)(c), (2)(d), (2)(e), (3)(a), (3)(b) or (3)(e) the means of benefiting from that exception or limitation, to the extent necessary to benefit from that exception or limitation and where that beneficiary has legal access to the protected work or subject-matter concerned." *Id*. art. 6(4). Copyright holders that use DRM on their works must set up voluntarily measures for users to bypass DRM in order to make a protected use, or EU states must adopt appropriate legal measures. Countries have adopted various legal measures to protect users: (1) lawful self-help; (2) arbitration; (3) cause of action in court; and (4) administrative or executive proceeding. *See* Gwen Hinze, *Brave New World, Ten Years Later: Reviewing the Impact of Policy Choices in the Implementation of the WIPO Internet Treaties' Technological Protection Measure Provisions*, 57 CASE W. RES. L. REV. 779, 810 (2007). Which approach is best?

7. *Bibliographic note*. Edward Lee, *Rules and Standards for Cyberspace*, 77 NOTRE DAME L. REV. 1275, 1356–1372 (2002); David Nimmer, *A Riff on Fair Use in the Digital Millennium Copyright Act*, 148 U. PA. L. REV. 673 (2000); Pamela Samuelson, *Intellectual Property and the Digital Economy: Why the Anti–Circumvention Regulations Need to Be Revised*, 14 BERKELEY TECH. L.J. 519 (1999).

I. SPECIAL DISCUSSION: ISP DUTIES, SAFE HARBORS, AND SECONDARY LIABILITY

PROBLEM 2–24

You are the General Counsel of Trinity Corp., a provider of broadband Internet access in Australia. The movie studios have approached Trinity to join other ISPs that have agreed to a voluntary set of "best practices" for ISPs formulated by the movie studios. Under the best practices, ISPs agree to undertake "mitigation measures" to help stop infringement by their users. Each time a notice of copyright infringement is sent by a copyright holder to an ISP for the activity of one of its broadband users, the ISP will send a "copyright alert" notice by email to the user. The alert notice, which is in a standardized form for all ISPs, will detail the allegation of infringement and warn the user to refrain from copyright infringement.

If a user receives over 6 copyright alert notices within any calendar year for repeated infringement, the ISP will use mitigation measures against the user. The measures include reducing the speed of the user's downloading through the service, and redirecting the user to a "landing page" before a download can be made that requires the user to call the ISP to discuss how to avoid copyright infringement or to watch a 15–minute educational video on proper copyright practices. The user may appeal a copyright notice to an independent arbitrator, who has the power to order the ISP to overrule the notice. The user must pay $35 for the appeal, but the fee is refunded if the user prevails. If Trinity agrees to implement these best practices, the movie studios have offered to sign a waiver of their right to sue Trinity for copyright infringement in the future as long as the ISP follows the industry agreement. Should Trinity agree to the movie studios' proposal? To evaluate this question, determine (i) how much copyright liability exposure Trinity has under Australian law currently, and (ii) how much liability exposure it may avoid under the movie studios' proposal. Is the proposal better for Trinity than its exposure to copyright liability or its ability to invoke the safe harbor under the current law? Consider the following discussion and case.

* * *

Secondary liability and ISPs. Secondary liability means holding an entity liable for the infringing activity of a primary or direct infringer, typically under theories of contributory or vicarious infringement. Under U.S. law, contributory infringement is based on the concept of aiding and abetting—an entity is held secondarily liable based on knowing contribution to a third party's direct infringement. Vicarious infringement is based on the concept of agency—an entity is held secondarily liable based on receiving a direct financial benefit from a third party's direct infringement, while having the ability to control or supervise the third part's actions. Other countries may have different standards, but they all consider the possibility of secondary liability. Curiously, neither TRIPS nor Berne appears to address secondary liability, despite its tremendous importance in modern copyright litigation. Copyright holders often find secondary liability claims more attractive because suing intermediaries is easier than suing thousands of individuals and is financially more attractive (i.e., suing a "deep pocket").

Given the ease with which unauthorized copies of copyrighted works can be shared on the Internet, all countries have faced a basic question whether to hold Internet service providers (ISPs) liable for the infringing conduct of their users. Services such as Facebook, Google, Twitter, and YouTube typically allow people to share and post content through an automated system, without human or prior review of the content. The open nature of these services allows third parties the freedom to share a vast amount of speech, but sometimes the sharing includes copies of works that constitute copyright infringement. Copyright industries have contended that ISPs should do more to police their sites for infringing activities, while ISPs have argued that to do so would be cost prohibitive and chill legitimate speech activities.

The TRIPS Agreement—effective as of 1995, well before the Internet's incredible growth—does not address this issue. Countries have had to deal with this issue on their own. In 1998, the U.S. enacted the Digital Millennium Copyright Act (DMCA), part of which established the DMCA safe harbors for ISPs. The DMCA safe harbors offer a way for ISPs to avoid monetary liability for the copyright infringement of their users. Four different activities of ISPs are protected by the DMCA safe harbors: (1) providing access to the Internet (conduit), (2) caching or temporary storage of Internet material, (3) providing storage to third-party materials (hosting), and (4) information location tools (e.g., search engines). *See* 17 U.S.C. § 512. Importantly, the DMCA does not impose any duty on ISPs to monitor their services "or affirmatively seek[] facts indicating infringing activity." *Id.* § 512(m)(1).

A key facet of the DMCA safe harbors is the establishment of the DMCA "notice-and-takedown" process. *Id.* § 512(c)(3). Under this process, a copyright holder files a DMCA notice with the ISP that alleges copyright infringement related to third-party content or links made available through the ISP's service. Once a proper notice is received, the ISP must remove expeditiously the allegedly infringing content either stored or linked to by the ISP in order to fall within the safe harbor. *Id.* § 512(c)(1)(C). (The notice-and-takedown process does not apply to an ISP that merely provides Internet access, and applies only in limited form to an ISP that engages in caching. For caching, the takedown duty does not arise until the copyright holder has successfully obtained the removal of the infringing content from the originating site. *Id.* § 512(b)(2)(E).) In order to protect the rights of users, the DMCA requires the ISP to give notice to the user who posted the material subject to takedown. For user content hosted by an ISP under § 512(c), but not for mere links under § 512(d), the user may file a counter notification alleging that the material was erroneously removed. *Id.* § 512(g)(3). If a counter-notice is received, the ISP must repost the content between 10 and 14 business days following its receipt unless the copyright holder informs the ISP that the copyright holder has filed an action seeking a court order to restrain the posting. *Id.* § 512(g)(2)(C). The DMCA also creates a cause of action for damages for material misrepresentations made by copyright holders or users. *Id.* § 512(f). Thus, if a copyright holder misrepresents that its content has been infringed, knowing it was not, the person who posted the content online may sue the copyright holder for damages.

In 2000, the EU soon followed with its own set of ISP safe harbors. Drawing on the U.S. approach, the Directive on Electronic Commerce ("E–Commerce Directive"), 2000/31/EC, recognizes safe harbors for 3 activities of ISPs: (1) providing access to the Internet (conduit), (2) caching, and (3) hosting of material. *Id.* arts. 12–14. Unlike the U.S. DMCA safe harbors, the E–Commerce Directive does not have an express safe harbor for providing information location tools (e.g., search engines), although the CJEU has interpreted Article 14 of the E–Commerce Directive, designed for passive hosting of material, to apply in some cases to search engines, or "internet referencing service providers." The safe harbor applies if the "service provider has not played an active role of such a kind as to give it knowledge of, or control over, the data stored. If it has not played such a role, that service provider cannot be held liable for the data which it has stored at the request of an advertiser, unless, having obtained knowledge of the unlawful nature of those data or of that advertiser's activities, it failed to act expeditiously to remove or to disable access to the data concerned." *Google France v. Louis Vuitton Malletier*, C–236/08, 238/08, ¶ 121(3) (2010).

The EU approach is different from the U.S. approach in several other respects. First, it is broader and applies not only to copyright infringement, but to claims under other areas of law, such as defamation and trademark infringement—taking the so-called "horizontal" approach to safe harbors. Second, the EU approach does not expressly set forth a notice-and-takedown process, instead choosing to leave the exact procedure to "voluntary agreements between all parties concerned" and the discretion of member states. E–Commerce Directive, 2000/31/EC, Recital 40; *see also id.* art. 14(1)(b) (ISP "acts expeditiously to remove or to disable access to the information"). The EU approach also allows greater injunctive relief against ISPs than the U.S. approach. Despite these differences, the general philosophy behind the EU safe harbors is very similar to the U.S. Both sets of safe harbors focus on specific activities of ISPs that may qualify for protection under the safe harbor. And, like the U.S. approach, the Directive expressly recognizes that the law "shall not impose a general obligation on providers . . . to monitor the information which they transmit or store, nor a general obligation actively to seek facts or circumstances indicating illegal activity." *Id.* art. 15.

In 2006, China enacted its own safe harbor, also influenced by the DMCA. Through the State Council, China adopted a regulation establishing safe harbors for ISPs for Internet access, caching, and storing or linking to third-party content. China Regulation on Protection of the Right to Network Dissemination of Information arts. 14–17, 20–24 (2006).* For hosting and linking, the safe harbors require a notice-and-takedown process similar to the U.S. approach. *Id.* arts. 14–18. However, one key difference is that China's counter-notification process applies to both hosting and linking, and requires the ISP to reinstate the material or the link that was taken down if the user files a proper counter-notification with "[p]reliminary materials that there has been no infringement." *Id.* arts. 16–17. Under Article 17, after counter-notice, the process of notice-and-takedown does not allow the copyright holder to seek another removal of the material from the ISP, as is allowed under the DMCA window of 10 to 14 business days in the U.S. *Id.* Presumably, the second removal of the content under China's law would require court action.

Other countries have recognized similar ISP safe harbors. The case below discusses Australia's adoption of ISP safe harbors in 2004 following the Free Trade Agreement with the United States.

ROADSHOW FILMS PTY LTD. v. IINET LIMITED

Federal Court of Australia.
[2011] 194 FCR 285.

EMMETT, J.

INTRODUCTION

One or other of the appellants (together the Copyright Owners) is the owner of copyright in one or more of a number of cinematograph films

---

* An English translation of China's law is available at translation at http://www.chinaitlaw. org/?%20p1=regulations & p2=060717003346.

(the Films). The respondent, iiNet Limited (iiNet), is a carriage service provider. That is to say, iiNet provides its customers with access to the internet. It is common ground that, by use of the internet access services provided to its customers by iiNet, the Copyright Owners' copyright in the Films has been infringed[.] The Copyright Owners claim that iiNet has authorised the acts of infringement done by the use of its services. Accordingly, they claim, iiNet itself has infringed their copyrights.

The Copyright Owners commenced a proceeding in the Court seeking relief against iiNet in respect of the alleged infringement by iiNet. [The main allegation was that some iiNet users used BitTorrent peer-to-peer software to share copyrighted movies illegally and that iiNet, as the Internet service provider, should also be held responsible.] A judge of the Court concluded that there was no infringement by iiNet and [alternatively, that iiNet fell within the Safe Harbor for ISPs]. The Copyright Owners have now appealed from those orders, saying that the primary judge erred in a number of respects.

AUTHORISATION

A person will authorise an act of infringement if the person sanctions, approves or countenances the act. Countenancing does not mean the same thing as approving and includes turning a blind eye and tolerating or permitting. The question is whether iiNet tolerated and permitted acts of infringement to continue.

iiNet was aware that allegations [by the copyright owners] that infringements by users of its services had occurred. To the extent that it could rely on the information provided by the Infringement Notices, it was in a position to determine the identity of the customers whose accounts were involved in the infringements. iiNet had the power to prevent further infringements involving those accounts by suspending or terminating the accounts. However, iiNet took no step to suspend or terminate any account in order to prevent or avoid the making of the communications that constituted subsequent infringements.

[W]hile the evidence supports a conclusion that iiNet demonstrated a dismissive and, indeed, contumelious, attitude to the complaints of infringement by the use of its services, its conduct did not amount to authorisation of the primary acts of infringement on the part of iiNet users. Before the failure by iiNet to suspend or terminate its customers' accounts would constitute authorisation of future acts of infringement, the Copyright Owners would be required to show that at least the following circumstances exist:

[1] iiNet has been provided with unequivocal and cogent evidence of the alleged primary acts of infringement by use of the iiNet service in question. Mere assertion by an entity such as AFACT, with whatever

particulars of the assertion may be provided, would not, of itself, constitute unequivocal and cogent evidence of the doing of acts of infringement. Information as to the way in which the material supporting the allegations was derived, that was adequate to enable iiNet to verify the accuracy of the allegations, may suffice. Verification on oath as to the precise steps that were adopted in order to obtain or discern the relevant information may suffice but may not be necessary.

[2] The Copyright Owners have undertaken:

to reimburse iiNet for the reasonable cost of verifying the particulars of the primary acts of infringement alleged and of establishing and maintaining a regime to monitor the use of the iiNet service to determine whether further acts of infringements occur, and to indemnify iiNet in respect of any liability reasonably incurred by iiNet as a consequence of mistakenly suspending or terminating a service on the basis of allegations made by the Copyright Owner.

They do not exist in the present case.

APPLICATION OF SAFE HARBOUR PROVISIONS

Division 2AA of Part V of the Copyright Act, which consists of §§ 116AA to 116J (the Safe Harbour Provisions), imposes limitations on the remedies available against carriage service providers for infringement of copyright. The Safe Harbour Provisions were inserted into the Copyright Act by the US Free Trade Agreement Implementation Act 2004 (Cth) (the US Free Trade Act). The purpose of the Safe Harbour Provisions is to limit the remedies that are available against a carriage service provider for infringements of copyright that relate to the carrying out of certain online activities by the carriage service provider.

Under § 116AC, a carriage service provider carries out a Category A activity by, relevantly, providing facilities or services for transmitting, routing or providing connections for a cinematograph film, or the intermediate and transient storage of a cinematograph film in the course of transmission, routing or provision of connections. Section 116AG(3) relevantly provides that, for an infringement of copyright that occurs in the course of the carrying out of a Category A activity, the relief that the Court may grant against a carriage service provider is limited to one or more of the following:

- an order requiring the carriage service provider to take reasonable steps to disable access to an online location outside Australia; and

- an order requiring the carriage service provider to terminate a specified account.

In deciding whether to make an order of the kind referred to in § 116AG(3), the Court must have regard to:

- the harm that has been caused to the owner of the copyright,

- the burden that the making of the order will place on the carriage service provider,

- the technical feasibility of complying with the order,

- the effectiveness of the order, and

- whether some other comparably effective order would be less burdensome.

The Court may also have regard to other matters that the Court considers relevant.

However, under § 116AG(1), before the limitations in § 116AG(3) apply, a carriage service provider must satisfy certain conditions. Relevantly, the conditions for category A activities of carriage service providers are set out in the table in § 116AH(1). The first condition in the table in s 116AH(1) is that the carriage service provider must adopt and reasonably implement a policy (Termination Policy) that provides for termination, in appropriate circumstances, of the accounts of repeat infringers.

Section 116AH(2) provides that nothing in those conditions is to be taken to require a carriage service provider to monitor its service or to seek facts to indicate infringing activity, except to the extent required by a standard technical measure that is the subject of an industry code. It is common ground that, at relevant times, there was no relevant industry code in force.

The Copyright Owners say that iiNet has not adopted or implemented a policy that satisfies the condition.

iiNet contends that its policy was to terminate the accounts of repeat infringers in three circumstances as follows:

- when iiNet was ordered to do so by a court;

- when an iiNet customer admitted to infringing copyright; or

- when an iiNet user was found by a court or other authority to have infringed.

It claims that its policy was evidenced by:

- The Internet Industry Association ICH and Safe Harbour guide;

- The iiNet copyright notice on its website; and

- iiNet's customer relationship agreement.

Mr. Malone said that iiNet's policy would be triggered where there was a court order, other legislative instrument or code, a finding of repeat infringement of copyright by a court in an action where iiNet was not a party or an admission by an account holder that the account holder had repeatedly infringed copyright. iiNet asserted that none of those situations had occurred and that, therefore, the policy had not been engaged.

iiNet receives thousands of unreliable robot notices per week alleging infringement and, in the case of the Infringement Notices, thousands of entries are contained in an unverified spreadsheet. iiNet says that it should not be required, in order to satisfy condition 1, to have a policy whereby it would be required, upon receipt of each robot notice or each of the Infringement Notices, to review, analyse and conduct secondary investigations of infringement allegations in order to ascertain whether the customer, or some other person using the customer's account, may or may not have infringed.

Thus, iiNet relies on the customer relationship agreement and the section of its website dealing with copyright. However, the customer relationship agreement provides no guidance as to the way iiNet will respond to copyright infringement. The copyright section of iiNet's website also provides no such guidance.

The explanatory memorandum published in connection with the US Free Trade Bill 2004 gives some guidance as to the purpose of the Safe Harbour Provisions. Thus, the Safe Harbour Provisions were intended to provide: [1] legal incentives for service providers to cooperate with copyright owners in deterring the unauthorised storage and transmission of copyright materials; and [2] limitations in the law regarding the scope and remedies available against service providers for copyright infringements that they do not control, initiate or direct and that take place through systems or networks controlled or operated by them or on their behalf.

The first element of iiNet's so-called policy is no more than a policy to obey the law. All three elements set thresholds that would excuse a service provider from acting on knowledge of copyright infringement, thus turning a blind eye to infringement that could be prevented. iiNet's so-called policy was not one for taking action in response to repeat infringement, and cannot constitute cooperation with Copyright Owners as required by the Safe Harbour Provisions. iiNet did not establish any processes to facilitate the operation of the so-called policy, in that it did not inform its customers of the existence of the policy. Indeed, iiNet claims it could not use information derived from the Infringement Notices, because of the operation of Part 13 of the Telco Act. Further, iiNet did not have an operational email address to receive notices from copyright owners as required by the Regulations. That is indicative of a failure to implement a policy.

Condition 1 of item 1 has at least two elements, being the implementation of a policy that provides for termination of accounts. That requires the identification of a relevant policy and its implementation. It may be that iiNet had a policy as formulated by Mr. Malone. It probably implemented that policy. The question, however, is whether that was a policy that provides for termination, in appropriate circumstances, of the account of a repeat infringer. The key concept in that phrase is "in appropriate circumstances." The circumstances of Mr. Malone's so called policy are not appropriate circumstances so as to satisfy the condition.

iiNet also says that, on the construction contended for by the Copyright Owners, it would be necessary for iiNet to terminate all accounts where an Infringement Notice purported to indicate any repeat infringement. It says that such a construction would give § 116AG(3)(b) no work to do, since there would be no accounts remaining for the Court to order to be terminated. The contention that an account holder would be authorising an infringement and therefore be an infringer is rejected by iiNet on the basis that that would require a construction that involves the complexity and questions raised in this proceeding as to the meaning of authorisation within the meaning of § 101.

The documents relied on by iiNet make no reference to repeat infringers or what iiNet may do in relation to such infringements. Customers were never made aware of the so-called policy and would be likely to argue that it formed no part of a contract for services and was therefore unenforceable. Merely attending meetings with the IIA and with other service providers, having its customer relationship agreement reviewed by lawyers and considering the issue internally does not amount to the implementation of a policy. iiNet had no processes in place that resemble a policy. There is no evidence that iiNet decided not to act on the Infringement Notices because they were not sworn or verified. For completely different reasons, iiNet decided not to act on the infringement notices, regardless of information they contained. Accordingly, if it were established that iiNet had authorised primary acts of infringement, iiNet would not be entitled to the benefit of the Safe Harbour Provisions in relation to those acts.

[The opinion of Justice Nicholas who was a part of the majority is omitted; under Australia's law, both opinions are considered precedential. The dissent of Justice Jagot is also omitted. *Ed.*]

NOTES AND QUESTIONS

1. *Internet service providers (ISPs).* In the United States, "ISP" is more commonly used to describe services that provide access to the Internet (e.g., AT&T, Comcast, and Time Warner). In Australia, as discussed in the *iiNet* case, this kind of ISP is also called a Carriage Service Provider (CSP). However, the definition of Internet "service provider" under the DMCA safe harbor in the U.S. is much broader. It includes not only ISPs like Comcast, but also Internet websites (e.g., Facebook, Google, and YouTube) that provide any service on the Internet. *See* 17 U.S.C. § 512(k) (definition of "service provider").

2. Is the Australian decision a victory for the copyright holders or the ISP? What should both do in the future in order to succeed in future copyright cases of this sort? In 2011, the case was on appeal to the High Court, with a decision expected soon.

3. The Australian safe harbors are modeled on the DMCA safe harbors, whose approach is included in the Free Trade Agreement secured by the U.S. with Australia. Like the DMCA safe harbors, the Australian safe harbor protect four activities of ISPs (known as Category A, B, C, and D). Which activity was at issue in *iiNet*? Does the safe harbor for this activity impose a

notice-and-takedown duty on ISPs? Under the decision, what steps should iiNet take to implement a repeat infringer policy?

4. *Judicial review before termination of Internet access.* Part of the *iiNet* dispute involved whether a person's access to the Internet should be terminated without a judicial order based on allegations by copyright holders that the person engaged in copyright infringement. The same issue arose in the context of the HADOPI law—popularly known as a "3 strikes" or graduated response law—in France. Ultimately, the French Constitutional Council ruled that revocation of a person's Internet access without prior judicial review violated an individual's freedom of speech and presumption of innocence guaranteed by Declaration of the Rights of Man and the Citizen of 1789. French Constitutional Council: Decision n° 2009–580 of June 10th 2009—Act furthering the diffusion and protection of creation on the Internet (10 June 2009). How did the Australian court view iiNet's policy of requiring a court order before terminating a user's account? Did that policy comport with the requirements of reasonable implementation of a repeat infringer policy under Australia's safe harbor?

5. *Notice and takedown.* The notice-and-takedown process, although influential around the world as a requirement for ISP safe harbors, has received criticisms on various fronts. Copyright industries complain that searching for infringement and filing notices with ISPs require considerable time, labor, and expense. Copyright industries want ISPs to have greater duties to police their sites on their own, especially if infringing activity is pervasive. On the other hand, public interest advocates have criticized the notice-and-takedown process as susceptible to erroneous and questionable removal of content that may be fair use or otherwise not infringing. ISPs have incentives to remove every material subject to a notice of infringement, without much, if any, question as to the legitimacy of the material. Typically, the ISP safe harbor protects an ISP for even erroneous removal of content that was not infringing as long as the ISP received a notice of infringement from a copyright owner. *See* Jennifer M. Urban & Laura Quilter, *Efficient Process of "Chilling Effects"? Takedown Notices Under Section 512 of the Digital Millennium Copyright Act*, 22 SANTA CLARA COMP. & HIGH TECH. L.J. 621, 666 (2006) (a third of DMCA notices in study were questionable). Which criticisms of notice-and-takedown are valid? Should the public have greater safeguards? For example, would you favor delaying takedown until the affected person has had a chance to file a counter-notification? Japan has such a "notice-wait-and-takedown" procedure, allowing seven days during which a user can file a counter-notice before any takedown is permitted.

6. *Graduated response.* Other countries have developed additional approaches, such as France's graduated response or 3 strikes approach under the HADOPI II law. The U.S. and other developed countries floated the idea of adopting "3 strikes" under the Anti–Counterfeiting Trade Agreement (ACTA), but the controversial idea was eventually abandoned. Do you think the WTO or WIPO should begin to develop an international standard for ISP safe harbors? Or should the issue be left, at least for now, to each country to decide its own standard?

7. *BitTorent.* The BitTorrent peer-to-peer technology has been the subject of numerous lawsuits. In 2011, the U.S. Copyright Group, a consortium of independent film studios that made *The Hurt Locker* and *The Expendables*, sued over 50,000 "John Doe" plaintiffs for allegedly using BitTorrent to share illegal copies of the movies. Julianne Pepitone, *50,000 BitTorrent Users Sued for Alleged Illegal Downloads*, CNN Money, June 10, 2011. The Group subpoenaed ISPs Comcast, Earthlink, Time Warner, and Verizon for the identities of the users suspected of infringement. Meanwhile, the founders of The Pirate Bay, a Swedish BitTorrent tracker site, were convicted of contributory copyright infringement, sentenced to one year in prison, and ordered to pay a fine of several million dollars. The judgment was appealed to Sweden's Supreme Court, but the Court declined to hear the appeal. All of these controversies involve individuals and entities other than the designers of the software for BitTorrent. To what extent should the software designers be held responsible?

8. *Bibliographic note.* Robert Burrell & Kimberlee Weatherall, *Exporting Controversy? Reactions to the Copyright Provisions of the U.S.–Australia Free Trade Agreement: Lessons for U.S. Trade Policy*, 2008 U. ILL. J.L. & TECH. & POL'Y 259 (2008); Jeremy de Beer & Christopher D. Clemmer, *Global Trends in Online Copyright Enforcement: A Non–Neutral Role for Network Intermediaries?*, 49 JURIMETRICS J. 375 (2009); Edward Lee, *Decoding the DMCA Safe Harbors*, 32 COLUM. J. OF LAW & ARTS 233 (2009); Jesse London, *China's Approaches to Intellectual Property Infringement on the Internet*, 38 RUTGERS L. REC. 1 (2010–11); Miquel Peguera, *The DMCA Safe Harbors and Their European Counterparts: A Comparative Analysis of Some Common Problems*, 32 COLUM. J.L. & ARTS 481 (2009); Peter Yu, *The Graduated Response*, 62 FLA. L. REV. 1373 (2010).

CHAPTER 3

PATENTS

■ ■ ■

A. INTRODUCTION

1. THE RIGHTS OF INVENTORS

Patents provide exclusive rights to inventors for their inventions. The first formal patent system is thought to have developed during the early Renaissance. In 1474, Venice enacted a statute that gave a patent to "every person who shall build any new and ingenious device in this City, not previously made in this Commonwealth," provided that the invention "has been reduced to perfection" and the inventor filed a notice of the invention with a General Welfare Board. A patent gave the inventor the exclusive right to make the invention for ten years within Venice, and to prevent others from copying the invention. The City, though, retained the right to use the invention at its discretion, recognizing that a larger societal interest may require the City's use of the invention.

Modern patent systems share many features with the ancient Venetian system. All patent systems today require that an invention be new (or novel) and have sufficient inventiveness, in order to qualify for a patent. An invention must also be useful and reduced to practice, meaning that it is sufficiently developed to allow someone to make and use the invention. All modern patent systems also require the filing of a patent application that is typically reviewed before a patent is granted or denied, although with varying degrees of scrutiny by the patent offices in different countries where an application is filed. The patent application today serves the added role of providing the public, particularly other inventors, with the essential know-how underlying an invention that people can freely use and build on, once the patent expires. In this regard, the grant of a patent is often described as a *quid pro quo* or bargain, with the patentee receiving exclusive rights to his or her invention for a limited time in exchange for the disclosure to the public of how to make and use the invention. Finally, modern systems recognize that patents should be limited in term, with the prevailing minimum standard under Article 33 of TRIPS lasting twenty years from the filing of the patent application. Although this term is twice as long as the Venetian patent term, it represents a relatively small increase over five hundred years of patent law development.

The predominant theory to justify patents is based on their relationship in creating economic incentives. By providing exclusive rights over new inventions, patents help to ensure that inventors receive compensation for their labor and investment in developing a new invention. Without patents, an inventor might invest a great amount of time, labor, and resources to develop a new technology, only to have a competitor copy the product with little cost to the competitor. Patents thus encourage innovation and technological development by providing legal incentives and protections for inventors. As the Venetian code recognized, by granting patents for new inventions, "more men would then apply their genius, would discover, and would build devices of great utility and benefit to our commonwealth."

Although this incentive-based rationale is the dominant theory of modern patent systems today, history has witnessed its share of patent abuses that have conflicted with this rationale. Perhaps the most notorious examples of abuse occurred in fifteenth and sixteenth century England, where the British Crown granted monopolies over many goods that had been already known and in public use in England, such as paper, brushes, drinking glasses, bottles, playing cards, vinegar, and starch. These patents were granted, not to encourage innovation, but simply to curry favors or raise money for the Crown. To end these abuses, Parliament passed the Statute of Monopolies in 1624, which prohibited the grant of monopolies except for new inventions and only for a term of fourteen years. The term correlated with the period of apprenticeship, during which an apprentice learned a trade under a master for seven years. A master who had obtained a patent would therefore have exclusive rights for two generations of apprentices. The patent abuses in England would later inform the Framers in the United States, who distrusted monopolies and limited Congress's power to grant exclusive rights under the Copyright and Patent Clause. Like the Statute of Monopolies, the first U.S. Patent Code enacted in 1790 allowed patents only to new inventions and only for a limited term of fourteen years.

Since their origin, patents have had an international dimension. Patents were often used to attract foreign artisans and craftsmen to introduce their skills into a territory. For example, the Venetian patent code required a "new" invention in the sense that it had not been "previously made in this Commonwealth." Existing foreign inventions that had not been made in Venice could, in other words, still qualify for a patent. This gave foreign inventors, who had developed inventions elsewhere, incentive to introduce their existing inventions into Venice. For example, in 1469, Venice granted John of Speyer a patent for introducing his printing device from Germany. Likewise, in sixteenth century England, the Crown gave patents to foreign artisans to bring their trade into England, including glassmakers and shipbuilders from Italy, ironworkers from France, and soapmakers from Spain. These patents to existing foreign inventions are known as "importation patents."

In order to ensure that foreign inventions would benefit the domestic market, many countries have historically imposed "working requirements" that required an inventor to manufacture the invention within the domestic market. If foreign inventors did not "work" their inventions within the domestic market within a certain time period, they could have their invention subject to compulsory licenses or possibly even to forfeiture. These working requirements enabled countries to use their patent laws to facilitate the transfer of technology into their own borders. As will be later examined, working requirements today remain a controversial part of patent systems. The patent system's role in attracting the transfer of foreign technology remains an ongoing, but disputed issue today, particularly for developing countries.

2. INTERNATIONAL AGREEMENTS: TRIPS, THE PARIS CONVENTION, AND THE PATENT COOPERATION TREATY

TRIPS

Article 2

Intellectual Property Conventions

1. In respect of Parts II, III and IV of this Agreement, Members shall comply with Articles 1 through 12, and Article 19, of the Paris Convention (1967).

2. Nothing in Parts I to IV of this Agreement shall derogate from existing obligations that Members may have to each other under the Paris Convention, the Berne Convention, the Rome Convention and the Treaty on Intellectual Property in Respect of Integrated Circuits.

As trade expanded internationally from the Renaissance and through the Industrial Revolution, the idea of providing legal protection for inventions in other countries followed, although with varying degrees of receptivity among countries. By the end of the nineteenth century, the divergences in patent laws among countries prompted developed countries to begin working out international standards for patents. The International Convention for the Protection of Industrial Property, more commonly known as the Paris Convention, represents the first major international agreement for intellectual property ever established. The Convention, which was first signed in 1883, covers "industrial property," a term commonly used in Europe to encompass patents, trademarks, industrial designs, and unfair competition.

In contrast with its reluctance to join the Berne Convention (or even to grant copyrights to foreign authors), the United States took a lead role in the development of the Paris Convention, perhaps due in part to the U.S.'s tremendous industrial growth during the Industrial Revolution.

The U.S. delegation to the Vienna conference in 1873 and the Paris convention in 1878 prevailed in convincing several European and Latin American countries that patents should be allowed for foreign inventors under national treatment. Important to the U.S. victory was persuading several continental European countries that favored the complete abolition of patents, such as Germany, Austria, and Switzerland, to accept the view that patents were desirable and should be treated as a form of property right for inventors. No doubt part of the U.S.'s success during the negotiations can be attributed to the common perception that the U.S.'s tremendous industrial growth stemmed in part from its strong patent system.

In 1884, ten countries were party to the Paris convention. Although a leading proponent of the Convention, the U.S. did not become a member until several years later in 1887. As of 2011, 173 countries have officially become members. Although the Paris Convention has been revised six times since its inception, it contains few provisions that set forth minimum standards. For patents, Article 4 establishes the important right of priority to file patent applications in other countries within one year of the first filing. Article 4*bis* recognizes the independent treatment of patents for the same invention in different countries—reinforcing the territorial approach to patents. A handful of other articles set limitations on forfeiture of patents, compulsory licenses, and working requirements. None, however, speaks to the substantive standards of patent subject matter, validity, rights, or term.

Just as in the case of the Berne Convention, the Paris Convention lacked an effective enforcement mechanism to handle any alleged violations of its provisions by member countries. In the same article, Article 28, the Paris Convention allows countries to raise disputes in the International Court of Justice, but also to declare themselves not bound by such proceedings. This is not to suggest that a member country had no means of exerting pressure on another country. Countries, such as Germany and the U.S., have sometimes, if not often, resorted to imposing tariffs and other trade sanctions on another country that failed to protect patents to their satisfaction.

Because the Paris Convention did not impose substantive minimum standards for patents, member countries had great freedom to tailor patent law according to their own needs and interests. Many countries excluded pharmaceuticals and biotechnology products and processes from patentability, based on the view that such medicine or health-related products should be more widely available at lower prices to their residents.

This gap in patent protection among many countries spurred the pharmaceutical and biotechnology industries, particularly in the United States, to mobilize to strengthen patent protection internationally. Because research and development costs for new pharmaceutical and biotechnology products can be enormous, these industries stood to lose millions of dollars annually if their products could not be patented in many countries—money that could affect not just their profits, but also their ability to conduct research and development for new products. India was one country that had long denied patents to pharmaceutical products. This allowed local manufacturers to copy drugs that others had patented in other countries and profit from their selling in India, albeit at much lower prices to consumers than charged by the patent holder. By 1986, when the Uruguay Round began and after several efforts to amend the Paris Convention had failed, the pharmaceutical and biotechnology industries made strengthening patents one of the top agenda items of the U.S. delegation. Developing countries, however, led by India strongly opposed the efforts to require expanded patent protection.

After eight years of intense negotiations during the Uruguay Round, with developed countries and developing countries often at odds on the issue of patents, the U.S. position, for the most part, won out. In addition to incorporating parts of the Paris Convention, the TRIPS Agreement sets forth a number of substantive minimum standards of patent protection, including the requirements that countries must allow for the patenting of processes and may not deny patents based on the field of technology. These provisions effectively prohibit a member country from categorically denying patents to pharmaceutical or biotechnology products and processes. TRIPS also delineates what exclusive rights a patent must entail and for how long, and puts limitations on when countries may enact exceptions or compulsory licenses to patents. The Agreement also requires countries to afford judicial review of any revocation or forfeiture of a patent. As discussed already, TRIPS is equipped with an elaborate enforcement mechanism under the auspices of the WTO, which allows, as a last resort, the imposition of trade sanctions against member countries that violate TRIPS.

The general approach under the Paris Convention and the TRIPS Agreement with respect to patents is similar to the approach for copyright. Patents are *territorial* in nature, meaning that they are effective only in the territory that created and granted the patent right. Article 4*bis* of the Paris Convention recognizes this principle by establishing the minimum standard that patents for the same invention applied for by the same person in different countries are to be treated "independent[ly], both as regards the grounds for nullity and forfeiture, and as regards their normal duration." The independent treatment of patent duration means that, unlike the Berne Convention's approach to copyrights (discussed in Chapter 2), there is no rule of the shorter term for patents. Articles 2 and 3 of Paris establish the principle of *national treatment* for inventors, which is buttressed by the national treatment requirement under Article 3 of TRIPS. Article 2 of Paris provides:

> Nationals of any country of the Union shall, as regards the protection of industrial property, enjoy in all the other countries of the Union the advantages that their respective laws now grant, or hereafter

grant, to nationals; all without prejudice to the rights specially provided for by this Convention.*

One major difference between the Berne Convention and the Paris Convention is their view of formalities. As you should recall from Chapter 2, Article 5(2) of the Berne Convention bars countries other than the country of origin from imposing formalities on a copyrighted work. By contrast, the Paris Convention presupposes patent systems in which patents are "applied for," as is the universal practice. Paris Conv. art. 4*bis*(1). Under Paris, an inventor who has acquired a patent under the national laws of a Paris Union country does not automatically acquire a patent in all other Paris Union countries. Rather, the inventor must typically file a separate patent application in every single country in which the inventor seeks a patent. In other words, the national treatment principle, as applied under Paris, does not overcome the limitations imposed by the territoriality principle and does not obviate the need to make a separate application for a patent in each national legal system. Each national patent authority retains the power to make its own determination on whether to grant the patent. The benefit of the national treatment principle under Paris is that a Union country cannot discriminate against foreign inventors by imposing more onerous requirements than those that apply to domestic inventors.

> Illustration 3–1. Ajay is an inventor and a national of the United Kingdom, a Paris Union country. Ajay obtains a patent under the laws of the UK. To obtain a patent in Australia, also a Union country, Ajay must make a separate application in Australia. If Australia charges higher filing fees and requires a heavier administrative burden for Ajay than for Australian inventors, Australia is in violation of the national treatment principle under the Paris Convention.

In this chapter, we will focus mainly on the patent provisions of the TRIPS Agreement and the Paris Convention, which are the two most important international patent agreements. Some attention will also be devoted to the Patent Cooperation Treaty (PCT), which is special agreement among members of the Paris Convention to help coordinate the procedures and deadlines for filing multiple patent applications for the same invention in different countries around the world.

NOTES AND QUESTIONS

1. *Non-retroactive.* Under Article 70(3) of TRIPS, countries have "no obligation to restore protection to subject matter which on the date of application of this Agreement for the Member in question has fallen into the public domain." As discussed in Chapter 2, an exception to this principle of

---

* The language of Article 2(1) of the Paris Convention is, of course, different from the "no less favourable" language in the national treatment provision under TRIPS Article 3. Presumably, though, the national treatment obligations are equivalent, although one WTO panel curiously avoided deciding the issue when it was raised. *See* European Communities—Protection of Trademarks and Geographical Indications for Agricultural Products and Foodstuffs, WT/DS174/R, 15 March 2005, at ¶ 7.216.

nonretroactivity is carved out for copyrights under Article 70(2) of TRIPS and Article 18 of the Berne Convention. What might justify applying a principle of nonretroactivity in the case of existing inventions that have fallen into the public domain? Would it be too disruptive to the public and business relations if inventions in the public domain are later subject to a restored patent? If so, doesn't the same problem arise with copyrighting works in the public domain?

2. *Industrial property*. Industrial property is the term historically used in European countries to distinguish literary and artistic rights from those rights associated with works of industry and utility, such as patents, trademarks, industrial designs, and unfair competition. Does the term "industrial property" make sense today when copyrighted works are often highly commercial and can be partly functional in nature? Does copyright stand apart from these other forms of intellectual property, or should we abandon the term altogether?

3. Why do you think the Paris Convention allows formalities for patents, while the Berne Convention does not for copyrights? Is there something so different about patents and copyrights, or the nature of the material they protect, that justifies the difference?

4. *Revisions of Paris Convention*. Since 1883, there have been six revisions of the Paris Convention, the last occurring in Stockholm, on July 14, 1967. Just as in the case of the Berne Convention, if a country is already a member of the Paris Convention, it does not have to ratify or be bound by a subsequent text or revision of the Convention. The vast majority of member countries, however, have ratified the most recent Stockholm text. A new member can only join the most recent text in force. Paris Conv. art. 23.

Even though the Paris Convention is the oldest international intellectual property agreement, it contains no minimum standards of substantive patent law. What might explain the absence of such standards in the Paris Convention? Wouldn't you expect that over the years member countries would be able to agree on some substantive minimum standards?

5. *Patents, incentives, and innovation*. The incentive-based rationale for patents is premised on a goal of spurring innovation and the development of new technology. While this theory is widely accepted as a legitimate justification for patents, how well a particular patent system meets this goal remains an ongoing question that recurs as the law and new technologies develop. In 2003, the U.S. Federal Trade Commission issued a report on the U.S. patent system, concluding that, although the U.S. system has, for the most part, worked well in promoting innovation, evidence also indicated that some questionable patents were being granted, whose effects harmed competition and innovation. FEDERAL TRADE COMMISSION, TO PROMOTE INNOVATION: THE PROPER BALANCE OF COMPETITION AND PATENT LAW AND POLICY (Oct. 2003). The FTC recommended, among other things, an amendment to the Patent Code that (i) would establish an opposition procedure by which third parties can challenge the validity of patents after they are granted by the Patent Office, and (ii) would lower the burden of proof to challenge the validity of a patent from clear and convincing evidence to a preponderance of the evidence. In 2011, following the FTC report, the America Invents Act (AIA) instituted a post-grant review procedure that enables third parties to challenge the

validity of a patent claim in the U.S. Patent Office, but only within a 9–month period after the grant of the patent. *See* AIA, H.R. 1249, § 6(d) (codified at 35 U.S.C. § 321 et seq.). Unlike litigation in which invalidity of a patent must be shown by clear and convincing evidence, the post-grant review is subject to a lower burden of proof showing "unpatentability by a preponderance of the evidence." *Id.* (codified at 35 U.S.C. § 326(e)). Do you agree with these patent reforms? What other measures could a country implement to reduce the granting of questionable patents?

6. *Incentive v. prospect theory.* In addition to the incentive-based rationale, another economic defense of patent systems is provided by the "prospect" theory advanced by Edmund Kitch. Edmund W. Kitch, *The Nature and Function of the Patent System*, 20 J. L. & ECON. 265 (1977). Under this theory, recognizing property rights to an invention can be justified on the grounds that it will facilitate the more efficient use of resources by centralizing control or management over the invention in one entity—who will have an economic interest in ensuring that it is used, maintained, licensed, and improved in an efficient manner.

7. *Natural rights theory of patents?* Natural rights theory has not had as prominent an influence on patent law as it has had on the author's right tradition under copyright law. While natural rights theory appears to have had at least some influence in Europe, very little formal recognition is ever made among countries that inventors are entitled to certain "moral rights." *See* Adam Mossoff, *Rethinking the Development of Patents: An Intellectual History, 1550–1800*, 52 HASTINGS L.J. 1255, 1294–1302 (2001); Fritz Machlup & Edith Penrose, *The Patent Controversy in the Nineteenth Century*, 10 J. ECON. HIST. 1, 10–11 (1950). In fact, in many circles, there was outright hostility to such a notion. What might explain the absence of such claims? Are inventors just less deserving than authors—or, as one journal in 1829 put it, "to talk of the natural rights of an inventor is to talk nonsense"? *See* Mossoff, *supra*, at 1256.

8. *Utility models.* Some countries also recognize what are called "utility models" or "petty patents" or "innovation patents." These utility models are subject to less onerous requirements (no inventive step needed) and to more speedy registration (with examination occurring typically afterwards). Small improvements to existing inventions may be a good candidate for utility models in countries where they are available. Although such countries vary in approach, utility models usually are much shorter than patents (typically, 7 to 10 years in duration). TRIPS does not directly address utility models. Could a WTO country adopt a system of utility models, but not patents, in compliance with TRIPS? *See* TRIPS Article 27(1).

9. *Bibliographic Note.* H.I. DUTTON, THE PATENT SYSTEM AND INVENTIVE ACTIVITY DURING THE INDUSTRIAL REVOLUTION, 1750–1852 (1984); ERICH KAUFER, THE ECONOMICS OF THE PATENT SYSTEM (1989); WILLIAM M. LANDES & RICHARD A. POSNER, THE ECONOMIC STRUCTURE OF INTELLECTUAL PROPERTY LAW 294–333 (2003); STEPHEN P. LADAS, THE INTERNATIONAL PROTECTION OF INDUSTRIAL PROPERTY (1930); Heinrich Kronstein & Irene Till, *A Reevaluation of the International Patent Convention*, 12 LAW & CONTEMP. PROBS. 765 (1947); Giulio Mandich, *Venetian Patents (1450–1550)*, 30 J. PAT. OFF. SOC'Y 166, 177 (1948); J.H.

Reichman, *The TRIPS Agreement Comes of Age: Conflict or Cooperation with the Developing Countries?*, 32 CASE W. RES. J. INT'L L. 441 (2000); Dominique S. Ritter, *Switzerland's Patent Law History*, 14 FORDHAM INTELL. PROP. MEDIA & ENT. L.J. 463 (2004).

3. PATENTS AND ECONOMIC DEVELOPMENT, THE ONGOING NORTH–SOUTH DEBATE

Patents are at the heart of some of the most contentious disagreements between developed and developing countries. One of the hot-button issues relates to access to medicines and the use of compulsory licenses on patented drugs, a topic discussed later in this chapter. The whole "Development Agenda" in WIPO, discussed in Chapter 1, stemmed in part as a counter-reaction by developing countries to the Substantive Patent Law Treaty (SPLT) negotiations led by the U.S., EU, and Japan. The SPLT was meant to harmonize substantive standards of patent law. In 2005, however, the developed countries' narrow focus on legal doctrine took a sharp turn. As WIPO reported, "The Delegation of Brazil, on behalf of the 'Friends of Development,' submitted a statement proposing the continuation of negotiations of the draft SPLT on the basis of the draft treaty as a whole and of other issues, such as provisions on the transfer of technology, anti-competitive practices, safeguarding of public interest flexibility as well as specific clauses on principles and objectives." *See* Substantive Patent Law Harmonization, at http://www.wipo.int/patent-law/en/harmonization.htm. Instead of focusing on patent harmonization, the discussions in WIPO shifted to development issues.

The North–South debate in the arena of patents shows no signs of letting up. In 2011, U.S. Ambassador to the UN Betty King suggested that the Development Agenda negotiations could lead to the ultimate demise of WIPO. King criticized proponents of the Development Agenda who seemed "hell-bent" on creating exceptions to patents or shorter terms. "[I]f we get to a system where the protection of patents are abrogated in the name of development, then we certainly will kill the organization," Ambassador King concluded. *See US Official Warns Patent Holders May Abandon WIPO*, WORLD INTELL. PROP. REPORT 21 (Feb. 2011). She added, "I am all pro-development, but I'm also committed to protecting the rights that were legally granted to American companies and other companies for the work that they do."

Given the contentiousness of the issue, the prospect that the North and the South will resolve their differences over the proper scope and role for patents seems remote. Part of the problem may be that, from an economic standpoint, a patent regime may have vastly different effects on a developing versus developed country. Consider the following problem and discussion.

PROBLEM 3–1

You are the adviser to the President of Elduxia, a developing country that has not yet joined the Paris Convention or the WTO. Elduxia has a rudimentary patent code that is considered weak by international standards. A number of MNEs have complained consistently that they have not been able to obtain patents in Elduxia for some of their inventions and that, in cases in which they have obtained patents, Elduxia lacks sufficient enforcement of the patents to stop infringement in Elduxia. Due to concern about Elduxia's patent laws, some MNEs will not sell any products containing their most advanced or core technologies to Elduxia. As for Elduxia's own inventors, they are few in number and have few, if any, foreign patents.

Elduxia's leading industry is tourism, but it also contains a variety of plants containing medicinal value that are drawing a lot of interest from multi-national pharmaceutical companies. Although the plants are promising, it appears that a great deal of research and development (R & D) will be needed to distill the plant into a commercially useful form. Because these plants die quickly once removed from their natural habitat, most of the needed R & D will have to done on the ground in Elduxia. Elduxia has also been undergoing rapid industrialization. Elduxia has made significant progress in recent years in expanding its educational system and has recently entered into a number of bilateral trade agreements. The President would like your analysis of the costs and benefits of joining the WTO and TRIPS both in the short term and the long term. In advising the President, consider the following article.

LESSONS FROM STUDYING THE INTERNATIONAL ECONOMICS OF INTELLECTUAL PROPERTY RIGHTS

Keith E. Maskus.
53 Vand. L. Rev. 2219, 2220, 2228–39 (2000).

I. Introduction

When the Uruguay Round negotiations began in 1986, the subject of intellectual property rights ("IPRs") was completely unfamiliar to international trade economists. Despite this general inattention, a small but growing literature has emerged in which trade economists have framed specific questions and applied theory and statistical analysis to them. In this Article, I provide an overview of what international economists have learned from studying IPRs in the global context. While progress has been made, many of the results remain subject to statistical and analytical uncertainty and wide areas of research remain insufficiently explored. There is much about the functioning of IPRs that we do not understand very well, particularly in the context of promoting economic development.

D. TRIPS Will Shift Income Among Countries

An interesting question is whether TRIPS will have an important short-run impact on the international distribution of patent rents. By making imitation more costly, stronger patents would permit higher license fees for inventors, generating higher net rent transfers abroad to the extent that licensors are foreign. In turn, the higher license fees on existing patents would cut the willingness of local firms to license, generating additional losses.

The [author's] computations [into 1995 dollars of Phillip McCalman's study of bilateral patent statistics and the implicit value of patent rights in 29 countries in 1988] demonstrate that the overwhelming share of rents transferred by stronger global patent rights would accrue to the United States. TRIPS required the United States to strengthen its patent regime only marginally, implying a small outward rent transfer on existing patents. However, American firms owned huge portfolios of patents abroad. The additional strength of patent laws in host countries would have transferred an additional $5.85 billion in rents, for a net gain to the United States of $5.76 billion. Other developed countries that would receive net inward transfers include Germany ($1.23 billion) France ($831 million), Italy ($277 million), Sweden ($217 million), and Switzerland ($36 million). The United Kingdom would experience a sizeable gross inward rent flow of around $588 million, but a larger outflow of $1.22 billion. The Japanese case was similar, with a net rent loss of $589 million. Among developed economies, Canada would realize the largest net loss from net changes in patent values, at $1.04 billion. Canadian patent changes would increase sharply the value of patents held there. However, foreign patents held by Canadian firms are overwhelmingly located in the United States and their value would not increase by much.

Among developing countries, the gross outward transfer would rise with the size of economies and the extent of patent reform. Because its citizens own so few patents, India would receive negligibly higher inward transfers, but the value of foreign-owned patents would rise by $430 million. The result for Korea was similar, with a net outward transfer of $454 million. However, this result is outdated because Korean firms have been granted far more patents abroad since 1988. Thus, applied to 2000 patent portfolios the gross inward transfer would be much larger. Brazil would experience the largest net outward transfer among all countries in the sample, at $1.7 billion.

These rent transfers are economically significant. Thus, for example, the rent-transfer gain on patents of $5.9 billion would complement U.S. short-run gains from standard trade liberalization in the Uruguay Round by 42%. Canada's short-run gains would be cut by 94 percent, from $1.106 billion to $66 million, and Brazil's by 76 percent, from $2.239 billion to $532 million. Accounting for the patent-valuation aspect of TRIPS, Mexico would actually experience a net welfare loss in the short run. Only the United States accrued large welfare gains, though France, Germany, and Italy registered small net benefits. Across all countries, the welfare losses induced by stronger patents amounted to as much as 20% of the global efficiency gains from trade liberalization.

E. *IPRs Stimulate International Economic Activity*

The preceding discussion suggests that for technology importing nations to benefit from stronger IPRs there must be dynamic gains that could emerge over time. Such gains could come from enhanced flows of international trade, investment, and technology transfer, which would augment growth prospects. The empirical literature is reasonably optimistic on this score.

1. *Patents and International Trade*

Intellectual property rights were taken up in the Uruguay Round on the grounds that weak and variable standards distort international trade. In theory, limited protection could raise or reduce trade, depending on demand characteristics, market structure, the ability of countries to prevent infringement, and other factors. It is also possible that highly protective IPRs could deter legitimate trade or facilitate collusive behavior that would limit competition through trade. The basic tradeoff when countries adopt stronger patents is between greater market power for rights-owning firms, permitting higher profits on lower trade volumes, and greater market demand for those firms as local imitators are made less competitive, inducing higher trade flows. Thus, no certain prediction may be made about the impacts of variable patent rights on trade volumes. A clear picture can emerge only from empirical analysis.

In a pair of studies, Maskus and Penubarti estimated the impact of patent rights on 1984 bilateral trade in manufacturing sectors. The authors found that within the group of large developing economies the strength of national patent laws exerted a statistically significant and positive effect on bilateral imports in many product categories. Thus, in these countries the market-expansion effect dominated. Put differently, weak patents in large developing economies are barriers to manufacturing exports from the OECD countries. The impacts were positive but weaker in the group of small developing countries, suggesting that net market-expansion effects largely operated in these nations as well. Interestingly, the pharmaceuticals sector registered positive impacts of patents on import volumes.

To assess the economic significance of these results, I computed the increases in international trade flows that the model would predict from changes in national patent rights. The coefficients were applied to crude estimates of the rise in patent indexes implied by implementation of the TRIPS Agreement. The scenarios entailed marked increases in the indexes of developing countries but did not impose full harmonization with laws in developed countries. The implied trade effects were long run in nature and would emerge only after TRIPS standards are phased in and markets adjust to the new policy regimes. Taking all manufacturing goods together, in the small developing economies as a group perhaps $2.7 billion in additional annual imports would be created. This came to 6.2% of total merchandise imports of this group in 1984. Manufacturing imports by the large developing countries would expand by between $14.7 billion and

$24.2 billion per year. These sums range from 5.4% to 8.9% of 1984 merchandise imports of these nations, suggesting that stronger patent rights would cause marked increases in import demand. Finally, the small policy changes envisioned in the developed economies would induce an additional $7.9 billion in imports, or perhaps 0.6% of merchandise imports.

Smith recently updated these studies by analyzing manufacturing exports of U.S. states to 96 countries in 1992. Smith attempted to identify market-power and market-expansion effects in countries distinguished by their abilities to imitate products. Her econometric results found that market-expansion effect dominated among the industrial countries, attesting to the effectiveness of their IPRs in deterring imitation. This was especially the case in patent-sensitive industries, such as chemicals and instruments. The market-expansion impact was pronounced in U.S. trade with middle-income economies displaying weak patent rights and strong imitation threats. Thus, countries such as Brazil and Malaysia should observe rising trade volumes as protection increases. Finally, the market-power effect dominated among the group of nations, primarily the least developed countries, with weak imitation and strong patent regimes.

These studies support two important conclusions. First, weak patent rights are significant barriers to manufacturing trade, particularly in IPRs-sensitive goods. However, this situation holds primarily within the group of industrializing economies that pose credible imitation threats. It is no surprise that these countries have been the main focus of complaints about weak intellectual property rights. As these countries strengthen their regimes, they should attract rising import volumes of high-technology goods, which may have a beneficial growth impact. Second, poor countries without much ability to imitate products are not a competitive threat. Thus, their weak patent regimes do not concern technology developers. As they adopt stronger patents their economies could be exposed to monopoly impacts with negative effects on their terms of trade.

2. *Patents and Foreign Direct Investment*

Economic theory suggests that the relationships between IPRs and Foreign Direct Investment ("FDI") are subtle and complex. Identifying these relationships requires empirical analysis. Despite their potential significance, few studies have included IPRs as a potential determinant of FDI.

Two recent studies find positive evidence, however. In the first, survey results were used to develop an index of perceived weakness of IPRs in destination countries on the part of U.S. firms. In the econometric model, the authors found that weak patents had a significantly negative impact on the location of American FDI. In the second, I argued that estimation should account for the joint decisions made by MNEs. In particular, multinational firms may choose to export, increase investment, or transfer technology directly in response to stronger patent rights. I estimated a simultaneous set of equations to capture these joint impacts, controlling for other relevant influences, for a set of 46 destination countries, using annual data from 1989–1992.

To summarize results, the level of patent strength in developing countries was positively associated with both exports to affiliates and affiliate sales. The coefficient on the patent index was negative and significant in the assets equation for developed economies, but the impact in developing countries was significantly positive. Thus, a one-unit increase in the patent index of the average developing economy would raise the asset stock of U.S. multinational affiliates by about 16%, or $1.9 billion. The evidence therefore suggests that U.S.-headquartered MNEs are sensitive to improvements in IPRs in developing countries in making foreign location decisions. However, these investments may come at the expense of reduced presence in developed economies, where a substitution effect between FDI and licensing becomes dominant once patent protection exceeds a particular level.

3. *Patents and Licensing*

Economic theory suggests that technology and product licensing also would be influenced ambiguously by stronger patent laws.

One recent study considered the real volumes of license fees for industrial processes, paid by unaffiliated foreign firms to U.S. firms, in 26 countries for the years 1985, 1990, and 1995. These volumes were regressed on the GP patent index in addition to several control variables. The authors found that unaffiliated royalties and license fees were positively and significantly affected by patent rights, but only once the patent index exceeded a critical value of 2.07 on a five-point scale. To the extent that license fees reflect the value of underlying technology, this finding supports the notion that technology transfer would rise with stronger patent rights in those countries that have enacted at least modest technology protection.

F. *The Statistical Correlation Between IPRs and Economic Growth Is Positive Under Some Circumstances*

One may question claims that the strength of intellectual protection is positively correlated with economic growth. After all, many countries have developed economically in the presence of weak IPRs, including Korea, Taiwan, Japan, and, arguably, the United States. Other countries have suffered stagnation in the presence of weak IPRs, including Brazil, Argentina, and India. Clearly there are many factors involved.

However, the economic evidence reviewed above provides scope for IP protection to enhance growth indirectly by promoting trade, FDI, and licensing. Each of these flows is a source of technology transfer. Imports of capital goods from technologically advanced nations have been shown to raise productivity in developing countries. Foreign direct investment has a similar impact, although the effect strengthens as countries expand their levels of education above some threshold level. Licensing directly transfers technology and know-how. Finally, patent applications may be read in order to develop competing products. Evidence exists that patenting activity among developed countries is strongly correlated with knowledge spillovers across borders.

While these processes are complex, two conclusions are supported by evidence. First, IPRs encourage growth more readily in economies that are open to international trade and investment. In addition to the direct positive impacts, competition from abroad encourages domestic firms to invest in technology and product quality. Moreover, firms in open economies are more likely to undertake the costs of technology transfer and adaptation when those investments are supported by IPRs. A recent study discovered that the impact of stronger patents in open economies was to raise growth rates by 0.66% on average in comparison with closed economies. Thus, market liberalization combined with stronger IPRs tends to increase growth.

Second, other relevant economic characteristics influence the effectiveness of IPRs. One study found no direct correlation between patent strength and growth, but there was a strong and positive impact of patents on physical investment and on R & D spending, which in turn raised growth performance. Another paper demonstrated that FDI raises growth performance in economies with sufficient stocks of human capital and skilled labor. These features are important for promoting local adaptation and learning new technologies.

Thus, IPRs, openness, investment, and human capital accumulation seem to work jointly in raising productivity and economic growth. Unfortunately, these impacts have taken little root in the least developed countries. They appear to become more complex and cumulative as countries grow richer. Thus, the role of IPRs in growth is intertwined with the details of complicated development processes.

G. Intellectual Property Rights Help Deepen Markets

One core reason for a sustained lack of economic development in poor countries is that institutions fail to support the development of extended markets. Weak IPRs may play a central role in this failure. Inadequate IPRs can stifle technical change even at low levels of economic development. Most innovation in developing countries involves small adaptations of existing technologies. These investments benefit from local patent or utility model protection. For example, utility models have been shown to improve productivity in farm-implement markets in Brazil and the Philippines.

A recent study analyzed how the Japanese patent system affected Japanese technical progress since the second world war. The system was designed to encourage incremental innovation and diffusion of knowledge into the economy through early disclosure of patent applications, utility models, and narrow claim requirements. The authors found that this system promoted large numbers of utility model applications for incremental inventions, which were based in part on laid-open prior applications for invention patents. In turn, utility models had a strongly positive impact on real productivity growth over the period. They concluded that utility models and patent applications were an important source of technical change and information diffusion in Japan.

Innovation through new product development and establishment of new firms may be discouraged by weak trademark protection in developing nations. A recent survey of trademark use in Lebanon provided evidence on this point. Firms in the apparel and food products industries wished to design clothing aimed at Middle Eastern markets. Attempts to do so were frustrated by trademark infringement by other firms in Lebanon and neighboring countries. Similar problems exist in China and retard the interprovincial marketing of products, as evidenced in another case study. Thus, new business activity may be restrained by trademark infringement targeted at domestic enterprises.

Entertainment and publishing firms in many developing countries tend to be small and often incapable of expanding their operations beyond minimal levels. In part, this problem is caused by extensive local piracy in the face of weakly enforced copyrights. However, a further structural difficulty is that inadequate copyrights cannot support the complex contracts that allocate rights in modern creative industries. For example, in China, the software industry has grown in the area of business applications, but has faced obstacles in developing fundamental program platforms. Thus, domestic commercial interests in stronger copyrights have emerged and are promoting enforcement. In contrast, India has long had a system of effective copyright protection, which is thought by many observers to have been important in developing and protecting its successful film and software industries.

III. Concluding Remarks

[T]he short-run impacts of TRIPS will be essentially redistributive between countries, with the bulk of gains accruing to the United States and other technology developers. Over the longer term, however, there are mechanisms that could enhance technical change and growth in the technology importing countries. To achieve those gains, developing nations should complement their stronger regimes with appropriate collateral policy reforms. While these conclusions seem warranted by the evidence marshaled to date, it is evident that much work remains to be done.

NOTES AND QUESTIONS

1. Of what significance is Professor Maskus's analysis that the U.S. benefited the most from the patent provisions of TRIPS, in the estimated amount of $5.76 billion in net rent transfer from patents? How does this compare to developing countries?

2. Professor Maskus suggests that, in order to benefit from stronger patent systems, developing countries need to have "enhanced flows of interna-

tional trade, investment, and technology transfer"? How exactly would these things be ensured? Does Maskus's theory suggest that TRIPS itself would be sufficient, or are other measures needed?

3. *Patents and least developed countries.* Are the potential beneficial effects of a patent system different for the least developed countries? Based on Professor Maskus's analysis, do you think a patent system can potentially benefit a least developed country? What if the infrastructure is so lacking that the country couldn't even have a patent office to review applications?

4. *Technology transfer.* Some empirical analysis indicates that stronger IP protection may lead to greater technology transfer to a developing country "in the domestic deployment of advanced technology by the affiliates of foreign firms." Lee G. Branstetter, *Do Stronger Patents Induce More Local Innovation?*, 7 J. INT'L ECON. L. 359, 359 (2004). Although stronger patent protection enabled greater rent extraction by patentees from a country, the study found an increase in licensing payments to U.S. multinationals from their affiliates in a country, or, alternatively, from third-party licensees. *Id.* at 368. R & D spending by patentees also tended to increase, suggesting the need to modify technology for transfer to the developing country. *Id.* at 369. Is this technology transfer to developing countries a positive benefit for developing countries? Does your answer depend on whether the transfer is to a foreign affiliate of a multinational entity or a third-party licensee?

5. *Bibliographic note.* Jean R. Homere, *Intellectual Property Rights Can Help Stimulate the Economic Development of Least Developed Countries*, 27 COLUM. J.L. & ARTS 277 (2004); Edwin Mansfield, Intellectual Property Protection, Direct Investment, and Technology Transfer (Int'l Finance Corp. Discussion Paper No. 27, 1995); Keith E. Maskus & Jerome H. Reichman, *The Globalization of Private Knowledge Goods and the Privatization of Global Public Goods*, 7 J. INT'L ECON. L. 279 (2004); A. Samuel Oddi, *The International Patent System and Third World Development: Reality or Myth?*, 1987 DUKE L.J. 831, 842 (1987); Carlos A. Primo Braga & Carsten Fink, *The Relationship Between Intellectual Property Rights and Foreign Direct Investment*, 9 DUKE J. COMP. & INT'L L. 163 (1998).

4. SPECIAL DISCUSSION: TRANSITIONAL PROVISIONS FOR DEVELOPING COUNTRIES

TRIPS attempts to accommodate the needs of developing countries, at least to some extent, by allowing a period of transition during which developing countries do not have to comply with certain TRIPS patent requirements. As a transitional measure, Article 65(1) and (2) allow all developing countries to enjoy a 5–year transition period from the date of entry into force of the WTO Agreement on January 1, 1995—meaning until January 1, 2000 to implement TRIPS obligations. Article 65(4) gives developing countries that had previously denied patents to certain fields of technology, such as pharmaceuticals, an additional period of five years—until January 1, 2005—to implement the new patent obligations of TRIPS.

Least developed countries were given 10 years from the date of application under Article 65(1)—until January 1, 2006—to comply with all TRIPS obligations; the date was later extended to July 1, 2013. The 2001 Doha WTO Ministerial granted least developed countries an additional 10 years—until January 1, 2016—to comply with the TRIPS provisions with regard to patenting of pharmaceutical products "without prejudice to the right of least-developed country members to seek other extensions of the transition periods as provided for in Article 66.1." What do you think was the reason for allowing these transitional arrangements?

During the period of transition, countries are still obligated to accept patent applications for pharmaceutical and agricultural chemical products upon joining the WTO under the "mailbox" rule of Article 70(8). The patent applications must be treated with the same priority as the original filing date. Exactly what the minimum standard under the mailbox rule entails became the subject of a dispute in the WTO shortly after its formation, as discussed next.

INDIA–PATENT PROTECTION FOR PHARMACEUTICAL AND AGRICULTURAL CHEMICAL PRODUCTS

Report of the Appellate Body, WTO. (Lacarte–Muro, Presiding Member; Bacchus and Beeby, Members). WT/DS50/AB/R (December 19, 1997).

[The United States brought an action in the WTO against India for allegedly failing to establish a "mailbox" under TRIPS Article 70.8 during the transition period that ended on January 1, 2005 in which India had to extend patent protection to pharmaceuticals and agricultural products. The panel agreed with the United States and ruled against India, which appealed to the Appellate Body, which rendered the decision below. *Ed.*]

VI.   Article 70.8

Article 70.8 states:

Where a Member does not make available as of the date of entry into force of the WTO Agreement patent protection for pharmaceutical and agricultural chemical products commensurate with its obligations under Article 27, that Member shall:

(a) notwithstanding the provisions of Part VI, provide as from the date of entry into force of the WTO Agreement a means by which applications for patents for such inventions can be filed;

(b) apply to these applications, as of the date of application of this Agreement, the criteria for patentability as laid down in this Agreement as if those criteria were being applied on the date of filing in that Member or, where priority is available and claimed, the priority date of the application; and

(c) provide patent protection in accordance with this Agreement as from the grant of the patent and for the remainder of the patent term, counted from the filing date in accordance with Article 33 of this Agreement, for those of these applications that meet the criteria for protection referred to in subparagraph (b).

With respect to Article 70.8(a), the Panel found that:

... Article 70.8(a) requires the Members in question to establish a means that not only appropriately allows for the entitlement to file mailbox applications and the allocation of filing and priority dates to them, but also provides a sound legal basis to preserve novelty and priority as of those dates, so as to eliminate any reasonable doubts regarding whether mailbox applications and eventual patents based on them could be rejected or invalidated because, at the filing or priority date, the matter for which protection was sought was unpatentable in the country in question.

In India's view, the obligations in Article 70.8(a) are met by a developing country Member where it establishes a mailbox for receiving, dating and storing patent applications for pharmaceutical and agricultural chemical products in a manner that properly allots filing and priority dates to those applications in accordance with paragraphs (b) and (c) of Article 70.8. India asserts that the Panel established an additional obligation "to create legal certainty that the patent applications and the eventual patents based on them will not be rejected or invalidated in the future." This, India argues, is a legal error by the Panel.

The introductory clause to Article 70.8 provides that it applies "[w]here a Member does not make available as of the date of entry into force of the WTO Agreement patent protection for pharmaceutical and agricultural chemical products commensurate with its obligations under Article 27 ..." of the TRIPS Agreement. Article 27 requires that patents be made available "for any inventions, whether products or processes, in all fields of technology," subject to certain exceptions. However, pursuant to paragraphs 1, 2 and 4 of Article 65, a developing country Member may delay providing product patent protection in areas of technology not protectable in its territory on the general date of application of the TRIPS Agreement for that Member until 1 January 2005. Article 70.8 relates specifically and exclusively to situations where a Member does not provide, as of 1 January 1995, patent protection for pharmaceutical and agricultural chemical products.

By its terms, Article 70.8(a) applies "notwithstanding the provisions of Part VI" of the TRIPS Agreement. Part VI of the TRIPS Agreement, consisting of Articles 65, 66 and 67, allows for certain "transitional arrangements" in the application of certain provisions of the TRIPS Agreement. These "transitional arrangements," which allow a Member to delay the application of some of the obligations in the TRIPS Agreement for certain specified periods, do not apply to Article 70.8. Thus, although there are "transitional arrangements" which allow developing country Members, in particular, more time to implement certain of their obligations under the TRIPS Agreement, no such "transitional arrange-ments" exist for the obligations in Article 70.8.

Article 70.8(a) imposes an obligation on Members to provide "a means" by which mailbox applications can be filed "from the date of entry into force of the WTO Agreement." Thus, this obligation has been in force since 1 January 1995. The issue before us in this appeal is not whether this obligation exists or whether this obligation is now in force. Clearly, it exists, and, equally clearly, it is in force now. The issue before us in this appeal is: what precisely is the "means" for filing mailbox applications that is contemplated and required by Article 70.8(a)? To answer this question, we must interpret the terms of Article 70.8(a)....

Issue

Paragraphs (b) and (c) of Article 70.8 constitute part of the context for interpreting Article 70.8(a). Paragraphs (b) and (c) of Article 70.8 require that the "means" provided by a Member under Article 70.8(a) must allow the filing of applications for patents for pharmaceutical and agricultural chemical products from 1 January 1995 and preserve the dates of filing and priority of those applications, so that the criteria for patentability may be applied as of those dates, and so that the patent protection eventually granted is dated back to the filing date. In this respect, we agree with the Panel that,

> ... in order to prevent the loss of the novelty of an invention ... filing and priority dates need to have a sound legal basis if the provisions of Article 70.8 are to fulfil their purpose. Moreover, if available, a filing must entitle the applicant to claim priority on the basis of an earlier filing in respect of the claimed invention over applications with subsequent filing or priority dates. Without legally sound filing and priority dates, the mechanism to be established on the basis of Article 70.8 will be rendered inoperational.

On this, the Panel is clearly correct. The Panel's interpretation here is consistent also with the object and purpose of the TRIPS Agreement. The Agreement takes into account, *inter alia*, "the need to promote effective and adequate protection of intellectual property rights."[38] We believe the Panel was correct in finding that the "means" that the Member concerned is obliged to provide under Article 70.8(a) must allow for "the entitlement to file mailbox applications and the allocation of filing and priority dates to them." Furthermore, the Panel was correct in finding that the "means" established under Article 70.8(a) must also provide "a sound legal basis to preserve novelty and priority as of those dates." These findings flow inescapably from the necessary operation of paragraphs (b) and (c) of Article 70.8.58.

However, we do *not* agree with the Panel that Article 70.8(a) requires a Member to establish a means "so as to eliminate any reasonable doubts regarding whether mailbox applications and eventual patents based on them could be rejected or invalidated because, at the filing or priority date, the matter for which protection was sought was unpatentable in the

---

38. Preamble to the *TRIPS Agreement*.

country in question." India is *entitled*, by the "transitional arrangements" in paragraphs 1, 2 and 4 of Article 65, to delay application of Article 27 for patents for pharmaceutical and agricultural chemical products until 1 January 2005. In our view, India is obliged, by Article 70.8(a), to provide a legal mechanism for the filing of mailbox applications that provides a sound legal basis to preserve both the novelty of the inventions and the priority of the applications as of the relevant filing and priority dates. No more.

But what constitutes such a sound legal basis in Indian law? To answer this question, we must recall first an important general rule in the TRIPS Agreement. Article 1.1 of the TRIPS Agreement states, in pertinent part:

> ... Members shall be free to determine the appropriate method of implementing the provisions of this Agreement within their own legal system and practice.

India insists that it has done that. India contends that it has established, through "administrative instructions,"[42] a "means" consistent with Article 70.8(a) of the TRIPS Agreement. According to India, these "administrative instructions" establish a mechanism that provides a sound legal basis to preserve the novelty of the inventions and the priority of the applications as of the relevant filing and priority dates consistent with Article 70.8(a) of the TRIPS Agreement. According to India, pursuant to these "administrative instructions," the Patent Office has been directed to store applications for patents for pharmaceutical and agricultural chemical products separately for future action pursuant to Article 70.8, and the Controller General of Patents Designs and Trademarks ("the Controller") has been instructed not to refer them to an examiner until 1 January 2005. According to India, these "administrative instructions" are legally valid in Indian law, as they are reflected in the Minister's Statement to Parliament of 2 August 1996. And, according to India:

> There is ... *absolute certainty* that India can, when patents are due in accordance with subparagraphs (b) and (c) of Article 70.8, decide to grant such patents on the basis of the applications currently submitted and determine the novelty and priority of the inventions in accordance with the date of these applications. (emphasis added)

India has not provided any text of these "administrative instructions" either to the Panel or to us.

Whatever their substance or their import, these "administrative instructions" were not the initial "means" chosen by the Government of India to meet India's obligations under Article 70.8(a) of the TRIPS Agreement. The Government of India's initial preference for establishing a "means" for filing mailbox applications under Article 70.8(a) was the Patents (Amendment) Ordinance (the "Ordinance"), promulgated by the President of India on 31 December 1994 pursuant to Article 123 of India's

---

42.   This is India's term for its measure. India's appellant's submission, p. 10.

Constitution. Article 123 enables the President to promulgate an ordinance when Parliament is not in session, and when the President is satisfied "that circumstances exist which render it necessary for him to take immediate action." India notified the Ordinance to the Council for TRIPS, pursuant to Article 63.2 of the TRIPS Agreement, on 6 March 1995. In accordance with the terms of Article 123 of India's Constitution, the Ordinance expired on 26 March 1995, six weeks after the reassembly of Parliament. This was followed by an unsuccessful effort to enact the Patents (Amendment) Bill 1995 to implement the contents of the Ordinance on a permanent basis. This Bill was introduced in the Lok Sabha (Lower House) in March 1995. After being passed by the Lok Sabha, it was referred to a Select Committee of the Rajya Sabha (Upper House) for examination and report. However, the Bill was subsequently not enacted due to the dissolution of Parliament on 10 May 1996. From these actions, it is apparent that the Government of India initially considered the enactment of amending legislation to be necessary in order to implement its obligations under Article 70.8(a). However, India maintains that the "administrative instructions" issued in April 1995 effectively continued the mailbox system established by the Ordinance, thus obviating the need for a formal amendment to the Patents Act or for a new notification to the Council for TRIPS.

With respect to India's "administrative instructions," the Panel found that "the current administrative practice creates a certain degree of legal insecurity in that it requires Indian officials to ignore certain mandatory provisions of the Patents Act"; and that "even if Patent Office officials do not examine and reject mailbox applications, a competitor might seek a judicial order to do so in order to obtain rejection of a patent claim."

[W]e must look at the specific provisions of the Patents Act. Section 5(a) of the Patents Act provides that substances "intended for use, or capable of being used, as food or as medicine or drug" are not patentable. "When the complete specification has been led in respect of an application for a patent," section 12(1) *requires* the Controller to refer that application and that specification to an examiner. Moreover, section 15(2) of the Patents Act states that the Controller "shall refuse" an application in respect of a substance that is not patentable. We agree with the Panel that these provisions of the Patents Act are mandatory. And, like the Panel, we are not persuaded that India's "administrative instructions" would prevail over the contradictory mandatory provisions of the Patents Act. We note also that, in issuing these "administrative instructions," the Government of India did not avail itself of the provisions of section 159 of the Patents Act, which allows the Central Government "to make rules for carrying out the provisions of [the] Act" or section 160 of the Patents Act, which requires that such rules be laid before each House of the Indian Parliament. We are told by India that such rulemaking was not required for the "administrative instructions" at issue here. But this, too, seems to be inconsistent with the mandatory provisions of the Patents Act.

We are not persuaded by India's explanation of these seeming contradictions. Accordingly, we are not persuaded that India's "administrative instructions" would survive a legal challenge under the Patents Act. And, consequently, we are not persuaded that India's "administrative instructions" provide a sound legal basis to preserve novelty of inventions and priority of applications as of the relevant filing and priority dates.

For these reasons, we agree with the Panel's conclusion that India's administrative instructions for receiving mailbox applications are inconsistent with Article 70.8(a) of the TRIPS Agreement.

NOTES AND QUESTIONS

1. If India had maintained the view that its law *did* preserve the priority and novelty of inventions whose applications had been filed under the mailbox rule, consistent with its obligations under TRIPS, why do you think the U.S. challenged India's law?

2. Did the Appellate Body view its role as including the interpretation of the law of India? If India maintained that its "administrative instructions" *did* preserve the novelty and priority of patent applications filed for pharmaceuticals and agricultural chemical products during the transition period, why did the Appellate Body find Indian law deficient? Should the Appellate Body (or the Panel below) have given greater deference to the explanation of the Indian government about its own law? Or was there a good reason to reject India's explanation of its own law?

3. Was it a mistake for India not to have provided the WTO panel with any text of the "administrative instructions"? But why didn't the WTO panel just ask for them or appoint an independent expert to opine on the issue? Would India's case have been strengthened had there been a judicial decision interpreting the "administrative instructions" by one of its courts?

4. What must India do to comply with its TRIPS obligations under the mailbox rule? Is this much different from the position taken by India before the WTO panel decision? Between 1999 and 2005, the Indian Parliament amended its patent code three times, recognizing the patentability of food, chemicals, and pharmaceutical inventions in the patent code. India reported its implementation to the WTO on April 28, 1999.

5. *Council for TRIPS.* Articles 68 and 71 establish a Council for TRIPS. The Council, which is open to all members, monitors the member countries' compliance with and implementation of the TRIPS Agreement. Under Article 63, member nations are obligated to notify the Council of "the laws and regulations" of their nation that implement their obligations under TRIPS. The Council reviews the implementing laws and identifies any perceived problems in the implementing laws. Would it be better for diplomacy and relations among countries if any initial objection to the adequacy of a country's law must first pass through a review by the Council of TRIPS?

6. *Bibliographic note.* Martin J. Adelman & Sonia Baldia, *Prospects and Limits of the Patent Provision in the TRIPS Agreement: The Case of India,* 29

VAND. J. TRANSNAT'L L. 507 (1996); Jerome H. Reichman, *Securing Compliance with the TRIPS Agreement after U.S. v. India*, 1 J. INT'L ECON. L. 585 (1998).

B. OWNERSHIP AND FORMALITIES: OBTAINING DOMESTIC AND FOREIGN PATENTS

Filing a patent application is a highly involved task, made more complicated by the prospect of filing applications in foreign countries and different languages. Historically, countries had considerable differences in what filings were required, but most, if not all, required the appointment of a local agent to carry out the filing in a particular country (a requirement still often true today). The cost of filing a patent also added considerably to the inventor's burden. In stark contrast, the securing of copyrights for an author's work under the Berne Convention is unhampered by any administrative formality. Unlike obtaining copyrights, the process for obtaining patents is complex, expensive, and filled with formalities in the filing and prosecuting of a patent application for the claimed invention. Just imagine the cost and burdens an inventor must face in filing 50 or more patent applications in different countries and languages around the world. In this section, we discuss the process of securing patents internationally.

PROBLEM 3–2

You have been hired as a consultant to the World Trade Organization to provide advice on whether its members should consider revising the patent provisions of TRIPS to adopt a single, universal patent system. Under such a universal patent system, all member countries would agree that international law developed under this new treaty would provide the sole, uniform law for patents. An inventor would only need to obtain one "universal" patent that would offer protection around the world, in all those countries that agreed to the proposal. One possible benefit of the universal patent is that it could avoid the need for a patentee to file parallel litigation in multiple jurisdictions (as is currently required) to enforce patents for the same invention against the same defendant. Are there any practical problems that would need to be addressed to implement such a system, such as agreeing on a single language or set of languages? Who might be in favor or against the idea? How would you compare the desirability of the proposal to the current territorial approach, in which each country grants patents that are effective only within its borders? In formulating your answer, consider the following discussion in section 1 on the current approach.

1. FILING FOR AND PROSECUTING PATENTS AROUND THE WORLD

a. The Period of Paris Priority

Paris Convention

Article 4

A.

(1) Any person who has duly filed an application for a patent, * * * in one of the countries of the Union, or his successor in title, shall enjoy, for the purpose of filing in the other countries, a right of priority during the periods hereinafter fixed.

(2) Any filing that is equivalent to a regular national filing under the domestic legislation of any country of the Union or under bilateral or multilateral treaties concluded between countries of the Union shall be recognized as giving rise to the right of priority.

(3) By a regular national filing is meant any filing that is adequate to establish the date on which the application was filed in the country concerned, whatever may be the subsequent fate of the application.

B.

Consequently, any subsequent filing in any of the other countries of the Union before the expiration of the periods referred to above shall not be invalidated by reason of any acts accomplished in the interval, in particular, another filing, the publication or exploitation of the invention, * * * and such acts cannot give rise to any third-party right or any right of personal possession. Rights acquired by third parties before the date of the first application that serves as the basis for the right of priority are reserved in accordance with the domestic legislation of each country of the Union.

C.

(1) The periods of priority referred to above shall be twelve months for patents and utility models, and six months for industrial designs and trademarks.

(2) These periods shall start from the date of filing of the first application; the day of filing shall not be included in the period.

(3) If the last day of the period is an official holiday, or a day when the Office is not open for the filing of applications in the country where protection is claimed, the period shall be extended until the first following working day.

(4) A subsequent application concerning the same subject as a previous first application within the meaning of paragraph (2), above, filed in the same country of the Union shall be considered as the first application, of which the filing date shall be the starting point of the

period of priority, if, at the time of filing the subsequent application, the said previous application has been withdrawn, abandoned, or refused, without having been laid open to public inspection and without leaving any rights outstanding, and if it has not yet served as a basis for claiming a right of priority. The previous application may not thereafter serve as a basis for claiming a right of priority. * * *

* * *

The major benefit of the Paris Convention, aside from the principle of national treatment, is the period of priority granted to qualifying patent applicants. For patents, Article 4 of Paris affords a 12–month period of priority. The 1–year period was viewed as a way for an inventor to gain more time to evaluate the commercial marketability of the invention, before deciding whether or not to incur the great expense of obtaining foreign patents. Inventors might decide to forego foreign patents altogether during that 1–year period if they decided their inventions would not likely have commercial success abroad.

However, if an inventor decides to seek patents internationally, Paris priority effectively allows an inventor to claim the earliest date of filing a patent application in any Paris country—the "Paris priority date"—as the date for *all* subsequently filed patent applications in other Paris countries within that 1–year period. The applicant will be entitled to two types of benefits for the priority period in every country of the Union: (1) the applicant can claim the benefit of the original filing date in priority disputes with other inventors claiming the same invention in a competing patent application and (2) the applicant is protected against certain acts committed by herself and third parties *after* the Paris priority date that would otherwise invalidate the patent.

To understand the benefit of Paris priority in priority disputes, one must understand that in most patent systems in the world, competing patent applications are decided under a *first-to-file* approach, i.e., an application that is first in time will prevail over an application that is later in time assuming that all other patent requirements are met. Under Paris priority, if the inventor files other patent applications in any other country in the Paris Union within the one-year period, *all* those applications are treated as if they were filed on the date of the first application filed—which could prove to be crucial in establishing that an inventor was the first to file in a particular country.

Illustration 3–2. On November 30, 2011, Alfreda is the first to file a patent application for a particular invention in the United Kingdom, a Paris Union country that follows the first-to-file approach. Alfreda did not reveal the invention to the public in any way. Based on her own independent research, Ulla files a patent application on February 1, 2012 for the same invention in Country Y, which also uses a first-to-file system. If Country Y is not a Paris Union country (or otherwise bound to apply Paris priority), Ulla's application in Country Y would, under the principle of territoriality and a first-to-file system, prevail over any subsequent application by Alfreda for the same invention in Country Y. Ulla would obtain the patent in Country Y, while Alfreda would obtain the patent in the UK. Each is considered the "first-to-file" in their respective countries.

Illustration 3–3. Under the same facts as above, except that Country Y is now a Paris Union country. Alfreda has one year from November 30, 2011, or until November 30, 2012, to file an application for the invention in Country Y. If Alfreda files an application by November 30, 2012, Alfreda is entitled to a priority date in Country Y of November 30, 2011, the date of the original filing in the UK, which establishes priority over Ulla's application (filed on February 1, 2012). The Paris priority date applies to all of Alfreda's patent applications for the same invention filed within the 1–year period. Alfreda would obtain the patent in Country Y, as well as in the UK.

In Illustration 3–3 above and in all cases involving Paris priority, there are at least two patent applications involved: (1) the first application establishes the original filing date, and (2) the second and subsequent application, if filed within one year, is entitled to claim the benefit of the original filing date as the effective filing date of the second application. Of course, a patentee can seek to file many other foreign patent applications in different countries within that Paris priority period.

A second benefit of Paris priority is that it effectively immunizes acts of the inventor or third parties that occur within the one-year period that could otherwise potentially defeat the novelty of the invention. As Article 4 states, "any subsequent filing in any of the other countries of the Union before the expiration of the periods . . . shall not be invalidated by reason of any acts accomplished in the interval, in particular, another filing, the publication or exploitation of the invention, the putting on sale of copies of the design, or the use of the mark, and such acts cannot give rise to any third-party right or any right of personal possession." Thus, inventors can avoid having their own activities during the 1–year period, such as marketing and selling their inventions to consumers, defeat the novelty of the inventions in countries in which they subsequently file patent applications during the Paris period of priority. Third party activities that occur after the inventor's first filed patent application also do not defeat the novelty of the inventions. The reason, in either case, is very simple: the Paris priority date (which is, by definition, earlier in time) will make all subsequent acts of the inventor or third parties within the 1–year Paris period totally irrelevant to measuring the novelty of the invention.

Illustration 3–4. Alfreda files a patent application in United Kingdom, a Paris Union country, on November 30, 2011. Alfreda's invention is discussed, with her permission, in full detail in a scientific magazine in Country Y on February 1, 2012. Alfreda files a patent application in Country Y on November 30, 2012. Does the Feb. 1, 2012 publication defeat the novelty of Alfreda's invention in Country Y? No. Under Country Y's patent law, the description of the invention in a publication prior to a patent application would normally defeat the novelty of the invention and disqualify the invention for a patent. However, in this case, if Country Y is a Paris Union country, then Alfreda's patent application in Country Y is accorded the earlier Paris priority date of November 30, 2011. Since the magazine was not published until after the Paris priority date, it cannot defeat the novelty of Alfreda's invention in Country Y.

U.S. switch to first-to-file system. For over 200 years, the U.S. patent system had a first-to-invent system, meaning priority of invention went to the first person to reduce the invention to practice. The U.S. approach—which differed from the rest of the world—was justified as a way to protect small-time inventors who lacked the resources to compete with corporations in the race to file in the patent office. However, in practice, the U.S. system sometimes resembled a first-to-file approach in cases in which the inventor could not or did not prove the actual date of invention with the requisite independent evidence corroborating the inventor's own testimony (e.g., contemporaneous records, eyewitnesses, and the like).* In such case, the inventor could rely on the date of *constructive reduction to practice* of the invention, which is the date of filing a patent application. Thus, proof of a Paris priority date may well be sufficient evidence for an inventor to prove she is entitled to a patent for an invention in a priority dispute in the U.S.

> Illustration 3–5. Alfreda files a patent application in the United Kingdom, a Paris Union country on November 30, 2011. Alfreda did not reveal the invention to the public in any way. Meanwhile, on February 1, 2012, Ulla reduces the same invention to practice in the U.S. and then files for a patent on March 5, 2012. Within the Paris priority period, on November 30, 2012, Alfreda files a patent application for the same invention in the U.S. In this priority dispute, Alfreda would be entitled to claim priority for the invention in the U.S. because Alfreda reduced the invention *before* Ulla, as evidenced by Alfreda's constructive reduction to practice on the Paris priority date of November 30, 2011. Even if Alfreda did not keep adequate records to prove the date of actual reduction to practice in the U.S., Alfreda would prevail over Ulla by virtue of Alfreda's Paris priority date. Alfreda gets the U.S. patent and the UK patent for the invention.

On September 16, 2011, the U.S. enacted major reforms to its patent law—indeed, the most sweeping changes to patent law since the current Act of 1952. The revision, known as the America Invents Act (AIA), Pub. L. No. 112–29, 125 Stat. 284 (2011), made numerous changes, including several designed to harmonize U.S. law with other countries. Most importantly for harmonization purposes, the AIA switched the U.S. patent system from a first-to-invent to a first-to-file system starting on March 16,

---

* *See* Mark A. Lemley & Colleen V. Chien, *Are the U.S. Patent Priority Rules Really Necessary?*, 54 HASTINGS L.J. 1299, 1317 (2003) (finding a significant percentage of priority disputes resolved simply by constructive reduction to practice and the filing date).

2013 (18 months after signing of the AIA). Thus, the new standard of inventorship based on the first-to-file the patent application for an invention in the U.S. applies to any patent application filed on or after March 16, 2013. AIA, § 3(n)(1). Practically speaking, this means that the prior first-to-invent standard will continue to have relevance for (i) all existing patents for their duration and (ii) any patent applications that are filed in the PTO before March 16, 2013. Thus, at least until probably 2035, the U.S. patent system will be a dual system of (1) a first-to-invent system for existing patents and applications filed before March 16, 2013 and (2) a first-to-file system for applications filed on March 16, 2013 or later.

The U.S. adopted a modified first-to-file system, allowing a 1–year grace period before the filing of the patent application for certain disclosures made by the inventor(s). A disclosure of the invention during that 1–year grace period will not be considered prior art if: "(A) the disclosure was made by the inventor or joint inventor or by another who obtained the subject matter disclosed directly or indirectly from the inventor or a joint inventor; or (B) the subject matter disclosed had, before such disclosure, been publicly disclosed by the inventor or a joint inventor or another who obtained the subject matter disclosed directly or indirectly from the inventor or a joint inventor." AIA, § 3(b). A similar 1–year grace period is provided for disclosures appearing in patents and applications. *Id.* The 1–year grace period for inventor disclosures is somewhat similar to the 1–year grace period under the statutory bars under the prior § 102(b), although the statutory bars even allowed activities by third parties during the 1–year grace period between invention and filing for a patent. It is unclear whether the permitted "disclosure" under the AIA also includes public use and sale of the invention as in the prior § 102(b).

The U.S. 1–year grace period is more generous to inventors than the European Patent Convention's approach. Article 55 of the EPC allows a very limited 6–month grace period for "non-prejudicial disclosures," meaning (1) unauthorized disclosures that constitute "an evident abuse in relation to the applicant" and (2) authorized disclosures of the invention "at an official . . . international exhibition falling within the terms of the Convention on international exhibitions signed at Paris on 22 November 1928."

Independent treatment. Note that Paris priority does not hinge on the granting of a patent in any country. The Paris Convention, like the Berne Convention, follows the principle of independent treatment and is not concerned with the effect or validity of rights under domestic law. To be entitled to the period of priority under Article 4, the applicant has to file an application under the national law of a Paris Union country and then later make a declaration in other Paris countries invoking priority for the subsequent patent applications filed within the Paris priority period. *See* Paris Conv. art. 4(D)(1). Whether the patent is eventually granted or denied in the first Paris country is of no importance in determining whether the applicant receives Paris priority. *See id.* art. 4(A)(3). The applicant is entitled to Paris priority so long as the filing is a "regular national filing" as determined under the domestic law of the Union country, and the proper declaration is made. *See id.* arts. 4(A)(2), 4(D)(1). Some countries, such as the United States, permit so-called provisional patent applications, which can later be converted into a regular filing that would entitle the applicant to the original date of the provisional filing. Under U.S. law, however, a provisional patent application is not treated as a "regular national filing" and is thus not entitled to Paris priority. 35 U.S.C. § 111(b)(7).

Of course, filing a patent application in one or several countries is only the first step of the process of obtaining a patent. Although patent prosecution is more a matter of domestic law and, therefore, will not be discussed in depth in this casebook, it is important to understand a few of the basics. Once an inventor files for a patent, the process of "prosecution" begins. In the U.S. and other countries, a patent examiner in the patent office will eventually review the application (out of the queue of patent applications) to determine whether the claimed invention qualifies for a patent. Particularly important is the examiner's review of the prior art to determine whether the claimed invention is already disclosed in the prior art. If it is disclosed in the prior art, the invention is not novel and cannot qualify for a patent; we shall return to novelty later below. During this period of patent prosecution, the examiner will identify any perceived problems in the application, including overly expansive claims, and will notify the inventor (or the patent attorney). The inventor then can defend or amend the application to address any problems raised by the examiner. This involved back-and-forth between examiner and inventor constitutes the "prosecution history" that later becomes relevant to determining the scope of the claims granted. The level of scrutiny a patent office devotes to a patent application may differ depending on the country. The U.S. Patent Office is considered to be relatively searching in its review. However, critics have pointed out that the U.S. patent examiner spends, on average, only eighteen hours reviewing any one application, and that patent examiners have incentives and institutional pressures to grant patents regardless of merit, due to the high number of applications each examiner must process and the fact that a grant typically requires less time than a rejection.[2]

PROBLEM 3–3

Anton files a patent application for his invention in Country Z on September 5, 2011. Brokaw files a patent application for the same invention in Country Y on August 1, 2012. Then, on September 5, 2012, Anton files a patent application for his invention in Country Y. But Anton's application is eventually rejected by the patent office of Z in early 2013. Both Y and Z are Paris Union countries. Who has priority to the patent for the invention in Country Y? Consult Article 4 of the Paris Convention and the discussion above.

---

2. *See* Mark A. Lemley, *Rational Ignorance at the Patent Office*, 95 Nw. U. L. Rev. 1495, 1496 n.3 (2001).

b. Filing an International Application Under the PCT

PROBLEM 3–4

Alexi, a Chinese national, files for a patent in the China Patent Office on November 30, 2011. On November 30, 2012, Alexi files an international application under the Patent Cooperation Treaty (PCT), automatically designating all PCT countries for the international application. Eighteen months later, Alexi decides to enter the national stage of the PCT process and files a national patent application (based on her PCT international application) in the United States Patent Office with a U.S. filing date of May 30, 2014. What, if any, priority date can Alexi claim for her U.S. patent application?

* * *

Although Paris priority was a monumental achievement at the time the Convention was adopted, it did little to ease the administrative burden of filing multiple patent applications for the same invention, often in different languages and under different requirements. By the 1960s, at the U.S.'s initiative, efforts began to streamline the process. The result was the signing of the Patent Cooperation Treaty (PCT) in 1970, which is a special agreement among Paris countries pursuant to Article 19 of the Paris Convention. The PCT attempts to ease at least some of the administrative burden of filing different patent applications for the same invention in different countries. The PCT is one of the most important conventions for patent practitioners today. In 1970, 28 countries were members of the PCT. As of 2011, 144 countries are PCT members.

The PCT is intended to reduce the burden an inventor faces in seeking patents around the world. The PCT does so in two key respects: (1) the PCT extends the time period before an inventor must file national applications in other countries, while still preserving Paris priority, and (2) the PCT establishes a common, uniform patent application form that must be accepted by every PCT country (with applicable translations and fees), thereby reducing the administrative burden of having to fill out applications in different formats.

To understand how the PCT operates, it is useful to recall the traditional route. Remember from our earlier discussion that under the traditional route under Paris, an inventor only has a 1–year period from the date of the first patent application to decide whether to pursue patent applications individually in other countries. By the end of the Paris priority period, the inventor has to file patent applications in other countries subject to their specific formality requirements (or risk losing any claim to the invention in those countries).

By contrast, if an inventor elects to go through the PCT process and files what is called an "international application" in the patent office or the International Bureau of WIPO within 12–months of the first patent filing for the invention under the Paris Convention, the inventor obtains a total of up to 30 months from the priority date to file a regular national application. (Under Article 39(1)(b), the PCT allows countries to "fix time limits which expire later than" 30 months. The European Patent Convention and a few countries have allotted 31 months from the priority date as the deadline to enter the national phase.) Under the PCT, the inventor is allowed effectively to delay a decision on whether to file a regular national application for an additional 18 months beyond the 12 months provided by the period of Paris priority. This is perhaps the most significant benefit of the PCT because it gives inventors who invoke Paris priority an additional 18 months in which to assess the commercial viability of the invention in certain markets before having to commit resources in applying for patents.

Illustration 3–6. *Traditional route under Paris.* Within a year after filing a patent application in the U.S., Donyell files separate applications with the patent offices of Australia, Belgium, and Canada. For each application, Donyell must now pay the requisite filing fee and provide whatever patent application form required by each national patent office in Australia, Belgium, and Canada. The forms in these countries could be different and require different information.

Illustration 3–7. *PCT route.* By contrast, under the PCT, if Donyell files an international application under the PCT within a year of filing his first application in the U.S., Donyell's international application preserves his Paris priority date while Donyell goes through the PCT process. During the PCT process, Donyell can wait 30 months from the priority date before having to decide whether to seek national patents in Australia, Belgium, and Canada. If Donyell decides to enter the PCT's national stage by 30 months from the priority date, Donyell's international PCT application can be used as the national patent applications in Australia, Belgium, and Canada (provided any required translations and fees are also met). Importantly, Donyell is still entitled to claim a priority date in Australia, Belgium, and Canada based on the international filing. With the Paris priority extended 18 months by the PCT process, Donyell is protected against any subsequent competing applications or any acts that might otherwise invalidate Donyell's application in Australia, Belgium, and Canada until the expiration of the 30–month period from the priority date.

The international application has the added benefit of being acceptable as a national application in all PCT countries, provided any required translation and fees are filed therewith in the national patent office. PCT art. 22. So, instead of having to fill out many different application forms, an inventor can use the international application as the basis for all subsequent filings.

The PCT can be broken down into two phases: (1) the international phase and (2) the national phase. To begin the international phase, an applicant files an international application with one of the national patent offices that has been designated as an International Search Authority (ISA). The patent offices of the United States, European Patent Office, Australia, Canada, Japan, Korea, and China, among others, are designated as ISAs. Under the 2004 amended Regulations to the PCT, the international application now automatically identifies all PCT states as designated states for the purposes of the application, a change from the old way of having the inventor elect the states to be designated. PCT Rule 4.9.[3]

---

3. A narrow exception is allowed for a PCT country whose law would treat the automatic designation of that state on the international application as defeating the priority of an earlier

So what happens during the PCT international process? It is an involved process. The following Diagram shows the basic features. As you read the following discussion, you may find it helpful to refer back to the Diagram.

Diagram 3–1: The Basic Timeline for the PCT Process: International Phase

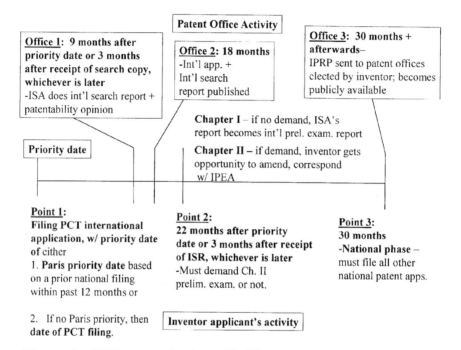

Patent Office Activity

Office 1: 9 months after priority date or 3 months after receipt of search copy, whichever is later
-ISA does int'l search report + patentability opinion

Office 2: 18 months
-Int'l app. +
Int'l search
report published

Office 3: 30 months +
afterwards–
IPRP sent to patent offices elected by inventor; becomes publicly available

Priority date

Chapter I – if no demand, ISA's report becomes int'l prel. exam. report

Chapter II – if demand, inventor gets opportunity to amend, correspond w/ IPEA

Point 1:
Filing PCT international application, w/ priority date of either
1. **Paris priority date** based on a prior national filing within past 12 months or

Point 2:
22 months after priority date or 3 months after receipt of ISR, whichever is later
-Must demand Ch. II prelim. exam. or not.

Point 3:
30 months
-National phase –
must file all other national patent apps.

2. If no Paris priority, then date of PCT filing.

Inventor applicant's activity

The entire PCT process begins with filing an international application—depicted as "Point 1" on the left-hand side in the Diagram above—that will establish a priority date. The priority date is crucial because all periods under the PCT are measured from the priority date. In the Diagram, all of the months designated are measured from the priority date for the international application unless otherwise noted. How the priority date is determined depends on whether the PCT application (1) is based on a prior national application or (2) is filed alone. *See* PCT art. 2 (definition of "priority date").

The more common route is (1): inventors file a national patent application in a Paris country and then file a PCT international application within 12 months of the first patent application. Because the PCT is a special agreement of the Paris Convention, PCT international applications, like all other regular patent applications in Paris countries, are subject to the period of priority contained in Article 4 of the Paris Convention. Like all Paris applications, the PCT international application can assert a priority claim based on a prior application. In such case, the "priority date" for the PCT application is the Paris priority date.

filed national application with "the same consequences as the withdrawal of the earlier national application." In such case, if the country files a reservation, the PCT application will not automatically designate that country if it would defeat the priority claim. Germany, Russia, and South Korea filed for this exception with the International Body of WIPO.

Illustration 3–8. On November 30, 2011, Donyell files a patent application in Germany, a Paris Union country. On November 30, 2012, within the 12–month period of Paris priority, Donyell files a PCT international application with the European Patent Office. Donyell's international application is allowed to claim a priority date of November 30, 2011.

While most PCT international applications are based on a prior national application, it is also possible—as noted in "Point 1" in the Diagram—for an inventor to file a PCT international application that does not assert Paris priority or the benefit of a previously filed national application. The PCT international application is effectively the first filing, and the "priority date" for the PCT application is simply the international filing date of the PCT application. One must bear in mind that the "priority date" under the PCT may not always be a Paris priority date, if the PCT application is not based on an earlier filing.

Illustration 3–9. On November 30, 2011, Donyell files a PCT international application in the USPTO. Donyell does not claim the benefit of a prior national application. The priority date of Donyell's PCT international application is November 30, 2011, the date of the PCT filing.

Once the priority date is determined, one can determine the rest of the timetable for proceeding under the PCT.

First, after the inventor files an international application, the ISA patent office conducts—under the Chapter I phase of the PCT process—an international prior art search related to the claimed invention, as depicted as "Office 1" (short for patent office activity) in the Diagram. The ISA then prepares a non-binding "international search report" evaluating the relevant prior art that exists that may potentially defeat the novelty of the invention. At the same time, under the current PCT rules, the ISA also prepares a written "opinion" on the patentability of the invention, analyzing whether the "claimed invention appears to be novel, to involve an inventive step (to be non-obvious), and to be industrially applicable." PCT Rule 43*bis*. If an inventor is invoking a Paris priority date (based on a prior national filing), the ISA typically completes the report and opinion by the end of 16 months after the priority date for the invention (which is typically 3 months after the receipt of the search copy of the application). *See* PCT Rule 42.[4] If the inventor is not relying on a Paris priority date, the ISA must typically complete the search report by 9 months after the PCT application filing date, which is the priority date of the application. After completing the report under either route, the ISA is then supposed to transmit the report and opinion to WIPO and the applicant. The search report, along with the international application, are then published by WIPO, "promptly" after the end of 18 months after the priority date, as depicted as "Office 2" in the Diagram. PCT art. 21. However, the written opinion on patentability remains confidential until the culmination of the entire PCT process.

---

4. The precise date may vary depending on the circumstances: the ISA has until 3 months after receiving the search copy of the application, or 9 months after the priority date, whichever is later. Thus, if an applicant waits until the very last day of the 12–month Paris priority period, usually the ISA will have 3 months after receiving the search copy to establish the report (occurring around the 16th month).

Once the international search report is complete, the applicant must decide whether to demand an "international preliminary examination" of the patentability of the claimed invention. PCT art. 31. This crucial point in the inventor's prosecution of a PCT application is depicted as "Point 2" in the Diagram. The inventor has until either 3 months after the receipt of the search report or 22 months after the priority date, whichever is later, to decide whether to make such demand. PCT Rule 54*bis*. Making such a demand requires the payment of further fees, but allows the applicant a second chance—in Chapter II of the PCT process—to make amendments to the application and to communicate with the International Preliminary Examining Authority (IPEA) that will issue the "international preliminary examination report" (IPER). PCT arts. 33–34. Under PCT Rule 66, the ISA's opinion on patentability in Chapter I serves as the IPEA's report in Chapter II. (If the IPEA is a different patent office than the one that conducted the search, the IPEA may elect to issue its own opinion on patentability, provided it notifies the International Bureau of WIPO. PCT Rule 66.1*bis*. In such case, the IPEA still must take into account the ISA's opinion.). The IPEA's non-binding patentability report is to be completed, subject to a few variations, by 28 months after the priority date. PCT Rule 69.2. The report is then transmitted to the International Bureau of WIPO and the applicant. PCT art. 36.

At "Point 3" in the Diagram, the applicant enters the national phase and must decide whether to proceed with national patent applications in other countries by 30 months after the priority date. Failing to do so within that 30–month period will jeopardize the applicant's right to the priority date—and potentially the ability of the applicant to obtain patents, given the publication of the application. Once the applicant has filed national patent applications, WIPO communicates the international patentability report to the national patent offices elected by the inventor, as depicted as "Office 3" in the Diagram.

Even if the inventor decides against making a demand for a patentability report (under Chapter II), instead choosing to stay within Chapter I after the international search report, the inventor has until 30 months after the priority date to decide to make any other national filings. *See* PCT art. 39; PCT Rule 76. In either case, the priority date is still preserved under the PCT process. This is a significant advantage created by the PCT: an inventor can obtain 18 months, on top of the 12 months already afforded by Paris priority, before having to decide whether it is worth obtaining foreign patents for her invention. Or, alternatively, if the inventor just files a PCT international application without Paris priority, the inventor obtains 30 months total before having to file national patent applications for the invention. Under Article 11 of the PCT, a properly filed PCT international application that is accorded "an international filing date shall have the effect of a regular national application in each designated State as of the international filing date, which date shall be considered to be the actual filing date in each designated State." Thus, the priority date established by the PCT international application becomes the national filing date in each designated state. In effect, the PCT international application is considered a single application that undergoes both an international phase and, if the applicant so wishes, a national stage in individual countries. The PCT application (with requisite translations and fees) serves as the national patent application, with the benefit of the same PCT priority date. Of course, each PCT country ultimately decides under its own laws whether to grant a patent or not. The PCT does not change substantive patent law in individual countries; it simply enhances the procedural advantages of Paris priority.

By using the PCT process, the applicant also gains the benefit of an independent evaluation concerning the prospects of obtaining a patent. Under current PCT procedure, the inventor will have both the international search report on prior art and the international preliminary report on patentability. Thus, the inventor has some formal (albeit nonbinding) evaluation on whether the claimed invention meets the general principles of novelty, inventive step, and industrial application, and whether the invention has been anticipated by the prior art. With such information, an inventor can better assess whether to go forward with the national patent applications in other countries around the world.

Whether the PCT reduces costs to the inventor, however, is more debatable. Once in the national phase, the inventor is just beginning the prosecution process in each of the countries elected. Thus, although the PCT affords an inventor significant benefits in terms of extra time to file national patent applications while preserving Paris priority, it may not necessarily reduce much, if any, of the cost. The inventor incurs filing fees and, most likely, attorney's fees, all along the way—for the first national filing, for the PCT filing, and then for every other national filing made in other countries. Of course, an inventor is under no obligation to go the PCT route, but instead, can choose to remain under the traditional route under Paris. Any inventor or patent attorney will have to consider carefully the trade-offs in proceeding under either route.

NOTES AND QUESTIONS

1. Is the PCT an improvement over filing multiple patent applications in different countries? If so, in what way has the PCT improved the process? If the PCT does not actually authorize the issuance of any patent, what good is it?

2. *Old PCT system, pre-April 1, 2002.* The applicable time limit for entering the national phase is now 30 months from the priority date. Under the prior practice, an applicant did not automatically receive that deadline. Instead, an applicant was entitled to a 20–month limit to enter national phase unless the applicant demanded an international preliminary examination in which case the applicant received an additional 10 months. Starting on April 1, 2002, the time limit has been extended to a uniform 30 months regardless of whether a preliminary examination is requested. However, only a few states (3 at this writing) continue to follow the former practice of a 20–month limit unless the applicant requests an international preliminary examination. These states are expected to conform their practices to the new 30–month limit in the future. *See* FAQs: Effects of Modification of PCT Article 22(1) Time Limit, at www.wipo.int/pct/en/faqs/article22_faq.htm.

3. *WIPO*. International PCT applications must be filed with a PCT prescribed patent office, which in turn must transmit a copy to the International Bureau of the World Intellectual Property Organization. The Bureau administers the Patent Cooperation Treaty, including the publication of international patent filings and search reports in the *PCT Gazette*. Valuable information about the PCT, including sample patent application forms, can be found on WIPO's website, at http://www.wipo.int/pct/en/.

Based on the number of filings of international applications, the PCT has been a huge success. By 2001, the total number of international PCT filings had increased fivefold from the past decade to over 100,000 applications. During that same period, the number of demands for international preliminary examinations increased close to eightfold to over 75,000 demands. *See* WIPO Publication No. 433 (E), at 11 (2002). In the past decade, the total number of PCT filings has steadily grown, with the exception of 2009 during the global economic downturn. In 2010, 162,900 PCT applications were filed. The U.S. remained the largest source of PCT applications (44,855 filed), followed by Japan (32,156 filed), Germany (17,171 filed), China (12,337 filed), and South Korea (9,686 filed). The most significant development in 2010 was the growth of filings from China and other Asian countries. China saw a 56% growth in PCT filings from the previous year, while South Korea (20.5%) and Japan (8%) also experienced growth. Asia surpassed Europe as the largest source of PCT filings by region. During this time, the U.S. and major European countries all saw declines in the number of PCT filings. Six of the top 10 PCT patent filers were from Northeast Asia in 2010. Another milestone for the PCT occurred in 2011: the two millionth PCT application was filed. *See* WIPO, *PCT: The International Patent System, Yearly Review 2010*, at www.wipo.int/export/sites/www/pct/en/activity/pct_2010.pdf.

4. *International Searching Authorities*. Under Article 16 of the PCT, the International Search Authority conducts an international prior art search for the applications filed. The ISA typically is the national patent office of any member country that has been designated to conduct prior art searches pursuant to the PCT. The ISAs include the patent offices of Austria, Australia, China, the European Patent Office, Japan, Korea, Russia, Sweden, and the United States. By 2009, 17 patent offices were authorized as ISAs. The patent offices in Europe, the U.S., and Japan historically have performed the most searches. In 2003, the EPO performed 60,767 searches; the U.S., 26,319; and Japan, 16,142. *See* WIPO Statistics, PCT Statistical Indicators Report (July 2004). However, since 2008, South Korea and China have seen a dramatic increase in ISA searches, while the number of searches in the U.S. has declined. In 2010, Korea performed 23,307 searches (14.2%); China, 13,298 (8.1%); and the U.S., 15,811 (9.6%). The EPO performed the most searches at 69,013 (42%), followed by Japan at 30,968 (18.8%). *See* WIPO, *PCT Yearly Review 2010*, at 44. What might explain the popularity of different offices for international searches? Why do you think searches in the U.S. has dropped to a level almost lower than China?

5. *International Preliminary Examination Report*. The patent offices that have been designated as ISAs also serve as International Preliminary Examining Authorities (IPEA). A patentee using the PCT method has the option of demanding an international preliminary examination report, al-

though under the current procedure a report is prepared in any event. What factors should the patentee consider in deciding whether to ask for such a report? Is there any reason to make a demand and pay additional fees under the current approach?

Just as with international prior art searches, the patent offices in Europe (52.7%), the U.S. (18.4%), and Japan (12.1%) have also performed the greatest number of international preliminary examinations thus far. In the report, the IPEA is asked to draw a fine line. Under Article 35, the IPEA is prohibited from making "any statement on the question whether the claimed invention is or seems to be patentable or unpatentable according to any national law." Instead, the IPEA "shall state, . . . in relation to each claim, whether the claim appears to satisfy the criteria of novelty, inventive step (non-obviousness), and industrial applicability, as defined for the purposes of the international preliminary examination." What standards of novelty, inventive step, and industrial application should an IPEA employ under this provision?

6. *Cost.* Filing PCT applications can be expensive, perhaps even more expensive than filing multiple applications outside the PCT. Having a patent attorney in the U.S. prepare the original patent application can cost in the neighborhood of $10,000 to $20,000 or more. Proceeding under the PCT involves additional expense. To have an attorney prepare the international application could typically add another $1,500 or more in legal fees and another $1,500 or so in PCT fees (basic, search, and transmittal fees). An international preliminary examination can cost between $600 and $750. Additional filing fees are incurred in each country that one files for a patent at the national stage. In the U.S., the fee is approximately $1,000. The patent fees in other countries vary, although they tend to be substantial. *See* PCT Fee Tables, at http://www.wipo.int/pct/en/fees.pdf.

Should the expense of filing for an international application raise a concern about disadvantaging individual (as opposed to corporate) inventors who may not have the wherewithal to secure foreign patents around the world? Under the PCT, "[a]n applicant who is a natural person and who is a national of and resides in a State whose per capita national income is below 3,000 US dollars is entitled to a reduction of 75% of certain fees, including the international fee." *See* WIPO Publication No. 433 (E), at 6 (2002). Does this adequately address the problem?

7. *The European Patent Convention and Efforts to Develop EU Patent.* The European Patent Convention, first signed in 1973, is the most important regional patent agreement today. Modeled on the PCT, the EPC establishes a common application procedure for obtaining patents in multiple European countries and a single prior art search conducted by a branch of the European Patent Office (EPO) at The Hague. The EPC does not displace the national patent laws of its member countries, but instead, provides a parallel, yet optional system that is intended to facilitate the securing of multiple patents across Europe. Thus, the EPC is *not* a Directive or law of the EU, such as in copyright or trademark law, that establishes a unitary law for the EU. Members of the EPC do not have to be EU members; in 2011, the EPC had 38 members, of which 27 are part of the EU. A patentee files a European patent application with the EPO in Munich, Germany, designating on the application

all member countries where it seeks to patent its invention. After reviewing the patent application and conducting a prior art search, the EPO has the authority pursuant to Article 97 of the EPC to grant or deny a "European patent" for the invention. Appeals of any patent denial are heard by the Board of Appeals. EPC art. 21.

The European patent functions as a collection of national patents of the member European countries. Once a European patent is granted, the national courts or agencies of each country designated in the application may require translations and filing fees, and may later evaluate the validity of the patent according to its own national law. The piecemeal approach under the EPC means that, in order to obtain the broadest protection, one has to obtain patents from 38 European countries in up to 29 different languages. Individual infringement suits are litigated in national courts where the infringement occurred. There is no supranational court (like the Court of Justice of the European Union) to resolve conflicting approaches to the European patent. Thus, it is conceivable that a European patent for an invention may be held valid in one country, but invalid in another. One important feature of the European patent is that it is available for designation in an international application under the PCT. An international patent application filed under PCT satisfies the format requirements of the European patent application.

For years, the EU countries have been considering the adoption of a Community-wide patent—"Compat," "Unitary Patent," or "EU Patent" for short—that would provide a unitary patent for an invention that would extend to all countries in the EU. The European patent was originally viewed as a precursor to a Community patent (under the Community Patent Convention), but the latter has yet to materialize. In recent years, the EU countries have undertaken renewed efforts to agree upon an EU patent. The EU patent would be governed by a uniform law and would be valid or invalid for the entire EU, not individual countries. Cases would be heard before a newly created EU Patent Court. The EU Patent could be obtained in addition to or instead of national patents or the European patent, and there would be a single fee for the EU Patent payable to the EPO.

So far, discussions over the EU Patent have stalled, in part, over the requirement of translations. Under one proposal, EU Patent applications must be filed in French, German, or English *and* then translated into the language of every country of the EU. This is similar to what is currently required under the EPC, which requires patent applications to be filed in one of the three official languages under Article 14 and allows countries to require translations under Article 65. Most do. According to the European Commission, because of translations, costs of filing patents in Europe are ten times more, on average, than filing in the U.S.

In 2011, the Court of Justice dealt a blow to the efforts to develop a unitary EU patent. The CJEU held that the draft proposal by the European Commission for a EU patent would violate EU law. See *Opinion on Draft Agreement—Creation of a Unified Patent Litigation System—European and Community Patents Court—Compatibility of the draft Agreement with the Treaties*, Avis 01/09 (2011). However, proceeding under the enhanced cooperation procedure, the EU Council considered and voted in favor of a revised proposal, with Spain and Italy objecting. Under the proposal, which still must be approved by the European Parliament, EU patent applications can be filed in any of the 20 official EU languages, with a translation into one of the 3 approved EPO languages (English, French, or German). Whether the EU Patent is passed and successfully implemented still remains to be seen.

Bibliographic note. J.B. van Benthem, *The European Patent System and European Integration*, 24 I.I.C. 435 (1993); Otto Bossung, *The Return of European Patent Law to the European Union*, 27 I.I.C. 287 (1996); Vincenzo Di Cataldo, *From the European Patent to a Community Patent*, 8 COLUM. J. EUR. L. 19 (2002); Christopher Heath, *Harmonizing Scope and Allocation of Patent Rights in Europe—Towards a New European Patent Law*, 6 MARQ. INTELL. PROP. L. REV. 11 (2002).

c. Priority Disputes

The patent systems of nearly all countries recognize that the inventor is the first to file the application for the invention in the patent office. In a first-to-file country, determining who among several competing inventors is entitled the patent rights to the invention is fairly easy, even if there are foreign or international filings claiming a Paris priority date.

> Illustration 3–10. Cole invents a new process for manufacturing methanol in Germany and files for a patent in Germany on November 30, 2011. Meanwhile, Dolores independently invents the same process in the United Kingdom and applies for a patent in the UK on December 1, 2011. A year later, Cole files for a patent in the UK on November 30, 2012. Who is entitled to the patent in the UK? Cole is. Given the Paris priority date of Cole's invention (November 30, 2011), Cole was the first to file in the United Kingdom and therefore has priority.

The sole exception to the first-to-file approach is the United States. For over 200 years, the United States took a different approach—a first-to-invent system that awarded priority to the first inventor to reduce the invention to practice (meaning that the inventor can show that the invention would work for its intended purpose). Neither TRIPS nor the Paris Convention speaks to the choice between first-to-file versus first-to-invent.

However, in 2011, the U.S.'s long adherence to the first-to-invent system finally ended. Starting with applications filed on March 16, 2013, the America Invents Act switches the U.S. to a modified first-to-file system (called a "first inventor to file" system). The modified system includes a one-year grace period allowing the inventor to make public disclosures of the invention one year before the filing date—similar to the one-year grace period under the statutory bars under the current Patent Code. *See* 35 U.S.C. § 102(b). Despite the change to a first-to-file system, all existing patents granted and applications filed before March 16, 2013 will continue to be governed by the prior standard of novelty and first-to-invent for the duration of their patent terms. Thus, patent attorneys in the U.S. will have to know both the prior and the new standard of novelty for years to come.

> Illustration 3–11. Cole invents a new process for manufacturing methanol in Germany and files for a patent in Germany on November 30, 2011. Cole, however, did not keep adequate records or other independent evidence to prove the date of his invention. Meanwhile, Edward independently invents the same process in the United States and reduces it to practice on November 29, 2011, keeping adequate records to prove the date of invention. Edward applies for a patent in the U.S. on December 1, 2011. A year later, Cole files for a patent in the U.S. on November 30, 2012. Who is entitled to the patent in the U.S.? Edward is. In the U.S., the date of the invention's reduction to practice is the critical date. In this case, Cole did not keep adequate records to prove in the U.S. the date of actual reduction to practice, so he must fall back on the date of filing (November 30, 2011 under Paris priority), which is also called the date of constructive reduction to practice. However, Edward did keep adequate records to prove the date of his actual reduction to practice on November 29, 2011, so he wins the priority dispute.

As should be evident by this example, U.S. law under the 1952 Patent Act differs from first-to-file countries in allowing inventors to prove and rely on their dates of actual reduction to practice, regardless of who filed for a patent first. U.S. law is somewhat similar to a first-to-file system, at least in the limited extent that a patentee can establish constructive reduction to practice by the filing date. Thus, in some priority disputes, both parties may rely on their filing dates to claim priority (similar to what might happen in a first-to-file country).

For applications filed on March 16, 2013 or later, the America Invents Act eliminates consideration of the date of actual reduction to practice. Instead, the date of filing will determine priority.

> Illustration 3–12. Doug invented a new, "green" technology in the U.S. on March 16, 2013 and filed for a patent on March 18, 2013. Erica independently invented the same invention in the U.S. a few weeks earlier on February 28, 2013, keeping adequate records to prove the date of invention. Erica, however, applied for a patent in the U.S. on April 1, 2013, several weeks *after* Doug. In this priority dispute, the new U.S. first-to-file system governs and Doug wins priority. Even though Erica was the first to reduce the invention to practice (with independent corroboration of the date), she was not the first to file in the U.S.

Notice that the result would have been different under the prior U.S. first-to-invent system. However, because Erica's application was filed after March 16, 2013, the new rules apply.

PROBLEM 3–5

On May 15, 2013, Amethyst invented a new cure for malaria. She filed her U.S. patent application on June 17, 2013 and a PCT application on June 17, 2014. Within the 18–month period allowed under the PCT, Amethyst filed her German application on November 25, 2015. Meanwhile, in Germany, Alka independently invented the same invention on June 6, 2013. Alka filed her German patent application on June 10, 2013 and a PCT application on June 10, 2014. Within the 18–month period allowed under the PCT, Alka filed her U.S. application on December 9, 2015. (i) Who is entitled to priority in the U.S.—Amethyst or Alka? (ii) What about in Germany? Consider the discussion above and the case below.

FRAZER v. SCHLEGEL

U.S. Court of Appeals for the Federal Circuit.
498 F.3d 1283 (Fed. Cir. 2007).

NEWMAN, CIRCUIT JUDGE.

Dr. Ian Frazer and Dr. Jian Zhou (together the interference party "Frazer") appeal the decision of the United States Patent and Trademark Office, Board of Patent Appeals and Interferences ("the Board") awarding priority to Dr. C. Richard Schlegel and Dr. A. Bennett Jenson (together the interference party "Schlegel"). The interference is between Frazer's United States patent application Serial No. 08/185,928 entitled "Papilloma Virus Vaccine," which claims priority from Australian and Patent Cooperation Treaty ("PCT") applications, and Schlegel's United States application Serial No. 08/216,506 entitled "Papillomavirus Vaccine."

DISCUSSION

The invention here contested relates to a vaccine for use against human papillomaviruses ("HPVs"), a class of viruses that can cause cervical cancer and other diseases. All HPVs have a similar structure: they have a core of disease-causing viral DNA, surrounded by an outer protein coat called a "capsid" that has an icosahedral, or twenty-sided, shape.

The facts are generally undisputed, although their significance is disputed. Dr. Frazer and Dr. Zhou, working at the University of Queensland in Australia and using procedures derived from recombinant DNA technology, succeeded in preparing what they call "papilloma virus (or virion)-like particles" that have the external icosahedral shape of the virus capsid and thereby mimic the papilloma virus, but lack the disease-causing genetic material. Their idea was to create a vaccine from such a virus-like particle, and thereby to stimulate the immune system to make antibodies that would deactivate any authentic papillomavirus that might enter the body. They first reported this work in a scientific article that was received by the journal *Virology* in California on May 21, 1991, entitled "Expression of Vaccinia Recombinant HPV 16 L1 and L2 ORF Proteins in Epithelial Cells Is Sufficient for Assembly of HPV Virion-like Particles," published at 185 *Virology* 251 (1991). The article included experimental details of the production of these virus-like particles, including photomicrographs of the products[.]

The text and experimental data from the article were included in a patent application filed in Australia on July 19, 1991, including electron micrographs of HPV virus-like particles, as shown in Fig. 5, Australian application PK 7322: [photo omitted].

The Australian application describes the recombinant DNA encoding the L1 and L2 proteins, and explains that the L1 and L2 genes may be included in the same or different DNA recombinant molecules. The application describes the amplification of the HPV–16 L1 and L2 genes using the polymerase chain reaction, identifies the two primers used, indicates the codons, and provides the procedures of extraction, purification, digestion, and subcloning. The application discusses sequencing of the resulting plasmid, its use to prepare the desired gene fragments, and its cloning into the specified site of the vaccinia vector. The purification and separation and identification of these virus-like particles are described.

Frazer's procedures for electron microscopy of the capsid particles, and analysis by immunoprecipitation and immunoblot, are also described in the Australian application, as are the methods of confirmation of L1 protein by autoradiography, and L2 transcription by northern blot of RNA extracted from infected CV–1 cells. The Australian application contains illustrations and electron micrographs showing approximately 40nm diameter virus-like particles in cell nuclei. The application discusses the fifty-six known human papillomavirus types and the diseases they cause, as well as immunotherapies and potential vaccines for papillomavirus infections. The application reports combinations of proteins that were and were not successful, and places the results in the context of the scientific knowledge then available, including citations to scientific articles and discussion of the advances made.

Drs. Frazer and Zhou presented this research on July 22, 1991 at the Papillomavirus Workshop, a scientific conference held in Seattle, Washington. The lecture by Dr. Frazer included the method of preparation of the virus-like particles, electron micrographs of the synthetic capsid, and a discussion of vaccine use of these VLPs. A written abstract by Dr. Zhou was distributed at the Workshop.

A PCT application was filed on July 20, 1992, claiming priority from the Australian application with additional text and experimental data[.]

Frazer's United States patent application, claiming the priorities of the PCT and Australian applications in accordance with statute, *see* 35 U.S.C. §§ 119, 363, was filed on January 19, 1994. This application was placed in interference with the Schlegel application and two other applications not here relevant.

Dr. Schlegel and Dr. Jenson of Georgetown University Medical Center on June 25, 1992 filed the United States patent application that is involved in the interference. It is not here disputed that the Schlegel and the Frazer applications are directed to the same subject matter. Schlegel was declared senior party, having the earlier United States filing date. Frazer was then granted the benefit of the Australian filing date, but that benefit was withdrawn by the patent examiner during the interference. This appeal turns on whether Frazer is entitled to rely on the filing date of the Australian application to show possession of the subject matter in interference.

The Interference

The Board held that Frazer is not entitled to the benefit of the Australian application's filing date, holding that the application's disclosure was inadequate. Thus the Board declared Schlegel the first inventor based on Schlegel's United States filing date.

We conclude that Frazer was entitled to the priority date of the Australian patent application. Since the Australian filing date antedates any date alleged by Schlegel, priority must be awarded to Frazer.

DISCUSSION

In accordance with United States law, when the priority claim is based on subject matter disclosed in a foreign patent application whose filing date is properly claimed, 35 U.S.C. § 119(a), the foreign application has the same effect as if filed in the United States. § 119(a), (e)(1). The invention must be "disclosed in the manner provided by the first paragraph of section 112." § 119(e)(1); *see Schur v. Muller*, 54 C.C.P.A. 1095, 372 F.2d 546, 551 (1967) (it is a "general principle" in interference proceedings that a party may claim the benefit of a foreign-filed priority document provided that it discloses all of the limitations of the count).

Constructive reduction to practice does not invoke different standards whether the priority document is foreign or domestic. When interference priority is at issue, constructive reduction to practice of a count may be established by disclosure of an embodiment within the count.

Although the Board analyzed the Australian application in terms of "conception," when reliance is on a patent document already filed, the question is whether the document discloses the invention of the count by meeting the written description and enablement requirements of 35 U.S.C. § 112 ¶ 1, for a filed application serves as a constructive reduction to practice of its content.

The Board held that Frazer's Australian application "did not provide a described and enabled anticipation under 35 U.S.C. § 102(g) of the subject matter of the count," Board op. at 43–44, because at the time the Australian application was filed "Frazer believed that both the L1 and L2 genes had to be expressed together from the same plasmid," whereas his "later work shows that only L1 protein was necessary." *Id.* at 53.

Although the Board acknowledged that "[t]he work reported in the Zhou manuscript [in *Virology*] and in the [Australian] application appears to be the first reports of particles comprised of coat protein from a papillomavirus obtained by recombinant techniques," *id.* at 51, the Board ruled that this did not show "conception" because Frazer stated in these documents that both the L1 and L2 genes were expressed, whereas Frazer later discovered, and reported in the PCT application, that expression of either the L1 gene alone, or the L1 and L2 genes together, form the virus-like particle. The Board also referred to an "unexplained" difference in particle size and shape between Frazer's initial and later observed VLP conformational epitope formation.

The Board stated that "[r]evising hypotheses in the face of evidence is a hallmark of well-conducted research," *id.* at 62–63, and ruled that Frazer was not entitled to any date of disclosure until he accurately and fully understood the mechanism. The Board referred to Dr. Frazer's "admission" that "it was impossible to determine, in 1991, whether the particles they produced had conformational epitopes of the native virions: 'at that time, the reagents that would be needed to do that work were not available.' " *Id.* at 55 (quoting Dr. Frazer's testimony). The Board ruled that neither the PCT application nor the ensuing United States application was entitled to the priority date of the Australian application.

We conclude that the Board erred in denying Frazer's entitlement to the date of the Australian patent application. The Australian application contained complete details of the method that is the subject of the interference count, and depicts the papillomavirus-like particle of the count with full disclosure of how to produce it. The specification also includes the DNA sequences encoding the papillomavirus L1 and L2 proteins. While Frazer in the Australian application reported the expression of both the papillomavirus L1 protein and the papillomavirus L2 protein, and he testified that at that time he believed both proteins were involved, his later discovery that either the L1 protein or both the L1 and L2 proteins led to capsid formation does not negate or contradict his disclosure and constructive reduction to practice of the method of the count that produced the papillomavirus-like particle of the count. Frazer correctly argues that the Australian application describes and enables the formation of the papilloma virus-like particles. The filing of a patent application is a constructive reduction to practice of the invention disclosed therein. *Hyatt v. Boone,* 146 F.3d 1348, 1352 (Fed. Cir. 1998); *see, e.g., Hybritech, Inc. v. Monoclonal Antibodies, Inc.,* 802 F.2d 1367, 1376 (Fed. Cir. 1986) ("constructive reduction to practice occurs when a patent application on the claimed invention is filed").

It is not disputed that Frazer's Australian application described virus-like particles and their production from recombinant vaccinia virus. Indeed, Dr. Frazer pointed out that this was new science, but acknowledgment of the complexities of the science does not negate the disclosure of the production of these virus-like particles. In *Genentech, Inc. v. Novo Nordisk A/S,* 108 F.3d 1361, 1367–68 (Fed. Cir. 1997), the court explained that "[w]here, as here, the claimed invention is the application of an unpredictable technology in the early stages of development, an enabling description in the specification must provide those skilled in the art with a specific and useful teaching," recognizing the stage of development of the technology. The Australian application was not "merely proposing an unproved hypothesis" or guess, *Rasmusson v. SmithKline Beecham Corp.,* 413 F.3d 1318, 1325 (Fed. Cir. 2005); it was an enabling disclosure.

Based on the constructive reduction to practice of an invention whose disclosure is in compliance with the requirements of § 112, Frazer is entitled to the priority benefit of the Australian filing date. That date predates Schlegel's earliest date. The award of priority to Schlegel is reversed, and priority is awarded to Frazer. We remand to the PTO for appropriate further proceedings.

   REVERSED and REMANDED.

NOTES AND QUESTIONS

1. *First-to-invent v. First-to-file Patent Systems.* What are the tradeoffs between a first-to-file system and a first-to-invent system? Which is easier to administer? Which more fair?

2. *Proving actual reduction to practice in the U.S.* For applications filed before March 16, 2013 in the U.S., inventors need more proof than their own testimony to prove actual reduction to practice under U.S. law. Any such testimony must be corroborated by independent evidence (such as contemporaneous records), which a court evaluates under a "rule of reason" considering all the evidence. *See Loral Fairchild Corp. v. Matsushita Elec. Indus. Co. Ltd.,* 266 F.3d 1358, 1363 (Fed. Cir. 2001). As noted above, an inventor can typically fall back on the date of filing a patent application to establish the date of constructive reduction to practice.

3. *Interference proceedings.* Under the U.S. Patent Code, an interference is a proceeding that the Patent Office may call if a patent application "would interfere with any pending application, or with any unexpired patent." 35 U.S.C. § 135. Typically, the interference involves a disputed claim for priority rights to the same invention. Interference proceedings have an involved set of procedures that attempt to determine who has priority to the claimed invention. For applications filed in the U.S. before March 16, 2013, priority can be established in two ways. First, an inventor who is the first to conceive the idea for the invention and the first to reduce the invention to practice will always have priority (except in the rare instance in which the inventor "abandoned, suppressed, or concealed it," *id.* § 102(g)(2)). Second, an inventor who is the first to conceive the invention, but who is last to reduce it to practice (compared to another), can still claim priority if the inventor exercised reasonable diligence in trying to reduce the invention to practice from the time before the other conceived the invention. 35 U.S.C. § 102(g). Would these elaborate priority rules be necessary in a first-to-file system?

4. Would the dispute over priority in *Frazer v. Schegel* still have arisen if the U.S. had in place at the time a first-to-file system and all the other facts

in the case remained the same? Would the result be different under a first-to-file system?

5. Go back over the dates of Frazer's various patent filings in Australia, PCT, and U.S. Verify that the filing dates were made within the deadlines to preserve priority for the U.S. filing.

6. Why did Frazer get the benefit of the Australian filing when it did not contain all the information that the PCT filing did (i.e., that only the L1 protein was necessary for capsid formation)? Without such disclosure in the Australian filing, did the application nonetheless provide an enabling disclosure of all elements of Frazer's invention?

2. WORKING REQUIREMENTS

Paris Convention

Article 5

[A. *Patents:* Importation of Articles; Failure to Work or Insufficient Working; Compulsory Licenses.]

A. (1) Importation by the patentee into the country where the patent has been granted of articles manufactured in any of the countries of the Union shall not entail forfeiture of the patent.

(2) Each country of the Union shall have the right to take legislative measures providing for the grant of compulsory licenses to prevent the abuses which might result from the exercise of the exclusive rights conferred by the patent, for example, failure to work.

(3) Forfeiture of the patent shall not be provided for except in cases where the grant of compulsory licenses would not have been sufficient to prevent the said abuses. No proceedings for the forfeiture or revocation of a patent may be instituted before the expiration of two years from the grant of the first compulsory license.

(4) A compulsory license may not be applied for on the ground of failure to work or insufficient working before the expiration of a period of four years from the date of filing of the patent application or three years from the date of the grant of the patent, whichever period expires last; it shall be refused if the patentee justifies his inaction by legitimate reasons. Such a compulsory license shall be non-exclusive and shall not be transferable, even in the form of the grant of a sub-license, except with that part of the enterprise or goodwill which exploits such license.

TRIPS Article 27(1)

Patentable Subject Matter

1. Subject to the provisions of paragraphs 2 and 3, patents shall be available for any inventions, whether products or processes, in all fields of technology, provided that they are new, involve an inventive step and are capable of industrial application. Subject to paragraph 4 of Article 65, paragraph 8 of Article 70 and paragraph 3 of this

Article, patents shall be available and patent rights enjoyable without discrimination as to the place of invention, the field of technology and whether products are imported or locally produced.

* * *

Countries differ on whether a foreign patent holder should be required to use the patent locally as a condition of retaining the patent. Some countries object to the practice of some foreign patent holders of acquiring a patent for an invention and then exporting the patented product into the country where the patent has been obtained, without manufacturing the product within the country. In some cases, a patentee might obtain patents from many foreign countries, but choose to sell the product in only a handful of those countries. A "working requirement" is a law that is intended to deal with this problem. Under a working requirement, a patentee may be obligated to produce and/or sell the patented good locally as a condition of the patent. Failure to work the invention may result in the grant of compulsory licenses for others to manufacture the patented good locally.

Illustration 3–13. Pharma, a multi-national pharmaceutical company based in the United States, obtains a patent for its drug in Country Z. Pharma manufactures the drug in its factory at home and then exports the drug to Country Z, where it is now protected from copying by the patent. Country Z believes that this one-sided arrangement mostly benefits Pharma, not the people of Country Z. Z is therefore considering implementing a local working requirement.

In Illustration 3–13, Z obtains the social benefit of the drug by purchasing it from Pharma, but Country Z may believe that Pharma enjoys most of the economic benefits of this arrangement. Z is the buyer-importer in this arrangement and Pharma is the seller-exporter. Z will pay Pharma, which will earn revenues and make a profit on its sales. The result is a transfer of wealth from Z to Pharma and the United States.

However, if Country Z imposes a local working requirement as a condition of granting or maintaining the patent, then Pharma may have to invest capital in order to build a manufacturing facility in Country Z, and transfer technology to Z by training local scientists and engineers on how to make the invention. Pharma's presence of a facility in Country Z will benefit the local economy by establishing jobs, and Country Z may be able to export some of the products manufactured by the Pharma foreign investment enterprise established in Country Z to other countries. Now Country Z is the seller-exporter, which earns revenues for the sale of its products. By requiring Pharma to work the patent locally, Country Z will not only have the benefit of the drug but will obtain a greater share in the economic exploitation of the patent.

Working requirements are controversial and countries tend to divide on the issue along the fault lines of the North–South debate. Developed countries do not favor working requirements and argue that they should be subject to strict restraints, if not abolished. The U.S., for example, imposes no working requirement on patentees. On the flip side, developing countries tend to view working requirements as a fair measure that allows them to share in some of the economic benefits of the patent. India, for example, has a working requirement for patented inventions. The rationale is explained in § 83 of the Patents Act:

> (a) that patents are granted to encourage inventions and to secure that the inventions are worked in India on a commercial scale and to the fullest extent that is reasonably practicable without undue delay;
>
> (b) that they are not granted merely to enable patentees to enjoy a monopoly for the importation of the patented article;
>
> (c) that the protection and enforcement of patent rights contribute to the promotion of technological innovation and to the transfer and dissemination of technology, to the mutual advantage of producers and users of technological knowledge and in a manner conducive to social and economic welfare, and to a balance of rights and obligations; * * *

Under § 84, failure to work the invention in India is a basis for the Controller General of Patents to grant a compulsory license for a third party to utilize the invention in India.

Article 5 of the Paris Convention regulates the extent to which countries may impose compulsory licenses and forfeiture of patents for failure to work an invention. Article 5(A)(1) prohibits countries from imposing the forfeiture of a patent based on an inventor's importation of the product into the country from another Paris country. To the extent forfeiture of a patent is ever allowed, Paris indicates that forfeiture cannot be imposed unless "the grant of compulsory licenses would not have been sufficient to prevent the said abuses" and at least two years have expired from the grant of the first compulsory license. Paris art. 5(A)(3).

At the same time, Article 5(A)(2) acknowledges that "[e]ach country of the Union shall have the right to take legislative measures providing for the grant of compulsory licenses to prevent the abuses which might result from the exercise of the exclusive rights conferred by the patent, for example, failure to work." But, in Article 5(A)(4), Paris dictates that "[a] compulsory license may not be applied for on the ground of failure to work or insufficient working before the expiration of a period of four years from the date of filing of the patent application or three years from the date of the grant of the patent, whichever period expires last." Because of the time it takes for an application to be reviewed, the later period of time will typically be three years from date of the grant of the patent. No compulsory license can be granted for failure to work "if the patentee justifies his inaction by legitimate reasons."

Although the Paris Convention expressly contemplates local working requirements, the TRIPS Agreement appears to qualify, if not prohibit, such practice even further. In Article 27(1), regarding subject matter of patents, TRIPS states in relevant part: "Subject to paragraph 4 of Article 65, paragraph 8 of Article 70 and paragraph 3 of this Article, patents shall be available and patent rights enjoyable without discrimination as to . . . whether products are imported or locally produced." This would seem to prohibit the complete forfeiture of patent rights in any case of a violation of a working requirement that requires the manufacture of the invention locally (as opposed to allowing the inventor to have the invention imported into the country to satisfy whatever working requirement that may exist). Whether or not a compulsory license ordered as a result a failure to work constitutes "discrimination" of the enjoyment of patent rights under TRIPS Article 27(1) is more debatable, however. Thus far, no WTO panel has decided the extent of this provision on working requirements. (TRIPS Article 31 also closely regulates the general conditions under which a compulsory license may be imposed. We will return to compulsory licenses at the end of this chapter.)

PROBLEM 3–6

Based on the facts of our Illustration 3–13 above, Country Z's Minister of Foreign Economic Cooperation has notified Pharma that unless Pharma establishes a local manufacturing facility or otherwise uses the patented good locally in Z within 4 years from the date of filing of the patent application or 3 years of the grant of the patent, whichever is later, Z will grant a compulsory license to local manufacturers so they can produce the drug more cheaply. If, within a reasonable time, the local manufacturers are unable to meet demand, Pharma's patent in Z will be forfeited to Country Z's Ministry of Foreign Economic Cooperation, which will assign it to SwissPharm, a competing MNE, which has indicated its willingness to manufacture the drug in Z in large quantities and at reasonable prices. Are these actions consistent with the Paris Convention Article 5? What about TRIPS Article 27?

NOTES AND QUESTIONS

1. What might be the rationale for a country to impose a local working requirement for the manufacture of a patented invention within the country? Do local working requirements benefit developing countries? What about developed countries? Are there costs to having patents for inventions that are never worked during their 20 year terms?

2. Are local working requirements for patents allowed under the Paris Convention? Are they allowed under TRIPS? If they are allowed under both Paris and TRIPS, is there any type of working requirement that would be prohibited under either the Paris Convention or TRIPS? A local manufacturing requirement? How about a requirement of selling the invention locally, whether imported or produced locally?

The effect of TRIPS on local working requirements has been the source of considerable debate, much of it divided. *Compare* J.H. Reichman, *The TRIPS Agreement Comes of Age: Conflict or Cooperation with the Developing Countries?*, 32 CASE W. RES. J. INT'L L. 441, 460–61 (2000) (arguing that TRIPS allows countries flexibility in imposing working requirements) *with* Ruth L. Gana, *Prospects for Developing Countries Under the TRIPS Agreement*, 29 VAND. J. TRANSNAT'L L. 735, 756 (1996) (arguing that TRIPS abolishes working requirements as a condition for the grant of a patent).

3. *Compulsory licenses and TRIPS Article 31.* TRIPS limits the conditions under which a country may order the grant of a compulsory license for a patented invention. This provision, Article 31, will be analyzed in greater depth later in the chapter, with the discussion of exceptions to rights.

3. OWNERSHIP

TRIPS Article 28(1) states that "[a] patent shall confer on its owner" certain exclusive rights and, under Article 28(3), the patent "owner" shall have the right to assign the patent to others. TRIPS, however, does not designate who the "owner" shall be. Article 4*ter* of the Paris Convention recognizes that "[t]he inventor shall have the right to be mentioned as such in the patent." But Paris, too, does not delineate any standard of initial ownership of a patent. At least formally, patent ownership is treated differently from the approach under the Berne Convention, which specifically grants the exclusive rights of copyright to "authors." *See* Berne Conv. art. 5. The lack of minimum standards on patent ownership in the international agreements presumably means that WTO countries have discretion to decide the issue. Because most patents stem from inventions produced in the employment context, an important issue is how a country's law determines the initial ownership of patent rights in the employment setting. Who initially owns the patent rights for an invention developed in the course of employment—the employer or the employee? Consider the following problem and discussion.

PROBLEM 3–7

Edgar, an employee of Hyde Chemical Industries, has invented a new chemical compound protected by a patent that has allowed Hyde to earn hundreds of millions of dollars in revenues. Edgar is given a letter of commendation, an annual raise of $500, and a one time bonus of $1,000 by Hyde as a form of thanks, but Edgar believes he is entitled to the patent rights instead. Does Edgar or Hyde obtain the ownership right to a patent in the following cases?

(a) Edgar is hired by Hyde under a contract providing that "all intellectual property rights in all work undertaken by employees in their course of employment vest in Hyde Chemical Industries."

(b) Edgar is hired by Hyde as a chemical engineer under an employee-at-will relationship with no written contract.

(c) Edgar is a hired by Hyde as an assistant in the copy office, and invents the compound (using his own knowledge from college) on the weekend in his own lab.

(A) If all of the activity above occurred in the U.S., who owns the patent rights in (a), (b), and (c) under U.S. law? Does the losing party obtain any rights related to the invention instead of a patent? *See Teets* below.

(B) What if all of the above activity occurred in Japan? Analyze the problem under Japanese law as discussed in *Nakamura* below and n. 6 on p. 313 following the case. Is there any difference in result?

TEETS v. CHROMALLOY GAS TURBINE CORPORATION

U.S. Court of Appeals for the Federal Circuit.
83 F.3d 403 (Fed. Cir. 1996).

RADER, CIRCUIT JUDGE.

Chromalloy Gas Turbine Corporation (Chromalloy) and J. Michael Teets dispute ownership of an invention called the hot forming process (HFP). Following a bench trial, the United States District Court for the Southern District of Florida concluded that Teets solely owned the HFP and enjoined Chromalloy from certain uses of the HFP. Because the district court erred in concluding Teets owned the process, this court reverses.

Background

The General Electric Aircraft Company (GE) developed a more power-ful and fuel efficient jet engine called the GE90. In conjunction with this development, GE designed a composite turbine engine fan blade which was lighter than existing metal fan blades. These lightweight blades, however, fractured more frequently from contact with birds, freezing rain, and other debris.

GE tried to solve this problem by fitting the leading edge of the blade with a hard protective covering of electroform nickel. After initially failing to manufacture the edge internally, GE asked DRB Industries, a division of Chromalloy, to devise a method of manufacturing the leading edge for the new composite blades. GE specified that DRB should make the leading edge of one piece of titanium. In fact, GE offered DRB a long-term contract if it was successful.

DRB labelled this project the GE90 Project. Less than a month later, in November 1991, Douglas R. Burnham, General Manager of DRB, assigned Teets as the Chief Engineer on the GE90 Project. Teets spent at least 70% of his time on the GE90 Project. At this time, Teets was an employee at will and had no written employment contract addressing ownership of inventive work. Burnham, on the other hand, had contractu-ally agreed to assign any inventive rights to DRB.

On November 1, 1991, DRB proposed several initial manufacturing designs. All the proposals involved welding or diffusion bonding several pieces together to form the leading edge. On November 12, 1991, GE agreed to purchase some welded and bonded fan blades. In that agreement, however, GE indicated its desire that DRB continue to work toward a one-piece leading edge.

In early 1992, GE discovered problems with DRB's weld method. The welds were porous, distorted, and suffered breakage at the joints. In response, GE ordered design changes. On March 12, 1992, Burnham and Teets met to discuss GE's required changes. During this meeting, Teets showed Burnham sketches he had drawn at home depicting Teets's initial idea for the HFP. Burnham thought the idea had potential. Nonetheless he instructed Teets to make changes in the welding process because GE would not alter its delivery schedule for design changes. Teets refined the HFP idea while still working on GE's changes to the welding process. Other employees at DRB assisted Teets in his refinement of the HFP process.

On April 21, 1992, Teets submitted a more detailed sketch of the HFP idea to Douglas Burnham and to Nigel Bond, GE's lead engineer on the GE90 Project. DRB also proposed other new approaches at this meeting. GE rejected all of the proposals.

In July 1992, GE tested the welded leading edges. Test results showed a complete composite failure. By August 1992, however, Teets had successfully tested the HFP at DRB. On the basis of this test data, DRB gained approval from GE. In October 1992, GE ordered 450 pieces using the HFP. Thereafter, GE continued to order one-piece leading edges manufactured with the HFP. In fact, GE still uses the HFP to manufacture leading edges for its GE90 engines.

In late 1992, Teets discussed with Burnham the need to seek patent protection for the HFP. On January 25, 1993, Teets sent a letter describing the HFP to Mitchell Bittman, patent counsel for Sequa Corporation, Chromalloy's parent company. In that letter, Teets states that DRB developed the HFP. On January 26, 1993, Teets and Burnham completed an invention disclosure form in preparation for a patent application. Teets identifies Burnham as co-inventor on that form. Both Teets and Burnham later assisted Bittman in the prosecution of a patent application for the HFP. The record in this appeal does not indicate if a patent has issued.

Teets first asserted sole ownership of the HFP process in April 1993. He, however, continued to assist in the prosecution of the patent application. On June 18, 1993, Teets filed this action against Chromalloy, seeking, among other things, a declaration of ownership of the HFP. On a summary judgment motion, the court concluded that Chromalloy held a shop right in the process. The district court then proceeded to try the issue of ownership. After a bench trial, the district court concluded that Teets solely owned the HFP and enjoined Chromalloy from licensing, selling, or transferring the HFP for third-party use.

Discussion

Ownership springs from invention. The patent laws reward individuals for contributing to the progress of science and the useful arts. *See* U.S.

Const. art. I, § 8. As part of that reward, an invention presumptively belongs to its creator. This simple proposition becomes more complex when one creates while employed by another person.

Consistent with the presumption that the inventor owns his invention, an individual owns the patent rights even though the invention was conceived and/or reduced to practice during the course of employment. At the same time, however, the law recognizes that employers may have an interest in the creative products of their employees. For example, an employer may obtain a shop right in employee inventions where it has contributed to the development of the invention. A shop right permits the employer to use the employee's invention without liability for infringement.

In addition, contract law allows individuals to freely structure their transactions and employee relationships. An employee may thus freely consent by contract to assign all rights in inventive ideas to the employer.

Without such an express assignment, employers may still claim an employee's inventive work where the employer specifically hires or directs the employee to exercise inventive faculties. When the purpose for employment thus focuses on invention, the employee has received full compensation for his or her inventive work. To apply this contract principle, a court must examine the employment relationship at the time of the inventive work to determine if the parties entered an implied-in-fact contract to assign patent rights.

An implied-in-fact contract is an agreement "founded upon a meeting of the minds, which, although not embodied in an express contract, is inferred, as a fact from conduct of the parties showing, in the light of the surrounding circumstances, their tacit understanding." By comparison, an implied-in-law contract is a "fiction of law where a promise is imputed to perform a legal duty, as to repay money obtained by fraud or duress."

[S]tate contract principles provide the rules for identifying and enforcing implied-in-fact contracts. Under these rules, a Florida employer can not claim ownership of an employee's invention "unless the contract of employment by express terms or unequivocal inference shows that the employee was hired for the express purpose of producing the thing patented." *State v. Neal*, 152 Fla. 582 (following *Bourne*). Thus, when an employer hires a person for general service and the employee invents on the side, the invention belongs to the employee. However, the employer may claim ownership of the invention if the employer hires a person for the "specific purpose of making the invention." *Id.* Even if hired for a general purpose, an employee with the specific task of developing a device or process may cede ownership of the invention from that task to the employer. *Id.*

The existence of an implied-in-fact contract to assign inventive rights is a question of fact. Consequently, we review the trial court's finding on this question of fact for clear error.

Returning now to Teets, the specific goal of his project was to develop a one-piece leading edge. GE approached DRB to propose ways to apply a leading edge to turbine blades in its new engine. GE specifically and repeatedly expressed a desire for a one-piece solution. Faced with GE's requests, DRB, through Burnham, assigned Teets as the chief engineer on the GE90 project. Teets spent 70% of his time on that project. After undertaking the GE90 project and attempting several solutions to GE's problem, Teets developed the HFP. Teets reduced the invention to practice using DRB's resources—DRB's employees, DRB's shop tools and materials, and DRB's time. DRB has paid and continues to pay for the prosecution of a patent application for the HFP.

Most important, as recognized by the trial court, Teets repeatedly acknowledged DRB's role in the development of the HFP. He stated "DRB devised or developed" the HFP. In fact, the patent application lists another DRB employee, Burnham, as a co-inventor. Thus, Teets himself recognized DRB's role in the inventive activity.

These undisputed facts show an implied-in-fact contract of assignment between Teets and DRB. DRB specifically directed Teets to devise a one-piece leading edge for GE. Having directed Teets to that task, compensated him for his efforts, paid for the refinement of the process, and paid for the patent protection, Chromalloy owns the patent rights in the HFP. The Florida Supreme Court's decision in *Neal* governs this case and compels the conclusion that Teets entered an implied-in-fact contract to assign patent rights to Chromalloy.

REVERSED.

NAKAMURA v. NICHIA KAGAKU KÔGYÔ K.K.

Tokyo District Court.
(Jan. 30, 2004).*

Facts

The plaintiff is a researcher who invented the blue light-emitting diode (Blue LED) when he was an employee of the defendant. The defendant is a leading manufacturer in the Blue LED industry and a registrant of a patent that covers the invention of the Blue LED. The plaintiff sued the defendant for a transfer of ownership of the patent by asserting that he never assigned his right to obtain a patent on his invention to the defendant. Also, the plaintiff secondarily asserted that, even if the right to obtain a patent was assigned to the defendant, the plaintiff was entitled to seek 20 billion yen from the defendant as a reasonable remuneration of assignment of the right.

Under the Japanese Patent Act, the inventor has the right to obtain a patent on his or her invention according to Sec. 29(1). On the other hand, according to Sec. 35(1)(2)(3), an employer may request assignment of the right to obtain a patent for the invention made by its employee, without

---

* Translation originally published in 35 IIC 941, 941–43 (2004). Reproduced with permission.

making any further separate assignment, under the following circumstances:

(1) such invention, by reason of its nature, falls within the scope of the business of the employer and fell within the present or past duties of the employer and fell within the present or past duties of the employee that were performed on behalf of the employer (hereinafter such invention is referred to as "service invention"); and

(2) the employer sets out a contract, a service regulation or any other stipulation according to which the employee shall assign the right to obtain a patent on his or her invention to the employer when the employee invents.

With respect to the issue of assignment of the right, the Tokyo District Court held, in its interlocutory decision of 19 September 2002, that the defendant was assigned the right to obtain a patent from the plaintiff under Sec. 35.

After the interlocutory decision, proceedings focused on the issue of deciding the "reasonable remuneration." When the right to obtain a patent is assigned to the employer, the employee shall have the right to a reasonable remuneration under Sec. 35(3). According to Sec. 35(4), the amount of such remuneration shall be determined by considering the profits which the employer will obtain from the invention and the degree of contribution of the employer in making the invention.

Findings

"The amount of profits that the employer will obtain from the invention" means the profits which the employer will obtain not by merely utilizing the invention but by monopolising the right to utilize the invention (hereinafter such profit is referred to as "monopolised profit").

The monopolised profit should be determined as follows:

(1) Where the employer licenses the right to utilize the invention to third parties, the monopolised profit means royalties that the employer will obtain from these licenses.

(2) Where the employer does not license the right to utilize the invention to anyone else and only the employer utilizes it, monopolised profits refer to profits that the employer will obtain by preventing third parties from the use of the invention until the patent expires. Specifically, these are profits that the employer will obtain from the sales amount by such monopoly, which is calculated by deducting the sales amount that the employer will obtain by licensing the right to third parties from the sales amount that the employer will obtain by monopolising the right.

Since the defendant has not licensed the right to anyone else, the monopolised profits are the profits the defendant will obtain from the direct sales under the monopolistic right, which is 120,860,120,000 yen (approximately 120 billion yen).

The degree of contribution made by the inventor to the invention correlates with that of the employer and should be evaluated as a numerical percentage.

While the defendant had neither know-how on Blue LED nor a researcher who could supervise or help the plaintiff, the plaintiff invented the invention all by himself based only on his conception. This case is completely exceptional because one employee hired by a small employer whose R & D power is quite weak made an invention that was recognised worldwide, outpacing worldwide research institutes. Considering these circumstances, the degree of contribution made by the plaintiff to the invention should not be less than 50%.

The plaintiff is entitled to get 60,430,060,000 yen (approximately 60 billion yen) as a reasonable remuneration, which is calculated by multiplying the monopolised profits (approximately 120 billion yen) by the percentage of the degree of contribution (50%) made by the plaintiff.

Since the plaintiff sought only 20 billion yen against the defendant, the court ordered the defendant to pay 20 billion yen.

HARMONIZING SCOPE AND ALLOCATION OF PATENT RIGHTS IN EUROPE—TOWARDS A NEW EUROPEAN PATENT LAW

Christopher Heath.
6 Marq. Intell. Prop. L. Rev. 11, 18–26 (2002).

A. Employees' Inventions

1. European Law

The EPC contains no harmonized rules concerning the allocation of rights in cases where the invention is created by an employee. Article 60(1) of the EPC only contains a rule concerning the conflict of laws: the question is determined according to the law of the Member State where the employee is a resident.

A harmonization of national patent laws with respect to employees' inventions would be desirable for several reasons: for joint cross-border projects, for the sake of multi-national enterprises, for a facilitated cooperation between enterprises of different nations, and for the sake of reaching a just and equitable solution for allocating profits between employer and employee.

2. National Legislation

i. Germany

The German rules for employees' inventions are codified in the Employees' Inventions Act of July 25, 1957, which deals with patentable inventions and technical improvement proposals. Both inventions that qualify as service inventions, as well as those made outside the sphere of employment, belong to the employee. The employee has to notify their employer, who then has the right to make use of the invention in exchange for payment of an equitable remuneration. The remuneration is calculated according to guidelines published by the Ministry of Labour. According to these guidelines, the value of an invention can be determined by way of a licensing analogy,[13] by the actual use of the employer, or by estimate. If actual licenses are granted, the value can be determined by either deducting all expenses from the royalty income or by a certain standard factor.

The value of the invention is only the first parameter used to determine the proper remuneration. The second is the "contributing factor," determined by considering the problem to be solved by the invention, the solution, and the duties and position of the employee within the company. The further the employee's duties are removed from the actual invention, the greater his contribution.[14] Accordingly, the lower the rank of an employee, the higher his contribution will be deemed, because those who are supposed to work on inventions already receive a salary in consideration thereof. For example, a cleaning woman who makes an invention will obtain a higher remuneration because contractually she was not supposed to engage in such activity.[15]

The Employees' Invention Act aims at maximizing social justice, yet it is perhaps rather cumbersome to apply.[16] In light of the shortcomings of the German Employees' Inventions Act, a reform is currently underway. In particular, five problems have been highlighted in connection with the current legal situation:

(1) Judged by international standards, a rule that gives 100% ownership of patentable employees' inventions to the employee, is rather unusual. Even in countries with rules favorable to the employee, the employer has at least the right to use the employees' inventions on a non-exclusive basis without remuneration.

(2) Current rules are fairly inflexible and require a high administrative burden without necessarily benefiting the employee. According to one study, handling an employee's invention leads to administrative costs of 2,200 Euro on average, while the economic gain of an employee's invention for the employer is only 1,000 Euro on average.

(3) If the employer wants to purchase the rights to the invention, a formal declaration is necessary, adding to the administrative burden.

---

13. The Guidelines on Employees' Inventions of 20 July 1959 (Richtlinien für die Vergütung von Arbeitnehmererfindungen im privaten Dienst) (hereinafter Guidelines) give some guidance on the royalty rate: 0.5% to 5% for inventions in the field of electronics, 0.33% to 10% in the field of machinery, 2% to 5% in the field of chemistry, and 2% to 10% in the field of pharmacy. *Id.* § 10.

14. The Guidelines distinguish between six categories. Guidelines § 31.

15. The Guidelines distinguish between eight groups of employees. *Id.* § 32.

16. SCHIPPEL, *supra* note 12, at 614 (acknowledging that "[t]o small and medium-sized enterprises, the rules on [remuneration] remained closed books").

(4) The employer's obligations to file the patent application, request permission to file patents abroad, and offer to re-transfer rights to the employee in countries where no protection is sought are rather cumbersome.

(5) Calculation of the proper remuneration is complicated, while the amount, as such, may well be justified.

A proposal published by the German Ministry of Justice in 1999 has proposed the following amendments:

(1) Presumption of ownership of an employee's invention in favor of the employer rather than the employee. This would also harmonize the rules for copyright law with those of patent and utility model law.

(2) Calculation of the proper remuneration of the employee in two phases, with the first being basic remuneration of 250 Euro for every patentable invention made by an employee. Subsequent payments then depend on the actual use of the invention by the employer and correspond to the economic benefits derived from such exploitation.

Disputes can be brought before an arbitration tribunal, and subsequently, before the courts.

ii. The United Kingdom

Until 1977, English law did not contain any specific rules concerning employees' inventions. Rather, consistent with the dogma of contractual freedom, the courts assumed that an invention made within the course of employment, based on a labor contract or contract of apprenticeship, belonged to the employer; while an invention by an employee or apprentice, made outside the sphere of employment, belonged to the employee. As the above was treated only as a presumption, both parties were free to stipulate different rules by contract.

As a concession to fairness, the 1977 Patent Act introduced rules more favorable to the employed inventor. In particular, sections 40 to 43 of the 1977 Patent Act introduced a statutory right to compensation in cases where the invention belonged to the employer. In order to avoid what was perceived as unnecessary red tape in the German rules, it was deemed that the employee should receive compensation when the employer either made exceptional profit from the invention or obtained an invention originally belonging to the employee at a "knock-down" price. While this helps to solve the majority of cases where a huge amount of paperwork would prove disproportionate when measured against the profits gained from the invention, the rules also have disadvantages. In cases where the employer's profits become indeed exceptional (which may well be years after the invention), there might not be sufficient documentary evidence concerning development costs, and so forth, or the employer's enterprise might have disappeared. Further, litigation is costly and contains a significant element of uncertainty, as there are no rules on how to calculate the employee's remuneration. It is unclear if the above rules also apply when the employer deliberately refrains from patenting an invention that is patentable.

iii. France

Until 1978, French patent law did not contain any specific rules for employees' inventions. Court precedent basically treated the matter as one of contract, and in the absence thereof, distinguished between inventions made in the course of employment, free inventions, and "mixed inventions." In the first category, the rights to inventions belonged to the employer. In the second category, the rights belonged to the employee, and in the third category the rights were jointly owned by employee and employer. The Patent Act of July 13, 1978 distinguishes between inventions that the employee was required to make under his employment contract and inventions that were made outside or in the absence of such a mandate. The law in the latter case distinguishes between (1) inventions made in the course of employment, yet without concrete mandate; (2) inventions within the scope of the enterprise's activities; and (3) inventions made by the employee while using either his specific knowledge of the enterprise or the enterprise's facilities. Only inventions in the first category (those mandated by the employer) automatically belong to the employer. Inventions in the second category, with its three alternatives, belong to the employee and yet may be claimed by the employer upon payment of compensation.

A remuneration for inventions made in the second category (those made without a mandate) requires adequate compensation when claimed by the employer. This compensation has to be calculated on the basis of the economic value of the invention in question.[25] In cases when the invention was made in the course of a concrete mandate (the first category), the remuneration was initially calculated on the basis of the employee's salary as a sort of additional remuneration to be specified by collective labor agreements.

A new decree in 2001 has only added to the general confusion about how to calculate proper remuneration. Again, the decree only applies to public servants, thus begging the question to what extent the courts would consider the same rules for private employees mutatis mutandis. In addition, the new decree bases calculation on the net profits of an invention, which is the turnover minus value added tax, minus all expenses in connection with the invention. The employee is entitled to receive half of this profit, up to the amount of his gross annual salary. When 50% of the net profits amount to more than the employee's annual salary, the employee would receive either a one-quarter of the sum superceding his annual salary, according to one interpretation, or 25% of the net profits of the invention, according to an alternative interpretation. The wording of the law is not clear as to which calculation is actually meant, and the Hansards seem to be untraceable.

---

25. Decision of the Commission Nationale des Inventions de Salariés (Arbitration Tribunal on Matters of Employees' Inventions) of 4 Feb. 1983, Case 85–2, Dossiers Brevets 1984.I.9.

iv. Other Countries

Italian patent law, under the Patent Act of 1939, is similar to the French Patent Act. Austrian patent law takes a position similar to the German rules, yet without the same amount of detail in calculating compensation. The rules of the Netherlands are similar to those of England, while the Nordic countries of Norway and Sweden enacted specific legislation for employees' inventions in 1970 and 1949, respectively. Specific legislation was also enacted in Denmark in 1972 and in Finland in 1967.

v. European Community Draft Rules

Finally, the Community made some proposals in its green paper on the Community patent and the patent system in June of 1997.[29] In fact, the paper is primarily meant to promote discussion on the topic rather than to make further proposals.

3. Analysis

Unfortunately, there is little common ground among European jurisdictions in the matter of employees' inventions beyond the understanding that inventing employees should receive some type of compensation.

These differences in perception reflect the wide gaps between European countries when it comes to defining the role of the employee in general. Still, finding equitable rules concerning employees' inventions is a task Brussels will not be able to shirk away from when harmonizing European patent law.

NOTES AND QUESTIONS

1. Neither the Paris Convention nor the TRIPS Agreement speaks to the issue of employee ownership of inventions created during employment. The European Patent Convention Article 60 leaves the issue to be decided by the "law of the State in which the employee is mainly employed." The issue, though, is of huge import, given that in most industrialized countries, the vast majority of inventors are employees, not solo inventors. Should the international patent conventions attempt to address the issue?

2. In *Teets*, did Mr. Teets agree to give up his patent rights to the HFP process? If so, when and to whom? What significance should be given to the fact that Mr. Burnham, the General Manager of DRB, had signed a written agreement to assign any patent rights to DRB, while Mr. Teets had not? Should DRB be rewarded with the patent even though it did not get an assignment in writing?

3. *Shop rights*. Even when an employee inventor is entitled to a patent on an invention developed at work, countries may recognize "shop rights" for the employer. Shop rights are nonexclusive licenses that allow the employer to

---

29. *See* Promoting Innovation Through Patents: Green Paper on the Community Patent and the Patent System in Europe, COM(97)314.

use the invention without permission. In some countries (e.g., the United States), shop rights are royalty free. In other countries (e.g., Germany), shop rights require the payment of royalties to the employee.

4. The approach to employee inventors of which country—the U.S., Japan, or Germany—is better for innovation? *See generally* Catherine L. Fisk, *Removing the "Fuel of Interest" from the "Fire of Genius": Law and the Employee–Inventor, 1830–1930*, 65 U. CHI. L. REV. 1127 (1998); Robert P. Merges, *The Law and Economics of Employee Inventions*, 13 HARV. J.L. & TECH. 1 (1999).

5. How did the Tokyo District Court determine the initial figure of "reasonable compensation" owed by Nichia Company to the inventor Nakamura? What about the final figure? Do you think the final amount was a fair and reasonable amount?

The amount of reasonable remuneration (20 billion yen) was the largest ever awarded to an inventor employee by a Japanese court under the patent code. Subsequently, Nakamura and Nichia Co. settled the case for the reported amount of 840 million yen (roughly 8 million U.S. dollars) in a court-mediated settlement by the Tokyo High Court. Why do you think Nakamura settled the case for such a smaller amount? Do you think the settlement was fair given that Nichia's profits from the invention were so large—120 billion yen (U.S. $1.07 billion)?

6. *Amendment to Japan's Law*. In the aftermath of the *Nakamura* case, the Japanese legislature amended § 35 of the Patent Act. The amended section allows employers to set, by contract or work rules, the method for determining "adequate remuneration" for employee inventions. The stipulated method set by contract will govern unless the amount given to the employee is "unreasonable," in which case the employee can seek statutory remuneration under § 35. Factors that can make the amount reasonable include (i) the employer's consultation with the employee regarding the establishment of the remuneration calculation; (ii) the employee had an opportunity to be heard on how the amount should be determined; and (iii) disclosure to employees of the standard of remuneration for their inventions. *See* Miyuki Hanai, *Employee Inventions in Japan*, IP OWNERSHIP, June/July 2005, at 49. The amendment appears to have discouraged the filing of § 35 lawsuits for adequate remuneration. Relatively few suits have been brought by employee inventors for statutory compensation in Japan. In 2007, 13 suits were brought; in 2008, 9 suits; and in 2009, only 4 suits. *See* AHUJA's World Patent & Trademark News (May–June 2010). Is Japan's amended § 35 an improvement over the law used in *Nakamura?*

C. PATENT REQUIREMENTS

TRIPS establishes several minimum standards related to the requirements for obtaining a patent for an invention. These requirements can be broken down into five areas: (1) subject matter, (2) novelty, (3) inventive step or nonobviousness, (4) capable of industrial application or utility, and (5) enablement. Each will be discussed in this section.

1. SUBJECT MATTER

TRIPS Agreement

Article 27

Patentable Subject Matter

1. Subject to the provisions of paragraphs 2 and 3, patents shall be available for any inventions, whether products or processes, in all fields of technology, provided that they are new, involve an inventive step and are capable of industrial application.[5] Subject to paragraph 4 of Article 65, paragraph 8 of Article 70 and paragraph 3 of this Article, patents shall be available and patent rights enjoyable without discrimination as to the place of invention, the field of technology and whether products are imported or locally produced.

2. Members may exclude from patentability inventions, the prevention within their territory of the commercial exploitation of which is necessary to protect *ordre public* or morality, including to protect human, animal or plant life or health or to avoid serious prejudice to the environment, provided that such exclusion is not made merely because the exploitation is prohibited by their law.

3. Members may also exclude from patentability:

(a) diagnostic, therapeutic and surgical methods for the treatment of humans or animals;

(b) plants and animals other than micro-organisms, and essentially biological processes for the production of plants or animals other than non-biological and microbiological processes. However, Members shall provide for the protection of plant varieties either by patents or by an effective *sui generis* system or by any combination thereof. The provisions of this subparagraph shall be reviewed four years after the date of entry into force of the WTO Agreement.

* * *

One of the most significant achievements of the TRIPS Agreement is its broad definition of patentable subject matter in Article 27. Patents must be available for "any inventions, whether products or processes, in all fields of technology," and "without discrimination as to the place of invention, the field of technology and whether products are imported or locally produced." This broad starting point for patentable subject matter effectively prohibits the practice of some countries that had excluded pharmaceuticals, chemicals, and processes from patents.

Article 27(2) and (3) recognize a country's right to exclude certain inventions from patents, however. Under Article 27(2), exceptions "neces-

---

5. For the purposes of this Article, the terms "inventive step" and "capable of industrial application" may be deemed by a Member to be synonymous with the terms "non-obvious" and "useful" respectively.

sary to protect *ordre public* or morality" are allowed under certain circumstances, "provided that such exclusion is not made merely because the exploitation is prohibited by their law." The proviso requires a justification other than "it's against the law," such as ethical or moral concerns. For example, Article 6 of the European Union Biotech Directive, 98/44/EC, prohibits patenting of "(a) processes for cloning human beings; (b) processes for modifying the germ line genetic identity of human beings; (c) uses of human embryos for industrial or commercial purposes; and (d) processes for modifying the genetic identity of animals which are likely to cause them suffering without any substantial medical benefit to man or animal, and also animals resulting from such processes." Each of the exclusions stems from ethical or moral concerns. The Court of Justice of the European Union has broadly interpreted the exclusion of inventions derived from uses of human embryos to bar also the patenting of "uses of human embryos for purposes of scientific research." *See Brüstle v. Greenpeace*, C–34–10, ¶ 39 (2011).

Under Article 27(3), medical, therapeutic, and surgical methods can be excluded from patentability, as can plants and animals other than microorganisms. Plant varieties, however, must be protected either through patents or *sui generis* protection.

Recently, several major controversies over patentable subject matter have arisen in a variety of important contexts: genetically engineered organisms, isolated DNA sequences, business methods, and computer software. The issues raised are among the most contentious in all of patent law today. Given their importance to the world economy, and the huge stakes involved to industries and society at large, we will study each issue in turn.

a. Special Discussion: Patentability of Higher Life Forms and DNA Sequences

1. *Higher Life Forms*

HARVARD COLLEGE v. CANADA (COMM'R OF PATENTS)

Supreme Court of Canada.
4 S.C.R. 45 (2002).

BASTARACHE, J.

I—Introduction

This appeal raises the issue of the patentability of higher life forms within the context of the *Patent Act*, R.S.C. 1985, C. P–4. The respondent, the President and Fellows of Harvard College, seeks to patent a mouse that has been genetically altered to increase its susceptibility to cancer, which makes it useful for cancer research. The patent claims also extend to all non-human mammals which have been similarly altered.

II—Factual Background

On June 21, 1985, the respondent, the President and Fellows of Harvard College ("Harvard"), applied for a patent on an invention entitled "transgenic animals." The invention aims to produce animals with a susceptibility to cancer for purposes of animal carcinogenic studies. The animals can be used to test a material suspected of being a carcinogen by exposing them to the material and seeing if tumours develop. Because the animals are already susceptible to tumour development, the amount of material used can be smaller, thereby more closely approximating the amounts to which humans are actually exposed. In addition, the animals will be expected to develop tumours in a shorter time period. The animals can also be used to test materials thought to confer protection against the development of cancer.

The technology by which a cancer-prone mouse ("oncomouse") is produced is described in the patent application disclosure. The oncogene (the cancer-promoting gene) is obtained from the genetic code of a non-mammal source, such as a virus. A vehicle for transporting the oncogene into the mouse's chromosomes is constructed using a small piece of bacterial DNA referred to as a plasmid. The plasmid, into which the oncogene has been "spliced," is injected into fertilized mouse eggs, preferably while they are at the one-cell stage. The eggs are then implanted into a female host mouse, or "foster mother," and permitted to develop to term. After the offspring of the foster mother are delivered, they are tested for the presence of the oncogene; those that contain the oncogene are called "founder" mice. Founder mice are mated with mice that have not been genetically altered. In accordance with Mendelian inheritance principles, 50 percent of the offspring will have all of their cells affected by the oncogene, making them suitable for the uses described above.

In its patent application, the respondent seeks to protect both the process by which the oncomice are produced and the end product of the process, i.e. the founder mice and the offspring whose cells are affected by the oncogene. The process and product claims also extend to all non-human mammals. In March 1993, by Final Action, a Patent Examiner rejected the product claims (claims 1 to 12) as being outside the scope of the definition of "invention" in § 2 of the *Patent Act*, but allowed the process claims (claims 13 to 26). In August 1995, after a review by the Commissioner of Patents and a hearing before the Patent Appeal Board, the Commissioner confirmed the refusal to grant a patent for claims 1 to 12. The Federal Court Trial Division dismissed the respondent's appeal from the decision of the Commissioner. The respondent's further appeal to the Federal Court of Appeal was allowed by a majority of the court, Isaac J.A. dissenting. The Commissioner of Patents appeals from that decision.

III—Relevant Statutory Provisions

Patent Act, R.S.C. 1985, c. P–4:

2. In this Act, except as otherwise provided, . . .

"invention" means any new and useful art, process, machine, manufacture or composition of matter, or any new and useful improvement in any art, process, machine, manufacture or composition of matter;

27. (1) The Commissioner shall grant a patent for an invention to the inventor or the inventor's legal representative if an application for the patent in Canada is filed in accordance with this Act and all other requirements for the issuance of a patent under this Act are met.

40. Whenever the Commissioner is satisfied that an applicant is not by law entitled to be granted a patent, he shall refuse the application and, by registered letter addressed to the applicant or his registered agent, notify the applicant of the refusal and of the ground or reason therefor.

V—Analysis

The Definition of Invention: Whether a Higher Life Form Is a "Manufacture" or a "Composition of Matter"

Having considered the relevant factors, I conclude that Parliament did not intend to include higher life forms within the definition of invention found in the *Patent Act.*

(1) The Words of the Act

The definition of invention in § 2 of the *Patent Act* lists five categories of invention: art, process, machine, manufacture or composition of matter. The first three, "art", "process" and "machine," are clearly inapplicable when considering claims directed toward a genetically engineered non-human mammal. If a higher life form is to fit within the definition of invention, it must therefore be considered to be either a "manufacture" or a "composition of matter."

Rothstein J.A. [writing for the majority of the Federal Court of Appeal] concluded that the oncomouse was a "composition of matter," and therefore did not find it necessary to consider whether it was also a "manufacture." In coming to this conclusion, he relied on the following definition of "composition of matter" adopted by the majority of the U.S. Supreme Court in *Diamond v. Chakrabarty*, 447 U.S. 303, 308 (1980)[.] In *Chakrabarty*, the majority attributed the widest meaning possible to the phrases "composition of matter" and "manufacture" for the reason that inventions are, necessarily, unanticipated and unforeseeable. Burger C.J., at p. 307, also referred to the fact that the categories of invention are prefaced by the word "any" ("*any* new and useful process, machine, manufacture, or composition of matter"). Finally, the Court referred to extrinsic evidence of Congressional intent to adopt a broad concept of patentability, noting at p. 309 that: "The Committee Reports accompanying the 1952 Act inform us that Congress intended statutory subject matter to 'include anything under the sun that is made by man.'"

I agree that the definition of invention in the *Patent Act* is broad. Because the Act was designed in part to promote innovation, it is only reasonable to expect the definition of invention to be broad enough to encompass unforeseen and unanticipated technology. I cannot however agree with the suggestion that the definition is unlimited in the sense that it includes "anything under the sun that is made by man." In drafting the *Patent Act*, Parliament chose to adopt an exhaustive definition that limits invention to any "art, process, machine, manufacture or composition of matter." Parliament did not define "invention" as "anything new and useful made by man." By choosing to define invention in this way, Parliament signalled a clear intention to include certain subject matter as patentable and to exclude other subject matter as being outside the confines of the Act.

With respect to the meaning of the word "manufacture" (*fabrication*), although it may be attributed a very broad meaning, I am of the opinion that the word would commonly be understood to denote a non-living mechanistic product or process. For example, the *Oxford English Dictionary* (2nd ed. 1989), vol. IX, at p. 341, defines the noun "manufacture" as the following:

> [T]he action or process of making by hand ... The action or process of making articles or material (in modern use, on a large scale) by the application of physical labour or mechanical power.

In *Chakrabarty*, *supra*, at p. 308, "manufacture" was defined as

> the production of articles for use from raw or prepared materials by giving to these materials new forms, qualities, properties, or combinations, whether by hand-labor or by machinery.

These definitions use the terminology of "article," "material," and "*objet technique*." Is a mouse an "article," "material," or an "*objet technique*"? In my view, while a mouse may be analogized to a "manufacture" when it is produced in an industrial setting, the word in its vernacular sense does not include a higher life form.

As regards the meaning of the words "composition of matter," I believe that they must be defined more narrowly than was the case in *Chakrabarty*, *supra*, at p. 308 namely "all compositions of two or more substances and ... all composite articles." If the words "composition of matter" are understood this broadly, then the other listed categories of invention, including "machine" and "manufacture," become redundant. This implies that "composition of matter" must be limited in some way. Although I do not express an opinion as to where the line should be drawn, I conclude that "composition of matter" does not include a higher life form such as the oncomouse.

First, the *Oxford English Dictionary*, *supra*, vol. III, at p. 625, defines the word "composition" as "[a] substance or preparation formed by combination or mixture of various ingredients," the *Grand Robert de la langue française*, *supra*, vol. 2, at p. 367, defines "*composition*" as [translation] "[a]ction or manner of forming a whole, a set by assembling several parts, several elements." Within the context of the definition of "invention," it does not seem unreasonable to assume that it must be the inventor who has combined or mixed the various ingredients. Owing to the fact that the technology by which a mouse predisposed to cancer is produced involves injecting the oncogene into a fertilized egg, the genetically altered egg would appear to be cognizable as "[a] substance or preparation formed by combination or mixture of various ingredients" or as [translation] "[a]ction or manner of forming a whole ... by assembling several parts." However, it does not thereby follow that the oncomouse itself can be understood in such terms. Injecting the oncogene into a fertilized egg is the but-for cause of a mouse predisposed to cancer, but the process by which a fertilized egg becomes an adult mouse is a complex process, elements of which require no human intervention. The body of a mouse is composed of various ingredients or substances, but it does not consist of ingredients or substances that have been combined or mixed together by a person. Thus, I am not satisfied that the phrase "composition of matter" includes a higher life form whose genetic code has been altered in this manner.

Patenting higher life forms would involve a radical departure from the traditional patent regime. Moreover, the patentability of such life forms is a highly contentious matter that raises a number of extremely complex issues. If higher life forms are to be patentable, it must be under the clear and unequivocal direction of Parliament.

(2) The Scheme of the Act

This interpretation of the words of the Act finds support in the fact that the patenting of higher life forms raises unique concerns which do not arise with respect to non-living inventions and which cannot be adequately addressed by the scheme of the Act. Unlike other inventions, biologically based inventions are living and self-replicating. In addition, the products of biotechnology are incredibly complex, incapable of full description, and can contain important characteristics that have nothing to do with the invention. In my view, the fact that the *Patent Act* in its current state is ill-equipped to deal appropriately with higher life forms as patentable subject matter is an indication that Parliament never intended the definition of invention to extend to this type of subject matter.

[S]everal of the issues raised by the interveners and in the literature are more directly related to patentability and to the scheme of the *Patent Act* itself. These issues, which pertain to the scope and content of the monopoly right accorded to the inventor by a patent, have been explored in depth by the Canadian Biotechnology Advisory Committee (CBAC), a body created in 1999 with a mandate to provide the government with advice on policy issues associated with biotechnology. In June 2002, the CBAC released its final report, *The Patenting of Higher Life Forms and Related Issues*. The report recommends that higher life forms should be patentable. Nonetheless, it concludes, at p. 7, that given the importance of issues raised by the patenting of higher life forms and the significant "values" content of the issues raised, Parliament and not the courts should determine whether and to what degree patent rights ought to extend to plants and animals.

Two of the issues addressed by the CBAC (farmers' privilege and innocent bystanders) arise out of the unique ability of higher life forms to self-replicate. Because higher life forms reproduce by themselves, the grant of a patent covers not only the particular plant, seed or animal sold, but also all of its progeny containing the patented invention. In the CBAC's view, this represents a significant increase in the scope of rights offered to patent holders that is not in line with the scope of patent rights provided in other fields.

Another concern identified by the CBAC in respect to self-replication pertains to infringement. The CBAC observes that since plants and animals are often capable of reproducing on their own, it must be recognized that they will not always do so under the control or with the knowledge of those who grow the plants or raise the animals. Patent law does not currently require a patent holder to prove that an alleged infringer knew or ought to have known about the reproduction of a patented invention. An "innocent bystander" may therefore be faced with high costs to defend a patent infringement suit and an award of damages for infringement without a countervailing remedy against the patent holder.

Finally, the respondent refers to the World Trade Organization's *Agreement on Trade Related Aspects of Intellectual Property Rights* (TRIPS), and the *North American Free Trade Agreement* (NAFTA), which both contain an article whereby members may "exclude from patentability" certain subject matter, including plants and animals other than microorganisms. The respondent argues that it is apparent from this provision that plants and animals are considered patentable, unless specifically excluded from patentability. I see little merit to this argument since the *status quo* position in Canada is that higher life forms are not a patentable subject matter, regardless of the fact that there is no explicit exclusion in the *Patent Act*. In my view, the fact that there is a specific exception in TRIPS and NAFTA for plants and animals does however demonstrate that the distinction between higher and lower life forms is widely accepted as valid.

As I remarked above, it is up to Parliament and not the courts to assess the validity of the distinction drawn by the Patent Office between higher life forms and lower life forms. For the reasons given above, the appeal is allowed.

BINNIE, J. (dissenting):

The oncomouse has been held patentable, and is now patented in jurisdictions that cover Austria, Belgium, Denmark, Finland, France, Germany, Greece, Ireland, Italy, Luxembourg, The Netherlands, Portugal, Spain, Sweden, the United Kingdom and the United States. A similar patent has been issued in Japan. New Zealand has issued a patent for a transgenic mouse that has been genetically modified to be susceptible to HIV infection. Indeed, we were not told of any country with a patent system comparable to Canada's (or otherwise) in which a patent on the oncomouse had been applied for and been refused.

Innovation is said to be the lifeblood of a modern economy. We neglect rewarding it at our peril. Intellectual property has global mobility, and states have worked diligently to harmonize their patent, copyright and trademark regimes. In this context, the Commissioner's approach to this case sounds a highly discordant note. Intellectual property was the subject matter of such influential agreements as the *Paris Convention* as early as 1883. International rules governing patents were strengthened by the *European Patent Convention* in 1973, and, more recently, the *Agreement on Trade–Related Aspects of Intellectual Property Rights* (TRIPS) in 1994. Legislation varies of course, from state to state, but broadly speaking Canada has sought to harmonize its concepts of intellectual property with other like-minded jurisdictions. The mobility of capital and technology makes it desirable that comparable jurisdictions with comparable intellectual property legislation arrive (to the extent permitted by the specifics of their own laws) at similar legal results.

In my view, the oncomouse is patentable subject matter. This does not mean that [the applicants'] claims must be allowed. They ought to be considered by the Commissioner in accordance with the usual patent principles. I would therefore have remitted the patent application to the Commissioner to have the specific claims considered and dealt with.

NOTES AND QUESTIONS

1. In *Diamond v. Chakrabarty*, 447 U.S. 303 (1980) (an important U.S. case discussed by the Canadian Supreme Court in *Harvard College*), the U.S. Supreme Court held that a genetically engineered bacterium that was used to clean up oil spills was patentable subject matter. *Chakrabarty* was the first case to allow a patent for a genetically-engineered life form and was a catalyst for the development of the biotechnology industry in the U.S. Following *Chakrabarty*, biotechnology patent applications flooded the USPTO. Biotechnology companies from around the world were eager to do business in the United States, resulting in the U.S. receiving the "lion's share" of the world's foreign direct investment for biotechnology. *See* Matthias Kamber, Note, *Coming Out of the Maze: Canada Grants the Harvard Mouse Patent*, 35 GEO. WASH. IN'T L. REV. 761, 783 (2003). *Chakrabarty* paved the way for the first Harvard Oncomouse patent, which was granted by the USPTO on April 12, 1988. *See id.* at 765.

2. How relevant is TRIPS or the Paris Convention to deciding the patentability of Harvard's invention? Is Canada's decision on the patentability of Harvard's invention consistent with its obligations under TRIPS and the Paris Convention?

3. Did the majority in the *Harvard* mouse case concede that a genetically altered egg could constitute either a "composition of matter" or "manufac-

ture"? If so, could Harvard have patented the genetically altered egg of the foster mouse?

4. How is the oncomouse created? Is there a difference between how the first oncomouse is created (foster mother) and how its subsequent offspring oncomice are created? Would it make a difference if oncomice reproduce on their own or by some human intervention?

5. Why did both the majority and dissent devote much discussion to the U.S. Supreme Court decision in *Chakrabarty*? Is U.S. patent law of greater relevance than other countries' laws because Canada had borrowed the language "composition of matter" and "manufacture" apparently from the U.S. Patent Code of 1793?

6. *Process v. product patent.* If Harvard was granted a patent in Canada for the process by which it created the oncomouse, why did it also seek to patent the oncomouse itself? How costly to Harvard was the denial of the patent on the oncomouse, if Harvard still has a process patent?

7. The dissent noted that no other country in which Harvard applied for a patent on the oncomouse denied Harvard a patent. What the dissent did not mention, however, is that Harvard probably could not have obtained patents for its oncomouse in a number of countries. As discussed below, a number of countries exclude animals from patentability. If the dissent relied on the practices of other jurisdictions that had allowed patents for the oncomouse, should it have also discussed those jurisdictions that do not allow patents for animals?

8. *Monsanto case.* In 2004, in another 5–4 decision, the Supreme Court of Canada revisited the issue of patenting of higher life forms, this time the validity of patents granted to Monsanto for (i) the process for creating a genetically engineered canola plant that was resistant to the herbicide "Roundup" and (ii) the cell derived from that process, but not the genetically modified plant itself. Although the majority acknowledged that plants and seeds are "unpatentable 'higher life forms' " under the holding of *Harvard College*, the majority found a difference with patenting just a gene or a cell. The Court upheld the lower court's determination that the defendant farmer, who cultivated Monsanto's Roundup Ready Canola after some seeds of the plant apparently had blown onto his farm, infringed Monsanto's patent by using the invention. *Monsanto Canada Inc. v. Schmeiser*, 2004 SCC 34 (2004). Is *Monsanto* consistent with *Harvard College*? Is it consistent to allow patents for a cell of a genetically engineered higher life form, but to hold, at the same time, that higher life forms are not patentable?

9. *Biotechnology patents in the EU.* In the 1980s, uncertainty about protection for biotechnology caused the EU to fall seriously behind the U.S. in attracting biotechnology research and industry. In a 1996 study, the EU found that the United States issued 65% of the world's patents for biotechnological research and had 1,300 biotechnology firms. By contrast, the EU had only a 15% share and 485 firms. *See Opinion of the Economic and Social Committee on the "Proposal for a European Parliament and Council Directive on the Legal Protection of Biotechnological Inventions,"* 1996 O.J. (C 295) 11 at §§ 1.2.2–1.3.2. Citing a need to avoid a "brain drain from Europe to America," the EU decided that it needed legal reform in the biotechnology sector.

See id. Ten years in the making, the EU Directive on the Legal Protection of Biotechnological Inventions (98/44/EC) was enacted on July 6, 1998.

The EU Directive takes the following approach. Article 1 requires member states to "protect biotechnological inventions under national patent law." Under Article 3, inventions cannot be denied simply because "they concern a product consisting of or containing biological material or a process by means of which biological material is produced, processed or used." Article 3 further states that "[b]iological material which is isolated from its natural environment or produced by means of a technical process may be the subject of an invention even if it previously occurred in nature." Article 4 excludes animal and plant varieties from patentability, but allows "[i]nventions which concern plants or animals ... if the technical feasibility of the invention is not confined to a particular plant or animal variety." Article 5 allows the patenting of human gene sequences, but requires that the "industrial application of a sequence or a partial sequence of a gene ... be disclosed in the patent application."

Like the European Patent Convention, the EU Directive introduces ethical concerns into the decision to grant a patent. Article 6(1) provides that inventions "shall be considered unpatentable where their commercial exploitation would be contrary to *ordre public* or morality." Article 6(2) provides specific examples of unpatentable inventions, including "processes for cloning human beings" and "processes for modifying the genetic identity of animals which are likely to cause them suffering without any substantial benefit to man or animal, and also animals resulting from such processes." The EU's emphasis on moral and ethical considerations sets it apart from the U.S. Under the U.S. approach, moral and ethical considerations are not explicitly mentioned in the U.S. Patent Act as part of the decision on whether to grant a patent.

10. *Plants, plant varieties, and sui generis protection.* Article 27 of TRIPS allows countries to exclude from patentability "plants and animals other than microorganisms." But members are required to "provide for the protection of plant varieties either by patents or by an effective *sui generis* system or by any combination thereof." Typically, *sui generis* protection for plant varieties in countries is less strong than a utility patent and obtainable under easier requirements. For example, the *sui generis* right for a plant variety typically would not include a right to prevent others from breeding the plant into a new hybrid.

Article 27 represents the deep division among countries about the patentability of life forms. Part of the division stems from a longstanding fault line between North and South countries. Developed countries have generally been receptive to recognizing patents for new plants and plant varieties. In the U.S., newly developed plants are eligible for a standard utility patent under the Patent Code, as well as for more limited forms of protection under the Plant Patent Act of 1930 (which grants a "plant patent" for asexually reproduced plants, e.g., by grafting or budding) and the Plant Variety Protection Act of 1970 (which grants a "plant variety protection" certificate for sexually reproduced plants, i.e., by seed). *See J.E.M. AG Supply, Inc. v.*

Pioneer Hi–Bred Int'l, Inc., 534 U.S. 124 (2001). Similarly, the EU has recognized that new plants (but not plant varieties) can be patented, consistent with Article 53 of the EPO's exclusion of "plant or animal varieties or essentially biological processes for the production of plants or animals." The EU has a separate law that creates a *sui generis* plant variety right under the Council Regulation on Community Plant Variety Rights (E.C. No. 2100/94), which was modeled on an earlier treaty first passed by several European countries in 1961, the International Convention for the Protection of New Varieties of Plants (UPOV).

By contrast, developing countries have been far less receptive to allowing patents for plants or other life forms due to various cultural and religious concerns. Countries in the South are relatively more genetically diverse in plant and biological resources. By some estimates, 25 percent of prescription drugs in the U.S. are derived in part from plants indigenous to South countries. The Community of Andean Nations (Bolivia, Columbia, Ecuador, Peru, and Venezuela), which are estimated as having 25 percent of the world's biodiversity, do not allow patents for plants or animals (other than microorganisms). Community of Andean Nations Decision 486 art. 20 (Dec. 1, 2000). China and India also prohibit patenting of such life forms. India Patents (Amendment) Act, Ch. II, § 3 (2005); Ruay Lian Ho, *Compliance and Challenges Faced by the Chinese Patent System Under TRIPS*, 85 J. PAT. & TRADEMARK SOC'Y 504, 509 (2003).

2. DNA Sequences and Gene Patents

In 1982, the U.S. Patent Office granted the first patent on an invention involving a human gene. The PTO considered DNA sequences or genes, including from humans, to be patentable subject matter if "isolated" from their naturally occurring composition in the body. Isolated genes are often useful to researchers in identifying mutations associated with diseases in order to develop possible cures or treatment. After the first gene patent, the floodgates opened in the U.S. Eventually, other developed states, including the EU and Japan, followed suit to varying degrees. For example, the EU Directive on Biotechnological Inventions, 98/44/EC (July 30, 1998), adopts the U.S. approach in allowing patents on isolated genes. *Id.* art. 5. Article 52(4) of the European Patent Convention strikes a counterbalance by excluding from patentability diagnostic methods performed on the human body—a departure from the U.S. approach. Despite these differences, isolated gene sequences were, for many years, readily accepted as patentable subject matter in the U.S., EU, and Japan. According to the National Academy of Sciences, by 2005, an estimated 40,000 DNA-related patents had been granted in the U.S. alone, encompassing 20 percent of the entire human genome, although some dispute the figure. In 2010, courts in the U.S. and EU began to question fundamental aspects of gene patents. Consider the following cases.

ASSOCIATION FOR MOLECULAR PATHOLOGY
v. U.S. PATENT AND TRADEMARK OFFICE

United States Court of Appeals for the Federal Circuit,
653 F.3d 1329 (Fed. Cir. 2011), judgment vacated by ___
S. Ct. ___, 2012 WL 986819 (Mar. 26, 2012).

LOURIE, CIRCUIT JUDGE. [Judge Moore joined the majority opinion as to patentability of the method claims and cDNA (complementary DNA) composition claims, but concurred only in the judgment related to the patentability of the isolated DNA sequences. Judge Bryson concurred in the same parts as Judge Moore, but dissented in part based on his view that isolated DNA sequences are unpatentable.]

BACKGROUND

Plaintiffs brought suit against Myriad, challenging the patentability of certain composition and method claims relating to human genetics. Specifically, Plaintiffs sought a declaration that fifteen claims from seven patents assigned to Myriad are drawn to patent-ineligible subject matter under 35 U.S.C. § 101. The challenged composition claims cover two "isolated" human genes, *BRCA1* and *BRCA2* (collectively, "*BRCA1/2*" or "*BRCA*"), and certain alterations, or mutations, in these genes associated with a predisposition to breast and ovarian cancers. The challenged claims thus relate to isolated gene sequences and diagnostic methods of identifying mutations in these sequences.

Mutations in the *BRCA* genes correlate with an increased risk of breast and ovarian cancer. The average woman in the United States has around a twelve to thirteen percent risk of developing breast cancer in her lifetime. Women with *BRCA* mutations, in contrast, face a cumulative risk of between fifty to eighty percent of developing breast cancer and a cumulative risk of ovarian cancer of between twenty to fifty percent. Diagnostic genetic testing for the existence of *BRCA* mutations is therefore an important consideration in the provision of clinical care for breast or ovarian cancer. This testing provides a patient with information on her risk for hereditary breast and ovarian cancers, and thus aids in the difficult decision regarding whether to undertake preventive options, including prophylactic surgery. Diagnostic results can also be an important factor in structuring an appropriate course of cancer treatment, since certain forms of chemotherapy are more effective in treating cancers related to *BRCA* mutations.

The inventors of the patents in suit identified the genetic basis of *BRCA1* and *BRCA2*-related cancers using an analysis called positional cloning. Relying on a large set of DNA samples from families with inherited breast and ovarian cancers, the inventors correlated the occurrence of cancer in individual family members with the inheritance of certain marker DNA sequences. This allowed the inventors to identify, or "map," the physical location of the *BRCA* genes within the human genome and to isolate the *BRCA* genes and determine their exact nucleotide sequences. This in turn allowed Myriad to provide *BRCA* diagnostic testing services to women.

Myriad filed the first patent application leading to the patents in suit covering isolated *BRCA1* DNA and associated diagnostic methods in August 1994. The first patent, the '473 patent, issued on December 2, 1997. Myriad filed the first application leading to the patents in suit covering isolated *BRCA2* DNA and associated diagnostic methods in December 1995, and the first patent, the '492 patent, issued on November 17, 1998.

Myriad, however, was not the only entity to implement clinical *BRCA* testing services. Starting in 1996, the University of Pennsylvania's Genetic Diagnostic Laboratory ("GDL"), co-directed by plaintiffs Haig H. Kazazian, Jr., M.D. and Arupa Ganguly, Ph.D., provided *BRCA1/2* diagnostic services to women. By 1999, however, accusations by Myriad that GDL's *BRCA* testing services infringed its patents forced the lab to stop providing such services. During this period, Myriad also initiated several patent infringement suits against entities providing clinical *BRCA* testing. Myriad filed suit against Oncormed Inc. in 1997 and again in 1998, *Myriad Genetics v. Oncormed,* Nos. 2:97–cv–922, 2:98–cv–35 (D.Utah), and the University of Pennsylvania in 1998, *Myriad Genetics v. Univ. of Pa.,* No. 2:98–cv–829 (D.Utah). Both lawsuits were later dismissed without prejudice after each defendant agreed to discontinue all allegedly infringing activity.

[In the current lawsuit,] [t]he district court held for Plaintiffs, concluding that the fifteen challenged claims were drawn to non-patentable subject matter and thus invalid under § 101. Myriad appealed.

DISCUSSION

II. Patentable Subject Matter

Plaintiffs challenge under § 101 Myriad's composition claims directed to "isolated" DNA molecules and method claims directed to "analyzing" or "comparing" DNA sequences. We address each in turn.

A. Composition Claims: Isolated DNA Molecules

The Supreme Court's decisions in *Chakrabarty* and *Funk Brothers* set out the framework for deciding the patent eligibility of isolated DNA molecules.

In *Chakrabarty,* the Court addressed the question whether a manmade, living microorganism is a patentable manufacture or composition of matter within the meaning of § 101. 447 U.S. at 305, 307. The Court held that the bacteria qualified as patentable subject matter because the "claim is not to a hitherto unknown natural phenomenon, but to a nonnaturally occurring manufacture or composition of matter—a product of human ingenuity 'having a distinctive name, character [and] use.' " *Id.* at 309–10.

To underscore the point, the Court compared Chakrabarty's engineered bacteria with bacteria inoculants found unpatentable in *Funk Brothers,* again casting this case decided on obviousness in terms of § 101. *See Parker v. Flook,* 437 U.S. 584, 591, (1978); *Benson,* 409 U.S. at 67. In *Funk Brothers,* the patentee discovered that certain strains of nitrogen-fixing bacteria associated with leguminous plants do not mutually inhibit each other. 333 U.S. at 129–30. Based on this discovery, the patentee produced (and claimed) mixed cultures of nitrogen-fixing species capable of inoculating a broader range of leguminous plants than single-species cultures. *Id.* The Court held that the bacteria's qualities of non-inhibition were, "like the heat of the sun, electricity, or the qualities of metals," the "work of nature," and thus not patentable. *Id.* at 130. The Court also held that application of the newly discovered bacterial trait of non-inhibition to create a mixed bacterial culture was not a patentable advance because no species acquired a different property or use. *Id.* at 131. The *Chakrabarty* Court thus concluded that what distinguished Chakrabarty's bacteria from those claimed in *Funk Brothers,* and made the former patent eligible, was that Chakrabarty's bacteria had "markedly different characteristics from any [bacterium] found in nature" based on the efforts of the patentee. *Chakrabarty,* 447 U.S. at 310.

The distinction, therefore, between a product of nature and a human-made invention for purposes of § 101 turns on a change in the claimed composition's identity compared with what exists in nature. Specifically, the Supreme Court has drawn a line between compositions that, even if combined or altered in a manner not found in nature, have similar characteristics as in nature, and compositions that human intervention has given "markedly different," or "distinctive," characteristics. *Id. Hartranft,* 121 U.S. at 615; *see also American Fruit Growers v. Brogdex Co.,* 283 U.S. 1, 11 (1931). Applying this test to the isolated DNAs in this case, we conclude that the challenged claims are drawn to patentable subject matter because the claims cover molecules that are markedly different—have a distinctive chemical identity and nature—from molecules that exist in nature.

It is undisputed that Myriad's claimed isolated DNAs exist in a distinctive chemical form—as distinctive chemical molecules—from DNAs in the human body, *i.e.,* native DNA. Native DNA exists in the body as one of forty-six large, contiguous DNA molecules. Each DNA molecule is itself an integral part of a larger structural complex, a chromosome. In each chromosome, the DNA molecule is packaged around histone proteins into a structure called chromatin, which in turn is packaged into the chromosomal structure.

Isolated DNA, in contrast, is a free-standing portion of a native DNA molecule, frequently a single gene. Isolated DNA has been cleaved (*i.e.,* had covalent bonds in its backbone chemically severed) or synthesized to consist of just a fraction of a naturally occurring DNA molecule. Accordingly, *BRCA1* and *BRCA2* in their isolated state are not the same molecules as DNA as it exists in the body; human intervention in cleaving or synthesizing a portion of a native chromosomal DNA imparts on that isolated DNA a distinctive chemical identity from that possessed by native DNA.

As the above description indicates, isolated DNA is not purified DNA. Purification makes pure what was the same material, but was previously impure. Although isolated DNA must be removed from its native cellular and chromosomal environment, it has also been manipulated chemically so as to produce a molecule that is markedly different from that which exists in the body. It has not been purified by being isolated. Accordingly, this is not a situation, as in *Parke–Davis & Co. v. H.K. Mulford Co.,* in which purification of adrenaline resulted in the *identical* molecule being "for every practical purpose a new thing commercially and therapeutically." 189 F. 95, 103 (C.C.S.D.N.Y.1911). Although, we note, Judge Learned Hand held the claimed purified "Adrenalin" to be patentable subject matter. *Id.* In this case, the claimed isolated DNA molecules do not exist as in nature within a physical mixture to be purified. They have to be chemically cleaved from their chemical combination with other genetic materials. In other words, in nature, isolated DNAs are covalently bonded to such other materials. Thus, when cleaved, an isolated DNA molecule is not a purified form of a natural material, but a distinct chemical entity. In fact, some forms of isolated DNA require no purification at all, because DNAs can be chemically synthesized directly as isolated molecules.

The district court in effect created a categorical rule excluding isolated genes from patent eligibility. *See SJ Op.,* at 228–29. But the Supreme Court has "more than once cautioned that courts 'should not read into the patent laws limitations and conditions which the legislature has not expressed,'" *Bilski,* 130 S. Ct. at 3226 (quoting *Diamond v. Diehr,* 450 U.S. 175, 182, (1981)), and has repeatedly rejected new categorical exclusions from § 101's scope, *see id.* at 3227–28 (rejecting the argument that business method patents should be categorically excluded from § 101); *Chakrabarty,* 447 U.S. at 314–17 (same for living organisms). We therefore reject the district court's unwarranted categorical exclusion of isolated DNA molecules.

III. Method Claims

We turn next to Myriad's challenged method claims. [W]e conclude that all but one of Myriad's method claims are directed to patent-ineligible, abstract mental processes, and fail the machine-or-transformation test.

A. Methods of "Comparing" or "Analyzing" Sequences

We conclude that Myriad's claims to "comparing" or "analyzing" two gene sequences fall outside the scope of § 101 because they claim only abstract mental processes. *See Benson,* 409 U.S. at 67 ("Phenomena of nature, ... mental processes, and abstract intellectual concepts are not patentable, as they are the basic tools of scientific and technological work."). The claims recite, for example, a "method for screening a tumor sample," by "comparing" a first *BRCA1* sequence from a tumor sample and a second *BRCA1* sequence from a non-tumor sample, wherein a difference in sequence indicates an alteration in the tumor sample. '001 patent claim 1. This claim thus recites nothing more than the abstract mental steps necessary to compare two different nucleotide sequences: look at the first position in a first sequence; determine the nucleotide sequence at that first position; look at the first position in a second sequence; determine the nucleotide sequence at that first position; determine if the nucleotide at the first position in the first sequence and the first position in the second sequence are the same or different, wherein the latter indicates an alternation; and repeat for the next position.

Myriad's claims ... do not include the step of "determining" the sequence of *BRCA* genes by, *e.g.*, isolating the genes from a blood sample and sequencing them, or any other necessarily transformative step. Rather, the comparison between the two sequences can be accomplished by mere inspection alone. Accordingly, Myriad's claimed methods of comparing or analyzing nucleotide sequences fail to satisfy the machine-or-transformation test, and are instead directed to the abstract mental process of comparing two nucleotide sequences. The claims thus fail to claim a patent-eligible process under § 101.

B.   Method of Screening Potential Cancer Therapeutics

Lastly, we turn to Myriad's method claim directed to a method for screening potential cancer therapeutics via changes in cell growth rates. '282 patent claim 20. Starting with the machine-or-transformation test, we conclude that the claim includes transformative steps, an "important clue" that it is drawn to a patent-eligible process. *Bilski,* 130 S. Ct. at 3227. Specifically, the claim recites a method that comprises the steps of (1) "growing" host cells transformed with an altered *BRCA1* gene in the presence or absence of a potential cancer therapeutic, (2) "determining" the growth rate of the host cells with or without the potential therapeutic, and (3) "comparing" the growth rate of the host cells. The claim thus includes more than the abstract mental step of looking at two numbers and "comparing" two host cells' growth rates. The claim includes the steps of "growing" transformed cells in the presence or absence of a potential cancer therapeutic, an inherently transformative step involving the manipulation of the cells and their growth medium. The claim also includes the step of "determining" the cells' growth rates, a step that also necessarily involves physical manipulation of the cells.

Moreover, the claim is tied to measuring a therapeutic effect on the cells solely by changes in the cells' growth rate. The claim thus presents "functional and palpable applications" in the field of biotechnology. *Id.* at 868; *see also Prometheus,* 628 F.3d at 1355 ("[T]he claims do not preempt all uses of the natural correlations; they utilize them in a series of specific steps."). Accordingly, we hold that claim 20 of the '282 patent claims patentable subject matter under § 101.

CONCLUSION

For the foregoing reasons, we affirm the district court's decision to exercise declaratory judgment jurisdiction over this case, we reverse the district court's grant of summary judgment with regard to Myriad's composition claims to isolated DNAs, we affirm the district court's grant of summary judgment with regard to Myriad's method claims to comparing or analyzing gene sequences, and we reverse the district court's grant of summary judgment with regard to Myriad's method claim to screening potential <u>cancer</u> therapeutics via changes in cell growth rates. AFFIRMED IN PART and REVERSED IN PART.

[Judge Moore joined Judge Lourie's opinion as to the patentability of isolated cDNA sequences, but concurred only in the judgment regarding the isolated DNA sequences. Because isolated cDNA (or complementary DNA) sequences are produced in the laboratory with introns removed and a sequence of nucleotides that are not exactly the same as the sequence of nucleotides in the cell DNA from which they are transcribed, Judge Moore concluded that the cDNA sequences present an easier case of patentable subject matter. However, Judge Moore concluded that DNA gene sequences that are isolated from the human body present a more difficult question. Judge Moore concluded: (1) "the claimed isolated DNA molecules, which are truncations (with different ends) of the naturally occurring DNA found as part of the chromosome in nature, are not naturally produced without the intervention of man"; and (2) "these differences impart a new utility [use in genetic testing] which makes the molecules markedly different from nature." Under Judge Moore's analysis, utility becomes a key question in deciding patentable subject matter of an isolated DNA sequence. *Ed.*]

[Judge Bryson's dissent concluded that an isolated DNA sequence is a product of nature. "The only material change to those genes from their natural state is the change that is necessarily incidental to the extraction of the genes from the environment in which they are found in nature.... In this respect, the genes are analogous to the 'new mineral discovered in the earth,' or the 'new plant found in the wild' that the Supreme Court referred to in *Chakrabarty*." *Ed.*]

NOTES AND QUESTIONS

1. Which patent claims of Myriad did the Federal Circuit find to be directed to patentable subject matter? Which claims were unpatentable? Do you think the decision will have a practical effect on medical diagnosis of breast cancer based on detection of mutations to the BRCA genes? After the decision, can third parties use the BRCA genetic testing without Myriad's permission if the testing requires isolation of the BRCA1 and BRCA2 genes?

2. *Isolated DNA sequences.* Judges Lourie, Moore, and Bryson disagreed on how to analyze the patentability of isolated DNA sequences that have the same nucleotide sequences as the part of the DNA from which they have been derived from the human body. Which judge's approach is the most persuasive?

3. *Change in U.S. government position.* One of the most remarkable aspects of the case was the amicus brief filed on appeal by the Department of Justice on behalf of the United States. Disagreeing with a long-standing position of the U.S. Patent Office, the Department of Justice (DOJ) agreed that isolated DNA sequences—that were unaltered from their naturally occurring state—were products of nature and, therefore, not patentable subject matter. By contrast, DOJ agreed that a cDNA (complementary DNA) sequence, which is produced in the lab without introns and with a different nucleotide sequence than that exists in the body, is patentable subject matter. What do you make of DOJ's disagreement with the PTO and the possibility that the PTO and Federal Circuit may have been applying the wrong standard for nearly 30 years? Given the position of the United States, the U.S. Supreme Court may eventually hear the case.

4. *European approach.* In the EU, Myriad's patents for the method of diagnosing breast cancer by the presence of mutations in the BCRA–1 gene were revoked during opposition proceedings, although two patents on the isolated BCRA–1 gene were allowed. *See* Anja von der Ropp & Tony Taubman, *Bioethics and Patent Law: The Case of Myriad,* WIPO Mag., at 8 (Aug. 2006). Is there a practical difference between allowing a patent on isolated genes and disallowing a patent on the method used with the isolated genes to diagnose patients? Should the WTO consider adopting a uniform approach to this issue, or is it too controversial?

5. *Bibliographic note.* Donna M. Gitter, *International Conflicts Over Patenting Human DNA Sequences in the United States and the European Union: An Argument for Compulsory Licensing and a Fair–Use Exception,* 76 N.Y.U. L. Rev. 1623 (2001).

MONSANTO TECHNOLOGY LLC v. CEFETRA BV.

Court of Justice of the European Union (Grand Chamber).
[2010] ERC I–06761, C–428/08 (July 6, 2010).

Judgment

  This reference for a preliminary ruling concerns the interpretation of Article 9 of Directive 98/44/EC of the European Parliament and of the Council of 6 July 1998 on the legal protection of biotechnological inventions (OJ 1998 L 213, p. 13) ('the Directive').

Legal context

European Union law

  Article 1 of the Directive [on Biotechnological Inventions] provides that Member States are to protect biotechnological inventions under national patent law and that, if necessary, they are to adjust the latter to take account of the provisions of that directive. It adds that the Directive is to be without prejudice to the obligations of the Member States pursuant, inter alia, to the TRIPS Agreement.* * *

The dispute in the main proceedings and the questions referred for a preliminary ruling

Monsanto is the holder of European patent EP 0 546 090 granted on 19 June 1996 relating to 'Glyphosate tolerant 5–enolpyruvylshikimate–3–phosphate synthases' ('the European patent'). The European patent is valid, inter alia, in the Netherlands.

Glyphosate is a non-selective herbicide. In a plant, it works by inhibiting the Class I enzyme 5–enol–pyruvylshikimate–3–phosphate synthase (also called 'EPSPS'), which plays an important role in the growth of the plant. The effect of glyphosate is that the plant dies.

The European patent describes a class of EPSPS enzymes which are not sensitive to glyphosate. Plants containing such enzymes survive the use of glyphosate, whilst weeds are destroyed. The genes encoding these Class II enzymes have been isolated from three different bacteria. Monsanto has inserted those genes into the DNA of a soy plant it has called RR (Roundup Ready) soybean plant. As a result, the RR soybean plant produces a Class II EPSPS enzyme called CP4–EPSPS, which is glyphosate-resistant. It thus becomes resistant to the herbicide 'Roundup'.

The RR soybean is cultivated on a large scale in Argentina, where there is no patent protection for the Monsanto invention. Cefetra and Toepfer trade in soy meal. Three cargoes of soy meal from Argentina arrived in the port of Amsterdam on 16 June 2005, 21 March and 11 May 2006. Vopak made a customs declaration for one of the cargoes. The three consignments were detained by the customs authorities pursuant to Council Regulation (EC) No 1383/2003 of 22 July 2003 concerning customs action against goods suspected of infringing certain intellectual property rights and the measures to be taken against goods found to have infringed such rights (OJ 2003 L 196, p. 7). They were released after Monsanto had taken samples. Monsanto tested the samples to determine whether they originated from RR soybeans.

Following the tests, which revealed the presence of CP4–EPSPS in the soy meal and the DNA sequence encoding it, Monsanto applied for injunctions against Cefetra, Vopak and Toepfler before the Rechtbank's–Gravenhage, on the basis of Article 16 of Regulation No 1383/2003, and for a prohibition of infringement of the European patent in all countries in which the patent is valid. The Argentine State intervened in support of the forms of order sought by Cefetra.

The Rechtbank's–Gravenhage considers that Monsanto has established the presence, in one of the disputed cargoes, of the DNA sequence protected by its European patent. It is nevertheless unsure as to whether that presence alone is sufficient to constitute infringement of Monsanto's European patent when the soy meal is marketed in the Community. The Rechtbank's–Gravenhage observes that Article 53a(3) of the 1995 Law, like Article 9 of the Directive, places all material in which the DNA is incorporated within the scope of the exclusive right of the proprietor of the patent if the genetic information is found in that material and performs its function therein. It concludes that the DNA cannot perform its function in soy meal, which is dead material.

The questions referred for a preliminary ruling

The first question

By its first question, the national court asks, essentially, whether Article 9 of the Directive is to be interpreted as conferring patent right protection in circumstances such as those of the case in the main proceedings, in which the patented product is contained in the soy meal, where it does not perform the function for which it was patented, but did perform that function previously in the soy plant, of which the meal is a processed product, or would possibly again be able to perform its function after it has been extracted from the soy meal and inserted into the cell of a living organism.

In that regard, it must be noted that Article 9 of the Directive makes the protection for which it provides subject to the condition that the genetic information contained in the patented product or constituting that product 'performs' its function in the 'material . . . in which' that information is contained. The usual meaning of the present tense used by the Community legislature and of the phrase 'material . . . in which' implies that the function is being performed at the present time and in the actual material in which the DNA sequence containing the genetic information is found.

In the case of genetic information such as that at issue in the main proceedings, the function of the invention is performed when the genetic information protects the biological material in which it is incorporated against the effect, or the foreseeable possibility of the effect, of a product which can cause that material to die.

The use of a herbicide on soy meal is not, however, foreseeable, or even normally conceivable. Moreover, even if it was used in that way, a patented product intended to protect the life of biological material containing it could not perform its function, since the genetic information can be found only in a residual state in the soy meal, which is a dead material obtained after the soy has undergone several treatment processes. It follows from the foregoing that the protection provided for in Article 9 of the Directive is not available when the genetic information has ceased to perform the function it performed in the initial material from which the material in question is derived.

It also follows that that protection cannot be relied on in relation to the material in question on the sole ground that the DNA sequence containing the genetic information could be extracted from it and perform its function in a cell of a living organism into which it has been transferred. In such a scenario, the function would be performed in a material which is both different and biological. It could therefore give rise to a right to protection only in relation to that material.

Monsanto argues, however, that its principal claim is for protection of its patented DNA sequence as such. It explains that the DNA sequence at issue in the case in the main proceedings is protected by the applicable national patent law, in accordance with Article 1(1) of the Directive. Article 9 of the Directive relates solely to an extension of such protection to other material in which the patented product is incorporated. In the case in the main proceedings, Monsanto is not, therefore, seeking to obtain the protection provided for by Article 9 of the Directive for the soy meal in which the patented DNA sequence is incorporated. This case concerns the protection of the DNA sequence as such, which is not linked to the performance of a specific function. Such protection is indeed absolute under the applicable national law, to which Article 1(1) of the Directive refers.

Such an analysis cannot be accepted. In that regard, it should be borne in mind that recital 23 in the preamble to the Directive states that 'a mere DNA sequence without indication of a function does not contain any technical information and is therefore not a patentable invention'. Moreover, the import of recitals 23 and 24 in the preamble to, and Article 5(3) of, the Directive is that a DNA sequence does not enjoy any protection under patent law when the function performed by that sequence is not specified.

Since the Directive thus makes the patentability of a DNA sequence subject to indication of the function it performs, it must be regarded as not according any protection to a patented DNA sequence which is not able to perform the specific function for which it was patented.

That interpretation is supported by the wording of Article 9 of the Directive, which makes the protection it provides for subject to the condition that the patented DNA sequence performs its function in the material in which it is incorporated.

An interpretation to the effect that, under the Directive, a patented DNA sequence could enjoy absolute protection as such, irrespective of whether or not the sequence was performing its function, would deprive that provision of its effectiveness. Protection accorded formally to the DNA sequence as such would necessarily in fact extend to the material of which it formed a part, as long as that situation continued. * * *

[A] DNA sequence such as that at issue in the main proceedings is not able to perform its function when it is incorporated in a dead material such as soy meal. Such a sequence does not, therefore, enjoy patent right protection, since neither Article 9 of the Directive nor any other provision thereof accords protection to a patented DNA sequence which is not able to perform its function.

Accordingly, the answer to the first question is that Article 9 of the Directive must be interpreted as not conferring patent right protection in circumstances such as those of the case in the main proceedings, in which the patented product is contained in the soy meal, where it does not perform the function for which it was patented, but did perform that function previously in the soy plant, of which the meal is a processed product, or would possibly again be able to perform that function after it had been extracted from the soy meal and inserted into the cell of a living organism. [The CJEU's ruling on the second and third questions is omitted.]

NOTES AND QUESTIONS

1. Did the CJEU's ruling go to the issue of patentable subject matter or the infringement of patent rights? Does the utility or function of an invention bear on patentable subject matter under the Biotech Directive?

2. According to the CJEU, why must a patented gene sequence be able to perform the specific function for which it was patented at the moment of infringement? Would the outcome be different if the shipment in the EU contained live soybean plants with the DNA sequence patented in Europe by Monsanto?

3. *Argentina.* Monsanto did not have patents on its invention in Argentina, where the genetically engineered Roundup Ready soybean plant was freely grown in great quantities. Argentina is one of the largest exporters of soybeans. Can the outcome in this case be explained as an application of the principle of territoriality?

4. *Roundup Ready 2.* Monsanto developed a second version of Roundup Ready soy that was more resistant to herbicides and pesticides. Monsanto patented this Roundup Ready 2 Yield soy in Argentina and elsewhere. But, wary of possible infringement in Argentina, where Roundup Ready 1 production was rampant, Monsanto preemptively sought licensing agreements from many Argentine farmers to pay for their use of Monsanto's second variety of soy. *See* Hugh Bronstein, *Monsanto Signs Royalty Deals with Argentine Farmers*, Reuters, Jun. 7, 2011. Is Monsanto's tactic a good business strategy?

b.   Special Discussion: Patentability of Business Methods

PROBLEM 3–8

You are a member of a WTO panel that is being asked to review the law of Country B, which categorically excludes both (i) business methods and (ii) computer programs from patentability. Are these exclusions in violation of TRIPS Article 27?

* * *

TRIPS Article 27 sets forth a broad scope of patentable subject matter: "patents shall be available for any inventions, whether products or processes, in all fields of technology, provided that they are new, involve an inventive step and are capable of industrial application."[5] Patents apply to *process* inventions, just as they do to product inventions. And patents shall be available without discrimination to the field of technology.

So where does this leave methods for doing business? Hard to say: TRIPS does not specifically address the issue, and countries have divided over

---

5. For the purposes of this Article, the terms "inventive step" and "capable of industrial application" may be deemed by a Member to be synonymous with the terms "non-obvious" and "useful" respectively.

whether methods for doing business should be considered patentable processes.

Just as in the case with genetically engineered organisms, the U.S. has been at the forefront of recognizing patents for business methods. For many years, U.S. case law had long held that business methods were not patentable subject matter. In 1998, however, the Federal Circuit in *State Street Bank & Trust Co. v. Signature Financial Group, Inc.*, 149 F.3d 1368 (Fed. Cir. 1998), held that business methods are patentable and rejected the prior bar against business methods that courts had recognized. The Federal Circuit distinguished business methods from pure abstract ideas, which are not patentable. *See, e.g., Diamond v. Diehr*, 450 U.S. 175, 185 (1981) ("laws of nature, natural phenomena, and abstract ideas" are unpatentable). But, when applied in a practical way to produce "a useful, concrete and tangible thing," an abstract idea or mathematical algorithm can be a part of method that *is* patentable under U.S. law. *State Street Bank*, 149 F.3d at 1373. The method must still satisfy the other patent requirements, such as utility, novelty, and nonobviousness (all of which are discussed later in this chapter).

State Street Bank resulted in a storm of controversy in the U.S. and elsewhere. Within two years of the decision, the number of business method patents the U.S. Patent Office granted more than doubled, to 1,006 patents. *See* John R. Allison & Emerson H. Tiller, *The Business Method Patent Myth*, 18 BERKELEY TECH. L.J. 987, 991 n.10 (2003). Two of the more celebrated patents included a patent for Amazon.com's "one-click" shopping and Priceline.com's patent for an online reverse auction or Dutch auction. *Id.* at 993. In response to concerns raised over business method patents, Congress enacted the First Inventor Defense Act, which creates a statutory defense to a patent infringement action for a business method if the defendant, "acting in good faith, actually reduced the subject matter to practice at least 1 year before the effective filing date of such patent, and commercially used the subject matter before the effective date of such patent." 35 U.S.C. § 273(b)(1) (2006). The provision creates a right akin to the general right for "prior users" recognized by many countries, which allows a prior inventor to keep on utilizing his or her invention even though someone else was the first to file a patent for the invention. In 2000, the U.S. Patent Office announced that it would undertake internal reforms to help ensure proper scrutiny of business method patents, including the hiring and training of examiners qualified in the relevant field and the conducting of a more searching prior art review. Allison & Tiller, *supra*, at 995. (In 2011, the U.S. expanded the exception for prior users of business methods in § 273 of the Patent Code to provide a general "prior user" defense for all inventions used in manufacturing or other commercial process. AIA, § 5. The defense becomes effective to any patent issued on September 16, 2011 or later. *Id.* § 5(c).)

In 2008, the Federal Circuit revisited its *State Street Bank* decision and the wisdom of its permissive approach to business method patents. *See In re Bilski*, 545 F.3d 943, 959–60 (Fed. Cir. 2008) (en banc). In a reversal, the Federal Circuit rejected its prior "useful, concrete, and tangible result" test of *State Street Bank* and held that the proper test was the "machine-or-transformation test": "(1) it is tied to a particular machine or apparatus, or (2) it transforms a particular article into a different state or thing." *Id.* at

954–55. The Federal Circuit attributed the test to Supreme Court precedent and appeared to create a much more difficult burden for business methods to qualify for a patent. However, the Supreme Court reviewed the Federal Circuit's decision and disagreed.

BILSKI v. KAPPOS

Supreme Court of the United States.
___ U.S. ___, 130 S. Ct. 3218 (2010).

JUSTICE KENNEDY delivered the opinion of the Court, except as to Parts II–B–2 and II–C–2.

The question in this case turns on whether a patent can be issued for a claimed invention designed for the business world. The patent application claims a procedure for instructing buyers and sellers how to protect against the risk of price fluctuations in a discrete section of the economy. Three arguments are advanced for the proposition that the claimed invention is outside the scope of patent law: (1) it is not tied to a machine and does not transform an article; (2) it involves a method of conducting business; and (3) it is merely an abstract idea. The Court of Appeals ruled that the first mentioned of these, the so-called machine-or-transformation test, was the sole test to be used for determining the patentability of a "process" under the Patent Act, 35 U.S.C. § 101.

I

Petitioners' application seeks patent protection for a claimed invention that explains how buyers and sellers of commodities in the energy market can protect, or hedge, against the risk of price changes. The key claims are claims 1 and 4. Claim 1 describes a series of steps instructing how to hedge risk. Claim 4 puts the concept articulated in claim 1 into a simple mathematical formula. Claim 1 consists of the following steps:

> "(a) initiating a series of transactions between said commodity provider and consumers of said commodity wherein said consumers purchase said commodity at a fixed rate based upon historical averages, said fixed rate corresponding to a risk position of said consumers;

> "(b) identifying market participants for said commodity having a counter-risk position to said consumers; and

> "(c) initiating a series of transactions between said commodity provider and said market participants at a second fixed rate such that said series of market participant transactions balances the risk position of said series of consumer transactions." App. 19–20.

The remaining claims explain how claims 1 and 4 can be applied to allow energy suppliers and consumers to minimize the risks resulting from fluctuations in market demand for energy.

II

A

Section 101 [of the Patent Act] specifies four independent categories of inventions or discoveries that are eligible for protection: processes, machines, manufactures, and compositions of matter. "In choosing such expansive terms . . . modified by the comprehensive 'any,' Congress plainly contemplated that the patent laws would be given wide scope." *Diamond v. Chakrabarty*, 447 U.S. 303, 308 (1980). Congress took this permissive approach to patent eligibility to ensure that " 'ingenuity should receive a liberal encouragement.' " *Id.*, at 308–309 (quoting 5 Writings of Thomas Jefferson 75–76 (H. Washington ed. 1871)).

The Court's precedents provide three specific exceptions to § 101's broad patent-eligibility principles: "laws of nature, physical phenomena, and abstract ideas." *Chakrabarty, supra,* at 309. While these exceptions are not required by the statutory text, they are consistent with the notion that a patentable process must be "new and useful." And, in any case, these exceptions have defined the reach of the statute as a matter of statutory *stare decisis* going back 150 years. The concepts covered by these exceptions are "part of the storehouse of knowledge of all men . . . free to all men and reserved exclusively to none." *Funk Brothers Seed Co. v. Kalo Inoculant Co.*, 333 U.S. 127, 130 (1948).

The § 101 patent-eligibility inquiry is only a threshold test. Even if an invention qualifies as a process, machine, manufacture, or composition of matter, in order to receive the Patent Act's protection the claimed invention must also satisfy "the conditions and requirements of this title." § 101. Those requirements include that the invention be novel, see § 102, nonobvious, see § 103, and fully and particularly described, see § 112.

B

1

Under the Court of Appeals' formulation, an invention is a "process" only if: "(1) it is tied to a particular machine or apparatus, or (2) it transforms a particular article into a different state or thing." This Court has "more than once cautioned that courts 'should not read into the patent laws limitations and conditions which the legislature has not expressed.' " *Diamond v. Diehr*, 450 U.S. 175, 182 (1981) (quoting *Chakrabarty, supra,* at 308; some internal quotation marks omitted).

Adopting the machine-or-transformation test as the sole test for what constitutes a "process" (as opposed to just an important and useful clue) violates these statutory interpretation principles. Section 100(b) provides that "[t]he term 'process' means process, art or method, and includes a new use of a known process, machine, manufacture, composition of matter, or material." The Court is unaware of any " 'ordinary, contemporary, common meaning,' " *Diehr, supra,* at 182, of the definitional terms "process, art or method" that would require these terms to be tied to a machine or to transform an article.

The Court of Appeals incorrectly concluded that this Court has endorsed the machine-or-transformation test as the exclusive test. It is true that *Cochrane v. Deener,* 94 U.S. 780, 788 (1877), explained that a "process" is "an act, or a series of acts, performed upon the subject-matter to be transformed and reduced to a different state or thing." More recent cases, however, have rejected the broad implications of this dictum; and, in all events, later authority shows that it was not intended to be an exhaustive or exclusive test. This Court's precedents establish that the machine-or-transformation test is a useful and important clue, an investigative tool, for determining whether some claimed inventions are processes under § 101. The machine-or-transformation test is not the sole test for deciding whether an invention is a patent-eligible "process."

C

1

Section 101 similarly precludes the broad contention that the term "process" categorically excludes business methods. The term "method," which is within § 100(b)'s definition of "process," at least as a textual matter and before consulting other limitations in the Patent Act and this Court's precedents, may include at least some methods of doing business. *See, e.g.,* Webster's New International Dictionary 1548 (2d ed. 1954) (defining "method" as "[a]n orderly procedure or process . . . regular way or manner of doing anything; hence, a set form of procedure adopted in investigation or instruction"). The Court is unaware of any argument that the " 'ordinary, contemporary, common meaning,' " *Diehr, supra,* at 182, of "method" excludes business methods. Nor is it clear how far a prohibition on business method patents would reach, and whether it would exclude technologies for conducting a business more efficiently.

The argument that business methods are categorically outside of § 101's scope is further undermined by the fact that federal law explicitly contemplates the existence of at least some business method patents. Under 35 U.S.C. § 273(b)(1), if a patent-holder claims infringement based on "a method in [a] patent," the alleged infringer can assert a defense of prior use. For purposes of this defense alone, "method" is defined as "a method of doing or conducting business." § 273(a)(3). In other words, by allowing this defense the statute itself acknowledges that there may be business method patents. Section 273's definition of "method," to be sure, cannot change the meaning of a prior-enacted statute. But what § 273 does is clarify the understanding that a business method is simply one kind of "method" that is, at least in some circumstances, eligible for patenting under § 101. A conclusion that business methods are not patentable in any circumstances would render § 273 meaningless. This would violate the canon against interpreting any statutory provision in a manner that would render another provision superfluous.

III.

In light of the[] Court's precedents, it is clear that petitioners' application is not a patentable "process." Claims 1 and 4 in petitioners' application explain the basic concept of hedging, or protecting against risk: "Hedging is a fundamental economic practice long prevalent in our system of commerce and taught in any introductory finance class." 545 F.3d, at 1013 (Rader, J., dissenting). The concept of hedging, described in claim 1 and reduced to a mathematical formula in claim 4, is an unpatentable abstract idea, just like the algorithms at issue in *Benson* and *Flook*. Allowing petitioners to patent risk hedging would pre-empt use of this approach in all fields, and would effectively grant a monopoly over an abstract idea.

Petitioners' remaining claims are broad examples of how hedging can be used in commodities and energy markets. *Flook* established that limiting an abstract idea to one field of use or adding token postsolution components did not make the concept patentable. That is exactly what the remaining claims in petitioners' application do. These claims attempt to patent the use of the abstract idea of hedging risk in the energy market and then instruct the use of well-known random analysis techniques to help establish some of the inputs into the equation. Indeed, these claims add even less to the underlying abstract principle than the invention in *Flook* did, for the *Flook* invention was at least directed to the narrower domain of signaling dangers in operating a catalytic converter.

Today, the Court once again declines to impose limitations on the Patent Act that are inconsistent with the Act's text. The patent application here can be rejected under our precedents on the unpatentability of abstract ideas. The Court, therefore, need not define further what constitutes a patentable "process," beyond pointing to the definition of that term provided in § 100(b) and looking to the guideposts in *Benson, Flook,* and *Diehr*.

And nothing in today's opinion should be read as endorsing interpretations of § 101 that the Court of Appeals for the Federal Circuit has used in the past. *See, e.g., State Street,* 149 F.3d, at 1373; *AT & T Corp.,* 172 F.3d, at 1357. It may be that the Court of Appeals thought it needed to make the machine-or-transformation test exclusive precisely because its case law had not adequately identified less extreme means of restricting business method patents, including (but not limited to) application of our opinions in *Benson, Flook,* and *Diehr*. In disapproving an exclusive machine-or-transformation test, we by no means foreclose the Federal Circuit's development of other limiting criteria that further the purposes of the Patent Act and are not inconsistent with its text. The judgment of the Court of Appeals is affirmed.

Nᴏᴛᴇs ᴀɴᴅ Qᴜᴇsᴛɪᴏɴs

1. Identify the test(s) the U.S. Supreme Court stated should be applied to determine whether a business method is patentable subject matter. Is it different from the Federal Circuit's approach?

2. *Categorical exclusion of business methods?* Four justices concurred in the judgment. Justice Stevens wrote the lengthy concurring opinion, which argued that "a claim that merely describes a method of doing business does not qualify as a 'process' under § 101." Justice Stevens recounted the historical development of patents in England and early United States, which showed, he argued, a long-standing recognition by courts and commentators that "[b]usiness methods are not patentable arts." Is this approach better for innovation?

* * *

Europe's Approach. While Article 52 of the European Patent Convention states that methods of "doing business" are not patentable "as such," there is some allowance, in practice, of patents for business methods with a "technical character." Countries in the Europe refer to the physical implementation of the business method as its "technical feature" or "technical character," and the pure abstract concept as the "non-technical" feature of the method. The term "technical" also connotes artificiality as opposed to something found in nature. Japan follows a similar approach, although in practice it appears to be more receptive to business method patents than Europe. To complicate matters further, the current law may be far from settled, since the debate over patenting business methods still wages on in most countries, including the U.S. and European countries. The next case explores Europe's approach.

European Patent Convention

Article 52

Patentable inventions

(1) European patents shall be granted for any inventions which are susceptible of industrial application, which are new and which involve an inventive step.

(2) The following in particular shall not be regarded as inventions within the meaning of paragraph 1:

    (a) discoveries, scientific theories and mathematical methods;

    (b) aesthetic creations;

    (c) schemes, rules and methods for performing mental acts, playing games or doing business, and programs for computers;

    (d) presentations of information.

(3) The provisions of paragraph 2 shall exclude patentability of the subject-matter or activities referred to in that provision only to the extent to which a European patent application or European patent relates to such subject-matter or activities as such.

(4) Methods for treatment of the human or animal body by surgery or therapy and diagnostic methods practised on the human or animal body shall not be regarded as inventions which are susceptible of industrial application within the meaning of paragraph 1. This provision shall not apply to products, in particular substances or compositions, for use in any of these methods.

HITACHI, LTD.

Technical Board of Appeal, European Patent Office.
T 0258/03–3.5.1 (April 21, 2004).

Summary of Facts and Submissions

The examining division decided that the main and first auxiliary requests before it were not allowable under Articles 123(2) and 83 EPC. Claim 1 of the second auxiliary request, found satisfactory in these respects, was refused on the ground that its subject-matter, an auction method, was a business method as such and therefore not regarded as an invention, pursuant to Article 52(2) and (3) EPC. Also the corresponding apparatus of claim 2 was found to be excluded from patentability since the claim defined subject-matter with a scope of protection equivalent to that of the method claim, and it would be formalistic to make a distinction in this respect between claims of different categories. The examining division added that even if the claimed subject-matter were an invention within the meaning of Article 52(1) EPC, it did not involve an inventive step as required by Article 56 EPC.

Reasons for the Decision

The invention according to claim 1 is an "automatic auction method executive in a server computer." In claim 3 a "computerized auction apparatus" comprising a server computer is defined, and in claim 4 a computer program for carrying out an auction. The features of the claims are closely related and in substance based on the same method steps.

The method can be described as follows. The auction starts with preliminary steps of data exchange between the client computers and the server computer in order to collect bids from the participants. Each bid comprises two prices, a "desired price" and a "maximum price in competitive state." After this initial phase the auction is automatic and does not require that the bidders follow the auction on-line. An auction price is set and successively lowered (which is typical for so-called Dutch auctions) until it reaches the level of the highest bid or bids as determined by the "desired price." In case of several identical bids the price is increased until only the bidder having offered the highest "maximum price" is left. He is declared successful. Claim 1 does not specify the exact price paid, nor the rules and conditions for determining the amounts of the product to be allotted.

Non-inventions pursuant to Article 52(2) EPC: The apparatus of claim 3

The idea behind the so-called contribution approach applied by earlier jurisprudence of the boards of appeal was that the EPC only permitted patenting *"in those cases in which the invention involves some contribution to the art in a field not excluded from patentability."* In other words, for assessing the first requirement, i.e., the presence of an invention within the meaning of Article 52(1) EPC, a criterion established which relied on meeting further requirements mentioned in that article, in particular novelty and/or inventive step. Thus, some prior art was taken into account when determining whether subject-matter was excluded under Article 52(2) and (3) EPC:

> *"In the above considerations concerning the question whether the claimed invention makes a technical contribution to the art, or involves technical considerations for its implementation which may be regarded as resulting in a technical contribution to the art, any specific prior art (other than general computer art, see point 3.4), for instance D1, has not been taken into account. If this is done, however, nothing in the above considerations will effectively be changed."* (T 769/92, OJ EPO 1995, 525, point 3.8).

However, in more recent decisions of the boards any comparison with the prior art was found to be inappropriate for examining the presence of an invention:

> *"Determining the technical contribution an invention achieves with respect to the prior art is therefore more appropriate for the purpose of examining novelty and inventive step than for deciding on possible exclusion under Article 52(2) and (3)."* (T 1173/97, OJ EPO 1999, 609, point 8).

This view is shared by the Board in its present composition.

Furthermore, in accordance with Article 52(3) EPC, the subject-matter mentioned in paragraph 2 of the same article is only excluded from patentability *as such*. It has long been recognized that, due to this stipulation, a mix of technical and non-technical features may be patentable. Therefore, taking into account both that a mix of technical and non-technical features may be regarded as an invention within the meaning of Article 52(1) EPC and that prior art should not be considered when deciding whether claimed subject-matter is such an invention, a compelling reason for not refusing under Article 52(2) EPC subject-matter consisting of technical and non-technical features is simply that the technical features may in themselves turn out to fulfill all requirements of Article 52(1).

Moreover, it is often difficult to separate a claim into technical and non-technical features, and an invention may have technical aspects which are hidden in a largely non-technical context (cf. point 5.8 below). Such technical aspects may be easier to identify within the framework of the examination as to inventive step, which, in accordance with the jurisprudence of the boards of appeal, is concerned with the technical aspects of an invention (cf. point 5.3 below). Thus, in addition to the restrictive wording of Article 52(3) EPC limiting the applicability of Article 52(2) EPC, there may be practical reasons for generally regarding mixes of technical and non-technical features as inventions in the meaning of Article 52(1) EPC.

For these reasons the Board holds that, contrary to the examining division's assessment, the apparatus of claim 3 is an invention within the meaning of Article 52(1) EPC since it comprises clearly technical features such as a "server computer," "client computers" and a "network."*

Non-inventions pursuant to Article 52(2) EPC: The method of claim 1

The reasoning above (point 3.5) is independent of the category of the claim. Thus, in the present case, also the method of claim 1 is not excluded from patentability under Article 52(2) EPC.

This conclusion is not in agreement with headnote II of decision T 931/95 which states: "A feature of a method which concerns the use of technical means for a purely non-technical purpose and/or for processing purely non-technical information does not necessarily confer a technical character to such a method."

However, in order to be consistent with the finding that the so-called "contribution approach," which involves assessing different patentability requirements such as novelty or inventive step, is inappropriate for judging whether claimed subject-matter is an invention within the meaning of Article 52(1) EPC, there should be no need to further qualify the relevance of technical aspects of a method claim in order to determine the technical character of the method. In fact, it appears to the Board that an assessment of the technical character of a method based on the degree of banality of the technical features of the claim would involve remnants of the contribution approach by implying an evaluation in light of the available prior art or common general knowledge.

From a practical point of view, this inconsistency becomes fully apparent when considering the question of whether technical character is conferred to a method using technical means for a purely non-technical purpose. In this case, following the approach taken in T 931/95, the mere presence of such means would not necessarily be sufficient to lend the method technical character. In the Board's opinion, any practical answer to this question would have to rely on some weighting of the importance of the features to determine the "core" of the invention, necessarily including considerations on their technical relevance, in particular possible novel or inventive contributions, with respect to the prior art. The Board would like to add that such weighting has already been rejected in early case law of the boards of appeal.

Finally, the Board in its present composition is not convinced that the wording of Article 52(2)(c) EPC, according to which "schemes, rules and methods for performing mental acts, playing games or doing business" shall not be regarded as inventions within the meaning of Article 52(1) EPC, imposes a different treatment of claims directed to activities and claims directed to entities for carrying out these activities. What matters

---

* Claim 3 is for a "computerized auction apparatus for performing an automatic auction via a network, among a plurality of bidders, the bidders using a corresponding plurality of client computers," the apparatus comprising means for performing the steps set out in claim 1.

having regard to the concept of "invention" within the meaning of Article 52(1) EPC is the presence of technical character which may be implied by the physical features of an entity or the nature of an activity, or may be conferred to a non-technical activity by the use of technical means. In particular, the Board holds that the latter cannot be considered to be a non-invention "as such" within the meaning of Article 52(2) and (3) EPC. Hence, in the Board's view, activities falling within the notion of a non-invention "as such" would typically represent purely abstract concepts devoid of any technical implications.

The Board is aware that its comparatively broad interpretation of the term "invention" in Article 52(1) EPC will include activities which are so familiar that their technical character tends to be overlooked, such as the act of writing using pen and paper. Needless to say, however, this does not imply that all methods involving the use of technical means are patentable. They still have to be new, represent a non-obvious technical solution to a technical problem, and be susceptible of industrial application.

It is therefore concluded that, in general, a method involving technical means is an invention within the meaning of Article 52(1) EPC.

[After analyzing (above) whether the business method was patentable subject matter, the Board of Appeal went on to evaluate whether the claimed invention possessed an *inventive step* (or was instead obvious) "by taking into account of only those features which contribute to a technical character." *Ed.*] [T]he Board is convinced that this way of ranking bids is a routine programming measure well within the reach of the skilled person. Thus, this feature, even if possibly constituting a technical solution to a problem would have been obvious to the person skilled in the art of data processing. It follows that the automatic auction method according to claim 1 does not involve an inventive step (Article 56 EPC).

NOTES AND QUESTIONS

1. Which approach to the patentability of business methods is better—the U.S. or EU?

2. According to the Board of Appeal of the European Patent Office, are patents for business methods ever allowed under Article 52 of the European Patent Convention? Can you explain what it means to exclude from patentability a non-invention "as such"? If patents for business methods are allowed, under what circumstances are they allowed?

3. What makes a method of "technical character" and how does the concept relate, if at all, to patentability and/or inventive step? Does the European Patent Office examine the prior art in determining the putative "technical character" of an invention for analysis of patentable subject matter?

4. Under the Board's analysis, would the "act of writing using pen and paper" be patentable subject matter?

5. *"Any hardware" and computer-implemented methods.* Under the EPO's approach, does incorporating the use of computers in implementing a

business method automatically give the method a technical feature to qualify it as a patentable subject matter? Subsequent decisions applying *Hitachi* suggest yes. *See Microsoft/Clipboard Formats I*, [2006] E.P.O.R. 414, 417; *Duns Licensing*, [2008] O.J.E.P.O. 46, 76. Commentators have characterized this approach as "any hardware": "[a] business method passes the Article 52 test as long as it is attached to 'any hardware.'" Susan J. Marsnik & Robert E. Thomas, *Drawing a Line in the Patent Subject–Matter Sands: Does Europe Provide a Solution to the Software and Business Method Patent Problem?*, 34 B.C. Int'l & Comp. L. Rev. 227, 290 (2011). Although this test seems easy to satisfy, remember that the test only bears on patentable subject matter. The EPO can still deny patent applications on other grounds, such as inventive step.

6. *Rejection of European Directive on Computer Implemented Inventions.* Because the decisions of the EPO are not binding on national patent offices, EU countries can take widely different approaches to the issue. The proposed Directive of the European Parliament and of the Council on the Patentability of Computer–Implemented Inventions was intended to provide legal certainty to the patentability (or not) of computer programs and business methods in EU countries by formally adopting the view of the European Patent Office regarding these issues. In the end, the proposed Directive proved to be too controversial. On July 6, 2005, the European Parliament rejected the proposed Directive by an overwhelming margin of 648 to 14. The rejection of the Directive leaves the issue for individual EU countries to decide under their national laws as before—a situation that allows for conflicting approaches.

7. *Harmonization?* Australia, Canada, China, Japan, the EPO, the UK, and the U.S. have allowed business method patents, but under different tests and levels of acceptance. India, whose patent law is still developing, has been skeptical of business method patents. *See* Eugene F. Derenyi et al., *Protection of Business Methods Patents Outside the United States*, 1 No. 5 Landslide 18 (2009). At one point, the U.S. delegation to the WTO sought to place business methods on the agenda for greater harmonization. Do you agree on the need for harmonization?

c. Special Discussion: Patentability of Computer Software and Computer–Implemented Methods

Problem 3–9

Facebook, co-founded in 2004 by Mark Zuckerberg, is the world's most popular social networking site, with over 800 million users. Facebook has applied for a patent on a method for "social mapping," or, as some might put it, a method for making friends. The application has the following claim:

Amended Claim:

1. (Currently Amended) A method for mapping a relationship between members of a social network, the method comprising:

> receiving profile data about a plurality of social network members, each member having a plurality of established relationships with other members of the social network; mapping an established relationship between

two members of the social network and all of the members who have established relationships with both of the two members, wherein the mapping comprises creating a listing of the established relationships shared between the two members, including with the listing at least one of a name, a picture, and a link to a member profile for the member who has the shared established relationship; and displaying on a social network display page at least a portion of the listing.

Please analyze whether Facebook's claim for a method for "social mapping" is patentable subject matter in (i) the U.S. and (ii) the European Union. What is the legal standard in each jurisdiction, and should the respective patent office conclude that the standard is satisfied (or not) under the facts? Does it matter if Facebook's claim does not expressly mention a machine or computer as a part of the process? In your analysis, consider whether a method for social mapping should be analogized to a business method. Limit your analysis to the issue of patentable subject matter. Consult *Bilski*, the European Patent Convention, *Hitachi*, and following discussion.

* * *

Before courts had to deal with the ongoing controversy over the patentability of business methods, they confronted the patentability of computer software. Because many business methods rely on computer software in their implementation, the two issues are often intertwined today. Many computer programs have nothing to do with business methods, so the issue of patenting computer software is different from the one discussed in the last section. A computer program is essentially a set of instructions for a computer to perform certain functions. The program consists of the "source code," which is written in a computer language understandable to the programmer. The source code is later translated by a computer into the "object code," which is written in binary language consisting of a bunch of 1's and 0's understandable to the machine. Given the rise of computers in our Information Economy, the question whether computer programs can be patented has profound importance. Yet countries have struggled for many years to answer that question.

U.S. approach. In the U.S., courts debated whether a computer program that was based in part on a mathematical algorithm or formula (which is often the case) was an unpatentable abstract idea. In 1981, nearly a decade after its first decision dealing with the patentability of computer programs, the Supreme Court ruled that computer programs that contain mathematical algorithms are not categorically ineligible for patents. Although a patent cannot be granted for a mathematical algorithm in the abstract, it can be granted "when a claim containing a mathematical formula implements or applies that formula in a . . . function which the patent laws were designed to protect (e.g., transforming or reducing an article to a different state or thing)." *Diamond v. Diehr*, 450 U.S. 175, 192 (1981). In applying this decision, the Federal Circuit has recognized that a computer program can create, in effect, a "new machine, because a general purpose computer . . . becomes a special purpose computer once it is programmed to perform particular functions pursuant to instructions from program software." *In re Alappat*, 33 F.3d 1526, 1545 (Fed. Cir. 1994). "Consequently, a computer operating pursuant to software *may* represent patentable subject matter, provided, of course, that the claimed subject matter meets all of the other requirements" of securing a patent. *Id.*

The permissive approach to patenting software may receive greater scrutiny after *Bilski,* ___ U.S. ___, 130 S. Ct. 3218 (2010). Although the Supreme Court's decision focused on business methods, parts of the ruling may apply to software as well. The "useful, tangible, and concrete" test of the Federal Circuit—under which software inventions were routinely granted—appears to be no longer good law. Although not the sole test, the machine-or-transformation test will likely be relevant to software inventions, as will the bar on "abstract ideas." Computer software that does not result in a "[t]ransformation and reduction of an article 'to a different state or thing' " might be open to greater scrutiny. In the first post-*Bilski* review of a software program, the Board of Patent Appeals and Interferences in the Patent Office ruled: "A claim that recites no more than software, logic or a data structure (i.e., an abstraction) does not fall within any statutory category. Significantly, 'Abstract software code is an idea without physical embodiment.' " *Ex parte Proudler,* 2010 WL 2727840 (BPAI 2010) (internal citations omitted). The invention, owned by HP, involved "[a] method of controlling the processing of data * * * comprising defining security controls for a plurality of data items, and applying individualised security rules to each of the data items based on a measurement of integrity of a computing entity to which the data items are to be made available." The BPAI rejected the patent application because it "is directed to software per se, abstract ideas, abstract concepts, and the like, including data per se, data items, data structures, usage rules, and the abstract intellectual processes associating them within the claims on appeal." *Id.*

In one case in 2011, the Federal Circuit applied the unpatentable mental process doctrine, in addition to the machine-or-transformation test, to uphold the denial of a patent to a method of detecting fraud in credit card transactions based on collection of IP addresses. *See CyberSource Corp. v. Retail Decisions, Inc.* 654 F.3d 1366 (Fed. Cir. 2011). The Federal Circuit held that the method could be performed all in the human mind, or on pencil and paper, and, therefore, was merely an unpatentable mental process. *Id.* at 1372. The court also held that putting the method on a computer program did not transform the method into patentable subject matter. *Id.* at 1375. The court explained: "the use of the machine 'must impose meaningful limits on the claim's scope.' In other words, the machine 'must play a significant part in permitting the claimed method to be performed.' " *Id.* But "merely claiming a software implementation of a purely mental process that could otherwise be performed without the use of a computer does not satisfy the machine prong of the machine-or-transformation test." *Id.*

CyberSource employs greater scrutiny to one software-implemented invention, post-*Bilski.* However, in a different case, the Federal Circuit appeared to take a more relaxed approach. *See Ultramercial, LLC v. Hulu LLC,* 657 F.3d 1323, 1328 (Fed. Cir. 2011) (method of distributing copyrighted works over Internet based on advertising model was patentable subject matter in part because it "purports to improve existing technology in the marketplace" and "invokes computers and applications of computer technology"). As more software cases are decided, the contours of the Federal Circuit's approach, post-*Bilski*, should become more developed.

Europe's "technical" approach. Article 52(2) of the European Patent Convention recognizes that, like business methods, "programs for computers" "as such" are not patentable subject matter. In 1986, the EPO Technical Board of Appeal allowed a patent for a program for digitally processing images, concluding that the program was more than just a pure mathematical algorithm producing pure numbers. Instead, the program involved a process that led to a physical change, instantiated in the images. *Computer-related Invention/VICOM*, T 208/84, 1987 OJ EPO 14 (1986). As in the *Hitachi* case excerpted above, to determine the patentability of computer programs, the patent office examines whether the program has a "technical character." The EPO's Guidelines for Examination § 2.3.6 (April 2010) explains:

> The basic patentability considerations in respect of claims for computer programs are in principle the same as for other subject-matter. While "programs for computers" are included among the items listed in Art. 52(2), if the claimed subject-matter has a technical character it is not excluded from patentability by the provisions of Art. 52(2) and (3). Moreover, a data-processing operation controlled by a computer program can equally, in theory, be implemented by means of special circuits, and the execution of a program always involves physical effects, e.g. electrical currents. According to T 1173/97, such normal physical effects are not in themselves sufficient to lend a computer program technical character.

> However, if a computer program is capable of bringing about, when running on a computer, a further technical effect going beyond these normal physical effects, it is not excluded from patentability. This further technical effect may be known in the prior art. A further technical effect which lends technical character to a computer program may be found, e.g., in the control of an industrial process or in processing data which represent physical entities or in the internal functioning of the computer itself or its interfaces under the influence of the program and could, for example, affect the efficiency or security of a process, the management of computer resources required or the rate of data transfer in a communication link. As a consequence, a computer program may be considered as an invention within the meaning of Art. 52(1) if the program has the potential to bring about, when running on a computer, a further technical effect which goes beyond the normal physical interactions between the program and the computer. A patent may be granted on such a claim if all the requirements of the EPC are met[.] Such claims should not contain program listings, but should define all the features which assure patentability of the process which the program is intended to carry out when it is run.

The EPO's discussion of its test(s) for identifying a "technical feature" of a computer program seems to take a permissive approach to patenting software and many computer programs can arguably qualify for patent protection. Patenting computer programs remains controversial among European countries, however. Commentators and courts have criticized the EPO's approach as inconsistent, if not incomprehensible. Perhaps feeling a need to respond to some of the criticisms, the EPO published a 2009 pamphlet titled "Patents for Software? European Law and Practice." The pamphlet defends the EPO's practice and grant of "high quality" patents. If the U.S. courts start scaling back the patentability of computer programs after *Bilski*, perhaps the EPO will revisit the issue. Time will tell.

NOTES AND QUESTIONS

1. How do you square the EPO's decisions allowing computer programs to be patented with Article 52 of the EPC? Is Article 52(2)'s exclusion of computer programs "as such" consistent with TRIPS Article 27's principle of non-discrimination?

2. The TRIPS Agreement requires countries to recognize computer programs as literary works for the purposes of copyright. TRIPS Agreement art. 10. Should the WTO resolve whether computer programs should be patentable subject matter as well?

3. Does widespread patenting of computer software raise any special concerns for innovation? Consider the following assessment written by Bill Gates, founder of Microsoft, on May 16, 1991:

PATENTS: If people had understood how patents would be granted when most of today's ideas were invented, and had taken out patents, the industry would be at a complete standstill today. I feel certain that some large company will patent some obvious thing related to interface, object orientation, algorithm, application extension or other crucial technique. If we assume this company has no need of any of our patents then they have a 17–year right to take as much of our profits as they want. The solution to this is patent exchanges with large companies and patenting as much as we can. Amazingly we haven't done any patent exchanges that I am aware of. Amazingly we haven't found a way to use our licensing position to avoid having our own customers cause patent problems for us. I know these aren't simple problems but they deserve more effort by both Legal and other groups. For example, we need to do a patent exchange with HP as part of our new relationship. In many application categories, straightforward thinking ahead allows you to come up with patentable ideas. A recent paper from the League for Programming Freedom (available from the Legal department) explains some problems with the way patents are applied to software.

Do you agree with Gates's concerns? How could software patents create a "standstill"? Would licensing take care of any such problem, according to Gates?

4. *India.* India has emerged as an important source of software development and industry. Yet it is not clear to what extent India allows patenting of computer programs. Under Section 3(k) of the Patent Act (amended in 2002), business methods and computer programs "per se" are not patentable. The Indian Patent Office has interpreted this exclusion to allow patenting of computer programs that have a "technical effect," solving a technical problem and containing "a hardware or machine limitation." *See* Vaibhav Choudhary, *The Patentability of Software Under Intellectual Property Rights: An Analysis*

of US, European, and Indian Intellectual Property Rights, 33 EIPR 435, 443–44 (2011). Does India's approach sound similar to the U.S. or EU approach?

2. UTILITY OR CAPABLE OF INDUSTRIAL APPLICATION

Under TRIPS Article 27, one of the requirements for any invention to qualify for a patent is that it be "capable of industrial application." In footnote 5, TRIPS explains that " 'capable of industrial application' may be deemed by a Member to be synonymous with the term[] . . . 'useful.' " This proviso in footnote 5 was necessary because different countries have adopted one or the other concept—industrial application or utility—as a benchmark for an invention. Industrial application is a concept that has been influential in European countries, while utility has been influential in the United States and Canada. Although TRIPS says the two terms can be considered "synonymous," are they? Are there any material differences? Consider the following article.

"INDUSTRIAL APPLICABILITY" AND "UTILITY" REQUIREMENTS: COMMONALITIES AND DIFFERENCES

WIPO, Standing Committee on the Law of Patents.
SCP/9/5 (March 17, 2003).*

IV. Commonalities and Differences Between the Industrial Applicability and the Utility Requirements

The scope of the term "industrial applicability" differs from one country to another, and so does the term "utility." Considerable overlaps, however, exist between these two requirements.

Commonalities

Focusing on the general common characteristics of the two requirements, an invention that is inoperative, for example, an invention which is clearly non-operable in view of well-established laws of nature, would not comply with both the industrial applicability and utility requirements. This type of invention is considered either having no application in industry or not being useful for any purpose, because it doesn't work.

Differences

One of the differences between the industrial applicability requirement and the utility requirement is that claimed inventions which could apply solely in the private or personal sphere for one's own needs, or which could be applied solely in association with a particular person, would not meet the industrial applicability requirement, even if the term

---

* Material provided by the World Intellectual Property Organization, and reproduced with permission. The Secretariat of WIPO assumes no responsibility with regard to any transformation of the data.

"industry" is interpreted in the broadest sense. Although not many examples of inventions falling under this category were suggested by the SCP members, it may be further explored how the patentability of these inventions is assessed in those countries which apply the utility requirement. At least in the submissions from Australia and Canada, with respect to "a manner of manufacture" and "utility," respectively, a commercial value in connection with benefits to the public was mentioned. It may be noted that at least some of the countries applying utility, although they grant patents for inventions applicable only for private use, provide some safeguards for limited uses of the invention, such as the *"de minimis"* doctrine.

As a general conclusion, an invention that is inoperative, for example, an invention which is clearly non-operable in view of well-established laws of nature, is not patentable on the grounds of both the industrial applicability requirement and the utility requirement. Under certain circumstances, an invention not having the requisite utility may be refused on the grounds of non-compliance with the industrial applicability requirement, where the invention could be made or used in any kind of industry, but could not show any practical or useful application. A clear difference exists between the industrial applicability requirement and the utility requirement as to inventions which could be solely used in the private and personal sphere, although the utility requirement applied in certain countries takes into account the public benefit of the invention.

V.   Alternatives in draft Article 12(4) of the SPLTs

As regards the industrial applicability and utility requirements, three alternative texts are proposed in draft Article 12(4) of the SPLT (see document SCP/9/2). Although a Contracting Party may use either the term "industrial applicability" or the term "utility" under the applicable law, the provision is intended to provide a single definition that could be expressed in either terms. The texts of the three alternatives are reproduced below:

"[Alternative A]

A claimed invention shall be industrially applicable (useful). It shall be considered industrially applicable (useful) if it can be made or used for exploitation in any field of [commercial][economic]activity.

"[Alternative B]

A claimed invention shall be industrially applicable (useful). It shall be considered industrially applicable (useful) if it can be made or used for exploitation in any kind of industry. "Industry" shall be understood in its broadest sense, as in the Paris Convention.

"[Alternative C]

A claimed invention shall be industrially applicable (useful). It shall be considered industrially applicable (useful) if it has a specific, substantial and credible utility."

According to Alternative A, the words "for exploitation in any field of [commercial][economic] activity" imply that the claimed invention has a practical or useful application, rather than that it could simply be made without any use, or could be simply used in a non-reasonable manner. The general rule as to what constitutes an invention with "practical or useful application" (or alternatively, what constitutes an invention without "practical or useful application") may be provided in the Practice Guidelines, if the SCP Members agreed that further elaboration is necessary. The expression "[commercial][economic] activity" attempts to capture the broad scope of the term "industry" that appears in many national and regional laws. Further, this expression is intended to exclude inventions that could be applied solely in connection with the personal and private sphere. In practice, according to the broad scope of the term "industry" in Alternative B, the term "any kind of industry" in Alternative B and the expression "any field of [commercial][economic] activity" may not be substantially different. Alternative A, however, aims at using an explicit term that covers the activities which could fall within the scope of "industry" in its broadest sense.

Alternative B reflects the standard wording of the industrial applicability requirement that appears in many national and regional laws. In addition to the question concerning the scope of the term "industry," the provision could be interpreted in a strict sense so that, for example, an invention concerning an isolated partial gene sequence may be considered as complying with the requirement under Alternative B, although no function of, or utility for, such a sequence is disclosed, apart from the general understanding that the sequence could be used as a probe.

The wording of Alternative C is modeled after the practice of the utility requirement, in particular, in the United States of America. In addition to the question as to the extent to which utility of the claimed invention should be required, Alternative C could be interpreted in a way that an invention that could be applied only in connection with personal needs or personal skills would be considered to comply with the industrial applicability/utility requirement as long as that invention has the required utility.

One possible way which may be explored by the SCP could be to first identify, based on this document, the commonalities between the two requirements. These elements, together with other requirements which overlap with industrial applicability/utility, may form the basis to attempt to elaborate a common requirement. The next step could be to identify and attempt to solve the existing differences. Finally, it may be noted that any terms chosen in respect of a new requirement would need to be clearly circumscribed, for example, in the Practice Guidelines. In any event, it should be ensured that such wording, if it had already been used in some jurisdictions, would not result in the importation of the case law and practices used in such jurisdiction in relation to that wording.

NOTES AND QUESTIONS

1. Putting aside the requirement under Article 27 of TRIPS, what theory or policy do you think underlies the requirement of utility or industrial application as a prerequisite for a patent?

2. Some countries that require "industrial application" for inventions interpret that requirement to not be satisfied if the invention is for purely personal use, such as a method of fixing a ski shoe, a method for smoking, and a method for application of a contraceptive. Countries that recognize "utility" do not have such a limitation, instead focusing on whether the invention is useful. Which is the better approach?

3. How does one determine what the minimum standard for "utility" or "capable of industrial application" is, if the concepts are not exactly the same? Based on the article by WIPO, can you articulate a minimum standard for this requirement?

4. Which of the three Alternative definitions of utility/industrial application proposed in the article do you think would be better for a patent system to adopt? Why? Do you have a different proposal or any other suggestions?

PROBLEM 3–10

You are a patent examiner in the United States. Evaluate the following inventions; do they have sufficient utility: (i) a commercial process for making crustless peanut butter jelly sandwiches by precutting the crust from bread, (ii) garbage bags made with a pumpkin face on the outside for decorative purposes in order to resolve the problem of unsightly garbage bags near the side of the street, and (iii) a juice dispenser that simulates the dispensing of fresh juice from a visible glass bowl, when in actuality the juice is dispensed from a container hidden from view? If you were a patent examiner applying industrial application in the United Kingdom, would your answer be different?

PROBLEM 3–11

Country X has brought a challenge before the WTO to the United States's and the European Union's treatment of utility for gene sequences. The basic complaint is that the patent laws of the United States and of the European Union create a higher standard of utility for gene sequences than for any other kind of invention. Country X claims that this differential treatment violates the principle of nondiscrimination in Article 27 of TRIPS. Country X points out that the U.S. and EU have given a number of patents for biotechnology inventions not involving gene sequences that are intended to be used for general research purposes (e.g., Harvard's oncomouse, whose benefit lies with cancer research). Country X argues that, under TRIPS Article 27, the same standard must be applied to the field of gene sequence inventions— otherwise, it is discrimination against the field of technology. Thus, as long as the gene sequence inventions are useful to researchers, utility for those inventions should be found. If you were to argue the case on behalf of Country

X, how would you go about developing your case? What different kinds of proof would you hope to offer to prove your case? If you were the representative for the U.S. or the EU, how would you respond?

3. NOVELTY

Article 27 of TRIPS requires an invention to be "new" or contain sufficient novelty to qualify for a patent. Of all the patent requirements, novelty is perhaps the most fundamental. The basic rationale is that the grant of patents should be reserved only for those inventions that are new, or add to the sum of useful knowledge.

Over the years, two different conceptions of novelty have evolved. One approach, as embodied in the European Patent Convention, is to place no geographical limitation on prior art. Thus, a prior foreign public use or knowledge of an invention anywhere in the world will defeat its novelty, assuming, of course, the prior use or knowledge can be proven.

The other approach is to restrict novelty by geography, in all or some respects. As you recall, Venice's first patent act contained such a geographical limitation to inventions "not previously made in this Commonwealth." This approach allowed what are sometimes called "importation patents," which lured foreign inventors to transfer their technology to the area. For many years, the United States followed a mixed approach that had some geographical limitation on novelty—foreign public uses or knowledge of an invention did not constitute prior art in the U.S. In 2011, the America Invents Act changed the standard of novelty in the U.S. for patent applications filed on March 16, 2013 or later, by removing the geographical limitation altogether. (Existing patents granted and applications filed before March 16, 2013 will be governed by the prior standard of novelty, with its geographical limitation, for their duration. Thus, patent attorneys in the U.S. must know both standards of novelty well into the future.) Under the new standard, the U.S. no longer excludes foreign public uses or knowledge from prior art. The amended § 102(a) treats as prior art circumstances in which "the claimed invention was patented, described in a printed publication, or in public use, on sale, or otherwise available to the public before the effective filing date of the claimed invention." AIA, § 3(b). Once implemented, the U.S. standard of novelty will become more like the European standard. In this section, we will compare the European and U.S. approaches.

a. Basic Doctrine

PROBLEM 3–12

Global Foods, a U.S. multi-national corporation in the food produce industry, has been seeking to develop a low starch brand of rice for the increasingly health conscious U.S. consumer. Global discovers that Varuni, an eccentric but brilliant professor in Sri Lanka, has refined and perfected a centuries old technique used by local tribes to make such a rice. Global sends a team of scientists to visit Varuni on the pretext of a scholarly exchange. For several weeks, the scientists attend the professor's lectures and demonstrations in her laboratory. Six months after the scientific team returns to the United States, Global files patent applications in the United States for a U.S. patent and in Europe for a European Patent within the Paris priority period, claiming both product and process patents for the low starch rice developed from the information learned from the professor in Sri Lanka. Outraged, the professor and the university contest the patent applications on the ground that Global's application is not novel. A number of students in the professor's classes can attest that they observed the presence of Global's scientists listening intently, busily taking copious notes, and asking probing questions in the professor's class and laboratory demonstrations. The students also have copies of their own notes that show the professor explaining the invention. However, the professor never published any publication disclosing her technique, and, to her knowledge, no printed publication has ever discussed it. (i) If Global filed an application in the U.S. before March 16, 2013, does Global get the patent in the U.S? What about the EU? (ii) If Global's application was filed in the U.S. after March 16, 2013, does the result change? Consider the discussion above and below.

European Patent Convention

Article 54 Novelty

(1) An invention shall be considered to be new if it does not form part of the state of the art.

(2) The state of the art shall be held to comprise everything made available to the public by means of a written or oral description, by use, or in any other way, before the date of filing of the European patent application.

(3) Additionally, the content of European patent applications as filed, of which the dates of filing are prior to the date referred to in paragraph 2 and which were published under Article 93 on or after that date, shall be considered as comprised in the state of the art. * * *

The Neem Tree

Photograph by Christopher Thiemann

EUROPEAN PATENT OFFICE, OPPOSITION DIVISION DECISION REVOKING THE EUROPEAN PATENT NO. EP–B–0436257

Feb. 13, 2001.

I. Summary of Facts and Submissions

European application no. 91305622.2 of the W.R. Grace & Co.–Conn., New York, US and the United States of America represented by the Secretary of Agriculture was filed on 20 December 1990. It claimed priority of the earlier US-application 456 762 (26.12.1989).

The patent was jointly opposed by Magda Alvoet, Brussels, BE, by Research Foundation For Science, Technology and Natural Resource Policy, New Delhi, India and by International Federation of Organic Agriculture Movements (IFOAM) Thorley–Theley, DE. The opponents filed a notice of opposition on 14 June 1995 requesting revocation of the patent in its entirety on grounds of lack of novelty (Article 54(1)(2) EPC), lack of inventive step (Article 56 EPC), insufficient disclosure (Article 83 EPC) and because it would be contrary to morality (Article 53(a) EPC).

II. Grounds for the Decision

Novelty with regard to a public prior use

The basic statement of Mr. Phadke both in the affidavit and his testimony was that there were field trials in summer 1985 and 1986 in the

Pune and Sangli districts of Maharashtra, Western India which were open to an unlimited number of local farmers. In the testimony he further specified that the fungicidal effect under discussion has been observed essentially in the months November and December and presented a list of 16 farmers plus their telephone numbers who were present at the trials. He further specified during the testimony that not only his employees carried out the trials, but also that he himself carried out some of the tests together with 2 farmers whose names he could present. Additionally, he stated that the farmers did not only watch the trials, but were given samples of the various extracts and the recipes to prepare them.

Accordingly, it is clearly established *when* and *where* the prior use took place. Additionally, it has been made clear that the trials in fact were made available to the public.

According to the affidavit and the testimony, the trials were performed in the following way: First of all a hydrophobic extract of neem oil was prepared by extracted neem seeds with a non-polar hydrophobic solvent, including hexane and others including aliphatic hydrocarbons. In a typical example, the extraction of 100 g of neem seeds resulted in 16 g of an extracted neem oil product. According to the testimony, this neem oil product was diluted by an amount of emulsifying surfactant chosen from synthetic emulsifiers like TWEEN® or natural extracts from *Acida Consina*. With respect to hexane as solvent, compositions were obtained containing less than 1% hexane, 90% neem oil and 10% emulsifier (synthetic one) or 85% neem oil and 15% emulsifier (natural one). For pest control 4–8 ml of the above produce were diluted with 1 L water in a concentration of about 0.4–0.8% neem oil and about 0.04–0.08% emulsifier.

Especially, the concentration of the neem oil as stated above and presented in the affidavit A7 differed since there a broad range of 0.5–5% was disclosed. However, the witness made clear that the affidavit concerns the whole period of testing whereas the above concentrations of 0.4–0.8% were applied in the first year.

As mentioned in the affidavit A7 and confirmed by testimony, agricultural crops like rice, lentils or sunflowers but also fruits and vegetable like grapes, tomatoes, strawberries, mangoes and pomegranates and beans were treated.

The target of the spraying were insects and diseases like powdery mildew, rust, brown patches, black spots and botrytis.

The opposition division considers the witness and his testimony as credible. The witness was able to elaborate on numerous details of the public prior use. He had several personal documents with him which related to the prior use and which he was able to present to the opposition division. While these documents as such were not included into the procedure, their presentation by the witness is a factor which, in the view of the opposition division, corroborates his credibility. Thus, the abovementioned facts form part of the prior act according to Article 54(1)(2) EPC.

Claims 1 and 7 of the patent suit are directed to methods for controlling fungi on plants comprising contacting the fungi (claim 1) or for protecting a plant from fungial infestation comprising contacting the plant (claim 7) with a neem oil formulation containing 0.1 to 10% of a hydrophobic extracted neem oil which is substantially free of azadirachtin, 0.005 to 5% of emulsifying surfactant and 0 to 99% of water.

According to the affidavit A7 and the testimony, extracts were prepared using hexane as a solvent, which is a typical hydrophobic and moreover preferred solvent of the patent in suit (cf. example 1). Therefore, the hexane extracts used in the above trials were also free of azadirachtin.

The prior art according to the affidavit A7 and the testimony had a concentration of the neem oil of 0.4–5% in the broadest sense, 1–2% as a preferred range and 0.4–0.8% as used in the first year of the trials and a concentration of the emulsifying agent of about 0.03–0.5% in the broadest sense and 0.04–0.08% in the first year of the trials.

Accordingly, the subject matter of present claims 1 and 7 as granted is clearly not novel over the prior art as represented by the affidavit A7 of Mr. Phadke and his testimony made during the oral proceedings and does thus not meet the requirements of Article 54(1)(2) EPC. In summary, the main request is considered not to be novel with respect to Article 54(1)(2) EPC in view of the above-discussed public prior use. [T]he patent is therefore revoked in accordance with Article 102(1) EPC.

NOTES AND QUESTIONS

1. *Opposition proceedings.* The European Patent Convention allows third parties to challenge the validity of a patent in an opposition proceeding before the patent office. The third parties are allowed to participate in the proceedings and present evidence. Under the America Invents Act of 2011, the U.S. finally instituted an opposition procedure in what is known as post-grant review. Within a 9–month period after the grant of the patent, third parties can challenge the validity of a patent claim in the U.S. Patent Office. *See* AIA, H.R. 1249, § 6(d) (codified at 35 U.S.C. § 321 et seq.). The EPC has a similar 9–month period for opposition. EPC § 99(1) (opposition must be "[w]ithin nine months of the publication of the mention of the grant of the European patent in the European Patent Bulletin"). Japan used to have a 6–month period for oppositions, but abolished oppositions in 2003. However, Japan recognizes an "invalidation trial" in the Japanese Patent Office that a party involved in a dispute related to the patent may seek to invalidate the patent. *See* Eric B. Cheng, Note, *Alternatives to District Court Patent Litigation: Reform by Enhancing the Existing Administrative Options*, 83 S. CAL. L. REV. 1135, 1146 (2010). China follows Japan's approach. *Id.* at 1148.

2. *Proof and corroboration of prior use.* How much evidentiary proof should be required to prove a prior use of an invention? Should the testimony of one witness be potentially sufficient? Should corroboration by written documents, other testimony, or evidence be required? What was the evidence of a prior use in the Neem case?

3. Do you think the EPO's decision would have been any different had the farmers been allowed to watch the field trials, but not to receive any samples of the neem-based fungicide?

4. *Grace's U.S. patent*. Grace obtained a patent in the United States for the same invention claimed in the European patent. Would the field trials in India in 1985 and 1986 defeat the novelty of the invention in the U.S.? The U.S. Patent Code (35 U.S.C. § 102 (2006)) applicable to Grace's patent states in relevant part:

U.S. Patent Code § 102. Conditions for patentability: novelty and loss of right to patent

A person shall be entitled to a patent unless—

(a) the invention was known or used by others in this country, or patented or described in a printed publication in this or a foreign country, before the invention thereof by the applicant for patent.
    * * *

If the field trials in India do not defeat the novelty of Grace's invention under U.S. law, does it make sense to allow a patent for the invention as novel in the U.S., but to disallow a patent for the invention due to lack of novelty in European countries? How can the same invention be both novel and not novel in the world at the same time?

5. *The U.S.'s complex approach to novelty*. The America Invents Act will eventually remove the geographical limits in the U.S. standard of novelty, starting with applications filed on March 16, 2013. As noted above, the old standard still applies to existing patents and applications filed before that date. Under the Act, the U.S. restricts novelty by geography in a rather complex way. Section 102 of the U.S. Patent Code does *not* recognize prior foreign knowledge or foreign use of an invention, in themselves, as novelty-defeating. Instead, in order to defeat novelty, prior disclosure of the invention must be patented in a foreign country or described in a foreign publication. 35 U.S.C. § 102(a) (2006). (An inventor, of course, can file a patent application in another country of the Paris Convention and still maintain the priority and novelty of his or her invention. *Id.* § 102(d)).

What explains this multivalent approach to novelty? Why don't foreign prior uses count as prior art in the U.S.? Are such prior uses in foreign countries somehow more difficult for an inventor to be able to find as prior art than a prior disclosure of an invention in a foreign publication? What if the foreign publication is an obscure doctoral thesis written in a foreign language and contained in a foreign university library (*see In re Hall*, 781 F.2d 897 (Fed. Cir. 1986))? Wouldn't such an obscure foreign publication be just as hard to find for an inventor in the U.S.? Or is the reason that prior foreign uses are more susceptible of fabrication or difficulties of proof than a printed publication, and therefore should not be considered prior art?

The first several U.S. Patent Acts, starting with the very first Act of 1790, did *not* contain a geographical limitation to novelty. *See* Patent Act of April 10, 1790, ch. 7, § 1, 1 Stat. 109–11; Patent Act of Feb. 21, 1793, ch. 11, § 1, 1 Stat. 318, 319. Prior foreign uses of an invention were considered to be novelty-defeating. *See Shaw v. Cooper*, 32 U.S. (7 Pet.) 292, 320 (1833). In essence, the America Invents Act will return the U.S. back closer to its original standard of novelty—and thereby harmonize U.S. law with the approach in other countries.

b. Patent Filings as Prior Art to Defeat Novelty

One aspect of prior art that deserves special attention is the extent to which patent applications filed in different countries constitute prior art. The question can be broken down into three parts: (1) do countries recognize filed patent applications as prior art; (2) if so, as of what date; and (3) in cases involving applications with a Paris priority date, does the Paris priority date apply as the date all the applications become prior art?

Domestic applications. As to the first question, the short answer is yes. Countries generally consider a filed patent application as establishing prior art. Foreign applications can constitute prior art, just as domestic applications can. Such an approach seems sensible enough: the patent application evidences that someone else has already invented the claimed invention, meaning that it was before the critical date as judged by a first-to-file or first-to-invent country.

However, the more difficult question is the second: what date does a patent application become prior art? To answer this question, we need to distinguish between domestic and foreign patent applications. Most countries treat the *filing date* of a domestic patent application as the date on which the patent application is treated as prior art so long as the patent application is later published or the patent is granted. In many first-to-file countries, the filing date of the patent application is treated retroactively as the effective date for the purposes of prior art once the patent application is published, usually within 18 months after the filing. *See* EPC art. 54(3) (treating the filing date of a European patent application later published as the effective date that the application "shall be considered as comprised in the state of the art").

> Illustration 3–14. Francis filed for a patent in France on Dec. 5, 2012. One day earlier, on December 4, 2012, Gil had filed for a patent for a different invention in France but the description in Gil's patent application also discloses the invention contained in Francis's application. Gil's patent application is published 18 months later. After Gil's patent application is published, can a third party use the December 4, 2012 filing date of Gil's patent application as prior art to defeat the novelty of Francis's invention in France? Yes. Even though Francis might not have been able to discover Gil's French patent application before it later became public, the French application forms part of the prior art. This is sometimes called "secret prior art," to the extent the prior art was not publicly available. (If the French application never became public, though, it would not be considered prior art.) The date of filing a patent application (that later becomes publicly available) is the date on which the application becomes prior art.

The U.S. approach is similar. The filing date of a domestic U.S. patent application is considered to be the effective date establishing the patent application as prior art, provided the application is later published or the patent is granted. *See* 35 U.S.C. § 102(e) (2006).

Foreign applications. Foreign patent applications, however, are treated differently by most countries. Foreign applications and patents are treated as prior art on the date on which they are published.

For example, under the 1952 Act in the U.S., foreign patent applications must fall within "printed publications" under § 102(a) in order to be prior art, while § 102(e) allows U.S. patent applications to be prior art as of the date of filing if later published. *Compare* 35 U.S.C. § 102(a) (2006) with *id.* § 102(e). The America Invents Act does not change this distinction in the amended § 102. AIA, § 3(b) (to be codified at 35 U.S.C. § 102(a)(1) (printed publication) and § 102(a)(2) (U.S. filed patents)).

As a matter of policy, one might attempt to justify the difference between domestic and foreign patents in terms of their effective prior art dates based on practical and fairness concerns: it might be both practically difficult and unfair to hold inventors to the knowledge contained in foreign patent applications that are not yet public. At least with domestic patents, the patent examiners presumably have access to the yet-to-be-published applications in their office. The EU and Japan follow a similar approach: foreign patent applications are not considered to be prior art until the date they become publicly available.

> Illustration 3–15. Uma invented her invention on Dec. 5, 2012 and immediately filed for a patent in the United States on the same date. But Gil had filed for a patent for the same invention in China, also a Paris Union country, on December 4, 2012, and Gil's application in China became publicly available 18 months later. Can a third party use the December 4, 2012 filing date of Gil's patent application in China as the effective date of the application as prior art to defeat the novelty of Uma's invention in the United States? No. In the United States, Gil's China patent application didn't become prior art until it was published—which was well after Uma invented her invention (18 months after December 4, 2012). The publication date, not the filing date, of the foreign patent application is the effective date of prior art.

Paris priority dates on prior art. Now we face the final question, which is the most difficult of all: what happens if an inventor filed several patent applications within the Paris priority period? Can a third party use the Paris priority date established by the first foreign filing as the date that the subsequent national applications became prior art? Historically, countries have divided over this issue—with the U.S. again being an outlier. In Europe and Japan, the answer is yes: a third party can rely on the Paris priority date in someone else's foreign patent application as the date on which all subsequent national filings become prior art, provided the foreign application is later published or a patent is granted. In Europe and Japan, when a foreign application establishes a priority date under the Paris Convention, the filing date of the foreign application, not its publication date, becomes the effective date for establishing prior art so long as the application is later published or a patent is granted.

Until the passage of the America Invents Act, the U.S. took the contrary view. Under the Hilmer doctrine, the U.S. rejected the offensive use of Paris priority to establish the date of prior art. In 2011, the U.S. finally did away with the Hilmer doctrine for applications filed on or after March 16, 2013. The amended § 102(d)(2) will use the Paris priority date on patents or applications for the purposes of prior art, thereby harmonizing U.S. law with Europe and Japan AIA, § 3(b). However, because the Hilmer doctrine still applies to existing patents and applications filed before March 16, 2013, U.S. patent attorneys still must know the doctrine for the foreseeable future. The Hilmer doctrine is discussed in the case below.

PROBLEM 3–13

Gil filed a patent application in Germany on November 30, 2011. Gil filed a second patent application in Country X, also a Paris Union country, for the same invention on November 30, 2012. Meanwhile, Lorena has independently invented the same invention and then filed a patent application for the invention in Country X on February 1, 2012. Lorena eventually obtained a patent that Lorena believes is now being infringed by Thurman. Thurman argues, however, that Lorena's patent in Country X is invalid because it was disclosed in the prior art contained in Gil's German patent application. What result under the following circumstances: (a) Country X is Japan or an EU country; (b) Country X is the United States. Would your answer for the United States change if the dates above are changed to November 30, 2014, November 30, 2015, and February 1, 2015, respectively? See the discussion above and below.

STUDIENGESELLSCHAFT KOHLE
mbH v. EASTMAN KODAK CO.

U.S. Court of Appeals for the Fifth Circuit.
616 F.2d 1315 (5th Cir. 1980).

COLEMAN, CHIEF JUDGE.

IV. The '792 PATENT

A. Validity

1. Prior Art

[Studiengesellschaft Kohle [SGK] brought a patent infringement action against Eastman Kodak for infringement of SGK's U.S. Patent '792. As a defense, Kodak claimed that SGK's patent was invalid because it was disclosed in the patent application filed in the United States by Professor Giulio Natta through which Natta eventually obtained U.S. Patent '987. Natta filed a foreign patent application for the same invention in Italy on

July 27, 1954 and then filed a U.S. patent application on June 8, 1955 within the period of Paris priority. Ziegler, the inventor of the '792 patent, filed a German application on August 3, 1954 and a U.S. application on June 8, 1955 within the period of Paris priority. Kodak does not own the patent obtained by Professor Natta, who is an unrelated third party to this litigation.]

The District Court held that claims 22 through 32 of SGK's '792 patent were invalid because they were anticipated by the disclosure of prior art as [in Natta's '987 patent.] The '987 patent discloses the same catalytic process as that at issue in Ziegler's '792 patent. According to the District Court, Natta's '987 patent had an Italian filing date of July 27, 1954, while the earliest possible effective invention date of the Ziegler '792 patent was August 3, 1954, the filing date of Ziegler's German application Z4348 covering the polymerization of propylene. Thus the Court found that the Natta patent was prior art, and the Ziegler claims were invalid.

Although the existence of a foreign patent is relevant as prior art, determining whether a particular foreign patent constitutes prior art for purposes of a challenge to the validity of another patent requires an examination of patent law and the judicial constructions placed on that law.

The patent laws outline a series of provisions which will defeat patentability of an invention. 35 U.S.C. § 102. Those which are relevant here are §§ 102(e) and 102(g). Section 102(e) provides that a person shall be entitled to a patent unless "the invention was described in a patent granted on an application for patent by another filed in the United States before the invention thereof by the applicant for the patent ..." Section 102(g) allows patentability unless "before the applicant's invention thereof the invention was made in this country by another who had not abandoned, suppressed, or concealed it."

Section 119 deals with filings in foreign countries and provides that an application for an American patent by a person who has previously filed a patent application in a foreign country "shall have the same effect as the same application would have if filed in this country on the date on which the application for patent for the same invention was first filed in such foreign country." Eastman contends that this means the Natta '987 patent is effective as a prior art reference as of its Italian filing date. Since that date precedes the filing date of Ziegler's German patent on polypropylene, Eastman argues, the Ziegler claims are invalid.

This Circuit has never explicitly addressed whether the filing date of a foreign patent may be used as the date of filing in the United States for the purposes of showing prior art under § 102(e) and (g). The Court of Customs & Patent Appeals has addressed this general issue, though in somewhat different contexts, on several occasions, and the District of Columbia Circuit has adopted the view articulated by that court. Although we may explore the issue on our own, we are reluctant to disagree with a court whose day-to-day activities require it to interpret and explicate patent law. This is particularly true, where, as here, the C.C.P.A.'s decision is a carefully reasoned examination of the relevant statutory provisions.

In an extensive inquiry into the effect of a foreign filing upon a U.S. patent used as a prior art reference, the Court of Customs and Patent Appeals held that a patent was not effective as a prior art reference under 35 U.S.C. § 102(e) as of its Swiss filing date. Rather, the patent was effective as prior art only as of the U.S. filing date. *Application of Hilmer*, 359 F.2d 859 (1966) (*Hilmer I*). In *Hilmer I* the appellants showed their earliest invention date as July 31, 1957, the date when they filed for a German patent. The patent relied upon as a prior art reference had a U.S. filing date of January 23, 1958, but also had a date of filing in Switzerland of January 23, 195[7]. The appellants thus could show that their invention occurred before the U.S. filing of the reference patent but they could not show their invention before the Swiss filing date of the U.S. patent. The Patent Office Board of Appeals gave the U.S. patent effect as prior art as of a foreign filing date. The Court of Customs and Patent Appeals reversed.

The Court pointed out that a patent may be entitled to a foreign filing date for some purposes and not for others. 359 F.2d at 863. Examining the language and legislative history of § 119, which allows a U.S. patent application to be effective as of its foreign filing date, the Court asserted that the purpose of § 119 was in establishing "priority" between parties directly competing for a patent on the same invention. The use of the foreign filing date as a priority right was "a protection to one who was trying to obtain patents in foreign countries, the protection being against patent-defeating provisions of national laws based on events intervening between the time of filing at home and filing abroad." 359 F.2d at 873.

Because § 119 was directed to priority between competing parties and § 102(e) was concerned with the elements which would defeat a patent, quite apart from priority disputes between parties, the Court refused to hold that the language in § 119 overrides the express requirement in § 102(e) that a patent relied on as a prior art reference be "filed in the United States before the invention" by current applicant. Thus under the *Hilmer I* doctrine, a prior art reference patent is effective only as of its U.S. filing date. The Court of Customs and Patent Appeals implicitly reaffirmed its position in *Hilmer II, Application of Hilmer*, 424 F.2d 1108 (1970), and *Application of McKellin*, 529 F.2d 1324 (Cust. & Pat. App. 1976). The Court of Appeals for the District of Columbia reached a similar conclusion in *Eli Lilly & Co. v. Brenner*, 375 F.2d 599 (D.C. Cir. 1967).

In *Hilmer II* the Court of Customs & Patent Appeals extended this interpretation to § 102(g). Just as in *Hilmer I* § 119 did not override the "filed in the United States" language of § 102(e), so in *Hilmer II*, § 119 did not remove § 102(g)'s limitation of "in this country." The essence of the Court's view is found in the following statement:

That (an alleged prior inventor), as an applicant, was entitled to the benefit of his (foreign) filing date does not mean that his invention acquires that same date under § 102(g) as patent-defeating prior art, in direct contravention of the "in this country" limitation of the section. 424 F.2d at 1113.

Eastman contends that our decision in *James B. Clow & Sons, Inc. v. United States Pipe & Foundry Co.*, 313 F.2d 46 (5th Cir. 1963) compels us to arrive at a different result. There, however, the issue was who was the first inventor under a priority claim between inventors. An interference between the two inventing parties had been privately settled in an allegedly fraudulent manner. In *Clow* we held that private parties could not conclusively settle the question of who the first inventor is, and we directed the trial court to see if the patent owner had properly won the interference, so as to be entitled to a valid patent. We pointed out that the foreign application was not being offered on the issue of anticipation or obviousness. Indeed, Eastman apparently concedes that *Clow* did not reach the issue. Thus our decision in *Clow* reflects the distinction which is at the heart of this issue in today's case between the use of a foreign application to determine priority and the use of a foreign application to establish prior art. We thus join our brethren in the Court of Customs & Patents Appeals in declaring that for purposes of determining whether a patent may serve as a prior art reference under § 102(e) or (g), the effective date is its date of filing in the United States.

Ziegler's German application covering the polymerization of polypropylene was filed August 3, 1954. Natta's U.S. filing occurred on June 8, 1955. Consequently, the Natta patent is not a reference of prior art and cannot render the Ziegler '792 patent invalid.

NOTES AND QUESTIONS

1. Why was SGK entitled to use the German filing date of August 3, 1954 as the U.S. filing date of the Ziegler '792 patent but Kodak was not entitled to use the Italian filing date of July 27, 1954 as the U.S. filing date of the Natta '987 patent?

2. *Priority date—Offensive versus Defensive Uses.* There are two kinds of uses of Paris priority dates. First, a "defensive use" occurs when an inventor invokes an earlier Paris priority date for her own patent applications to establish priority. An applicant is unquestionably allowed under the Paris Convention to use the prior filing date of a foreign patent application as the priority date of the national application if the national application is filed within one year of the foreign application. This is a "defensive" use of the Paris priority date because the applicant is protected from subsequent events that might otherwise invalidate the national patent application for the period of Paris priority. Second, as discussed in *Hilmer*, an "offensive" use of priority dates exists when a *third party* seeks to invoke the Paris priority date on some unrelated inventor's patent for the inventor's later filed applications to use those applications as prior art. This use of Paris priority is often

referred to as an "offensive use" by a third party to "knock out" someone else's patent.

Do you agree with the Fifth Circuit's resolution of the issue? Should it make a difference whether a person is attempting to use the earliest foreign filing date for defensive purposes to protect its own patent or for offensive purposes to knock out someone else's patent?

3. *The Hilmer rule and U.S. treatment of foreign applications.* As *Eastman Kodak* indicates, the leading U.S. case on the use of foreign patent applications as prior art from Paris countries is the *Hilmer* case. The "Hilmer rule" was controversial. Can you think of policy or other reasons that might justify the rule? Is one plausible reason that typically the publication of patent applications takes time, which means that, for some period after filing, the applications will not even be accessible to the public?

In a 1992 Report, an Advisory Commission evaluated whether the Hilmer rule should be changed, but cautioned against it:

> Change in the "Hilmer rule" would open up an additional one year of prior art because those U.S. applications claiming foreign priority would be effective as prior art references up to one year earlier against pending applications. Hence, changing the "Hilmer rule" would allow such foreign-originated U.S. applications to "knock out" more U.S. patent applications, whether themselves U.S.-originated or foreign-originated, than is presently the case. The effect would be fewer patents granted in the U.S.

Advisory Comm'n on Patent Law Reform, A Report to the Secretary of Commerce (1992).

Do you agree with the Advisory Commission's recommendation for the U.S. not to harmonize its patent law with other countries? Why do you think Congress in 2011 decided in the America Invents Act to abrogate the Hilmer rule and harmonize U.S. law with the other countries?

4. *Patent applications in Europe and Japan.* European countries and Japan have taken a different approach, recognizing that prior art can be established by foreign patent filings, going back to the earliest filing date of a patent application under Paris priority. The use of patent applications for prior art is limited, however, to defeating the novelty (but not the nonobviousness) of an invention. In 2011, the U.S. finally harmonized its approached with the EU and Japan with the enactment of the America Invents Act.

5. *Patent Cooperation Treaty (PCT) applications.* Article 11(3) of the PCT requires that "any international application fulfilling the requirements [of the PCT] and accorded an international filing date shall have the effect of a regular national application in each designated State as of the international filing date, which date shall be considered to be the actual filing date in each designated State." This provision is qualified by Article 64, which allows countries to *not* treat an international filing date (through Paris priority) as "an actual filing in that State for prior art purposes." The U.S. had made such a reservation, which allowed it under § 102(e) of the Patent Code of 1952 to treat PCT applications as prior art as of the date of their PCT filing "only if the international application designated the United States and was published under Article 21(2) of such treaty in the English language." 35

U.S.C. § 102(e) (2006). The America Invents Act removes these limitations. AIA, § 3(b) (to be codified at 35 U.S.C. § 102(d)(2)).

c. Special Discussion: Patenting or Biopiracy?

The Neem plant controversy discussed on pp. 357–60 above raises questions that go well beyond the concept of novelty. At the heart of the controversy is a larger debate about the propriety of foreign entities, often corporations, claiming patents for uses of plants or other biological organisms that are indigenous to one country or area. If anyone is to have patent rights to uses of the Neem plant, shouldn't it be the people of India, particularly if they have first used the Neem plant in the very same way as later claimed in Grace's foreign patents? Or, alternatively, should countries all agree that the known uses of the Neem plant should not be patentable at all because they are already in the prior art? More fundamentally, are the foreign developers' efforts to claim patents over products or methods derived from another country's indigenous life a form of "biopiracy," as a number of developing countries would charge? If so, should patent or other law be interpreted or amended to address the problem of biopiracy? Consider the following discussion.

Since 2001, WIPO has delegated to the Intergovernmental Committee on Intellectual Property and Genetic Resources, Traditional Knowledge and Folklore (IGC) the task of studying the problems of biopiracy and commercial exploitation of traditional knowledge (TK), traditional cultural expression (TCE) (i.e., folklore), and genetic resources (GR). Carrying out its mandate from the WIPO General Assembly in 2010, the IGC has been working on a draft text "of an international legal instrument . . . which will ensure the effective protection of GRs, TK and TCEs." By 2011, the IGC had drafted separate texts for the protection of (1) folklore, (2) traditional knowledge, and (3) genetic resources. The texts are working drafts, available on WIPO's website, with options and alternative language proposed by various member states and stakeholders for further debate.

The three texts related to TK and GR are most relevant to stopping biopiracy. The TK draft in 2011 proposed a *sui generis* form of protection of TK to benefit indigenous peoples and local communities. The draft contains 3 alternatives for legal protection: (1) beneficiaries of TK rights would share "exclusive collective rights" in the utilization of their TK; (2) beneficiaries would be entitled to "adequate and effective legal means/measures" to protect their TK; or (3) prior informed consent and proper attribution would be required before use of TK. Although several alternatives were proposed for adequate remedies in the event of violations of the requirements under the proposal, they all afford much discretion to member states. By contrast, the draft text recognized only 2 options for the duration of TK protection, both of which lasted indefinitely, as long as the TK satisfied some criterion. The GR draft text outlines various options for adopting 5 objectives and principles for GR. A key focus of the 5 objectives is the intersection of biopiracy with intellectual property, especially patents.

PROBLEM 3–14

Sora is a tribal leader in Country Z, a populous Southeast Asian country with dense and fertile rain forests. Sora has just learned that two delegations of business executives of two MNEs will visit Country Z next month to meet with the tribe and government officials. The first delegation is from Home Supercenter, a large department store specializing in lumber and other materials for the self-starter home owner seeking to make upgrades. The second delegation is from Nature's Cure, a consumer products company that promotes a strategy for a long healthy life based on organic vitamins, food supplements, and a line of health care products based on subtropical fruits and vegetation. The government officials are eager to meet with the business delegations, and the governor of the region has already made plans to build a lavish new private mansion and to buy a private airplane. Sora is nervous and is not exactly sure what the MNEs are planning and is not even sure he wants to meet with either group. Sora would like your advice on what the MNEs are up to, whether he should meet with them, and whether he should try to form any allegiances and strategic partnerships. Are any of these alternatives risk free?

PROBLEM 3–15

You have been commissioned by the IGC of WIPO to evaluate the various proposals for Objective 2 listed below, which deal with the intersection between biopiracy and intellectual property. Evaluate each option for Objective 2, with accompanying explaining principles. Provide a report with your recommendation on which option or set of options, if any, would be best for the international community to adopt. For background, you may find helpful Prof. Dwyer's article below.

INTERGOVERNMENTAL COMMITTEE ON INTELLECTUAL PROPERTY AND GENETIC RESOURCES, TRADITIONAL KNOWLEDGE AND FOLKLORE

Draft Objectives and Principles Relating to Intellectual Property and Genetic Resources

OBJECTIVE 2

Objective 2–Options 2 and 6 NEW CONSOLIDATED TEXT

Prevent intellectual property rights involving the access and utilization of genetic resources, their derivatives and/or associated traditional knowledge from being granted where there is no prior informed consent, mutually agreed terms and/or fair and equitable benefit-sharing, and disclosure of origin.

Objective 2—Option 3

Prevent patents from being granted in error for inventions that are not novel or inventive in light of genetic resources and associated traditional knowledge.

Objective 2—Option 4

Prevent intellectual property rights from being granted in error and/or bad faith for intellectual property applications relating to genetic resources, their derivatives and/or associated traditional knowledge that do not satisfy the eligibility conditions.

Objective 2—Option 5

Ensure that no patents on life and life forms are granted for genetic resources and associated traditional knowledge, because they do not comply with the requirements of novelty and inventive step.

Objective 2—Option 7

Increase transparency in access and benefit-sharing.

PRINCIPLES OF OBJECTIVE 2

Principles of Objective 2—Option 1

Patent applicants should not receive exclusive rights on inventions that are not new or inventive. The patent system should provide certainty of rights for legitimate users of genetic resources.

Principles of Objective 2—Option 2

The intellectual property system should provide certainty of rights for legitimate users and providers of genetic resources, their derivatives and/or associated traditional knowledge. The intellectual property system must provide for mandatory disclosure requirements ensuring that the intellectual property offices become key checkpoints for disclosure and monitoring the utilization of genetic resources, their derivatives and/or associated traditional knowledge. Administrative and/or judicial authorities shall have the right to (a) prevent the further processing of the intellectual property applications or (b) prevent the granting of intellectual property rights, as well as (c) revoke intellectual property rights subject to Article 32 of the TRIPS Agreement and render unenforceable intellectual property rights when the applicant has either failed to comply with the objectives and principles or provided false or fraudulent information.

Principles of Objective 2—Option 6

Intellectual property rights applicants should not receive exclusive rights where free, prior and informed consent and fair and equitable benefit-sharing requirements for accessing and using genetic resources have not been met.

Principles of Objective 2—Option 7

Persons applying for intellectual property rights involving the use of genetic resources and/or associated traditional knowledge have a duty of good faith and candor to disclose in their applications all background information relating to the genetic resources and associated traditional knowledge, including the country of source or origin.

BIOPIRACY, TRADE, AND SUSTAINABLE DEVELOPMENT
Lorna Dwyer.
19 Colo. J. Int'l Env. L. & Pol'y 219 (2008).*

I. Introduction

Only recently has traditional knowledge (TK) of PGRs [plant genetic resources] and their medicinal and agricultural uses created social, economic, and legal issues. "PGRs consist of seeds, plants, and plant parts useful in crop breeding and their medical value, which are explored for their genetic attributes." PGRs can be "raw" or "worked," where the latter are altered by human intervention. Before the development of biotechnology in the 1980s, the global community did not take into account the ethical and economic consequences of using indigenous knowledge. The impact of globalization on indigenous societies has many facets, but the focus of this article is one of economic concern. In 1995, the estimated market value of pharmaceutical derivatives from TK was $43 billion; this represents almost thirteen percent of worldwide profits from pharmaceuticals. Developing countries use several expressions to refer to the appropriation of TK by industries of developed countries. "Biopiracy" is the term most commonly used when multinational corporations profit from the medicinal and agricultural uses of plants known to indigenous or native societies and fail to compensate those communities. Access to PGRs is an important issue because these resources fulfill many pharmaceutical and agricultural needs of the global community. As a result, many competing interests attempt to control the appropriation and use of PGRs; states, indigenous communities, and farming communities in developing countries usually compete with private multinational corporations and individuals from the developed world. Additionally, non-governmental organizations (NGOs) and international organizations sometimes intervene in defense of particular interests, groups, or communities.

III. Illustrative Examples of Biopiracy

A. Rosy Periwinkle (Catharanthus Roses)

Scientists from developed nations engineered the cancer-fighting medicines vinblastine and vincristine from the rosy periwinkle plant, found in Madagascar. Vinblastine has increased the chance of surviving childhood leukemia and is used to treat Hodgkins' disease. The U.S. pharmaceutical company Eli Lilly has patented and generated huge profits from Vincristine despite the fact that none of the financial benefits have gone to Madagascar or to the indigenous group that first made use of the plant.

The difficulty with this situation is that the pharmaceutical industry took rosy periwinkle out of Madagascar and used it in ways other than initially suggested by the indigenous people. This example illustrates the difficulties inherent in the protection of TK and biodiversity, especially

---

when the final pharmaceutical use differs from the use suggested by indigenous communities.

* * *

C. The Enola Bean

Larry Proctor, an American executive in the agricultural industry, traveled to Mexico on vacation and bought a bag of different varieties of beans that he found interesting because of their yellow color. Upon his return to the United States, Proctor began a selective breeding program, and two years later he received a patent for one of the beans, which he named the Enola bean. Proctor's company, POD–NERS LLC, admitted that its Enola bean was a descendent from a traditional Mexican bean called Mayacoba. The company argued, however, that its bean had a "better" yellow color and consistency than the Mayacoba. Proctor aggressively defended his patent by suing other companies that grow the bean and by asking for royalties on imports from Mexico. Proctor's appropriation seriously impacted Mexican farmers: export sales dropped over ninety percent, causing severe economic damage to more than 22,000 farmers in northern Mexico who depended on sales from this bean.

Proctor claimed that the "new" characteristic of his Enola bean was its color. Questions remained, however, as to whether Proctor's Enola bean was patentable (i.e., whether he had changed the plant in a way that created a "new" variety). Scientific studies concluded that "probability calculations of matching the specific Enola fingerprint showed that the most likely origin of Enola is by direct selection within pre-existing yellow-bean cultivars from Mexico, most probably 'Azufrado Peruano 87.'" Experts thus have recognized that Proctor's Enola bean is identical to the Mexican bean.

Armed with the expert studies, Action Aid, an NGO, protested the U.S. patent for Proctor's Enola bean. The Colombia-based International Center for Tropical Agriculture (CIAT), with support from FAO, also challenged the patent in 2000. In May 2008, the United States Patent and Trademark Office (USPTO) rejected all of the patent claims for Enola bean. Despite the NGO victory, Proctor and his company profited from the patent for more than seven years prior to the challenge; one-third of the twenty-year patent term.

D. Other Examples

Other examples of biopiracy include: (1) the commercialization of Hagen abyssinica products as a treatment for cancer after Ethiopians had used the plant for centuries; (2) the use of the ayahuasca plant from the Amazonian rainforest, for which a patent was granted to an American scientist but later rescinded by the PTO, in response to action taken by 400 indigenous groups; (3) the proposed patenting of basmati rice and a later finding that the term is a generic one; (4) the revocation of a patent for using Indian turmeric for wound healing; and (5) the aborted patenting of Bolivian quinoa by two American researchers. These are just a few examples of the multiple reported biopiracy claims; there are many others.

A recent report presented at a meeting of the Convention of Biological Diversity (CBD) denounced thirty-six examples of medicines, cosmetics, and agricultural products that originated in African countries but had resulted in products patented without the consent of, or benefit to, the countries of origin. The African Center of Biosafety took only one month to identify these cases. Developing countries, therefore, can expect that with a more detailed analysis on current patents, there will be more cases reported. India conducted a study of the USPTO, the United Kingdom Patent Office (UKPO), and the European Patent Office (EPO) databanks in 2000 and found 4,896 references to medical plants, eighty percent of which originated in India. By 2003, the number of patents based upon TK had risen to 15,000. A study based on a random selection of these patents showed that forty-nine percent were based on TK.

Additionally, crop-breeders and agro-biotech corporations in developing countries have obtained IPRs by exploiting PGRs within the public domain and those collected by the Consultative Group of International Agricultural Research (CGIAR) ex situ seed banks. This practice raises concerns about food security, the accessibility and adequacy of food, and the exclusion of natural and original suppliers. Even more, it affects traditional farming practices in indigenous communities, makes communities dependent on industrialized countries for most of their food, threatens the world's biodiversity, and raises the possibility that modification will lead to the loss of original genetic information.

In summary, it cannot be disputed that biopiracy practices are advancing in a way that cause great concern over public health and food security in the developing world.

[The article's discussion of various international treaties is omitted. *Ed.*]

VI. Proposed Solutions

[The article discusses a variety of proposed ways to protect against biopiracy, including (i) a "checklist" approach modeled on the CBD that requires the disclosure of information related to TK, prior consent before exploitation of TK, and benefit-sharing from use of TK, (ii) use of watchdog groups, (iii) *sui generis* forms of legal protection, such as limited common property (LCP), (iv) international treaty harmonization, (v) participation of indigenous peoples, and (vi) patent reexamination. Below is the article's discussion of "self-help."]

E. Self–Defense Mechanisms

Self-defense is always the best defense. Local governments should use their police and regulatory powers to prevent and control the misappropriation of TK. Individual nations should use their domestic immigration, intellectual property, criminal, and other laws as important tools for self-defense. Defense should be proactive and not reactive. Once a local community loses control of its TK and PGRs, the damage may be inevitable and the potential benefits unrealizable. Consequently, the precautionary approach is the most desirable option.

Enactment of IP legislation that seeks to defend TK and PGRs is sorely needed. A recent WIPO survey asked forty-seven countries if they had enacted legislation to protect TK, and most responded they had not. Some developing countries, including Costa Rica, Panama, and Nigeria, are enacting regulations on the utilization of PGRs that seek to achieve equitable PGR benefit sharing, sustainable PGR conservation, and prior informed consent requirements. In 2001 Brazil enacted a similar law, but was persuaded to modify it in 2005 because researchers criticized that it had a chilling effect on research and development.

Perhaps, most importantly, however, local TK research and management efforts are best suited to address existing TK shortcomings: first, to acknowledge the content, extension, and potential economic uses of TK; second, to correctly address the protection of PGRs and prevent their extinction; and finally, to document TK and establish it as a "prior art" developed by indigenous communities. As explained above, some countries have already taken steps in that direction. In Colombia, for instance, the Botanic Garden Jose Celestino Mutis, named after the Spanish botanist who in colonial times dedicated his life to the "Botanic Expedition of the New World," could be used for these purposes. This institution could provide a leadership example by reassuming the mission to create a databank of known and recently discovered plants, as reported by indigenous communities. It could demonstrate that local databases could be compared to and integrated into international databases and create a means for patent examiners to identify what is novel in reference to TK. Efforts to create an international database were recently pursued by WIPO, however, the global pharmaceutical industry opposed the effort, and argued that it would discourage research and development. Local efforts could strengthen the case for the WIPO database, assist in its content development, and provide a counterforce to industry opposition.

Developing countries should additionally focus on improving their negotiation skills with multinational pharmaceutical companies that seek the discovery of new PGRs. Some countries have been successful in improving their bargaining power and negotiating more favorable deals. For instance, in 2004 the Samoan government signed an agreement with the University of California to equally share the profits from a potential anti-HIV drug called "Prostratin," derived from the bark of the Samoan mamala tree. Paul Alan Cox, Director of the Institute for Ethnobotany at the National Tropical Botanical Garden in Hawaii, stated, "This may be the first time that indigenous people have extended their national sovereignty over a gene sequence." Developing countries should take heart and follow the Samoan example.

Another example of successful negotiation involved the Costa Rican government, which entered into an agreement with Merck & Co., wherein the multinational company agreed to provide financial support, share profits, and build research facilities in return for TK. From these examples it is clear that developing countries must establish unambiguous rules regarding representation of indigenous communities in order to negotiate successfully. * * *

NOTES AND QUESTIONS

1. Based on the examples and evidence cited in Prof. Dwyer's article, do you think biopiracy is a problem? As she notes elsewhere in her article, some critics contend that biopiracy claims are exaggerated, and that overprotection to stop biopiracy could deter innovation particularly in medicines. For a forceful argument that "biopiracy" is not a problem, see Jim Chen, *There's No Such Thing as Biopiracy,* ... *And It's a Good Thing Too,* 37 McGEORGE L. REV. 1 (2006) (contending that developing countries have the power to control, at the physical layer, the amount of bioprospecting within their borders).

2. *Novelty.* How, if at all, do the concerns about traditional knowledge and biopiracy relate to the issue of novelty, such as in the Neem case?

3. *New Uses of Known Plants.* Might allowing the grant of patents for certain uses of certain indigenous plants be justified on economic or other ground? What if the uses of a well known plant were either new or improvements?

4. *The Traditional Knowledge Digital Library (TKDL).* To combat biopiracy, India has spearheaded efforts to construct the Traditional Knowledge Digital Library, a database that will store thousands and thousands of ancient healing arts known as *ayurveda, unani,* and *siddha,* as well as yoga poses and other traditional knowledge. The creators of the database hope that it will stop biopirates from patenting traditional practices and inventions that have been known in India for hundreds, if not thousands, of years. The database will be accessible to patent offices for their prior art searches on a secure website. *See* John Lancaster, *India Digitizes Age–Old Wisdom,* WASH. POST, Jan. 8, 2006, at A22. What do you think of the TKDL as a way to combat biopiracy? Visit the TKDL: www.tkdl.res.in/tkdl/langdefault/common/Home. asp?GL=Eng.

5. *CBD.* As a part of the United Nations Convention on Biological Diversity (CBD), signed in 1992, 168 countries (but not the U.S.) agreed to recognize that states have "the sovereign right to exploit their own resources pursuant to their own environmental policies" (Art. 3). The CBD recognizes principles for sustainable use of resources, including (i) prior informed consent and (ii) revenue sharing in the exploitation of genetic resources from a region.

6. *Swakopmund Protocol.* In 2010, the African Regional Intellectual Property Organization (ARIPO), comprised of 17 countries, adopted the Swakopmund Protocol, a regional treaty to protect traditional knowledge (TK) and traditional cultural expressions (TCE). A fundamental principle of the Protocol is that local and traditional communities are the collective custodians of their TK and TCE and have legal rights to protect both. *See* Swakopmund Protocol, at www.aripo.org/images/Swakopmun_Protocol.pdf. ARIPO submit-

ted the Protocol to the IGC of WIPO as a model for the drafting of the IGC text on these issues.

7. *The U.S. Position.* The U.S. has attempted to walk a fine line in negotiations with developing countries over their proposals for strengthening protection against biopiracy under TRIPS (such as by incorporating features of the United Nations' Convention on Biodiversity (CBD), an agreement that the U.S. has yet to ratify). Bolivia, Brazil, Cuba, Ecuador, India, Pakistan, Peru, Thailand, and Venezuela have called for adoption of a specific agenda (or "checklist") for biopiracy topics at WTO negotiations. In a move that is a role reversal from the initial negotiations of TRIPS, the U.S. has suggested that WIPO, not the WTO, is a better forum to discuss biopiracy problems. Is the U.S. being hypocritical in its position on biopiracy? Can the U.S. credibly demand stronger IP enforcement around the world if it is "soft" on biopiracy?

4. NONOBVIOUSNESS OR INVENTIVE STEP

In addition to novelty, Article 27 of TRIPS also requires that inventions satisfy the related concept of "inventive step." Footnote 5 then explains that WTO members may deem "inventive step" as synonymous with "non-obvious." The concept of inventive step or nonobviousness is based on a rationale similar to novelty, i.e., in protecting against the grant of patents for things already in the sum of public knowledge. Under the requirement of inventive step or nonobviousness, an invention can be new, in the sense of not ever having been made before, but still fail to qualify for a patent if it is obvious to a person of ordinary skill in the art relevant to the putative invention. The rationale is that neither an old invention nor an obvious invention adds to innovation or the state of the art.

Just as in the case of proving lack of novelty, proving that an invention is obvious or lacking an inventive step involves examination of the prior art. For first-to-file countries, the critical date is the date of filing. For the U.S., the critical date for existing patents or applications filed before March 16, 2013 is the date of invention or reduction of practice (unless such date cannot be corroborated by independent evidence, in which case the date of filing provides the date of constructive reduction to practice). For applications filed on or after March 16, 2013, the critical date is the date of filing. How easy do you think it is for a patent examiner or court to determine that an invention is obvious? Consider the respective approaches of the United States and the United Kingdom in the following two cases.

U.S. Patent Code

Sec. 103. Conditions for patentability; non-obvious subject matter

(a) A patent may not be obtained though the invention is not identically disclosed or described as set forth in section 102 of this title, if the differences between the subject matter sought to be patented and the prior art are such that the subject matter as a whole would have been obvious at the time the invention was made to a person having ordinary skill in the art to which said subject matter pertains. Patentability shall not be negatived by the manner in which the invention was made. . . . *

KSR INTERNATIONAL CO. v. TELEFLEX INC.

Supreme Court of the United States.
550 U.S. 398 (2007).

JUSTICE KENNEDY delivered the opinion of the Court.

Teleflex Incorporated and its subsidiary Technology Holding Company—both referred to here as Teleflex—sued KSR International Company for patent infringement. The patent at issue, United States Patent No. 6,237,565 B1, is entitled "Adjustable Pedal Assembly With Electronic Throttle Control." The patentee is Steven J. Engelgau, and the patent is referred to as "the Engelgau patent." Teleflex holds the exclusive license to the patent.

Claim 4 of the Engelgau patent describes a mechanism for combining an electronic sensor with an adjustable automobile pedal so the pedal's position can be transmitted to a computer that controls the throttle in the vehicle's engine. When Teleflex accused KSR of infringing the Engelgau patent by adding an electronic sensor to one of KSR's previously designed pedals, KSR countered that claim 4 was invalid under the Patent Act, 35 U. S. C. § 103, because its subject matter was obvious.

In *Graham v. John Deere Co. of Kansas City*, 383 U.S. 1 (1966), the Court set out a framework for applying the statutory language of § 103, language itself based on the logic of the earlier decision in *Hotchkiss v. Greenwood*, 11 How. 248 (1851), and its progeny. *See* 383 U.S., at 15–17. The analysis is objective:

> "Under § 103, the scope and content of the prior art are to be determined; differences between the prior art and the claims at issue are to be ascertained; and the level of ordinary skill in the pertinent art resolved. Against this background the obviousness or nonobviousness of the subject matter is determined. Such secondary considerations as commercial success, long felt but unsolved needs, failure of others, etc., might be utilized to give light to the circumstances surrounding the origin of the subject matter sought to be patented." *Id.*, at 17–18.

While the sequence of these questions might be reordered in any particular case, the factors continue to define the inquiry that controls. If a court, or patent examiner, conducts this analysis and concludes the claimed subject matter was obvious, the claim is invalid under § 103.

---

* The America Invents Act amended § 103 for applications filed on March 16, 2013 or later. Adjusting to the switch to a first-to-file system, the amended § 103 measures obviousness at the effective filing date of the claimed invention (instead of the date of invention as under the 1952 Act). AIA, § 3(c) (to be codified at 35 U.S.C. § 103).

Seeking to resolve the question of obviousness with more uniformity and consistency, the Court of Appeals for the Federal Circuit has employed an approach referred to by the parties as the "teaching, suggestion, or motivation" test (TSM test), under which a patent claim is only proved obvious if "some motivation or suggestion to combine the prior art teachings" can be found in the prior art, the nature of the problem, or the knowledge of a person having ordinary skill in the art. KSR challenges that test, or at least its application in this case. Because the Court of Appeals addressed the question of obviousness in a manner contrary to § 103 and our precedents, we granted certiorari, 547 U.S. 902 (2006). We now reverse.* * *

II

A

We begin by rejecting the rigid approach of the Court of Appeals. Throughout this Court's engagement with the question of obviousness, our cases have set forth an expansive and flexible approach inconsistent with the way the Court of Appeals applied its TSM test here.

For over a half century, the Court has held that a "patent for a combination which only unites old elements with no change in their respective functions ... obviously withdraws what is already known into the field of its monopoly and diminishes the resources available to skillful men." *Great Atlantic & Pacific Tea Co. v. Supermarket Equipment Corp.*, 340 U.S. 147, 152 (1950). This is a principal reason for declining to allow patents for what is obvious. The combination of familiar elements according to known methods is likely to be obvious when it does no more than yield predictable results.

The principles underlying the[] cases [dealing with obviousness] are instructive when the question is whether a patent claiming the combination of elements of prior art is obvious. When a work is available in one field of endeavor, design incentives and other market forces can prompt variations of it, either in the same field or a different one. If a person of ordinary skill can implement a predictable variation, § 103 likely bars its patentability. For the same reason, if a technique has been used to improve one device, and a person of ordinary skill in the art would recognize that it would improve similar devices in the same way, using the technique is obvious unless its actual application is beyond his or her skill. [A] court must ask whether the improvement is more than the predictable use of prior art elements according to their established functions.

Following these principles may be more difficult in other cases than it is here because the claimed subject matter may involve more than the simple substitution of one known element for another or the mere application of a known technique to a piece of prior art ready for the improvement. Often, it will be necessary for a court to look to interrelated teachings of multiple patents; the effects of demands known to the design community or present in the marketplace; and the background knowledge possessed by a person having ordinary skill in the art, all in order to determine whether there was an apparent reason to combine the known elements in the fashion claimed by the patent at issue. To facilitate review, this analysis should be made explicit. As our precedents make clear, however, the analysis need not seek out precise teachings directed to the specific subject matter of the challenged claim, for a court can take account of the inferences and creative steps that a person of ordinary skill in the art would employ.

B

When it first established the requirement of demonstrating a teaching, suggestion, or motivation to combine known elements in order to show that the combination is obvious, the Court of Customs and Patent Appeals captured a helpful insight. *See Application of Bergel*, 292 F.2d 955, 956–957 (1961). As is clear from cases such as *Adams*, 383 U.S. 39 (1966) a patent composed of several elements is not proved obvious merely by demonstrating that each of its elements was, independently, known in the prior art. Although common sense directs one to look with care at a patent application that claims as innovation the combination of two known devices according to their established functions, it can be important to identify a reason that would have prompted a person of ordinary skill in the relevant field to combine the elements in the way the claimed new invention does. This is so because inventions in most, if not all, instances rely upon building blocks long since uncovered, and claimed discoveries almost of necessity will be combinations of what, in some sense, is already known.

Helpful insights, however, need not become rigid and mandatory formulas; and when it is so applied, the TSM test is incompatible with our precedents. The obviousness analysis cannot be confined by a formalistic conception of the words teaching, suggestion, and motivation, or by overemphasis on the importance of published articles and the explicit content of issued patents. The diversity of inventive pursuits and of modern technology counsels against limiting the analysis in this way. In many fields it may be that there is little discussion of obvious techniques or combinations, and it often may be the case that market demand, rather than scientific literature, will drive design trends. Granting patent protection to advances that would occur in the ordinary course without real innovation retards progress and may, in the case of patents combining previously known elements, deprive prior inventions of their value or utility.

C

The flaws in the analysis of the Court of Appeals relate for the most part to the court's narrow conception of the obviousness inquiry reflected in its application of the TSM test.

The first error of the Court of Appeals in this case was to foreclose this reasoning by holding that courts and patent examiners should look only to the problem the patentee was trying to solve. The Court of Appeals failed to recognize that the problem motivating the patentee may be only one of many addressed by the patent's subject matter. The question is not whether the combination was obvious to the patentee but whether the combination was obvious to a person with ordinary skill in the art. Under the correct analysis, any need or problem known in the field of endeavor at the time of invention and addressed by the patent can provide a reason for combining the elements in the manner claimed.

The second error of the Court of Appeals lay in its assumption that a person of ordinary skill attempting to solve a problem will be led only to those elements of prior art designed to solve the same problem. The primary purpose of Asano was solving the constant ratio problem; so, the court concluded, an inventor considering how to put a sensor on an adjustable pedal would have no reason to consider putting it on the Asano pedal. Common sense teaches, however, that familiar items may have obvious uses beyond their primary purposes, and in many cases a person of ordinary skill will be able to fit the teachings of multiple patents together like pieces of a puzzle. Regardless of Asano's primary purpose, the design provided an obvious example of an adjustable pedal with a fixed pivot point; and the prior art was replete with patents indicating that a fixed pivot point was an ideal mount for a sensor. The idea that a designer hoping to make an adjustable electronic pedal would ignore Asano because Asano was designed to solve the constant ratio problem makes little sense. A person of ordinary skill is also a person of ordinary creativity, not an automaton.

The same constricted analysis led the Court of Appeals to conclude, in error, that a patent claim cannot be proved obvious merely by showing that the combination of elements was "obvious to try." When there is a design need or market pressure to solve a problem and there are a finite number of identified, predictable solutions, a person of ordinary skill has good reason to pursue the known options within his or her technical grasp. If this leads to the anticipated success, it is likely the product not of innovation but of ordinary skill and common sense. In that instance the fact that a combination was obvious to try might show that it was obvious under § 103.

The Court of Appeals, finally, drew the wrong conclusion from the risk of courts and patent examiners falling prey to hindsight bias. A factfinder should be aware, of course, of the distortion caused by hindsight bias and must be cautious of arguments reliant upon ex post reasoning. *See Graham,* 383 U.S., at 36 (warning against a "temptation to read into the prior art the teachings of the invention in issue" and instructing courts to " 'guard against slipping into the use of hindsight' "). Rigid preventative rules that deny factfinders recourse to common sense, however, are neither necessary under our case law nor consistent with it.

III

When we apply the standards we have explained to the instant facts, claim 4 must be found obvious. We agree with and adopt the District

Court's recitation of the relevant prior art and its determination of the level of ordinary skill in the field. As did the District Court, we see little difference between the teachings of Asano and Smith and the adjustable electronic pedal disclosed in claim 4 of the Engelgau patent. A person having ordinary skill in the art could have combined Asano with a pedal position sensor in a fashion encompassed by claim 4, and would have seen the benefits of doing so. * * * The judgment of the Court of Appeals is reversed, and the case remanded for further proceedings consistent with this opinion.

European Patent Convention

Article 56

Inventive step

An invention shall be considered as involving an inventive step if, having regard to the state of the art, it is not obvious to a person skilled in the art. If the state of the art also includes documents within the meaning of Article 54, paragraph 3, these documents are not to be considered in deciding whether there has been an inventive step.

Article 54, paragraph 3

Novelty

(3) Additionally, the content of European patent applications as filed, of which the dates of filing are prior to the date referred to in paragraph 2 and which were published under Article 93 on or after that date, shall be considered as comprised in the state of the art.

SANDOZ GmbH v. ROCHE DIAGNOSTICS GmbH

High Court of Justice Chancery Division (Eng. & Wales).
[2004] EWHC 1313 (Ch), HC–2003–03648.*

MR. JUSTICE PATTEN:

Introduction

This is an action for the revocation of European Patent (UK) No 0,607,156. The patent teaches ways in which injectable liquid formulations (commonly known as parenterals) which have proteins as their active ingredient can be effectively preserved when prepared for multi-dose application. As granted the claim specified the use of three antimicrobial preservatives (chlorobutanol, benzyl alcohol and benzalkonium chloride) either alone or in combination at a concentration of up to 2% in the solution but the Defendant, Roche Diagnostics GmbH ("Roche") does not seek to maintain the granted claims and has applied to amend the patent in order to restrict the claims to formulations which contain one particular protein, erythropoietin ("EPO") and which utilise a combination of

---

* Reproduced by permission.

two or more of the three specified preservatives rather than any one of them singly.

Priority is claimed from 15th August 1991. The sole question for determination in relation to the amended patent is whether the process set out in the amended claims involving the combination of low concentrations of two or more of the three selected preservatives was obvious as at the priority date. The Claimant's case is that the amended claims did not disclose any inventive step and that in August 1991 the suggested combination of preservatives was an obvious experiment to try.

The Tests of Obviousness

The general principles to be applied are not in dispute. Section 3 of the Patents act 1977 provides that:

> "An invention shall be taken to involve an inventive step if it is not obvious to a person skilled in the art, having regard to any matter which forms part of the state of the art by virtue only of section 2(2) above (and disregarding section 2(3) above)."

In this case the state of the art has to be considered by reference to the published art referred to earlier in paragraph 3 and both principal experts dealt with it in their evidence. The now generally accepted approach to assessing the question of obviousness as set out in the Judgment of Oliver LJ in *Windsurfing International Inc. v. Tabur Marine (Great Britain) Ltd* [1985] RPC 59, at pp. 73–4, involves four steps:

> "The first is to identify the inventive concept embodied in the patent in suit. Thereafter, the court has to assume the mantle of the normally skilled but unimaginative addressee in the art at the priority date and to impute to him what was, at that date, common general knowledge in the art in question. The third step is to identify what, if any, differences exist between the matter cited as being 'known or used' and the alleged invention. Finally, the court has to ask itself whether, viewed without any knowledge of the alleged invention, those differences constitute steps which would have been obvious to the skilled man or whether they require any degree of invention."

In general I propose to deal with the issues in that way although stages 2 and 4 will need modification to accommodate the plea of obviousness over common general knowledge.

The Inventive Concept

There is no dispute about this. The inventive concept of Claim 1 is the use of one of the specified combinations of the three preservatives in order to produce a multi-dose formulation of EPO. The inventive concept of Claim 3 is the use of the combination of benzyl alcohol and benzalkonium chloride. The inventive concept of Claims 6 and 7 is the use of that particular combination in the low concentrations specified.

The Person Skilled in the Art

The attributes of the person skilled in the art have been the subject of repeated judicial comment and analysis. The latest attempt to describe this fictional character was by Jacob LJ in *Rockwater v. Technip France SA* [2004] EWCA Civ. 381 who said that the skilled man, if real, would be "very boring—a nerd." Not every member of the Court of Appeal was happy to accept this term which the dictionary defines as "a person who lacks social skills or is boring and studious." Pill LJ preferred to stick to Lord Reid's statement in *Technograph v. Mills and Rockley* [1972] RPC 346 at page 355:

"The hypothetical addressee is a skilled technician who is well acquainted with workshop technique and who has carefully read the relevant literature. He is supposed to have an unlimited capacity to assimilate the contents of, it may be, scores of specifications but to be incapable of a scintilla of invention. When dealing with obviousness, unlike novelty, it is permissible to make a 'mosaic' out of the relevant documents, but it must be a mosaic which can be put together by an unimaginative man with no inventive capacity."

The choice between the two descriptions is more a matter of taste than substance. The standard which the law is seeking to apply to judge the inventiveness of the Patent in suit is not a particularly high one. As Jacob LJ said in paragraphs 8 and 9 of his judgment in the *Rockwater* case the skilled person:

"Reads all the prior art, but unless it forms part of his background technical knowledge, having read (or learnt about) one piece of prior art, he forgets it before reading the next unless it can form an uninventive mosaic or there is a sufficient cross-reference that it is justified to read the documents as one. He does on the other hand, have a very good background technical knowledge—the so-called common general knowledge. Luxmoore J's happy phrase 'common stock of knowledge' conveys the flavour of what this notional man knows. Other countries within the European Patent Convention apply, so far as I understand matters, essentially the same standard."

In the present case there are disputes both as to the identity of the skilled person and in relation to what constituted common general knowledge at the time. The first of these issues arises because the Claimant's expert, Professor Michael Allwood, considers that the Patent is not addressed to a single individual but to a team. His evidence is that pharmaceutical companies employ people with a wide range of scientific expertise and experience in order to develop new or existing products.

The Defendant's expert, Professor Theodore Randolph, takes a slightly different view. His evidence is that the skilled person at the time would have been one of what he describes as the new breed of formulation chemists involved in this field.

Professor Randolph said that the skilled person in the shape of the protein formulation chemist would have had access to a microbiology support group which would be able to test the efficacy of the preservatives and could (with support from a separate clinical group) have been able to define doses and other patient related issues. Advice on regulatory matters would also have been available.

The skilled person can of course be a team. In such cases one is hypothesising "an assembly of nerds with different basic skills, all unimaginative": see *Rockwater* per Jacob LJ at paragraph 10. In the end however there was far less between the experts on this topic than their witness statements might at first suggest.

In the light of this evidence it seems to me that it may be unnecessary to choose between Professor Randolph's model of the protein formulation scientist and Professor Allwood's model based on a team. If a choice had to be made my own preference would be for the protein formulation scientist envisaged by Professor Randolph—because (as I shall indicate later) he was more likely to be used to develop a product based on recombinant proteins but in substance this is unlikely to make much difference. I say that because even if one postulates a team comprising three players; the formulation scientist, the protein scientist and the microbiologist; it is clear that the role and views of the protein scientist are likely to be pivotal in relation to the course of the project. The Patent in its amended (and even unamended) form is concerned with the preservation of a protein based solution. The effectiveness of the product depends upon being able to deliver the protein to the patient in a multi-dose formulation which does not degrade or reduce the effectiveness of the active ingredient. Expertise in formulating parenterals with an effective preservative content only provides the general background against which the creation of a suitable preservative regime for use in connection with proteins can be considered. It would be to the protein scientist that the team would look for guidance as to which in any list of preservatives were worth testing in the relation to the protein that was to be used.

Common General Knowledge

Common general knowledge is described by Luxmoore J in *British Acoustic Films* 53 RPC 221 at p. 250 as "what is generally known and accepted without question by the bulk of those who are engaged in the particular art." It therefore excludes, for example, articles in scientific journals even if widely circulated and read unless their contents have become received wisdom. This principle also underlies the distinction between common general knowledge and prior art. In *Raychem Corporations's Patents* [1998] RPC 31 p. 40 Laddie J. referred to the matter this way:

"The court is trying to determine in a common sense way how the average skilled but non-inventive technician would have reacted to the pleaded prior art if it had been put before him in his work place or laboratory. The common general knowledge is the technical background of the notional man in the art against which the prior art must be considered. This is not limited to material he has memorised and has at the front of his mind. It includes all that material in the field he is working in which he knows exists, which he would refer to as a matter of course if he cannot remember it and which he understands is generally regarded as sufficiently reliable to use as a foundation for further work or to help understand the pleaded prior art. In many cases common general knowledge will include or be reflected in readily available trade literature which a man in the art would be expected to have at his elbow and regard as basic reliable information.''

The Claimant relies on the contents of eight works which Professor Allwood says in his first report were current in 1991 and would have formed part of the common general knowledge of the skilled addressees. They are: (i) The Handbook of Pharmaceutical Excipients ("the HPE"); (ii) Remington's Pharmaceutical Sciences; (iii) The Pharmaceutical Handbook ("the Handbook"); (iv) Martindale: the Extra Pharmacopoiea; (v) The Guide to Microbiological control in Pharmaceuticals ("the Guide") edited by S.P. Denyer and R.M. Baird; (vi) The British Pharmacopoiea; (vii) The European Pharmacopoiea; and (viii) The United States Pharmacopoiea.

Obviousness over Common Knowledge

The Claimant's case is postulated on the basis that it would have been obvious to any formulation scientist (including his team) in 1991 that it was worth trying to combine what were conventional preservatives and test their reaction upon a protein based formulation. Professor Allwood's evidence in chief was that benzalkonium chloride, benzyl alcohol and chlorobutanol were part of a recognised group of about ten preservatives commonly in use in 1991 and that at the time the benefits of using the preservatives in combination to achieve synergy were well known.

The critical step is the use of the chosen preservatives in combination. Professor Allwood says that it would have been routine for the skilled addressees to have tried a range of preservatives and to have tested synergistic combinations of conventional preservatives as part of that process.

I think that however obvious it may now seem a decade later to have tested these combinations, that is very much the product of hindsight. I believe that the skilled person in 1991 would have taken a selective and conservative approach designed to identify which of the preservatives known to be of use with proteins would provide the most effective longer term protection for the solution. There is nothing in the evidence which convinces me that based on his common knowledge the skilled addressee would have regarded it as obvious to use a combination of preservatives which he had previously rejected for single use. On the contrary I believe he would have qualified his knowledge that the combination of (for example) benzyl alcohol and benzalkonium chloride could produce a better microbial effect with an assumption that they would retain their same chemical characteristics if applied to a protein. He would not therefore have regarded it as obvious to test whether that assumption was correct. That is the province of general experimentation which is the very thing which the skilled addressee with his lack of inventive capacity is supposed not to indulge in. The claim based on obviousness over common knowledge fails in relation to Claims 1 and 3 and also therefore to claims 6 and 7.

Conclusions

For these reasons the claim fails and will be dismissed. In the absence of agreement I will hear counsel on the form of the order and on costs.

NOTES AND QUESTIONS

1. How do the approaches to nonobviousness compare under U.S. and UK law? Which opinion—*KSR* or *Sandoz*—did you find more helpful in explaining how a court is supposed to analyze nonobviousness under their respective countries' laws? Can you suggest a possible minimum standard for nonobviousness based on the two countries' approaches?

2. *Prior art references.* As demonstrated in both *KSR* and *Sandoz*, courts (or the patent offices) typically examine prior art contained in printed material in order to determine whether an invention was obvious. Both cases speak about the use of a combination or "mosaic" of several different prior art references, none of which in itself discloses the entire invention. Does U.S. and UK patent law permit several prior art references to be pieced together in a way that can establish the obviousness of an invention? If so, are there any limits on when piecing together of prior art references can be properly used under either U.S. or UK law?

3. *Teaching-suggestion-motivation to combine (TSM) test.* Explain the TSM test. How does it relate to prior art? Did the U.S. Supreme Court reject the use of the TSM test in obviousness determinations?

4. *South Korean approach.* A year after *KSR* was decided in the U.S., the South Korean Supreme Court decided an important case of inventive step. Reversing the Patent Court's finding that 3M's prism film lacked an inventive step based on the combination of two prior art references, the Korean Supreme Court ruled that the prior art contained no suggestion or motivation to combine the two prior art references. Combining the two references was based on improper hindsight bias. *See 3M Company v. LMS Corp.*, 2010 Hu 2698 (2011). Commentators have characterized the Court's test as comparable to the TSM test from the Federal Circuit in the U.S., now discredited, to some extent, in *KSR*.

5. *Common sense and common knowledge.* Do the U.S. and UK decisions allow patent examiners to rely on "common sense" or "common knowledge" in finding an invention obvious?

6. *Hindsight.* The courts' wariness to the use of common sense and common knowledge under both U.S. and UK law stems from a worry that

inventions will mistakenly seem obvious in hindsight based on unsubstantiated assertions of "common sense" or "common knowledge." Do you agree with this worry, or do you trust the ability of patent examiners and reviewing courts to determine what would be common sense or common knowledge?

7. *Person of Ordinary Skill in the Art (POSA).* Why is obviousness measured from the viewpoint of the "person of ordinary skill in the art" (POSA)? What exactly is a "person of ordinary skill in the art," and how does a patent examiner or a court adopt that viewpoint? Is it possible for a court or patent examiner to assume the mindset or perspective of this hypothetical person? Should POSA be viewed as someone who is just a "skillful mechanic" (as suggested by U.S. law in *Hotchkiss*), or someone who is just a "very boring" "nerd" (as suggested by UK law in *Sandoz*)?

What do you think of the argument in *Sandoz* that the person having ordinary skill in the art would be a *research team* of several scientists of different expertise? If several people having ordinary skill in different arts work as a team, wouldn't it be more likely to imagine that the team would think to combine their respective basic knowledge? Isn't teamwork meant to be collaborative and synergistic?

8. *No Paris priority dates for obviousness purposes.* The U.S., the EU, and Japan generally agree that the Paris priority date of a foreign application should *not* be used to establish the date on which it becomes prior art in the domestic country for purposes of determining nonobviousness. Why do you think countries have rejected "offensive" use of Paris priority for the purposes of determining nonobviousness of an invention? Could part of the reason be that countries have typically been more permissive in allowing the combination of several prior art references for nonobviousness review, but have typically required that novelty review be limited to finding a single prior art reference that contains all elements of the invention? Would allowing courts to combine prior art references *and* to use Paris priority dates offensively for prior art be undesirable?

5. ENABLEMENT

Article 29 of TRIPS establishes a final requirement for countries to impose before patents are allowed for inventions—enablement and the disclosure of the invention in the patent application. Unlike the requirements of subject matter, utility, novelty, and nonobviousness, however, enablement is less of a substantive requirement, and more of a procedural or administrative requirement—meaning that if an invention satisfies the four previously discussed substantive requirements, the inventor (or the hired patent attorney) presumably should be able to fulfill the process of describing adequately the invention in a patent application, at least if careful attention is paid to the drafting of the patent application.

Under TRIPS Article 29, countries must require that "an applicant for a patent . . . disclose the invention in a manner sufficiently clear and complete for the invention to be carried out by a person skilled in the art." The rationale behind this rule goes back to the *quid pro quo* underlying patent law: inventors get patent rights to their invention, in exchange for their public disclosure of the know-how underlying their inventions.

Article 29 also gives countries the option to require the applicant to provide (i) "the best mode for carrying out the invention known to the inventor at the filing date," (ii) the priority date of the application if priority is claimed, and (iii) "information concerning his corresponding foreign applications and grants." The U.S. Patent Code has a best mode requirement that requires the inventor to "set forth the best mode contemplated by the inventor of carrying out his invention," but the America Invents Act changed the requirement so as no longer to be the basis for invalidating a patent upon lack of compliance. AIA, § 15 (codified at 35 U.S.C. § 282).

NOTES AND QUESTIONS

1.   Can a WTO country impose even more exacting standards for the patent application than the ones required or allowed under Article 29 of TRIPS? For example, what happens if a country requires a level of specificity in the patent application even beyond one that is "sufficiently clear and complete for the invention to be carried out by a person skilled in the art"?

2.   Some critics of recent Federal Circuit decisions in the U.S. might argue that U.S. law goes beyond the TRIPS standard. The Federal Circuit has held that U.S. patent law requires an adequate written description of the invention *separate and apart from* the enablement requirement. *See Regents of the Univ. of Cal. v. Eli Lilly & Co.*, 119 F.3d 1559, 1567 (Fed. Cir. 1997); *Enzo Biochem, Inc. v. Gen–Probe Inc.*, 323 F.3d 956, 968 (Fed. Cir. 2002); *University of Rochester v. G.D. Searle & Co.*, 358 F.3d 916 (Fed Cir. 2004). Under U.S. law, the written description in the application must establish that the inventor truly "possessed the invention at the time of original filing," judged from the standard of the person of ordinary skill in the art. *See Moba B.V. v. Diamond Automation, Inc.*, 325 F.3d 1306, 1320 (Fed. Cir. 2003). Thus, it might be possible under U.S. law that an application satisfies the enablement requirement, but not the written description requirement.

Assume for this question that the U.S. written description is more onerous to patentees than the standard set forth in Article 29 of TRIPS. *Cf.* Janice M. Mueller, *The Evolving Application of the Written Description Requirement to Biotechnological Inventions*, 13 BERKELEY TECH. L.J. 615, 617 (1998) (describing "[t]he *Lilly* court's elevation of written description to an effective 'super enablement' standard"). Does the U.S. have discretion to impose a more stringent standard that has the effect of denying a greater number of patents? Should Article 29 be read to allow such discretion? If so, should there be any limit to a country's discretion in imposing higher standards in patent drafting under Article 29? What happens if a country required patent applicants to draft their claims in at least 500 pages, and to be sufficiently understandable to the average layperson, explaining every single scientific or technical term in footnotes?

6. SPECIAL DISCUSSION: FUTURE HARMONIZATION OF PATENT LAWS AND PROCEDURES

a. The Need for More Patent Harmonization?

PATENT LAW HARMONIZATION: THE TIME IS NOW

David J. Kappos, Under Secretary of Commerce for Intellectual Property and Director of the U.S. Patent and Trademark Office, excerpts of article from 2011.

Our patent laws ... are stuck in the last century and have not kept up with a technological and commercial system that has become global, with ideas and technology, and with products and services, moving across borders. In addition, the laws governing patenting of these inventions vary markedly from country to country. This leaves the patent system, ironically, as something of a laggard among commercial legal regimes. In order to meet the challenges presented by a mounting backlog of patent applications, the patent system must become significantly more harmonized.

Harmonization—the alignment of laws and procedures among intellectual property (IP) systems to ensure consistency and clarity of rights for the world's innovators—is a prerequisite to maximizing the development and dissemination of innovation and thereby improving quality of life for all the world's people. Harmonization is also absolutely essential to reducing the global patent backlog and reducing the amount of time it takes innovators around the world to get a patent.

Substantive patent law harmonization is a critical step in the process of reducing application backlogs worldwide. Harmonization enables worksharing—the critical processes that allow IP offices to maximize cooperation and avoid the inefficient and costly duplication of efforts between offices. Harmonization will create certainty around rights and help ensure consistent IP outcomes for domestic firms in foreign offices and courts. And harmonization will ensure faster review of applications, allowing companies to take their innovative products into the global marketplace without fear of misappropriation.

As in the United States, Europe, Japan, and other major trading partners are reconsidering whether their patent systems are suited to meet the challenges of the new economy. Developing countries also are looking at ways to adapt the international patent system to meet their needs in promoting greater socioeconomic development and to provide more opportunities for their citizens to share in the wealth of technological progress.

To be sure, harmonization is not about imposing the will of any country or group of countries onto another or about challenging patent sovereignty. These efforts also are not about imposing higher levels of patent protection on developing countries. Rather, harmonization efforts are aimed at achieving the best policies and the best practices to improve the global patent system for all stakeholders.

Past Attempts at Harmonization

Substantive patent law harmonization is not a new concept. Indeed, it has been the subject of discussion in international fora for the better part of 50 years. Unfortunately, past attempts at harmonization have been marked by periods of intensive activity followed by disappointing results. There have been notable successes—the Patent Cooperation Treaty, the WTO TRIPS Agreement, and the Patent Law Treaty (PLT) have been milestones on the road to rationalizing the international patent system. But the objective of deeper harmonization of other areas of substantive patent law, such as prior art, novelty, and nonobviousness—the areas on which decisions on patentability usually depend—remains elusive.

Part of the reason for lack of success has been the inability to reconcile differing perspectives on the objectives of the patent system. When talks on the Substantive Patent Law Treaty (SPLT) were launched at the World Intellectual Property Organization (WIPO) in 2000, there was optimism that the recently and successfully concluded procedural PLT would serve as a catalyst for major progress on harmonizing substantive law. It quickly became apparent, however, that developing and developed countries had very different views as to the objectives of substantive harmonization, including whether it was an appropriate goal. As a result, discussions at WIPO effectively broke down in 2005.

Now there can be little doubt; innovative firms are setting up shop and moving their goods and services into markets with consistent IP protection. Developing countries realize they can no longer afford to sit on the sidelines and watch the benefits of IP systems accrue only to the developed world. Similarly, companies cannot afford to ignore expansive consumer markets in the developing world. Consistent IP protection will allow those firms to bring goods and services that enhance quality of life to those markets and set price points that ensure profitability for companies as well as access to life-changing goods and services for people.

Another factor limiting progress has been the view that harmonization should be seen as a negotiated trade-off rather than an adoption of global best practices. This was the issue in "Group B+," the group of experts that was formed outside of WIPO in 2005 to continue discussions on substantive harmonization following the collapse of the SPLT discussions. Group B+ came to an impasse in 2006—2007 after failure to agree on what should be included or excluded from the "reduced package" of prior art-related provisions then under discussion, particularly differences with regard to a U.S.-style 12–month grace period and 18–month period before publication of pending applications.

Another important factor behind the lack of progress over the last decade has been the context in which the discussions were held. Discussions in WIPO and Group B+ were not animated by a sense of economic urgency, like today. Rather, the climate was one of relative global economic optimism and prosperity. The length and depth of the recession, however, has shattered that view. Government and business frustration with the status quo has resulted in a renewed interest in constructing a sensible, streamlined, and effective international patent system.

The Time Is Now

The time for substantive harmonization is now. We are operating in a global economy, business innovation is happening across borders. The IP system needs to be supportive of this new reality. We can no longer afford to ignore new economic realities and the role the patent system plays in them.

Therefore, the question at this time is not whether, but how, to move the process forward. There are two essential components to achieving this. The first component, as the participants agreed, is that as harmonization is a global matter affecting global trade and interests, the discussion "must be taken global and also must continue to include both developing and developed members." Taking into account the views of interested developing countries is going to be critical to the success of this effort. Equally critical will be the participation of our European colleagues. Europe is in the midst of a historic debate concerning the establishment of a unitary European patent system, one that could replace the current system of individually validated and enforceable patent rights in each European country. Harmonization of patent law between Europe and the United States would not only help reduce patent pendency but also would significantly boost trade and open markets.

The second component critical to progress is the need to focus not on trade-offs but on best practices. [The America Invents Act] will contribute significantly to the discussions in this regard, as it demonstrates the willingness of the United States to move unilaterally to what it considers to be global best practices. These include long-standing "asks" from other countries that the United States switches from first-to-invent to first-inventor-to-file and that it make changes to its prior art and novelty regimes to move away from more parochial interests towards a system reflecting the global nature of business and trade. [T]he United States will move to a first-inventor-to-file system because that is what is best for inventors and best serves the IP system. First-inventor-to-file is a best practice that that will add certainty to the system and help businesses, large and small, to make better and more certain decisions around their IP assets.

Global best practices in the areas of grace period, definitions of prior art, patentability standards, submissions of art by third parties, and disclosure requirements can and should emerge from an open dialogue aimed at creating the best IP systems possible.

NOTES AND QUESTIONS

1. Do you agree with Director Kappos on the need for greater harmonization in patent laws and procedures? Is the global economic downturn in 2008 a relevant factor to consider?

2. Are you convinced that developing countries will or should agree to further patent harmonization?

3. How does patent harmonization, or the lack thereof, affect the backlog of patent applications, in Director Kappos's view?

4. Is harmonization of patent procedures in the 21st century just as important as harmonization of substantive patent law?

b. Trilateral Review in EPO, JPO, and USPTO

The Trilateral Office is an organization set up to enhance cooperation between the United States Patent Office (USPTO), the European Patent Office (EPO), and the Japanese Patent Office (JPO), which handle the vast majority of patent filings in the world. Established in 1983, the Trilateral Office coordinates projects aimed at streamlining and harmonizing the patent prosecution process in all three offices. It also organizes a conference every year. *See* www.trilateral.net.

Objectives. The Trilateral Office has several objectives: (1) enhance work sharing to reduce patent application backlogs; (2) develop the Patent Cooperation Treaty (PCT); (3) harmonize classifications of inventions; (4) develop translations tools for patent documents; (5) harmonize prosecution for biotechnology; (6) enhance information sharing between offices; (7) enhance training for examiners; and (8) achieve interoperability in technology systems.

The Patent Prosecution Highway (PPH), probably the most widely known initiative, allows a patent application to be examined by one of the member patent offices. If the claims are deemed allowable, the file is forwarded to other participating offices. The results of the Office of First Filing (OFF) are used for an expedited or fast-track examination in the Office of Second Filing (OSF). A trial PPH program was started in September 2008. The USPTO has bilateral PPH programs now with 18 other patent offices, including from Australia, Korea, Mexico, and Russia. The USPTO indicates that fast-track examination in its office will occur within 2 to 3 months of the request, and that more than 90 percent of PPH applications are allowed during fast track if the OFF allowed the claim.

Significantly, the PPH program has been expanded to include a pilot PPH–PCT that allows fast-track examinations during the national phase after the international phase of the PCT is complete. Thus, if an applicant receives a favorable international preliminary report on patentability from an eligible PCT office, the applicant can request the patent application receive a fast-track examination in the USPTO under the PCT–PPH program. The fast-track examination in the USPTO has the potential to change dramatically how applications are reviewed by increasing the weight of PCT examinations, which, in the past, may have received little, if any, weight.

Other notable programs include a program to standardize technology to allow better communication among the offices, as well as training and exchanges for the examiners of each office. The Trilateral Office developed a secure network—called TRINet—for the transfer of data among all the member offices. The Trilateral Office programs have begun to include other nations. The network now also connects to the Canadian Intellectual Property Office, the Korean Intellectual Property Office (KIPO), and IP Australia (IPAU). The Trilateral Office invited the other members of the "IP5," KIPO, and the State Intellectual Property Office of China (SIPO), to the PPH trials.

Comparative studies. The Trilateral Review also conducts studies among the three different patent offices. In 2009, the Trilateral Review submitted case studies to the USPTO, the EPO, and the JPO. The review did two sets of case studies. In one set, the different offices were asked to determine novelty, focusing on features that are implicitly or inherently disclosed in the prior art. In the second set, the offices were asked to make a determination of inventiveness or nonobviousness. Some of these cases were real, and some were hypothetical. The Review then compared the results of each office.

In half of the six cases, the three offices disagreed on the novelty of the invention. Each office was in the minority once, meaning it disagreed with the other two offices' determination of novelty. *See* Trilateral Office, *Comparative Study on Hypothetical/Real Cases: Novelty* 41–45 (Nov. 2009). One of the case studies is excerpted below. The six cases studies dealt with difficult cases involving possible inherent anticipation of an invention in the prior art. For prior art to anticipate an invention, it must disclose each and every element of the claimed invention—either expressly or implicitly. An implicit disclosure is one in which the prior art does not explicitly contain at least one element of the claimed invention, but can be said to disclose the invention implicitly or inherently. Of course, the key question is how to determine if something is "inherent" or "implicit" in prior art— a question that has confounded courts for some time. *See* Janice M. Mueller & Donald S. Chisum, *Enabling Patent Law's Inherent Anticipation Doctrine*, 45 Hous. L. Rev. 1101 (2008).

The three patent offices agreed on the determination of inventive step or nonobviousness. Out of the six case studies, the offices only disagreed once. The JPO determined a claimed invention did not have an inventive step over the prior art, while the other two offices determined that there was an inventive step. *See* Trilateral Office, *Comparative Study on Hypothetical/Real Cases: Inventive Step/Non-obviousness* 53–55 (Nov. 2008). The Review concluded that while the substantive tests that the offices use are slightly different, they mostly reached the same result. The basic standard was whether a person of ordinary skill in the art would have a reasonable basis for arriving at the claimed invention from the prior art.

COMPARATIVE STUDY ON HYPOTHETICAL/REAL CASES: NOVELTY

Trilateral Office (Nov. 2009).

3.5. Case 5

(1) Outline of the Application (US 08/187,111)

[Claim]

A dispensing top for passing only several kernels of a popped popcorn at a time from an open-ended container filled with popped popcorn, having a generally conical shape and an opening at each end, the opening at the reduced end allows several kernels of popped popcorn to pass through at the same time, and means at the enlarged end of the top to embrace the open end of the container, the taper of the top being uniform and such as to by itself jam up the popped popcorn before the end of the cone and permit the dispensing of only a few kernels at a shake of a package when the top is mounted on the container.

[Description]

The invention is directed to a device for dispensing popped popcorn. The device is conically shaped with a large opening that fits on a container and a smaller opening at the opposite end that allows popped popcorn to pass through when the device is attached to a popcorn container and turned upside down.

[Drawings]

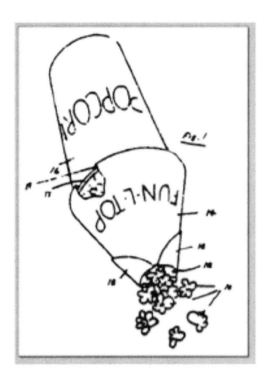

(2) Outline of the Prior Art Swiss Patent No. 172,689 to Harz (January 16, 1935)

The Harz patent discloses "a spout for nozzle-ready canisters," which may be tapered inward in a conical fashion, and it states that the spout is useful for purposes such as dispensing oil from an oil can. [See Figure 5 below.]

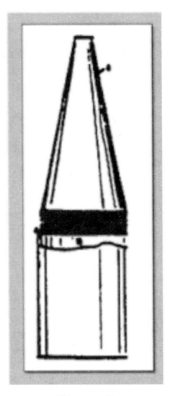

Figure 5

(3) Assessments of Novelty by each Office

[EPO]

The EPO considers that the claimed dispensing top is not anticipated by the Swiss Patent CH 172689 to Harz. This document, figure 5, discloses a dispensing top having all the technical features of claim 1, except for the following functional feature: "the opening at the reduced end allows several kernels of popped popcorn to pass through at the same time."

Indeed, although the EPO fully agrees to the court's statements that "the recitation of a new use for an old product does not make a claim to that old product patentable" and that "contrary to Schreiber's suggestion, the structure disclosed in Harz is not limited to use as an oil can dispenser", the EPO is not able to find a clear basis in the Swiss Patent for the examiner's affirmation that "the opening of a conically shaped top as disclosed in Harz is inherently of a size sufficient to allow several kernels of popped popcorn to pass through at the same time."

The only information given in the Harz Patent which is relevant to the above functional feature seems to be:

–... due to its cone shape, the discharge port (6) can be introduced the ingot mouth of a conventional car's oil tank..." (page 1, left column, lines 11–14 of the Swiss Patent).

From this information, it can be deduced that the cone shape is such that not all kernels of popped popcorn pass through the dispensing top at once but is such "as to by itself jam up the popped popcorn before the end of the cone" (as claimed in the claim). However, it would appear that it cannot be deduced from the Harz patent that the size of the open end is sufficient to let several kernels of popped kernels pass through at a time, i.e. at least 10 mm.

It is noted that novelty according to Article 54 EPC is a strict and narrow concept in the sense that all claimed features must be disclosed unambiguously by the prior art document. Lack of novelty may not be based on probabilities. Inherent or intrinsic disclosure is only acknowledged in case that it would not be possible for the skilled person to interpret the feature in the prior art document in another way as claimed. However, in the present case, the skilled person could interpret the dispensing top of the Harz Patent such as to comprise an open end of less than 10 mm.

[JPO]

The JPO considers that the claimed invention seems to be novel. The cited document (Harz patent) discloses the dispensing top whose shape is similar to the claimed invention in terms of following points:

> having a generally conical shape
> opening at each end
> having means at the enlarged end of the top to embrace the open end of the container
> the taper of the top being uniform

On the other hand, the cited document fails to disclose that the dispensing top is "permitting the dispensing of only a few kernels of popped popcorn at a shake of package" (In other word, the dispensing top allows several kernels of popped popcorn to pass through at the same time).

When a claim includes a limitation of use and the claimed invention can be construed as an invention based on discovering an unknown attribute of a product and finding that the product is suitable for new use due to the presence of such attribute, the limitation of use should be regarded as having a meaning that specifies the claimed invention and it is appropriate to construe the claimed invention by including the aspect of the limitation of use. In such case, the claimed invention is novel unless the cited document discloses the limitation of use. However the claimed invention in Case 5 isn't considered to be such case.

Instead, the claimed invention is construed as having a structure which is suitable for permitting the dispensing of only a few kernels of popped popcorn at a shake of package. Thus, if the cited document discloses the suitable structure, even though the limitation of use is not literally disclosed, the claimed invention lacks the novelty. As mentioned above, the shape of dispensing top in the cited document is similar to the claimed invention. So, whether the size of the dispensing top in the cited document is suitable for permitting the dispensing of only a few kernels of popped popcorn at a shake of package is an important issue.

However, the cited document merely discloses the dispensing top is introduced the ingot mouth of a conventional car's oil tank and its size isn't clear. As a result, the cited document can't be considered to disclose the structure which is suitable for permitting the dispensing of only a few kernels of popped popcorn at a shake of package and the claimed invention seems to be novel.

[USPTO]

Claim 1 is rejected under 35 U.S.C. § 102(b) as being anticipated by Harz. In Figure 5, Harz discloses a dispensing top for an open ended container. The top is conical in shape with means at the enlarged end to embrace the container shown as threads in Figure 5. The taper of the top is uniform to each end. The dispensing top of Harz is capable of functioning and of being used to dispense popped popcorn in the manner set forth in claim 1.

Note that the examiner's rejection was affirmed by both the Board of Patent Appeals and Interferences and the Federal Circuit in *In re Schreiber*, 44 USPQ2d 1429 (Fed. Cir. 1997). The court stated that "[t]o anticipate a claim, a prior art reference must disclose every limitation of the claimed invention, either explicitly or inherently ... the question whether a claim limitation is inherent in a prior art reference is a factual issue on which evidence may be introduced." The court went on to say that "[a]lthough Schreiber is correct that Harz does not address the use of the disclosed structure to dispense popcorn, the absence of a disclosure relating to function does not defeat the Board's finding of anticipation. It is well settled that the recitation of a new intended use for an old product does not make a claim to that old product patentable." *Schreiber* at 1431. The court stated that "[t]he examiner and the Board both addressed the question whether the functional limitations of Schreiber's claim gave it patentable weight and concluded that they did not, because those limitations were found to be inherent in the Harz prior art reference ... an embodiment according to Harz (Fig. 5) and the embodiment depicted in figure 1 of Schreiber's application have the same general shape. For that reason, the examiner was justified in concluding that the opening of a conically shaped top as disclosed by Harz is inherently of a size sufficient to 'allow [ ] several kernels of popped popcorn to pass through at the same time' and that the taper of Harz's conically shaped top is inherently of such a shape 'as to by itself jam up the popped popcorn before the end of the cone and permit the dispensing of only a few kernels at a shake of a package when the top is mounted on the container.' The examiner therefore correctly found that Harz established a *prima facie* case of anticipation." *Schreiber* at 1432. In addition, the court stated that "contrary to Schreiber's suggestion, the structure disclosed in Harz is not limited to use as an oil can dispenser. While that use is given as the principal example of the uses to which the invention could be put, nothing in the Harz patent suggests that the invention is in any way limited to that use. In sum, Schreiber's declaration fails to show that Harz inherently lacks the functionally defined limitations recited in claim 1 of the application. Accordingly, we agree with the Board that Schreiber has failed to rebut the *prima facie* case of anticipation identified by the examiner. The Board's factual finding on the issue of anticipation is therefore *affirmed." Schreiber* at 1433.

NOTES AND QUESTIONS

1.   Why did the U.S. Patent Office come out with a different result than the EPO and JPO in Case Study 5? What did the USPTO view differently? Which patent office's analysis on the novelty of the popcorn dispenser is most persuasive?

2.   Should the goals of the Trilateral Review be expanded to a Multilateral Review and include interested patent offices in other WTO countries?

3.   Would there be a need for Trilateral Review if the WTO had a universal patent system with a unitary law for all patents around the world? Does a universal patent system offer any advantages in terms of prosecution of patents that the Trilateral Office can never attain, no matter how much work-sharing occurs among the patent offices?

4.   Is it a violation of national treatment or the most-favored nation principle for the U.S. to extend the PPH fast-track application process to a few WTO countries, but not others?

c.   Peer-to-Patent Projects

Another interesting initiative to improve patent examination is the Peer-to-Patent Project. Proposed by Professor Beth Noveck, Peer-to-Patent allows individuals in the community to assist the patent office in finding relevant prior art pertaining to a patent application. By using crowdsourcing techniques, patent examination may become better at winnowing out nonmeritorious inventions.

The United States Patent and Trademark Office (USPTO) conducted the first and second Peer-to-Patent trials from June 2007 to June 2009. The trials were open only to software and business method inventions, and had a maximum of 400 patent application slots. 189 patents were submitted to the process by their applicants. The benefit of submitting a patent to the trial is that the patent goes to the beginning of the patent examination line. Under the process, patent applications are posted to the Peer-to-Patent website. Registered members from the public can join a patent discussion group and submit potential prior art. The group then votes on the prior art and the top prior art gets forwarded to the examiner in the USPTO. This public examination period lasts 90 days. Only the prior art the community agrees on is forwarded to the examiner. The community submitted 603 pieces of prior art. Based on the community's submission of prior art, 30 patent applications received rejections. In 15 of these rejections, the examiner did not find the relevant prior art in an independent search. The third trial started in October 2010 and was scheduled to run through September 2011. The trial now also includes chemistry and telecommunications inventions. *See* New York Law School Center for Patent Innovation, *Peer to Patent First Anniversary Report*, June 2008; New York Law School Center for Patent Innovation, *Peer to Patent Second Anniversary Report*, June 2009.

Other countries, including the UK, South Korea, Australia, and Japan, have started or plan to start their own Peer-to-Patent project. In addition, WIPO is currently implementing its own system as a part of the PCT application process. The WIPO Patent Cooperation Treaty ('PCT') Working Group has been meeting to discuss a system of allowing third party observations to be submitted to the International Bureau to be included in files sent to national offices. Submissions would be reviewed by the International Bureau and screened for relevance. Notably, however, the WIPO system would not have the crowd-sourcing element of community review and collective decisionmaking on prior art that is characteristic of the Peer-to-Patent model. The WIPO trial website was scheduled to become operational in early 2012. *See* Patent Cooperation Treaty Working Group, *Third Party Observation System; Quality Feedback System,* (April 29, 2011); Patent Cooperation Treaty Working Group, *Draft Report,* at ¶ 124 (July 11, 2011).

NOTES AND QUESTIONS

1. Should all patent offices adopt a Peer-to-Patent review? For all classes of inventions?

2. Are there any dangers in allowing third party submissions of prior art to patent examiners? Might it slow down the process?

3. Do you agree with WIPO's proposed inclusion of peer review in the PCT process? Should it incorporate the crowdsourcing techniques of the U.S. Peer-to-Patent project? Or is it better to allow the patent office, instead of a community vote, decide what peer submissions are relevant.

D. EXCLUSIVE RIGHTS

TRIPS

Article 28

Rights Conferred

1. A patent shall confer on its owner the following exclusive rights:

 (a) where the subject matter of a patent is a product, to prevent third parties not having the owner's consent from the acts of:

making, using, offering for sale, selling, or importing[6] for these purposes that product;

(b) where the subject matter of a patent is a process, to prevent third parties not having the owner's consent from the act of using the process, and from the acts of: using, offering for sale, selling, or importing for these purposes at least the product obtained directly by that process.

2. Patent owners shall also have the right to assign, or transfer by succession, the patent and to conclude licensing contracts.

1. PATENT RIGHTS

For well over a hundred years and counting, the Paris Convention has lacked any provision concerning what exclusive rights for inventors countries must protect under patent law. That gap in coverage was addressed finally in 1994 with the adoption of Article 28 of the TRIPS Agreement, which sets forth the minimum standards for patent rights. Article 28's clarity and simplicity in encapsulating the five basic rights under patent— "making, using, offering for sale, selling, or importing" the invention— stands in stark contrast with the piecemeal enumeration of exclusive rights under the Berne Convention, as discussed in the copyright chapter. The simplicity with which the patent rights are stated may belie, however, the complexity often presented in patent cases that involve conduct that spans several different countries. Consider the following problem and case.

PROBLEM 3–16

You have been hired to provide legal advice concerning the following dispute. Vandelay Industries is a multinational corporation with offices and business in both the U.S. and Korea. An engineer of Vandelay obtained a publicly available copy of the U.S. patent for a robotic cat, which was made by one of its U.S. competitors, Cosmo Enterprises. The patent contained the claims describing the invention and a written description enabling one to make the robotic cat. From its U.S. office, Vandelay sent these materials on how to make the robotic cat to its engineers in Korea. Cosmo Enterprises holds a U.S. patent on the robotic cat, but was denied a patent on the invention in Korea for lack of industrial application. Vandelay Industries proceeded to manufacture the robotic cat in Korea and sell it to many countries around the world (except the U.S.) based on the know-how disclosed in Cosmo's U.S. patent. Can Cosmo Enterprises stop Vandelay Industries from making and selling its robotic cat under U.S. law as interpreted in *Pellegrini* below? Are there any alternatives other than U.S. law that Cosmo could turn to for help?

---

6. This right, like all other rights conferred under this Agreement in respect of the use, sale, importation or other distribution of goods, is subject to the provisions of Article 6.

PELLEGRINI v. ANALOG DEVICES, INC.

U.S. Court of Appeals for the Federal Circuit.
375 F.3d 1113 (Fed. Cir. 2004).

LOURIE, CIRCUIT JUDGE.

Gerald Pellegrini appeals from the decision of the United States District Court for the District of Massachusetts granting partial summary judgment in favor of Analog Devices, Inc. ("Analog") in a patent infringement suit. Because there are no genuine issues of material fact in dispute and Analog is entitled to partial judgment as a matter of law, we affirm.

Background

Pellegrini is the sole inventor and owner of U.S. Patent 4,651,069, directed to brushless motor drive circuits. Analog develops and fabricates integrated circuit chips, including a line of chips called "ADMC" chips. In August 2002, Pellegrini sued Analog, alleging direct infringement and inducement of infringement of the '069 patent, contending that certain claims of the '069 patent read on the combination of ADMC chips and other components in brushless motors. Both parties moved for summary judgment.

It is undisputed that the ADMC chips are manufactured exclusively outside of the United States.[1] It is also undisputed that most of those chips are sold and shipped to customers outside the United States.[2] Noting that the U.S. patent laws do not have extraterritorial effect, the district court granted Analog's motion for partial summary judgment with respect to products containing those chips (hereinafter, "ADMC products") sold and shipped to non-U.S. customers, and the court denied Pellegrini's motion. The district court rejected Pellegrini's argument that, because Analog's headquarters are located in the United States and instructions for the production and disposition of the ADMC chips emanate from the United States, the chips should be regarded as having been "supplie[d] or cause[d] to be supplied in or from the United States" and Analog should be liable as an infringer under 35 U.S.C. § 271(f)(1). Accordingly, the district court entered separate and final judgment in Analog's favor with respect to Pellegrini's claim under § 271(f)(1). Pellegrini timely appealed to this court.

Discussion

This case presents the question whether components that are manufactured outside the United States and never physically shipped to or from the United States may nonetheless be "supplie[d] or cause[d] to be supplied in or from the United States" within the meaning of 35 U.S.C. § 271(f)(1) if those components are designed within the United States and the instructions for their manufacture and disposition are transmitted

---

1. The ADMC chips are manufactured by Analog in Ireland and by two independent contractors hired by Analog in Taiwan.

2. Analog concedes that it has imported a small number of ADMC chips into the United States, *e.g.*, for testing purposes, but those chips are not the subject of the summary judgment on appeal.

from within the United States. This is a matter of first impression for this court. According to § 271(f)(1),

> Whoever without authority supplies or causes to be supplied in or from the United States all or a substantial portion of the components of a patented invention, where such components are uncombined in whole or in part, in such a manner as to actively induce the combination of such components outside the United States in a manner that would infringe the patent if such combination occurred within the United States shall be liable as an infringer.

Section 271(f)(1) was enacted in the wake of the United States Supreme Court's decision in *Deepsouth Packing Co. v. Laitram Corp.*, 406 U.S. 518 (1972), in which the Court acknowledged that unauthorized manufacturers of patented products could avoid liability for infringement under the then-existing law by manufacturing the unassembled components of those products in the United States and then shipping them outside the United States for assembly. Congress enacted § 271(f) in order to close that loophole. *Rotec Indus., Inc. v. Mitsubishi Corp.*, 215 F.3d 1246, 1250 n.2 (Fed. Cir. 2000). As explained in the Congressional Record:

> Section 101 [of the Bill] makes two major changes in the patent law in order to avoid encouraging manufacturers outside the United States....

> [Section 271(f)] will prevent copiers from avoiding U.S. patents by supplying components of a patented product in this country so that the assembly of the components may be completed abroad. This proposal responds to the ... decision in *Deepsouth* ... concerning the need for a legislative solution to close a loophole in patent law.

130 Cong. Rec. H10525 (1984).

On appeal, Pellegrini asserts that the district court failed to consider, or at least did not address, certain relevant facts and that the court misapplied and incorrectly interpreted controlling case law. In his first argument, Pellegrini contends that the record shows that Analog is incorporated in the United States and has executive, marketing, and product line responsibilities for ADMC products; that Analog conceived and designed the ADMC products; that Analog is the exclusive manufacturer of ADMC products; that Analog makes all development and production decisions for ADMC products; that Analog is responsible for the fabrication, assembly, and testing of ADMC products; that ADMC uses, subcontracts with, and pays others for the express purpose of the proprietary fabrication, assembly, and testing of ADMC products; that Analog's ADMC products are capable of motor control; that Analog sets budgetary pricing and receives payment for ADMC products sold worldwide; and that Analog receives purchase orders from and invoices customers worldwide for ADMC products and increases production levels for ADMC products in response to those purchase orders. According to Pellegrini, these facts satisfy the "supplies" requirement of § 271(f)(1) because they evidence acts of infringement occurring inside the United States.

Analog responds that Pellegrini's facts are not supported by the record, but, even if they are credited, they are irrelevant because they do not demonstrate that the accused ADMC chips at issue were "supplied in or from the United States." According to Analog, § 271(f)(1) is simply inapplicable to products manufactured outside the United States and never shipped to or from the United States.

We agree with Analog that § 271(f)(1) does not apply to the facts of this case. First, § 271(f)(1) is clear on its face. It applies only where components of a patent invention are physically present in the United States and then either sold or exported "in such a manner as to actively induce the combination of such components outside the United States in a manner that would infringe the patent if such combination occurred within the United States." Secondly, as Pellegrini himself recognizes, we explained in *North American Philips v. American Vending Sales, Inc.*, 35 F.3d 1576 (Fed. Cir. 1994), that "the 'tort' of patent infringement occurs where the offending act [making, using, selling, offering for sale, or importing] is committed and not where the injury is felt." *Id.* at 1579. There is no dispute that the ADMC chips are not made, used, sold, or offered for sale in the United States. The plain language of § 271(f)(1) focuses on the location of the accused components, not the accused infringer. Pellegrini contends that it is irrelevant that the chips within the scope of the partial summary judgment never enter the United States, because to impose a location requirement would lead to a "seemingly contradictory construction of § 271(f)(1)." According to Pellegrini, "it is difficult to understand how the combination of such components outside the United States can occur if they are inside the United States." However, the language of § 271(f)(1) clearly contemplates that there must be an intervening sale or exportation; there can be no liability under § 271(f)(1) unless components are shipped from the United States for assembly.

As stated above, Analog does not make, use, sell, or offer to sell ADMC products in the United States, and it does not import ADMC products into the United States. Analog also does not supply ADMC chips in or from the United States, and does not cause ADMC chips to be supplied in or from the United States. Thus, 35 U.S.C. § 271(f)(1) is inapplicable. "[S]uppl[ying] or caus[ing] to be supplied" in § 271(f)(1) clearly refers to physical supply of components, not simply to the supply of instructions or corporate oversight. In other words, although Analog may be giving instructions from the United States that cause the components of the patented invention to be supplied, it is undisputed that those components are not being supplied in or from the United States.

Finally, Pellegrini contends that the district court's reliance on our decision in *Rotec* was incorrect and misplaced. Pellegrini points out that in *Rotec,* no U.S. defendant was alleged to be the manufacturer or seller of the accused components, whereas it is undisputed that Analog is the exclusive manufacturer of the ADMC products sold worldwide or that Analog invoices and receives payment for those products. Although factually correct, that distinction is legally unavailing. The present case is analogous to *Rotec* in the only sense that matters here: Analog's ADMC chips within the scope of the summary judgment, like the crane and conveyor belt system components at issue in *Rotec,* are not made in, used in, sold in, offered for sale in, or imported into the United States, 215 F.3d at 1247, 1256, and they are therefore outside of the reach of U.S. patent laws. As in *Rotec*, the present record "contains no evidence that any Defendant 'supplied or caused to supply' any component of a patented invention in or from the United States." *Id.* at 1256. Pellegrini speculates that "had there been admissible evidence to show an 'offer for sale' occurring in the United States [in *Rotec*], the Court would have judged otherwise." Be that as it may, there is no evidence of record here that Analog has offered to sell the ADMC chips domestically. Although Analog receives purchase orders, has responsibility for worldwide manufacturing and sales of ADMC products, and has marketing and product line responsibilities for ADMC products, there is no evidence of record that any of that manufacturing occurs in the United States or that Analog offers to sell those products in the United States. As the Supreme Court explained in *Dowagiac Mfg. Co. v. Minnesota Moline Plow Co.*, 235 U.S. 641 (1915), "the right conferred by a patent under our law is confined to the United States and its territories, and infringement of this right cannot be predicated on acts wholly done in a foreign country." *Id.* at 650.

We have considered Pellegrini's other arguments and find them unpersuasive.

Conclusion

Because there is no genuine issue of material fact and Analog is entitled to judgment as a matter of law with respect to the ADMC products that are not manufactured in the United States and are never shipped to or from the United States, the decision of the district court is *AFFIRMED.*

NOTES AND QUESTIONS

1. If Analog made chips that were the same as Pellegrini's U.S. invention, shouldn't Pellegrini be allowed to stop Analog from making the chips? Why wouldn't Analog's conduct fall within the exclusive rights under Article 28 of TRIPS, such as "making" or "selling" the invention? Is the U.S. approach in *Pellegrini* consistent with TRIPS?

2. *Evasion of patent law or dissemination of technology*? How do you view the business practices of Analog alleged by Pellegrini? Do the allegations suggest conduct that was devious evasion of the U.S. patent law through offshoring? Or do the allegations suggest conduct that was a perfectly acceptable effort to mass produce a competitor's chip in places where it was not patented?

3. Supposing Analog were to concede that it imported some ADMC chips into the United States allegedly for testing purposes as suggested in footnote

2, can Analog be liable for patent infringement? Was the trial court right to sever this issue from the decision under § 271(f)(1) that was on appeal? If the trial court found that Analog's importation for testing purposes *was* an infringement, should it order Analog to pay damages for all profits derived from or related to such importation and testing, including any activity of Analog in selling the chips abroad? Would your answer depend on whether Analog's testing of the ADMC chips in the U.S. materially contributed to its sale of the chips abroad? *Cf. Sheldon v. Metro–Goldwyn Pictures Corp.*, 106 F.2d 45 (2d Cir. 1939) (allowing recovery of lost profits from copyright infringement, including from extraterritorial activity, based on showing that infringement in U.S. facilitated the extraterritorial activity). *But cf. Los Angeles News Serv. v. Reuters Television Int'l, Ltd.*, 340 F.3d 926, 930–32 (9th Cir. 2003) (not allowing recovery of actual damages for extraterritorial activity that was legal abroad, where no actual damages resulted from domestic copyright infringement).

4. Apparently, Pellegrini did not seek foreign patents for his invention. Do you have any guess why he didn't?

5. What if a master copy of a computer software program that infringes a U.S. patent is sent by the defendant to a foreign country where secondary copies of the program are made from the master copy and installed on computers sold in the foreign country? The master copy from the U.S. is not itself installed on the foreign-made computers, however. Are the foreign-installed copies of the software program a "component" of a U.S. patented invention "supplie[d] ... from the United States" under § 271(f)(1)? *See Microsoft Corp. v. AT & T Corp.*, 550 U.S. 437, 442 (2007) (yes as to component, but no as to supplied from the United States).

6. *Offer to sell.* The U.S. Patent Code did not recognize the exclusive rights of offering to sell or importation until after the TRIPS Agreement was formed. *See* Pub. L. No. 103–465, §§ 532(a), 533(a), 108 Stat. 4809 (1994). The *Rotec* decision, which is discussed by the *Pellegrini* court, recognized that an "offer to sell" a U.S. patented invention that takes place in the United States can be an infringement, even if the contemplated sale is to be completed abroad with the manufacture and delivery of the item all taking place outside the U.S. *See Rotec Indus., Inc. v. Mitsubishi Corp.*, 215 F.3d 1246, 1253–57 (Fed. Cir. 2000). *But see id.* at 1258–59 (Newman, J., concurring in judgment) (arguing that an "offer to sell" constitutes infringement only when the contemplated sale itself (if effectuated) would be infringing in the U.S.).

Just as with the issue raised by § 271(f)(1), the controversy over what constitutes an "offer to sell" within the U.S. revolves around the question whether U.S. law should reach certain predicate acts (e.g., directions to make or an offer to sell someone else's U.S. patented product) that occur in the U.S., but that do not lead to the manufacture or sale of any infringing product in the U.S. As a matter of policy, how should the law approach this issue, where the allegedly infringing product is made, sold, or used abroad? If the actual sale or manufacture of the disputed invention occurs abroad, where a U.S. patent has no force, is there any reason U.S. law should attempt to proscribe such conduct?

2. EXCEPTIONS TO PATENT

TRIPS

Article 30

Exceptions to Rights Conferred

Members may provide limited exceptions to the exclusive rights conferred by a patent, provided that such exceptions do not unreasonably conflict with a normal exploitation of the patent and do not unreasonably prejudice the legitimate interests of the patent owner, taking account of the legitimate interests of third parties.

CANADA–PATENT PROTECTION OF PHARMACEUTICAL PRODUCTS

Report of the Panel, WTO. (Chairman: Robert Hudec;
Members: Mihaly Ficsor, Jaime Sepulveda).
WT/DS114/R (March 17, 2000).

FINDINGS

A. MEASURES AT ISSUE

At issue in this dispute is the conformity of two provisions of Canada's *Patent Act* with Canada's obligations under the *Agreement on Trade–Related Aspects of Intellectual Property Rights* ("the TRIPS Agreement"). The two provisions in dispute, Sections 55.2(1) and 55.2(2) of the Patent Act, create exceptions to the exclusive rights of patent owners.

(1) SECTION 55.2(1): THE REGULATORY REVIEW EXCEPTION

Section 55.2(1) provides as follows:

"It is not an infringement of a patent for any person to make, construct, use or sell the patented invention solely for uses reasonably related to the development and submission of information required under any law of Canada, a province or a country other than Canada that regulates the manufacture, construction, use or sale of any product."

Section 55.2(1) is known as the "regulatory review exception." It applies to patented products such as pharmaceuticals whose marketing is subject to government regulation in order to assure their safety or effectiveness. The purpose of the regulatory review exception is to permit potential competitors of the patent owner to obtain government marketing approval during the term of the patent, so that they will have regulatory permission to sell in competition with the patent owner by the date on which the patent expires. Without the regulatory review exception, the patent owner might be able to prevent potential competitors from using the patented product during the term of the patent to comply with testing requirements, so that competitors would have to wait until the patent expires before they could begin the process of obtaining marketing approval. This, in turn, would prevent potential competitors from entering the market for the additional time required to complete the regulatory approval process, in effect extending the patent owner's period of market exclusivity beyond the end of the term of the patent.

Since patent applications are generally filed as quickly as possible after the invention has been made, actual marketing of the patented product is frequently delayed for a certain period of time because time is required for development of the product in commercial form, after which additional time is required to complete the testing required for government approval. According to the information supplied by Canada, the process of development of the drug and regulatory approval for new patented pharmaceuticals normally takes approximately eight to 12 years. The long development and approval process means that, for most patented pharmaceuticals, the 20–year patent term results in an actual period of market exclusivity of only some 12 to eight years. After a pharmaceutical patent expires, it is common for other producers to enter the market supplying copies of the patented product at lower prices. These lower-priced copies, known as "generic" pharmaceuticals, often constitute a large part of the supply of pharmaceuticals in national markets. Generic pharmaceuticals must also comply with the government approval process. According to Canada's information, for generic producers the process of developing their version of the drug and obtaining regulatory approval takes approximately three to six-and-a-half years, with development taking some two to four years and the regulatory process itself one to two-and-a-half years. If none of the development process could be performed during the term of the patent, generic producers could be forced to wait the full three to six-and-a-half years after the patent expires before being able to enter the market in competition with the patent owner. To the extent that some development activity might be permitted, consistently with Article 30 of the TRIPS Agreement, under other exceptions such as the traditional exception for experimental use of the patented product, the delay in entering the market would be correspondingly less. The regulatory review exception in Section 55.2(1) would allow generic producers to complete both development and regulatory approval during the term of the patent, thus allowing them to enter the market as soon as the patent expires.

(2) SECTION 55.2(2): THE STOCKPILING EXCEPTION

Section 55.2(2) of the Patent Act, which is referred to as "the stockpiling exception," reads as follows:

> "It is not an infringement of a patent for any person who makes, constructs, uses or sells a patented invention in accordance with subsection (1) to make, construct or use the invention, during the applicable period provided for by the regulations, for the manufacture and storage of articles intended for sale after the date on which the term of the patent expires."

The provision allows competitors to manufacture and stockpile patented goods during a certain period before the patent expires, but the goods cannot be sold until the patent expires. Without this exception, the patent owner's right to exclude any person from "making" or "using" the patented good would enable the patent owner to prevent all such stockpiling.

The exception created by Section 55.2(2) does not become effective until implementing regulations are issued. The only regulations issued to date under the stockpiling exception have been regulations making the exception operative with regard to pharmaceutical products. The period during which pharmaceutical products can be made and stockpiled is six months immediately prior to the expiration of the patent. * * *

E.   Section 55.2(2) (The Stockpiling Exception)

(1) APPLICATION OF ARTICLE 28.1 AND ARTICLE 30 OF THE TRIPS AGREEMENT

The TRIPS Agreement contains two provisions authorizing exceptions to the exclusionary patent rights laid down in Article 28—Articles 30 and 31. Of these two, Article 30—the so-called limited exceptions provision—has been invoked by Canada in the present case. It reads as follows:

> "Exceptions to Rights Conferred
>
> Members may provide limited exceptions to the exclusive rights conferred by a patent, provided that such exceptions do not unreasonably conflict with the normal exploitation of the patent and do not unreasonably prejudice the legitimate interests of the patent owner, taking account of the legitimate interests of third parties."

Both parties agreed upon the basic structure of Article 30. Article 30 establishes three criteria that must be met in order to qualify for an exception: (1) the exception must be "limited"; (2) the exception must not "unreasonably conflict with normal exploitation of the patent"[382]; (3) the exception must not "unreasonably prejudice the legitimate interests of the patent owner, taking account of the legitimate interests of third parties." The three conditions are cumulative, each being a separate and independent requirement that must be satisfied. Failure to comply with any one of the three conditions results in the Article 30 exception being disallowed.

(c) "Limited Exceptions"

The Panel agreed with the EC that, as used in this context, the word "limited" has a narrower connotation than the rather broad definitions cited by Canada. Although the word itself can have both broad and narrow definitions, the narrower being indicated by examples such as "a mail train taking only a limited number of passengers"[393], the narrower

---

382. The parties disagreed over whether this second condition also includes the final phrase of Article 30—"taking account of the legitimate interests of third parties." For reasons explained below, the Panel found it unnecessary to resolve this disagreement.

393. The Shorter Oxford English Dictionary at p. 1216.

definition is the more appropriate when the word "limited" is used as part of the phrase "limited exception." The word "exception" by itself connotes a limited derogation, one that does not undercut the body of rules from which it is made. When a treaty uses the term "limited exception," the word "limited" must be given a meaning separate from the limitation implicit in the word "exception" itself. The term "limited exception" must therefore be read to connote a narrow exception—one which makes only a small diminution of the rights in question.

The Panel agreed with the EC interpretation that "limited" is to be measured by the extent to which the exclusive rights of the patent owner have been curtailed. The full text of Article 30 refers to "limited exceptions to the exclusive rights conferred by a patent." In the absence of other indications, the Panel concluded that it would be justified in reading the text literally, focusing on the extent to which legal rights have been curtailed, rather than the size or extent of the economic impact.

In the Panel's view, the question of whether the stockpiling exception is a "limited" exception turns on the extent to which the patent owner's rights to exclude "making" and "using" the patented product have been curtailed. The right to exclude "making" and "using" provides protection, additional to that provided by the right to exclude sale, during the entire term of the patent by cutting off the supply of competing goods at the source and by preventing use of such products however obtained. With no limitations at all upon the quantity of production, the stockpiling exception removes that protection entirely during the last six months of the patent term, without regard to what other, subsequent, consequences it might have. By this effect alone, the stockpiling exception can be said to abrogate such rights entirely during the time it is in effect.

In view of Canada's emphasis on preserving commercial benefits *before* the expiration of the patent, the Panel also considered whether the market advantage gained by the patent owner in the months after expiration of the patent could also be considered a purpose of the patent owner's rights to exclude "making" and "using" during the term of the patent. In both theory and practice, the Panel concluded that such additional market benefits were within the purpose of these rights. In theory, the rights of the patent owner are generally viewed as a right to prevent competitive commercial activity by others, and manufacturing for commercial sale is a quintessential competitive commercial activity, whose character is not altered by a mere delay in the commercial reward. In practical terms, it must be recognized that enforcement of the right to exclude "making" and "using" during the patent term will necessarily give all patent owners, for all products, a short period of extended market exclusivity after the patent expires. The repeated enactment of such exclusionary rights with knowledge of their universal market effects can only be understood as an affirmation of the purpose to produce those market effects.

For both these reasons, the Panel concluded that the stockpiling exception of Section 55.2(2) constitutes a substantial curtailment of the exclusionary rights required to be granted to patent owners under Article 28.1 of the TRIPS Agreement. Without seeking to define exactly what level of curtailment would be disqualifying, it was clear to the Panel that an exception which results in a substantial curtailment of this dimension cannot be considered a "limited exception" within the meaning of Article 30 of the Agreement.

F. SECTION 55.2(1) (THE REGULATORY REVIEW EXCEPTION)

(1) APPLICATION OF ARTICLE 28.1 AND ARTICLE 30 OF THE TRIPS AGREEMENT

(a) "Limited Exceptions"

Canada asserted that the regulatory review exception of Section 55.2(1) can be regarded as "limited" because the rights given to third parties do not deprive the patent holder of his right to exclude all other "commercial sales" of the patented product during the term of the patent.

In the Panel's view, Canada's regulatory review exception is a "limited exception" within the meaning of TRIPS Article 30. It is "limited" because of the narrow scope of its curtailment of Article 28.1 rights. As long as the exception is confined to conduct needed to comply with the requirements of the regulatory approval process, the extent of the acts unauthorized by the right holder that are permitted by it will be small and narrowly bounded. Even though regulatory approval processes may require substantial amounts of test production to demonstrate reliable manufacturing, the patent owner's rights themselves are not impaired any further by the size of such production runs, as long as they are solely for regulatory purposes and no commercial use is made of resulting final products.

In sum, the Panel found that the regulatory review exception of Section 55.2(1) is a "limited exception" within the meaning of Article 30 of the TRIPS Agreement.

(b) "Normal Exploitation"

The Panel considered that "exploitation" refers to the commercial activity by which patent owners employ their exclusive patent rights to extract economic value from their patent. The term "normal" defines the kind of commercial activity Article 30 seeks to protect. The ordinary meaning of the word "normal" is found in the dictionary definition: "regular, usual, typical, ordinary, conventional."[411] As so defined, the term can be understood to refer either to an empirical conclusion about what is common within a relevant community, or to a normative standard of entitlement. The Panel concluded that the word "normal" was being used in Article 30 in a sense that combined the two meanings.

---

411. The New Shorter Oxford English Dictionary, p. 1940.

The normal practice of exploitation by patent owners, as with owners of any other intellectual property right, is to exclude all forms of competition that could detract significantly from the economic returns anticipated from a patent's grant of market exclusivity.

Canada has raised the argument that market exclusivity occurring after the 20–year patent term expires should not be regarded as "normal." The Panel was unable to accept that as a categorical proposition. Some of the basic rights granted to all patent owners, and routinely exercised by all patent owners, will typically produce a certain period of market exclusivity after the expiration of a patent. For example, the separate right to prevent "making" the patented product during the term of the patent often prevents competitors from building an inventory needed to enter the market immediately upon expiration of a patent. There is nothing abnormal about that more or less brief period of market exclusivity after the patent has expired.

The Panel considered that Canada was on firmer ground, however, in arguing that the additional period of de facto market exclusivity created by using patent rights to preclude submissions for regulatory authorization should not be considered "normal." The additional period of market exclusivity in this situation is not a natural or normal consequence of enforcing patent rights. It is an unintended consequence of the conjunction of the patent laws with product regulatory laws, where the combination of patent rights with the time demands of the regulatory process gives a greater than normal period of market exclusivity to the enforcement of certain patent rights. It is likewise a form of exploitation that most patent owners do not in fact employ. For the vast majority of patented products, there is no marketing regulation of the kind covered by Section 55.2(1), and thus there is no possibility to extend patent exclusivity by delaying the marketing approval process for competitors.

In sum, the Panel found that the regulatory review exception of Section 55.2(1) does not conflict with a normal exploitation of patents, within the meaning of the second condition of Article 30 of the TRIPS Agreement. The fact that no conflict has been found makes it unnecessary to consider the question of whether, if a conflict were found, the conflict would be "unreasonable." Accordingly, it is also unnecessary to determine whether or not the final phrase of Article 30, calling for consideration of the legitimate interests of third parties, does or does not apply to the determination of "unreasonable conflict" under the second condition of Article 30.

(c) "Legitimate Interests"

The third condition of Article 30 is the requirement that the proposed exception must not "unreasonably prejudice the legitimate interests of the patent owner, taking into account the legitimate interests of third parties."

(ii) Definition of "legitimate interests"

The word "legitimate" is commonly defined as follows:

(a) Conformable to, sanctioned or authorized by, law or principle: lawful; justifiable; proper;

(b) Normal, regular, conformable to a recognized standard type.[418]

To make sense of the term "legitimate interests" in this context, that term must be defined in the way that it is often used in legal discourse— as a normative claim calling for protection of interests that are "justifiable" in the sense that they are supported by relevant public policies or other social norms. This is the sense of the word that often appears in statements such as "X has no legitimate interest in being able to do Y." We may take as an illustration one of the most widely adopted Article 30– type exceptions in national patent laws—the exception under which use of the patented product for scientific experimentation, during the term of the patent and without consent, is not an infringement. It is often argued that this exception is based on the notion that a key public policy purpose underlying patent laws is to facilitate the dissemination and advancement of technical knowledge and that allowing the patent owner to prevent experimental use during the term of the patent would frustrate part of the purpose of the requirement that the nature of the invention be disclosed to the public. * * * While the Panel draws no conclusion about the correctness of any such national exceptions in terms of Article 30 of the TRIPS Agreement, it does adopt the general meaning of the term "legitimate interests" contained in legal analysis of this type.

In sum, after consideration of the ordinary meaning of the term "legitimate interests," as it is used in Article 30, the Panel was unable to accept the EC's interpretation of that term as referring to legal interests pursuant to Article 28.1. Accordingly, the Panel was unable to accept the primary EC argument with regard to the third condition of Article 30. It found that the EC argument based solely on the patent owner's legal rights pursuant to Article 28.1, without reference to any more particular normative claims of interest, did not raise a relevant claim of non-compliance with the third condition of Article 30.

(iii) Second claim of "legitimate interest"

After reaching the previous conclusion concerning the EC's primary argument under the "legitimate interests" condition of Article 30, the Panel then directed its attention to another line of argument raised in statements made by the EC and by one third party. This second line of argument called attention to the fact that patent owners whose innovative products are subject to marketing approval requirements suffer a loss of economic benefits to the extent that delays in obtaining government approval prevent them from marketing their product during a substantial part of the patent term. According to information supplied by Canada, regulatory approval of new pharmaceuticals usually does not occur until approximately eight to 12 years after the patent application has been filed,

---

418. New Shorter Oxford Dictionary, page 1563.

due to the time needed to complete development of the product and the time needed to comply with the regulatory procedure itself. The result in the case of pharmaceuticals, therefore, is that the innovative producer is in fact able to market its patented product in only the remaining eight to 12 years of the 20–year patent term, thus receiving an effective period of market exclusivity that is only 40–60 per cent of the period of exclusivity normally envisaged in a 20–year patent term. The EC argued that patent owners who suffer a reduction of effective market exclusivity from such delays should be entitled to impose the same type of delay in connection with corresponding regulatory requirements upon the market entry of competing products.

The type of normative claim put forward by the EC has been affirmed by a number of governments that have enacted *de jure* extensions of the patent term, primarily in the case of pharmaceutical products, to compensate for the de facto diminution of the normal period of market exclusivity due to delays in obtaining marketing approval. According to the information submitted to the Panel, such extensions have been enacted by the European Communities, Switzerland, the United States, Japan, Australia and Israel. The EC and Switzerland have done so while at the same time allowing patent owners to continue to use their exclusionary rights to gain an additional, de facto extension of market exclusivity by preventing competitors from applying for regulatory approval during the term of the patent.* The other countries that have enacted *de jure* patent term extensions have also, either by legislation or by judicial decision, created a regulatory review exception similar to Section 55.2(1), thereby eliminating the possibility of an additional de facto extension of market exclusivity.

This positive response to the claim for compensatory adjustment has not been universal, however. In addition to Canada, several countries have adopted, or are in the process of adopting, regulatory review exceptions similar to Section 55.2(1) of the Canadian Patent Act, thereby removing the de facto extension of market exclusivity, but these countries have not enacted, and are not planning to enact, any *de jure* extensions of the patent term for producers adversely affected by delayed marketing approval.[426] When regulatory review exceptions are enacted in this manner, they represent a decision not to restore any of the period of market exclusivity due to lost delays in obtaining marketing approval. Taken as a whole, these government decisions may represent either disagreement with the normative claim made by the EC in this proceeding, or they may simply represent a conclusion that such claims are outweighed by other equally legitimate interests.

On balance, the Panel concluded that the interest claimed on behalf of patent owners whose effective period of market exclusivity had been reduced by delays in marketing approval was neither so compelling nor so

---

* The EU has since adopted a regulatory review exception. *See* Directive 2004/EC/27, art. 10(6). *Ed.*

426. See replies of Poland and Thailand to questions asked by the Panel to third parties. See First Submission of Canada, paragraphs 115, 116 (Hungary, Argentina).

widely recognized that it could be regarded as a "legitimate interest" within the meaning of Article 30 of the TRIPS Agreement. Notwithstanding the number of governments that had responded positively to that claimed interest by granting compensatory patent term extensions, the issue itself was of relatively recent standing, and the community of governments was obviously still divided over the merits of such claims. Moreover, the Panel believed that it was significant that concerns about regulatory review exceptions in general, although well known at the time of the TRIPS negotiations, were apparently not clear enough, or compelling enough, to make their way explicitly into the recorded agenda of the TRIPS negotiations. The Panel believed that Article 30's "legitimate interests" concept should not be used to decide, through adjudication, a normative policy issue that is still obviously a matter of unresolved political debate.

(iv) Conclusion with regard to compliance of Section 55.2(1) with Article 30

Having reviewed the conformity of Section 55.2(1) with each of the three conditions for an exception under Article 30 of the TRIPS Agreement, the Panel concluded that Section 55.2(1) does satisfy all three conditions of Article 30, and thus is not inconsistent with Canada's obligations under Article 28.1 of the TRIPS Agreement.

CONCLUSIONS

In light of the findings above, the Panel has concluded as follows:

(1) Section 55.2(1) of Canada's *Patent Act* is not inconsistent with Canada's obligations under Article 27.1 and Article 28.1 of the TRIPS Agreement.

(2) Section 55.2(2) of Canada's *Patent Act* is not consistent with the requirements of Article 28.1 of the TRIPS Agreement.

Accordingly, the Panel recommends that the Dispute Settlement Body request that Canada bring Section 55.2(2) into conformity with Canada's obligations under the TRIPS Agreement.

Notes and Questions

1. *TRIPS Article 30*. What is the test for determining whether an exception to patent rights under national law is consistent with Article 30 of TRIPS? Is it different from the 3–part test for limited exceptions to copyrights under Article 13, as elaborated by the WTO Panel in the *United States–110(5)* case discussed in the copyright chapter? In comparing the language of these two articles, Articles 13 and 30 of TRIPS, do you think the tests for determining limited exceptions under the articles should be different or substantially the same? If you believe there are or should be differences, is either test better formulated as a matter of policy, or more helpful and easy to administer in practice?

2. *Limited exceptions*. How does the Panel determine if an exception to patent rights is "limited"? Why did the Panel find the stockpiling exception

not limited, even though it applied to a generic drug maker for only a 6–month period before the expiration of the patent on a pharmaceutical? Why did the Panel find the regulatory review exception *limited*, even though it could potentially apply for a period of 3 to 6 years, if not more, while a generic drug maker was seeking drug approval for an anticipated generic drug that was based on a patented drug? Are these conclusions reconcilable? Do you agree with the Panel's reasoning? Can you propose a more specific list of factors to help future panels determine whether an exception is limited?

3. *Unreasonably conflict with a normal exploitation of patent.* How does the Panel determine if an exception "unreasonably conflict[s] with a normal exploitation of the patent"? Can the "normal" exploitation involve activity for a patent holder *after* the patent expires? In evaluating the regulatory review exception, the Panel appears to focus on the effects of the exception after a patent expires. Should this be the correct inquiry? Wouldn't the key activity of generic drug makers invoking the regulatory review exception take place *during* the patent on the drug, *before* it expired, when the generic drug makers are "making" the drug for drug approval without authorization of the patent holder? And, in such case, wouldn't there be an arguable conflict with the normal exploitation of the drug patent by allowing others to make and use the drug without authorization? If you were on the Panel, would you have decided the second element on the "reasonableness" or not of the putative conflict, instead of saying there was no conflict at all?

4. *Unreasonably prejudice the legitimate interests of the patent owner.* How does the Panel determine if an exception "unreasonably prejudice[s] the legitimate interests of the patent owner, taking into account of the legitimate interests of third parties"? What is a "legitimate" interest? In the Panel's view, did the "regulatory review" exception violate a legitimate interest of Canadian patent holders?

5. *Canadian drug review system.* If the regulatory review of a new pharmaceutical drug in Canada is so time consuming that it reduces the effective period of a patent for the drug by 12 to 8 years, would not the regulatory review exception allowed to generic drug manufacturers during the term of a patented drug prejudice the patent holders of the pharmaceuticals? Does this disparate treatment of drug manufacturers make any sense?

6. Putting aside the regulatory review and stockpiling exceptions, could the European Union have challenged Canada's patent law based on the fact that its drug safety review effectively diminishes the patents for new drugs to a term of 8 to 12 years? If so, under what provision(s) of TRIPS? What would the argument(s) be? Given the WTO panel's analysis in the *Canadian Pharmaceutical* case, do you think such a challenge would be successful?

7. *Experimental use exceptions.* The WTO panel in *Canadian Pharmaceutical* describes "experimental use" exceptions as "one of the most widely adopted Article 30–type exceptions in national patent laws," but stops short of drawing any conclusion as to their compliance with Article 30. As explained by the panel, an experimental use exception is an "exception under which use of the patented product for scientific experimentation, during the term of the patent and without consent, is not an infringement."

U.S. patent law has recognized a judicially created "experimental use" exception, but courts have given the doctrine an exceedingly narrow scope, allowing it only for experimentation undertaken "for [one's] amusement, to satisfy idle curiosity, or for strictly philosophical inquiry." Business related experimentation does not qualify for an exemption; nor does any experiment with the "slightest commercial implication." *Madey v. Duke Univ.*, 307 F.3d 1351, 1362 (Fed. Cir. 2002). *See* John R. Thomas, *Scientific Research and the Experimental Use Privilege in Patent Law*, CRS Report for Congress, Oct. 28, 2004; Rebecca S. Eisenberg, *Patents and the Progress of Science: Exclusive Rights and Experimental Use*, 56 U. CHI. L. REV. 1017 (1989); Janice M. Mueller, *The Evanescent Experimental Use Exemption from United States Patent Infringement Liability: Implications for University and Nonprofit Research and Development*, 56 BAYLOR L. REV. 917 (2004).

In 1984, Congress passed the Hatch–Waxman Act, which creates a patent exemption comparable to the "regulatory review" exemption discussed in the Canadian case. Under the exemption, 35 U.S.C. § 271(e)(1), there is a patent exemption for acts "reasonably related to the development and submission of information under a Federal law which regulates the manufacture, use, or sale of drugs." The U.S. Patent Code also has a patent term extension to offset the loss of time on a patent for inventions, such as pharmaceuticals, subject to federal regulatory review for approval. *Id.* § 156. As discussed in the *Canadian Pharmaceutical* case, Canada's Patent Code had no such term extension for inventions subject to regulatory review.

PROBLEM 3–17

The WTO members would like more guidance on permissible patent exemptions than TRIPS Article 30 provides. You have been asked to propose a list of examples of permissible patent exceptions that countries should be allowed to recognize under Article 30. Consider whether the following should be recognized as acceptable exemptions under TRIPS:

A. Exemptions for generic drug makers (as in the *Canadian Pharmaceutical* case) to make and use the patented drug without authorization in preparation for regulatory review of the generic drug;

B. Experimental use exemptions that allow third parties to make and use a limited number of copies of a patented invention for research, experimental, or scientific use, as long as not used publicly or in the sale of the patented item while the patent is in effect;

C. Prior use exemptions allowing a nonexclusive license for an inventor in situations where the inventor had developed the same invention but eventually lost out to another party who qualified for the patent rights; and

D. Employment-related exemptions such as an employer's shop rights to a patented invention developed by one of its employees (such as under U.S. law), or an employee's right to reasonable compensation (such as under Japanese law) for developing an invention ultimately owned by the employer.

Should these all be considered as permissible patent exceptions and allowed under Article 30? Would it be helpful if TRIPS specifically recognizes the validity of any of the above exemptions?

3. COMPULSORY LICENSES

A compulsory license creates an exception to the exclusive rights of the patent owner by allowing a third party to use the patent without the owner's permission. We introduced the compulsory license in our earlier discussion of local working requirements at pp. 298–302 as a measure used by some countries to control what they perceive to be abuses by some patent owners. However, compulsory licenses are not limited to cases in which a foreign patent owner refuses to work the patent locally—they are also used to curb other perceived abuses.

> Illustration 3–16. Pharma, a multi-national pharmaceutical company, establishes a manufacturing plant in Country Z and makes a patented drug for malaria locally. Country Z finds that Pharma charges monopoly prices that are so high that most citizens in Country Z are denied access to the drug. In the midst of a national epidemic of malaria, Country Z decides to issue a compulsory license that will authorize local third party manufacturers to produce cheap generic versions of the drug.

As we shall discuss below, compulsory licenses in the patent context are heavily regulated under TRIPS, much more so than in the copyright context. Why is this so? A compulsory license in the context of patents is a form of forced technology transfer, which is controversial and elicits strong reactions from both sides of the debate. Patent owners view the compulsory license as highly disadvantageous for a number of reasons. Most patent owners, as well as other IP owners, are highly protective of their proprietary technology as it is one of their most valuable business assets. While patent owners will give access to their technology to third parties under the right conditions, such access always carries some risks. The third party might misuse the technology or even misappropriate it. For this reason, patent owners will carefully scrutinize any potential license to ensure that the licensee is trustworthy and responsible. In addition, most licensing arrangements involve a long term working relationship between the patent owner and the licensee. Authorizing the licensee to use the patent is usually the first step in a continuing business relationship in which scientists, engineers, and managers from the patent owner will work with counterparts from the licensee to ensure that the licensee is able to use the technology properly and is able to adopt the technology for the particular market and the particular uses contemplated by the license. In many cases, the most important part of the licensing arrangement is not the authorization itself but the continuing working relationship between the patent owner and the licensee. For all of these reasons, patent owners are careful in their selection of licensees and view the imposition of a licensee by a foreign government with great disfavor. In fact, many patent owners would rather offer concessions, such as a reduction in price, than submit to a forced licensing arrangement.

On the flip side, some developing countries believe that some patent owners, mostly MNEs, abuse the monopoly power granted by the patent by charging exorbitant prices. These concerns reach what may be their zenith in connection with access to patented life-saving medicines, which we will study in depth below. But the concerns related to compulsory licenses on both sides of the debate arise with respect to many other types of patents as well. As in the case of working requirements, the debate over compulsory licenses is arrayed along the North–South default lines. Developing countries favor a broad authorization to issue compulsory licenses, while developed countries seek to subject compulsory licenses to clear limitations. For now, consider how the balance between the concerns on both sides was struck in TRIPS.

a. General Doctrine

PROBLEM 3–18

Country R is a developing country in sub-Saharan Africa that has struggled mightily with social and political problems since it gained its independence from colonial rule in 1955. Among its other problems, the mortality rate among newborn infants in Country R is 3 times the average rate for developed countries. However, the problem is only one of many facing Country R; in fact, it is considered by the government to be relatively minor in comparison to various other health and political issues. Recently, Innovatrition has obtained a patent in Country R for a vaccine that can reduce the infant mortality rate significantly. It sells the vaccine at $500 per dose, which is far more than R's citizens can afford. Country R sent Innovatrition a letter notifying Innovatrition that Country R will immediately impose a compulsory license on Innovatrition's patented drug, which would allow third party manufacturers to produce the drugs for Country R's market and other countries in the sub-Saharan region. Country R will provide Innovatrition a one time payment of $15,000 as a licensing fee—a payment that Country R can make only after receiving debt relief and foreign aid from developing countries. All compulsory licenses will be nonexclusive and nonassignable, and subject to review by the Prime Minister. Innovatrition claims that it cost $1 billion to develop the vaccine. Is Country R in compliance with TRIPS Article 31 below? Consider the following Article and accompanying notes.

TRIPS

Article 31

Other Use Without Authorization of the Right Holder

Where the law of a Member allows for other use[7] of the subject matter of a patent without the authorization of the right holder, including use by the government or third parties authorized by the government, the following provisions shall be respected:

(a) authorization of such use shall be considered on its individual merits;

---

7. "Other use" refers to use other than that allowed under Article 30.

(b) such use may only be permitted if, prior to such use, the proposed user has made efforts to obtain authorization from the right holder on reasonable commercial terms and conditions and that such efforts have not been successful within a reasonable period of time. This requirement may be waived by a Member in the case of a national emergency or other circumstances of extreme urgency or in cases of public non-commercial use. In situations of national emergency or other circumstances of extreme urgency, the right holder shall, nevertheless, be notified as soon as reasonably practicable. In the case of public non-commercial use, where the government or contractor, without making a patent search, knows or has demonstrable grounds to know that a valid patent is or will be used by or for the government, the right holder shall be informed promptly;

(c) the scope and duration of such use shall be limited to the purpose for which it was authorized, and in the case of semi-conductor technology shall only be for public non-commercial use or to remedy a practice determined after judicial or administrative process to be anti-competitive;

(d) such use shall be non-exclusive;

(e) such use shall be non-assignable, except with that part of the enterprise or goodwill which enjoys such use;

(f) any such use shall be authorized predominantly for the supply of the domestic market of the Member authorizing such use;

(g) authorization for such use shall be liable, subject to adequate protection of the legitimate interests of the persons so authorized, to be terminated if and when the circumstances which led to it cease to exist and are unlikely to recur. The competent authority shall have the authority to review, upon motivated request, the continued existence of these circumstances;

(h) the right holder shall be paid adequate remuneration in the circumstances of each case, taking into account the economic value of the authorization;

(i) the legal validity of any decision relating to the authorization of such use shall be subject to judicial review or other independent review by a distinct higher authority in that Member;

(j) any decision relating to the remuneration provided in respect of such use shall be subject to judicial review or other independent review by a distinct higher authority in that Member;

(k) Members are not obliged to apply the conditions set forth in subparagraphs (b) and (f) where such use is permitted to remedy a practice determined after judicial or administrative process to be anti-competitive. The need to correct anti-competitive practices may be taken into account in determining the amount of remuneration in such cases. Competent authorities shall have the authority to refuse termination of authorization if and when the conditions which led to such authorization are likely to recur;

(l) where such use is authorized to permit the exploitation of a patent ("the second patent") which cannot be exploited without infringing another patent ("the first patent"), the following additional conditions shall apply:

(i) the invention claimed in the second patent shall involve an important technical advance of considerable economic significance in relation to the invention claimed in the first patent;

(ii) the owner of the first patent shall be entitled to a cross-licence on reasonable terms to use the invention claimed in the second patent; and

(iii) the use authorized in respect of the first patent shall be non-assignable except with the assignment of the second patent.

NOTES AND QUESTIONS

1. *Duty to bargain.* One of the requirements under TRIPS Article 31 is a requirement that an entity seeking a compulsory license must make prior "efforts to obtain authorization from the right holder on reasonable commercial terms * * * and that such efforts have not been successful within a reasonable period of time." What policy or theory supports such a requirement?

2. *National emergency, extreme urgency, public non-commercial use.* Article 31 exempts members from the duty to bargain in cases of "national emergency or other circumstances of extreme urgency or in cases of public non-commercial use." Why shouldn't countries be required to make efforts to bargain in these cases? Perhaps in a national emergency or matter of extreme urgency, bargaining will be impracticable, but what about in cases of public non-commercial use?

What do you think should qualify as a national emergency? How about an anthrax scare in which a country fears the threat of anthrax contaminated letters? What about the avian bird flu scare? Should countries have the right to consider such situations national emergencies based on a few isolated incidents, so that they can stockpile drugs to prevent a public health crisis (which has yet to materialize)?

3. *Patent holder's right to adequate remuneration.* Article 31(h) expressly recognizes the patent holder's right to "be paid adequate remuneration in the circumstance of each case, taking into account the economic value of the authorization." Any decision relating to the amount of remuneration "shall be subject to judicial review or other independent review by a distinct higher authority in that Member." TRIPS art. 31(j). Should there be a minimum standard under TRIPS on what constitutes "adequate" remuneration? How should countries go about determining what is "adequate"? The market price? A reduced market price? A reduced market price at the level comparable to the prices of similar goods in the country where a compulsory license is sought?

b. Special Discussion: Access to Medicines, the Doha Declaration, and the Implementation Decision

1. *Compulsory Licenses and Patented Life–Saving Medicines*

As the preceding section indicates, the compulsory licensing provision of TRIPS is subject to some important conditions that may in practice restrict the ability of members to issue compulsory licenses. In recent years, the debate concerning Article 31 reached a new level of intensity in connection with the issue of access to life-saving medicines.

Soon after the WTO was established in 1995, MNEs became the target of fierce criticism over access to medicines needed to combat deadly epidemic diseases such as AIDS. Many critics charged that the effect of patents was to allow MNEs to charge monopoly prices that were out of reach of those populations that were in most dire need of the medicines. Most of the countries with the most severe health problems are also among the world's poorest nations, which lack the resources to pay for these medicines:

> Of the three million worldwide deaths from AIDS in 2000, 2.4 million occurred in sub-Saharan Africa. At least 12 million African children have been orphaned by AIDS, a number that could soar to 40 million by 2010 without more effective HIV control. Of an estimated 36 million people now living with HIV worldwide, 95 percent live in developing countries. Twenty-five million—more than two-thirds—abide in Africa, and about four million of these suffer from advanced HIV related illness. Yet only 10,000 to 30,000 Africans receive anti-retroviral therapy, the state-of-the-art drug treatment that has transformed AIDS from a sure, short-term killer into a disease with which one can live indefinitely.

M. Gregg Bloche & Elizabeth R. Jungman, *Health Policy and the WTO*, 31 J.L. MED. & ETHICS 529, 534–535 (2003).

Multi-national pharmaceutical companies argue that they must charge prices that allow them to recoup the cost of developing the drugs, to earn a fair return for their shareholders, and to create an incentive to develop additional drugs and treatments for the future. MNEs cite as support the high costs of research and development, which is estimated by the drug industry to exceed $800 million for each drug that is successfully brought to market. Developing countries and Non–Governmental Organizations (NGOs) engaged in public health issues view these claims with considerable skepticism. They allege that MNEs seek to maximize their profits by charging the highest price that the market will bear without any regard for social or ethical concerns. MNEs place profits over people, these critics contend.

Undeterred by the intense criticism by developing countries and NGOs, a number of MNEs boldly and aggressively sought to protect their patent rights in the late 1990s in a number of highly publicized challenges to compulsory licensing schemes. On June 8, 2000, the United States filed a petition with the WTO Dispute Settlement Body challenging the validity of the compulsory licensing provisions contained in Article 68 of the Brazilian Industrial Property Law. This challenge generated a great deal of concern on the part of developing countries and NGOs as Brazil's compulsory licensing provision provided negotiating leverage for its highly successful nationwide program that had reduced the mortality rates among the approximately 536,000 Brazilians infected with HIV by 50%. A number of NGOs viewed the Brazilian program as model for other countries around the world that could be undermined by the U.S. challenge. A number of U.S. pharmaceutical companies, however, argued that the law (reproduced below) was inconsistent with Article 31 of TRIPS:

Brazil Industrial Property Law, Article 68

Compulsory License

68.   The titleholder shall be subject to having the patent licensed on a compulsory basis if he exercises his rights derived therefrom in an abusive manner, or by means thereof engages in abuse of economic power, proven pursuant to law in an administrative or judicial decision.

(1) The following also occasion a compulsory license:

> I.   non-exploitation of the object of the patent within the Brazilian territory for failure to manufacture or incomplete manufacture of the product, or also failure to make full use of the patented process, except cases where this is not economically feasible, when importation shall be permitted; or

> II.   commercialization that does not satisfy the needs of the market.

(2) A license may be requested only by a person having a legitimate interest and having technical and economic capacity to effectively exploit the object of the patent, that shall be destined predominantly for the domestic market, in which case the exception contained in Item I of the previous Paragraph shall be extinguished.

(3) In the case that a compulsory license is granted on the grounds of abuse of economic power, the licensee who proposes local manufacture shall be assured a period, limited to the provisions of Article 74, to import the object of the license, provided that it was introduced onto the market directly by the titleholder or with his consent.

(4) In the case of importation to exploit a patent and in the case of importation as provided for in the preceding Paragraph, third parties shall also be allowed to import a product manufactured according to a process or product patent, provided that it has been introduced onto the market by the titleholder or with his consent.

(5) The compulsory license that is the subject of Paragraph 1 shall only be required when 3 (three) years have elapsed since the patent was granted.

* * *

Can you make an argument on behalf of the U.S. pharmaceutical companies as to why Article 68 of the Brazilian Industrial Property Law may be inconsistent with Article 31 of TRIPS? What might be the response of the Brazilian government to such an argument?

Although the United States government initially pursued the WTO dispute on behalf of the U.S. pharmaceutical industry with fervor, the U.S. delegation to the WTO soon lost its enthusiasm as the following indicates:

BRAZIL–MEASURES AFFECTING PATENT PROTECTION

WT/DS199/4 (July 19, 2001).

Notification of Mutually Agreed Solution

The following communication, dated 5 July 2001, from the Permanent Mission of the United States and the Permanent Mission of Brazil to the Chairman of the Dispute Settlement Body, is circulated pursuant to Article 3.6 of the DSU.

The United States of America and Brazil wish to notify the Dispute Settlement Body that they have reached a mutually satisfactory solution to the matter raised by the Government of the United States in WT/DS199/1 (Brazil—Measures Affecting Patent Protection), dated 8 June 2000.

Please find attached the text of the exchange of letters of 19 and 25 June 2001 on this subject. We would ask you to circulate this notification and attachment to the relevant Councils and Committees, as well as to the Dispute Settlement Body.

Letter from Mr. José Alfredo Graça Lima, Under–Secretary–General for Integration, Economic and External Trade Matters to Ambassador Peter Allgeier, Deputy USTR, dated 19 June 2001

1. I refer to the panel initiated by your Government questioning the compatibility of Article 68 of Brazil's Industrial Property Law (Law 9.279/96) with the TRIPS Agreement. In the view of Brazil, as you are aware, Article 68 is fully compatible with the TRIPS Agreement.

2. Nevertheless, in the spirit of the proposal made by Ambassador Robert Zoellick to Minister Celso Lafer in their recent meeting in Geneva for a common endeavor to find a mutually satisfactory solution for the dispute, and following up on our recent conversation about the same subject in Washington D.C., on May 24, I would like to convey to you the following proposal.

3. Should the U.S. withdraw the WTO panel against Brazil concerning the interpretation of Article 68, the Brazilian Government would agree, in the event it deems necessary to apply Article 68 to grant compulsory license on patents held by the U.S. companies, to hold prior talks on the matter with the U.S. Government. These talks would be held within the scope of the U.S.—Brazil Consultative Mechanism, in a special session scheduled to discuss the subject.

4. I look forward to receiving your response to this proposal.

Letter from Mr. Peter F. Allgeier, Executive Office of the President, Deputy United States Trade Representative to Mr. José Alfredo Graça Lima, Under–Secretary–General for Integration, Economic and External Trade Matters, Ministry of Foreign Affairs, Brazil, dated 25 June 2001

Thank you for your letter, which referred to the panel initiated by the United States regarding the consistency of Article 68 of Brazil's Industrial Property Law (Law 9.279/96) with the TRIPS Agreement.

As Ambassador Zoellick mentioned during his meeting with Minister Celso Lafer, we are interested in finding a mutually satisfactory solution to this dispute. Your letter conveyed a proposal that should lead to such a solution. I am pleased to report that my government will agree to terminate the WTO panel proceeding without prejudice concerning the interpretation of Article 68, based on your government's commitment to hold prior talks with the United States with sufficient advance notice to permit constructive discussions in the context of a special session of the US—Brazil Consultative Mechanism, should Brazil deem it necessary to apply Article 68 to grant a compulsory license on patents held by U.S. companies. While we had real concerns regarding the potential use of Article 68 of Brazil's Industrial Property Law, we note that this provision has never been used to grant a compulsory license. In addition, we would expect Brazil not to proceed with further dispute settlement action regarding sections 204 and 209 of the U.S. patent law.

As Ambassador Zoellick noted during his meeting with Minister Lafer, the United States' concerns were never directed at your government's bold and effective program to combat HIV/AIDS. Our ability to find a mutually satisfactory solution to this WTO dispute will allow our conversation regarding this scourge to turn to our shared goal of defeating the HIV/AIDS virus.

We will make the necessary arrangements to notify the WTO Secretariat of our decision as soon as possible.

NOTES AND QUESTIONS

1. Why did the United States challenge Article 68 of Brazil's patent law if it had apparently never been used to grant a compulsory license? If few countries have authorized a compulsory license for a patented invention since TRIPS was formed, why do you think there is such a controversy over granting compulsory licenses for patented inventions?

2. *Dispute Resolution.* Just as in the case of litigation, the WTO dispute settlement process allows countries to settle their disputes informally, before a formal decision of a WTO panel is even rendered. Indeed, Article 3(7) of the Dispute Settlement Understanding of the WTO states that "[a] solution mutually acceptable to the parties to a dispute and consistent with the covered agreements is clearly to be preferred." What are the benefits of encouraging the mutual settlement of disputes related to TRIPS? Is there any potential downside to encouraging these kind of settlements without a formal decision of a WTO panel or Appellate Body?

3. *Consultations.* The exchange of letters by U.S. and Brazilian officials appears to indicate that, in exchange for Brazil's agreeing to consult with the U.S. before issuing a compulsory license, the U.S. would withdraw its WTO petition. It is a normal practice, however, for U.S. trading partners that enjoy a good relationship with the United States to notify and engage in a dialogue with the U.S. before they undertake any action that might damage trading ties. In this case, Brazil had never actually issued a compulsory license, but instead could have used the threat of issuing a compulsory license as a negotiation tool to pressure pharmaceutical companies to lower their prices. This suggests that Brazil would not simply unilaterally issue a compulsory license: Brazil was likely to notify the U.S. in any event before seeking to impose a compulsory license, even without the settlement. So what exactly did the U.S. get out of the WTO dispute settlement? Added assurance from Brazil? Brazil's agreement "not to proceed with further dispute settlement action regarding sections 204 and 209 of the U.S. patent law" (discussed in the settlement above and below in Problem 3–19)? Or was the U.S. driven to settle the case because of public relations concerns over access to medicines, which will be discussed in the next section?

4. Would the same kind of prior notice and discussions contemplated in the settlement for U.S. companies have to be extended by Brazil to companies of other WTO countries before Brazil imposed any compulsory license on patents held by those other companies? Would such a result be required by TRIPS Article 31? Even in cases of national emergency? Would such a result be required by the most favored nation principle, TRIPS Article 4?

5. *Bibliographical note.* Ubirajara Marques, Valeska Guimaraes, Caitlin Sternberg, *Brazil's Aids Controversy: Antiretroviral Drugs, Breaking Patents, and Compulsory Licensing*, 60 FOOD & DRUG L.J. 471 (2005); Mary Ann Liebert, *Brazil, Abbott Reach Tentative Deal on Kaletra: Threat to Suspend Antirevoviral Patents in Abeyance for Now*, 24 BIOTECHNOLOGY L. REP. 583 (2005).

PROBLEM 3–19

On Jan. 31, 2001, Brazil requested WTO consultations with the U.S. over two provisions of the U.S. Patent Code, §§ 204 and 209. As referenced in the U.S.–Brazil settlement discussed above, the U.S. understood that Brazil would not proceed forward with its challenge as a part of the settlement. But what if Brazil had proceeded with its challenge? For this problem, focus only on § 204 excerpted below. Brazil claimed that § 204 was inconsistent with TRIPS

Articles 27 and 28 because it limits the ability of small business or nonprofit organizations to license any of their patented inventions developed with federal funding unless the license stipulates that the invention "will be manufactured substantially in the United States."

§ 204. Preference for United States industry

Notwithstanding any other provision of this chapter, no small business firm or nonprofit organization which receives title to any subject invention and no assignee of any such small business firm or nonprofit organization shall grant to any person the exclusive right to use or sell any subject invention in the United States unless such person agrees that any products embodying the subject invention or produced through the use of the subject invention will be manufactured substantially in the United States. However, in individual cases, the requirement for such an agreement may be waived by the Federal agency under whose funding agreement the invention was made upon a showing by the small business firm, nonprofit organization, or assignee that reasonable but unsuccessful efforts have been made to grant licenses on similar terms to potential licensees that would be likely to manufacture substantially in the United States or that under the circumstances domestic manufacture is not commercially feasible.

N.B. Under § 201(e), "[t]he term 'subject invention' means any invention of the contractor conceived or first actually reduced to practice in the performance of work under a [federal] funding agreement."

What specific provisions under TRIPS Article 27 and 28 might be implicated by the U.S. provision? Why would a federal law that regulated the ability of patent holders to license any inventions developed by small businesses with federal funding (i.e., by imposing a requirement of substantial manufacturing in the U.S. in the license) raise any issue under TRIPS? Shouldn't a country be allowed to dictate certain licensing terms for inventions developed in part with government funding? Just as any venture firm can presumably stipulate by contract conditions on an inventor the firm funded, shouldn't the government be allowed to do the same by imposing stipulations on an inventor in exchange for the receipt of federal funding?

2. The Doha Declaration

Around the same time that the United States filed a dispute settlement petition against Brazil's compulsory licensing provision with the WTO, U.S. pharmaceutical companies, along with other international MNEs, filed a lawsuit in South Africa challenging the legality of the compulsory licensing provisions in the South African Medical and Related Substances Control Act of 1997. In both the Brazilian and South African disputes, U.S. pharmaceutical companies initially had the strong support of the United States government. However, as the negative publicity and adverse reaction to these challenges mounted, the U.S. government began to waiver in its support of the pharmaceutical industry. Advocacy and public interest group drew embarrassing attention to U.S. government officials on the U.S. position in several highly publicized incidents. The U.S. government soon withdrew its support for the challenge to the South

African law. And, without the support of the U.S. government, the U.S. plaintiffs withdrew their lawsuit. Three months later, the U.S. also withdrew its petition against Brazil with the WTO.

The U.S. position on compulsory licenses lost further credibility as a result of actions taken in the aftermath of the terrorist attacks of September 11, 2001. In response to a scare that terrorists might launch a biological attack (such as an anthrax scare), the United States threatened to issue a compulsory license for the antibiotic Cipro manufactured by Bayer AG Corporation if Bayer did not lower its prices for the drug. In other words, the U.S. was threatening to engage in the very same tactics that it had condemned: using the threat of a compulsory license to pressure a multi-national pharmaceutical company to lower its prices in order to make a drug available to a general population.

By the time of the WTO Fourth Ministerial Conference held in Doha, Qatar in 2001, developing countries had managed to place the issue of access to medicines as a priority on the work agenda. Showing both political skill and organization, developing countries were able to obtain the following "Doha Declaration" from the WTO ministers set forth below.

PROBLEM 3–20

Using the facts in Problem 3–18, analyze Country R's compulsory license in light of the Doha Declaration. Is Country R in compliance with Article 31 as interpreted by the Doha Declaration?

DOHA WTO MINISTERIAL 2001: TRIPS
WT/MIN(01)/DEC/2 (November 20, 2001).

1. We recognize the gravity of the public health problems afflicting many developing and least-developed countries, especially those resulting from HIV/AIDS, tuberculosis, malaria and other epidemics.

2. We stress the need for the WTO Agreement on Trade–Related Aspects of Intellectual Property Rights (TRIPS Agreement) to be part of the wider national and international action to address these problems.

3. We recognize that intellectual property protection is important for the development of new medicines. We also recognize the concerns about its effects on prices.

4. We agree that the TRIPS Agreement does not and should not prevent members from taking measures to protect public health. Accordingly, while reiterating our commitment to the TRIPS Agreement, we affirm that the Agreement can and should be interpreted and implemented in a manner supportive of WTO members' right to protect public health and, in particular, to promote access to medicines for all.

In this connection, we reaffirm the right of WTO members to use, to the full, the provisions in the TRIPS Agreement, which provide flexibility for this purpose.

5. Accordingly and in the light of paragraph 4 above, while maintaining our commitments in the TRIPS Agreement, we recognize that these flexibilities include:

a. In applying the customary rules of interpretation of public international law, each provision of the TRIPS Agreement shall be read in the light of the object and purpose of the Agreement as expressed, in particular, in its objectives and principles.

b. Each member has the right to grant compulsory licences and the freedom to determine the grounds upon which such licences are granted.

c. Each member has the right to determine what constitutes a national emergency or other circumstances of extreme urgency, it being understood that public health crises, including those relating to HIV/AIDS, tuberculosis, malaria and other epidemics, can represent a national emergency or other circumstances of extreme urgency.

d. The effect of the provisions in the TRIPS Agreement that are relevant to the exhaustion of intellectual property rights is to leave each member free to establish its own regime for such exhaustion without challenge, subject to the MFN and national treatment provisions of Articles 3 and 4.

6. We recognize that WTO members with insufficient or no manufacturing capacities in the pharmaceutical sector could face difficulties in making effective use of compulsory licensing under the TRIPS Agreement. We instruct the Council for TRIPS to find an expeditious solution to this problem and to report to the General Council before the end of 2002.

7. We reaffirm the commitment of developed-country members to provide incentives to their enterprises and institutions to promote and encourage technology transfer to least-developed country members pursuant to Article 66.2. We also agree that the least-developed country members will not be obliged, with respect to pharmaceutical products, to implement or apply Sections 5 and 7 of Part II of the TRIPS Agreement or to enforce rights provided for under these Sections until 1 January 2016, without prejudice to the right of least-developed country members to seek other extensions of the transition periods as provided for in Article 66.1 of the TRIPS Agreement. We instruct the Council for TRIPS to take the necessary action to give effect to this pursuant to Article 66.1 of the TRIPS Agreement.

NOTES AND QUESTIONS

1. One of the requirements of Article 31 of TRIPS is a duty to bargain with the patent owner prior to issuing a compulsory license. However, the duty to bargain "may be waived by a member in the case of a national emergency or other circumstances of extreme urgency." How, if at all, is the duty to bargain affected by the Doha Declaration. See paragraph 5(c).

2. TRIPS Article 31(h) further provides that even where a compulsory license is issued, the patent owner must "be paid adequate remuneration." How, if at all, does the Doha Declaration affect this obligation? See paragraph 5(b).

3. *The Implementation Decision*

The Doha Declaration acknowledged that it left one significant issue unresolved and urged the Council of TRIPS to resolve the issue expeditiously. The issue concerned the plight of certain least developed countries that are unable to make effective use of a compulsory license even if one were granted. Some countries are at such a low level of development that they lack the economic and technological capacity to use the patent. For example, some countries simply do not have the capital to invest in a manufacturing facility, a supply of raw materials, and enough trained scientists and engineers to use a patent effectively. These countries may also be unable to import generic drugs from other countries making the generics under a compulsory license. Article 31(f) of TRIPS provides that a compulsory license must be used predominantly for the supply of the domestic market in the country where the compulsory license is granted. In other words, a developing country that is capable of using a compulsory license to manufacture a drug may not be allowed to export the drug to a least developed country, which lacks the capability of using a compulsory license effectively.

Recognizing the seriousness of this problem, the Doha Declaration directs the Council of TRIPS to find an expeditious solution. The Council agreed to the following:

IMPLEMENTATION OF PARAGRAPH 6 OF THE DOHA DECLARATION ON THE TRIPS AGREEMENT AND PUBLIC HEALTH

Decision of the WTO General Council.
WT/L/520 (August 30, 2003).

The General Council ... [d]ecides as follows:

1. For the purposes of this Decision:

(a) "pharmaceutical product" means any patented product, or product manufactured through a patented process, of the pharmaceutical sector needed to address the public health problems as recognized in paragraph 1 of the Declaration. It is understood that active ingredients necessary for its manufacture and diagnostic kits needed for its use would be included:

(b) "eligible importing Member" means any least-developed country Member, and any other Member that has made a notification to the Council for TRIPS of its intention to use the system as an importer, it being understood that a Member may notify at any time that it will use the system in whole or in a limited way, for example only in the case of a national emergency or other circumstances of extreme urgency or in cases of public non-commercial use. It is noted that some Members will not use the system set out in this Decision as importing Members[5] and that some other Members have stated that, if they use the system, it would be in no more than situations of national emergency or other circumstances of extreme urgency;

(c) "exporting Member" means a Member using the system set out in this Decision to produce pharmaceutical products for, and export them to, an eligible importing Member.

2. The obligations of an exporting Member under Article 31(f) of the TRIPS Agreement shall be waived with respect to the grant by it of a compulsory licence to the extent necessary for the purposes of production of a pharmaceutical product(s) and its export to an eligible importing Member(s) in accordance with the terms set out below in this paragraph:

(a) the eligible importing Member(s) has made a notification to the Council for TRIPS, that:

(i) specifies the names and expected quantities of the product(s) needed;

(ii) confirms that the eligible importing Member in question, other than a least-developed country Member, has established that it has insufficient or no manufacturing capacities in the pharmaceutical sector for the product(s) in question in one of the ways set out in the Annex to this Decision; and

(iii) confirms that, where a pharmaceutical product is patented in its territory, it has granted or intends to grant a compulsory licence in accordance with Article 31 of the TRIPS Agreement and the provisions of this Decision;

(b) the compulsory licence issued by the exporting Member under this Decision shall contain the following conditions:

(i) only the amount necessary to meet the needs of the eligible importing Member(s) may be manufactured under the licence and the entirety of this production shall be exported to the Member(s) which has notified its needs to the Council for TRIPS;

(ii) products produced under the licence shall be clearly identified as being produced under the system set out in this Decision through specific labeling or marking. Suppliers should distinguish such products through special packing and/or special colouring/shaping of the products themselves, provided that such distinction is feasible and does not have a significant impact on price; and

(iii) before shipment begins, the licensee shall post on a website the following information:

---

5. Australia, Austria. Belgium, Canada, Denmark, Finland, France, Germany, Greece, Iceland, Ireland, Italy, Japan, Luxembourg, the Netherlands, New Zealand, Norway, Portugal, Spain, Sweden, Switzerland, the United Kingdom and the United States.

- the quantities being supplied to each destination as referred to in indent (i) above, and

- the distinguishing features of the product(s) referred to in indent (ii) above;

(c) the exporting Member shall notify the Council for TRIPS of the grant of the licence, including the conditions attached to it. The information provided shall include the name and address of the licensee, the product(s) for which the licence has been granted, the quantity(ies) for which it has been granted, the country(ies) to which the product(s) is (are) to be supplied and the duration of the licence. The notification shall also indicate the address of the website referred to in subparagraph (b)(iii) above. . . .

5. Members shall ensure the availability of effective legal means to prevent the importation into, and sale in, their territories of products produced under the system set out in this Decision and diverted to their markets inconsistently with its provisions, using the means already required to be available under the TRIPS Agreement. If any Member considers that such measures are proving insufficient for this purpose, the matter may be reviewed in the Council for TRIPS at the request of that Member. * * *

11. This Decision, including the waivers granted in it, shall terminate for each Member on the date on which an amendment to the TRIPS Agreement replacing its provisions takes effect for that Member. The TRIPS Council shall initiate by the end of 2003 work on the preparation of such an amendment with a view to its adoption within six months. * * *

NOTES AND QUESTIONS

1. How does the Implementation Decision address the concerns of the least developed countries in the world with no manufacturing capacity?

2. Are the Doha Declaration and Implementation Agreement an adequate solution to the controversy over the availability of HIV–AIDs drugs in sub-Saharan Africa and other least developed countries, at least in terms of the patent issues raised by the controversy? What was at stake in treating the issue under Article 31 of TRIPS, instead of Article 30? Do you think it is more likely that countries will grant compulsory licenses for patented pharmaceuticals after the Doha Declaration and Implementation Agreement?

3. What legal status should be accorded to the Doha Declaration and Implementation Agreement within the WTO? Their precise status was somewhat unclear, although a 2005 vote of the WTO General Council has helped to clarify their status. Technically, the Declaration and Implementation do not have the same force of the TRIPS Agreement or Agreement Establishing the WTO, which can be amended only through the proper WTO amendment process. In that sense, the Doha Declaration and Implementation Agreement would not be binding authority on WTO members or a WTO panel consider-

ing a challenge. Even if technically nonbinding, should they nevertheless be considered persuasive interpretations of TRIPS? For further discussion of these and other issues related to the Doha Declaration, see Bryan C. Mercurio, *TRIPS, Patents, and Access to Life–Saving Drugs in the Developed World*, 8 MARQ. INTELL. PROP. L. REV. 211 (2004).

4. In late 2005, the WTO General Council voted to make permanent, for pharmaceuticals, the Implementation's waiver of TRIPS Article 31(f)'s restriction on compulsory licenses to be used "predominantly for the supply of the domestic market of the Member authorizing such use." If the WTO states ratify the General Council's decision, a new Article 31*bis* will be added to TRIPS containing essentially the same waiver as the Implementation. In addition, an Annex will also be added to TRIPS with definitions of key terms in the new Article 31*bis*, notification requirements, and a method for evaluating a least developed country's manufacturing capacity. The practical effect of the new Article would be to allow (as is the case under the Implementation) countries to grant compulsory licenses on patented pharmaceuticals to be produced for export to eligible least developed countries.

5. *Canada's Experience as Exporter.* Canada is the first and only country thus far to invoke the Implementation Decision to export drugs under a compulsory license to a developing country. In 2004, Parliament passed Canada's Access to Medicines Regime (CAMR), which permits compulsory licenses on drugs for exportation. In 2007, the Commissioner of Patents authorized a compulsory license on the HIV/AIDS drug TriAvir to Apotex, a Canadian drug company, for shipment to Rwanda. Unfortunately, Canada's compulsory license process proved to be too complex and time-consuming. Apotex took four years to send its first shipment of the drug. Afterwards, Apotex criticized the lengthy process. In 2011, Parliament considered a bill (C–393) to amend CAMR to make the process more streamlined. For further discussion, see Tania Bubela et al., *Wicked Issues for Canada at the Intersection of Intellectual Property and Public Health: Mechanisms for Policy Coherence*, 4 MCGILL J.L. & HEALTH 3, 11–14 (2011).

6. *Seizure of In–Transit Generic Drugs.* Access to medicines raises issues beyond Article 31 and compulsory licenses. In 2010, Brazil and India, two large producers of generic drugs, requested consultations with the EU and Netherlands for their "in transit" seizure of pharmaceuticals in the EU destined for a country outside the EU. Brazil and India maintain that the generic drugs are legal both in the country of production and in the country of final destination. The EU contends, however, the drugs violate patents in Europe. (Such differences may exist because of the territorial approach to patents, plus differences in exhaustion rules.) The drugs involved were for treating blood pressure, heart conditions, HIV/AIDS, and mental illness, including schizophrenia and dementia. As summarized by the WTO DSB: "India alleges that the measures at issue are . . . inconsistent . . . with the obligations of the European Union and the Netherlands under Articles V and X of GATT 1994 and under various provisions of the TRIPS Agreement, namely, Article 28 read together with Article 2, Articles 41 and 42, and Article 31 read together with the provisions of the August 2003 Decision on TRIPS and Public Health." *See* Case Summary, European Union and a Member State—Seizure of Generic Drugs in Transit, DS408, DS409 (WTO website). If

the consultations break down, India and Brazil could file a WTO challenge. In late 2010, the EU reportedly reached a tentative settlement with India, but India said it would not withdraw its case until all EU countries amended their laws. Even if the EU settles with India, Brazil's challenge could still proceed.

c. Special Discussion: Thailand's Compulsory Licenses and Retaliation

Over a decade has passed since the WTO Doha Declaration was adopted, yet the controversy over providing greater access to medicines remains. Relatively few compulsory licenses for medicines have been authorized, and even fewer for export under the Implementation Decision. By one estimate, only ten countries have invoked Article 31 to authorize compulsory licenses for patented drugs.[1] Some commentators suggest that a reason for the low number of compulsory licenses for medicines is the discouragement and retaliation by drug companies and developed countries to dissuade other countries from authorizing compulsory licenses. Consider the following problem and discussion.

PROBLEM 3–21

Developing countries have put on the agenda in the current WTO round of negotiations an amendment to the TRIPS Agreement that prohibits "any threat or retaliation by a WTO member against a developing country to deter the country from issuing a compulsory license on a patented drug as permitted under Article 31 or 31*bis*." An alleged violation of the proposed amendment would be handled as any other WTO complaint before the Dispute Settlement Body, subject to the same remedies including possible trade sanctions. The WTO has asked you to provide an assessment of (i) whether the proposed amendment is necessary or desirable, (ii) if so, whether retaliation by a drug company should be attributable to country where it is headquartered for the purposes of the WTO challenge, and (iii) whether any changes should be made to the proposal.

PATENT BREAKING OR BALANCING?: SEPARATING STRANDS OF FACT FROM FICTION UNDER TRIPS

Cynthia M. Ho.
34 N.C. J. Int'l L. & Com. Reg. 371 (2009).

IV. Thailand's Compulsory Licenses

A. Chronology

Thailand has a national mandate to provide universal access to essential medicine to all its citizens pursuant to the National Health Security Act of 2002 and access to antiretrovirals for all AIDS patients since 2003. While some suggest that universal access to necessary drugs

---

1. *See* Donald Harris, *TRIPS After Fifteen Years: Success or Failure, as Measured by Compulsory Licensing*, 18 J. INTELL. PROP. L. 367, 388 (2011).

was a mere populist measure, others including the WHO praise Thailand as a leader in providing treatment for HIV patients. However, the WHO and the World Bank predict that Thailand will face dramatic price increases in treating their HIV population because HIV patients normally become resistant to initial treatments and need to switch to newer, patented drugs. In fact the World Bank specifically notes that compulsory licenses of second-line HIV treatment would be one way for Thailand to provide cost-effective treatment, although it recognizes that it will require "high-level political commitment" to deal with the implications.

Thailand issued compulsory licenses to achieve its mandate of providing access to essential drugs, including antiretroviral drugs that cannot otherwise be provided despite increases in the public health budget after years of negotiation with patent owners that failed to yield price cuts beyond the level of currency appreciation. Although Thailand asserts that it engaged in prior negotiations with the patent owners, each of its compulsory licenses stated that it could grant compulsory licenses without prior negotiations in the case of public use based on the "right to ... protect ... public health" as supported by the Doha Public Health Declaration. The licenses were issued to cover only Thai citizens who are supported by government funded insurance and not the small percent of Thai citizens who are capable of paying the premium patent prices for the drugs. Accordingly, the licenses should expand revenue for patent owners who can continue to sell their drugs at a premium to wealthy Thai citizens in addition to obtaining compulsory license royalties for the drugs provided to low-income citizens.

On November 29, 2006, Thailand issued a compulsory license to its Government Pharmaceutical Organization (GPO) on Merck's patented drug Efavirenz (sold by the patent owner under the brand name Stocrin), an effective first line treatment for AIDS that has fewer adverse side effects, including life-threatening side effects, than the generic antiretroviral Nevirapine. Thailand's license stated that it was for non-commercial purposes and for the public interest to help achieve its policy of universal access to antiretrovirals for the 500,000 Thai citizens that need them for long-term use.

A Thai compulsory license on the AIDS drug Kaletra was issued to the GPO on January 25, 2007. Kaletra is a patented combination of two antiretrovirals that is often used for patients that become resistant to basic formulations of HIV medications, such as Efavirenz. The Thai government estimated that around ten percent of patients require second-line treatments such as Kaletra within the first few years, or else such patients will die. Prior to the compulsory license, Kaletra was priced at $2200 per patient per year by patent owner Abbott, a cost that is close to the yearly income of a Thai citizen.

On the same day, January 25, 2007, Thailand issued a compulsory license to the GPO for Bristol Myers' anti-platelet drug Plavix, a drug useful for treating heart disease. According to the license, heart disease is one of the top three causes of death in Thailand and although some non-drug preventative measures could be taken there is a need for drug treatment to prevent unnecessary mortality. Without the license only twenty percent of government insured patients could access the medicine, which is inconsistent with the Thai policy of providing universal coverage of essential medicine.

Even though controversy never subsided regarding the initial licenses, Thailand continued to explore additional compulsory licenses. In June 2007, Thailand established two exploratory committees to consider possible compulsory licenses on cancer medications considered necessary for the universal healthcare scheme. At the same time, Thailand was pressured against perceived broad use of compulsory licenses by E.U. Trade Commissioner Peter Mandelson, as well as by the U.S. Ambassador to Thailand, Ralph Boyce. Thailand began negotiations for lower prices on patented cancer drugs in October 2007. Although initial signs were promising, the negotiations eventually broke down in December 2007.

Thailand then issued licenses on four cancer drugs in January 2008, on the eve of a change in government administration. Thailand asserted that they were necessary because cancer is currently the number one cause of death in Thailand, and most effective cancer treatments are patented, not covered on the Thai List of Essential Drugs due to their high cost, and thereby inaccessible to Thai citizens. Thailand asserted that cancer is no less serious than HIV/AIDS, accounting for 30,000 deaths a year with 100,000 new cases diagnosed each year. Moreover, Thailand noted that the licenses were critical to prevent either severe economic hardship, including bankruptcy or certain death, without treatment.

However, unlike the initial compulsory licenses, Thailand delayed implementation of the signed licenses to enable continued negotiations. The continued negotiations yielded a successful outcome in one case; patent owner Novartis agreed to provide its drug Glivec at no cost to Thai citizens meeting certain income requirements, and Thailand revoked the license on Glivec. On the other hand, Thailand was not satisfied with the prices of other patented drugs. Although the other patent owners offered discounts of up to one third the original price, Thailand stated that it would impose a compulsory license unless patent owners offered prices no more than five percent higher than those offered by generic competitors.

* * *

[The Article's extensive analysis in Part V examining whether Thailand's compulsory licenses satisfied TRIPS Article 31, including the public non-commercial use and adequate remuneration requirements, is omitted. *Ed.*]

VI. Concerns Beyond TRIPS

Although Part V concluded that Thailand's licenses could be reasonably considered within the scope of TRIPS Article 31, there are important related issues that must be considered by Thailand, as well as any other country interested in considering compulsory licenses. In particular, retaliatory acts against Thailand cast a troubling shadow over TRIPS' legitimacy that needs to be addressed.

A. Retaliation and Repercussions Beyond TRIPS

1. Drug Company Retaliation

One important problem with issuing compulsory licenses is that patent owners may retaliate by withdrawing other drugs from the marketplace. Thailand, like most countries, requires drug manufacturers to establish that new drugs are safe and effective before they can be sold. After Thailand issued a compulsory license on Abbott's HIV drug Kaletra, Abbott announced that it was withdrawing its application to sell seven new drugs in Thailand including its new HIV drug, Aluvia, that was well-suited to Thailand's climate. Abbott's action is believed to be the first such retaliation by a drug company to a compulsory license; prompting substantial criticism, calls for boycotts, and protests at Abbott's shareholder meeting. Although Abbott eventually decided to register Aluvia and offer it at a discounted rate to Thailand, it has not changed its position on the other drugs.

Abbott's decision not to introduce certain drugs in Thailand is beyond the reach of TRIPS. TRIPS requires nations to patent certain drugs but does not require patented drugs to be sold. Accordingly, despite the fact that TRIPS provides the flexibility of using a compulsory license, that flexibility may be illusory if patent owners can respond by withdrawing other drugs from the market. After all, what good is a compulsory license of one drug for a relatively small population of 50,000 (the number for which Kaletra was licensed), if it results in half a dozen other drugs being unavailable to all citizens of a country? The scope of the risk may be a function of what drugs are at issue—although Abbott remains steadfast in declining to sell certain drugs in Thailand, most of the drugs were not unique.

Abbott's action underscores that whether patients have access to medicine does not solely depend on patent issues, but also on whether a patent owner elects to seek permission to sell the patented drug. Technically, any entity that has a compulsory license could seek permission to sell a patented drug. However, the relevant laws to approve the sale of a new drug entail a substantial investment of time and resources; multiple stages of clinical testing of the drug in the laboratory, in animals, as well as in humans must be completed—a process that generally takes years and millions of dollars. A company launching a newly patented drug can recover these expenses by charging more for the new drug. However, if a second company seeks to sell a drug already on the market, the second company can often rely on the safety and efficacy studies of the first company's drug and then simply establish bioequivalence to the first drug, entailing minimal cost and time. This bioequivalence is important with respect to compulsory licenses because licenses are generally issued for drugs already sold, such that the approval costs are low. On the other hand, if a compulsory license is issued for a drug that has never been previously sold, the license may be ineffective in reducing final costs to consumers because the necessary market approval tests may be expensive enough that the licensed company cannot sell drugs at a price that is both accessible to consumers and yields a profit.

2. Unilateral Trade Sanction—Retaliation by Individual Countries

Another very real implication of compulsory licenses is that countries may be subject to unilateral economic sanctions, or at least political pressure, imposed by individual countries even if a license is TRIPS-compliant. Economic implications are a major problem since any cost-saving from issuing a compulsory license may be dwarfed by more substantial economic sanctions.

The United States, for example, has enacted a number of trade laws that permit it to investigate other countries and potentially impose economic sanctions for a variety of perceived infractions, including intellectual property laws that are viewed as inadequate. In particular, the United States can withdraw trade benefits or impose duties on goods for a country that fails to provide "adequate and effective" protection for U.S. intellectual property rights. By statute, the U.S. Office of Trade Representatives (USTR) must issue an annual report, called the "Special 301" report that lists countries with inadequate levels of intellectual property protection. The worst offenders are labeled priority countries and are automatically subject to investigations that may result in the withdrawal of trade benefits. Countries can and have been listed on the Special 301 report even if they are in full compliance with TRIPS and other international commitments.

Thailand provides a useful illustration—Thailand's compulsory licenses were noted as an issue in the 2007 and 2008 Special 301 reports, but Thailand was not alleged to have violated any specific provision of TRIPS. Indeed, the United States may have no interest in asserting that Thailand violates TRIPS because the WTO rules concerning disputes for all WTO agreements require that individual nations not impose unilateral economic sanctions for violations of TRIPS; rather, nations are to use the WTO dispute settlement proceedings to settle any alleged violations of TRIPS. However, as the Thailand case illustrates, a nation may be in compliance with TRIPS yet nonetheless vulnerable to unilateral trade sanctions—or, at least the threat of such sanctions, which includes pressure to enter into bilateral trade agreements that are likely unfavorable to Thailand. This situation may seem particularly unfair to developing countries because many of them entered into TRIPS with the assumption that the agreement would end unilateral trade sanctions. Prior drafts of the WTO dispute settlement rules had broader language prohibiting any use of unilateral trade sanctions. However, the final wording is much more limited, thus subjecting a country such as Thailand to the potential whim of other countries' rules. * * *

1. Should other developing countries consider following Thailand's lead in issuing compulsory licenses on patented medicines in order to ensure adequate health care?

2. Analyze whether Thailand's compulsory licenses satisfied the requirements of TRIPS Article 31. Assume Thailand did not engage in prior negotiations for Efavirenz, Kaletra, or Plavix, but did so before issuing the compulsory licenses on the cancer drugs. The earlier licenses for the first group of drugs granted only .5% of the net sales to the patentees, while the compulsory licenses for the cancer drugs granted 2% to the patentees.

3. What do you make of the reactions of drug company Abbott and the U.S. in response to Thailand's compulsory licenses? Were these legitimate responses, or acts of retaliation? Should the WTO forbid such responses against a country that exercises its rights under Article 31 to issue compulsory licenses?

4. PATENT TERM

TRIPS

Article 33

Term of Protection

The term of protection available shall not end before the expiration of a period of twenty years counted from the filing date.[8]

The minimum standard for the patent term is 20 years from the date of filing. Although the standard allows for longer terms, nearly all countries follow the 20–year term. Unlike in the copyright context, patent terms have not been subject to increasing pressures to extend the term.

In *Canada–Term of Patent Protection*, WT/DS170/AB/R (September 18, 2000), a WTO panel concluded that the 20–year term of patent under TRIPS Article 33 applied to all existing patents in WTO members that had not yet expired, even if granted before the effective date of TRIPS. The WTO panel explained:

> Article 70.2 applies the obligations of the *TRIPS Agreement* to "all subject matter existing ... and which is protected" on the date of application of the *TRIPS Agreement* for a Member. A Member is required, as from that date, to implement *all* obligations under the *TRIPS Agreement* in respect of such existing subject matter. This includes the obligation in Article 33. We see no basis in the text for isolating or insulating the obligation in Article 33 relating to the duration of a patent term from the other obligations relating to patents that are also found in Section 5 of the *TRIPS Agreement*.

---

8. It is understood that those Members which do not have a system of original grant may provide that the term of protection shall be computed from the filing date in the system of original grant

[The panel rejected the argument that Article 70.1 should be read as "not giv[ing] rise to obligations in respect of" existing patents. The panel concluded that existing patents are not "acts which occurred before" the effective date of TRIPS because the patents are still ongoing.]

NOTES AND QUESTIONS

1. *Application to Existing Patents.* Canada was not alone in needing to change its patent term to comply with the minimum standard of 20 years from the date of filing the patent application contained in Article 33. Many developing countries and even developed countries (including the United States, Germany, Australia, and New Zealand) had previously had shorter patent terms. *See* Joseph Straus, *Implications of the TRIPS Agreement in the Field of Patent Law, in* FROM GATT TO TRIPS—THE AGREEMENT ON TRADE-RELATED ASPECTS OF INTELLECTUAL PROPERTY RIGHTS 160, 199–200 (Friedrich-Karl Beier & Gerhard Schricker eds., 1996).

2. What policy rationale can justify the extension of a patent term for already existing patents? Since the invention is already in existence, does the inventor need any more incentive? Isn't adding more years to an existing patent pure windfall to the patentee? What extra benefit does the public receive? International harmonization?

CHAPTER 4

TRADEMARKS AND GEOGRAPHICAL INDICATIONS

■ ■ ■

A. INTRODUCTION

1. THE RIGHTS IN MARKS FOR GOODS AND SERVICES

a. Trademarks

Merchants have used marks to identify—or "brand"—their products and services probably dating back close to the beginning of commerce. The ancient Greeks used marks to identify their goods, as did the Romans. Trademarks can be used to identify a good such as a cereal, or a service such as a hotel. Historically, the latter kind of mark was called a "service mark," although today it is also commonly referred to as a trademark.

The law of trademark developed to deal with the problem created when several businesses started using the same mark, a situation that might create confusion among consumers. Some cases involve blatant "passing off" in which a competitor of a trademark holder used the holder's mark on its own products to pass them off as the holder's goods. The public might suffer harm if the "passed off" products were of inferior quality. And, if the trademark holder had built up considerable goodwill among customers, the competitor would be free riding on the trademark holder's mark and investment. Other trademark cases, however, involve two or more companies that started using the same mark in good faith, operating in different areas or without notice of each other. The question in these cases is priority—who has the right to use the mark.

A primary justification for protecting trademarks is to protect the consuming public. If a mark properly identifies the source of the product, the public can know the quality of the source's goods and begin to make decisions based on past purchasing experience. If Créme de la Créme Company's donuts tasted good when purchased and eaten last week, they

441

are likely to be good when purchased and eaten this week. Trademark law also helps to prevent deception of the consuming public by third parties who falsely "pass off" goods or who use a mark that is likely to cause confusion among consumers.

One might also justify trademark law completely apart from considerations of the consuming public. Instead, trademark law may be seen as a form of business ethics (similar to the concerns of trade secret law, discussed in Chapter 5) to regulate wasteful or harmful forms of free riding on the goodwill built up in another's mark. Here, the concern is less on the consuming public than it is on protecting a business's goodwill and deterring unsavory forms of misappropriation.

In economic terms, trademarks help to reduce the search costs of consumers that would arise if they had to check the quality of every product or service purchased each time they purchased it. Instead, consumers can avoid search costs once they determine whether ABC Company's goods are of sufficient quality or not. Trademarks also prevent the free riding that takes place when a third party "passes off" its product as the product of a trademark holder who has established a large consumer base.

As this discussion indicates, the historical development of trademark law has been linked to tort law or unfair competition, with the ultimate goal of protecting the consuming public. Unlike copyright or patent, a trademark holder did not receive a bundle of exclusive rights to the mark under traditional trademark law; rather, the trademark holder's rights were contingent upon showing that a third party was using the mark in a way that was likely to cause confusion. Today, however, trademarks and brands are increasingly viewed as creating property rights. Trademark owners and MNEs view their trademarks as among their most valuable business assets. What has caused this shift towards a property theory? Consider the following discussion of branding by businesses:

> [B]rands have been taking center stage in a sweeping shift that some compare to the wave of mass marketing that occurred in the years following World War II.
>
> * * * That's why companies that once measured their worth strictly in terms of tangibles such as factories, inventory, and cash have realized that a vibrant brand, with its implicit promise of quality, is an equally important asset.

The Best Global Brands, BUSINESSWEEK, Aug. 6, 2001, at 53–54. The world's most valuable brands, measured by the value of the brand alone as a revenue-producing business asset, are as follows:

The World's 10 Most Valuable Brands in 2011

Rank	Brand	2011 Brand Value ($Billions)
1	Apple	153.3
2	Google	111.5
3	IBM	100.8
4	McDonald's	81.0
5	Microsoft	78.2
6	Coca–Cola	73.8
7	AT&T	69.9
8	Marlboro	67.5
9	China Mobile	57.3
10	GE	50.3

Source: *BrandZ Top 100 Most Valuable Global Brands* (2011).

The recognition of the value of brands as business assets and the importance of their management to business success has been one of the major developments of the new millennium. Keep this development in mind as we explore recent changes in trademark law and geographical indications, discussed below, that may reflect this shift.

b. Geographical Indications (GIs)

Geographical indications (GIs) are defined in the TRIPS Agreement Article 22 as "indications which identify a good as originating in the territory of a Member, or a region or locality in that territory, where a given quality, reputation or other characteristic of the good is essentially attributable to its geographical origin." GIs are very important for wines, other beverages, cheeses, and foods that use the name of a geographical region, such as Bordeaux, Chablis, Chianti, Rocquefort cheese, Florida orange juice, Colombian coffee, and Parma ham. Theoretically, a GI is limited to use by producers located within that geographical region. This means that GIs are collective marks in the sense that several producers, as long as from the region, can use the GI, for example, "Napa Valley wine."

The Paris Convention does not specifically mention GIs, but Article 10's prohibition on the importation of goods that use "a false indication of the source of the goods" arguably encompasses misuse of geographical indications by others outside the region. Paris Conv. art. 10. The lack of express coverage, however, led France to push for the adoption of the Madrid Agreement for the Repression of False or Deceptive Indications of

Source on Goods, first signed in 1891 ("the Madrid Agreement for GIs"). Although formed at the same time as the Madrid Agreement Concerning the International Registration of Marks (discussed in the next section), the Madrid Agreement for GIs has not elicited much international support. As of 2011, only 35 countries have signed the Agreement—the United States being one of the most noticeable countries not to sign on. One of the more controversial provisions of the Madrid Agreement is Article 4, which forbids countries from deeming GIs for wines to be generic. *See* Madrid Agreement for GIs art. 4. Another attempt was made to secure greater protection for GIs in the Lisbon Agreement for the Protection of Appellations of Origin and Their International Registration, first signed in 1958. As of 2011, however, only 27 countries agreed to the Lisbon Agreement—with the U.S. again declining to join. The Lisbon Agreement attempts to establish an international registration system for GIs and requires countries to protect GIs that have been registered. No country can deem a GI generic if it is protected in the country of origin. *See* Lisbon Agreement for the Protection of Appellations of Origin and Their International Registration art. 6. The robust protection required for GIs under Lisbon made it unattractive to countries that adopt a less expansive view of GIs.

Against this historical backdrop, the inclusion of a separate section for the protection of GIs within the TRIPS Agreement was a monumental achievement—particularly for countries, such as France, that have long been pushing for greater international protection of GIs. The inclusion of GIs within TRIPS did not occur without considerable debate and division, much of which still remains today. Article 24(1) acknowledges this division by requiring members to engage in further negotiations on GIs, specifically instructing them to "be willing to consider the continued applicability of these provisions to individual geographical indications whose use was the subject of such negotiations." TRIPS art. 24(1). Already, several challenges have been brought before the Dispute Settlement Body to enforce parts of the current provision of TRIPS. And the WTO continues to debate aspects of protecting GIs, including (i) establishing an international registry for GIs of wines and spirits and (ii) expanding the higher level of protection for wines and spirits under Article 23 to all GIs. It would be no exaggeration to characterize the protection of GIs as one of the most controversial topics covered in TRIPS—often pitting the U.S. against the EU.

2. INTERNATIONAL AGREEMENTS: TRIPS, THE PARIS CONVENTION, AND THE MADRID PROTOCOL

The Paris Convention's treatment of trademarks shares many of the same features of its treatment of patents. As discussed in Chapter 3, Article 2 of the Paris Convention requires countries to provide national treatment for foreign nationals of member countries with respect to "the protection of industrial property," including both patents and trademarks. Paris Conv. art. 2. Trademarks also may require the filing of an application in different countries, as is the case with patents. This, of course, is different from copyright. As we saw in Chapter 2, the Berne Convention bars formalities on copyrights for works outside the country of origin. By contrast, the trademark owner can be subject to formalities, such as the filing of application for registration to obtain protection. Of course, the national treatment principle prohibits nations from discriminating against foreign trademark owners, such as by imposing fees or administrative requirements that do not apply to local owners.

Article 4 also sets forth the right of Paris priority. In the case of trademarks, however, the period of priority lasts only 6 months. Paris Conv. art. 4(C)(1). Just as with the grant of patents, Paris requires countries to allow registration of marks *independent* of whatever protection may exist for the same mark in different countries. *Id.* art. 6(3). For example, a Paris country cannot refuse to register a mark of a foreign national of another Paris country just because the mark has not been registered in the country of origin. *Id.* art. 6(2). However, Paris does recognize some benefits to registering a mark in the country of origin under Article 6*quinquies*, commonly called the "telle quelle" (meaning "as is") provision. Under this provision, once a mark is duly registered in the country of origin, other countries are supposed to register the mark "as is"—not questioning any aspect of the form of the mark. *Id.* art. 6*quinquies*(A)(1). What this limitation means precisely will be examined later in this chapter.

Article 2(1) of TRIPS requires member countries to adhere to Articles 1–12 and 19 of the Paris Convention (1967 Stockholm text). TRIPS art. 2(1). In addition, in Articles 15–21 for trademarks and 22–24 for geographical indications, TRIPS adds its own minimum standards. One noticeable change from the Paris Convention is that TRIPS now expressly elevates service marks to the same status as trademarks. Article 6*sexies* of the Paris Convention expressly allows countries the discretion whether or not to have registration for service marks. Paris Conv. art. 6*sexies*. However, Articles 15 and 16 of TRIPS now effectively treat service marks the same as marks for goods; both fall within the term "trademark." TRIPS arts. 15, 16. Thus, under TRIPS, countries must also allow for registration of service marks.

Article 19 of the Paris Convention allows members to enter into "special agreements for the protection of industrial property," as long as they do not derogate from the provisions of the Convention. As we have already studied, the Patent Cooperation Treaty is a special agreement for patent law. In trademark law, the two main special agreements are the Madrid Agreement Concerning the International Registration of Marks (1891) (commonly referred to as the "Madrid Agreement") and the Madrid Protocol Relating to the Madrid Agreement Concerning the International Registration of Marks (1989) (commonly referred to as the "Madrid Protocol"). Both attempt to establish a common international registration system, somewhat similar to the aims of the PCT for patent filings. As of 2011, 56 countries had agreed to the Madrid Agreement, while 84 countries had joined the Madrid Protocol. Although the Madrid Agreement is older, the Madrid Protocol may be gaining preeminence with the U.S.'s recent accession to the Protocol (but not to the Madrid Agreement). In fact, the Madrid Protocol was drafted as a codicil to the Madrid Agreement, with the goal of revising some of the perceived shortcomings of the Madrid Agreement. A Paris country can join either or both trademark agreements (or decide not to join at all).

In this chapter, we will focus our attention on three international agreements—TRIPS, the Paris Convention, and the Madrid Protocol. Some discussion will also be given to the Madrid Agreement. As you read the chapter, consider whether the international standards for trademarks are any more complete or well organized than the international standards for copyright or patent we have studied.

NOTES AND QUESTIONS

1. Do you think it makes a difference whether trademark law is considered a form of tort or unfair competition, or a form of property? Could it contain elements of both?

2. "Branding" is now a major business strategy for governments, businesses, universities, and individuals. Why is branding so important and what is the difference between a brand and a trademark? Do you think that a trademark that is not very distinctive or well known among consumers can be a brand?

3. According to BrandZ, Apple is the top brand in the world. Do you think Apple would ever sell its trademarks for $153.3 billion?

4. William Landes and Richard Posner suggest that trademark law also creates incentives for businesses to invent new words and symbols. WILLIAM M. LANDES & RICHARD A. POSNER, THE ECONOMIC STRUCTURE OF INTELLECTUAL PROPERTY LAW 168–69 (2003). Although this is not one of the traditional justifications for trademark law, should it be one of the reasons to protect trademarks? How does it compare to copyright law's policy goal of creating incentives to create, yet its exclusion of short phrases from any protection?

5. What are the differences between a trademark and a geographical indication? Should geographical indications be protected to the same extent as (if not greater than) trademarks? Are the policy reasons for protecting GIs different than those for trademarks? Does the fact that a geographical indication is tied to a geographical region—and its people and heritage—give it a stronger, or at least different type of, claim for protection than trademark?

6. *The Unworldly Consumer?* At least part of the controversy over protecting GIs stems from the United States's and other countries' reluctance to protect GIs that may not necessarily be recognized by consumers in their countries as indicating a geographical source. For example, some people may not know that "Champagne" is a province in France where champagne is

produced. If the consuming public in a country is, by and large, ignorant of the geographical significance of an indication, should it nevertheless be protected as long as the GI is recognized in the country of origin? We will return to this discussion later in this chapter.

7. *Bibliographic note.* STEPHAN P. LADAS, PATENTS, TRADEMARKS, AND RELATED RIGHTS: NATIONAL AND INTERNATIONAL PROTECTION 965–1267 (1975); WILLIAM M. LANDES & RICHARD A. POSNER, THE ECONOMIC STRUCTURE OF INTELLECTUAL PROPERTY LAW 166–209 (2003); Paul J. Heald, *Trademarks and Geographical Indications: Exploring the Contours of the TRIPS Agreement*, 29 VAND. J. TRANSNAT'L L. 635 (1996); Joanna Schmidt–Szalewski, *The International Protection of Trademarks After the TRIPS Agreement*, 9 DUKE J. COMP. & INT'L L. 189 (1998); Molly Torsen, *Apples and Oranges (and Wine): Why the International Conversation Regarding Geographic Indications Is at a Standstill*, 87 J. PAT. & TRADEMARK OFF. SOC'Y 31 (2005).

B. TRADEMARKS

1. FORMALITIES, REGISTRATION, AND USE REQUIREMENTS

TRIPS, Article 15

Protectable Subject Matter

1. Any sign, or any combination of signs, capable of distinguishing the goods or services of one undertaking from those of other undertakings, shall be capable of constituting a trademark. Such signs, in particular words including personal names, letters, numerals, figurative elements and combinations of colours as well as any combination of such signs, shall be eligible for registration as trademarks. Where signs are not inherently capable of distinguishing the relevant goods or services, Members may make registrability depend on distinctiveness acquired through use. Members may require, as a condition of registration, that signs be visually perceptible.

2. Paragraph 1 shall not be understood to prevent a Member from denying registration of a trademark on other grounds, provided that they do not derogate from the provisions of the Paris Convention (1967).

3. Members may make registrability depend on use. However, actual use of a trademark shall not be a condition for filing an application for registration. An application shall not be refused solely on the ground that intended use has not taken place before the expiry of a period of three years from the date of application.

4. The nature of the goods or services to which a trademark is to be applied shall in no case form an obstacle to registration of the trademark.

5. Members shall publish each trademark either before it is registered or promptly after it is registered and shall afford a reasonable

opportunity for petitions to cancel the registration. In addition, Members may afford an opportunity for the registration of a trademark to be opposed.

Article 19

Requirement of Use

1. If use is required to maintain a registration, the registration may be cancelled only after an uninterrupted period of at least three years of non-use, unless valid reasons based on the existence of obstacles to such use are shown by the trademark owner. Circumstances arising independently of the will of the owner of the trademark which constitute an obstacle to the use of the trademark, such as import restrictions on or other government requirements for goods or services protected by the trademark, shall be recognized as valid reasons for non-use.

2. When subject to the control of its owner, use of a trademark by another person shall be recognized as use of the trademark for the purpose of maintaining the registration.

Article 20

Other requirements

The use of a trademark in the course of trade shall not be unjustifiably encumbered by special requirements, such as use with another trademark, use in a special form or use in a manner detrimental to its capability to distinguish the goods or services of one undertaking from those of other undertakings. This will not preclude a requirement prescribing the use of the trademark identifying the undertaking producing the goods or services along with, but without linking it to, the trademark distinguishing the specific goods or services in question of that undertaking.

Paris Convention, Article 6

Marks: Conditions of Registration; Independence of Protection of Same Mark in Different Countries

(1) The conditions for the filing and registration of trademarks shall be determined in each country of the Union by its domestic legislation.

(2) However, an application for the registration of a mark filed by a national of a country of the Union in any country of the Union may not be refused, nor may a registration be invalidated, on the ground that filing, registration, or renewal, has not been effected in the country of origin.

(3) A mark duly registered in a country of the Union shall be regarded as independent of marks registered in the other countries of the Union, including the country of origin.

* * *

Countries have differed over two basic approaches to how trademarks are secured. Civil law countries tend to have trademark systems based on *registration* of a mark—meaning that the first to register a mark in the country's trademark office is entitled to the mark, without any requirement of the registrant's prior use of the mark in commerce. In first-to-register countries, such as France and other continental European countries, the examination process tends to be modest, and registrations are allowed for any registrable mark that has not previously been registered for the particular type of good or service.

By contrast, historically, common law countries had trademark systems based on the *prior use* of a mark in commerce—meaning that the first to use a mark in a geographical area was entitled to use the mark in that area (for that type of product or service in which it was used), without any requirement of the user's registration of the mark. However, common law countries have also now adopted registration systems that enable the trademark user to obtain additional rights or benefits upon registration. For example, under U.S. trademark law, if the user of a mark registers the mark in the Trademark Office, the registrant can defeat the claims of all subsequent or "junior" users of the mark in the entire United States. Registration effectively establishes constructive notice and use of the mark in the United States, thereby "conferring a right of priority, nationwide in effect, on or in connection with the goods or services specified in the registration." Lanham Act, § 7(c), 15 U.S.C. § 1057(c).

For the most part, Article 15 of TRIPS avoids taking a side between first-to-register and first-to-use trademark systems. Article 15 does require countries to have a registration system in place for individuals to register their trademarks. Given this requirement, even use-based trademark systems must have a system of registration. At the same time, Article 15 recognizes that "[m]embers may make registrability depend on use"— providing even greater recognition of use-based trademark systems than Article 6 of the Paris Convention, which generally acknowledges that each country may decide the "conditions" of registration. TRIPS qualifies this provision, however, stating: "*actual use* of a trademark shall *not* be a condition for filing an application for registration. An application shall not be refused solely on the ground that intended use has not taken place before the expiry of a period of three years from the date of application." TRIPS art. 15(3) (emphasis added).

This latter proviso effectively requires first-to-use countries, such as the United States, to allow applications for registration of trademarks based on the *intent to use* the mark in commerce. *See, e.g.*, Lanham Act, § 1(b), 15 U.S.C. § 1051(b). Under U.S. law, a registrant who registers a mark based on an intent to use the mark is required to use the mark (as verified in a statement of use filed in the Trademark Office) within a specified time in order to perfect the registration. *Id.* Nonuse for 3 consecutive years is "prima facie evidence of abandonment" of the mark. Lanham Act, § 45, 15 U.S.C. § 1127. However, as will be discussed below, applications based on prior foreign applications from the country of origin are entitled to registration in the U.S., without any requirement of use or a statement of use in the U.S. Lanham Act, § 44, 15 U.S.C. § 1126.

Paris Article 5(D) expressly forbids countries from requiring mention of the registration of the trademark on the good (as holders commonly do with the symbol "®") as a condition of protection of the trademark. Paris Conv. art. 5(D).

NOTES AND QUESTIONS

1. Which, if any, system of trademarks is preferable—a system that accords rights to [i] the first to use a mark in commerce or [ii] the first to register the mark in the trademark office? What are the advantages and disadvantages of each approach? What interests does each serve?

2. *Mixed systems.* Some countries have systems that incorporate features of both the first-to-register and the first-to-use systems. For example, the United States has recognized an "intent-to-use" registration of a mark, which makes the predominantly use-based system in the U.S. closer to a registration system. Conversely, some countries, such as Venezuela, have predominantly registration-based systems, but recognize that a prior user can defeat a later (even if the first) registrant's claim to a mark. But, under Venezuela law, the only way that a user can establish the "right to exclusive use" of the mark in Venezuela is by registration of the mark. *See Babbit Elec., Inc. v. Dynascan Corp.*, 38 F.3d 1161, 1168–70 (11th Cir. 1994) (discussing Venezuela trademark law). Instead of a pure first-to-register or pure first-to-use system, would you prefer some form of mixed system like the U.S. or Venezuela? If so, should the trademark system give greater priority to establishing rights based on use or on registration of a mark, or neither?

3. *Relationship to copyright systems.* Would it be imaginable to get rid of all formalities in patents and trademarks? Does the reliance on registration and application systems in both patent and trademark law provide any greater insight(s) to the desirability of having no formalities in copyright law under the Berne Convention Article 5(2)? Should this provision in Berne be revisited?

4. *Bibliographic note.* INTERNATIONAL TRADEMARK ASSOCIATION (INTA), COUNTRY GUIDES: BASIC INFORMATION ON TRADEMARK REGISTRATION WORLDWIDE (3d ed. 2002); STEPHAN P. LADAS, PATENTS, TRADEMARKS, AND RELATED RIGHTS: NATIONAL AND INTERNATIONAL PROTECTION 1041–1059 (1975).

PROBLEM 4–1

As discussed above, the United States has amended its trademark law to recognize an alternative to registration of a mark based on use. An applicant may file an "intent-to-use" application, which must be later supported by a "verified statement" indicating that the mark has been used in commerce within a certain period of time. Registration is not to be granted by the U.S. Trademark Office until the verified statement of use is filed. Lanham Act, § 1(b), 15 U.S.C. § 1051(b). The only exception is that a foreign registrant in a Paris country may register a mark in the U.S. regardless of any use or verified statement, if the registrant has registered the mark in the country of origin. Lanham Act, § 44, 15 U.S.C. § 1126. However, if the foreign registrant has not registered the mark in its country of origin, the foreign registrant must file a U.S. application based on either (i) use of the mark in commerce or (ii) an intent-to-use that complies with § 1 of the Lanham Act, which is quoted in relevant part below.

You are the Minister of Intellectual Property Law for Country A. You question whether U.S. trademark law, particularly its verified statement of use requirement, complies with its obligations under TRIPS Article 15(3). You are not concerned with the exception under U.S. law described above for Paris filings based on applications from the country of origin. You are concerned instead about cases in which foreign businesses and persons file for trademark registration in the U.S. directly with an "intent to use" application as the first filing. You have learned that the U.S. Trademark Office's issuance of a notice of an allowance for a trademark can take 6 months to a year from the date of filing of the application. Please evaluate whether the U.S. law potentially violates TRIPS Article 15(3). What arguments could you make on behalf of Country A that U.S. law violates TRIPS Article 15(3)? What counter-arguments would you anticipate from the U.S. representative? Which side has the better argument? The following is the relevant portion of U.S. law (Lanham Act, § 1(b), 15 U.S.C. § 1051).

(b) Application for bona fide intention to use trademark

(1) A person who has a bona fide intention, under circumstances showing the good faith of such person, to use a trademark in commerce may request registration of its trademark on the principal register hereby established by paying the prescribed fee and filing in the Patent and Trademark Office an application and a verified statement, in such form as may be prescribed by the Director.

(2) The application shall include specification of the applicant's domicile and citizenship, the goods in connection with which the applicant has a bona fide intention to use the mark, and a drawing of the mark.

(3) The statement shall be verified by the applicant and specify—

> (A) that the person making the verification believes that he or she, or the juristic person in whose behalf he or she makes the verification, to be entitled to use the mark in commerce;

> (B) the applicant's bona fide intention to use the mark in commerce;

> (C) that, to the best of the verifier's knowledge and belief, the facts recited in the application are accurate; and

> (D) that, to the best of the verifier's knowledge and belief, no other person has the right to use such mark in commerce either in the identical form thereof or in such near resemblance thereto as to be likely, when used on or in connection with the goods of such other person, to cause confusion, or to cause mistake, or to deceive.

Except for applications filed pursuant to section 1126 of this title [which governs applications filed after registration in the country of origin], no mark shall be registered until the applicant has met the requirements of subsections (c) and (d) of this section. * * *

(d) Verified statement that trademark is used in commerce

(1) Within six months after the date on which the notice of allowance with respect to a mark is issued under section 1063(b)(2) of this title to an applicant under subsection (b) of this section, the applicant shall file in the Patent and Trademark Office, together with such number of specimens or facsimiles of the mark as used in commerce as may be required by the Director and payment of the prescribed fee, a verified statement that the mark is in use in commerce and specifying the date of the applicant's first use of the mark in commerce and those goods or services specified in the notice of allowance on or in connection with which the mark is used in commerce. Subject to examination and acceptance of the statement of use, the mark shall be registered in the Patent and Trademark Office, a certificate of registration shall be issued for those goods or services recited in the statement of use for which the mark is entitled to registration, and notice of registration shall be published in the Official Gazette of the Patent and Trademark Office. Such examination may include an examination of the factors set forth in subsections (a) through (e) of section 1052 of this title. The notice of registration shall specify the goods or services for which the mark is registered.

(2) The Director shall extend, for one additional 6–month period, the time for filing the statement of use under paragraph (1), upon written request of the applicant before the expiration of the 6–month period provided in paragraph (1). In addition to an extension under the preceding sentence, the Director may, upon a showing of good cause by the applicant, further extend the time for filing the statement of use under paragraph (1) for periods aggregating not more than 24 months, pursuant to written request of the applicant made before the expiration of the last extension granted under this paragraph. Any request for an extension under this paragraph shall be accompanied by a verified statement that the applicant has a continued bona fide intention to use the mark in commerce and specifying those goods or services identified in the notice of allowance on or in connection with which the applicant has a continued bona fide intention to use the mark in commerce. Any request for an extension under this paragraph shall be accompanied by payment of the prescribed fee. The Director shall issue regulations setting forth guidelines for determining what constitutes good cause for purposes of this paragraph.

(3) The Director shall notify any applicant who files a statement of use of the acceptance or refusal thereof and, if the statement of use is refused, the reasons for the refusal. An applicant may amend the statement of use.

(4) The failure to timely file a verified statement of use under paragraph (1) or an extension request under paragraph (2) shall result in abandonment of the application, unless it can be shown to the satisfaction of the Director that the delay in responding was unintentional, in which case

the time for filing may be extended, but for a period not to exceed the period specified in paragraphs (1) and (2) for filing a statement of use.

2. PARIS PRIORITY AND REGISTERING TRADEMARKS IN DIFFERENT COUNTRIES

a. Paris Priority: Article 4

PROBLEM 4–2

You've been hired by Sam Wilson, a jazz musician, to register the mark "Dulcet Enterprises" for a new record label. Sam applied for U.S. registration in the Patent & Trademark Office (PTO) on January 25 of this year (assume it is a weekday), using the PTO's electronic application system (TEAS). The USPTO rejected Sam's application, however, as Sam has never used the trademark in commerce and has not submitted an affidavit of an intent to use. Sam also plans to register the mark in several EU countries with strong markets for English language music, but has discovered a company began selling music under the same mark on September 10 of the previous year and has been continuously marketing music under the mark up to the present. The company also filed trademark registrations for the mark in a number of EU countries on June 10. It is now June 17 of the same year. With respect to the European market, what should Sam do and why? Also, besides the filing date, what factor(s) should Sam consider in deciding whether to seek registrations in other countries and in how many other countries? Please advise your client.

SCM CORP. v. LANGIS FOODS LTD.

U.S. Court of Appeals for the District of Columbia Circuit.
539 F.2d 196 (D.C. Cir. 1976).

McGOWAN, CIRCUIT JUDGE:

This case presents the issue whether a corporate foreign national, which has applied for a trademark registration in its home country, has priority in registering that trademark in the United States over a domestic corporation when: (1) the foreign national filed a trademark application in its home country without prior use of the trademark in any country; (2) the foreign national subsequently filed a timely application to register the trademark in the United States based upon the earlier application in its home country; (3) the foreign national used the trademark in its home country, but not in the United States prior to filing its United States application; and (4) the domestic corporation used the trademark in the United States after the foreign national's home country application was filed but before the foreign national's United States application was filed. The District Court concluded that the domestic corporation was entitled to registration of the trademark. For the reasons set forth below, we reverse.

I

On March 28, 1969, appellant Langis Foods, a Canadian corporation, filed applications to register three trademarks in Canada APPLE TREE, ORANGE TREE, and LEMON TREE.[1] Shortly thereafter, on May 15, 1969, Langis used these marks in Canada. Appellee SCM Corporation, a domestic corporation, apparently started to use the LEMON TREE trademark in this country on the same day.[4] Both Langis and SCM subsequently applied to the United States Patent Office to register these trademarks: SCM's application, filed on June 18, 1969, requested registration of the LEMON TREE trademark; Langis's application, filed on September 19, 1969, requested registration of three trademarks LEMON TREE, ORANGE TREE, and APPLE TREE. While these applications were pending in the Patent Office, SCM began using the marks ORANGE TREE and LIME TREE in the United States in June of 1970, and on July 22 of that year applied to the Patent Office to register those marks.

In August of 1971, the Patent Office published Langis's trademarks APPLE TREE and ORANGE TREE in its "Official Gazette" for purposes of opposition. Two months later, the Office issued a registration to Langis for the trademark LEMON TREE. SCM Corporation then instituted oppositions to the APPLE TREE and ORANGE TREE applications, and also filed a petition to cancel the LEMON TREE registration. On May 7, 1973, the Trademark Trial and Appeal Board denied the petition to cancel and dismissed the oppositions on the ground that, pursuant to section 44(d) of the Trademark Act of 1946, "(Langis) is entitled herein as a matter of right to rely upon the filing dates of its Canadian applications, i.e., March 28, 1969, and hence that it possesses superior rights in its marks as against (SCM)."

SCM then filed a complaint in the District Court seeking to have the LEMON TREE registration canceled and the APPLE TREE and ORANGE TREE registrations denied. The District Court granted SCM's motion for summary judgment on the ground that "prior right in a trademark in the United States depends on priority of use in the United States and is not affected by priority of use in a foreign country." Since Langis used the marks in Canada but not in the United States, the court canceled the LEMON TREE registration and remanded the proceedings opposing ORANGE TREE and APPLE TREE to the Board. This appeal is taken from that final order.

II

Appellee SCM directs our attention to section 2(d) of the Trademark Act of 1946 (Lanham Act), 15 U.S.C. § 1052(d) (Supp. IV, 1974), which appears to preclude registration of the disputed trademarks by Langis. That section provides that "(n)o trade-mark ... shall be refused registra-

---

1. The trademarks were to cover dry crystals which, when mixed with water, would produce a fruit beverage.

4. SCM used the trademark with respect to a fruit beverage similar to that of Langis.

tion on the principal register on account of its nature unless it (d) Consists of or comprises a mark which so resembles ... a mark or trade name *previously used in the United States by another* and not abandoned, as to be likely, when applied to the goods of the applicant, to cause confusion, or to cause mistake, or to deceive...." *Id.* (emphasis added). Langis has admitted that SCM was the first to use the marks in the United States, and nowhere suggests that SCM has abandoned them. Therefore, SCM argues, section 2(d) is "in *haec verba* a complete bar to Langis obtaining or maintaining registrations for its marks."

This argument must, however, be evaluated in light of legislative attempts to reconcile differences between the American and foreign systems of trademark registration. In the United States, federal registration under the Lanham Act is generally based upon first use. Canada, however, employs a system which allows registration of a trademark without prior use. Certain provisions of the Lanham Act were designed to provide some protection to trademarks already registered elsewhere by foreign nationals, and Langis relies for protection specifically on section 44(d), which provides in relevant part that a trademark registration application filed by a foreign national "shall be accorded the same force and effect as would be accorded to the same application if filed in the United States on the same date on which the application was first filed in (the) foreign country...." 15 U.S.C. § 1126(d).

Both SCM and Langis recognize that section 44(d) protects trademarks for which registration applications have first been filed in a foreign country. The dispute in this case goes only to the precise scope of that statutory protection. SCM contends that section 44(d) gives a foreign applicant a constructive filing date in the United States as of the date of the foreign filing; the filing date is important because the party with the later filing date bears the burden of proving that it possesses the prior right to the mark. SCM would concede that it had the burden of proof in this proceeding with respect to the right to register LEMON TREE since its actual filing date was subsequent to Langis's "constructive filing date" of March 28, 1969. The District Court accepted this view of section 44(d), and since Langis admitted that it had not used the mark in the United States, granted summary judgment for SCM.

Appellant Langis offers a second and, in our view, more plausible interpretation of section 44(d). Langis suggests that section 44(d) grants a foreign applicant which has used the trademark in its home country after the foreign filing but prior to the actual United States filing a constructive use date as of the date of the foreign filing. Under this view, Langis would have priority since its constructive use date of March 28, 1969 preceded SCM's actual use date of May 15, 1969.

We think the structure of the Lanham Act reinforces Langis's interpretation of section 44(d). In the first place, section 1 of the Act, 15 U.S.C. § 1051(a)(1), requires an applicant for registration to indicate the date the trademark was first used in commerce in the United States; but foreign nationals applying pursuant to section 44(d) are exempted from that requirement, *id.* § 1126(d)(2). Moreover, the 1946 Act deals specifically with the protection to be accorded to rights acquired by third parties, and it expressly protects only those "rights acquired by third parties before the date of the filing of the first application in the foreign country...." *Id.* § 1126(d)(3). The Lanham Act also provides that nothing in section 44(d) "shall entitle the owner of a registration granted under ... section (44) to sue for acts committed prior to the date on which his mark was registered in this country unless the registration is based on use in commerce." *Id.* § 1126(d)(4). The clear implication is that section 44 recognizes registration based on something other than "use in commerce," namely, a foreign registration. *See id.* § 1126(e).

An examination of the relevant international treaty the International Convention for the Protection of Industrial Property (the Paris Union Treaty) resolves whatever doubt we may have concerning the reach of section 44(d).

As revised in London in 1934, Article 4 of the Paris Union Treaty provides:

A. (1) Any person who has duly applied for ... the registration of a ... trade mark in one of the countries of the Union ... shall enjoy for the purposes of registration in other countries a right of priority during the periods hereinafter stated (six months for trademarks).

(2) Any filing having the value of a formal national filing by virtue of the internal law of each country of the Union or of international treaties concluded among several countries of the Union shall be recognized as giving rise to a right of priority.

B. Consequently, *subsequent filing in one of the other countries of the Union before the expiration of these periods shall not be invalidated through any acts accomplished in the interval, as, for instance, by another filing, ... or by use of the trade mark, and these facts cannot give rise to any right of third parties or any personal possession. The rights acquired by third parties before the day of the first application on which priority is based shall be reserved by the internal legislation of each country of the Union.*

53 Stat. 1748, T.S. 941 (emphasis added). This revised version clearly provides that an intervening use during the priority period cannot give rise to rights on the part of third parties. The only rights of third parties specifically protected are "(those) rights acquired by third parties before the day of the first application on which priority is based." Thus, to the extent that the property rights in this case depend on the Paris Union Treaty, Article 4 reinforces our conclusion that a foreign applicant's mark must be protected in this country from the date of the foreign application even as against an intervening first use by another in the United States.

III

Our holding in this case is that section 44(d) of the Trademark Act of 1946, which implements Article 4 of the Paris Union Treaty, accorded appellant Langis a "right to priority" for the six months following the filing of its Canadian application for registration, that is to say, from March 28, 1969 to September 27, 1969; and that an intervening use in the United States during that period cannot invalidate Langis's right to registration in this country pursuant to an application filed on September 19, 1969.[12] We recognize that section 2(d) prohibits registration of a trademark "previously used in the United States by another," 15 U.S.C. 1052(d), but we cannot read that section in isolation from the context of the rest of the statute. Our task is to endeavor to harmonize and give full effect to both sections 2(d) and 44(d). We need only interpret the word "previously" in section 2(d) to mean "before the filing date in the Convention country" in order to give meaning to both statutory provisions. As our earlier discussion indicates, both the structure of the Act and its legislative history support such an interpretation.

Since in our view Langis is entitled to a valid federal trademark registration, we reverse the decision of the District Court and remand the case with directions to dismiss the complaint.

It is so ordered.

NOTES AND QUESTIONS

1. Does the D.C. Circuit's interpretation of the Lanham Act in *SCM Corp.* make U.S. law consistent with its obligations under Paris Article 4?

---

12. There are three possible positions that can be argued with respect to the use requirements applicable to section 44 filings by foreign nationals: (1) foreign nationals must allege use in commerce; (2) though use in commerce is not required, foreign nationals must nevertheless allege use somewhere; or (3) foreign nationals are not required to allege use at all. Section 44(d)(2) of the 1946 Act clearly exempts section 44(d) applications from the section 1 requirement that applications allege use in commerce. 15 U.S.C. § 1051(a)(1); *id.* § 1126(d)(2). As to the other two possible positions, the official policy of the Patent Office has shifted with some regularity. *See British Insulated Callender's Cables Ltd.*, 83 U.S.P.Q. 319 (Comm'r 1949) (there must be an allegation of use "somewhere"), *overruled in Societe Fromageries Bel*, 105 U.S.P.Q. 392 (Comm'r 1955) (the "Merry Cow" case) (there is no use requirement), *overruled in Certain Incomplete Trademark Applications*, 137 U.S.P.Q. 69 (Comm'r 1963) (there must be an allegation of use somewhere). And there has been considerable disagreement among commentators on that issue. Compare Ladas, *What Does the Vienna Trademark Registration Treaty Mean to the United States?*, 63 T.M.Rep. 551, 559–63 (1973) (there must be use somewhere) with Zelnick, *Foreign Trademark Applicants and Registrants and the Requirement of Use: The Right to Register*, 52 T.M.Rep. 641, 650–51 (1962) (there is no use requirement).

The Trademark Trial and Appeal Board opinion in the instant case erroneously states that appellant Langis "had made no use of the marks 'LEMON TREE,' 'ORANGE TREE,' or 'APPLE TREE' ... prior to the filing of its applications in this country." Nevertheless, the Board, citing the Merry Cow case, supra, upheld Langis's registration, thus overruling Certain Incomplete Trademark Applications, supra, and reinstating the policy that there is no use requirement.

In the de novo proceeding below, the District Court reviewed the Paris Union Treaty and the Trademark Act of 1946 and concluded that "(t)he decision of the Board ... which reverts to the 'Merry Cow' doctrine ... is ... in error." In this respect, the opinion of the District Court is dictum. The record in the District Court clearly indicates that the applications filed by Langis with the Patent Office alleged use of the marks in Canada, during the applicable six month period, and there was thus no reason for the District Court to rule on the Merry Cow issue. The fact that the Trademark Trial and Appeal Board found it necessary to reach that question given its misstatement of the facts does not mean that, despite a record indicating to the contrary, the question was presented to the District Court. Appellee SCM contends that the "Merry Cow" issue is not presented by this case, Brief at 4–6, and we agree.

What if the D.C. Circuit had adopted the interpretation of the district court—would such a ruling have been consistent with the U.S.'s obligations under Paris Article 4? Was the *SCM Corp.* court's decision based on an interpretation of U.S. law or of the Paris Convention, or both?

2.   Does the effect of the *SCM Corp.* ruling mean that foreign trademark holders may be treated more favorably under U.S. trademark law? If so, in what respect(s)? Assuming U.S. law is more favorable to foreign trademark applicants, what might explain this favoritism? Can you think of an instance in either copyright or patent law that we have studied already in which U.S law treated foreign intellectual property rights holders *more* favorably than U.S. nationals?

3.   *Comparison with patent systems.* As we have studied, Article 4 of the Paris Convention gives a period of 12–months for priority—meaning that a rights holder that has filed a patent application in a Paris country has a year in which to decide whether to file patent applications in other Paris countries. Why do you think the Paris Convention allows only half as much time for trademark holders? (And, if the PCT process is considered, patentees have 30 months within which to decide to file subsequent national applications compared to the 6 months allowed for trademarks under Paris.) Do you think six months is an adequate amount of time for priority of a trademark filing?

4.   Would the result in *SCM Corp.* have been different had SCM Corp., the U.S. corporation, first used the mark "LEMON TREE" in the United States *before* Langis filed its trademark application in Canada?

5.   *Section 44 Applications under Lanham Act.* As the *SCM Corp.* explained, § 44 of the Lanham Act governs trademark applications filed in the U.S. pursuant to Paris priority based on a prior registration filed in the country of origin. These "Section 44 applications" produced some confusion over whether an allegation of use of the mark somewhere in the world was required, as the court noted in footnote 12. Today, the Trademark Office's position is that *no* use of the mark need be alleged for Section 44 applications. *See Crocker Nat'l Bank v. Canadian Imperial Bank of Commerce,* 223 U.S.P.Q. 909 (T.T.A.B. 1984); *see also In re Compagnie Generale Maritime,* 993 F.2d 841, 844 (Fed. Cir. 1993). However, under the current version of Section 44, an applicant is now required to state that "the applicant has a bona fide intention to use the mark in commerce." 15 U.S.C. § 1126(d). But such an applicant (with Paris priority) is exempted from the requirements of filing a verified statement of use. *Id.* § 1051(b)(3).

What if U.S. law took the opposite approach and required a use of the mark somewhere in the world before it could be registered in the U.S., even for Section 44 applications? Would such a requirement be consistent with Paris Articles 4 and 6? Would it be consistent with TRIPS Articles 15 and 19? After reading the next section, we will consider whether such an approach would be consistent with Article 6*quinquies* of the Paris Convention.

6.   *Trademark availability search.* Most new businesses deciding what to call themselves or one of their new products hire a professional search service to suggest possible names that have not been used as trademarks by others. The search firm can also search logos, in addition to word marks. Of course, the basic starting point is searching the registry in the Trademark Office,

which is available on the Internet for the U.S. Trademark Office (www.uspto. gov). A professional search firm usually searches databases going beyond trademark registrations, to include telephone, Dun & Bradstreet, and other directories, secretary of state filings, domain names, and Internet searches. The cost of the search depends on its scope. A full availability U.S. search of a word mark might cost approximately $700, and a full U.S. search of a design or logo might cost over $1,000. The search can also be expanded to consider the use of the potential mark in unrelated goods or services, which may double the cost. Of course, searches for other countries will add even greater expenses for each country sought. Some firms may offer package rates for multi-country screenings and search of Madrid Protocol countries (the Madrid Protocol is discussed later in this chapter).

7. *Bibliographic note.* STEPHAN P. LADAS, PATENTS, TRADEMARKS, AND RELATED RIGHTS: NATIONAL AND INTERNATIONAL PROTECTION 1196–1211 (1975); Daniel R. Bereskin & Aaron Sawchuk, Crocker *Revisited: The Protection of Foreign Nationals in the United States*, 93 Trademark Rep. 1199 (2003).

b. Paris *Telle Quelle*/"As Is" Provision: Article 6*quinquies*

PROBLEM 4–3

Countries A and B are both members of the Paris Convention and the WTO. Sweet Spa Corp., which is based in Country A, obtains a trademark registration for the smell of a certain kind of incense popular at Sweet Spa's health spas. Within six months, Sweet Spa files an application to register the same incense as a trademark in Country B. Country B, however, denies registration because smells are not eligible for trademark under Country B's law.

Is Country B's law consistent with the Paris Convention, Article 6*quinquies*? Would your answer be the same if Country B's law expressly stated: "Trademarks cannot be granted to any subject matter in the form of smells"? Would it be different if it stated instead: "Smells cannot be granted trademark registration because they lack sufficient distinctiveness."? How, if at all, does TRIPS Article 15(1)'s recognition that "[m]embers may require, as a condition of registration, that signs be visually perceptible" bear on the issue? To answer this problem, consider the following provision and case.

Paris Convention

Article 6*quinquies*

Marks: Protection of Marks Registered in One Country of the Union in the Other Countries of the Union

A.

(1) Every trademark duly registered in the country of origin shall be accepted for filing and protected as is in the other countries of the Union, subject to the reservations indicated in this Article. Such countries may, before proceeding to final registration, require the production of a certificate of registration in the country of origin, issued by the competent authority. No authentication shall be required for this certificate.

(2) Shall be considered the country of origin the country of the Union where the applicant has a real and effective industrial or commercial establishment, or, if he has no such establishment within the Union, the country of the Union where he has his domicile, or, if he has no domicile within the Union but is a national of a country of the Union, the country of which he is a national.

B.

Trademarks covered by this Article may be neither denied registration nor invalidated except in the following cases:

(1) when they are of such a nature as to infringe rights acquired by third parties in the country where protection is claimed;

(2) when they are devoid of any distinctive character, or consist exclusively of signs or indications which may serve, in trade, to designate the kind, quality, quantity, intended purpose, value, place of origin, of the goods, or the time of production, or have become customary in the current language or in the bona fide and established practices of the trade of the country where protection is claimed;

(3) when they are contrary to morality or public order and, in particular, of such a nature as to deceive the public. It is understood that a mark may not be considered contrary to public order for the sole reason that it does not conform to a provision of the legislation on marks, except if such provision itself relates to public order.

This provision is subject, however, to the application of Article 10*bis*.

C.

(1) In determining whether a mark is eligible for protection, all the factual circumstances must be taken into consideration, particularly the length of time the mark has been in use.

(2) No trademark shall be refused in the other countries of the Union for the sole reason that it differs from the mark protected in the country of origin only in respect of elements that do not alter its distinctive character and do not affect its identity in the form in which it has been registered in the said country of origin.

D.

No person may benefit from the provisions of this Article if the mark for which he claims protection is not registered in the country of origin.

E.

However, in no case shall the renewal of the registration of the mark in the country of origin involve an obligation to renew the registration in the other countries of the Union in which the mark has been registered.

F.

The benefit of priority shall remain unaffected for applications for the registration of marks filed within the period fixed by Article 4, even if registration in the country of origin is effected after the expiration of such period.

As should be evident, Article 6*quinquies* of the Paris Convention is a very complicated provision. It regulates the extent to which Paris countries may deny applications for trademark registrations filed after the trademark has been duly registered in the country of origin in a Paris country. Although Article 6(3) of Paris generally requires independent treatment of a mark duly registered in different Paris countries (including the country of origin), Article 6*quinquies* creates a special benefit for any mark that has been duly registered in its country of origin (as defined in subsection (2) of the same article). The special benefit under Article 6*quinquies* is, in other words, dependent on a proper registration in the country of origin: Once a mark has been duly registered in its country of origin, all other Paris countries must accept the mark for filing and protection "as is"—meaning that the particular *form* of the mark cannot be questioned by another country or used as a basis for denying the registration. *See* Paris Conv. art. 6*quinquies*(A)(1). What constitutes the "form" of a mark is discussed in the following WTO decision. Article 6*quinquies* is commonly known as the *"telle quelle"* provision because it requires Paris countries to accept and protect a trademark that has been duly registered in the country of filing "as is" (in French, *"telle quelle"*), subject to a few reservations.

Article 6*quinquies*(B) sets forth three permissible bases to deny a registration of a mark under the *"telle quelle"* provision: (i) the mark infringes the rights of a party in the country where protection is claimed; (ii) the mark lacks "distinctive character"; and (iii) the mark is deceptive or "contrary to morality or public order." Paris Conv. art. 6*quinquies*(B). The precise meaning of "as is" and the *telle quelle* provision has been disputed, however. Consider the following WTO case.

UNITED STATES—SECTION 211 OMNIBUS APPROPRIATIONS ACT OF 1998

Report of the Appellate Body, WTO. (Ehlermann, Presiding
Member; Bacchus and Lacarte–Muró, Members).
WT/DS176/AB/R (Jan. 2, 2002).

[This case involves a long-standing controversy over the mark "Havana Club." For the history of the dispute, see pp. [36–42] in Chapter 1. On June 30, 2000, the European Union filed a challenge in the WTO to the U.S. law (Section 211), raising numerous challenges. The Appellate Body's discussion of the *telle quelle* provision is excerpted below, while the notes following the decision discuss the Appellate Body's finding with respect to national treatment and most favored nation. *Ed.*]

The Nature of the Measure

A number of the legal issues raised in this appeal turn on the meaning or nature of Section 211. We begin our consideration of this pivotal issue by noting that Section 211(a)(1) provides:

> Notwithstanding any other provision of law, no transaction or payment shall be authorized or approved pursuant to section 515.527 of title 31, Code of Federal Regulations, as in effect on September 9, 1998, with respect to a mark, trade name, or commercial name that is

the same as or substantially similar to a mark, trade name, or commercial name that was used in connection with a business or assets that were confiscated unless the original owner of the mark, trade name, or commercial name, or the bona fide successor-in-interest has expressly consented.

The Panel concluded that "the language of Section 211(a)(1) indicates that it is a measure that deals with ownership of trademarks used in connection with confiscated assets." The Panel concluded also that Section 211(a)(1) "regulates ownership" [and therefore was not inconsistent with Article 15.1 of the TRIPS Agreement].

On appeal, the participants continue to disagree about the nature of Section 211. In our view, a measure such as the one before us that conditions rights on obtaining the express consent of the original owner is, unquestionably, a measure that deals with ownership. [T]he mere fact that Section 211(a)(1) does not affirmatively establish ownership does not, in and of itself, render that measure one that does not deal with ownership. Further, we agree with the United States that, although Section 211(a)(1) does not determine who does own a trademark, it can, in the particular circumstances in which it applies, determine who does not. To us, this alone is sufficient to make Section 211(a)(1) a measure that, in its nature, relates to the ownership of trademarks and trade names.

V. Article 6*quinquies* of the Paris Convention (1967)

We turn now to the claims of the European Communities as they relate to Article 6*quinquies* of the Paris Convention (1967). Article 6*quinquies* A(1) reads:

Every trademark duly registered in the country of origin shall be accepted for filing and protected as is in the other countries of the Union, subject to the reservations indicated in this Article. Such countries may, before proceeding to final registration, require the production of a certificate of registration in the country of origin, issued by the competent authority. No authentication shall be required for this certificate.

Before the Panel, the European Communities claimed that Section 211(a)(1) is inconsistent with Article 2.1 of the TRIPS Agreement in conjunction with Article 6*quinquies* A(1) of the Paris Convention (1967), an allegation contested by the United States.

The Panel found:

The ordinary meaning of the term "as is" and read in its context and as confirmed by the negotiating history indicates that Article 6*quinquies* A(1) addresses the form of the trademark; that is, those trademarks duly registered in one country, even when they do not comply with the provisions of domestic law of a Member concerning the permissible form of trademarks, have nevertheless to be accepted for filing and protection in another country.... Section 211(a)(1) is a measure that regulates ownership and does not deal with the form of the signs of which the trademark is composed. For these reasons, Section 211(a)(1) is not inconsistent with Article 6*quinquies* A(1) of the Paris Convention (1967).

The European Communities appeals this finding and argues on appeal, as before the Panel, that Article 6*quinquies* A(1) requires that a trademark duly registered in a country of origin that is a country of the Paris Union must be accepted for registration and protected "as is" in every respect in other countries of the Paris Union, subject only to the specific exceptions set forth in that Article. Thus, the European Communities sees Article 6*quinquies* A(1) as applying to more than merely the form of a trademark. According to the European Communities, Section 211(a)(1) violates Article 6*quinquies* A(1) because it does not permit the filing and protection of the trademark "as is." Rather, it prevents the owner of a trademark registered in another country from acquiring or maintaining a trademark registration in the United States by preventing the payment of the required fees necessary for registration and renewal in the United States, unless the original owner or the bona fide successor-in-interest has expressly consented.

Before examining the text of Article 6*quinquies*, we note that the Paris Convention (1967) provides two ways in which a national of a country of the Paris Union may obtain registration of a trademark in a country of that Union other than the country of the applicant's origin: one way is by registration under Article 6 of the Paris Convention (1967); the other is by registration under Article 6*quinquies* of that same Convention.

Article 6(1) of the Paris Convention (1967) provides:

The conditions for the filing and registration of trademarks shall be determined in each country of the Union by its domestic legislation.

Article 6(1) states the general rule, namely, that each country of the Paris Union has the right to determine the conditions for filing and registration of trademarks in its domestic legislation. This is a reservation of considerable discretion to the countries of the Paris Union—and now, by incorporation, the Members of the WTO—to continue, in principle, to determine for themselves the conditions for filing and registration of trademarks. Thus, in our view, the general rule under the Paris Convention (1967) is that national laws apply with respect to trademark registrations within the territory of each country of the Paris Union, subject to the requirements of other provisions of that Convention. And, likewise, through incorporation, this is also now the general rule for all WTO Members under the TRIPS Agreement.

Therefore, an applicant who chooses to seek registration of a trademark in a particular foreign country under Article 6 must comply with the conditions for filing and registration specified in that country's legislation. Such an applicant is not obliged to register a trademark first in its country of origin in order to register that trademark in another country of the Paris Union. However, that applicant must comply with the conditions of that other country where registration is sought.

Article 6 is not the only way to register a trademark in another country. If an applicant has duly registered a trademark in its country of origin, Article 6*quinquies* A(1) provides an alternative way of obtaining protection of that trademark in other countries of the Paris Union.

This alternative way of seeking acceptance in another country of the Paris Union of a trademark registered in the applicant's country of origin, afforded by Article 6*quinquies* A(1), is subject to two prerequisites. First, that trademark must be duly registered according to the domestic legislation of the country of origin, and, second, it must be registered in the applicant's country of origin, as defined in Article 6*quinquies* A(2). Article 6*quinquies* D confirms that the recognition of a trademark in another country of the Paris Union under Article 6*quinquies* is dependent on registration in the country of origin. These two prerequisites though are not at issue in this appeal. The issue in this appeal relates to the extent of the obligations established by Article 6*quinquies* A(1), assuming that these two prerequisites have been met.

By virtue of Article 6*quinquies* A(1), WTO Members are obliged to confer an exceptional right on an applicant in a Paris Union country other than its country of origin, one that is over and above whatever rights the other country grants to its own nationals in its domestic law. A national who files for registration of a trademark in his own country must comply fully with the conditions for filing and registration as determined by the national legislation of that country. But, if that country is a Member of the Paris Union—and, now, of the WTO—then an applicant from another WTO Member who seeks registration in that country of a trademark duly registered in its country of origin has the additional rights that WTO Members are obliged to confer on that applicant under Article 6*quinquies* A(1).

The participants to this dispute disagree on the scope of the requirement imposed by Article 6*quinquies* A(1) to accept for filing and protect trademarks duly registered in the country of origin "as is." Looking first to the text of Article 6*quinquies* A(1), we see that the words "as is" (or, in French, "telle quelle") relate to the trademark to be "accepted for filing and protected" in another country based on registration in the applicant's country of origin. The ordinary meaning of the words "as is" is "in the existing state." The French term "telle quelle" can be defined as "sans arrangement, sans modification." This suggests to us that the requirement of Article 6*quinquies* A(1) to accept for filing and protect a trademark duly registered in the applicant's country of origin relates at least to the form of the trademark as registered in the applicant's country of origin. The question before us is whether the scope of this requirement also encompasses other features and aspects of that trademark as registered in the country of origin.

According to one expert:

... whenever a trademark is duly registered in the country of origin, the other countries of the Union are obliged to accept and protect it, even if, as regards its form, that is, with regard to the signs of which it is composed, such trademark does not comply with the requirements of the domestic legislation, subject to the additional rules, particularly the grounds for refusal or invalidation of any mark, considered on its individual merits, established in the Article. This rule will therefore apply to trademarks consisting of numbers, letters, surnames, geographical names, words written or not written in a certain language or script, and other signs of which the trademark is composed.[81]

However, this view is not determinative of the question before us. To resolve this question, we look to the context of Article 6*quinquies* A(1). We find that there is considerable contextual support for the view that the requirement to register a trademark "as is" under Article 6*quinquies* A(1) does not encompass all the features and aspects of that trademark. As we have stressed, Article 6(1) of the Paris Convention (1967) reserves to the countries of the Paris Union the right to determine the conditions for filing and registration of trademarks by their domestic legislation. Article 6(1) confirms that the countries of the Paris Union did not relinquish their right to determine the conditions for filing and registration of trademarks by entering into the Paris Convention (1967)—subject, of course, to the other obligations of Paris Union countries under the Paris Convention (1967). Clearly, if Article 6quinquies A(1) were interpreted too broadly, the legislative discretion reserved for Members under Article 6(1) would be significantly undermined.

To illustrate this point, we will assume for the moment, and solely for the sake of argument, that, as the European Communities argues, Article 6*quinquies* A(1) does require other countries to accept for filing and to protect duly registered trademarks in respect of all their aspects, including those other than the form of a trademark. If this were so, an applicant who is a national of a country of the Paris Union would have two choices: that applicant could request trademark registration under Article 6 in another country of the Paris Union—in which case, that registration would be subject to the trademark law of that other country. Or, that applicant could register the trademark in its country of origin and then invoke the right, pursuant to Article 6*quinquies* A(1), to request acceptance of that trademark for filing and protection in another country. In the latter case, that registration would be governed by the trademark law, not of the country in which the applicant sought registration under Article 6*quinquies* A(1), but of the applicant's country of origin. The "conditions" for registration imposed in the law of the other country of the Paris Union where registration was sought under Article 6*quinquies* A(1) would be irrelevant. If this were so, any such applicant would be able to choose between trademark registration under Article 6 and trademark registra-

---

81. See, Bodenhausen, G.H.C, Guide to the Application of the Paris Convention for the Protection of Industrial Property as revised at Stockholm in 1967, (hereinafter "Guide to the Paris Convention"), United International Bureaux for the Protection of Intellectual Property, (1968, reprinted 1991), pp. 110–111.

tion under Article 6*quinquies*, depending on which conditions for filing and registration were viewed by the applicant as more favourable to the applicant's interests. Consequently, within the territory of any country of the Paris Union other than the applicant's country of origin, a national of a country of that Union could ensure that it would be subject to either the domestic trademark registration requirements of the country of origin (through recourse to Article 6*quinquies*) or the domestic trademark registration requirements of the other country where trademark registration is sought (through recourse to Article 6)—whichever it preferred. In other words, a national of a Paris Union country could circumvent the "use" requirements of a particular regime by registering in the jurisdiction that does not impose "use" requirements.

We are persuaded that the drafters of the Paris Convention did not intend such a result. If, even today, WTO Members have—as the European Communities concedes—reserved the right under the TRIPS Agreement to maintain domestic regimes of trademark ownership based on use, then it does not seem credible to us to contend—as the European Communities does—that many of those very same countries intended more than a century ago, in concluding the Paris Convention, or on the occasion of one of the subsequent Revision Conferences of the Paris Convention, to establish a global system for determining trademark ownership that could circumvent, and thereby undermine, a domestic regime of trademark ownership based on use.

We have already stated that we agree with the Panel that Section 211(a)(1) is a measure dealing, in the particular circumstances in which it applies, with the ownership of a defined category of trademarks. We also agree that the obligation of countries of the Paris Union under Article 6*quinquies* A(1) to accept for filing and protect a trademark duly registered in the country of origin "as is" does not encompass matters related to ownership. For these reasons, we uphold the finding of the Panel in paragraph 8.89 of the Panel Report that Section 211(a)(1) is not inconsistent with Article 2.1 of the TRIPS Agreement in conjunction with Article 6*quinquies* A(1) of the Paris Convention (1967).

NOTES AND QUESTIONS

1. What was the Appellate Body's interpretation of the *telle quelle* provision? Does the *telle quelle* provision limit the types of grounds on which Paris countries can deny registration of trademarks filed during Paris priority after having been duly registered in the country of origin? If so, what kinds of grounds are impermissible? In the Body's view, did the U.S. law violate the *telle quelle* provision?

2. *Revisiting use.* Under the Appellate Body's interpretation of the *telle quelle* provision, could the United States deny registration of a mark that has been duly registered in its country of origin (which is a first-to-register Paris country) if no use of the mark has been made in the U.S.? Would such a use requirement be consistent with the *telle quelle* provision in Paris? Would it be

consistent with Articles 15 and 19 of TRIPS? You may find it useful to revisit the *SCM Corp.* decision above.

3. *London Text of 1934.* The London Text of the Paris Convention (1934) had the following version of Article 6*quinquies*: "Every trade-mark registered in the country of origin shall be admitted for registration and protection in the form originally registered in other countries of the Union under the reservations indicated below." Does this provide further support for the Appellate Body's interpretation? Which language is more helpful—(i) the "form" of the trademark "originally registered" or (ii) "as is"? What does either mean?

4. *Appellate Body's decision on national treatment and most-favored nation.* The Appellate Body rejected 10 of the European Union's 12 challenges to § 211 of the U.S. law. But the two violations were significant. First, the Appellate Body concluded that Section 211(a)(2) and (b)'s application to "designated nationals" treated foreign nationals less favorably than U.S. nationals (who were not subject to § 211's restrictions), in that foreign nationals would be required to withstand the additional hurdle of a § 211 proceeding to claim status as a legitimate "successor in interest." Second, for similar reasons, the Body found the U.S. law violated the most favored nation principle of Article 4 of TRIPS by effectively treating non-Cubans better than Cubans. The Appellate Body rejected the U.S.'s argument that the discriminatory effect of § 211 was "offset" by another provision that the U.S. contended effectively made up for any discriminatory treatment by putting foreign nationals on equal footing. According to the Appellate Body, the United States failed to present sufficient evidence substantiating that the second provision "would offset the inherently less favourable treatment present in Sections 211(a)(2) and (b) in each and every case."

In concluding, the Body felt obliged to state:

362. We wish to emphasize that this ruling is not a judgment on confiscation as that term is defined in Section 211. The validity of the expropriation of intellectual or any other property rights without compensation by a WTO Member within its own territory is not before us. Nor do we express any view, nor are we required to express any view in this appeal, on whether a Member of the WTO should, or should not, recognize in its own territory trademarks, trade names, or any other rights relating to any intellectual or other property rights that may have been expropriated or otherwise confiscated in other territories.

363. However, where a WTO Member chooses not to recognize intellectual property rights in its own territory relating to a confiscation of rights in another territory, a measure resulting from and implementing that choice must, if it affects other WTO Members, comply with the TRIPS Agreement, by which all WTO Members are voluntarily bound. In such a measure, that WTO Member must accord "no less favourable treatment" to the nationals of all other WTO Members than it accords to its own nationals, and must grant to the nationals of all other WTO Members "any advantage, favour, privilege or immunity" granted to any other WTO Member. In such a measure, a WTO Member may not discriminate in a way that does not respect the obligations of national treatment and

most-favoured-nation treatment that are fundamental to the TRIPS Agreement.

Given the political situation between the U.S. and Cuban governments, do you think it was proper for the WTO Appellate Body to find the U.S. in violation of TRIPS? Could the U.S. justify § 211 as a measure for national security under TRIPS Article 73? Can the U.S. revise § 211 to comply with TRIPS? If so, how? In 2005, two bills were proposed in Congress to amend § 211 by striking any reference to "designated national or its successor in interest"? Would that fix the TRIPS violations with respect to national treatment and most favored nation? Alternatively, Congress considered two bills seeking the complete repeal of the bar on Cuban trademark claims. By 2011, Congress had yet to pass any amendment.

5. *Bibliographic note*. STEPHAN P. LADAS, PATENTS, TRADEMARKS, AND RELATED RIGHTS: NATIONAL AND INTERNATIONAL PROTECTION 1211–1240 (1975); Donald R. Dinan, *An Analysis of the United States—Cuba "Havana Club" Rum Case Before the World Trade Organization*, 26 FORDHAM INT'L L.J. 337 (2003); Robert Dufresne, *Assessing Clashes and Interplays of Regimes from a Distributive Perspective: IP Rights Under the Strengthened Embargo Against Cuba and Agreement on TRIPS*, 24 MICH. J. INT'L L. 767 (2003).

c. Filing an International Application Under the Madrid System

PROBLEM 4–4

Andover Co. files a trademark application for "wowweezany toys" in the United States, a Paris Union country, on December 30, 2011. Andover subsequently files an international application under the Madrid Protocol with the United States Patent and Trademark Office (USPTO) on June 15, 2012. The USPTO reviews the application, finds some problems with the application that are then cured by Andover, and forwards it to the International Bureau of WIPO, which receives the application on September 3, 2012. The application designates, among other states, Country X, also a Paris Union country. Meanwhile, Brill Co. has filed an application in Country X for the same trademark, "wowweezany toys," on February 1, 2012. If Country X has a first-to-file system, who is entitled to the trademark registration in Country X? What if WIPO had received the international application from the USPTO on August 3, 2012, instead of September 3, 2012? See the discussion below.

PROBLEM 4–5

Colette obtained an international trademark registration through the Madrid System in the International Bureau of WIPO on January 3, 2011. Her registration has designated Country Z, among other states. On February 1, 2011, Drew starts to make counterfeit copies of Colette's trademark in Country Z. Colette's international application was based on a basic registration for the trademark issued by Colette's home country's trademark authority on Sept. 1, 2006. In May 2011, Colette's trademark in its home country is declared invalid by the trademark authority. Who wins in Colette's trademark infringement lawsuit against Drew in Country Z? What advice do you have for Colette as her attorney?

* * *

So how does a trademark holder obtain rights to a mark internationally? We know from earlier chapters that the process of obtaining copyrights is fairly easy, but for patents, the process is rather difficult and expensive. Trademark probably falls somewhere in between.

Under the principles of territoriality and independence of trademarks, a trademark owner traditionally had to seek registration in every country in which protection was desired. This, of course, entailed significant expenditure of time and costs. Eventually, a number of nations decided to simplify the process of obtaining trademark protection in different countries through a single procedure with the creation of the Madrid System for the International Registration of Marks (Madrid System). The Madrid System parallels the way that nations simplified the process of obtaining patents internationally through the Patent Cooperation Treaty, although the approaches adopted in the two systems differ in some respects as discussed below.

The basic concept of the Madrid System is that the owner of a trademark can obtain, through a registration of the trademark in the International Register, protection for the trademark in each of the contracting states to the Madrid System for which an "extension of protection" is sought. Under the Madrid System, the designated contracting states in which protection is sought do not issue national registrations for the trademark. Rather, the trademark is registered in the International Register maintained by WIPO and is entitled to protection under national law as if the trademark had obtained a national registration in each of the designated countries. Each designated contracting state must extend protection under its national laws to an international registration of a mark under the Madrid System.

The Madrid System consists of two treaties, the Madrid Agreement, which has been in existence since 1891,[1] and the Madrid Protocol, which was formed much later in 1989.[2] As noted earlier, the Madrid Protocol has garnered greater participation than the earlier Agreement, in large part due to the U.S.'s joining of the Protocol (but not the Madrid Agreement). A country can be a member of both the Agreement and Protocol, or just one (being subject only to its rules). As of 2011, the Protocol had 28 more signatories than the Agreement.

Under the Madrid Protocol, which became effective in the U.S. on November 2, 2003, a U.S. trademark owner or a trademark owner in any contracting state to the Madrid Protocol can obtain, through a single procedure, trademark protection and the equivalent of a national registration in 80 other countries of the world. The streamlined process can result in substantial cost savings when compared to filing separate applications in each country, although the overall cost can still be expensive. A color logo registered in all Madrid countries would cost approximately $15,000 in filing fees, not includ-

---

1. Madrid Agreement Concerning the International Registration of Marks, April 14, 1891.

2. Protocol Relating to the Madrid Agreement Concerning the International Registration of Marks, June 27, 1989.

ing attorney or local agent costs that may be incurred if a national office denies a registration. WIPO provides a schedule of fees on its website. *See* www.wipo.int/madrid/en/fees/sched.html.

Filing for international registration. All international applications under the Madrid System are based upon an existing basic application in the home country. For example, in order to file an international application to obtain trademarks in multiple countries under the Madrid Protocol, a U.S. applicant must also file a U.S. application. The U.S. application can be either what is called a "basic application" or a "basic registration." Under a basic application, the U.S. applicant files an international application with the USPTO on the basis of an existing pending application for a U.S. trademark. (The basic application can be filed with the USPTO at the same time that the U.S. applicant files the international application under the Madrid Protocol.) Or, in the alternative, the U.S. applicant can file an international application with the USPTO on the basis of a "basic registration," i.e., an existing U.S. registered trademark.

The Madrid Protocol allows for greater ease of filings than under the older Madrid Agreement, which requires the applicant to file based upon a basic registration only. The United States objected to this requirement on the grounds that it is more difficult to obtain a registration in the United States than in many other countries. This was one reason why the United States refused to join the Madrid Agreement. By contrast, under the Madrid Protocol, the U.S. applicant can file for an international application on the basis of one or more existing U.S. applications that are still pending and that have not yet resulted in registrations. The mark and the owner of the basic international application must be the same as the mark and the owner of the basic registration. The international application must also include a list of goods and services for the mark identical or narrower than that claimed in the basic application.

The trademark holder designates on the international application the various contracting states to the Madrid System where protection is sought. In the case of the EU, the application can either designate separate individual nations within the EU or the EU as a whole. If the international application is filed in the U.S., the USPTO will examine the application to determine whether the application contains the same information as that contained in the U.S. basic application or basic registration. If the USPTO decides that this requirement is met, it will then certify the application and forward it to the International Bureau of WIPO in Geneva. The speed with which the USPTO can complete its review and forward the international application to WIPO is important. Under Madrid Protocol Article 3(4), if WIPO receives the international application within two months of the filing with the USPTO, the date of the international registration is the date of receipt of the international application in the USPTO. If WIPO does not receive the international application within 2 months of the date of receipt in the USPTO, the date of the international registration will be the later, actual date of receipt by WIPO. *See* Madrid Protocol art. 3(4); Madrid Agreement art. 3(4). The date of the international registration is important because most countries in the world today follow a first-to-file approach in determining priority among competing trademark applications. An international application can be subject to priority rights in one or more of the designated contracting states if a prior application had been made for the same trademark. The date of international registration establishes the priority date in the case of competing applications.

Of course, the period of priority under the Paris Convention for trademarks is available for applications under the Madrid System. Under Article 4 of the Paris Convention, a trademark owner who has filed a trademark application with a Paris Union country is permitted to assert the benefit of the original filing date for all subsequent applications filed with other Union countries if the subsequent application is filed within six months of the original filing. This benefit is also available if the subsequent application is an international application filed under the Madrid System.

Illustration 4–1. On December 14, 2012, Zoe files a basic application with the trademark office in Country Z, a Paris Union country. If Zoe files an international application with the home country trademark office under the Madrid System by June 14, 2013, Zoe will be entitled to a priority date of December 14, 2012 for the international application in all designated contracting states.

International Bureau action. Once WIPO has received the international application from the USPTO or other home country trademark office, the International Bureau of WIPO will review the international application to determine whether it meets the Madrid System filing requirements. If the requirements are met, WIPO will then immediately register the mark in WIPO's International Register and will publish it in WIPO's Gazette of International Marks. Once WIPO registers the mark in the International Register, the effect of the international registration is that "the protection of the mark in each of the Contracting Parties concerned shall be the same as if the mark had been deposited direct with the Office of that Contracting Party." Madrid Protocol art. 4(1)(a); *see also* Madrid Agreement art. 4(1). The effect of the international registration will vary for contracting states depending upon whether a state follows an examination system for trademarks or not. In those states that do not follow an examination system, all trademark applications are automatically registered upon filing. In such states, the trademark authority does not examine the validity of the trademark and the issue of its validity does not arise until later, if and when the trademark is challenged. The effect of the international registration under the Madrid System is that a trademark is entitled to protection immediately as of the date of the international registration in these contracting states.

National offices' actions. The process is more complicated in states following an examination procedure. Article 5(1) of the Madrid Protocol provides that "[w]here the applicable legislation so authorizes," a contracting state is entitled to notify WIPO of its refusal to extend protection to the international registration. *See also* Madrid Agreement art. 5(1). States that have an examination procedure are permitted under Article 5(1) of the Madrid Protocol to refuse to extend protection to the international registration so long as the notice of refusal is communicated to WIPO within a period of 18 months of the date the notice of extension of protection was sent by WIPO. *See* Madrid Protocol art. 5(2). Failure to do so within that time period will result in the automatic extension of protection for the mark in that country (subject, however, to the standard procedures for invalidation of a mark within that country). *See, e.g.,* Lanham Act, § 69(c)(4), 15 U.S.C. § 1141h(c) ("If a notification specified in paragraph (1) or (2) is not sent to the International Bureau within the time period set forth in such paragraph with respect to a request for extension of protection, the request for extension of protection shall not be refused and the Director shall issue a certificate of extension of protection pursuant to the request."). By contrast, under the Madrid Agreement, a designated contracting state must notify WIPO of a refusal within 12 months of transmittal, or protection must be automatically extended. The United States objected to the 12 month period under the Madrid Agreement on the grounds that determining whether to grant registration under U.S. is more complex and time consuming than in many other countries.

Once the notice of refusal to extend protection is submitted to WIPO by a contracting state, WIPO must forward the notice of refusal without delay to the holder of the international registration. The holder is entitled to the same remedies under national law as if the holder had filed a national application directly in the contracting state refusing to extend protection. *See* Madrid Protocol art. 5(3); Madrid Agreement art. 5(3).

Duration and validity of international registration. An international registration under the Madrid Protocol lasts 10 years in each designated contracting state that has extended protection and may be renewed indefinitely for additional ten-year periods. *See* Madrid Protocol arts. 6(1), 7(1). A renewal of the international registration applies to all countries (including the home country) where protection was obtained, thus simplifying the renewal to a single filing. The applicant can also later apply to extend the reach of the international application to additional designated contracting states.

Registrations under the Madrid System are subject to what is known as "central attack." The basic idea behind central attack is that the Madrid registration is based upon an underlying application or registration *from the home country*. If the basic application or the basic registration, as the case may be, is invalidated or fails at any time during the first five years of the international registration, then the entire international registration is cancelled. Once the basic application or basic registration is invalidated, the office of origin is required to request the International Bureau to cancel the international registration. This would mean that the trademark loses protection in all of the designated contracting states if the basic application or basic registration fails. However, if the home country application or registration is not invalidated or does not fail within the first five years, the international registration becomes independent of the home country application or registration. Once that happens, the validity (or not) of the home country registration has absolutely no bearing on the validity of the international registration.

A successful central attack may seem to produce a harsh result. After all, trademark registrations are generally treated independently of one another. Why should the invalidation of the home country application within the first five years cause the invalidation of others? The Madrid Protocol attempts to soften the harshness of such an approach. Under the Madrid Protocol Article 9*quinquies*, the applicant is allowed to transform the international registration into national applications by filing separate national applications in each of the countries in which the international registration had effect. Each of these national applications will be entitled to a filing date as of the date of the (now invalid) international registration, provided that (i) "such application is filed within three months from the date on which the international registration was cancelled"; (ii) the national application is for goods or services already "contained in the international registration in respect of the Contracting Party concerned"; and (iii) the national application "complies with all requirements of the applicable law, including the requirements concerning fees." Madrid Protocol art. 9*quinquies*. Such a procedure to convert a cancelled international registration into national applications is not available under the older Madrid Agreement; under the Agreement, the cancellation of a home country registration necessarily dooms the international application in all designated contracting states. The inability to cure or ameliorate the effects of a central attack is another reason why the United States chose not to participate in the Madrid Agreement.

International searches. The existence of the Madrid System requires all applicants for trademarks to do an international search with WIPO. For a fee, WIPO will provide any person with a copy of entries in the International Register concerning a specific mark. *See* Madrid Protocol art. 5*ter*(1); Madrid Agreement art. 5*ter*. An international search is important because a search of the national trademark registry may not necessarily uncover international registrations.

NOTES AND QUESTIONS

1. Do you think the Madrid Protocol is an improvement over having to file individual registrations in each country?

2. *Comparison with Patent Cooperation Treaty.* While Paris priority is available under both the Madrid System and the Patent Cooperation Treaty for patents (see Chapter 3 at pp. 282–289), there is an important distinction. The Patent Cooperation Treaty provides a period of up to 30 months after the original priority date during which the patent applicant can decide whether to proceed with the patent application for each contracting state. This is one of the most important benefits of the PCT: the patent applicant is given an extended period in which to assess the desirability of going forward and paying the fees and costs of undergoing the processing of the patent application by national patent authorities. No such extended period exists under the Madrid System. A second difference is that under the PCT, each designated state must issue a patent under its own national legal system. Under the Madrid System, no national registrations are ever issued. Instead, national protection is extended to the trademark based upon the international registration. What might account for these differences?

3. *Popularity of Madrid System.* As of 2011, the Madrid Protocol had 84 signatories. By comparison, the Madrid Agreement had only 56 members. (To compare trademarks with patents, the Patent Cooperation Treaty had 144 members in 2011.) The Madrid System has garnered a significant number of international filings. According to WIPO, 39,687 international applications

were filed and 37,533 international registrations made in 2010. In that same year, the International Register had over a half million active registrations (526,674). *See* WIPO, *Madrid System for the International Registration of Marks, Report for 2010.*

4. *Costs.* The USPTO charges a certification fee of $100 per application if the international application is based on a single U.S. application or registration and $150 per application if the international application is based on more than one U.S. application or registration. Additional fees are due for each designated contracting state in which trademark protection is sought. *See* Trademark Electronic Application System, http://teasi.uspto.gov/.

5. *Bibliographic note.* Jeffrey M. Samuels & Linda B. Samuels, *International Trademark Protection Streamlined: The Madrid Protocol Comes into Force in the United States,* 12 J. INTELL. PROP. L. 151 (2004).

d. Community Trade Mark (CTM)

PROBLEM 4–6

You are the General Counsel of AlterMatrix Co., a start-up company based in Silicon Valley. The Company manufactures computer and electronic games, and is in its third month of operation. There are only ten employees, and the Company has cash reserves of only $1 million. The Company was founded by two college dropouts, Stan and Fran, who are brilliant programmers. They have asked you to figure out "if we need to do any trademark registrations, or what not." "But don't run up huge legal fees, because we're strapped for cash," they tell you. But you are most concerned about giving the best legal advice to the Company.

Please advise Stan and Fran on the following: (1) whether the Company should hire a trademark search firm to conduct a national and international search of any registrations or uses of "AlterMatrix"; (2) assuming no federal registration of the mark exists, whether the Company should file a registration of "AlterMatrix" in the U.S.; and (3) whether the Company should seek an international registration under the Madrid Protocol. You may assume that the U.S. filing would cost at least $2,000 or more (for basic trademark search fees, attorney fees, and registration fees), and that each additional filing would add additional costs.

In your answer, be sure to advise the Company on (i) the general timetable for filings; (ii) how many countries should be designated for extension of protection if an international registration is sought; and (iii) whether the Company should designate a Community Trade Mark or proceed individually in those European countries. Please also advise the Company on the possible tradeoffs involved in filing for registration in the U.S., but not filing an international registration. In answering this problem, you should refer back to the previous discussion on the Madrid Protocol and the following discussion on the Community Trade Mark.

ENFORCEMENT OF CTMS IN THE EU: THE REAL TEST OF THEIR COMMERCIAL VALUE

Michael Fammler & Christopher Aide.
86 J. Pat. & Trademark Off. Soc'y 135, 135–49 (2004).

1. Introduction

Uniformity. Uniformity. If there is one word that summarises the desired purpose of the European Community legislators in creating the Community Trade Mark ("CTM") system, that is it. A CTM registration is to have uniform protection and effect across the entire area of the European Union ("EU"). This principle is explicitly set forth in Article 1(2) of the European Council Regulation No. 40/94 (the "CTM Regulation"):

> A Community trademark shall have a unitary character. It shall have equal effect throughout the Community: it shall not be registered, transferred or surrendered or be subject of a decision revoking the rights of the proprietor or declaring it invalid, nor shall its use be prohibited, save in respect of the whole Community. This principle shall apply unless otherwise provided in this Regulation.

Specifically, as of on April 1, 1996, the CTM Regulation introduced the CTM system that offers Europeans and most non-Europeans (including North American companies and individuals) a unitary system of registration and protection for their marks throughout the (then) 15 EU Member States [now 27 members]. CTM applications can be filed by EU nationals as well as any other nationals who belong to World Trade Organization countries, Paris Convention countries and/or countries that extend to EU nationals the same trademark rights as to their own nationals (this includes North American companies and individuals). Under the CTM Regulation, a single application with the Office for Harmonization in the Internal Market (Trade Marks and Designs) ("OHIM") in Alicante, Spain leads to a trademark registration that is valid in the entire EU.

The number of CTM applications filed has exceeded initial expectations and is rising at a rapid pace. In summary, this is so because there are a number of significant benefits in obtaining a CTM registration, including cost and administrative benefits in consolidating a trade mark portfolio covering the EU and maintaining the validity of a CTM through use.

However, obtaining a CTM registration is only the first step. As the number of CTM registrations increases, so does the scope for CTM infringement proceedings. To have "real teeth," however, a CTM, once registered, must be able to be readily enforced as against infringers. Thus, while the introduction of CTMs has been widely welcomed, the ability to enforce CTMs is the real test of their commercial value. This paper outlines the options open to a proprietor of a CTM who wishes to enforce his rights.

2. Background

The rights which a unitary CTM confers may be enforced in a "CTM Court" in an individual EU Member State. An action commenced in a Member State may be in respect of acts of infringement committed in that Member State or, in some circumstances, in respect of acts of infringement committed in other Member States. This is possible because the CTM Courts have extra-territorial jurisdiction, provided certain conditions are met. The CTM proprietor will, therefore, often be faced with a choice of courts in which to enforce rights. The onus is on the proprietor of a CTM to ensure that the CTM Court chosen is the appropriate one in given all the circumstances.

The enforcement of CTMs, of course, is also governed by the CTM Regulation, as well as the Brussels Convention on Jurisdiction and the Enforcement of Judgments in Civil and Commercial Matters 1968 (the "Brussels Convention"). The core of the procedural provisions in the CTM Regulation are issues of jurisdiction (functional and international) and the designation of special CTM Courts.

However, the CTM Regulation contains significant gaps, leaving it to the national trademark and procedure laws of the EU Member States to govern the details of enforcement and remedies. Whereas the substantive provisions of the CTM Regulation coupled with the harmonized material rules of the national trade mark laws of the respective EU Member States provide for a highly unitary system as regards the obtaining of a CTM; however, the use and limitations of a CTM are far from being uniform: this includes, at least partially, the transfer and licensing aspects thereof, as well as the procedural aspects of enforcement proceedings, and the consequences of an infringement of a CTM are far from being uniform. Only the claim of the CTM owner against the infringer for injunctive relief (Article 9(1) and Article 98(1)) and the claim for reasonable compensation in respect of infringing acts between publication of an application and the publication of a registration (Article 9(3)) are regulated. The CTM Regulation also provides for sanctions against the reproduction of a CTM in dictionaries (Article 10) and prohibits the use of a CTM registered in the name of an agent or representative. However, the CTM Regulation is silent as regards damage claims, claims for information and rendering of account, seizure, removal and/or destruction, nor publication of judgements or criminal sanctions. Also not addressed in the CTM Regulation are the availability of temporary injunction proceedings and the enforcement of judgements.

4. CTM Courts

Rather than creating a special Community court to deal with CTM litigation, the CTM Regulation provides that enforcement of CTMs is to be dealt with by national courts. Specifically, under the CTM Regulation, enforcement of a CTM registration is a matter for an appointed national court of the defendant if the defendant is domiciled or has a business establishment in one of the EU Member States, or, if not applicable, enforcement may be sought in a court of the Member State in which the infringement has occurred. The test as to whether infringement has occurred will be established by the law of the jurisdiction in which the action is commenced. The procedures and tactics of such enforcement proceedings are discussed below.

4.1 Designated Courts

Jurisdiction for disputes concerning the infringement or validity of CTMs lies exclusively with the respective national courts of the EU Member States. Article 91(1) of the Regulation requires the Member States to designate as limited a number as possible of courts of first and second instance to serve as CTM Courts. These CTM Courts were to be identified and communicated to the European Commission by March 15, 1997, i.e., three years after the entry into force of the CTM Regulation. In Member States failing to comply with this deadline (and only a handful of Member States have done so to date), jurisdiction for CTM disputes has been assigned to those national courts that have jurisdiction over proceedings relating to the national trade marks of that state.

While the idea to implement a limited number of specialized CTM Courts should encourage a uniform application of the CTM Regulation and, hence, further promote the uniformity of the CTM system; such concepts have already been weakened to a certain extent. For example, whereas in the UK, only the High Court is designated as a (first instance) CTM Court (at least as regards in England, Wales and Northern Ireland), each German Federal State (Bundesland) has appointed at least one CTM Court, so that there are more than 20 CTM Courts in Germany.

The designated CTM Courts of each Member State are required to apply the provisions of the CTM Regulation wherein possible and to apply their own trade mark law only in relation to matters not covered by the CTM Regulation. The procedure to be followed when conducting proceedings in a CTM Court is the same as that which applies to national proceedings in respect of national trade mark rights (Article 97).

In order to enforce their rights, CTM proprietors must bring proceedings in the designated CTM Courts.

5. Forum Shopping

Under the CTM Regulation's rules of jurisdiction, the jurisdiction of the CTM Courts of the Member States where an infringement or an unauthorised use of the CTM occurred may or may not coincide with the jurisdiction based on domicile, establishment, location of OHIM, consent of the defendant with a non-competent venue, or choice of venue. If jurisdictions do not coincide, the plaintiff can choose the forum most favourable to its interests.

The CTM Regulation tries to prevent forum shopping by stipulating that, for claims other than those to cease and desist or for indemnification for infringements following the publication of the CTM application (i.e.

claims the CTM Regulation specifically notes), sanctions for infringements are subject to the laws of the Member State where the infringement occurred (Article 98(2)). Still, the CTM proprietor may want to investigate whether various available options exist, if available, to take advantage of procedural peculiarities some jurisdictions offer that others do not. The CTM Courts apply their respective national procedural laws, which, of course, differ from country to country. As a consequence, for example, the practice of granting preliminary injunctions in one country may well differ from practices of other countries, or particularly effective measures of enforcement may be available in one country as compared with the others.

5.1   National Relief

A CTM proprietor has various options available, depending upon the relief required. Should it wish to obtain recourse in only one Member State, it can commence proceedings in any Member State in which an act of infringement has occurred, regardless of whether the claimant or defendant is domiciled or has an establishment in that Member State. The CTM Court will, however, only have jurisdiction in respect of those acts of infringement occurring within its jurisdiction. If successful, the CTM proprietor will obtain relief in that Member State only (see Articles 93(5) and 94(2)).

5.2   Pan–European Relief

In most circumstances, however, a CTM proprietor will have the option of obtaining pan-European relief, provided proceedings are brought in the correct CTM Court. In order to grant pan-European relief, the CTM Court in which proceedings are brought must have extraterritorial jurisdiction, that is jurisdiction over acts of infringement in other Member States. Articles 93 and 94 govern the extra-territorial jurisdiction of the CTM Courts. The CTM proprietor must apply the following rules in order to obtain pan-European relief:

i.   The basic rule is that an action must be brought in the Member State in which the defendant is domiciled or, if he is not domiciled in any of the Member States, the Member State in which he has an establishment.

ii.   If the defendant is not domiciled, or does not have an establishment in any Member State, the action must be brought in the Member State in which the claimant is domiciled. If the claimant has no domicile in the EU, the action must be brought in a Member State in which the claimant has an establishment.

iii.   If neither the claimant nor the defendant has a domicile or establishment in a Member State, the appropriate court for commencing proceedings is the court of the Member State in which OHIM is located, that is the Spanish Court.

The appropriate court can, however, be designated by agreement between the parties. In this case, Article 17 of the Brussels Convention applies and that court will have jurisdiction.

In addition, if proceedings are brought in a court which would not normally have jurisdiction, and the defendant does not challenge jurisdiction and takes steps in those proceedings, then that court will have jurisdiction and may grant pan-European relief.

There will be a few circumstances in which a CTM proprietor will have recourse to only one CTM Court:

i. where the infringer has a domicile or establishment in one Member State and is only infringing in that one Member State;

ii. where the infringer has neither a domicile nor an establishment in any Member State and is only infringing in the Member State in which the claimant has a domicile or his only establishment;

iii. where neither the infringer no[r] the claimant has a domicile or an establishment in any Member State, and the infringer is only infringing in Spain (the country of residence of OHIM).

It must be noted that the plaintiff has no choice between the above rules that apply in a strict sequence of priority.

In other cases, the claimant will have a choice of CTM Courts in which to commence proceedings. Should the infringement be widespread, or if the infringer and/or claimant has many establishments, the choice of courts will increase.

6. Remedies

Upon a finding of infringement, the CTM Court is required by Article 98 of the CTM Regulation to make an order (subject to any special reasons for not doing so) prohibiting the defendant from proceeding with the acts that infringe or would infringe the CTM. It is also obliged to take such measures in accordance with its national law as are aimed at ensuring that the defendant complies with this prohibition.

In all other respects, the CTM Court must apply national law. It follows that remedies such as damages and delivery up of infringing products will be subject to national variations. The award of costs will also be subject to the laws of the individual Member States. This will be a factor in deciding the most appropriate court in which to bring an action.

As regards interim and protective measures such as interim injunctions, Article 99 of the CTM Regulation allows the CTM Court to grant such relief as is available under the laws of the Member State. A CTM Court that has extra-territorial jurisdiction may grant pan-European provisional relief. The 1998 Spice Girls case in Italy saw the first use of a CTM Court's power to grant a pan-European injunction on an interim basis. The case demonstrated the ability of a CTM Court to grant pan-European interim injunctions, as well as in respect of trade mark applications, since under Italian law (but not, for example, under German or

English law) it is possible to obtain interim relief upon the basis of a trade mark application.

8. Avoiding Conflicting Decisions by OHIM and the CTM Courts on the Validity of Identical CTMS

Upon application by certain third parties, OHIM can declare a CTM invalid. A CTM Court may also declare a CTM invalid upon a counterclaim filed by the defendant in an infringement action. To avoid conflicting decisions of those bodies regarding the same CTM, the following rules apply:

Under Article 95 of the Regulation, the CTM Courts must regard a CTM as valid unless the defendant in an infringement action files a counterclaim for revocation or for a declaration of invalidity, or the defendant in infringement actions and actions over the unauthorised use between the publication of the application and the publication of the registration (Article 9(3) of the CTM Regulation) claims that the CTM could be revoked for the lack of use, or could be declared invalid on account of an earlier right of the defendant.

Once a decision by OHIM becomes final, counterclaims for revocation or for a declaration of invalidity of a CTM that relate to the same subject matter and involve the same parties must be dismissed by the CTM Courts.

When a decision by OHIM has not yet become final, or when proceedings before OHIM and the CTM Court were initiated in parallel, the following rules on the stay of proceedings apply:

Under Article 96(7) of the CTM Regulation, the CTM Court may stay the proceedings when it is hearing a counterclaim for revocation or for a declaration of invalidity of a CTM. It does stay the proceedings upon request from the CTM proprietor, after hearing the other parties, and orders the defendant to submit an application for revocation or for a declaration of invalidity to OHIM within a certain time limit. If the defendant fails to submit the application to OHIM within the time limit, the counterclaim will be deemed withdrawn, and the proceedings continue. For the duration of the stay, the CTM Court may order provisional and protective measures.

Under Article 100(2) of the CTM Regulation, when OHIM hears an application for a revocation or for a declaration of invalidity of a CTM, it will stay the proceedings if the validity of the CTM is already being challenged in a counterclaim before a CTM Court, unless there are special grounds for continuing the hearing. OHIM may order a stay on its own motion after hearing the parties or at the request of one party after hearing the other parties. Even if proceedings before the CTM Court have started prior to those before OHIM, the CTM Court may order a stay of its proceedings at the request of one party after hearing the other parties. In this event, OHIM continues its proceedings.

Under Article 100(1) of the CTM Regulation, a CTM Court hearing infringement or compensation actions will stay the proceedings if the validity of the CTM is already being challenged before another CTM Court in a counterclaim, or if an application for revocation or for a declaration of invalidity has already been filed with OHIM. The CTM Court stays the proceedings on its own motion after hearing the parties, or at the request of one party after hearing the others.

NOTES AND QUESTIONS

1. What are the benefits, if any, of the Community Trade Mark (CTM)? Is it similar to the European patent? Is it different in any way? In evaluating the CTM, does it make you change your opinion on either the feasibility or desirability of moving toward a "universal" trademark system in which one trademark would be effective around the world?

2. What do you make of the authors' suggestion that countries in the EU may differ in their national laws with respect to trademark remedies for the CTM, as well as with respect to issues related to pronunciation of marks for the CTM? Are such differences good or bad for the CTM system, which purports to establish a "unitary" trademark that applies throughout the EU?

3. *New Accessions to the European Union.* Ten new countries joined the European Union in 2004. CTMs that had been previously registered were automatically extended protection in the 10 new countries, without any further fees. The countries are Cyprus, the Czech Republic, Estonia, Hungary, Latvia, Lithuania, Malta, Poland, Slovak Republic, and Slovenia. However, the extension of CTMs to these 10 countries of accession is subject to third party rights established in the marks before the date of accession. If a trademark holder had established and registered rights before accession, for example, the holder can prevent the use of the CTM within that territory. *See* Eva Szigeti & Zsofia Klauber, *Enlargement of the European Union: Trade Mark Issues in Hungary and Other New EU States*, 94 TRADEMARK REP. 924, 926–27 (2004).

4. *Max Planck Study in 2011.* The European Commission enlisted the Max Planck Institute for Intellectual Property and Competition Law to write a report on the CTM. The report, titled "Study on the Overall Functioning of the European Trade Mark System," provided a comprehensive analysis of the CTM's implementation fifteen years after its adoption. The report found that 41 percent of proprietors and 59 percent of agents "are using the national systems and file national trade marks, either simultaneously with CTMs or only on the national level," while "38 percent of proprietors and 24 percent of agents say that the filing only as a CTM is their prevailing practice." *Id.* at 255. Major recommendations of the Study include: (1) abolishing the requirement of graphical representation for a trade mark to be eligible for protection, particularly to accommodate nontraditional marks (*id.* at 264), a topic we consider later; (2) harmonizing the standard of "genuine use" to maintain a CTM, with a significant use of the CTM even in only a small part of the EU (e.g., one country) being potentially sufficient (*id.* at 135–36) (the CJEU will decide the issue in *Onel v. Omel*, 200.057.983/01); and (3) extending the

period of time to establish a genuine use from 5 to 15 years after registration (*id.* at 136).

5. *Popularity of CTMs.* The CTM has been incredibly popular. In 2010, more than 98,000 applications were filed. After 16 years, nearly 1 million total applications have been filed, with over 700,000 resulting in registrations. *See* http://oami.europa.eu/rw/pages/OHIM/statistics.en.do.

6. *Bibliographic note.* ERIC GASTRUEL & MARK MILFORD, THE LEGAL ASPECTS OF THE COMMUNITY TRADE MARK (2001).

DHL EXPRESS FRANCE SAS v. CHRONOPOST SA.

Court of Justice of the European Union (Grand Chamber).
[2011] E.T.M.R. 33, Case C–235/09 (April 12, 2011).

Judgment

This reference for a preliminary ruling concerns the interpretation of Article 98 of Council Regulation (EC) No 40/94 of 20 December 1993 on the Community trade mark (OJ 1994 L 11, p. 1), as amended by Council Regulation (EC) No 3288/94 of 22 December 1994 (OJ 1994 L 349, p. 83; 'Regulation No 40/94'). The reference has been made in proceedings between DHL Express France SAS ('DHL Express France'), successor to DHL International SA ('DHL International'), and Chronopost SA ('Chronopost') concerning the use by DHL International of Chronopost's French and Community trade marks WEBSHIPPING, the prohibition of that use and the coercive measures attached to that prohibition.

The dispute in the main proceedings and the questions referred for a preliminary ruling

Chronopost is the proprietor of the French and Community trade marks for the sign 'WEBSHIPPING.' The Community trade mark, applied for in October 2000, was registered on 7 May 2003 in respect of, inter alia, services relating to: logistics and data transmission; telecommunications; transport by road; collecting mail, newspaper and parcels; and express mail management.

It is apparent from the documents before the Court that, having noted that one of its principal competitors, DHL International, had used the signs 'WEB SHIPPING,' 'Web Shipping' and/or 'Webshipping' in order to designate an express mail management service accessible via the Internet, on 8 September 2004 Chronopost brought an action against that company before the Tribunal de grande instance de Paris (Regional Court, Paris, France)—which heard the case as a Community trade mark court within the meaning of Article 91(1) of Regulation No 40/94—alleging, in particular, infringement of the Community trade mark WEBSHIPPING. By its judgment of 15 March 2006, that court found, inter alia, that DHL Express France, successor to DHL International, had infringed Chronopost's French trade mark WEBSHIPPING, although it did not adjudicate upon the infringement of the Community trade mark.

The order for reference states that, by a judgment of 9 November 2007, the Cour d'appel de Paris (Court of Appeal, Paris)—acting as a second-instance Community trade mark court on the appeal brought against the judgment of 15 March 2006 by Chronopost—prohibited DHL Express France, subject to a periodic penalty payment in the event of infringement of the prohibition, from continuing to use the signs 'WEB-SHIPPING' and 'WEB SHIPPING' in order to designate an express mail management service accessible, inter alia, via the Internet. The Cour d'appel de Paris regarded such use as infringing the French and Community trade mark WEBSHIPPING.

[I]n the course of the same proceedings before the Cour de cassation (Court of Cassation), Chronopost has brought a cross-appeal in which it submits that the judgment of 9 November 2007 infringes Articles 1 and 98 of Regulation No 40/94 in so far as the prohibition against further infringement of the Community trade mark WEBSHIPPING, subject to a periodic penalty payment, issued by the Cour d'appel de Paris does not extend to the entire area of the European Union. Since it had doubts as to the interpretation, in that context, of Article 98 of Regulation No 40/94, the Cour de cassation decided to stay proceedings and to refer the following questions to the Court of Justice for a preliminary ruling[.]

Consideration of the questions referred

Preliminary observations

The first sentence of Article 98(1) provides that where a Community trade mark court hearing a case finds that there have been acts of infringement or threatened infringement of a Community trade mark, it is to issue an order prohibiting the defendant from proceeding with such acts. The second sentence of Article 98(1) provides that that court is required to take such measures in accordance with its national law as are aimed at ensuring that that prohibition is complied with.

The first question

By its first question the national court asks, in essence, whether Article 98(1) of Regulation No 40/94 must be interpreted as meaning that the prohibition against further infringement or threatened infringement issued by a Community trade mark court has effect as a matter of law throughout the entire area of the European Union.

It must be observed that the territorial scope of a prohibition against further infringement or threatened infringement of a Community trade mark, as provided for in Article 98(1) of Regulation No 40/94, is to be determined both by the territorial jurisdiction of the Community trade mark court issuing that prohibition and by the territorial extent of the Community trade mark proprietor's exclusive right which is adversely affected by the infringement or threatened infringement, as that extent results from Regulation No 40/94.

As regards, first, the territorial jurisdiction of a Community trade mark court, it must be noted at the outset that under Article 14(1) and (3) of Regulation No 40/94, infringement of a Community trade mark is to be governed by the national law relating to infringement of a national trade mark in accordance with the provisions of Title X of that regulation. The rules of procedure to be applied are to be determined in accordance with the provisions of Title X, headed 'Jurisdiction and procedure in legal actions relating to Community trade marks' and comprising Articles 90 to 104 of that regulation.

Article 92(a) of Regulation No 40/94 provides that the Community trade mark courts are to have exclusive jurisdiction to adjudicate upon all infringement actions and—if they are permitted under national law—actions in respect of threatened infringement relating to Community trade marks.

In the present case, it is apparent from the written observations submitted to the Court by Chronopost that the action was brought before the Community trade mark court pursuant to Article 93(1) to (4) of Regulation No 40/94. According to those observations, the application to bring the infringement or threatened infringement to an end is not based on Article 93(5).

Under Article 93(1) to (4) of Regulation No 40/94, read in conjunction with Article 94(1) of that regulation, a Community trade mark court, which is established in accordance with Article 91 of that regulation in order to protect the rights conferred by a Community trade mark, is to have jurisdiction, in particular, in respect of acts of infringement committed or threatened within the territory of any of the Member States.

Therefore, a Community trade mark court, such as that hearing the case in the main proceedings, has jurisdiction in respect of acts of infringement committed or threatened within the territory of one or more Member States, or even all the Member States. Thus, its jurisdiction may extend to the entire area of the European Union.

Second, the exclusive right of a Community trade mark proprietor, conferred under Regulation No 40/94, extends, as a rule, to the entire area of the European Union, throughout which Community trademarks enjoy uniform protection and have effect.

In accordance with Article 1(2) of that regulation, a Community trade mark is to have a unitary character. Having equal effect throughout the European Union, it may not, in accordance with that provision, be registered, transferred or surrendered or be the subject of a decision revoking the rights of the proprietor or declaring it invalid, nor may its use be prohibited, save in respect of the whole of the European Union. This principle is to apply unless otherwise provided in that regulation.

The unitary character of the Community trade mark is also apparent from the fifteenth and sixteenth recitals in the preamble to Regulation No 40/94. These state, first, that the effects of decisions regarding the validity and infringement of Community trademarks must cover the entire area of the European Union, in order to prevent inconsistent decisions on the part of the courts and OHIM and to ensure that the unitary character of Community trademarks is not undermined, and, second, that contradictory judgments should be avoided in actions which involve the same acts and the same parties and which are brought on the basis of a Community trade mark and parallel national trade marks.

In addition, the Court has already held, at paragraph 60 of the judgment in Case C–316/05 *Nokia* [2006] ECR I–12083, that the objective of Article 98(1) of Regulation No 40/94 is the uniform protection, throughout the entire area of the European Union, of the right conferred by the Community trade mark against the risk of infringement. In order to ensure that uniform protection, a prohibition against further infringement or threatened infringement issued by a competent Community trade mark court must therefore, as a rule, extend to the entire area of the European Union.

However, the territorial scope of the prohibition may, in certain circumstances, be restricted. The exclusive right of a Community trade mark proprietor, as provided for under Article 9(1) of Regulation No 40/94, is conferred in order to enable that proprietor to protect his specific interests as such, that is, to ensure that the trade mark is able to fulfil its functions. The exercise of that right must therefore be reserved to cases in which a third party's use of the sign affects or is liable to affect the functions of the trade mark (see, to that effect, Joined Cases C–236/08 to C–238/08 *Google France and Google* [2010] ECR I–0000, paragraph 75 and the case-law cited).

It follows, as the European Commission has pointed out, that the exclusive right of a Community trade mark proprietor and, hence, the territorial scope of that right, may not extend beyond what that right allows its proprietor to do in order to protect his trade mark, that is, to prohibit only uses which are liable to affect the functions of the trade mark. The acts or future acts of a defendant (namely the person whose use of the Community trade mark is complained of) which do not affect the functions of the Community trade mark, cannot therefore be prohibited.

Accordingly, if a Community trade mark court hearing a case in circumstances such as those of the main proceedings finds that the acts of infringement or threatened infringement of a Community trade mark are limited to a single Member State or to part of the territory of the European Union, in particular because the applicant for a prohibition order has restricted the territorial scope of its action in exercising its freedom to determine the extent of that action or because the defendant proves that the use of the sign at issue does not affect or is not liable to affect the functions of the trade mark, for example on linguistic grounds, that court must limit the territorial scope of the prohibition which it issues.

Lastly, it must be stated that the territorial scope of a prohibition against further infringement or threatened infringement of a Community trade mark can extend to the entire area of the European Union. That said, in accordance with Article 90 of Regulation No 40/94, which is concerned with the application of the Brussels Convention, read in conjunction with Article 33(1) of Regulation No 44/2001, the other Member States are, as a rule, required to recognise and enforce the judgment, thereby conferring on it a cross-border effect.

Consequently, the answer to the first question is that Article 98(1) of Regulation No 40/94 must be interpreted as meaning that the scope of the prohibition against further infringement or threatened infringement of a Community trade mark, issued by a Community trade mark court whose jurisdiction is based on Articles 93(1) to (4) and 94(1) of that regulation, extends, as a rule, to the entire area of the European Union. [The CJEU's ruling on the other questions is omitted. The CJEU ruled that a coercive measure, such as payments, ordered by a Community trade mark court to ensure compliance with a prohibition against further infringement extends to other EU Member States and must be enforced in equivalent manner, even if a Member State does not have the same coercive measure. *Ed.*]

NOTES AND QUESTIONS

1. Is the Court of Justice's allowance of EU-wide injunctions to stop infringement of a Community Trade Mark consistent with the unitary nature of a CTM?

2. Do courts in EU states always have to order EU-wide injunctions to stop infringement of a CTM, or are narrower injunctions permitted?

3. Would EU-wide injunctions be desirable to stop copyright or patent infringement in the EU as well? If so, evaluate the merits of adopting a unitary approach to copyrights and patents.

3. OWNERSHIP AND TRANSFER OF TRADEMARKS

Ownership of trademarks begins with satisfying the relevant requirements for obtaining trademark and priority rights—whether it be the first to use the mark or the first to register the mark in a country. As discussed above, these requirements will depend on the countries in which trademark protection is sought. A business or entity that successfully obtains trademark rights, however, cannot presume that it has perpetual ownership rights or that it can freely license or assign away its mark however it sees fit. Historically, trademark law has regulated the conditions under which trademarks may be assigned, licensed, and left in nonuse. This section examines these issues.

Paris Convention

Article 6*quater*

Marks: Assignment of Marks

(1) When, in accordance with the law of a country of the Union, the assignment of a mark is valid only if it takes place at the same time as the transfer of the business or goodwill to which the mark belongs, it shall suffice for the recognition of such validity that the portion of the business or goodwill located in that country be transferred to the assignee, together with the exclusive right to manufacture in the said country, or to sell therein, the goods bearing the mark assigned.

(2) The foregoing provision does not impose upon the countries of the Union any obligation to regard as valid the assignment of any mark the use of which by the assignee would, in fact, be of such a nature as to mislead the public, particularly as regards the origin, nature, or essential qualities, of the goods to which the mark is applied.

TRIPS

Article 21

Licensing and assignment

Members may determine conditions on the licensing and assignment of trademarks, it being understood that the compulsory licensing of trademarks shall not be permitted and that the owner of a registered trademark shall have the right to assign the trademark with or without the transfer of the business to which the trademark belongs.

* * *

An assignment of a trademark transfers ownership of the mark to the assignee. By contrast, a trademark license does not transfer ownership, but instead allows the licensee to use the mark while the trademark holder still retains ownership over the mark.

Let us first focus on assignments of trademarks. Historically, countries divided over whether a trademark holder should be allowed to assign away a trademark in itself, without any transfer of business assets or the goodwill related to the mark. Such an assignment—without any transfer of business assets or goodwill—is commonly referred to as an "assignment in gross." Recognizing this division among countries without resolving it, Paris Convention Article 6*quater* establishes a geographical minimum standard for countries that do choose to require a transfer of either business assets or goodwill to effectuate a trademark assignment: in such countries, "it shall suffice for the recognition of such validity that the portion of the business or goodwill located in that country be transferred to the assignee, together with the exclusive right to manufacture in the said country, or to sell therein, the goods bearing the mark assigned." Paris Conv. art. 6*quater*. By implication, the Paris Convention does not prohibit a country from allowing assignments in gross: countries are free to choose whether to allow assignments in gross, or prohibit them and be subject to the minimum standard of Article 6*quater*. But, of course, notwithstanding any assignment in gross, countries must still prohibit misleading uses of a trademark under Article 10*bis*(3), a requirement reinforced by Article 6*quater*(2). *See id.* art. 10*bis*(3).

Countries revisited the issue of assignments in gross in the formation of TRIPS. TRIPS Article 21 gives countries the discretion to determine any conditions for trademark assignment and licensing. In addition, TRIPS Article 21 establishes two minimum standards. First, it prohibits compulsory licensing of trademarks. Second, it states that "the owner of a registered trademark shall have the right to assign the trademark with or without the transfer of the business to which the trademark belongs." TRIPS art. 21. The second requirement specifically prohibits a WTO country from requiring the transfer of "the business"—presumably referring to business assets—as a part of a trademark assignment. Some countries argued, even further, for a prohibition on any requirement of the transfer of goodwill in trademark assignments, but the U.S. and other countries rejected the proposal. Article 21 only bars countries from requiring the transfer of business assets in trademark assignments. Thus, WTO countries can choose to require the transfer of the goodwill associated with the mark. But what constitutes the goodwill apart from any business assets? Consider the following case, which defines the U.S. approach.

VITTORIA NORTH AMERICA, L.L.C.
v. EURO–ASIA IMPORTS, INC.

U.S. Court of Appeals for the Tenth Circuit.
278 F.3d 1076 (10th Cir. 2001).

EBEL, CIRCUIT JUDGE.

In this case we are called upon to interpret provisions of the Tariff Act of 1930 designed to protect domestic owners of trademarks affixed to goods produced overseas by foreign manufacturers. Plaintiff–Appellee Vittoria North America, L.L.C., ("VNA"), an Oklahoma limited liability company, alleges that it is the U.S. owner of the trademark Vittoria, which designates a well-known brand of bicycle tires. VNA alleges that Defendant–Appellant Euro–Asia Imports, a California sole proprietorship, has purchased Vittoria-branded tires overseas and imported them into the United States in violation of VNA's trademark rights. VNA sued Euro–Asia Imports and its sole proprietor Robert Hansing (collectively "EAI") under § 526 of the Tariff Act (codified at 19 U.S.C. § 1526) ("the Act") seeking damages as well as an injunction to prevent EAI from continuing to import Vittoria bicycle tires into the United States. The Act states:

> Except as provided in subsection (d) of this section, it shall be unlawful to import into the United States any merchandise of foreign manufacture if such merchandise, or the label, sign, print, package, wrapper, or receptacle, bears a trademark owned by a citizen of, or by a corporation or association created or organized within, the United States, and registered in the Patent and Trademark Office by a

person domiciled in the United States, under the provisions of sections 81 to 109 of Title 15, and if a copy of the certificate of registration of such trademark is filed with the Secretary of the Treasury, in the manner provided in section 106 of said Title 15, unless written consent of the owner of such trademark is produced at the time of making entry.

19 U.S.C. § 1526. In other words, the Act provides so-called "gray market"[2] protection to U.S. owners of trademarks associated with goods of foreign manufacture, prohibiting any other person or entity from importing goods bearing that trademark into the United States without the consent of the trademark owner. *See, e.g., K Mart Corp. v. Cartier, Inc.*, 486 U.S. 281, 288–89 (1988).

The district court granted VNA partial summary judgment, holding that the evidence showed that VNA owns and has properly registered the Vittoria trademark in the United States, that Vittoria-branded bicycle tires are manufactured overseas, and that EAI has imported Vittoria tires into the United States without VNA's consent. EAI now appeals, arguing that the evidence was insufficient to support summary judgment on the issue of whether VNA is the U.S. owner of the Vittoria trademark. EAI further argues that VNA is not entitled to protection under the Act because VNA is controlled by the foreign manufacturer of Vittoria tires. We AFFIRM.

I. Background

On November 25, 1992, VNA's predecessor Hibdon Tire Center entered into an agreement ("the 1992 Agreement") with Vittoria S.p.A. ("Vittoria Italy"), a company organized under the laws of Italy and with headquarters in Bergamo, Italy. Hibdon Tire Center agreed to form VNA as a North American distributor of Vittoria tires, and Vittoria Italy agreed to designate VNA as its exclusive distributor in the United States, Canada, and Mexico. VNA distributed Vittoria-branded bicycle tires in the United States from that time forward. In February 1999, Vittoria Italy entered into an agreement ("Assignment Agreement") with VNA purporting to assign VNA "all right, title and interest in and to the United States Trademark 'VITTORIA' and the registration therefore ..., together with the goodwill of the business connected with the use of and symbolized by said Trademark, as well as the right to sue for infringement of the Trademark or injury to said goodwill." The Assignment Agreement stated that "[t]he purpose of this Agreement is to permit Assignee [VNA] to act against infringers and unauthorized importers of Vittoria trademarked products into the United States." Vittoria Italy retained the right to retake title to the Trademark and its associated goodwill upon giving thirty days' written notice to VNA.

---

2. "Gray market goods" are defined to include "[f]oreign-manufactured goods, bearing a valid United States trademark, that are imported without the consent of the U.S. trademark holder." *Black's Law Dictionary* 701 (6th ed. 1990).

Shortly thereafter, VNA filed suit against EAI alleging that it infringed on VNA's trademark rights by importing Vittoria tires into the United States without first gaining VNA's consent. EAI concedes that it has been purchasing Vittoria-branded tires overseas and importing the tires into the United States since the early 1980s. VNA's suit seeks damages, an injunction to prevent further importation by EAI, and confiscation of EAI's inventory of Vittoria-branded products.

The district court granted VNA's motion for partial summary judgment, holding that undisputed facts in the case established VNA's right to protection under 19 U.S.C. § 1526. The district court therefore enjoined EAI from further importation of Vittoria-branded products into the United States, although it did not address the issue of damages in its order. EAI now appeals the district court's injunction.

II. Discussion

B. Transfer of Vittoria Trademark to VNA

We next consider EAI's contention that VNA is not entitled to gray market protection under the Act. In order to prove entitlement to protection under the Act, VNA must show that it is a corporation or association created or organized within the United States, that it owns the Vittoria trademark in the United States, that the trademark is registered in the Patent and Trademark Office of the United States Customs Service, and that EAI is, without VNA's consent, importing Vittoria-branded goods of foreign manufacture. 19 U.S.C. § 1526(a). The district court found that undisputed evidence sufficiently established each of these points.

EAI contests whether the evidence demonstrates that VNA owns the Vittoria trademark in the United States.

EAI asserts that the transfer was invalid because the Assignment Agreement failed to transfer the goodwill associated with the trademark along with the trademark itself. Courts have consistently held that a valid assignment of a trademark or service mark requires the transfer of the goodwill associated with the mark. *See, e.g., Sands, Taylor & Wood Co. v. Quaker Oats Co.*, 978 F.2d 947, 956 (7th Cir. 1992) ("[T]he transfer of a trademark apart from the goodwill of the business which it represents is an invalid 'naked' or 'in gross' assignment, which passes no rights to the assignee."); *Premier Dental Prods.*, 794 F.2d at 853 (transfer of goodwill is necessary to transfer ownership of a trademark). "A trademark symbolizes the public's confidence or 'goodwill' in a particular product. However, it is no more than that, and is insignificant if separated from that confidence. Therefore, a trademark 'is not the subject of property except in connection with an existing business.' " *Id.* at 853 (quoting *United Drug Co. v. Theodore Rectanus Co.*, 248 U.S. 90, 97 (1918)) (footnote omitted).

EAI points to several perceived distinctions between *Premier Dental Prods.* and the facts of this case to suggest that goodwill did not transfer under the Assignment Agreement. EAI notes that the assignee in *Premier Dental Prods.* was not created expressly for the purpose of marketing goods bearing the trademark at issue, and that the assignee was the exclusive distributor of such goods in the United States, whereas here VNA was created pursuant to the 1992 Agreement, and VNA competed with EAI prior to the Assignment Agreement. Moreover, EAI points out that it has been distributing Vittoria-branded bicycle tires in the United States for a longer period of time than VNA, and that EAI never obtained its products directly from VNA.

The purpose for requiring transfer of goodwill along with the transfer of the trade or service mark is to ensure that consumers receive accurate information about the product or service associated with the mark. *Sugar Busters LLC v. Brennan*, 177 F.3d 258, 265 (5th Cir. 1999) ("The purpose of the rule prohibiting the sale or assignment of a trademark in gross is to prevent a consumer from being misled or confused as to the source and nature of the goods or service that he or she acquires.").

Transfer of assets is not a *sine qua non* for transferring the goodwill associated with a trademark. The *Restatement (Third) of Unfair Competition* explains:

> [C]ourts now evaluate each assignment in light of the circumstances of the particular case, including both the terms of the transfer and the nature of the assignee's subsequent use. Recent decisions recognize that the central enquiry is whether the use of the mark by the assignee is likely to confuse prospective purchasers by departing from the expectations created by the presence of the trademark. The traditional requirement of accompanying transfer of goodwill can thus be understood as requiring that the assignment not disrupt the existing significance of the mark to consumers.

Restatement (Third) of Unfair Competition § 34 cmt. b (1995). "The courts have upheld such assignments if they find that the assignee is producing a product or performing a service substantially similar to that of the assignor and that the consumers would not be deceived or harmed." *Marshak*, 746 F.2d at 930 (citations omitted); *see also Sugar Busters*, 177 F.3d at 266; *Defiance Button Mach. Co. v. C & C Metal Prods. Corp.*, 759 F.2d 1053, 1059 (2d Cir. 1985) ("[A] trademark may be validly transferred without the simultaneous transfer of any tangible assets, as long as the recipient continues to produce goods of the same quality and nature previously associated with the mark.").

In this case, VNA's actions both prior and subsequent to the transfer of the Vittoria trademark were calculated to maintain continuity in the use of the mark and the public's perceptions of the products associated with it. The record shows that VNA took significant steps throughout its use of the trademark to ensure that the mark continued to signify high-end racing tires for bicycles. VNA placed advertisements, sponsored professional athletes, attended trade shows, and developed a marketing network consisting of 25 to 30 sales representatives who promoted these tires to approximately 6,000 bicycle dealers. Significantly, EAI has never alleged any sort of disruption in the kind or quality of the products associated with the Vittoria trademark, and we could find no evidence of any such break upon our independent review of the record. We therefore hold the Assignment Agreement constitutes a valid transfer of the rights to use the Vittoria trademark in the United States.

For the reasons set forth herein, we AFFIRM the grant of partial summary judgment for VNA.

NOTES AND QUESTIONS

1. In an omitted part of the opinion, the court considered whether the gray market tires could be imported into the United States without the consent of VNA under an exception to the § 526 of the Tariff Act called the common control exception. The court found that the common control exception did not apply to a mere exclusive distributor such as VNA, which the court found to be independent of Vittoria Italy, and the goods of Vittoria Italy sold abroad could therefore be excluded. *See* 278 F.3d at 1085–86. We defer a full discussion of gray market goods until Chapter 6.

2. In order for VNA to establish that it received ownership of the U.S. trademark to VITTORIA from Vittoria Italy, must VNA prove that it had received a transfer of (i) goodwill of the business and/or (ii) the assets of the business from Vittoria Italy? If so, what level of proof is required and what purpose does such a requirement serve? Does either the Paris Convention or the TRIPS Agreement require such proof for ownership of trademarks discussed in the *Vittoria* case? Does either Paris or TRIPS forbid countries from requiring such proof?

3. *Assignment v. Licensing.* The *Vittoria* case dealt with one of the more common types of conditions recognized by countries to effectuate the assignment of a trademark accompanied by the transfer of the goodwill associated with the mark. An analogous condition for *licensing* is imposed by some countries, such as the United States, to ensure that customers will not be confused by licensed trademarks. Under U.S. law, for example, a trademark holder who licenses its marks for third parties to use must maintain some level of quality control over the product on which its mark is being used, in order to ensure that the licensee is marketing a product that is not different from (or inferior to) the quality of the trademark holder's product. *See Dawn Donut Co. v. Hart's Food Stores, Inc.*, 267 F.2d 358, 367–68 (2d Cir. 1959). Failure to maintain quality control constitutes "naked licensing" of the mark and results in the trademark holder's abandonment of rights to the mark. *Id.* Thus, in the case of assignment of a trademark, the quality control might be effectuated by the requirement that the assignee receives a transfer of the goodwill associated with the trademark in order to ensure a consistent product. By contrast, in the case of licensing, the quality control might be effectuated by the trademark holder's contractual stipulations and actual inspections related to the use of the mark by the licensee.

4. Why not allow assignments in gross and naked licensing? Wouldn't the market and incentives of businesses correct any problems with inferior or changed products bearing the same trademark? If the assignee or licensee's product was inferior, wouldn't consumers and reviewers be able to tell and

then refuse to buy the product? *See* Irene Calboli, *Trademark Assignment "With Goodwill": A Concept Whose Time Has Gone*, 57 FLA. L. REV. 771 (2005).

4. SUBJECT MATTER AND DISTINCTIVENESS

a. General Approach for Trademarks

Article 15 of TRIPS takes an expansive view on what subject matter must be eligible for trademarks. It states: "Any sign, or any combination of signs, capable of distinguishing the goods or services of one undertaking from those of other undertakings, shall be capable of constituting a trademark. Such signs, in particular words including personal names, letters, numerals, figurative elements and combinations of colours as well as any combination of such signs, shall be eligible for registration as trademarks. Where signs are not inherently capable of distinguishing the relevant goods or services, Members may make registrability depend on distinctiveness acquired through use. Members may require, as a condition of registration, that signs be visually perceptible." TRIPS art. 15(1).

The key is that the mark must be *distinctive* to identify the source of the product or service, or be "capable of distinguishing the goods or services of one undertaking from those of other undertakings." *Id.* Article 15 specifically allows countries the option of excluding signs that are not visually perceptible—such as smells or sounds—from registration. *Id.* In addition, Article 15(2) allows countries the discretion to "deny[] registration of a trademark on other grounds, provided that they do not derogate from ... the Paris Convention (1967)."

As discussed in this section, marks that are words or logos tend not to present any controversy as potentially eligible subject matter (provided distinctiveness is met). Nontraditional marks, however, such as colors, sounds, smells, and three-dimensional shapes present more difficult questions as indicated by the materials later below.

OFFICE FOR HARMONISATION IN THE INTERNAL MARKET (OHIM) v. BORCO–MARKEN–IMPORT MATTHIESEN GmbH & CO. KG

Court of Justice of the European Union (First Chamber).
[2011] E.T.M.R. 4, C–265/09 (Sept. 9, 2010).

Judgment

Background to the dispute

On 14 September 2005, BORCO–Marken–Import Matthiesen GmbH & Co. KG ('BORCO') filed an application for registration of the sign

as a Community trade mark.

The goods in respect of which registration was sought are in Class 33 of the Nice Agreement concerning the International Classification of Goods and Services for the Purposes of the Registration of Marks of 15 June 1957, as revised and amended, and correspond to the description 'alcoholic beverages (except beers), wines, sparkling wines and beverages containing wine'.

By decision of 31 May 2006, the examiner refused the application for registration on the ground that the sign at issue lacked distinctive character, on the basis of Article 7(1)(b) of Regulation No 40/94. The examiner found that the mark applied for constituted a faithful reproduction of the Greek lower-case letter 'α', without graphical modifications, and that Greek-speaking purchasers would not detect in that sign an indication of the commercial origin of the goods described in the trade mark application.

On 15 June 2006, BORCO lodged an appeal with OHIM against that decision. That appeal was dismissed by the contested decision on the ground that the sign at issue was devoid of the distinctive character required under Article 7(1)(b) of Regulation No 40/94.

The action before the General Court and the judgment under appeal

On 5 February 2007, BORCO brought an action before the General Court seeking the annulment of the contested decision[.] As regards the analysis carried out in the case by that Board of Appeal, the General Court stated, in paragraphs 40 to 52 of the judgment under appeal, that the Board of Appeal had refused, in breach in particular of Article 4 of Regulation No 40/94, to accept that single letters can have distinctive character without undertaking the examination based on the facts mentioned above.

[T]he General Court concluded:

'It follows from all of the foregoing that, by assuming from its lack of graphical modifications or ornamentations that, by definition, the sign at issue lacked distinctive character in relation to the Times New Roman character font, without carrying out an examination as to whether, on the facts, that sign is capable of distinguishing, in the mind of the reference public, the goods at issue from those of [BORCO's] competitors, the Board of Appeal misapplied Article 7(1)(b) of Regulation No 40/94.'

The appeal

OHIM claims that, contrary to the General Court's assessment, the examination of the distinctive character of a sign on the basis of Article 7(1)(b) of Regulation No 40/94 does not always imply a determination of whether that sign is capable of distinguishing the different goods in the context of an examination, based on the facts, focused on those goods.

Findings of the Court

As a preliminary point, it should be recalled that, according to Article 4 of Regulation No 40/94, letters are among the categories of signs of which a Community trade mark may consist, provided that they are capable of distinguishing the goods or services of one undertaking from those of other undertakings.

However, the fact that a sign is, in general, capable of constituting a trade mark does not mean that the sign necessarily has distinctive character for the purposes of Article 7(1)(b) of the regulation in relation to a specific product or service (Joined Cases C–456/01 P and C–457/01 P *Henkel* v *OHIM* [2004] ECR I–5089, paragraph 32). Under that provision, marks which are devoid of any distinctive character are not to be registered.

According to settled case-law, for a trade mark to possess distinctive character for the purposes of that provision, it must serve to identify the product in respect of which registration is applied for as originating from a particular undertaking, and thus to distinguish that product from those of other undertakings.

It is settled case-law that that distinctive character must be assessed, first, by reference to the goods or services in respect of which registration has been applied for and, second, by reference to the perception of them by the relevant public. Furthermore, the Court has held, as OHIM points out in its appeal, that that method of assessment is also applicable to an analysis of the distinctive character of signs consisting solely of a colour per se, three-dimensional marks and slogans.

However, while the criteria for the assessment of distinctive character are the same for different categories of marks, it may be that, for the purposes of applying those criteria, the relevant public's perception is not necessarily the same in relation to each of those categories and it could therefore prove more difficult to establish distinctiveness in relation to marks of certain categories as compared with marks of other categories.

As the Advocate General observed at point 47 of his Opinion, the requirement of an examination as to whether, on the facts, the sign in question is capable of distinguishing the goods or services designated from those of other undertakings, allows for the accommodation of the ground for refusal laid down in Article 7(1)(b) of Regulation No 40/94 with the general capacity of a sign to constitute a trade mark recognised in Article 4 thereof.

In that regard, it should be pointed out that, even though it is apparent from the case-law cited that the Court has recognised that there are certain categories of signs which are less likely prima facie to have distinctive character initially, the Court, nevertheless, has not exempted the trade mark authorities from having to carry out an examination of their distinctive character based on the facts.

In relation, more particularly, to the fact that the sign at issue consists of a single letter with no graphic modifications, it should be borne in mind that registration of a sign as a trade mark is not subject to a finding of a specific level of linguistic or artistic creativity or imaginative-ness on the part of the proprietor of the trademark.

It follows that, particularly as it may prove more difficult to establish distinctiveness for marks consisting of a single letter than for other word marks, OHIM is required to assess whether the sign at issue is capable of distinguishing the different goods and services in the context of an examination, based on the facts, focusing on those goods or services.

Therefore, in ascertaining whether the Fourth Board of Appeal of OHIM carried out an examination as to whether, on the facts, the sign at issue was capable of distinguishing the goods designated from those of other undertakings, the General Court correctly applied Article 7(1)(b) of Regulation No 40/94. It follows that the first part of the single plea must be rejected as unfounded.

NOTES AND QUESTIONS

1. According to the Court of Justice, can the alpha symbol (α) be eligible for a trademark?

2. What test did the CJEU use to determine if a symbol can be distinctive?

3. Does TRIPS Article 15 speak to the issue of trademarking of a symbol like the alpha letter (α)?

4. *U.S. Approach*. The U.S. takes a similarly expansive approach to trademarks. A basic letter or shape may also be treated as inherently distinctive—and thus a trademark—if it is sufficiently stylized, such as in shading, border, or thickness, such that it is unique or unusual in the relevant market. *See Star Indus., Inc. v. Bacardi & Co., Ltd.*, 412 F.3d 373 (2d Cir. 2005) ("O" on vodka was stylized and inherently distinctive). Even when a symbol is not inherently distinctive, it may become distinctive (or acquire "secondary meaning") based on use of the symbol in a particular market.

b. Product Designs as Trademarks

Given the broad scope countries have given to trademarks for tradi-tional marks, such as words and logos, it should not be surprising that businesses have attempted to assert trademarks in a wide variety of things—color, smell, 3-dimensional shapes, sound, touch, holograms, and motion—that go well beyond the traditional mark. These so-called "non-traditional marks" have tested the boundaries of trademark law. This section discusses product designs, while the next section discusses other non-traditional marks. Consider whether the WTO should expressly in-clude within Article 15(1) any class of nontraditional marks.

PROBLEM 4–7

Lego manufactures "Lego" toys, which consist of plastic building blocks that can be snapped together in order to build various objects. The standard

Lego brick is rectangular and depicted below. The raised circular tabs on top allow the brick to be snapped into the bottoms of other bricks. You may assume that the Lego shape is distinctive—and, indeed, famous—among consumers. Lego obtained patents in the EU and U.S. for the Lego brick that expired in 1988. Can the shape of the Lego brick be trademarked today in the EU and U.S.?

PROBLEM 4–8

Apple manufactures a popular tablet called the "iPad," which is sold in countries around the world, including the U.S. and Europe. The iPad now comes in a white model, in addition to the standard black model. The display of the tablet is 9.7 inches (diagonal) and has multi-touch technology allowing the user to touch the screen to enter commands. The iPad itself is 9.50 inches by 7.31 inches, and .37 inches thick. On the white model, a white, rectangular border of roughly 1 inch surrounds the front of the display screen. The back of the iPad is silver in color, with a black Apple logo in the center. Among Apple consumers, white has become a popular color that many identify with Apple products, such as the white iPhone, white iPod music player, and the all-white MacBook laptop, which was extremely popular, but is now discontinued. Apple's earpieces are also in white, with white ear buds and wires.

You are the General Counsel for TTT Corp., which is headquartered in Europe, but sells its products worldwide. TTT Corp. would like to manufacture a tablet that is encased with a white, rectangular border of approximately 1 inch on the front display, plus an entirely white plastic casing on back. TTT would like to manufacture the white tablet in a rectangular shape in roughly the same dimensions as the iPad, since, in TTT's view, the size has become the industry standard. All of the software within TTT's tablet was created by its own developers. Apple has not registered white as a trademark, but, in the U.S., registration is not required. Nor is registration required for well-known marks under the Paris Convention Article 6*bis*.

TTT Corp. wants to know whether it can manufacture and sell the white tablet described above without fear of any trademark lawsuit. Please analyze the following: (i) what is the likelihood that Apple could claim trademark or trade dress protection for the iPad's shape and white color in the U.S. and the EU; (ii) whether TTT should market its white tablet in the U.S. and/or the EU; and (iii) what, if any, other factual information would be helpful to your decision. In answering this problem, limit your analysis to trademark law, and consider the following two cases and accompanying notes.

KONINKLIJKE PHILIPS ELECTRONICS NV v. REMINGTON CONSUMER PRODUCTS LTD.

European Court of Justice.
[2002] ECR I–5475, Case C–299/99 (June 18, 2002).

By order of 5 May 1999, received at the Court on 9 August 1999, the Court of Appeal (England and Wales) (Civil Division) referred for a preliminary ruling under Article 234 EC seven questions concerning the interpretation of Articles 3(1) and (3), 5(1) and 6(1)(b) of First Council Directive 89/104/EEC of 21 December 1988 to approximate the laws of the Member States relating to trade marks (OJ 1989 L 40, p. 1, hereinafter the Directive).

 Community legislation

The purpose of the Directive is, as the first recital in its preamble states, to approximate the laws of the Member States on trade marks in order to remove existing disparities which may impede the free movement of goods and freedom to provide services and may distort competition within the common market.

Article 2 of the Directive provides, under the heading Signs of which a trademark may consist:

A trademark may consist of any sign capable of being represented graphically, particularly words, including personal names, designs, letters, numerals, the shape of goods or of their packaging, provided that such signs are capable of distinguishing the goods or services of one undertaking from those of other undertakings.

Article 3 of the Directive, which lists the grounds for refusal or invalidity of registration, provides:

1.   The following shall not be registered or if registered shall be liable to be declared invalid:

(a) signs which cannot constitute a trade mark;

(b) trade marks which are devoid of any distinctive character;

(c) trade marks which consist exclusively of signs or indications which may serve, in trade, to designate the kind, quality, quantity, intended purpose, value, geographical origin, or the time of production of the goods or of rendering of the service, or other characteristics of the goods or service;

(d) trade marks which consist exclusively of signs or indications which have become customary in the current language or in the bona fide and established practices of the trade;

(e) signs which consist exclusively of:

—the shape which results from the nature of the goods themselves, or

—the shape of goods which is necessary to obtain a technical result, or

—the shape which gives substantial value to the goods; * * *

3. A trade mark shall not be refused registration or be declared invalid in accordance with paragraph 1(b), (c) or (d) if, before the date of application for registration and following the use which has been made of it, it has acquired a distinctive character. Any Member State may in addition provide that this provision shall also apply where the distinctive character was acquired after the date of application for registration or after the date of registration. * * *

The main proceedings and the questions referred

In 1966, Philips developed a new type of three-headed rotary electric shaver. In 1985, Philips filed an application to register a trade mark consisting of a graphic representation of the shape and configuration of the head of such a shaver, comprising three circular heads with rotating blades in the shape of an equilateral triangle. That trade mark was registered on the basis of use under the Trade Marks Act 1938.

In 1995, Remington, a competing company, began to manufacture and sell in the United Kingdom the DT 55, which is a shaver with three rotating heads forming an equilateral triangle, shaped similarly to that used by Philips. Philips accordingly sued Remington for infringement of its trade mark. Remington counter-claimed for revocation of the trade mark registered by Philips.

The High Court of Justice of England and Wales, Chancery Division (Patents Court) (United Kingdom), allowed the counter-claim and ordered revocation of the registration of the Philips trade mark on the ground that the sign relied on by Philips was incapable of distinguishing the goods concerned from those of other undertakings and was devoid of any distinctive character. The High Court also held that the trade mark consisted exclusively of a sign which served in trade to designate the intended purpose of the goods and of a shape which was necessary to obtain a technical result and which gave substantial value to the goods. It went on to hold that, even if the trade mark had been valid, it would not have been infringed.

Philips appealed to the Court of Appeal against that decision of the High Court. As the arguments of the parties raised questions relating to the interpretation of the Directive, the Court of Appeal (England and Wales) (Civil Division) decided to stay proceedings and to refer the following questions [analyzed below] to the Court of Justice for a preliminary ruling[.]

The first question

By its first question the referring court seeks to know whether there is a category of marks which is not excluded from registration by Article 3(1)(b), (c) and (d) and Article 3(3) of the Directive which is none the less excluded from registration by Article 3(1)(a) thereof on the ground that such marks are incapable of distinguishing the goods of the proprietor from those of other undertakings.

Findings of the Court

First of all, Article 2 of the Directive provides that all signs may constitute trademarks provided that they are capable both of being represented graphically and of distinguishing the goods or services of one undertaking from those of other undertakings.

Second, under the rule laid down by Article 3(1)(b), (c) and (d), trademarks which are devoid of any distinctive character, descriptive marks, and marks which consist exclusively of indications which have become customary in the current language or in the bona fide and established practices of the trade are to be refused registration or declared invalid if registered.

Finally, Article 3(3) of the Directive adds a significant qualification to the rule laid down by Article 3(1)(b), (c) and (d) in that it provides that a sign may, through use, acquire a distinctive character which it initially lacked and thus be registered as a trade mark. It is therefore through the use made of it that the sign acquires the distinctive character which is a prerequisite for its registration. [I]t is clear from the wording of Article 3(1)(a) and the structure of the Directive that that provision is intended essentially to exclude from registration signs which are not generally capable of being a trade mark and thus cannot be represented graphically and/or are not capable of distinguishing the goods or services of one undertaking from those of other undertakings.

Accordingly, Article 3(1)(a) of the Directive, like the rule laid down by Article 3(1)(b), (c) and (d), precludes the registration of signs or indications which do not meet one of the two conditions imposed by Article 2 of the Directive, that is to say, the condition requiring such signs to be capable of distinguishing the goods or services of one undertaking from those of other undertakings. It follows that there is no class of marks having a distinctive character by their nature or by the use made of them which is not capable of distinguishing goods or services within the meaning of Article 2 of the Directive.

The second question

By its second question, the national court seeks to know whether the shape of an article is capable of distinguishing for the purposes of Article 2 of the Directive only if it contains some capricious addition, such as an embellishment which has no functional purpose.

Findings of the Court

First, it is clear from Article 2 of the Directive that a trade mark has distinctive character if it serves to distinguish, according to their origin, the goods or services in respect of which registration has been applied for. It is sufficient for the trade mark to enable the public concerned to distinguish the product or service from others which have another commercial origin, and to conclude that all the goods or services bearing it have originated under the control of the proprietor of the trade mark to whom responsibility for their quality can be attributed. In particular, the Directive in no way requires that the shape of the article in respect of which the sign is registered must include some capricious addition.

The third question

[T]he answer to the third question must be that, where a trader has been the only supplier of particular goods to the market, extensive use of a sign which consists of the shape of those goods may be sufficient to give the sign a distinctive character for the purposes of Article 3(3) of the Directive in circumstances where, as a result of that use, a substantial proportion of the relevant class of persons associates that shape with that trader and no other undertaking or believes that goods of that shape come from that trader. However, it is for the national court to verify that the circumstances in which the requirement under that provision is satisfied are shown to exist on the basis of specific and reliable data, that the presumed expectations of an average consumer of the category of goods or services in question, who is reasonably well-informed and reasonably observant and circumspect, are taken into account and that the identification, by the relevant class of persons, of the product as originating from a given undertaking is as a result of the use of the mark as a trade mark.

The fourth question

By its fourth question the referring court is essentially asking whether Article 3(1)(e), second indent, of the Directive must be interpreted to mean that a sign consisting exclusively of the shape of a product is unregistrable by virtue of that provision if it is established that the essential functional features of the shape are attributable only to the technical result. It also seeks to know whether the ground for refusal or invalidity of the registration imposed by that provision can be overcome by establishing that there are other shapes which can obtain the same technical result.

Findings of the Court

The rationale of the grounds for refusal of registration laid down in Article 3(1)(e) of the Directive is to prevent trade mark protection from granting its proprietor a monopoly on technical solutions or functional characteristics of a product which a user is likely to seek in the products of competitors. Article 3(1)(e) is thus intended to prevent the protection conferred by the trade mark right from being extended, beyond signs which serve to distinguish a product or service from those offered by competitors, so as to form an obstacle preventing competitors from freely offering for sale products incorporating such technical solutions or functional characteristics in competition with the proprietor of the trade mark.

As regards, in particular, signs consisting exclusively of the shape of the product necessary to obtain a technical result, listed in Article 3(1)(e), second indent, of the Directive, that provision is intended to preclude the registration of shapes whose essential characteristics perform a technical function, with the result that the exclusivity inherent in the trade mark right would limit the possibility of competitors supplying a product incorporating such a function or at least limit their freedom of choice in regard to the technical solution they wish to adopt in order to incorporate such a function in their product.

As Article 3(1)(e) of the Directive pursues an aim which is in the public interest, namely that a shape whose essential characteristics perform a technical function and were chosen to fulfil that function may be freely used by all, that provision prevents such signs and indications from being reserved to one undertaking alone because they have been registered as trade marks.

As to the question whether the establishment that there are other shapes which could achieve the same technical result can overcome the ground for refusal or invalidity contained in Article 3(1)(e), second indent, there is nothing in the wording of that provision to allow such a conclusion. In refusing registration of such signs, Article 3(1)(e), second indent, of the Directive reflects the legitimate aim of not allowing individuals to use registration of a mark in order to acquire or perpetuate exclusive rights relating to technical solutions. Where the essential functional characteristics of the shape of a product are attributable solely to the technical result, Article 3(1)(e), second indent, precludes registration of a sign consisting of that shape, even if that technical result can be achieved by other shapes.

The referring court makes clear that consideration of the questions relating to the infringement would not be required if its interpretation of Article 3 were to be upheld by the Court of Justice. As the answer to the fourth question confirms that interpretation, there is no need to reply to the fifth, sixth and seventh questions. * * *

TRAFFIX DEVICES, INC. v. MARKETING DISPLAYS, INC.

Supreme Court of the United States.
532 U.S. 23 (2001).

JUSTICE KENNEDY delivered the opinion of the Court.

Temporary road signs with warnings like "Road Work Ahead" or "Left Shoulder Closed" must withstand strong gusts of wind. An inventor named Robert Sarkisian obtained two utility patents for a mechanism built upon two springs (the dual-spring design) to keep these and other outdoor signs upright despite adverse wind conditions. The holder of the now-expired Sarkisian patents, respondent Marketing Displays, Inc. (MDI), established a successful business in the manufacture and sale of sign stands incorporating the patented feature. MDI's stands for road signs were recognizable to buyers and users (it says) because the dual-spring design was visible near the base of the sign.

This litigation followed after the patents expired and a competitor, TrafFix Devices, Inc., sold sign stands with a visible spring mechanism that looked like MDI's. MDI and TrafFix products looked alike because they were. When TrafFix started in business, it sent an MDI product abroad to have it reverse engineered, that is to say copied. Complicating matters, TrafFix marketed its sign stands under a name similar to MDI's. MDI used the name "WindMaster," while TrafFix, its new competitor, used "WindBuster."

MDI brought suit under the Trademark Act of 1946 (Lanham Act), 60 Stat. 427, as amended, 15 U.S.C. § 1051 *et seq.,* against TrafFix for trademark infringement (based on the similar names), trade dress infringement (based on the copied dual-spring design), and unfair competition. TrafFix counterclaimed on antitrust theories. After the United States District Court for the Eastern District of Michigan considered cross-motions for summary judgment, MDI prevailed on its trademark claim for the confusing similarity of names and was held not liable on the antitrust counterclaim; and those two rulings, affirmed by the Court of Appeals, are not before us.

II

It is well established that trade dress can be protected under federal law. The design or packaging of a product may acquire a distinctiveness which serves to identify the product with its manufacturer or source; and a design or package which acquires this secondary meaning, assuming other requisites are met, is a trade dress which may not be used in a manner likely to cause confusion as to the origin, sponsorship, or approval of the goods. In these respects protection for trade dress exists to promote competition. As we explained just last Term, see *Wal–Mart Stores, Inc. v. Samara Brothers, Inc.,* 529 U.S. 205 (2000), various Courts of Appeals have allowed claims of trade dress infringement relying on the general provision of the Lanham Act which provides a cause of action to one who is injured when a person uses "any word, term name, symbol, or device, or any combination thereof . . . which is likely to cause confusion . . . as to the origin, sponsorship, or approval of his or her goods." Congress confirmed this statutory protection for trade dress by amending the Lanham Act to recognize the concept. Title 15 U.S.C. § 1125(3) (1994 ed., Supp. V) provides: "In a civil action for trade dress infringement under this chapter for trade dress not registered on the principal register, the person who asserts trade dress protection has the burden of proving that the matter sought to be protected is not functional." This burden of proof gives force to the well-established rule that trade dress protection may not be claimed for product features that are functional. *Qualitex Co. v. Jacobson Products Co.*, 514 U.S. 159, 164–65 (1995); *Two Pesos, Inc. v. Taco Cabana, Inc.*, 505 U.S. 763, 775 (1992). And in *Wal–Mart, supra*, we were careful to caution against misuse or overextension of trade dress. We noted that "product design almost invariably serves purposes other than source identification." *Id.* at 213.

The principal question in this case is the effect of an expired patent on a claim of trade dress infringement. A prior patent, we conclude, has vital significance in resolving the trade dress claim. A utility patent is strong evidence that the features therein claimed are functional. If trade dress protection is sought for those features the strong evidence of functionality based on the previous patent adds great weight to the statutory presumption that features are deemed functional until proved otherwise by the party seeking trade dress protection. Where the expired patent claimed the features in question, one who seeks to establish trade dress protection must carry the heavy burden of showing that the feature is not functional, for instance by showing that it is merely an ornamental, incidental, or arbitrary aspect of the device.

In the case before us, the central advance claimed in the expired utility patents (the Sarkisian patents) is the dual-spring design; and the dual-spring design is the essential feature of the trade dress MDI now seeks to establish and to protect. The rule we have explained bars the trade dress claim, for MDI did not, and cannot, carry the burden of overcoming the strong evidentiary inference of functionality based on the disclosure of the dual-spring design in the claims of the expired patents.

The fact that the springs in this very different-looking device fall within the claims of the patents is illustrated by MDI's own position in earlier litigation. In the late 1970's, MDI engaged in a long-running intellectual property battle with a company known as Winn–Proof. Although the precise claims of the Sarkisian patents cover sign stands with springs "spaced apart," U.S. Patent No. 3,646,696, col. 4; U.S. Patent No. 3,662,482, col. 4, the Winn–Proof sign stands (with springs much like the sign stands at issue here) were found to infringe the patents by the United States District Court for the District of Oregon, and the Court of Appeals for the Ninth Circuit affirmed the judgment. *Sarkisian v. Winn–Proof Corp.*, 697 F.2d 1313 (1983). Although the Winn–Proof traffic sign stand (with dual springs close together) did not appear, then, to infringe the literal terms of the patent claims (which called for "spaced apart" springs), the Winn–Proof sign stand was found to infringe the patents under the doctrine of equivalents, which allows a finding of patent infringement even when the accused product does not fall within the literal terms of the claims. *Id.* at 1321–22. In light of this past ruling—a ruling procured at MDI's own insistence—it must be concluded the products here at issue would have been covered by the claims of the expired patents.

The rationale for the rule that the disclosure of a feature in the claims of a utility patent constitutes strong evidence of functionality is well illustrated in this case. The dual-spring design serves the important purpose of keeping the sign upright even in heavy wind conditions; and, as confirmed by the statements in the expired patents, it does so in a unique and useful manner. As the specification of one of the patents recites, prior art "devices, in practice, will topple under the force of a strong wind." U.S. Patent No. 3,662,482, col. 1. The dual-spring design allows sign stands to resist toppling in strong winds. Using a dual-spring design rather than a single spring achieves important operational advantages. For example, the specifications of the patents note that the "use of a pair of springs . . . as opposed to the use of a single spring to support the frame structure prevents canting or twisting of the sign around a vertical axis," and that, if not prevented, twisting "may cause damage to the spring structure and may result in tipping of the device." U.S. Patent No. 3,646,696, col. 3. In the course of patent prosecution, it was said that "[t]he use of a pair of spring connections as opposed to a single spring connection . . . forms an important part of this combination" because it "forc[es] the sign frame to tip along the longitudinal axis of the elongated ground-engaging members." App. 218. The dual-spring design affects the cost of the device as well; it was acknowledged that the device "could use three springs but this would unnecessarily increase the cost of the device." *Id.*, at 217. These statements made in the patent applications and in the course of procuring the patents demonstrate the functionality of the design.

III

In finding for MDI on the trade dress issue the Court of Appeals gave insufficient recognition to the importance of the expired utility patents, and their evidentiary significance, in establishing the functionality of the device. Discussing trademarks, we have said " '[i]n general terms, a product feature is functional,' and cannot serve as a trademark, 'if it is essential to the use or purpose of the article or if it affects the cost or quality of the article.' " *Qualitex*, 514 U.S. at 165 (quoting *Inwood Laboratories, Inc. v. Ives Laboratories, Inc.*, 456 U.S. 844, 850 n.10 (1982)). Expanding upon the meaning of this phrase, we have observed that a functional feature is one the "exclusive use of [which] would put competitors at a significant non-reputation-related disadvantage." 514 U.S. at 165. The Court of Appeals in the instant case seemed to interpret this language to mean that a necessary test for functionality is "whether the particular product configuration is a competitive necessity." This was incorrect as a comprehensive definition. As explained in *Qualitex*, *supra*, and *Inwood*, *supra*, a feature is also functional when it is essential to the use or purpose of the device or when it affects the cost or quality of the device. The *Qualitex* decision did not purport to displace this traditional rule. Instead, it quoted the rule as *Inwood* had set it forth. It is proper to inquire into a "significant non-reputation-related disadvantage" in cases of esthetic functionality, the question involved in *Qualitex*. Where the design is functional under the *Inwood* formulation there is no need to proceed further to consider if there is a competitive necessity for the feature. In *Qualitex* by contrast, esthetic functionality was the central question, there having been no indication that the green-gold color of the laundry press pad had any bearing on the use or purpose of the product or its cost or quality.

There is no need, furthermore, to engage, as did the Court of Appeals, in speculation about other design possibilities, such as using three or four springs which might serve the same purpose. Here, the functionality of the spring design means that competitors need not explore whether other spring juxtapositions might be used. The dual-spring design is not an arbitrary flourish in the configuration of MDI's product; it is the reason the device works. Other designs need not be attempted.

Because the dual-spring design is functional, it is unnecessary for competitors to explore designs to hide the springs, say, by using a box or framework to cover them, as suggested by the Court of Appeals. The dual-spring design assures the user the device will work. If buyers are assured the product serves its purpose by seeing the operative mechanism that in itself serves an important market need. It would be at cross-purposes to those objectives, and something of a paradox, were we to require the manufacturer to conceal the very item the user seeks.

In a case where a manufacturer seeks to protect arbitrary, incidental, or ornamental aspects of features of a product found in the patent claims, such as arbitrary curves in the legs or an ornamental pattern painted on the springs, a different result might obtain. There the manufacturer could perhaps prove that those aspects do not serve a purpose within the terms of the utility patent. The inquiry into whether such features, asserted to be trade dress, are functional by reason of their inclusion in the claims of an expired utility patent could be aided by going beyond the claims and examining the patent and its prosecution history to see if the feature in question is shown as a useful part of the invention. No such claim is made here, however. MDI in essence seeks protection for the dual-spring design alone. The asserted trade dress consists simply of the dual-spring design, four legs, a base, an upright, and a sign. MDI has pointed to nothing arbitrary about the components of its device or the way they are assembled. The Lanham Act does not exist to reward manufacturers for their innovation in creating a particular device; that is the purpose of the patent law and its period of exclusivity.

The judgment of the Court of Appeals is reversed, and the case is remanded for further proceedings consistent with this opinion.

NOTES AND QUESTIONS

1. How similar are the approaches of EU and U.S. trademark laws to protecting three-dimensional product shapes? Are there any differences?

2. *Functionality.* Should there be a concern about granting trademark protection for a part of a product that has a functional purpose? What if the

product shape serves *both* functional and ornamental purposes? Shouldn't a trademark be allowed as long as the relevant consumers associate the shape with the source of the product? Or is there a danger in allowing trademarks for things that also serve a useful function, which is typically the domain of patent law?

What is the test of functionality in *Philips*? In *TrafFix*? Under which standard, if any, would it be easier for someone to prove that a product shape is *not* functional—EU or U.S. law?

3. *Trademark v. patents*. Why did the U.S. Supreme Court in *TrafFix* discuss the patent status of the product for which trade dress protection was asserted? How is patent law relevant to a trademark issue?

4. *Colors*. The U.S. and EU take somewhat similar approaches with respect to whether a color or colors are eligible to be trademarked. In *Qualitex Co. v. Jacobson Products Co.*, 514 U.S. 159 (1995), the U.S. Supreme Court held that a color alone can fall within the broad definition of "trademark" under the Lanham Act, which "includes any word, name, symbol, or device, or any combination thereof." 15 U.S.C. § 1127. The Supreme Court noted that shapes, sounds, and fragrances had already been allowed as trademarks under U.S. law, and there was no principled basis to exclude colors. *Id.* at 162. The Court ruled that a color alone—such as the gold-green color used in Qualitex's dry cleaning press pads since the 1950s—can constitute a trademark, but *only if* the color has attained *secondary meaning* (i.e., the color identifies the source of the product in the minds of consumers). *Id.* at 163. Responding to the objection that trademarking colors would cause "color depletion," the Court said that such concerns would likely be alleviated by the functionality doctrine, which disallows a trademark for an item that is (i) "essential to the use or purpose of the article," (ii) "affects [its] cost or quality," or (iii) "if exclusive use of the feature would put competitors at a significant non-reputation-related disadvantage." *Id.* at 169.

Likewise, in *Libertel Groep BV v. Benelux–Merkenbureau*, [2003] ECR I–3793, C–104/01, the European Court of Justice held that a color in itself—such as orange for Libertel's telecommunication services—can constitute a trademark within the meaning of Article 2 of the Trademark Directive, 89/104/EEC. Just as under the U.S. approach, the color must be shown "to distinguish the goods or services concerned as originating from a particular undertaking." *Id.* ¶ 62. Moreover, the EU Directive requires that the mark be "capable of being represented graphically"—meaning that it is "clear, precise, self-contained, easily accessible, intelligible, durable and objective." *Id.* ¶¶ 9, 29. In a subsequent case, the ECJ explained the reason for this requirement: "economic operators must be able to acquaint themselves, with clarity and precision, with registrations or applications for registration made by their actual or potential competitors, and thus to obtain relevant information about the rights of third parties." *Heidelberger Bauchemie GmbH*, [2003] ECR 00, C–49/02, ¶ 30. A mere sample of the color on paper cannot satisfy this requirement because it may fade over time and is therefore not durable. *Id.* ¶¶ 31–33. However, (i) a literal description of the color could be durable enough, but whether it satisfies the other requirements of graphic representation must be judged based on the particular facts. One may also attempt to satisfy the graphic representation requirement by (ii) a combination of color sample and literal description, (iii) designation of color using an internationally recognized identification code, or (iv) a combination of the above.

The ECJ seemed more concerned about "color depletion" than the U.S. Supreme Court in *Qualitex*. The ECJ concluded "the fact that the number of colours actually available is limited means that a small number of trade mark registrations for certain services or goods could exhaust the entire range of the colours available." *Id.* ¶ 54. The ECJ admonished: "[I]n assessing the potential distinctiveness of a given colour as a trade mark, regard must be had to the general interest in not unduly restricting the availability of colours for the other traders who offer for sale goods or services of the same type as those in respect of which registration is sought." *Id.* ¶ 59.

The eligibility of color as a possible trademark, of course, does not mean that a color can automatically be trademarked. As discussed above, both the U.S. and the EU require proof that the color has become distinctive, meaning that relevant consumers associate the color with the source of the product or service.

5. *Sounds and smells.* The U.S. Supreme Court in *Qualitex* discussed with approval the decisions of the U.S. Trademark Office recognizing that a distinctive sound (NBC's three chimes) or smell (plumeria blossoms on sewing thread) may constitute a trademark under the Lanham Act. *Qualitex*, 514 U.S. at 162. In the EU, distinctive sounds can constitute a trademark, but smells cannot. The reason goes back to the requirement of graphical representation under the Trademark Directive. The ECJ has held that sounds can satisfy the graphical representation requirement (they can be written in sheet music, with "a clef, musical notes and rests whose form indicates the relative value and, where necessary, accidentals"), whereas smells cannot. *See Shield Mark BV v. Kist (trading as Memex)*, [2003] ECR I–14313, C–283/01, ¶ 62 (sounds); *Sieckmann v. Deutsches Patent-und Markenamt*, [2002] ECR I–11737, C–273/00 (smells—"in respect of an olfactory sign, the requirements of graphic representability are not satisfied by a chemical formula, by a description in written words, by the deposit of an odour sample or by a combination of those elements"). Which approach to trademarking smells do you think is better—the U.S. or the EU approach?

What about taste, such as coffee or a flavor of ice cream alleged to be distinctive of one producer? Do you think the U.S. or the EU would allow a taste to be trademarked?

6. *State emblems, official hallmarks, and emblems of intergovernmental organizations.* Article 6*ter* of the Paris Convention requires member countries to "refuse or to invalidate the registration" of "armorial bearings, flags, and other State emblems, of the countries," as well as "official signs and hallmarks indicating control and warranty adopted by them."

7. *Bibliographic note.* STEPHAN P. LADAS, PATENTS, TRADEMARKS, AND RELATED RIGHTS: NATIONAL AND INTERNATIONAL PROTECTION 974–1037 (1975); Robert Burrell & Michael Handler, *Making Sense of Trade Mark Law*, 4 I.P.Q. 388 (2003); Seiko Hidaka *et al.*, *A Sign of the Times? A Review of Key Trade Mark Decisions of the European Court of Justice and Their Impact Upon National Trade Mark Jurisprudence in the EU*, 94 TRADEMARK REP. 1105 (2004);

Catherine Seville, *Trade Mark Law: The Community's Thinking Widens and Deepens*, 53 INT'L & COMP. L.Q. 1013 (2004).

c. Other Nontraditional Marks

PROBLEM 4–9

Lamborghini is an Italian sports car manufacturer. It applies for a trademark registration in the U.S. on "the unique motion in which the door of a vehicle is opened." As depicted in the diagram in the case below, the doors move upward toward the front of the car. Should the U.S. Trademark Office consider the motion or movement of the doors within the scope of trademark subject matter and eligible for a trademark? Assume the Trademark Office has not yet considered whether motion can serve as a trademark. In *Qualitex Co. v. Jacobson Products Co.*, 514 U.S. 159 (1995), the Supreme Court held that color alone can be a trademark because "the Lanham Act describes that universe in the broadest of terms. It says that trademarks 'includ[e] any word, name, symbol, or device, or any combination thereof.' Since human beings might use as a 'symbol' or 'device' almost anything at all that is capable of carrying meaning, this language, read literally, is not restrictive." *Id.* at 1302–03. The Court ruled that as long as the color was shown to be distinctive as to source, it can serve as a trademark unless it was also functional—meaning "use of a product's feature as a trademark ... will put a competitor at a significant disadvantage because the feature is 'essential to the use or purpose of the article' or 'affects [its] cost or quality.' " *Id.* at 1306. In answering this problem, consider the analysis from *Qualitex* above, and, if you find relevant, the following decision on Lamborghini's asserted mark under the Community Trade Mark.

AUTOMOBILI LAMBORGHINI HOLDING S.P.A.'S APPLICATION

Office for Harmonisation in the Internal Market (OHIM) (First Board of Appeal).
Case R 772/2001–1 (Sept. 23, 2003) [2005] E.T.M.R. 43.

DECISION

Summary of the facts

By an application received by the Office on 26 November 1999 Automobili Lamborghini Holding S.p.A. ("the appellant") sought to register a trade mark which, under the heading "Other type of mark" in the application form, was described as "other" and depicted as follows:

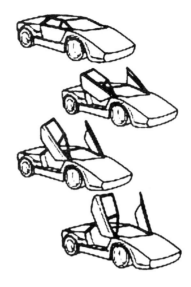

The application contained the following description: "The trademark refers to a typical and characteristic arrangement of the doors of a vehicle. For opening the doors are 'turned upwardly,' namely around a swiveling axis which is essentially arranged horizontally and transverse to the driving direction." The trademark applied for related to the following list of goods: Class 12—Automobiles and construction parts thereto; Class 28—Scale model vehicles. The application claimed priority of a trade mark applied for in Germany on 17 July 1999.

In a decision of 10 August 2001 the examiner refused the application in accordance with Art. 7(1)(b) and (e)(ii) [Community Trade Mark Regulation] CTMR. With regard to the grounds for refusal under Art. 7(1)(b) CTMR* the examiner asserted that although the arrangement of vehicle doors applied for by the appellant may well be unusual in the mass-produced car market, it nevertheless had to be taken into consideration that the door mechanism in question was also used by the appellant's competitors in the restricted market of exclusive sports cars targeted by the appellant. This was evident from the Internet printouts attached to the decision, which showed that manufacturers such as Saleen, Vector, Bugatti, McLaren, Ultima and Mercedes also offered cars with upwards-swivelling doors. The examiner also commented that the date of application was not the only relevant point in time when assessing eligibility for registration. The preconditions for registration did not just have to be in place on the date of application, but also at the end of the examination procedure. The comment that competitors only used door constructions similar to the application after the date of priority was not therefore relevant to any decision, since the door construction in question was now widely used in the relevant trade circles. The trade mark was therefore

* CTMR Article 7(1)(b) states: "The following shall not be registered: (b) trade marks which are devoid of any distinctive character." *Ed.*

not suited to acting as an allusion to a specific business establishment in the sector concerned.

As far as the grounds for refusal under Art. 7(1)(e)(ii) CTMR** were concerned, the examiner maintained that in accordance with more recent legal opinion, such as was evident for example from the final submissions of the Solicitor–General in the preliminary ruling procedure of the CJEC in Case C–299/99 (Philips v Remington), this provision was to be interpreted to the effect that any shape, the essential functional features of which were attributable only to the technical result, had to be viewed as a sign consisting solely of the shape of the product which was required to achieve a technical result, regardless of whether it was also possible to achieve this result with another shape. Even if the subject-matter for which the present application seeks protection was the movement of a car door and it was not the shape of the door itself that was applied for, it nevertheless involved the shape or technical arrangement of goods, the essential characteristic of which only served to achieve a technical result, namely the opening of a door. The protection applied for also solely involved this characteristic, since the application did not display any other distinctive elements.

On 22 August 2001 the appellant filed an appeal against this decision and set out the grounds therefore in a letter of 26 November 2001. In its statement of grounds for appeal the appellant asserts that the subject-matter of the trade mark application is "a movement mark, namely the movement of a vehicle door, which can be swivelled forward from its closed position to an open position within a perpendicular plane lying in the longitudinal direction of travel."

The Board is aware of the fact that the concept of the "movement mark" has been adopted into German trade mark legal doctrine. In his book *Markenrecht* (1997 ed.) Dr Karl–Heinz Fezer asserts that the subject-matter of the trade mark protection of a stylised movement mark as a motive mark is not only a concrete sequence of images, but also a stylised movement. A precondition of the suitability of such a motive mark to becoming a trademark as a stylised movement mark is its ability to be depicted graphically. In the case at hand the Office assumed that the trade mark applied for was graphically depicted in accordance with the regulations, since the examiner dropped the original opposition based on Art. 7(1)(a) CTMR. According to the contested decision, the application was rejected solely on the basis of Art. 7(1)(b) and (e)(ii) CTMR.

Re grounds for refusal of Art. 7(1)(e)(ii) CTMR

In its statement of grounds for appeal the appellant argues that the grounds for refusal of Art. 7(1)(e) CTMR cannot apply, since this provision refers explicitly and exclusively to trademarks that consist of the shape of the goods, and the trade mark applied for does not consist of the shape of the goods in question. The Board of Appeal is not convinced by this formal

---

** CTRM Article 7(1)(e)(ii) states: "The following shall not be registered: e) signs which consist exclusively of: (ii) the shape of goods which is necessary to obtain a technical result."

argument. According to the appellant's depiction, the trademark consists of a movement, namely of a forwards and upwards swivelling of the doors. The trademark is therefore necessarily three-dimensional in nature, and if it is not based on a specific shape amounts to nothing more than a characteristic mechanical movement which in the opinion of the Board equates to a technical function of a car door.

In its judgment of 18 June 2002 in Case C–299/99, Koninklijke Philips Electronics NV v Remington Consumer Products Ltd, the Court of Justice of the European Communities stated with regard to Art. 3(1)(e), second indent, of the First Council Directive to approximate the laws of the Member States relating to trade marks, the content of which corresponds to that of Art. 7(1)(e), second indent CTMR, that the provision is intended to preclude "the registration of shapes whose essential characteristics perform a technical function, with the result that the exclusivity inherent in the trademark right would limit the possibility of competitors supplying a product incorporating such a function or at least limit their freedom of choice in regard to the technical solution they wish to adopt in order to incorporate such a function in their product" (at [79] of the judgment). The Board is of the opinion that the principle expressed here does not only apply to "shapes whose essential characteristics perform a technical function," but also, indeed a fortiori, to the actual arrangement of such a technical function. The provisions of Art. 7(1)(e) CTMR do explicitly refer to trade marks consisting of the shape of the product. It is not, however, disputed that this wording refers to the category of "three-dimensional trademarks." Thus, in para. 8.6 of the Examination Guidelines published by the OHIM (O.J. OHIM 9/96, p. 1308), which is devoted to Art. 7(1)(e) CTMR, the Office refers to the "three-dimensional trademark" meant by this provision. The opinion expressed by the examiner in the contested decision that the trademark applied for by the appellant is subject to the provision of Art. 7(1)(e)(ii) CTMR therefore does not appear nonsensical, since by its very nature the trade mark applied for unmistakably represents a three-dimensional sign. This is evident from the fact that the sign can only be perceived if the door of the goods thus characterised is actually swivelled.

In the opinion of the Board, the movement of the doors of a vehicle applied for by the appellant belongs to the "technical solutions or functional characteristics" mentioned by the Court, which under Art. 7(1)(e) CTMR are precluded from trade mark protection, in the same way as, for example, a functional movement when opening the roof of a cabriolet would be.

The Court emphasises in this connection that the provisions under discussion reflect the legitimate aim of not allowing individuals to use registration of a mark in order to acquire or perpetuate exclusive rights to technical solutions.

Re grounds for refusal of Art. 7(1)(b) CTMR

As far as the grounds for refusal under Art. 7(1)(b) CTMR also used by the examiner as a basis for his decision are concerned, the opinion of the appellant must first be confirmed that, first, the goods and services applied for and secondly, the perception by the relevant trade circles are to be taken into account when examining the distinctive character of a trade mark.

In the contested decision the examiner maintained that several competitors in the automobile sector offer cars with upwards-swivelling doors, and that the use of upwards-swivelling doors was a particularly normal feature in the market of high-performance sports cars. In that observation of 4 December 2000 the examiner literally stated: "Car doors which open by swivelling upwards are also used by other manufacturers (*e.g.* BMW Z9 Gran Turismo, Mercedes–Benz Vision SLR Roadster)". In so doing the examiner had not only indicated that several references were available, but that it must be assumed that the development of competitors' models on the specialised market of high-performance sports cars was fully known to the appellant.

With regard to the examiner's argument that upwards-swivelling car doors were also used by other manufacturers, the appellant first responded in its observation of 11 January 2001 that it was correct that doors opening in this way had been known since the 1950s—and had at that time been labelled "gull-wing doors"—but that the previous doors swivelled about an axis arranged in the driving direction, whereas the trade mark application involved a swivelling axis arranged transverse to the driving direction. This unusual type of swivelling axis arrangement had previously been used on only two other models, namely from the makes Bugatti and Audi, which both belonged to the same group of companies as the appellant, before the application's date of priority. The Mercedes Benz Vision alluded to by the examiner was only introduced to the public after the date of priority. In its statement of grounds for appeal the appellant also points out that the contested decision did not address this last argument.

The appellant also argues in its statement of grounds for appeal that the models referred to by the examiner in the contested decision are all, with the exception of the Bugatti, prototypes, which are therefore unavailable on the market and had therefore remained previously unknown even to the appellant. Finally, the appellant submits a press article from the Handelsblatt of 1 November 2001 which is devoted to presenting the new Lamborghini "Murciélago" model, and in which the description of the characteristics of the vehicle explicitly states: "Like its predecessor, the opening of the upwards-swivelling gull-wing doors is spectacular." This is a further indication that the unusual quality of the swivelling door movement on which the trade mark application is based has been preserved until now.

The Board would first like to emphasise that the examiner did indeed address the objection raised by the appellant that one of the car models alluded to by the examiner had only appeared after the date of priority of the application. The examiner adopted the following stance in this respect in the contested decision: "The decisive point in time when assessing the eligibility of a trade mark for registration is not solely the date of application. The application must have been eligible for registration on the date of application, but the preconditions for registration must also be in place at the end of the examination procedure."

Moreover, in its observation of 11 January 2001, the appellant explicitly confirmed the examiner's conclusion that car doors which opened by swivelling upwards were also used by other manufacturers. The appellant even added that such doors had been used on the Mercedes 300 SL in the 1950s. Furthermore, in the contested decision the examiner referred to five other manufacturers that also offer cars with upwards-swivelling doors. Based on these facts the Board concludes that upwards-swivelling car doors are perceived by the relevant trade circles as a characteristic feature of a category of (sports) cars and not as a trade mark of a particular manufacturer of these cars.

With regard to the appellant's assertion that the relevant trade circles still associate the door movement under discussion with Lamborghinis, the Board wishes to point out that the website submitted by the examiner and devoted to the Saleen not only states, as the appellant emphasises, that the car resembles a Lamborghini Diablo, but also contains a photo of a Saleen with open doors, with the legend: "Like the famous Mercedes–Benz Gullwings, the doors of the Saleen cantilever skyward when opened."

In the Board's opinion, the subject of the application, as defined by the appellant in the description applied for, is therefore devoid of the distinctive character required under Art. 7(1)(b) CTMR. Accordingly, the contested decision is to be upheld and the appeal dismissed.

NOTES AND QUESTIONS

1. What was the unusual way in which Lamborghini's car doors opened? How was it different from other cars with upward-opening doors?

2. On what basis did OHIM refuse to grant a registration for Lamborghini's car door motion mark? Based on the ruling, can motion ever be trademarked under the Community Trade Mark?

3. *What is a motion mark?* OHIM's Board of Appeal spent much attention dissecting what the claimed mark was. Lamborghini argued that its intended mark was motion, but not the shape of its doors, and therefore the limitations of functionality of shapes in Article 7(1)(e) of the Community Trade Mark Regulation simply did not apply. How did OHIM resolve the issue?

4. *Functionality.* Did the existence of alternative and more popular ways to open a car door make the unusual motion of Lamborghini's car door not functional? Was OHIM's decision similar to the U.S. Supreme Court's analysis of the issue in *TrafFix* above?

5. Why did OHIM consider the car industry's use of upward-opening doors *after* the date of priority claimed by Lamborghini? If Lamborghini could establish the distinctiveness of its door motion by the priority date, wouldn't competitors' subsequent doors adopting the same motion be infringing? Should OHIM also have considered that third-party vendors who sell and install "kit" parts for cars commonly refer to this upward-opening style of door as "Lambo doors"?

d. Generic Marks

PROBLEM 4–10

MegaFoods Corp. has applied to register various trademarks with the USPTO using words from the language of the Togu tribe, who live contentedly with few material possessions on an obscure and insular island nation in the South Pacific. No member of tribe has left the island in over thirty years, and there is no Internet access or modern telecommunications system. The Togu tribe speaks an ancient language that is based on pictograms and uses no alphabet. The pictograms that MegaFoods would like to register as marks from the Togu language are the Togu pictograms and their transliterations for "water," "mineral" and "spring" for a new line of spring mineral water to be marketed as a sports drink. MegaFoods maintains that no one in the United States has even heard of the Togu tribe, so these pictograms are arbitrary in the English language. Should the USPTO issue the trademarks? Would your answer change if the ancient Togu language had become an essentially "dead" language in Togu that was understood and studied only by a few linguistic professors at the local university after the Togu tribe had adopted English as its standard language? See the case below and the accompanying notes.

OTOKOYAMA CO. LTD. v. WINE OF JAPAN IMPORT, INC.

U.S. Court of Appeals for the Second Circuit.
175 F.3d 266 (2d Cir. 1999).

LEVAL, CIRCUIT JUDGE:

This is a trademark dispute between two importers of Japanese sake. Otokoyama Co. Ltd., the registered owner of four U.S. trademarks for the word "otokoyama" and Japanese language pictograms signifying that word, filed suit against Wine of Japan Import, Inc., alleging, *inter alia*, that defendant infringed its trademark in violation of the Lanham Act, 15 U.S.C. § 1051 *et seq.,* by importing a brand of sake labelled "Mutsu Otokoyama." Defendant counterclaimed, seeking to cancel plaintiff's trademarks under § 14 of the Lanham Act, 15 U.S.C. § 1064. Defendant contended that 1) otokoyama is a generic term signifying a type of sake and is therefore ineligible for trademark protection, and 2) plaintiff's trademarks were "obtained fraudulently" within the meaning of 15 U.S.C. § 1064(3).

After a hearing, the district court granted plaintiff's motion for a preliminary injunction. On appeal from that order, defendant argues that the district court erred when it refused to consider evidence of the meaning and usage of otokoyama in Japan and refused to consider a ruling of the Japanese trademark office denying plaintiff's application for trademark protection on the ground that otokoyama is generic. We agree that the district court erred in both respects. Applying the correct legal standard and crediting defendant with the improperly excluded evidence, we find that defendant raises sufficient doubt as to the validity of plaintiff's trademark to overcome plaintiff's showing of likelihood of success. We therefore vacate the preliminary injunction.

Background

Plaintiff, a Japanese corporation, has been brewing sake—a Japanese wine made from fermented rice—on the northern island of Hokkaido since the 1930s. In Japan, its sake is sold under the name "Hokkai Otokoyama," Hokkai being a reference to the island of Hokkaido. Since 1984, plaintiff has imported its sake into the U.S., where it is marketed and sold as "Otokoyama" brand sake. Plaintiff registered the English transliteration of otokoyama and three trademarks of Japanese pictograms comprising otokoyama with the U.S. Trademark Office.

Defendant is a domestic corporation, which imports various brands of sake into the U.S. Defendant's importation and sale of sake under the designation "Mutsu Otokoyama," begun in or around 1997, is the subject of this suit. As noted, plaintiff claims the defendant's use of otokoyama infringes plaintiff's trademark, while defendant claims that because otokoyama is a generic word for a type of sake, it is not eligible for use as a trademark for sake.

In Japanese pictograms, the word otokoyama is comprised of the characters for "man" and "mountain." The parties dispute the meaning and history of the word in relation to sake, but they agree that its use in Japan in relation to sake dates back at least to the Edo period, which began in the seventeenth century. Paintings from the period show samurai warriors drinking from sake barrels displaying the characters for otokoyama. In Japan, between ten and twenty brewers in addition to plaintiff designate sake as "otokoyama," often (like plaintiff) adding a geographical modifier.

Plaintiff has been unsuccessful in its attempts to obtain trademark rights in Japan for otokoyama. In 1962 (then doing business under the name Yamazaki Shuzo K.K.) plaintiff sought to register the characters for "Hokkai Otokoyama" as a trademark in Japan. The application was rejected, and in 1966 the Japanese Patent Office ("JPO") affirmed the rejection. The JPO issued a written decision, whose exact translation is disputed, but which apparently signified that the word otokoyama was not eligible for trademark protection because of its longstanding use as a designation for sake by other traders in the industry.

In 1984, plaintiff became the first company to market sake labelled otokoyama in the United States. Two years later, plaintiff petitioned the United States Patent and Trademark Office ("USPTO") to register the Kanji characters for otokoyama. In processing plaintiff's application, the USPTO asked plaintiff to provide an English translation of the characters. Plaintiff responded with a sworn statement that "to applicant's knowledge, the mark is an arbitrary, fanciful term. Accordingly, the mark cannot be translated." The USPTO granted plaintiff's request to register the mark in 1988.

Between 1992 and 1995, plaintiff sought and obtained U.S. registrations for three other otokoyama trademarks: one each for the Katakana and Hiragana[2] characters for otokoyama, and one for the English transliteration. Again the USPTO asked for English translations, to which plaintiff again responded in sworn declarations that otokoyama is "an arbitrary, fanciful" term that "has no meaning and cannot be translated."

In April, 1997, plaintiff wrote to defendant demanding that it cease importation, distribution, advertisement and sale of "Mutsu Otokoyama." Defendant replied that it believed plaintiff's trademarks were invalid, and refused.

Plaintiff filed suit, alleging trademark infringement, unfair competition, and false designation of origin under the Lanham Act, as well as state law violations, and moved for a preliminary injunction. At the preliminary injunction hearing, the court declined to consider any meaning the word otokoyama might have outside the United States, stating that "[t]he meaning of a term outside of the United States is irrelevant" to a determination of entitlement to the protection of the U.S. trademark laws. The court also declined to consider defendant's proffer of the 1966 decision of the Japanese Patent Office which denied plaintiff's request to register otokoyama in Japan. Concluding that plaintiff had shown both irreparable harm and likelihood of success on the merits, the court granted the preliminary injunction.

Discussion

I.

It is a bedrock principle of the trademark law that no trader may acquire the exclusive right to the use of a term by which the covered goods or services are designated in the language. Such a term is "generic." Generic terms are not eligible for protection as trademarks; everyone may use them to refer to the goods they designate. This rule protects the interest of the consuming public in understanding the nature of goods offered for sale, as well as a fair marketplace among competitors by insuring that every provider may refer to his goods as what they are.

The same rule applies when the word designates the product in a language other than English. This extension rests on the assumption that

---

2. Katakana, Hiragana, and Kanji are apparently three different writing systems in the Japanese language.

there are (or someday will be) customers in the United States who speak that foreign language. Because of the diversity of the population of the United States, coupled with temporary visitors, all of whom are part of the United States marketplace, commerce in the United States utilizes innumerable foreign languages. No merchant may obtain the exclusive right over a trademark designation if that exclusivity would prevent competitors from designating a product as what it is in the foreign language their customers know best. Courts and the USPTO apply this policy, known as the doctrine of "foreign equivalents," to make generic foreign words ineligible for private ownership as trademarks. *See Weiss Noodle*, 290 F.2d at 846–47 (applying ban on trademarking generic names to foreign equivalents, and holding that "ha-lush-ka," phonetic spelling of Hungarian word for "egg noodles," is non-protectible); *see also In re Le Sorbet, Inc.*, 228 U.S.P.Q. 27, 28 (T.T.A.B. 1985) ("sorbet," French word for fruit ice, held non-protectible); *In re Hag Aktiengesellschaft*, 155 U.S.P.Q. 598, 599–600 ("kaba," coffee in Serbian and Ukranian, held non-protectible).

This rule, furthermore, does not apply only to words that designate an entire species. Generic words for sub-classifications or varieties of a good are similarly ineligible for trademark protection. *See, e.g., Genesee Brewing Co., Inc. v. Stroh Brewing Co.*, 124 F.3d 137, 148–49 (2d Cir. 1997) ("honey brown" held generic for type of ale); *In re Cooperativa Produttori Latte E Fontina Valle D'Acosta*, 230 U.S.P.Q. 131, 134 (T.T.A.B. 1986) ("fontina" held generic for a type of cheese); *In re Northland Aluminum Prods.*, 221 U.S.P.Q. 1110, 1112 (T.T.A.B. 1984) ("bundt" held generic for variety of ring-shaped coffee cake), *aff'd*, 777 F.2d 1556, 1561 (Fed. Cir. 1985); *Italian Swiss Colony v. Italian Vineyard Co.*, 158 Cal. 252, 257 ("tipo" held generic Italian word for a chianti wine). A word may also be generic by virtue of its association with a particular region, cultural movement, or legend. *See Holland v. C. & A. Import Corp.*, 8 F. Supp. 259, 260 (S.D.N.Y. 1934) ("Est Est Est" held generic for wine from Italy's Montefiascone region); *In re Ricci–Italian Silversmiths, Inc.*, 16 U.S.P.Q.2d 1727, 1729 (T.T.A.B. 1990) ("art deco" held generic for flatware made in design style introduced at L'Exposition Internationale des Arts Decoratifs et Industriels Modernes in Paris); *In re Bauhaus Designs Canada Ltd.*, 12 U.S.P.Q.2d 2001, 2003 (T.T.A.B. 1989) ("Bauhaus" held generic for style of furniture developed at Germany's Bauhaus school of design); *see also* Restatement (Third) of Unfair Competition, § 15 cmt. a.

The defendant contended in the district court that the word "otokoyama" falls within the generic category. It claimed that in Japanese, otokoyama has long been understood as designating a variety of "dry, manly sake" that originated more than 300 years ago. The district court, however, declined to accord any significance to the Japanese meaning of the word. The court stated that the Japanese meaning of otokoyama is "irrelevant to the U.S. PTO's determination of [plaintiff's] trademark rights.... [T]he meaning of the term 'otokoyama' in Japan is not relevant to this action."

For the reasons explained above, this was error. If otokoyama in Japanese signifies a type of sake, and one United States merchant were given the exclusive right to use that word to designate its brand of sake, competing merchants would be prevented from calling their product by the word which designates that product in Japanese. Any Japanese-speaking customers and others who are familiar with the Japanese terminology would be misled to believe that there is only one brand of otokoyama available in the United States.

The meaning of otokoyama in Japanese, and particularly whether it designates sake, or a type or category of sake, was therefore highly relevant to whether plaintiff may assert the exclusive right to use that word as a mark applied to sake. Defendant should have been allowed to introduce evidence of otokoyama's meaning and usage in Japan to support its claim that the mark is generic and therefore ineligible for protection as a trademark. In light of this error, the district court's finding that plaintiff is likely to succeed on the merits cannot be sustained.

II.

Defendant also challenges the district court's exclusion of the ruling of the Japanese Patent Office denying plaintiff trademark rights in Japan. The district court, citing *Vanity Fair Mills, Inc. v. T. Eaton Co.*, 234 F.2d 633, 639 (2d Cir. 1956), ruled that the JPO decision was irrelevant. We disagree.

We disagree first with the district court's understanding of the precedent it cited. It is true that a claimant's rights (or lack of rights) to a trademark in the United States cannot be established by the fact that the claimant was found by a foreign court to have (or not to have) rights over the same mark in a foreign country. That is what the *Vanity Fair* opinion meant by its broad statement to the effect that "the decisions of foreign courts concerning the respective trade-mark rights of the parties are irrelevant and inadmissible." *Id.* at 639. It does not follow, however, that foreign court decisions are *never* relevant or admissible for any purpose in a U.S. trademark dispute. Indeed, as authority for the quoted proposition, the *Vanity Fair* opinion cited our ruling in *George W. Luft Co. v. Zande Cosmetic Co.*, 142 F.2d 536, 539 (2d Cir. 1944), which ruled that foreign decisions *were* relevant and admissible. In *Luft,* the defendant offered various foreign registrations of the disputed mark to prove that the defendants might lawfully use the mark within the foreign country that granted the registration. The district court had excluded them in reliance on *City of Carlsbad v. Kutnow*, 68 F. 794 (S.D.N.Y.), *aff'd,* 71 F. 167 (2d Cir. 1895). The *Luft* Court pointed out that in *Carlsbad,* "the purpose of introducing the English registration was to prove that the defendants were privileged to use [the mark] on sales in the United States. *On this issue* a foreign trade-mark was rightly held irrelevant, for clearly the English law could not confer [a trademark right] which our courts were bound to recognize." 142 F.2d at 539 (emphasis added). The opinion goes on, however, to say "We do not think that the *Carlsbad* case controls the case at bar." *Id.* Because "the purpose of offering the foreign registrations was not to establish the privilege of using the [mark] in the United States but to prove that the defendants might lawfully use it within the foreign country which granted the registration," *id.,* the court found that the foreign decisions were relevant and admissible and the district court had erred in failing to consider them.

Whether a foreign decision is relevant in a trademark case in our courts depends on the purpose for which it is offered. The fact that a litigant has been awarded or denied rights over a mark in a foreign country ordinarily does not determine its entitlement to the mark in the United States. The foreign court decision is not admissible if that is the purpose of the offer. But if, as in *Luft,* the foreign decision is competent evidence of a relevant fact, it is relevant and admissible to prove that fact.

Defendant offered the decision of the JPO for two purposes. First, it was offered to prove the fact assertedly found by the JPO that the word otokoyama in Japanese refers to a type or class of sake. Second, it was offered as evidence supporting defendant's claim that plaintiff committed fraud on the trademark office in the prosecution of its application for registration. The theory of this offer was to show plaintiff's awareness that the word otokoyama was not an "arbitrary, fanciful term ... [that] cannot be translated," as plaintiff represented to the trademark examiner. Both purposes are relevant to defendant's claims. It was error to exclude the JPO decision on grounds of relevance.

Our reversal of the preliminary injunction awarded to plaintiff should not be construed as an indication that defendant should necessarily prevail on the merits. The question whether otokayama is a generic term for sake or a type of sake in the Japanese language will turn on the strength of the evidence defendant presents at trial once given the opportunity. The evidence defendant sought unsuccessfully to introduce at the preliminary injunction hearing was sufficient to undermine plaintiff's likelihood of success on the merits, but was not necessarily sufficient to carry the defendant's burden of proving that otokoyama is generic. The preliminary injunction in plaintiff's favor is hereby vacated. The case is remanded for trial.

NOTES AND QUESTIONS

1.   What defines when a mark has become generic? Why does trademark law forbid individuals from claiming rights to generic marks? What policy is served by such a doctrine?

2.   Why is the generic status of a mark in a foreign country relevant to whether the mark can be registered in the United States, according to the Second Circuit? Is this a departure from the principle of territoriality? What if the mark otokoyama was shown to be *not* generic in the U.S., *and* the public associated it with Otokoyama Company's product? Would Otokoyama be entitled to the mark in the U.S. under the Second Circuit's ruling? Should it be?

3. Is the doctrine of foreign equivalents under U.S. law inconsistent or at least in tension with Paris Convention Article 6, which requires the independent treatment of the same mark registered in different countries?

4. *Problem of genericide.* The issue of the genericness of a mark can arise in two situations: (i) in the first instance, when an individual is seeking to use for the first time a mark that is already generic (as alleged in *Otokoyama*); and (ii) later, after a mark has been validly used or registered, a valid mark may *become generic* if the public uses the mark primarily—such as "yoyo," "thermos," and "nylon,"—to describe the *type* of product, not its source. In theory, no valid trademark is immune from the possibility of becoming generic one day. It all depends on how the public uses the mark—as a source identifier or a generic term. That is why trademark holders often spend considerable resources "policing" their marks, not only to stop infringement but also to prevent *genericide*, or the loss of rights to their mark through the public's use of it as a generic term.

5. *Generic marks under Paris and TRIPS.* Although neither the Paris Convention nor the TRIPS Agreement expressly mentions the term "generic" or "generic mark," the concept is described as one of the bases on which countries may deny or invalidate a mark under the *telle quelle* provision. Article 6*quinquies* of the Paris Convention states in relevant part: trademarks may be denied "when they are devoid of any distinctive character, or consist exclusively of signs or indications which may serve, in trade, to designate the kind . . . of the goods, . . . or have become customary in the current language or in the bona fide and established practices of the trade of the country where protection is claimed." Paris Conv. art. 6*quinquies*(B)(2). The concept of "customary" is often used interchangeably with generic. *Cf.* TRIPS art. 24(6) (member countries may deny protection for geographical indications that are "identical with the term customary in common language as the common name for such goods or services in the territory of that Member"). Does Article 6*quinquies* require Paris countries to deny protection for generic marks?

TRIPS Article 15 also speaks to generic marks, at least tacitly. Article 15 recognizes trademark subject matter for "[a]ny sign, or any combination of signs, capable of distinguishing the goods or services of one undertaking from those of other undertakings." TRIPS art. 15(1). Does Article 15 forbid countries from allowing trademarks for generic marks? Or should it be understood as a minimum standard requiring countries to protect, at the very least, marks that are "capable of distinguishing the goods or services of one undertaking," but allowing discretion to protect generic marks?

5. EXCLUSIVE RIGHTS

a. General Approach for Trademarks

Trademark infringement is typically shown by proof that the defendant's use of a mark is "likely to cause confusion" with the plaintiff's mark for which the plaintiff has priority. TRIPS Article 16(1) codifies that standard. The following discussion analyzes the EU's test for likelihood of confusion.

TRIPS

Article 16(1)

1. The owner of a registered trademark shall have the exclusive right to prevent all third parties not having the owner's consent from using in the course of trade identical or similar signs for goods or services which are identical or similar to those in respect of which the trademark is registered where such use would result in a likelihood of confusion. In case of the use of an identical sign for identical goods or services, a likelihood of confusion shall be presumed. The rights described above shall not prejudice any existing prior rights, nor shall they affect the possibility of Members making rights available on the basis of use.

EC Trade Marks Directive (89/104/EEC)

Article 5(1)

1. The registered trade mark shall confer on the proprietor exclusive rights therein. The proprietor shall be entitled to prevent all third parties not having his consent from using in the course of trade:

a. any sign which is identical with the trade mark in relation to goods or services which are identical with those for which the trade mark is registered;

b. any sign where, because of its identity with, or similarity to, the trade mark and the identity or similarity of the goods or services covered by the trade mark and the sign, there exists a likelihood of confusion on the part of the public, which includes the likelihood of association between the sign and the trade mark.

SABEL BV v. PUMA AG

European Court of Justice.
[1997] ECR I–6191, Case C–251/95 (November 11, 1997).

Grounds

By order of 29 June 1995, received at the Court on 20 July 1995, the Bundesgerichtshof (Federal Court of Justice) referred to the Court for a preliminary ruling under Article 177 of the EC Treaty a question on the interpretation of Article 4(1)(b) of First Council Directive 89/104/EEC of 21 December 1988 to approximate the laws of the Member States relating to trade marks (OJ 1989 L 40, p. 1, hereinafter "the Directive").That question was raised in proceedings between the Dutch company SABEL BV (hereinafter "SABEL") and the German company Puma AG, Rudolf Dassler Sport (hereinafter "Puma") concerning an application to register the IR mark 540 894, depicted below,

in Germany, inter alia for goods in classes 18 "Leather and imitation leather, products made therefrom not included in other classes bags and handbags" and 25 "Clothing, including tights, hosiery, belts, scarves, ties/cravats and braces footwear hats."

Puma lodged opposition to the registration of that mark on the ground, in particular, that it was the proprietor of the pictorial mark depicted below,

which was of earlier priority and registered in Germany (under No 1 106 066), inter alia for "leather and imitation leather, goods made therefrom (bags) and articles of clothing."

The Deutsches Patentamt (German Patent Office) considered there to be no resemblance for the purposes of trade-mark law between the two marks and rejected the opposition. Puma therefore appealed to the Bundespatentgericht (Federal Patents Court) which partially upheld its application and held that there was a resemblance between the two marks with respect to SABEL's goods in classes 18 and 25, which it regarded as being identical or similar to the goods on the list of articles covered by the Puma mark. SABEL then appealed to the Bundesgerichtshof for annulment of the decision refusing its application.

The Bundesgerichtshof provisionally considered that, applying the principles applied hitherto under German law for determining whether there is a likelihood of confusion for trade-mark purposes, no such likelihood existed as regards the two marks in question.

Nonetheless, the Bundesgerichtshof seeks to ascertain the importance to be accorded to the semantic content of the marks (in the present case, a "bounding feline") in determining the likelihood of confusion. That difficulty is occasioned, in particular, by the ambiguous wording of Article 4(1)(b) of the Directive, in terms of which the likelihood of confusion "includes the likelihood of association with the earlier trade mark." The question therefore arises for the national court whether the mere association which the public might make between the two marks, through the idea of a "bounding feline," justifies refusing protection to the SABEL mark in Germany for products similar to those on the list of articles covered by Puma's priority mark.

The Directive, which was implemented in Germany by the Gesetz uber den Schutz von Marken und sonstigen Kennzeichen (Law on the Protection of Trade Marks and Other Signs) of 25 October 1994 (BGBl I, p. 3082), contains, in Article 4(1)(b), the following provision:

> "A trade mark shall not be registered or, if registered, shall be liable to be declared invalid:
>
> (a) . . .
>
> (b) if because of its identity with, or similarity to, the earlier trade mark and the identity or similarity of the goods or services covered by the trade marks, there exists a likelihood of confusion on the part of the public, which includes the likelihood of association with the earlier trade mark."

The Bundesgerichtshof decided to stay proceedings and to refer the following question to the Court for a preliminary ruling[.] In its question the Bundesgerichtshof is essentially asking whether the criterion of the "likelihood of confusion . . . which includes the likelihood of association with the earlier trade mark" contained in Article 4(1)(b) of the Directive is to be interpreted as meaning that the mere association which the public might make between the two marks as a result of a resemblance in their semantic content, is a sufficient ground for concluding that there exists a likelihood of confusion within the meaning of that provision, taking into account that one of those marks is composed of a combination of a word and a picture, whilst the other, consisting merely of a picture, is registered for identical and similar goods, and is not especially well known to the public.

Article 4(1)(b) of the Directive, which sets out the additional grounds on which registration may be refused or a registered mark declared invalid in the event of conflict with earlier marks, provides that a trade mark conflicts with an earlier trade mark if, because of the identity or similarity of both the trade marks and the goods or services covered, there exists a likelihood of confusion on the part of the public, which includes the likelihood of association between the two marks.

The Belgian, Luxembourg and Netherlands Governments claimed that the term "likelihood of association" was included in those provisions of the Directive at their request, in order that they should be construed in the same manner as Article 13a of the Uniform Benelux Law on Trade Marks which adopts the concept of resemblance between marks, rather than that of likelihood of confusion, in defining the scope of the exclusive right conferred by a trade mark.

Those governments refer to a judgment of the Benelux Court holding that there is resemblance between a mark and a sign when, taking account of the particular circumstances of the case, in particular the distinctiveness of the mark, the mark and the sign, considered separately and together, present, aurally, visually or conceptually, a similarity such as to establish an association between the sign and the mark (judgment of 20 May 1983 in Case A 82/5 Jullien v Verschuere, Jur. 1983, vol. 4, p. 36). That decision is based on the idea that, where a sign is likely to give rise to association with a mark, the public makes a connection between the sign and the mark. Such a connection may be prejudicial to the earlier mark not only if it gives the impression that the products have the same or a related origin, but also where there is no likelihood of confusion between the sign and the mark. Since perception of the sign calls to mind, often subconsciously, the memory of the mark, associations made between a sign and a mark can result in the "goodwill" attached to the earlier mark being transferred to the sign and dilute the image linked to that mark.

It must therefore be determined whether, as those governments claim, Article 4(1)(b) can apply where there is no likelihood of direct or indirect confusion, but only a likelihood of association in the strict sense. Such an interpretation of the Directive is contested by both the United Kingdom Government and by the Commission.

In that connection, it is to be remembered that Article 4(1)(b) of the Directive is designed to apply only if, by reason of the identity or similarity both of the marks and of the goods or services which they designate, "there exists a likelihood of confusion on the part of the public, which includes the likelihood of association with the earlier trade mark." It follows from that wording that the concept of likelihood of association is not an alternative to that of likelihood of confusion, but serves to define its scope. The terms of the provision itself exclude its application where there is no likelihood of confusion on the part of the public.

Furthermore, the interpretation given in paragraph 18 of this judgment is not inconsistent with Article 4(3) and (4)(a) and Article 5(2) of the Directive, which permit the proprietor of a trade mark which has a reputation to prohibit the use without due cause of signs identical with or similar to his mark and do not require proof of likelihood of confusion, even where there is no similarity between the goods in question.

In that respect, it is sufficient to note that, unlike Article 4(1)(b), those provisions apply exclusively to marks which have a reputation and on condition that use of the third party's mark without due cause takes unfair advantage of, or is detrimental to, the distinctive character or the repute of the trade mark.

Article 4(1)(b) of the Directive does not apply where there is no likelihood of confusion on the part of the public. In that respect, it is clear from the tenth recital in the preamble to the Directive that the appreciation of the likelihood of confusion "depends on numerous elements and, in particular, on the recognition of the trade mark on the market, of the association which can be made with the used or registered sign, of the degree of similarity between the trade mark and the sign and between the goods or services identified." The likelihood of confusion must therefore be appreciated globally, taking into account all factors relevant to the circumstances of the case.

That global appreciation of the visual, aural or conceptual similarity of the marks in question, must be based on the overall impression given by the marks, bearing in mind, in particular, their distinctive and dominant components. The wording of Article 4(1)(b) of the Directive— "... there exists a likelihood of confusion on the part of the public ..." — shows that the perception of marks in the mind of the average consumer of the type of goods or services in question plays a decisive role in the global appreciation of the likelihood of confusion. The average consumer normally perceives a mark as a whole and does not proceed to analyse its various details.

In that perspective, the more distinctive the earlier mark, the greater will be the likelihood of confusion. It is therefore not impossible that the conceptual similarity resulting from the fact that two marks use images with analogous semantic content may give rise to a likelihood of confusion where the earlier mark has a particularly distinctive character, either per se or because of the reputation it enjoys with the public.

However, in circumstances such as those in point in the main proceedings, where the earlier mark is not especially well known to the public and consists of an image with little imaginative content, the mere fact that the two marks are conceptually similar is not sufficient to give rise to a likelihood of confusion.

The answer to the national court's question must therefore be that the criterion of "likelihood of confusion which includes the likelihood of association with the earlier mark" contained in Article 4(1)(b) of the Directive is to be interpreted as meaning that the mere association which the public might make between two trade marks as a result of their analogous semantic content is not in itself a sufficient ground for concluding that there is a likelihood of confusion within the meaning of that provision.

NOTES AND QUESTIONS

1. *Likelihood of confusion.* Article 16 of TRIPS recognizes the well-accepted standard of "likelihood of confusion" as the test for trademark infringement. Article 16 further states that "[i]n case of the use of an identical sign for identical goods or services, a likelihood of confusion shall be presumed." TRIPS art. 16(1). Why should likelihood of confusion be the standard, and not *actual* confusion by consumers? Are trademark holders harmed if there is only a likelihood of confusion, but no actual confusion by consumers? Does the likelihood of confusion standard allow for unsubstantiated speculation by courts or juries?

2. *EU Approach.* When the EC Trade Mark Directive was ratified, some thought that one could prove a likelihood of confusion by showing "the likelihood of association between the sign [in question] and the trade mark." How does the Court of Justice resolve that issue? Is proof of likelihood of association enough to establish likelihood of confusion? What factors must a court consider under the CJEU's approach to likelihood of confusion? What do you think the Court meant in stating that likelihood of confusion must be "appreciated globally"?

When we discuss trademark dilution in the following section, we will revisit the notion of protecting against certain types of mental associations created by a mark similar or identical to a famous mark; for dilution, likelihood of confusion is not required.

3. Did the CJEU's ruling appear to help or hurt Puma's chances of prevailing in its opposition of Sabel's trademark?

4. *Comparison with U.S. approach.* How different are the factors the Court of Justice considers to be relevant for analyzing likelihood of confusion from the "Polaroid" factors relied upon by many U.S. courts in analyzing the issue under U.S. law? The Polaroid factors are: (1) the strength of the senior mark; (2) the degree of similarity between the two marks; (3) the proximity of the products; (4) the likelihood that the prior owner will "bridge the gap"; (5) actual confusion; (6) the defendant's good faith or bad faith in adopting its own mark; (7) the quality of defendant's product; and (8) the sophistication of the buyers. *Polaroid Corp. v. Polarad Electronics Corp.*, 287 F.2d 492, 495 (2d Cir. 1961); *see also* Barton Beebe, *An Empirical Study of the Multifactor Tests for Trademark Infringement*, 94 CAL. L. REV. 1581 (2006).

In the U.S., likelihood of confusion is typically proven with the aid of elaborate consumer surveys conducted by survey firms, usually at great expense to any party that hires them. Do you think there is any better way of establishing likelihood of confusion other than a survey? If not, would you make a survey a requirement of proof?

5. *Bibliographic note.* Ann Bartow, *Likelihood of Confusion*, 41 SAN DIEGO L. REV. 721 (2004) (critiquing U.S. law); Seiko Hidaka *et al.*, *A Sign of the Times? A Review of Key Trade Mark Decisions of the European Court of Justice and Their Impact Upon National Trade Mark Jurisprudence in the EU*, 94 TRADEMARK REP. 1105 (2004).

b. Special Protections for Well-known or Famous Marks

Well-known or famous marks receive special protections under Paris Convention Article 6*bis* and TRIPS arts. 16(2), (3). Paris Article 6*bis* allows a well-known mark (also called a famous mark) to establish priority over other marks once it has become well-known in that country, even absent use or registration of the mark in that country. The owner of a famous mark in a country in which the mark has achieved fame (but has not been registered) can prohibit the registration or use of the same or similar marks that are likely to create confusion with the famous mark used on identical or similar goods.

TRIPS Article 16(2) expands Paris Article 6*bis* protection to service marks. More controversially, Article 16(3) expands 6*bis* protection for *registered* well-known marks "to goods or services which are *not similar* to those in respect of which a trademark is registered" if (i) "use of that trademark in relation to those goods or services would indicate a connection between those goods or services and the owner of the registered trademark" and (ii) "the interests of the owner of the registered trademark are likely to be damaged by such use." TRIPS art. 16(3) (emphasis added). The precise meaning of Article 16(3), especially "likely to be damaged," is unclear. Part of the confusion stems from Article 16(3)'s incorporation of Article 6*bis* of Paris "mutatis mutandis" to TRIPS. As you recall, Article 6*bis* is based on a likelihood of confusion. WTO countries have disagreed over whether Article 16(3) means that countries must recognize protection for famous marks against dilution versus some lesser protection based on trademark infringement in unrelated goods or services. This section discusses the special protection of priority for famous marks under Paris Article 6*bis*, while the next section discusses dilution.

PROBLEM 4–11

To take advantage of Country Z's new openness to foreign direct investment, Rex has set up a company named "All–World Marks" to register the famous trademarks of successful MNEs from around the world. Rex's strategy is based on the following: many MNEs refused to do any business in Country Z for a long period due to its poor record on human rights and the environment, and therefore have never registered their trademarks in Country Z. However, as Country Z has enacted a number of new laws that redress these concerns, many MNEs are now eager to enter Z's market. Under Z's first-to-file system, All–World Marks has now registered hundreds of well-known marks of MNEs that were never previously registered in Country Z.

You are the General Counsel of a Fortune 200 company with internationally famous marks in the consumer products business—or, at least, the Company is pretty confident its marks are well known in most of the major markets in the world based on its ads, promotions, and sales. You have just received a letter from All–World with the following demand: "Pay us $1 million to buy your marks registered by All–World in Country Z within 30 days, or we will transfer them free of charge to several ambitious local companies from a wide variety of industries eager to use the marks for their products." All–World's demand couldn't have come at a worse time for your Company: the marketing department had just finished a strategic plan to begin selling in Country Z this year. Do you pay the $1 million to All–World for the rights to the registered mark in Country Z? Or is All–World's demand just "extortion," as one of your assistants claims? Are there any facts that you would like to determine before making your recommendation on what the Company should do? Assume that Country Z's trademark laws are modeled on the laws of South Africa as set forth in the *McDonald's* case below.

Paris Convention

Article 6*bis*

(1) The countries of the Union undertake, ex officio if their legislation so permits, or at the request of an interested party, to refuse or to cancel the registration, and to prohibit the use, of a trademark which constitutes a reproduction, an imitation, or a translation, liable to create confusion, of a mark considered by the competent authority of the country of registration or use to be well known in that country as being already the mark of a person entitled to the benefits of this Convention and used for identical or similar goods. These provisions shall also apply when the essential part of the mark constitutes a reproduction of any such well-known mark or an imitation liable to create confusion therewith.

(2) A period of at least five years from the date of registration shall be allowed for requesting the cancellation of such a mark. The countries of the Union may provide for a period within which the prohibition of use must be requested.

(3) No time limit shall be fixed for requesting the cancellation or the prohibition of the use of marks registered or used in bad faith.

TRIPS

Article 16(2), (3)

2. Article 6*bis* of the Paris Convention (1967) shall apply, *mutatis mutandis*, to services. In determining whether a trademark is well-known, Members shall take account of the knowledge of the trademark in the relevant sector of the public, including knowledge in the Member concerned which has been obtained as a result of the promotion of the trademark.

3. Article 6*bis* of the Paris Convention (1967) shall apply, *mutatis mutandis*, to goods or services which are not similar to those in respect of which a trademark is registered, provided that use of that trademark in relation to those goods or services would indicate a connection between those goods or services and the owner of the registered trademark and provided that the interests of the owner of the registered trademark are likely to be damaged by such use.

McDONALD'S CORP. v. JOBURGERS DRIVE-INN RESTAURANT (PTY) LTD.

1997 South African Reports 1.
Appellate Division, Case No. 547/95 1996.

E M GROSSKOPF, JA

This is a dispute about the use and continued registration of the appellant's trademarks. The appellant, to which I shall refer to as McDonald's, is a corporation incorporated in the state of Delaware in the United States of America. It is one of the largest franchisers of fast food restaurants in the world, if not the largest. It first commenced business in the United States of America in 1955 and has carried on business internationally since 1971. McDonald's obtained registration of its trade marks in South Africa in 1968, 1974, 1979, 1980, 1984 and 1985. It is now the registered proprietor of fifty-two marks. Of these, twenty-seven consist of or incorporate the word "McDonald" or "McDonald's." When the present proceedings commenced, McDonald's had not traded in South Africa nor, we may assume for present purposes, had it used any of its trade marks here.

Joburgers Drive–Inn Restaurant (Pty) Limited ("Joburgers") is a South African company with its principal place of business in Johannesburg. Its managing director is Mr. George Sombonos. Mr. Sombonos has been engaged in the fast food industry since 1968. In 1979 he registered a company called Golden Fried Chicken (Pty) Limited ("Chicken Licken"). He holds 90% of the shares in the company and is its managing director. In 1979 Chicken Licken applied for the registration of a number of trademarks, including Chicken Licken. Since then it has franchised the Chicken Licken business so that today there are more than 177 stores throughout South Africa. Mr. Sombonos says that Chicken Licken is the biggest fried chicken fast food franchise chain in the world not having its origins in the United States of America.

During 1992 Mr. Sombonos on behalf of Joburgers decided to establish fast food outlets and restaurants using the trade marks McDonald's, Big Mac and the golden arches design. In 1993 Mr. Sombonos applied for the registration of these and some other McDonald's marks. At the same time he applied to the Registrar of Trade Marks in terms of Section 36(1)(a) and (b) of the Trade Marks Act, No. 62 of 1963 ("the old Act") for the expungement of the trademarks which are held by McDonald's. McDonald's opposed these applications and filed its counter-statements in the expungement applications during August 1993. During the same period McDonald's applied again for the registration of all the trade marks in its name.

On 1 May 1995 the Trade Marks Act, No. 194 of 1993 ("the new Act") came into force. Section 35 of the new Act provides for the protection of "well-known" trademarks emanating from certain foreign countries. On 20 June 1995 McDonald's brought an application against Joburgers under Sec. 35 of the new Act. It claimed that all 52 of its trade marks were well-known marks in terms of the section, and sought an order that Joburgers be interdicted and restrained from imitating, reproducing or transmitting those marks in the Republic of South Africa. I shall call this the "well-known marks application."

The three applications were heard together by Southwood J. He found in favour of Joburgers. Accordingly, in the Joburgers application, the application by McDonald's for an interdict was dismissed and Joburgers' counter-application for expungement granted; and the well-known marks application by McDonald's was refused. With the leave of the court a quo McDonald's now appeals against these orders.

Section 35 of the new Act reads as follows:

"(1) References in this Act to a trade mark which is entitled to protection under the Paris Convention as a well-known trade mark, are to a mark which is well-known in the Republic as being the mark of—

(a) a person who is a national of a convention country; or

(b) a person who is domiciled in, or has a real and effective industrial or commercial establishment in, a convention country, whether or not such person carries on business, or has any goodwill, in the Republic.* * *

(3) The proprietor of a trade mark which is entitled to protection under the Paris Convention as a well-known trade mark is entitled to restrain the use in the Republic of a trade mark which constitutes, or the essential part of which constitutes, a reproduction, imitation or translation of the well-known trade mark in relation to goods or services which are identical or similar to the goods or services in respect of which the trade mark is well known and where the use is likely to cause deception or confusion."

The essential dispute between the parties was what level of awareness in the public mind is required for a mark to qualify as "well-known" in terms of section 35.

The Paris Convention, to which reference is made in § 35, is the Paris Convention on the Protection of Industrial Property of 20 March 1883 as revised or amended from time to time (§ 2 of the Act). [The court quotes Paris, art. 6*bis* set forth above—*Ed.*]

Although art 6*bis* was inserted into the convention as far back as 1925, neither Britain nor South Africa gave legislative effect to it until recently—South Africa in § 35 of the new Act, and Britain in § 56 of the Trade Marks Act, 1994 (42 & 43 Elizabeth 2 C. 26). The reason why Britain did not legislate earlier was that previously it claimed to be honouring the article by means of its common law of passing off. The protection granted to foreign marks by the law of passing off was limited, however, by the requirement that a plaintiff had to establish a goodwill in the country.

It seems clear that § 35 of the new Act and the corresponding provision in the United Kingdom were intended to remedy this lack. Thus § 35(1) pertinently extends protection to the owner of a foreign mark "whether or not such person carries on business, or has any goodwill, in the Republic." It is against this background that the expressions "well-known trade mark" and "well known in the Republic" must be interpreted. This [case] raises two questions, namely

(a) must the mark be well-known to all sectors of the populations; and

(b) whatever the relevant sector of the population may be, what degree of awareness within that sector is required before a mark can properly be described as well-known.

The answer to question (a) is, I think, clear. Section 35 of the new Act was intended to provide a practical solution to the problems of foreign businessmen whose marks were known in South Africa but who did not have a business here. The South African population is a diverse one in many respects. There are wide differences in income, education, cultural values, interests, tastes, personal life styles, recreational activities, etc. This was obviously known to the legislature when it passed the new Act. If protection is granted only to marks which are known (not to say well-known) to every segment of the population (or even to most segments of the population) there must be very few marks, if any, which could pass the test. The legislation would therefore not achieve its desired purpose. Moreover, there would not appear to be any point in imposing such a rigorous requirement. In argument we were referred as example to a mark which might be very well known to all persons interested in golf. Why should it be relevant, when deciding whether or not to protect such a mark, that non-golfers might never had heard of it? I consider therefore that a mark is well-known in the Republic if it is well-known to persons interested in the goods or services to which the mark relates.

The next question then is: how well should it be known to such persons? (question (b) above). On behalf of McDonald's it was argued that the test in this regard is qualitative and not a quantitative one. The question is not, it was argued, how many of the relevant persons know the mark, but how profound the knowledge of the mark is among those who do know it. In my view this argument is untenable. I suppose that knowledge of a mark could be so vague or superficial as hardly to count as knowledge at all, but apart from that I would not have thought that there would normally be great differences in the degree of knowledge of the mark by members of the public, or that such differences, if they existed, would be of any relevance. In the present context the important practical question is not whether a few people know the mark well but rather whether sufficient persons know it well enough to entitle it to protection against deception or confusion.

How many people are sufficient? The only guideline provided by the legislature lies in the expression "well-known." This is in itself so vague as hardly to provide any assistance at all.

It seems to me that McDonald's contention must be sustained. The legislature intended to extend the protection of a passing off action to foreign businessmen who did not have a business or enjoy a goodwill inside the country provided their marks were well-known in the Republic. It seems logical to accept that the degree of knowledge of the marks that is required would be similar to that protected in the existing law of passing off. The concept of a substantial number of persons is well established. It provides a practical and flexible criterion which is consistent with the terms of the statute.

I turn now to the evidence concerning the extent to which the McDonald's trade marks are known in the Republic. At the end of 1993 there were 13,993 McDonald's restaurants spread over 70 countries. The annual turnover of McDonald's restaurants amounts to some $23,587 million. McDonald's trademarks are used extensively in relation to its own restaurants as well as to those that are franchised. The level of advertising and promotion which has been carried out by McDonald's, its subsidiaries, affiliates and franchisees in relation to McDonald's restaurants exceeds the sum of $900 million annually. Their international marketing campaigns have included sponsorship of the 1984 Los Angeles and 1992 Barcelona Olympics. McDonald's has also been a sponsor of the 1990 soccer World Cup Tournament in Italy and the 1994 World Cup Soccer Tournament in the United States of America. Mr. Paul R Duncan, the vice president and general counsel of McDonald's, stated on affidavit that, in view of the vast scale of his organization's operations, the McDonald's trademarks are in all probability some of the best known trade marks in the world. This was not denied. Although there was no evidence on the extent to which the advertising outside South Africa spilled over into this country through printed publications and television, it must, in all probability, be quite extensive. In addition the McDonald's trademarks would be known to many South Africans who have travelled abroad. This again would not be an insignificant number.

During September 1993 Mr. Corder was instructed to conduct a market survey on behalf of McDonald's. He was informed that the objectives of the study were to establish awareness of the name McDonald's, to measure recognition of the McDonald's trademarks, to ascertain the association of McDonald's with certain products or types of business undertakings, and to establish the awareness of McDonald's hamburgers. The method used by him was the conducting of personal interviews using a structured questionnaire and interviewing aids. The interviewing aids consisted of two text show cards and one colour picture show card featuring the main McDonald's trademarks. Copies of the questionnaires and show cards were before the Court.

The universe for the survey was defined as white adult males and females, aged 16 years and over, living in houses in high income suburbs of Pretoria, Verwoerdburg, Johannesburg, Bedfordview, Randburg and Sandton. A sample of 202 persons was taken. The fieldwork was conducted from 7 December to 24 December 1993 by trained interviewers under the supervision of field supervisors. The relevant conclusions were set out as follows:

> "A large majority of respondents were aware of the name McDonald's, and/or the McDonald's logos/trademarks (77%). More than half had heard of both McDonald's, and knew the logos/trademarks too (57%).
>
> Most respondents spontaneously associated McDonald's with hamburgers, knew of "McDonald's Hamburgers" (80%).
>
> The results indicate that the majority of white adults, aged 16 and over, living in households in high income suburbs of Johannesburg

and Pretoria are aware of the McDonald's brand name, and associate McDonald's with hamburgers."

During January and February 1995 a similar survey was conducted among white males and females, aged 16 years and over, living in selected higher income suburbs of Durban. [The second survey yielded similar results. *Ed.*]

On behalf of McDonald's it was contended, correctly in my view, that there are two categories of such persons—potential customers and potential franchisees. Potential customers would cover a wide field. It would include all persons who like fast food of this type and have the money to buy it. Since the cost is not high there would be many such people. Potential franchisees would be a smaller group, namely persons who can finance and run a McDonald's franchise, or consider that they can.

The evidence adduced by McDonald's leads, in my view, to the inference that its marks, and particularly the mark McDonald's, are well known amongst the more affluent people in the country. People who travel, watch television, and who read local and foreign publications, are likely to know about it. They would have seen McDonald's outlets in other countries, and seen or heard its advertisements there or its spillover here in foreign journals, television shows, etc. Although the extent of such spillover has not been quantified, it must be substantial. Moreover, as has been shown, McDonald's has also received publicity in the local media. The market survey evidence specifically related to two groups of adult white persons living in relatively affluent suburbs of Gauteng and KwaZulu Natal. It is reasonable to suppose that much the same results would be achieved elsewhere among persons of all races who have a similar financial and social background. These are also the type of people who would have heard about McDonald's and its marks from Collins, or who would have discussed these matters with him, or would have written to McDonald's to solicit a franchise agreement.

By the same token, people who are poor, do not travel abroad, do not read foreign publications or, possibly do not read at all, and are not exposed to television, are likely not to have heard of McDonald's or its marks. It is accordingly not surprising that market surveys commissioned by Joburgers showed a low awareness of McDonald's and its marks among black persons generally.

These conclusions must be applied to the relevant categories among the public. Potential franchisees, I consider, would be the type of persons who would almost without exception have heard of McDonald's and know its marks. Among potential customers the level of awareness would be lower. Many people who would be interested in buying a hamburger would not have heard of McDonald's. However, a certain degree of financial well-being is required for the purchase of prepared food. Extremely poor people are not likely to patronise McDonald's establishments. Of the persons who are likely to do so, at least a substantial portion must be of the category who would probably have heard of McDonald's and know its marks, or some of them. This inference is supported by the zeal shown by Joburgers to appropriate these marks for themselves.

I consider therefore that at least a substantial portion of persons who would be interested in the goods or services provided by McDonald's know its name, which is also its principal trade mark. [I]f the McDonald's mark is used as contemplated by Joburgers in relation to the same type of fast food business as that conducted by McDonald's, it would cause deception or confusion within the meaning of § 35(3) of the new Act. In the result the following order is made. In the well-known marks application (case number 11700/95): The First and Second Respondents are hereby inter-dicted and restrained, with costs, from imitating, reproducing or translat-ing in the Republic of South Africa any of the Applicant's trade marks in which the word McDonald or McDonald's appears.

EMPRESA CUBANA DEL TABACO v. CULBRO CORP.

U.S. Court of Appeals for the Second Circuit.
399 F.3d 462 (2d Cir. 2005).

STRAUB, CIRCUIT JUDGE.

This appeal arises from a dispute between Cubatabaco, a Cuban company, and General Cigar, an American company, over who has the right to use the COHIBA mark on cigars.

Background

In 1963 the United States imposed an embargo on Cuba. The Cuban Asset Control Regulations ("Embargo Regulations" or "Regulations"), 31 C.F.R. § 515.201 *et seq.,* which were promulgated pursuant to Section 5(b) of the Trading with the Enemy Act of 1917, ch. 106, § 5(b), 40 Stat. 415, contain the terms of the embargo. In 1996 Congress codified the Regula-tions in the Cuban Liberty and Democratic Solidarity Act of 1996 ("LI-BERTAD Act"). The Secretary of the Treasury has the authority to administer the Cuban embargo, which he has delegated to the Office of Foreign Assets Control ('OFAC'). The Embargo Regulations prevent Cu-ban entities, such as Cubatabaco, from selling cigars in the United States. Despite its inability to sell cigars here, Cubatabaco claims that it owns the COHIBA mark in the United States and that General Cigar's sale of COHIBA cigars in the United States unlawfully infringes its mark.

In 1969 Cubatabaco filed an application to register the COHIBA mark in Cuba. Throughout the 1970s it sold COHIBA cigars in Cuba. By January 1978 Cubatabaco had applied to register the COHIBA mark in seventeen countries, including most Western European countries, but did not apply to register the mark in the United States. In 1982 Cubatabaco began selling COHIBA cigars outside of Cuba. In 1983 Cubatabaco consid-ered registering its COHIBA mark in the United States but learned that General Cigar had already obtained the United States registration. On February 22, 1985, Cubatabaco filed an application with the United States Patent and Trademark Office ("PTO") to register its BEHIQUE mark in the United States with the same trade dress that it used on its COHIBA cigars elsewhere. In 1987 Cubatabaco considered challenging General Cigar's 1981 COHIBA registration, but chose not to take any action.

General Cigar first learned of the name "Cohiba" in the late 1970s after General Cigar executives read a *Forbes* magazine article stating that Cubatabaco was planning to sell its COHIBA cigars outside of Cuba. General Cigar filed an application to register the COHIBA mark with the PTO on March 13, 1978, with a claimed first use date of February 13, 1978. The application was unopposed, and General Cigar obtained the registration on February 17, 1981. General Cigar sold COHIBA cigars in the United States from 1978 until late 1987.

In February 1992 *The Wine Spectator* magazine published articles describing COHIBA as Cuba's "finest" cigar and "*the* hot brand." In September 1992, the premier issue of *Cigar Aficionado* magazine, which had a United States circulation of 115,000 copies, featured a story about Cubatabaco's Cuban COHIBA cigars. The magazine rated cigars and gave the Cubatabaco's COHIBA Robusto the highest ranking. Shortly thereafter, General Cigar decided to use COHIBA on a new premium cigar, which it launched on November 20, 1992. The District Court noted that General Cigar "acknowledges that the reintroduction was at least in part a response to *Cigar Aficionado's* coverage of the Cuban COHIBA." General Cigar filed for a second COHIBA registration on December 30, 1992, and the application was granted without opposition in 1995.

In late 1992 and early 1993 General Cigar considered seeking permission to use Cubatabaco's registered trade dress. In a January 1993 memo, General Cigar's then in-house counsel wrote that having permission to use the trade dress would help General Cigar "to exploit the popularity, familiarity, brand recognition and overall success of the Cuban Cohiba." General Cigar did not pursue further the plan to seek permission to use the trade dress.

In late January or February 1997 General Cigar decided to launch a new cigar under the COHIBA name. General Cigar acknowledges that the Cuban COHIBA was well known to U.S. cigar consumers by the time General Cigar launched its new product in the fall of 1997. The District Court noted that "[t]he 1997 advertising for the General Cigar COHIBA attempted to create an association in the consumer's mind to Cuba and the Cuban COHIBA."

In January 1997 Cubatabaco commenced a proceeding in the Trademark Trial and Appeal Board to cancel General Cigar's registration of the COHIBA mark. On November 12, 1997, Cubatabaco filed this action alleging thirteen claims against General Cigar. The court held a bench trial on various dates between May 27, 2003, and June 23, 2003. On March 26, 2004, the District Court found that Cubatabaco was entitled to prevail on its claim of trademark infringement under Section 43(a) of the Lanham Act. The court's finding of trademark infringement rested on its adoption of the famous marks doctrine.

After oral argument in this Court we invited the United States Departments of Justice and Treasury ("government") to submit a brief as *amicus curiae* addressing the question of whether the Embargo Regulations barred Cubatabaco's acquisition of the COHIBA mark in the United States via the famous marks doctrine. On November 12, 2004, the government filed its letter brief. There, the government asserts that the Regulations bar Cubatabaco's acquisition of the mark via the famous marks doctrine and that the District Court's finding of trademark infringement under Section 43(a) must therefore be reversed. In addition, the government reasons that the portion of the District Court's order requiring General Cigar to deliver merchandise and other materials bearing the COHIBA mark to Cubatabaco is barred by the Regulations. According to the government, however, the Regulations do not bar the portion of the District Court's order that cancels General Cigar's registration and enjoins its use of the COHIBA mark. The government notes that Cubatabaco's ownership of the U.S. COHIBA mark is not required for a Section 43(a) claim, and expresses the view that, given the District Court's factual findings, the cancellation of General Cigar's mark and the injunction against General Cigar's use of the mark is appropriate relief.

Discussion

For the reasons explained below, we hold that the Embargo Regulations bar Cubatabaco's acquisition of property rights in the U.S. COHIBA trademark through the famous marks doctrine.

I. CLAIMS UNDER SECTIONS 43(a), 44(b), AND 44(h) OF THE LANHAM ACT BASED ON "FAME" OF THE CUBAN COHIBA MARK.

　　A. The Trademark Infringement Claim Fails Because Acquisition of the Mark Via the Famous Marks Doctrine Is Prohibited by the Embargo Regulations

　　1. The Embargo Regulations

Unless otherwise authorized, the Embargo Regulations prohibit a broad range of transactions involving property in which a Cuban entity has an interest. 31 C.F.R. § 515.201(b) (2005). Section 515.201(c) provides that "[a]ny transaction for the purpose or which has the effect of evading or avoiding any of the prohibitions set forth in paragraphs (a) or (b) of this section is hereby prohibited." *Id.* § 515.201(c); *see also Havana Club Holding, S.A. v. Galleon S.A.*, 203 F.3d 116, 122 n.3 (2d Cir.), *cert. denied*, 531 U.S. 918 (2000). [After examining the regulations,] [w]e hold that Cubatabaco's acquisition of the U.S. COHIBA mark through the famous marks doctrine would constitute a transfer that is prohibited by § 515.201(b), and such transfers are not authorized by a general or specific license.

B. Cubatabaco's Claims for Injunctive Relief Based on Section 43(a) and the Paris Convention Fail Because They Entail a Transfer of Property Rights to Cubatabaco in Violation of the Embargo

Cubatabaco argues that even if the Regulations bar its acquisition of the U.S. COHIBA mark, it is entitled to obtain cancellation of General Cigar's registration of the COHIBA mark and an injunction preventing General Cigar from using the mark in the United States because its mark was famous in the United States before General Cigar recommenced its use in November 1992. Cubatabaco maintains that this relief is warranted under Section 43(a) of the Lanham Act, as well as under Article 6*bis* of the Paris Convention, which it claims is implemented by Sections 44(b) and (h) of the Lanham Act even if full transfer of the COHIBA mark to Cubatabaco is prohibited.

1. Section 43(a) Claim for Unfair Competition

Cubatabaco's theory is that General Cigar's sale of COHIBA cigars in the United States violates Section 43(a) because it is likely to cause consumer confusion as to the source or attribution of those cigars. The confusion alleged by Cubatabaco in support of its Section 43(a) claim is derived solely from General Cigar's use of the COHIBA mark. Cubatabaco cannot obtain relief on a theory that General Cigar's use of the mark causes confusion, because, pursuant to our holding today, General Cigar's legal right to the COHIBA mark has been established as against Cubatabaco. General Cigar has a right to use the mark in the United States because it owns the mark in the United States.

2. Article 6*bis* Paris Convention

Cubatabaco maintains that even if the Regulations bar its acquisition of the mark, and even if it cannot obtain relief for an unfair competition claim under Section 43(a), it has a right under Article 6*bis* of the Paris Convention, in conjunction with Sections 44(b) and (h) of the Lanham Act, to obtain cancellation of General Cigar's mark and an injunction against its use. Both the United States and Cuba are parties to the Paris Convention.

According to Cubatabaco, Sections 44(b) and (h) incorporate treaty provisions relating to the "repression of unfair competition," and rights under Article 6*bis* fall into that category. Section 44(b) provides that:

> Any person whose country of origin is a party to any convention or treaty relating to trademarks, trade or commercial names, or the repression of unfair competition, to which the United States is also a party, or extends reciprocal rights to nationals of the United States by law, shall be entitled to the benefits of this section under the conditions expressed herein to the extent necessary to give effect to any provision of such convention, treaty or reciprocal law, in addition to the rights to which any owner of a mark is otherwise entitled by this chapter.

15 U.S.C. § 1126(b). Therefore, Cubatabaco is entitled to the benefits of Section 44, "under the conditions expressed herein," but only to the extent necessary to give effect to any provision of a treaty. Section 44(h) provides:

Any person designated in subsection (b) of this section as entitled to the benefits and subject to the provisions of this chapter shall be entitled to effective protection against unfair competition, and the remedies provided in this chapter for infringement of marks shall be available so far as they may be appropriate in repressing acts of unfair competition.

Id. § 1126(h). "Rights under Section 44(h) are co-extensive with treaty rights under section 44(b), including treaty rights 'relating to ... the repression of unfair competition.'" *Havana Club*, 203 F.3d at 134 (quoting 15 U.S.C. § 1126(b)); *see also Mattel, Inc. v. MCA Records, Inc.*, 296 F.3d 894, 907 (9th Cir. 2002) (" '[T]he grant in subsection (h) of effective protection against unfair competition is tailored to the provisions of the unfair competition treaties by subsection (b), which extends the benefits of section 44 only to the extent necessary to give effect to the treaties.' Subsection 44(h) creates a federal right that is coextensive with the substantive provisions of the treaty involved." (quoting *Toho Co. v. Sears, Roebuck & Co.*, 645 F.2d 788, 792 (9th Cir. 1981) (citation omitted))).

Cubatabaco may be correct that Sections 44(b) and (h) incorporate Article 6*bis* and allow foreign entities to acquire U.S. trademark rights in the United States if their marks are sufficiently famous in the United States before they are used in this country. That is the view expressed by some commentators. *See* 4 *McCarthy on Trademarks and Unfair Competition* § 29:4 (4th ed. 2004).

However, we need not decide that broad question here because even assuming that the famous marks doctrine is otherwise viable and applicable, the embargo bars Cubatabaco from acquiring property rights in the U.S. COHIBA mark through the doctrine. The Embargo Regulations do not permit Cubatabaco to acquire the power to exclude General Cigar from using the mark in the United States. We do not read Article 6*bis* and Section 44(b) and (h) of the Lanham Act to require cancellation of General Cigar's properly registered trademark or an injunction against its use of the mark in the United States under these circumstances.

For the foregoing reasons, [w]e vacate those portions of the District Court's order that cancel General Cigar's registration, enjoin its use of the mark, order it to deliver materials to Cubatabaco, and require it to recall from retail customers and distributors products bearing the mark, and to inform customers and distributors that they cannot sell General Cigar's COHIBA-labeled products in the United States.

NOTES AND QUESTIONS

1. *Use versus registration.* Does Article 6*bis* of the Paris Convention take a stance on whether a well-known mark must be registered or used in the territory of a member country before it can receive protection in that country? Do well-known marks get any additional benefits in protection under Paris that regular marks do not receive? What about under TRIPS Article 16(2) and (3)?

2. McDonald's had registered its marks in South Africa, starting in 1968. But, at the time of the case in 1996, McDonald's had never used its marks in South Africa or done business there. Why do you think that was so? How does McDonald's have any legal basis to assert trademark rights in South Africa?

3. If the holder of a famous mark has voluntarily chosen not to use the mark in a foreign country for an extended period of time, shouldn't someone else be allowed to make productive uses of the mark in commerce as arguably was the case with George Sombonos's attempt to use McDonald's? Contrast the *McDonald's* case with a case of a "squatter," who registers marks in order to sell them for a profit. For example, in 2002, a Russian attorney—who was in the business of registering the famous marks of others—had the Russian registration of Starbucks Corp. from 1997 invalidated on the ground the "Starbucks" mark had been abandoned through nonuse. The Russian attorney then registered "Starbucks" in Russia in 2004 and eventually offered to sell the registered mark to the U.S. company for $600,000. Ultimately, however, the Russian trademark office invalidated the registration and restored rights to the U.S. Starbucks company, a decision upheld on appeal.

4. How did the South African court determine whether "McDonald's" was well-known? What is the relationship between fame and the expenditure of resources on advertising and promotion?

5. *U.S. Approach to Famous Marks*. There are two potential sources of protection for famous marks in the United States—one statutory, and the other, common law.

The Lanham Act was amended in 1996 to expressly recognize a cause of action for dilution of "famous" marks. (Dilution claims, including the definition of "famous marks," are discussed in the next section.)

The other basis for protection of famous marks is the common law doctrine of famous or well-known marks, which relates to priority and the Paris Convention Article 6*bis*. Although the Second Circuit in the Cohiba case declined to consider whether the doctrine should be recognized, other federal courts and the Trademark Trial and Appeal Board (TTAB) have recognized the doctrine. *See Grupo Gigante SA De CV v. Dallo & Co., Inc.*, 391 F.3d 1088, 1094 (9th Cir. 2004); *Empresa Cubana del Tabaco v. Culbro Corp.*, 2004 WL 602295, at *30 (S.D.N.Y. 2004) (collecting cases), *rev'd*, 399 F.3d 462 (2d Cir. 2005); *Vaudable v. Montmartre, Inc.*, 193 N.Y.S.2d 332, 335 (N.Y. Sup. Ct. 1959). To prove a mark is "famous" under the common law, the Ninth Circuit has held that a trademark holder must show: (i) the mark has secondary meaning, i.e., the public identifies the mark primarily as representing the source of the product, and (ii) "that a substantial percentage of consumers in the relevant American market is familiar with the foreign mark," as shown by such factors as "the intentional copying of the mark by the defendant, and whether customers of the American firm are likely to think they are patronizing the same firm that uses the mark in another country." *Grupo Gigante*, 391 F.3d at 1098.

6. Do you believe the result in the Cohiba case was correct? Should Cubatabaco lose the ability to assert that its mark is famous in the U.S.? Was Cubatabaco (which was barred by U.S. law from using its mark in the U.S.)

any less deserving of an opportunity to assert that its mark was famous than McDonald's (which chose not to use its mark in South Africa for many years)?

7. Is the decision of the Second Circuit in the Cohiba case consistent with the U.S.'s obligations under the Paris Convention Article 6*bis*? What about Article 3? Does it violate any of the standards of TRIPS, such as national treatment, most favored nation, or the minimum standard for use requirements under Article 19? Should the Second Circuit have considered the WTO decision in *Havana Club* (discussed above) before issuing its ruling in the Cohiba case?

8. *Bibliographic note.* Luiz Henrique do Amaral, *Famous Marks: The Brazilian Case*, 83 TRADEMARK REP. 394 (1993); Horst–Peter Gotting, *Protection of Well–Known, Unregistered Marks in Europe and the United States*, 31 I.I.C. 389 (2000); Frederick W. Mostert, *Well–Known and Famous Marks: Is Harmony Possible in the Global Village?*, 86 TRADEMARK REP. 103 (1996); Charles Webster, *The* McDonald's *Case: South Africa Joins the Global Village*, 86 TRADEMARK REP. 576 (1986); WIPO JOINT RECOMMENDATION CONCERNING PROVISIONS ON THE PROTECTION OF WELL-KNOWN MARKS (Sept. 20–29, 1999); WIPO MEMORANDUM ON PROTECTION OF WELL-KNOWN MARKS (Int'l Bureau), Third Session, Geneva, October 20 to 23, 1997.

PROBLEM 4–12

You are deputy general counsel of a multinational corporation, Pilgrim Technology, Inc., which does business in parts of Asia, Europe, and the United States. You have been invited to speak at a joint conference between WTO and WIPO members on the topic of the protection of well-known marks.

The CEO of Pilgrim Technology has asked you to come up with some proposal that will provide greater protection of well-known marks and on a simpler basis. Here are some ideas you have been considering: (i) expressly allowing the well-known status of a mark in a substantial part of the WTO to constitute well-known status in *all* WTO countries, even if not well-known in those other parts, (ii) expressly exempting well-known marks from any use requirements, or, alternatively, allowing use in one country to constitute use in all countries; (iii) expressly exempting well-known marks from any registration requirements; and (iv) expressly forbidding member countries from requiring that a mark be well-known to the entire public at large in a member country. Which, if any, of these would you most like to see adopted and why? What counterarguments or criticisms would you expect the proposal to elicit? What would your responses be?

c. Dilution Claims

TRIPS Article 16(3) provides some form of protection to registered well-known or famous marks in goods or services not similar to those for which the mark is registered. Because the language in Article 16(3) is unclear, countries have disagreed over its meaning. The EU and U.S. believe it requires protection against dilution, while some other countries disagree. In 1999, the U.S. led an effort in WIPO to clarify obligations of countries to protect against dilution. WIPO produced a Joint Recommendation Concerning Provisions on the Protection of Well–Known Marks ("Joint Recommendation") that recommended that WIPO countries protect famous marks from three kinds of third-party uses of the mark:

(i) the use of that mark would indicate a connection between the goods and/or services for which the mark is used, is the subject of an application for registration, or is registered, and the owner of the well-known mark, and would be likely to damage his interests;

(ii) the use of that mark is likely to impair or dilute in an unfair manner the distinctive character of the well-known mark;

(iii) the use of that mark would take unfair advantage of the distinctive character of the well-known mark.

Joint Recommendation art. 4(1)(b). The Joint Recommendation is not a binding treaty, however, and a number of WIPO members disagree with it. In addition, the Joint Recommendation of WIPO cannot alter the TRIPS Agreement, so the controversy over the meaning of TRIPS Article 16(3) remains unresolved. This section considers the U.S. approach to dilution.

PROBLEM 4–13

You are a counsel in the Office of the United States Trade Representative (USTR). The USTR has asked you to draft a preliminary proposal for an amendment to TRIPS that would specifically recognize dilution type claims for trademarks. The USTR would like to submit an amendment that distinguishes dilution from trademark infringement as much as possible and asks you to draft the amendment with this goal in mind. Please advise on the following: (i) how the amendment should define dilution (for example, should it be available for competing products and should it incorporate aspects of consumer confusion); (ii) what level of proof should be required (actual or likelihood of dilution); (iii) whether dilution claims should be limited to famous marks or apply to all trademarks; and (iv) how the U.S. can respond to the critics of dilution claims to explain why your proposal is necessary and desirable.

United States Lanham Act, Section 43(c): Dilution Claims

15 U.S.C. § 1125(c)

(c) Dilution by blurring; dilution by tarnishment

(1) Injunctive relief

Subject to the principles of equity, the owner of a famous mark that is distinctive, inherently or through acquired distinctiveness, shall be entitled to an injunction against another person who, at any time after the owner's mark has become famous, commences use of a mark or trade name in commerce that is likely to cause dilution by blurring or dilution by tarnishment of the famous mark, regardless of the presence or absence of actual or likely confusion, of competition, or of actual economic injury.

(2) Definitions

(A) For purposes of paragraph (1), a mark is famous if it is widely recognized by the general consuming public of the United States as a designation of source of the goods or services of the mark's owner. In determining whether a mark possesses the requisite degree of recognition, the court may consider all relevant factors, including the following:

(i) The duration, extent, and geographic reach of advertising and publicity of the mark, whether advertised or publicized by the owner or third parties.

(ii) The amount, volume, and geographic extent of sales of goods or services offered under the mark.

(iii) The extent of actual recognition of the mark.

(iv) Whether the mark was registered under the Act of March 3, 1881, or the Act of February 20, 1905, or on the principal register.

(B) For purposes of paragraph (1), "dilution by blurring" is association arising from the similarity between a mark or trade name and a famous mark that impairs the distinctiveness of the famous mark. In determining whether a mark or trade name is likely to cause dilution by blurring, the court may consider all relevant factors, including the following:

(i) The degree of similarity between the mark or trade name and the famous mark.

(ii) The degree of inherent or acquired distinctiveness of the famous mark.

(iii) The extent to which the owner of the famous mark is engaging in substantially exclusive use of the mark.

(iv) The degree of recognition of the famous mark.

(v) Whether the user of the mark or trade name intended to create an association with the famous mark.

(vi) Any actual association between the mark or trade name and the famous mark.

(C) For purposes of paragraph (1), "dilution by tarnishment" is association arising from the similarity between a mark or trade name and a famous mark that harms the reputation of the famous mark.

(3) Exclusions

The following shall not be actionable as dilution by blurring or dilution by tarnishment under this subsection:

(A) Any fair use, including a nominative or descriptive fair use, or facilitation of such fair use, of a famous mark by another person other than as a designation of source for the person's own goods or services, including use in connection with—

(i) advertising or promotion that permits consumers to compare goods or services; or

(ii) identifying and parodying, criticizing, or commenting upon the famous mark owner or the goods or services of the famous mark owner.

(B) All forms of news reporting and news commentary.

(C) Any noncommercial use of a mark. * * *

LEVI STRAUSS & CO. v. ABERCROMBIE & FITCH TRADING CO.

United States Court of Appeals for the Ninth Circuit.
633 F.3d 1158 (9th Cir. 2011).

RIPPLE, SENIOR CIRCUIT JUDGE:

Levi Strauss & Co. ("Levi Strauss") seeks review of a district court judgment that Abercrombie & Fitch Trading Co. ("Abercrombie") did not dilute Levi Strauss's trademarked "Arcuate" design in violation of the Trademark Dilution Revision Act of 2006 ("TDRA"), 15 U.S.C. § 1125(c). Levi Strauss maintains that the district court applied an incorrect legal standard in evaluating its dilution claim, namely that the junior mark be "identical or nearly identical" to the senior one. We agree with Levi Strauss that the "identical or nearly identical" standard did not survive Congress's enactment of the TDRA and that the district court's use of the incorrect standard was not harmless error. Accordingly, we reverse the judgment of the district court and remand the case for further proceedings consistent with this opinion.

BACKGROUND

A. The Stitched Designs

Levi Strauss created, and began selling, blue jeans in the 1870s. Since 1873, the company has stitched the back pocket of its jeans with two connecting arches that meet in the center of the pocket; Levi Strauss holds a federally registered trademark on this "Arcuate" design. Sales of garments bearing the Arcuate mark have accounted for more than ninety-five percent of Levi Strauss's revenue over the past thirty years, totaling roughly fifty billion dollars. Levi Strauss actively monitors use of competing stitching designs and enforces its trademark rights against perceived infringers.

In 2006, Abercrombie began using a stitching design on the back pockets of its jeans that, according to Levi Strauss, "incorporates the distinctive arcing elements of the Arcuate trademark." Abercrombie's "Ruehl" design consists of two less-pronounced arches that are connected by a "dipsy doodle," which resembles the mathematical sign for infinity. The design on the Abercrombie jeans sits lower on the pocket than Levi Strauss's Arcuate design.

Levi Strauss's "Arcuate" design   Abercrombie's "Ruehl" design

DISCUSSION

Levi Strauss submits that the district court erred in requiring it to establish that its mark was identical or nearly identical to the Ruehl design. Levi Strauss looks to the plain language of 15 U.S.C. § 1125(c) and notes that the terms "identical or nearly identical" appear nowhere in the language of the statute. The statute, it maintains, does not require a prima facie showing of substantial similarity before a district court balances the dilution factors listed in § 1125(c)(2)(B). Instead, "degree of similarity" is one of several factors that a district court must balance in order to determine whether dilution has occurred and whether, therefore, a plaintiff is entitled to injunctive relief.

To properly evaluate the parties' contentions, we must look at the origins of the "identical or nearly identical" standard, how it has been employed and whether it remains viable after the enactment of the TDRA. * * *

E.   Interpretation of the TDRA

1.

Beginning with subsection (c)(1) of 15 U.S.C. § 1125, Congress provided that "the owner of a famous mark . . . shall be entitled to an injunction against another person who . . . commences use of *a* mark or trade name in commerce that is likely to cause dilution." 15 U.S.C. § 1125(c) (emphasis added). When referring to the junior mark, Congress did not authorize an injunction against another person who commences use of "the" mark; use of the definite article "the" clearly would have signaled that the junior mark had to be the same as the senior. Instead, Congress employed the indefinite article "a," which indicates that any number of unspecified, junior marks may be likely to dilute the senior mark.

Turning to the language of subsection (c)(2)(B), the TDRA defines "dilution by blurring" as the "association arising from the *similarity* between a mark and a trade name and a famous mark that impairs the distinctiveness of the famous mark." *Id.* § 1125(c)(2)(B) (emphasis added). Congress did not require an association arising from the "substantial" similarity, "identity" or "near identity" of the two marks. The word chosen by Congress, "similarity," sets forth a less demanding standard than that employed by many courts under the FTDA.

This analysis of the language of the statute, and our comparison of this language with the now-repealed statute, are further supported by Congress's decision to employ, in subsection (c)(2)(B), a non-exhaustive list of relevant factors to determine when dilution has occurred. Congress's implementation of such a methodology is simply not compatible with a determination that identity, near identity or substantial similarity are necessary to constitute a threshold showing for relief under § 1125(c). Indeed, Congress chose instead to make the "degree of *similarity* between the mark or trade name and the famous mark," *id.* § 1125(c)(2)(B)(i) (emphasis added), to be the first of the six (or more) relevant factors to be considered.

No doubt, similarity has a special role to play in the implementation of the new statute's multifactor approach. After all, dilution by blurring is defined by the statute as an "association arising from the similarity between a mark ... and a famous mark." *Id.* § 1125(c)(1)(B). It is also the *first* factor listed in the multifactor approach. Nevertheless, Congress's decision to make "degree of similarity" one consideration in a multifactor list strongly suggests that it did not want "degree of similarity" to be the necessarily controlling factor.

Finally, we believe that it is significant that, in adopting the TDRA, Congress decided to re-write 15 U.S.C. § 1125(c), as opposed to altering discrete wording or subsections. This action suggests that Congress did not wish to be tied to the language or interpretation of prior law, but instead crafted a new approach to our consideration of dilution-by-blurring claims.

Thus, the plain language of 15 U.S.C. § 1125(c) does not require that a plaintiff establish that the junior mark is identical, nearly identical or substantially similar to the senior mark in order to obtain injunctive relief. Rather, a plaintiff must show, based on the factors set forth in § 1125(c)(2)(B), including the degree of similarity, that a junior mark is likely to impair the distinctiveness of the famous mark.

Our interpretation of the TDRA is compatible with the case law of the only other court of appeals to have addressed squarely the question whether the requirement of identity or substantial similarity survives the TDRA. In *Starbucks*, the company brought a federal dilution claim against Wolfe's based on its use of the term "Charbucks" in connection with one of its coffee blends. The district court found that "the marks were not substantially similar" and "that '[t]his dissimilarity alone is sufficient to defeat [Starbucks's] blurring claim.'" *Starbucks*, 588 F.3d at 107. The Second Circuit disagreed. It acknowledged that, pre-TDRA, it had required plaintiffs to show that the marks were " 'very' or 'substantially similar' " before they could prevail on a federal dilution claim. *Id.* This was no longer the case under the TDRA, the court explained:

> The post-TDRA federal dilution statute, however, provides us with a compelling reason to discard the "substantially similar" requirement for federal trademark dilution actions. The current federal statute defines dilution by blurring as an "association arising from the similarity between a mark ... and a famous mark that impairs the distinctiveness of the famous mark," and the statute lists six non-exhaustive factors for determining the existence of an actionable claim for blurring. 15 U.S.C. § 1125(c)(2)(B). Although "similarity" is an integral element in the definition of "blurring," we find it significant that the federal dilution statute does not use the words "very" or "substantial" in connection with the similarity factor to be considered in examining a federal dilution claim.

Id. at 108. Furthermore, the court continued, in addition to leaving out any modifier for "similarity," Congress also employed specific language that cannot be reconciled with a requirement of substantial similarity; the court stated:

> [O]ne of the six statutory factors informing the inquiry as to whether the allegedly diluting mark "impairs the distinctiveness of the famous mark" is "[t]he *degree* of similarity between the mark or trade name and the famous mark." 15 U.S.C. § 1125(c)(2)(B)(i) (emphasis added). Consideration of a "degree" of similarity as a factor in determining the likelihood of dilution does not lend itself to a requirement that the similarity between the subject marks must be "substantial" for a dilution claim to succeed.

Id.

F.   The District Court's Error Was Not Harmless

Abercrombie also submits that, even if the district court erred in applying the "identical or nearly identical" requirement, the judgment nonetheless should be affirmed because any error was harmless. According to Abercrombie, the district court determined the Arcuate mark and the Ruehl design were not visually similar. Because "similarity" is the correct standard under the TDRA, Levi Strauss suffered no prejudice as a result of the district court's application of the incorrect standard. Abercrombie also notes that, in assessing the likelihood of dilution, the district court not only considered whether the marks were identical, but also took into account the other five factors set forth in § 1125(c)(2)(B). Abercrombie maintains that, because the court engaged in a weighing of all of the factors, the "similarity" requirement played only an insignificant role in its determination.

Abercrombie presents a very strained view of the district court's opinion. In its order entering judgment for Abercrombie, the court noted that "[t]he advisory jury found that the Ruehl design and the Arcuate mark were not identical or nearly identical." *Levi Strauss & Co.*, 2009 WL 1082175, at *7. It also observed that the test for similarity in a dilution context "is more stringent than in the infringement context." *Id.* After evaluating the visual depictions of the designs, the court concluded that "[t]his evidence demonstrates that a significant segment of the target group of customers would not view the marks as *essentially the same.*" *Id.* at *8 (emphasis added). The court then reviewed Dr. Sood's testimony and concluded that, given the survey shortcomings, there was insufficient evidence that target customers would "see the Ruehl design and the Arcuate mark as *essentially the same.*" *Id.* (emphasis added). In summary, the court stated: "[T]he Court concludes, consistent with the advisory jury's finding, that [Levi Strauss] has not established that [Abercrombie] is making commercial use of a mark that is identical or nearly identical to the Arcuate mark." *Id.* at *9. Use of the "identical or nearly identical" standard permeated the court's analysis and provided the basis upon which the court evaluated the evidence.

This standard also played a pivotal role in the court's determination that the Ruehl design was not likely to dilute the Arcuate mark. With respect to the similarity of the marks, the court observed that the two marks must be essentially the same and that, "[f]or the reasons set forth above, the Court finds that the Ruehl design and the Arcuate mark are not visually similar." *Id.* In other words, the court equated similarity with sameness and employed the latter, more stringent definition when entering its findings of fact.

Finally, our review of the district court's balancing of the relevant factors convinces us that application of the incorrect standard affected its dilution determination. According to the district court, degree of similarity was only one of three factors that weighed in Abercrombie's favor. The district court assumed, without deciding, that Levi Strauss also had two factors—acquired distinctiveness and degree of recognition—that weighed in its favor. Thus, application of the correct, less-demanding standard could have tipped the balance in favor of Levi Strauss. The degree of similarity between the Ruehl and Arcuate marks may be insufficient to support a likelihood of dilution, but that conclusion can come only after consideration of the degree of similarity in light of all other relevant factors and cannot be determined conclusively by application of an "essentially the same" threshold.

Given the relative balance of the parties' positions, we cannot say, with any confidence, that the district court would have reached the same result absent the legal error. We therefore must reverse the judgment of the district court with respect to Levi Strauss's claim under the TDRA. REVERSED and REMANDED.

NOTES AND QUESTIONS

1. Review the U.S. dilution provision above. What are the two forms of dilution recognized under U.S. law? How are they different?

2. What is the rationale for having a claim for "dilution" of a mark? How is it different from trademark infringement? What kind of situations, if any, would a dilution claim cover that a trademark infringement claim would not?

3. Does TRIPS Article 16(3) apply to the scenario in the *Levi* case between direct competitors for the same type of goods (jeans)? Should dilution claims be limited to non-competitors who do not sell in the same market?

4. In your view, do the two jeans' stitchings (Levi's versus Abercrombie's) have any similarity? Do you think Abercombie's stitching is likely to cause any harm or damage to Levi's mark?

5. *Likelihood of dilution.* In 2006, after intense lobbying by the International Trademark Association (INTA), the U.S. Congress enacted the Trademark Dilution Revision Act, which changed the standard of dilution in the U.S. from actual dilution to the lower standard of likelihood of dilution. *See* 15 U.S.C. § 1125(c). The EU Trade Marks Directive is somewhat similar in approach. Although Article 4(a) of the Directive requires a use of a later mark that "would take unfair advantage of, or be detrimental to" a famous mark as a ground for refusing or invalidating registration of the later mark, the Court of Justice has interpreted the provision so as not to require actual injury, but instead, a serious risk of future injury. *See Intel Corp. v. CPM*, [2008] ECR I–8823, No. C–252/07, ¶¶ 38–39. In addition, the Court interpreted similar language "would take unfair advantage" in Article 5(2) as not even requiring proof of likelihood of detriment. It would be enough, in a comparative ad making reference to a famous mark, for the trademark owner to show the defendant "seeks by that use to ride on the coat-tails of the mark with a reputation in order to benefit from the power of attraction, the reputation and the prestige of that mark and to exploit, without paying any financial compensation, the marketing effort expended by the proprietor of the mark in order to create and maintain the mark's image." *L'Oreal SA v. Bellure NV*, [2009] ECR I–5185, C–487/07, ¶ 81(1). Do you have any concerns about the expansion of dilution claims?

6. *National fame, not niche fame.* While the TDRA made dilution easier to prove, it also required a higher standard for marks to qualify as famous marks. The mark must be "widely recognized by the general consuming public in the United States" for it to qualify for a dilution claim, thereby rejecting niche fame in one area as a basis for dilution. *Id.*

7. *EU Approach to Marks with a "Reputation."* Article 5(2) of the EU Trade Marks Directive applies to marks that have a "reputation" in the member state where the mark is registered. *See* EU Trade Marks Directive 89/104, art. 5(2). In *General Motors v. Yplon SA* (also known as the "Chevy" case), the European Court of Justice described the standard for showing "reputation" as follows: the mark must "be known by a significant part of the public concerned by the products or services covered by that mark." *General Motors Corp. v. Yplon SA*, [1999] ECR I–05421, Case C–375/97, ¶ 26 (Sept. 14, 1999). In other words, "a sufficient degree of knowledge of that mark that the public, when confronted by the later trade mark, may possibly make an association between the two trade marks, even when used for non-similar products or services, and ... the earlier trade mark may consequently be

damaged." *Id.* ¶ 23. The reputation does not have to extend throughout the entire member state; it is sufficient if the reputation is shown to exist in a "substantial part" of the member state. *Id.* ¶ 28. In determining whether a reputation exists, courts "must take into consideration all the relevant facts of the case, in particular the market share held by the trade mark, the intensity, geographical extent and duration of its use, and the size of the investment made by the undertaking in promoting it." *Id.* ¶ 27.

How does the EU concept of reputation compare with the U.S. approach to famous marks? Which requirement is easier to satisfy?

8. *Exceptions to Dilution.* Critics of expansive dilution claims argue that they threaten to remove important words from public discourse and unrelated areas of commerce by propertizing them. For example, Facebook has sought to trademark "Face" and also "Book" in various trademark uses. How does the U.S. provision for dilution attempt to address this problem? Are the exceptions adequate? For more discussion of this issue, see Lisa P. Ramsey, *Free Speech and International Obligations to Protect Trademarks*, 35 YALE J. INT'L L. 405 (2010). Interestingly, Congress has devoted more thought and attention to the exceptions to the recent dilution provision than to basic infringement. *See* Graeme B. Dinwoodie, *Developing Defenses in Trademark Law*, 13 LEWIS & CLARK L. REV. 99 (2009).

d. Special Discussion: The Internet and Keyword Advertising Controversy

PROBLEM 4–14

Prada is a high-end fashion designer of men's and women's clothing and accessories based in Milan, Italy. Its mark is famous in the European Union and most developed countries around the world. Prada's general counsel has learned that Google is selling the term "prada" as a keyword for third parties to purchase in relationship to a sponsored link on Google through Google's AdWords program. If an advertiser purchases the keyword "prada," the advertiser's own sponsored link ad will appear whenever someone types in "prada" for a search on Google. Prada's general counsel has learned that numerous low-end clothing manufacturers have purchased the keyword "prada" on Google. Thus, whenever someone searches for "prada" on Google, Google displays not only Prada's website as the first search listing, but also "Ads" for low-end clothing manufacturers on the right side bar of Google. The "Ads" are so indicated by Google. Prada's general counsel has hired you to prepare a legal analysis of whether Prada can prevail in a trademark infringement lawsuit against Google in the EU. In answering this question, please advise whether Prada can undertake any steps or inquiries to strengthen its possible case against Google. Consider the following discussion and cases.

* * *

The Internet has raised challenges for trademark law. In 2010, WIPO's Standing Committee on the Law of Trademarks (SCT) issued a report on "Trademarks and the Internet" to address some of these challenges, including its 2001 Joint Recommendation by the Assemblies of the Paris Union and WIPO General Assembly Concerning Provisions on the Protection of Marks on the Internet.

As the WIPO report identified, one of the most contentious issues is whether keyword ads online that contain trademarks of others infringe the rights of the trademark owners. Internet search engines, such as Google, allow third parties to buy search terms or keywords that trigger a third-party ad to be displayed on the search engine when a user enters that term into a search. Trademark holders object, however, to the use of their marks by others in keyword advertising. Numerous lawsuits have been brought around the world. Countries have taken varying approaches to the issue, ranging from generally allowing keyword advertising to holding Internet search engines liable. Consider the approach of the European Union below. The first case discusses liability against the Internet search engine, and the second case, liability against the entity placing the keyword ad.

GOOGLE FRANCE SARL v. LOUIS VUITTON MALLETIER SA

Court of Justice of the European Union (Grand Chamber).
[2010] E.T.M.R. 30, C–236/08, C–237/08, C–238/08 (March 23, 2010).

Judgment

II—The disputes in the main proceedings and the questions referred for a preliminary ruling

A—The 'AdWords' referencing service

Google operates an internet search engine. When an internet user performs a search on the basis of one or more words, the search engine will display the sites which appear best to correspond to those words, in decreasing order of relevance. These are referred to as the 'natural' results of the search. In addition, Google offers a paid referencing service called 'AdWords.' That service enables any economic operator, by means of the reservation of one or more keywords, to obtain the placing, in the event of a correspondence between one or more of those words and that/those entered as a request in the search engine by an internet user, of an advertising link to its site. That advertising link appears under the heading 'sponsored links,' which is displayed either on the right-hand side of the screen, to the right of the natural results, or on the upper part of the screen, above the natural results.

That advertising link is accompanied by a short commercial message. Together, that link and that message constitute the advertisement ('ad') displayed under the abovementioned heading. A fee for the referencing service is payable by the advertiser for each click on the advertising link. That fee is calculated on the basis, in particular, of the 'maximum price per click' which the advertiser agreed to pay when concluding with Google the contract for the referencing service, and on the basis of the number of times that link is clicked on by internet users.

A number of advertisers can reserve the same keyword. The order in which their advertising links are then displayed is determined according to, in particular, the maximum price per click, the number of previous clicks on those links and the quality of the ad as assessed by Google. The advertiser can at any time improve its ranking in the display by fixing a higher maximum price per click or by trying to improve the quality of its ad. Google has set up an automated process for the selection of keywords and the creation of ads. Advertisers select the keywords, draft the commercial message, and input the link to their site.

B—Case C–236/08

Vuitton, which markets, in particular, luxury bags and other leather goods, is the proprietor of the Community trade mark 'Vuitton' and of the French national trade marks 'Louis Vuitton' and 'LV.' It is common ground that those marks enjoy a certain reputation.

At the beginning of 2003, Vuitton became aware that the entry, by internet users, of terms constituting its trade marks into Google's search engine triggered the display, under the heading 'sponsored links,' of links to sites offering imitation versions of Vuitton's products. It was also established that Google offered advertisers the possibility of selecting not only keywords which correspond to Vuitton's trademarks, but also those keywords in combination with expressions indicating imitation, such as 'imitation' and 'copy.' Vuitton brought proceeding against Google with a view, inter alia, to obtaining a declaration that Google had infringed its trademarks.

Google was found guilty of infringing Vuitton's trade marks by a judgment of 4 February 2005 of the Tribunal de grande instance de Paris (Regional Court, Paris), and subsequently, on appeal, by judgment of 28 June 2006 of the Cour d'appel de Paris (Court of Appeal, Paris). Google has brought an appeal on a point of law (cassation) against that latter judgment. In those circumstances, the Cour de cassation (French Court of Cassation) decided to stay the proceedings and to refer the following questions to the Court for a preliminary ruling[.]

III—Consideration of the questions referred

A—Use, in an internet referencing service, of keywords corresponding to trademarks of other persons

By application of Article 5(1)(a) of Directive 89/104 or, in the case of Community trademarks, of Article 9(1)(a) of Regulation No 40/94, the proprietor of a trademark is entitled to prohibit a third party from using, without the proprietor's consent, a sign identical with that trade mark when that use is in the course of trade, is in relation to goods or services which are identical with, or similar to, those for which that trade mark is registered, and affects, or is liable to affect, the functions of the trade mark.

a) Use in the course of trade

The use of a sign identical with a trademark constitutes use in the course of trade where it occurs in the context of commercial activity with a view to economic advantage and not as a private matter.

With regard, firstly, to the advertiser purchasing the referencing service and choosing as a keyword a sign identical with another's trademark, it must be held that that advertiser is using that sign within the meaning of that case-law. From the advertiser's point of view, the selection of a keyword identical with a trademark has the object and effect of displaying an advertising link to the site on which he offers his goods or services for sale. Since the sign selected as a keyword is the means used to trigger that ad display, it cannot be disputed that the advertiser indeed uses it in the context of commercial activity and not as a private matter.

With regard, next, to the referencing service provider, it is common ground that it is carrying out a commercial activity with a view to economic advantage when it stores as keywords, for certain of its clients, signs which are identical with trademarks and arranges for the display of ads on the basis of those keywords. It is also common ground that that service is not supplied only to the proprietors of those trademarks or to operators entitled to market their goods or services, but, at least in the proceedings in question, is provided without the consent of the proprietors and is supplied to their competitors or to imitators.

Although it is clear from those factors that the referencing service provider operates 'in the course of trade' when it permits advertisers to select, as keywords, signs identical with trademarks, stores those signs and displays its clients' ads on the basis thereof, it does not follow, however, from those factors that that service provider itself 'uses' those signs within the terms of Article 5 of Directive 89/104 and Article 9 of Regulation No 40/94. In that regard, suffice it to note that the use, by a third party, of a sign identical with, or similar to, the proprietor's trade mark implies, at the very least, that that third party uses the sign in its own commercial communication. A referencing service provider allows its clients to use signs which are identical with, or similar to, trademarks, without itself using those signs.

That conclusion is not called into question by the fact that that service provider is paid by its clients for the use of those signs. The fact of creating the technical conditions necessary for the use of a sign and being paid for that service does not mean that the party offering the service itself uses the sign. To the extent to which it has permitted its client to make such a use of the sign, its role must, as necessary, be examined from the angle of rules of law other than Article 5 of Directive 89/104 and Article 9 of Regulation No 40/94, such as those referred to in paragraph 107 of the present judgment [dealing with liability of intermediary service providers].

Consequently, the conditions relating to use 'in relation to goods or services' and to the effect on the functions of the trademark need to be examined only in relation to the use, by the advertiser, of the sign identical with the mark. [The Court of Justice ruled that an advertiser that uses another's trademark in keyword advertising could be directly liable for trademark infringement "on the basis of a keyword identical with that trademark which that advertiser has, without the consent of the proprietor, selected in connection with an internet referencing service, goods or services identical with those for which that mark is registered, in the case where that ad does not enable an average internet user, or enables that user only with difficulty, to ascertain whether the goods or services referred to therein originate from the proprietor of the trademark or an undertaking economically connected to it or, on the contrary, originate from a third party." *Ed.*]

B—The liability of the referencing service provider

By its third question in Case C–236/08, its second question in Case C–237/08 and its third question in Case C–238/08, the Cour de cassation asks, in essence, whether Article 14 of Directive 2000/31 [Directive on Electronic Commerce] is to be interpreted as meaning that an internet referencing service constitutes an information society service consisting in the storage of information supplied by the advertiser, with the result that that information is the subject of 'hosting' within the meaning of that article and that the referencing service provider therefore cannot be held liable prior to its being informed of the unlawful conduct of that advertiser.

Section 4 of Directive 2000/31, comprising Articles 12 to 15 and entitled 'Liability of intermediary service providers,' seeks to restrict the situations in which intermediary service providers may be held liable pursuant to the applicable national law. It is therefore in the context of that national law that the conditions under which such liability arises must be sought, it being understood, however, that, by virtue of Section 4 of that directive, certain situations cannot give rise to liability on the part of intermediary service providers.

The restriction on liability set out in Article 14(1) of Directive 2000/31 applies to cases '[w]here an information society service is provided that consists of the storage of information provided by a recipient of the service' and means that the provider of such a service cannot be held liable for the data which it has stored at the request of a recipient of that service unless that service provider, after having become aware, because of information supplied by an injured party or otherwise, of the unlawful nature of those data or of activities of that recipient, fails to act expeditiously to remove or to disable access to those data.

[T]he legislature defined the concept of 'information society service' as covering services which are provided at a distance, by means of electronic equipment for the processing and storage of data, at the individual request of a recipient of services, and normally in return for remuneration. Regard being had to the characteristics of the referencing service at issue in the cases in the main proceedings, the conclusion must be that that service features all of the elements of that definition.

In order for the storage by a referencing service provider to come within the scope of Article 14 of Directive 2000/31, it is further necessary that the conduct of that service provider should be limited to that of an 'intermediary service provider' within the meaning intended by the legislature in the context of Section 4 of that directive. In that regard, it follows from recital 42 in the preamble to Directive 2000/31 that the exemptions from liability established in that directive cover only cases in which the activity of the information society service provider is 'of a mere technical, automatic and passive nature,' which implies that that service provider 'has neither knowledge of nor control over the information which is transmitted or stored.'

Accordingly, in order to establish whether the liability of a referencing service provider may be limited under Article 14 of Directive 2000/31, it is necessary to examine whether the role played by that service provider is neutral, in the sense that its conduct is merely technical, automatic and passive, pointing to a lack of knowledge or control of the data which it stores.

With regard to the referencing service at issue in the cases in the main proceedings, it is apparent, with the help of software which it has developed, Google processes the data entered by advertisers and the resulting display of the ads is made under conditions which Google controls. Thus, Google determines the order of display according to, inter alia, the remuneration paid by the advertisers.

It must be pointed out that the mere facts that the referencing service is subject to payment, that Google sets the payment terms or that it provides general information to its clients cannot have the effect of depriving Google of the exemptions from liability provided for in Directive 2000/31. Likewise, concordance between the keyword selected and the search term entered by an internet user is not sufficient of itself to justify the view that Google has knowledge of, or control over, the data entered into its system by advertisers and stored in memory on its server.

By contrast, the role played by Google in the drafting of the commercial message which accompanies the advertising link or in the establishment or selection of keywords is relevant. It is in the light of the foregoing considerations that the national court, which is best placed to be aware of the actual terms on which the service in the cases in the main proceedings is supplied, must assess whether the role thus played by Google corresponds to [the standard that "its conduct is merely technical, automatic and passive, pointing to a lack of knowledge or control of the data which it stores."]

It follows that the answer to the third question in Case C–236/08, the second question in Case C–237/08 and the third question in Case C–238/08 is that Article 14 of Directive 2000/31 must be interpreted as meaning that the rule laid down therein applies to an internet referencing service provider in the case where that service provider has not played an active role of such a kind as to give it knowledge of, or control over, the data stored. If it has not played such a role, that service provider cannot be held liable for the data which it has stored at the request of an advertiser, unless, having obtained knowledge of the unlawful nature of those data or of that advertiser's activities, it failed to act expeditiously to remove or to disable access to the data concerned.

NOTES AND QUESTIONS

1. Was the case a victory for Louis Vuitton or Google, or both?

2. *Trademark use.* The Court of Justice considered whether (i) an Internet service provider that sells keyword ads and (ii) a third party that purchases a keyword ad identical to another's trademark from the ISP "use" the trademark in the ad for the purposes of proving a trademark infringement claim. How did the CJEU rule? Was there a "use" of the trademark contained in a keyword associated with a search engine? If so, a use by whom?

3. *ISP safe harbor in EU.* ISPs might be subject to claims of secondary liability based on the keyword advertising of one of its clients. The CJEU thus considered the application of the ISP safe harbor under the E–Commerce Directive Article 14(1) in the keyword ad context. Based on the CJEU's ruling, is an ISP like Google immune from liability when selling keyword ads? If not, when might Google be held liable?

4. *U.S. approach.* After initial uncertainty, U.S. courts have held that such keyword uses of trademarks are used in commerce under U.S. law. *See Rescuecom Corp. v. Google Inc.*, 562 F.3d 123 (2d Cir. 2009) (Internet search engine use); *Network Automation, Inc. v. Advanced Systems Concepts*, 638 F.3d 1137, 1144 (9th Cir. 2011) (advertiser use). In these cases, U.S. courts have held the keyword ad constitutes a "use in commerce" by both the Internet search engine and the advertiser. Thus, the central question in these disputes is whether the keyword ad is likely to cause confusion with the trademark—an issue that is fact-specific and requires the consideration of the likelihood of confusion factors. Some courts have found no likelihood of confusion, while others have found the opposite. *Compare Rosetta Stone Ltd. v. Google, Inc.*, 730 F. Supp. 2d 531, 540–46 (E.D. Va. 2010) (no likelihood of confusion in keyword containing "Rosetta Stone" for "sponsor link" ads on Google) with *Storus Corp. v. Aroa Marketing, Inc.*, 2008 WL 449835, at *3–*7 (N.D. Cal. 2008) (likelihood of confusion based on competitor's use of keyword "smart money clip" (identical to plaintiff's trademark) for ad on Google, with "smart money clip" also appearing in the ad itself for the same type of product as plaintiff). Is the U.S. approach more or less protective of Internet search engines than the EU's approach?

5. *Other countries.* For summaries of other countries' approaches, including China, India, Argentina, and Australia, see Standing Committee on the Law of Trademarks, Industrial Designs and Geographical Indications, WIPO (Nov. 1–4, 2010). Should the WTO attempt to harmonize the different approaches to keyword advertising among countries?

INTERFLORA INC. v. MARKS & SPENCER PLC

Court of Justice of the European Union (First Chamber).
[2012] E.T.M.R. 1, C–323/09 (2011).

Judgment

This reference for a preliminary ruling concerns the interpretation of Article 5 of First Council Directive 89/104/EEC of 21 December 1988 to approximate the laws of the Member States relating to trademarks (OJ 1989 L 40, p. 1) and Article 9 of Council Regulation (EC) No 40/94 of 20 December 1993 on the Community trade mark (OJ 1994 L 11, p. 1).

Interflora Inc., a company incorporated in the State of Michigan (United States), operates a worldwide flower-delivery network. Interflora British Unit is a licensee of Interflora Inc. The network of Interflora Inc. and Interflora British Unit (together 'Interflora') is made up of florists with whom customers may place orders in person or by telephone. Interflora also has websites that enable orders to be placed via the internet, those orders then being fulfilled by the network member closest to the place where the flowers are to be delivered. The address of the main website is www.interflora.com. That site redirects to country-specific websites such as www.interflora.co.uk. INTERFLORA is a national trademark in the United Kingdom and also a Community trademark. It is common ground that, so far as the flower-delivery service is concerned, those marks have a substantial reputation both in the United Kingdom and in other Member States of the European Union.

M & S, a company governed by English law, is one of the main retailers in the United Kingdom. It retails a wide range of goods and supplies services through its network of shops and via its website www. marksandspencer.com. One of those services is the sale and delivery of flowers. That commercial activity is in competition with that of Interflora. Using the 'AdWords' [of Google] referencing service, M & S selected as keywords the word 'Interflora,' as well as variants made up of that word with minor errors and expressions containing the word 'Interflora' ('Interflora Flowers,' 'Interflora Delivery,' 'Interflora.com,' 'interflora co uk' and so forth). Consequently, when internet users entered the word 'Interflora' or one of those variants or expressions as a search term in the Google search engine, an M & S advertisement appeared under the heading 'sponsored links.'

Consideration of the questions referred

The questions concerning Article 5(1)(a) of Directive 89/104 and Article 9(1)(a) of Regulation No 40/94

[T]he sign selected by an advertiser as a keyword in the context of an internet referencing service is the means used by the advertiser to trigger the display of its advertisement and is thus used in the course of trade within the meaning of Article 5 of Directive 89/104 and Article 9 of

Regulation No 40/94 (Joined Cases C–236/08 to C–238/08 *Google France and Google* [2010] ECR I–2417, paragraphs 49 to 52).

The case in the main proceedings falls within the situation referred to in Article 5(1)(a) of Directive 89/104 and Article 9(1)(a) of Regulation No 40/94, namely the so-called 'double identity' situation, in which use by a third party of a sign identical with the trade mark is made in relation to goods or services which are identical with those for which the trade mark is registered. Indeed, it is not in dispute that M & S made use in relation to its flower-delivery service, of, inter alia, the sign 'Interflora,' which is in substance identical with the word mark INTERFLORA, registered for flower-delivery services. In that situation, the proprietor of the trademark is entitled to prevent that use only if it is liable to have an adverse effect on one of the functions of the mark.

Adverse effect on the function of indicating origin

The question whether a trademark's function of indicating origin is adversely affected when internet users are shown, on the basis of a keyword identical with the mark, a third party's advertisement, such as that of a competitor of the trade mark proprietor, depends in particular on the manner in which that advertisement is presented. That function is adversely affected if the advertisement does not enable reasonably well-informed and reasonably observant internet users, or enables them only with difficulty, to ascertain whether the goods or services referred to by the advertisement originate from the proprietor of the trade mark or an undertaking economically connected to it or, on the contrary, originate from a third party (*Google France and Google*, paragraphs 83 and 84).

Where a third party's advertisement suggests that there is an economic link between that third party and the proprietor of the trademark, the conclusion must be that there is an adverse effect on that mark's function of indicating origin. Similarly, where the advertisement, while not suggesting the existence of an economic link, is vague to such an extent on the origin of the goods or services at issue that reasonably well-informed and reasonably observant internet users are unable to determine, on the basis of the advertising link and the commercial message attached thereto, whether the advertiser is a third party vis-à-vis the proprietor of the trade mark or whether, on the contrary, it is economically linked to that proprietor, the conclusion must be that there is an adverse effect on that function of the trade mark (*Google France and Google*, paragraphs 89 and 90).

It is for the referring court to assess whether, on the facts of the dispute before it, the trade mark's function of indicating origin as described in the preceding paragraphs is, or is liable to be, adversely affected. For the purposes of that assessment, the fact that the referencing service provider has not permitted trademark proprietors to prevent the selection of a sign identical with that trademark as a keyword is irrelevant.

By contrast, a situation such as that described in question 4(a) may be relevant for the purpose of applying the rule set out in Article 5(1)(a) of Directive 89/104 and Article 9(1)(a) of Regulation No 40/94. Indeed, if the referring court's assessments of the facts were to show that M & S's advertising, displayed in response to searches performed by internet users using the word 'Interflora,' may lead those users to believe, incorrectly, that the flower-delivery service offered by M & S is part of Interflora's commercial network, it would have to be concluded that that advertising does not allow it to be determined whether M & S is a third party in relation to the proprietor of the trade mark or whether, on the contrary, it is economically linked to that proprietor. In those circumstances, the function of the INTERFLORA trade mark of indicating origin would be adversely affected. In that context, the relevant public comprises reasonably well-informed and reasonably observant internet users. Therefore, the fact that some internet users may have had difficulty grasping that the service provided by M & S is independent from that of Interflora is not a sufficient basis for a finding that the function of indicating origin has been adversely affected.

In carrying out its examination of the facts, the referring court may choose to assess, first, whether the reasonably well-informed and reasonably observant internet user is deemed to be aware, on the basis of general knowledge of the market, that M & S's flower-delivery service is not part of the Interflora network but is, on the contrary, in competition with it and, second, should it become apparent that that is not generally known, whether M & S's advertisement enabled that internet user to tell that the service concerned does not belong to the Interflora network. In particular, the referring court may take into account that, in the present case, the commercial network of the trade mark proprietor is composed of a large number of retailers which vary greatly in terms of size and commercial profile. The Court considers that, in such circumstances, it may be particularly difficult for the reasonably well-informed and reasonably observant internet user to determine, in the absence of any indication from the advertiser, whether or not the advertiser—whose advertisement is displayed in response to a search using that trade mark as a search term—is part of that network.

Having regard to that situation and to the other matters that it may consider relevant, the referring court will, in the absence of any general knowledge, have to determine whether or not the use of words such as 'M & S Flowers' in an advertisement such as the one set out [above] is sufficient to enable a reasonably well-informed and reasonably observant internet user who has entered search terms including the word 'Interflora' to tell that the flower-delivery service offered does not originate from Interflora.

Adverse effect on the advertising function

With regard to the advertising function, the Court has already had occasion to state that use of a sign identical with another person's trademark in a referencing service such as 'AdWords' does not have an adverse effect on that function of the trademark. Internet advertising on the basis of keywords corresponding to trade marks constitutes such a practice in that its aim, as a general rule, is merely to offer internet users alternatives to the goods or services of the proprietors of those trademarks (see, to that effect, *Google France and Google*, paragraph 69).

Adverse effect on the 'investment' function

Although that function of a trade mark—called the 'investment function'—may overlap with the advertising function, it is none the less distinct from the latter. Indeed, when the trademark is used to acquire or preserve a reputation, not only advertising is employed, but also various commercial techniques. When the use by a third party, such as a competitor of the trade mark proprietor, of a sign identical with the trade mark in relation to goods or services identical with those for which the mark is registered substantially interferes with the proprietor's use of its trade mark to acquire or preserve a reputation capable of attracting consumers and retaining their loyalty, the third party's use must be regarded as adversely affecting the trade mark's investment function.

However, it cannot be accepted that the proprietor of a trademark may—in conditions of fair competition that respect the trademark's function as an indication of origin—prevent a competitor from using a sign identical with that trademark in relation to goods or services identical with those for which the mark is registered, if the only consequence of that use is to oblige the proprietor of that trademark to adapt its efforts to acquire or preserve a reputation capable of attracting consumers and retaining their loyalty. Likewise, the fact that that use may prompt some consumers to switch from goods or services bearing that trade mark cannot be successfully relied on by the proprietor of the mark.

The question relating to Article 5(2) of Directive 89/104 and Article 9(1)(c) of Regulation No 40/94 [Marks with a Reputation]

By point (b) of question 3, read in conjunction with questions 1 and 2, the referring court asks, in essence, whether Article 5(2) of Directive 89/104 and Article 9(1)(c) of Regulation No 40/94 must be interpreted as meaning that the proprietor of a trade mark with a reputation is entitled to prevent a competitor from basing its advertising on a keyword corresponding to that trademark which the competitor has, without the proprietor's consent, selected in an internet referencing service.

The types of injury against which Article 5(2) of Directive 89/104 and Article 9(1)(c) of Regulation No 40/94 provide protection are, first, detriment to the distinctive character of the trademark, second, detriment to the repute of that mark and, third, unfair advantage taken of the distinctive character or the repute of the mark, just one of those types of injury sufficing for the rule set out in those provisions to apply.

Detriment to the distinctive character of a mark with a reputation, also referred to as, inter alia, 'dilution,' is caused when that mark's ability to identify the goods or services for which it is registered is weakened, whilst detriment to the repute of the mark, also referred to as, inter alia, 'tarnishment,' is caused when the goods or services for which the identical or similar sign is used by the third party may be perceived by the public in such a way that the trade mark's power of attraction is reduced.

For its part, the concept of 'taking unfair advantage of the distinctive character or the repute of the trade mark,' also referred to as, inter alia, 'free-riding,' relates not to the detriment caused to the mark but to the advantage taken by the third party as a result of the use of the identical or similar sign. It covers, in particular, cases where, by reason of a transfer of the image of the mark or of the characteristics which it projects to the goods identified by the identical or similar sign, there is clear exploitation on the coat-tails of the mark with a reputation.

Detriment to the distinctive character of a trade mark with a reputation (dilution)

[D]etriment is caused to the distinctive character of a trademark with a reputation when the use of a sign identical with or similar to that mark reduces the ability of the mark to distinguish the goods or services of its proprietor from those which have a different origin. At the end of the process of dilution, the trade mark is no longer capable of creating an immediate association, in the minds of consumers, with a specific commercial origin. For the proprietor of a trademark with a reputation to be effectively protected against that type of injury, Article 5(2) of Directive 89/104 and Article 9(1)(c) of Regulation No 40/94 must be interpreted as entitling the proprietor to prevent all use of a sign identical with or similar to that trade mark which reduces the distinctiveness of the mark, without it being required to wait for the end of the process of dilution, that is to say, the total loss of the trade mark's distinctive character.

In support of its contention that detriment is caused to its trademark's distinctive character, Interflora maintains that the use by M & S and other undertakings of the word 'Interflora' within a referencing service such as that at issue in the main proceedings gradually persuades internet users that the word is not a trademark designating the flower-delivery service provided by florists in the Interflora network but is a generic word for any flower-delivery service.

It is true that the use, by a third party in the course of trade, of a sign identical with or similar to a trade mark with a reputation reduces the latter's distinctiveness and is thus detrimental to the distinctive character of that trade mark for the purposes of Article 5(2) of Directive 89/104 or, in the case of a Community trade mark, of Article 9(1)(c) of Regulation No 40/94, when it contributes to turning the trademark into a generic term. However, contrary to Interflora's contention, the selection of a sign which is identical with or similar to a trade mark with a reputation as a keyword within an internet referencing service does not necessarily contribute to such a development.

Thus, when the use, as a keyword, of a sign corresponding to a trade mark with a reputation triggers the display of an advertisement which enables the reasonably well-informed and reasonably observant internet user to tell that the goods or services offered originate not from the proprietor of the trademark but, on the contrary, from a competitor of that proprietor, the conclusion will have to be that the trademark's distinctiveness has not been reduced by that use, the latter having merely served to draw the internet user's attention to the existence of an alternative product or service to that of the proprietor of the trademark.

If, on the other hand, the referring court were to conclude that the advertising triggered by the use of the sign identical to the INTERFLORA trade mark did not enable the reasonably well-informed and reasonably observant internet user to tell that the service promoted by M & S is independent from that of Interflora and if Interflora were to seek moreover from the referring court, in addition to a finding that the mark's function of indicating origin has been adversely affected, a finding that M & S has also caused detriment to the distinctive character of the INTERFLORA trade mark by contributing to turning it into a generic term, it would fall to the referring court to determine, on the basis of all the evidence submitted to it, whether the selection of signs corresponding to the trademark INTERFLORA as keywords on the internet has had such an impact on the market for flower-delivery services that the word 'Interflora' has come to designate, in the consumer's mind, any flower-delivery service.

Unfair advantage taken of the distinctive character or the repute of the trade mark (free-riding)

It is clear from those particular aspects of the selection as internet keywords of signs corresponding to trademarks with a reputation which belong to other persons that such a selection can, in the absence of any 'due cause' as referred to in Article 5(2) of Directive 89/104 and Article 9(1)(c) of Regulation No 40/94, be construed as a use whereby the advertiser rides on the coat-tails of a trademark with a reputation in order to benefit from its power of attraction, its reputation and its prestige, and to exploit, without paying any financial compensation and without being required to make efforts of its own in that regard, the marketing effort expended by the proprietor of that mark in order to create and maintain the image of that mark. If that is the case, the advantage thus obtained by the third party must be considered to be unfair.

As the Court has already stated, that is particularly likely to be the conclusion in cases in which internet advertisers offer for sale, by means of the selection of keywords corresponding to trademarks with a reputation, goods which are imitations of the goods of the proprietor of those marks (*Google France and Google*, paragraphs 102 and 103).

By contrast, where the advertisement displayed on the internet on the basis of a keyword corresponding to a trademark with a reputation puts forward—without offering a mere imitation of the goods or services of the proprietor of that trade mark, without causing dilution or tarnishment and without, moreover, adversely affecting the functions of the trademark concerned—an alternative to the goods or services of the proprietor of the trademark with a reputation, it must be concluded that such use falls, as a rule, within the ambit of fair competition in the sector for the goods or services concerned and is thus not without 'due cause' for the purposes of Article 5(2) of Directive 89/104 and Article 9(1)(c) of Regulation No 40/94.

Advertising on the basis of such a keyword is detrimental to the distinctive character of a trade mark with a reputation (dilution) if, for example, it contributes to turning that trademark into a generic term. By contrast, the proprietor of a trademark with a reputation is not entitled to prevent, inter alia, advertisements displayed by competitors on the basis of keywords corresponding to that trademark, which put forward—without offering a mere imitation of the goods or services of the proprietor of that trademark, without causing dilution or tarnishment and without, moreover, adversely affecting the functions of the trade mark with a reputation—an alternative to the goods or services of the proprietor of that mark.

On those grounds, the Court (First Chamber) hereby rules:

1. Article 5(1)(a) of First Council Directive 89/104/EEC of 21 December 1988 to approximate the laws of the Member States relating to trademarks and Article 9(1)(a) of Council Regulation (EC) No 40/94 of 20 December 1993 on the Community trade mark must be interpreted as meaning that the proprietor of a trade mark is entitled to prevent a competitor from advertising—on the basis of a keyword which is identical with the trademark and which has been selected in an internet referencing service by the competitor without the proprietor's consent—goods or services identical with those for which that mark is registered, where that use is liable to have an adverse effect on one of the functions of the trade mark. Such use:

—adversely affects the trade mark's function of indicating origin where the advertising displayed on the basis of that keyword does not enable reasonably well-informed and reasonably observant internet users, or enables them only with difficulty, to ascertain whether the goods or services concerned by the advertisement originate from the proprietor of the trade mark or an undertaking economically linked to that proprietor or, on the contrary, originate from a third party;

—does not adversely affect, in the context of an internet referencing service having the characteristics of the service at issue in the main proceedings, the trademark's advertising function; and

—adversely affects the trade mark's investment function if it substantially interferes with the proprietor's use of its trade mark to acquire or preserve a reputation capable of attracting consumers and retaining their loyalty.

2. Article 5(2) of Directive 89/104 and Article 9(1)(c) of Regulation No 40/94 must be interpreted as meaning that the proprietor of a trade mark with a reputation is entitled to prevent a competitor from advertising on the basis of a keyword corresponding to that trademark, which the competitor has, without the proprietor's consent, selected in an internet referencing service, where the competitor thereby takes unfair advantage of the distinctive character or repute of the trademark (free-riding) or where the advertising is detrimental to that distinctive character (dilution) or to that repute (tarnishment).

Advertising on the basis of such a keyword is detrimental to the distinctive character of a trademark with a reputation (dilution) if, for example, it contributes to turning that trademark into a generic term.

By contrast, the proprietor of a trade mark with a reputation is not entitled to prevent, inter alia, advertisements displayed by competitors on the basis of keywords corresponding to that trademark, which put forward—without offering a mere imitation of the goods or services of the proprietor of that trade mark, without causing dilution or tarnishment and without, moreover, adversely affecting the functions of the trademark with a reputation—an alternative to the goods or services of the proprietor of that mark.

NOTES AND QUESTIONS

1. Was the decision a victory for Interflora or M & S, or both?

2. Did the CJEU establish a low or high standard for trademark owners to prove trademark infringement based on keyword advertising? What about for dilution? How might Interflora prove the keyword ad here constituted infringement or dilution of its mark?

3. *Reasonably well-informed and reasonably observant Internet users.* The CJEU held that trademark infringement might arise from a keyword ad "if the advertisement does not enable reasonably well-informed and reasonably observant internet users, or enables them only with difficulty, to ascertain whether the goods or services referred to by the advertisement originate from the proprietor of the trade mark or an undertaking economically connected to it or, on the contrary, originate from a third party." How might a trademark owner show this standard is met?

4. *Three functions of trademarks.* The CJEU elaborated three functions of trademarks: origin, advertising, and investment. Explain the differences and how they bear on whether a keyword advertisement involving a trademark can constitute infringement.

5. *Famous marks.* In the second part of the decision, the CJEU considered dilution and other claims that may be brought by owners of famous marks (i.e., marks with "reputation"). How can famous trademark owners prove keyword advertising containing their marks violates their rights?

6. ABANDONMENT

Article 19 of the TRIPS Agreement provides a minimum standard for those countries that opt to require use of the trademark to maintain registration. It states in part: "If use is required to maintain a registration, the registration may be cancelled only after an uninterrupted period of at least three years of non-use, unless valid reasons based on the existence of obstacles to such use are shown by the trademark owner." It also recognizes a justification for nonuse of a trademark arising from factors beyond the holder's will: "Circumstances arising independently of the will of the owner of the trademark which constitute an obstacle to the use of the trademark, such as import restrictions on or other government requirements for goods or services protected by the trademark, shall be recognized as valid reasons for non-use." TRIPS art. 19(1).

As mentioned above, some countries also recognize abandonment and loss of trademark rights when the trademark holder engages in naked licensing of the mark, which is licensing without adequate quality control over the product on which the mark is used. The level of quality control required tends to be rather modest, however.

PROBLEM 4–15

You have examined three cases in which trademark holders did not use their marks for extended periods of time: (1) McDonald's in South Africa; (2) Pernod–Ricard's joint venture in the U.S. (the mark HAVANA CLUB); and (3) Cubatabaco in the U.S. (the mark COHIBA). Which of these circumstances, if any, should fall within the minimum standard for justified non-use under Article 19 of TRIPS? Which, if any, should not? In answering these questions, what significance should be given to the fact that McDonald's and Pernod–Ricard had registered their marks in the respective countries, but Cubatabaco had not? Is Article 19 still applicable where no registration had been effected?

7. EXCEPTIONS TO RIGHTS

TRIPS

Article 17

Exceptions

Members may provide limited exceptions to the rights conferred by a trademark, such as fair use of descriptive terms, provided that such exceptions take account of the legitimate interests of the owner of the trademark and of third parties.

TRIPS Article 17 regulates the extent to which countries can recognize exceptions to trademarks. There has been only one WTO dispute involving Article 17, but the dispute involved the special circumstance involving the intersection of trademarks and geographical indications

(GIs). We will study that WTO dispute (challenging the EU's Regulation for GIs) and the test for Article 17 of TRIPS later in this chapter when we discuss GIs. In addition, Article 21 of TRIPS expressly forbids countries from allowing compulsory licenses for trademarks. In both copyright and patent, however, they are not prohibited (although subject to minimum standards).

Trademark law has historically afforded weaker forms of protection than patent or copyright. Some commentators argue that trademark developed, not as a distinct type of property or exclusive right, but instead as a protection from unfair competition or passing off. As we have studied, a claim for trademark infringement typically is based on the "likelihood of confusion." Under this standard, a wide variety of uses of a trademark, such as for commentary, comparative advertising, and use of the term to describe one's own product, may well not create any likelihood of confusion. What happens when a fair use of a trademarked term does create a likelihood of confusion? Should fair use still protect the use of the term because it is necessary for description? Consider the following case, which discusses the U.S. approach.

KP PERMANENT MAKE–UP, INC. v. LASTING IMPRESSION I, INC.

Supreme Court of the United States.
543 U.S. 111 (2004).

JUSTICE SOUTER delivered the opinion of the Court.

The question here is whether a party raising the statutory affirmative defense of fair use to a claim of trademark infringement, 15 U.S.C. § 1115(b)(4), has a burden to negate any likelihood that the practice complained of will confuse consumers about the origin of the goods or services affected. We hold it does not.

I

Each party to this case sells permanent makeup, a mixture of pigment and liquid for injection under the skin to camouflage injuries and modify nature's dispensations, and each has used some version of the term "micro color" (as one word or two, singular or plural) in marketing and selling its product. Petitioner KP Permanent Make–Up, Inc., claims to have used the single-word version since 1990 or 1991 on advertising flyers and since 1991 on pigment bottles. Respondents Lasting Impression I, Inc., and its licensee, MCN International, Inc. (Lasting, for simplicity), deny that KP began using the term that early, but we accept KP's allegation as true for present purposes; the District and Appeals Courts took it to be so, and the disputed facts do not matter to our resolution of the issue. In 1992, Lasting applied to the United States Patent and Trademark Office (PTO) under 15 U.S.C. § 1051 for registration of a trademark consisting of the words "Micro Colors" in white letters separated by a green bar within a black square. The PTO registered the mark to

Lasting in 1993, and in 1999 the registration became incontestable. § 1065.

It was also in 1999 that KP produced a 10–page advertising brochure using "microcolor" in a large, stylized typeface, provoking Lasting to demand that KP stop using the term. Instead, KP sued Lasting in the Central District of California, seeking, on more than one ground, a declaratory judgment that its language infringed no such exclusive right as Lasting claimed. Lasting counterclaimed, alleging, among other things, that KP had infringed Lasting's "Micro Colors" trademark.

KP sought summary judgment on the infringement counterclaim, based on the statutory affirmative defense of fair use, 15 U.S.C. § 1115(b)(4). After finding that Lasting had conceded that KP used the term only to describe its goods and not as a mark, the District Court held that KP was acting fairly and in good faith because undisputed facts showed that KP had employed the term "microcolor" continuously from a time before Lasting adopted the two-word, plural variant as a mark. Without inquiring whether the practice was likely to cause confusion, the court concluded that KP had made out its affirmative defense under § 1115(b)(4) and entered summary judgment for KP on Lasting's infringement claim.

On appeal, 328 F.3d 1061 (2003), the Court of Appeals for the Ninth Circuit thought it was error for the District Court to have addressed the fair use defense without delving into the matter of possible confusion on the part of consumers about the origin of KP's goods. The reviewing court took the view that no use could be recognized as fair where any consumer confusion was probable, and although the court did not pointedly address the burden of proof, it appears to have placed it on KP to show absence of consumer confusion.

We granted KP's petition for certiorari to address a disagreement among the Courts of Appeals on the significance of likely confusion for a fair use defense to a trademark infringement claim, and the obligation of a party defending on that ground to show that its use is unlikely to cause consumer confusion. We now vacate the judgment of the Court of Appeals.

II

A

The Trademark Act of 1946, known for its principal proponent as the Lanham Act, 60 Stat. 427, as amended, 15 U.S.C. § 1051 et seq., provides the user of a trade or service mark with the opportunity to register it with the PTO, §§ 1051, 1053. If the registrant then satisfies further conditions including continuous use for five consecutive years, "the right . . . to use such registered mark in commerce" to designate the origin of the goods specified in the registration "shall be incontestable" outside certain listed exceptions. § 1065.

The holder of a registered mark (incontestable or not) has a civil action against anyone employing an imitation of it in commerce when "such use is likely to cause confusion, or to cause mistake, or to deceive." § 1114(1). Although an incontestable registration is "conclusive evidence . . . of the registrant's exclusive right to use the . . . mark in commerce," § 1115(b), the plaintiff's success is still subject to "proof of infringement as defined in section 1114," § 1115(b). And that, as just noted, requires a showing that the defendant's actual practice is likely to produce confusion in the minds of consumers about the origin of the goods or services in question. This plaintiff's burden has to be kept in mind when reading the relevant portion of the further provision for an affirmative defense of fair use, available to a party whose "use of the name, term, or device charged to be an infringement is a use, otherwise than as a mark, . . . of a term or device which is descriptive of and used fairly and in good faith only to describe the goods or services of such party, or their geographic origin. . . ." § 1115(b)(4).

Two points are evident. Section 1115(b) places a burden of proving likelihood of confusion (that is, infringement) on the party charging infringement even when relying on an incontestable registration. And Congress said nothing about likelihood of confusion in setting out the elements of the fair use defense in § 1115(b)(4).

Starting from these textual fixed points, it takes a long stretch to claim that a defense of fair use entails any burden to negate confusion. It is just not plausible that Congress would have used the descriptive phrase "likely to cause confusion, or to cause mistake, or to deceive" in § 1114 to describe the requirement that a markholder show likelihood of consumer confusion, but would have relied on the phrase "used fairly" in § 1115(b)(4) in a fit of terse drafting meant to place a defendant under a burden to negate confusion.

Finally, a look at the typical course of litigation in an infringement action points up the incoherence of placing a burden to show nonconfusion on a defendant. If a plaintiff succeeds in making out a prima facie case of trademark infringement, including the element of likelihood of consumer confusion, the defendant may offer rebutting evidence to undercut the force of the plaintiff's evidence on this (or any) element, or raise an affirmative defense to bar relief even if the prima facie case is sound, or do both. But it would make no sense to give the defendant a defense of showing affirmatively that the plaintiff cannot succeed in proving some element (like confusion); all the defendant needs to do is to leave the factfinder unpersuaded that the plaintiff has carried its own burden on that point. A defendant has no need of a court's true belief when agnosticism will do. Put another way, it is only when a plaintiff has shown likely confusion by a preponderance of the evidence that a defendant could have any need of an affirmative defense, but under Lasting's theory the defense would be foreclosed in such a case. Nor would it make sense to provide an affirmative defense of no confusion plus good faith, when merely rebutting the plaintiff's case on confusion would entitle the defendant to judgment, good faith or not.

B

Since the burden of proving likelihood of confusion rests with the plaintiff, and the fair use defendant has no free-standing need to show confusion unlikely, it follows (contrary to the Court of Appeals's view) that some possibility of consumer confusion must be compatible with fair use, and so it is. The common law's tolerance of a certain degree of confusion on the part of consumers followed from the very fact that in cases like this one an originally descriptive term was selected to be used as a mark, not to mention the undesirability of allowing anyone to obtain a complete monopoly on use of a descriptive term simply by grabbing it first. *Canal Co. v. Clark, supra,* at 323–24, 327. The Lanham Act adopts a similar leniency, there being no indication that the statute was meant to deprive commercial speakers of the ordinary utility of descriptive words. "If any confusion results, that is a risk the plaintiff accepted when it decided to identify its product with a mark that uses a well known descriptive phrase." *Cosmetically Sealed Industries, Inc. v. Chesebrough–Pond's USA Co.,* 125 F.3d at 30. This right to describe is the reason that descriptive terms qualify for registration as trademarks only after taking on secondary meaning as "distinctive of the applicant's goods," 15 U.S.C. § 1052(f), with the registrant getting an exclusive right not in the original, descriptive sense, but only in the secondary one associated with the markholder's goods, 2 McCarthy, *supra,* § 11:45 ("The only aspect of the mark which is given legal protection is that penumbra or fringe of secondary meaning which surrounds the old descriptive word").

While we thus recognize that mere risk of confusion will not rule out fair use, we think it would be improvident to go further in this case, for deciding anything more would take us beyond the Ninth Circuit's consideration of the subject. It suffices to realize that our holding that fair use can occur along with some degree of confusion does not foreclose the relevance of the extent of any likely consumer confusion in assessing whether a defendant's use is objectively fair.

III

Because we read the Court of Appeals as requiring KP to shoulder a burden on the issue of confusion, we vacate the judgment and remand the case for further proceedings consistent with this opinion.

NOTES AND QUESTIONS

1. *U.S. law of trademark fair use.* U.S. law recognizes two types of trademark fair use: (i) classic fair use occurs when a third party uses the mark (which is allegedly descriptive) to describe the third party's own products, *see Zatarains, Inc. v. Oak Grove Smokehouse, Inc.,* 698 F.2d 786, 796 (5th Cir. 1983) (holding that use of the term "fish fry" to describe fish frying batter was fair use, notwithstanding plaintiff's registered mark "fish-fri"); and (ii) nominative fair use occurs when a third party uses the mark to describe the trademark holder's products because the mark is "the only word

reasonably available to describe a particular thing," *New Kids on the Block v. News America Publ'g, Inc.*, 971 F.2d 302, 308 (9th Cir. 1992) (holding that USA Today poll asking question about "New Kids on the Block" was nominative fair use). What policy reason(s) might underlie the two types of fair use?

Which type of fair use was at issue in the *KP Permanent* case? Can you explain how KP's use of "microcolor" was alleged to be a fair use—what exactly is a microcolor?

2. What did the U.S. Supreme Court hold in *KP Permanent*? Can a plaintiff's showing of a likelihood of confusion ever negate a defendant's showing of fair use under § 1115(b)(4)? Do you agree with the Court's analysis? If there is some likelihood of confusion among consumers by the defendant's descriptive use of a term, should fair use be allowed according to the Court? If so, why?

3. *TRIPS Article 17.* TRIPS Article 17 specifically recognizes "fair use of descriptive terms" as an example of a permissible "limited exception[]" to trademark—"provided that such exception[] take[s] account of the legitimate interests of the owner of the trademark and of third parties." Does the U.S. approach in *KP Permanent* satisfy this proviso? Does U.S. law on fair use take into account the legitimate interests of the trademark owner and third parties? For further discussion of TRIPS Article 17, see European Communities—Protection of Trademarks and Geographical Indications for Agricultural Products and Foodstuffs, WT/DS174/R (15 March 2005), excerpted below at pp. 603–09.

4. *Fair use for trademark dilution.* The federal dilution provision in the Lanham Act recognizes fair use as follows: "Any fair use, including a nominative or descriptive fair use, or facilitation of such fair use, of a famous mark by another person other than as a designation of source for the person's own goods or services, including use in connection with—

(i) advertising or promotion that permits consumers to compare goods or services; or

(ii) identifying and parodying, criticizing, or commenting upon the famous mark owner or the goods or services of the famous mark owner."

15 U.S.C. § 1125(c)(3)(A).

Notice that the dilution exemptions may be broader than the fair use defenses for trademark infringement. This may have been due to the perception that dilution claims substantially broadened the scope of rights for famous marks, so some corresponding broadening of permissible exemptions should be recognized as well. Practically speaking, nominative fair use may overlap with some of the same kinds of uses of the mark under the dilution exemptions above, such as comparative advertising. For trademark infringement claims, however, parody is not a separate defense of fair use, but is typically analyzed as a factor in the likelihood of confusion analysis. *See Eli Lilly & Co. v. Natural Answers, Inc.*, 233 F.3d 456, 463 (7th Cir. 2000) ("[A] parody ... still runs afoul of the trademark laws if it is likely to confuse consumers."). In contrast, for trademark dilution claims, parody is a recognized defense. 15 U.S.C. § 1225(c)(3)(A); *see Mattel, Inc. v. MCA Records*, 296

F.3d 894, 905–07 (9th Cir. 2002). In addition, the dilution provision also exempts: "(B) All forms of news reporting and news commentary. (C) Any noncommercial use of a mark."

5. *Comparison with copyright.* It is important to bear in mind that trademark fair use is not equivalent to copyright fair use under U.S. law. Copyright fair use tends to be broader and more open-ended, as adjudged by the four fair use factors under 17 U.S.C. § 107.

8. TERM OF TRADEMARK REGISTRATION

Technically, there is no term of a "trademark," at least not in the same sense as a limited term for copyright or patent. Under Article 18 of TRIPS, countries are obligated to allow a term for *registrations* to last at least 7 years and to be renewable *indefinitely* for subsequent terms of such length (typically, with the payment of registration fees). Thus, as long as a trademark has distinctiveness in identifying the source of the product, protection for the trademark could potentially last forever.

NOTES AND QUESTIONS

1. What policy reason(s) might support allowing trademarks to be registered and renewed indefinitely? Does such a system raise any concerns?

2. *Comparison with copyright and patent.* William Landes and Richard Posner have proposed adopting a similar system of indefinitely renewable copyrights. *See* William Landes & Richard Posner, *Indefinitely Renewable Copyright*, 70 UNIV. CHI. L. REV. 471, 484–86 (2003). Are there differences between copyright and trademarks that might make this proposal questionable in the copyright context? What about a system of indefinitely renewable patents? Should a system of indefinitely renewable terms for patents also be recognized? Why or why not?

9. OTHER TYPES OF MARKS: COLLECTIVE MARKS AND TRADE NAMES

Paris Convention

Article 7bis

Marks: Collective Marks

(1) The countries of the Union undertake to accept for filing and to protect collective marks belonging to associations the existence of which is not contrary to the law of the country of origin, even if such associations do not possess an industrial or commercial establishment.

(2) Each country shall be the judge of the particular conditions under which a collective mark shall be protected and may refuse protection if the mark is contrary to the public interest.

(3) Nevertheless, the protection of these marks shall not be refused to any association the existence of which is not contrary to the law of the

country of origin, on the ground that such association is not established in the country where protection is sought or is not constituted according to the law of the latter country.

Article 8

Trade Names

A trade name shall be protected in all the countries of the Union without the obligation of filing or registration, whether or not it forms part of a trademark.

* * *

Under Article 7*bis* of Paris, countries are obligated to protect collective marks. A collective mark is a mark that indicates a collective group or association, usually comprised of several businesses. The mark therefore identifies the association itself, not the individual businesses. (The collective mark is to be contrasted with the certification mark, which some associations may issue as a "guarantee" of compliance with a certain industry standard.) Article 7*bis* allows denial of registration of a collective mark if the collective mark is contrary to the law of the country of origin or contrary to the public interest in the country where protection is sought. However, countries may not refuse registration "on the ground that such association is not established in the country where protection is sought or is not constituted according to the law of the latter country." TRIPS does not alter (much less speak to) these minimum standards for collective marks under Paris.

Paris Convention Article 8 requires countries to protect trade names (i.e., names of businesses)—"without the obligation of filing or registration, whether or not it forms part of a trademark." The TRIPS Agreement incorporates this requirement of Paris for all WTO members. *See* United States Section 211 Omnibus Appropriations Act of 1998, WT/DS176/AB/R, ¶¶ 338–41. Article 8 does not specify how countries are to protect trade names. Presumably, countries are free to do so under trademark law, unfair competition, a special statute, or some other law.

Notes and Questions

1. Is there a difference between the minimum standard of protection for trade names under Article 8 of the Paris Convention and the minimum standard for protection of trademarks under Paris Article 6 and TRIPS Article 16? If so, what is the difference? Are there any similarities?

2. Why might the business owner of a trade name also seek to register it as a trademark? If trade names are to be protected "without the obligation of filing or registration" in Paris countries, what more can be gained by securing trademark registration?

C. GEOGRAPHICAL INDICATIONS

We have already introduced the topic of geographical indications (GIs) at the outset of this chapter. Article 22 of TRIPS defines geographical indications as "indications which identify a good as originating in the territory of a Member, or a region or locality in that territory, where a given quality, reputation or other characteristic of the good is essentially attributable to its geographical origin." Unlike the typical trademark owned by one entity, a GI—such as "Parma ham"—is commonly used by several, if not many, qualifying entities from that particular geographical region. Thus, instead of identifying a particular source of the product as in the case of a trademark, a GI indicates the region from which the product originates. The European Union, a major producer of foodstuffs and wines, has been at the forefront of attempting to strengthen the international protection of GIs. The U.S., however, has languished far behind in its willingness to adopt stronger GI protection. As you read the following section, try to identify the pros and cons of adopting stronger GI protection. Why do you think the U.S.—which has been a leader in strengthening other IP protections—is so slow to embrace stronger protections for GIs?

1. BASIC APPROACH: RIGHTS AND EXCEPTIONS

a. TRIPS Agreement Article 22

PROBLEM 4–16

Big Apple Fine Wines and International Foods, based in New York, NY, is a gourmet food company that produces and sells fine wines and foods. In its catalogue, Big Apple boasts that it sells the "Finest Swiss Cheese" and that its "Big Apple Cuban Cigars" should be savored with a cup of its "gourmet Colombian Coffee." In fact, all cheeses sold by Big Apple are produced in Pennsylvania. The cigars are produced by Big Apple's tobacco growers in the Dominican Republic. Big Apple's coffee beans come from a small town called Colombia, Venezuela. None of Big Apple's customers has ever complained about the quality of its products, or of being misled. For this problem, assume that Swiss Cheese, Cuban Cigars, and Colombian Coffee are all geographical indications in their respective country of origin. Is Big Apple in violation of TRIPS? What additional facts, if any, would be helpful to your analysis? Consider TRIPS Articles 22 and 24, and the discussion below.

TRIPS Agreement

Article 22

Protection of Geographical Indications

1. Geographical indications are, for the purposes of this Agreement, indications which identify a good as originating in the territory of a Member, or a region or locality in that territory, where a given quality,

reputation or other characteristic of the good is essentially attributable to its geographical origin.

2. In respect of geographical indications, Members shall provide the legal means for interested parties to prevent:

(a) the use of any means in the designation or presentation of a good that indicates or suggests that the good in question originates in a geographical area other than the true place of origin in a manner which misleads the public as to the geographical origin of the good;

(b) any use which constitutes an act of unfair competition within the meaning of Article 10*bis* of the Paris Convention (1967).

3. A Member shall, *ex officio* if its legislation so permits or at the request of an interested party, refuse or invalidate the registration of a trademark which contains or consists of a geographical indication with respect to goods not originating in the territory indicated, if use of the indication in the trademark for such goods in that Member is of such a nature as to mislead the public as to the true place of origin.

4. The protection under paragraphs 1, 2 and 3 shall be applicable against a geographical indication which, although literally true as to the territory, region or locality in which the goods originate, falsely represents to the public that the goods originate in another territory.

Article 24

Exceptions

* * *

3. In implementing this Section, a Member shall not diminish the protection of geographical indications that existed in that Member immediately prior to the date of entry into force of the WTO Agreement. * * *

5. Where a trademark has been applied for or registered in good faith, or where rights to a trademark have been acquired through use in good faith either:

(a) before the date of application of these provisions in that Member as defined in Part VI; or

(b) before the geographical indication is protected in its country of origin;

measures adopted to implement this Section shall not prejudice eligibility for or the validity of the registration of a trademark, or the right to use a trademark, on the basis that such a trademark is identical with, or similar to, a geographical indication.

6. Nothing in this Section shall require a Member to apply its provisions in respect of a geographical indication of any other Member with respect to goods or services for which the relevant indication is identical with the term customary in common language as the common name for such goods or services in the territory of that Member. * * *

7. A Member may provide that any request made under this Section in connection with the use or registration of a trademark must be presented

within five years after the adverse use of the protected indication has become generally known in that Member or after the date of registration of the trademark in that Member provided that the trademark has been published by that date, if such date is earlier than the date on which the adverse use became generally known in that Member, provided that the geographical indication is not used or registered in bad faith.

8. The provisions of this Section shall in no way prejudice the right of any person to use, in the course of trade, that person's name or the name of that person's predecessor in business, except where such name is used in such a manner as to mislead the public.

9. There shall be no obligation under this Agreement to protect geographical indications which are not or cease to be protected in their country of origin, or which have fallen into disuse in that country.

* * *

Article 22 provides the minimum standard of protection for geographical indications (GIs). Countries are obligated to "refuse or invalidate the registration of a trademark which contains or consists of a geographical indication with respect to goods not originating in the territory indicated, if use of the indication in the trademark for such goods in that Member is of such a nature as to mislead the public as to the true place of origin." TRIPS art. 22(3). Notice that GIs can effectively trump a (non-grandfathered, see below) trademark registration of a mark that contains a GI on a good "not originating in the territory indicated," if use of the trademark "is of *such a nature as to mislead the public as to the true place of origin.*" In addition, countries are obligated to protect against any use of a GI that "constitutes an act of unfair competition within the meaning of Article 10*bis* of the Paris Convention (1967)." *Id.* art. 22(b). Although there is some controversy over the precise scope of unfair competition under Article 10*bis*, it is generally perceived to cover "passing off" claims.

The basic protections for GIs under Article 22 of TRIPS are qualified by several exceptions under Article 24. First, Article 24(5) requires countries to "grandfather" in trademarks registered, applied for registration, or used in good faith before the effective date of TRIPS in the member country or before the GI in question is protected in its country of origin. Trademarks (applied for, registered, or used in good faith) before either of these dates are to remain valid—and cannot be denied "on the basis that such a trademark is identical with, or similar to, a geographical indication." TRIPS art. 24(5).

Second, Article 24(6) allows countries the discretion to deny protection to any GI that is generic in the member country where protection is sought—meaning that "the relevant indication is identical with the term customary in common language as the common name for such goods or services in the territory of that Member." TRIPS art. 24(6). Third, Article 24(9) exempts countries from having to protect any GI that is no longer protected in its country of origin or has fallen into disuse there. *Id.* art. 24(9). Finally, Article 24(8) recognizes that the GI protections under TRIPS "in no way prejudice the right of any person to use, in the course of trade, that person's name or the name of that person's predecessor in business, except where such name is used in such a manner as to mislead the public." *Id.* art. 24(8).

NOTES AND QUESTIONS

1. *Standard for GI protection.* Does protection of GIs under Article 22 of TRIPS hinge on proof that the mark in question (i) misleads the public or (ii) is likely to mislead the public as to the true place of origin? Is the standard for GI protection different from the likelihood-of-confusion standard under TRIPS Article 16(1) for trademark infringement?

2. *Dilution claims?* Would a better way to protect GIs be to recognize protection against the *dilution* of established GIs, regardless of any misleading uses of the mark? Isn't dilution just as great a concern for GIs as it is for trademarks?

3. *Exceptions.* Which of the exceptions in Article 24 discussed above are discretionary and which are mandatory? Could, for example, a country choose to give GI protection to a geographical indication, even though it is generic? Which of the exceptions do you think would have the greatest potential to undercut the protection of GIs?

4. *Reverse doctrine of foreign equivalents?* Does allowing a country to refuse protection for GIs if the country deems the GI generic possibly reward the past *lack of prior GI protection* in that country? Does it reward countries that have less geographically knowledgeable consumers? Would a better standard be to require GI protection in all member countries as long as the GI is protected in the country of origin? In the *Otokoyama* case, the court recognized, under the doctrine of foreign equivalents, that a foreign word would be considered generic in the U.S. if it is generic in its country of origin. *See, supra,* at pp. 515–520. Wouldn't a "reverse doctrine of foreign equivalents"—recognizing worldwide protection if the GI is protected in the country of origin—be a better rule for geographical origins, given the special connection between the GI and the country of origin? A similar approach was adopted in Article 6 of the Lisbon Agreement. Lisbon Agreement for the Protection of Appellations of Origin and Their International Registration art. 6 (Oct. 31, 1956), as amended at Stockholm on July 14, 1967, and amended Sept. 28, 1979.

5. *Bibliographic note.* Albrecht Conrad, *The Protection of Geographical Indications in the TRIPS Agreement,* 86 TRADEMARK REP. 11 (1996); Christine Haight Farley, *Conflicts Between U.S. Law and International Treaties Concerning Geographical Indications,* 22 WHITTIER L. REV. 73 (2000); Paul J. Heald, *Trademarks and Geographical Indications: Exploring the Contours of the TRIPS Agreement,* 29 VAND. J. TRANSNAT'L L. 635 (1996); Thomas Helbling, *The Term "Swiss" on Trade Goods: A Denomination of Origin and Its Legal Protection in the United Kingdom,* 19 EUR. INTELL. PROP. REV. 51 (1997).

b. GI Regulation in the EU

PROBLEM 4–17

Assuming a proper registration, which of the following practices would most likely be permitted under the specification for the GI "Prosciutto di Parma" discussed in the case below? How is the result in each of these situations consistent with the goals behind protecting the term "Prosciutto di Parma"?

(1) Joe's English Pub in London imports Parma ham in bricks and slices it in its open air kitchen before serving the ham to its customers.

(2) Harry's English Deli in Newcastle on Tyne imports Parma ham in bricks and slices the ham for its customers in accordance with their instructions in the meat department in the back of its store.

(3) Hygrade Foods based in England employs a group of Italian workers with 20 years experience in slicing and packaging ham who have emigrated from the Parma region of Italy to England to slice and package the ham in London.

(4) Hygrade imports Parma ham in marked bricks and sells it in bulk to retail consumers who then slice the ham for themselves at home before consuming it.

* * *

Other than the basic definition of "geographical indications," TRIPS does not speak to any formalities or prerequisites for countries to impose on those seeking to qualify for a GI. Presumably, WTO countries are free to decide what, if any, requirements should be imposed under national law. Of course, countries favoring strong GI protection have an interest in requiring some standards, in order to ensure that "a given quality, reputation or other characteristic of the good is essentially attributable to its geographical origin" within the meaning of TRIPS Article 22. In this section, we will study European law because Europe is the leader in GI protection and regulation. In 1992, the EU established protection for geographical indications and designations of origin for agricultural products and foodstuffs. Council Regulation 2081/92.* EU countries have over 700 domestically registered GIs. To qualify for a GI under EU law, one must satisfy numerous requirements. Consider the following case.

CONSORZIO DEL PROSCIUTTO DI PARMA v. ASDA STORES LTD.

European Court of Justice.
[2003] ECR I–5121, Case C–108/01 (May 20, 2003).

By order of 8 February 2001, received at the Court on 7 March 2001, the House of Lords referred to the Court for a preliminary ruling under

---

* The regulation has been superseded by Council Regulation 510/2006, On the Protection of Geographical Indications and Designations of Origin for Agricultural Products and Foodstuffs, 2006 O.J. (L 93) 12 (EC).

Article 234 EC a question on the interpretation of Council Regulation (EEC) No 2081/92 of 14 July 1992 on the protection of geographical indications and designations of origin for agricultural products and food-stuffs (OJ 1992 L 208, p. 1), as [later] amended (OJ 1994 C 241, p. 21, and OJ 1995 L 1, p. 1) ("Regulation No 2081/92"), and of Commission Regulation (EC) No 1107/96 of 12 June 1996 on the registration of geographical indications and designations of origin under the procedure laid down in Article 17 of Regulation No 2081/92 (OJ 1996 L 148, p. 1).

That question was raised in proceedings between Consorzio del Prosciutto di Parma ("the Consorzio"), an association of producers of Parma ham, established in Italy, and Salumificio S. Rita SpA ("Salumificio"), a company also established in Italy, a producer of Parma ham and a member of the Consorzio, of the one part, and Asda Stores Ltd ("Asda"), a company established in the United Kingdom, an operator of supermarkets, and Hygrade Foods Ltd ("Hygrade"), also established in the United Kingdom, an importer of Parma ham, of the other part, concerning the marketing in the United Kingdom under the protected designation of origin "Prosciutto di Parma" ("the PDO 'Prosciutto di Parma'") of Parma ham sliced and packaged in that Member State.

The main proceedings

Asda operates a chain of supermarkets in the United Kingdom. It sells among other things ham bearing the description "Parma ham," purchased pre-sliced from Hygrade, which itself purchases the ham boned but not sliced from an Italian producer who is a member of the Consorzio. The ham is sliced and hermetically sealed by Hygrade in packets each containing five slices. The packets bear the wording "ASDA A taste of Italy PARMA HAM Genuine Italian Parma Ham." The back of the packets states "PARMA HAM All authentic Asda continental meats are made by traditional methods to guarantee their authentic flavour and quality" and "Produced in Italy, packed in the UK for Asda Stores Limited."

On 14 November 1997 the Consorzio brought proceedings by writ in the United Kingdom against Asda and Hygrade seeking various injunctions against them, essentially requiring them to cease their activities, on the ground that they were contrary to the rules applicable to Parma ham.

[After the lower courts dismissed the action,] [t]he Consorzio and Salumificio thereupon appealed to the House of Lords. Since the House of Lords considered that the outcome of the case depended on the interpretation of Regulation No 2081/92 and Regulation No 1107/96, it decided to stay the proceedings and refer the following question to the Court for a preliminary ruling:

As a matter of Community law, does Council Regulation (EEC) No 2081/92 read with Commission Regulation (EC) No 1107/96 and the specification for the PDO "Prosciutto di Parma" create a valid Community right, directly enforceable in the court of a Member State, to restrain the retail sale as "Parma ham" of sliced and packaged ham derived from hams duly exported from Parma in compliance with the conditions of the PDO but which have not been thereafter sliced, packaged and labelled in accordance with the specification?

The question referred for a preliminary ruling

Article 29 EC prohibits all measures which have as their specific object or effect the restriction of patterns of exports and thereby the establishment of a difference in treatment between the domestic trade of a Member State and its export trade, in such a way as to provide a particular advantage for national production or for the domestic market of the State in question.

As noted above, the specification of the PDO "Prosciutto di Parma" expressly mentions the requirement of slicing and packaging the product in the region of production for ham marketed in slices. In registering the PDO "Prosciutto di Parma," Regulation No 1107/96 thus makes slicing and packaging in the region of production a condition for the use of the PDO "Prosciutto di Parma" for ham marketed in slices. That condition has the consequence that ham produced in the region of production and fulfilling the other conditions required for use of the PDO "Prosciutto di Parma" cannot be sliced outside that region without losing that designation.

By contrast, Parma ham transported within the region of production retains its right to the PDO if it is sliced and packaged there in accordance with the rules referred to in the specification. Those rules thus have the specific effect of restricting patterns of exports of ham eligible for the PDO "Prosciutto di Parma" and thereby establishing a difference in treatment between the domestic trade of a Member State and its export trade. They therefore introduce quantitative restrictions on exports within the meaning of Article 29 EC.

Whether the condition that the product is sliced and packaged in the region of production is justified.

The Consorzio, Salumificio, the Spanish and Italian Governments and the Commission submit that in Belgium v Spain the Court held that a measure having equivalent effect to a quantitative restriction on exports, constituted by the obligation to bottle a wine with a designation of origin in the region of production in order to be able to use the designation of origin, was justified in that its aim was to preserve the reputation of the designation by guaranteeing, in addition to the authenticity of the product, the maintenance of its qualities and characteristics. They consider that the reasoning in that judgment may be applied to the condition that Parma ham be sliced and packaged in the region of production, as that condition is justified for the purpose of guaranteeing the authenticity and quality of the product. The French Government observes that the condition makes it possible to guarantee that the product originates in the geographical area.

Asda, Hygrade and the United Kingdom Government assert that the slicing and packaging operations do not affect the quality of Parma ham or damage its authenticity.

It should be noted that, in accordance with Article 30 EC, Article 29 EC does not preclude prohibitions or restrictions on exports which are justified inter alia on grounds of the protection of industrial and commercial property.

Designations of origin fall within the scope of industrial and commercial property rights. The applicable rules protect those entitled to use them against improper use of those designations by third parties seeking to profit from the reputation which they have acquired. They are intended to guarantee that the product bearing them comes from a specified geographical area and displays certain particular characteristics. They may enjoy a high reputation amongst consumers and constitute for producers who fulfil the conditions for using them an essential means of attracting custom. The reputation of designations of origin depends on their image in the minds of consumers. That image in turn depends essentially on particular characteristics and more generally on the quality of the product. It is on the latter, ultimately, that the product's reputation is based. For consumers, the link between the reputation of the producers and the quality of the products also depends on his being assured that products sold under the designation of origin are authentic.

The specification of the PDO "Prosciutto di Parma," by requiring the slicing and packaging to be carried out in the region of production, is intended to allow the persons entitled to use the PDO to keep under their control one of the ways in which the product appears on the market. The condition it lays down aims better to safeguard the quality and authenticity of the product, and consequently the reputation of the PDO, for which those who are entitled to use it assume full and collective responsibility.

Against that background, a condition such as at issue must be regarded as compatible with Community law despite its restrictive effects on trade if it is shown that it is necessary and proportionate and capable of upholding the reputation of the PDO "Prosciutto di Parma."

Parma ham is consumed mainly in slices and the operations leading to that presentation are all designed to obtain in particular a specific flavour, colour and texture which will be appreciated by consumers. The slicing and packaging of the ham thus constitute important operations which may harm the quality and hence the reputation of the PDO if they are carried out in conditions that result in a product not possessing the organoleptic qualities expected. Those operations may also compromise the guarantee of the product's authenticity, because they necessarily involve removal of the mark of origin of the whole hams used.

By the rules it lays down and the requirements of the national provisions to which it refers, the specification of the PDO "Prosciutto di Parma" establishes a set of detailed and strict rules regulating the three stages which lead to the placing on the market of prepackaged sliced ham.

The first stage consists of boning the ham, making bricks, and refrigerating and freezing them for slicing. The second stage corresponds to the slicing operations. The third stage is the packaging of the sliced ham, under vacuum or protected atmosphere.

First, after checking the authenticity of the hams used, a selection must be made from them. Only hams which satisfy additional, more restrictive conditions, relating in particular to weight, length of aging, water content, internal humidity rate and lack of visible faults, may be sliced and packaged. Further selections are made at the various stages of the process, if anomalies in the product which cannot be detected before boning or slicing appear, such as dots resulting from micro-haemorrhages, areas of blankness in the muscle or the presence of excess intra-muscular fat.

Second, all operators in the region of production who intend to slice and package Parma ham must be approved by the inspection structure, which also approves the suppliers of packaging.

Third, representatives of the inspection structure must be present at each of the three stages in the process. They monitor permanently compliance with all the requirements of the specification, including the marking of the product at each stage. When the operations are completed, they certify the number of packages produced.

During the various stages there are technical operations and strict checks relating to authenticity, quality, hygiene and labelling. Some of these require specialist assessments, in particular during the stages of refrigeration and freezing of the bricks.

In this context, it must be accepted that checks performed outside the region of production would provide fewer guarantees of the quality and authenticity of the product than checks carried out in the region of production in accordance with the procedure laid down in the specification. First, checks performed in accordance with that procedure are thorough and systematic in nature and are done by experts who have specialised knowledge of the characteristics of Parma ham. Second, it is hardly conceivable that representatives of the persons entitled to use the PDO could effectively introduce such checks in other Member States.

The risk to the quality and authenticity of the product finally offered to consumers is consequently greater where it has been sliced and packaged outside the region of production than when that has been done within the region. That conclusion is not affected by the fact, pointed out in the present case, that the ham may be sliced, at least under certain conditions, by retailers and restaurateurs outside the region of production. That operation must in principle be performed in front of the consumer, or at least the consumer can require that it is, in order to verify in particular that the ham used bears the mark of origin. Above all, slicing and packaging operations carried out upstream of the retail sale or restaurant stage constitute, because of the quantities of products concerned, a much more real risk to the reputation of a PDO, where there is inadequate control of the authenticity and quality of the product, than operations carried out by retailers and restaurateurs.

Consequently, the condition of slicing and packaging in the region of production, whose aim is to preserve the reputation of Parma ham by strengthening control over its particular characteristics and its quality, may be regarded as justified as a measure protecting the PDO which may be used by all the operators concerned and is of decisive importance to them. The resulting restriction may be regarded as necessary for attaining the objective pursued, in that there are no alternative less restrictive measures capable of attaining it.

The PDO "Prosciutto di Parma" would not receive comparable protection from an obligation imposed on operators established outside the region of production to inform consumers, by means of appropriate labelling, that the slicing and packaging has taken place outside that region. Any deterioration in the quality or authenticity of ham sliced and packaged outside the region of production, resulting from materialisation of the risks associated with slicing and packaging, might harm the reputation of all ham marketed under the PDO "Prosciutto di Parma," including that sliced and packaged in the region of production under the control of the group of producers entitled to use the PDO.

Accordingly, the fact that the use of the PDO "Prosciutto di Parma" for ham marketed in slices is conditional on the slicing and packaging operations being carried out in the region of production may be regarded as justified, and hence compatible with Article 29 EC.

[The Court of Justice ruled that the condition of slicing and packaging in the region of production could not be relied by the Consorzio due to a technical issue. The Consorzio failed to provide proper notice to economic operators in accordance with Regulation No. 110796. *Ed.*]

NOTES AND QUESTIONS

1. What do you think of the EU's elaborate regulations on Parma ham, and how and where it is prepared, sliced, and packaged? How might the location of slicing a Parma ham affect its quality, if at all? What does the court mean by "organoleptic qualities?"

2. What is the effect of the Court of Justice's ruling in the Parma ham case? Did the Court rule that the slicing and packaging requirements for Parma ham were justified restrictions? If so, can that restriction be applied against Asda Stores in the United Kingdom?

3. If Asda Stores' ham came from Parma, Italy, why shouldn't it be allowed to use the GI "Parma ham"? Is the EU regulation fair and justifiable? Does TRIPS Article 22 speak to who is entitled to use a GI for a product that is undeniably from the geographical region indicated? Does it seem somewhat anomalous that (i) some countries in which GIs are highly regulated, such as in the European Union, might deny a producer from using the GI for a product that in fact originates from the geographical region, while (ii) other

countries with lax GI requirements and protections, such as the U.S., might allow another producer to use a GI, even though the product does not originate from the geographical region indicated in the GI?

4. *Audit.* The EU system for GIs is widely perceived to be the strongest in the world. In 2011, however, the European Court of Auditors reviewed the EU system and concluded that the EU did not have adequate minimum requirements for checks of member states' compliance with GI specifications. *See* EUROPEAN COURT OF AUDITORS, DO THE DESIGN AND MANAGEMENT OF THE GEOGRAPHICAL INDICATIONS SCHEME ALLOW IT TO BE EFFECTIVE? (2011).

PROBLEM 4–18

The European Council Regulation discussed in the Parma ham case (Regulation (EEC) No. 2081/92, July 24, 1992) establishes an elaborate set of rules for the protection of GIs. Article 12 of the Regulation deals with protection for GIs from countries outside the EU. Please evaluate whether the following portion of Article 12 of the Regulation is consistent with TRIPS. It states in part:

1. Without prejudice to the international agreements, this Regulation may apply to an agricultural produce or foodstuff from a third country provided that:

—the third country is able to give guarantees identical or equivalent to those referred to in Article 4,*

—the third country concerned has inspection arrangements equivalent to those laid down in Article 10,*

—the third country concerned is prepared to provide protection equivalent to that available in the Community to corresponding products for foodstuffs coming from the Community.

2. If a protected name of a third country is identical to a Community protected name, registration shall be granted with due regard for local and traditional usage and the practical risk of confusion. Use of such name shall be authorized only if the country of origin of the product is clearly and visibly indicated on the label.

Imagine you are a member of the WTO panel in the proceedings in which the above EU Regulation 2081/92 is being challenged. Do you think the Regulation advantages or disadvantages certain nationals? If so, how? Does the provision violate national treatment under TRIPS? The EU defends its Regulation by pointing out (i) that it specifically is "[w]ithout prejudice to the international agreements"; and (ii) GI protection for products made within

---

* Article 4 of the Regulation requires as a prerequisite for GI protection that the product must comply with a "product specification," requiring at least eight pieces of information (such as geographical area, evidence that the foodstuff originates from there, a description of obtaining the foodstuff, details of inspection structures provided for in Article 10 to show the contours and worthiness of the geographical indication in question). *Ed.*

* Article 10 requires member states of the EU to institute "inspection structures," whose function "shall be to ensure that agricultural products and foodstuffs bearing a protected name meet the requirements laid down in the specifications." *Ed.*

the EU are available to entities—whether domestic or foreign—on an equal basis. How would you rule?

THE FEDERAL REPUBLIC OF GERMANY AND THE KINGDOM OF DENMARK v. COMMISSION OF THE EUROPEAN COMMUNITIES

European Court of Justice (Grand Chamber).
[2005] ECR I-9178, C-465/02, C-466/02 (October 25, 2005).

The Federal Republic of Germany and the Kingdom of Denmark have applied for annulment of Commission Regulation (EC) No 1829/2002 of 14 October 2002 amending the Annex to Regulation (EC) No 1107/96 with regard to the name "Feta" (OJ 2002 L 277, p. 10) ("the contested regulation"). Article 2(1) to (3) of Council Regulation (EEC) No 2081/92 of 14 July 1992 on the protection of geographical indications and designations of origin for agricultural products and foodstuffs (OJ 1992 L 208, p. 1) ("the basic regulation") provides:

"1. Community protection of designations of origin and of geographical indications of agricultural products and foodstuffs shall be obtained in accordance with this Regulation.

2. For the purposes of this Regulation:

(a) designation of origin: means the name of a region, a specific place or, in exceptional cases, a country, used to describe an agricultural product or a foodstuff:

—originating in that region, specific place or country, and

—the quality or characteristics of which are essentially or exclusively due to a particular geographical environment with its inherent natural and human factors, and the production, processing and preparation of which take place in the defined geographical area;

(b) geographical indication: means the name of a region, a specific place or, in exceptional cases, a country, used to describe an agricultural product or a foodstuff:

—originating in that region, specific place or country, and

—which possesses a specific quality, reputation or other characteristics attributable to that geographical origin and the production and/or processing and/or preparation of which take place in the defined geographical area.

3. Certain traditional geographical or non-geographical names designating an agricultural product or a foodstuff originating in a region or a specific place, which fulfil the conditions referred to in the second indent of paragraph 2(a) shall also be considered as designations of origin."

Article 3(1) of the same regulation provides:

"Names that have become generic may not be registered.

For the purposes of this Regulation, a "name that has become generic" means the name of an agricultural product or a foodstuff which, although it relates to the place or the region where this product or foodstuff was originally produced or marketed, has become the common name of an agricultural product or a foodstuff.

To establish whether or not a name has become generic, account shall be taken of all factors, in particular:

—the existing situation in the Member State in which the name originates and in areas of consumption,

—the existing situation in other Member States,

—the relevant national or Community laws."

Facts

On 14 October 2002, the Commission adopted the contested regulation. Under that regulation, the name "feta" was registered as a protected designation of origin.

It is common ground in the present proceedings that the term "feta" is derived from the Italian word "fetta," meaning "slice," which entered the Greek language in the seventeenth century. It is also common ground that "feta" is not the name of a region, place or country within the meaning of Article 2(2)(a) of the basic regulation. Accordingly, the term cannot be registered as a designation of origin pursuant to that provision. At most, it may be registered under Article 2(3) of the basic regulation, which extends the definition of designation of origin, in particular, to certain traditional non-geographical names. It was on that basis that the term "feta" was registered as a designation of origin by the contested regulation. According to the 35th recital in the preamble thereto, "the name 'Feta' is a traditional non-geographical name within the meaning of Article 2(3) of [the basic regulation]."

In order to be protected under that provision, a traditional non-geographical name must, inter alia, designate an agricultural product or a foodstuff "originating in a region or a specific place." Article 2(3) of the basic regulation, moreover, in referring to the second indent of Article 2(2)(a) of the same regulation, requires that the quality or characteristics of the agricultural product or foodstuff be essentially or exclusively due to a particular geographical environment with its inherent natural and human factors, and that the production, processing and preparation of that product take place in the defined geographical area. It follows from a combined reading of those two provisions that the place or region referred to in Article 2(3) must be defined as a geographical environment with specific natural and human factors and which is capable of giving an agricultural product or foodstuff its specific characteristics. The area of origin referred to must, therefore, present homogenous natural factors which distinguish it from the areas adjoining it.

As the Commission based itself on the Greek legislation governing the matter, it is appropriate to consider Article 1 of Ministerial Order No

313025/1994 of 11 January 1994 recognising the protected designation of origin (PDO) of feta cheese, which provides:

> "1.   The name 'feta' is recognised as a protected designation of origin (PDO) for white cheese soaked in brine traditionally produced in Greece, more specifically ('syngekrimena') in the regions mentioned in paragraph 2 of this article, from ewes' milk or a mixture of ewes' milk and goats' milk.
>
> 2.   The milk used for the manufacture of 'feta' must come exclusively from the regions of Macedonia, Thrace, Epirus, Thessaly, Central Greece, Peloponnese and the department (Nomos) of Lesbos."

The geographical area thus defined for the production of feta covers only mainland Greece and the department of Lesbos. It does not include the island of Crete or certain Greek archipelagos, namely the Sporades, the Cyclades, the Dodecanese Islands and the Ionian Islands. These areas which have been excluded from this geographical area cannot be considered as negligible. Thus the area defined by the national legislation for the production of cheese bearing the name "feta" does not cover the entire territory of the Hellenic Republic. It is therefore not necessary to consider whether Article 2(3) of the basic regulation allows the geographical area connected with a name to cover the entire territory of a country.

It is nevertheless appropriate to consider whether the area in question was determined in an artificial manner. According to the information submitted to the Court, and particularly to the specifications sent by the Greek Government to the Commission on 21 January 1994 with a view to registering the name "feta" as a designation of origin, the effect of that provision, read together with Article 1 of the same Ministerial Order, is to define the geographical area covered by reference, inter alia, to geomorphology, that is, the mountainous or semi-mountainous nature of the terrain; to the climate, that is, mild winters, hot summers and a great deal of sunshine; and to the botanical characteristics, namely the typical vegetation of the Balkan medium mountain range.

Those factors adequately indicate that the area has homogenous natural features which distinguish it from the adjoining areas. The case-file indicates that the areas of Greece which are excluded from the defined area do not display the same natural features as the area in question. It is thus apparent that the area in question in the present case was not determined in an artificial manner.

The third plea

The German Government submits that the contested regulation infringes Article 3(1) of the basic regulation [because] "Feta" is a generic name within the meaning of Article 3(1). As to the argument put forward by the Danish Government to the effect that the term "feta" refers to a type of cheese originating from the Balkans, it is common ground that white cheeses soaked in brine have been produced for a long time, not only in Greece but in various countries in the Balkans and the southeast of the

Mediterranean basin. However, as noted in point B(a) of the scientific committee's opinion, those cheeses are known in those countries under other names than "feta." As regards the production situation in the Hellenic Republic itself, the Danish Government submits, without being contradicted on this point, that, until 1988, cheese produced from cow's milk according to methods other than the traditional Greek methods was imported into Greece under the name "feta" and that, until 1987, feta cheese was produced in Greece using non-traditional methods, in particular from cow's milk.

It must be recognised that, if such operations were to persist, they would tend to confer a generic nature on the name "feta." The Court nevertheless notes that, by Ministerial Order No 2109/88 of 5 December 1988 approving the replacement of Article 83 "Cheese products" in the Food Code, the definition of the geographical area of production based on traditional practices was established. In 1994, Ministerial Order No 313025 codified all of the rules applicable to feta cheese. Furthermore, all of that legislation created a new situation in which such operations should no longer take place.

As to the production situation in the other Member States, the Court notes that it held in paragraph 99 of the judgment in Denmark and Others v Commission, cited above, that the fact that a product has been lawfully marketed under a name in some Member States may constitute a factor which must be taken into account in the assessment of whether that name has become generic within the meaning of Article 3(1) of the basic regulation.

The Commission acknowledges, moreover, that feta is produced in Member States other than the Hellenic Republic, namely the Kingdom of Denmark, the Federal Republic of Germany and the French Republic. According to the 13th to the 17th recitals in the preamble to the contested regulation, the Hellenic Republic produces approximately 115,000 tonnes annually. In 1998, almost 27,640 tonnes were produced in Denmark. From 1988 to 1998, production in France varied between 7,960 tonnes and 19,964 tonnes. Production in Germany has varied between 19,757 and 39,201 tonnes since 1985. According to those same recitals, the production of feta commenced in 1972 in Germany, in 1931 in France and in the 1930s in Denmark.

Moreover, it is common ground that the cheese thus produced could be lawfully marketed, even in Greece, at least until 1988. Although the production in the other countries has been relatively large and of substantial duration, the Court notes, as pointed out by the scientific committee in the first indent of the conclusion in its opinion, that the production of feta has remained concentrated in Greece. The fact that the product has been lawfully produced in Member States other than the Hellenic Republic is only one factor of several which must be taken into account pursuant to Article 3(1) of the basic regulation.

As regards the consumption of feta in the various Member States, as opposed to its production, the Court notes that the 19th recital in the preamble to the contested regulation indicates that more than 85% of Community consumption of feta, per capita and per year, takes place in Greece. As noted by the scientific committee, the consumption of feta is therefore concentrated in Greece.

The information provided to the Court indicates that the majority of consumers in Greece consider that the name "feta" carries a geographical and not a generic connotation. In Denmark, by contrast, the majority of consumers believe that the name is generic. The Court does not have any conclusive evidence regarding the other Member States. The evidence adduced to the Court also shows that, in Member States other than Greece, feta is commonly marketed with labels referring to Greek cultural traditions and civilisation. It is legitimate to infer therefrom that consumers in those Member States perceive feta as a cheese associated with the Hellenic Republic, even if in reality it has been produced in another Member State.

Those various factors relating to the consumption of feta in the Member States tend to indicate that the name "feta" is not generic in nature. As to the national legislation, it must be borne in mind that, according to the 18th and 31st recitals in the preamble to the contested regulation, the Kingdom of Denmark and the Hellenic Republic were the only Member States at the time which had legislation specifically relating to feta. The Danish legislation does not refer to "feta" but to "Danish feta," which would tend to suggest that in Denmark the name "feta," by itself, has retained a Greek connotation.

It follows from the foregoing that several relevant and important factors indicate that the term has not become generic. In the light of the foregoing, the Court finds that the Commission could lawfully decide, in the contested regulation, that the term "feta" had not become generic within the meaning of Article 3 of the basic regulation. On those grounds, the Court (Grand Chamber) hereby dismisses the actions.

Notes and Questions

1. What does the word "feta" mean? Is it even Greek? Does it indicate or imply a certain region or a place? If not, then can it qualify as a geographical indication?

2. The EU Regulation protects both "designations of origin" and "geographical indications" as defined by the Regulation. What's the difference? Would both satisfy TRIPS Article 22(1)'s definition of geographical indication?

3. How did the ECJ rule on whether "feta" had become a generic term? What factors and evidence did the court consider? If the production and consumption of feta cheese are heavily concentrated in Greece, should that be enough to negate a finding that the term is generic? How, if at all, should consumer perceptions of "feta" factor in?

4. In your mind, which, if any, has more of a geographical connotation in the U.S.: feta cheese or Swiss cheese? Should both or either be protected as GIs in the U.S.?

2. HEIGHTENED PROTECTION FOR WINES AND SPIRITS AND EXCEPTIONS

TRIPS Article 23 establishes a heightened level of protection specifically for GIs involving wines and spirits, in addition to the basic protections for GIs under Article 22 that apply generally to all GIs, including those for wines and spirits. France led the charge to secure greater protection for wines and spirits. Article 23 does not hinge protection of GIs on any concept of a "misleading" use. Instead, Article 23(1) requires protection against use of a GI on a product that did not originate from that geographical region, regardless if "misleading" or not. Moreover, Article 23(1) applies even where a third party attempts to use a disclaimer of sorts, by indicating on the wine or spirit "the true origin of the goods" and using someone else's protected GI only "in translation or accompanied by expressions such as 'kind', 'type,' 'style,' 'imitation' or the like." TRIPS art. 23(1). Under Article 23(2), countries are obligated to deny or invalidate registration of any marks bearing the GI if the wines or spirits do not originate from the geographical region. *Id.* 23(2).

The minimum standards of GI protection for wines and spirits are subject to the same general exceptions in Article 24 discussed above in the preceding section. In addition, Article 24(4) recognizes an additional "grandfather" provision for GIs on wines and spirits. A country can allow the continued use of a GI by nationals or domiciliaries who have used the GI on wines or spirits "in a continuous manner with regard to the same or related goods or services in the territory of that Member either (a) for at least 10 years preceding 15 April 1994 or (b) in good faith preceding that date." TRIPS art. 24(4). Thus, even if the GI is used on a product that does not originate from the geographical region mentioned in the GI, a member country may allow the continued use of the GI by the national or domiciliary of the country if the use qualifies under the exception based on a "grandfathered" use under Article 24(4). And this is irrespective of whether the national or domiciliary has obtained or applied for any trademark rights in the GI at issue (as required for the other grandfather exemption in Article 24(5)). In addition, Article 24(6) gives countries the discretion whether to allow continued uses of indications that are identical with "the customary name of a grape variety existing in the territory of that Member as of the date of entry into force of the WTO Agreement." *Id.* art. 24(6). Pinot Noir, Merlot, Chardonnay, and Cabernet Sauvignon are examples of well-known grape varieties.

PROBLEM 4–19

Apparently invoking Footnote 4 to TRIPS Article 32, which permits a member to enforce GIs for wines and spirits by "administrative action," the

U.S. has delegated some of the responsibility for GI protection to the Bureau of Alcohol, Tobacco, Firearms and Explosives (ATF) to regulate the labeling of wines with geographical names. The ATF has issued the following regulation that classifies geographical names into 3 categories: (1) generic, (2) semi-generic, and (3) non-generic. Whether manufacturers not from a geographical region can use the geographical term depends on the category the term falls into. Review the categories below.

§ 4.24   Generic, semi-generic, and non-generic designations of geographic significance.

(a)(1) A name of geographic significance which is also the designation of a class or type of wine, shall be deemed to have become generic only if so found by the appropriate ATF officer.

(2) Examples of generic names, originally having geographic significance, which are designations for a class or type of wine are: Vermouth, Sake.

(b)(1) A name of geographic significance, which is also the designation of a class or type of wine, shall be deemed to have become semi-generic only if so found by the appropriate ATF officer. Semi-generic designations may be used to designate wines of an origin other than that indicated by such name only if there appears in direct conjunction therewith an appropriate appellation of origin disclosing the true place of origin of the wine, and if the wine so designated conforms to the standard of identity, if any, for such wine contained in the regulations in this part or, if there be no such standard, to the trade understanding of such class or type. See § 24.257(c) of this chapter for exceptions to the appropriate ATF officer's authority to remove names from paragraph (b)(2) of this section.

(2) Examples of semi-generic names which are also type designations for grape wines are Angelica, Burgundy, Claret, Chablis, Champagne, Chianti, Malaga, Marsala, Madeira, Moselle, Port, Rhine Wine (syn. Hock), Sauterne, Haut Sauterne, Sherry, Tokay.

(c)(1) A name of geographic significance, which has not been found by the appropriate ATF officer to be generic or semi-generic may be used only to designate wines of the origin indicated by such name, but such name shall not be deemed to be the distinctive designation of a wine unless the appropriate ATF officer finds that it is known to the consumer and to the trade as the designation of a specific wine of a particular place or region, distinguishable from all other wines.

(2) Examples of nongeneric names which are not distinctive designations of specific grape wines are: American, California, Lake Erie, Napa Valley, New York State, French, Spanish. Additional examples of foreign nongeneric names are listed in subpart C of part 12 of this chapter.

(3) Examples of nongeneric names which are also distinctive designations of specific grape wines are: Bordeaux Blanc, Bordeaux Rouge, Graves, Medoc, Saint–Julien, Chateau Yquem, Chateau Margaux, Chateau Lafite, Pommard, Chambertin, Montrachet, Rhone, Liebfraumilch, Rudesheimer, Forster, Deidesheimer, Schloss Johannisberger, Lagrima, and Lacryma Christi. A list of foreign distinctive designations, as determined by the Director, appears in subpart D of part 12 of this chapter.

In 2006, the U.S agreed with the EU in the Wine Trade Agreement to limit the class of semi-generic names to the ones listed above and to not allow any new users of the semi-generic names. Those wine makers that had been using the semi-generic names in the U.S. prior to the 2006 law were allowed to continue to use the names under a "grandfathering" provision. *See* 26 U.S.C. § 5388(c).

Please evaluate whether the ATF's regulation is consistent with Articles 23 and 24 of TRIPS? Go through subsections (a), (b), and (c), and evaluate their compliance with TRIPS. Which subsection, if any, is the most questionable?

PROBLEM 4–20

Big Apple Fine Wines and International Foods also produces wines. Due to the spectacular success in the United States of a new table wine from the Normandy region of France introduced by French vineyards in 2004, Big Apple wants to sell a similar wine produced locally under the label "Big Apple Normandy Red Table Wine." Big Apple's best selling label is "Big Apple Champagne—Finest Since 1977," while it also sells "Chablis," an expensive and popular wine using grapes from the Chablis Winery in Napa Valley, California. For each of these wines, analyze (i) whether Big Apple can invoke the above ATF Regulation for generic and semi-generic indications in Problem 4–19, and (ii) whether Big Apple's use of "Big Apple Normandy Red Table Wine," "Big Apple Champagne—Finest Since 1977," and "Chablis" would be consistent with TRIPS? In answering these questions, consider the following provisions, discussion, and notes.

TRIPS Agreement

Article 23

Additional Protection for Geographical Indications for Wines and Spirits

1. Each Member shall provide the legal means for interested parties to prevent use of a geographical indication identifying wines for wines not originating in the place indicated by the geographical indication in question or identifying spirits for spirits not originating in the place indicated by the geographical indication in question, even where the true origin of the goods is indicated or the geographical indication is used in translation or accompanied by expressions such as "kind," "type," "style," "imitation" or the like.[4]

2. The registration of a trademark for wines which contains or consists of a geographical indication identifying wines or for spirits which contains or consists of a geographical indication identifying spirits shall be refused or invalidated, *ex officio* if a Member's legislation so permits or at the request of an interested party, with respect to such wines or spirits not having this origin.

3. In the case of homonymous geographical indications for wines, protection shall be accorded to each indication, subject to the provisions of

---

4. Notwithstanding the first sentence of Article 32, Members may, with respect to these obligations, instead provide for enforcement by administrative action.

paragraph 4 of Article 22. Each Member shall determine the practical conditions under which the homonymous indications in question will be differentiated from each other, taking into account the need to ensure equitable treatment of the producers concerned and that consumers are not misled. * * *

Article 24

Exceptions [parts specific to wines and spirits*]

4.   Nothing in this Section shall require a Member to prevent continued and similar use of a particular geographical indication of another Member identifying wines or spirits in connection with goods or services by any of its nationals or domiciliaries who have used that geographical indication in a continuous manner with regard to the same or related goods or services in the territory of that Member either (a) for at least 10 years preceding 15 April 1994 or (b) in good faith preceding that date.

6.   * * * Nothing in this Section shall require a Member to apply its provisions in respect of a geographical indication of any other Member with respect to products of the vine for which the relevant indication is identical with the customary name of a grape variety existing in the territory of that Member as of the date of entry into force of the WTO Agreement.

NOTES AND QUESTIONS

1.   *Standard for GI protection on wines and spirits.* Is the standard for protection for GIs on wine and spirits different from the standard for other GIs? If so, why do you think this is the case? Are wine and spirits deserving of different protection than foods?

2.   *GI-imitations.* Do agree with Article 23's prohibition on the use of "kind," "type," "style," "imitation" coupled with a GI on a wine or spirit not from the geographical region indicated? For example, what if a wine producer in Europe used "California style" wine on a bottle of wine that also clearly indicated that the product originated from Europe? Should that be allowed? What about a U.S. wine producer that uses "Champagne style" on a bottle of sparking wine that also clearly indicated that the product originated in the U.S.?

3.   *Exceptions.* Are the exceptions in Article 24(4) and (6) discussed above discretionary or mandatory for countries to recognize? Do you agree with each of the exceptions, or would you have altered them in any way?

4.   *Jurisdiction.* Which jurisdiction should have the ultimate power to regulate who should qualify for a geographical indication? The locality or state in which the region is located? The national government in which the region is located? Should the WTO and TRIPS have any authority to set limits on a locality's, state's, or country's ability to determine who qualifies to use a geographical indication?

---

* Note the general exceptions in Article 24 described earlier in the preceding section also apply to GIs for wines and spirits, but will not be repeated again here. *Ed.*

For example, should the state of California be allowed to require that, for any use of the term "Napa" on wines, 75 percent of the grapes used be from Napa County. Cal. Bus. & Prof. Code § 25241; *see Bronco Wine Co. v. Jolly*, 33 Cal.4th 943, 95 P.3d 422 (2004), *cert. denied*, 544 U.S. 922, 125 S.Ct. 1646 (2005). What if the state law overrides a federal law that allows a "grandfather" exception to a similar federal requirement that 75 percent of the grapes must come from the region? Under the federal grandfather exception, a wine producer could use Napa even though it used less than 75 percent of grapes from Napa "if the brand name was in use prior to July 7, 1986, *and* the front label also discloses the true geographic source of the grapes used to make the wine contained in the bottle." *Id.* at 953. Doesn't California have a greater claim to define the conditions under which a wine producer can use "Napa" than the United States government—or anyone else, for that matter?

3. UNRESOLVED ISSUES RELATING TO GIs

Articles 23 and 24 of TRIPS are unique in expressly requiring WTO members to negotiate in the future. Article 23 requires negotiations to consider establishing a registration system for GIs for wines. Article 24 requires negotiations "aimed at increasing the protection of individual geographical indications under Article 23." For several years, the WTO Director–General led a consultative process with members. By 2011, talks appeared to be going nowhere. As the Director–General reported: "Delegations continued to voice the divergent views that have characterized this debate, with no convergence evident on the specific question of extension of Article 23 coverage: some Members continued to argue for extension of Article 23 protection to all products; others maintained that this was undesirable and created unreasonable burdens." *See* Report by the Director–General, WT/GC/W/633 (21 April 2011). The following discussion examines some of the major areas of disagreement among countries.

PROBLEM 4–21

The WTO Council has proposed the following notification and registration system for geographical indications (GIs). The key features of the proposal are:

(1) An international system of notification and registration for all GIs shall be established. Registration in the system will entitle the GI to standards of protection in accordance with Article 23 of TRIPS in all WTO countries.

(2) GIs shall be available to designate any agricultural or food product from a particular region whose quality, reputation, or other characteristic is attributable to its geographical origin.

(3) A government designated entity from the geographical region in which the GI originates will serve as the "owner" of the GI, but any person or entity shall be allowed to use the GI with the consent and approval of the government entity.

Is this proposal for GI protection good for developing countries that seek to protect traditional knowledge and their local nature resources from biopiracy? What about for the U.S.? If you were to devise a system of GI registration, what else might you adopt instead of or in addition to the features outlined above? For example, what, if any, review and opposition process should be adopted in the registration system? Who should administer the registration system? Shall registration apply "WTO-wide," entitling the registrant to GI protection in all WTO countries? In addition to the readings so far, consider the materials below.

TRIPS

Article 23

4.   In order to facilitate the protection of geographical indications for wines, negotiations shall be undertaken in the Council for TRIPS concerning the establishment of a multilateral system of notification and registration of geographical indications for wines eligible for protection in those Members participating in the system.

Article 24

International Negotiations; Exceptions

1.   Members agree to enter into negotiations aimed at increasing the protection of individual geographical indications under Article 23. The provisions of paragraphs 4 through 8 below shall not be used by a Member to refuse to conduct negotiations or to conclude bilateral or multilateral agreements. In the context of such negotiations, Members shall be willing to consider the continued applicability of these provisions to individual geographical indications whose use was the subject of such negotiations.

2.   The Council for TRIPS shall keep under review the application of the provisions of this Section; the first such review shall take place within two years of the entry into force of the WTO Agreement. Any matter affecting the compliance with the obligations under these provisions may be drawn to the attention of the Council, which, at the request of a Member, shall consult with any Member or Members in respect of such matter in respect of which it has not been possible to find a satisfactory solution through bilateral or plurilateral consultations between the Members concerned. The Council shall take such action as may be agreed to facilitate the operation and further the objectives of this Section.

TRIPS AGREEMENT: TOWARDS A BETTER PROTECTION FOR GEOGRAPHICAL INDICATIONS?

Jose Manuel Cortes Martin.
30 Brook. J. Int'l L. 117, 132, 141–45, 147–69 (2004).

IV.   Negotiations for a Multilateral System of Registration

A.   *Terms of Reference in Article 23.4: Facilitate; Voluntariness; Registration and its Legal Effects; Wines and Spirits*

Under the TRIPS system, WTO Members must open negotiations in the TRIPS Council to establish a multilateral notification and registration system for GIs. The precise terms of this obligation are in Article 23.4, which states that "(i)n order to facilitate the protection of geographical indications for wines, negotiations shall be undertaken in the Council for TRIPS concerning the establishment of a multilateral geographical system of notification and registration of geographical indications for wines eligible for protection in those Members participating in the system."

B. *Differing Proposals on the Nature of the Registration System*

The submissions that have been presented at the TRIPS Council for the establishment of a multilateral notification and registration system for GIs can be divided into two camps. The first is a minimalist approach defended by the United States, Australia, New Zealand, Japan, along with many Latin American countries.

The second group advocates a maximalist approach. Members of the European Union, Switzerland, former Eastern bloc countries, and a selection of developing countries champion this view.

1. *The Minimalist Approach*

i) The United States-led Proposal

The primary proposal advocating a minimalist approach was presented by the United States, Canada, Chile and Japan (U.S.-led Proposal). The system of notification and registration of GIs urged in this approach is characterized solely by its informative nature. The system proposed would not create legal rights, and consequently, the inscription of a GI would not require protection by other Members. Under this proposal, registration follows receipt by the administering body of notifications from participating Members. It includes notification in a searchable database of all GIs for wines and spirits and affirms the principle that GIs are territorial rights and, therefore, the conditions for granting and exercising them must be established in national legislations of WTO Members. For that reason, the minimalist approach conceives of a voluntary system of notification and registration. This means that any GI for wines or spirits established in accordance with national legislation is entitled to protection under Part II, Section 3, of the TRIPS, regardless of whether it is registered in the WTO database.

Members wishing to participate in this system submit to the Secretariat a list of domestic GIs eligible for protection under their national legislation, indicating the date, if any, on which protection will expire. Subsequent notifications include additional domestic GIs eligible for protection under a Member's national legislation and any previously-notified GIs no longer eligible for such protection. Following receipt of notifications, the Secretariat will compile a database of all notified GIs for wines and spirits and distribute copies to all Members. After the initial notification, the Secretariat will revise the database of notified GIs, adding or deleting indications in accordance with Members' notifications. Moreover, the proposal states that, in accordance with Article 23.3, identical or similar GIs may be submitted by more than one WTO Member, provided that the GI is recognized by each notifying WTO Member in accordance with its national regime for protecting GIs.

With regard to the effects under national legislation, participants would be legally bound to consult the database, along with other sources of information, when making decisions regarding the recognition and protection of GIs for wines and spirits. Registration in the multilateral system would not give rise to any presumption regarding eligibility for protection given the territorial nature of GIs and the application of Article 24 exceptions, which would remain in force under national law. Non-participants would be encouraged to refer to the database, along with other sources of information, in making such decisions under their national legislation. Thus, Members' participation would be limited to receiving these lists, among other sources of information, when they must make decisions on the protection in their territories of GIs of other Members.

With regard to appeals or objections, the proposal sets out that decisions concerning protection for GIs, regardless of whether the WTO is notified, should occur at the national level at the request of interested parties. Should any appeal or objection result in a final decision that a domestic GI is ineligible for protection, that Member should notify the Secretariat during the subsequent notification period.

iii) Shortcomings of the Minimalist Approach

A multilateral register clearly implies multilateral protection, and this must be the key element in establishing such a register. However, the U.S.-led Proposal is limited to creating a record rather than a true registration, as it only refers to legal effects under national legislation. The system does not provide for a mechanism to filter out names that should not be protected and, therefore, risks creating more confusion than clarity. The proposal is silent on the need for elements of proof, for the assessment of eligibility, or for an opposition procedure—elements which are indispensable to a future multilateral register. It is impossible under this approach to ensure that terms that do not meet the provisions of Articles 22.1 or 24.9, or which fall under one of the exceptions provided for in Article 24, are denied eligibility.

The U.S.-led Proposal also does not establish procedures to resolve possible litigation, an indispensable procedure for any future multilateral register. At the same time, the proposal leaves open the possibility for Members to end or interrupt their participation without legal ramifications. The great uncertainty regarding the legal effects of the system may thus increase litigation and, consequently, administrative costs.

As to the voluntary system upon which the U.S.-led Proposal insisted, it is unclear whether non-participating Members would be bound to give protection according to Article 23. If non-participating Members were not bound, the protections announced in Article 23.4 would be undermined. The literal meaning of the U.S.-led Proposal is based on a political commitment without legal force: authorities would be bound to refer to the register, yet the register gives rise to no national legal commitment. The U.S.-led Proposal also does not provide for any monitoring mechanism which requires national authorities to "refer" to the lists of GIs on the database. As a result, these national authorities will not know whether to rely on the information included in the system when making a determination on the protection of a GI.

For these reasons, it is difficult to understand how the mandate to facilitate the protection of GIs established in Article 23.4 would be fulfilled through this system. This proposal would establish a mere juxtaposition of existing national protection systems in a database without legal effects. As such, its value would be minimal. Assuredly, Article 23.4 calls for more ambitious action than this proposal offers. The proposal concentrates on the first part of the job, namely the establishment of a notification system, while the register would simply compile participating Members' information. This does not satisfy the requirement of producing legal effects that registration inherently entails in the context of intellectual property rights. A database which national authorities might or might not be required to refer to does not constitute a registration system in the intellectual property context. The costs of establishing and operating such a system should not be measured in absolute terms but, rather, in relation to the benefit offered by the system. If transparency alone is the only advantage offered by the proposed U.S.-led system, it might not be sufficient to justify its costs. To "facilitate" the legal protection of GIs under Article 23.4, a multilateral system should help administering bodies implement, and producers and consumers avail themselves of, legal protection.

2. *The Maximalist Approach*
i) The EC Proposal

The proposal advocating maximum protection and legal effect for the GI registration and notification system was presented by the EC and its Member States (EC Proposal). This proposal provides for a full registration system and combines elements from the Lisbon Agreement and EC Regulation 2081/92. This proposal favors clarity and legal certainty on the protection of GIs by advocating for the creation of a system that has several stages. In the first stage, Members notify their domestic GIs together with regional, bilateral, or multilateral agreements protecting such GIs and proof of compliance with the definition of GIs to the Secretariat. In the second stage, the Secretariat notifies all Members of the submission. The Members then have an eighteen-month period in which to examine the submission. During that period, each Member may challenge the registration of the GI on any of the following four grounds for opposition: non-compliance with the general definition of a GI; absence of protection in the country of origin, genericness, and that the use of the GI would be misleading. During the eighteen months following the publication by the Secretariat, the Members would be able to examine the GI's legitimacy by requesting explanations from the Member who presented the registration request. During this period, if a Member properly challenged the protection of a proposed GI, bilateral negotiations would be undertaken with the aim of reaching an agreement.

As far as who must demonstrate the grounds for opposition, the EC Proposal establishes that, in accordance with the TRIPS provisions and the normal legal practice in the WTO, the Member invoking the benefit must demonstrate that it has fulfilled the necessary conditions. According to this principle, Members must invoke the exception and prove its applicability if the Member trying to register the GI does not agree.

Once the period of eighteen months from publication ends, the GI would be inscribed in the register. If, during that time, there has been no opposition, the EC Proposal establishes that no Member will be able to reject the protection alleging that it does not fulfill the conditions demanded in the general definition. Members also may not allege that the GI, although literally true as to the territory in which the goods originated, falsely represents that the goods originated in another territory. Moreover, Members may not allege that the GI deals with a generic term. It is possible, however, to deduce sensu contrario that the other exceptions to the protection will continue to be allowed to be demanded by any Member.

From its inscription in the register, the GI would benefit from unconditional protection in the markets of all Members, as it would then be considered prima facie compatible with the definition in Article 22.1 and consequently deserving of protection. Nevertheless, such presumption could be refuted if use of a GI was the object of a controversy before a national tribunal. The register would protect GIs of other Members, since national jurisdictions and trademarks offices would have concise and clear information at their disposition. The list of GIs that had been registered would be published so that all the operators might know the inscription in the register. Consequently, the GIs would benefit from the presumption of protection. In addition, the EC Proposal mandates that Members will have to establish legal means so that the interested parties use the registration as a presumption of GI protection.

ii) Critical Appraisal: Why the EC Proposal Works Best

The EC Proposal is the only one that facilitates multilateral GI protection as Article 23.4 prescribes. The principal characteristic of the EC Proposal is its concept of a full registration system. Although voluntary, the system proposed by the EC would provide that once a GI was registered it would bind all WTO Members. Rights to oppose registration would counterbalance this legal obligation. It, therefore, does not create new obligations, as any Member would have the opportunity to oppose a registration under the EC Proposal.

But, is a system which creates legal effects at the international level really necessary to facilitate protection? There are several reasons why it is necessary, but the most important is that international legal effects would make GI protection easier to implement by providing that registered GIs benefit from a presumption of eligibility for protection. The system would enable producers to reduce costs as they would have easier access to the legal means available to them to secure and enforce the level of protection prescribed in Articles 22 and 23. Producers would not feel compelled to seek protection of their GIs by way of prevention in Member countries. Occasional free-riding of a notified GI would be discouraged because producers using GIs registered by other countries would have to bear the burden of proof and incur litigation costs.

In case of litigation, the register would be a tool for these producers to "facilitate" the protection of their GIs by shifting the burden of proof. This could be particularly valuable for producers in developing countries who might not otherwise have the means to assert their rights in all markets. The notification, examination, and opposition phases should therefore be considered an investment in the system's viability; the costs involved would be offset by the benefit that would be derived from effective protection. Without a presumption of eligibility, in most cases it would be difficult, if not impossible, for the average right-holder of a GI to enforce his rights under Article 23, because he would have to build a case from scratch before local courts. In certain cases, litigants would be thousands of kilometers from home and under completely different legal systems. This inconvenience would threaten the Members' clear intention to provide Article 23–level protection to GIs for wines and spirits. Under the EC Proposal, producers with a policy of international expansion would be able to save costs when defending their names around the world.

Public administrations would have timely information that allows them, for example, not to register trademarks containing such GIs, as prescribed by Article 23.2. As a result, a system with legal effects at the international level is necessary to facilitate protection because usurpation would diminish and, in turn, litigation and administration costs would decrease. Again, this means that the EC Proposal would make GI protection easier to implement. Under the proposal, registered GIs benefit from a presumption of eligibility for protection; moreover, piracy is discouraged. These two features benefit all parties: producers, consumers, and administrations.

V. Expansion of the System: Additional Protection for Products Other than Wines and Spirits

The second battleground over GIs is the expansion of Article 23 protection for products other than wines and spirits. Indeed, a large group of WTO Members, especially developing countries, have proposed before the TRIPS Council the elimination of existing deficiencies in the sphere of GI protection with a view to applying the same level of protection of wines and spirits to all other products. As a result of the pressure exerted by developing countries, this issue ranks very high on the negotiating agenda of the WTO.

B. Advocating for Expansion of GI Protection to Other Products

The benefits resulting from extension would foster the development of local rural communities and encourage a high-quality agricultural and industrial policy. As is the case for products protected via trademarks, those benefiting from adequate GI protection would be in a better position to benefit from enhanced access to third-world markets. As such, a strong GI regime would bring economic benefits to producers worldwide, and not only to producers in countries where the local protection of GIs is already stronger than in the WTO.

When considering extending GI protection, it is imperative to emphasize that the proposal presented by the sponsors of additional protection for products other than wines and spirits does not seek to require re-appropriation of terms and indications considered generic. The exceptions provisions of Article 24.6 would continue to apply to such indications. The goal of the extension proposal is to prevent GIs, which are not generic, from becoming generic. The proposal presented by these WTO Members also concerns other disadvantages resulting from the insufficient protection provided by Article 22, such as the burden of proof required under that provision to defend a GI against misuse.

However, many countries, including Argentina, Australia, Canada, Chile, Japan, Mexico, New Zealand, and the United States, have strongly opposed extension, partly because they believe there is no evidence that protection currently available for products other than wines and spirits is inadequate. They also object because they feel that extending protections would create unnecessary obligations, be significantly costly, and generate limited benefits, if any. Additionally, New Zealand, for example, believes that an extension to the scope of goods covered by Article 23 would be premature. The majority of these countries has been consistently obstinate about giving strong protection to GIs. While these countries wish to approach negotiations over protection for GIs and expansion of TRIPS slowly, Members that could benefit the most are ready to move full speed ahead.

NOTES AND QUESTIONS

1. *Old World v. New World?* Do the disagreements over GI protection discussed by Professor Martin reflect deeper cultural divisions over the importance attributed by a country to GIs versus prior trademarks and/or the free use of generic terms? If so, do you see any way for WTO countries to bridge the divide? What do you think of Professor Martin's suggestion that developing countries could play an important part in the negotiations? Do you think the developing countries—such as those from Africa, Asia, and Latin America—side unanimously with one approach or the other, the U.S. camp or the EU camp? If not, would that diminish or enhance the ability of developing countries to help reach some greater level of harmonization?

2. *Diversity of approaches.* What about just maintaining the current approach to GI protection under TRIPS? Could, in effect, countries just agree to disagree on this issue? Or does the current approach provide virtually no protection for GIs, causing harm to the legitimate interests of GI holders?

3. What do you think of the "built in" negotiation provisions in Articles 23(4) and 24(1), (2) of TRIPS? Are these provisions mandatory or voluntary?

If mandatory, should they be enforceable against a country that chooses to stop negotiating? Can the country be "ordered" to negotiate? Is there a time limit for how long the duty lasts? What if a country negotiates for five years, but then finds it futile? Do you believe it should be required to negotiate further?

4. *Registration system.* Would an international registry for GIs be desirable? What should the objectives of a multilateral registration system be? Can you answer that question without answering the basic question on how much you think GIs should be protected?

Voluntary or mandatory. Should participation in the registry be required of all WTO countries, or should it be voluntary? Do you favor the U.S. proposal, the EU proposal, or neither? What rights will the owner of a GI obtain as a result of registration under the U.S. approach? What about under the EU approach? What are the advantages and shortcomings (if any) of the U.S. and EU approaches?

Legal effect. What scope of protection among countries should be afforded to an internationally registered GI? Should an international registration carry with it a presumption of validity? Should the current exemptions for grandfathering and generic GIs remain in place?

Logistics. Who should decide who is entitled to register a GI and upon what kind of formality or application? Who should administer the international registry? Should there be a formal examination of each application for registration to verify the claimed GI in the country of origin? Do you like the 18–month process to contest an application for registration of a GI proposed by the EU?

5. *Expanding wine/spirit level of protection to all GIs.* Does it make any sense for WTO countries to debate expanding GI protection if they cannot agree on whether to have an international registry? Do not the divisions over a registry reflect basic disagreements over the scope of GI protection that only become more pronounced in considering the expansion of all GI protection to the heightened level for wines and spirits?

6. *Bibliographic note.* Burkhart Goebel, *Geographical Indications and Trademarks—The Road from Doha*, 93 TRADEMARK REP. 964 (2003); Molly Torsen, *Apples and Oranges (and Wine): Why the International Conversation Regarding Geographic Indications Is at a Standstill*, 87 J. PAT. & TRADEMARK OFF. SOC'Y 31 (2005).

D. THE RELATIONSHIP BETWEEN TRADEMARKS AND GEOGRAPHICAL INDICATIONS

As should be evident, trademarks and geographical indications are rather different in purpose and rationale. Notwithstanding these differences, it is possible, as TRIPS Article 24(5) contemplates, that both forms of protection could apply to identical or similar words. Perhaps the most famous example involves the longstanding worldwide dispute between the owner of the trademarks "Budweiser" and "Bud" for the American beer and the owner of the GIs for "Budejovické pivo," "Ceskobudejovické pivo," and "Budejovický met'anský var" for the Czech beer that is brewed in Ceské Budejovické, a city in the Czech Republic. Historically, the city has also been called "Budweis" in German, given its substantial German-speaking population. Almost from the start of both breweries' use of "Budweiser" in the early 1900s, the parties have contested ownership of the mark and have waged, more recently, numerous lawsuits around the world, with victories and defeats for both sides.[3] In 2011, the Court of Justice of the European Union agreed with the United Kingdom courts' ruling that both sides could have concurrent registration of "Budweiser" in the UK. Budíjovický Budvar v. Anheuser–Busch Inc., [2012] E.T.M.R. 2, C–482/09. The CJEU explained: "Article 4(1)(a) of Directive 89/104 must be interpreted as meaning that the proprietor of an earlier trade mark cannot obtain the cancellation of an identical later trade mark designating identical goods where there has been a long period of honest concurrent use of those two trade marks where, in circumstances such as those in the main proceedings, that use neither has nor is liable to have an adverse effect on the essential function of the trade mark which is to guarantee to consumers the origin of the goods or services." *Id.* ¶ 84. It remains to be seen whether the decision will end the century-long dispute between the two sides, as other litigation continues in Europe.

We have already discussed how TRIPS Articles 22, 23, and 24 generally regulate the protection of GIs. Now let us examine more closely how TRIPS addresses the situation that arises when someone obtains a GI for something that another party has already trademarked.

PROBLEM 4–22

In Canada, a Canadian producer had registered the trademark for "Parma ham" prior to the effective date of TRIPS. For a number of years, the Canadian producer sold hams in Canada bearing the label "Parma ham," even though the hams were made in Canada. You are the Trade Representative for the European Union. Evaluate the EU's chances of prevailing in the WTO's Dispute Settlement Body on a claim that Canada's trademark law violates Article 22 of TRIPS. What counterarguments do you expect the representatives from Canada to raise? Is there any further factual discovery relevant to the EU's claim that might bolster its chances of prevailing?

One of your attorney advisors recommends that one of the EU's alternative arguments should be that Articles 22 and 24 must be read, at the very least, in such a way to balance the interests of both legitimate GI holders and legitimate trademark holders. Under this theory, Article 24(5) must be read to allow at least the *coexistence* of (i) a legitimate trademark owned by A and (ii) a legitimate GI owned by B in Canada, even though the trademark and the GI are the same. In other words, although A's registered trademark would remain valid if it falls within TRIPS Article 24(5), B should be allowed to

---

3. For further discussion, see Richard M. Terpstra, *Which Bud's for You: An Examination of the Trademark Dispute Between Anheuser–Busch and Budejovicky Budvar in English Courts*, 18 TEMP. INT'L & COMP. L.J. 479 (2004).

continue to use the GI in Canada—and not be stopped by A. What do you think of this argument? Does TRIPS require Canada to adopt the coexistence approach? Consider the following WTO case.

EUROPEAN COMMUNITIES—PROTECTION OF TRADE-MARKS AND GEOGRAPHICAL INDICATIONS FOR AG-RICULTURAL PRODUCTS AND FOODSTUFFS

Report of the Panel, WTO.
(Chair: Miguel Rodríguez Mendoza; Members: Prof. Seung Wha Chang, Peter Kam-fai Cheung).
WT/DS174/R (March 15, 2005).

[The United States and Australia filed separate complaints in the Dispute Settlement Body against the European Communities, specifically challenging, on numerous grounds, the EU's Regulation No. 2081/92 (14 July 1992) regulating geographical indications in the EU. Although the complaints were heard before a single WTO panel, the panel issued two separate, lengthy reports.

One part of the case involved the relationship between GI protection and protection for prior trademarks similar to or identical with the GI in question (i.e., "grandfathered" or prior trademarks under TRIPS Article 24(5)). Article 14(2) of the EU Regulations dealt with prior trademarks as follows:

2.   With due regard to Community law, a trademark the use of which engenders one of the situations indicated in Article 13 and which has been applied for, registered, or established by use, if that possibility is provided for by the legislation concerned, in good faith within the territory of the Community, before either the date of protection in the country of origin or the date of submission to the Commission of the application for registration of the designation of origin or geographical indication, *may continue to be used notwithstanding the registration of a designation of origin or geographical indication*, provided that no grounds for its invalidity or revocation exist as specified by Council Directive 89/104/EEC of 21 December 1998 to approximate the laws of the Member States relating to trade marks and/or Council Regulation (EC) No 40/94 of 20 December 1993 on the Community trade mark. (emphasis added)

Under the EU Regulation, the grandfathered trademark and a similar or identical GI can "coexist"—meaning that the trademark holder can enforce its trademark against third parties, but not against the GI holder. Thus, the trademark holder loses the right to stop the use of the GI, even though, in some cases, it may cause a likelihood of confusion. Although Article 14(3) of the EU Regulation does recognize that "[a] designation of origin or geographical indication shall not be registered where, in the light of a trade mark's reputation and renown and the length of time it has been used, registration is liable to mislead the consumer as to the true identity of the product," Article 14(3) does not enable a grandfathered trademark holder to prevent all uses of a similar or identical GI.

Below is an excerpt from the WTO panel's report in the U.S. case, analyzing the European Communities' arguments that the EU Regulation can be justified on the basis of TRIPS Article 24(5) (exceptions to GIs) and Article 17 (exceptions to trademarks). *Ed.*]

[TRIPS Article 24(5) Analysis]

It is evidently the position under the European Communities' domestic law that an implied positive right to use a registered GI prevails over the negative right of a prior trademark holder to prevent confusing uses. However, such an interpretation of the TRIPS Agreement is not possible without a suitable basis in the treaty text. The text of Article 24.5 expressly preserves the right to use a trademark—which is not expressly provided for in the TRIPS Agreement—and is silent as to any limitation on the trademark owner's exclusive right to prevent confusing uses of signs—which is expressly provided for in the TRIPS Agreement—when the sign is used as a GI.

The ordinary meaning of the terms in their context must also be interpreted in light of the object and purpose of the agreement. The object and purpose of the TRIPS Agreement, as indicated by Articles 9 through 62 and 70 and reflected in the preamble, includes the provision of adequate standards and principles concerning the availability, scope, use and enforcement of trade-related intellectual property rights. This confirms that a limitation on the standards for trademark or GI protection should not be implied unless it is supported by the text.

Therefore, the Panel concludes that, under Article 16.1 of the TRIPS Agreement, Members are required to make available to trademark owners a right against certain uses, including uses as a GI. Article 24.5 of the TRIPS Agreement is inapplicable and does not provide authority to limit that right.

[TRIPS Article 17 analysis]

The Panel will now consider the European Communities' argument that its particular regime of coexistence between GIs and prior trademarks is justified under Article 17 of the TRIPS Agreement. Article 17 provides as follows:

"Exceptions

Members may provide limited exceptions to the rights conferred by a trademark, such as fair use of descriptive terms, provided that such exceptions take account of the legitimate interests of the owner of the trademark and of third parties."

The ordinary meaning of the terms indicates that an exception must not only be "limited" but must also comply with the proviso in order to satisfy Article 17. The structure of Article 17 differs from that of other exceptions provisions to which the parties refer. It can be noted that Articles 13, 26.2 and 30 of the TRIPS Agreement, as well as Article 9(2) of the Berne Convention (1971) as incorporated by Article 9.1 of the TRIPS Agreement, also permit exceptions to intellectual property rights and all contain, to varying degrees, similar language to Article 17. However, unlike these other provisions, Article 17 contains no reference to "conflict with a [or the] normal exploitation," no reference to "unreasonabl[e] prejudice to the legitimate interests" of the right holder or owner, and it not only refers to the legitimate interests of third parties but treats them on par with those of the right holder. Therefore, whilst it is instructive to refer to the interpretation by two previous panels of certain shared elements found in Articles 13 and 30, it is important to interpret Article 17 according to its own terms.

Limited exceptions

The first issue to decide is the meaning of the term "limited exceptions" as used in Article 17. The Panel agrees with the views of the Panel in Canada–Pharmaceutical Patents, which interpreted the identical term in Article 30, that "[t]he word 'exception' by itself connotes a limited derogation, one that does not undercut the body of rules from which it is made." The addition of the word "limited" emphasizes that the exception must be narrow and permit only a small diminution of rights. The limited exceptions apply "to the rights conferred by a trademark." They do not apply to the set of all trademarks or all trademark owners. Accordingly, the fact that it may affect only few trademarks or few trademark owners is irrelevant to the question whether an exception is limited. The issue is whether the exception to the rights conferred by a trademark is narrow.

There is only one right conferred by a trademark at issue in this dispute, namely the exclusive right to prevent certain uses of a sign, provided for in Article 16.1. Therefore, it is necessary to examine the exception on an individual "per right" basis. There is no indication in the text of Article 17 that this involves an economic assessment, although economic impact can be taken into account in the proviso. In this regard, we note the absence of any reference to a "normal exploitation" of the trademark in Article 17, and the absence of any reference in Section 2, to which Article 17 permits exceptions, to rights to exclude legitimate competition.

The overriding requirement is that the exception must be "limited" and it must also satisfy the proviso, considered below. These elements provide a useful framework for an assessment of the extent to which an exception curtails the right provided for in Article 16.1.

The example in the text, "fair use of descriptive terms," provides guidance as to what is considered a "limited exception," although it is illustrative only. Fair use of descriptive terms is inherently limited in terms of the sign which may be used and the degree of likelihood of confusion which may result from its use, as a purely descriptive term on its own is not distinctive and is not protectable as a trademark. Fair use of descriptive terms is not limited in terms of the number of third parties who may benefit, nor in terms of the quantity of goods or services with respect to which they use the descriptive terms, although implicitly it only applies to those third parties who would use those terms in the course of trade and to those goods or services which those terms describe. The number of trademarks or trademark owners affected is irrelevant, although implicitly it would only affect those marks which can consist of, or include, signs that can be used in a descriptive manner. According to the text, this is a "limited" exception for the purposes of Article 17.

Turning to the Regulation, it curtails the trademark owner's right in respect of certain goods but not all goods identical or similar to those in respect of which the trademark is registered. It prevents the trademark owner from exercising the right to prevent confusing uses of a sign for the agricultural product or foodstuff produced in accordance with the product specification in the GI registration. The trademark owner's right against all other goods is not curtailed. We note that there is no limit in terms of the quantity of goods which may benefit from the exception, as long as they conform to the product specification. However, this cannot prevent the limitation on rights of owners of trademarks subject to Article 14(2) from constituting a limited exception for the purposes of Article 17, as fair use of descriptive terms implies no limit in terms of quantity either, and the text indicates that it is a limited exception for the purposes of Article 17. The quantity of goods which benefits from an exception may be related to the curtailment of the rights to prevent the acts of making, selling or importing a product, but these are not rights conferred by a trademark.

Under the Regulation, once a GI has been registered and a trademark is subject to the coexistence regime under Article 14(2), the GI may, in principle, be used without regard to the likelihood of confusion that it may cause. However, the Regulation refers to the likelihood or risk of confusion, with a given mark, which would result from use as a GI of an identical or similar sign, in Articles 7(5)(b), 12b(3) and 12d(3), in relation to the decision on whether to register a GI where an objection is admissible. Article 7(4) and, hence, Article 12b(3), provide a ground for objection where registration would jeopardize the existence of a mark, and Article 14(3) provides a ground for refusal of registration which refers to the trademark's reputation and renown and the length of time it has been used. Furthermore, the European Communities has explained that the use of a name registered as a GI is subject to the applicable provisions of the food labelling and misleading advertising directives so that the ways in which it may be used are not unlimited. For the above reasons, the Panel finds that the Regulation creates a "limited exception" within the meaning of Article 17 of the TRIPS Agreement.

The proviso to Article 17

Limited exceptions must satisfy the proviso that "such exceptions take account of the legitimate interests of the owner of the trademark and of third parties" in order to benefit from Article 17. Given that Article 17 creates an exception to the rights conferred by a trademark, the "legitimate interests" of the trademark owner must be something different from full enjoyment of those legal rights. The "legitimate interests" of the trademark owner are also compared with those of "third parties," who have no rights conferred by the trademark. Therefore, the "legitimate interests," at least of third parties, are something different from simply the enjoyment of their legal rights.

We agree with the following view of the Panel in Canada–Pharmaceutical Patents, which interpreted the term "legitimate interests" of a patent owner and third parties in the context of Article 30 as follows:

> "To make sense of the term 'legitimate interests' in this context, that term must be defined in the way that it is often used in legal discourse—as a normative claim calling for protection of interests that are 'justifiable' in the sense that they are supported by relevant public policies or other social norms."

In our view, this is also true of the term "legitimate interests" of a trademark owner and third parties in the context of Article 17.

The legitimacy of some interest of the trademark owner is assumed because the owner of the trademark is specifically identified in Article 17. The TRIPS Agreement itself sets out a statement of what all WTO Members consider adequate standards and principles concerning trademark protection. Although it sets out standards for legal rights, it also provides guidance as to WTO Members' shared understandings of the policies and norms relevant to trademarks and, hence, what might be the legitimate interests of trademark owners. The function of trademarks can be understood by reference to Article 15.1 as distinguishing goods and services of undertakings in the course of trade. Every trademark owner has a legitimate interest in preserving the distinctiveness, or capacity to distinguish, of its trademark so that it can perform that function. This includes its interest in using its own trademark in connection with the relevant goods and services of its own and authorized undertakings. Taking account of that legitimate interest will also take account of the trademark owner's interest in the economic value of its mark arising from the reputation that it enjoys and the quality that it denotes.

Turning to the Regulation, the evidence shows that the owner's legitimate interest in preserving the distinctiveness, or capacity to distinguish, of its trademark can be taken into account in various ways. Article 7(4) of the Regulation provides that a statement of objection shall be admissible inter alia if it shows that the registration of the proposed GI would "jeopardize the existence . . . of a mark." This requires GI registration to be refused. Article 14(3) also requires the refusal of GI registration in light of a trademark's reputation and renown and the length of time it has been used, if a particular condition is fulfilled. This addresses the distinctiveness, or capacity to distinguish, of prior trademarks and can ensure that, in cases where trademark owners' legitimate interests would be most likely to be affected, the exception in Article 14(2) simply does not apply.

In the one instance in which Article 14(3) has been applied, the European Communities informs the Panel that its authorities [denied GI registration.] This indicates to the Panel that Article 14(3) of the Regulation was, in fact, applied to take account inter alia of the legitimate interest of the trademark owners to protect the distinctiveness of their respective marks. In the other instance to which the parties refer, the registration of the three Czech beer GIs contains an endorsement that they apply "without prejudice to any beer trademark or other rights existing in the European Union on the date of accession." Although the European Communities has confirmed that such an endorsement is unique and it has not explained in what other circumstances such an endorsement might be possible, this example does show that, at least in this case, not only the legitimate interests of trademark owners, but also their rights, have been taken into account.

In the light of the provisions of Articles 7(4) and 14(3), we are satisfied that where the likelihood of confusion is relatively high, the exception in Article 14(2) will not apply. In any event, even where the exception does apply, Article 14(2) expressly provides that the trademark may continue to be used, on certain conditions. We also note that the proviso to Article 17 requires only that exceptions "take account" of the legitimate interests of the owner of the trademark, and does not refer to "unreasonabl[e] prejudice" to those interests, unlike the provisos in Articles 13, 26.2 and 30 of the TRIPS Agreement and Article 9(2) of the Berne Convention (1971) as incorporated by Article 9.1 of the TRIPS Agreement. This suggests that a lesser standard of regard for the legitimate interests of the owner of the trademark is required.

For these reasons, the Panel considers that the exception created by the Regulation takes account of the legitimate interests of the owner of the trademark within the meaning of Article 17. This finding is confirmed by responses to a question from the Panel which revealed that, of over 600 GIs registered under the Regulation over a period of eight years, the complainants and third parties are unable to identify any that, in their view, could be used in a way that would result in a likelihood of confusion with a prior trademark, with four exceptions. Three of these are the Czech beer GIs, the registration of which is subject to the endorsement set out above. The only remaining example is "Bayerisches Bier," in respect of which the complainants have not shown an example of actual likelihood of confusion with a prior trademark.

[The WTO panel also concluded that the EU regulation adequately considered the interests of third party consumers in avoiding confusion over trademarks and GIs.]

Therefore, the Panel concludes that, with respect to the coexistence of GIs with prior trademarks, the Regulation is inconsistent with Article 16.1 of the TRIPS Agreement but, on the basis of the evidence presented to the Panel, this is justified by Article 17 of the TRIPS Agreement. Article 24.3 and Article 24.5 of the TRIPS Agreement are inapplicable.

NOTES AND QUESTIONS

1. Did the WTO panel conclude that the EU's approach to the "coexistence" of GIs and grandfathered trademarks was consistent with TRIPS or not? Did the decision render a reasonable interpretation of TRIPS and a good compromise between the aims of protecting GIs and trademarks?

2. *Two-step test?* What test did the WTO panel apply to determine if the EU Regulation was a permissible exception to trademark under Article 17? How, if at all, is that test different from the test for exceptions to copyright under Article 13 elaborated in the *Section 110(5)* case (see pp. 187–195) and the test for exceptions to patent under Article 30 elaborated in the *Canada–Patent Protection of Pharmaceutical Products* case (see pp. 407–417).

3. *Rest of WTO panel's decision.* In a lengthy discussion (not excerpted), the WTO panel concluded that other parts of the EU Regulation violated the requirement of national treatment under TRIPS. Review Problem 4–18 to reconsider one part of the EU Regulation that was problematic.

E. SPECIAL DISCUSSION: INTERNET DOMAIN NAMES AND TRADEMARK DISPUTES

Historically, new technologies have raised challenges for protecting intellectual property. With the advent of the Internet in the mid '90s, trademark law was beset with thousands of controversies involving Internet domain names and trademark rights. Initially, these disputes were litigated in courts as trademark infringement and dilution disputes. In 1999, the World Intellectual Property Organization (WIPO) recommended the establishment of a uniform policy to address domain name disputes by the Internet Corporation for Assigned Names and Numbers (ICANN), a non-profit corporation instituted in 1998 to oversee the domain name registry. By October 24, 1999, ICANN formulated the Uniform Dispute Resolution Policy (UDRP), at http://www.icann.org/udrp/udrp-policy–24oct 99.htm.

The UDRP is a form of alternative dispute resolution (ADR). Anyone who registers a domain name agrees to be subject to a "mandatory administrative proceeding" for UDRP disputes. The disputes are to be decided by either one arbitrator or, if either party requests it, a panel of three arbitrators administered by WIPO. *See* Rules for UDRP, ¶ 6(c), at http://www.icann.org/dndr/udrp/uniform-rules.htm. If the complainant chooses one arbitrator, but the respondent elects to have three arbitrators, the respondent "shall be required to pay one-half of the applicable fee for a three-member Panel." *Id.* ¶ 5(c).

In a UDRP dispute, the complainant must allege and prove a "bad faith" registration of a domain name by establishing the following three elements:

(i) [the] domain name is identical or confusingly similar to a trademark or service mark in which the complainant has rights; and

(ii) [the person who registered the domain name] ha[s] no rights or legitimate interests in respect of the domain name; and

(iii) [the] domain name has been registered and is being used in bad faith.

UDRP ¶ 4(a). Notice that a UDRP dispute is limited to claims involving "bad faith" registration and use of the domain name. In cases involving no bad faith, the UDRP does not govern.

Since bad faith is the *sine qua non* of a UDRP claim, it is important to understand the concept. Bad faith is defined in ¶ 4(b) as follows:

b. Evidence of Registration and Use in Bad Faith. For the purposes of Paragraph 4(a)(iii), the following circumstances, in particular but without limitation, if found by the Panel to be present, shall be evidence of the registration and use of a domain name in bad faith:

(i) circumstances indicating that you have registered or you have acquired the domain name primarily for the purpose of selling, renting, or otherwise transferring the domain name registration to the complainant who is the owner of the trademark or service mark or to a competitor of that complainant, for valuable consideration in excess of your documented out-of-pocket costs directly related to the domain name; or

(ii) you have registered the domain name in order to prevent the owner of the trademark or service mark from reflecting the mark in a corresponding domain name, provided that you have engaged in a pattern of such conduct; or

(iii) you have registered the domain name primarily for the purpose of disrupting the business of a competitor; or

(iv) by using the domain name, you have intentionally attempted to attract, for commercial gain, Internet users to your web site or other on-line location, by creating a likelihood of confusion with the complainant's mark as to the source, sponsorship, affiliation, or endorsement of your web site or location or of a product or service on your web site or location.

As should be evident by the above factors, bad faith may involve the so-called "cyber-squatter" who attempted to register a domain name with an existing trademark in order to sell it back to a trademark holder at a higher price (see factor (i) above). But bad faith can involve other conduct, such as disrupting or preventing the businesses of others by registering their domain names, or attempting to attract customers to one's website by using a domain name that is likely to cause confusion with a trademark.

Decisions rendered by WIPO panels under the UDRP are not binding on any court. UDRP ¶ 4k. A complainant or respondent could, therefore, bring a traditional lawsuit after losing a UDRP administrative decision. However, the nonbinding nature of UDRP decisions has not decreased the popularity of this alternative form of dispute resolution. As of October 2011, after eleven years of existence, the UDRP has handled over 21,500 domain name disputes by administrative decision. Each year from 2007 to 2011, WIPO resolved over 2,000 UDRP cases. Under the UDRP, ICANN has the authority "to cancel, transfer or otherwise make changes to domain name registrations" based on an administrative decision. UDRP ¶ 3.

PROBLEM 4–23

Michael Jordan, a 45–year–old salesman and avid fisherman living in Cleveland with the same name as the famous retired basketball player, sets up an Internet site, michaeljordan.net. The site features news stories and commentary on the best places to fish in the Great Lakes region of northern Ohio. The site has no advertising at all. Nor does it conduct any transactions. On the right hand column of the website, there are several links to the Cleveland salesman's favorite websites, including CNN, ESPN, and Playboy. The Playboy link goes to an adult website for men. The michaeljordan.net website has the following disclaimer at the bottom of the home page, in 12–point font: "This site is not affiliated or sponsored in any way by the basketball player Michael Jordan. He's no relation."

When associates of the retired basketball player, who owns the website michaeljordan.com, discovered the .net website, they immediately called the Cleveland salesman demanding the transfer of the domain name. Jordan, the salesman, replied, "I don't see any reason to transfer the domain name since I have just as much right to my name as your client does to his. I just want to be left alone, do you understand? I don't want to deal with lawyers and agents. You can tell Mike I will only deal with him. If my website is so valuable to him, MJ will have to show me the money himself. But I'm not going to be bought. I never liked MJ as a player. Tell him I'm a Cleveland Cavs fan, and I don't care if I disrupt his business."

Michael Jordan, the former NBA basketball star, uses his name on a variety of products and services, including restaurants, cafes, and clothing— but none related to fishing. The website of Michael Jordan, the salesman, attracts just as many visitors (numbering in the tens of thousands each day), but probably many of the visitors go to the site by mistake, searching for the basketball player's site. You are the attorney for the retired basketball player Michael Jordan. Evaluate your client's likelihood of prevailing in a UDRP dispute to get the transfer of the domain name michaeljordan.net. Would you advise your client to meet with the Cleveland salesman about the domain name? If so, should your client make an offer for the domain name? Consider the two cases below.

MADONNA CICCONE, p/k/a MADONNA v. DAN PARISI AND "MADONNA.COM"

Administrative Panel Decision.
WIPO Case No. D2000–0847 (October 12, 2000).

Mark V.B. Partridge, Presiding Panelist; James W. Dabney, Panelist, David E. Sorkin, Panelist.

4. Factual Background

Complainant is the well-known entertainer Madonna. She is the owner of U.S. Trademark Registrations for the mark MADONNA for entertainment services and related goods (Reg. No. 1,473,554 and 1,463,-601). She has used her name and mark MADONNA professionally for entertainment services since 1979. Complainant's music and other entertainment endeavors have often been controversial for featuring explicit sexual content. In addition, nude photographs of Madonna have appeared in Penthouse magazine, and Complainant has published a coffee-table book entitled "Sex" featuring sexually explicit photographs and text.

Respondent is in the business of developing web sites. On or about May 29, 1998, Respondent, through its business Whitehouse.com, Inc., purchased the registration for the disputed domain name [Madonna.com] from Pro Domains for $20,000. On June 4, 1998, Respondent registered MADONNA as a trademark in Tunisia. On or about June 8, 1998, Respondent began operating an "adult entertainment portal web site." The web site featured sexually explicit photographs and text, and contained a notice stating "Madonna.com is not affiliated or endorsed by the Catholic Church, Madonna College, Madonna Hospital or Madonna the singer." By March 4, 1999, it appears that Respondent removed the explicit sexual content from the web site. By May 31, 1999, it appears that the site merely contained the above notice, the disputed domain name and the statement "Coming soon Madonna Gaming and Sportsbook."

On June 9, 1999, Complainant, through her attorneys, objected to Respondent's use of the Madonna.com domain name. On June 14, 1999, Respondent through its counsel stated: "As I assume you also know, Mr. Parisi's website [sic] was effectively shut down before you sent your letter, and is now shut down altogether. He is in the process of donating his registration for the domain name."

The word "Madonna," which has the current dictionary definition as the Virgin Mary or an artistic depiction of the Virgin Mary, is used by others as a trademark, trade name and personal name. After Respondent's receipt of Complainant's objection, it appears that Respondent had communication with Madonna Rehabilitation Hospital regarding the transfer of the domain name to the Hospital. It further appears that Respondent has not identified all of its communications on this matter. Nevertheless, the transfer had not taken place at the time this proceeding was commenced.

By his own admission, Respondent has registered a large number of other domain names, including names that matched the trademarks of others. Other domain names registered by Respondent include <walls-treetjournal.com> and <edgaronline.com>.

6. Discussion and Findings

A. The Evidentiary Standard For Decision

Paragraph 4(a) of the Policy directs that the complainant must prove each of the following:

(i) that the domain name registered by the respondent is identical or confusingly similar to a trademark or service mark in which the complainant has rights; and,

(ii) that the respondent has no legitimate interests in respect of the domain name; and,

(iii) that the domain name has been registered and used in bad faith.

Since these proceedings are civil, rather than criminal, in nature, we believe the appropriate standard for fact finding is the civil standard of a preponderance of the evidence (and not the higher standard of "clear and convincing evidence" or "evidence beyond a reasonable doubt"). Under the "preponderance of the evidence" standard a fact is proved for the purpose of reaching a decision when it appears more likely than not to be true based on the evidence.

B.   Similarity of the Disputed Domain Name and Complainant's Mark

As noted above, Respondent does not dispute that its domain name is identical or confusingly similar to a trademark in which the Complainant has rights. Accordingly, we find that Complainant has satisfied the requirements of Paragraph 4(c)(i) of the Policy.

C.   Lack of Rights or Legitimate Interests In Domain Name

Complainant has presented evidence tending to show that Respondent lacks any rights or legitimate interest in the domain name. Respondent's claim of rights or legitimate interests is not persuasive.

First, Respondent contends that its use of the domain name for an adult entertainment web site involved prior use of the domain name in connection with a bona fide offering of goods or services. The record supports Respondent's claim that it used the domain name in connection with commercial services prior to notice of the dispute. However, Respondent has failed to provide a reasonable explanation for the selection of Madonna as a domain name. Although the word "Madonna" has an ordinary dictionary meaning not associated with Complainant, nothing in the record supports a conclusion that Respondent adopted and used the term "Madonna" in good faith based on its ordinary dictionary meaning. We find instead that name was selected and used by Respondent with the intent to attract for commercial gain Internet users to Respondent's web site by trading on the fame of Complainant's mark. We see no other plausible explanation for Respondent's conduct and conclude that use which intentionally trades on the fame of another can not constitute a "bona fide" offering of goods or services. To conclude otherwise would mean that a Respondent could rely on intentional infringement to demonstrate a legitimate interest, an interpretation that is obviously contrary to the intent of the Policy.

Second, Respondent contends that it has rights in the domain name because it registered MADONNA as a trademark in Tunisia prior to notice of this dispute. Certainly, it is possible for a Respondent to rely on a valid trademark registration to show prior rights under the Policy. However, it would be a mistake to conclude that mere registration of a trademark creates a legitimate interest under the Policy. If an American-based Respondent could establish "rights" vis a vis an American Complainant through the expedient of securing a trademark registration in Tunisia, then the ICANN procedure would be rendered virtually useless. To establish cognizable rights, the overall circumstances should demonstrate that the registration was obtained in good faith for the purpose of making bona fide use of the mark in the jurisdiction where the mark is registered, and not obtained merely to circumvent the application of the Policy.

Here, Respondent admits that the Tunisia registration was obtained merely to protect his interests in the domain name. Respondent is not located in Tunisia and the registration was not obtained for the purpose of making bona fide use of the mark in commerce in Tunisia. Under the circumstances, some might view Respondent's Tunisian registration itself as evidence of bad faith because it appears to be a pretense to justify an abusive domain name registration. We find at a minimum that it does not evidence a legitimate interest in the disputed name under the circumstances of this case.

Third, Respondent claims that its offer to transfer the domain name to the Madonna Hospital in Lincoln, Nebraska, is a legitimate noncommercial use under Paragraph 4(c)(iii) of the Policy. We disagree. The record is incomplete on these negotiations. It also appears that the negotiations started after Complainant objected to Respondent's registration and use of the domain name. These circumstances do not demonstrate a legitimate interest or right in the domain name, and instead suggest that Respondent lacks any real interest in the domain name apart from its association with Complainant. Further, we do not believe these circumstances satisfy the provisions of Paragraph 4(c)(iii), which applies to situations where the Respondent is actually making noncommercial or fair use of the domain name. That certainly was not the situation at the time this dispute arose and is not the situation now.

Respondent cites examples of other parties besides Complainant who also have rights in the mark MADONNA, but that does not aid its cause. The fact that others could demonstrate a legitimate right or interest in the domain name does nothing to demonstrate that Respondent has such right or interest. Based on the record before us, we find that Complainant has satisfied the requirements of Paragraph 4(a)(ii) of the Policy.

D. Bad Faith Registration and Use

Under Paragraph 4(b)(iv) of the Policy, evidence of bad faith registration and use of a domain name includes the following circumstances:

(iv) by using the domain name, you have intentionally attempted to attract, for commercial gain, Internet users to your web site or other on-line location, by creating a likelihood of confusion with the complainant's mark as to the source, sponsorship, affiliation, or endorsement of your web site or location or of a product or service on your web site or location.

The pleadings in this case are consistent with Respondent's having adopted <madonna.com> for the specific purpose of trading off the name and reputation of the Complainant, and Respondent has offered no alternative explanation for his adoption of the name despite his otherwise detailed and complete submissions. Respondent has not explained why <madonna.com> was worth $20,000 to him or why that name was thought to be valuable as an attraction for a sexually explicit web site. Respondent notes that the complainant, identifying herself as Madonna, has appeared in Penthouse and has published a "Sex" book. The statement that "Madonna" is a word in the English language, by itself, is no more of a defense than would be the similar statement made in reference to the word "coke." Respondent has not even attempted to tie in his web site to any dictionary definition of madonna. The only plausible explanation for Respondent's actions appears to be an intentional effort to trade upon the fame of Complainant's name and mark for commercial gain. That purpose is a violation of the Policy, as well as U.S. Trademark Law.

Respondent's use of a disclaimer on its web site is insufficient to avoid a finding of bad faith. First, the disclaimer may be ignored or misunderstood by Internet users. Second, a disclaimer does nothing to dispel initial interest confusion that is inevitable from Respondent's actions. Such confusion is a basis for finding a violation of Complainant's rights.

The Policy requires a showing of bad faith registration and use. Here, although Respondent was not the original registrant, the record shows he acquired the registration in bad faith. The result is the equivalent of registration and is sufficient to fall within the Policy. Indeed, Paragraph 4(b)(i) of the Policy treats acquisition as the same as registration for the purposes of supporting a finding of bad faith registration. We therefore conclude that bad faith acquisition satisfies the requirement of bad faith registration under the Policy.

Respondent asserts that we should reject Complainant's claims because she has been disingenuous in claiming that her reputation could be tarnished by Respondent's actions. Respondent suggests that her reputation cannot be tarnished because she has already associated herself with sexually explicit creative work. That argument misses the point. Even though Complainant has produced sexually explicit content of her own, Respondent's actions may nevertheless tarnish her reputation because they resulted in association with sexually explicit content which Complainant did not control and which may be contrary to her creative intent and standards of quality. In any event, we do not rely on tarnishment as a basis for our decision.

7. Decision

Under Paragraph 4(i) of the Policy, we find in favor of the Complainant. The disputed domain name is identical or confusingly similar to a trademark in which Complainant has rights; Respondent lacks rights or legitimate interests in the domain name; and the domain name has been registered and used in bad faith. Therefore, we decide that the disputed domain name <madonna.com> should be transferred to the Complainant.

BRUCE SPRINGSTEEN v. JEFF BURGAR AND BRUCE SPRINGSTEEN CLUB

Administrative Panel Decision.
Case No. D2000–1532 (January 25, 2001).

Gordon D. Harris, Presiding Panelist

A. Michael Froomkin, Panelist

4.   Factual Background

The Complainant is the famous, almost legendary, recording artist and composer, Bruce Springsteen. Since the release of his first album in 1972 he has been at the top of his profession, selling millions of recordings throughout the world. As a result, his name is instantly recognisable in almost every part of the globe. There is no assertion made on behalf of Bruce Springsteen that his name has been registered as a trade mark but he rather relies upon common law rights acquired as a result of his fame and success.

The domain name at issue [brucespringsteen.com] was registered by Mr. Burgar apparently on 26 November 1996 according to the Who–Is search at exhibit 1 to the complaint. It appears that the domain name at issue was registered under the name "Bruce Springsteen Club" with Mr. Burgar identified as the administrative point of contact.

5.   Parties' Contentions

In relation to the issue of bad faith, Mr Springsteen's representatives point to the fact that Mr. Burgar is the owner of around 1,500 names, and that many of those names, including the domain name at issue, take the internet user to his own site, "celebrity1000.com." They therefore point to the fact that this constitutes bad faith under paragraphs 4(b)(ii) and (iv) of the UDRP. They further assert that he has registered this domain name, and others, using a fictitious name. In this case the fictitious name is "Bruce Springsteen Club."

In relation to the question of identicality of name, Mr. Burgar says that Bruce Springsteen's representatives have given no evidence of any common law rights. He points to the fact that the name has already been registered in a domain name, namely "brucespringsteen.net" and, that his use does not besmirch or denigrate the name of Bruce Springsteen to any extent. He refers to other websites which feature the name in question, including, for example, "artistplace.com/brucespringsteen."

6. Panel's Findings

The first question to be considered is whether the domain name at issue is identical or confusingly similar to trademarks or service marks in which the Complainant has rights.

It is common ground that there is no registered trade mark in the name "Bruce Springsteen." In most jurisdictions where trademarks are filed it would be impossible to obtain a registration of a name of that nature. Accordingly, Mr. Springsteen must rely on common law rights to satisfy this element of the three part test. It appears to be an established principle from cases such as Jeanette Winterson, Julia Roberts, and Sade that in the case of very well known celebrities, their names can acquire a distinctive secondary meaning giving rise to rights equating to unregistered trademarks, notwithstanding the non-registerability of the name itself. It should be noted that no evidence has been given of the name "Bruce Springsteen" having acquired a secondary meaning; in other words a recognition that the name should be associated with activities beyond the primary activities of Mr. Springsteen as a composer, performer and recorder of popular music.

In the view of this Panel, it is by no means clear from the UDRP that it was intended to protect proper names of this nature. As it is possible to decide the case on other grounds, however, the Panel will proceed on the assumption that the name Bruce Springsteen is protected under the policy; it then follows that the domain name at issue is identical to that name.

It is a clearly established principal that the suffix ".com" does not carry the domain name away from identicality or substantial similarity.

The second limb of the test requires the Complainant to show that the domain name owner has no rights or legitimate interests in respect of the domain name. The way in which the UDRP is written clearly requires the Complainant to demonstrate this, and the mere assertion that the Respondent has no such rights does not constitute proof, although the panel is free to make reasonable inferences. That said, a Respondent would be well advised to proffer some evidence to the contrary in the face of such an allegation. Paragraph 4(c) of the UDRP sets out specific circumstances to assist the Respondent in demonstrating that he or she has legitimate rights or legitimate interests in the domain name. The circumstances are stated to be non-exclusive, but are helpful in considering this issue.

Dealing with each in turn as follows:

(i) The first circumstance is that, before any notice of the dispute to the Respondent, the Respondent had shown demonstrable preparations to use the domain name in connection with a bona fide offering of goods or services. In this case, there is no suggestion that the domain name <brucespringsteen.com> had in fact been used in this way prior to notification of the complaint. Instead, the domain name resolved to another website belonging to Mr. Burgar, namely "celebrity1000.com."

(ii) The second circumstance is that the Respondent has "been commonly known by the domain name, even if he has acquired no trade mark or service mark rights." This is much more problematic. Mr. Burgar would say that the domain name at issue was registered in the name of "Bruce Springsteen Club" and consequently that the proprietor of the domain name has "been commonly known by the domain name" as required in the UDRP. The question in this case involves the meaning of the words "commonly" and "known by."

(iii) It is hard to say that the mere use of the name "Bruce Springsteen Club" can give rise to an impression in the minds of internet users that the proprietor was effectively "known as" Bruce Springsteen. It is even more remote that it could be said that the proprietor was "commonly" recognised in that fashion. Accordingly the Panel finds that this circumstance in paragraph 4(c) is not met.

The third circumstance is that the Respondent is "making a legitimate non-commercial or fair use of the domain name, without intent for commercial gain to misleadingly divert customers or to tarnish the trade mark or service mark at issue." There are a number of concepts contained within this "circumstance" which make it a complex issue to resolve. For example, at what point does use of a domain name become "commercial" or alternatively what amounts to "fair use" since those concepts appear to be in the alternative.

An internet search using the words "Bruce Springsteen" gives rise to literally thousands of hits. It is perfectly apparent to any internet user that not all of those hits are "official" or "authorized" sites. The user will browse from one search result to another to find the information and material which he or she is looking for in relation to a search item, in this case the celebrity singer Bruce Springsteen. It is therefore hard to see how it can be said that the registration of the domain name at issue can be "misleading" in its diversion of consumers to the "celebrity1000.com" website.

There have been examples in other cases of blatant attempts, for example, by the use of minor spelling discrepancies to entrap internet users onto sites which have absolutely no connection whatsoever with the name which is being used in its original or slightly altered form. In this case, the internet user, coming upon the "celebrity1000.com" website would perhaps be unsurprised to have arrived there via a search under the name "Bruce Springsteen." If the internet user wished to stay longer at the site he or she could do so, or otherwise they could clearly return to their search results to find more instructed material concerning Bruce Springsteen himself.

Accordingly, it is hard to infer from the conduct of the Respondent in this case an intent, for commercial gain, to misleadingly divert consumers. There is certainly no question of the common law rights of Mr. Springsteen being "tarnished" by association with the "celebrity1000.com" website. The Panelists' own search of that site indicates no links which would have that effect, for example connections to sites containing pornographic or other regrettable material.

Accordingly the Panel finds that Bruce Springsteen has not satisfied the second limb of the three part test in the UDRP.

Moving on to the question of bad faith, once again the UDRP contains helpful guidance as to how the Complainant may seek to demonstrate bad faith on the part of the Registrant. The four, non-exclusive, circumstances are set out in paragraph 4(b) of the UDRP, and can be dealt with as follows:

(i) The first circumstance is that there is evidence that the Registrant obtained the domain name primarily for the purpose of selling, renting or otherwise transferring it to the Complainant or to a competitor. This can be dealt with swiftly. There is simply no evidence put forward by the Complainant that there has been any attempt by Mr. Burgar to sell the domain name, either directly or indirectly.

(ii) The second circumstance is that the Registrant obtained the domain name in order to prevent the owner of the trade mark or service mark from reflecting that mark in a corresponding domain name, provided that there has been a pattern of such conduct. In this case, Bruce Springsteen's representatives point to the many other celebrity domain names registered by Mr. Burgar as evidence that he has indulged in a pattern of this conduct.

However, Mr. Burgar is clearly experienced in the ways of the internet. When he registered the domain name at issue in 1996, he would have been well aware that if he had wanted to block the activities of Bruce Springsteen or his record company in order to extract a large payment, or for whatever other reason there may be in creating such a blockage, he could, at nominal cost, have also registered the domain names <brucespringsteen.net> and <brucespringsteen.org>. He did not do so, and indeed subsequently in 1998 Mr. Springsteen's record company registered the name <brucespringsteen.net> which has been used as the host site for the official Bruce Springsteen website since that time. It appears in the top five items in a search on the internet under the name "Bruce Springsteen."

Nothing that has been done by Mr. Burgar has prevented Bruce Springsteen's official website at <brucespringsteen.net> being registered and used in his direct interests. That is surely a "corresponding domain name" for these purposes, as the expression "corresponding domain name" clearly refers back to the words "trade mark or service mark" rather than the domain name at issue referred to in the first line of paragraph 4(b)(ii).

(iii) The third circumstance is that the Registrant has obtained the domain name "primarily for the purpose of disrupting the business of a competitor." This can be dealt with very swiftly as there is no suggestion that that is the case in the present complaint.

(iv) The fourth circumstance is that, by using the domain name, the Registrant has "intentionally attempted to attract, for commercial gain, internet users to his website or other online location, by creating a likelihood of confusion with the Complainant's mark as to the source, sponsorship, affiliation or endorsement of the website or location or of a product or a service on the website or location."

As indicated above, a simple search under the name "Bruce Springsteen" on the internet gives rise to many thousands of hits. As also indicated above, even a relatively unsophisticated user would be clearly aware that not all of those hits would be directly associated in an official and authorised capacity with Bruce Springsteen himself, or his agents or record company. The nature of an internet search does not reveal the exact notation of the domain name. Accordingly, the search result may read "Bruce Springsteen—discography," but will not give the user the exact address. That only arises on a screen once the user has gone to that address. The relevance of this is that it is relatively unlikely that any user would seek to go straight to the internet and open the site <brucespringsteen.com> in the optimistic hope of reaching the official Bruce Springsteen website. If anyone sufficiently sophisticated in the use of the internet were to do that, they would very soon realise that the site they reached was not the official site, and consequently would move on, probably to conduct a fuller search.

The Panel therefore finds that none of the circumstances in paragraph 4(b) of the UDRP are met in this case. For all the reasons set out above, the users of the internet do not expect all sites bearing the name of celebrities or famous historical figures or politicians, to be authorised or in some way connected with the figure themselves. Users fully expect domain names incorporating the names of well known figures in any walk of life to exist independently of any connection with the figure themselves, but having been placed there by admirers or critics as the case may be.

Accordingly, in all the circumstances the Panel does not believe that Bruce Springsteen has met the necessary criteria to sustain a complaint under the URRP. The Panel orders that the registration of the domain name be left as it stands.

Richard W. Page, Dissenting Panelist

The Dissenting Panelist concludes that the average internet user would not sift through thousands of hits searching for information on Bruce Springsteen. Instead, the internet user would devise shortcuts. One obvious shortcut is to go directly to <brucespringsteen.com> with the expectation that it would lead to the official website. Respondent alludes to the phenomenon that "postponing the creation of other Tld's until the '.com' name space dominated the world just sort of happened." The dominance of the ".com" name space is reflected in the common usage of the phrase ".com" as being synonymous with commercial activity on the

Internet. Given a vast array of information on the performer Bruce Springsteen, the internet user is more likely than not to associate <brucespringsteen.com> with commercial activity and with an official domain name, resolving to an official website. Therefore, the Dissenting Panelist concludes that that resolution of the domain name <brucespringsteen.com> into Respondent's website www.celebrity1000.com is misleading.

NOTES AND QUESTIONS

1.   Do you believe the Madonna case was correctly decided? How about the Bruce Springsteen case? Why is it that Madonna has a right to madonna.com, but Springsteen does not have a right to brucespringsteen.com? Shouldn't the outcomes be exactly reverse, given that "Madonna" is a common name, while "Bruce Springsteen" is not? Are the two decisions consistent? If so, how can they be explained?

2.   What is the UDRP trying to protect against? Confusion of domain names with existing trademarks? Tarnishment or dilution of trademarks? Free riding on trademarks? Bad faith business practices? Some or all of the above?

3.   In the *Bruce Springsteen* case, the majority seems to question whether personal names are protected under the UDRP, but assumes without deciding that they would be. Based on your knowledge of trademarks, is there any reason a personal name (such as Bruce Springsteen) could not constitute a trademark if it has secondary meaning or distinctiveness? After all, what's the difference between a personal name, a business name, and a name for a product? If they all are associated by consumers with a certain product or service, shouldn't that be enough to establish a trademark? TRIPS art. 15(1).

4.   *Creation of more Top–Level Domains (TLDs).* In 2000, ICANN approved the creation of seven additional top-level domains (TLDs), to add to the original seven TLDs (.com, edu, .gov, .int, .mil, .net, and .org). In 2001 and 2002, the new TLDs became operational, including four TLDs that are unsponsored and available for anyone to register: .biz, .info, .name, and .pro. In 2011, ICANN approved .xxx for pornographic websites. How, if at all, should the creation of new TLDs change the analysis under the UDRP? Does the existence of several additional alternatives for Madonna, Bruce Springsteen, and others to register domain names containing their trademarked names—such as "madonna.biz" or "brucespringsteen.info"—undermine their claim to the exclusive use or registration of the ".com" domain name? For example, what significance should be given to the fact that Bruce Springsteen has his own website established at "brucespringsteen.net"? If Madonna could have registered "madonna.net" or now "madonna.biz," should her case have come out differently?

5.   *Sophistication of search engines.* How should the greater sophistication of search engines today—such as Google and Bing—factor into the UDRP cases? What if today's search engines greatly increase the likelihood that an Internet user searching for Madonna's, Bruce Springsteen's, or any trademark holder's website will be able to find the site on the very first try? Does

this undermine the claim of a likelihood of confusion by the trademark holder?

6. Why do you think, as noted above, that the UDRP has been so popular as a way to resolve thousands of domain name disputes? Although the decisions are not binding and the disputes could be litigated anew in court, most UDRP disputes do not appear to end up in court.

7. *Pro-trademark holder bias?* Notwithstanding the Bruce Springsteen decision, WIPO panels have more often found in favor of complainants (typically, trademark holders) in UDRP disputes. From 1999 to 2011, complainants prevailed in approximately 86% of the 16,414 disputes that were litigated (and not settled). *See* WIPO, Cases Outcomes by Year(s), http://www.wipo.int/amc/en/domains/statistics/outcome.jsp.

Based on a study conducted in 2002, 83% of single-member panel UDRP decisions were decided in favor of the complainant, while 60% of three-member panel decisions were decided in favor of the complainant. Michael Geist, *Fair.com?: An Examination of the Allegations of Systematic Unfairness in the ICANN UDRP*, 27 BROOK. J. INT'L L. 903, 911 (2002). The study also found that National Arbitration Forum (NAF), an ICANN-accredited provider of arbitrators, assigned the lion's share of their single-member UDRP cases (56%) to *only six arbitrators*. Are these numbers disturbing? If so, should three-member panels be required in every dispute and complainants (not respondents) be required to pay the cost? Should the pool of arbitrators and the randomness of their assignment be more closely regulated by ICANN? Should the UDRP include an appellate process?

8. *Bibliographic note.* For additional commentary on the UDRP, see Jay P. Kesan, *Private Internet Governance*, 35 LOY. U. CHI. L.J. 87, 108–09 n.63 (2003) (collecting sources). *See also* Laurence R. Helfer, *Whither the UDRP: Autonomous, Americanized, or Cosmopolitan?*, 12 CARDOZO J. INT'L & COMP. L. 493 (2004); Laurence R. Helfer & Graeme B. Dinwoodie, *Designing Non-National Systems: The Case of the Uniform Domain Name Dispute Resolution Policy*, 43 WM. & MARY L. REV. 141, 155–56 (2001).

CHAPTER 5

UNFAIR COMPETITION AND TRADE SECRETS

■ ■ ■

A. UNFAIR COMPETITION

Unfair competition is somewhat of a contested term. It may mean different things in different countries. In common law countries, such as the United States and the United Kingdom, unfair competition originated from the cause of action for "passing off" of another's trademark—thus making consumer confusion with respect to trademarks the principal worry of unfair competition. Although unfair competition in common law countries eventually evolved to include other claims, such as false or deceptive advertising, unfair competition still tends to be more limited in scope when compared to unfair competition in continental European countries, such as Germany. In Europe, unfair competition encompasses not only "passing off" claims for trademark, but a whole panoply of claims against "unfair" conduct in business or commercial dealing, such as bribery and different forms of competitive and promotional advertising. This broad understanding of unfair competition recognizes claims against unfair business practices that are not limited to situations involving the likelihood of consumer confusion, or even trademarks. But if consumer confusion is not the linchpin of unfair competition in continental Europe, what exactly defines "unfair" competition there? Consider the following discussion and excerpt.

1. NATIONAL APPROACHES

PROBLEM 5–1

You are a first-year associate in an international law firm. In each of the hypotheticals below, you represent the first named party. The senior partner, Sydney Bristow, has assigned you to provide a "quick, preliminary" assessment of whether anyone in the following situations might have violated the law of unfair competition in the United States (i.e., the common law approach) and in continental Europe (i.e., the civil law approach). Bristow has asked you to hold off on any legal research, but instead to give your "initial impression" based on the discussion above, and the following article and principal case. In assessing U.S. law, you should not consider any additional federal or state regulations of commercial activity; just focus on the common law approach discussed in this chapter. The senior partner would find it most helpful if you can provide an initial assessment of whether each of the situations below is (i) likely or (ii) unlikely to be considered unfair competition in the U.S. and the EU, assuming the same conduct occurred in both places.

(1) Harold's Department Store breaks a supply contract with Advanced Design, a manufacturer of flat screen panel displays, after New Age Graphics, a fierce competitor to Advanced Design, informed Harold's that Advanced Design "cuts corners" on its manufacturing process. Harold's subsequently enters into a new supply contract with New Age for the screens. It turns out that Advanced Design and New Age use the exact same production process for their products.

(2) Super Digital Media starts a new media campaign in print and television promising a 40% discount for one year's digital TV service for all customers who switch from Capital Cable, a competitor. Super Digital employees also randomly call Capital's current customers asking them to switch. Super Digital does in fact give 40% discounts as claimed, and makes no false or misleading statements in its phone campaign.

(3) Luigi's Dollar Fashions makes inexpensive copies of high-end luxury dresses shown at fall fashion shows and sells the imitations at a fraction of the cost in discount stores. For various reasons, the luxury designs do not qualify for copyright, patent, or trademark protection.

DOES THE UNITED KINGDOM OR THE EUROPEAN COMMUNITY NEED AN UNFAIR COMPETITION LAW?

Aidan Robertson & Audrey Horton.
17 Eur. Intell. Prop. Rev. 568, 568–69, 574–76 (1995).*

English law has traditionally refused to deal in concepts such as fairness or good faith in business, leaving the market-place to determine its own morality without the force of legal sanction. However, during the passage of the Trade Marks Act 1994 there was much lobbying from certain sections of industry to create new rights against unfair competition. This was resisted by the Government and the new Act does not explicitly create any general right to restrain unfair competition. That lobbying can be expected to continue in an attempt to keep unfair competition high on the law reform agenda.

UK Law

English law is difficult to summarise succinctly, as it depends on the interaction of a number of torts, each of which has been developed in largely piecemeal fashion. As a broad generalization, it could be said that English law prevents unfair competition in three principal ways.

---

* Published by Sweet & Maxwell, reproduced with permission.

(1) *Passing off.* A may be restrained from misappropriating B's reputation in its goods by misleading B's customers, for example, by suggesting a connection or association with B's business. This is done by B bringing an action for passing off against A. The essence of this action is customer confusion. Unless B can show that its customers have been or are likely to be misled into confusing A's for B's goods or into making a false connection or association with B's business, it will not succeed.

(2) *Inducing breach of contract and unlawful interference with contractual relations.* A may be restrained from acquiring B's customers through unlawful means. This applies where A induces B's customers to break their contracts with B or otherwise unlawfully interferes with B's contractual relations.

(3) *Defamation and injurious falsehood.* A may be restrained from acquiring B's customers by telling lies to B's customers about B or B's goods. In the case of lies about B, there is an action for defamation. In the case of lies about B's goods, there are actions for slander of goods or injurious falsehood.

Seen in this way, the law emphasizes the role of the customer. It is unfair competition to acquire customers by causing them to transfer their custom by (1) confusing them as to with whom they are doing business; (2) inducing them to break existing contracts with competitors, or (3) lying to them about competitors. Beyond these limits, attempts to attract customers from other competitors are considered legal.

The focus of English law relevant to unfair competition (as distinct from contract law) is to prevent customers being confused. Provided customers have available correct information about what and with whom they are dealing, and that bargains once struck are adhered to, the law is prepared to leave the proper functioning of the market to the free play of market forces. A similar attitude is taken by US federal and state laws.

In continental Europe, while civil law jurisdictions also prevent customer confusion, unfair competition law starts from the basis that its rationale is to enforce the "honest usages" of the market-place. Beier summarises this as meaning that a trader was granted "the right to restrain his competitors from causing him injury by unfair conduct." Thus the focus is not just on customer confusion, but on what is fair or ethical commercial conduct. English law has eschewed this approach, and continues to focus on customer confusion, as two recent decisions of English courts demonstrate.

National Unfair Competition Laws in Europe

A survey of unfair competition cases reported in English reveals much apparent activity in most jurisdictions under this name. Most attention in the literature available on this topic in English is focused on German unfair competition law, owing principally to the fact that it is seemingly often the most strict and rigid and therefore is the most eye-catching, not to say startling, for a common lawyer. However, it is possible to summarise more generally the content of civil unfair competition laws.

Ulmer identified a coherent body of unfair competition law across Europe, which, despite national differences, could be said to have a unifying objective. This is described by Beier as being the interest

> of the honest trader in having the right to restrain his competitors from causing him injury by unfair conduct. The test was whether a competitor's conduct complied with "honest usages" of the trade, the "usages honnêtes" (Article 10*bis* Paris Convention), the "correttezza professionale" (Article 2598 Codice Civile) or the "bonos mores" ("gute Sitten") in the course of trade (Article 1, German law against Unfair Competition 1999).

Beier takes the view that this "classical" unfair competition law has, in more recent times, been "shattered [as u]nfair competition law has become a playground for special interests and competences, uncoordinated and lacking any clear vision." However, from a common law perspective the similarities in the civil law approach remain more striking than the differences and while there are undeniably very distinct national differences, the following common elements of unfair competition law can be identified:

Prohibition on Unfair Conduct

This includes laws regulating comparative advertising, special offers, low prices (including loss-leading), prohibiting disparaging competitors, and a general prohibition on discriminatory sales conditions, including price discounting.

In France, it was held that a supermarket is permitted to advertise its prices as against those of competitors only in relation to identical products and under precisely similar conditions. Thus it would not be possible to have a price comparison between a supermarket and a small shop. In Germany, Ford was held to have contravened unfair competition law by inviting Opel drivers to trade in their "good old Opels" for a "well-designed Sierra, a sports Capri or a comfortable Granada." This was regarded as comparative advertising, implicitly denigrating a competitor's products.

Low prices were condemned as unfair competition in Italy, where a court held that sale is not fair if the seller does not charge all costs plus a reasonable profit. Similarly, the Hague Appeal Court condemned as unfair competition an attempt by Dutch daily newspapers to queer the pitch of a new weekly sports newspaper which was to come out on Monday mornings by distributing free their normal Monday evening sports sections some hours earlier on Monday mornings. Such sports sections, it was held, could only be legitimately distributed at a reasonable price.

Its capacity for novel applications is illustrated by a case in France in which a software company was restrained from selling software which would enable users to evade anti-copying protection included in other software. Enabling infringement of copyright was considered an act of unfair competition. Similarly, a Dutch court held that sales of pirate decoders for subscription television was an act of unfair competition, even though not an infringement of any intellectual property right. Importing bootleg compact discs into the Netherlands, though not an infringement under Dutch intellectual property law nor in the country of manufacture, was held to be unfair competition.

An example of the German courts' extensive interpretation of what contravenes "bonos mores" is afforded by the Federal Supreme Court's condemnation on this ground of telephone solicitation, without prior approval from the person concerned to be phoned. Similar condemnation has also been made of telex or fax solicitation methods.

Prohibition on Deceptive Advertising and Marketing

A classic example of deceptive marketing of goods was condemned as unfair competition by a Swedish court which ordered a spaghetti importer not to sell its product in a packet larger than was necessary for its contents. Beier notes that the suppression of deceptive advertising still poses great difficulties in Italy, as courts refer to the principle of Roman law *omnis mercator mendax*, viewing the Italian consumer as suspicious and vigilant enough to exclude the possibility of deception. The Italian judiciary's view of its consumers is to be contrasted with that of German judges with their concern to protect, in Schricker's words, "purchasers with below average talent."

The German Federal Supreme Court has condemned, for example, the sort of promotional advertising which requires returning a lucky winning ticket for a prize, if potential participants are excessively enticed by being misled as to the chances of winning a prize. Indeed, it was held in the same case that the distribution of money-off coupons as a promotional tool can infringe the law on rebates which forbids discounts on goods and services of more than 3 percent. The Federal Supreme Court regarded as unfair competition anything that tied a prize to the purchase of a product. In another case, it was held that a promotional game which required contestants to enter the defendant's shops to collect a sticker required to play the game would make them feel morally obliged to buy something and thus was contrary to fair competition. Similar promotional devices such as restaurant guides including vouchers for two main courses for the price of one and American Express card air miles points in return for expenditure charged to the card account have also been held to be in contravention of this law.

An advertising description of a mineral water as "A Champagne among Mineral Waters" was condemned by the German Federal Supreme Court as *contra bonos mores*, since the defendant was devaluing the plaintiff champagne producers' product by comparing champagne to water (the ultimate in trade mark dilution perhaps?), unless the slogan was permitted under French law, since this was the country of origin of both products. This can be compared with an Italian Supreme Court decision in which a Champagne producer failed to prevent a bath foam producer using champagne shaped bottles, on the basis that it had not been shown either that there would be confusion between customers nor that use of the same type of bottle would cause customers to think less of the Champagne producer's product. Similarly, in France, the same producer failed to stop a publicity campaign advertising its product as a prize to winners of a draw, on the basis that it was disparagement of their trade mark.

Prohibition on False Indications of Origin

In Belgium, a Scotch whisky producer was able to obtain an injunction preventing a Belgian blend of Scotch whisky and Belgian alcohol from using a name and get-up suggestive of Scottish origin.

In France, a perfume company was restrained by injunction from calling its perfume "Champagne," the action being brought by two French state-controlled organizations, the Institut National des Appellations d'Origine and the Comité Interprofessional du Vin de Champagne.

Prohibition on Slavish Copying

In Denmark, slavish copying of an item not protected by copyright or patent may be an act of unfair competition.

In Italy, protection against slavish copying has been granted to protect colours used in packaging a product in circumstances which might well not amount to passing off under English law, although it was stressed that protection depended on evidence of customer confusion. Confusingly similar packaging (*in casu* a petroleum additive packaged in a way similar to beer and soft drinks cans) was condemned as unfair competition in a German court on the grounds of consumer protection. However, in another Italian case, an injunction was granted to prevent slavish copying (*in casu* an opera libretto copied from the original score, now out of copyright) even though it was specifically found that there was no risk of customer confusion.

In the Netherlands, the style of a particular artist in illustrating children's books was protected under unfair competition even in the absence of copyright infringement.

Protection for Distribution Networks

This is illustrated by two Greek cases. In one, an injunction was ordered against an unauthorized trader refilling the plaintiff's butane gas cylinders, this being held to give an unfair advantage over the appointed agent who had to bear costs of repairing damaged cylinders. In the second, an injunction was granted to exclusive distributor of "Lacoste" products in Greece preventing parallel imports of genuine Dutch Lacoste goods. However, the Italian courts reached the opposite conclusion in a case involving parallel imports of "Christian Dior" perfumes, applying notions of privity of contract familiar to the common law.

However, German unfair competition law did not prevent a German importer of computer games from Japan selling them in the absence of an authorized German distributor.

German law seemingly goes further than other civil laws in two principal ways. First, it allows a wider class of plaintiffs to enforce unfair competition laws. Competitors and trade associations may sue even without proof of direct injury. Secondly, in assessing deceptiveness, German courts place great reliance on the public's opinion of whether something would be false or misleading, rather than judging such issues on the basis of legislative intent or on an assessment of competing interests.

PROBLEM 5–2

Joe's Club, a large discount store located in the United States with stores in Europe, is considering the following slogans for its advertisements for its stores in London:

(1) "In a blind taste test involving 500 randomly selected people, 99 percent of all consumers found that Joe's Discount Cola tasted just the same as Coca–Cola." In fact, Joe's claim is true and Joe's has supporting data that substantiate these results.

(2) "Why pay more? Joe's Discount Cola costs half as much as the leading brand and tastes just as good."

(3) "We sell Coca–Cola. We also sell Joe's Discount Cola in the next aisle at half the price."

Are these comparative advertising claims permitted under EU law? What about in the United States? Consult the case and notes below.

L'ORÉAL SA v. BELLURE NV

England and Wales Court of Appeal.
[2010] RPC 23, [2010] ETMR 47.

[In December 2003, L'Oréal SA, Lancôme parfums et beauté & Cie SNC and Laboratoire Garnier & Cie brought a suit in an English court against Bellure and other defendants for using comparative advertisements that claimed that defendants' inexpensive perfumes smelled just like the high priced luxury perfumes of the plaintiffs. For example, defendants ran the advertisement "Stitch No 7 smells like Trésor." The advertisements identified the perfumes (Trésor owned L'Oreal) of the plaintiffs by name. There was no claim by the plaintiffs that either professionals or the public would be misled by the advertisements into confusing the defendants' inexpensive products with the luxury perfumes sold by the plaintiffs. The plaintiffs also did not claim that their brands would be tarnished by comparison to inexpensive imitations. The plaintiffs raised a number of claims that the advertisements violated both EU Trademark Directive, 89/104/EEC and the EU Directive 84/450/EEC2 on misleading and comparative advertising (EU Comparative Advertising Directive).

In the first litigation, the Court of Appeal referred several issues concerning EU trademark and comparative advertising law to the Court of Justice. The CJEU issued an opinion, L'Oreal SA v Bellure NV, Case C–487/070 (2010) and the case resumed in the England and Wales Court of Appeal. Applying the opinion of the CJEU, the Court of Appeal found that the use of plaintiffs' trademarks by defendants in their advertisements violated Article 5(1)(a) of the EU Trademark Directive because the use was not purely descriptive. A purely descriptive use, such as "I can supply a diamond cut in the same shape as Spirit Sun," would be permitted under the EU Trademark Directive, but the Court of Appeals felt compelled to find under the CJEU opinion that the use of plaintiff's trademarks in this instance was not purely descriptive but was for advertising purposes (such as in price comparisons). However, an advertisement that infringes trademark law could be lawful if it is protected by the EU Comparative Advertising Directive. But the CJEU held: "since, under Directive 84/450, comparative advertising which presents the advertiser's products as an imitation of a product bearing a trade mark is inconsistent with fair competition and thus unlawful, any advantage gained by the advertiser through such advertising will have been achieved as the result of unfair competition and must, accordingly, be regarded as taking unfair advantage of the reputation of that mark." The excerpt below focuses on the comparative advertising issues once they returned back in the UK court. *Ed.*]

JACOB LJ

[T]he defendants have three ranges of products called Stitch, Creation Lamis and Dorrall. Each member of the range smells like a famous, luxury branded perfume known by a well known registered trade mark. L'Oréal alleges that the defendants' use of comparison lists for each of the defendants' ranges of product, showing which products correspond to which L'Oréal perfume, infringed its registered trademarks for those perfumes. Originally it also contended that some of the packaging used for the Creation Lamis and Dorrall ranges also infringed other registered trademarks. No complaint was made about the packaging of the Stitch range.

Thus we are left only with the comparison lists. As to the impact of these in the market I set the factual findings out in the earlier judgment [2008] RPC 196, paras 55 and 63:

"55. So the factual position can be summarised thus: (i) It is lawful to make and sell a smell-alike product. (ii) The best and only practical way to describe its smell is to inform people that it smells like X. (iii) That is done by the use of the comparison lists. (iv) The defendants get a major promotional advantage from using such lists. (v) Neither customers nor ultimate consumers are deceived as a result of the use of the lists. (vi) Neither the image nor the distinctiveness of the trade mark for the comparable fine fragrance is impaired by the use of the lists-there is no tarnishment or blurring. (vii) Sales of the corresponding fine fragrance are not affected by the use of the lists."

"63. I would add that a touch of reality is called for here. Consumers are not stupid. They will not see the cheap copy as being the same in quality as the original. They will see it for what it is and no more."

The problem, stated at its most general, is simple. Does trademark law prevent the defendants from telling the truth? Even though their perfumes are lawful and do smell like the corresponding famous brands, does trade mark law none the less muzzle the defendants so that they cannot say so?

I have come to the conclusion that the Court of Justice's ruling is that the defendants are indeed muzzled. My duty as a national judge is to follow EU law as interpreted by the Court of Justice. I think, with regret, that the answers we have received from the Court of Justice require us so to hold. Before I consider why in detail I wish to say why I regret those answers.

My own strong predilection, free from the opinion of the Court of Justice, would be to hold that trademark law did not prevent traders from making honest statements about their products where those products are themselves lawful.

I have a number of reasons for that predilection. First and most generally is that I am in favour of free speech—and most particularly where someone wishes to tell the truth. There is no good reason to dilute the predilection in cases where the speaker's motive for telling the truth is his own commercial gain. Truth in the market place matters—even if it does not attract quite the strong emotions as the right of a journalist or politician to speak the truth.

The Court of Justice's decision in this case means that poor consumers are the losers. Only the poor would dream of buying the defendants' products. The real thing is beyond their wildest dreams. Yet they are denied their right to receive information which would give them a little bit of pleasure; the ability to buy a product for a euro or so which they know smells like a famous perfume.

Moreover there is no harm to the trade mark owner—other than possibly a "harm" which, to be fair, L'Oréal has never asserted. That "harm" would be letting the truth out—that it is possible to produce cheap perfumes which smell somewhat like a famous original. I can understand that a purveyor of a product sold at a very high price as an exclusive luxury item would not like the public to know that it can be imitated, albeit not to the same quality, cheaply—there is a bit of a message that the price of the real thing may be excessive and that the "luxury image" may be a bit of a delusion. But an uncomfortable (from the point of view of the trade mark owner) truth is still the truth: it surely needs a strong reason to suppress it.

My second reason is more specific. It is about freedom to trade—indeed, potentially in other cases, to compete honestly. (This case is a fortiori for the parties' respective products are not in competition with each other.) If a trader cannot (when it is truly the case) say "my goods are the same as Brand X (a famous registered mark) but half the price", I think there is a real danger that important areas of trade will not be open to proper competition.

Comparative Advertising Directive

[Defendants' comparative advertisement] will escape infringement (i.e., be within article 6(1)(b)) if it complies with all the conditions set forth in article 3a(1) of the Comparative Advertising Directive.

The only conditions remaining in issue and the subject of the reference were (g) and (h) [of the Comparative Advertising Directive) which I will, for convenience, set out again:

> "(g) it does not take unfair advantage of the reputation of a trade mark, trade name or other distinguishing marks of a competitor or of the designation of origin of competing products; (h) it does not present goods or services as imitations or replicas of goods or services bearing a protected trade mark or trade name."

Although these are two distinct conditions which one might have thought required distinct consideration, the Court of Justice chose to provide a composite answer, [2010] Bus LR 303, para 80:

> "article 3a(1) of Directive 84/450 must be interpreted as meaning that an advertiser who states explicitly or implicitly in comparative advertising that the product marketed by him is an imitation of a product bearing a well known trade mark presents 'goods or services as imitations or replicas' within the meaning of article 3a(1)(h). The advantage gained by the advertiser as a result of such unlawful comparative advertising must be considered to be an advantage taken unfairly of the reputation of that mark within the meaning of article 3a(1)(g)." In short, if in a comparative advertisement you do not comply with (h) you are taking unfair advantage within the meaning of (g). Actually, of course, if you fail to comply with (h) it does not matter whether or not you comply with (g)—you will not have complied with all the conditions anyway.

Thus it is upon (h) which the court concentrated—and so we must do likewise. One might have thought that the court would have given this a narrow construction in accordance with its own principle laid down in Toshiba Europe GmbH v Katun Germany GmbH (Case C–112/99) [2002] All ER (EC) 325, and Pippig Augenoptik GmbH & Co KG v Hartlauer Handlesgesellschaft mbH (Case C–44/01) [2004] All ER (EC) 1156, that "the conditions required of comparative advertising must be interpreted in the sense most favourable to it" (the Toshiba case, para 37, the Pippig Augenoptik case, para 42).

However the court departed from its own "most favoured" principle. It gave condition (h) a wide meaning. The defendants argued that (h) was confined to counterfeits—that that is what "imitations or replicas" means. But the court said [2010] Bus LR 303, paras 75–76:

"75. The particular object of the condition laid down in article 3a(1)(h) of Directive 84/450 is to prohibit an advertiser from stating in comparative advertising that the product or service marketed by him constitutes an imitation or replica of the product or the service covered by the trademark. In that regard, as the Advocate General stated in para 84 of his opinion, it is not only advertisements which explicitly evoke the idea of imitation or reproduction which are prohibited, but also those which, having regard to their overall presentation and economic context, are capable of implicitly communicating such an idea to the public at whom they are directed.

"76. It is not in dispute that the object and effect of the comparison lists at issue in the main proceedings are to draw the attention of the relevant public to the original fragrance of which the perfumes marketed by Malaika and Starion are purportedly an imitation. Those lists thus attest to the fact that those perfumes are imitations of the fragrances marketed under certain marks belonging to the claimants, and they consequently present the goods marketed by the advertiser as being imitations of goods bearing a protected trade mark within the meaning of article 3a(1)(h) of Directive 84/450. As the Advocate General stated in para 88 of his opinion, it is irrelevant in that regard whether the advertisement indicates that it relates to an imitation of the product bearing a protected mark as a whole or merely the imitation of an essential characteristic of that product such as, in the present case, the smell of the goods in question."

So even saying, truthfully, that the defendant's product has an essential characteristic (in the instant case the smell) of the trade mark owner's product amounts to saying the product is an "imitation or replica" and so outside the protection of the Comparative Advertising Directive. I am forced so to conclude.

I can actually see no rational basis for such a rule. Indeed I can see no rational commercial or economic basis for article 3a(1)(h) at all—on any construction. If a man trades in *lawful* replicas or in *lawful* copies, why should he not be able to inform the public what they are? And why should the truth be kept from the public? If, as I think there should be, there is to be reform of the law, this aspect of the Comparative Advertising Directive should be reconsidered. And in my view it should be made explicit that telling the truth about a lawful product does not involve any "unfair advantage" (the phrase used in article 3a(1)(g)).

As I have said I do not agree with or welcome this conclusion—it amounts to a pointless monopoly. But my duty is to apply it. For by the use of the comparison lists there is clearly free-riding of the sort condemned by the court.

NOTES AND QUESTIONS

1. Comparative advertising is a staple of the U.S. advertising industry. Naming a competitor for the purposes of comparison is permitted as a nominative fair use under trademark law, and comparative advertising claims in general are permissible so long as they can be substantiated and are not deceptive or misleading. Compare the U.S. approach to comparative advertising with the EU approach. What are the differences? Which approach to unfair competition do you think is better for business competition?

2. Why did the UK court apply a legal rule that it found anticompetitive, inconsistent with free speech, and lacking any rational basis?

3. *Relationship between unfair competition and other IP.* What should the relationship be between unfair competition and other forms of intellectual property, such as copyright and patent? As the Robertson and Horton article notes, some European countries recognize unfair competition claims against "slavish copying" in instances in which the copying of subject matter that falls within the scope of copyright or patent would not be prohibited by copyright or patent law—such as in the case of an expired copyright. Under this understanding, unfair competition functions almost as a residual backstop, to protect against copying that does not violate other forms of intellectual property.

By contrast, in the United States, federal copyright and patent law may preempt such claims of unfair competition, effectively permitting people to copy copyrightable or patentable subject matter where such copying does not violate a copyright or patent. As the U.S. Supreme Court explained, "when an article is unprotected by a patent or a copyright, state law may not forbid others to copy that article. To forbid copying would interfere with the federal policy, found in Art. I, § 8, cl. 8, of the Constitution and in the implementing federal statutes, of allowing free access to copy whatever the federal patent and copyright laws leave in the public domain." *Compco Corp. v. Day–Brite Lighting, Inc.,* 376 U.S. 234, 237 (1964). Which approach do you favor?

4. *Bibliographic note.* Frauke Henning–Bodewig & Gerhard Schricker, *New Initiatives for The Harmonisation of Unfair Competition Law in Europe,* 24 EUROPEAN INTELL. PROP. REV. 271 (2002); Gerhard Schricker, *Twenty Five Years of Protection Against Unfair Competition,* 26 INT'L REV. OF INDUS. PROP. & COPYRIGHT L. [IIC] 782 (1995); Friedrick–Karl Beier, *The Law of Unfair Competition in the European Community, Its Development and Present Status,* 16 IIC 139 (1985); Eugen Ulmer, *Unfair Competition Law in the European Economic Community,* 4 IIC 188 (1973).

2. THE PARIS CONVENTION AND THE TRIPS AGREEMENT

PROBLEM 5–3

You are a special counsel to the USTR and have been asked to prepare an assessment of the following issues: (i) what are the current minimum standards of unfair competition required by TRIPS and the Paris Convention; and

(ii) what areas of unfair competition (if any) should the WTO seek further harmonization in the next round of negotiations? In discussing (i), can you propose a minimalist interpretation of the relevant provisions of TRIPS and Paris that would allow the United States to argue that its current position on unfair competition, based on consumer confusion, is consistent with its treaty obligations? You should anticipate and attempt to respond to counterarguments that would support a broad obligation on the part of the U.S. to include claims against commercial bribery, promotional advertising, and discount pricing as part of unfair competition. Consider the treaty provisions below, *General Motors*, and the following notes.

Paris Convention

Article 10*bis*

Unfair Competition

(1) The countries of the Union are bound to assure to nationals of such countries effective protection against unfair competition.

(2) Any act of competition contrary to honest practices in industrial or commercial matters constitutes an act of unfair competition.

(3) The following in particular shall be prohibited:

(i) all acts of such a nature as to create confusion by any means whatever with the establishment, the goods, or the industrial or commercial activities, of a competitor;

(ii) false allegations in the course of trade of such a nature as to discredit the establishment, the goods, or the industrial or commercial activities, of a competitor;

(iii) indications or allegations the use of which in the course of trade is liable to mislead the public as to the nature, the manufacturing process, the characteristics, the suitability for their purpose, or the quantity, of the goods.

Article 10*ter*

Marks, Trade Names, False Indications, Unfair Competition: Remedies, Right to Sue

(1) The countries of the Union undertake to assure to nationals of the other countries of the Union appropriate legal remedies effectively to repress all the acts referred to in Articles 9, 10, and 10*bis*.

(2) They undertake, further, to provide measures to permit federations and associations representing interested industrialists, producers, or merchants, provided that the existence of such federations and associations is not contrary to the laws of their countries, to take action in the courts or before the administrative authorities, with a view to the repression of the acts referred to in Articles 9, 10, and 10*bis*, in so far as the law of the country in which protection is claimed allows such action by federations and associations of that country.

TRIPS Agreement

Article 22

Protection of Geographical Indications

In respect of geographical indications, Members shall provide the legal means for interested parties to prevent: * * * (b) any use which constitutes an act of unfair competition within the meaning of Article 10*bis* of the Paris Convention (1967).

Section 7: Protection of Undisclosed Information

Article 39

(1) In the course of ensuring effective protection against unfair competition as provided in Article 10*bis* of the Paris Convention (1967), Members shall protect undisclosed information in accordance with paragraph 2 and data submitted to governments or governmental agencies in accordance with paragraph 3.

(2) Natural and legal persons shall have the possibility of preventing information lawfully within their control from being disclosed to, acquired by, or used by others without their consent in a manner contrary to honest commercial practices[10] so long as such information:

> (a) is secret in the sense that it is not, as a body or in the precise configuration and assembly of its components, generally known among or readily accessible to persons within the circles that normally deal with the kind of information in question;

> (b) has commercial value because it is secret; and

> (c) has been subject to reasonable steps under the circumstances, by the person lawfully in control of the information, to keep it secret.
> * * *

* * *

Article 10bis of Paris Convention. The same basic question over the scope of unfair competition that arises in the context of national laws (discussed in the preceding section) arises under Article 10*bis* of the Paris Convention. Article 10*bis* requires countries "to assure to nationals of such countries effective protection against unfair competition." Paris Conv. art. 10*bis*(1). It defines unfair competition as "[a]ny act of competition contrary to honest practices in industrial or commercial matters." *Id*. art. 10*bis*(2). Subsection 3 of Article 10*bis* then specifies three types of unfair competition that must be prohibited by member countries:

> (i) all acts of such a nature as to create confusion by any means whatever with the establishment, the goods, or the industrial or commercial activities, of a competitor;

---

10. For the purpose of this provision, "a manner contrary to honest commercial practices" shall mean at least practices such as breach of contract, breach of confidence and inducement to breach, and includes the acquisition of undisclosed information by third parties who knew, or were grossly negligent in failing to know, that such practices were involved in the acquisition.

(ii) false allegations in the course of trade of such a nature as to discredit the establishment, the goods, or the industrial or commercial activities, of a competitor;

(iii) indications or allegations the use of which in the course of trade is liable to mislead the public as to the nature, the manufacturing process, the characteristics, the suitability for their purpose, or the quantity, of the goods.

The Paris Convention appears to leave unanswered whether Article 10*bis* obligates countries to prohibit any other acts not enumerated in subsection 3. Countries have differed over this question—some countries taking a narrow view of unfair competition, while other countries (predominantly in continental Europe) taking a much broader view.

TRIPS Article 39 and Trade Secrets. The TRIPS Agreement clarified, to some extent, the scope of unfair competition, specifically including trade secrets within the rubric of unfair competition. This marked the first time trade secrets have been expressly included within the coverage of an international intellectual property agreement. Although developing countries initially resisted the inclusion of trade secrets within TRIPS on the ground that it was not a traditional form of intellectual property, they eventually agreed to its inclusion in a proposal led by Switzerland and the United States. *See* MICHAEL BLAKENEY, TRADE RELATED ASPECTS OF INTELLECTUAL PROPERTY RIGHTS: A CONCISE GUIDE TO THE TRIPS AGREEMENT 102 (1996). TRIPS ties trade secret protection to unfair competition under Article 10*bis* of the Paris Convention. Article 39(1) of TRIPS states: "In the course of ensuring effective protection against unfair competition as provided in Article 10*bis* of the Paris Convention (1967), Members shall protect undisclosed information in accordance with paragraph 2 and data submitted to governments or governmental agencies in accordance with paragraph 3." TRIPS art. 39(1).

Article 39(2) deals with the general standard for trade secret protection. A trade secret constitutes information that (a) is secret—"in the sense that it is not, as a body or in the precise configuration and assembly of its components, generally known among or readily accessible to persons within the circles that normally deal with the kind of information in question;" (b) has commercial value because it is secret; and (c) has been subject to reasonable secrecy measures. *Id.* art. 39(2).

If a trade secret is established, TRIPS requires that trade secret holders "have the possibility of preventing information lawfully within their control from being disclosed to, acquired by, or used by others without their consent in a manner contrary to honest commercial practices." TRIPS art. 39(2). Not surprisingly, the standard "contrary to honest commercial practices" has raised some controversy. Footnote 10 states that the term "means at least practices such as breach of contract, breach of confidence and inducement to breach, and includes the acquisition of undisclosed information by third parties who knew, or were grossly negligent in failing to know, that such practices were involved in the acquisition." Some commentators have criticized this provision for failing to expressly include acquiring a trade secret by improper means, such as through espionage or other forms of deception or skullduggery. *See, e.g.,* Christopher G. Blood, *Holding Foreign Nations Civilly*

Accountable for Their Economic Espionage Practices, 42 IDEA 227, 234–35 (2002).

The following case discusses the scope of unfair competition under (i) the Paris Convention and (ii) the U.S. Lanham Act. Are they equivalent, or not?

GENERAL MOTORS CORP. v. LOPEZ DE ARRIORTUA

U.S. District Court of the Eastern District of Michigan.
948 F. Supp. 684 (E.D. Mich. 1996).

EDMUNDS, DISTRICT JUDGE.

I. Facts

Plaintiffs, General Motors Corporation ("GM") and Adam Opel AG ("Opel"), brought suit against Defendants alleging theft of trade secrets and conspiracy. GM is an American corporation and Opel is a German corporation wholly owned by GM. Defendants include:

1. Volkswagen AG, a German corporation ("VW")

2. Volkswagen of America, Inc., wholly owned by Volkswagen AG ("VWOA")

3. The "Lopez Group," including the following individuals who worked at GM or its subsidiaries until March of 1993 when they left and joined VW:

Jose Ignacio Lopez, a former executive at GM Espana, Opel, and GM (Europe) AG. On February 1, 1993 he became group vice president of GM. Subsequently, on March 10, 1993, he resigned from GM and moved to Germany. On March 16, he joined VW and was appointed to its management board.

Jose Manuel Gutierrez, executive director of purchasing with GM Espana (based in Spain). He quit on March 22, 1993. He moved to Germany and joined VW as a division head.

Jorge Alvarez, a platform manager for the S–Car and the O–car for Opel when he quit on March 22, 1993. He then joined VW's subsidiary SEAT, in Spain, as a purchasing director.

Rosario Piazza, a sourcing specialist for Opel when he quit on March 22, 1993. He then joined VW in Spain as head of forward sourcing.

Hugo Van der Auwera, executive director of worldwide purchasing, metallic commodity group, for GM Continental (based in Belgium) when he quit on March 22, 1993. He joined VW as a division head.

Francisco Garcia–Sanz, executive director of worldwide purchasing, electrical commodity group, for GM when he quit on March 22, 1993. He joined VW as a division head.

Andries Versteeg, manager-European liaison, advance purchasing and global sourcing, for GM when he quit on March 22, 1993. He joined VW as a division head.

Willem Admiraal, an employee of GM when he quit on March 22, 1993. He then joined VW. He is married to Lopez's daughter, Irene.[2]

4. The "VW Group" including:

Ferdinand Piech, the chairman of the board of VW;

Jens Neumann, a member of VW's management board and member of the VWOA board;

Jaero Wicker, a VW employee in Wolfsburg and later, when Lopez was hired by VW, an administrative assistant to Lopez; and

H.W. Lytle, executive director of human resources for VWOA.

Plaintiffs allege that while Lopez was a high level GM executive, he secretly communicated with VW representatives and agreed to leave GM and join VW. He agreed to bring confidential business plans and trade secret information with him. Lopez worked with the other Lopez Group Defendants to secretly collect confidential information. In March of 1993, the Lopez Group Defendants left GM and Opel to join VW where they were paid significantly higher salaries. They allegedly took over 20 cartons of stolen documents with them. Plaintiffs allege that Defendants copied the documents and entered them into VW computers, and then proceeded to shred the documents and cover up the theft.

On March 7, 1996, Plaintiffs filed this suit. Counts 3 and 4 of their complaint allege that Defendants violated the Lanham Act, 15 U.S.C. § 1126, and that Defendants violated the Copyright Act, 17 U.S.C. § 101 et seq. The complaint further alleges that VW has used and continues to use the trade secret information to reduce its costs and to increase its market share. Defendants moved to dismiss count 3 (Lanham Act) and count 4 (Copyright Act). For the reasons set forth below, Defendants' motions are denied.

III. Analysis

A. *Lanham Act*

All Defendants (except Alvarez, Piazza, and Versteeg who have not been served) have moved to dismiss count 3 of the complaint. Count 3 alleges that Defendants violated the substantive terms of the Paris Convention, an international agreement incorporated into section 44 of the Lanham Act, 15 U.S.C. § 1126. Defendants contend that the Lanham Act does not incorporate any substantive provisions of the Paris Convention, and thus that Plaintiffs have failed to state a viable claim for relief. They argue that the Paris Convention only required that signatory nations provide the same trademark protection to foreign citizens that they provide to their own citizens. Courts are split on the issue of whether section 44(b) of the Lanham Act incorporates substantive rights set forth in the Paris Convention.

---

2. Defendants allege that Alvarez, Piazza, Garcia–Sanz, Versteeg, and Admiraal all had employment contracts with Opel in Germany, not with GM in the U.S.

Generally, the Lanham Act prohibits two types of unfair competition: trademark infringement (15 U.S.C. § 1114) and false designation of origin or "passing off" (15 U.S.C. § 1125). In addition, the Lanham Act provides rights stipulated by international conventions respecting unfair competition. 15 U.S.C. § 1127. Section 1127 provides:

> The intent of this chapter is ... to provide rights and remedies stipulated by treaties and conventions respecting trade-marks, trade names, and unfair competition entered into between the United States and foreign nations.

This purpose is implemented in sections 44(b), (h), and (i). Section 44(b) provides:

> Any person whose country of origin is a party to any convention or treaty relating to trademarks ... to which the United States is also a party ... shall be entitled to the benefits of this section under the conditions expressed herein *to the extent necessary to give effect to any provision of such convention [or] treaty ... in addition to the rights to which any owner of a mark is otherwise entitled* by this chapter.

15 U.S.C. § 1126(b) (emphasis added). Under section 44(h), foreign citizens are entitled to protection against unfair competition as follows:

> Any person designated in subsection (b) of this section as entitled to the benefits and subject to the provisions of this chapter shall be entitled to effective protection against unfair competition, and the remedies provided in this chapter for infringement of marks shall be available so far as they may be appropriate in repressing acts of unfair competition.

15 U.S.C. § 1126(h). The Act specifically provides under section 44(i) that United States citizens shall have the same rights as foreigners. "Citizens or residents of the United States shall have the same benefits as are granted by this section to persons described in subsection (b) of this section." 15 U.S.C. § 1126(i).

One treaty incorporated by this section is the International Convention for the Protection of Industrial Property, the Paris Convention. 24 U.S.T. 2140 (July 14, 1967). The Paris Convention requires signatory nations to prohibit unfair competition:

> (1) The countries of the Union are bound to assure to nationals of such countries effective protection against unfair competition.

> (2) Any act of competition contrary to honest practices in industrial or commercial matters constitutes an act of unfair competition.

Paris Convention, article 10*bis*. The broad concept of unfair competition set forth in the Paris Convention has been described as follows:

> Article 10*bis* is not premised upon the narrow meaning of "unfair competition" as it was understood in American common law, but adopts the more liberal construction of the European countries such as France, Germany and Switzerland ... The statement that unfair

competition is competition "contrary to honest practice" is not a definition; it merely expresses the concept that a particular act of competition is to be condemned as unfair because it is inconsistent with currently accepted standards of honest practice. It impliedly affirms that unfair competition is too broad a concept to be limited to any narrow definition such as for instance, passing off.

4A Rudolf Callmann, *The Law of Unfair Competition, Trademarks and Monopolies,* § 2610 (4th ed. 1994). The United States and Germany are both signatories to the Paris Convention.

Defendants concede that the Lanham Act incorporates the Paris Convention. However, they contend that the Paris Convention does not provide substantive rights, and that it only requires "national treatment." One authority on trademark law explained this interpretation of the Convention:

> The Paris Convention is essentially a compact between the various member countries to accord in their own countries to citizens of the other contracting parties' trademark and other rights comparable to those accorded their own citizens by their domestic law. *The underlying principle is that foreign nationals should be given the same treatment in each of the member countries as that country makes available to its own citizens ["national treatment"].* The Convention is not premised upon the idea that the trademark laws of each member nation shall be given extraterritorial application, but on exactly the converse principle that each nation's law shall have only territorial application.

In re Compagnie Generale Maritime, 993 F.2d 841, 850 (Fed. Cir. 1993) (Nies, J., dissenting) (quoting 1 McCarthy, *Trademarks and Unfair Competition*, § 19:24, at 927 (2d ed. 1984) (emphasis added)).

[O]ther courts have held that the Lanham Act incorporates international agreements. In *Toho Co. v. Sears, Roebuck & Co.*, 645 F.2d 788, 792 (9th Cir. 1981), a Japanese company brought suit against Sears, an American company, alleging unfair competition. The court explained that sections 44(b) and (h) incorporated the provisions of a treaty between the United States and Japan. "The federal right created by subsection 44(h) is coextensive with the substantive provisions of the treaty involved.... [S]ubsections (b) and (h) work together to provide federal rights and remedies implementing federal unfair competition treaties." *Toho*, 645 F.2d at 792. The U.S.–Japan treaty only required national treatment. Thus, the court reasoned that the Japanese company was entitled to bring the same claims as an American company would be entitled to bring: both claims for trademark infringement and false designation of origin under the Lanham Act as well as a claim for unfair competition under state law.

> Domestic companies are entitled to federal protection against trademark infringement, 15 U.S.C. § 1114 (1976), and passing off, 15 U.S.C. § 1125(a) (1976). They are also entitled to the protection accorded them by any applicable state law of unfair competition.

Subsection 44(h) requires only that Toho be granted these same protections because it extends only as far as is necessary to give effect to the treaty. *Thus, the practical effect of section 44 and this treaty is to provide a federal forum in which Toho can pursue its state claims.*

Toho, 645 F.2d at 793 (emphasis added).

Still other courts have taken *Toho* one step further and have held that the Lanham Act incorporates the substantive provisions of the Paris Convention and thus creates a federal law of unfair competition applicable in international disputes. In *Maison Lazard et Compagnie v. Manfra, Tordella & Brooks, Inc.*, 585 F. Supp. 1286, 1289 (S.D.N.Y. 1984), a French company brought suit against an American company, alleging that the American company sold commemorative Olympic coins overseas in violation of the plaintiff's exclusive right to make such sales. In essence, the French company claimed that the defendant misappropriated an exclusive right and that this constituted unfair competition under the Paris Convention. The court followed *Toho*, holding that the Lanham Act incorporated the Convention. Because the Paris Convention provides broad protection from unfair competition, the court held that the plaintiff had a valid federal claim for misappropriation of an exclusive right.

The court is persuaded that *Toho* and *Maison Lazard* properly interpret the Lanham Act as incorporating the substantive provisions of the Paris Convention. The express purpose of the Lanham Act dictates this result. "The intent of this chapter is . . . to provide rights and remedies stipulated by treaties and conventions. . . ." 15 U.S.C. § 1127. The Paris Convention provides that signatory countries must protect individuals from unfair competition. Article 10*bis*. Subsection (b) of the Lanham Act implements this concept by providing that foreigners are entitled to benefits "to the extent necessary to give effect to any provision" of a convention. Subsection (h) specifies that foreigners are entitled "to protection against unfair competition."

Opel seeks the right to sue for unfair competition pursuant to 44(h), and GM seeks to enforce the same rights pursuant to section 44(i). Because the Lanham Act incorporates the Paris Convention's broad prohibition against unfair competition, Plaintiffs have stated a claim.

Defendants also claim that the Lanham Act does not reach extraterritorial acts. This is incorrect. Congress has the power to regulate even entirely foreign commerce where it has a substantial effect on commerce between the states or between the United States and foreign countries. *Vanity Fair*, 234 F.2d at 641. "Particularly is this true when a conspiracy is alleged with acts in furtherance of that conspiracy taking place in both the United States and foreign countries." *Id. See also Steele v. Bulova Watch Co.*, 344 U.S. 280 (1952) (holding U.S. citizen who sold infringing watches only in foreign countries liable under Lanham Act).

[The court denied the defendants' motion to dismiss.]

NOTES AND QUESTIONS

1. The *Lopez* case involves a claim under the Lanham Act, which is (at least primarily) a federal statute for trademark protection in the U.S. If the plaintiffs in *Lopez* are not alleging any violations of trademark law, how do they attempt to rely on the Lanham Act? What is the theory of their cause of action?

2. In *Lopez*, two legal questions were raised: (i) what is the scope of unfair competition under § 44 of the Lanham Act, and (ii) does § 44 incorporate whatever understanding of unfair competition is embodied in Paris Convention Article 10*bis*? How did the district court answer these questions?

Do you agree with the *Lopez* court's conclusion that § 44h's recognition of "effective protection against unfair competition" is "substantially similar" to the prior version that the congressional subcommittee rejected, which stated: "All acts of unfair competition in commerce are declared to be unlawful . . ."? Couldn't one draw the opposite inference to the one drawn by the *Lopez* court—i.e., as evidenced in the legislative history, Congress considered a broad prohibition on "all acts of unfair competition" similar to Paris Article 10*bis*(2), but chose not to adopt it.

3. Assuming the *Lopez* court was correct in its interpretation of § 44 of the Lanham Act, would § 44 also encompass theft of trade secrets, commercial bribery, and promotional advertising recognized as unfair competition in Europe? Or should each country have the discretion to decide what constitutes an act of unfair competition above and beyond the three types of acts enumerated under subsection 3?

Cf. G.H.C. BODENHAUSEN, GUIDE TO THE APPLICATION OF THE PARIS CONVENTION FOR THE PROTECTION OF INDUSTRIAL PROPERTY 144 (1968) (favoring the latter interpretation); WIPO, PROTECTION AGAINST UNFAIR COMPETITION 18 (1994) (Article 10*bis*(2) "leaves the determination of the notion of 'commercial honesty' to the national courts and administrative authorities"). *But cf.* WIPO, MODEL PROVISIONS ON PROTECTION AGAINST UNFAIR COMPETITION n. 1.02 (suggesting that, for a proposed model provision following Article 10*bis*, "honest practices" should take into account "conceptions of honest practices that are established in international trade" in disputes between parties of different countries).

4. As the *Lopez* court notes, there is a split of authority on whether the Lanham Act incorporates a broad cause of action for unfair competition that encompasses European notions of unfair competition. The *Lopez* court is in the minority.

The majority view is that the Lanham Act does not incorporate any substantive rights under the Paris Convention beyond those already independently recognized by the Lanham Act. *See Vanity Fair Mills, Inc. v. T. Eaton Co.*, 234 F.2d 633, 644 (2d Cir. 1956) (§ 44 meant to adopt principle of national treatment); *Scotch Whisky Ass'n v. Majestic Distilling Co., Inc.*, 958 F.2d 594, 597 (4th Cir. 1992) (§ 44 limited to unfair competition within scope of § 43(a) of Lanham Act); *Kemart Corp. v. Printing Arts Research Labs., Inc.*, 269 F.2d 375, 389 (9th Cir. 1959) ("the Paris Convention was not intended to define the substantive law in the area of 'unfair competition' of the signatory countries"); *International Café, S.A.L. v. Hard Rock Café Int'l (U.S.A.), Inc.*, 252 F.3d 1274, 1278 (11th Cir. 2001) (same). *See also L'Aiglon Apparel v. Lana Lobell, Inc.*, 214 F.2d 649, 652 (3d Cir. 1954) ("Congress manifested an intent to fashion a remedy to coincide with rights growing from the respective international agreements," but concluding § 44 does not proscribe unfair competition between domestic parties—§ 43(a) may apply to that situation); *Toho Co. v. Sears, Roebuck & Co.*, 645 F.2d 788, 792 (9th Cir. 1981) (§ 44 gives foreigners cause of action to pursue federal unfair competition as defined by Lanham Act and state law).

5. *TRIPS and trade secrets.* TRIPS Article 39 requires members to provide trade secret protection under unfair competition laws as provided in Paris Article 10*bis*. Does TRIPS then provide further support for the *Lopez* decision? On the one hand, the plaintiffs could argue that TRIPS Article 39 provides an additional definition of unfair competition for Paris Article 10*bis*, which should be incorporated into § 44 of the Lanham Act. On the other hand, § 44 specifically addresses unfair competition in the context of a "treaty relating to trademarks," and does not appear to contemplate trade secrets. It might be a stretch to argue that the Lanham Act, primarily a trademark statute, has been expanded to encompass a federal trade secret statute after TRIPS. Trade secret is, by and large, a creation of state (not federal) law in the United States. Given these state law protections for trade secrets, the U.S. arguably is in compliance with its obligations under TRIPS Article 39, regardless of how § 44 of the Lanham Act is interpreted.

6. *Trade secret laws in Europe.* The protection of trade secrets—or undisclosed "know how," as it commonly referred to—in Europe varies among countries, at least in form if not in substance. Civil law countries in continental Europe, such as Germany and France, tend to treat misappropriation of trade secret under unfair competition law or general code provisions. By contrast, in the United Kingdom, trade secret law developed under the common law (similar to the U.S.). Eastern European countries that only recently have protected trade secrets, such as Ukraine, Armenia, and the Czech and Slovak Republics, have enacted express provisions in their civil codes protecting trade secrets. *See* Salem M. Katsh & Michael P. Dierks, *Globally, Trade Secrets Are All Over the Map*, Vol. 7, No. 11 J. PROPRIETARY RTS. 12 (1995). Compared to the harmonization efforts in copyright, patent, trademark, and geographical indications, the EU's efforts for harmonization of trade secret law has been modest. Although EU law has adopted regulations governing the know-how licensing of trade secrets, exempting such licenses from competition laws, the EU has not adopted or proposed any comprehensive harmonization of trade secret laws in Europe. *See* EC Regulation on Know-how Licensing, Reg. No. 556/89, 1989 O.J. (L. 61) 1; EC Regulation No. 240/96, 1996 O.J. (L. 31) 2. *See generally* JERRY COHEN & ALAN S. GUTTERMAN, TRADE SECRETS PROTECTION AND EXPLOITATION 75–78, 86–97 (Supp. 2000). The lack of formal harmonization of trade secret laws in the EU mirrors the lack of such formal harmonization of unfair competition laws more generally in the EU. *See* Frauke Henning–Bodewig & Gerhard Schricker, *New Initiatives for The Harmonisation of Unfair Competition Law in Europe* 24 EUROPEAN INTELL. PROP. REV. 271, 271 (2002); Gerhard Schricker,

Twenty Five Years of Protection Against Unfair Competition, 26 I.I.C. 782, 795 (1995).

7. *Trade Secret v. Patent.* One recurring question that businesses face is whether to protect their know-how under trade secret law by keeping it a secret, or whether to seek a patent and disclose their know-how in the patent application. The tradeoffs are several. First, a trade secret lasts indefinitely as long as the know-how is secret, while a patent lasts only for 20 years. Second, a trade secret provides relatively modest protection, given that reverse engineering and independent discovery by a competitor are valid acts that can defeat a trade secret. By contrast, reverse engineering and independent discovery by competitors will not defeat a patent. Third, a trade secret is relatively cheap and easy to obtain, in that no application or approval must be sought (although reasonable secrecy measures must be undertaken to protect the trade secret). By contrast, prosecuting a patent application is expensive, time-consuming, and fraught with pitfalls and hurdles on both the national and international level.

Research suggests that the preference in the U.S. for patent or for trade secret may vary by industry. *See* WESLEY M. COHEN ET AL., PROTECTING THEIR INTELLECTUAL ASSETS: APPROPRIABILITY CONDITIONS AND WHY U.S. MANUFACTURING FIRMS PATENT (OR NOT) 9–11 (Nat'l Bureau of Econ. Research, Working Paper No. 7552, 2000); RICHARD C. LEVIN ET AL., APPROPRIATING THE RETURNS FROM INDUSTRIAL RESEARCH AND DEVELOPMENT, in 1987 Brookings Papers on Econ. Activity 783, 794–97 (1987); *see also* Dan L. Burk & Mark A. Lemley, *Policy Levers in Patent Law*, 89 VA. L. REV. 1575, 1584 (2003) ("some industries rely more heavily on trade secrets than on patents to protect their innovation, particularly the chemical industry, which emphasizes process innovation").

What are the tradeoffs for developing countries to protect trade secrets v. patents? Assuming a country has not protected either in the past, which form of intellectual property would be easier to administer and protect?

8. *Criminal law.* More so than other forms of intellectual property, theft of trade secrets is increasingly viewed as a criminal act, a form of "economic espionage." This association may be due in part to the fact that trade secret theft often may involve acts of deception, clandestine operations, and other kinds of skullduggery—sometimes allegedly committed or sponsored by governments against other countries. It also may be due in part to the amount of money at stake in the protection of a trade secret, the theft of which could cause great loss to a corporation, if not a country's economy. Recognizing these concerns, the U.S. Congress enacted the Economic Espionage Act of 1996 (EEA), which criminalizes certain acts of economic espionage if committed intending or knowing that "the offense will benefit any foreign government, foreign instrumentality, or foreign agent." 18 U.S.C. § 1831. The EEA also criminalizes certain acts of intentional trade secret theft involving a trade secret "that is related to or included in a product that is produced for or placed in interstate or foreign commerce." *Id.* § 1832.

Problem 5–4

You have been assigned by the WTO to prepare a report on potential revisions to countries' obligations to protect trade secrets. (i) What, if anything, would you recommend changing in TRIPS Article 39? Please draft any suggested change, and explain the reason why it should be adopted. (ii) Would you recommend including theft of trade secrets as the subject of criminal procedures within TRIPS Article 61, which currently requires criminal sanctions only for trademark counterfeiting and copyright piracy?

B. PROTECTION FOR UNDISCLOSED TEST DATA FOR PHARMACEUTICALS AND AGRICULTURAL CHEMICAL PRODUCTS

TRIPS Article 39(3)

(3) Members, when requiring, as a condition of approving the marketing of pharmaceutical or of agricultural chemical products which utilize new chemical entities, the submission of undisclosed test or other data, the origination of which involves a considerable effort, shall protect such data against unfair commercial use. In addition, Members shall protect such data against disclosure, except where necessary to protect the public, or unless steps are taken to ensure that the data are protected against unfair commercial use.

TRIPS Article 39(3) deals with the special problem of submitting undisclosed test or other data regarding pharmaceuticals and agricultural chemical products to government agencies as a required part of government approval for the product. The United States was a strong proponent of adding such a provision, given its importance to the pharmaceutical industry. TRIPS requires that countries "shall protect such data against unfair commercial use," if the origination of the data "involves a considerable effort." "In addition, Members shall protect such data against disclosure, except where necessary to protect the public, or unless steps are taken to ensure that the data are protected against unfair commercial use." Thus, Article 39(3) expressly allows public disclosure of such data in two instances: (i) "where necessary to protect the public" or (ii) if "steps are taken to ensure that the data are protected against unfair commercial use."

Just as in the case of TRIPS Article 39(2)'s "contrary to honest commercial practices," Article 39(3)'s "unfair commercial use" has been the source of criticism for its lack of specificity and clarity. The term may be even more ambiguous than "contrary to honest commercial practices," which at least is partially defined in footnote 10. *Compare* Carlos Maria Correa, *Unfair Competition Under the TRIPS Agreement: Protection of Data Submitted for the Registration of Pharmaceuticals*, 3 Chi. J. Int'l L. 69, 78 (2002) ("unfair commercial use" is left to the discretion of each country) *with* Aaron Xavier Fellmeth, *Secrecy, Monopoly, and Access to*

Pharmaceuticals in International Trade Law: Protection of Marketing Approval Data Under the TRIPS Agreement, 45 HARV. INT'L L.J. 443, 460–67 (2004) ("unfair commercial use" establishes a minimum standard of trade secret-type protection).

What exactly is at stake in the protection of test data for pharmaceuticals and agricultural chemical products? How might the issue relate to generic drug manufacturers and whether they can rely on the brand drug manufacturer's test data for market approval? Consider the following articles.

SECRECY, MONOPOLY, AND ACCESS TO PHARMACCEUTICALS IN INTERNATIONAL TRADE LAW: PROTECTION OF MARKETING APPROVAL DATA UNDER THE TRIPS AGREEMENT

Aaron Xavier Fellmeth.
45 Harv. Int'l L.J. 443, 468–77 (2004).

III.   Secrecy, Monopoly, and Access to Medicines

Preclinical testing for drug marketing approval typically encompasses feeding a drug to, injecting the drug into, or otherwise testing the drug on non-human mammals. Following evaluation of the toxicity, pharmacokinetics, and pharmacodynamics of the drug on animals, the agencies usually demand testing on human subjects in varying conditions and over varying periods of time. In the last stages of testing before approval, several hundred human test subjects may be required. These studies tend to last several years and require the expenditure of millions of dollars before the conditions for marketing approval are satisfied. In the United States, the most recent statistics suggest that the cost of obtaining marketing approval averages $403 million out of pocket and $802 million fully capitalized (i.e., accounting for the time value of money). Although these figures are probably greatly exaggerated because they fail to account for significant cost offsets and overstate the costs of studies conducted by private drug developers, it is beyond doubt that the marketing approval process is risky, laborious, and expensive.

The arguments in favor of data exclusivity advanced by large drug developers and the WTO members that represent their interests are based on both economic and equitable considerations. The economic argument arises from the claim that, without such exclusivity, drug developers will have insufficient incentive to conduct the costly clinical research and trials necessary to obtain marketing approval. The equitable argument is based on the view that, because generic drug manufacturers and other subsequent registrants do not produce the test and clinical data upon which they rely, they are unfairly benefiting from the "sweat of the brow" of the initial registrant.

A.   *Economic Incentives for Marketing Approval*

The assertion that data exclusivity is a necessary incentive to seeking marketing approval, while often advanced, is an unproven empirical claim.

In at least some circumstances, it is possible that the benefit of being the first registrant will outweigh the cost of obtaining marketing approval, especially if drug developers achieve brand-name recognition for their products early, such that competing generic drugs either are unknown to consumers or seem like inadequate or inferior substitutes. However, as noted above, the cost of obtaining marketing approval is quite high, while the marginal cost of manufacturing pharmaceuticals is usually low. Thus, the first-mover advantage for registering a drug would need to be significant to overcome the negative price effects of competition from drug manufacturers that free ride on the initial registrant's marketing approval. Accordingly, it is argued that, without a temporary monopoly, the developers of new drugs will have no incentive to incur regulatory approval costs.

It is also possible that drugs not requiring the grant of a monopoly to motivate marketing approval represent a very small minority of cases. However, given the unusually high growth in sales and returns on equity of large drug developers, skepticism of this position appears justified. As of July 2003, the median return on equity (net of research expenses) of the nine pharmaceutical companies listed in the top 300 of the Fortune 500 was over four times that of the remaining 277 companies. Average return on equity for the drug developers was even greater in proportion to that of other companies of comparable size (52% versus 11%).

Relative Economic Performance of Large Pharmaceutical Companies (July 2003)		
	Median Return on Equity	Average Return on Equity
Pharmaceutical developers in the Fortune 300	58.5%	52.1%
All Fortune 300 companies	13.4%	11.4%

More generally, the value of the U.S. pharmaceutical industry's worldwide sales has grown by a factor of more than thirty-two since 1970. Since 1990, the industry has grown twice as fast as the U.S. economy. This is hardly the picture of a suffering industry.

Although many countries do not grant data exclusivity, large drug developers do benefit from five or more years of data exclusivity (plus whatever market power their patent rights may confer) in their largest markets—the United States, Canada, Europe, and Japan. The United States offers a five-year period of data exclusivity to new drug registrants,[128] and the European Union offers between six and ten years of

---

128. See Drug Price Competition and Patent Term Restoration Act of 1984, Pub. L. No. 98–417, 98 Stat. 1585 (1984) (codified in Titles 15, 21, 28, and 35 of the U.S. Code).

exclusivity.[129] (Nearly half of all EC members grant ten years of exclusivity by default.) In each jurisdiction, not only does the initial registrant have exclusive access to the data submitted, but the regulatory authority may not rely on the data to approve subsequent applications to market the same drugs.[131] The returns on equity that form the basis of the calculations above undoubtedly reflect, at least to some degree, the market power conferred by data exclusivity. Whether drug developers would be as profitable without such exclusivity is an open question. Until better empirical evidence is available, the safest route may be to assume that some, but certainly not all, foreign marketing approvals would not be sought without adequate compensation for the costs of obtaining such approval.

The "solution" to the problem of duplicative testing that has been adopted in the United States, Europe, and several other developed countries is to preclude competition in a drug altogether for five to ten years after an initial registration, even in the absence of a patent. This kind of cure may be worse than the disease since it does not allow competitors the option of undergoing the duplicative testing, even when such testing is economically efficient (i.e., when it results in lower-priced drugs). Considering that many drugs are not discretionary purchases, but correlate highly with the quality and even preservation of human life, an unnecessary monopoly such as that conferred by unqualified data exclusivity should be eschewed.

B. Equitable Considerations

The debate about the equity of allowing subsequent applicants to free ride on the drug testing data of the initial registrant has relevance only with respect to drugs upon which the patent has expired, or to those that are unpatentable, such as certain kinds of therapeutic biologics. Registrants of patented drugs generally need not concern themselves with competition because subsequent registrants are precluded from competing in the relevant market for the term of the patent (usually twenty years after the filing date). Unpatented drugs, such as drugs invented under conditions precluding patentability, can benefit, at best, from trade secret protection under the TRIPS Agreement. This lack of patent protection becomes especially problematic where a slow patenting process significantly eats into the period of patent protection, which generally runs from the date of filing and not from the date the patent is granted. Economically developed countries have already begun solving the delay problem by negotiating a "patent credit" in bilateral and multilateral FTAs for delay in marketing approval. Several years ago, the United States began requiring its FTA partners to extend the period of patent protection to compensate for the delay in obtaining marketing approval.

---

129. Council Directive 65/65, 1965–66 O.J. SPEC. ED. 24 (EC), as amended by Council Directive 87/21, art. 1(a)(iii), O.J. (L 015) 36 (EC).

131. Council Directive 65/65, supra note 129, art. 8, as amended by Council Directive 87/21, supra note 129, art. 1.

Assuming the delay problem is adequately addressed, proponents of data exclusivity observe that, where patent protection is lacking, there is no significant barrier to the subsequent registration of generic drugs based on the initial marketing approval. A patent blocks unlicensed manufacturers from manufacturing or testing the drug for commercial purposes, forcing would-be competitors to forego competition entirely or to undertake the expensive, lengthy, and risky process of inventing around the patented drug. In the absence of a patent, then, there is little to prevent generic drug manufacturers from free riding on the initial registrant's marketing approval. The initial registrant is forced to disclose its otherwise protected trade secret in order to obtain marketing approval; by disclosing this secret to competitors or allowing them to rely on the data, the WTO member is, in effect, expropriating the registrant's trade secret. Subsequent registrants can maintain prices lower than the initial registrant because they benefit from the trade secret without having to recoup the costs of performing extensive testing to obtain marketing approval. To prevent such purportedly inequitable use of the data, drug developers argue that both data confidentiality and data exclusivity should be maintained. Clearly, if the concept of unfair use of a trade secret covers anything beyond fraud or deception, it should cover free riding by competitors.

Opponents of data exclusivity reply that an unpatentable drug is ipso facto unworthy of protection by the government. The U.S. strategy of persuading or coercing its trading partners into granting data exclusivity is, in this view, a "backdoor attempt[ ] to convey private monopoly power for drugs that do not qualify for patent protection." Such drugs are either not new or not inventive, and drug developers may not seek patent-like protection over such drugs by the indirect means of monopolizing their testing data. The cost of obtaining marketing approval, in this view, is the forfeiture of trade secret rights in the data, or at least of the exclusive right to benefit from the data. It is certainly the case that having exclusive rights to a drug on one hand, and being required to demonstrate the drug's safety, efficacy, and quality on the other, are conceptually unrelated.

The foregoing objection to data exclusivity does not deny that drug developers have an equitable basis for seeking economic incentives to share drug marketing approval data. It simply denies that data exclusivity is the most equitable solution. It was noted above that the duplicative testing that may be occasioned by a rule of data exclusivity is economically wasteful. However, duplicative testing is worse than wasteful—it is unethical. Animal testing of drugs causes the suffering and death of many millions of animals every year. Duplicative research caused by lack of access to confidential marketing approval data increases the number of animals unnecessarily subjected to testing. It may also subject humans to suffering in the form of side effects or prolonged unameliorated symptoms where some indications of the drug, though known to the drug regulatory authority by virtue of a prior registration for the drug, remain unknown to the subsequent applicant.

However, the solution adopted by those WTO members that refuse to register competing drugs at all during the exclusivity period is open to the same moral criticism. It is no more ethical to allow persons in need of drugs to pay higher costs during the exclusivity period than it is for the state to expropriate a drug company's marketing approval data. Higher costs mean that at least some people in need of drugs will go without them, resulting in unnecessary suffering and death. Although even more suffering and death will undoubtedly occur if the drug developers lack adequate financial incentive to obtain marketing approval, a balance must be struck between providing incentives for drug marketing and preventing monopolistic behavior. As noted above, WTO members recognized in the Doha Declaration on the TRIPS Agreement and Public Health that these goals must be balanced. In the context of international trade negotiations, the balance is often thought to weigh more heavily toward access. Companies that stand to profit from data exclusivity tend to pay their dividends to the world's richest populations, while the consumers who pay the higher prices to finance these dividends often come from the world's poorest countries. The WHO has accordingly contended that "poorer populations in developing countries should not be expected to pay the same price as do the wealthy for newer essential drugs." In any case, if it is possible to avoid unfair use of the initial registrant's data by competitors while avoiding imposing monopoly prices on consumers, such a policy should be preferred strongly to unqualified data exclusivity.

C. Public Health and Transparency Considerations

Finally, there is the question of whether disclosure and nonexclusivity practices endanger public health. Disclosure of marketing approval data honors the public's interest in being informed about the safety and effectiveness of an approved drug and allows independent observers, such as academics and public interest groups, to conduct further testing and to verify or dispute the accuracy and impartiality of the data submitted by the registrant. It is sometimes observed that drug developers have an incentive to suppress unfavorable results from their drug testing or to exaggerate their efficacy findings. The lack of access to testing data seriously impedes third parties from uncovering bias, inaccurate or incomplete results, and false claims based on that data. The public may thereby be defrauded and public health exposed to unnecessary danger. By refusing to disclose drug testing information, the drug regulatory authority may prevent the discovery of undetected side effects, dangers, counterindications, or even the inefficacy of an approved drug. Whether such independent assessment is "necessary to protect the public"[154] may be arguable in any given instance, but disclosure is certainly more helpful to that end than nondisclosure. As one commentator observed, nondisclosure "facilitates the circulation and use of substandard drugs."

---

154. See TRIPS AGREEMENT art. 39.3.

Article 39.3 of the TRIPS Agreement implicitly recognizes that public health considerations may necessitate disclosure of marketing approval data, but requires WTO members to protect against unfair commercial use of the data. The public disclosure of such data is perfectly compatible with protection against unfair commercial use under a rule of data exclusivity that disallows competing registrations during the exclusivity period. It is also, however, compatible with other models for preventing unfair commercial use. The public disclosure of data is independent of granting drug marketing approval; it can be done regardless of whether marketing approval has been granted or denied. [I]t is possible to craft a regime in which drug manufacturers must fulfill requirements in addition to showing that their drugs are safe and effective in order to obtain marketing approval. These requirements can be tailored to address the economic and equity concerns advanced by drug developers.

D. Conclusions

The considerations discussed above lead to the conclusion that nondisclosure and data exclusivity are undesirable, but that some arrangement is necessary to provide economic incentives for drug companies to seek marketing approval and to prevent unfair commercial use of the data by their competitors. The problem with the exclusivity model is that it treats data as the exclusive property of the drug developer when the public also has a clear interest in the data by virtue of the very same marketing approval. The ethical and public-health implications of trade secrets in drug marketing approval data argue against both data exclusivity and nondisclosure. A better solution than secrecy and monopoly must be invented. The drug regulatory authority, rather than treating the data as fortuitously in its possession and subject to its total discretion, might be considered a trustee of the initial registrant's trade secret.

DESPITE VOW, DRUG MAKERS STILL WITHHOLD DATA

Alex Berenson.
The New York Times, May 31, 2005, at A1, C3.*

* * * When the drug industry came under fire last summer for failing to disclose poor results from studies of antidepressants, major drug makers promised to provide more information about their research on new medicines. But nearly a year later, crucial facts about many clinical trials remain hidden, scientists independent of the companies say.

Within the drug industry, companies are sharply divided about how much information to reveal, both about new studies and completed studies for drugs already being sold. The split is unusual in the industry, where companies generally take similar stands on regulatory issues.

Eli Lilly and some other companies have posted hundreds of trial results on the Web and pledged to disclose all results for all drugs they sell. But other drug makers, including Merck and Pfizer, release less information and are reluctant to add more, citing competitive pressures.

As a result, doctors and patients lack critical information about important drugs, academic researchers say, and the companies can hide negative trial results by refusing to publish studies, or by cherry-picking and highlighting the most favorable data from studies they do publish.

"There are a lot of public statements from drug companies saying that they support the registration of clinical trials or the dissemination of trial results, but the devil is in the details," said Dr. Deborah Zarin, director of clinictrials.gov, a Web site financed by the National Institutes of Health that tracks many studies.* * *

In August, GlaxoSmithKline agreed to pay $2.5 million to settle a suit by Eliot Spitzer, the New York attorney general, alleging that Glaxo had hidden results from trials showing that its antidepressant Paxil might increase suicidal thoughts in children and teenagers. At a House hearing in September, Republican and Democratic lawmakers excoriated executives from several top companies, including Pfizer and Wyeth, for hiding study results. In response, many companies promised to do better.

At the same time, Merck and Pfizer have been criticized for failing to disclose until this year clinical trial results that indicated that cox–2 painkillers like Vioxx might be dangerous to the heart.

Drug makers test their medicines in thousands of trials each year, and federal laws require the disclosure of all trials and trial results to the F.D.A. While too complex for many patients to understand, the trial results are useful to doctors and academic scientists, who use them to compare drugs and look for clues to possible side effects. But companies are not required to disclose trial results to scientists or the public.

Some scientists and lawmakers say new rules are needed, and a bill that would require the companies to provide more data was introduced in the Senate in February. So far no hearings have been scheduled on the legislation. The bill's prospects are uncertain, said a co-sponsor, Senator Christopher J. Dodd, Democrat of Connecticut.* * *

In September, Pharmaceutical Research and Manufacturers of America, an industry lobbying group known as PhRMA, said it would create a site for companies to post the results of completed trials. Then, under pressure from the editors of medical journals, the major drug companies in January agreed to expand the number of trials registered on clinicaltrials.gov, the N.I.H. site, which was originally created so patients with life-threatening diseases could find out about clinical trials.

But Merck, Pfizer and GlaxoSmithKline, three of the six largest drug companies, have met the letter but not the spirit of that agreement, Dr. Zarin said.

The three companies have filed only vague descriptions of many studies, often failing even to name the drugs under investigation, Dr. Zarin said. For example, Merck describes one trial as a "one-year study of an investigational drug in obese patients." * * *

Pfizer, Merck and GlaxoSmithKline say that they disclose their largest trials, which determine whether a drug will be approved. Though they would not discuss their policies in detail, executives and press representatives at the companies said generally that disclosing too much information about early-stage trials might reveal business or scientific secrets.* * *

All the companies were meeting the group's guidelines for the site, said Dr. Alan Goldhammer, associate vice president for regulatory affairs at PhRMA. The lobbying group requires only that its members post a notice that a trial has been completed and a link to a published study or a summary of an unpublished study, he said. Studies completed before October 2002 are exempt from the requirements, and PhRMA has not set penalties for companies that do not comply.* * *

The continued gaps in disclosure have caused some lawmakers to call for new federal laws. The bill introduced in February by Mr. Dodd and Senator Charles E. Grassley, Republican of Iowa, would convert clinicaltrials.gov into a national registry for both new trials and results and impose civil penalties of up to $10,000 a day for companies that hide trial data. But Mr. Dodd said that the chances the bill would pass in this Congress were even at best.* * *

Dr. David Fassler, a psychiatry professor at the University of Vermont and a longtime proponent of more disclosure, said that trial reporting had improved in the last two years. But he said that a central federally run site, as opposed to the current mix of government and industry efforts, was the only long-term solution.

NOTES AND QUESTIONS

1. *Rethinking TRIPS Article 39(3)?* Do the practices of pharmaceutical companies discussed in the N.Y. Times article suggest the need to rethink the logic of TRIPS Article 39(3)? If pharmaceutical companies are under no obligation to publicly disclose such test data, and if TRIPS requires countries to protect the data from disclosure ("except where necessary to protect the public, or unless steps are taken to ensure that the data are protected against unfair commercial use"), should pharmaceutical companies be faulted for not voluntarily disclosing their test data to the public—even if the information is relevant to public safety?

2. What are the policy reasons for and against Article 39(3)'s standard of protecting "such data against disclosure"? Why is nondisclosure the default approach? Is it good policy to have a default approach that stops other researchers from using or scrutinizing test data related to medicines that affect human lives? If drug manufacturers seek patents on drugs for which regulatory approval is sought, in the hopes of selling them to the public one

day, wouldn't public disclosure of the underlying test data be consistent with the *quid pro quo* rationale of patents—the patentee gets a 20–year monopoly on the drug, but the public gets the know-how related to the drug? Or is there a difference between such test data to seek approval for the marketability of a drug and the know-how for the invention (i.e., drug) itself?

3. *Disclosure of test data.* Article 39 allows for disclosure of test data "[i] where necessary to protect the public, or [ii] unless steps are taken to ensure that the data are protected against unfair commercial use." TRIPS art. 39(3). Presumably, such disclosures can be public. Assuming a country invokes either exception and requires public disclosure of test data, would the test data become ineligible for protection as a trade secret?

The N.Y. Times article discusses possible reforms that were raised in Congress after incidents involving the nondisclosure of tests related to possible harmful side effects of certain antidepressants and cox–2 painkillers. What disclosures of test data could the U.S. government require of the drug makers for these and other drugs consistent with TRIPS Article 39(3)? Could the U.S. government require a federal registry of all test data that was accessible to all on the Internet? What if U.S. law also took "steps" to protect against unfair commercial use, such as (i) recognizing a 5–year period of exclusivity for the test data, as already exists under U.S. law, and/or (ii) requiring competitors to pay a fee to the data's originator under a mandatory license in order to use the test data. Would this satisfy Article 39(3)'s standard for disclosure of test data?

4. *NAFTA.* The North American Free Trade Agreement signed by the U.S., Canada, and Mexico also sets forth minimum standards for trade secret protection. North American Free Trade Agreement, U.S.–Can.–Mex., art. 1711, Dec. 17, 1992, 32 I.L.J. 612. In fact, a number of the provisions in Article 39 of TRIPS, including subsection 3, are modeled on NAFTA Article 1711. However, one key difference is that NAFTA contains additional or more specific minimum standards governing the protection of test data submitted for pharmaceutical approval and the data's use by other drug manufacturers:

> Each Party shall provide that for data subject to paragraph 5 that are submitted to the Party after the date of entry into force of this Agreement, no person other than the person that submitted them may, without the latter's permission, rely on such data in support of an application for product approval during a reasonable period of time after their submission. For this purpose, a reasonable period shall normally mean not less than five years from the date on which the Party granted approval to the person that produced the data for approval to market its product.…

The U.S. had attempted to secure a provision within TRIPS similar to the one in NAFTA, but ultimately failed. However, the U.S. Trade Representative has maintained the position that some period of exclusivity over the data is required by TRIPS, and has negotiated bilateral agreements or Free Trade Agreements (FTAs) with a host of developing countries requiring them to recognize a 5–year data exclusivity period for such test data. Fellmeth, *supra*, at 45 HARV. INT'L L.J. at 455–56.

5. The 5–year period of data exclusivity runs *concurrent* with any patent (if obtained) for the pharmaceutical. Doesn't this render the 5–year period of

exclusivity of little, if any, importance for patented drugs, given that patents grant inventors exclusive rights that last for 20 years? If so, why would the U.S. press so hard for adoption of a 5–year period of data exclusivity in FTAs? *See* Bruce N. Kuhlik, *The Assault on Pharmaceutical Intellectual Property*, 71 U. Chi. L. Rev. 93, 98–99 (2004). Might part of the reason be that "drugs that are off patent or otherwise denied retroactive patent protection under TRIPS may nonetheless remain off limits to would be generic producers in developing countries for the specified period of marketing exclusivity"? Jerome H. Reichman, *Rethinking the Role of Clinical Trial Data in International Intellectual Property Law: The Case for a Public Goods Approach*, 13 Marq. Intell. Prop. L. Rev. 1, 26 (2009).

6. *Developing Countries*. From the start of negotiations of the TRIPS Agreement, developing countries have been skeptical of trade secret protection, especially in the context of test data for pharmaceuticals. One of the main bones of contention revolves around the U.S. position that some period of exclusivity is required for such test data. Why would developing countries disagree with the U.S. position during the negotiations of TRIPS? Is it about securing more affordable access to medicines? If so, why do you think some developing countries (such as Sri Lanka, Ecuador, Laos, Cambodia, Vietnam, Singapore, and Chile) would later agree to the U.S. position requiring a 5–year exclusivity period in subsequent bilateral trade agreements secured by the U.S.?

C. TRANSNATIONAL LAWSUITS: PROTECTING TRADE SECRETS INTERNATIONALLY

Given the forces of globalization in commercial activities, courts are under increasing pressure to deal with transnational activity under domestic law. Consider the following problem and case.

PROBLEM 5–5

Ultra Reality (UR), a company specializing in virtual reality computer games, has just discovered that Tom Chen, one of its former employees in its China joint venture based in Beijing, has left the company to set up a competing company. Before Chen left UR, UR had developed a brand new and exciting 3–D computer game all through work done in China. Chen's company is now making computer games that UR believes are based on its trade secrets developed in China and selling the games in China as well as exporting the games to the United States and the EU. UR believes that Chen has left with an armful of documents containing trade secrets and other proprietary information developed by UR's staff in China. UR is contemplating bringing a lawsuit against China under China's Anti–Unfair Competition Law prohibiting the theft of trade secrets, but notes that plaintiffs rarely win these cases in China due to lack of probative evidence or the unwillingness of courts to enforce the law. A second option would be to sue Chen in the United States, where he maintains a small branch office consisting of a desk and supplies in a small rented office. UR is worried about jurisdictional issues, however. Even if successful in a U.S. court, UR might have to seek to enforce the judgment in China, which is difficult to obtain because most courts in China may simply refuse to recognize the foreign judgment. UR comes to your law firm and asks what other options are available? Chen's company is planning a large shipment of his new computer games to the United States in the next year. Can anything else be done?

TIANRUI GROUP COMPANY LTD. v. INTERNATIONAL TRADE COMMISSION

U.S. Court of Appeals for the Federal Circuit.
661 F.3d 1322 (Fed.Cir. 2011).

BRYSON, CIRCUIT JUDGE.

This appeal arises from a determination by the International Trade Commission that the importation of certain cast steel railway wheels violated section 337 of the Tariff Act of 1930, 19 U.S.C. § 1337. The Commission found that the wheels were manufactured using a process that was developed in the United States, protected under domestic trade secret law, and misappropriated abroad. We are asked to decide whether the Commission's statutory authority over "[u]nfair methods of competition and unfair acts in the importation of articles ... into the United States," as provided by section 337(a)(1)(A), allows the Commission to look to conduct occurring in China in the course of a trade secret misappropriation investigation. We conclude that the Commission has authority to investigate and grant relief based in part on extraterritorial conduct insofar as it is necessary to protect domestic industries from injuries arising out of unfair competition in the domestic marketplace.

[Amsted Industries is a U.S. company that manufactured cast steel railway wheels by two processes that are protected by trade secrets in the U.S. After failing to secure a license from Amsted, TianRui Group, a Chinese company, hired away nine employees from Amsted's licensee in China. The employees hired by TianRui allegedly misappropriated Amsted's trade secrets and violated their duty of confidentiality as to the secret processes in their employment agreements. Amsted filed a Section 337 complaint against TianRui in the International Trade Commission to stop imports of TianRui-made cast steel railway wheels into the United States. The ITC ruled in favor of Amsted. *Ed.*]

The main issue in this case is whether section 337 authorizes the Commission to apply domestic trade secret law to conduct that occurs in part in a foreign country.

Section 337 authorizes the Commission to exclude articles from entry into the United States when it has found "[u]nfair methods of competition [or] unfair acts in the importation of [those] articles." 19 U.S.C. § 1337(a)(1)(A). The Commission has long interpreted section 337 to apply to trade secret misappropriation. TianRui does not challenge that interpretation. Nor does it dispute the Commission's factual finding that proprietary information belonging to Amsted was disclosed to TianRui in breach of obligations of confidentiality imposed on the former Datong employees or the finding that the information was used in manufacturing the imported railway wheels. Instead, TianRui focuses on the fact that the disclosure of the trade secret information occurred in China. According to TianRui, section 337 cannot apply to extraterritorial conduct and therefore does not reach trade secret misappropriation that occurs outside the United States.

The presumption against extraterritoriality does not govern this case, for three reasons. First, section 337 is expressly directed at unfair methods of competition and unfair acts "in the importation of articles" into the United States. As such, "this is surely not a statute in which Congress had only 'domestic concerns in mind.' " *Pasquantino v. United States,* 544 U.S. 349, 371–72 (2005).

Second, in this case the Commission has not applied section 337 to sanction purely extraterritorial conduct; the foreign "unfair" activity at issue in this case is relevant only to the extent that it results in the importation of goods into this country causing domestic injury. In light of the statute's focus on the act of importation and the resulting domestic injury, the Commission's order does not purport to regulate purely foreign conduct.

Third, the legislative history of section 337 supports the Commission's interpretation of the statute as permitting the Commission to consider conduct that occurs abroad. Congress first enacted a prohibition against "unfair methods of competition" in the Federal Trade Commission Act, Pub.L. No. 63–203, § 5, 38 Stat. 717, 719 (1914), codified as amended at 15 U.S.C. § 45. Congress chose that phrase because it was "broader and more flexible" than the traditional phrase "unfair competition," which had acquired a narrow meaning in its common law usages.

TianRui argues that the Commission should not be allowed to apply domestic trade secret law to conduct occurring in China because doing so would cause improper interference with Chinese law. We disagree. In the first place, as we have noted, the Commission's exercise of authority is limited to goods imported into this country, and thus the Commission has no authority to regulate conduct that is purely extraterritorial. The Commission does not purport to enforce principles of trade secret law in other countries generally, but only as that conduct affects the U.S. market. That is, the Commission's investigations, findings, and remedies affect foreign conduct only insofar as that conduct relates to the importation of articles into the United States. The Commission's activities have not hindered TianRui's ability to sell its wheels in China or any other country.

Second, TianRui has failed to identify a conflict between the principles of misappropriation that the Commission applied and Chinese trade secret law. Indeed, in its forum non conveniens motion TianRui argued that Chinese trade secret law would provide a "more than adequate" remedy for any alleged misappropriation. In addition, China has acceded to the Agreement on Trade–Related Aspects of Intellectual Property Rights ("TRIPS"). We cannot discern any relevant difference between the misappropriation requirements of TRIPS article 39 and the principles of trade secret law applied by the administrative law judge in this case. We therefore detect no conflict between the Commission's actions and Chinese law that would counsel denying relief based on extraterritorial acts of trade secret misappropriation relating to the importation of goods affecting a domestic industry. *AFFIRMED*. [Judge Moore's dissent is omitted.]

NOTES AND QUESTIONS

1. Does the Federal Circuit's decision amount to an extraterritorial application of U.S. trade secret law?

2. Are you persuaded that the decision does not interfere with China's ability to regulate trade secret protection in China?

3. How should the fact that TianRui's wheels were about to be imported to the United States affect the extraterritoriality analysis?

4. How does Article 39 of the TRIPS Agreement factor into the court's analysis? Are you persuaded that Article 39 supports the court's approach?

CHAPTER 6

INTERNATIONAL ENFORCEMENT OF INTELLECTUAL PROPERTY RIGHTS

■ ■ ■

A. INTRODUCTION

We began our discussion of international intellectual property in Chapter 1 with debate of the potential limits of international law. Are the elaborate structure and obligations created by TRIPS just a mirage—to be followed when it serves a country's interest, but ignored when it does not? In this chapter, we revisit this question but in the context of enforcement procedures. The preceding chapters have focused mainly on substantive international legal standards established by TRIPS and other intellectual property treaties. Such substantive standards, however, do not automatically ensure protection of intellectual property, or the enforcement of rights in a particular country. Even if the "law on the books" conforms to the standards of TRIPS, intellectual property rights are illusory if there are no means to enforce them.

The WTO recognized this problem of enforcement. Developed countries, led by the U.S., argued forcefully for the need to establish an effective enforcement mechanism for intellectual property owners to enforce their rights through private means. Of considerable concern to developed countries was the increase of international commercial piracy, particularly in terms of unauthorized copying of copyrighted and trade-marked goods. In recognition of the specific challenges posed by commercial piracy, Part III of TRIPS established detailed enforcement obligations on all WTO members to create judicial means that permit an intellectual property owner to enforce its rights through private action before judicial authorities. These international enforcement standards are a first: prior to TRIPS, no international intellectual property treaty addressed the issue of effective enforcement.

As discussed in previous chapters, the WTO also establishes a dispute settlement process on issues of compliance by WTO members with their treaty obligations. The dispute settlement process can be used by a complaining nation to bring an offending nation that has not met its TRIPS obligations into compliance. The WTO dispute settlement process is set forth in the WTO Dispute Settlement Understanding (DSU), which was a major achievement of the Uruguay Round. Throughout the earlier chapters, we have seen opinions issued by panels and the Appellate Body under the auspices of the DSU.

In addition, as discussed in Chapter 1, the United States, Australia, the EU, Japan, and several other nations agreed to the Anti–Counterfeiting Trade Agreement (ACTA) in 2011. ACTA requires "TRIPS-plus" measures for these countries, in order to provide stronger protections against counterfeiting and piracy.

In this chapter, however, our focus is on enforcement by intellectual property owners of their rights through private means, such as litigation or administrative measures within domestic legal systems. In contrast to a country's compliance with TRIPS or treaties at the macro level, private enforcement of IP rights by individuals might be characterized as enforcement at the micro level. The intellectual property owner is primarily concerned with obtaining a remedy against an infringer, which usually consists of compelling the infringer by a court judgment or administrative order to cease the offending activity and to pay compensation. In some cases, an intellectual property owner (or the state authorities) will also seek criminal penalties against an infringer.

Although a country's compliance with TRIPS at the macro level is certainly important, private enforcement may be more of a concern of businesses on a day-to-day level. The issue of TRIPS compliance is raised by a government in its sovereign capacity, not by a private party, through WTO dispute settlement procedures. A private party has no standing to bring a dispute before the WTO, and, of course, the WTO has no jurisdiction over a private dispute concerning the infringement of intellectual property rights. Accordingly, our focus in this chapter is on the process and practical issues involved when an intellectual property owner in one nation is faced with a violation of its intellectual property rights in one or more foreign nations.

B. COMMERCIAL PIRACY

1. OVERVIEW OF PROBLEMS FACED BY BUSINESSES TO PROTECT IP

To obtain an overview of the enforcement issues facing IP owners, let us take the hypothetical case of Apex Corporation, a large diversified multi-national enterprise with its headquarters in the United States and business operations around the world. As MNEs are owners of the world's most commercially valuable intellectual property, an examination of Apex's efforts to protect its global intellectual property portfolio will illustrate the many challenges and issues involved.

Apex is engaged in two main and related lines of business: (i) consumer products and (ii) pharmaceutical and other medical products. Apex's consumer products line includes several well-known international brands of shampoos, soaps, lotions, and cosmetics. Apex is also in the medical field with a line of non-prescription drugs, such as cough medicine, bandages, and pain relievers. Apex has a substantial research and development department that supports its product lines and also a marketing department that promotes its products around the world. Apex spends many millions of dollars not only on research and development, but also on advertising and promotion.

Apex's combination of cutting-edge research and development, advanced technology, and aggressive marketing has made Apex products some of the most recognizable and successful in the world. Like many MNEs today, Apex's intellectual property is critical to its success on a worldwide basis. While Apex has substantial capital reserves and smart managers, the key to Apex's success is in the quality of its advanced technology, which is protected by patents and copyrights, in its marketing of its brands or trademarks, and in its business know-how. Some of Apex's technology is proprietary, and some of its brands now have strong consumer loyalty and goodwill on a worldwide basis. Like many other companies, Apex considers its intellectual property portfolio—primarily copyrights, trademarks, and patents, but in some cases, trade secrets—to be one of its most valuable business assets. Apex is committed to aggressively protecting these rights around the world.

Like many MNEs, Apex has a large in-house legal department located in its headquarters that is responsible for managing Apex's worldwide legal issues. Some members of the in-house legal department specialize in intellectual property rights protection. The IP group has followed all procedures to protect Apex's intellectual property rights in the United States by registering all patents and trademarks. Apex has given clear instructions to its lawyers and agents around the world to make sure that all of the registrations are in Apex's name. Apex wants to ensure that it is the registered and legal owner of its patents, trademarks, and copyrights in all countries of the world. Once these intellectual property rights are registered in Apex's name under local law, Apex will license these rights to its foreign subsidiaries, joint ventures, or in some cases to third party manufacturers, but Apex, as the licensor, remains the owner of the rights. As a general rule, Apex will never register one of its global trademarks or patents in the name of a foreign entity, even if it is a wholly owned subsidiary. This is a fundamental principle of the way that Apex, like most other MNEs, handles its intellectual property rights around the world: the MNE owns all intellectual property rights and authorizes their use by its own subsidiaries or by third parties. The rationale behind this approach is that Apex wants to ensure that there is never a dispute or question of who is the owner of Apex's most important business assets, its intellectual property rights.

Although Apex has long conducted business abroad, its foreign operations grew substantially beginning in the 1980s with the disintegration of the Soviet Union and its eastern block of influence and the emergence of the People's Republic of China as one of the world's largest and most significant markets. For the first time, Apex also targeted developing countries as a key strategic market for its products. As the process of globalization deepened in the 1990s, Apex's business operations also witnessed significant growth. At the same time Apex came under increasing competition as other MNEs and smaller competitors rushed into untapped markets.

As a result of heavy advertising and promotion campaigns, Apex's brands in the consumer products business have acquired significant consumer recognition and goodwill in many countries, and its pharmaceuticals and health care products also command a significant share of the market in developing countries. To satisfy the increasing demand for its products, Apex began to establish foreign sales offices and foreign facilities abroad. Apex now has established a formidable presence in many foreign markets due primarily to the success of its technology, brands, and marketing. More than ever, Apex realizes that its intellectual property is the key to its commercial success in international business.

As Apex expanded its operations abroad during the last decades of the twentieth century, Apex also witnessed a sharp increase in the unauthorized copying, infringement and theft of its intellectual property abroad, particularly in China and other parts of Asia. To some extent, Apex, like many other owners of commercially valuable intellectual property, is a victim of its own success. Apex has found that as its products generate higher sales and achieve higher levels of fame and recognition, they increasingly become the target of unauthorized copying around the world. Some of Apex's problems are legitimate business disputes involving a lawful competitor that can be resolved by negotiation, informal dispute settlement, or as a last recourse by litigation.

Aside from these disputes, Apex finds that its problems fall into two main categories: (i) commercial piracy and (ii) gray market goods. We turn our attention here to the problem of commercial piracy, leaving the problem of gray market goods for the end of this chapter. Entities in foreign nations may be making unauthorized copies of Apex's products for sale locally in the foreign nation. Apex believes that these counterfeits and copycat products lead to lost sales revenue for its genuine products. These "pirates" in foreign nations may also make unauthorized copies for export to other nations abroad, including the United States. Apex now realizes that commercial piracy has become a global problem and that counterfeits from China and other parts of Asia appear in many countries around the world. In fact, Apex is becoming increasingly concerned over the influx of imported counterfeits in the United States of many of its products, including its pharmaceuticals.

While Apex has a number of concerns about intellectual property, it has recently grown alarmed about the threat that commercial piracy poses to its worldwide business. Apex estimates that it loses billions of dollars each year to commercial piracy. Apex is not unusual as many other MNEs claim similar losses. As a whole, MNEs claim that worldwide annual losses from commercial piracy are now $650 billion, more than the GDP of many countries. (Of course, as discussed later, some question the accuracy of these figures.)

Under instructions from the CEO, Apex, like many other MNEs, has now formed a corporate team that serves as the company's brand and IP protection group. In addition to the legal department, the corporate team now consists of members from the following departments: government affairs, marketing and advertising, sales, research and development, and corporate security. The head of the brand protection group at Apex is the global general counsel, who, as the head of the corporate legal department, is also a senior vice president and part of the company's most senior management and leadership team. Each of the departments mentioned above delegates a member to serve on the brand protection group and each department brings different expertise to the problem. The government affairs department helps to establish contacts with government officials, such as police, customs, and the various intellectual property agencies in the United States and abroad. Some counterfeit products are so well made that they require laboratory analysis to determine whether they are authentic or counterfeit, so a member of the research and development department is added to the team. Research and development is also helpful as Apex is considering using technological advances in product design and manufacture to foil unauthorized copying and to facilitate detection of fakes. The sales department, with its worldwide sales force, is most often the first point of contact with counterfeit and pirated products as Apex's sales force works in the field where it encounters counterfeits being sold. The sales force brings back on-the-ground knowledge about the scope of the problem. The marketing and advertising department can help to educate governments and consumers about the harm that is caused by pirated and counterfeit products. The marketing department is considering several advertising campaigns for television and other media about the dangers posed by counterfeit products and is working with government health authorities to promote a number of educational programs. The corporate security department is involved because Apex suspects that, as is often the case, some of its own employees or independent contractors may be involved in theft of its intellectual property. Apex has found that in some countries pirated products appear on the market within days of the market launch of the genuine products and that some of the packaging used on the counterfeits is second quality but genuine packaging that was produced by third party contract manufacturers. Apex has found that some of the ingredients used in counterfeit shampoos and lotions are identical to its genuine products. Apex suspects that there is a breach of internal corporate security at one or more of its foreign subsidiaries in China and other parts of Asia. The corporate security department will need to review all internal security measures to detect a breach within the company and will help, along with the legal department, to implement new security measures throughout all of the company's foreign subsidiaries.

The commercial piracy problem has grown so serious that the brand and IP protection group now meets once a month at Apex's corporate headquarters to review strategy and options to combat piracy. At its most recent meeting, the brand and IP protection group has decided that it must take more aggressive action by pursuing legal action against "pirates." Accordingly, the group instructed the Apex legal department to prepare a number of options to enforce its rights worldwide against counterfeiters and pirates, and to develop an overall strategy for the enforcement of its IP generally. Apex is not interested in seeking the assistance of the United States government in raising this issue before the WTO, but is interested in directly enforcing its rights through private means such as litigation and administrative enforcement in the United States and abroad. The in-house legal department has begun to analyze the options and the issues that are involved in private enforcement.

In legitimate business disputes concerning intellectual property, Apex will be dealing with a lawful business entity that is licensed and registered. Apex will be able to serve legal papers on the defendant and the defendant will be required to appear in court to assert a defense or a counterclaim. We will discuss some of the procedural and substantive hurdles that Apex will face in litigation at the end of this chapter.

In the case of pirates and counterfeiters, however, Apex will usually find that the identity of the perpetrator is unknown. Most counterfeiters and pirates work in illegal underground factories in order to hide their identities to avoid detection. Pirates usually leave no official business records or will create false identities in order to facilitate escape. As there is usually no question of guilt or liability, most counterfeiters are not anxious to vindicate themselves in court but flee at the first sign of detection. This creates a problem with the use of court based litigation as it becomes difficult to serve papers and to require defendants to appear in court. Some special procedural mechanisms have been created and are now required by TRIPS to deal with the issues of unknown defendants who flee at the first sign of trouble.

A second issue is that counterfeiters and pirates are not only adept at eluding capture but are also quite resourceful in disguising the origin of their goods, creating difficult evidentiary problems. In the global trade in counterfeit and pirated goods today, tracing the source of the contraband to its origin can be quite difficult. Counterfeiters in China, which accounts for about 80% of all counterfeit and pirated goods in the world, are adept at using fraudulent shipping documents and using transshipment through third countries to elude detection. For example, counterfeit auto parts are often shipped from China to South American countries, which have less vigilant border controls, where they are then repackaged and then shipped to the United States. Tracing these goods back to their origin becomes more difficult once clever pirates divert shipments through third party states. As the trade in counterfeit and pirated goods has become a truly global one, TRIPS now has specific border enforcement measures that are designed to stop the influx of contraband products.

A third issue that creates special concerns is the role of organized crime in commercial piracy. Criminal organizations in Asia have been drawn to commercial piracy by the relatively low-risk nature of the crime and the high profits that can be earned. The same criminal organizations that are involved in smuggling of goods and people, gambling, narcotics, and prostitution have now moved into commercial piracy. As we shall see in a later section, profit margins from some forms of commercial piracy can rival or exceed similar margins for illegal narcotics. But while drug trafficking can routinely result in draconian penalties—including the death penalty in some Asian countries—commercial piracy can often lead to penalties that do not create fear or deterrence. The involvement of criminal organizations in commercial piracy means that Apex and other intellectual property owners are faced with a formidable adversary: the mastermind behind any commercial piracy problem may be a large, well-financed, intelligent, and ruthless foe willing to commit any crime to evade detection and capture. In recognition of the criminal nature of commercial piracy, TRIPS requires criminal sanctions.

There also may be corrupt foreign government officials, who only compound the problem. As commercial piracy has become a highly lucrative activity, some foreign governments, particularly at the local level, have become directly or indirectly involved in supporting or defending the trade in counterfeit goods. If Apex brings a lawsuit or an enforcement action against a counterfeiter in the foreign nation, Apex may find that local judges and enforcement officials will protect local pirates by refusing to fully enforce the laws. If Apex obtains a court judgment in the U.S. and attempts to enforce it in the foreign nation where the defendant has assets, Apex may find that local courts refuse to recognize the judgment. An especially daunting obstacle is created if, as is often the case, criminal organizations involved in commercial piracy also enjoy the protection of corrupt government officials.

Even with the help of law-abiding government officials and law enforcement officers, detection of counterfeiters and pirates is difficult. As we have noted, counterfeiters and pirates often are difficult to detect as they operate underground and outside the purview of the law and may be affiliated with clandestine criminal organizations. In cases involving exported goods, the IP owner may not even know the source of the goods. IP owners will need to first identify the source of goods before they can bring any type of enforcement action. Public law enforcement authorities in most countries, including the United States, are reluctant to commit resources to detect counterfeiters in routine cases. While some IP owners use their own staff to track down counterfeiters, most IP owners hire professional private investigation agencies to track down and identify counterfeiters and pirates. Many investigation companies employ former police, FBI, and customs officials who have some background in law enforcement to do what can be dangerous work. The use of private investigation agencies is an additional expense that the IP owner will need to incur in addition to fees for lawyers. Many IP owners also hire outside counsel to supervise private investigation agencies and to handle the legal aspects of the enforcement action. The need for outside counsel is especially acute in foreign nations as the in-house lawyers of the IP owner may be unfamiliar with local laws. Outside counsel are needed to supervise the activities of enforcement agencies because these agencies have been known to act outside the law in hunting down counterfeiters and pirates.

In many countries, the private investigation industry operates at the periphery of the law and is populated by many colorful and nefarious characters. For example, private investigation agencies have been known to enter private premises without permission, to confiscate and destroy private property without legal authority, and to make bribes to government enforcement officials to induce them to bring an enforcement action. Some private investigators have even been known to impersonate law enforcement officials to extort counterfeiters for money and property. As much of the activities of private investigation companies occur in the field and out of sight of the IP owner, the use of questionable or illegal tactics can be quite common. To curb these abuses, some IP owners hire local outside counsel who monitor the activities of private investigation agencies. Local counsel is also needed to represent the interests of the IP owner before local courts and enforcement agencies. To complicate matters even further, some local lawyers in some foreign countries have been known to engage in illegal tactics themselves, such as bribing the police, prosecutor, or judge. In these situations, Apex's in-house lawyers must closely monitor the foreign local lawyers.

These hypothetical problems for Apex are the kind that many MNEs claim they face today. Just imagine if you were advising Apex on trying to protect its IP rights in a global market where havens of infringement exist. How should Apex deal with the problem?

2. MAGNITUDE OF COMMERCIAL PIRACY—INDUSTRY ESTIMATES

As this discussion suggests, the economic costs of commercial piracy can be myriad and can mount quickly. There are the lost sales attributable to the counterfeit and pirated products, i.e., the sales revenue generated by the sale of genuine products that the IP owner would have otherwise gained but for the presence of the counterfeit and pirated product. In addition, there are the costs of private investigation agencies and legal fees for outside local counsel. In China, home of the world's most serious commercial piracy problem, it would not be unusual for a simple enforcement action involving an investigation, seizure and confiscation of pirated goods, and follow-up to cost between $7,500 and $15,000, and for a complex case involving months of investigation to cost $60,000 or more. Many companies have hundreds of cases every year. These companies now have multi-million dollar annual budgets for protecting global IP rights.

MNEs often bemoan that they are in an uneven fight where they are at a serious disadvantage—while counterfeiters and pirates feel no compunction in breaking the law to steal intellectual property assets and evade detection, IP owners who pursue them must do so within the constraints of the law. Moreover, IP owners also complain that they suffer double economic losses from commercial piracy—the costs of lost sales and the high costs of enforcement, which are usually unrecoverable. Recent studies by industry groups now estimate worldwide annual losses from all forms of commercial piracy have reached crisis levels at $650 billion annually. *See* Estimating the Global Economic and Social Impacts of Counterfeiting and Piracy, Frontier Economics (February 2011).

Although industry estimates point to losses from commercial piracy that are staggering, industry groups continue to express frustration over what they believe is a lax public attitude towards commercial piracy. Many consumers believe that the only victims of commercial piracy are wealthy MNEs that earn fewer profits. Some consumers consider the purchase of counterfeits to be harmless and fun. MNEs argue, however, that commercial piracy also results in the loss of jobs as the plentiful supply of counterfeits reduces demand for legitimate goods and leads to a reduction in production and manufacturing capacity, which in turn leads to a reduction in the workforce. MNEs claim that millions of dollars in tax revenues are also lost. Counterfeiters and pirates do not pay taxes and legitimate IP owners lose sales to counterfeits on which they would have otherwise paid taxes to government authorities. MNEs also claim that commercial piracy funds organized crime and terrorist groups. We will take a closer look at some of these claims in the materials that follow.

a. Copyright Piracy

Copyright piracy refers to the unauthorized copying of the content of some fixed medium of expression such as books, digital music files, DVDs containing movies, business and entertainment computer software, and other audio-visual media products. In copyright piracy, there is normally no attempt to disguise the unauthorized nature of the copy—the consumer is interested in the content and is not concerned that the copy was not made or authorized by the original manufacturer and copyright owners. The availability of highly sophisticated and inexpensive copy technology means that pirates can make high quality copies at relatively low cost. Copyright owners are now also at higher risk because the availability of sophisticated copy technology means that even one authorized copy can become the basis of a massive amount of pirated copies.

As the chart below indicates, most of the estimated losses from copyright piracy are concentrated in the business and entertainment software, music, and motion picture industries. By far the most pirated sector is business software applications:

Worldwide Losses from Copyright Piracy to U.S. Companies (U.S. $ millions)

	2010	2009	2008	2007	2006	2005	2004
Business Software Applications	58,754	51,443	15,940	12,940	10,345	8,028	6,448
Records & Music	-	-	1,756	1,618	2374	2,563	2,657
Entertainment Software	-	-	-	2,656	1,866	2,653	1,744
Motion Pictures	-	-	-	-	-	1,976	1,801
Books	-	-	-	531	583	607	571

Sources: IIPA's Special 301 Reports on Copyright Protection and Enforcement to the U.S. Trade Representative, and the Eighth Annual BSA and IDC Global Software Piracy Study (2011).

The highest rates of copyright piracy occur in the developing world with the highest rates at over 90 percent. Piracy rates tend to be much lower in developed countries, such as the United States, which have stronger enforcement regimes.

10 Countries with the Highest Software Piracy Rates

Country	2008	2010
Georgia	95%	93%
Zimbabwe	92%	91%
Bangladesh	92%	90%
Moldova	90%	90%
Yemen	89%	90%
Armenia	92%	89%
Venezuala	86%	88%
Libya	87%	88%
Azerbaijan	90%	88%
Indonesia	85%	87%

Source: Eighth Annual BSA and IDC Global Software Piracy Study (2011).

In general, the estimated piracy rate is a better indication of the severity of the problem than the figure of estimated total losses. One way to understand the relationship of piracy losses to the piracy rate is to compare the developed world with developing countries. As the illustration below indicates, the legitimate software market in developed countries is about six times the size of the market in developing countries, yet the amount of piracy losses is less than twice as much.

Legitimate vs. Pirated Market

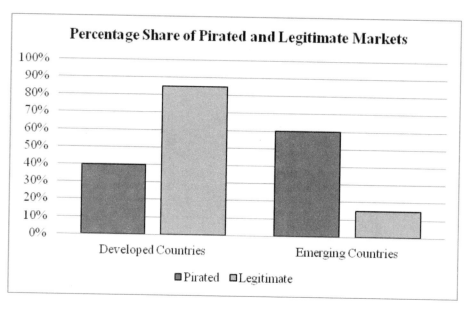

Source: Sixth Annual BSA and IDC Global Software Piracy Study (2008).

An even more stark comparison emerges between the United States, the country with the world's lowest piracy rate, and China, which until recently had the world's highest software piracy rate. In 2010 software piracy losses in the United States totaled $9.5 billion, the highest in the world but the piracy rate in the United States is 20%, the lowest in the world. *See* Eighth Annual BSA and IDC Global Software Piracy Study 6 (2011). The high volume of piracy losses is attributable to the large size of the U.S. market. By contrast, China had the world's second largest piracy losses at $7.8 billion but a 78% piracy rate in 2010. By most accounts, China has the most serious software piracy problem in the world due to the potent combination of the amount of losses (the second highest in the world) with the piracy rate. In 2011, Microsoft CEO Steve Ballmer claimed that the company lost billions of dollars due to software piracy in China, which, despite being nearly the biggest PC market in the world in 2011, generated less revenues for Microsoft than even the sparsely populated country of the Netherlands. *See* Owen Fletcher & Jason Dean, *Ballmer Bares China Travails*, WALL ST. J., May 26, 2011.

b. Trademark Counterfeiting

Trademark counterfeiting refers to the unauthorized copying of a trademark owned by another and placing the trademark on similar or identical goods. Unlike copyright piracy (where consumers may commonly know a copy is unauthorized), trademark counterfeiting involves passing off an illegal unauthorized copy for a genuine product. In many cases, a counterfeit product will not only display an identical or substantially similar trademark owned by another, but the packaging will include the name and the address of the lawful manufacturer as well. For example, just imagine that a store sells new golf clubs with the trademark "Taylor-Made" on them, even though they are counterfeits. How is the average consumer to tell that the golf clubs are not really TaylorMades if they look exactly like the genuine product? While consumer deception as to the origin of the goods is often not an issue in copyright piracy, consumer deception can be an element of trademark counterfeiting as some consumers are deceived into believing that they are purchasing an authentic product when they purchase a fake. However, not all consumers who purchase counterfeit products are deceived. Depending on the category of goods, some consumers may knowingly purchase a counterfeit product. For example, in the area of high-end luxury items such as clothing, watches, handbags, many consumers knowingly purchase counterfeits of "Gucci" bags, "Rolex" watches, and the like, as they are seeking the prestige of the brand without having to pay the expense of the authentic product. Another area in which trademark counterfeiting differs from copyright piracy is in the area of consumer health and safety. Consumers have suffered injuries and even death from unsafe and inferior quality counterfeits, such as food items and pharmaceuticals.

Most experts believe that trademark counterfeiting is the most serious form of commercial piracy today and that the bulk of the $650 billion annual losses from commercial piracy can be attributed to trademark counterfeiting. One reason why trademark counterfeiting leads to higher losses is that copyright piracy occurs primarily in a limited category of products: audio-visual products that contain movies, music, and computer programs. By contrast, trademark counterfeiting now occurs in any category of goods or services protected by a trademark: the variety of products that are counterfeited is limited only by whether the counterfeiter can make a profit by selling fakes. As the next section on counterfeiting in China makes clear, the type of products subject to counterfeiting by enterprising criminals is seemingly unlimited—even cars can be counterfeited.

All commercial piracy is driven by a strong economic incentive. In the area of trademark counterfeiting, the economic incentive may be the most compelling. Take, for example, an entrepreneur in a developing country that is considering entering into the consumer products business that is now dominated by famous brands owned by MNEs. The entrepreneur may find the market entry barriers to be so costly as to be prohibitive. The MNE may have spent substantial resources in research and development to create high quality and high performance products. The MNE may also have spent significant sums in television and media advertising to create goodwill for its brands with local consumers. Even if a competitor expended significant resources, a new product might be unable to compete with an established brand that now enjoys strong consumer loyalty. Counterfeiters, however, have low market entry costs. A counterfeit of the famous brand will be able to "free ride" on the goodwill that the MNE has created for the brand. A counterfeit of a famous brand will have an established demand and market. As fierce global competition has now forced MNEs to expend millions of dollars to differentiate their products through branding, certain established brands are now more commercially valuable than ever and have created an even greater economic incentive to copy.

Because commercial piracy has now become a highly lucrative global trade requiring organizations with substantial resources and an international reach, large scale criminal organizations have become involved in trademark counterfeiting. Take, for example, the trade in counterfeit cigarettes. High profits, relatively low risk, and low cost have made the trade in counterfeit cigarettes highly attractive to criminal organizations. With a profit margin of more than ten to one, the trade in counterfeit cigarettes rivals that for narcotics, but the risks are much lower. Under the U.S. Trademark Counterfeiting Act of 1984, the maximum term of imprisonment is ten years, whereas prison sentences for drug trafficking are routinely much higher. And, while enforcement against drug trafficking is a high level priority in every country in the world, enforcement against counterfeiting is often given a much lower priority by some law enforcement officials. Even in the United States, which has the strongest enforcement regime for intellectual property in the world, brand owners often bemoan the lack of priority given to their interests by U.S. Customs and other enforcement agencies.

Most of the counterfeit cigarettes in the United States are manufactured in China. To effectively carry out this trade, it is necessary to be able to produce and manufacture the cigarettes in China, to package and ship them to the United States using false documentation so the containers can enter the U.S. undetected, and to be able to distribute the cigarettes to reach the consumer. As most legitimate cigarette manufacturers use only large qualified distributors in the United States, it becomes necessary to locate "soft spots" in the market or those secondary distributors or "sub-jobbers" (sub-distributors) who receive their supplies from the qualified distributor but who are also willing to mix counterfeit cigarettes into their supply of genuine products. The size and scope of this trade takes organization, planning, and resources that can only be supplied by large scale criminal organizations. Customs officials in the U.S. believe that criminal organizations in Asia have "foot soldiers" in China, Hong Kong, and the United States all coordinating the trade in counterfeit cigarettes goods. Because of the high profits involved, these Asian criminal organizations are considered to be every bit as ruthless and violent as the South American cartels dealing in drug trafficking.

Not only are profits high, but the costs of the trade in counterfeit cigarettes are also much lower than the costs involved in drug trafficking. Narcotics must always be hidden from sight even when they are consumed. This means that special arrangements must be made for storage, transportation, and distribution. Counterfeit cigarettes, however, can be transported in plain sight, use ordinary storage facilities, and can be consumed in public.

As the table below indicates, seizures of counterfeit and other infringing products at ports of entry in the United States by U.S. Customs officials have risen sharply in the past several years.

Number and Domestic Value of IPR Seizures

Fiscal Year	Value of Seizures	Number of Seizures
2010	$188,125,346	19,959
2009	$260,697,937	14,841
2008	$272,728,879	14,992
2007	$196,754,377	13,657
2006	$155,369,236	14,675
2005	$93,234,510	8,022

Source: Intellectual Property Rights 2010 Seizure Statistics—Final Report, U.S. Customs Office.

According to the U.S. government statistics in the chart below, most of the counterfeits and other infringing goods originate in China, which accounts for 79% of the total. If seizures from Hong Kong, through which many counterfeits and other infringing goods made in China are trans-shipped, are also included, China accounts for nearly 90% or $232 million of the $261 million worth of counterfeits and other infringing goods seized by U.S. Customs. Of course, what is seized by Customs can represent only a tiny fraction of what actually enters the United States. At present, U.S. Customs conducts full inspections on less than 5% of all containers that enter U.S. ports of entry. One reason is the lack of sufficient resources to perform wider-scale random inspections; another reason is that delay caused by inspections may impede the flow of commerce and trade. In most cases, U.S. Customs officials will not conduct a full inspection, which involves opening up the container. Instead, Customs officials typically perform a physical search only when there is some reason to believe that illegal products are involved. This type of information assumes that the brand owner has accurate intelligence that is gathered through the use of private investigation companies. Otherwise, it is likely that the containers will enter the United States without undergoing inspection.

U.S. Customs and Border Protection and U.S. Immigration and Customs Enforcement
FY 2009 Top Trading Partners for IPR Seizures

Trading Partner	Domestic Value	Percent of Total Seizures
China	$204,656,093	79%
Hong Kong	$26,887,408	10%
India	$3,047,311	1%

Trading Partner	Domestic Value	Percent of Total Seizures
Taiwan	$2,453,914	Less than 1%
Korea	$1,510,443	Less than 1%
Paraguay	$1,496,043	Less than 1%
Philippines	$1,479,958	Less than 1%
Switzerland	$1,277,646	Less than 1%
Pakistan	$710,658	Less than 1%
Vietnam	$603,529	Less than 1%
All Others	$16,573,934	6%

Source: Intellectual Property Rights 2010 Seizure Statistics—Final Report, U.S. Customs Office 99.

c. Patent Infringements

Patent infringements refer to the unauthorized copying, manufacture, use, and sale of products protected by patents owned by another. Patent infringements are sometimes distinguished from commercial piracy involving copyright infringement and trademark counterfeiting. Part III of TRIPS includes heightened enforcement requirements only for trademark and copyright piracy, but not patent infringement. During the TRIPS negotiations, patent infringement was not perceived as a "commercial piracy" problem. The difference in perception stems in part from the fact that patent infringement lawsuits more typically involve business disputes between legitimate competitors. Moreover, the worst cases of possible patent infringement in the past often involved cases in which countries simply did not provide patent protection before TRIPS, such as in the case of pharmaceuticals in many developing countries where as much as 60% of all pharmaceuticals are unauthorized copies. Instead of dealing with any of these patent controversies under the rubric of commercial piracy, WTO countries chose to address them in the basic patent provisions in Articles 27 through 34, and later in the Doha Declaration and Implementation Agreement. The reluctance of WTO countries to characterize the unauthorized manufacture of pharmaceuticals as "commercial piracy" no doubt stemmed from heightened sensitivities to the role medicines play in public health and saving lives. The issue continues to be a topic of intense debate and controversy within the WTO.

PROBLEM 6–1

You are the CEO of MovieMax, an independent film studio based in Hollywood. Your studio also licenses rights to Computer Arts Corp. to make video games based on action movies your studio produces. MovieMax has had a tremendously successful year with one futuristic martial arts blockbuster *Dragon Reloaded*, which brought in $180 million in profits from theatre viewings in the U.S. Critics raved about the movie, and millions of viewers flocked to the box office to see the movie, some even several times. More profits are expected once the movie hits theatres abroad. Profits from the video game for the movie brought in $200 million more in this year alone. But so far, MovieMax, which just opened up shop two years ago, has spent virtually no resources on combating piracy.

As MovieMax anticipates the release of *Dragon Reloaded* on DVD, your General Counsel has informed you that unauthorized hard copies of the movie and video game can already be found among unauthorized street sellers in big cities in the U.S. (especially New York and LA), Asia, and Europe, and digital copies can be found on many unauthorized websites on the Internet. The GC recommends pouring in at least $30 million to build immediately a "corporate security department" to combat piracy worldwide.

However, an independent consultant who specializes in piracy detection and who has been hired by the Company advises: "You'll always have piracy. You'll never put an end to it. It's like slaying the hydra. Cut off one head, another one grows. Unless you think the piracy is so great that it has taken away most of your profits—which does not appear to be the case, you might spend your money more wisely by developing another blockbuster movie. Your *Dragon* movie proves that millions of people will pay to see a good movie. . . . Don't get me wrong I'd be happy to take more of your money to help you combat piracy, but I would be remiss if I didn't give you a realistic picture of the problem."

As the CEO of MovieMax, what would you do? Whose advice—your GC's or the independent consultant's—would you follow? If you believe MovieMax should devote more resources to combating piracy, how much would you expend?

NOTES AND QUESTIONS

1. *Market Share.* The figures and tables above present a picture of a formidable problem where counterfeit and pirated products can obtain a large market segment or dominate the market for certain types of products. What method do industry groups use to arrive at these figures?

Most IP owners use the following method, or a variant: A brand owner will first determine the total amount of products, genuine and counterfeit, in any given market by conducting a market survey. The brand owner will then determine how much genuine product is present in the market by checking its own distribution records. If there is more product in any given market than has been supplied by the brand owner, the difference will be attributed to counterfeits. For example, suppose that a brand owner hires a marketing and research company to conduct a market survey in the field on the quantities of its trademarked high-end luxury handbag in a large urban area, and it is determined that there are 10,000 handbags in the market with the brand owner's famous logo. The brand owner then checks its distribution records that show that the brand owner shipped 7,500 handbags to the market in question. The brand owner will conclude that there are 2,500 counterfeit handbags in the market or that 25% of the market is occupied by counterfeits. Or suppose that a computer software company manufactures a software program that is a computer operating system. The IP owner will conduct a survey to determine the total number of computers sold in a given market and then determine how many genuine software applications it supplied to the location. The difference between the number of computers in a market and the number of genuine software applications supplied to the location equals the number of pirated copies of the computer software operating system. For example, the software company determines that there were 10,000 computers sold in a given area and that it has supplied 1,000 authorized software applications to that market. The company will conclude that 9,000 applications are pirated or that the piracy rate is 90%.

2. *Losses.* Industry groups claim that losses from commercial piracy are $650 billion annually, which is certainly an impressive and daunting number. What is the method used by industry groups to arrive at this figure?

Most use the following method: they simply multiply the number of estimated counterfeited items by the retail price of the items. Returning to our earlier examples set forth above, if a brand owner determines that there are 10,000 handbags in the market and that 25% or 2,500 pairs of these handbags are counterfeit, the brand owner will then conclude that it has lost the revenue that it would have otherwise earned from the sale of 2,500 genuine handbags at the retail price. Assuming a retail of $500 per handbag (about average for a high-end luxury bag) the losses from counterfeiting are $1.25 million for that market. In the software example above, if the price of an authorized software application is $200 and 9,000 applications are pirated, then the software company will conclude that it has lost $1.8 million in sales revenue for that market.

3. What do you think of the method used by companies to estimate the losses and the size of the commercial piracy problem? Do you believe the claim that every sale of pirated copy blocks the sale of a genuine product at the retail price? For a skeptical view of the methods and losses claimed by multinational companies, see Daniel Chow, *Counterfeiting as an Externality Imposed by Multinational Companies on Developing Countries*, 51 VA. J. INT'L L. 785, 787 (2011).

3. SPECIAL DISCUSSION: COUNTERFEITING IN CHINA

PROBLEM 6–2

The United States has been leading the efforts at developing the Free Trade Area of the Americas (FTAA), a free trade area encompassing all countries in North and South America. A free trade area allows goods from any member country of the area to travel without the payment of customs duties to any other country in the entire area. For goods that originate outside of the free trade area, the importer pays one set of customs duties when the goods first enter a country of the free trade area. From that point forward the goods are allowed to transit duty-free throughout the entire area and under simplified customs procedures. Discussions on the FTAA have stalled, however. It looks as if a free trade area will be created in piecemeal fashion now, if at all. You represent a coalition of brand owners in the United States and have just learned that China has recently been pressuring some its trading partners, particularly countries in South America, to simplify the procedures for clearing Chinese-made goods through customs. Should this be a concern to your group? Would your answer change depending on whether or not the FTAA is eventually established? What if China is able to secure a free trade area with other countries, including from South America?

* * *

In the discussion of commercial piracy in the previous section, one country stands out: the People's Republic of China (China or PRC). Not only does China have the world's most serious copyright piracy problem, but many observers now believe that China accounts for as much as 70–80% of all counterfeit trademark products in the world today. What is remarkable is that until the 1990s, commercial piracy in China was not an international issue at all. How did such a problem of this size and magnitude emerge in such a short period? The next set of readings explores this issue.

STATEMENT OF PROFESSOR DANIEL CHOW BEFORE THE U.S. SENATE GOVERNMENT OVERSIGHT AND MANAGEMENT SUBCOMMITTEE, APRIL 20, 2004

In terms of size, scope, and magnitude, trademark counterfeiting in China is considered by many to be the most serious counterfeiting problem in world history. A recent study by the PRC State Council Research and Development Center reported that in 2001 the PRC economy was flooded with between $19–$24 billion worth of counterfeit goods. Brand owners in China estimate that 15 to 20% of all well-known brands in China are counterfeit and estimate their losses to be in the tens of billions of dollars per year. Counterfeiting is estimated to now account for approximately 8% of China's gross domestic product.

China has also become the platform for the export of counterfeit products to other countries in Asia, Europe, and the United States. In 2003, China accounted for 66% or over $62 million of the $94 million of all counterfeit and other types of infringing goods seized by the US Customs Service at ports of entry into the United States. An ominous development is that beginning in 2004, exports of counterfeits from China to the United States and other parts of the world may begin to increase significantly for the foreseeable future.

There are several explanations for the unprecedented size and scope of counterfeiting in China:

(1) *Foreign Direct Investment and Advanced Technology*. In recent years, China's economy has enjoyed unprecedented growth for an economy of its size with growth rates of 9.8% from 1980–92 and at 9% more recently. According to some estimates, China is on track to have the world's largest economy in the first decades of the twenty-first century. This is a remarkable achievement for a nation that was mired in backwardness and poverty just several decades ago.

This economic growth has been fueled in large part by foreign direct investment from multi-national enterprises. In the 1990s, China emerged as the world's second largest recipient of foreign direct investment behind only the United States and in 2002, China surpassed the United States to become the world's largest recipient of foreign direct investment with $50 billion of foreign capital inflows. FDI is the best means in the world today for the transfer of advanced technology, intellectual property, and other forms of valuable information. In many cases today the intellectual property component of a FDI in the form of patents, copyrights, and trademarks is the most important component of the foreign investment. For example, the value of the Coca–Cola trademark in China is worth many more times to that company than the millions of dollars in capital that it has invested in China. The same is true for the patents and copyrights owned by pharmaceutical companies and software companies doing business in China today. However, while MNEs are creating a transfer of technology through FDI that is being absorbed into China's legitimate economy through joint ventures and wholly foreign owned enterprises, some of this intellectual property is also being diverted into China's illegitimate economy as pirates steal this technology to engage in counterfeiting and other forms of commercial piracy. It is no coincidence that China, the world's largest recipient of FDI, advanced technology, and intellectual property also has the world's most serious commercial piracy problem.

(2) *State Support of Counterfeiting and Local Protectionism.* No problem of this size and scope could exist without the direct or indirect involvement of the state. In China, the national government in Beijing appears to be sincere in its recognition of the importance of protecting intellectual property rights, but national level authorities are policy and law-making bodies whereas enforcement occurs on the ground at the local level. At this level, local governments are either directly or indirectly involved in supporting the trade in counterfeit goods. Counterfeiting has become so important that this illegal trade now supports entire local economies and a crackdown on counterfeiting would result in a shutdown of the local economy with all of the attendant costs of unemployment, dislocation, social turmoil, and chaos. Because the costs of a crackdown at the local level can be so severe, counterfeiting is heavily defended at local levels.

(3) *Ineffective Legal Enforcement and Lack of Deterrence.* China has a developing legal system that is weak in many respects by comparison to legal systems in advanced industrialized countries such as the United States. While China's intellectual property laws are now considered by most observers to be in compliance with the standards set by TRIPS, enforcement of these laws remains inadequate and fails to create sufficient deterrence to counterfeiting.

The combination of these factors—the world's largest influx of foreign direct investment and widespread access to advanced technology, direct or indirect government involvement and support of the counterfeit trade, and a weak legal system that does not create sufficient deterrence for counterfeiters in a very lucrative trade—has resulted in a counterfeiting and commercial piracy problem that is unprecedented in world history.

NOTES AND QUESTIONS

1. If history is any guide, most nations appear to experience a surge in commercial piracy at some point in their history when they reach a certain stage of economic development. The United States was the leading pirate nation of the day in the nineteenth century as copies of books published by Charles Dickens and other foreign authors were made available in the U.S. without payment of royalties. *See* Oded Shenkar, THE CHINESE CENTURY 82 (2005). Why shouldn't China have the same opportunity to accelerate its economic growth that the U.S. had in the nineteenth century by copying technology free of charge just as the U.S. did? Are the United States and other developed countries being consistent in their treatment of China and much of the developing world?

2. Professor Chow notes that exports of counterfeit goods from China may increase dramatically now and in the future. Why? The increase in counterfeit goods may stem in large part from China's reform of export laws to liberalize trade consistent with its WTO obligations.

Under China's prior laws, only certain state-owned trading companies had the right to export or import goods. To export, a counterfeiter had to engage a compliant state trading company to handle an export transaction for a fee. As a result of China's entry into the WTO in 2001, however, China had to eliminate the state monopoly on trading rights as a measure to further liberalize its economy. China amended the Foreign Trade Law effective as of July 1, 2004, which eliminated the state monopoly on export rights. With the exception of certain kinds of goods, such as crude oil, cotton, and some foodstuffs, which must be traded by the government, all business operators now have the right to export directly. One unintended consequence of the reform in law: the amendment of the Foreign Trade Law effectively allows counterfeiters to export on their own without the assistance of an intermediary and without the payment of extra fees. While there was no shortage of compliant state trading companies willing to assist in the export of counterfeits, the use of a state trading company involved an extra step of finding an intermediary and the payment of a fee. In addition, while the sale of counterfeit goods in China is subject to criminal laws, there may be a loophole that would exempt exports of counterfeits from criminal liability under PRC law. Thus, perhaps paradoxically, China's elimination of the state monopoly and liberalization of trade policies consistent with WTO obligations has created an environment in which exports of counterfeits from China might rise sharply. A comparison of U.S. government statistics on p. 673 supra shows that the value of counterfeit goods seized by U.S. Customs more than doubled from $93 million in 2005 to $188 million in 2010.

3. *WTO Challenge.* The U.S. challenged China's law "relating to the importation into China, and/or distribution within China, of certain products consisting of reading materials, audiovisual products, sound recordings, and

films for theatrical release." China–Measures Affecting Trading Rights and Distribution Services for Certain Publications and Audiovisual Entertainment Products, WT/DS363/AB/R (Dec. 21, 2009), ¶ 125. According to the United States, China restricted U.S. entities from importing or distributing such works in China except through Chinese state-owned or state-approved channels, in violation of China's Protocol of Accession to the WTO, the General Agreement on Tariffs and Trade (GATT) 1994, and the General Agreement on Trade in Services (GATS). Both the Panel and the Appellate Body agreed with the U.S. argument and recommended that China bring its law into conformity. *Id.* ¶ 417.

* * *

Commercial piracy may raise concerns that go beyond intellectual property rights. Consider the following reading.

ORGANIZED CRIME, LOCAL PROTECTIONISM, AND THE TRADE IN COUNTERFEIT GOODS IN CHINA

Daniel C.K. Chow.
14 China Economic Review 473–484 (2003).*

This paper examines the role of organized crime and local protectionism in promoting and protecting the trade in counterfeit goods in the People's Republic of China ("PRC" or "China"). By "organized crime," this paper refers to a group of persons or entities acting in concert to engage in criminal conduct within an overall organizational structure and under the direction of an individual or group of individuals. "Local protectionism" refers to the role of local governments in protecting illegal activity by failing to fully enforce the law. Note that under the definitions set forth above some forms of local protectionism may also be considered forms of organized crime.

The Role of Organized Crime and Local Protectionism

The illegal trade in counterfeit goods in China can be divided into two components: manufacture and distribution. Criminal organizations play a significant role in the manufacturing side whereas local governments are involved in the distribution side. Local governments also protect the illegal but useful economic activity of counterfeiters through the imposition of light fines and penalties, which do not serve as a deterrent to further counterfeiting by the same offender.

A. *Manufacture and Organized Crime*

The manufacture of counterfeits appears to be concentrated in the southeastern region of China, mostly in Fujian and Guangdong Provinces. Fujian, located across the China Straits from Taiwan, is the ancestral home of many Taiwanese. Guangdong Province is adjacent to Hong Kong

and the ancestral home of many Hong Kongese. Both Guangdo.
Fujian Provinces were some of the first areas opened to foreign in.
ment in China and were some of the first locations for sino-foreign ju
ventures and wholly foreign owned enterprises engaged in the manufac
ture of famous international brands of consumer products. Both of these
areas were among the first areas in China to legally acquire foreign
technology used in the production and manufacture of famous brands.
Some of this technology and know-how has been acquired for illegal
purposes. In a pattern that appears throughout other parts of China, an
area where legitimate manufacturing is concentrated has given rise to
illegal underground factories manufacturing counterfeits of the genuine
products that are manufactured in nearby factories under the authority of
the intellectual property owner.

Criminal organizations based in Hong Kong and Taiwan who have
maintained connections with their ancestral homelands often provide the
financing for the underground factories that manufacture illegal counterfeits in Guangdong and Fujian province. Anecdotal evidence indicates that
these are the same criminal organizations that are involved in smuggling
products into China, narcotics, prostitution, and pornography.

These criminal organizations promoting the counterfeit trade in China benefit from the jurisdictional and legal issues that are created by the
international borders that separate Hong Kong and Taiwan from mainland China. As Hong Kong is an autonomous administrative unit of China,
it continues to maintain its own police force, system of courts, and laws.
As a result, police in China must work together with police in Hong Kong
to pursue Hong Kong criminal organizations that support counterfeiting
in Guangdong. The involvement of more than one set of enforcement
authorities, laws, and legal systems create practical and logistical problems that impede law enforcement. In the case of Taiwan-based criminal
organizations, the political problems that continue to divide China and
Taiwan result in little or no law enforcement cooperation across the China
Straits and Taiwan enforcement authorities have shown little interest in
pursuing Taiwan persons or corporations for illegal activity on mainland
China. Many Taiwan organizations feel that they can act with relative
impunity in China.

(1) Exports: Counterfeit Cigarettes

Recent investigations by US tobacco companies have revealed that
these criminal organizations are heavily involved in the export of counterfeit cigarettes made in China to the United States.

A carton of genuine premium cigarettes sells in the United States for
about $35.00 in many states; a high quality carton of counterfeits pro-
duced in China can sell for as much as $30.00 in the U.S. while the cost of
producing a counterfeit carton is $3.00. [A]t a recent meeting, U.S.
Customs officials reported that every day containers of counterfeit cigarettes produced in China are unloaded from ships in Los Angeles port and
enter the United States under false import documents as U.S. officials are

682

...ue to detect and seize all of these containers. Each container that is ...ized has a street value of $1–$1.5 million dollars, yet the cost of producing the counterfeit product in the container to the manufacturer is about $80,000. In the same meeting, U.S. Customs officials estimated that as many as 8–10 containers pass through Los Angeles Customs undetected everyday. On the basis of the street value of each container at $1–1.5 million, the trade in counterfeit cigarettes produced in China and exported to the United States through Los Angeles port alone likely exceeds $1 billion per year. Criminal organizations with entities active in the United States, China, and Hong Kong are known to be behind this highly successful trade.

B. Distribution and Local Protectionism

The manufacture of counterfeit products is of little use if the products cannot be delivered to the end-use consumer. For this reason, the distribution of counterfeit products to retail levels of commerce is crucial to the counterfeit trade in China as elsewhere in the world. Large, legitimate wholesale distributors deliver products to state-owned stores or foreign-owned chain stores. Counterfeits cannot enter retail markets through these regular channels.

In China, the distribution of counterfeit products occurs through a series of large open-air or partially enclosed wholesale markets located in densely populated areas with convenient transportation access. These markets are often massive in size and can contain more than one thousand outlets, each a wholesale distributor, occupying a stall or a semi-finished storefront. In the author's experience there is no wholesale market in China that does not carry counterfeit and infringing goods for sale. Many wholesale dealers have counterfeit goods on open display while others will display genuine products but have counterfeits in a back room or under the counter and available for the asking. In the heart of Beijing, hundreds of small retail vendors swarm the Tianyi wholesale market everyday and use three wheel bicycles, lorries, and small trucks to furnish the street stalls, open air kiosks, and small retail stores with abundant supplies of counterfeit and infringing products.

These wholesale markets are established and regulated by the local Administration of Industry and Commerce (AIC), a branch of the local government responsible for promoting, regulating, and policing commercial activity. In a typical situation, AICs will invest their own funds in establishing the wholesale market and will collect rent from each of the individual wholesale distributors. In addition, AICs will issue business licenses for a fee to each individual proprietor. Once the business is in operation, AICs will also collect a management fee from each individual proprietor. In a large wholesale market such as Tianyi, the operating revenues to the local AIC can easily exceed $100,000 per year. As noted above, many if not most of these wholesale distributors deal in counterfeit goods. As AICs are also one of the primary government entities in China charged with the enforcement against counterfeiting, AICs are faced with a conflict of interest as they are charged with policing and enforcing the very markets in which AICs and the local government have a substantial investment and financial interest. Shutting down these wholesale markets would not only result in a direct loss of revenue to the AIC but would also have many repercussions as many retail businesses, hotels, restaurants, and nightclubs are all supported by the trade in counterfeit goods. In some cities, such as Yiwu discussed below, the entire local economy is connected to the trade in counterfeits.

[T]here are at least five major wholesale markets in China: Hanzhen Jie in Wuhan City, Hubei Province; Linyi Market in Linyi, Shandong Province; Nansantiao Market in Shijiazhuang in Hebei Province; China Small Commodities City in Yiwu City, Zhejiang Province; and Wuai Market in Shenyang, Liaoning Province. Together these markets serve the entire coastal region of China and its most populous urban areas including Guangzhou in the south, to Shanghai in the east and Beijing and Tianjin in the northeast. A branch of the China Small Commodities City market of Yiwu located in Wulumuqi in Xinjiang Province serves as an export post for the Middle East and Eastern Europe. These markets (represented by circles) and their relationship to the manufacturing centers (shaded areas) are set forth in the map below:

Major Distributors and Manufacturers of Counterfeit Goods in China

1. The Zhejiang China Small Commodities City Group, Ltd.

A sense of the formidable size, scope, organization, and resources of these wholesale markets is provided by a review of the China Small Commodities City wholesale market in Yiwu, Zhejiang Province, one of the most highly organized and successful wholesale markets for counterfeit and infringing goods in China.

In 1982, the Yiwu Administration of Industry and Commerce established the Zhejiang China Small Commodities City Group, Ltd. (hereinafter CSCG), a wholesale market specializing in trading small commodities.[1] By its own estimates, the Yiwu City AIC invested US$10 million to establish this market, which immediately experienced rapid and sustained growth. Recognizing the potential for further growth and the potential for expanding into related businesses, the Yiwu City AIC and related government entities decided to privatize the management and operation of the wholesale markets by forming the CSCG as a limited liability stock company in 1993. Privatization extended to management only but not to ownership of the CSCG. A majority interest in the CSCG continues to be held by state and collective enterprises and a substantial minority interest is held by individuals.

a. Privatization

Privatization has served a critical strategic purpose for the CSCG. Under previous practice so long as the markets were under the direct management of the AIC or other local government entities, all revenues derived from such operations had to be transferred to the national government treasury with some portion of the funds returned as a type of rebate to the local government. After privatization, the company became responsible for its own profits and losses and company revenues and profits can be distributed in any manner in accordance with management directives. An additional advantage of privatization is that the company can now branch out into other related business[es] that are beyond the scope of the AIC's jurisdiction, which is limited to regulating markets. This allows the privatized company to form a conglomerate of different businesses and to benefit from the synergy that such a combination creates. Forming a conglomerate of different businesses was far more difficult to accomplish so long as the markets were directly under the management of the AIC with its circumscribed jurisdiction. Privatization has served the key function of allowing the shareholders of the company direct access to the substantial wealth generated by the company and has created the framework for aggressive expansion.

The CSCG is unique among the wholesale markets in China described in this paper in that it is the only distribution center to the author's knowledge to have privatized its operations.

---

1. The information in this section was gathered through the course of several weeks of investigation in Yiwu by the author working with a private investigation company.

b. Ties with Local Government

Although ostensible efforts were made to sever direct connections between government entities and the business operations of the CSCG, there are still strong ties between the CSCG and local government. In practice, the process of privatization meant that many of the same government officials responsible for forming and operating the CSCG left their government posts and assumed leadership roles within the corporation as private citizens. The lines between government and private spheres, however, continue to be blurred. The CSCG Chairman is a former vice mayor of Yiwu who continues to maintain office space in the Yiwu city government building. The Director of the Yiwu City AIC was also at the same time the legal representative of the CSCG's largest corporate shareholder. The Director is said to have resigned from all CSCG offices and is currently a director of one of Yiwu's four municipal offices, but his name continues to be listed second on a list of the CSCG's top executives in the CSCG's internal documents. The Vice–Director of the Yiwu City Government Municipal offices uses a name card that also bears the logo and the name of the Small Commodities City Market. It appears to be a common practice for Yiwu government officials to use name cards with the China Small Commodities City logo. In practice, the CSCG conducts its affairs as if it carries government authority. In the case of the CSCG, as in many other instances in China, the line between a private enterprise and government authority is blurred.

Given the historical and present links between the Yiwu government and the CSCG and the CSCG's importance to the local economy, it is reasonable to assume that there is a *de facto* partnership between the Yiwu government and the CSCG. This partnership is likely to be a significant cause of the CSCG's remarkable growth from US$470,000 in sales in 1982 to US$2.2 billion in 1996—a growth of 4,700% in 14 years. It is also reasonable to assume that the CSCG and the Yiwu City government are well aware of the size and magnitude of the traffic in counterfeit goods in the CSCG markets and elsewhere in Yiwu.

c. Shareholding and Corporate Structure

With a total registered capital of US $14 million, the CSCG currently has six corporate shareholders, all state owned or collectively owned enterprises, which own 55.59% of all shares. The shareholders and their respective shareholder's interest in percentage terms and value in RMB are:

(1) Zhejiang Yiwu China Small Commodities City Hengda Development Corp. Capital Contribution RMB 43,211,300 (37%);

(2) Yiwu City Financial Development Corp. Capital Contribution: RMB 6,600,000 (5.7%);

(3) Zhejiang Province International Trust Investment Corp. Capital Contribution: RMB 5,500,000 (4.7%);

(4) Zhejiang Province Financial Development Corp. Capital Contribution: RMB 5,500,000 (4.7%);

(5) Zhongxin Trading Corp. Capital Contribution: RMB 2,200,000 (1.9%);

(6) Shanghai Shenyin Bond Corp. Capital Contribution: RMB 2,200,000 (1.9%).

Individual shareholders own 41% of all total shares worth RMB 47,401,200 and employees of the CSCG own 2.5% of all total shares worth RMB 2,887,500.

The CSCG operates through a board of directors, with a president, and a CSCG parent holding company that has a president's office, and separate departments for marketing, development, finance and securities. The CSCG parent holding company operates through a series of 14 wholly owned subsidiaries that have expanded into other businesses, most of which directly or indirectly support its trading operations through its wholesale markets, which seems to remain the CSCG's core business. These subsidiaries are as follows:

(1) China Small Commodities Market ("CSCM") Management Company

(2) CSCM Property Management Company

(3) CSCM Information Internet Company

(4) CSCM Hengda Development Company

(5) CSCM Trading Development Company

(6) Yindu Hotel Limited Liability Company

(7) Shangcheng Hotel

(8) Yiwu City Finance Development Company

(9) CSCM Real Estate Company

(10) CSCM Advertising Company

(11) Shangcheng Urban Credit Cooperative

(12) Yiwu City Property Right Exchange

(13) CSCM Highway Construction Co., Ltd.

(14) CSCM Exhibition Company

One CSCG subsidiary, the CSCM Management Company, actually engages in the trading of counterfeit goods and serves a major role in distribution of these products to the CSCG's branch markets. The CSCM internet company has set up a website advertising numerous small commodities for sale, creating worldwide access to goods sold in Yiwu and attracting buyers worldwide. Notable among the other subsidiaries is the Yindu Hotel Limited Liability Company, which operates a four star hotel that is by far the best hotel in Yiwu and that is part of a complex also housing the corporate headquarters of the CSCG, which includes a nightclub and karaoke bar in the lower level of the hotel. The CSCG has also set up a trade development subsidiary that has been exploring the establishment of representative branches in countries abroad, although the recent economic downturn seems to have curtailed these expansion efforts for the time being.

d. The CSCG Yiwu Wholesale Markets

The CSCG manages the China Small Commodities City, which has been by far the largest wholesale market in the PRC for the past six successive years. In 1996, the last year for which statistics published by the Yiwu City AIC are available, the market reached a floor space of over 500,000 square meters and had over 24,000 booths. The CSCG rents these booths to individual proprietors who hold individual business licenses. Over 50,000 business people operate in this market and over 200,000 people visit the market each day to conduct business. Based upon the author's own experience, at least 90% of the products sold in the China Small Commodities Market are either counterfeit or infringing products.

During a four year period in the 1990's, the wholesale market grew at a rate of over 100% annually and its average annual growth rate through the entire history of the market is 90%. From 1991 to 1996, total volume of business in the market grew 22 times from US$100 million in 1991 to US$2.2 billion in 1996. No official data are available after 1997, but even assuming a modest growth rate, total sales for the China Small Commodities City wholesale market should reach nearly US$3 billion in 2003. Revenues at this level would place the CSCG above the largest multinational enterprises doing business in China.

Given its rapid growth, the China Small Commodity Cities has quickly assumed a major role in supporting the entire local economy. In the 1990's, the tax revenues from the wholesale market operations have averaged 26% of the entire tax revenues for the city of Yiwu. CSCG's total annual revenue from rental fees alone paid by the 30,000 wholesalers and 3,500 stores is about US$55 million. Total annual management fees paid by individual businesses to the local AIC are about US$6 million. Total local taxes paid by individual businesses in the CSCG wholesale markets to the Yiwu city government are approximately US$8 million. The CSCG appears to be involved in virtually every aspect of the local economy with over 50 pages of listings in the local 112 page phone book related to the CSCG. The remarkable growth of the CSCG's trade in counterfeit goods and the growth of other wholesale markets parallel the recent sharp rise in the amount of counterfeiting in the PRC.

15 YEAR DEVELOPMENT OF CHINA SMALL COMMODITY CITY WHOLESALE MARKET

	1982	1983	1984	1985	1986	1987	1988	1989	1990	1991	1992	1993	1994	1995	1996
Number of Booths	750	1050	1874	2874	5500	5600	6130	8400	10500	10500	13910	13910	22731	15747	24069
Business Area (m² in 1000's)	4.252	4.252	4.252	13.59	13.59	57	57	57	57	57	103	103	269	269	500.1
Business Vol (RMB, million)	3.92	14.44	23.21	61.90	100.29	153.8	265	390	606	1025	2054	4515.2	10212	15200	18468
Business Vol Annual Growth (%)	/	268	61	167	62	54	72	47	55	67	99	120	126	49	21.5
Tax Volume (RMB 1000)	160	380	640	1290	2840	5650	9360	14870	19760	42050	42350	55750	52100	61640	/
Tax Volume Annual Growth (%)	/	137	68	102	120	99	66	59	33	113	0.7	32	-0.7	18	/
% of Total YIWU Tax Revenues	0.64	1.12	1.02	2.03	5.24	9.45	11.09	17.45	24.1	28	31	25.14	24.69	23.8	/

e. *Role of Yiwu in Distribution*

Yiwu serves as a central distribution center for counterfeit goods to markets around the country. At the center of town, two large transportation companies occupy two open area transport areas, both the size of football fields. Around the perimeter of these areas are representative local transport offices from cities and towns all over China. Operating continuously day and night, trucks and lorries unload counterfeit products made in southern China in factories financed by criminal organizations in Hong Kong and Taiwan in one open transport area for storage and sale in Yiwu's wholesale markets. In the other open transport area, other trucks and lorries load counterfeit products already bought from these wholesale markets for delivery to all parts of China.

f. *Importance of the CSCG to the Local Economy*

As this brief examination of the CSCG indicates, the trade in counterfeit goods has become an integral part of the Yiwu economy. Businesses that engage in the sale of counterfeit products pay taxes to the local government, which support public services for the local economy. This point is worth emphasizing because brand owners have argued that China suffers from a loss of tax revenues on counterfeit goods that otherwise would be paid by legitimate manufacturers on sales that are lost to counterfeiting. In Yiwu, local businesses operating within the CSCG markets negotiate a flat tax rate that becomes a substantial portion of the tax revenue of the city, thus helping to integrate the economic benefits of counterfeiting into the local economy. The myriad other businesses operated by the CSCG all depend directly or indirectly on the robust trade in counterfeit goods. The second point worth emphasizing is the close link between the CSCG, composed of former or current government officials,

and the Yiwu government. This link suggests that the operations of the CSCG will be strongly defended at local levels.

* * *

PROBLEM 6–3

You are an industry consultant to MNCs that are frustrated with the counterfeiting problem in China, but enthusiastic about the "get tough" approach discussed in the excerpt below. You have been asked: (1) How might this approach backfire and actually make the counterfeiting problem in China worse, inciting counterfeiting to higher levels? (2) How might the enforcement-based approach create incentives for the private enforcement industry that encourages perpetuating counterfeiting in China instead of eradicating it? Consult the article below.

ANTI–COUNTERFEITING STRATEGIES OF MULTINATIONAL COMPANIES IN CHINA

Daniel Chow.
41 Geo. J. Int'l L. 749, 760–65 (2010).

1. Brand Protection Units

Many MNCs have established their own dedicated brand protection units that specialize in the enforcement of intellectual property rights. MNCs that have set up internal brand protection units usually establish the unit under the corporate security department and not the legal department because anti-counterfeiting is viewed as a type of investigative and enforcement activity that is similar to police work. These units are supervised by a brand protection manager. Within many MNCs, brand protection managers (members of the corporate security department) report to brand managers or general managers (members of the business or marketing department). Many MNCs have a business manager of a particular brand or trademarked product. Within an MNC in China, a business manager will be assigned to manage the advertising, marketing, and sales of a famous trademarked or branded product and will be evaluated based upon the total sales revenue and market penetration of the product. The brand manager performs a core function for MNCs in the consumer products business and outranks the brand protection manager in the corporate hierarchy of most MNCs. The brand protection manager supports the brand manager.

Brand protection units assist the PRC authorities in enforcement. Only PRC government entities are permitted by law to engage in actual enforcement. However, MNCs use their brand protection units, sometimes with the help of private investigation companies, to support PRC government enforcement entities in locating and identifying the counterfeiter. Armed with the appropriate intelligence, the MNC's representatives (accompanied by private investigators or outside lawyers) go directly to the

PRC authorities and ask for a raid. If the parties are familiar with each other because of a prior business relationship, the PRC authorities will often, within fifteen minutes to half an hour, initiate a raid. The MNCs representatives are usually allowed to accompany PRC authorities. The MNCs representatives sit in the vans or trucks used by the enforcement authorities and give directions to the counterfeiter's location (the location is not revealed until the raid is in motion to avoid tip offs). Representatives of the MNC are usually present at the raid to identify the counterfeit products for PRC officials.

Brand protection managers have vowed to take off the kid gloves and "get tough" in dealing with counterfeiting. The corporate security departments of MNCs have hired ex-military commandos, former special-forces agents from the U.S. military, former FBI agents, and ex-police officials to lead their internal anti-counterfeiting units. These business officials in charge of anti-counterfeiting use a paramilitary approach, vowing to crush counterfeiters by focusing almost entirely on enforcement and intimidation. Their actions consist of raiding counterfeiting sites, "roughing up" suspected counterfeiters found on the premises, seizing counterfeit goods, destroying machinery on the spot, and pursuing criminal sanctions. Some brand protection managers have divided China into "war zones" with persons within the brand protection units and outside contractors referred to as "soldiers" or "warriors." Many brand protection managers within MNCs want to portray anti-counterfeiting as a "war," and issue harsh threats to counterfeiters about the consequences of getting caught. Many brand protection managers want to project an image of toughness, bravado, and swagger.

This "get tough" approach advocated by brand protection managers appears to receive strong support from senior management within many MNCs. This approach creates the impression that MNCs have reached or exceeded their limits of tolerance for counterfeiting and are taking the problem seriously. This approach also promises immediate, tangible results in the form of seized counterfeit goods and equipment.

Within MNCs, many brand managers take the position that every seized counterfeit product results in the recovery of a sale of an authentic product that would have otherwise been lost due to the sale of the counterfeit. Brand managers are constantly putting pressure on brand protection managers for more seizures of counterfeit products. Brand managers are acutely focused on short-term statistics; there is a running week-by-week tally of the number of raids, the number of counterfeits seized, and the amount of equipment destroyed. Brand managers within MNCs act as if each quarter's revenue and profits can be improved by smashing the counterfeiters.

Many of the assumptions underlying this approach are seriously flawed: the notion that consumers would have purchased a genuine product at retail price but for the existence of a counterfeit on the market is highly questionable, since many counterfeits cost a fraction of the price

of a real product. A consumer who purchases a counterfeit luxury watch for $30 will not purchase a genuine article for $3000 but for the existence of the counterfeit on the market. The same is true for a purchaser of counterfeit business or entertainment software, luxury goods, and many other counterfeit items, which are sold at a tiny fraction of the cost of the genuine product. Many consumers who purchase counterfeits would not be willing or be able to pay for the genuine product. Moreover, most consumers who purchase counterfeit products are actively looking to purchase fakes, not genuine products. In China, it is widely known that counterfeits are sold in street markets and small retail stores. Counterfeits are never found in large department stores that purchase only from qualified distributors that are able to exercise tight control over the channels of distribution in order to prevent penetration by counterfeiters. The price of the fake and the place where it is purchased are sure indications that the product is not genuine. Most consumers are rarely deceived into purchasing a counterfeit when they are seeking to purchase a genuine product.

As questionable as these assumptions may be, many MNCs operate their anti-counterfeiting strategies based upon them. Currently, MNCs are actively engaged in raids and seizures on a continuing basis with the assistance of PRC administrative authorities. Some MNCs conduct two or three raids and seizures per week. Many MNCs budget several million dollars per year for anti-counterfeiting activity; almost all of it is concentrated on paying for the costs of enforcement.

2. Private Investigation Companies and Law Firms

The emphasis on enforcement by MNCs has resulted in the rise of a vast and highly lucrative support industry established in recent years to assist MNCs in their battle against counterfeiting. As noted earlier, the PRC authorities conduct the actual raid with the assistance of the MNC, but the preparation that is required for setting up a raid can be extensive because it involves identifying the counterfeiter and finding the location of the counterfeiter's factory or storage facilities. Counterfeiters work underground and are constantly on the move to avoid detection; gathering the intelligence necessary to set up an enforcement action can be time consuming, expensive, and dangerous.

To assist in this investigative work, an entire industry of private investigation companies has risen to offer their services to MNCs. Those MNCs that do not have their own internal units outsource all of their work to third-party private investigators. Even MNCs who have their own internal brand protection units outsource some work because the business of investigation can be quite dangerous. Tracking down counterfeiters involves weeks or months of investigative work and often requires the use of operatives who assume false identities to gain the trust of counterfeiters and infiltrate counterfeiting rings. PRC enforcement authorities do not have the resources to conduct these investigations, and as a result, a large number of investigation companies have been established to complete this work.

Taking their cues from their MNC clients, private investigation companies based in Hong Kong or China also tend to hire managers who have a police or military background. There appears to be a shared culture of "toughness" and swagger that has developed, linking MNC brand protection managers and the private investigation industry.

The private investigation industry in China has grown at a dramatic pace, but there are a number of issues that continue to plague the industry. As a technical legal matter, private companies and individuals are not allowed under PRC law to conduct investigations into illegal activity. These private entities are engaging in what might be viewed as police work, which is reserved to PRC government authorities. However, PRC officials tolerate or accept investigation companies because these officials realize that they lack the resources (or the willingness) to conduct the painstaking investigative work. As a result, these private investigation companies obtain business licenses as "market survey" companies, although it is widely known that they are really engaged in private detective work for MNCs. In China, observers refer to the uncertain status of the private investigation industry as falling in a "gray" area, a euphemism describing an industry that is unregulated, unlicensed, and in which abuses, such as giving bribes to government officials and extorting money from counterfeiters, are commonplace. However, despite its uncertain status (or perhaps because of it), the private investigation industry is highly lucrative and offers opportunities for wealth and advancement for persons with little formal education (since street guile is more important than formal education). Thus, it continues to grow at a steep rate.

Law firms in the PRC and Hong Kong have also developed a role in the anti-counterfeiting business. Lawyers may be necessary to obtain copies of trademark registration certificates to show to PRC authorities, and some brand owners use lawyers to pursue criminal actions against suspected counterfeiters. Some of the law firms involved in the anti-counterfeiting business are multinational firms, with headquarters in the United States or Europe and offices in China. Others are specialized intellectual property law firms established by local PRC lawyers. Some MNCs directly hire law firms and the law firms then hire private investigation companies. Other law firms have established their own private investigation companies that function essentially as a department of the law firm. Some law firms will hire independent private investigation companies to locate the counterfeiter, but insist on conducting the raids themselves in order to seize evidence and collect higher fees from their MNC clients.

The emphasis placed by MNCs on enforcement has given rise to a massive support industry consisting of private investigation firms and law firms.

NOTES AND QUESTIONS

1.   What do you think about the "get tough" approach by MNCs? Might such an approach create legal problems?

2.   Why are local enforcement officials reluctant to shut down counterfeiting? What would happen if China's central leaders ordered a national crackdown on counterfeiting? Brand owners often claim that as counterfeiters pay no taxes, China loses the tax revenue that it would earn from the sales of genuine products that are displaced by counterfeits. Review the chart on page 688. What do you think of this claim? What strategic purpose is served by the payment of taxes by the CSGC, which became the single largest taxpayer in Yiwu?

3.   Most brand owners acknowledge that the issue of enforcement in China does not concern the level of enforcement activity. Rather, the issue has to do with the penalties and sanctions that are meted out to counterfeiters once an enforcement action is concluded. China's State Administration of Industrial and Commerce (AIC), which has local branches with primary responsibility for enforcement of trademark rights, has provided the following statistics for penalties between 1997 and 2009:

AIC TRADEMARK ENFORCEMENT ACTIVITY, 2001–2009

Year	Cases	Average Fine	Criminal Prosecutions
2001	22,813	$1,150	86 total (1 in 265 cases)
2002	23,539	$1,136	59 total (1 in 399 cases)
2003	26,488	$1,142	45 total (1 in 589 cases)
2004	40,171	$834	96 total (1 in 418 cases)
2005	49,412	$1,017	91 total (1 in 542 cases)
2006	50,534	$1,158	252 total (1 in 200 cases)
2007	50,318	$1,220	229 total (1 in 220 cases)
2008	56,634	$1,212	137 total (1 in 413 cases)
2009	51,044	$1,112	92 total (1 in 554 cases)
2010	56,034	$1,149	175 total (1 in 320 cases)

Source: State Administration of Industry and Commerce Annual Statistics.

Based on the statistics, what issues do you see for brand owners?

PROBLEM 6–4

You are general counsel of Ultrasoft, a multi-national consumer products company, headquartered in Country Z, an advanced industrialized country. Country Z does not have a law against making bribes to foreign government officials like the U.S. Foreign Corrupt Practices. You have identified and located the boss and the inner circle of the criminal organization that operates the entire counterfeiting operations for all of your products in China. You have approached the local Public Security Bureau, China's police agency, to make arrests. The police official says, "Sure, we can do that. But we would like a bonus of RMB 80,000 (about $10,000) per arrest, plus we would like an expenses paid weekend stay for five in a luxury hotel in Macau so we can do some research at the local law libraries. There's no room for negotiation here. No payments, no hotel, no arrests."

Your anti-counterfeiting budget in China is $10 million per year. Accordingly, you can afford the payments to the inner circle consisting of the boss and about ten lieutenants. Covering the cost of the weekend stay in Macau would not be a problem, although you seem to recall that Macau is noted for its casinos and nightclubs and doesn't even have a law library. As you are considering the offer, you get word that the counterfeiting boss is getting suspicious and is checking into flights for Europe. Should you pay? Why or why not? Would your answer change depending on whether Country Z is also subject to U.S. law? What do you think about the suggestion made by some experts that Ultrasoft should try either to qualify the counterfeiter to make genuine products or to form a joint venture in China with the counterfeiter?

C. ENFORCEMENT OBLIGATIONS UNDER TRIPS

TRIPS was drafted with special concerns about commercial piracy and the perceived need for improved enforcement of intellectual property around the world. Part III of TRIPS, Articles 41–61, creates enforcement obligations on all WTO members, a first in the history of intellectual property law treaties. The United States was one of the driving forces behind the adoption of Articles 41–61, and much of the U.S.'s concern—as is evident in Article 51 and 52—was to create an effective mechanism to combat the growing problem of the international trade in copyright piracy and trademark counterfeiting.

Part III of TRIPS is divided into five sections: (i) general obligations, (ii) civil procedures and remedies, (iii) provisional measures, (iv) border controls, and (iv) criminal sanctions. Sections 1 through 3 create general provisions of enforcement under TRIPS that apply to all intellectual property rights covered by TRIPS, while Sections 4 and 5 create heightened enforcement requirements to deal with commercial piracy involving copyrighted and trademarked goods. Let us start first with Article 41, which sets forth the general obligations of enforcement all countries must follow:

TRIPS

Article 41

1.   Members shall ensure that enforcement procedures as specified in this Part are available under their law so as to permit effective action against any act of infringement of intellectual property rights covered by this Agreement, including expeditious remedies to prevent infringements and remedies which constitute a deterrent to further infringements. These procedures shall be applied in such a manner as

to avoid the creation of barriers to legitimate trade and to provide for safeguards against their abuse.

2. Procedures concerning the enforcement of intellectual property rights shall be fair and equitable. They shall not be unnecessarily complicated or costly, or entail unreasonable time-limits or unwarranted delays.

3. Decisions on the merits of a case shall preferably be in writing and reasoned. They shall be made available at least to the parties to the proceeding without undue delay. Decisions on the merits of a case shall be based only on evidence in respect of which parties were offered the opportunity to be heard.

4. Parties to a proceeding shall have an opportunity for review by a judicial authority of final administrative decisions and, subject to jurisdictional provisions in a Member's law concerning the importance of a case, of at least the legal aspects of initial judicial decisions on the merits of a case. However, there shall be no obligation to provide an opportunity for review of acquittals in criminal cases.

5. It is understood that this Part does not create any obligation to put in place a judicial system for the enforcement of intellectual property rights distinct from that for the enforcement of law in general, nor does it affect the capacity of Members to enforce their law in general. Nothing in this Part creates any obligation with respect to the distribution of resources as between enforcement of intellectual property rights and the enforcement of law in general.

PROBLEM 6–5

The Republic of Karnia is a large southeast Asian country with a massive counterfeiting problem, one of the worst in the world. Karnia joined the WTO in 2001 and now has laws on the books that comply with or exceed the letter of TRIPS, including laws providing for generous compensatory damages, injunctions, border controls, and severe criminal enforcement for willful IP infringements. Karnia is an impoverished country, however, so it lacks a developed judicial system. Karnia has only a few rudimentary courts that command little, if any respect, within Karnia's own system of government. Most of the judges in Karnia's courts are not lawyers, but are instead retired army generals with no legal training who are seeking a sinecure instead of retirement. Karnia relies mainly on administrative agencies and local police to enforce its laws. Many of Karnia's administrative and police officials have no training in intellectual property at all and do not understand even the most basic concepts of intellectual property. Moreover, most of Karnia's administrative and police officials are engaged in fighting violent crimes and have little interest in pursuing counterfeiting, which they consider to be a harmless economic crime. As a result, counterfeiting is rampant in Karnia. Counterfeiters act brazenly and have no fear whatsoever of the law. MNEs are outraged and are calling for international action. Is Karnia in violation of Article 41?

1. CIVIL/PROVISIONAL REMEDIES (TRIPS ARTICLES 42–50)

TRIPS Articles 42–50 (Sections 2 and 3 of TRIPS Part III) require WTO members to provide for tools for effective civil enforcement against commercial piracy. The drafters of TRIPS had in mind private enforcement through civil litigation, which plays an important role in enforcement in developed countries such as the United States. Among other obligations, members are to create evidentiary presumptions against defendants who destroy evidence (Article 43), make available injunctions that prevent the entry into commerce of imported infringing goods after customs clearance (Article 44), provide damages adequate to compensate the right holder for infringement of intellectual property rights (Article 45), and create a mechanism for the disposal of infringing goods, materials, and implements used to create those goods outside the channels of commerce (Article 46).

Among the most important tools for private enforcement against commercial piracy is the availability of injunctive relief. Article 50 provides for provisional measures:

TRIPS

Article 50

1. The judicial authorities shall have the authority to order prompt and effective provisional measures:

> (a) to prevent an infringement of any intellectual property right from occurring, and in particular to prevent the entry into the channels of commerce in their jurisdiction of goods, including imported goods immediately after customs clearance;

> (b) to preserve relevant evidence in regard to the alleged infringement.

2. The judicial authorities shall have the authority to adopt provisional measures *inaudita altera parte* where appropriate, in particular where any delay is likely to cause irreparable harm to the right holder, or where there is a demonstrable risk of evidence being destroyed.

3. The judicial authorities shall have the authority to require the applicant to provide any reasonably available evidence in order to satisfy themselves with a sufficient degree of certainty that the applicant is the right holder and that the applicant's right is being infringed or that such infringement is imminent, and to order the applicant to provide a security or equivalent assurance sufficient to protect the defendant and to prevent abuse.

4. Where provisional measures have been adopted *inaudita altera parte*, the parties affected shall be given notice, without delay after the execution of the measures at the latest. A review, including a

right to be heard, shall take place upon request of the defendant with a view to deciding, within a reasonable period after the notification of the measures, whether these measures shall be modified, revoked or confirmed.

5. The applicant may be required to supply other information necessary for the identification of the goods concerned by the authority that will execute the provisional measures.

6. Without prejudice to paragraph 4, provisional measures taken on the basis of paragraphs 1 and 2 shall, upon request by the defendant, be revoked or otherwise cease to have effect, if proceedings leading to a decision on the merits of the case are not initiated within a reasonable period, to be determined by the judicial authority ordering the measures where a Member's law so permits or, in the absence of such a determination, not to exceed 20 working days or 31 calendar days, whichever is the longer.

7. Where the provisional measures are revoked or where they lapse due to any act or omission by the applicant, or where it is subsequently found that there has been no infringement or threat of infringement of an intellectual property right, the judicial authorities shall have the authority to order the applicant, upon request of the defendant, to provide the defendant appropriate compensation for any injury caused by these measures.

* * *

Article 50 reflects the practice of the United States, where civil litigation has become an effective tool used by IP owners against infringers. Article 50(2) requires countries to recognize "provisional measures *inaudita altera parte* where appropriate, in particular where any delay is likely to cause irreparable harm to the right holder, or where there is a demonstrable risk of evidence being destroyed." *Inaudita altera parte* means without granting a hearing to the other side.

This provision is modeled on U.S. practice, which allows for provisional pre-trial relief. Under procedures set forth in Rule 65 of the Federal Rules of Civil Procedure, an IP owner is able to appear ex parte before a federal district court and seek a Temporary Restraining Order (TRO) and seizure order against a suspected counterfeiter. In cases where the IP owner is unaware of the name or identity of the counterfeiter, some district courts will issue a "John Doe" TRO. When the federal district court issues the TRO, the court will send a copy of the TRO to the United States Attorney's Office, so that federal prosecutors can decide whether to initiate a criminal prosecution. With the TRO in hand, the IP owner will go to the site of the suspected counterfeiter accompanied by a federal marshal and serve a copy of the TRO and order on the suspected counterfeiter. If the counterfeiter is not present, the IP owner can post the TRO and order in a conspicuous place or use other circumscribed means of providing legally effective notice. The seizure order allows the federal marshal to seize any illegal goods found on the premises. The service of the order serves as notice to the defendant that the IP owner will seek a preliminary injunction at a hearing at the earliest possible time in accordance with Rule 65(b) of the Federal Rules of Civil Procedure.

In the meanwhile, the TRO prevents the defendant from engaging in any further illegal activity until the hearing on the preliminary injunction. As the TRO is issued based upon an ex parte application, it is a form of extraordinary relief that is permitted for a temporary period not to exceed ten days before a plenary hearing on the case can be held where both sides can be heard. At the hearing, the court will hear arguments from both sides on whether a court should issue a preliminary injunction, which would take effect as soon as the TRO expires. If the court then issues a preliminary injunction at the hearing, the preliminary injunction will prohibit the defendant from engaging in any further illegal activity pending the outcome of the litigation. When the district court enters its final judgment, the court can also issue a final and permanent injunction against the defendant in addition to damages and other relief. In most cases involving counterfeiting, however, the issuance of the TRO and seizure order effectively resolves the case. Counterfeiters do not usually have any basis for contesting the claims by the plaintiff and often do not even appear in court. If the counterfeiter does appear in court, a consent decree is usually entered and a trial becomes unnecessary.

The procedures discussed above provide an effective enforcement mechanism because once IP owners locate a counterfeiter, IP owners are able to completely stop any illegal activity pending the final resolution of the case. (Locating the counterfeiter, of course, is no easy matter and will usually involve the use of private investigators, as discussed at pp. 666–667 supra.) A critical feature of this procedure is the availability of ex parte injunctive relief. Counterfeiters usually flee at the first sign of trouble, so preserving the element of surprise is critical in any effective enforcement action. The availability of ex parte relief may allow an IP owner to obtain a TRO without any prior notice to the counterfeiter or infringer. The first time that the counterfeiter becomes aware of the TRO is when it is being served along with a seizure order. The availability of ex parte provisional relief serves the critical role of preserving the element of surprise. The importance of ex parte relief is underscored by the willing-ness of the United States to challenge the laws of countries that provide for injunctive relief, but not on an ex parte basis. *See, e.g.* Notification of Mutually Agreed Solution (June 1, 2001) of Denmark—Measures Affecting the Enforcement of Intellectual Property Rights, WT/DS83/1 (May 14, 1997) (reaching mutually satisfactory solution after Denmark agreed to make available provisional measures *inaudita altera parte* in civil proceed-ings involving intellectual property rights).

In 2004, the European Parliament issued a directive designed at harmonizing enforcement measures for intellectual property rights throughout the EU that requires all Member States to provide that provisional injunctive relief can "be taken without the defendant having been heard." Article 9(4), Corrigendum to Directive 2004/48/EC of the European Parliament and of the Council of April 29, 2004 on the Enforcement of Intellectual Property Rights (OJ L 157) (April 30, 2004). The Directive recognized that Member States, despite TRIPS, still had major disparities in enforcement measures and is designed to harmonize the enforcement of intellectual property rights throughout the EU.

PROBLEM 6–6

Country Y, a member of the WTO since its formation, has a severe counterfeiting and copyright piracy problem. To carry out its obligations under Part III of TRIPS, Y passed several enforcement provisions under its domestic law, including the following: "Injunctions *inaudita altera parte* shall be available to protect intellectual property rights. A plaintiff who seeks an injunction *inaudita altera parte* in civil proceedings involving intellectual property rights shall first file a complaint initiating a civil action against the defendant. After or simultaneous with the submission to the court of proof that a copy of the complaint and summons has been served on the defendant, the plaintiff may apply *inaudita altera parte* to obtain a temporary injunction against the defendant where there is a risk that evidence will be destroyed. The temporary injunction shall be in effect for a maximum period of ten days."

You are the Assistant USTR in charge of intellectual property rights. How, if at all, is Country Y's practice different from the U.S.'s? Do you think Country Y's statute will be an effective tool in the fight against commercial piracy? Do you believe the statute is consistent with TRIPS Article 50?

2. CRIMINAL SANCTIONS (TRIPS ARTICLE 61)

TRIPS once again broke new ground in providing for mandatory criminal penalties for commercial piracy. Article 61 provides:

TRIPS

Article 61

Members shall provide for criminal procedures and penalties to be applied at least in cases of wilful trademark counterfeiting or copyright piracy on a commercial scale. Remedies available shall include imprisonment and/or monetary fines sufficient to provide a deterrent, consistently with the level of penalties applied for crimes of a corresponding gravity. In appropriate cases, remedies available shall also include the seizure, forfeiture and destruction of the infringing goods and of any materials and implements the predominant use of which has been in the commission of the offence. Members may provide for criminal procedures and penalties to be applied in other cases of infringement of intellectual property rights, in particular where they are committed wilfully and on a commercial scale.

The mandatory requirement for all WTO members to establish criminal sanctions is a major breakthrough. Many observers agree that criminal sanctions, specifically imprisonment, provide the single most effective deterrent against commercial piracy. Civil litigation and administrative remedies are of limited utility in many countries of the world, especially in developing countries such as China, Vietnam, and other countries in Southeast Asia and Eastern Europe. Awards of compensatory damages in civil cases in developing countries are extremely low by U.S. standards and create practically no deterrent to those who are engaging in a highly lucrative trade. In contrast, imprisonment, even for short terms, can serve as a powerful deterrent, some policy makers contend.

TRIPS Article 61 now requires countries to impose criminal penalties for "cases of wilful trademark counterfeiting or copyright piracy on a commercial scale." Countries are given the discretion to apply criminal sanctions in other areas of IP infringement, "in particular where they are committed wilfully and on a commercial scale." Countries are also given the discretion whether to impose "imprisonment and/or monetary fines," as long as "sufficient to provide a deterrent, consistently with the level of penalties applied for crimes of a corresponding gravity." U.S. law provides for criminal liability for trafficking in counterfeit goods or services, *see* 18 U.S.C. § 2320, and for willful copyright violations. *See* 17 U.S.C. § 506 (criminal offenses).

Some IP owners still complain, however, that obtaining criminal convictions that result in imprisonment is difficult, even though the law on the books may allow imprisonment for commercial piracy. A criminal case must typically be brought by the state prosecutor, which requires the government to expend its own resources. The statistics on criminal enforcement in China on page 693 supra provide some indication of the frustrations that IP owners face in developing countries. Some IP owners argue that there is insufficient criminal enforcement even in countries such as the United States, where law enforcement officials may have other pressing priorities such as fighting terrorism, drug trafficking, and violent crimes.

The United States challenged China's criminal laws under TRIPS Article 61, with the following result.

CHINA–MEASURES AFFECTING THE PROTECTION AND ENFORCEMENT OF INTELLECTUAL PROPERTY RIGHTS

Report of the Panel, WTO.
(Macey, Chairperson; Porzio and Tiwari, Members).
WT/DS362/R (January 26, 2009).

[In August 2007, the United States brought several challenges of China's laws relating to intellectual property. In the portion excerpted below, the WTO Panel considers the U.S. claim that China's thresholds for criminal procedures and penalties are inconsistent with Article 61 of TRIPS. *Ed.*]

A. CRIMINAL THRESHOLDS

1. Description of the measures at issue

[Articles 213 through 218 of China's Criminal Law make it a crime to use counterfeit trademarks, sell counterfeit trademark goods, or engage in criminal copyright infringement, provided that such conduct reaches a certain "serious" or "large" level. The Supreme People's Court and the Supreme People's Procuratorate have further defined these provisions with certain quantitative thresholds triggered, e.g., by the monetary value of the illegal sales or gains. *Ed.*]

For example, Article 1 of Judicial Interpretation No. 19 [2004] interprets the phrase "the circumstances are serious" in Article 213 of the Criminal Law and may be translated as follows:

> "Whoever, without permission from the owner of a registered trademark, uses a trademark which is identical with the registered trademark on the same kind of commodities, in any of the following circumstances which shall be deemed as 'the circumstances are serious' under Article 213 of the Criminal Law, shall be sentenced to fixed-term imprisonment of not more than three years or criminal detention for the crime of counterfeiting registered trademark, and shall also, or shall only, be fined:
>
> (1) the *illegal business operation volume* of not less than 50,000 Yuan[1] or the *amount of illegal gains* of not less than 30,000 Yuan;
>
> (2) in the case of counterfeiting two or more registered trademarks, the *illegal business operation volume* of not less than 30,000 Yuan or the *amount of illegal gains* of not less than 20,000 Yuan;
>
> (3) other serious circumstances." (emphasis added)

Likewise, Article 5 of Judicial Interpretation No. 19 [2004] interpreted the phrases "the amount of illegal gains is relatively large" and "there are other serious circumstances" under Article 217 of the Criminal Law and may be translated as follows:

> "Whoever, for the purpose of making profits, commits any of the acts of infringement of copyright under Article 217 of the Criminal Law, with the *amount of illegal gains* of not less than 30,000 Yuan which shall be deemed as 'the amount of illegal gains is relatively large'; in any of the following circumstances which shall be deemed as 'there are other serious circumstances,' shall be sentenced to fixed-term imprisonment of not more than three years or criminal detention for the crime of infringement of copyright, and shall also, or shall only, be fined:
>
> (1) the *illegal business operation volume* of not less than 50,000 Yuan;
>
> (2) reproducing [/] distributing, without permission of the copyright owner, a written work, musical work, cinematographic work, televi-

---

1. This corresponds to US$6,250 at average market exchange rates (¥8.013/US$ for 2004–2007).

sion or other video works, computer software and other works of not less than 1,000[2] in total;

(3) other serious circumstances." (emphasis added)

[T]he Panel concludes that, whilst the structure of the thresholds and the method of calculation of some of them can take account of various circumstances, acts of trademark and copyright infringement falling below *all* the applicable thresholds are not subject to criminal procedures and penalties. The Panel will now consider whether any of those acts of infringement constitute "wilful trademark counterfeiting or copyright piracy on a commercial scale" within the meaning of Article 61 of the TRIPS Agreement.

2.   Claim under the first sentence of Article 61 of the TRIPS Agreement

This claim is brought under the first sentence of Article 61 of the TRIPS Agreement. [The Panel reviews the various parts of TRIPS Article 61, and focused on the language in Article 61 that members must "provide for criminal procedures and penalties for wilful trademark and copyright piracy "on a commercial scale." The United States argued that China's laws were in violation of Article 61 because they did not provide for criminal sanctions for certain acts of piracy on a commercial scale. According to the Panel, the key issue was the meaning of "commercial scale." The Panel analyzes this issue below.]

(i)   "on a commercial scale"

[The Panel rejected the argument by the United States that "on a commercial scale" should be interpreted to mean any commercial activity. *Ed.*] The provisions of the Paris Convention (1967) incorporated by Article 2.1 of the TRIPS Agreement include uses of the word "commercial" in the phrase "industrial or commercial establishment" (in the singular or plural)[3] and in the phrases "industrial or commercial matters" and "industrial or commercial activities."[4] The provisions of the Berne Convention (1971) incorporated by Article 9.1 of the TRIPS Agreement include the phrase "any commercial purpose."[5]

The context shows that the negotiators chose to qualify certain activities, such as rental, exploitation and use, as "commercial." They also chose to qualify various nouns, such as "terms," "value," "nature" and "interests," as "commercial" or "non-commercial." In a similar way, they could have agreed that the obligation in the first sentence of Article 61 would apply to cases of wilful and "commercial" trademark counterfeiting or copyright piracy. This would have included all commercial activity. Indeed, the records of the negotiation of the TRIPS Agreement show that

---

2.   The number "1000" has been superseded by "500."

3.   Articles 3, 5C(3), 6*quinquies*A(2) and 7*bis*(1)) of the Paris Convention (1967). This phrase also appears in footnote 1 to the TRIPS Agreement.

4.   Article 10*bis* of the Paris Convention (1967).

5.   Articles II(9)(a)(iv) and IV(4)(c)(iii) of the Appendix to the Berne Convention (1971).

this formulation was in fact suggested (by the United States) at an early stage.[6]

Instead, the negotiators agreed in Article 61 to use the distinct phrase "on a commercial scale." This indicates that the word "scale" was a deliberate choice and must be given due interpretative weight. "Scale" denotes a relative size, and reflects the intention of the negotiators that the limitation on the obligation in the first sentence of the Article depended on the *size* of acts of counterfeiting and piracy. Therefore, whilst "commercial" is a qualitative term, it would be an error to read it solely in those terms. In context it must indicate a quantity.[7]

The Panel finds that a "commercial scale" is the magnitude or extent of typical or usual commercial activity. Therefore, counterfeiting or piracy "on a commercial scale" refers to counterfeiting or piracy carried on at the magnitude or extent of typical or usual commercial activity with respect to a given product in a given market. The magnitude or extent of typical or usual commercial activity with respect to a given product in a given market forms a benchmark by which to assess the obligation in the first sentence of Article 61. It follows that what constitutes a commercial scale for counterfeiting or piracy of a particular product in a particular market will depend on the magnitude or extent that is typical or usual with respect to such a product in such a market, which may be small or large. The magnitude or extent of typical or usual commercial activity relates, in the longer term, to profitability.

(ii) Conformity of the measures at issue with respect to the level of the thresholds

The Panel has reviewed the measures [at issue] and agrees that, on their face, they do exclude certain commercial activity from criminal procedures and penalties. For example, some of the criminal thresholds are set in terms that refer expressly to commercial activity, such as "illegal business operation volume," which is defined in terms of "manufacture, storage, transportation, or sales" of infringing products, and "illegal gains" which is defined in terms of profit. However, based solely on the measures on their face, the Panel cannot distinguish between acts that, in China's marketplace, are on a commercial *scale*, and those that are not.

Certain thresholds are set in monetary terms, ranging from ¥20,000 profit to ¥50,000 turnover or sales. The measures, on their face, do not indicate what these amounts represent as compared to a relevant commercial benchmark in China.[8] Each of these amounts represents a range of

---

6. The United States suggested in October 1988 a provision applying to trademark counterfeiting and copyright infringement that were "wilful and commercial" (see document MTN. GNG/NG11/W/14/Rev.1). This suggestion was not taken up. A later US proposal, like certain other proposals, used the phrase "on a commercial scale" (see document MTN.GNG/NG11/W/70).

7. The Panel is not required, for the purposes of this claim, to express a view as to whether "commercial" also indicates certain qualitative factors, such as a profit-seeking purpose.

8. The parties agree that the thresholds should be assessed in the form in which they appear in China's measures, namely *Renminbi* (¥), which is the local currency used in China's marketplace: see their respective responses to Question No. 5.

volumes of goods, which vary according to price. Another factor to take into account is the period of time over which infringements can be cumulated to satisfy these thresholds. One threshold is set not in monetary terms but rather at 500 ("copies" for the sake of simplicity). Whilst it is reasonably clear to the Panel how many goods that comprises with respect to certain traditional media, this is not, on its face, related to any relevant market benchmark in China either.

The Panel has noted the United States' repeated assertions that certain amounts constitute counterfeiting or piracy on a commercial scale. The most recurrent example concerns 499 copyright-infringing "copies," although it is not related to the same product in all examples or, sometimes, to any product. The only facts in these examples are amounts equal to, or slightly less than, those in the measures themselves. Those amounts, in combination with the monetary thresholds and the factors used in the thresholds, demonstrate the class of acts for which China does not provide criminal procedures and penalties to be applied. Those numbers and factors do not, in themselves, demonstrate what constitutes a commercial scale for any product or in any market in China.

[T]he United States did not provide data regarding products and markets or other factors that would demonstrate what constituted "a commercial scale" in the specific situation of China's marketplace.

In its rebuttal of China's assertion regarding the scale of commerce in China, the United States noted that the "commercial scale" standard was a relative one. It commented on the Economic Census statistics submitted by China but at the same time dismissed their relevance as they are aggregate statistics related to undefined average economic units. It also recalled an earlier assertion that the Chinese market, including the market for many copyright and trademark-bearing goods, is fragmented and characterized by a profusion of small manufacturers, middlemen, distributors, and small outlets at the retail level.

The Panel has reviewed the evidence in support of this assertion. The evidence comprises a quote from a short article from a US newspaper, the *San Francisco Chronicle*, titled *"30,000–Store Wholesale Mall Keeps China Competitive"* regarding the number of stores in a particular mall in Yiwu and the physical dimensions of some stalls; a statistic quoted from an extract from a management consultant report titled *"The 2005 Global Retail Development Index"* that the top ten retailers in China hold less than 2 per cent of the market, and another statistic that the top 100 retailers have less than 6.4 per cent[9]; and a quote from an article in *Time* magazine titled *"In China, There's Priceless, and for Everything Else, There's Cash"* that a shopping mall in Luohu spans six floors of small stores.[10]

---

9. A.T. Kearney: "Destination: China" in *The 2005 Global Retail Development Index* in Exhibit US–29.

10. Exhibit US–30. An article from the London *Daily Telegraph* is also submitted in Exhibit US–31.

The Panel finds that, even if these sources were suitable for the purpose of demonstration of contested facts in this proceeding, the information that was provided was too little and too random to demonstrate a level that constitutes a commercial scale for any product in China.

The United States also submitted other press articles to illustrate points in its first written submission, particularly regarding the calculation of certain thresholds. The Panel has reviewed the press articles and notes that none of them are corroborated, nor do they refer to events or statements that would not require corroboration. Whilst the publications are reputable, most of these particular articles are brief and are quoted either for general statements or random pieces of information. Most are anecdotal in tone, some repeating casual remarks about prices of fake goods, anonymous statements or speculation. They have titles including *"Fake Pens Write Their Own Ticket," "Chasing copycats in a tiger economy," "Hollywood takes on fake Chinese DVDs," "Film not out yet on DVD? You can find it in China"* and *"Inside China's teeming world of fake goods."* Most of the press articles are printed in US or other foreign English-language media that are not claimed to be authoritative sources of information on prices and markets in China. There are four press articles from Chinese sources, one from Xinhua News Agency and three from the English-language *China Daily*. Two are quoted simply to demonstrate the existence of certain goods in China[11]; another quotes a vague statement from unnamed "market insiders" on how illegal publishers tend to work; and the other quotes an "insider" for the maximum and minimum prices of a range of pirated and genuine goods. One other alleged "recent news account" is not attributed to any source at all.[12]

The Panel emphasizes that, in the absence of more reliable and relevant data, it has reviewed the evidence in the press articles with respect to a central point in this claim that is highly contested. The credibility and weight of that evidence are therefore critical to the Panel's task. For the reasons set out above, the Panel does not ascribe any weight to the evidence in the press articles and finds that, even if it did, the information that these press articles contain is inadequate to demonstrate what is typical or usual in China for the purposes of the relevant treaty obligation.

In light of the Panel's findings above, the Panel concludes that the United States has not established that the criminal thresholds are inconsistent with China's obligations under the first sentence of Article 61 of the TRIPS Agreement.

NOTES AND QUESTIONS

1. Both the United States and China agreed that "on a commercial scale" in this case must be determined by reference to China's marketplace,

---

11. A Xinhua News Agency article refers to goods with high turnover and relatively low cost, in Exhibit US–26, and a *China Daily* article refers to the existence of HDVDs, in Exhibit US–39.

12. United States' first written submission, para. 136, citing the price of a *Spider Man 3* DVD.

specifically for each specific market and each product that is the subject of wilful trademark counterfeiting or copyright piracy. What kind of evidence about specific markets and products of piracy or counterfeiting in China did the United States present? Go through each piece of evidence presented. Was the evidence credible? The parties in the best position to provide evidence of the size of counterfeiting in China are multinational companies that have operations in China. Yet, MNCs have been quite reluctant to come forward to provide detailed information about their losses. Why? *See* China: Effects of Intellectual Property Infringement and Indigenous Innovation Policies on the U.S. Economy, 38–41 (Int'l Trade Comm'n June 10, 2010) (testimony of Professor Daniel Chow).

2. For all of the United States's public outcry about rampant piracy in China, does the result of the WTO's decision surprise you? Will the decision encourage China to be more lenient towards piracy?

3. After the WTO decision, Dan Glickman, the Chairman and CEO of the Motion Picture Association of America, stated: "We are disappointed that the WTO did not accept the strength of the US argument that China's thresholds for taking criminal action do not deter rampant piracy, which is evident. Yet, we are pleased that the panel did not say China's thresholds meet international standards." Do you agree with Glickman's characterization?

4. *ACTA.* Undaunted by its loss before the WTO as to the meaning of "on a commercial scale" under TRIPS, the United States persuaded other countries in the Anti–Counterfeiting Trade Agreement (ACTA) to adopt a different meaning. Article 23 of ACTA requires criminal penalties for wilful trademark counterfeiting or copyright piracy on a commercial scale and provides that "acts carried out on a commercial scale include at least those carried out as commercial activities for direct or indirect economic or commercial advantage." Is the definition of "on a commercial scale" in ACTA the same one the WTO rejected under TRIPS? Remember that ACTA is a treaty concluded outside of the WTO. Is the U.S. creating an alternative option to the WTO? Is this a positive development?

3. BORDER CONTROLS (TRIPS ARTICLES 51–60)

a. TRIPS Minimum Standards

The global trade in counterfeit and pirated goods prompted the drafters of TRIPS to include specific border enforcement obligations in Articles 51–60, which provide additional mandatory requirements to deal with copyright piracy and trademark counterfeiting. Just as in the case of Article 61 and criminal liability, countries have the discretion to apply the border control requirements to infringements of other IP rights, such as patents or trade secrets. Note, however, that articles place obligations only on the country of importation of the illegal goods and not on the country of exportation. The basic border control measure is as follows:

Article 51

Suspension of Release by Customs Authorities

Members shall, in conformity with the provisions set out below, adopt procedures to enable a right holder, who has valid grounds for suspecting that the importation of counterfeit trademark or pirated copyright goods may take place, to lodge an application in writing with competent authorities, administrative or judicial, for the suspension by the customs authorities of the release into free circulation of such goods. Members may enable such an application to be made in respect of goods which involve other infringements of intellectual property rights, provided that the requirements of this Section are met. Members may also provide for corresponding procedures concerning the suspension by the customs authorities of the release of infringing goods destined for exportation from their territories.

Many observers believe that the lack of border control requirements for the country of exportation was a major oversight in TRIPS. The port of exportation and the port of importation are two "choke" points in the international trade of illegal goods: Focusing only on the country of importation could therefore leave a gap in the enforcement. Just imagine that one country is a haven for commercial piracy and is exporting counterfeit goods to 25 other countries. It may be easier or more efficient to try to shut down the source of counterfeit goods in the country of exportation by having the goods seized even before they leave port. Article 51 of TRIPS does not require customs seizures in the country of exportation, but instead leaves it up to each country to decide whether to adopt "corresponding procedures concerning the suspension by the customs authorities of the release of infringing goods destined for exportation from their territories." TRIPS art. 51.

So what explains the TRIPS limitation to the country of importation? The short answer is that WTO countries were unable to agree on a set of export border controls. While countries recognized the need to protect their internal markets from imports of counterfeits, they were less concerned with exports because exports lead to a favorable trade balance with a transfer of wealth from the importing country to the exporting country. Exports also allow some countries to earn hard currency as they can demand payment in U.S. dollars. For these reasons, many countries were wary of imposing border controls on the export transaction. While the controls required under Article 51 are targeted at illegal fakes, countries were nevertheless concerned that export controls might also impede or add to the expense of exports of genuine goods and hinder legitimate trade.

In the country of importation, TRIPS Article 51 requires the country to allow a copyright or trademark holder to file a written application seeking seizure of infringing goods by customs authorities. Article 52 requires such application to be supported by "adequate evidence to satisfy the competent authorities that, under the laws of the country of importation, there is prima facie an infringement of the right holder's intellectual property right." The applicant must also "supply a sufficiently detailed description of the goods to make them readily recognizable by the customs authorities."

TRIPS also provides that authorities shall be able to require an applicant to provide a security or equivalent assurance to protect the defendant (Article 53) and to order the applicant to pay compensation for an injury caused by the wrongful detention of the goods (Article 56). Under Article 55, a suspension of the release of the goods cannot exceed ten working days unless a decision on the merits has been initiated by the applicant or steps have been taken with the authorities to prolong the suspension. Otherwise, the goods must be released.

Under TRIPS Article 59 (Remedies), competent authorities shall have the right "to order the destruction or disposal of infringing goods in accordance with the principles set out in Article 46." "In the case of trademark counterfeit goods, authorities shall not allow the re-exportation of the goods in an unaltered state or subject them to a different customs procedure, other than in exceptional circumstances."

Earlier, we examined the U.S. challenge to China's criminal laws under Article 61. The United States also challenged China's compliance with the border controls required by TRIPS Articles 59 and 46 with the following result.

CHINA–MEASURES AFFECTING THE PROTECTION AND ENFORCEMENT OF INTELLECTUAL PROPERTY RIGHTS

Report of the Panel, WTO.
Chairperson: Adrian Macey; Members: Marino Porzio, Sivakant Tiwari
WT/DS362/R.

A. C<small>USTOMS</small> M<small>EASURES</small>

3. Description of the measures at issue

This Section of the Panel's findings concerns three of China's Customs measures. The Regulations on Customs Protection of Intellectual Property Rights ("Customs IPR Regulations") were enacted by the Standing Committee of the State Council in November 2003 and entered into force in March 2004. Article 27 provides for the confiscation of goods determined to have infringed an intellectual property right and, in the third paragraph, sets out different options for the disposal or destruction of such goods. The parties agreed to translate the relevant text as follows:

> "Where the confiscated goods which infringe on intellectual property rights can be used for the social public welfare undertakings, Customs shall hand such goods over to relevant public welfare bodies for the use in social public welfare undertakings. Where the holder of the intellectual property rights intends to buy them, Customs can assign them to the holder of the intellectual property rights with compensa-

tion. Where the confiscated goods infringing on intellectual property rights cannot be used for social public welfare undertakings and the holder of the intellectual property rights has no intention to buy them, Customs can, after eradicating the infringing features, auction them off according to law. Where the infringing features are impossible to eradicate, Customs shall destroy the goods."

[The other measures are implementing regulations and are similar in substance to the basic law above.]

[The United States challenged China's law on various grounds. The Panel rejected the U.S. argument "that Customs lacks authority to donate goods to social welfare bodies in such a manner as to avoid any harm to the right holder caused by lower quality goods," allegedly in violation of TRIPS Articles 59 and 46. *Ed.*] The Red Cross distributes donated goods itself, outside the channels of commerce, including in disaster relief projects, where it cannot simply be assumed that the recipients are misled as to the origin of the goods. The recipients do not choose the goods in the way that ordinary consumers do, nor can it be assumed that the recipients are potential consumers of the genuine goods. [The WTO Panel also noted that China had a Customs–Red Cross Memorandum that imposed restrictions on the donated goods to prevent their return into the stream of commerce. Accordingly, the Panel rejected the U.S. challenge to China's donation of confiscated goods to the Red Cross. The Panel considered the U.S.'s other challenge below. *Ed.*]

4.   Claim under Article 59 of the TRIPS Agreement

(a)   Main arguments of the parties

(ix) Auction and authority to order the destruction of infringing goods

The United States claims that the competent Chinese authorities lack the scope of authority to order the destruction or disposal of infringing goods required by Article 59 of the TRIPS Agreement. The measures at issue create a "compulsory scheme" so that the Chinese customs authorities cannot exercise their discretion to destroy the goods and must give priority to disposal options that allow infringing goods to enter the channels of commerce or otherwise cause harm to the right holder. *Donation to social welfare bodies* can be harmful to a right holder and nothing appears to prevent such bodies from selling the infringing goods; *sale to the right holder* harms the right holder in the amount that the right holder pays for the infringing goods; and *auction* does not constitute disposal outside the channels of commerce and, absent his consent, may harm the right holder. Where any of these three options is available, the authorities are not authorized to order *destruction* of the infringing goods.

The [United States] claim is that the measures, on their face, treat auction (and the other disposal methods) as "compulsory prerequisites" to destruction and create a "compulsory sequence of steps" that renders auction mandatory in certain circumstances. China responds that the Regulations express a "preference" for certain disposition methods and that the Implementing Measures confirm this prioritization. China argues that the measures vest Customs with "considerable discretion" to determine what method is appropriate and that Customs has the legal authority to order any of the four disposition methods.

The Panel begins by examining the measures on their face. The Customs IPR Regulations set out four disposition methods in Article 27, of which auction is the third. With respect to auction, Article 27 provides as follows:

> "Where the confiscated goods infringing on intellectual property rights cannot be used for social public welfare undertakings and the holder of the intellectual property rights has no intention to buy them, Customs *can*, after eradicating the infringing features, auction them off according to law." (emphasis added)

This phrase provides for the auction of infringing goods. It is conditional on the non-application of the first two methods, i.e. donation to social welfare bodies and sale to the right holder. This phrase uses a modal verb translated as "can" (or "may"). This indicates that the Customs IPR Regulations impose no obligation to auction infringing goods even where the first two disposition methods are not applied.

The succeeding phrase on destruction provides that "[w]here the infringing features are impossible to eradicate, Customs shall destroy the goods." This indicates that the provision that Customs shall destroy the goods is conditional upon whether "the infringing features are impossible to eradicate." That condition, on its face, does not imply that there is any lack of authority to destroy the goods where the infringing features are *not* impossible to eradicate.

The United States submits that if none of the first three options is viable, "Customs *may, then and only,* proceed to the third item: destruction of the goods" (emphasis added). However, in the Panel's view, this misreads the text which provides that if none of the first three options is viable, Customs shall destroy the goods. It does not state that Customs *shall not* destroy the goods in other situations.

Accordingly, the Panel finds that the United States has not established that the Customs measures on their face oblige Customs to order the auction of infringing goods. The Panel concludes that the United States has not established that the Customs measures are inconsistent with Article 59 of the TRIPS Agreement, as it incorporates the principles set out in the *first* sentence of Article 46 of the TRIPS Agreement (i.e., "In order to create an effective deterrent to infringement, the judicial authorities shall have the authority to order that goods that they have found to be infringing be, without compensation of any sort, disposed of outside the channels of commerce in such a manner as to avoid any harm caused to the right holder, or, unless this would be contrary to existing constitutional requirements, destroyed.").

(x) Auction and "simple removal of the trademark unlawfully affixed"

The Panel recalls its finding that "the principles set out in Article 46" as incorporated by Article 59 of the TRIPS Agreement include the *fourth* sentence of Article 46. That sentence provides as follows:

> "In regard to counterfeit trademark goods, the simple removal of the trademark unlawfully affixed shall not be sufficient, other than in exceptional cases, to permit release of the goods into the channels of commerce."

It seems clear from this provision that the eradication of infringing features is a condition attached to auction of goods confiscated by Customs. Article 27 of the Customs IPR Regulations is implemented and confirmed by Article 30(2) of the Implementing Measures and is expressly confirmed by the first operative paragraph of Public Notice No. 16/2007 which provides, relevantly, as follows:

> "Where the confiscated infringing goods are auctioned by Customs, Customs shall completely eradicate all infringing features on the goods and the packaging thereof strictly pursuant to Article 27 of the Regulations, including eradicating the features infringing trademarks, copyright, patent and other intellectual property rights."

It is undisputed that in all cases in which Customs auctions goods that it has confiscated under the measures at issue, Customs first removes the infringing features.

The Panel notes that the fourth sentence of Article 46, by its specific terms, is not limited to an action to render goods non-infringing, which the simple removal of the trademark would achieve. Rather, the fourth sentence of Article 46 imposes an additional requirement beyond rendering the goods non-infringing in order to deter further acts of infringement with those goods. Therefore, it is insufficient, other than in exceptional cases, to show that goods that have already been found to be counterfeit are later unmarked. The release into the channels of commerce of such goods, while they may no longer infringe upon the exclusive rights in Article 16 of the TRIPS Agreement, will not comply with the requirement in the fourth sentence of Article 46, as incorporated by Article 59.

[T]he Panel considers that, in regard to counterfeit trademark goods, China's Customs measures provide that the simple removal of the trademark unlawfully affixed is sufficient to permit release of the goods into the channels of commerce. Therefore, the Panel considers that, in regard to counterfeit trademark goods, China's Customs measures provide that the simple removal of the trademark unlawfully affixed is sufficient to permit release of the goods into the channels of commerce in more than just "exceptional cases." [T]he Customs measures are inconsistent with Article 59 of the TRIPS Agreement, as it incorporates the principle set out in the *fourth* sentence of Article 46 of the TRIPS Agreement.

1. Explain the U.S. position that Chinese authorities did not have the unrestricted power under China's law to destroy infringing goods as required by Article 59 of TRIPS but could only do so if certain other methods of disposal were unavailable. What exactly was the United States's complaint about the law?

2. Why was the procedure used by China in eradicating the trademark on counterfeit goods and then selling them inconsistent with Articles 59 and 46 of TRIPS?

3. Considering how this entire WTO case was resolved (i.e., criminal thresholds, disposal of infringing goods, and copyright for censored works), which country prevailed on the most important issues: the United States or China?

b. U.S. Approach to Border Controls

As evident in the *China–Measures* dispute above, the TRIPS Agreement affords countries a certain amount of flexibility in implementing the border control measures under Articles 51–60. Not surprisingly, the U.S. approach is different from China's—and stricter, for example, in terms of setting a default approach of destroying any counterfeit goods that are confiscated unless the trademark owner consents to an alternative and the goods are not unsafe. 19 U.S.C. § 1526(e). Below is a brief overview of the U.S. approach.

The United States has implemented a complex set of laws and regulations that reflect the TRIPS requirements for border enforcement measures. These measures concentrate on the prevention of entry into the U.S. of goods that violate trademarks and copyrights and are based on relevant laws contained in various sections in Titles 15 (Trademarks), 17 (Copyright), 18 (Criminal Provisions), and 19 (Customs) of the U.S. Code. These provisions allow U.S. trademark and copyright owners to prevent the entry into the U.S. of goods that violate trademark and copyrights and, under certain conditions, parallel imports or gray market goods. Trademark and copyright (but not patent) owners in the United States are provided a set of simple procedures in 19 C.F.R. Chapter 1, subparts C & D to enlist the aid of U.S. Customs to prevent the entry into the U.S. of counterfeit and pirated goods.

Under 19 CFR § 133.22, an owner of a registered U.S. trademark can record the trademark with Customs under procedures set forth in 19 C.F.R. §§ 133.1–133.4. Once the mark is recorded, the trademark owner is entitled to the help of U.S. Customs in protecting the mark at the border. In protecting the recorded trademark, Customs makes a fundamental distinction between goods bearing a counterfeit trademark, i.e., an identical or substantially indistinguishable trademark, and goods bearing a merely infringing trademark (short of a counterfeit), i.e., a confusingly similar trademark.

Customs must seize and forfeit all goods that counterfeit the recorded mark. Counterfeit goods that are seized are destroyed unless the trademark owner consents to allow their disposition other than by destruction. If the counterfeit goods are not unsafe and the trademark owner consents, the Customs authorities "may obliterate the trademark where feasible and dispose of the goods seized" by (1) donation to federal, state, or local government agencies, (2) donation to charities, or (3) public auction. *See* 19 U.S.C. § 1526(e). Even if the trademark is not registered or recorded, Customs has the authority to seize and forfeit counterfeit goods because of the existence of a federal criminal statute against the trafficking in counterfeit goods. *See* Anti–Counterfeiting Consumer Protection Act, 18 U.S.C. § 2320 (2002).

Infringing goods that are detained are subject to a 30–day detention period under 19 U.S.C. § 1499(c). During this period, the importer can seek to obtain entry of the goods under various means. For example, the importer can ask Customs for permission to remove or obliterate the mark by grinding it off or removing the plates that bear the mark. Despite the objections of trademark owners, Customs has allowed importers to import goods bearing an infringing mark if the importer obliterates or removes the offending mark. Goods that bear a mark that infringes a trademark that is not recorded with Customs are not prohibited from entry into the United States. Customs has an internal directive that instructs Customs officers to allow the goods to be imported. *See* Customs Directive 2310–010A (Dec. 11, 2000). The trademark owner will have to take action civilly against the offending goods and cannot rely on Customs for enforcement. The distinction between counterfeit and infringing marks is further discussed in *Ross Cosmetics*, the principal case below.

A similar procedure exists for copyright owners. A copyright owner must first register the copyright with the U.S. Copyright Office and then record the registered copyright with U.S. Customs. Customs will then seize or detain any pirated or infringing products. As in the case of trademarks, Customs has the authority to seize pirated copies even though the copyright has not been recorded. Where the copyright is unrecorded, however, Customs will act only against "clearly piratical goods," i.e., unauthorized copies that are overwhelmingly similar to the copyrighted work and will not take action against "possibly piratical" goods. *See* Customs Directive No. 2310–005B (Dec. 12, 2001).

Importers and other interested parties who are concerned that a shipment of goods may be seized or detained by Customs are allowed under 19 CFR Part 177 to seek advance rulings from Customs on whether the shipment violates rights of recorded trademarks or copyrights. An advanced ruling will alert the importer of the possibility of a seizure. Importers are able to appeal an adverse ruling by Customs to the court of international trade. The case below provides a good example of the operation of these procedures.

ROSS COSMETICS DISTRIBUTION CENTERS INC. v. UNITED STATES

U.S. Court of International Trade.
18 C.I.T. 979, 34 U.S.P.Q.2d 1758 (Ct. Int'l Trade 1994).

DiCarlo, C.J.

Plaintiff, an importer of cosmetics, toiletries, and related products, requested Customs to issue a pre-importation ruling regarding whether its packaging for certain bath oils and fragrance oils proposed for importation conformed with Customs-administered laws and regulations relating to trademarks, trade names, and similar intellectual property rights. Specifically, plaintiff's packages for its bath oil products GORGEOUS, LOVE BIRDS, WHISPER, OBLIVION, OSCENT, and MORNING DREAM bear language inviting customers to compare these products to the well-known products of GIORGIO, L'AIR DU TEMPS, OMBRE ROSE, OPIUM, OSCAR, and YOUTH DEW respectively. Plaintiff's products are sold at a fraction of the price of the well-known products.

[Customs' original ruling was overturned by the court of international trade for failing to make a proper determination that the allegedly infringing copies were counterfeits or would cause consumer confusion.]

On November 10, 1993, Customs issued its remand determination. The remand determination ruled: (1) plaintiff's products using the trademarks "OMBRE ROSE," "OPIUM," and "OSCAR" are admissible as non-infringing goods; and (2) plaintiff's products using the trademarks "GIORGIO," "YOUTH DEW," and "L'AIR DU TEMPS" are considered to infringe the rights of the respective trademark owners, and constitute a counterfeit use of these trademarks. Because "GIORGIO" and "YOUTH DEW" are recorded with Customs and "L'AIR DU TEMPS" is not, products using the trademarks "GIORGIO" and "YOUTH DEW," if imported, would be subject to seizure and forfeiture under 19 U.S.C. § 1526(e) and products using the trademark "L'AIR DU TEMPS," if imported, would be subject to seizure and forfeiture under 19 U.S.C. § 1595a(c). *Remand Determination*, at 28.

Plaintiff now contests Customs' remand determination concerning plaintiff's use of the trademarks "GIORGIO" and "L'AIR DU TEMPS."

Discussion

1. The Products

a. "GIORGIO" v. "GORGEOUS" The trademark "GIORGIO" is owned by Giorgio Beverly Hills, Inc., which has three valid trademark registrations with both the PTO and Customs for GIORGIO perfume and toiletry products: (1) the word mark "GIORGIO"; (2) a GIORGIO crest design; and (3) a design of alternating yellow and white vertical stripes. The GIORGIO packages use the stripe design as background, and bear[]

the GIORGIO crest and the word mark "GIORGIO" in various styles and sizes.

The proposed package of plaintiff's product GORGEOUS invites the consumer to compare GORGEOUS to GIORGIO. The package of GORGEOUS uses diagonal yellow and white stripes as the background. A crest design appears above the name "GORGEOUS." At the top of the front panel is the language "COMPARE TO GIORGIO YOU WILL SWITCH TO ...," in which the word mark "GIORGIO" is followed by the registered trademark symbol and appears in a bold and larger size print than the rest of the words. At the bottom of the front panel is a disclaimer: "OUR PRODUCTS IS [sic] IN NO MANNER ASSOCIATED WITH, OR LICENSED BY, THE MAKERS OF GIORGIO." The word mark "GIORGIO" is again followed by the registered trademark symbol. All words in the disclaimer appear to be in the same size print.

b. "L'AIR DU TEMPS" v. "LOVE BIRDS" The trademark "L'AIR DU TEMPS" is owned by Nina Ricci, S.A.R.L., and is registered with the PTO, but is not recorded with Customs. In addition to the word mark "L'AIR DU TEMPS," Nina Ricci has two valid trademark registrations with the PTO, each with a design mark of a swirled glass bottle with a closure, with one topped by one three-dimensional dove, and the second topped by two three-dimensional doves. The sample box of L'AIR DU TEMPS shows a yellow background, a golden oval containing two white doves in flight in a prominent position on the front panel, a golden band across the bottom of the front panel, and the word mark "L'AIR DU TEMPS" in gold print between the oval and the band.

The proposed packaging for plaintiff's product LOVE BIRDS has a primarily yellow background with thin white stripes. The front panel of the box shows an orange oval in a prominent position and an orange band across the bottom. The orange oval contains four birds in flight and the words "LOVE BIRDS," all in gold color. At the top of the front panel is the language "COMPARE TO L'AIR DU TEMPS YOU WILL SWITCH TO ...," in which the word mark "L'AIR DU TEMPS" is followed by the registered trademark symbol and appears in a bold and larger size print than the rest of the words. At the bottom of the front panel and within the orange band is a disclaimer: "OUR PRODUCTS IS [sic] IN NO MANNER ASSOCIATED WITH, OR LICENSED BY, THE MAKERS OF L'AIR DU TEMPS." The word mark "L'AIR DU TEMPS" in the disclaimer is also followed by the registered trademark symbol. All words in the disclaimer appear to be in the same size print.

2. Statutory and Regulatory Scheme; Customs Policy

a. Applicable Statutory Violations

Section 42 of the Lanham Act, 15 U.S.C. Section 1124, forbids importation of any goods that "copy or simulate" a trademark registered with the PTO. "A 'copying or simulating' mark" is either "an actual counterfeit of the recorded mark or name[,] or is one which so resembles it as to be likely to cause the public to associate the copying or simulating mark with the recorded mark or name." 19 C.F.R. Section 133.21(a) (1993).

Section 43(b) of the Lanham Act, 15 U.S.C. Section 1125(b), forbids importation of any goods "marked or labeled in contravention of" section 3(a). Section 3(a) provides in pertinent part:

Any person who, on or in connection with any goods ... or any container for goods, uses in commerce *any word, term, name, symbol, or device, or any combination thereof,* or any false designation of origin, false or misleading description of fact, or false or misleading presentation of fact, which—

(1) *is likely to cause confusion, or to cause mistake, or to deceive as to the affiliation, connection, or association* of such person with another person, *or as to the origin, sponsorship or approval* of his or her goods ... by another person, or

(2) in commercial advertising or promotion, misrepresents the nature, characteristics, qualities, or geographic origin of his or her or another person's goods ...,

shall be liable in a civil action by any person who believes that he or she is or is likely to be damaged by such act.

15 U.S.C. Section 1125(a) (emphasis added). By virtue of this broad coverage of section 43, Customs' protection of trademark rights extends to all trademarks and trade dresses, regardless of whether they are registered with the PTO or recorded with Customs.

b. Penalties

Under 19 U.S.C. Section 1526(e), any merchandise "bearing a counterfeit mark" imported into the United States in violation of 15 U.S.C. Section 1124 "shall be seized and, in the absence of the written consent of the trademark owner, forfeited for violations of the customs laws." A "counterfeit" is defined as "a spurious mark which is identical with, or substantially indistinguishable from, a registered mark." 15 U.S.C. Section 1127 (1988).

Under 19 U.S.C. Section 1595a(c), any merchandise imported into the United States "may be seized and forfeited" if the merchandise or its packaging violates section 1124, 1125, or 1127 of title 15 of the United States Code, or section 2320 of title 18 of the United States Code, which imposes criminal liability on any person who intentionally traffics in counterfeit goods. 19 U.S.C. Section 1595a(c)(2)(C).

c. Counterfeit v. Confusingly Similar

In order to facilitate the enforcement of trademark protection at the border, Customs currently divides trademark infringement cases into two categories: those which bear a "counterfeit" mark, and those which bear a "confusingly similar" mark. A "counterfeit" mark is defined in accordance with 15 U.S.C. Section 1127. A "confusingly similar" mark is defined by Customs as one "that is likely to cause confusion, or to cause mistake, or to deceive the consumer as to the origin, affiliation, or sponsorship of the goods in question." *Remand Determination*, at 4. This definition appears to track the language contained in section 43(a) of the Lanham Act. In addition, Customs draws a distinction between trademarks that are registered and recorded with Customs, and trademarks that are registered but not recorded with Customs.

Thus, imported articles bearing "counterfeit" versions of marks recorded with Customs are subject to seizure and forfeiture under 19 U.S.C. Section 1526(e). Imported articles bearing "counterfeit" versions of marks not recorded with Customs are subject to seizure and forfeiture under 19 U.S.C. Section 1595a(c) for violation of 18 U.S.C. Section 2320.

Imported articles bearing "confusingly similar" versions of marks recorded with Customs are ultimately subject to seizure and forfeiture for violation of 15 U.S.C. Section 1124. Imported articles bearing "confusingly similar" versions of marks not recorded with Customs are currently not prohibited for importation. *Id.*

3. *Counterfeit v. Mere Infringement*

Under Customs' laws and regulations, goods that infringe upon rights of trademark owners are classified into two categories. The first category consists of counterfeit merchandise which bears "a spurious mark which is identical with, or substantially indistinguishable from, a registered mark." 15 U.S.C. Section 1127. Usually, "counterfeit merchandise is made so as to imitate a well-known product in all details of construction and appearance so as to deceive customers into thinking that they are getting genuine merchandise." 3 J. Thomas McCarthy, McCarthy on Trademarks and Unfair Competition Section 25.01[5][a] (3d ed. 1992).

The second category consists of "merely infringing" goods which are not counterfeits but bear marks likely to cause public confusion. This category includes merchandise which bears a mark that "copies or simulates" a registered mark so as to be likely to cause the public to associate the copying or simulating mark with the registered mark. Also included in this category is merchandise which uses any word, name, symbol, or any combination thereof, in such a manner that is likely to cause public confusion as to the origin, sponsorship, or approval of the merchandise by another person.

The significance of the distinction between counterfeits and merely infringing goods lies in the consequences attached to the two categories. Counterfeits must be seized, and in the absence of the written consent of the trademark owner, forfeited. Merely infringing goods, on the other hand, *may* be seized and forfeited. Under Customs regulations, merely infringing goods may be imported if the "objectionable mark is removed or obliterated prior to importation in such a manner as to be illegible and incapable of being reconstituted." 19 C.F.R. Section 133.21(a), (c)(4).

4. Whether Plaintiff's Use of Registered Trademarks Constitutes Counterfeit Use

Customs determined that plaintiff's use of the word marks "GIOR-GIO" and "L'AIR DU TEMPS" on the packaging of its own products constituted a counterfeit use of these marks, because plaintiff applied marks "identical to the registered trademarks" to its goods without the authorization of the trademark owners. The court disagrees. It is clear that plaintiff's products are not counterfeits. Plaintiff's products GOR-GEOUS and LOVE BIRDS do not imitate the well-known products GIOR-GIO and L'AIR DU TEMPS in all details of construction and appearance. Rather, plaintiff uses the marks "GIORGIO" and "L'AIR DU TEMPS" to market its products GORGEOUS and LOVE BIRDS.

The use of another person's trademark in the context of marketing one's own product is not prohibited by law unless it creates a reasonable likelihood of confusion as to the source, identity, or sponsorship of the product. Thus, at issue is not whether plaintiff may use the marks "GIORGIO" and "L'AIR DU TEMPS" on the packaging of its own products, but whether such use is likely to cause consumer confusion. If a likelihood of confusion exists, plaintiff's use of the marks would constitute trademark infringement, but not a counterfeit use of the marks.

In reaching the conclusion that plaintiff's use of the marks constitutes a counterfeit use, Customs misapplied 15 U.S.C. Section 1127, which defines a counterfeit as a spurious mark "identical with, or substantially indistinguishable from, a registered mark." According to Customs, any reference to another person's mark in the context of marketing one's own goods (whether a parallel use or comparative advertising) would constitute counterfeit use if a likelihood of confusion is found. This is because, under Customs' reasoning, the mark used in such a context would be necessarily "identical" to the registered mark. Customs' application of the statutory definition of counterfeit ignores the distinction between counterfeit and mere infringement, and therefore is not in accordance with law.

5. Whether Plaintiff's Use of Registered Trademarks Constitutes Infringement

Having held that plaintiff's use of the marks "GIORGIO" and "L'AIR DU TEMPS" does not constitute a counterfeit use, the court must now address whether such use nevertheless infringes the rights of the trademark owners.

The basic test for statutory trademark infringement "likelihood of confusion," which has been construed by courts to mean a probability of confusion rather than a possibility of confusion. In order to determine whether a likelihood of confusion exists, courts apply and balance multiple factors. The commonly used factors include: the degree of resemblance between the conflicting marks; the similarity of the marketing methods and channels of distribution; where the goods are not directly competitive, the likelihood that the senior user will expand into the field of the junior user; the degree of distinctiveness of the mark; the characteristics of the prospective purchasers and the degree of care they exercise; the intent of the alleged infringer; and evidence of actual confusion.

Although courts may also consider an alleged infringer's use of a disclaimer stating that it is not connected with the trademark-owner, the mere presence of a disclaimer does not necessarily prevent consumer confusion. In fact, under certain circumstances, use of a disclaimer may even aggravate brand confusion. Generally, the relative location and size of the disclaimer within the overall context of the advertisement is an important consideration in evaluating the effectiveness of a disclaimer.

In this case, Customs applied commonly accepted factors, and determined that the use of the marks "GIORGIO" and "L'AIR DU TEMPS" on the packaging of GORGEOUS and LOVE BIRDS is likely to cause confusion, and that the disclaimers on the packaging are insufficient to dispel the likelihood of confusion. Plaintiff agrees that the factors Customs used to determine the likelihood of confusion are appropriate. Plaintiff asserts, however, that Customs incorrectly applied these factors to the two packages, and that Customs was arbitrary in finding the disclaimers ineffective.

a. "GIORGIO" v. "GORGEOUS"

Applying the list of factors relevant to the determination of likelihood of confusion, Customs found the following:

(a) The word mark "GIORGIO," as used on fragrance and toiletry products, is inherently distinctive, and is therefore a strong mark entitled to a broad scope of protection. *Remand Determination*, at 12.

(b) "GORGEOUS" and "GIORGIO" are used on identical products—perfumes and toiletries are listed in the same class for the purposes of the Trademark Office. This factor enhances the likelihood of confusion. *Id.*

(c) There is a high degree of similarity between the two packages. GIORGIO is covered by a pattern of alternating vertical white and yellow stripes; GORGEOUS by a pattern of alternating diagonal white and yellow stripes, of the same width as the GIORGIO stripes. GIORGIO has the red, black, and gold GIORGIO crest; GORGEOUS a red and gold crest. On the GIORGIO packaging, the word "GIORGIO" appears slightly above the center of the front panel and in close proximity to the GIORGIO crest; on the GORGEOUS packaging, the word "GORGEOUS" also appears slightly above the center of the front panel and in close proximity to its crest. In addition, the words "GORGEOUS" and "GIORGIO" share consonants, vowels, and sounds in their pronunciation.

(d) The fact that plaintiff selected and combined the three design elements utilized on GIORGIO boxes for use on its packaging (the word mark "GIORGIO," the image of a crest, and the yellow and white stripes), and the fact that the word mark "GIORGIO" appears in a prominent location on the front panel and in a darker and bigger print than the surrounding language inviting comparison, strongly suggest that plaintiff intentionally designed its packaging to be similar to GIORGIO, and thus did not develop its design in good faith.

(e) Since the quality of GORGEOUS is not comparable to that of GIORGIO, GORGEOUS would be sold in discount and low-end retail stores, whereas GIORGIO is normally sold in boutiques and fine department stores. However, there is a possibility GIORGIO would be sold in the same store as GORGEOUS. Customs' survey revealed that both GIORGIO and plaintiff's products were sold by a WalMart store, and that a major retail drug store chain sold both GIORGIO products and various brands of "smell-alike" products. The possibility that the two products could be sold in the same stores enhances the likelihood of confusion.

(f) While a typical buyer of GIORGIO products may be expected to exercise care before purchasing because of the higher prices involved, a typical buyer of GORGEOUS would be less likely to make more than a cursory inspection of the product because low-priced items are often the subject of impulse purchasing. The nature of plaintiff's product as a target of impulse purchasing enhances the likelihood of confusion.

On balance, Customs found the factors that enhance the likelihood of confusion outweigh the factors that diminish the likelihood of confusion. Therefore, "there is a substantial likelihood that consumers could be confused as to the source of the Ross product." *Id.* at 16.

Customs then examined whether the disclaimer used is sufficient to eliminate the confusion. Customs found that the disclaimer on the package of GORGEOUS is located at the bottom of the front panel, far from the word mark "GIORGIO" which appears in a prominent position at the top of the panel, and that the disclaimer is written in a smaller type size than any other words on the box. Customs concluded that the disclaimer could be easily overlooked by consumers and therefore is insufficient to dispel the likelihood of confusion. *Id.* at 18.

The court holds that Customs properly applied the relevant factors in determining a likelihood of confusion, and that Customs' examination of the adequacy of the disclaimer was consistent with the applicable law. Although the court may not necessarily come to the same conclusion if reviewing the case de novo, it finds there is a rational connection between the facts found and the determination made by Customs.

The court sustains Customs' finding of a likelihood of confusion with respect to plaintiff's packaging for GORGEOUS. Accordingly, packages identical to that of GORGEOUS shall be denied entry and, if imported, are subject to seizure and forfeiture.

[The court of appeals found that "LOVE BIRDS" was also confusingly similar to "L'AIR DU TEMPS for similar reasons.]

Conclusion

For the reasons stated above, the court holds that Customs' determination that plaintiff's proposed packages of GORGEOUS and LOVE

BIRDS infringe the rights of the trademark owners of "GIORGIO" and "L'AIR DU TEMPS" is not arbitrary, capricious, or an abuse of discretion, and is otherwise in accordance with law. Further, the court holds Customs' conclusion that plaintiff's use of the trademarks "GIORGIO" and "L'AIR DU TEMPS" is a counterfeit use is not in accordance with law.

NOTES AND QUESTIONS

1. *Patents and ITC.* While U.S. law provides a simple procedure for the seizure of goods that violate trademarks and copyrights at the border, a similar procedure is not available for products that infringe patents and trade secrets. For a U.S. industry to prevent the entry of goods infringing a patent at a port of entry, a patent holder must file an action for an exclusion order under Section 337 of the Tariff Act of 1930 before the International Trade Commission. The ITC will hold an adversary (Section 337) proceeding where the plaintiff will be allowed to present evidence of the infringement and the defendant will have an opportunity to contest the plaintiff's case. Although ITC proceedings (typically resolved in 1 year) are much quicker than litigation in court, they can be expensive. Should a simpler procedure, such as described in *Ross* for trademarks, be available for patents? What practical differences are there between determining whether a trademark is counterfeit or confusingly similar and whether a patent infringement exists?

2. While U.S. law provides for a simple recordation procedure, you should not assume that it is easy to stop counterfeit and pirated products at the border. To the contrary, even in the best of circumstances, a strategy that relies on sealing off the borders of a country from the entry of illegal goods will have only a limited effect. In the case of counterfeit and pirated goods, the rights holder will still need to obtain intelligence identifying a specific shipment of infringing goods in order to take advantage of the Customs procedures outlined above. Without such information, it will not be possible for Customs to seize the goods. As counterfeiters generally use false shipping documentation, such information is difficult to obtain. Moreover, while Customs has authority on its own to seize counterfeit goods, U.S. Customs officials have placed their priorities since 9/11 on detecting and preventing the entry into the United States of materials that can pose a terrorist threat. For these reasons, many observers believe that large quantities of counterfeit and pirated products enter the U.S. undetected every day.

c.   The European Union Approach to Border Controls

In accordance with its TRIPS obligations, the EU has implemented border enforcement measures for counterfeit trademarked goods and pirated copyright goods that must be adopted for Customs authorities throughout the EU. *See* Council Regulation (EC) No. 1383/2003 (OJ L. 196) (July 22, 2003); *see also* Corrigendum to Directive 2004/48/EC of the European Parliament and of the Council of 29 April 2004 on the Enforcement of Intellectual Property Rights (OJ L 157). Under Regulation No. 1383/2003, a rights holder can lodge an application in writing to the relevant customs authorities to seek the suspension of goods that are suspected of infringing trademarks, copyrights, neighboring rights, patents, and geographical indications. *See* EC Regulation, No. 1383/2003, Articles 2 & 4. Customs authorities must prevent goods found to infringe intellectual property rights from release for free circulation and must destroy or forfeit them. *See* Articles 16 & 17. Customs authorities can also act on their own initiative to suspend the release of goods suspected of infringing intellectual property rights. Notice is then given to rights holders who can submit an application in accordance with Article 4.

The issue of how to deal with the traffic in goods that violate intellectual property rights in the EU, however, is complicated by the basic principle of the freedom of movement of goods that is a fundamental principle of the common market. The EU recognizes the importance of enforcement against the transnational flow of counterfeit and pirated goods, but the imposition of border controls can also frustrate the fundamental goal of establishing a common market. The following case illustrates this conflict.

PROBLEM 6–7

La Belle Jeunesse, a French manufacturer of luxury goods has been alerted by a private investigation company that a large shipment of counterfeit handbags made in China is destined for England with a final destination in France. The shipment will not pass through English customs but will undergo repackaging in a bonded facility in England and then will then be shipped to their final destination in France. No customs duties will be paid in England as the bond facility is a transit zone. The French company files an application with English customs authorities with detailed information concerning the shipment of counterfeit bags as required by Article 4 of the EC Regulation, supra. The shipment coincidentally arrives during a World Cup soccer match between England and Germany. At the time, English customs authorities—busy on other matters—did not seize the shipment, but instead issued documents allowing the goods to enter the country. La Belle Jeunesse has located the goods in one of four bonded facilities near a port in Southern England bound for France and now asks the English authorities to seize the goods. What result? Do you believe that English customs authorities must seize the allegedly counterfeit handbags under EU law? See *Rioglass* below. What advice do you have for La Belle Jeunesse?

ADMINISTRATION des DOUANES et DROITS INDIRECTS v. RIOGLASS SA, TRANSREMAR SL

European Court of Justice.
[2003] ECR 00000, Case C–115/02 (October 23, 2003).

By judgment of 26 March 2002, received at the Registry of the Court on 2 April 2002, the Cour de cassation (Court of cassation) (France) referred to the Court for a preliminary ruling under Art. 234 EC a question on the interpretation of Art. 28 EC.

That question has been raised in proceedings between the Administration des douanes et droits indirects (Customs and Indirect Taxes Administration, the customs authority) and Rioglass SA (Rioglass) and Transremar SL (Transremar), both companies registered under Spanish law, concerning the detention in France, on suspicion of infringement of trade mark, of spare parts for cars manufactured in Spain and being transported to Poland.

National law

Article L.716–8 of the Code de la propriété intellectuelle (Intellectual Property Code) introduced by Art. 11 of Law 94–102 of 5 February 1994 ([1994] Journal Officiel de la République Française 2151) provides:

> The customs authority may, as part of its controls, upon a written request from the owner of a registered trade mark or the holder of an exclusive export right, detain goods which the latter alleges are supplied under a trade mark which infringes his registered trade mark or in respect of which he holds an exclusive right of use.
>
> Where the customs authority detains goods it shall forthwith notify that fact to the Procureur de la République (state prosecutor), the person requesting such detention and the person declaring or in possession of the goods.
>
> Unless within ten working days of the notification of the detention of the goods the person requesting the detention provides the customs authority with evidence either:
>
>> —of an order of the President of the Tribunal de Grande Instance (Regional Court) for interim measures; or
>>
>> —that the person requesting the detention has instituted civil or criminal proceedings and provided the security required to cover any liability where the infringement is not upheld in final proceedings . . .
>
> the measure by which the goods are detained shall be discharged.

The dispute in the main proceedings and the question referred for a preliminary ruling

Rioglass manufactures and sells windows and windscreens for all makes of car. According to the file, it was approved by Sogédac, responsible, in its capacity as agent and central purchaser, for the approval of suppliers to the car manufacturers Peugeot, Citroen and Renault, as a supplier to those manufacturers.

In November 1997, Rioglass sold to Jann, a company registered in Poland, a consignment of windows and windscreens, lawfully produced in Spain, intended for various makes of car. Transremar was given responsibility for the transport of those goods. The goods were exported from Spain to Poland under cover of a Community transit certificate EX T2 issued on 24 November 1997, and thus qualified for the duty-suspension arrangements which allow movement between two points in the customs territory of the Community and Poland free of import duty, tax or commercial policy measures. Some of the windows and windscreens, intended for use in Peugeot, Citroň or Renault models, bore the logo or trade mark of those constructors alongside the manufacturer's trade mark.

On the same day, French customs officers carried out an inspection of Transremar's lorry near Bordeaux. On 25 November 1997 and 27 November 1997, the customs officers drew up, respectively, a report of detention of the goods and a report of seizure of the goods on suspicion of infringement of trade mark.

Rioglass and Transremar applied for interim relief seeking an order that the detention and seizure measures be lifted. By two orders of 8 December 1997 and 8 January 1998, the judge hearing the application for interim relief dismissed the applications, whereupon the applicants brought appeal proceedings against those orders. Their appeals were upheld by the Cour d'appel de Bordeaux (Bordeaux Court of Appeal) which ruled, in its judgment of 22 November 1999, that the detention of the lorry, the windscreens and the windows constituted a clear infringement of the right to private property and ordered the customs authority to return the goods, documents and deposits.

The customs authority lodged an appeal against that judgment before the Cour de cassation.

The Cour de cassation referred in that context to the judgment in Case C–23/99 *Commission v France* [2000] E.C.R. I–7653, in which the Court of Justice held that, by implementing, pursuant to the Code de la propriété intellectuelle, procedures for detention by the customs authorities of goods lawfully manufactured in a Member State of the European Community which are intended, following their transit through French territory, to be placed on the market in another Member State, where they may be lawfully marketed, the French Republic had failed to fulfil its obligations under Art. 28 EC.

The Cour de cassation formed the view, however, that resolution of the dispute called for an interpretation of Community law in order to determine whether the solution adopted in that judgment also applied in the present case, and decided to stay the proceedings and refer the following question to the Court for a preliminary ruling:

> Is Art. 30 of the Treaty, now Art. 28 EC, to be interpreted as meaning that it precludes the implementation, pursuant to the Code de la propriété intellectuelle, of procedures for detention by the customs authorities of goods lawfully manufactured in a Member State of the European Community which are intended, following their transit through French territory, to be placed on the market in a non-member country, in the present case, Poland?

The question referred for a preliminary ruling

Reply of the Court

It should be noted as a preliminary point that the fact that the goods in question in the main proceedings were intended for export to a non-member country does not necessarily lead to the conclusion that, in a situation such as that in the present case, those goods do not fall within the scope of the EC Treaty provisions on the free movement of goods between Member States.

Given that, as is apparent from the file, the present case involves goods lawfully manufactured in one Member State in transit within another Member State, it must be pointed out that, according to settled case law, the Customs Union established by the EC Treaty necessarily implies that the free movement of goods between Member States should be ensured. That freedom could not itself be complete if it were possible for Member States to impede or interfere in any way with the movement of goods in transit. It is therefore necessary, as a consequence of the Customs Union and in the mutual interest of the Member States, to acknowledge the existence of a general principle of freedom of transit of goods within the Community. That principle is, moreover, confirmed by the reference to transit in Art. 30 EC.

The Court has moreover already held that Arts. 28 to 30 EC are applicable to goods in transit through a Member State but intended for a non-member country.

It follows that, even if goods in transit are intended for a non-member country, they come within the scope of Arts. 28 to 30 EC and the question referred for a preliminary ruling must accordingly be examined in the light of those provisions.

The Court is bound to conclude in that connection, firstly, that a measure of detention under customs control such as that in issue in the main proceedings, which delays the movement of goods and, if the competent court rules that they are to be confiscated, may block their movement completely, has the effect of restricting the free movement of goods and therefore constitutes an obstacle to that freedom.

Therefore, given that the detention under customs control in issue in the main proceedings was carried out on the basis of the Code de la propriété intellectuelle, it is necessary to determine whether the obstacle to the free movement of goods created by that detention under customs control may be justified by the need to ensure the protection of industrial and commercial property referred to in Art. 30 EC.

In order to answer that question it is necessary to take account of the purpose of that exception, which is to reconcile the requirements of the free movement of goods and the right of industrial and commercial property, by avoiding the maintenance or establishment of artificial barriers within the common market. Article 30 EC allows derogations from the fundamental principle of the free movement of goods within the common market only to the extent to which such derogations are justified for the purpose of safeguarding rights which constitute the specific subject-matter of such property.

According to the judgment for reference, the goods in issue in the present case were detained on suspicion of infringement of trade mark.

With respect to trade marks, it is settled case law that the specific subject-matter of a trade mark is, in particular, to guarantee to the owner that he has the exclusive right to use that mark for the purpose of putting a product on the market for the first time and thus to protect him against competitors wishing to take unfair advantage of the status and reputation of the trade mark by selling products illegally bearing it.

The implementation of such protection is therefore linked to the marketing of the goods.

Transit, such as that in issue in the main proceedings, which consists in transporting goods lawfully manufactured in a Member State to a non-member country by passing through one or more Member States, does not involve any marketing of the goods in question and is therefore not liable to infringe the specific subject-matter of the trade mark.

Furthermore, that conclusion holds good regardless of the final destination of the goods in transit. The fact that the goods are subsequently placed on the market in a non-member country and not in another Member State does not alter the nature of the transit operation which, by definition, does not constitute a placing on the market.

Therefore, a measure of detention under customs control, such as that in issue in the main proceedings, cannot be justified on the ground of protection of industrial and commercial property within the meaning of Art. 30 EC.

In those circumstances, the answer to the question referred for a preliminary ruling must be that Art. 28 EC is to be interpreted as precluding the implementation, pursuant to a legislative measure of a Member State concerning intellectual property, of procedures for detention by the customs authorities of goods lawfully manufactured in another Member State and intended, following their transit through the territory of the first Member State, to be placed on the market in a non-member country.

NOTES AND QUESTIONS

1. In *Rioglass*, French Customs officials detained goods manufactured by Rioglass on suspicion of trademark infringement. What were the acts committed by Rioglass that led French officials to conclude that it may have engaged in a violation of trademarks owned by Peugeot, Citroen, or Renault?

2. How did the ECJ rule on whether French officials could detain the goods? Why is it significant that goods that are in transit are not placed on the market in the country of transit?

3. *Comparison with United States law.* In *United States v. Watches, Watch Parts, Calculators & Misc. Parts*, 692 F.Supp. 1317 (S.D. Fla. 1988), the defendants shipped watches and watch parts from Hong Kong into the U.S. bearing counterfeit marks of U.S. registered trademarks. The shipment was in transit through the U.S. with a final destination in Paraguay. The defendants argued that as the shipment was in transit, the goods had not been imported into the U.S. and were not subject to seizure under U.S. trademark law. The district court disagreed, and allowed goods in transit through the U.S. to be subject to seizure and detention. Compare the U.S. approach with the EU approach in *Rioglass*. What do you think accounts for the difference in approach? How is the EU concept of a common market and free movement of goods relevant? Is the approach of the EU consistent with TRIPS? See footnote 13 of TRIPS Article 51.

D. PRIVATE ENFORCEMENT—PROCEDURAL AND SUBSTANTIVE CONCERNS

Even if countries faithfully implement enforcement mechanisms consistent with their TRIPS obligations and combat commercial piracy, IP rights holders still face many procedural and substantive concerns in attempting to enforce their rights internationally. In this final section, we revisit our hypothetical company Apex's difficulties in seeking and litigating to enforce IP rights internationally. We discuss the following topics: (1) choice of forum, jurisdiction, and choice of law, (2) recognition and enforcement of foreign court judgments, and (3) exhaustion of IP rights and gray market goods. Each of these issues raises challenges for enforcing IP rights internationally—challenges which derive in part from the longstanding territorial approach to intellectual property. In this section, we discuss the first two sets of issues. The issue of exhaustion is discussed in the next section.

1. CHOICE OF FORUM, JURISDICTION, AND CHOICE OF LAW

For any IP lawsuit involving transnational activity or elements, Apex must consider three distinct but related concepts: (1) the choice of forum, (2) a court's jurisdiction over the claim(s) and defendant(s), and (3) the choice of law that governs the claim(s). The forum's law typically will provide the rules of jurisdiction and conflicts of laws. MNEs, such as Apex with its headquarters in the United States, often have a strong preference for choosing a forum of the home nation, assuming all other factors to be equal. Filing an action in the United States will allow Apex to use U.S. legal procedures with which Apex's legal department is familiar. But a party's choice of forum does not necessarily mean that a court will entertain the lawsuit: a court must have jurisdiction over a lawsuit in order to hear the lawsuit. In cases involving the international trade in counterfeit and pirated goods, the choice of the United States as the forum may not even be an option.

The key in choosing a forum in which to sue is finding a court that has jurisdiction over (i) the defendant(s) and (ii) the IP claim(s). TRIPS does not establish any governing principles for jurisdiction, and countries vary somewhat in their approaches. Countries have attempted to create a uniform set of rules for jurisdiction in civil cases under the proposed Hague Convention on Jurisdiction and Foreign Judgments in Civil and Commercial Matters (1999), which is modeled on the European approach in the Brussels (1968) and the Lugano (1988) Conventions on Jurisdiction and Enforcement of Judgments in Civil and Commercial Matters. Such efforts, however, have stalled. Consequently, parties must consult the laws of each country where suit is brought to determine issues of jurisdiction.

U.S. approach to jurisdiction. In the U.S., jurisdiction is broken down into (i) personal jurisdiction over the defendant(s) and (ii) subject matter jurisdiction over the claim(s). First let us consider personal jurisdiction over the defendant. Territorial jurisdiction over the defendant is a fundamental requirement because under international law no court can render a valid and enforceable judgment adjudicating rights against a defendant over which the court has no jurisdiction. The United States approach allows a U.S. court to assert jurisdiction over a defendant consistent with the requirements of the Due Process Clause of the U.S. Constitution if the defendant has certain minimum contacts with the forum. This principle was established long ago in the landmark case *International Shoe Co. v. State of Washington*, 326 U.S. 310 (1945) and was developed in a long line of U.S. Supreme Court cases. *See, e.g., Hanson v. Denckla*, 357 U.S. 235, 253 (1958) (minimum contacts are established when defendant purposefully avails itself of the privilege of conducting activities within the forum state invoking the privilege and benefit of its laws). Although *International Shoe* involved a domestic dispute, U.S. courts use the same approach based on minimum contacts for an international dispute where a defendant is located in a foreign nation. *See Asahi Metal Industry Co., Ltd. v. Superior Court*, 480 U.S. 102 (1987) (dismissing tort case arising from a motorcycle accident brought against defendant Japanese valve manufacturer for lack of territorial jurisdiction).

Even if jurisdiction over a defendant is established, subject matter jurisdiction and choice of law must also be considered. Generally, the country where the alleged infringing activity occurred both (i) creates the governing IP law to proscribe the infringing activity and (ii) has jurisdiction to entertain IP claims for activity within its border. This is, in part, a reflection of the territorial approach to IP laws that we discussed in Chapter 1. As the initial starting point in determining what country's IP law to invoke, one must determine where the alleged infringing activity occurred. The law of the country where the infringement occurred will typically govern. Take the following simple example:

> Illustration 6–1. Competitor X infringes Apex's patented and trademarked products in the U.S. What law governs Competitor X's infringing activity? U.S. patent and trademark law govern because the infringement is in the U.S. Do U.S. federal courts have subject matter

jurisdiction to hear Apex's lawsuit against Competitor X? Yes, U.S. courts have the authority to hear U.S. patent and trademark claims.

Things become more complicated, however, when infringing activity spans several countries. Consider the following two examples:

Illustration 6–2. Competitor X infringes Apex's patented and trademarked products in Europe and Japan. Can Apex sue Competitor X in the U.S. for patent and trademark infringement? In the typical case, no. Apex's U.S. patent and U.S. trademark do not typically have effect outside of the U.S., and, for a number of reasons, U.S. courts traditionally have not entertained foreign patent or trademark claims. However, trademark claims under the Lanham Act may reach extraterritorial conduct if the conduct produces a substantial effect within the United States. *Steele v. Bulova Watch Co.*, 344 U.S. 280 (1952).

Illustration 6–3. Competitor X infringes Apex's patented and trademarked products in the U.S., Europe, and Japan. Can Apex sue Competitor X in the U.S. for patent and trademark infringement? Yes, but typically only for the infringing activity in the U.S. Even though the U.S. court has jurisdiction over the U.S. patent and trademark claims, U.S. courts traditionally have not entertained supplemental jurisdiction over foreign patent or trademark claims.

Illustration 6–3 provides a good example of why enforcing IP rights internationally may be expensive and burdensome. Traditionally, most countries do not hear foreign patent or trademark claims, even where a court has jurisdiction over a domestic patent or trademark claim involving a related course of infringing conduct. Part of the reason for this doctrine, as discussed in *London Films* below, is the perception that a patent or trademark lawsuit might involve a defense challenging the validity of the particular foreign patent or trademark, a matter best left for the foreign country that granted the IP right to decide. Under various doctrines, such as comity, forum non conveniens, and the act of the state doctrine, countries have been reluctant to entertain foreign patent and trademark claims, in order to avoid passing on the (in)validity of patents or trademarks granted by a foreign country.

By contrast, the U.S. and other countries have appeared to be more receptive to allowing their own courts to hear foreign copyright claims. Does the difference in approach between foreign patent/trademark claims versus foreign copyright claims make sense? Consider the following U.S. cases.

LONDON FILM PRODUCTIONS LIMITED v. INTERCONTINENTAL COMMUNICATIONS, INC.

U.S. District Court for the Southern District of New York.
580 F. Supp. 47 (S.D.N.Y. 1984).

CARTER, DISTRICT JUDGE.

This case presents a novel question of law. Plaintiff, London Film Productions, Ltd. ("London"), a British corporation, has sued Intercontinental Communications, Inc. ("ICI"), a New York corporation based in New York City, for infringements of plaintiff's British copyright. The alleged infringements occurred in Chile and other South American countries. In bringing the case before this Court, plaintiff has invoked the Court's diversity jurisdiction. 28 U.S.C. § 1332(a)(2). Defendant has moved to dismiss plaintiff's complaint, arguing that the Court should abstain from exercising jurisdiction over this action.

Background

London produces feature motion pictures in Great Britain, which it then distributes throughout the world. ICI specializes in the licensing of motion pictures, produced by others, that it believes are in the public domain. London's copyright infringement claim is based mainly on license agreements between ICI and Dilatsa S.A., a buying agent for Chilean television stations. The agreements apparently granted the latter the right to distribute and exhibit certain of plaintiff's motion pictures on television in Chile. London also alleges that ICI has marketed several of its motion pictures in Venezuela, Peru, Ecuador, Costa Rica and Panama, as well as in Chile. Plaintiff alleges that the films that are the subjects of the arrangements between Dilatsa S.A. and defendant are protected by copyright in Great Britain as well as in Chile and most other countries (but not in the United States) by virtue of the terms and provisions of the Berne Convention.

Determination

There seems to be no dispute that plaintiff has stated a valid cause of action under the copyright laws of a foreign country. Also clear is the fact that this Court has personal jurisdiction over defendant; in fact, there is no showing that defendant may be subject to personal jurisdiction in another forum. Under these circumstances, one authority on copyright law has presented an argument pursuant to which this Court has jurisdiction to hear the matter before it. M. Nimmer, 3 *Nimmer on Copyright,* (1982). It is based on the theory that copyright infringement constitutes a transitory cause of action, and hence may be adjudicated in the courts of a sovereign other than the one in which the cause of action arose. That theory appears sound in the absence of convincing objections by defendant to the contrary.

Although plaintiff has not alleged the violation of any laws of this country by defendant, this Court is not bereft of interest in this case. The Court has an obvious interest in securing compliance with this nation's laws by citizens of foreign nations who have dealings within this jurisdiction. A concern with the conduct of American citizens in foreign countries is merely the reciprocal of that interest. An unwillingness by this Court to hear a complaint against its own citizens with regard to a violation of foreign law will engender, it would seem, a similar unwillingness on the part of a foreign jurisdiction when the question arises concerning a violation of our laws by one of its citizens who has since left our jurisdiction. This Court's interest in adjudicating the controversy in this case may be indirect, but its importance is not thereby diminished.

The facts in this case confirm the logic of Nimmer's observation. The British films at issue here received copyright protection in Great Britain simply by virtue of publication there. Chile's adherence to the Berne Convention in 1970 automatically conferred copyright protection on these films in Chile. Therefore, no "act of state" is called into question here. Moreover, there is no danger that foreign courts will be forced to accept the inexpert determination of this Court, nor that this Court will create "an unseemly conflict with the judgment of another country." *See Packard Instrument Co. v. Beckman Instruments, Inc.,* 346 F. Supp. 408, 410 (N.D. Ill. 1972). The litigation will determine only whether an American corporation has acted in violation of a foreign copyright, not whether such copyright exists, nor whether such copyright is valid.

With respect to defendant's *forum non conveniens* argument, it is true that this case will likely involve the construction of at least one, if not several foreign laws.[6] However, the need to apply foreign law is not in itself reason to dismiss or transfer the case. Moreover, there is no foreign forum in which defendant is the subject of personal jurisdiction, and an available forum is necessary to validate dismissal of an action on the ground of *forum non conveniens,* for if there is no alternative forum "the plaintiff might find himself with a valid claim but nowhere to assert it." *Farmanfarmaian v. Gulf Oil Corp.,* 437 F. Supp. 910, 915 (S.D.N.Y. 1977) (Carter, J.), *aff'd,* 588 F.2d 880 (2d Cir. 1978).

For all of the above reasons, the Court finds it has jurisdiction over the instant case and defendant's motion to dismiss is denied.

VODA v. CORDIS CORP.

U.S. Court of Appeals for the Federal Circuit.
476 F.3d 887 (Fed. Cir. 2007).

GAJARSA, CIRCUIT JUDGE.

I. BACKGROUND

The plaintiff-appellee Voda is a resident of Oklahoma City, Oklahoma. The defendant-appellant Cordis is a U.S.-based entity incorporated in Florida. None of the several foreign Cordis affiliates is a party to the present action, and we note that they appear to be separate legal entities. [All of the Cordis companies, both U.S. and foreign, are members of the Johnson & Johnson family of companies.] These foreign affiliates have not been joined to this action. To prevent confusion, we refer to the defendant-appellant as "Cordis U.S."

---

6. Plaintiff has alleged infringements in Chile, Venezuela, Peru, Ecuador, Costa Rica and Panama. Since, under the Berne Convention, the applicable law is the copyright law of the state in which the infringement occurred, defendant seems correct in its assumption that the laws of several countries will be involved in the case.

The patents at issue relate generally to guiding catheters for use in interventional cardiology. Voda's U.S. patents stem from a common continuation-in-part ("CIP") application filed in October 1992, which provides the written description common to the three U.S. patents at issue in this case. The foreign patents issued from a common Patent Cooperation Treaty ("PCT") application. The PCT application designated the European Patent Office ("EPO") and Canada as recipients. Voda's EPO patent application eventually generated European Pat. No. 0 568 624, British Pat. No. GB 568 624, French Pat. No. FR568624, and German Pat. No. DE 69 23 20 95. The PCT application also ultimately led to the issuance of Canadian Pat. No. CA 2,100,785.

Voda sued Cordis U.S. in the United States District Court for the Western District of Oklahoma alleging infringement of his three U.S. patents. Cordis U.S. answered by asserting noninfringement and invalidity of the U.S. patents. Voda then moved to amend his complaint to add claims of infringement of the European, British, Canadian, French, and German foreign patents. Cordis U.S. has admitted that "the XB catheters have been sold domestically and internationally since 1994. The XB catheters were manufactured in Miami Lakes, Florida from 1993 to 2001 and have been manufactured in Juarez, Mexico since 2001."

A proper exercise of subject matter jurisdiction pursuant to § 1367 requires both the presence of jurisdiction under subsection (a) and an appropriate decision to exercise that jurisdiction under subsection (c). For the reasons discussed below, we conclude that the district court erred under subsection (c).

III.   DISCUSSION

A.   *Asserted Statutory Basis*

1.   *Authorization*

[The majority acknowledged that supplemental jurisdiction can be exercised over foreign law claims under Section 1367(a) when they arise under the same "common nucleus of operative fact" as a claim over which a court has proper jurisdiction but decided not to reach this issue because the court found that the district court abused its discretion under 1367(c). *Ed.*]

2.   *Discretion*

Section 1367 "reaffirms that the exercise of supplemental jurisdiction is within the discretion of the district court." *Mars,* 24 F.3d at 1374. We conclude that the district court's exercise of supplemental jurisdiction over Voda's foreign patent infringement claims is independently limited by subsection (c).

Section 1367(c) provides: "The district courts may decline to exercise supplemental jurisdiction over a claim under subsection (a) if—" * * * (4) in exceptional circumstances, there are other compelling reasons for declining jurisdiction." 28 U.S.C. § 1367(c). We find that considerations of comity, judicial economy, convenience, fairness, and other exceptional circumstances constitute compelling reasons to decline jurisdiction under § 1367(c) in this case and therefore, hold that the district court abused its discretion by assuming jurisdiction.

Article VI of the Constitution proclaims that "all treaties made, or which shall be made, under the authority of the United States, shall be the supreme law of the land." U.S. Const. art. VI, cl. 2.

The United States entered into Articles 13 through 30 of the Paris Convention for the Protection of Industrial Property ("Paris Convention") on September 5, 1970 and Articles 1 through 12 of the Paris Convention on August 25, 1973. Article 4 *bis* of the Paris Convention states that U.S. patents "shall be independent of patents obtained for the same invention in other countries" and that the "foregoing provision is to be understood in an unrestricted sense, . . . both as regards the grounds for nullity and forfeiture." In addition, Article 2(3) of the Paris Convention states that the "provisions of the laws of each of the countries of the Union relating to judicial and administrative procedure and to jurisdiction, . . . which may be required by the laws on industrial property are expressly reserved." The Paris Convention thus clearly expresses the independence of each country's sovereign patent systems and their systems for adjudicating those patents. Nothing in the Paris Convention contemplates nor allows one jurisdiction to adjudicate the patents of another, and as such, our courts should not determine the validity and infringement of foreign patents.

Subsequently, the United States adopted the Patent Cooperation Treaty ("PCT") on January 24, 1978. As with the Paris Convention, the text of the PCT maintains the independence of each country's patents.

On January 1, 1995, the United States joined the World Trade Organization, which binds all of its members to the Agreement on Trade–Related Aspects of Intellectual Property Rights ("TRIPS"). The Agreement on TRIPS contains several provisions regarding the enforcement of patents. Article 41 § 1 of the Agreement on TRIPS specifies that each country "shall ensure that enforcement procedures as specified in this Part are available under their law so as to permit effective action against any act of infringement of intellectual property rights." In addition, § 4 states that "[p]arties to a proceeding shall have an opportunity for review by a judicial authority of final administrative decisions and, subject to jurisdictional provisions in a Member's law concerning the importance of a case," and § 5 states "[i]t is understood that this Part does not . . . affect the capacity of Members to enforce their law in general." *See also id.,* art. 41–49. Like the Paris Convention, nothing in the PCT or the Agreement on TRIPS contemplates or allows one jurisdiction to adjudicate patents of another.

Voda asserts and one of the amicus curiae briefs suggests that these international treaties evince a trend of harmonization of patent law and thus, that allowing the exercise of supplemental jurisdiction over Voda's foreign patent infringement claims furthers the harmonization goals underlying the treaties. Regardless of the strength of the harmonization trend, however, we as the U.S. judiciary should not unilaterally decide either for our government or for other foreign sovereigns that our courts will become the adjudicating body for any foreign patent with a U.S. equivalent "so related" to form "the same case or controversy." Permitting our district courts to exercise jurisdiction over infringement claims based on foreign patents in this case would require us to define the legal boundaries of a property right granted by another sovereign and then determine whether there has been a trespass to that right.

Based on the international treaties that the United States has joined and ratified as the "supreme law of the land," a district court's exercise of supplemental jurisdiction could undermine the obligations of the United States under such treaties, which therefore constitute an exceptional circumstance to decline jurisdiction under § 1367(c)(4).

VACATED and *REMANDED.*

NEWMAN, CIRCUIT JUDGE, dissenting.

[The dissent noted cases in which the exercise of jurisdiction over foreign patents was contemplated. *Ed.*] [I]n *Ortman v. Stanray,* 371 F.2d 154 (7th Cir. 1967) the court approved the exercise of supplemental jurisdiction of counts concerning the corresponding Canadian, Brazilian, and Mexican patents. In *Medigene AG v. Loyola Univ. of Chicago,* No. 98 C 2026, 2001 WL 1636916 (N.D. Ill. Dec. 19, 2001) the district court declined to dismiss the issue of inventorship of foreign patent applications, stating that "in appropriate circumstances Section 1367 permits exercise of supplemental jurisdiction over a claim for infringement of a foreign patent." *Id.* at *1.

I respond to the several other justifications offered in the majority opinion, for they also are flawed:

The Facts as Pled Support the District Court's Action

The accused catheter is the same in all five countries; it is manufactured by Cordis Corporation in a single plant, initially at Miami Lakes, Florida and now in Mexico. Cordis manages the Mexican plant and arranges for shipment to the Cordis companies in the five countries where infringement is charged, *viz.,* Cordis Corporation (US), Cordis S.A. (France), Cordis G.m.b.H (Germany), Cordis UK Limited, and Cordis in Canada. All of the Cordis companies are related to the Johnson & Johnson Company. The patents in the five countries show that they are of common origin. A PCT application, based on the United States application, was filed in the Canadian and European Patent Offices.

The Role of Patent Treaties

The panel majority proposes that it would violate the Paris Convention for the Protection of Industrial Property, the Patent Cooperation Treaty, and the TRIPS Agreement of the World Trade Organization, if the

United States were to consider the validity and infringement of Dr. Voda's foreign patents. None of these treaties prohibits resolution by a national court of private disputes that include foreign patent rights.

Comity, Harmonization, and the Future

Proponents of patent "harmonization" point to the similarity of the policies that underlie patent law of all industrialized nations, and stress that for most technologies the same scope of practical protection is available to industrial development in all nations. It would be anomalous indeed for the United States now to rule that the courts cannot understand patent principles as applied in other nations. From my colleagues' extreme limitation and bar on the district court's exercise of discretion to receive and resolve foreign patent issues, I respectfully dissent.

Notes and Questions

1. What was the basis of subject matter jurisdiction over the copyright claims in *London Film*? Should the same approach be available for patents or trademarks?

2. In a part of her dissent not reproduced above, Judge Newman noted that some courts such as in Japan have exercised jurisdiction over foreign patent law claims. These cases are the exception, however. Most courts refuse to hear foreign patent claims. Should the increased efforts to achieve substantive and procedural patent harmonization—led by the United States and discussed in Chapter 3—be extended so that countries can entertain foreign patent claims?

3. *European approach to jurisdiction.* Although the U.S. is not a party to a multi-lateral treaty on jurisdiction in civil matters, the EU concluded the Brussels Convention on Jurisdiction and the Enforcement of Judgments in Civil and Commercial Matters, 1972 O.J. (L299) (1990) (originally signed in 1968 and applicable among all EU member states) and the almost identical Lugano Convention on Jurisdiction and the Enforcement of Judgments in Civil and Commercial Matters, 1988 O.J. (L319) 28 I.L.M. 620 (1989) (applicable among EU states and the European Free Trade Association). Although the U.S. was a major participant in negotiations for the proposed Hague Convention, differences among countries thus far have not been resolved.

Under the Brussels Convention Article 2, parties can be sued in any country (i.e., contracting state) where they are domiciled. Under Article 5, parties can also be sued in other contracting states outside of their domicile in certain defined circumstances, such as "in matters relating to tort, delict or quasidelict, in the courts for the place where the harmful event occurred"—a provision that covers intellectual property claims. The Brussels Convention follows a similar approach to the U.S. in terms of patents and trademarks. "[I]n proceedings concerned with the registration or validity of patents, trade marks, designs, or other similar rights required to be deposited or registered," Article 16 creates exclusive jurisdiction in "the courts of the Contracting State in which the deposit or registration has been applied for, has taken place or is under the terms of an international convention deemed to have taken place."

The Court of Justice interpreted this provision to require exclusive jurisdiction of the validity of a patent in the country that granted the patent, irrespective of how invalidity is raised. *See Gesellschaft für Antriebstechnik mbH & Co. KG (GAT) v. Lamellen und Kupplungsbau Beteiligungs KG (LuK),* Case C–4/03, 2006 E.C.R. I–6509.

2. RECOGNITION AND ENFORCEMENT OF FOREIGN COURT JUDGMENTS

PROBLEM 6–8

Max Goods, a multi-national consumer products company with its headquarters in the United States, has recently found that a flood of counterfeits of its products are being imported into the U.S. through false documentation. Max Goods has traced the original production of the goods to Eastern and Southern China through the use of diligent private investigations, but has not yet identified the particular entity who is counterfeiting Max Goods' products. Nor has Max Goods determined whether the source of the counterfeits in China was responsible for or even authorized the shipment to the U.S., as opposed to some third party distributor in the stream of commerce. The CEO of Max Goods, who finished one year of law school before switching to business, has just read *London Film* and asks you, the general counsel, the following, "I've been told how hard it is to enforce IP rights in China and that the courts are very weak. Let's sue the counterfeiter in federal district court in the United States just as the plaintiffs did in *London Film*. What do you think about my plan?" In answering the CEO's question, be sure to provide advice on the following four issues:

(1) Can a U.S. court establish personal jurisdiction over the original source of the counterfeited products from China based on the facts known so far?

(2) Can Max Goods bring a U.S. trademark claim against the original source of the counterfeited products from China based on the facts known so far?

(3) Would you recommend that Max Goods spend more resources trying to ascertain the identity of (a) who was responsible for the shipment of counterfeits into the U.S. and/or (b) who was responsible for the production of counterfeits in China?

(4) For this question only, assume that Max Goods later successfully brought a U.S. trademark claim against the source of the counterfeited products from China, but the defendant had no assets in the U.S. How likely do you think it will be for Max Goods to enforce the U.S. judgment in China, where the defendant does have assets?

Consider the following section on the enforcement of judgments, as well as the prior discussion on jurisdiction on pp. 727–736 supra.

* * *

In some cases, even where a U.S. or foreign court can assert territorial jurisdiction over a defendant, it may become necessary to enforce any judgment obtained against the foreign defendant in a different jurisdiction, such as the defendant's home country, if the defendant does not have any assets in the forum state. Recognition and enforcement of judgments is not usually an issue in the case of domestic disputes in the United States where a defendant has assets. Courts in the United States will generally recognize a valid judgment from a court in another state or by a U.S. federal court.

In an international context, however, enforcement of a judgment rendered by a court of one nation in another nation can pose some difficult problems. For example, assume that Apex is able to establish territorial jurisdiction over a foreign defendant in a U.S. court and is able to recover a judgment against the defendant. If the defendant has no assets in the United States, Apex may be compelled to seek to enforce the judgment in a foreign nation where the defendant has assets. In order to enforce the judgment, Apex will need to ask a court in the foreign nation to recognize the U.S. court judgment. As a general matter, court judgments, like intellectual property laws and national laws, are also bounded by the principle of territoriality. Unless the countries involved have entered into a multilateral or bilateral treaty, domestic courts will recognize foreign court judgments as a matter of international comity, which does not create a binding legal obligation but allows a domestic court to exercise its discretion in whether to recognize a foreign court judgment. A common approach to international comity followed by many countries, including the United States, is to examine a foreign judgment to determine (1) if the court had jurisdiction, (2) if the defendant was properly served, (3) if the proceedings were invalidated by fraud, and (4) if the foreign judgment is inconsistent with some public policy of the forum.

While the United States will generally recognize foreign judgments that meet the four requirements set forth above, many foreign states have not been as willing to recognize U.S. judgments. Part of their reluctance can be traced to the monetary awards in U.S. judgments, which are considerably higher than monetary awards in many countries of the world. In part for this reason, the U.S. has been the leading proponent of the proposed Hague Convention on the Recognition and Enforcement of Civil and Commercial Judgments. The Hague Convention, if and when it becomes effective, would create binding treaty obligations on the part of contracting states to recognize foreign judgments. As mentioned earlier, the EU follows the Brussels Convention on Jurisdiction and the Enforcement of Judgments in Civil and Commercial Matters, 1972 O.J. (L299) (1990), which establishes uniform rules for the enforcement of judgments in addition to jurisdiction. The proposed Hague Convention attempts to do the same. Although the U.S. has been relatively slow to join international agreements in this area, it has joined, in the area of arbitration, the United Nations Convention on the Recognition and Enforcement of Foreign Arbitral Awards, (New York, June 10, 1958) 330 U.N.T.S. 38 (1959). The U.S. would like to create a similarly reliable enforcement system for court judgments. To date, however, disagreement over the proposed Hague Convention has stalled negotiations.

Even in countries that normally enforce foreign judgments either out of principles of comity or treaty, most typically recognize a "public policy" exception. For example, Article 27 of the Brussels Convention states a "judgment shall not be recognized . . . if such recognition is contrary to public policy in the State in which recognition is sought." The following case provides a good illustration of the U.S. approach.

SARL LOUIS FERAUD INTERNATIONAL
v. VIEWFINDER, INC.

U.S. Court of Appeals for the Second Circuit.
489 F.3d 474 (2007).

POOLER, CIRCUIT JUDGE.

[Plaintiff-appellants were two French companies Sarl Louis Feraud International (Feraud) and S.A. Pierre Balmain (Balmain) in the business of designing high fashion clothing for women. Feraud and Balmain claimed that Viewfinder, a Delaware corporation, had posted photographs of their fashion shows on a website owned by Viewfinder. Feraud and Balmain filed suit against Viewfinder in France for breach of their intellectual property rights and unfair competition and recovered a default judgment when Viewfinder failed to appear. Feraud and Balmain then attempted to enforce the French court judgment in federal district court in New York. The district court refused to enforce the judgment on the grounds that enforcement would violate the public policy of New York because it would violate Viewfinder's First Amendment rights. Feraud and Balmain appealed to the Second Circuit, which rendered the opinion below. *Ed.*]

DISCUSSION

The question presented by this appeal is whether the district court properly found that the French Judgments were unenforceable under New York law. In order to address this question, we begin with the language of the relevant state statute: "A foreign country judgment need not be recognized if . . . the *cause of action* on which the judgment is based is repugnant to the public policy of this state." N.Y. C.P.L.R. § 5304(b)(4) (emphasis added). As the plain language of the statute makes clear, the first step in analyzing whether a judgment is unenforceable under Section 5304(b)(4) is to identify the "cause of action on which the judgment is based." The district court never identified the French statutes that underlie the judgments at issue in this case. Nor does Viewfinder do so in its submission. The default judgments issued by the French court explicitly state that Viewfinder's actions violated "articles L 716–1 and L 122–4 of the Intellectual Property Code." Article L 122–4 is in Book I, Title II, Chapter II of the French Intellectual Property Code, which are entitled "Copyright," "Authors' Rights," and "Patrimonial Rights," respectively. *See* Code de la propriete intellectuelle art. L 122–4(Fr.), *available at http:// www. legifrance. gouv. fr.* Article L 122–4 provides: "Any complete or partial performance or reproduction made without the consent of the author or of his successors in title or assigns shall be unlawful." *Id.* This is analogous to the United States Copyright Act, which defines a copyright infringer as one "who violates any of the exclusive rights of the copyright owner," 17 U.S.C. § 501, including the rights of reproduction, performance, and public display. 17 U.S.C. § 106. Under French copyright law, the "creations of the seasonal industries of dress and articles of fashion" are entitled to copyright protection. Code de la propriete intellectuelle art. L 112–2(Fr.), *available at http:// www. legifrance. gouv. fr.** The French court found that Viewfinder's publication of numerous photographs depicting plaintiffs' design collections violated plaintiffs' copyrights. Furthermore, the French Judgments concluded that Viewfinder's reproduction and publication of plaintiffs' designs were "without the necessary authorization." Thus, it is apparent that the French Judgments were based in part on a finding of copyright infringement.

We cannot second-guess the French court's finding that Viewfinder's actions were "without the necessary authorization." Viewfinder had the opportunity to dispute the factual basis of plaintiffs' claims in the French court, but it chose not to respond to the complaint. Thus, for the purposes of this action, we must accept that Viewfinder's conduct constitutes an unauthorized reproduction or performance of plaintiffs' copyrighted work infringing on plaintiffs' intellectual property rights, and the only question to consider is whether a law that sanctions such conduct is repugnant to the public policy of New York.

The "public policy inquiry rarely results in refusal to enforce a judgment unless it is inherently vicious, wicked or immoral, and shocking to the prevailing moral sense." *Sung Hwan Co. v. Rite Aid Corp.*, 7 N.Y.3d 78, 82 (N.Y. 2006). Furthermore, "it is well established that mere divergence from American procedure does not render a foreign judgment unenforceable." *Pariente v. Scott Meredith Literary Agency, Inc.*, 771 F. Supp. 609, 616 (S.D.N.Y. 1991). "Under New York law[,] ... foreign decrees and proceedings will be given respect ... even if the result under the foreign proceeding would be different than under American law." *Id.*; *see also Ackermann*, 788 F.2d at 842 ("We are not so provincial as to say that every solution of a problem is wrong because we deal with it otherwise at home.") Thus, "[o]nly in clear-cut cases ought [the public policy exception] to avail defendant." *Ackermann*, 788 F.2d at 841.

Laws that are antithetical to the First Amendment will create such a situation. Foreign judgments that impinge on First Amendment rights will be found to be "repugnant" to public policy. *See, e.g., Bachchan v. India Abroad Publ'ns Inc.*, 585 N.Y.S.2d 661, 662 (N.Y. Sup. Ct. 1992) ("[I]f ... the public policy to which the foreign judgment is repugnant is embodied in the First Amendment to the United States Constitution or the free speech guaranty of the Constitution of this State, the refusal to recognize the judgment should be, and it is deemed to be, 'constitutionally mandatory.' "); *Yahoo!, Inc. v. La Ligue Contre Le Racisme et L'Antisemitisme*, 169 F. Supp. 2d 1181, 1189–90 (N.D. Cal. 2001) (holding unenforceable French judgment rendered under law prohibiting Nazi propaganda because such law would violate the First Amendment), *rev'd on other grounds*, 433 F.3d

---

* By contrast, fashion designs typically are not copyrightable in the United States because they are designs that are often inseparable from the useful articles in which they are embodied. *Ed.*

1199 (9th Cir. 2006) (in banc). The district court in this case reached the conclusion that the French Judgments were unenforceable because they impinged on Viewfinder's First Amendment rights. In doing so, however, it appears not to have conducted the full analysis for us to affirm its decision.

The district court's decision appears to rest on the assumption that if Viewfinder is a news magazine reporting on a public event, then it has an absolute First Amendment defense to any attempt to sanction such conduct. The First Amendment does not provide such categorical protection. Intellectual property laws co-exist with the First Amendment in this country, and the fact that an entity is a news publication engaging in speech activity does not, standing alone, relieve such entities of their obligation to obey intellectual property laws. While an entity's status as a news publication may be highly probative on certain relevant inquiries, such as whether that entity has a fair use defense to copyright infringement, it does not render that entity immune from liability under intellectual property laws.

Rather, because Section 5304(b) requires courts to examine the cause of action on which the foreign judgment was based, the district court should have analyzed whether the intellectual property regime upon which the French Judgments were based impinged on rights protected by the First Amendment. This is consistent with the two-step analysis courts apply in deciding whether foreign libel judgments are repugnant to public policy: (1) identifying the protections deemed constitutionally mandatory for the defamatory speech at issue, and (2) determining whether the foreign libel laws provide comparable protection. *See, e.g., Bachchan,* 585 N.Y.S.2d at 663–65; *Abdullah v. Sheridan Square Press, Inc.,* No. 93 Civ. 2515, 1994 WL 419847, at *1 (S.D.N.Y. May 4, 1994). For instance, in *Bachchan,* the defamatory speech at issue related to a matter of public concern. Because the First Amendment requires a plaintiff to bear the burden of proving falsity when the speech involves matters of public concern, the New York court refused to enforce a British libel judgment because the British laws failed to provide this protection, placing the burden of proof on the defendant to prove the truth. *Bachchan,* 585 N.Y.S.2d at 664. The same analysis is appropriate here. In deciding whether the French Judgments are repugnant to the public policy of New York, the district court should first determine the level of First Amendment protection required by New York public policy when a news entity engages in the unauthorized use of intellectual property at issue here. Then, it should determine whether the French intellectual property regime provides comparable protections.

With regard to the protections provided by the First Amendment for the unauthorized use of copyrighted material, this court has held that absent extraordinary circumstances, "the fair use doctrine encompasses all claims of first amendment in the copyright field." *Twin Peaks Prods., Inc. v. Publ'ns Int'l, Ltd.,* 996 F.2d 1366, 1378 (2d Cir. 1993) (holding that book containing detailed synopses of episodes of television show "Twin

Peaks" would, absent a fair use defense, infringe copyright on television show); *see also Nihon Keizai Shimbun, Inc. v. Comline Bus. Data, Inc.,* 166 F.3d 65, 74 (2d Cir. 1999) ("We have repeatedly rejected First Amendment challenges to injunctions from copyright infringement on the ground that First Amendment concerns are protected by and coextensive with the fair use doctrine."); *Wainwright Sec., Inc. v. Wall St. Transcript Corp.,* 558 F.2d 91, 95 (2d Cir. 1977) ("Conflicts between interests protected by the first amendment and the copyright laws thus far have been resolved by application of the fair use doctrine."). Because the fair use doctrine balances the competing interests of the copyright laws and the First Amendment, some analysis of that doctrine is generally needed before a court can conclude that a foreign copyright judgment is repugnant to public policy. Factors that must be considered in determining fair use are:

(1) the purpose and character of the use, including whether such use is of a commercial nature or is for nonprofit educational purposes;

(2) the nature of the copyrighted work;

(3) the amount and substantiality of the portion used in relation to the copyrighted work as a whole; and

(4) the effect of the use upon the potential market for or value of the copyrighted work.

17 U.S.C. § 107. In this case, the district court dispensed with the issue of fair use in a single sentence: "Similarly, even were plaintiffs' designs copyrightable, the copyright law similarly provides, as a matter of First Amendment necessity, a 'fair use' exception for the publication of newsworthy matters." *Viewfinder,* 406 F. Supp. 2d at 284. To the extent the district court believed that Viewfinder's use was necessarily fair use because it was publishing "newsworthy matters," this was erroneous. *See, e.g., Harper & Row,* 471 U.S. at 557 (finding that The Nation's use of verbatim quotes from upcoming Gerald Ford memoir regarding Watergate scandal was not fair use even though material related to matter of public importance); *see also Roy Exp. Co. Establishment v. Columbia Broad. Sys.,* 672 F.2d 1095, 1099 (2d Cir. 1982) (rejecting argument from CBS that a "generalized First Amendment privilege" regarding "newsworthy events" precluded liability for copyright infringement); *Iowa State Univ. Research Found., Inc. v. Am. Broad. Cos.,* 621 F.2d 57, 61 (2d Cir.1980) ("The fair use doctrine is not a license for corporate theft, empowering a court to ignore copyright whenever it determines the underlying work contains material of possible public importance."). Whether the material is newsworthy is but one factor in the fair use analysis.

While both parties urge this court to resolve the issue of fair use, the record before us is insufficient to determine fair use as a matter of law. For instance, the record is unclear as to the percentage of plaintiffs' designs that were posted on firstView.com. While the French Judgments do provide some information as to the number of photographs posted by Viewfinder, that information is both incomplete and unclear because it does not indicate what proportion of plaintiffs' designs were revealed by these photographs. Such factual findings are relevant in determining whether Viewfinder's use would constitute "fair use" under United States law. If the publication of photographs of copyrighted material in the same manner as Viewfinder has done in this case would not be fair use under United States law, then the French intellectual property regime sanctioning the same conduct certainly would not be repugnant to public policy. Similarly, if the sole reason that Viewfinder's conduct would be permitted under United States copyright law is that plaintiffs' dress designs are not copyrightable in the United States, the French Judgment would not appear to be repugnant. However, without further development of the record, we cannot reach any conclusions as to whether Viewfinder's conduct would fall within the protection of the fair use doctrine.

CONCLUSION

For the foregoing reasons, we vacate the judgment of the district court and remand for further proceedings consistent with this opinion. Because we remand for a new analysis by the district court, we do not address the other grounds of alleged error raised by plaintiffs.

NOTES AND QUESTIONS

1. According to the Second Circuit, what was the error committed by the district court when it found that the French court judgment was repugnant to the policy of the United States? Suppose that on remand, the district court finds that French copyright law provides protections comparable to U.S. First Amendment protections for news agencies. Would the judgment be enforceable? Since the fashions in this case would mostly likely not be protected by copyright under U.S. law, is the granting of copyright protection by the French courts repugnant to the public policy of the United States and a basis for denying recognition of the French court judgment?

2. The approach followed by *Feraud* is similar to that followed by many countries in the world. Courts will not recognize foreign court judgments that are inconsistent with some important public policy or interest of the forum. How predictable is the enforcement of foreign judgments under this standard? Should there be any limits placed on the public policy exception, or is this one area in which countries must be afforded wide latitude?

3. What if enforcement of judgments (subject to public policy and other exceptions) became a TRIPS obligation for WTO countries? Do you think the U.S. would favor such an approach? What about other countries?

E. EXHAUSTION OF RIGHTS AND GRAY MARKET GOODS

Let us return now to our hypothetical company Apex. One of its main concerns beyond commercial piracy is with gray market goods. Apex finds that some of its genuine goods that it manufactures abroad for sale at cheaper prices in a foreign country are being purchased by foreign distributors and then shipped to other foreign markets, including the United States. Gray market goods may pose a significant business problem for Apex, which like most MNEs, engages in price discrimination among different markets. For example, Apex charges higher prices for its goods in its two largest markets, North America and Europe, than in Southeast Asia and South America, its next two largest markets. If a distributor can purchase less expensive Apex goods in Southeast Asia and then import them into Europe and North America, the distributor can undercut Apex's higher prices in its two largest markets and Apex will lose the benefits of price differentials between markets.

Parallel imports or gray market goods are different from commercial piracy. Gray market goods or parallel imports are authentic goods that are intended for a foreign market but that are diverted or imported without permission of the IP owner into a country where the IP owner has valid intellectual property rights. Unlike counterfeit or pirated goods, which are fakes made without the authorization of the owner, gray market goods are genuine goods made with the authorization of the IP owner. The issue in most situations involving gray market goods is whether the IP owner has the right to prevent the importation of gray market goods by parties who do not have the consent of the IP owner. Unlike counterfeits, gray market goods may not be illegal, depending on the law of the relevant jurisdiction on exhaustion of rights.

> Illustration 6–4. Universal Electronics (UE), with its headquarters in Country Z, manufactures high-end electronic goods both for the market in Z and for sales to foreign markets around the world. A consumer goes to a large discount store where the consumer sees UE products that are being sold for up to 50% less than the normal retail price. The goods have an English language label pasted on the foreign language labeling. These are genuine UE goods that were intended to be sold in a foreign market. The discount store has taken advantage of currency exchange rates to purchase the UE products first sold abroad in a foreign market and has imported them into Z. UE seeks to prevent the entry of the gray market goods into Z. Whether UE can exclude the gray market goods or not depends on Z's approach to the exhaustion of intellectual property rights.

Countries have been unable to agree on a uniform approach to gray market goods. The lack of consensus can be traced to a disagreement on the exhaustion of intellectual property rights. In Illustration 6–4 above, whether UE can exclude the gray market goods from entry into Country Z depends on whether the first sale of the goods abroad exhausts UE's intellectual property rights to control the subsequent sale and distribution of the particular goods sold. If Country Z follows a doctrine of *international exhaustion*, then the first sale of the goods anywhere in the world exhausts UE's rights to control the subsequent sale and distribution of the particular goods sold and UE will have no right to prevent the importation of the goods into Country Z. If Country Z follows a doctrine of *national exhaustion*, then exhaustion occurs only if the first sale of the goods occurs within Country Z. As the first sale in Illustration 6–4 occurs abroad, under a national exhaustion approach, UE's rights are not exhausted and UE can prevent the importation of the goods. The EU follows a third approach: *regional exhaustion*. If Country Z is a member of the EU, then the crucial question is whether the first sale occurred within the EU, which will result in exhaustion of the IP owner's rights in the goods sold in all EU countries.

The issue of exhaustion can arise whether the intellectual property rights involved are patents, trademarks, or copyrights. Some countries, such as the United States, adopt a different approach with respect to each of these types of rights, while the EU adopts a common approach.

The inability of nations to agree on an international approach to exhaustion is reflected in TRIPS Article 6, which provides that "nothing in this Agreement shall be used to address the issue of the exhaustion of intellectual property rights." Subject to the requirements of the national treatment principle and the most favored national principle, WTO members are allowed to determine their own rules governing gray market goods. We explore the approaches of the EU and the United States below in greater detail below. Traditionally, IP courses have analyzed exhaustion in isolation, looking at trademarks, copyrights, and patents separately. Because modern business practice routinely involves items protected by several IP forms, we think the better approach is to examine the principles of exhaustion from all the major IP forms together as a unit. As you read each section, consider whether the rules for exhaustion differ across IP forms.

Notes and Questions

1. How do consumers benefit from gray market goods? If consumers benefit from gray market goods, why should trademark owners and other IP owners ever be able to prevent their importation?

2. Why would UE or another IP owner object to gray market goods?

3. Which approach to exhaustion—national, regional, or international—is most consistent with the overall goals of the World Trade Organization and the TRIPS Preamble's statement that members "*desir[e]* to reduce distortions and impediments to international trade, and tak[e] into account the need to promote effective and adequate protection of intellectual property rights, and to ensure that measures and procedures to enforce intellectual property rights do not themselves become barriers to legitimate trade"?

1. EXHAUSTION OF TRADEMARKS

Historically, the most complex exhaustion issues arose in connection with the gray market importation of trademarked goods. Exhaustion issues involving trademarks tended to be more complex because trademarks, more so than patents or copyrights, were often used simultaneously by the registered trademark owner and other affiliated or unaffiliated entities. With the growth of international business and trade in the past several decades, MNEs now have established even more subsidiaries and affiliated entities around the globe in order to penetrate foreign markets for their products. The expansion of MNEs has created a complex international corporate structure where many different affiliated corporate entities are involved in selling the same or modified products. The use of a single trademark by all of these entities becomes essential to indicate a single source of the origin of these goods. To decide whether exhaustion has occurred, countries examine a number of factors, including whether A is affiliated with B or can otherwise exercise control over the goods manufactured by B.

a. Approach in the EU

PROBLEM 6–9

La Nuit est Encore Jeune (La Nuit) is a French distributor of trendy fashion items directed at youthful consumers. La Nuit has purchased, from two different distributors, shipments of jeans manufactured by Wasted Youth, a U.S. clothing manufacturer. The Wasted label is a world famous brand and a pair of Wasted jeans can retail for as much as $600 in the United States. Wasted has obtained trademark registrations for the mark in many countries of the world, including the United States and all countries of the EU. La Nuit has obtained (i) a shipment of jeans originally sold by Wasted in Germany to a German distributor and (ii) a shipment originally sold by Wasted in the United States to a U.S. distributor located in New York. La Nuit wants to market those shipments now in Paris. Wasted's French headquarters for its EU business objects to La Nuit's sale of both shipments in France. Does Wasted have a legal basis to stop La Nuit? To advise Wasted, see the case below.

PROBLEM 6–10

Under EU law, which of the following (if any) would exhaust the trademark rights of Company A for its registered trademark in the EU:

  i. Company A's parent company or subsidiary sells the trademarked product in Germany;

  ii. Company A's licensee or exclusive distributor sells the trademarked product in France;

  iii. Company B, which is economically linked to Company A, sells the trademarked product in the United Kingdom;

  iv. Company C, which has received a complete assignment of all trademark rights from Company A in Spain, sells the trademarked product in Spain.

What test applies to determine whether these situations create exhaustion? Consult the following case.

IHT INTERNATIONALE HEIZTECHNIK GmbH v. IDEAL STANDARD GmbH

European Court of Justice.
[1994] ECR I–2789, Case C–9/93 (June 22, 1994).

[This dispute arose from a sale of the French trademark "Ideal Standard" used for heating equipment by the French subsidiary of American Standard, a US company, to Societe Generale de Fonderie ("SGF"), which then assigned the trademark to another French company, CICh. Both SGF and CICh have no affiliation with American Standard or any of its subsidiaries.

[American Standard also had a German subsidiary, Ideal–Standard GmbH, which used the German trademark "Ideal Standard" in Germany for heating equipment and sanitary fittings. Another German company, IHT, a subsidiary of CICh, imported heating equipment manufactured in France under the "Ideal Standard" trademark and sold the equipment in Germany. Ideal–Standard GmbH subsequently sought to enjoin IHT from marketing heating equipment in Germany under the "Ideal Standard" trademark on the grounds that such marketing would cause consumer confusion. The lower court in Germany entered the injunction on the grounds that it was consistent with two authorities: Case 192/73 Van Zuylen v HAG [1974] (HAG I) and Case C–10/89 CNL–SUCAL v. Hag [1990] ECR I–3711 (HAG II). The appeal court in Germany believed enjoining the French company from marketing its products in Germany might violate Articles 30 and 36 of the EEC Treaty prohibiting restrictions on trade within the common market. Article 30 prohibits quantitative restrictions on products traveling between EU countries. Article 36 allows exceptions when necessary to protect intellectual property rights. The German appeals court referred the case to the ECJ, which rendered the opinion below. *Ed.*]

It is common ground that a prohibition on the use in Germany by IHT of the name "Ideal Standard" for heating equipment would constitute a measure having equivalent effect to a quantitative restriction under Article 30. The question is, therefore, whether that prohibition may be justified under Article 36 of the Treaty.

The case-law on Articles 30 and 36, trade-mark law and parallel imports

On the basis of the second sentence of Article 36 of the Treaty the Court has consistently held:

"Inasmuch as it provides an exception to one of the fundamental principles of the common market, Article 36 in fact only admits of derogations from the free movement of goods where such derogations are justified for the purpose of safeguarding rights which constitute the specific subject-matter of this property.

An obstacle to the free movement of goods may arise out of the existence, within a national legislation concerning industrial and commercial property, of provisions laying down that a trade mark owner's right is not exhausted when the product protected by the trade mark is marketed in another Member State, with the result that the trade mark owner can [oppose] importation of the product into his own Member State when it has been marketed in another Member State.

Such an obstacle is not justified when the product has been put onto the market in a legal manner in the Member State from which it has been imported, by the trade mark owner himself or with his consent, so that there can be no question of abuse or infringement of the trade mark.

In fact, if a trade mark owner could prevent the import of protected products marketed by him or with his consent in another Member State, he would be able to partition off national markets and thereby restrict trade between Member States, in a situation where no such restriction was necessary to guarantee the essence of the exclusive right flowing from the "trade mark" (see Case 16/74 Centrafarm v Winthrop [1974] ECR 1183, paragraphs 7 to 11).

So, application of a national law which would give the trade-mark owner in the importing State the right to oppose the marketing of products which have been put into circulation in the exporting State by him or with his consent is precluded as contrary to Articles 30 and 36. This principle, known as the exhaustion of rights, applies where the owner of the trade mark in the importing State and the owner of the trade mark in the exporting State are the same or where, even if they are separate persons, they are economically linked. A number of situations are covered: products put into circulation by the same undertaking, by a licensee, by a parent company, by a subsidiary of the same group, or by an exclusive distributor.

There are numerous instances in national case-law and Community case-law where the trade mark had been assigned to a subsidiary or to an exclusive distributor in order to enable those undertakings to protect their national markets against parallel imports by taking advantage of restrictive approaches to the exhaustion of rights in the national laws of some States.

Articles 30 and 36 defeat such manipulation of trade-mark rights since they preclude national laws which enable the holder of the right to oppose imports.

In the situations described above the function of the trade mark is in no way called in question by freedom to import. As was held in HAG II: "For the trade mark to be able to fulfil [its] role, it must offer a guarantee that all goods bearing it have been produced under the control of a single undertaking which is accountable for their quality." In all the cases mentioned, control was in the hands of a single body: the group of companies in the case of products put into circulation by a subsidiary the manufacturer in the case of products marketed by the distributor the licensor in the case of products marketed by a licensee. In the case of a licence, the licensor can control the quality of the licensee's products by including in the contract clauses requiring the licensee to comply with his instructions and giving him the possibility of verifying such compliance. The origin which the trade mark is intended to guarantee is the same: it is not defined by reference to the manufacturer but by reference to the point of control of manufacture (see the statement of grounds for the Benelux Convention and the Uniform Law, Bulletin Benelux, 1962–2, p. 36).

Articles 30 and 36 thus debar the application of national laws which allow recourse to trade-mark rights in order to prevent the free movement of a product bearing a trade mark whose use is under unitary control.

The situation where unitary control of the trade mark has been severed following assignment for one or several Member States only

The problem posed by the [German appeals court's] question is whether the same principles apply where the trade mark has been assigned, for one or several Member States only, to an undertaking which has no economic link with the assignor and the assignor opposes the marketing, in the State in which he has retained the trade mark, of products to which the trade mark has been affixed by the assignee.

That situation must be clearly distinguished from the case where the imported products come from a licensee or a subsidiary to which ownership of the trade-mark right has been assigned in the exporting State: a contract of assignment by itself, that is in the absence of any economic link, does not give the assignor any means of controlling the quality of products which are marketed by the assignee and to which the latter has affixed the trade mark.

The Commission has submitted that by assigning in France the trade mark "Ideal Standard" for heating equipment to a third company, the American Standard group gave implied consent to that third company putting heating equipment into circulation in France bearing that trade mark. Because of that implied consent, it should not be possible to prohibit the marketing in Germany of heating equipment bearing the assigned trade mark.

That view must be rejected. The consent implicit in any assignment is not the consent required for application of the doctrine of exhaustion of rights. For that, the owner of the right in the importing State must, directly or indirectly, be able to determine the products to which the trade mark may be affixed in the exporting State and to control their quality. That power is lost if, by assignment, control over the trade mark is surrendered to a third party having no economic link with the assignor.

The insulation of markets where, for two Member States of the Community, there are separate trade-mark owners having no economic links is a result that has already been accepted by the Court in HAG II. However, since that was a case where unitary ownership was divided following sequestration, it has been submitted that the same result does not have to be adopted in the case of voluntary division.

That view cannot be accepted because it is contrary to the reasoning of the Court in HAG II. The Court stressed that in that case the determinant factor was absence of consent of the proprietor of the trade mark in the importing State to the putting into circulation in the exporting State of products marketed by the proprietor of the right in the latter State. It concluded that free movement of the goods would undermine the essential function of the trade mark: consumers would no longer be able to identify for certain the origin of the marked goods and the proprietor of the trade mark could be held responsible for the poor quality of goods for which he was in no way accountable.

IHT in particular has submitted that the owner of a trade mark who assigns the trade mark in one Member State, while retaining it in others, must accept the consequences of the weakening of the identifying function of the trade mark flowing from that assignment. By a territorially limited assignment, the owner voluntarily renounces his position as the only person marketing goods bearing the trade mark in question in the Community.

That argument must be rejected. It fails to take account of the fact that, since trade-mark rights are territorial, the function of the trade mark is to be assessed by reference to a particular territory.

IHT has further argued that the French subsidiary, Ideal–Standard SA, has adjusted itself in France to a situation where products (such as heating equipment and sanitary fittings) from different sources may be marketed under the same trade mark on the same national territory. The conduct of the German subsidiary of the same group which opposes the marketing of the heating equipment in Germany under the trade mark "Ideal Standard" is therefore abusive.

That argument cannot be upheld either.

First of all, the assignment was made only for France. The effect of that argument, if it were accepted, would, as the German Government points out, be that assignment of the right for France would entail permission to use the device in Germany, whereas assignments and licences always relate, having regard to the territorial nature of national trade-mark rights, to a specified territory.

Moreover, and most importantly, French law, which governs the assignment in question here, permits assignments of trade marks confined to certain products, with the result that similar products from different sources may be in circulation on French territory under the same trade mark, whereas German law, by prohibiting assignments of trade marks confined to certain products, seeks to prevent such co-existence. The effect of IHT's argument, if it were accepted, would be to extend to the importing State whose law opposes such co-existence the solution prevailing in the exporting State despite the territorial nature of the rights in question.

Starting from the position that assignment to an assignee having no links with the assignor would lead to the existence of separate sources within a single territory and that, in order to safeguard the function of the trade mark, it would then be necessary to allow prohibition of export of the assignee's products to the assignor's territory and vice versa, unified laws, to avoid creating such obstacles to the free movement of goods, render void assignments made for only part of the territory covered by the rights they create. By limiting the right to dispose of the trade mark in this way, such unified laws ensure single ownership throughout the territory to which they apply and guarantee free movement of the product.

RULING

There is no unlawful restriction on trade between Member States within the meaning of Articles 30 and 36 where a subsidiary operating in Member State A of a manufacturer established in Member State B is to be enjoined from using as a trade mark the name "Ideal Standard" because of the risk of confusion with a device having the same origin, even if the manufacturer is lawfully using that name in his country of origin under a trade mark protected there, he acquired that trade mark by assignment and the trade mark originally belonged to a company affiliated to the undertaking which, in Member State A, opposes the importation of goods bearing the trade mark "Ideal Standard."

NOTES AND QUESTIONS

1. Who originally held the trademark rights to "Ideal Standard" in Germany and France in 1984? Were the rights originally held by one company, related companies, or unrelated companies?

2. Now trace how the French company CICh eventually obtained the trademark rights to "Ideal Standard" in France, and how the German company Ideal–Standard GmbH obtained the trademark rights in Germany. Were CICh and Ideal–Standard GmbH affiliated in any way?

3. What is the result of this case? Can the German Ideal–Standard GmbH stop IHT from importing into Germany heating equipment under the Ideal Standard trademark produced by CICh in France?

4. *Regional exhaustion of rights in the EU.* In the EU, the straightforward case of exhaustion occurs when the trademark owner consents to the sale of its trademarked goods anywhere in the EU. After a first sale, the trademark owner loses its distribution or importation rights to those sold goods in the EU. In other words, the owner's rights to the particular goods sold are exhausted "Community-wide" throughout the EU. EU Trade Mark Directive art. 7 (First Council Directive 89/104/EEC). First sales outside the EU, however, do not count for the purposes of exhaustion under Article 7(2) of the EU Directive, which applies only to a good put "on the market in the Community" with the consent of the trademark holder. *Id.*; *see Silhouette*

Int'l Schmied GmbH & Co. KG v. Hartlauer Handlesgesellschaft mbH, [1998] ECR I–4799, Case C–355/96 (1998).

b. Approach in the U.S.

Like the EU, the United States considers the authorized first sales by related companies to constitute exhaustion of distribution rights under trademark law. The U.S. approach is broader than the EU's approach in adopting what amounts to international exhaustion. Sales of the trademarked good anywhere by an entity under the "common control" of the U.S. trademark owner will trigger exhaustion. Sales by independent third parties will not. However, the U.S. concept of "common control" is narrower than the EU concept of "economically linked" entities. The U.S. notion of common control would not typically treat a mere licensee or an exclusive distributor as an entity under the common control. *See Vittoria North America, L.L.C. v. Euro–Asia Imports*, 278 F.3d 1076, 1085–86 (10th Cir. 2001). U.S. law of exhaustion for trademark law is based on a complex patchwork of a trade statute, Customs regulations, and case law. Consider the following problem and discussion.

PROBLEM 6–11

Advanced Metrix Technologies (AMT), with its headquarters in Dearborn, Michigan, is the owner of a registered U.S. trademark for a handheld organizer called "The Dateon" that is popular with young professionals. AMT has a subsidiary based in Belgium that manufactures the organizer for the EU market. The organizer for Europe has slightly smaller buttons and a clicking device that is located at the bottom of the organizer not at the top as in AMT's organizers manufactured in the U.S. AMT also licenses a Taiwan-based company to manufacture and sell the product in Asia. The organizers manufactured in Taiwan are identical in design and features to the U.S. organizer. Big–Mart, a large discount chain, has begun to import organizers purchased by third party distributors in Europe and Asia. AMT now comes to your law office and wants advice on whether it can prevent the importation of these goods into the United States. What advice do you have? Consult *K Mart*, *Lever Brothers*, and the accompanying notes.

K MART CORP. v. CARTIER, INC.

Supreme Court of the United States.
486 U.S. 281 (1988).

JUSTICE KENNEDY announced the judgment of the Court and delivered the opinion of the Court with respect to Parts I, II–A, and II–C, and an opinion with respect to Part II–B, in which WHITE, J., joined.

A gray-market good is a foreign-manufactured good, bearing a valid United States trademark, that is imported without the consent of the United States trademark holder. These cases present the issue whether the Secretary of the Treasury's regulation permitting the importation of certain gray-market goods, 19 CFR § 133.21 (1987), is a reasonable agency interpretation of § 526 of the Tariff Act of 1930 (1930 Tariff Act), 46 Stat. 741, as amended, 19 U.S. C. § 1526.

I

A

The gray market arises in any of three general contexts. The prototypical gray-market victim (case 1) is a domestic firm that purchases from an independent foreign firm the rights to register and use the latter's trademark as a United States trademark and to sell its foreign-manufactured products here. Especially where the foreign firm has already registered the trademark in the United States or where the product has already earned a reputation for quality, the right to use that trademark can be very valuable. If the foreign manufacturer could import the trademarked goods and distribute them here, despite having sold the trademark to a domestic firm, the domestic firm would be forced into sharp intrabrand competition involving the very trademark it purchased. Similar intrabrand competition could arise if the foreign manufacturer markets its wares outside the United States, as is often the case, and a third party who purchases them abroad could legally import them. In either event, the parallel importation, if permitted to proceed, would create a gray market that could jeopardize the trademark holder's investment.

The second context (case 2) is a situation in which a domestic firm registers the United States trademark for goods that are manufactured abroad by an affiliated manufacturer. In its most common variation (case 2a), a foreign firm wishes to control distribution of its wares in this country by incorporating a subsidiary here. The subsidiary then registers under its own name (or the manufacturer assigns to the subsidiary's name) a United States trademark that is identical to its parent's foreign trademark. The parallel importation by a third party who buys the goods abroad (or conceivably even by the affiliated foreign manufacturer itself) creates a gray market. Two other variations on this theme occur when an American-based firm establishes abroad a manufacturing subsidiary corporation (case 2b) or its own unincorporated manufacturing division (case 2c) to produce its United States trademarked goods, and then imports them for domestic distribution. If the trademark holder or its foreign subsidiary sells the trademarked goods abroad, the parallel importation of the goods competes on the gray market with the holder's domestic sales.

In the third context (case 3), the domestic holder of a United States trademark *authorizes* an independent foreign manufacturer to use it. Usually the holder sells to the foreign manufacturer an exclusive right to use the trademark in a particular foreign location, but conditions the right on the foreign manufacturer's promise not to import its trademarked goods into the United States. Once again, if the foreign manufacturer or a third party imports into the United States, the foreign-manufactured goods will compete on the gray market with the holder's domestic goods.

B

Until 1922, the Federal Government did not regulate the importation of gray-market goods, not even to protect the investment of an independent purchaser of a foreign trademark, and not even in the extreme case where the independent foreign manufacturer breached its agreement to refrain from direct competition with the purchaser. That year, however, Congress was spurred to action by a Court of Appeals decision declining to enjoin the parallel importation of goods bearing a trademark that (as in case 1) a domestic company had purchased from an independent foreign manufacturer at a premium. See *A. Bourjois & Co.* v. *Katzel*, 275 F. 539 (2d Cir. 1921), rev'd, 260 U.S. 689 (1923).

In an immediate response to *Katzel*, Congress enacted § 526 of the Tariff Act of 1922, 42 Stat. 975. That provision, later reenacted in identical form as § 526 of the 1930 Tariff Act, 19 U.S.C. § 1526, prohibits importing

"into the United States any merchandise of foreign manufacture if such merchandise ... bears a trademark owned by a citizen of, or by a corporation or association created or organized within, the United States, and registered in the Patent and Trademark Office by a person domiciled in the United States ..., unless written consent of the owner of such trademark is produced at the time of making entry." 19 U.S.C. § 1526(a).

The regulations implementing § 526 for the past 50 years have not applied the prohibition to all gray-market goods. The Customs Service regulation now in force provides generally that "foreign-made articles bearing a trademark identical with one owned and recorded by a citizen of the United States or a corporation or association created or organized within the United States are subject to seizure and forfeiture as prohibited importations." 19 CFR § 133.21(b) (1987). But the regulation furnishes a "common-control" exception from the ban, permitting the entry of gray-market goods manufactured abroad by the trademark owner or its affiliate:

"(c) *Restrictions not applicable.* The restrictions ... do not apply to imported articles when:

"(1) Both the foreign and the U.S. trademark or trade name are owned by the same person or business entity; [or]

"(2) The foreign and domestic trademark or trade name owners are parent and subsidiary companies or are otherwise subject to common ownership or control...."

The Customs Service regulation further provides an "authorized-use" exception, which permits importation of gray-market goods where

"(3) the articles of foreign manufacture bear a recorded trademark or trade name applied under authorization of the U.S. owner...."
19 CFR § 133.21(c) (1987).

Respondents, an association of United States trademark holders and two of its members, brought suit in Federal District Court in February 1984, seeking both a declaration that the Customs Service regulation, 19 CFR §§ 133.21(c)(1)–(3) (1987), is invalid and an injunction against its enforcement. *Coalition to Preserve the Integrity of American Trademarks* v. *United States*, 598 F. Supp. 844 (D.D.C. 1984). They asserted that the common-control and authorized-use exceptions are inconsistent with § 526 of the 1930 Tariff Act. Petitioners K mart and 47th Street Photo intervened as defendants.

The District Court upheld the Customs Service regulation, 598 F. Supp. at 853, but the Court of Appeals reversed[,] holding that the Customs Service regulation was an unreasonable administrative interpretation of § 526. We granted certiorari, 479 U.S. 1005 (1986), to resolve a conflict among the Courts of Appeals.

A majority of this Court now holds that the common-control exception of the Customs Service regulation, 19 CFR §§ 133.21(c)(1)–(2) (1987), is consistent with § 526. See *post*, at 309–310 (opinion of BRENNAN, J.). A different majority, however, holds that the authorized-use exception, 19 CFR § 133.21(c)(3) (1987), is inconsistent with § 526. See *post*, at 328–329 (opinion of SCALIA, J.). We therefore affirm the Court of Appeals in part and reverse in part.

II

A

In determining whether a challenged regulation is valid, a reviewing court must first determine if the regulation is consistent with the language of the statute. "If the statute is clear and unambiguous 'that is the end of the matter, for the court, as well as the agency, must give effect to the unambiguously expressed intent of Congress.' . . . The traditional deference courts pay to agency interpretation is not to be applied to alter the clearly expressed intent of Congress." *Board of Governors, FRS* v. *Dimension Financial Corp.*, 474 U.S. 361, 368 (1986).

Following this analysis, I conclude that subsections (c)(1) and (c)(2) of the Customs Service regulation, 19 CFR §§ 133.21 (c)(1) and (c)(2) (1987), are permissible constructions designed to resolve statutory ambiguities. All Members of the Court are in agreement that the agency may interpret the statute to bar importation of gray-market goods in what we have denoted case 1 and to permit the imports under case 2a. . . . As these writings state, "owned by" is sufficiently ambiguous, in the context of the statute, that it applies to situations involving a foreign parent, which is case 2a. This ambiguity arises from the inability to discern, from the statutory language, which of the two entities involved in case 2a can be said to "own" the United States trademark if, as in some instances, the domestic subsidiary is wholly owned by its foreign parent.

A further statutory ambiguity contained in the phrase "merchandise of foreign manufacture," suffices to sustain the regulations as they apply to cases 2b and 2c. This ambiguity parallels that of "owned by," which sustained case 2a, because it is possible to interpret "merchandise of foreign manufacture" to mean (1) goods manufactured in a foreign country, (2) goods manufactured by a foreign company, or (3) goods manufactured in a foreign country by a foreign company. Given the imprecision in the statute, the agency is entitled to choose any reasonable definition and to interpret the statute to say that goods manufactured by a foreign subsidiary or division of a domestic company are not goods "of foreign manufacture."

Subsection (c)(3), 19 CFR § 133.21(c)(3) (1987), of the regulation, however, cannot stand. The ambiguous statutory phrases that we have already discussed, "owned by" and "merchandise of foreign manufacture," are irrelevant to the proscription contained in subsection (3) of the regulation. This subsection of the regulation denies a domestic trademark holder the power to prohibit the importation of goods made by an independent foreign manufacturer where the domestic trademark holder has authorized the foreign manufacturer to use the trademark. Under no reasonable construction of the statutory language can goods made in a foreign country by an independent foreign manufacturer be removed from the purview of the statute.

We hold that the Customs Service regulation is consistent with § 526 insofar as it exempts from the importation ban goods that are manufactured abroad by the "same person" who holds the United States trademark, 19 CFR § 133.21(c) (1) (1987), or by a person who is "subject to common ... control" with the United States trademark holder, § 133.21(c)(2). Because the authorized-use exception of the regulation, § 133.21(c)(3), is in conflict with the plain language of the statute, that provision cannot stand.

LEVER BROTHERS CO. v. UNITED STATES

U.S. Court of Appeals for the District of Columbia Circuit.
981 F.2d 1330 (D.C. Cir. 1993).

Lever Brothers Company ("Lever US" or "Lever"), an American company, and its British affiliate, Lever Brothers Limited ("Lever UK"), both manufacture deodorant soap under the "Shield" trademark and hand dishwashing liquid under the "Sunlight" trademark. The trademarks are registered in each country. The products have evidently been formulated differently to suit local tastes and circumstances. The U.S. version lathers more, the soaps smell different, the colorants used in American "Shield" have been certified by the FDA whereas the colorants in British "Shield" have not, and the U.S. version contains a bacteriostat that enhances the deodorant properties of the soap. The British version of "Sunlight" dishwashing soap produces less suds, and the American version is formulated to work best in the "soft water" available in most American cities, whereas the British version is designed for "hard water" common in Britain.

The packaging of the U.S. and UK products is also somewhat different. The British "Shield" logo is written in script form and is packaged in foil wrapping and contains a wave motif, whereas the American "Shield" logo is written in block form, does not come in foil wrapping and contains a grid pattern. There is small print on the packages indicating where they were manufactured. The British "Sunlight" comes in a cylindrical bottle labeled "Sunlight Washing Up Liquid." The American "Sunlight" comes in a yellow, hourglass-shaped bottle labeled "Sunlight Dishwashing Liquid."

Lever asserts that the unauthorized influx of these foreign products has created substantial consumer confusion and deception in the United States about the nature and origin of this merchandise, and that it has received numerous consumer complaints from American consumers who unknowingly bought the British products and were disappointed. Lever argues that the importation of the British products was in violation of section 42 of the Lanham Act, 15 U.S.C. § 1124 which provides that with the exception of goods imported for personal use:

> No article of imported merchandise which shall copy or simulate the name of the [sic] any domestic manufacture, or manufacturer ... or which shall copy or simulate a trademark registered in accordance with the provisions of this chapter ... shall be admitted to entry at any customhouse of the United States.

Id. The United States Customs Service ("Customs"), however, was allowing importation of the British goods under the "affiliate exception" created by 19 C.F.R. § 133.21(c)(2), which provides that foreign goods bearing United States trademarks are not forbidden when "the foreign and domestic trademark or trade name owners are parent and subsidiary companies or are otherwise subject to common ownership or control."[3]

In *Lever I,* we concluded that "the natural, virtually inevitable reading of section 42 is that it bars foreign goods bearing a trademark identical to the valid U.S. trademark but physically different," without regard to affiliation between the producing firms or the genuine character of the trademark abroad. 877 F.2d 101, 111 (D.C. Cir. 1989). * * *

After reviewing the submissions of the parties, the District Court found that Customs' administrative practice was "at best inconsistent" and, in any event, had "never addressed the specific question of physically different goods that bear identical trademarks." *Lever Bros. Co. v. United States,* 796 F. Supp. 1, 5 (D.D.C. 1992). The District Court concluded that "section 42 ... prohibits the importation of foreign goods that ... are physically different, regardless of the validity of the foreign trademark or the existence of an affiliation between the U.S. and foreign markholders." *Id.* The court accordingly concluded that "neither the legislative history of the statute nor the administrative practice of the Customs Service clearly

---

3. This case does not involve a dispute between corporate affiliates. Neither Lever US nor Lever UK has authorized the importation which is being conducted by third parties. *See Lever I,* 877 F.2d at 103.

contradicts the plain meaning of section 42" and granted summary judgment against the government. *Id.* at 13.

Customs' main argument from the legislative history is that section 42 of the Lanham Act applies only to imports of goods bearing trademarks that "copy or simulate" a registered mark. Customs thus draws a distinction between "genuine" marks and marks that "copy or simulate." A mark applied by a foreign firm subject to ownership and control common to that of the domestic trademark owner is by definition "genuine," Customs urges, regardless of whether or not the goods are identical. Thus, any importation of goods manufactured by an affiliate of a U.S. trademark owner cannot "copy or simulate" a registered mark because those goods are *ipso facto* "genuine."

This argument is fatally flawed. It rests on the false premise that foreign trademarks applied to foreign goods are "genuine" in the United States. Trademarks applied to physically different foreign goods are not genuine from the viewpoint of the American consumer. As we stated in *Lever I:*

> On its face ... section [42] appears to aim at deceit and consumer confusion; when identical trademarks have acquired different meanings in different countries, one who imports the foreign version to sell it under that trademark will (in the absence of some specially differentiating feature) cause the confusion Congress sought to avoid. The fact of affiliation between the producers in no way reduces the probability of that confusion; it is certainly not a constructive consent to importation.

877 F.2d at 111.

There is a larger, more fundamental and ultimately fatal weakness in Customs' position in this case. Section 42 on its face appears to forbid importation of goods that "copy or simulate" a United States trademark. Customs has the burden of adducing evidence from the legislative history of section 42 and its administrative practice of an exception for materially different goods whose similar foreign and domestic trademarks are owned by affiliated companies. At a minimum, this requires that the specific question be addressed in the legislative history and administrative practice. The bottom line, however, is that the issue of materially different goods was not addressed either in the legislative history or the administrative record. It is not enough to posit that silence implies authorization, when the authorization sought runs counter to the evident meaning of the governing statute. Therefore, we conclude that section 42 of the Lanham Act precludes the application of Customs' affiliate exception with respect to physically, materially different goods.

For the foregoing reasons, we affirm the District Court's ruling that section 42 of the Lanham Act, 15 U.S.C. § 1124, bars the importation of physically different foreign goods bearing a trademark identical to a valid U.S. trademark, regardless of the trademark's genuine character abroad or affiliation between the producing firms.

1.   Explain how the rule in *K Mart* operates as a principle of international exhaustion for trademarks.

2.   The *Lever* decision dealt with a comparable "common control" or "affiliate" exception under the then-Customs Service regulation, 19 C.F.R. § 133.21(c)(2). Did the *Lever* court allow the Customs Service to apply the "common control" exception to Lever US and Lever UK? Or did the *Lever* court create, in effect, an exception to the "common control" exception?

3.   After the decisions in *K Mart* and *Lever Brothers*, the Customs Service amended its regulations. The current regulation, 19 CFR § 133.23, provides:

(a) *Restricted gray market articles defined.* "Restricted gray market articles" are foreign made articles bearing a genuine trademark or trade name identical with or substantially indistinguishable from one owned and recorded by a citizen of the United States or a corporation or association created or organized within the United States and imported without the authorization of the U.S. owner. "Restricted gray market goods" include goods bearing a genuine trademark or trade name which is:

(1) *Independent licensee.* Applied by a licensee (including a manufacturer) independent of the U.S. owner, or

(2) *Foreign owner.* Applied under the authority of a foreign trademark or trade name owner other than the U.S. owner, a parent or subsidiary of the U.S. owner, or a party otherwise subject to common ownership or control with the U.S. owner ... from whom the U.S. owner acquired the domestic title or to whom the U.S. owner sold the foreign titles(s); or

(3) *"Lever Rule."* Applied by the U.S. owner, a parent or subsidiary of the U.S. owner or a party otherwise subject to common ownership or control with the U.S. owner ... to goods that the Customs Service has determined to be physically and materially different from the articles authorized by the U.S. trademark owner for importation or sale in the U.S.

(b) *Labeling of physically and materially different goods.* Goods determined by the Customs Service to be physically and materially different [and] bearing a genuine mark applied under the authority of the U.S. owner, a parent or subsidiary of the U.S. owner, or a party otherwise subject to common ownership and control with the U.S. owner ... shall not be detained where the merchandise or its packaging bears a conspicuous and legible label designed to remain on the product until the first sale to a retail consumer in the United States stating that: "This product is not a product authorized by the United States trademark owner for importation and is physically and materially different from the authorized product."

(c) *Denial of Entry.* All restricted gray market goods imported into the United States shall be denied entry and subject to detention.

How, if at all, did the Customs Service respond in the above regulation to the *Lever* decision?

2. EXHAUSTION OF COPYRIGHT: APPROACH IN THE EU AND THE UNITED STATES

The regional exhaustion approach adopted by the European Union in trademark law applies also to copyright and patent law. Thus, the consent approach articulated by the Court of Justice in *Ideal Standard* is also applicable to other IP regimes. The Information Society Directive, Directive 2001/29/EC, expressly codifies this approach for copyrights in Article 4(2): "The distribution right shall not be exhausted within the Community in respect of the original or copies of the work, except where the first sale or other transfer of ownership in the Community of that object is made by the rightholder or with his consent." The Court of Justice has interpreted this provision to preclude a principle of international exhaustion (or exhaustion based on sales of copyrighted works outside the EU). *See Laserdisken APS v. Kulturministeriet,* Case C–479/04 (Sept. 12, 2006) (EU regional exhaustion applies under InfoSoc Directive).

By contrast, instead of taking one approach to exhaustion for all IP forms, the U.S. approach to copyright exhaustion is narrower than its approach to trademark exhaustion. Copyright exhaustion or the first-sale doctrine under 17 U.S.C. § 109(a) has been interpreted by courts to resemble a form of national exhaustion, although some recent challenges have advanced an interpretation of § 109(a) that would amount to international exhaustion. Because of these challenges and the conflicting approaches taken by the lower courts to national exhaustion, the Supreme Court may eventually resolve the issue. The Court had an opportunity to clarify the issue, but divided equally. *See Costco Wholesale Corporation v. Omega S.A.,* ___ U.S. ___, 131 S. Ct. 565 (2010). The narrower scope of exhaustion for U.S. copyright law, at least as interpreted by the lower courts, has led some brand owners to take advantage of copyright law by using copyrighted logos on their goods. Thus, instead of international exhaustion under trademark law, these brand owners seek national exhaustion under copyright law. Consider the following problems and U.S. cases.

PROBLEM 6–12

Advanced Metrix Technologies (AMT) has a copyright for the software used in the organizers. AMT's Dearborn manufacturing facility has just shipped a large supply of the organizers to Big–Mart stores in Canada. Big–Mart has overestimated demand in Canada and is now shipping the surplus to its stores in Michigan and Minnesota. AMT has also discovered that AMT–Canada, a joint venture between AMT and a Canadian electronics company, is selling Canadian manufactured organizers identical to the U.S. model directly to stores in Ohio and Indiana. AMT's U.S. general manager asks your law firm the following questions: "Can we exclude these two gray market shipments on the basis of trademark law? What about copyright?" What advice do you have? For trademark exhaustion, review the discussion above. For copyright exhaustion, consult *Quality King* below.

PROBLEM 6–13

Digital Dreams, Inc. (DDI), a U.S. company, has trademarks and copyrights from the U.S. and other WTO countries where it markets its various media products, including computer games. DDI has licensed the manufacture of its products to an independently owned factory in Italy. Under the license, the foreign manufacturer ships the DDI products to DDI's foreign subsidiary for sale in foreign markets. A wholesale distributor in Florence has purchased a large supply of the products from DDI's foreign subsidiary and plans to export them to the United States. The price of the goods in Italy are much cheaper than they are in the U.S. Can DDI block the imports on the basis of its copyright? *See Quality King* and *Costco* below. What about trademark? *See KMart* and 19 CFR § 133.23, *supra.*

QUALITY KING DISTRIBUTORS, INC. v. L'ANZA RESEARCH INTERNATIONAL, INC.

Supreme Court of the United States.
523 U.S. 135 (1998).

JUSTICE STEVENS delivered the opinion of the Court.

Section 106(3) of the Copyright Act of 1976 (Act), 17 U.S.C. § 106(3), gives the owner of a copyright the exclusive right to distribute copies of a copyrighted work. That exclusive right is expressly limited, however, by the provisions of §§ 107 through 120. Section 602(a) gives the copyright owner the right to prohibit the unauthorized importation of copies. The question presented by this case is whether the right granted by § 602(a) is also limited by §§ 107 through 120. More narrowly, the question is whether the "first sale" doctrine endorsed in § 109(a) is applicable to imported copies.

I.

Respondent, L'anza Research International, Inc. (L'anza), is a California corporation engaged in the business of manufacturing and selling shampoos, conditioners, and other hair care products. L'anza has copyrighted the labels that are affixed to those products. In the United States, L'anza sells exclusively to domestic distributors who have agreed to resell within limited geographic areas and then only to authorized retailers such as barber shops, beauty salons, and professional hair care colleges. L'anza has found that the American "public is generally unwilling to pay the price charged for high quality products, such as L'anza's products, when they are sold along with the less expensive lower quality products that are generally carried by supermarkets and drug stores." L'anza promotes the domestic sales of its products with extensive advertising in various trade magazines and at point of sale, and by providing special training to authorized retailers.

L'anza also sells its products in foreign markets. In those markets, however, it does not engage in comparable advertising or promotion; its prices to foreign distributors are 35% to 40% lower than the prices charged to domestic distributors. In 1992 and 1993, L'anza's distributor in the United Kingdom arranged the sale of three shipments to a distributor in Malta; each shipment contained several tons of L'anza products with copyrighted labels affixed. The record does not establish whether the initial purchaser was the distributor in the United Kingdom or the distributor in Malta, or whether title passed when the goods were delivered to the carrier or when they arrived at their destination, but it is undisputed that the goods were manufactured by L'anza and first sold by L'anza to a foreign purchaser.

It is also undisputed that the goods found their way back to the United States without the permission of L'anza and were sold in California by unauthorized retailers who had purchased them at discounted prices from Quality King Distributors, Inc. (petitioner). There is some uncertainty about the identity of the actual importer, but for the purpose of our decision we assume that petitioner bought all three shipments from the Malta distributor, imported them, and then resold them to retailers who were not in L'anza's authorized chain of distribution.

After determining the source of the unauthorized sales, L'anza brought suit against petitioner and several other defendants. The complaint alleged that the importation and subsequent distribution of those products bearing copyrighted labels violated L'anza's "exclusive rights under 17 U.S.C. §§ 106, 501 and 602 to reproduce and distribute the copyrighted material in the United States." App. 32. The District Court rejected petitioner's defense based on the "first sale" doctrine recognized by § 109 and entered summary judgment in favor of L'anza. Based largely on its conclusion that § 602 would be "meaningless" if § 109 provided a defense in a case of this kind, the Court of Appeals affirmed.

II.

This is an unusual copyright case because L'anza does not claim that anyone has made unauthorized copies of its copyrighted labels. Instead, L'anza is primarily interested in protecting the integrity of its method of marketing the products to which the labels are affixed. Although the labels themselves have only a limited creative component, our interpretation of the relevant statutory provisions would apply equally to a case involving more familiar copyrighted materials such as sound recordings or books. Indeed, we first endorsed the first sale doctrine in a case involving a claim by a publisher that the resale of its books at discounted prices infringed its copyright on the books. *Bobbs–Merrill Co.* v. *Straus*, 210 U.S. 339 (1908).

In that case, the publisher, Bobbs–Merrill, had inserted a notice in its books that any retail sale at a price under $1.00 would constitute an infringement of its copyright. The defendants, who owned Macy's department store, disregarded the notice and sold the books at a lower price without Bobbs–Merrill's consent. We held that the exclusive statutory right to "vend"[4] applied only to the first sale of the copyrighted work:

> "What does the statute mean in granting 'the sole right of vending the same'? Was it intended to create a right which would permit the holder of the copyright to fasten, by notice in a book or upon one of the articles mentioned within the statute,' a restriction upon the subsequent alienation of the subject-matter of copyright after the owner had parted with the title to one who had acquired full dominion over it and had given a satisfactory price for it? It is not denied that one who has sold a copyrighted article, without restriction, has parted with all right to control the sale of it. The purchaser of a book, once sold by authority of the owner of the copyright, may sell it again, although he could not publish a new edition of it."

> "In this case the stipulated facts show that the books sold by the appellant were sold at wholesale, and purchased by those who made no agreement as to the control of future sales of the book, and took upon themselves no obligation to enforce the notice printed in the book, undertaking to restrict retail sales to a price of one dollar per copy." 210 U.S. 339 at 349–350.

The statute in force when *Bobbs–Merrill* was decided provided that the copyright owner had the exclusive right to "vend" the copyrighted work. Congress subsequently codified our holding in *Bobbs–Merrill* that the exclusive right to "vend" was limited to first sales of the work. Under the 1976 Act, the comparable exclusive right granted in 17 U.S.C. § 106(3) is the right "to distribute copies ... by sale or other transfer of ownership." The comparable limitation on that right is provided not by judicial interpretation, but by an express statutory provision. Section 109(a) provides

> "Notwithstanding the provisions of section 106(3), the owner of a particular copy or phonorecord lawfully made under this title, or any person authorized by such owner, is entitled, without the authority of the copyright owner, to sell or otherwise dispose of the possession of that copy or phonorecord...."

The *Bobbs–Merrill* opinion emphasized the critical distinction between statutory rights and contract rights. In this case, L'anza relies on the terms of its contracts with its domestic distributors to limit their sales to authorized retail outlets. Because the basic holding in *Bobbs–Merrill* is now codified in § 109(a) of the Act, and because those domestic distribu-

---

4. In 1908, when *Bobbs–Merrill* was decided, the copyright statute provided that copyright owners had "the sole liberty of printing, reprinting, publishing, completing, copying, executing, finishing, and *vending*" their copyrighted works. Copyright Act of 1891, § 4952, 26 Stat. 1107 (emphasis added).

tors are owners of the products that they purchased from L'anza (the labels of which were "lawfully made under this title"), L'anza does not, and could not, claim that the statute would enable L'anza to treat unauthorized resales by its domestic distributors as an infringement of its exclusive right to distribute copies of its labels. L'anza does claim, however, that contractual provisions are inadequate to protect it from the actions of foreign distributors who may resell L'anza's products to American vendors unable to buy from L'anza's domestic distributors, and that § 602(a) of the Act, properly construed, prohibits such unauthorized competition. To evaluate that submission, we must, of course, consider the text of § 602(a).

III

The most relevant portion of § 602(a) provides:

"Importation into the United States, without the authority of the owner of copyright under this title, of copies or phonorecords of a work that have been acquired outside the United States is an infringement of the exclusive right to distribute copies or phonorecords under section 106, actionable under section 501...."

It is significant that this provision does not categorically prohibit the unauthorized importation of copyrighted materials. Instead, it provides that such importation is an infringement of the exclusive right to distribute copies "under section 106." Like the exclusive right to "vend" that was construed in *Bobbs–Merrill*, the exclusive right to distribute is a limited right. The introductory language in § 106 expressly states that all of the exclusive rights granted by that section—including, of course, the distribution right granted by subsection (3)—are limited by the provisions of §§ 107 through 120. One of those limitations, as we have noted, is provided by the terms of § 109(a), which expressly permit the owner of a lawfully made copy to sell that copy "notwithstanding the provisions of section 106(3)."

After the first sale of a copyrighted item "lawfully made under this title," any subsequent purchaser, whether from a domestic or from a foreign reseller, is obviously an "owner" of that item. Read literally, § 109(a) unambiguously states that such an owner "is entitled, without the authority of the copyright owner, to sell" that item. Moreover, since § 602(a) merely provides that unauthorized importation is an infringement of an exclusive right "under section 106," and since that limited right does not encompass resales by lawful owners, the literal text of § 602(a) is simply inapplicable to both domestic and foreign owners of L'anza's products who decide to import them and resell them in the United States.

IV.

[The Court rejected the argument that its interpretation rendered the importation right under § 602(a) superfluous with § 602(b).] Even in the absence of a market allocation agreement between, for example, a publisher of the United States edition and a publisher of the British edition of the same work, each such publisher could make lawful copies. If the author of the work gave the exclusive United States distribution rights—enforceable under the Act—to the publisher of the United States edition and the exclusive British distribution rights to the publisher of the British edition,[20] however, presumably only those made by the publisher of the United States edition would be "lawfully made under this title" within the meaning of § 109(a). The first sale doctrine would not provide the publisher of the British edition who decided to sell in the American market with a defense to an action under § 602(a) (or, for that matter, to an action under § 106(3), if there was a distribution of the copies).

The argument that the statutory exceptions to § 602(a) are superfluous if the first sale doctrine is applicable rests on the assumption that the coverage of that section is coextensive with the coverage of § 109(a). But since it is, in fact, broader because it encompasses copies that are not subject to the first sale doctrine—*e.g.,* copies that are lawfully made under the law of another country—the exceptions do protect the traveler who may have made an isolated purchase of a copy of a work that could not be imported in bulk for purposes of resale. As we read the Act, although both the first sale doctrine embodied in § 109(a) and the exceptions in § 602(a) may be applicable in some situations, the former does not subsume the latter; those provisions retain significant independent meaning.

The judgment of the Court of Appeals is reversed.

JUSTICE GINSBURG, concurring.

This case involves a "round trip" journey, travel of the copies in question from the United States to places abroad, then back again. I join the Court's opinion recognizing that we do not today resolve cases in which the allegedly infringing imports were manufactured abroad.

OMEGA S.A. v. COSTCO WHOLESALE CORPORATION

U.S. Court of Appeals for the Ninth Circuit.
541 F.3d 982, aff'd by an equally divided court, ___ U.S. ___, 131 S. Ct. 565 (2010).

SMITH, JR., CIRCUIT JUDGE:

Omega manufactures watches in Switzerland and sells them globally through a network of authorized distributors and retailers. Engraved on the underside of the watches is a U.S.-copyrighted "Omega Globe Design."

Costco obtained watches bearing the copyrighted design from the "gray market" in the following manner: Omega first sold the watches to authorized distributors overseas. Unidentified third parties eventually purchased the watches and sold them to ENE Limited, a New York

---

20. A participant in a 1964 panel discussion expressed concern about this particular situation. Copyright Law Revision Part 4: Further Discussion and Comments on Preliminary Draft for Revised U.S. Copyright Law, 88th Cong., 2d Sess., 119 (H.R. Judiciary Comm. Print 1964) (statement of Mrs. Pilpel)[.]

company, which in turn sold them to Costco. Costco then sold the watches to consumers in California. Although Omega authorized the initial foreign sale of the watches, it did not authorize their importation into the United States or the sales made by Costco.

Omega filed a lawsuit alleging that Costco's acquisition and sale of the watches constitute copyright infringement under 17 U.S.C. §§ 106(3) and 602(a), and subsequently moved for summary judgment. Costco filed a cross-motion on the basis of 17 U.S.C. § 109(a), arguing that, under the first sale doctrine, Omega's initial foreign sale of the watches precludes claims of infringing distribution and importation in connection with the subsequent, unauthorized sales. The district court ruled without explanation in favor of Costco on both motions. This appeal followed.

DISCUSSION

[Omega argued that in order for exhaustion to occur under § 109(a), the copies had to be "lawfully made under this title," meaning that the copies had to be made in the United States. According to Omega, because its watches were made overseas and first sold overseas, no exhaustion occurred under § 109(a) and Costco's importation of the watches violated §§ 602(a) and 106(3). The Ninth Circuit considered the validity of this argument below. *Ed.*]

A.   Current Rule in the Circuit

Omega's position was clearly correct under pre-*Quality King* Ninth Circuit precedent. Under these cases, Costco would not be entitled to summary judgment on the basis of § 109(a). The statute would not apply because Omega made copies of the Omega Globe Design in Switzerland and Costco sold the copies without Omega's authority in the United States. The district court's unexplained grant of summary judgment on the basis of § 109(a) was at odds with *BMG Music* [and other precedents.]

B.   The Impact of Quality King

It is clear that *Quality King* did not directly overrule *BMG Music* [and other precedents]. *Quality King* involved "round trip" importation: a product with a U.S.-copyrighted label was manufactured inside the United States, exported to an authorized foreign distributor, sold to unidentified third parties overseas, shipped back into the United States without the copyright owner's permission, and then sold in California by unauthorized retailers. 523 U.S. at 138–39. The Court held that § 109(a) can provide a defense to an action under § 602(a) in this context. *Id.* at 144–52. However, because the facts involved only domestically manufactured copies, the Court did not address the effect of § 109(a) on claims involving unauthorized importation of copies made abroad. *See id.* at 154 (Ginsburg, J., concurring) ("[W]e do not today resolve cases in which the allegedly infringing imports were manufactured abroad."). Moreover, the Court never discussed the scope of § 109(a) or defined what "lawfully made under this title" means.

The common understanding of the presumption against extraterritoriality is that a U.S. statute "appl[ies] only to conduct occurring within, or having effect within, the territory of the United States, unless the contrary is clearly indicated by the statute." Restatement (Second) of Foreign Relations Law of the United States § 38 (1965). Recognizing the importance of avoiding international conflicts of law in the area of intellectual property, however, we have applied a more robust version of this presumption to the Copyright Act, holding that the Act presumptively does not apply to conduct that occurs abroad even when that conduct produces harmful effects within the United States. *See Subafilms,* 24 F.3d at 1096–98.

Given this understanding of the presumption, the application of § 109(a) to foreign-made copies would impermissibly apply the Copyright Act extraterritorially in a way that the application of the statute after foreign sales does not. Under the latter application, the statute merely acknowledges the occurrence of a foreign event as a relevant fact. The former application would go much further. To characterize the making of copies overseas as "lawful[ ] . . . under [Title 17]" would be to ascribe legality under the Copyright Act to conduct that occurs entirely outside the United States, notwithstanding the absence of a clear expression of congressional intent in favor of extraterritoriality.

Other significant parts of *Quality King*'s analysis are also consistent with *BGM Music*'s limitation of § 109(a) to domestically made copies. The Court found that copies of a work copyrighted under Title 17 are not necessarily "lawfully made under [Title 17] even when made by the owner of the copyright: The category of copies covered by § 602(a), it was explained, encompasses "copies that were 'lawfully made' not under the United States Copyright Act, but instead, under the law of some other country." 423 U.S. at 147. Because § 602(a) extends to such copies, but on its terms permits an infringement action only by the "owner of copyright under [Title 17]," copies of a work can be lawfully made "under the law of some other country," rather than "under [Title 17], even when the copies are protected by a U.S. copyright. In short, copies covered by the phrase "lawfully made under [Title 17] in § 109(a) are not simply those which are lawfully made by the owner of a U.S. copyright. Something more is required. To us, that "something" is the making of the copies *within the United States,* where the Copyright Act applies. *See* 2–8 Nimmer on Copyright § 8.12(B)(6)(c), at 8–178.4(6)–(7).

Finally, in the decision's only direct language on the issue, Justice Ginsburg's concurrence cited a copyright treatise for the proposition that "lawfully made under this title" means "lawfully made in the United States." 523 U.S. at 154 (citing W. Patry, Copyright Law and Practice 166–70 (1997 Supp.)). The majority opinion did not dispute this interpretation, which aligns closely with the one adopted by our circuit. *See BMG Music,* 952 F.2d at 319.

[The court of appeals recognized an exception that treats some foreign made copies as subject to the first sale doctrine, in order to prevent an "offshoring" loophole that would otherwise be created. *Ed.*] Perhaps most compelling is the objection that *BMG Music* would provide substantially greater copyright protection to foreign-made copies of U.S.-copyrighted works. A U.S. copyright owner, for example, would be unable to exercise distribution rights after one lawful, domestic sale of a watch lawfully made in South Dakota, but, without the limits imposed by § 109(a), the same owner could seemingly exercise distribution rights after even the tenth sale in the United States of a watch lawfully made in Switzerland. The difference would likely encourage U.S. copyright owners to outsource the manufacturing of copies of their work overseas. *Drug Emporium* and *Denbicare,* however, resolved this problem by clarifying that parties can raise § 109(a) as a defense in cases involving foreign-made copies so long as a lawful domestic sale has occurred. *See Drug Emporium,* 38 F.3d at 481; *Denbicare,* 84 F.3d at 1150.

In summary, our general rule that § 109(a) refers "only to copies legally made ... in the United States," *id.,* is not clearly irreconcilable with *Quality King* and, therefore, remains binding precedent. Under this rule, the first sale doctrine is unavailable as a defense to the claims under §§ 106(3) and 602(a) because there is no genuine dispute that Omega manufactured the watches bearing the Omega Globe Design in Switzerland. *Id.;* Fed. R. Civ. P. 56(c); *see also Swatch S.A. v. New City, Inc.,* 454 F. Supp. 2d 1245, 1253–54 (S.D. Fla. 2006) (concluding that *Quality King* is consistent with the interpretation that "lawfully made under this title" means "legally made ... in the United States"); 2 Goldstein on Copyright § 7.6.1, at 143–44 (concluding that Quality King "indicates an intention not to disturb lower court holdings that the first sale defense is unavailable to importers who acquire ownership of gray market goods made abroad"). REVERSED AND REMANDED.

NOTES AND QUESTIONS

1. *Circuit split.* The Supreme Court affirmed the *Costco* decision by a 4–4 vote. *See* 131 S. Ct. 565 (2010). Justice Kagan was recused because she worked on the case as Solicitor General. The split vote means that the Ninth Circuit decision in *Costco* stands, but the Supreme Court decision has no precedential value. After *Costco* was decided, the Second Circuit took a different approach, holding that copyright exhaustion applies only to U.S. manufactured works even if first sale occurred in the U.S. *See John Wiley & Sons, Inc. v. Kirtsaeng,* 654 F.3d 210 (2d Cir. 2011). Thus, under the Second Circuit approach, the offshoring loophole to the first sale doctrine is allowed. Given the circuit split and the confusion over the meaning of *Quality King,* the Supreme Court may revisit the issue.

2. Why couldn't L'anza attempt to exclude the goods on the basis of trademark law? Hint: where were the goods manufactured? What measures, if any, can L'anza take in light of *Quality King* to protect against the sale of low priced gray market goods of L'anza at discount stores?

3. Do you think shampoo bottles and watches were supposed to be analyzed under copyright law? Does it make sense for the U.S. to have different exhaustion rules under trademark and copyright if brand owners can simply affix a copyrighted label on their goods?

4. *No common control exception for copyright.* As discussed in *K Mart* and *Lever*, trademark law recognizes exhaustion based on the foreign sales of a trademarked product by an entity under the common control with the U.S. trademark holder. By contrast, no exhaustion occurs based on the foreign sales of a copyrighted product by an entity under the common control with the U.S. copyright holder. *See Parfums Givenchy, Inc. v. Drug Emporium, Inc.*, 38 F.3d 477, 483–84 (9th Cir. 1994). The "common control" exception under the Lanham Act for trademarks was intended (i) to protect U.S. companies that purchase trademarks from foreign manufacturers for use in the U.S. and (ii) to protect consumers from confusion as to goods made by foreign manufacturers independent of the U.S. trademark holder. *Id.* at 484–85. Such policy goals do not apply to copyright, however. *Id.* In any event, if foreign sales do not constitute copyright exhaustion under U.S. law, the consideration of foreign affiliates is unnecessary to the analysis.

3. EXHAUSTION OF PATENTS: APPROACH IN THE EU AND THE UNITED STATES

The EU takes the same approach of regional exhaustion for patents. The U.S. adopts national exhaustion. Consider the following problems and cases. As the *Merck* case demonstrates, pharmaceuticals are one area in which patent exhaustion is significant.

PROBLEM 6–14

Zenos, a multi-national electronics company that holds U.S. and European patents, sells two large shipments of its patented product, an expensive and highly advanced digital camera, to a distributor in the U.S. and to a distributor in Frankfurt, Germany. The sales contracts for both shipments contain a clause prohibiting the sale of the cameras to low priced discount stores and street markets. The U.S. distributor subsequently sells the cameras to discount stores in the United States. The distributor in Frankfurt sells the camera to discount stores throughout the European Union. Zenos objects to the sales in discount stores in the U.S. and the European Union as it believes that such sales will hurt the image of Zenos's camera as an expensive item reserved for the upper end of the market. Can Zenos prevent these sales? *See Merck & Co. v. Primecrown* and *Jazz Photo* below.

PROBLEM 6–15

Pharmacacia is a U.S. drug company that produces a patented "wonder" drug for acne and anti-aging of the skin. It intends to sell its drug in the U.S. and Canada. Pharmacacia intends to sell the drug for $200 per package in the U.S., but for only $50 per package in Canada due to the Canadian price controls. Pharmacacia has just learned that Congress may amend the current food, drug, and safety laws to allow importation of prescription drugs from Canada into the U.S. Pharmacacia has hired you to provide advice on whether U.S. patent law would allow it to stop the importation of its drugs from Canada into the U.S. Can Pharmacacia structure its business to avoid parallel importation of its drugs? *See Jazz Photo* below.

MERCK & CO. v. PRIMECROWN LTD.

European Court of Justice.
[1996] ECR I–6285, Case C–267/95 (December 5, 1996).

Grounds

[T]he High Court of Justice of England and Wales, Chancery Division, Patents Court, referred to the Court for a preliminary ruling under Article 177 of the EC Treaty questions concerning the interpretation of Article 47 and Article 209 of the Act concerning the Conditions of Accession of the Kingdom of Spain and the Portuguese Republic and the Adjustments to the Treaties (hereinafter "the Act of Accession") and of Articles 30 and 36 of the EC Treaty. [Article 30 prohibits quantitative restrictions on goods at the border while Article 36 makes an exception for measures necessary to protect intellectual property rights. *Ed.*]

Merck claims that Primecrown has infringed its United Kingdom patents for a hypertension drug marketed under the trade mark Innovace in the United Kingdom and under the trade mark Renitec elsewhere, for a drug prescribed in prostrate treatment, marketed under the trade mark Proscar, and for a glaucoma drug marketed under the trade mark Timoptol. It complains that Primecrown has carried out parallel imports of those products into the United Kingdom. Renitec and Proscar have been imported from Spain whilst Timoptol has been imported from Portugal. [Likewise,] Beecham has brought an action against Europharm for infringing its United Kingdom patents covering an antibiotic called Augmentin in the United Kingdom and Augmentine in Spain. Beecham complains that Europharm has imported this product from Spain into the United Kingdom with a view to applying to the competent authorities for an import licence which would allow it to import more of the product.

Merck and Beecham consider that they are entitled to oppose parallel imports of a drug for which they hold patents when, as in these cases, those imports come from a Member State where their products are marketed but were not patentable there.

[T]he national court explains that the present disputes have arisen because the holders of the patents in question do not have, and never could have got, patent protection in Spain or Portugal for the drugs concerned. Prices in those Member States are lower than elsewhere in the European Union, and medicines sold by the patent holders to wholesalers there, instead of going to Spanish or Portuguese consumers, are immediately exported.

The third question

By its third question the national court asks whether Articles 30 and 36 of the Treaty preclude application of national legislation which grants the holder of a patent for a pharmaceutical product the right to oppose importation by a third party of that product from another Member State in circumstances where the holder first put the product on the market in that State after its accession to the European Community but before the product could be protected by a product patent in that State.

In substance, the High Court is seeking to ascertain whether it is necessary to reconsider the rule in *Merck v. Stephar* or whether, having regard to the specific circumstances mentioned, its scope should be limited. It is first necessary to recall the Court's reasoning in *Merck*. In that judgment, the Court referred to its judgment in Case 15/74 *Centrafarm v. Sterling Drug* [1974] ECR 1147 in which it held that as an exception, on grounds of the protection of industrial and commercial property, to one of the fundamental principles of the common market, Article 36 of the Treaty admitted such derogation only in so far as it was justified for the purpose of safeguarding rights constituting the specific subject-matter of that property, which, as regards patents, is, in particular, in order to reward the creative effort of the inventor, to guarantee that the patentee has the exclusive right to use an invention with a view to manufacturing industrial products and putting them into circulation for the first time, either directly or by the grant of licences to third parties, as well as the right to oppose infringements.

In paragraphs 9 and 10 of *Merck*, the Court then stated that it followed from the definition of the specific purpose of a patent that the substance of a patent right lies essentially in according the inventor an exclusive right to put the product on the market for the first time, thereby allowing him a monopoly in exploiting his product and enabling him to obtain the reward for his creative effort without, however, guaranteeing such reward in all circumstances.

The Court held, finally, in paragraphs 11 and 13 of *Merck* that it was for the holder of the patent to decide, in the light of all the circumstances, under what conditions he would market his product, including the possibility of marketing it in a Member State where the law did not provide patent protection for the product in question. If he decides to do so, he must then accept the consequences of his choice as regards free movement of the product within the common market, this being a fundamental principle forming part of the legal and economic circumstances which the holder of the patent must take into account in determining how to exercise his exclusive right. Under those conditions, to permit an inventor to invoke a patent held by him in one Member State in order to prevent the importation of the product freely marketed by him in another Member State where that product was not patentable would cause a partitioning of national markets contrary to the aims of the Treaty.

For the reasons set out below, the arguments for reconsideration of the rule in *Merck* are not such as to call in question the reasoning on which the Court based that rule. [T]he situations addressed by the ruling in *Merck* are set to disappear since pharmaceutical products are now patentable in all the Member States. Merck's and Beecham's argument that judgments given by the Court after Merck, in particular those in Case 19/84 *Pharmon v. Hoechst* ([1985] ECR 2281) and in Case 158/86 *Warner Brothers and Metronome Video v. Christiansen* ([1988] ECR 2605), support their point of view must be rejected.

Contrary to their contention, the judgment in *Pharmon* shows that the Court confirmed the principles laid down in *Merck*. In *Pharmon*, the Court emphasized the importance of the patentee's consent to the product in question being put into circulation. At paragraph 25 it held that, where the authorities of a Member State grant a third party a compulsory licence allowing him to carry out manufacturing and marketing operations which the patentee would normally have the right to prevent, the patentee cannot be deemed to have consented to those operations and he may therefore oppose importation of products made by the holder of the compulsory licence.

Unlike the cases now under consideration, *Warner Brothers* concerned legislation of the importing State which allowed the author of a musical or cinematographic work not only to control the initial sale but also to oppose the hiring out of videos of that work for as long as he refused specific consent for such hiring out. In that judgment, the Court held that, since there was a specific market for hiring out distinct from the market for sales, such a specific right would lose its substance if the proprietor of the work were unable to authorize hiring out, even in the case of video cassettes already put into circulation with his consent in another Member State whose legislation allowed the author to control the initial sale without giving him the right to prohibit hiring out.

Merck and Beecham maintain in particular that, in the circumstances mentioned in the order for reference, their right to decide freely on the conditions in which they market their products is removed or considerably reduced. In their view, it follows from *Pharmon* that the rule in *Merck* does not apply in the present cases.

As to that, although the imposition of price controls is indeed a factor which may, in certain conditions, distort competition between Member States, that circumstance cannot justify a derogation from the principle of free movement of goods. It is well settled that distortions caused by different price legislation in a Member State must be remedied by measures taken by the Community authorities and not by the adoption by another Member State of measures incompatible with the rules on free movement of goods.

The next question which must be examined is how far the rule in *Merck* applies where patentees are legally obliged to market their products in the exporting State.

In answering that question it is to be remembered, first, that in *Merck* the Court emphasized the importance of the fact that the patentee had taken his decision to market his product freely and in full knowledge of all relevant circumstances and, second, that it follows from *Pharmon* that a patentee who is not in a position to decide freely how he will market his products in the exporting State may oppose importation and marketing of those products in the State where the patent is in force.

It follows that, where a patentee is legally bound under either national law or Community law to market his products in a Member State, he cannot be deemed, within the meaning of the ruling in Merck, to have given his consent to the marketing of the products concerned. He is therefore entitled to oppose importation and marketing of those products in the State where they are protected. It is for the patentee to prove, before the national court from which an order prohibiting imports is sought, that there is a legal obligation to market the product concerned in the exporting State. He must in particular show, for example by reference to decisions of the competent national authorities or courts or of the competent Community authorities, that there is a genuine, existing obligation.

According to the information given to the Court in these proceedings and as the Advocate General observes in points 152 and 153 of his Opinion, such obligations can hardly be said to exist in the case of the imports in question.

RULING

Articles 30 and 36 of the EC Treaty preclude application of national legislation which grants the holder of a patent for a pharmaceutical product the right to oppose importation by a third party of that product from another Member State in circumstances where the holder first put the product on the market in that State after its accession to the European Community but before the product could be protected by a patent in that State, unless the holder of the patent can prove that he is under a genuine, existing legal obligation to market the product in that Member State.

JAZZ PHOTO CORP. v. INTERNATIONAL TRADE COMMISSION

U.S. Court of Appeals for the Federal Circuit.
264 F.3d 1094 (Fed. Cir. 2001).

NEWMAN, CIRCUIT JUDGE.

The Patented Inventions

The LFFP [lens fitted film package] is a relatively simple camera, whose major elements are an outer plastic casing that holds a shutter, a shutter release button, a lens, a viewfinder, a film advance mechanism, a film counting display, and for some models a flash assembly and battery.

The casing also contains a holder for a roll of film, and a container into which the exposed film is wound. At the factory a roll of film is loaded into the camera. The casing is then sealed by ultrasonic welding or light-tight latching, and a cardboard cover is applied to encase the camera.

LFFPs are intended by the patentee [Fuji Photo Film Co.] to be used only once. After the film is exposed the photo-processor removes the film container by breaking open a pre-weakened portion of the plastic casing which is accessed by removal of the cardboard cover. Discarded LFFPs, subsequently purchased and refurbished by the respondents, are the subject of this action.

The parts of an LFFP are illustrated in Figure 8 of the '087 patent:

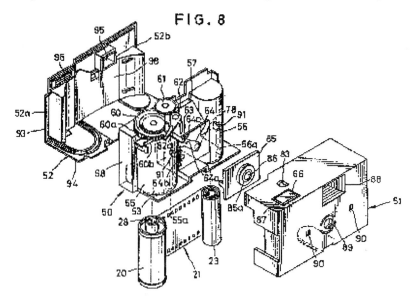

It is not disputed that the imported refurbished cameras contain all of the elements of all or most of the [patent] claims in suit.

The Accused Activities

The appellants [Jazz Photo Corp.] import used LFFPs that have been refurbished by various overseas entities (called "remanufacturers" in the International Trade Commission proceeding). Some of the remanufacturers refused discovery entirely or in part, and some presented evidence that the (Administrative Law Judge) ALJ found incomplete or not credible. The Commission explains: "Since so little was known about the accused infringing processes, the ALJ considered the common steps that each participating respondent admitted during the hearing were part of their processes." ITC Brief at 15–16. The ALJ summarized these common steps as follows:

- removing the cardboard cover;

- opening the LFFP body (usually by cutting at least one weld);

- replacing the winding wheel or modifying the film cartridge to be inserted;
- resetting the film counter;
- replacing the battery in flash LFFPs;
- winding new film out of a canister onto a spool or into a roll;
- resealing the LFFP body using tape and/or glue;
- applying a new cardboard cover.

Initial Determination at 108–109. The Commission held that these activities constitute prohibited reconstruction. In view of this holding, it was not material to the Commission's ruling that the full extent of various respondents' activities was not made known, for in all events the importation would be infringing and unlawful.

The appellants argue that they are not building new LFFPs, but simply replacing the film in used cameras. They argue that the LFFPs have a useful life longer than the single use proposed by Fuji, that the patent right has been exhausted as to these articles, and that the patentee can not restrict their right to refit the cameras with new film by the procedures necessary to insert the film and reset the mechanism. Unless these activities are deemed to be permissible, infringement of at least some of the patents in suit is conceded.

The unrestricted sale of a patented article, by or with the authority of the patentee, "exhausts" the patentee's right to control further sale and use of that article by enforcing the patent under which it was first sold. In *United States v. Masonite Corp.*, 316 U.S. 265, 278, the Court explained that exhaustion of the patent right depends on "whether or not there has been such a disposition of the article that it may fairly be said that the patentee has received his reward for the use of the article." Thus when a patented device has been lawfully sold in the United States, subsequent purchasers inherit the same immunity under the doctrine of patent exhaustion. However, the prohibition that the product may not be the vehicle for a "second creation of the patented entity" continues to apply, for such re-creation exceeds the rights that accompanied the initial sale.

Fuji states that some of the imported LFFP cameras originated and were sold only overseas, but are included in the refurbished importations by some of the respondents. The record supports this statement, which does not appear to be disputed. United States patent rights are not exhausted by products of foreign provenance. To invoke the protection of the first sale doctrine, the authorized first sale must have occurred under the United States patent. *See Boesch v. Graff*, 133 U.S. 697, 701–03 (1890) (a lawful foreign purchase does not obviate the need for license from the United States patentee before importation into and sale in the United States). Our decision applies only to LFFPs for which the United States patent right has been exhausted by first sale in the United States. Imported LFFPs of solely foreign provenance are not immunized from infringement of United States patents by the nature of their refurbishment.

[The Court went on to hold that, under the first sale doctrine, for those LFFPs that Fuji first sold in the U.S., the appellants' reimportation of those products back into the U.S. were not infringing to the extent the appellants had engaged only in limited repair (as opposed to reconstruction) of Fuji's sold products. The appellants' importation of LFFPs that Fuji first sold abroad, however, were infringing of Fuji's right of importation under U.S. law, since the first sale doctrine did not apply to first sales abroad.]

[In later proceedings after remand, the Federal Circuit clarified what it meant by "solely foreign provenance." *Fuji Photo Film Co., Ltd. v. Jazz Photo Corp.,* 394 F.3d 1368, 1376 (Fed. Cir. 2005). The excerpt below is from the court's opinion. *Ed.*]

This court does not construe the "solely foreign provenance" language [in *Jazz Photo*] or the *Boesch* citation to dictate a narrow application of the exhaustion principle. Specifically, this court does not read *Boesch* or the above language to limit the exhaustion principle to unauthorized sales. *Jazz* therefore does not escape application of the exhaustion principle because Fuji or its licensees authorized the international first sales of these LFFPs. The patentee's authorization of an international first sale does not affect exhaustion of that patentee's rights in the United States. Moreover, the "solely foreign provenance" language does not negate the exhaustion doctrine when either the patentee or its licensee sells the patented article abroad.

Read in full context, this court in *Jazz* stated that only LFFPs sold within the United States under a United States patent qualify for the repair defense under the exhaustion doctrine. Moreover, Fuji's foreign sales can never occur under a United States patent because the United States patent system does not provide for extraterritorial effect. *Int'l Rectifier Corp. v. Samsung Elecs. Co.,* 361 F.3d 1355, 1360 (Fed. Cir. 2004) ("Further, it is well known that United States patent laws 'do not, and were not intended to, operate beyond the limits of the United States,'" quoting *Brown v. Duchesne,* 60 U.S. 183, 195 (1856)). In *Jazz,* therefore, this court expressly limited first sales under the exhaustion doctrine to those occurring within the United States. *Fuji Photo,* 394 F.3d at 1368 (additional citations omitted).

NOTES AND QUESTIONS

1. What is the EU's approach to exhaustion of patent rights based on the sale of a patented item? What is the U.S.'s approach? Is either approach more advantageous to patent holders? To consumers? Does one approach favor developed countries or developing countries?

2. *EU free movement of goods.* How does the European Union's recognition of the principle of the free movement of goods within the EU relate to the

issue of patent exhaustion? Under the ruling of *Merck Co. v. Primecrown Ltd.*, are there any circumstances in which the first sale of a patented item in a country within the EU would *not* result in the exhaustion of patent rights to that item?

3. *Exhaustion of process patents.* In *Quanta Computer, Inc. v. LG Electronics, Inc.*, 553 U.S. 617, 638 (2008), the U.S. Supreme Court held that an authorized first sale (presumably in the U.S.) of a product substantially embodying a patented *process* exhausted the distribution rights as to the process.

4. Should the U.S. follow the EU's approach in adopting one principle of exhaustion that applies to all IP forms—trademarks, copyrights, and patents?

5. *Bibliographic note. See* Ako Shimada Williams, *International Exhaustion of Patent Rights Doctrine: Is Japan's Move a Step Forward or Back from the Current Harmonization Effort?*, 7 J. INT'L L. & PRAC. 327, 345–54 (1998) (discussing *Jap–Auto Products v. BBS Kraftahrzeug Technik* (Sup. Ct. July 1, 1997)).

INDEX

References are to Pages